BRITISH FOREIGN POLICY UNDER
SIR EDWARD GREY

BRITISH FOREIGN POLICY UNDER
SIR EDWARD GREY

EDITED BY
F. H. HINSLEY
PROFESSOR OF THE HISTORY OF INTERNATIONAL RELATIONS
UNIVERSITY OF CAMBRIDGE
AND PRESIDENT OF ST JOHN'S COLLEGE, CAMBRIDGE

CAMBRIDGE UNIVERSITY PRESS
CAMBRIDGE
LONDON · NEW YORK · MELBOURNE

Published by the Syndics of the Cambridge University Press
The Pitt Building, Trumpington Street, Cambridge CB2 1RP
Bentley House, 200 Euston Road, London NW1 2DB
32 East 57th Street, New York, NY 10022, USA
296 Beaconsfield Parade, Middle Park, Melbourne 3206, Australia

First published 1977

Printed in Great Britain at the
University Press, Cambridge

Library of Congress cataloguing in Publication Data
Main entry under title:
British foreign policy under Sir Edward Grey.
Bibliography p.
Includes index
1. Great Britain – Foreign relations – 1901–10 – Addresses, essays, lectures. 2. Great
Britain – Foreign relations – 1910–1936 – Addresses, essays, lectures. 3. European
War, 1914–1918 – Diplomatic history – Addresses, essays, lectures. 4. Grey, Edward
Grey, 1st Viscount, 1862–1933 – Addresses, essays, lectures.
I. Hinsley, Francis Harry, 1918–
DA570.B73   327.41   76-19631
ISBN 0-521-21347-9

CONTENTS

PREFACE

As a result of the operation of the rule by which the archives of British government departments were at the time opened to the public after the passage of fifty years, a new phase in the study of British foreign policy in the period from 1905 to 1916 began in the 1950s. By 1970 it was coming to an end: diplomatic historians, their ranks reinforced by increasing numbers of research students, had completed the scrutiny of the archives up to 1916 and, further encouraged by the decision to replace the fifty-year rule by a thirty-year rule, were turning their attention to those of later years. This volume, written mainly by scholars who first came forward as research students at the time, summarises the work that was done and presents its findings as a comprehensive account of the subject.

In my duties as general editor I have been assisted throughout by the individual contributors to the volume. Other contributors as well as myself have discussed each chapter with its author or authors in an attempt to keep duplication to a minimum and to arrive at consistency of treatment. In addition, Mrs Steiner has undertaken the task of compiling and checking the bibliography.

October 1975   F. H. HINSLEY

THE CONTRIBUTORS

F. R. Bridge, Reader in International History, University of Leeds

P. A. R. Calvert, Reader in Politics, University of Southampton

R. J. Crampton, Lecturer in History, University of Kent at Canterbury

M. L. Dockrill, Lecturer in the Department of War Studies, King's College, University of London

E. W. Edwards, Senior Lecturer in History, University College, Cardiff

Michael G. Ekstein, Lecturer in History, The New University of Ulster, Coleraine

K. A. Hamilton, Lecturer in International Politics, University College of Wales, Aberystwyth

Marian Kent, Reader in History, Deakin University, Victoria, Australia

R. T. B. Langhorne, Fellow of St John's College, Cambridge

The late C. J. Lowe, Professor of History, University of Alberta

Arthur Marsden, Senior Lecturer in Modern History, University of Dundee

C. M. Mason, Lecturer in Politics, University of Glasgow

I. H. Nish, Reader in International History, London School of Economics and Political Science

Clive Parry, Professor of International Law, University of Cambridge

K. G. Robbins, Professor of History, University College of North Wales, Bangor

D. W. Sweet, Senior Lecturer in Modern History, University of Durham

Jonathan Steinberg, Lecturer in History and Fellow of Trinity Hall, Cambridge

Zara Steiner, Fellow of New Hall, Cambridge

Beryl Williams, Lecturer in History, University of Sussex

INTRODUCTORY

1

The Foreign Secretary, the Cabinet, Parliament and the parties

K. G. ROBBINS

In the period before 1914, it was widely accepted that, at any rate in the long run, public opinion could vitally influence the course of foreign policy. But there was remarkably little constitutional provision that it should do so. Dicey, for example, believed that it was 'not Parliament, but the Ministry, who direct the diplomacy of the nation, and virtually decide all questions of peace or war'. He was in the happy position of feeling certain that 'the Ministry in all matters of discretion carry out, or tend to carry out, the will of the House'.[1] While this might indeed be so, there was no certainty, and Radicals placed little reliance on such tacit understandings. They deplored the extent to which the House of Commons and the country were at the mercy of the Cabinet. While it was the case that treaty negotiations frequently led to a government statement in the Commons, it was the prevailing legal opinion that parliamentary sanction was not needed, either for signing, or ratifying, treaties, so long as no changes in the law of the land were involved. All that was required for agreements to be valid was the signature of the Powers concerned – the ratification by the Sovereign and counter-signing by the Foreign Secretary. The sanction of Parliament was required only for treaties which incurred financial obligations or ceded territory in time of peace. The majority of political agreements were signed and ratified without the assent of Parliament, though they were normally published soon afterwards. The exclusion of certain articles from the published version of the Anglo–French agreement of 1904 was an exception to the normal practice of publishing the terms of treaties in full.[2] Such a situation clearly left immense potential power in the hands of the Cabinet, however much it was normally tempered by conventions of disclosure and debate.

In addition to this constitutional position, external circumstances seemed to strengthen the executive just at the time when pleas for greater democratic control were gaining ground. For it was becoming clear that British freedom of action in foreign policy was no longer what it had once been. There were those who continued to resist this conclusion but, broadly speaking, the mental climate of 'splendid isolation' was passing. The effect of this uncertainty was to strengthen the position of the Cabinet. In protesting against its powers, many critics were in fact protesting against the changes in the international system which reduced Britain's freedom of manoeuvre.[3]

These external constraints were inevitable, but both the Campbell-Bannerman and Asquith Governments suffered from the peculiar circumstances surrounding the formation of the Liberal Cabinet in December 1905. The divisions in the Liberal Party at the time of the Boer War had not resulted in the open split which many at one time had forecast. Nevertheless, suspicions generated at that time had not been forgotten. When it had seemed likely that the Unionist Government would not last much longer, Asquith, Grey and Haldane pledged themselves to force Campbell-Bannerman to take a peerage as the price for their own acceptance of office. When the crisis came, however, the compact did not work. Asquith was the first to be seduced by the prospect of office and when Campbell-Bannerman made it clear that he did not intend to be blackmailed in the formation of his Cabinet, Haldane and Grey eventually fell into line. The despised Sir Henry gained an unexpected triumph and the plotters were trounced.[4] It is possible that their discomfiture would have been greater if the government had been formed after the General Election of January 1906, which gave the Liberals their unexpectedly large majority. Three of the most prominent 'Liberal Imperialists' were in important positions – at the Foreign Office, the War Office and the Treasury.[5] Other members of the Cabinet, and of the party at large, believed that the 'Liberal Imperialists' had captured the Cabinet. Such allegations go too far. In the first place, too great a cohesion has been attributed to the 'Liberal Imperialists' as a group. They happened to be close personal friends, but not such friends as to make them indifferent to their own individual interests – the failure of their compact shows this. Secondly, it is by no means clear that their objections to Campbell-Bannerman (and his to them) were particularly the product of disagreement over foreign policy. They felt that he would not be an effective leader if he remained in the Commons at his age; he felt that they were mischievous and too ambitious. Thirdly, as far as such things matter, Campbell-Bannerman's own personal sympathies were probably 'pro-French' rather than 'pro-German'. Whatever the truth, the Cabinet was widely believed to be divided between 'Liberal Imperialists' and the rest. But this simple division makes little sense of the Cabinet's behaviour over the next decade.[6] The Government was composed of an unusually high number of ambitious men who, at different junctures, formed different alliances with seemingly unlikely colleagues. In this situation, attempts to fix individuals in particular groups are misleading.[7]

It is impossible to tell what Campbell-Bannerman might have achieved if his Ministry had lasted longer, and he had been free from family and personal illness. Initially, however, his authority as a leader surprised his critics. He had no great interest in foreign affairs, but clearly did not wish to abdicate all responsibility for them. In the first great issue of foreign policy – the nature of the Anglo–French relationship and the military conversations – he must take the main responsibility for the failure to bring the matter before the Cabinet. After all, Campbell-Bannerman and the elder statesman, Lord Ripon, both had experiences of previous Cabinets; Grey and Haldane had not. After many years of Cabinet experience, Grey himself subsequently concluded that he ought to have asked for a discussion when Campbell-Bannerman gave him the opportunity. In his memoirs, Grey says that no record has survived of his reply to the Prime Minister's invitation. However, on 22 January, Grey asked that no Cabinet on the French question should be fixed until they had had the opportunity of a personal discussion.[8] Presumably after such a conversation, possibly at Windsor in the presence of the King, it was agreed that Grey should see Cambon without a Cabinet.[9] The Foreign Secretary clearly preferred not to discuss the matter in the Cabinet, though he could hardly have objected in principle if Campbell-Bannerman had insisted upon it. Sir Henry also saw the record of these conversations and decided that, although he was not completely happy with them, it was as well to hope for the best.[10] The fatal accident to Lady Grey then called the Foreign Secretary back to Northumberland. Sir Edward's conversations with Cambon were not discussed in the Cabinet and records of them were not circulated. It has been surmised that Campbell-Bannerman, concerned for the unity of the party, did not want to see the matter debated and divisions revealed. But it is an exaggeration to claim that Grey was in the Cabinet not only as an individual, but also as the representative of a party too strong for the Prime Minister to defy.[11] Sir Henry had just won a great victory which was believed to have strengthened his wing of the party. Even before this, he had made it clear both to Haldane and Grey that they were expendable. Aware of Haldane as a backstairs operator, albeit a somewhat clumsy one, and finding 'Master' Grey not beyond suspicion, the Prime Minister is hardly likely to have given in to them, and thus set a bad precedent, if he had been seriously alarmed himself.

Lord Ripon had told Grey on his coming into office that there were always some Foreign Office papers that were sent to the Prime Minister and not circulated to the Cabinet, at any rate in the first instance. Besides, it would have been physically impossible to circulate all the private correspondence to each member of the Cabinet. Ministers were not very assiduous in reading those despatches which they did receive. The new Cabinet was a large one, and while there was no formally constituted inner Cabinet, it seems sensible to conclude that the Prime Minister (a former Secretary for War) was content with the arrangement whereby a small group of men in relevant Ministries knew of the position.[12] Since, as seems most likely, Asquith was not informed, it is difficult to believe that Haldane, Asquith and Grey were 'hunting in a pack' in the Cabinet.[13] Furthermore, despite the fact that Grey stayed in Haldane's house in London after his wife's death, this did not prevent a disagreement between them concerning policy towards Germany in the autumn of 1906. Grey then felt that Haldane's intended visit to Germany would upset the French, '...I want to preserve the entente with France, but it isn't easy, and

if it is broken up I must go.'[14] Rosebery rightly complained subsequently
to Haldane that the French had been rather sharp in pressing Grey so soon
after his arrival in office.[15] But then, Rosebery, the exemplar of 'Liberal
Imperialism', was the leading opponent of the Anglo-French entente.

Grey himself held a very high view of the nature and powers of his office.
He did not believe that the Cabinet should control foreign policy, if by that
was meant close supervision in detail by its members of all aspects of foreign
policy. The fact that such control was also administratively impossible reinforced his convictions. He consulted the Prime Minister quite often, and
decided with him what items it was appropriate to bring before their colleagues. Because of this system, Parliament often knew little of what was
going on. In any case, during this first crucial two and a half months of the
Liberal Government, Parliament was not sitting. Such a situation did not alarm
Grey. In October 1905, he had gone out of his way to emphasize publicly his
belief in 'continuity' as regards foreign policy.[16] It would be too much to expect
that the parties could agree in every detail, but it was essential that the basic
foreign policy arrangements should not be disputed between the parties. This
was partly because the 'national interest' could be conceived as lying beyond
the realm of party political exchanges, and partly because any fundamental
changes of attitude would unsettle the international situation and place grave
doubts against Britain's reliability. It was not, in fact, difficult to maintain the
doctrine of 'continuity' in Parliament. While there had been a very few
distinguished critics of the Anglo–French entente, it would be true to say that
the arrangement had been accepted by all the political parties. No one
seriously proposed the reversal of the entente, but there was considerable
Liberal anxiety that it might be transformed into a binding commitment to
assist France. The Liberal backbenches contained a considerable number of
men who regarded themselves, often with justification, as experts on foreign
policy in general, or at least on certain specific areas. The presence of these
men was to mean that the Government would receive more criticism from its
own backbenches than it did from the Opposition. Yet, while a large section
of the party, perhaps one might say a third, shared a 'Radical' outlook, the
negative voice of this group was more prominent than its positive. Radicals
felt that a Liberal Government ought to be committed to reducing arms
expenditure, but apart from a general agreement in principle, there was little
unanimity on the best way to achieve it. The 'Radicals' also found themselves
in an awkward dilemma. They sniffed anxiously for the least trace of a
continental entanglement and at the same time opposed a high level of
defence expenditure. To be a reductionist might be sensible. To be an
isolationist might be sensible. But was it possible to be both?

Many of the newly-elected younger generation of Radicals with interests in
foreign policy were also keenly interested in social questions. Indeed the chief
objection to an accelerated naval programme was that it diverted resources
which would be more usefully employed in social welfare programmes. Yet,

however disappointed some of them might feel with their party's achievements, they did not believe that the Tories would do better. So, when it came
to debate over foreign policy, they pressed their disagreements so far, but no
further. Finally, it was often the case that while general criticism of the
Government's policy was easy, when it came to details, as for example in the
Balkans, the critics differed almost as much amongst themselves. The fact
that, on the whole, the Radicals were largely unsuccessful in their campaigns,
tended to heighten their sense of moral superiority, and belief that Government and Opposition were in collusion in the interests of the 'governing class'.
Each defeat in battle therefore strengthened their determination to win the
war. It was apparent by 1914 that criticism of specific policy decisions had
broadened into a general attack on the structure of Government.

Criticism of policy was not, however, confined to the back benches. In July
1906, hardly in distress, Grey commented to Ripon that 'Foreign policy has
been discussed so little at the Cabinet.'[17] The Foreign Secretary preferred to
operate through a small group of Ministers who received all the important
despatches. Campbell-Bannerman rarely took issue with him and, though this
is not often admitted, it must be presumed that he was content with the
general course of developments. Lloyd George has, of course, painted a
picture of Cabinet meetings in which only a select few elder statesmen were
expected to comment on the arcane mysteries of foreign affairs. His criticism
suffers from a failure to make specific charges about particular years. Certainly, for Grey's early period there seems to be truth in the accusation.[18] But,
apart from the inherent unlikelihood of Lloyd George being silenced if his
interest was really engaged, the other members of the Cabinet were formally
deeply involved in their own departmental responsibilities. However, it cannot
be denied that Grey gave a restricted circulation to a number of important
telegrams; how malevolent his purposes were is another matter. As far as the
Anglo–Russian agreement was concerned, Grey seems to have worked in close
collaboration with the Prime Minister, Ripon, Asquith and Morley. Grey's
method of operation was not, in fact, so markedly different from that of his
immediate predecessors. While Salisbury and Lansdowne consulted the full
Cabinet more than Grey, they also made use of a small inner group of
Ministers. As regards the Anglo–Russian agreement, nothing was kept from
the Cabinet, although Grey was not anxious for Morley to see the full European
implications of what was being done.[19] The Foreign Secretary acknowledged
that the Secretary of State for India's support was vital. 'Without Morley,' he
wrote to the Prime Minister, 'we should have made no progress at all, for the
Govt. of India would have blocked every point; Morley has removed moun-
tains in the path of the negotiations.' [20] Fortunately for Grey while Morley
expressed his reservations about 'anti-Germans' in the Foreign Office, his
character was sufficiently complex for him to find pleasure in being regarded
as a 'strong man' and not a mere 'doctrinaire'.[21] Morley's approval of the
agreement went some way towards disarming Radical criticisms, but the agree-

ment as a whole led to the first major clash in Parliament between the Government and some of its own supporters – not to mention the Opposition.

Grey defended his conclusion of the agreement at a time of Russian constitutional crisis. Foreign policy should not be used to interfere, one way of the other, in the internal problems of a country. Those Liberals who had strong sympathies for the Russian constitutional movement profoundly disagreed with him. A Liberal Government which treated with those who suppressed the Duma was not worthy the name. Moreover, what about the 'independence' of Persia? Speakers pointed out that peaceful revolution was proceeding in Persia when the convention was signed. Placing the capital of the country and the centres of the reform movement within the Russian sphere was tantamount to handing over the Persian reform movement to the tender mercies of a foreign despotism. Grey replied that the agreement would lead to better relations with Russia at the relatively small cost of losing some trading possibilities in Northern Persia. He professed to believe that the agreement would be kept in good faith, but this was the element of which his critics saw little sign. If the Russians did honour their part of the bargain, then perhaps the parts of the settlements which offended the Liberal conscience, both as regards Russia itself and Persia, might reluctantly be accepted. But if the Russians should misbehave, then the full fury of the critics would turn upon Grey.

The Foreign Secretary also contended that as far as Russia and North Persia were concerned, Britain might have been able to obstruct her progress for a time, but in the long run the concessions made under the agreement could not have been prevented. Other critics, chiefly Conservative, raised little 'ideological' objection. Taking their cue from Curzon's speech in the House of Lords, they argued that too much had been given away in return for too little solid benefit. Balfour was critical of details and procedure, but while he did not believe the convention a great diplomatic success, he thought it brought substantial advantages.[22] The bi-partisan tradition was therefore maintained. In turn, when Asquith became Prime Minister in 1908, he invited Balfour to serve on a sub-committee of the Committee of Imperial Defence. Balfour accepted – a step amounting to a constitutional innovation – although Asquith later denied that Balfour was, properly speaking, a member of the C.I.D.[23]

Confronted by this front-bench consensus, it was left to the Labour Party to make gestures of dissent. The Anglo-Russian Convention remained the chief target of Labour and Radical criticism. When Grey informed the Commons that the King was to meet the Tsar of Russia in the summer of 1908 on the Baltic, a critical motion was brought before the House by Keir Hardie. It failed by 225 votes to 59. The King was displeased and in retaliation banned Keir Hardie and Victor Grayson from the next Windsor Castle Garden Party. He was particularly angry with Arthur Ponsonby, Campbell-Bannerman's successor as Member for Stirling. Ponsonby, as a son of Queen Victoria's private secretary, should have known better than to vote against the Russian meeting. The visit duly took place, although the Labour Party continued to criticize.[24] In the hands of spokesmen like MacDonald, Snowden and Henderson, Labour's attitude to foreign affairs was hardly distinguishable from that of the Liberal Radicals. They merely insisted more frequently upon the evils of capitalism and the inevitability of war while such a system continued. MacDonald, whose knowledge of foreign countries was considerable, praised the Socialist Congresses when they declared that international strife was the result of capitalist activity. These assemblies, in his view, represented the nucleus of the coming 'parliament of man'. But there were other Labour propagandists who did not share this taste for radical rhetoric when it came to foreign affairs. Robert Blatchford and his *Clarion* probably influenced more Labour men than any other figure, but he spoke strongly of the need for national defence, advocated conscription and warned of the German menace. Even among the more orthodox Marxists, divisions on the question of national defence were apparent and 'social patriots' were subsequently to be found lurking in high places.[25] In any case, one suspects that the overwhelming concern of the Labour rank and file was with domestic questions and that the internationalist stance of the leadership was not strongly reflected at the grass roots.

The mood of the Liberal Government after the death of Campbell-Bannerman was one of some depression. Although it had been in office for two years, it had achieved disappointingly little. While Asquith was the obvious successor, he did not excite great enthusiasm. Nor did future prospects seem encouraging. The Liberals, to their great dismay, came into office at a time of technological innovation. This played havoc with their good intentions, originally shared by Asquith as much as by Campbell-Bannerman. In departing from the Cawdor programme, laid down by the previous Government, the Prime Minister lost Britain the margin of naval superiority which might have prevented future alarms. As it was, however, the German supplementary naval law of late 1907 prompted Lord Tweedmouth, the First Lord, to ask for increases in the 1908–9 naval estimates.[26] The first of the recurrent naval crises then ensued. This clash also led to the first serious challenge to his authority which Grey had experienced. The promotion of Lloyd George to the Exchequer and of Churchill to the Board of Trade brought into greater prominence two energetic men who were both worried by the Government's mediocre performance. In the interests of domestic social reform, they vigorously opposed Tweedmouth's estimates and, though unsuccessful, for a time they seriously imperilled the Government's unity.

Although Grey supported the naval programme, he was aware of the strength of Liberal feeling on the question. He did not oppose exploratory discussions with the Germans, on condition that both naval supremacy and the ententes were preserved intact. In July 1908, he suggested to Metternich, the German Ambassador, the possibility of mutual reductions in naval expenditure.[27] In August, Hardinge raised with the Emperor the possibility of discussions on the subject.[28] The Germans did not respond, and Grey decided to await a more favourable occasion. Lloyd George, however, decided to take on the problem himself. He made a number of public speeches on the need for a rapprochement with Germany.[29] These were followed by a visit to Germany to study social legislation. At the same time, he offered to discuss naval questions with German politicians despite his previous promise to Asquith to refrain from making public statements on this matter. Grey, anxious both about his own status and French reactions, protested to the Prime Minister, who ordered Lloyd George to desist.[30] 'I don't think any harm has been done by recent utterances', Grey wrote to Lord Sanderson, 'But I have taken occasion to point out the risk that is involved in them.' Some of his colleagues apparently did not believe in the existence of brick walls and it did no harm to let Lloyd George run his head against German examples, 'but there is always the danger that if foreign on-lookers do not understand what is going on there may be direct consequences, which are inconvenient.'[31] Similarly, he had a dispute with Churchill in December 1908 when the latter intimated his willingness to have talks in Paris on a forthcoming visit. Churchill was told that in Paris only the Prime Minister and himself were regarded by those in authority as 'exponents of the views of H.M. Government in questions of foreign policy'. His interviews might give rise to misunderstandings.[32] There was no doubt that the 'responsible men' in London were determined to maintain their authority!

Grey's touchiness on this matter was partly accounted for by the international situation and partly by continuing tension over the navy. In a public speech, Grey had warned of the need to maintain a clear-cut supremacy; there was no half-way house between 'complete safety and absolute ruin'. In face of rumours and evidence of acceleration in the German programme, it was clear that some further step would have to be decided. But, in view of the previous friction, could the Cabinet agree, keep the party with it, and gain an acceptable vote in Parliament? Early in February 1909, Churchill circulated a memorandum to the Cabinet stating his view that the German challenge was much exaggerated.[33] Lloyd George warned Asquith that endless discussions on the Naval Estimates were likely to destroy the spirit of the Government's supporters in the country. The Prime Minister reported to the King that the Cabinet was divided on whether to lay down six Dreadnoughts with an option of two additional ships according to German plans for construction, or to lay down four. On the side of the former proposal were Grey, Runciman, Crewe, McKenna and Buxton, and on the latter, Churchill, Harcourt, Burns and Morley.[34] A small committee, consisting of Asquith, Morley, Grey and Lloyd George, was appointed to try to reach a settlement. At the Cabinet on 24 February, the Prime Minister took the initiative. It was agreed that four ships be laid down at once, with power to order four more by April 1910, if German construction appeared to make such a step necessary.[35]

It was only with difficulty that the Cabinet survived this crisis. Grey and McKenna had threatened to resign if, as at one time seemed likely, the 'economists' had their way. A year later McKenna acknowledged that 'but for him [Grey] I should have been beaten on the Navy Estimates...'[36] Sir Edward believed that the crucial time for the navy would come in 1912–13, and he was not willing to see his foreign policy jeopardized by weakness at that juncture. At one stage in the conflict, Asquith wrote to his wife that he was disposed summarily to cashier both Lloyd George and Churchill for their attitudes, but that Grey had proved a great stand-by.[37] Lloyd George, Churchill and Morley meditated resignation – as Asquith commented to Grey, 'the two former cannot help reflecting how they would have looked at this moment if they had resigned with (as Winston Churchill predicted) "90 per cent of the Liberal party behind them"'.[38] Such an estimate was a considerable exaggeration. In fact, after listening to Asquith in the Commons, J. E. Ellis, one of the 'economists' recorded: 'Our men scattered like sheep. I do not think that at that moment five Liberals would have voted against increase.'[39] The critics reluctantly acquiesced, although both sides put their own construction upon the compromise. Asquith wrote that its effect would be 'to make us stronger in 1912 than McKenna's original proposal would have done'.[40] He was going to have eight and that settled the matter. Others, however, laid stress upon the fact that the four Dreadnought campaigners had 'won' and discounted the possibility of the four contingent ships ever being ordered. Some backbenchers felt that they had been tricked, but there was no need for the Government to rely on Tory votes to get the extra four ships as some had predicted would be necessary.[41] Whatever his rank and file might think, Asquith knew that, whether justifiably or not, the country was rattled. The Government had to face the vote of censure from the Opposition on 29 March for its shipbuilding policy. Grey spoke in strong terms: 'There is no comparison between the importance of the German Navy to Germany, and the importance of our Navy to us. Our Navy is to us what their Army is to them...'[42] Balfour was not content. He demanded the extra four ships there and then. As he was speaking, the result of the Croydon by-election became known in the House – an election in which the 'Dreadnought' issue was widely believed to have helped increase the Unionist vote. It was better to risk the wrath of less than a hundred of his own supporters than that of the country as a whole. Although some regretted that the position of the Navy, and hence the security of the country, should become an occasion for direct antagonism between the parties, Balfour, afflicted with his self-imposed responsibility for keeping Liberalism 'safe', was determined to keep the question in the forefront. And public opinion, at least as far as the existing electorate reflected it, was probably with him.[43]

At the Cabinet of 24 July, the further four ships were approved, apparently without much debate. The Cabinet accepted McKenna's request, and did not question him too closely. But some sheep who had scattered in the spring came back into the fold in the summer. Seventy-nine Liberals voted against the 'contingent' ships. They argued that the need had not been sufficiently established. In addition, they wanted to know the place of Parliament in this affair. They had assumed, rather optimistically, that there would be a prolonged discussion on the further orders. The Cabinet saw no such need. As Grey had noted in conversation with Fisher back in March, all that would be required would be 'to give notice to Parliament that we intended to give the orders when necessary...'[44] As some members had feared at the time, there was no provision for Parliament to make any further contribution. Cabinet Government was in operation. Some Liberal members concluded that this was 'rather the culmination of a not very dignified tactical manoeuvre than a conclusion forced upon minds by the emergence of new factors'.[45]

Bethmann Hollweg's appointment as German Chancellor in July 1909, and his proposal on 21 August that negotiations for a naval and political agreement should be opened, seemed to open up new possibilities. Grey gave the proposal a cautious welcome.[46] He was convinced that German naval reductions were the only way of accomplishing a real improvement in Anglo-German relations. Britain's existing ententes should not be brought into the discussion. Grey grew pessimistic when he found that the Germans were only offering a reduction in the tempo of naval building in return for a neutrality and non-aggression pact – and even this offer was later withdrawn as superfluous in view of the improved climate which, in itself, a pact would create. Late in the spring of 1910, Grey came to the conclusion that the basic German objective in these talks was to damage the Triple Entente.[47] Nevertheless, the Radicals were determined to keep up their pressure on the Government. In July 1910, the Lord Chancellor, Lord Loreburn, a close friend of the late Prime Minister (though of hardly anyone else), raised in Cabinet the possibility of a closer political understanding between Britain and Germany. Grey, who had agreed to the subject being discussed, reported that the conversations were continuing, but again stressed the inexpediency of entering into any engagements with Germany which might jeopardize French and Russian friendship.[48] Loreburn's anxieties, and they were shared, in general terms, by Lloyd George, Churchill, Burns and Harcourt, were not allayed. At the next meeting of the Cabinet, the Foreign Secretary submitted a memorandum drawn up for the guidance of the Ambassador in Berlin, which was slightly amended before its despatch.[49] But the discussion of foreign affairs in the Cabinet seems to have been of this spasmodic, hit-or-miss character. This was, perhaps, in large part, because of the rather haphazard organization of government then prevailing – lack of system was not confined to discussion of foreign affairs.

Lloyd George and Churchill were growing restless at the lack of governmental success. The Chancellor of the Exchequer complained of the slow progress being made in the talks, and he did not restrict his criticisms to private comments.[50] Haldane found Lloyd George 'irritating in the extreme' to be giving interviews to the press during the course of these conversations.[51] It is against this background of disquiet that the Prime Minister decided to appoint a Cabinet Committee on Foreign Affairs, with himself as Chairman. The members were Grey, Morley, Crewe, Runciman and Lloyd George.[52] Lloyd George was at this time Grey's strongest critic, occasionally supported by Morley, and possibly by Runciman; the others normally agreed with the Foreign Secretary. The Committee was unprecedented, and alarmed many Foreign Office officials. Its immediate task was to draw up a memorandum for the Cabinet on relations with Germany. An initial draft was amended by Lloyd George, but Grey was able to keep to his contention that the political and naval agreements were to be concluded simultaneously. When the proposals were finally presented to the Cabinet, they were, in substance, little different from those which had been on the table since 1909. However, in deference to the Radicals, the Cabinet stressed the importance of giving the reply to Germany a tone of 'unmistakable cordiality'. At the same time, nothing was to be said which could lead to misinterpretation in France and Russia. Finally, there was the difficulty, which would 'ultimately have to be encountered', of finding a formula for general acceptance by the Powers, 'in view of the impossibility of France openly abandoning, as against Germany, the policy of "revanche"'. Asquith reported to the King that the memorandum had been gone through 'sentence by sentence'.[53] Similarly, after the German reply had been received, it was discussed in the Cabinet and the terms of the British reply agreed upon. Then came Agadir.

The Cabinet reviewed the situation at a special meeting on 4 July. It was the sole subject of discussion. It was clearly felt to be undesirable to reply to this provocative proceeding by any action of a similar character. Even if Grey himself had wanted to do this, he soon realized that his colleagues would not agree. The German Ambassador was to be told that Britain could not allow the future of Morocco to be settled behind her back. The French were to be told that some concessions on their part would be expected since, by their own action, they had made a return to the status quo impossible. The situation was again discussed at the Cabinet on 11 and 19 July. It was then agreed that the German proposals for the virtual absorption of the French Congo were such that France could not possibly accept them. The French were to be urged to submit counter-proposals. Grey urged the calling of a conference and Germany should be told that in the event of a refusal, steps would be taken to protect British interests. This was going too far for Loreburn. Morley, Burns and Harcourt were also unhappy. The Lord Chancellor counter-attacked by claiming that direct British interest in Morocco was negligible and intervention might end in war. The discussion then became long and animated. It was agreed to postpone a communication to Germany. In the meantime, the French were to be asked whether they were prepared to resist *à outrance* the admission of Germany into Morocco – an admission which, under proper conditions, would not be deemed fatal to British interests and which would not in itself constitute a casus belli. There was still no acknowledgement from Germany of the British note sent on 4 July.[54] The Cabinet's desire for delay worried Sir Edward, but he felt unable to resist it.[55] On 21 July, there still having been no reply from Germany, the Cabinet took a firmer line and Grey was instructed to inform the German Ambassador that Britain would welcome an agreement between Germany and France on the basis of concessions in the French Congo – but, failing that, she would recognize no Moroccan settlement in which she did not participate.[56] In the evening, Lloyd George spoke at the Mansion House.

The Chancellor's speech was perhaps the most surprising development of a surprising summer.[57] It still has not been entirely explained. His declaration that British interests could never be ignored had been approved beforehand both by Asquith and Grey. In conversation with C. P. Scott, of the *Manchester Guardian*, Lloyd George claimed that the Cabinet 'up to a certain point' was practically unanimous. The only exception was Loreburn. Scott, who obtained much of his information from Loreburn, had just been warned by him: 'Always remember that this is a Liberal League Government. The Government of France is a tinpot Government: Germany has but to stamp her foot and they will give way... It would suit them admirably that we should be involved in a war with Germany...' Lloyd George dismissed Loreburn as petulant and unreasonable. He also dismissed the 'Liberal League' charge – there had been a great change over the previous couple of years, which he attributed to the campaign over the Budget.[58] Lloyd George's speech shattered for the moment the common assumptions about the structure of opinion in the Liberal Party. The early Radical reaction to the crisis had been one of criticizing France for taking action in Fez. The German response, though exaggerated, was deemed understandable. It was assumed by many Radicals that Lloyd George, together with Morley, Harcourt and Burns, would take the same position in the Cabinet. Instead, the official Cabinet Foreign Affairs Committee seems to have faded from sight at this point, and Lloyd George, together with Asquith, Grey, Churchill and Haldane met frequently throughout the rest of the summer to discuss the situation.

The 'betrayal' by Lloyd George gave added impetus to the activities of the recently formed Liberal Foreign Affairs Group, a parliamentary body which claimed some seventy members and more sympathizers. The leaders were Noel Buxton and Arthur Ponsonby. While some were anxious about the fate of the Moroccans, most were concerned to reprimand France and ensure that Germany should get her 'fair share' of colonies. In his memorial to Grey, Buxton stated that if, in relation to France, 'We had laid ourselves under treaty duties so incredible there is nothing for it but to stand by them. But till convinced that we are under the obligation of a promise, Liberals of all classes, and not Liberals alone, are bound to protest against a policy of "hemming Germany in" from a share in the colonial world.'[59]

The crisis dragged on throughout the summer. Amongst political circles in

London, it triggered off a series of questions about the precise state of Anglo–French relations. Grey either informed or reminded the Prime Minister of the military conversations with France which had been authorized in 1906. He said little about what had happened to them since – which may be a sign of discretion or ignorance.[60] This was in April 1911, but the Cabinet as a whole was still not informed.[61] A special meeting of the C.I.D. was held on 23 August, 1911, called by Asquith to determine British military and naval strategy in the event of war. The Cabinet had not been informed of this meeting and no 'dissenter' was present since, besides Asquith, the only politicians to attend were Grey, Haldane, Churchill, McKenna and Lloyd George. On the whole, they supported the desire of the General Staff to send an expeditionary force to France in the event of war. McKenna, as First Lord, took the navy's part and disagreed strongly with this tendency.[62] This secret meeting did not remain secret for long. The other members of the Cabinet, dispersed through they were, soon became alarmed. Runciman wrote confidently to Harcourt on 24 August that 'in the most unexpected quarters I find something more than a merely negative attitude, *a positive desire for conflict*'. One knew where one was with Grey and Haldane, whatever one felt about their views. But now, 'the stability or balance of opinion of the Cabinet cannot now be relied on by us'. The one thing to keep the 'rampageous strategists' in check was a definite decision of the Cabinet that under no circumstances would the present crisis lead to the landing of a single British soldier on the continent.[63] Harcourt, too, was alarmed. He told Runciman of the C.I.D. meeting and the fact that neither he nor Morley had been invited to it. 'It was to decide on where and how British troops could be landed to assist a French Army on the Meuse!!!' Long before such criminal folly had been embarked upon, Harcourt declared that he would have returned to a back bench.[64] Whether or not Churchill was 'going out of his mind with military mania', he was now bombarding his colleagues with memoranda and schemes. He and Lloyd George exchanged estimates and plans with the enthusiasm of neophytes. On a visit to Balmoral at the end of September, it was rumoured that the Chancellor had told their majesties that it would be a great pity if war did not come there and then.[65] Asquith himself was somewhat perturbed at the prospect of conversations between Joffre and the Army – 'The French ought not to be encouraged in present circumstances to make their plans on any assumptions of this kind.'[66] Grey argued that while the talks implied no commitment, to stop them would in fact have signalled a change of policy and alienated the French. Clearly the Cabinet could not go on with this state of affairs unresolved.

It was an angry Morley who insisted on debating the subject at the Cabinet meeting on 1 November 1911.[67] Those 'small fry' who had been excluded from the 'packed' committee on 23 August were undoubtedly furious.[68] It was left to Haldane to explain the origin of the military conversations. Asquith declared that all questions of policy had been and would be reserved for the

Cabinet. Grey concurred. But their sole supporters on this occasion seem to have been Lloyd George and Churchill.[69] The Cabinet broke up without coming to any conclusion. A fortnight later, when tempers had cooled a little, the subject of the military talks was resumed. Grey, who must have been the main target of the critics, declared that at no stage had freedom of decision and action by Britain, in the event of war between France and Germany, been compromised. Confronted by this strong feeling, Asquith hit upon a formula whereby it was agreed that no communication should take place between the British General Staff and other Staffs which could, directly or indirectly, commit the country to military or naval intervention.[70] Even so, Loreburn wanted to resign and only decided against doing so when Morley and Harcourt refused to join him.[71] After these sessions, the number of Cabinet Ministers who regularly attended the C.I.D. went up.

The Cabinet crisis was paralleled by a crisis in the party. Agadir had sparked this off, but discontent with British policy in Persia in the summer and autumn of 1911 increased its importance. All the latent antagonism towards the Anglo–Russian Entente amongst Liberals came to the surface. Grey had said that the Russians would honour the agreement, but they did not seem to be doing so, and Britain was, to say the least, acquiescing in the destruction of the Persian reform movement. The Radicals pressed successfully for a foreign affairs debate. Just three days in advance of it, the Foreign Office released the unpublished secret articles of the 1904 Entente.[72] In the debate on 27 November, Grey narrated the course of the Moroccan crisis and defended the part he had taken in it. On general grounds, he argued that no British Government would make secret agreements on matters of first-rate importance. No British Government could embark upon a war without public opinion behind it. British friendship with France and Russia was a guarantee that these powers would not act aggressively towards Germany, for they knew that British public opinion would not support them in such action. Germany was rightly proud of her strength, but it was natural that the growth of her fleet would arouse apprehensions. The kernel of his argument was that new friendships worth having were not made by deserting old ones.[73] The new Conservative leader, Bonar Law, following Grey, reiterated his party's determination 'to keep foreign affairs out of the scope of party politics'. He declared that 'the change in the leadership of our party makes no change in our attitude on foreign politics.[74]

It was then the turn of the Government's critics. Ramsay MacDonald rejected the principle of continuity. If previous policies were bad, there was nothing to be said for maintaining them. John Dillon, the Irish nationalist, claimed that when it was said that a satisfactory settlement had been reached, the only people whose satisfaction had not been considered were the Moroccans.[75] Other speakers made similar points about Persia. Noel Buxton wondered why it was not possible to bring about a rapprochement with Germany without in any way rupturing relations with France.[76] But while they attacked the Government on specific issues, most speakers had another theme: 'it is about time for this House to insist upon knowing something more about foreign affairs than it has done hitherto'.[77] Arthur Ponsonby made the same point in his attack on secrecy during the resumed debate on 14 December. What influence, he wanted to know, had Parliament exerted over the Moroccan crisis?[78] The question was largely rhetorical. The members were fully aware of the fact that it had been the Government which had permitted the debate and that the survey given by Grey was retrospective. The Radicals found that question-time offered insufficient scope for the fundamental analysis of foreign policy as a whole. They found Grey notably reluctant to burden the House with Blue Books. They also attacked the structure and composition of the Foreign Office, but at the same time had an uneasy suspicion that the more it was reformed, the more efficient it became, and the more influence it had over Ministers.[79] Parliament would once again be downgraded. Their cry was the perennial cry of the impotent back bencher. The previous thirty years had witnessed the tightening of parliamentary procedure, with the reduction of opportunities for extended debate and questioning. The rights of the private member were curtailed by the growth of party discipline and government management. Since both front benches were agreed on 'continuity', the field was left to the private member 'whose influence was as great as his authority was slight'.[80] The Radicals had a remedy for this situation in the creation of a Foreign Affairs Committee. Precise formulations varied, but the general idea was to appoint a group of about fifty members with power of scrutiny, who would, if necessary, interview the Foreign Secretary in secret session. Parliament would be reassured, while in turn the Cabinet would be more fully aware of the views of members. From 1912 onwards, some variant of this idea was regularly suggested by critics of the established policy-making process.[81] But both the Prime Minister and the Foreign Secretary resisted the idea and it made little progress. Once again, both front benches shared this view. When the matter was discussed in 1914 before a Commons select committee on procedure, Balfour declared that to give Parliament more power would be undesirable. He held that the basic reason for the decline in the fervour and frequency of foreign affairs debates was that there was now substantial inter-party agreement on foreign policy. It was a conclusion, of couse, which Ponsonby rejected.[82]

Yet while the Foreign Secretary undoubtedly faced his biggest public crisis in late 1911 and early 1912, his survival, and that of the Government, was never really in doubt. This was in part because, whatever he might say in public, in defence of his Near Eastern policy, he was in private far from pleased with Russian action. Moreover, in his dealings with St Petersburg, it was invaluable to him for the existence of a substantial volume of back-bench criticism to be known. He warned the Russian ambassador that the formal Russian military occupation of Northern Persia would mean a revision of the Anglo–Russian agreement. He reported the steps he had taken to the Cabinet, which agreed that the Russian demands for the removal of the American financial adviser to the Persian Government, Shuster, were 'not unreasonable' and could not be opposed.[83] Grey's passage was also helped by the fact that some of his fiercest critics, Loreburn for example, felt that the Persians were 'a miserable lot' and not worth spending much time on.

Partly because of disenchantment with Russia, Grey also recognized the advantages of détente with Germany. An opportunity arose when Churchill was invited to visit Berlin early in 1912. It was decided that Haldane should go instead, and the agenda for his conversations was drawn up by Haldane, Grey, Lloyd George and Churchill during January. Haldane did not, however, succeed in persuading the Germans to offer reduced naval estimates. He himself hinted that Britain might discuss the question *after* the conclusion of a non-aggression pact.[84] Haldane and Harcourt were most anxious that the negotiations should not lapse, and Grey was not only prepared to let them continue but showed an uncharacteristic lack of concern for French susceptibilities.[85] On 12 March, the Germans offered to withdraw the naval Novelle, if the British Cabinet would agree to a suitable political convention.[86] Grey and Haldane, who had seen Metternich, reported to their colleagues on 14 March that it seemed, at least for the moment, that Bethmann-Hollweg had got the better of Tirpitz, and that if Berlin was offered an acceptable 'formula', it would not press the controversial part of the new naval law. The question for the Cabinet was whether this 'formula' should include a promise of neutrality.[87] Harcourt and Haldane pressed Grey privately on 14 March to agree to such a clause, but Grey would not budge. The use of the word 'neutrality', would tie Britain's hands in the event of war, and would certainly alienate France.[88] The lobbying continued, but on 30 March, Asquith reported to the King that the latest German 'formula' was found to be 'full of equivocation and pitfalls' and further clarification was demanded.[89] The Prime Minister was becoming 'more and more doubtful as to the wisdom of prolonging these discussions with Germany about a formula. Nothing, I believe, will meet her purpose which falls short of a promise on our part of neutrality, a promise we cannot give.'[90] The talks broke down.

This failure did not mean that Grey abandoned the hopes of reducing Anglo–German tension. He had never been very sanguine about the chances of a direct naval agreement. More might be achieved by local agreements, such as those concerning colonies and the Baghdad Railway. In his speech in the House of Commons in November 1911, Grey was at pains to make clear that Britain had no further colonial ambitions in Africa. One of his critics, the Colonial Secretary, Harcourt, followed this up by urging, in December 1911, that 'Anglo–German relations could be permanently improved if we had "conversations" leading to exchanges of territory which might give Germany "a place in the sun" without injury to our Colonial or Imperial interests.'[91] Grey agreed that Portugal would do well to sell her colonies, and agreed that Harcourt should explore the possibilities throughout 1912. The negotiations on this complicated subject lasted until August 1913, when an agreement with Germany was initialled but never signed.[92] Grey was relieved when the Germans refused the conditions for publication because he felt that the proceedings were somewhat discreditable to Britain. In any case, the talks had now served his wider purpose.[93] Harcourt was less pleased with this final failure and, in an angry exchange of letters, accused Grey of possessing an unwavering pro-entente orientation.[94] But, while he did not wish to alter his relations with France and Russia, Grey's behaviour in this instance seems to show a greater willingness to risk their displeasure in the interests of a rapprochement with Germany than he had hitherto shown. Similarly, in 1913, the Baghdad Railway question, which had dragged on for years, was brought to a satisfactory conclusion as far as Britain and Germany were concerned. Britain did not oppose the Baghdad Railway system, which was to terminate at Basra. Germany did not oppose British control of the navigation of the Mesopotamian rivers and undertook not to establish a port or railway terminus on the Persian Gulf without British agreement. Equally, during the Balkan crisis in 1913, Grey deliberately set himself up as 'honest broker' – to the annoyance of the French and Russians, not to mention his own officials. As a result of all these moves, Anglo–German relations improved, though whether on a false basis is another matter.

However important this flanking strategy pursued by Grey, the fact remains that the naval question and Anglo–French relations obstinately remained at the centre of the stage. The breakdown of the Anglo–German naval and political talks in March 1912 led to a further reappraisal of the position, and to further controversy. Churchill continued to exude his prodigious enthusiasm for the Navy. He enunciated the new principle of a sixty per cent advantage in Dreadnoughts over Germany, as long as she adhered to her existing declared programme, and two keels to one for every additional ship she laid down.[95] Churchill proposed that the British battle fleet in the Mediterranean should be withdrawn and concentrated in future in the North Sea against Germany. He gave expense as the justification for this proposal; unless there was some concentration, the Navy Estimates would soar. The Admiralty hoped that the French would concentrate their fleet in the Mediterranean. The French requested talks on the naval question and the whole matter was discussed at various Cabinets in May and June. Churchill had to face opposition on various grounds. While some Foreign Office opinion welcomed the increased intimacy with France which such a transfer would necessarily involve, other officials lamented the loss of British influence in the Mediterranean. Grey himself stressed the close connexion between naval policy and general policy.[96] Haldane and the War Office correspondingly complained that a much greater military establishment would be needed to protect Britain's Mediterranean possessions.[97] McKenna, Morley and Harcourt claimed that the navy could continue to maintain its position without further increases in ships and without political intimacy with France.[98] At a specially summoned meeting of the C.I.D., on 4 July, no one supported Churchill completely and a formula was accepted whereby Britain pledged the maintenance of the one-power standard in the Mediterranean.[99] But some form of co-operation with France still seemed necessary and, after sharp debate, naval conversations were authorized on 13 July, though their non-binding nature was emphasized to the French.[100] Churchill began negotiations but, not unexpectedly, found the French unwilling to transfer their fleet without some pledge of intervention by Britain in a continental war. At the end of July, Churchill still felt the non-committal proviso, 'perfectly fair', but in August, while still feeling the need to safeguard 'our freedom of choice', he felt that 'we have the obligations of an alliance without its advantages, and above all without precise definitions.'[101] Grey, however, refused to give a pledge to France, pleading the ascendancy in the Cabinet of the anti-French group.[102] He was also aware of the pressure in the Liberal party against a formal alliance even if, as is doubtful, he himself favoured it. Eventually, in October and November 1912, the Cabinet thrashed out the formula put forward by Cambon to express the relations between the two countries. The famous Grey–Cambon exchange of letters of 22–3 November 1912 reiterated that consultation between experts did not commit the Governments.[103] This was a collective Cabinet decision. Dissent from it was surely a matter of resignation, but no resignation took place.

Against this background, it is probably true to say that the Cabinet was more united on foreign policy in 1913 than it had been for many years past. In this final period, there is little justification for Lloyd George's contention that 'The Cabinet as a whole were never called into genuine consultation upon the fundamental aspects of the foreign situation.'[104] No member of the Cabinet had any excuse for failing to be aware of the extent and nature of British commitments. Grey had appeased his critics to some degree – though in 1912–13 F. W. Hirst and Sir John Brunner were busy turning the National Liberal Federation into an anti-Grey organization. He opposed efforts to revive the naval conversations with Germany, not because he feared agreement, but because he was afraid that such talks only exacerbated Anglo–German relations. Not that he came to trust Germany. Whatever his irritation with Russian policy in Persia or with France, he was not going to give the Germans an easy victory by letting his relations with these Powers collapse. By and large, most of his colleagues shared this view. Indeed, Grey's personal position, as a result of his successful diplomacy during the Balkan crisis, was stronger than it had been for some time. Asquith reported to the King that Grey's colleagues had 'warmly congratulated' him on his skill in 'piloting the European ship through troubled waters'.[105]

There remained one further Cabinet crisis – again over Naval Estimates – before the arguments broke out over British intervention in the war. As in the other naval crises, the line-up of the Cabinet was different though the issue remained the same. When Churchill outlined his Naval Estimates in December

1913, the Cabinet would not accept them. He was made to produce a lower figure, although it was agreed that the supplementary estimate should be raised by £2½ million and that four capital ships (not the two the critics thought sufficient) should be laid down. Grey seems to have supported Churchill, though perhaps not as vigorously as Churchill had anticipated. Grey was annoyed by Lloyd George's interview on 1 January 1914 for the *Daily Chronicle*, in which he called for reduced estimates, on the grounds that Anglo–German relations were so good that a quarrel was unlikely. But his annoyance may well have been caused by Lloyd George's failure to consult him in advance rather than by the sentiments themselves.[106] Certainly, they exchanged friendly letters a few weeks later concerning German press exaggerations of the interview.[107] The Cabinet dispute was settled in February by an agreement between Churchill and Lloyd George, whereby the Estimates were to be increased in 1914, in return for a promise from Churchill that he would produce substantial savings in the following year. The other 'economists', Samuel, Hobhouse, Beauchamp, Pease, Runciman, McKenna and Simon, acquiesced.[108]

Perhaps the Cabinet had now returned to its 'proper balance'. In any case, it would seem that the seriousness of the Ulster situation prevented the row over the Estimates becoming too grave. Ireland dominated the Cabinet's time and energies in the two months before the outbreak of war. Foreign affairs were hardly touched on in Cabinet. There seemed little cause for anxiety about them. Bertie reported on 25 June 1914 that 'Grey thinks that the German Government are in a peaceful mood and that they are very anxious to be on good terms with England, a mood he wishes to encourage.'[109] The greatest challenge to the unity of the Cabinet was, of course, shortly to burst upon this scene of tranquillity. Yet, in recounting the history of the Liberal Cabinet's handling of foreign affairs, it is perhaps worth recalling the commonplace that conflict attracts more attention than co-operation. Writing to Lloyd George in the summer of 1913, Grey believed that the 'personal relations of all of us have not only stood the strain but have gained in attachment to an extent that must be very rare if not unprecedented in the history of Cabinets'.[110]

2

The Foreign Office
under Sir Edward Grey, 1905–1914

ZARA STEINER

It was under Sir Edward Grey that the Foreign Office reached the peak of its pre-war reputation. The diplomatic situation in which Britain found herself at the beginning of the twentieth century was far too intricate to be mastered by any one man. The days of Olympian detachment were clearly over and the relatively static world in which the country had once played the dominant role was rapidly disappearing. In almost every part of the globe the British were faced with an increasingly competitive commercial and political situation, while on the continent alterations in the relative strengths of the great powers were already creating new international tensions. Technical changes in armaments were occurring which, however, imperfectly understood, were reshaping diplomatic as well as domestic strategic calculations. The new divisions of these years proved so difficult and exacting a process that a new professionalism was needed in policy-making. The very range and complexity of the questions which had to be settled assured the Foreign Office an enhanced position within the governmental framework.

Grey was fully aware of these new dimensions. Though somewhat diffident at the start of his term at the Foreign Office. Grey rapidly gained in self-confidence and won not only the regard but the respect of his officials. He was industrious and carefully scrutinised the contents of his despatch boxes but the very pressure of events encouraged the new Foreign Secretary to seek advice and to listen closely to the counsels of his own department. Unlike Salisbury and Lansdowne, Grey sat in the Commons. Even when his parliamentary responsibilities were reduced to a minimum, they still remained numerous and time-consuming. Moreover, Grey found himself involved in the many domestic clashes of the period – the coal strike, the House of Lords debate and Ulster – and there were times when the daily business of the Foreign Office had to be left to others. Grey's personal qualities as well as the exigencies of the time opened the way for the permanent officials. He encouraged discussion and did not shrink from debate within the walls of the Foreign Office. Moreover, as his biographers have noticed, Grey was somewhat ambivalent about his public role. He was never totally at home in his Foreign Office room or in the Commons and his laments about the burdens of office became increasingly frequent after the Liberal success of 1910.

Trends within the Foreign Office accelerated the expansion of the role of the permanent officials. The introduction of the new registry system on 1 January 1906 represented a final step in the general modernisation of the department which had begun under Lansdowne.[1] The purely formal work of registering, indexing, copying and circulating despatches formerly done by members of the diplomatic establishment in the political departments was now performed by men of the second division staff in a Central and three Sub-Registries. This important administrative reform had two major purposes. It was to increase the efficiency of the Foreign Office which had been seriously over-taxed as the number of despatches and telegrams soared and the Treasury refused to sanction any significant increase in number of staff. Secondly, it was hoped that the members of the Diplomatic Establishment, now freed from their clerical functions, would take a more active part in the diplomatic concerns of the office. Senior officials would have the time to concentrate on their advisory functions while juniors were urged 'to take an active interest in their work and to develop political initiative and a sense of responsibility'.[2] An over-due alteration in the registering and docketing of papers gave the members of each political department an opportunity to express their views in the form of minutes and memoranda which went up the Foreign Office hierarchy and, if of any importance, were seen by Grey himself. A short minute by a junior was generally followed by a minute from the head of the department and the supervising under-secretary and Grey had at his command a constant source of written advice. The under-secretaries and senior clerks were encouraged to take their own decisions whenever this was possible.

It has been argued, with some justice, that the involvement of the junior clerks in the writing of despatches and the participation of the senior officials in the decision-making process predated the 1905–6 reforms.[3] This process of devolution would have undoubtedly continued without the introduction of the registry system and the active encouragement of Grey and the new permanent under-secretary, Charles Hardinge. Nevertheless, the Registry system did act as a catalyst which confirmed and accelerated earlier developments. Contemporaries attest to the changed atmosphere in the Foreign Office and the release from the more time-consuming work was warmly welcomed by the juniors. In regard to the writing of minutes and memoranda, what had once been a sporadic practice, more common in the non-European than in the European departments, became an established part of Foreign Office procedure. If the minutes by juniors were of limited importance, individuals did develop special areas of competence. Advice from more senior officials was treated with greater seriousness. It was up to Grey to accept or reject their suggestions but an additional source of information and advice was now available on a daily routine basis.

The men at the Foreign Office who served Grey varied considerably in importance and in ability. During the last years of Lansdowne's administration, a number of changes in personnel had brought a group of men with similar views into positions of prominence.[4] Thomas Sanderson, who had served for forty-seven years in the Foreign Office, retired and was replaced by Charles Hardinge, an energetic diplomat and a capable administrator who, from the start, was determined to have an active say in the direction of affairs. Sanderson had participated in the formulation of policy but he never considered his advisory role to be of paramount importance. This was to change under Hardinge. Similarly, both Salisbury and Lansdowne had been served by the same private secretary, Eric Barrington, Barrington, very much a figure of the old Foreign Office, had played a considerable part in the administration of the diplomatic service particularly with regard to assignments and promotions. He rarely discussed political questions with his chiefs and did not consider his views to be relevant to the actual course of policy. Grey's private secretaries, Louis Mallet and William Tyrrell, saw their roles in a different light. Mallet openly tried to influence Grey and Tyrrell became Grey's closest Foreign Office confidant and played, as will be shown, a crucial diplomatic role during the last years of peace. If the assistant under-secretaries of the non-European departments were still accorded a greater measure of independence than their European colleagues, one Foreign Office figure, Eyre Crowe, first as senior clerk and then as an assistant under-secretary, voiced his views clearly in a continuous series of minutes and memoranda which were always read by his seniors with attention if not with full agreement.

Hardinge, Mallet, Tyrrell and Crowe as well as other less prominent personalities provided an excellent reservoir of talent for the Foreign Secretary. It is important to realise, however, that Grey and almost all of his senior officials shared a common view of Britain's diplomatic position. The very factors which made a greater division of responsibility inevitable also determined the main outlines of Foreign Office thinking. Few of these men believed any longer in the fixity or security of Britain's world stance. Most assumed that the older concepts of the European concert of power would have to take into account the rise and decline of the member states. In their awareness of Britain's exposed position and in their belief that Britain's safety rested on a powerful fleet and on agreements with France and Russia, the Foreign Secretary and his office were at one. Though they might differ on specific solutions, there was general agreement that Germany was the power most likely to upset the status quo and that such a change could only be to Britain's detriment. This basic reading of the European situation underlined the cooperation of Grey with his officials and also limited the range of possible responses in the period between 1905 and 1914. Imperial problems which had so pre-occupied Grey's predecessor, though still of some moment, were no longer at the centre of Foreign Office concern and were rarely considered in isolation but against the background of the European balance of power. In this respect, too, Grey and his officials acted on a common set of shared assumptions.

Nor were these views restricted to Whitehall. The men appointed by Lansdowne and Grey, Francis Bertie at Paris, Arthur Nicolson at St Petersburg, Edward Goschen first at Vienna and then at Berlin and Fairfax Cartwright in Vienna, were even more outspoken in their suspicion of German ambitions, and in their support for the policies of the ententes. The exceptions at home and abroad were few. Lord Fitzmaurice, Grey's parliamentary undersecretary from 1905 until 1908, remained more deeply concerned with the advance of Russia in Central Asia than with the threat posed by a restless Germany and an enlarged German fleet.[5] In Berlin, Frank Lascelles, ambassador from 1895 until 1908, continued to work for a rapprochement with Germany even after it became clear that his interventions were scarcely welcomed by his London colleagues. Ralph Paget, a younger man of undoubted ability, was suspected by Hardinge of an over-optimistic view of German intentions and was sent off to Belgrade until the climate of opinion shifted. A few individuals, particularly those who had to deal directly with the Russians in Central Asia, were more irritated by Russian aggression than by German blackmail. In the case of Cecil Spring Rice, who was to become minister in Persia, this distaste increased his dislike of the German who had forced the British 'to sup with the devil'. Those who opposed the prevailing mood at the Foreign Office were acutely conscious of their isolation. Sanderson left the office early in 1906 though he was to repeat his warnings of the dangers of the new anti-German mood in his commentary on Crowe's memorandum of 1907. Fitzmaurice felt that he could only indirectly influence Grey (through Lord Ripon) and welcomed his promotion to Lord Privy Seal in 1908. Lascelles' recommendations were often disregarded and the Foreign Office was pleased to be able to replace him in 1908 with the more sympathetic Goschen.

How far did the Foreign Office and Diplomatic Service influence the Foreign Secretary? Can one reach any positive conclusions about the contributions of the senior officials to the making of policy? The relationship between minister and civil servant was clearly understood. The Foreign Secretary determined and was responsible for the conduct of British foreign relations. In practice, the civil servants were making decisions which in previous years had been reserved to the Foreign Secretary but even those most conscious of this altering balance never challenged the ultimate division of authority. The influence of the officials was exercised within the Foreign Office hierarchy and no civil servant, no matter how highly placed, would have pursued an independent policy in direct opposition to Grey's wishes. Diplomats, particularly those stationed outside of Europe, might stretch the limits of their discretion until the Foreign Office actively intervened. But there was no 'eminence grise' at Whitehall and only limited scope for any individual with such ambitions. The point is an important one, for elsewhere, particularly in Berlin, this fundamental fact was sometimes ignored and the real springs of British diplomacy somewhat misunderstood.

Though Grey enjoyed a very special position within the Liberal party, he was faced with a far from united cabinet whose differences extended to foreign policy issues. In general, he could successfully maintain his own course but the frequent if sporadic interventions of his colleagues were of considerable importance in determining Grey's tactics. Grey was acutely conscious of the boundaries within which he had to operate. Some of the daily differences between Grey and his senior officials resulted from Grey's greater awareness of these political parameters. Foreign Office officials were, for the most part, jealous of the prerogatives of their department and suspicious of the intervention of outsiders whether they were politicians, journalists or members of other departments. Grey was the bridge between this self-conscious professional elite and the wider political framework within which both he and the Foreign Office had to operate. Grey was the final court of appeal for the civil servant in the Foreign Office; there were very few occasions when outside support was solicited. On the contrary, cabinet government reinforced the administrative restrictions on the members of the Foreign Office.

A study of the role of the Foreign Office really implies a study of specific individuals and policies. If it is taken for granted that the permanent officials operated within a defined area of responsibility, some generalisations about the decision-making process can be reached. The most important personage at the Foreign Office remained the permanent under-secretary. Charles Hardinge exploited the traditional powers of his office and took full advantage of the new opportunities resulting from Grey's willingness to consult his advisors. Freed from direct departmental responsibilities by the 1905–6 reform, Hardinge could concentrate on more general administrative and diplomatic problems. The permanent under-secretary became the main channel of communication between Grey, the Office and the diplomats. Almost all important despatches (particularly those from the Eastern and Western departments) were seen by Hardinge before they were forwarded to Grey. It was Hardinge rather than the Foreign Secretary who maintained regular contact with British diplomats abroad. Whereas Grey's letters did not compare in volume or in importance with those of his predecessors, Hardinge's long, detailed explanations make Sanderson's irregular and short notes seem insignificant. The return correspondence also came to Hardinge, though key letters were seen by Grey and even by the Prime Minister. Hardinge's access to these various sources of outside information placed him in a central position.

The new head of the Foreign Office was a seasoned diplomat and Grey respected his knowledge and political tact. The two men discussed many general topics in private; the Foreign Secretary was to miss these informal conversations when Hardinge left for India. It is indicative of Hardinge's position that he should have known about the military conversations with France before either the C.I.D. or most of the cabinet were informed of these proceedings.[6] Grey utilised Hardinge's royal connections and trips with Edward VII to explore possibilities difficult to raise through the usual diplomatic channels. Hardinge's interviews with the Kaiser and Franz Joseph as well as his conversations with their foreign secretaries were useful to a man who, like most foreign secretaries of his time, did not travel and was somewhat shy of royal encounters. Grey never resented Hardinge's closeness to the King nor did he object to that slightly imperious tone which so irritated Hardinge's subordinates.[7] Hardinge's comments were read with care and disagreements were argued out with a minimum of personal friction. For his part, Hardinge was loyal to Grey though he was less than enthusiastic about the Liberal government and distrustful of Asquith whom he never liked.[8] He appreciated Grey's difficult cabinet position and was particularly careful to avoid any hint of disagreement at the Foreign Office. It was certainly to Grey's advantage that his chief advisor had a keen sense of politics and that the latter's suggestions were framed with an eye to the possible as well as to the desirable. 'Hardinge himself is not a courtier', wrote Cecil Spring Rice, 'but is a good business man and perfectly fearless and decided.'[9]

Hardinge reached the peak of his diplomatic career during this pre-war period. His views like those of Grey, had already been formulated before he came back to London from St Petersburg and soon became the prevailing Foreign Office orthodoxy. He believed that the German naval-building programme represented an intended challenge to British supremacy at sea and, in subsequent years, repeatedly returned to the brief that this supremacy was a 'condition which must be regarded as an absolute sine qua non'.[10] This was Britain's ultimate weapon; the French entente and any future agreement with Russia would serve only to give British diplomacy greater strength and flexibility in Europe and in the Middle East. According to Hardinge there was but one response to the German naval laws and that was a clear demonstration of Britain's overwhelming naval superiority. If Germany were sincere in her declarations of pacific intent, the German naval programme would be cut and Britain's control of the seas acknowledged. The German army was already the strongest in Europe: a decision to build a great navy as well could only be received as an indication of aggressive intent.

Hardinge's willingness to engage in some form of dialogue with the Germans, despite the dangers of entanglement, was based on an accurate assessment of the strength of the radicals. The passage of a supplementary German naval law in January 1906 led to the first of a series of sharp cabinet disputes which at various times seriously strained the unity of the government. Hardinge knew that Grey could not turn a deaf ear to this pressure. The permanent under-secretary, undoubtedly at Grey's request, raised the naval question with the Kaiser at Cronberg in 1908 though with little success. He concluded that the German government left the Liberals no choice but to go on building more ships. Even after the victory of the 'big navalists', continued intervention by Lloyd George and Churchill indicated that the battle was far from won.

The most dramatic phase in this chapter of the naval quarrel occurred at the end of 1908 when rumours circulated that the Germans were accelerating their building programme. Hardinge and Grey believed these rumours to be true and the former even distrusted the compromise solution won by Asquith in February. Hardinge felt the government would not commission the approved eight ships and believed Grey had been bested by Churchill.[11] Subsequent events proved Hardinge erroneous in his judgement but confirmed his reading of the domestic situation. He was clearly surprised (given the public outcry and mutual recriminations of 1909) when in the spring of that year the Germans began to campaign for an agreement between the two countries. Hardinge thought that an Anglo-German entente would serve only to open the way for German control over the continent of Europe but he rightly predicted that this new approach would encourage the radical campaign for an agreement with Berlin. On 30 April, therefore, he sent a circular letter to all heads of missions instructing them not to use the phrase 'triple entente' in despatches as 'some of the Cabinet Ministers are a little sensitive on the subject and think it might offend Germany'.[12] Early in May, considering a new approach from the German embassy, Hardinge concluded that a renewal of negotiations would lead to further pressure for cuts in the naval construction programme. Yet, unlike some of his subordinates, Hardinge was again realistic enough to realise that Grey could not afford to ignore German hints and that some positive benefit might be derived from a genuine naval compact. Hardinge and Grey were agreed on their goals. Any such arrangement must leave Britain's naval edge intact and must not encourage Germany to proceed as she wished on the European continent.

It was political realism rather than optimism which led Hardinge to examine Bethmann-Hollweg's proposals in August 1909. The former prepared a long memorandum for Grey's use in which he outlined a declaration of pacific policy towards Germany which would preserve the existing balance of power. Hardinge's formula was a fine example of diplomatic finesse but it could scarcely have satisfied the Germans. Bethmann-Hollweg's reply on 14 October did not encourage further exchanges. Neither an offer of slowing down the rate of naval construction nor a Baltic agreement type of arrangement was acceptable to the Foreign Office. Political events in London prevented further talks. The permanent under-secretary was delighted with the election results; the moderate wing of the Liberal party had been strengthened and the pro-navy men had won a decisive victory. Yet the Germans again returned to the charge in the spring of 1910 with a proposal for a neutrality formula and an accommodation on the Baghdad railway and Persian questions. As Hardinge remained convinced that Germany was the only element of danger to the peace of Europe, the possibility of renewed conversations filled him with alarm. 'I fully believe in the theory of Germany's intention, if possible, to dominate

Europe to which we are the only stumbling block',[13] Hardinge wrote to his hand-picked successor, Arthur Nicolson.

From the start, the Russian entente had for Hardinge both a European and a Middle Eastern importance. Hardinge and Nicolson predicted that Russia would soon be able to put her finances in order and rebuild her army. A Germany hemmed in between Russia and France might be discouraged from embarking on an ambitious policy in Europe. In the Middle East, Anglo–Russian cooperation was essential. 'Our whole future in Asia is bound up with the possibility of maintaining the best and most friendly relations with Russia', Hardinge argued when defending the new entente.[14] He had gone after all, to St Petersburg in 1904 to lay the groundwork for this understanding and it was one of the chief reasons why he had accepted the under-secretaryship in 1905. He played a crucial role in the drafting of the terms of the conventions and his contribution to its success was fully acknowledged by Grey and Nicolson. Already in 1907, Hardinge suggested that the King should meet the Tsar at Reval as a gesture of goodwill. Despite Grey's doubts, the Cabinet's hesitation and a public uproar, the meeting between the monarchs was a success and Hardinge used the occasion for a friendly and far-reaching talk with Isvolsky not only about the Macedonian reform question but about the military role Russia could play on the continent of Europe. Hardinge clearly encouraged Isvolsky to think of the relations between Britain and Russia in the same terms as those which existed between London and Paris.[15]

There were difficulties. The cabinet was less enthusiastic than the permanent under-secretary; the entente was unpopular with the radical wing of the Liberal party, with the Labour party and even with sections of the Conservative party. If these domestic problems could be ignored, there were crucial areas in which Anglo–Russian interests did not coincide and which needed to be carefully watched if the entente was to survive. Events in Persia, in Turkey and, above all, in the Balkans were to tax Hardinge's patience and ingenuity. Persia, in particular, absorbed a disproportionate amount of Grey's and Hardinge's energies. The truth was that the Russians had the upper hand in this decaying state. The Persian convention had salvaged for the British what Grey believed was the most essential requirements for the safety of the Persian Gulf and India. Nevertheless, Grey was pledged, as were the Russians, to the maintenance of the independence of Persia and he could not permit a formal division into spheres of influence or a Russian take-over at Tehran. Russian intervention at the capital provoked numerous embarrassing questions in Parliament and Hardinge admitted 'we have had to suppress the truth and resort to subterfuge at times to meet hostile public opinion'.[16] At first, German interference in Persia helped strengthen the new Anglo–Russian partnership and Hardinge was optimistic about the future. Soon, however, revolutionary troubles divided the two partners who supported opposing factions. Hardinge had no doubts about the proper order of priorities. He was willing to pay a high price in Persia to maintain the agreement though even he became increasingly annoyed as repeated quarrels at Tehran embittered Anglo–Russian relations. During 1910, disorders broke out in the south; British traders complained that the weaknesses of the central government were due to the Russian occupation of the north. Grey's protests only irritated the Russians and the Foreign Secretary moderated in private what he said in public. The British and Russian ministers quarrelled openly in Persia and at one point Hardinge feared for the safety of the entente. These worries were magnified when rumours of a meeting between the Russian and German Emperors began to circulate through the European chancelleries.

More crucial to the entente than the perennial question of Persia were the problems raised by events in Constantinople and in the Balkans. Britain's traditional policy of supporting Turkey had to be brought in line with the improvement of relations with Russia. As the British were out of favour with the Sultan's government, Hardinge felt it might be possible to take a stronger hand in the Balkans than earlier. In fact, during 1908, the permanent undersecretary encouraged Grey to ignore the concert and to support a joint Anglo-Russian policy in Macedonia. Hardinge believed that Britain should exploit the rift in Austro-Russian relations and use the question of the Macedonian reforms to cement the newly created entente.[17] His hopes proved to be ill-founded and he was only too pleased when the Young Turk revolution of 1908 temporarily brought the Macedonian problem to an end.

Both Hardinge and Grey welcomed the Young Turk revolution and hoped to see a restoration of the British position in Turkey. 'We intend to do all we can to be on the best of terms with a strong and regenerate Turkey', Hardinge wrote Bertie.[18] Yet even before the annexationist crisis, it had become difficult to maintain the links with both Turkey and Russia. The crisis itself brought the British to the Russian side. Whatever his reservations about Isvolsky, Hardinge argued that it was essential to assist the Russian minister in all possible ways. He and Grey prodded the cabinet to find some face-saving answer to the Russian demand for a revision of the Straits Convention and a compromise was finally secured. Yet this was not enough to satisfy the Russians. Hardinge might rail against 'that wretched little Serbia who is bent on mischief' but he knew that Grey would have to champion her cause to conciliate St Petersburg.

At the same time, the British wanted to help Turkey. Hardinge, like other Foreign Office officials, hoped to encourage the formation of a Balkan bloc based on an agreement between Turkey and Bulgaria which would 'spell checkmate' to Aehrenthal's policy of establishing Austrian supremacy in the Balkans. Much to Hardinge's disgust, the Turks refused to cooperate and the British ambassador in Constantinople bore the brunt of Hardinge's irritation.[19] By early 1909, a war between Austria and Bulgaria against Turkey and Serbia seemed inevitable. Above all, London wanted peace in the Balkans.

Accordingly, backed by Hardinge, Grey turned down a Turkish bid for an alliance and, with more reluctance, parried a Russian enquiry as to the British position in a Balkan struggle. Hardinge feared that if the Turks were beaten, the British navy would have to defend Constantinople. Worse still, if Serbia were attacked, the Russians would intervene and the Anglo–Russian entente severely strained. Hardinge might hint that it would be difficult for Britain to stay out of a general war but he knew that the cabinet would never sanction involvement in a Balkan clash.

Under such circumstances it is not surprising that Hardinge welcomed all peace moves and that he became increasingly irritated with the Turkish government which proved unexpectedly intransigent about accepting them. To add to Hardinge's discomfiture, the Russians raised questions about British loyalty in the Near East. Grey was furious and Hardinge found Ivolsky's attitude 'very trying'.[20] Neither at home nor abroad did the situation look particularly encouraging and Hardinge began to search for a way of retreat. As each of Hardinge's suggestions proved unsatisfactory, he and Grey realised that Serbia (for whom they had little pity and even less sympathy) would have to be sacrificed though the decision had to be disguised to avoid offending the Russians. Fortunately for them, Isvolsky, too, urged Serbia to drop her demands for territorial compensation. Hardinge's bitterness over Russia's final capitulation to Germany hardly masked his ultimate relief that peace and the entente had been preserved.

British policy had suffered a set-back despite Hardinge's efforts to gloss over the effects of the protracted crisis. Anglo–Turkish relations were seriously damaged. Hardinge came to accept Lowther's pessimistic appraisal of the young Turks who had proved to be as dictatorial and pro-German as the old leaders. The new government refused to cooperate with the British either in the Persian Gulf or on the Baghdad railway question and this stand in turn complicated Anglo–German relations in a way which Hardinge deplored. At St Petersburg, the British reaped little reward for their anti-Austrian stance during the annexationist crisis and Hardinge was forced to calm Nicolson who was convinced that the Russians would desert the entente and settle with the Germans. The crisis had shown the limited nature of British support and the impossibility of turning the entente into an alliance. Hardinge's memorandum of May 1909, drawn up at Grey's request, summed up the existing situation in the most realistic terms.[21] He argued that an alliance with Russia was neither necessary nor desirable and that British public opinion would never accept such a binding engagement with the Tsarist regime. Fortunately, even in the face of European isolation, Britain's safety would be secured by her naval supremacy. Hardinge admitted that the present position was fraught with difficulties and dangers but the existing ententes remained the best possible arrangements under the prevailing political and diplomatic conditions. The alternative – an arrangement with Germany – was far more perilous for the nation's safety. The understanding with Russia was to be maintained but it need not be strengthened. 'My sole aim is to keep things going on the present lines so long as this present Government remains in office', Hardinge wrote to the uneasy ambassador.[22]

It was during these years that people outside the Foreign Office began to speak of its influence. W. T. Stead and E. D. Morel, in particular, singled Hardinge out as the object of their attacks. They charged that Grey had lost control of his department and was dominated by his permanent officials and that Hardinge was unduly influencing the course of Grey's diplomacy. Stead attributed the failure of the Second Hague Peace Conference to the power of the Foreign Office while Morel concentrated his efforts on securing Hardinge's support for his campaign over the Belgian Congo. When the Foreign Office wavered, Morel attacked the permanent under-secretary and the whole system by which policy was formulated and executed. Yet there is little evidence that Hardinge persuaded Grey to follow any course which the latter disliked or seriously questioned.[23] It is true that the partnership between Grey and Hardinge was more one of equals than of chief and subordinate. The bond which connected them, however, was a general concurrence of views both in regard to Germany and Russia. The strength of their relationship rested on a similar reading of the European and imperial scenes and in their almost identical order of priorities. Hardinge was a powerful figure at Whitehall but he did not dominate Grey nor did he shape Grey's thinking or policies.

Hardinge was in a unique position; the permanent under-secretary, since the days of Lord Hammond, had enjoyed a special relationship with the Foreign Secretary. But even at the next level of the Foreign Office there were men who, while less influential than Hardinge, contributed to the shaping of Grey's diplomacy. The pressure of events and the complications of the British position abroad had created a need for professional advice which had led inevitably to a further devolution of responsibility. The private secretary and the assistant under-secretaries all extended their spheres of action with regard to the daily business of their departments. Louis Mallet, Grey's first private secretary, had been appointed in 1905 as a result of Hardinge's promptings. Mallet's political views were well-known. He had urged Grey to underwrite the French during the Algeciras Conference and was subsequently obsessed by the fear that the French or Russians would take umbrage at any Anglo–German conversations.[24] With his promotion to an under-secretaryship (again sponsored by Hardinge against some internal opposition) in 1907, Mallet became involved in the affairs of the Eastern and American departments. His general opinions did not alter. He continued to forecast a German bid for the supremacy of Europe and he was even more outspoken than Hardinge in his condemnation of talks with Berlin. Mallet had warmly welcomed the French entente and later argued that the Russian agreement was even more essential to Britain than to Russia. His many minutes on Balkan and

Middle Eastern affairs suggest that Mallet was unduly suspicious of German intervention and tended to exaggerate the dependence of Vienna on Berlin. In both areas, he underwrote Hardinge's pro-Russian orientation. Nevertheless, he was fully aware of the fragility of the link with St Petersburg and ultimately preferred to rely on the French connection as an obstacle to German power and as an insurance policy against a Russo–German bargain.

Mallet was yet another Foreign Office voice pointing out the dangers of German ambitions and the necessity of the entente policies. Yet he was increasingly absorbed in the technical problems in his departments. Questions raised by the Macedonian reforms, the Turco–Persian frontier dispute, concessions in Mesopotamia and relations with the Emir of Afghanistan left little time for general speculation. Mallet was to some extent overshadowed by Hardinge who took such an active part in these matters; there are few important despatches which do not carry minutes from both men. The two were generally in agreement but Mallet undoubtedly played the secondary role.

This is not true of F. A. Campbell, the assistant under-secretary who supervised the Far Eastern department. Campbell was Grey's chief advisor on Far Eastern affairs until his death in December 1911. His department had always enjoyed a large measure of independence and, except in moments of crisis, previous Foreign Secretaries had allowed its head a good deal of initiative. Though the area had ceased to be the storm centre for European rivalries, the British remained in a defensive position in both economic and political terms and there was a great deal of diplomatic activity throughout the Liberal period. Grey took a close interest in these developments and all the broad policy decisions were his own. Nevertheless, he relied heavily on Campbell (who had been senior clerk and assistant under-secretary in the department since the days of Lord Salisbury) for advice and guidance. Campbell wrote most of the key memoranda and handled the negotiations with the Hongkong and Shanghai Bank and other firms active in this area. There was a whole range of secondary questions which Campbell settled directly with John Jordan, the minister in China, or with Claude Macdonald, the ambassador in Tokio. Numerous letters were exchanged with the diplomats in the Far East paralleling Hardinge's correspondence with European-based diplomats. As railway concessions and loans dominated both Chinese and Japanese relations with Britain, it was inevitable that Campbell and the local British representative should enjoy key positions in the daily decision-making process.

Campbell's view of British interests in China coincided with those of Grey.[25] Both wanted to uphold British commercial interests particularly in the Yangtse Valley and yet wished to avoid dismemberment of the country. Even before the Liberals came to power, Campbell had welcomed international financial cooperation and had encouraged the formation of an Anglo–French group to invest in Chinese railways. The assistant under-secretary felt that given the reluctance of British capitalists to invest in China, a multinational approach to the building of railways was essential for the promotion of British trade. Though Campbell shared Foreign Office fears about Germany's future intentions, he acquiesced in the admission of Germany to the Anglo–French group in 1909. Economic considerations would have to prevail over diplomatic preferences. When international cooperation failed to serve British commercial interests, Campbell took a firmer stand. For instance, he advised against the admission of the United States to the Three Power Consortium in 1909, though events forced him to abandon his opposition. In general, Campbell's advice was for multi-national participation and his arguments influenced Grey in this direction. The under-secretary even succeeded in temporarily convincing the influential Jordan who, however, remained deeply suspicious about the intentions of all financiers (particularly the Hongkong and Shanghai Bank) not to speak of the political ambitions of other nations and would have preferred a more assertive stand.

Walter Langley who had served under Campbell in the Far Eastern department became an assistant under-secretary in 1907. He was first placed in charge of the Western department though he occasionally substituted for Campbell and took over the latter's post in 1912. Langley too, believed that the real danger to peace lay with Berlin and that the maintenance of the ententes was essential for preserving the status quo. He expected little to result from either the 1909 or 1910 talks with Berlin and was to continue to deprecate all such efforts in the period before the war. He was, however, inclined to defer to his senior clerk, Eyre Crowe, and rarely amended Crowe's far more detailed and conclusive minutes. His tone was more moderate than Crowe's though his advice pointed in the same direction. Campbell took an active part in handling the many disputes with France which punctuated Anglo–French relations throughout this period – Madagascar, New Hebrides, Newfoundland fishing rights and above all Morocco. His irritation with France mounted as it became clear that she was approaching Germany for a sharing of the economic spoils to the exclusion of Britain. Langley listened sympathetically to Spanish complaints against French policy in Morocco but conceded that 'we cannot throw the French overboard to please Spain'. In Langley's eyes, the entente with France was far too important to be compromised however unwelcome French behaviour might be. Langley was a perfectly competent civil servant though he played a minor and supporting role.

The same generalisations may be made of the two other assistant under-secretaries serving under Hardinge. Eric Barrington held only a brief (eighteen months) appointment just prior to retirement. Barrington supervised the Western and African departments but left few minutes and made little impact on policy. His promotion was a reward for past services. It also cleared the way for Mallet's appointment as Grey's private secretary. Eldon Gorst, the remaining under-secretary, was expected to take a leading role at the office. When he first came to the department in 1904 (having been sent by Cromer from Egypt to assist in the Anglo–French negotiations) he was spoken of as a possible replacement for the ailing Sanderson. Yet Gorst was very much an 'outside man' and though highly intelligent never lived up to the expectations of his contemporaries. He did the usual work of an under-secretary in the American and Eastern departments but almost all of his minutes were restricted to points of immediate concern. Gorst's appointment to succeed Cromer in Cairo in 1907 ended his London career.

The senior clerks continued to be the Foreign Office specialists. These were men who had come up the Foreign Office ladder and who remained in these positions for eight or more years. They saw that drafts were properly prepared (routine drafting was now done in the sub-registries) and that directions for future action were properly carried out. They read the despatches and their juniors' comments and added their own minutes if the papers had to go further up the Foreign Office hierarchy. Suggestions made by senior clerks carried a special weight. Men like R. P. Maxwell (who refused an assistant under-secretaryship) and Arthur Larcom in the Eastern and American departments were experienced and knowledgeable. Walter Langley and Beilby Aston knew almost as much about Far Eastern matters as their supervisory under-secretaries. Algernon Law, a dull man and a strict disciplinarian, who ran the Commercial and Sanitary department and Lord Dufferin, a 'kindly, well-meaning but lethargic official with a passion for neatness and red ink', were the main links between the Foreign Office and consular service.[26] Eyre Crowe, appointed as senior clerk in the Western department at the start of 1906 carved out a special position for himself. He had previously served as Sir Clement Hill's assistant in the African Protectorates department. When this department was disbanded (the Protectorates were handed over to the Colonial Office), Crowe, instead of being re-assigned to the Consular depart-ment which needed an assistant, was asked to solve the practical administrative problems created by the introduction of the Registry system. In the winter of 1906, Crowe became the driving force behind the new reforms. His efforts brought promotion to senior clerk and an assignment to the Western Depart-ment followed. Within a year, Crowe had become the leading expert on German affairs.[27] He was totally bi-lingual, having been born and raised in Germany until his father's transfer to Paris as commercial attache for Europe. Through his mother, and wife, he was related to Admiral von Holtzendorf and other members of the German establishment, with whom he was in constant contact. His knowledge gave his minutes and memoranda an authority unusual even for a senior clerk. Except when he was absent, there was hardly an important despatch from Germany which escaped Crowe's attention. As he was particularly interested in military and naval matters his services were also utilised during the Second Hague Peace Conference and than at the International Maritime Conference which produced the abortive Declaration of London.

Because German affairs were the major pre-occupation of the Foreign Office during these years, Crowe's advice merited special attention. He was undoubtedly, the most logical and consistent believer in the German threat to the peace of Europe and the security of the British Empire. He was fully aware of Germany's power and the sources of its political and social malaise. His minutes often reflected impatience with the naivety of his own countrymen who either under-estimated German strength or failed to understand what had happened on the European continent since 1871. Crowe's memorandum of 1907 was read with approval by Grey and Hardinge and was considered significant enough to be circulated to a small circle of politicians (Asquith, Morley, Ripon and Haldane), and officials. Crowe argued that Germany would not be content with her current European position but would strive to alter it using the methods and tactics which had brought her to her great-power status. Such a change would not only upset the European balance of power but would challenge Britain's imperial position. Crowe did not argue that Berlin was consciously aiming at world domination but that, given her Bismarckian inheritance, and a weak, vacillating and confused government, she might well resort to force to establish her primacy. Crowe's reasoning led him to contrast the Pax Britannica, based on naval power, with a German conquest of Europe by arms in the Prussian tradition.

It is true that Crowe was not anti-German in any narrow sense of the word and that he had a high opinion of Germany's cultural inheritance as well as her economic resources and managerial capabilities. But his advice, based on a realistic appraisal of German ambitions, left little room for any accommodation with this growing and restless power. Crowe thought that any change in the status quo could only take place at British expense. From his review of Germany's conduct in the past, Crowe concluded that the Germans would push as far and as hard as they could and that this pressure must be resisted. He wrote, 'to give way to the blackmailer's menace enriches him, but it had been proved by uniform experience that, although this may secure for the victim temporary peace, it is certain to lead to renewed molestation and higher demands after ever shortening periods of amicable forebearance'.[28] Elsewhere, Crowe was to argue that British commerce had much to learn from German practice and that trade rivalry was not an unhealthy sign. But in the diplomatic world the status quo had to be maintained and British rights and interests upheld with 'unbending determination'. The balance-of-power doctrine which Crowe restated in this powerfully argued 1907 memorandum was based on a static conception of world power which contrasted sharply with Crowe's own highly developed historical perspective. It reveals the strongly defensive cast of mind which characterised so many of the clerks and diplomats of this period. The older view, as shown in Thomas Sanderson's critique of Crowe's memorandum, exhibited a greater flexibility and a striking awareness of the need to find room for a restless power who always found the British lion in her path.[29] In fact, the room for manoeuvre had become too constricted for Sanderson's hopes to be realised; the dangers of German pressure evoked a sharp and negative response from the Foreign Office.

From the time he came to the Western Department, Crowe's minutes were read with attention and respect, Hardinge rarely challenged his analyses of German behaviour and Langley deferred to his judgement. Crowe's critiques of Lascelles, the sympathetic ambassador at Berlin, were echoed by Hardinge and Grey. His critical comments on reports from the military and naval attachés stationed in Germany were forwarded to their respective service ministries. His memoranda were often circulated to the members of the Cabinet. Though Crowe was not to have an easy time within the Foreign Office, his intellectual ability and fearless expositions commanded wide admiration.

Crowe was entirely consistent in his attitude towards Berlin. He saw in the German challenge at Morocco a strong bid to break up the Anglo–French entente and applauded the firm stand taken by Grey during the Algeciras Conference. He had little sympathy with those anxious to seek a rapprochement with Germany on naval questions and bitterly resented Lloyd George's intervention in foreign affairs during 1908. Crowe's experience at the Hague and during the maritime conference in London convinced him that the German fleet was intended as a challenge to Britain. But he did not exaggerate the importance of this rivalry. Unlike Hardinge, Crowe saw the naval race as only an outward symptom of Germany's determination to establish her hegemony in Europe. He was, therefore, less patient than Hardinge or Grey with an accommodation on the naval issue in return for some form of political arrangement. In fact, he believed that any attempt to reach such a compromise was doomed to failure. 'I believe we must reckon with it as a hard fact that whatever the cost the German government will build the big and powerful navy...which they have so systematically planned.'[30] Crowe understood that the navy, far more than the army, had a wide social appeal and that the domestic situation in Germany made it 'quite certain that no responsible German statesman – with the possible exception of a second Bismarck – could carry through a policy which would involve a repeal of the German Navy Act'. He deplored radical pressure for an arrangement with Berlin during the spring of 1909 and repeatedly criticised Bethmann-Hollweg's proposals in the following year.

When assessing Crowe's influence it is important to stress that though his intimate knowledge of German affairs and crystal-clear presentation of his views gave him a special place in the Foreign Office hierarchy, he was only a senior clerk. Even when his minutes were approved, his advice was not always followed. Grey did not accept his clerk's proposals during the Algeciras Conference nor did he cut off negotiations in 1909 or in 1910 which Crowe thought useless and dangerous. Grey was, of course, responding to political pressures with which Crowe had little concern or patience. Grey and even

Hardinge saw the German problem against a wider framework. Crowe repeatedly urged decisive action; Grey tended to draw back from final steps. This difference in approach was not restricted to German affairs. Crowe handled many of the disputes with France and though a warm supporter of the entente was often irritated by French behaviour both in Newfoundland waters and in Morocco. But when he urged Grey to take a firmer line, the latter often refused to follow his lead, always more concerned with the ultimate implications of the quarrel than its immediate solution. Hardinge was the intermediary between Crowe and Grey. Until 1913, the senior clerk showed little interest in Russian affairs and took no role in the conflicts in the Balkans or in the Middle East. His centre of concern was Western Europe.

Crowe's focus was a narrow one albeit one which reinforced Grey's own order of concern. As in the case of Hardinge, Crowe's views, sharply defined and cogently argued, reflecting the prevailing attitude at the senior levels of the Foreign Office. But Grey could not share Crowe's rigid appraisal of the future course of Anglo–German relations however much he might agree with his clerk's basic premises. It is important to see Crowe within a Foreign Office context. Senior clerks, however able, were not the final determiners of policy and Crowe's influence on Grey has been considerably exaggerated.[31]

'I am sorry to hear that the anti-German current still flows and I can only hope that no incidents will arise to increase its strength', Lascelles wrote to Fitzmaurice in the autumn of 1906.[32] His hopes proved illusory. Hardinge, Mallet, Crowe and to a lesser extent Langley and Campbell concurred in their suspicious appraisal of German intentions and subsequent events only served to confirm them in their beliefs. Another influential figure at the Foreign Office, William Tyrrell, Grey's precis-writer (1905–7) and then private secretary (1907–15) must also be counted in this group. Long before Grey took office, the private secretary's department had earned a reputation of being an 'imperium in imperio' and the private secretary had become responsible for recommending candidates for examination and for the administration of the diplomatic service. Though a Board of Selection had been established as part of the new reforms scheme. Tyrrell remained the key figure in this Board which screened recruits for both the Foreign Office and Diplomatic Service. He rapidly assumed control over the appointments, transfers and promotions of members of the diplomatic service.[33] Tyrrell, again like his predecessors but on a wider scale, was the Foreign Office contact with the press. The private secretary delighted in these informal conversations and Valentine Chirol, for one, found him an excellent source of information. But Tyrrell, who probably saw Grey daily and had access to all the telegrams and despatches coming into the Foreign secretary, also thought of himself as an advisor on policy.

Tyrrell's pre-war role remains a shadowy one. His personal closeness to Grey precluded the writing of minutes or memoranda (the volume of Crowe's writing is an indication that this was the only means by which he could make his views known to Grey). By nature Tyrrell was lazy about paper work and his notes to diplomats were short and highly personal. In distinction to Crowe, with whom he was on excellent terms, Tyrrell was irritated by red tape and office routine and much preferred private meetings to official encounters. He had wit and charm and was approachable to a wide variety of people at a time when the Foreign Office frowned on outsiders.[34] Like Crowe, Tyrrell had been educated in Germany and spent many of his vacations with Prince Radolin. But whereas Crowe's views are revealed in the Foreign Office archives, Tyrrell's have to be pieced together from a variety of sources, many of them unofficial and often untrustworthy.

The task is somewhat easier during Tyrrell's earlier years as private secretary. He made no secret of his fears about Germany and his belief in the need to maintain the agreements with France and Russia. In more than one letter, Tyrrell expanded on his conviction that the Prussians would attempt one day to settle the score with their British competitors.[35] The private secretary shared Hardinge's conviction that the naval question was the key to Anglo–German relations. He too, distrusted German offers to negotiate and deplored Lloyd George's incursions into these muddied waters. In the summer of 1909, he was worried by Grey's apparent willingness to examine Bethmann-Hollweg's proposals for a naval and political agreement and Hardinge's memorandum on the subject increased his uneasiness.[36] Recapitulating Hardinge's earlier arguments, Tyrrell warned Grey that the German offer was calculated to strengthen the hands of the radicals and an arrangement might lead to a reduction in the naval estimates. He believed that Germany would inform France and Russia of these pourparlers and thus purposely weaken the ententes. Grey yielded, somewhat reluctantly, to his officials' insistence that France and Russia be informed despite Bethmann-Hollweg's request for secrecy.

Tyrrell, though not enthusiastic about the Anglo–Russian convention, particularly the Persian agreement, thought it the best the British could obtain. During the annexationist crisis, Tyrrell assumed that the Germans were involved and were 'trying some dirty tricks' in Turkey. He supported Grey's efforts on Isvolsky's behalf during these anxious months and shared the Foreign Secretary's indignation when the latter charged Grey with disloyalty. 'As you know the Chief is the soul and essence of loyalty himself and this quality has been the keynote of his attitude towards France and Russia and he resents any suspicions as almost an imputation of his honour' Tyrrell wrote Nicolson.[37]

It can only be conjectured that Tyrrell and Grey were growing increasingly intimate. The two men complemented each other and personal liking seems to have strengthened their official ties. Grey was reserved, self-enclosed and uneasy with outsiders while Tyrrell, a far more extroverted personality, moved easily in domestic and foreign circles. Hints that he was Grey's closest confident spread beyond the walls of Whitehall. Grey also frequently dined with his parliamentary private secretary, Arthur Murray, a Liberal M.P., and the brother of the Master of Elibank, the Chief Whip of the party. Murray really performed the functions of a social secretary on the political side and had little directly to do with Foreign Office business as such.

Even after the 1905 reforms, assistant and junior clerks had little say in matters of policy. If no longer 'glorified copying clerks' their responsibilities remained limited and they were still involved in a good deal of routine work. Assistant clerks might be asked to deal with a special issue or dispute and were often required to prepare memoranda for the use of the Foreign Secretary or cabinet. It was on Crowe's suggestion, for instance, that Gerard Spicer, his assistant at the Western department, drew up a precis of 'the correspondence showing the attitudes of the German government towards the question of the limitation of naval armaments'.[38] Both Spicer and G. H. Villiers, a junior in the Western Department were as suspicious of German intentions as Crowe and frequently reminded Grey of the risks involved in any talks with Berlin.[39] The members of the Eastern Department shared their head's (R. P. Maxwell) views and were over-optimistic about the future of the Young Turks and the possibility of a pro-British Balkan bloc. The dockets show an occasional minute or query penned by a junior though these were rarely of any length. Most of the non-routine drafting was done by the juniors and as they were frequently moved about they soon became familiar with the workings of the Foreign Office. There was a hierarchy of preference based on the work of the department and on the reputation of the senior clerk who ran it. The Western department led the list; the Consular department remained the 'Cinderella' of the office. James Murray's complaint in 1860 that 'there is not a man who is put into the Consular Department who does not, from that moment, try to get out of it again' was reiterated half a century later by Bruce Lockhart.[40]

Well before Grey took office, the balance between the Foreign Office and the diplomatic service had tipped in the former direction. Each service continued to be separately recruited and administered; exchanges were on a voluntary basis and had to be privately arranged. It was generally acknowledged that the Foreign Office was attracting the abler candidates and that the need for an independent income and the pressures of a continuous life abroad were restricting entry into the diplomatic service. There had been no reform of the overseas service in 1905 and no devolution of responsibility followed. Seasoned diplomats continued to perform routine functions which were handled in London by second-division staff. The more talented and ambitious found the long, slow ladder of promotion discouraging and the round of minor posts enervating. But it was not only a question of personnel and their terms of service. In the Foreign Office, Grey had an alternative source of professional advice. Incoming reports were read by men who considered themselves competent judges even when, as was frequently the case, they had no first-hand knowledge of the countries under their supervision. Ambassadorial advice was questioned, judgements contradicted and alternative courses of action proposed. Lascelles in Berlin, Cartwright in Vienna, Lowther at Constantinople all had reason to complain of such treatment. The protests of successive British ministers at Tehran were either moderated or ignored on the grounds of local myopia and an inability to see the wider pattern of Anglo–Russian relations. Diplomats in more remote territories might well wonder if their reports were read at all.

The speeding-up of communications and the use of the telegraph limited the scope for independent action. Grey's tight control over the reins of policy, the importance of London as a centre for diplomatic negotiations as well as the growing prestige of the senior men in Whitehall left less room for diplomatic initiative. New appointments were carefully discussed and the men selected were expected to give advice but also to carry out instructions. Lascelles' attempts in Berlin to improve the tone of Anglo-German relations were sharply checked and he was retired as early as possible.[41] His far more Germanophobe successor, Edward Goschen, selected after considerable difficulty, proved a far more loyal interpreter of Grey's policy. In a small service where the private secretary and the permanent under-secretary kept close contact with their colleagues abroad, it was relatively easy not only to recognise ability but to establish a consistency in policy at the ambassadorial level.

It would be a mistake to think that diplomats were cyphers or were without influence in their respective capitals. Francis Bertie, for instance, was in a class by himself. Forthright in his views and actions, the 'Bull' played a critical part in strengthening the French entente. Though he was somewhat more effective in Paris than in London, his prestige was such that the Foreign Office openly enlisted his support during the Agadir crisis and in the course of the Anglo–French naval negotiations. Sir Fairfax Cartwright, who also came from an old and rich Oxfordshire family, was equally independent particularly when he thought Grey erroneous in his estimate of Aehrenthal's policy.[42] During the Serbian crisis in March 1909, it was Cartwright who, by exceeding his instructions and acting on his own initiative, broke the deadlock and helped Aehrenthal find a solution.[43] These examples could easily be multiplied. Distance and the complexities of a local situation often provided opportunities for action which could not be referred back to London. In the Far East, for instance, where communication was still relatively slow, Grey was served by two experienced diplomats, Claude MacDonald in Tokyo and John Jordan in Peking. Grey deferred to the advice of the men on the spot, particularly to Jordan's for he was 'quite exceptional in his knowledge of Chinese, his skill in negotiation and his personal acquaintance with successive Chinese leaders.'[41] No-one in the Far Eastern Department could match such a record and it was natural that Jordan's views should carry special authority.

In St Petersburg and Washington, it was not only a question of distance but of the peculiar nature of the respective governmental situations. Both Nicolson and Buchanan established excellent relations with Isvolsky and Sazonov; Nicolson's pacing of the Anglo–Russian entente negotiations is a text-book model for aspiring diplomats while Buchanan's tactful nursing of the entente itself considerably eased Grey's path. In Washington, a great deal depended on having the right political contacts and finding the right tone. Mortimer Durand was a disaster. Bryce, a rather unconventional appointment, proved to be a great success and managed to solve a number of pressing disputes which clouded Anglo–American relations. Spring-Rice, who had known Theodore Roosevelt well, found the Democrats less congenial and even before the outbreak of war never really found his entrance into the Wilson–House circle. Because of domestic complications both in Russia and in the United States it was easier to negotiate abroad rather than in London and this gave a special importance to the British representative there. The same can be said of capitals where the ambassador or minister was engaged in commercial and economic negotiations though the degree of local success often depended on general diplomatic relations rather than on the ability of the ambassador. Constantinople is a case in point; neither Lowther nor Mallet were able to establish the position which the Foreign Office sought. The most successful negotiations with the Turks in this period, the Baghdad Railway agreement, were conducted in London.

However remote the area or complex the problem, what is surprising is the degree of control which Grey exercised. Even when the issues themselves were of secondary importance, as often was the case in China or in the United States, Grey kept a careful check on his agents and hammered out their general lines of action. The diplomatic service, like the Foreign Office, was very much the servant of its political master.

The Foreign Office scene did not alter when Arthur Nicolson replaced Hardinge at the end of 1910. Sixty-one years of age, Nicolson suffered from arthritis and rheumatism and from the first had doubts about his suitability for this post. After the initial flush of excitement, the daily routine of a Whitehall bureaucrat began to wear and the red despatch boxes 'filled him with nausea and despair. Never had any man so cordially disliked being Permanent under-Secretary'.[45] Nicolson had been a great success at St Petersburg and the Anglo–Russian entente owed a great deal to his diplomatic skill and perseverance. But the new appointee had little patience with the numerous administrative concerns of the Foreign Office and found that the top-heavy administrative machine which Hardinge had created was difficult to run. Within eighteen months of his arrival, Nicolson petitioned Grey for relief. He first asked for the Vienna embassy and then for Constantinople but was put off both times. It was only in early 1913 that Grey finally promised him Paris and then the war was to cheat him of his final reward.

Despite protests from the Germans and Austrians both Grey and Hardinge were anxious to have Nicolson in the top position in London. He was a passionate defender of the ententes, particularly the Russian entente which he hoped to see converted into an alliance. The new permanent under-secretary was pessimistic by nature. Influenced by a rather crude form of social-darwinism, he was convinced that war was inevitable and feared that Britain might well find herself on the losing side. At some level, perhaps, Nicolson was less worried by the German threat than by the potential hostility of an enlarged and strengthened Russian empire. Germany, he declared more than once, 'would give us plenty of annoyance but it cannot really threaten any of our more important interests, while Russia especially could cause us extreme embarrassment and, indeed, danger in the Mid-East and on our Indian frontier, and it would be most unfortunate were we to revert to the state of things which existed before 1904 and 1907'.[46] It was the nightmare of a Russo-German combination which haunted Nicolson whose faith in the Anglo-French entente was somewhat shaken after his experience with French policy during the annexationist crisis. The Russians, if not convinced of British loyalty or if courted by the Germans, might well combine with the Dual Alliance powers and swing the balance in Europe and in the east against Britain.

Like Hardinge, but with less finesse, Nicolson opposed all conversations with Berlin and was openly hostile to the Liberal cabinet particularly its radical wing. For him, as for others, the cabinet committee on German affairs created in January 1911 was a device intended to limit the powers of the Foreign Secretary and check the influence of permanent officials. 'I am sorry for Nicolson's position under the new system' Hardinge wrote from India; 'He will practically have no power at all.'[47] Nicolson did his best to strengthen Grey's stand against the radicals and there was something of a tug of war between the committee (whose members represented more diversified views than Nicolson or Hardinge assumed) and the senior officials. Few people in Britain, Nicolson argued, realised the importance of the triple entente for Britain's safety or understood that each German overture was a step towards the isolation of France. In the latter view, Nicolson was seconded by Crowe who also watched the exchanges in the spring of 1911 with mounting suspicion.[48] Their fears were exaggerated; the cabinet committee's answer to Bethmann-Hollweg while friendly in tone was limited in substance.

Nicolson remained apprehensive. He deplored the visit of the German Emperor to London in May and little incidents were blown up into sharp if temporary crises. Nicolson grew somewhat calmer during June but was not sorry when the Adagir crisis exposed 'the real aims of German diplomacy'.[49] This crisis represented the high point of Anglo-German tension during Grey's tenure of office. It illustrated Grey's independence, the differences in approach between the Foreign Secretary and his senior advisors and the ultimate limitations of the influence of even his most intimate officials. Throughout that

tense summer, Nicolson and Crowe pressed Grey for a strong commitment
to France. They feared that the French would collapse under German pressure
and the whole policy of the ententes would be shattered. Their alarm, which
almost bordered on panic, was shared by Tyrrell and Langley and above all
by Bertie in Paris. But Grey, after some hesitation, rejected their more
extreme advice (e.g. sending a warship to a port near Agadir) and mindful
of the mood of the Cabinet sought a way to bring the crisis to a close through
diplomatic compromise. When the extent of the German demands in Africa
became known, Crowe pictured the struggle as a 'trial of strength in which
concession meant defeat'.[50] Grey did not see the situation in such terms;
Britain need not become involved in a war with Germany to underwrite the
French position in Morocco. Nicolson and Crowe were despondent; the
Cabinet's indecision made the latter 'ashamed as well as angry'.[51] Tyrrell
hoped that a visit from Bertie might encourage Grey to take a firmer stand
against his radical colleagues.[52]

Lloyd George's Mansion House speech brought delight to the Foreign
Office. Nicolson and Tyrrell were particularly pleased by Lloyd George's
conversion and the latter became an overnight hero. With the defection of
both Lloyd George and Churchill, the radicals would be in disarray. Yet even
as an inner group of cabinet ministers met and preparations were made
to organise British defences, Grey continued to pursue his own line: support
for the entente but no promises which would encourage French provocation
or obstinacy. At the Foreign Office, the officials recovered their equilibrium.
Nicolson would have liked a dramatic gesture made and complained of the
apathy at the Admiralty. But he was feeling much more confident. In
September, he wrote Goschen that 'the French would not now flinch from
accepting war with Germany...We also have been making preparations very
quietly, and if need be, we shall be quite prepared to render very efficient aid
to the French troops.'[53] The permanent under-secretary was doubtless aware
of the schemes for sending an Expeditionary Force to France and fully
supported the War Office commitment to a 'Continental strategy'. Indeed,
Nicolson was enjoying one of his very rare moments of optimism. The cabinet
had closed ranks; the 'Potsdam party' was in retreat, the King was sound and
even the 'furiously pro-German Stamfordham' had modified his views. The
French army was in excellent shape and the Russians loyal. The Austrians were
uninterested in Morocco and the Italians would remain neutral.[54] The net
effect of the crisis was to give new teeth to the entente.

Tyrrell shared Nicolson's satisfaction with the current position and told
Balfour's private secretary that 'for many reasons it would be better for war
to come now rather than later; but that it would not come now but later'.[55] Only
Crowe did not fully share the new enthusiasm; his suspicions about French
duplicity and his fears for the future were not entirely put to rest. Nor did
Nicolson relax his efforts until the Franco–German conversations were concluded. He pressed Grey with 'all the vigour of which I am capable' not to

force arbitration on the French if the Franco–German talks failed for a French refusal might rouse British public opinion.[56] The permanent under-secretary also dissuaded Grey from following Goschen's advice to caution the French against too stiff a stand. When the stalemate in the Franco–German talks continued, Grey reversed this decision with some degree of success.[57]

Even after these negotiations ended, relations between London and Paris remained tense. The French tried to make up for their losses by bullying Spain in Morocco and words were exchanged between Bertie and Caillaux in November which had to be kept out of the confidential print. It was a storm in a teacup but led Crowe to record his views in a general memorandum on the Agadir crisis early in 1912. He reiterated his earlier claim that there had been a bargain between Caillaux and Kiderlen which had only been thwarted by a violent upsurge of French public opinion.[58] The real danger, Crowe argued, lay not in French unreliability; the recent check to German ambitions would leave that government more restless and ambitious than ever. If the present European equilibrium was to be preserved, and it was in Britain's interest to see it preserved, then the British would have to remain Germany's chief adversary and must 'hold fast to the entente with France and Russia in order to maintain the balance of power'.[59]

Nicolson and Crowe again joined forces in the spring of 1912 to strengthen the entente with Paris. It was well known in diplomatic and military circles that both men would have preferred an alliance but that the cabinet would never sanction such a move. The renewal of Anglo–German talks after Haldane's visit to Berlin in early 1912 alarmed the French and both Bertie and Nicolson warned their chief of French fears. Neither deterred Grey from his unsuccessful search for a formula to satisfy the Germans. When Cambon approached Nicolson for reassurance on the 15 April, the latter cautioned his friend that the moment was inauspicious for any clearer definition of the entente. Cabinet differences on the size and distribution of the fleet, however, did suggest a possible way of tightening the links.

On 18 March, Churchill announced his new proposals for the fleet which involved a shifting of naval forces from the Mediterranean to home waters.[60] The matter was discussed in the C.I.D., and the Foreign Office (Nicolson, Crowe and Mallet) became a centre of opposition to the new scheme. Nicolson protested to Grey against any reduction in force; Crowe submitted a memorandum to the C.I.D. on 8 May outlining the disastrous consequences of such a withdrawal on Britain's diplomatic position. In forwarding this memorandum, Nicolson suggested that the only alternative was a naval arrangement with the French. At a crucial meeting of the C.I.D. on 4 July, a compromise solution was reached based on a one-Power standard in the Mediterranean excluding France. Grey and Nicolson felt that they had achieved a victory for the decision involved building additional dread-noughts and left open the way for talks with the French.

Even before the Cabinet had turned its attention to Churchill's proposals, Cambon had raised the subject of renewing the Anglo–French naval conversations which had lapsed during the winter of 1912. The somewhat surprised Nicolson, who knew nothing of these talks, saw Grey and was told that conversations had begun but committed neither government to go to war.[61] The 4 July compromise suggested a means of renewing and expanding this earlier connection. Yet there was little hope of turning the entente into an alliance through this particular back-door. Radical pressure against the new measures mounted; numerous meetings were held during the summer to deal with the question. Nicolson complained that, in Grey's absence, he was left without information and feared that the recent C.I.D. decision might be reversed. When the cabinet finally came to discuss the terms of a naval arrangement with the French, it was clear that a solid majority opposed any exchange which would curtail Britain's future freedom of action. While Nicolson and Crowe pressed for an understanding which would have the character of a defensive alliance, Grey rejected proposals made first by Nicolson and then by Bertie which pointed in this direction.

Bertie hurried over from Paris and fought stubbornly for a clear commitment to the French. After further talks with Nicolson, Tyrrell and Churchill, however, the ambassador abandoned his efforts and sought to salvage what he could out of the situation. The pro-French group had won half a victory; the exchange of notes between Grey and Cambon did mark 'one further stage' in the definition of the entente. The naval agreement, the notes and the subsequent technical arrangements opened a 'Pandora's box of troubles' which left open the question of Britain's moral as distinct from her purely legal obligations to the French.[62] If Harcourt and the radicals assumed that the British had safeguarded their independence, there were grounds for the French assumption that some form of commitment had been given. Grey had once more chosen the middle course which ultimately could hardly satisfy either the radicals or his senior officials.

Nicolson argued that if a collision did occur between France and Germany, Britain would waver until it was too late.[63] Though Crowe was later to insist that the naval agreements had created a moral obligation for the British to come to the aid of her partner, he, too, would have preferred a clearer statement than Grey thought necessary or possible. Quarrels in various parts of the globe – Madagascar, Muscat and Morocco – added to Crowe's worries. 'The French are unbearable', he complained.[64] Nor was it only Crowe who feared that French hostility to Britain would play into the hands of the anti-entente radicals. Even Grey was conscious of the need to make light of these differences.

The Foreign Office had grounds for concern. There had been a very sharp reaction after the Agadir crisis and Grey was the object of a personal attack from a great variety of sources. All the liberal papers with the exception of the *Westminster Gazette* joined the 'Grey-must-go' chorus. Ponsonby, Noel

Buxton, E. D. Morel and the Persia Committee each had their own complaints about Grey's policies and methods. The Foreign Office, which did not escape from the general denunciation, rose to Grey's defence. Nicolson protested that the movement was most unjust as no-one had pursued a straighter nor more moderate line of action than Grey. Crowe was scathing in his comments on articles appearing in the *Daily News* and *Contemporary Review*. It has been argued that these attacks did not move Grey, and, if anything, convinced him to stay at the Foreign Office despite increasing weariness and a certain disenchantment with political life.[65] Nevertheless, it is true that during 1912 the Foreign Office was once more engaged in conversations with Berlin.

It is difficult to judge just what Grey expected the Haldane Mission to accomplish. There is, however, no doubt about the Foreign Office reaction. Nicolson objected to the trip and bitterly opposed the political and naval talks which followed. Crowe was appalled by the informal and 'highly questionable' background to the exchanges and could find little in Haldane's reports which warranted any departure from previous policies. 'It would be a political mistake of the first magnitude to allow the German government to squeeze concessions out of us and leave them quite free to pursue the policy of carefully preparing their inevitable war against us', he concluded.[66] As Grey was involved in the coal-strike settlement, Nicolson had to work directly with Haldane in the search for a satisfactory political formula. Nicolson assured the anxious Bertie that he was doing his best 'to get us out of this quagmire into which we are plunged, and into which we have been led by our unscrupulous adversaries and our singularly naive and feeble negotiators'.[67] He was ably seconded by Crowe whose attacks on the German proposals grew increasingly strident. At various times Crowe stressed the one-sided nature of the colonial proposals, the dangers of all political formulas, the unreliability of German assurances and the disastrous effects of the exchanges on France and Russia.[68] As in the spring of 1911, the Foreign Office was excessively apprehensive. The naval talks collapsed first and German demands for a clear declaration of neutrality proved unacceptable to Grey and to a majority in the cabinet. Nevertheless, Nicolson and Crowe were horrified that the cabinet should contemplate such a formula. Even when the talks lapsed, Nicolson complained that the cabinet was walking around the question without coming to a definite decision and pleaded with Grey to terminate the negotiations in a more decisive manner.

'Formulas are dangerous – and I have never been able to understand why we should give to Germany what we have never given to France or Russia', Nicolson told Grey.[69] Nicolson thought the path was an obvious one, 'not to tie our hands in any way with anyone, to remain the sole judges of our actions, to keep on the close and intimate terms we have hitherto maintained with France and Russia, and which have been the best guarantees of peace'.[70] Goschen congratulated Nicolson for his work in opposing the political understanding and even Valentine Chirol, the ex-foreign-editor of *The Times* who had often complained of Nicolson's lack of influence felt the latter had 'played up splendidly'.[71] Nicolson was less sure of the extent of his triumph. He knew there were many in the cabinet who would go to almost any lengths to secure the 'so-called good will' of Germany.[72] Moreover, he believed that though Grey opposed a neutrality formula, he was less adverse to a colonial bargain which might reduce the diplomatic fever chart.

The talks between the German and British colonial offices had already begun in late 1911 and received a fresh impetus from the renewed efforts in both countries to come to an arrangement. Discussions about the Belgian Congo and Katanga did not lead to any definite conclusions; Crowe found the talks morally distasteful in the extreme.[73] But the posssibility of a bargain over the Portuguese colonies proved more fruitful.[74] With Grey's consent, Harcourt and Kühlmann began discussions for a revision of the 1898 agreement. The officials at the Foreign Office distrusted Harcourt and resented their initial exclusion from the main arena. Nicolson was pleased, he claimed, to have nothing to do with such discreditable proceedings. Crowe, who never wavered in his opposition to the treaty, was soon involved in the daily exchanges between the negotiators.

By the time the details of the bargain were concluded, Grey's main aim as well as Harcourt's, the improvement of relations with Berlin, had been achieved and the Foreign Secretary initialled the revised agreement even before securing cabinet approval. There is no doubt that he had moral qualms about the proceedings and both he and Harcourt agreed with Crowe that all the relevant treaties would have to be published before the new agreement could be ratified. German queries about British intentions led to delays and Nicolson and Crowe urged Grey to capitalise on the German opposition to publication and abandon the treaty entirely. Grey temporised; the Germans were not required to choose between publication and the treaty. The Foreign Secretary preferred not to force the issue in the summer of 1914. Nicolson took little comfort from Grey's refusal to act.

These colonial talks confirmed Nicolson's belief that little was to be expected of a 'radical-socialist' cabinet and that the pro-German forces were continuing to grow in power and appeal. He was, at the same time unduly nervous about the French entente: neither Cambon nor Bertie left him in any doubt of French fears. Worse still, in Nicolson's eyes, at the same time as the Anglo-German conversations were causing anxiety in Paris, there were continued difficulties with Russia. As the architect of the Anglo-Russian convention, Nicolson took more than an official interest in all matters affecting its perilous existence. As in the case of how Germany was to be treated, however, the differences between Grey and Nicolson over Persia and the Balkans were one of degree rather than substance.

Persia was a source of constant tension. As crisis followed crisis and Grey twisted in all directions to satisfy the conflicting demands of the Government of India, the radicals, the Russians and the Persians, the situation in Tehran continued to deteriorate. Nicolson feared for the future of the entente; he thought Persia was in a hopeless state and that the British were 'ploughing into the sands'. He felt that Grey should support the Russians and take a strong line against the Shuster–Stokes attempt to revive the feeble Persian government. Grey finally did intervene to force the Persians to comply with Russia's demands but did not cease in his protests against the Russian intervention in the Persian capital. The Foreign Secretary used the complaints of the Persia Committee as an excuse to warn Benckendorff that if the Russians occupied Tehran he would have to resign. These warnings had some effect – Russian troops did not move and the Persians capitulated. Nicolson was so exhausted by these events that he was ordered abroad for a six week rest by his physician.

The domestic campaign against Grey's Russian policy continued throughout the winter of 1912. Though Nicolson claimed it had little effect on the Foreign Secretary the situation in Persia gave the radical critics fresh ammunition. Russian pressure on the constitutionalists weakened their authority and there were disorders in the south as well as in the neutral zone. Nicolson pressed for intervention; Grey and the India Office decided to evacuate the British consuls and subjects from the inland to the coastal towns so that similar pressure might be brought on the Russians in the north. In April 1912, Russian troops bombarded a Moslem shrine in Meshed; Grey protested vigorously to Sazonov. Nicolson once more took fright and he repeatedly intervened to moderate the wording of instructions given to Buchanan.

Grey had few weapons at his command. The Indian government thought he had already sacrificed too much for the sake of the entente and was particularly concerned about the Trans-Persian railway scheme which Grey had supported to avoid offending the Russians. Nicolson thought partition inevitable and regretted the sharp tone of Grey's exchanges with Sazonov. As Persia lapsed into total chaos, Grey was 'bombarded with letters from people here who want me to break with Russia over Persia; how on earth can we help Persia if we do?'[75] Grey's meeting with Sazonov in September 1912 was friendly but indecisive. It was clear that the Russian offensive in Persia, as well as in Afghanistan, Tibet and other parts of Chinese Central Asia would continue to strain an entente which was never popular in parliamentary circles.

The breakdown in the Balkan equilibrium posed equally difficult problems for the entente. Before he came to London, Nicolson had taken little interest in the Turkish Empire except as it affected Russia. Though he had only limited confidence in the Young Turks, he recommended reversing Hardinge's unsuccessful policy of pressuring Turkey and turned to a policy of conciliation. He urged Grey to offer concessions in the Gulf, including the recognition of Turkish sovereignty over Kuwait, in return for a compromise

on the Baghdad railway question. In March 1911 the Turks offered to inter-
nationalise the Gulf section, allotting 40 per cent of the shares to herself and
20 per cent each to Germany, France and England. Hardinge, Goschen and
Bertie opposed the offer which they believed the Germans had inspired
and which they feared would make a German-sponsored Turkey master in the
Gulf area. Neither Grey nor Nicolson intended to accept such adverse terms;
they proposed a new settlement which would give the triple entente a majority
of the shares. But, differently from Hardinge, they were willing to reduce the
British demands in order to conciliate the Turks and to secure British entry
into the Baghdad railway project. Meanwhile, there were new rumblings
within the Turkish empire but the Foreign Office, determined not to become
involved in Balkan affairs again, refused to intervene. Nicolson was not unduly
alarmed: 'Personally I would view with equanimity the break up of the
Turkish regime and Turkish empire in Europe – I have no desire to see either
consolidated and consider that should they become too strong they would be
a menace to every Power with Mussulman subjects and especially to us who
hold Egypt and India.'[76]

Faced with the actualities of the situation, neither Nicolson nor Grey could
view the disintegration of Turkey-in-Asia with anything but apprehension.
The Foreign Office favoured a policy of strict neutrality in the Italian–Turk
conflict and intervened to quiet the press which was notoriously anti-Italian.
Grey rejected a Turkish plea for mediation and for an alliance. Though he
was considerably irritated by the Italian action and then by her inability to
bring the war to a successful end, he did not wish to alienate the Rome
government.[77] To complicate the picture, the Russians tried to exploit Turkish
weakness by persuading her to open the Straits to Russian warships. 'We do
not want another question on our hands', Nicolson noted, 'and I think we
could pour baths of cold water on it.'[78] The under-secretary also condemned
the Tcherykov proposals of October 1912 as a source of future trouble. The
rapid shifts of Russian policy at Constantinople exasperated the British and
Nicolson was plainly relieved when the Tripoli question was settled without
international intervention.

Despite fears in London to the contrary, the Balkan states remained inactive
during this war. The Russians, however, fished in the troubled waters and the
newly formed Balkan League owed much to their initiative. Nicolson
complained that Sazonov was the primary cause of these new troubles and
thought the Russians were playing a game which would end in disaster.
Though he assumed a Russian takeover in this area inevitable, he wished to
postpone the day of reckoning. When the Balkan War broke out, Nicolson
whole-heartedly supported Grey's efforts to promote Austro–Russian co-
operation. The extent of the Turkish debacle took the Foreign Office by
surprise. Grey stepped up his efforts to localise the conflict through action by
the Concert powers. Nicolson became more depressed than usual. He doubted
whether the Concert could preserve the general peace. He anticipated an

Austro–Russian rupture, a possible defeat for the Russians and a deterioration in Britain's relations with her Moslem subjects whatever the outcome of the Balkan war. With German assistance, Grey sought a peaceful solution of the Albanian clash between Austria and Russia. The much-feared threat to Constantinople subsided when the Bulgarians failed to capture the city. Grey succeeded, moreover, in persuading the interested powers to join in an ambassadorial conference in London to settle questions which affected their mutual interests while leaving the Balkan states to work out their individual problems. During the winter, Grey's prestige soared as, seconded by the Germans, successive crises were settled without a general European conflagration.

Nicolson remained despondent. He feared the consequences of the new Anglo–German partnership in the Balkans and the results of Grey's self-appointed role as honest broker.[79] The under-secretary warned Grey about Germany's efforts to weaken the triple entente. 'What Nicolson is concerned at', Chirol reported to Hardinge, 'is not so much...that actual policy hitherto adopted with regard to the different phases of the Balkan War, but the under-currents which have accompanied it.'[80] Nicolson thought that the new policy of cooperation with Berlin would not only alienate the Russians but would encourage the pro-German wing of the London cabinet. Early in 1913, he explained that 'the party in favour of intimate relations with Germany has increased and strengthened'.[81]

As so often during these years, Nicolson's alarm was excessive. Grey was fully aware of the dangers of his new Balkan partnership. As British interests were not actively engaged in this area, he had everything to gain from German cooperation as long as the Germans would restrain their Austrian allies. Even during the Scutari dispute, moreover, when Grey persuaded the reluctant Sazonov to allow the port to go to Albania, it was clear that Grey would ultimately support the entente when its interests clashed with those of the Concert.[82] Nevertheless, Nicolson, remained troubled by Grey's neutral stance and reputation for impartiality. Russian restiveness confirmed his worst forebodings.

During the next year, Nicolson found himself in an increasingly isolated position. There were not the same close ties with Grey which had characterised the Foreign Secretary's relations with Hardinge. In part, Grey no longer needed the kind of advice and support which Hardinge had provided. But some of the difficulty must be attributed to Nicolson's personality and political persuasions. His tendency towards despondency and his open contempt for the Liberals did not make for an easy partnership. Nicolson was deeply frightened by the changes in British society which had occurred during his long years abroad. He found the Liberal government unduly weak in its handling of the various domestic crises. He was not above informing the French that they had little to hope for from the present cabinet of 'financiers, pacifists, faddists and others' and went on to assure Cambon that 'the cabinet will not last, it is done for and with the Conservatives you will get something precise'.[83]

Nicolson was a vehement Ulsterman. 'For some reason – perhaps because he talks too much Ulster, his wife still more and...he has absolutely lost Grey's confidence', Chirol wrote Hardinge, 'and he does not conceal the fact that he is sick of it all.'[84] Nicolson believed that Liberal policy in Ireland would provoke a civil war, weaken the army and undermine British influence in Europe. As Ulster became the dominant issue of the day during the spring of 1914, personal relations with Grey became increasingly strained.

It is not surprising that Nicolson increasingly felt his advice was being discounted. The only man to report that Grey 'ought to say no to Nicolson more often' was William Tyrrell, reputedly the most influential figure at the Foreign Office and Nicolson's chief critic.[85] At the time of the Agadir crisis, the two men had worked in harmony. Tyrrell shared the Foreign Office view that Germany was intent on wrecking the French entente and was one of the leaders of the extreme pro-German group.[86] Early in 1912, Tyrrell deplored the 'curious hankering every British government has of wishing to talk to Germany'.[87] Yet in the spring of that year, von Kühlmann visited him and considered the private secretary friendly to the idea of a colonial bargain.[88] In October 1912, Kühlmann reported that in a 'Tischunterhaltung' (Kiderlen's description) Tyrrell made 'a serious and decisive proposal' suggesting co-operation in the Balkans and in China, Persia, Turkey and Africa.[89] It seems highly probable, particularly in the light of British fears about the Balkans, that Tyrrell, with Grey's knowledge, did discuss the possibility of a common policy. The conversation was general and informal and Tyrrell might well have ranged the globe without feeling he was making any concrete offer. Kühlmann's telegram to Berlin repeated the private secretary's warning that he had been expressing Grey's personal views and that neither Nicolson nor Goschen had been told. Later in the month, Grey and Kühlmann met and agreed to exchange views and information about the Balkan crisis and subsequent Anglo–German action followed.[90] Yet no further efforts were made to enter into a more general arrangement.

Valentine Chirol, alerted by Nicolson, sought an explanation of Tyrrell's volte face. 'He is convinced...that we are relieved, at least for a long time to come, from the German menace and can therefore take up a somewhat firmer line with Russia without compromising the Entente', Chirol reported to Hardinge.[91] Tyrrell felt that the Russians were being unduly troublesome. He had already asked Chirol, who accompanied a parliamentary delegation to Russia in February 1912, to warn the Russians that British public opinion distrusted their methods. 'I cannot help thinking that you cannot do enough to make this point of view clear to them and to make them realise that in Europe they are as much in need of our cooperation as we, in Asia, are in need of theirs with regard to India.'[92]

The private secretary, re-assured by the established margin of naval

superiority and the efforts being made by the Germans to stabilise the
Balkan situation may have felt that the British had a breathing space. Nicolson
denied that Tyrrell had joined the pro-Germans but warned that the
private secretary's line of reasoning could bring Britain into the Berlin orbit.[93]
Hardinge, too, was alarmed by Chirol's account 'since I know well the
influence he [Tyrrell] enjoys with Edward Grey, who temperamentally is
quite ready to listen to German blandishments influenced as he is by Haldane
in his views'.[94] Hardinge's misgivings were unjustified; it is not even clear
that Tyrrell's opinions were reported accurately. It seems most probable that
the private secretary did not want a repetition of the 1908 crisis and felt
that the Russians should not be encouraged in the Balkans. There was a
good deal to be said for a British policy of non-involvement. He was undoubtedly irritated by Sazonov's unwillingness to compromise in Central Asia
and might have hoped that an improvement of relations with Berlin would
strengthen Grey's hand in Persia. What is not clear is how far Tyrrell was
willing to go in the German direction and how far he influenced his chief.
The Germans, at least, considered Tyrrell sympathetic to the idea of a
detente.

Tyrrell's assessment of the Russian situation led to an open clash with
Nicolson who 'wanted to leave the Russians to pipe the tune and us to dance
to it whatever may be'.[95] There were differences between the two men on the
policies to be followed in Persia and Central Asia and the Foreign Office
gossips reported that Tyrrell was in high favour and 'was everything to Grey'.
In the autumn of 1913, Tyrrell was sent to Washington to discuss a wide range
of diplomatic problems, particularly the Mexican question which was
becoming increasingly critical. His stay in Washington, during Spring-Rice's
illness, added considerably to Tyrrell's stature and reputation. He was received
by House and Wilson as Grey's personal representative and closest intimate.
In London, it was thought that Tyrrell might either take Nicolson's place at
the Foreign Office or be sent to Berlin to replace Goschen (a rumour denied
by Tyrrell himself). In fact, it was Tyrrell who accompanied Grey on the
latter's visit to Paris in the spring of 1914 and a second trip abroad, this time
to Germany, was being planned.

Nicolson's eclipse may explain the vehemence with which he expounded his
views during the last year of peace. He continued to feel that only the existing
division of powers would preserve the peace and that if Germany were
convinced the British might remain neutral in a European war she would adopt
a very different policy. Nicolson was highly sensitive to French worries about
the post-Agadir improvement in Anglo-German relations and believed that
the new German rapprochement would convince Paris that the British were
'fair-weather' friends.

'I am afraid that should war break out on the continent the likelihood of
our despatching any expeditionary force is extremely remote, and it was on
such an expeditionary force being sent that France at one time was basing

her military measures. I believe that of late she has gradually abandoned the hope of ever receiving prompt and efficient military aid from us.'[96]

Nicolson was even more concerned by the obvious weakness of the Russian entente; his Russomania irritated Bertie and Goschen as well as Tyrrell. Nicolson shared Buchanan's impression that Russia had entered a period of rapid growth and could, if she wished, take the offensive in Central Asia. 'This to me is such a nightmare', Nicolson wrote, 'that I would at almost any cost keep Russia's friendship.'[97] She would, moreover, soon be a formidable factor in Europe and the Germans, conscious of Russian strength might either move against her before the Russian army was ready or come to an agreement. 'I am also haunted by the same fear as you', Nicolson wrote Buchanan, 'lest Russia become tired of us and strike a bargain with Germany.'[98]

Nicolson's daily activities only increased his sense of impending doom. Anglo–Russian tension in Central Asia and Grey's courting of Turkey threatened the whole fabric of Anglo–Russian relations. During the winter of 1913, the Russians consolidated their hold over northern Persia, and prepared to extend their control over the neutral zone which, with the discovery of extensive oil deposits, had become of vital importance to the British navy. Already in the previous May, Sazonov, annoyed by Grey's repeated complaints, had suggested a revision of the 1907 convention but Grey and Crewe, aware of the opposition both in the Cabinet and from the Government of India, were not anxious to acknowledge the partition of Persia. Nicolson, backed by Buchanan, argued that such a step could not be avoided and that the Russian initiative might be used to secure a general agreement in Central Asia as well as in Persia.

In April 1914, the Simla Convention (which placed Outer Tibet under British influence) was signed and the moment seemed an appropriate one for new conversations at St Petersburg. 'All along the line we want something, and have nothing to give', Grey warned. 'For these reasons, I hesitate to propose a general discussion at present, though I realise that events are forcing us nearer to it.'[99] Nicolson was impatient at Grey's procrastination; Sazonov became increasingly irritable and the patient Buchanan had a difficult time with the Russian foreign minister. Nicolson once more intervened to rewrite the Persian despatches going to St Petersburg. Further exchanges only illustrated the extent of the Russian appetite and the weakness of the British position. On 28 July 1914, Nicolson warned Buchanan 'our relations with Russia are now approaching a point where we shall have to make up our minds as to whether we should become really intimate and permanent friends, or else diverge into another path'.[100]

Events in the near east were hastening this day of reckoning. The Second Balkan War disgusted both Nicolson and Grey who agreed on a policy of non-involvement. Though Nicolson cared little for Albania or the Aegean islands, he was concerned for the future of Asiatic Turkey. He still hoped to postpone the breakdown of the Empire and was prepared to make yet another attempt to challenge the German hold over the Turkish government. Sazonov's aims were not entirely clear; Russia was not ready for a division of the Empire but she was contemplating the banquet. Once again, with regard to Turkey, British and Russian aims were divergent.

There was a clash over the problem of Armenian reforms. Sazonov proposed a scheme which the Foreign Office was convinced would open the way for a Russian occupation of the territories nearest her borders. The Russians, on the other hand, would not accept the Turkish reform proposals. Mallet, even while he was in London, urged a stronger line at St Petersburg and support for any scheme of reform which had a chance of acceptance at Constantinople. Nicolson wanted the question dealt with 'calmly and temperately' and optimistically predicted that Sazonov would not prove unreasonable.[101] In the autumn of 1913, Mallet was sent to Constantinople to make a new effort at establishing British influence. From the start, his efforts were frustrated by Russian reluctance to see the Empire successfully reformed. Caught between conflicting desires to satisfy both the Turks and the Russians, Grey abandoned the Armenian reform scheme despite Mallet's protests.

The only major British enterprise in Turkey, the re-equipping and re-training of the Turkish fleet, found little favour in Russian eyes. Grey's subsequent failure to strongly under-write Russian complaints over the appointment of Liman von Sanders led to another clash. At the start, Nicolson encouraged Grey to support Sazonov; particularly 'at this moment when some misgivings exist as to our intimacy with Germany it was important that we should not appear to be indifferent or sympathetic to the German action'.[102] As the complications of the British position became clear, such a stand became impossible and Nicolson admitted that Grey would look foolish if 'we took the question up warmly and then found that Sazonov more or less deserted us...In fact there is a certain disinclination on our part to pull the chestnuts out of the fire for Russia.'[103]

Given this mood, it is hardly surprising that Nicolson warmly welcomed Sazonov's attempt to strengthen the Anglo–Russian entente. Frightened by the German appearance in Turkey and the lukewarm attitude of the British, Sazonov suggested an exchange of views between the respective naval staffs. Buchanan warned Nicolson that the Russians were tiring of their 'so-called friends' and unless the entente was enlarged it would be difficult to maintain. Nicolson and Crowe urged Grey to act but the Foreign Secretary was reluctant to disturb the existing disposition of diplomatic alignments. Grey had noted Germany's preoccupation with Austria's growing weakness and her fears of a Russian offensive. He was particularly adverse to any step which would alarm the 'war party' in Berlin. The French, who distrusted Grey's diplomacy (hence

the British state visit to Paris) pressed Grey and the latter reluctantly agreed
to raise the matter with the cabinet. 'I do fear – and I know the French are
haunted with the same apprehension – that if we do not try to tighten up the
ties with Russia she may become weary of us and throw us overboard',
wrote the ever-anxious under-secretary.[104]

Just the situation Grey dreaded occurred. A French leak and an inspired
but accurate report of the naval talks in the *Berliner Tageblatt* led to German
protests and embarrassing questions in the Commons.[105] Nicolson wanted Grey
to ignore the German complaint; instead Grey, intensely irritated by the
leakage, tried to reassure Lichnowsky. Grey had every intention of keeping
his line to St Petersburg but he also wanted to maintain his good relations with
Bethmann-Hollweg. This careful balancing act and Grey's 'over-ambitious'
diplomacy filled Nicolson with apprehensions about the future. He deplored
the government's failure to arm for an inevitable war; its disastrous policy in
Ireland was weakening British prestige abroad. 'My views are so entirely
divergent with those of the present government', he wrote Hardinge, 'that
I think it better to limit myself to talking on those matters which are strictly
within my province.'[106] By the summer of 1914, Nicolson was Grey's chief
advisor in name only.

No single assistant under-secretary became the dominating voice within the
department. Each had an influence within his own special geographical area.
Louis Mallet, whom Hardinge hoped might succeed Nicolson, continued to
represent the views of the extreme anti-Germans. He was active during the
Agadir crisis and strongly deprecated subsequent efforts made to come to an
arrangement with Berlin. He even wrote to Balfour's secretary in March 1912
suggesting that 'a little plain speaking on the international situation would do
a lot of good' as no one seemed to understand that the best way of improving
relations with Germany was to be on better terms with France and Russia.[107]
Deeply impressed by the Russian revival, Mallet was a strong supporter of
the Russian entente though, as head of the Eastern department, his involvement in Turkish affairs resulted in a more critical attitude towards Russian
policy.

Like others in his department, Mallet started with exaggerated hopes for
the Young Turks and thought that a Baghdad railway compromise and a
revival of British influence were possible. The war with Italy revealed how
weak the Empire was. Mallet placed his hopes on an alliance between Turkey
and the Balkan states which might save what was left of European Turkey.
This illusion, too, was shattered and Mallet was thrown back on the Concert
and Austro–Russian cooperation. The assistant under-secretary reviewed the
limited possibilities when a second Turkish request for support reached
London in June 1913. Mallet argued that an alliance was not within the realm
of practical politics and would arouse German hostility: to abstain completely
would throw Turkey into the waiting arms of the Triple Alliance. All that could

be proposed was a joint guarantee of Turkish independence and the mutual participation of all the powers in the reform and financial rehabilitation of the Empire.[108]

Mallet remained convinced that the dissolution of Asiatic Turkey would be dangerous for Britain's imperial and European position and he was annoyed when Sazonov failed to give the Concert the backing it required at Constantinople. Mallet felt the Russians were preparing to carve up the dying state and thought it worth the risk of a sharp word at St Petersburg and even a conciliatory attitude towards the Germans to underwrite its continued existence. It was better to have some measure of reform than no reform at all.[109] With the successful conclusion of the Baghdad railway negotiations, Mallet became more hopeful that Britain might yet play a role in the regeneration of Turkey. It was, in part, for these reasons that Grey selected him to replace the unsuccessful Lowther whom even the Foreign Secretary admitted had been asked to make bricks without straw.

In addition to his responsibilities in the Eastern department, Mallet also supervised the American department. Anglo–American relations had been punctuated by a number of small disputes which culminated in a conflict over the question of the recognition of General Huerta in Mexico.[110] It was generally assumed in London that the United States would try to extend its control over its revolutionary southern neighbour in the same way as it had over Nicaragua. While the British did not want to encourage American expansion in a country where they had numerous economic interests (including the new Cowdray oil concessions) they could not directly challenge the Americans on their own continent. Nicolson, in particular was afraid of offending Wilson but Mallet pressed for a more independent line. On the recognition question, Mallet argued that the murder of the Mexican ex-president and the means by which Huerta came to power were irrelevant.[111] The real question was whether the new government was legally established and if it could maintain law and order. Grey had come to a similar conclusion and decided on the provisional recognition of the Huerta government just when it became clear that the Americans would withhold recognition on moral grounds. Grey and Mallet were irritated by Wilson's moralism; Grey, was, however, not willing to press his defence of British interests too far (the Americans exaggerated the influence of Cowdray on Foreign Office thinking). By the time Mallet left the Foreign Office both Wilson and Grey had moderated their respective lines of diplomacy.

Mallet's appointment to Constantinople came as a shock to the assistant under-secretary, though it confirmed earlier suspicions: 'I have felt, ever since you left, that the chances of my succeeding Nicolson were not very secure. Tyrrell never really accepted the solution...and Crowe naturally thought himself the better candidate...I am heartily sick of being an Assistant Under Secretary, especially under Nicolson with whom, however, my personal relations are excellent.'[112] Nicolson, himself, confirmed Mallet's impression that his embassy was a 'second prize' and that his appointment was intended to clear the way for Crowe's promotion to Nicolson's position. It was a sign of the times that Mallet was replaced by Ralph Paget, whose pro-German sympathies had so irritated Hardinge.[113] Paget took on the American and Treaty departments but was too junior to make any mark on policy before the outbreak of war.

Eyre Crowe was finally appointed to an assistant under-secretaryship in 1912 and given the highly regarded Western department. His elevation did not increase his influence and though his responsibilities multiplied his views did not always prevail. Enough has been said to indicate that Crowe never wavered from the conviction that the Germans would try, if given the chance, to make themselves masters of Europe. Like Nicolson, he would have liked the ententes strengthened or converted into alliances. He regarded all political negotiations with Germany highly dangerous and deplored the efforts of 'amateur diplomatists, peace mongers and meddlesome busybodies' who were endeavouring to bring the two countries closer together. He was relieved when the naval talks were dropped and, like Grey, believed that good relations between the two countries could be attributed to the lack of such negotiations. Again, like Grey, he disliked Churchill's 'naval holiday' proposals and when, in early 1914, the First Lord reversed his stand and pressed for supplementary naval estimates, Crowe supported the 'big navy' men more energetically than Grey.

Crowe's role during the Kühlmann-Harcourt talks showed the reasons for the assistant under-secretary's high reputation within the Foreign Office. He never disguised his opposition to the talks and openly criticised Harcourt's proceedings even when he knew these critiques were read with some degree of irritation. In the detailed exchanges which followed, Crowe fought tenaciously to counteract Harcourt's liberality with the colonies of Britain's oldest ally. In the spring of 1914 when the Germans refused to agree to the publication of the initialled agreement, Crowe again returned to the charge and pressed Grey to bury the treaty. It is true that Crowe supported Parker's efforts to conclude arrangements over the Baghdad Railway and other concessions in Mesopotamia but this was the kind of *quid pro quo* bargain which Crowe had always favoured. An improvement of relations with Berlin was a far less important motive in these exchanges than in the simultaneously-conducted colonial talks.

During the spring and summer of 1913, Crowe was seriously ill and away from the Foreign Office a great deal of the time. Though not fully recovered, he returned in the early autumn to take temporary charge of the Far Eastern department while Langley was on holiday and to assume responsibility for the Eastern (as well as the Western) department on Mallet's departure. This put Crowe in the central Office position; nevertheless it was Balkan affairs which absorbed most of his attention. In these tangled matters, Crowe tried to implement Grey's Concert policy but the Austro-Italian partnership in Albania and the continued Italian–Greek–Turkish dispute over the Aegean islands placed impossible pressures on any form of international cooperation. The victory of the Serbians in the Second Balkan War – during which the Foreign Office opted for a policy of strict non-involvement – had increased Serbian ambitions and led to their military intervention in north-west Albania. The Austrians intervened successfully but unilaterally and Crowe denounced Berchtold's move as an anti-Concert gesture. With regard to the southern Albanian frontier, the Austrians and Italians joined forces and issued an ultimatum to the occupying Greeks, again demonstrating the fragility of the Concert. By the end of 1913, Crowe was advocating withdrawal both on practical and moral grounds.

When the Prince of Weid (over whose candidature there had been endless dispute) demanded a large loan and Italy and Austria fell out over the way Albania was to run, Crowe urged that Britain withdraw leaving the Triple Alliance to fight it out among themselves and forcing Germany to decide between her two partners. Grey's own inclination was in the same direction particularly as British interests were not involved but the Russians felt such a withdrawal would confirm the victory of their rivals. In the spring of 1914 Crowe minuted 'to remain in the concert on these terms is neither useful nor dignified'.[114] Given the Irish troubles at home, this was not the moment for a 'Quixotic crusade' in Albania. Grey was in the process of disengaging when the assassination crisis began.

Grey tried to link the Albanian and Aegean islands question. He suggested that the Greeks should retire from southern Albania and occupy instead the Aegean islands including those taken by Greece which under the terms of the Treaty of Lausanne were to be returned to Turkey. His Albanian proposal was acceptable but the Aegean solution brought a storm of protest from both the Italians and Turks. The latter, fearing Concert coercion, turned to the Germans who immediately disclaimed any intention of such action which, indeed, the British had never proposed. Crowe pointed out that the Germans were less than helpful in this matter and were relapsing into their old policy of sowing discord among the other Powers to confirm their own position in Constantinople. Once again, while the islands question remained unresolved, Austria and Italy in a joint action demanded that the Greeks withdraw their forces from Albania. Though the Germans tried to keep the Concert together during this crisis, the Foreign Office was rapidly retreating from any form of participation in this matter as well.

Crowe also inherited the unresolved Armenian reform programme and reviewed the various efforts being made to secure the survival of Turkey-in-Asia. At first, he hoped that a new Russian proposal (which the British had already considerably modified) might prove acceptable to the Germans and consequently to the Turks.[115] But the Germans, not unexpectedly, refused to bring any pressure on the Turkish government and Crowe doubted whether any joint action could be arranged. Crowe thought Mallet might succeed where Lowther had failed but was always balancing the need to reform Asiatic Turkey (and the disagreeable policy of cooperation with Berlin) against the requirements of the Anglo–Russian connection.

Crowe was less Russophile than Nicolson and did not share the latter's nightmares about the possibility of a Russo–German combination. Nor did he think that Russian loyalty had to be bought by a policy of subservience to Russian demands. He believed that the Russian foreign minister had considerably exaggerated the importance of von Sanders' appointment at Constantinople; Sazonov's complaints about the lack of British support were unjustified and 'his opinions almost incredibly jejune'.[116] This dispute, coming at the same time as the difficulties in Persia and Central Asia (which also concerned Crowe as head of the Eastern department) raised the whole problem of Anglo–Russian relations. Brushing aside Nicolson's excessive concern with Russian sensitivity, Crowe came to argue for a more decisive stand against the Russian penetration of Persia. If British interests were to be secured in the neutral zone as well as in the south, the fiction of an independent Persia must be abandoned and the Anglo–Russian convention renegotiated. During June, the Foreign Office began to take a far sharper line with regard to Persia: Crowe had some caustic comments to make about Sazonov's tactics and reply to Grey's tentative approach in early June.[117] Serious discussions had begun when the July crisis transformed the scene.

Despite Crowe's hardening attitude towards St Petersburg, he was anxious, nevertheless, to see the entente sustained. For instance, he welcomed Sazonov's initiative with regard to a naval agreement and was somewhat disappointed by Grey's reluctance to act.[118] Given the impasse in Persia, Crowe believed that a general reconstruction of the convention was essential and an exchange of views between naval experts might soothe relations during the tense time of re-negotiation. Crowe was so preoccupied with Balkan and Persian affairs that there was little time for long minutes on general policy. He obviously continued to think that Germany was the main threat to Britain's security and had little confidence in the expressions of goodwill emanating from Berlin. He did not believe that a peace party could prevail in the capital and did not share Grey's hopes that von Jagow would prove more trustworthy than previous foreign secretaries. Like Nicolson, he watched the detente with Berlin with deep misgivings and deplored the government's unwillingness to prepare for a conflict he believed was inevitable. He would have preferred a clearer definition of Britain's obligations towards France but his views on this subject were well known and Grey continued to pursue his own line of action.

The assistant under-secretary had assumed many of the administrative burdens which Nicolson disliked and took the initiative in suggesting various ways of reorganising the office so that the work might be despatched more efficiently. After Mallet's departure, he became the acting head of office when Grey and Nicolson were away and was generally expected to inherit Nicolson's post. With Hardinge's exception, no one questioned Crowe's ability nor his suitability for the permanent under-secretaryship though it was felt that Tyrrell was personally closer to Grey and ultimately more influential. Crowe was always conscious of the limited power of the civil servant and though fearless never attempted to over-step his position.

The third assistant under-secretary, Walter Langley, was not a dominating figure and continued to play a secondary role. As head of the African department, he opposed the Colonial Office negotiations with Kühlmann. He sensed that 'the Colonial Office will not be as careful as we are about the foreign – especially French – susceptibilities and it will be we who will have to bear the brunt of their displeasure'.[119] After Campbell's death in 1912, Langley's main concern was with the Far Eastern department.[120] Here he continued his predecessor's policies – support for the Anglo–Japanese alliance, international cooperation in China and a working partnership with C. S. Addis and the Hongkong and Shanghai Bank. There were, however, others in the department, notably Beilby Alston (senior clerk) and J. D. Gregory (assistant), who had different ideas and gradually influenced Grey's thinking. Alston was sent out to Pekin on two occasions, in 1912 and 1913, to act as chargé during Jordan's leaves. This was an unusual procedure and a tribute to Alston's expertise. Alston reacted sharply to Japanese activity in the Yangtse Valley during the Sun Yat-sen rebellion in the summer of 1913 and his alarmed reports, though balanced by the more restrained assessments from the ambassador in Tokio, made a deep impression at home.

Gregory also favoured a more independent policy in China. Like Alston, he opposed cooperation on industrial loans and favoured strong counteraction against the Japanese and French offensives in the British sphere of influence. His arguments were warmly echoed by Jordan who continued to be held in high regard by Grey. Finally Langley acquiesced in the decision to proclaim a special British interest in the heart of the Yangtse. By 1914 Gregory had become the key figure in the department and, with Jordan's support, succeeded in convincing Grey to take a stronger independent line.[121] The war was to again alter the situation.

Not all senior clerks achieved the position of a Crowe or Gregory. Factors of personality remained important and some departments enjoyed a greater measure of initiative and independence than others. 'If all the assistant under-secretaries are ill'. Grey wrote to Nicolson who was particularly distressed by Crowe's absence, 'we must rely upon the heads of the respective Departments, who seem to me quite capable of doing the work well.'[122] While Crowe remained senior clerk of the Western department, he had done the

major share of minute writing. His assistant, Alwyn Parker, was given specific
questions to handle, e.g. the Declaration of London, the problem of the
Flushing fortifications. After 1912, the Western department had a somewhat
lighter work load than usual and there was a rapid turn-over of heads. Eric
Drummond and G. R. Clerk were each transferred after a year, the latter's
experience (two years in Constantinople) was needed in the pressed Eastern
department. Clerk became involved in the problems associated with the Balkan
Wars. He, like Crowe, urged Grey to withdraw from the Concert in Albania
and was prepared to take a sharp line with the Turks over the Aegean islands.
Clerk did much of the drafting for the Eastern department though he was
ably seconded by Henry Norman and Robert Vansittart, the latter a specialist
on the Aegean islands.

The Eastern department had two assistants after 1912; Alwyn Parker, one
of the two, enjoyed a very special position. Even while he had been in the
Western department, Parker was known as the Office expert on railway
matters and had been urging with little success that the British decide what
they wanted with regard to the Baghdad railway and make a choice between
alternatives. Most papers on such questions came to him: 'I minute with some
diffidence...because I do feel very strongly indeed that our policy in regard
to these negotiations [Baghdad railway] should not be merely passive and
expectant, – but since my previous minutes to this effect have not been approved, I am not sure whether insistence from my subordinate position will
be welcomed.'[123] In time, Parker's advice did have effect and when a new
attempt was made to come to terms with Turkey, he became the chief British
negotiator. Despite clashes with Hardinge, Parker worked amicably with the
India Office on the terms of the proposals and then conducted the discussions
with Hakki Pasha, the Turkish ambassador. At one point, Parker was working
twelve hours a day for a five week period without a break.[124] By the end of
August 1913, Britain had secured the bulk of her demands from the Turkish
ambassador. Parker then embarked on a series of parallel talks with Kühlmann
and English representatives who had interests in Mesopotamia and in the
Gulf.[125] Oil discoveries complicated the picture but Parker utilised the new
mood in Anglo–German relations to create a new company on a fifty–fifty basis
to exploit this all-important resource.[126]

Though each stage of the discussions was reported to Parker's superiors,
he was responsible for the shape and contents of both sets of agreements
and amply merited Grey's praise for his tenacity and perseverance. Grey could
not have spared the time for such talks and an under-secretary would have
had to abandon all other tasks to conduct the negotiations properly. In an
earlier age, the British ambassador at Constantinople might have taken the
leading role but the international complications of the commercial interests
involved made it highly desirable for one man in Whitehall to have undivided
responsibility.

Among the other clerks, some were more forthcoming than others. R. P.

Maxwell, the experienced Eastern department head who retired in 1913, rarely did more than address himself to the specific problem at hand. His successor, George Clerk, was less reticent and was already building the reputation which made him a leading voice in Balkan affairs during the war. Even juniors like Norman and Vansittart who dealt with Persian as well as Balkan matters often gave vent to their irritation with Russian demands and methods. This close participation in the decision-making process, customary in the Far Eastern department and necessary in the Eastern department, was also noticeable in the American department. Spicer, its head, pressed the case for the recognition of Huerta in a series of important minutes. Rowland Sperling, the assistant, and Orme Sargent, a junior, wrote penetrating assessments of the American domestic and external situations which Grey read with care. Even one of the most junior clerks, Knatchbull Hugessen, did not hesitate to pen his views about the recognition question. In such matters, it was always Grey who determined policy but the advice of his officials was an important factor in his deliberations.

It is difficult to speak of a Foreign Office view in 1914. The issues of the day were too complex to elicit general pronouncements and there were no major European clashes which provoked such discussions. Even Eyre Crowe was too concerned with Balkan problems to press his Cassandra-like fears on the Foreign Secretary, If the officials were united in their basic support for Grey's entente policies, there were a variety of contending answers to the daily questions which constituted the bulk of departmental business. There were men who would have preferred a tighter connection with the entente powers than Grey thought politically wise or diplomatically useful. Tyrrell on the other hand, wished to maintain the existing detente in Anglo–German relations. Grey was undoubtedly aware of these cross-currents which were exacerbated by some measure of personal animosity. During the spring and summer of 1914, the feud between Tyrrell and Nicolson was particularly bitter; the former charged the permanent under-secretary with disloyalty towards Grey and inattention to the duties of his office. There were quarrels between Nicolson and Crowe and even between Crowe and Tyrrell.

Though Nicolson was anxious to leave, Grey made no final decision as to when he was to go and Bertie was determined to hang on to his Paris post. Nicolson's unwillingness or inability to cope with the huge volume of paperwork left a vacuum which others, particularly Crowe, had to fill. There was endless speculation about the next appointment to Nicolson's post. 'The majority regard Crowe's success as certain', Mark Oliphant wrote. 'I feel there may be a battle of giants between him and Tyrrell.'[127] A visiting diplomat reported that Tyrrell was in high favour and that 'both he and Grey were very Germanophile'.[128] It was fortunate that the spring was an unusually quiet one on the foreign front and that the Office could run on its own momentum. Grey, preoccupied with Ulster and already having trouble with his eyes, did nothing to resolve this internal situation. Bertie charged him with being too weak to make a decisive move but it seems more likely that Grey was not unduly bothered by whatever tensions these rumours provoked.

At the purely administrative level, too, there were signs that the 1905 reforms had not gone far enough. The period had been one of consolidation rather than innovation and the formal structure of the Foreign Office barely changed during these nine years of Liberal rule.[129] Between 1906 and 1913, however, the volume of Foreign Office business increased 36% while there was only a slight increase in staff (less than 10%) and no expansion in accommodation. The Registry system failed to live up to the hopes of the reformers. The Central Registry proved to be a giant bottle-neck and even after improvements in indexing were introduced during 1910 the sub-registries were often inefficient and their indices and registers in arrears. The political departments complained of inadequate dockets, delays in submitting papers even of an urgent nature and a general failure to produce past papers when they were needed. It was discovered by an intra-departmental committee that all papers were summarised four times during their trip from the registries to the Library. This duplication of effort compounded by lack of staff threatened clerical chaos.

To make matters worse, the second division staff was growing increasingly restive with inadequate opportunities for promotion and pay raises. The staff (with the exception of those employed in the Chief Clerk's department) petitioned Grey and receiving no satisfaction pressed the matter before the 1914 Royal Commission on the Civil Service which was scrutinising the Foreign Office in the early summer of 1914.[130] Nothing was done before the war broke out and then the huge expansion of clerical staff and the employment of women created even more difficult problems for the authorities.[131]

Few outsiders knew about these internal matters, It was symptomatic of the times and of the changing base of the Liberal party that Grey and the Foreign Office were coming under increasing criticism during these years. To a surprising degree Grey was able to maintain his image as a figure above politics, trusted by both Liberals and Conservatives. Nevertheless, his freedom of action was repeatedly circumscribed by the factional character of his party and by the divisions in the cabinet. If the Foreign Office took umbrage, Grey trimmed his diplomatic sails. The detente with Germany and Grey's adroit handling of the First Balkan War disarmed some of his critics; though the members of the Liberal Foreign Affairs Committee sporadically attacked the isolation and social bias of the Foreign Office, Ponsonby's protests barely dented the combined Liberal–Conservative defence of Grey. A Royal Commission was created to investigate the complaints not only about the Foreign Office but about the diplomatic and consular services; its hearings took place during the summer of 1914. Though it is true that foreign affairs still concerned only a few in the body politic, the charges of aristocratic bias, social snobbery and bureaucratic power had their echo beyond the walls of Westminster.

There was a good deal of substance to the radical charges. The Foreign Office, and even more, the diplomatic service, continued to represent a social elite of the narrowest kind. Neither the alteration in the examination process nor the institution of a Board of Selection altered the recruitment of 'the right sort of gentleman'. Successful applicants came from aristocratic and gentry families, most of whom had already entered the service of the state. Only a few candidates with mercantile backgrounds competed: a considerable number of Catholics, but almost no nonconformists and, of course, no Jews. Almost all had attended one of the better public schools (with Eton still leading the list) and had gone on to Oxford and Cambridge. The hopeful entrant spent some time abroad perfecting his French and German before the traditional cramming for the highly competitive entrance examination. Many knew each other before they entered the Foreign Office; there were few real 'outsiders'. When Owen O'Malley joined the Western department in 1911, four of its six members were the scions of noble familes. It is not surprising that there was an air of unconscious superiority which permeated some of the diplomatic correspondence and that private letters were rich in the customary allusions to Latins, Levantines and Semites. Like most of their European counterparts, the Foreign Office had successfully withstood the middle-class invasion of the domestic bureaucracy.

This social and educational exclusiveness had important consequences. The similarity in background and upbringing allowed for a comfortable partnership between the Foreign Secretary and his advisors. These men, some fifty in number, shared a common tradition and language which promoted comprehension and speed. The best of these officials could master the most complex problems and reduce them to manageable proportions. They were eager for responsibility and open in their expressions of dissent however unwelcome to their political superiors. The weak or inept were recognised and though protected were found appropriate slots so that the level of competence at the Foreign Office made it much respected both at home and abroad. To some degree shared assumptions arising from class and profession transcended national boundaries. Europe remained the centre of the diplomatic world and the distinction between great and small powers was understood and rigidly maintained (hence the ambiguity of Italian foreign policy). As a group, the European diplomats believed that conflicting interests could be resolved through negotiation and that a resort to force represented a breakdown in the normal order and a defeat for the professional. Outward forms and manners remained important and were essential for the proper working of the international system.

There was, of course, another side to the coin. Officials and diplomats moved in narrow social and professional circles. This shaped their attitudes, reinforced their prejudices, affected their reporting and coloured their advice.

Diplomats cultivated those already in power and deliberately isolated themselves from the more dynamic and revolutionary elements in their host nations. There was a narrowness of interest and of vision which cut officials off from some of the major currents of their day. Even Eyre Crowe, distinguished from his fellow clerks by his intense intellectual preoccupations and by his modest way of life, never felt totally accepted by this narrow establishment world. But the problem went deeper. The domestic political scene of which the Foreign Office was a necessary part had changed far more rapidly than its administrative institutions. Hardinge and Nicolson were undoubtedly extreme examples of the Foreign Office preoccupaton with the leftward drift of British politics but many shared their sense of living in an alien and hostile world. It was a mark of Grey's singularity that he was often more radical in his domestic sympathies than most of his officials who viewed the policies of the left with rising distaste and alarm. Such men watched the entrance of the 'new man' into the governing classes with undisguised hostility. There was a sharp and developing social gulf between those who controlled Britain's foreign relations and those shaping the course of home affairs. The Foreign Office did not know how to deal with the new popular currents. It reacted by becoming increasingly sensitive to any manifestations of public debate and by insisting on its independence from public scrutiny even when such tactics were unnecessary and harmful.

This sense of social defensiveness was strengthened by the Foreign Office pride in its professionalism. The greater need for expertise had enhanced the importance of the permanent official and had increased his sense of power. Diplomacy was a specialist's craft which would only be properly practised by those qualified to give advice. Officials were quick to resent the interference of other cabinet ministers and departments not to speak of even more unwelcome outsiders. The open dislike of Lloyd George and Churchill, and after Agadir, Harcourt, stemmed not only from their pro-German sympathies but from their repeated interventions in Foreign Office matters. Neither Grey nor his subordinates felt called upon to explain or defend their policies to a wider public. Only once did the opposition force Grey to make a statement in the Commons and his officials were outraged at this 'unjust attack' upon their chief. Grey shared their view that the daily issues with which they dealt were far too complex and intricate to be properly understood by the public. He deplored the tendency of the new members to ask questions and raise debates about issues which 'had much better be left alone'.[132] Parliamentary questions absorbed valuable time; blue-books, the number and value of which noticeably diminished in this period, had to be carefully edited; the travelling M.P. was a universal nuisance. Newspapers, too, were regarded with considerable distaste, particularly the powerful and popular press controlled by Northcliffe; the newcomers, men who stood apart from the traditional ruling elite, did not accept the rules of the club. Individual editors and correspondents of the old school – Valentine Chirol or Wickham Steed – were welcome friends and important sources of information and advice. But press campaigns, even in *The Times*, were deplorable for they added an irrational and irrelevant dimension to the conduct of diplomacy. Repeatedly, it was argued that the decision-making process was distorted by the requirements of parliamentary and political life. The relative isolation of the Foreign Office permitted a detachment from the demands and passions of the moment but also created a fundamental public misunderstanding of the causes of the war and the nature of British war aims.

The definition of the diplomatic context was a narrow one. The social and professional elitism of the Office helped to perpetrate a traditional view of international relations. The worlds of diplomacy and commerce remained separate. There were still snobberies about commercial matters which ill-suited a nation of shop-keepers.[133] The contempt in which the Consular Service was held, its isolation and low status, were outward reflections of a deep distrust of the commercial world, its representatives and needs. It is true that in the battle for concessions, British diplomats could hold their own. The non-European departments, moreover, were acutely aware of the economic race and the Office far from reticent when it came to using economic means to achieve political ends. It was often the Foreign Office which brought pressure on the City to invest or provide loans to countries where returns were problematical and less attractive to financiers than to diplomats. There were individual contacts with the leading financial houses; few of the prejudices against traders extended to the Rothschilds or Barings. Yet old traditions died hard and the beliefs inherited from a less competitive age still prevailed. The Foreign Office accepted the view of much of the commercial world that the development and exploitation of trade should be left to the business community. Indeed, it was often felt at Whitehall that exporters were unduly complacent and that German and American competition might stir them out of their lethargy. The Anglo–German commercial rivalry did not seriously alarm the Foreign Office. British firms had recovered from their moment of shock and their pressure for support overseas was sporadic and ill-organised. Some of the more successful Anglo–German negotiations of this period were initiated or supported by financial and business groups on both sides. The existence of this rivalry complicated the international scene and increased the general sense of uneasiness but it was only during the war that German trade expansion became 'black villainy' and that an energetic group within the Foreign Office insisted that trade and finance should be considered a normal part of diplomatic work.

Other weaknesses of the pre-war Foreign Office stemmed from this narrowness of focus. Diplomacy was still divorced from strategy. Grey's misunderstanding of the nature of a British involvement in a continental war was shared by his subordinates. Few challenged the assumption that naval power would determine the outcome of any struggle in which Britain was involved. Though Nicolson and Crowe welcomed the close military links with France, neither explored the long-range consequences of the adoption of a continental strategy. Individual members of the Foreign Office sat on the sub-committees of the C.I.D.; the Foreign Office was active in the fight for increased naval expenditure; Crowe, for one, took a deep interest in military tactics and technological advances. Nevertheless, there was a general assumption that planning and priorities should be left to the services; the contradictory intentions of the Admiralty and War Office did not concern the masters of diplomacy. Few really understood the extent to which all the great powers were circumscribed in their policies by military and strategic considerations. Grey, in fact, welcomed the gap between diplomatic and strategic planning for it gave him an illusion of freedom. While there were those in the Office who were troubled by this semi-committed position, its full implications were never clearly understood.

There is a final dimension to the problem only indirectly connected with the social and professional conservatism of the Foreign Office. In diplomatic terms, Britain was the natural defender of the status quo for she had more to fear than to gain from any readjustment in world power. Both the ententes stemmed from an awareness of competition and a sense of weakness. In time, these new links brought Britain more firmly into the anti-German camp and decreased her freedom of action. It is not surprising that Grey often drew back from accepting the full implications of his own policies despite the pleading of his own officials. The Foreign Office may have exaggerated the strength of their competitors as well as the weakness of their own country. Driven by the danger of a German advance in a direction which was never clearly defined, the officials were willing to pay a high price for French and Russian solidarity. The nature of the German challenge was recognised but the solutions suggested left little room for accommodation. It remains debatable whether a more flexible approach would have allayed German apprehensions or curbed her need to expand. The next generation of officials was to become preoccupied with just this question. But Grey's advisors suggested but one path, a solution which increased German apprehensions without diminishing her appetite and which tied Britain to the actions of her partners. Historans will continue to debate whether any other course of action could have preserved the peace. The clerks argued that only the threat of war itself would check a German advance and that only the combined action of the entente partners could sustain the status quo. We are dealing with men who were on the defensive in diplomatic terms.

Under Sir Edward Grey, the Foreign Office, reached a new stage in its development. His officials, among whom were men of powerful personality, long years of experience, and undoubted ability, had expanded their area of responsibility and were an essential part of the policy-making process. Within clear limits, Grey's clerks shaped as well as enacted the decisions of their chiefs. The ability and dedication of these men allowed the Foreign Office to handle an ever-increasing range of problems in all areas of the world at a time when

Britain's position was under attack. The situation demanded skill and speed for, as the July crisis was to demonstrate, the diplomatic machine itself was slow and cumbersome. That it worked as well and as long as it did was a tribute to the competence of its operators. It was, however, the Foreign Secretary and not his staff, who determined and was responsible for its success or failure. The advice of officials, however strongly urged, was but one element in Grey's deliberations. If the civil servant was no longer a scribe, his sphere of action remained clearly defined. Sir Edward Grey was his own master.

3

Public opinion, the press and pressure groups

K. G. ROBBINS

Sir Edward Grey, of course, believed that 'public opinion' existed. References to it appear both in his speeches and despatches. He sometimes gave 'public opinion' as a reason for taking action or for declining to do so. But Grey was not a speculative man. He never published a detailed picture of the structure of public opinion as he conceived it from his position of power. A behavioural scientist will look in vain for a model of the policy-making process from him.

Certainly, in general terms, public opinion was felt to play a part in the making of British foreign policy. Foreign secretaries before Grey had rather paraded the insular factor of 'public opinion' in their dealings with continental statesmen who were supposed not to have knowledge of the phenomenon. Britain's reputation abroad for fickleness and unreliability, where this feeling existed, was at least in part supposed to derive from the nature of the British constitution. Lord Salisbury, for example, professed to believe that 'The British Government cannot undertake to declare war, for any purpose, unless it is a purpose of which the electors of this country would approve... The course of the English Government in [every] crisis must depend on the view taken by public opinion in this country, and public opinion would be largely, if not exclusively, governed by the nature of the "*Casus belli*".'[1] Lord Lansdowne, similarly, had occasion to warn the German Ambassador in 1905 that it was 'impossible to foresee the lengths to which public opinion in England would press the government to support France.'[2] And in the course of his conversations with the French Ambassador, Cambon, in January 1906, Grey declared that he could promise nothing to any foreign power unless it was subsequently to receive the whole-hearted support of public opinion if the occasion arose.

Such statements all have in common the presumption that in Britain, 'public opinion', at any rate when it came to the ultimate question of resorting to war or maintaining peace, was supreme. In effect, British promises were declared to be worth what the papers said about them. In this situation, foreign countries were meant to console themselves with the thought that when Britain did act, her assistance could be relied upon because it would represent a truly national decision. While it might be true that formally speaking, the commitments made by other states were more firm, this reliability might but mask potentially serious internal divisions.

Nevertheless, it is one thing to read testimonies to the importance of public opinion, another to see how this opinion operated in practice. There is a significant difference of emphasis in these quoted remarks. Lansdowne speaks as if public opinion was capable of forcing the Government to adopt a course of action which it was reluctant to undertake. On this analysis, the function of public opinion was not confined to passing judgment on a Government decision; it was actually capable of taking the initiative itself, making its view plain, and having a direct impact. But of course, public opinion is rarely such a unitary whole, capable of mobilizing itself in such an unambiguous form. It must, in any case, be remembered that these eminent remarks were all made within a specific context. In each case, the Foreign Secretary was not making a normative statement about the 'place of public opinion in the foreign policy-making process', he was using public opinion in talks with a representative of a foreign power to explain his refusal to make a firm commitment. Conceivably, public opinion may indeed have been the reason for this reluctance, but it is as likely to have been a convenient excuse for a refusal which was, in fact, made on other grounds. It seemed to be the case that somewhere in Britain a public opinion could always be located of sufficient importance to block any course of action to which the British Government objected. Most Foreign Secretaries also talked about the future; they rarely said at any given moment that public opinion was the cause of a specific action in the present. It is, in any case, very hard to decide how Foreign Secretaries made up their minds as to what public opinon was at any special time. Grey was not immune from a general tendency among politicians to believe that public opinion corresponded with their own inclinations.

The use of public opinion as a device was not, however, inconsistent with the recognition that at some stage in its formulation and execution British foreign policy had to meet with popular approval. This did not mean that public opinion either could, or should, exercise democratic control over foreign policy. It was the business of the Government to govern. The function of 'public opinion', insofar as it was represented in microcosm in Parliament, was to accept or reject the Government's proposals. Just as the Opposition could not initiate legislation, public opinion had to respond to Government initiatives. Moreover, the Foreign Secretary had succeeded in establishing for himself a position in which it was quite proper for him to appear less partisan than his Cabinet colleagues. As if to symbolize this aloofness, Grey's late-nineteenth-century predecessors had sat in the House of Lords. By remaining in the Commons, Grey was more accessible to public opinion as channelled through the members. In practice, both personal inclination and the pressures of office restricted Grey's attendances in the Commons.

Such a view of the relationship between the Cabinet and the Commons could be defended on two grounds. Firstly, the Foreign Secretary and the Foreign

Office were alone in possession of all relevant facts and able to form a relevant policy on the basis of them. Public opinion might wish to disagree with the policy which resulted, starting from supposed first principles. This was quite legitimate, but it could not have enough information at its disposal to be able to suggest a well-grounded alternative. Secondly, while the virtues of secrecy in foreign policy could be exaggerated, they could not be dismissed. There might well be certain pieces of information which should be kept from an enemy, and which therefore necessarily had to be kept from the public.[3] It was argued that this seemingly irreducible element of secrecy made the relations between Government and public opinion rather different in the sphere of foreign politics from what it might become in domestic politics. While the structure and organization of the Foreign Office might be reformed, that would not in itself alter the need for secrecy and discretion.

Grey himself does not seem to have felt a need to convince public opinion of the merits of his own policy. His position in the successive Liberal Governments was a strong one, indeed impregnable, but it was not based upon a regular following in the country. In contrast to some of his colleagues, he eschewed public speaking whenever possible. While he did have surprisingly strong views on certain aspects of domestic politics, he was usually content to make them known privately. The notion that the Foreign Secretary had a responsibility to 'sell' his policy to the country was foreign to someone of Grey's background and methods, He demanded trust and confidence in himself as a person. While he did not refuse to see representatives of the press if they called, he took no particular steps to cultivate their good offices.[4] The belief that he was remote and aloof was one which he was little interested in changing. In a sense, therefore, it was public deference to his office which sustained Grey.

Not surprisingly, however, most opinion-makers were not content with this view of the role of public opinion. In their view, it should express itself at a much earlier stage in the policy-making process. It was not enough to point to the freedom of action which, in theory, Parliament retained in the summer of 1914. If Parliament was to do anything other than legitimate the decisions of the executive, there would need to be a sustained and informed public, interested in the issues involved long before the moment of decision arrived. But even when such a foreign affairs 'community' can be said to exist, the patterns of mutual interaction between it and the Government are difficult to trace. And there is a strong case for supposing that in this period a developed public opinion of this nature was largely lacking. The study of international history as such was not developed in British universities – it was only in the inter-war period that chairs in this field were established. *The Round Table* was perhaps the nearest approach to a journal entirely devoted to international affairs, but that concentrated on the British Empire and had an avowed point of view to propagate.[5] Certainly, individual academic figures took a keen interest in foreign affairs, but there was no organized forum for their activities comparable to the later Royal Institute of International Affairs.[6] Nor were there organized gatherings composed of members of the Foreign Office and interested laymen to discuss problems of foreign affairs. Access to the Foreign Secretary or the Foreign Office depended rather more on personal contact than on professional status. Whether the Liberal Governments should be censured for failing to stimulate that kind of public opinion, or sympathized with in its absence, is another matter.

The opinion-makers on foreign affairs were therefore restricted to the editors and journalists of the daily and weekly press, writers on public affairs generally, and specialists in the history of one or other country. But there were, of course, very different conceptions of duty and responsibility. It was for the first time possible to distinguish between the 'serious' and 'popular' press, but less easy to measure the impact of either type of paper on its readership. In the absence of attitude surveys, such as would now be deemed essential, any attempt to measure the impact of the press must be extremely tentative. There is no means of ascertaining whether sections of newspapers relating to foreign affairs were read or ignored, nor is it possible to presuppose that purchase of a particular paper implied agreement with its views on foreign affairs. Clearly, there would have been very little knowledge of the details of foreign policy in the mass public. But this public might, nevertheless, readily embrace certain assumptions about Britain's place in the world. In simple terms, such a public might well have answered that the basic objective of British foreign policy was the advancement and projection of British interests. The sole objection to this consensus would have come from class-conscious Socialists, for whom the concept of the 'national interest' had no relevance.[7] They only identified themselves with the concept of international class solidarity, Yet such a general assumption is clearly capable of widely differing degrees of emphasis. There was a patriotism which was accepted as natural without being mawkish or self-conscious. In terms of its own propaganda and self-image, the Unionist Party liked to see itself as the *national* party par excellence. In the event of an inter-state conflict, a Conservative Government would put what it identified as the national interest before every other consideration. The Liberal Party also saw itself as the guardian of the national interest, but it tended to stress the necessity and possibility of reconciling the national interest with wider goals. Liberals, for example, felt in some vague way that the pursuit of the national interest should be combined with a concern for the fate of peoples not blessed with the good fortune of being governed by liberal principles. A Liberal Government admitted the necessity of international competition, but denied the necessity of international conflict.

Was this concern with the national interest a mere façade, hiding the reality of a blatant 'Jingoism'? Was public opinion, at its lower levels, a mass of xenophobic sentiment? It is, once again, extremely difficult to do more than generalize on a precarious basis. Certainly, the casual mention of the 'influence' of Seeley or Kipling will not tell one much about the predispositions of many English working men who never read a serious book in their lives.[8] The self-educated working man was likely to be Gladstonian in his outlook, but while Will Crooks might remark that if the sun never set on the British Empire, it never rose in many parts of his London constituency, it would be odd if pride in the Empire was not present in a vague way among large sections of the working class. While their own status might be low, it was a consolation to know that the British were better than the continentals and certainly superior to the non-European peoples. The fact that the Liberal Government never repealed the Aliens Act is an indication of the limits beyond which popular tolerance of immigration would not go.[9] Workers in certain trades and industries which obviously benefited from a 'strong' foreign policy, such for example as shipbuilding, arms manufacture, the metal trades generally, as well as those in dockyard towns and naval bases, could normally be expected to endorse it. Some parts of the United Kingdom may have been more inclined than others to 'Jingoism', and big cities rather more than country areas. On the other hand, it has recently been observed that strict attention to the words of the song which inspired the concept of 'Jingoism' reveals that they do not express a rampant desire for warfare.[10]

Would this public opinion ever desire war, or was war something for the Captains and the Kings, and not for the 'people'? The Boer War had been a recent reminder to Englishmen of the reality of fighting. It had been won by volunteer soldiers but hardly in a manner likely to encourage a general enthusiasm for further British triumphs. Haldane's reorganization of the Army necessarily assumed that the great mass of the nation would be prepared to fight, but most assumed that the Army would only be called upon to act in national self-defence. The reluctance to contemplate aggression was partly because Britain was a 'satisfied' power, anxious to preserve the status quo, and partly because Britain's insular situation meant that the term 'defence' could have a strict connotation. Hence, in some measure, the reluctance to depart from a 'Blue Water' strategy. It was one thing to ask a man to defend his country from attack, another to ask him to believe that this defence involved fighting on the continent. The notion that a preventive war could be justified was, in all probability, confined to a small number of no doubt influential people. But against the speculations of Fisher and others on this subject must be reckoned the fact that it was received doctrine that public opinion would not tolerate such an exercise. The notion of conscription as the best method of ensuring self-defence was anathema to large sections of 'public opinion' and not confined to the Liberal and Labour parties. Liberal opinion, for the most part, persisted in identifying conscription with 'militarism'. To resort to conscription would be to defeat the integrity of the civilization which one would be fighting to preserve. Nevertheless, in the years just before the war, the issue of conscription was being seriously debated. Although Lord Roberts was disappointed with the response his campaigns evoked, the membership of his National Service League grew from 16,000 in March 1908 to over 91,000 three years later. To some extent, the very fact that Haldane was forced to write an attack on compulsory service shows that the movement was making some impact.[11]

It is extremely difficult to judge how widespread and serious was the belief that war was inevitable – or how far the prospect of war was actually welcomed.[12] Again, it is a question of the level of opinion with which one is concerned. Bernard Bosanquet's *Philosophical Theory of the State*, in Halévy's words, 'soon took its place as a classic', but it is a different matter to suppose that it shaped mass opinion. No one would dispute that changes were taking place in the philosophical climate of the period, but to pick on one volume as epitomizing a general mood is a hazardous enterprise. In any case, it might be argued that the philosophical climate only tells one about the philosophical climate. For example, it has been suggested that G. E. Moore's *Principia Ethica*, in considerable measure was responsible for the 'pacifism' of the Bloomsbury group. Survivors of the group have, however, denied reading Moore or even if they did read him, believed that their pacifism had a quite different basis.[13] Similarly with the influence of Social Darwinism, in its various and varying manifestations. The language of the 'struggle for existence', as much between nations as individuals, and the images of 'dying' and 'living' nations certainly can be found in many contexts. The writings of Kidd, Pearson and others must have circulated among the Edwardian middle-class and 'influenced' it; but opinions must differ on the extent to which the popular mind can be said to have made these differing opinions their own.[14] The assumptions and attitudes of many popular fiction writers, particularly of stories for boys, have been laid bare, in a somewhat humourless way. The sense of superiority, the excitement of adventure, and the code of honour, need not be interpreted as symptoms of an aggressive malaise. That there was unease and 'decadence' can readily be conceded, but the precise connexion with any particular policies is difficult to establish. Undoubtedly, however impressive was the façade of Empire, it was widely sensed to be an uncertain foundation of British greatness. Yet, if not the Empire, on what else was Britain's position founded? In terms of population and resources, Britain was being overtaken by Germany and the United States, and there was considerable alarm about the future development of Russia. There was a great deal of discussion (and myth-making) about the 'Great Depression' and the long-term future of British industry. Whether or not 'Splendid Isolation' had ever strictly existed, Britain's relationship to the continent was clearly changing. Some of the assumptions underlying the pattern of alignment which Britain should seek were undoubtedly racial in character. The notion of 'Anglo-Saxondom', for example, with Britain, the United States and Germany as natural associates, was widespread. No two nations were believed to resemble each other more closely than the English and the Germans. Against this, however, there was a growing interest in Russia and the Slav world. Nor was it unknown for English travellers to prefer taking a room with a view in France or Italy. It is a far jump from the tracing of cultural influences and fashion to the formulation of foreign policy.[15]

There were those who felt that great sections of public opinion with strong national views on foreign policy were being manipulated by sinister forces bent on furthering their own economic ends. The most cogent expression of this view came from J. A. Hobson. British foreign policy, he believed, was primarily 'a struggle for profitable markets of investment'. While it was true that 'an ambitious statesman, a frontier soldier, an overzealous missionary, a pushing trader, may suggest or even initiate a step of imperial expansion, may assist in educating patriotic public opinion to the urgent need of some fresh advance...the final determination rests with the financial power.' He elaborated the view that 'the industrial and financial forces of Imperialism, operating through the party, the press, the church, the school, mould public opinion and public policy by the false idealization of those primitive lusts of struggle, domination, and acquisitiveness which have survived throughout the eras of peaceful industrial order and whose stimulation is needed once again for the work of imperial aggression.'[16] These views were echoed by H. N. Brailsford, for whom it was a perversion of the objects for which the State existed 'that the power and prestige for which all of us pay, should be used to win profits for private adventurers'. In Turkey, for example, he believed that embassies inextricably mixed their politics and finance.[17] The public should not be exploited in the interests of the few.

This view was challenged by Norman Angell. Class interests were no doubt served by the 'patriotic outbursts', but 'those interests did not, and could not, create the sentiment throughout the numerous classes whose material interests were in no way touched by the national action in the events concerned'. The feeling itself was 'non-rational' and precluded the idea that it could have its origin in a 'limited clique whose motives are intensely rationalistic. At the most we can assume that the vested interests merely exploited an already existing sentiment.' It was this universal sentiment which was of real importance to the student of politics. Angell felt that it was too simple to believe that the Harmondsworth or any other press, could have created these 'disorders of the public mind'.[18] On the other hand, the Press had done little to restrain public sentiment. Abuse of the Press Lords, however, was not very helpful. If the mass public would not read the 'better' newspaper, how could it be reached? Could the unsensational be made sensational?

Angell then began an association with Northcliffe as editor of the continental *Daily Mail*. Ramsay MacDonald thought he was being 'used' by accepting such an appointment. Angell replied, 'My mission is evidently to the heathen – the unconverted. That is why I use the "Mail". If I knew of a paper more jingo, or rather more successfully jingo, I would use that.'[19] He also attempted to bring about a revolution in public opinion. In *Europe's Optical Illusion*, and its more elaborate sequel, *The Great Illusion*, he took issue with what he held to be the prevailing assumption about the nature and rewards of war. He seized on the glib contemporary talk about the collapse of the British Empire and the 'ruin' which would then ensue. It seemed to be axiomatic that if British security were placed in jeopardy, British commerce and industry would decline, and with it, the nation as a whole. He noted Frederic Harrison's assertion that talk about industrial reorganization was hollow 'until we have secured our country against a catastrophe that would involve untold destruction and misery on the people in the mass – which would paralyse industry and raise food to famine prices, whilst closing our factories and our yards'.[20] In particular, Angell tilted at the monthly *National Review*, edited by L. J. Maxse, which regularly threatened dire consequences for Britain from the German challenge.[21] In reply to such fears, Angell advanced two basic propositions: that Germany could only destroy British trade by destroying the British population, and that if she could destroy the population (which was inconceivable) then she would destroy one of her most valuable markets. While the current political philosophy in Europe remained unchanged, Angell did not urge the reduction of the British defence budget by a single sovereign – but the whole philosophy was grossly antiquated. By making political conceptions 'rational', and seeing exactly what armaments and conquests could and could not do, a state of mind could be produced in Europe 'which will render it no more necessary to arm nationally than it is necessary for an individual Anglo-Saxon of our day to arm individually in order to fight duels to defend his honour'.[22] Not that Angell was free from his own illusions. He never reckoned with the possibilities of transfer of population, mass destruction or forcible de-nationalization. Nevertheless, 'Norman Angellism' was the most talked about notion relating to international affairs in Britain, if not in the world, in the years just before the First World War. His book was constantly revised and reprinted. Norman Angell Societies mushroomed. A monthly journal appeared to spread his ideas. Perhaps no other book in this field was as widely reviewed – though by no means always favourably. King Edward VII read it, Lord Esher espoused it, and Sir Edward Grey pronounced it full of thought. The Foreign Secretary acknowledged that Angell's ideas had met with great success in Britain and he hoped that they would do so in time on the Continent. But he believed that it was not enough to get ideas into people's heads – feelings as well as minds had to be changed.[23]

Naturally, it was through the press that both men's minds and emotions were reached, and as Francis Williams remarks: 'After 1896 the world of journalism was never to be quite the same.'[24] The launching by Northcliffe of the *Daily Mail* marked a further extension of the daily national newspaper into households which had previously not taken a newspaper regularly. Although this step did mark the beginning of the 'popular' newspaper, it would be a mistake to exaggerate its circulation. The Education Acts of 1870, 1876 and 1880 undoubtedly improved the standards and extent of literacy, but spare money was needed in the pockets of large sections of the working class before advertisement could be attracted for the biggest mass market of all. The *Daily*

Mail seems basically to have appealed to the self-improving lower middle-class, a rapidly expanding and ambitious section of the population. Francis Williams describes it as an ignorant public, though eager to learn, 'ill-informed on public affairs and not deeply interested in politics, particularly of a party kind...'[25] No evidence is presented for this assertion. The *Daily Mail*, of course, was not left alone on its pinnacle for long, though no rival succeeded in toppling it during this period. The *Daily Express*, founded by Pearson in 1900, was the first British newspaper to print news on its front page. When Beaverbrook took an interest in its affairs in 1913, it was, even with a circulation of just over 275,000 copies, a losing concern.[26] The other existing newspapers were inevitably affected. The *Daily Telegraph*, which had itself previously made the running, and had a circulation of more than 300,000 in 1896, lost between 50,000 and 60,000 readers almost at once and never recovered them. The *Standard*, which had flourished during Lord Salisbury's prime, had been sold to Pearson in 1904. He tried to save it by imitating *Mail* methods, but without success, and it expired towards the end of the First World War. Similarly the *Morning Post* was suffering from a fall in circulation, and it only found salvation in a post-war merger with the *Telegraph*.[27] The *Daily News* and the *Daily Chronicle* both left the ranks of the penny press and came out at a halfpenny in the partially successful attempt to gain increased circulation. But both papers were in financial difficulties.[28]

Other papers tried to ride out the changes and pretend that they did not need to adapt to the new circumstances. Naturally, therefore, in order to survive, they depended on the services of a patron, motivated by social ambition or desire to serve a political cause. The most noteworthy of this group were the *Westminster Gazette*, the *St James Gazette*, the *Pall Mall Gazette* and the *Globe* – all of them London evening papers with small circulations designed basically for Clubland and 'informed' opinion. The normal circulation of the *Westminster Gazette*, for example, did not rise above 20,000. It was financed after 1908 by a group of wealthy Liberals, and at least one shareholder was a nominee for the Liberal Party itself.[29] Equally magisterial, but in an equally perilous position, was *The Times* which remained at 3d. but which was losing circulation and was in financial difficulties. When Northcliffe took it over in 1908, it had a circulation of but 38,000. He reduced the price to 2d. in 1912 and the sale rose by 10,000, and to 1d. early in 1914, when the circulation climbed to 165,000 copies,[30] Northcliffe also rescued the *Observer* which, when he bought it in May 1905, had an average circulation of some 3,000 copies. When he sold it in April 1911, the circulation was not far short of the 40,000 which Northcliffe believed necessary to make a profit.[31]

The search for profit was probably more important than it had ever been. Previously, owners of newspapers had, within limits, foregone in many instances the maximization of profits in return for the pleasures and influence of ownership. Now, while this still remained the case with some newspapers, Northcliffe's dynamic approach had led to a more stringent application of the profit yardstick. In many cases, ownership became commercialized and, under these conditions, 'money came before public policy'.[32] This is, perhaps, to overstate the position. Northcliffe, and his editors, and they were not alone, continued to believe that they had a policy and an opportunity to influence public opinion. But it may be that the very nature of the instruments of their greatness prevented them from having an influence with Governments, who resented, and perhaps did not understand, this spawning industry. In any case, C. P. Scott's comments on Northcliffe, that his tragedy was that 'though he knew how to create the instruments not only of profit but of power he had not the least idea what to do with his power when he got it' are not altogether inaccurate.[33] On the other hand, it should be remembered that it was possible to launch national newspapers on a precarious basis with very little money – as the pre-war struggles of the *Daily Herald* and the *Daily Citizen* demonstrated.[34]

Another result of the search for profitability was the gradual domination of the London press over the country as a whole. Again, the *Daily Mail* was first in the field, establishing a printing office in Manchester. The tentacles of London even spread to Scotland. Other newspapers similarly set up subordinate printing offices. The old-established provincial dailies took a heavy battering and many were forced to close down, or were swallowed up, then or later, by the national giants. As a result of this process, public opinion became more of a genuinely national entity and Ensor believed that 'Hitherto the larger provincial centres followed each their own public opinion, often saner and less febrile than London's. Now the passions of the metropolis infected the country.' This latter is, of course, an obvious value judgment of somewhat doubtful validity. Not that all the leading provincial papers were forced to submit to the domination of the capital. The *Yorkshire Post*, the *Liverpool Daily Post* and the *Birmingham Daily Post* all survived, as did the *Scotsman* and *Glasgow Herald* in Scotland. The *Manchester Guardian*, under C. P. Scott, was the most distinguished provincial daily paper and already developing its national pretensions. Yet it is dangerous to assume too readily a correspondence between the fact that the *Guardian* was a provincial paper in Manchester and its particular approach to foreign affairs. As C. E. Montague observed, the *Manchester Guardian*, under Scott, was moving against the stream of its local public opinion. He converted a 'Whig journal into an organ of advanced Liberalism, while a large proportion of its readers, sons and grandsons of the followers of Cobden and Bright, were pretty obviously destined to pass through the antechamber of Liberal Unionism into the Conservative household...'[35]

Such a point raises the obvious question of the extent to which it is possible to regard the press in this period as creating 'public opinion'. With a secure, though never easily gained, financial base, Scott could to a large extent go his own way. Other editors and papers did not so much bend public opinion as be bent by it. H. W. Massingham was exaggerating when he wrote of the transformation of journals of opinion into 'organs of business, supplying the wares they think their customers want, and changing them whenever a new demand arises', but this seemed to be the way things were going.[36] Moulding opinion seemed a straightforward business – except when one was actually sitting in an editorial chair. One might have expected that the situation of journals would have been better than newspapers. The weeklies were concerned with interpreting the news rather than being the first to give it. The editor of the *Spectator*, J. St Loe Strachey, was far from believing that periodicals could direct opinion in any easy fashion.[37] The great days of the nineteenth century periodicals were in fact over. The common stock of a cultural and political heritage which they had refined and perpetuated was giving place to the specialized disciplines of the twentieth century. Not that there were no fresh periodicals. The *Speaker* had emerged as a radical weekly to speak for the 'pro-Boers', and it continued to be a lively journal until it was wound up in 1907. The *Nation* then took its place with substantially the same contributors and general outlook. It probably reached a circulation of over 3,000 – as did the *Saturday Review*. The *Contemporary Review* and the *Nineteenth Century and After* usually carried a good range of articles on foreign and military policy. Circulation figures were normally not available, but it would seem that the *Spectator* headed the list – though it declined from the figure of 22,000 in 1903 to 13,500 in 1922. Ensor claims that it alone made a profit. The *New Age*, edited by A. R. Orage, had a circulation of just under 3,000. The *New Statesman*, founded in 1913, had about the same figure. Then there was the *Economist*, edited with fierce Cobdenite rigour by Francis Hirst. But even with these small circulations, it was possible to run such a sixpenny weekly without losing much more than £2,000 a year. Other weeklies which began in this period and which did not reach 3,000 copies found survival a more difficult task. It is clear from these figures that whatever the intrinsic merit of the articles, the journals themselves could have played little part in moulding mass opinion. Their circulation (possibly overlapping) must primarily have been among the professional classes.[38]

It was once fashionable to place the behaviour of the press high on the list of the reasons for war in 1914.[39] But it is difficult to believe that the press 'created', for example, the naval scare of the spring of 1909. Certainly the press did nothing to subdue the panic. The Conservative newspapers were unanimous in supporting a larger programme of building: 'We want eight and we won't wait.'[40] *The Times* also supported the construction of the four 'contingent' ships to guard againt the possibility of German hegemony. The Liberal press was in a deep dilemma. To accept the need for an acceleration was extremely distasteful, and went against all the convictions of progressive opinion. Therefore, while no Liberal newspaper challenged the principle of naval superiority over Germany, most commentators were anxious to delay the construction of the extra ships as long as possible. Only Spender in the *Westminster Gazette* gave his government entire support. But some sections of

the press were not detached observers of the crisis. Fisher, in a totally abandoned manner, gave information on the struggle in the Cabinet to Garvin of
the *Observer* who published it. Fisher's activities came near to being exposed
in a sharp exchange of letters between the Foreign Secretary and Garvin.[41]
When, at the end of July 1909, the laying down of the four ships was
announced, the *Economist* denounced the move as 'very provocative in
character'.[42] At a local level, while one of the Croydon newspapers deprecated
'dragging the Navy into the cockpit of politics' the local Liberals were forced
to admit that it was the chief object of concern in the by-election. The
Conservatives doubled their majority. It was a clear warning to the Government that there were deep popular anxieties which could not be ignored.

There were no official contacts between the Foreign Office and Fleet Street.[43]
Grey did not encourage interviews and could only be said to be on terms of
any intimacy with J. A. Spender, though he also corresponded with St Loe
Strachey, chiefly about the United States.[44] However, William Tyrrell, Grey's
private secretary from 1908 to 1915 went out of his way to cultivate relations
with the Press. Editors found Tyrrell a more subtle man than the Foreign
Secretary. Spender has recorded that when he wanted 'more sophisticated'
material he went from Grey to Tyrrell who 'played over the same subject with
a keen and brilliant wit and the surest eye for its personal equations.'[45] In
addition to Spender, Tyrrell saw Bell, Buckle and Chirol of the *Times*,
amongst others. For its part, the Foreign Office possessed a list of papers to
whom information was sent, and offending newspapers could be taken off the
circulation list.[46] It sometimes went further. For example, Tyrrell intervened
with Moberley Bell in the summer of 1908, and successfully prevented Steed
from being transferred from Vienna to Berlin because he feared that Steed's
anti-German attitudes would further embitter Anglo–German relations.[47]
Nicolson, when he was permanent under-secretary, urged the press to moderate its anti-Italian tone during the Turco–Italian war, and only the *Daily
News* refused.[48] But in general, interventions were few and requests were only
made on a personal basis. The Foreign Secretary himself rarely acted, but both
the permanent under-secretary and his own private secretary placed items,
asked for changes, and used interviews in order to influence the leader
writers. They were not, of course, invariably successful in their attempts.
Indeed, the paradox of Grey's relations with the press was that with the
exception of Spender, he could normally expect to be opposed on most issues
by writers on foreign affairs in the Liberal press – by H. Sidebotham in the
Manchester Guardian, H. W. Massingham and H. N. Brailsford in the *Nation*,
A. G. Gardiner in the *Daily News* and F. W. Hirst in the *Economist*.[49]

This assault was never more clearly demonstrated than at the end of 1911
with particular reference to Persian policy. The *Daily News* claimed that Grey
was 'not flouting Liberal opinion only, but the opinion of all parties in this
country who believe that our word is our bond'.[50] The *Economist* lamented
that the quarrels of diplomatist with diplomatist stood in the way of a proper

arrangement with Germany. And British policy in Persia had done little more than back up Russian encroachments. Such talk played a part in gaining the foreign debates at the end of 1911. The explanations then given by Grey did not satisfy his press critics. In an editorial entitled 'Grey must be stopped', Massingham declared that 'public opinion has not authorized the government which acts in its name to follow a policy so mean and weak as this'.[51] At this point, the press campaign merged with attempts by pressure groups to secure a fundamental change of policy, if not the overthrow of Grey himself, and its significance will be assessed later. Asked whether he minded the abuse, Grey replied in February 1912: 'Well really I haven't time to read my papers except Times, Westminster Gazette & Spectator & I have seen very little of the abuse. I get the drift of it from what is told me & from extracts sent me, but I have too much to do to mind...'[52]

There was, of course, one newspaper which was widely regarded abroad as the mouthpiece of the Government, and that was *The Times*. Such a position was disclaimed both by the paper and the Foreign Office. Yet, apart from Spender, it was representatives of *The Times* who were the most frequently received visitors at the Foreign Office. Valentine Chirol, for example, was in a special position. He had himself formerly served in the Foreign Office and used his links with Hardinge and others to good effect for the paper. Charles Repington, the military correspondent of *The Times* also had extremely good contacts, largely stemming from his own previous service as an officer. The status of *The Times* was therefore *sui generis*.

The leading critics of government policy were, of course, protean. The same names appear in many different contexts, and their activities are perhaps best considered in the context of the pressure groups which they led. Edwardian England possessed a great many societies of journalists, scholars, politicians and clergymen whose activities had some bearing on foreign policy. These groups were by no means co-ordinated, even if, as was by no means always the case, they were agreed on their precise objectives. The broad field of Anglo-German reconciliation occupied the attention of many people in different organizations, As early as 1905, the Anglo–German Friendship Society was founded, chaired by Lord Avebury, the veteran scientist and politician. Apparently an attempt by the Society to insert, in its address of welcome to the Kaiser in 1907, a clause urging mutual reduction of armaments, was ruled out by Count Metternich with tears in his eyes.[53] This does not seem to indicate great strength on the part of the Society. Nevertheless, it did its best to arrange exchanges 'to promote greater understanding'. It was widely felt, even in the years of acute tension on the naval question, that Britain and Germany resembled each other very closely and that the prospect of a clash was intolerable for this very reason. The crisis of 1911 led to fresh efforts at reconciliation. Leading churchmen sponsored exchanges with their German brethren and published a journal, the *Peacemaker*. It would try to prevent 'the irreparable disaster to Christendom of a collision between the two great

Teutonic peoples'.[54] The eminent church historian, Harnack, felt that after Agadir it rested with England to convince Germany 'by deeds that our experience during the past year was an episode'. Other German churchmen declared that they could 'no longer believe in the friendship of England'. In the autumn of 1912, an Anglo–German Understanding conference was held, sponsored by the National Peace Council, the British–German Friendship Society and the Associated Councils of Churches in Britain and Germany.[55] Most prominent in these activities was J. Allen Baker, M.P. Grey refused to accept that if there was international tension the Triple Alliance was alone without blame. In fact, writing at the end of December 1912, he expressed the view that relations between the two countries were excellent.[56] The churchmen agreed, writing in the spring of 1913 that the clouds were dispersing. By the summer of 1914, they found it 'almost difficult to realize that there were still unresolved problems affecting the relations of the two countries'.[57] Other organizations also claimed some share in achieving this detente – Sir Ernest Cassel, for example, who was a German Jew by birth and intimate of King Edward, founded an Anglo–German Institute in 1911 to assist young Englishmen in Germany and Germans in England. Cassel was, on occasion, used as an intermediary between Britain and Germany.

Efforts of this kind were not concerned exclusively with Anglo–German relations. Sir Thomas Barclay, a distinguished jurist, was not alone in believing that the Anglo–French entente constituted something new in international relations, because, allegedly, it found its most congenial soil among the business and popular elements of the two nations. Every attempt, he believed, should be made to strengthen the ties 'in every branch of the public and local activities of the two nations – in that way public opinion would ensure that the relationship was indestructible. Once this had been assured, there was nothing to stop similar links being constructed with Germany. The Institut Français du Royaume Uni was the product of this kind of public relations activity.[58] Attempts to assess the relative strength of Germanophil and Francophil sentiment must be somewhat tentative. One gets the impression, perhaps paradoxically, that there were more extensive links with Germany, but this may be because they were felt to be more vital insofar as it was with Germany that relations were strained. In any case, it may be argued that these attempts to develop public opinion to public opinion relations, albeit initially at an élite level, were but scratching the surface and absurdly pretentious in their claims and activities. Perhaps the most bizarre of these exchanges was that of the pressmen themselves. A party of German journalists were entertained in England in June 1906 and the visit reciprocated in the following year. Nothing substantial seems to have followed these events.[59]

The Anglo–Russian convention could hardly fail to be strongly attacked. The Society of Friends of Russian Freedom had a distinguished and long record of concern for the progress of constitutional government in Russia.[60] It had been patronized by Liberals of all kinds. The conclusion of an agreement with Russia seemed to many Radicals to call for active opposition. Outside support was enabling the Tsar to recover and there was now a vested interest in England in his survival. 'The time has come' Brailsford proclaimed in 1912 'for public opinion to end this alliance of subservience and complicity.' The people of Britain had no wish to be entangled in a continental system with a Power which 'hanged its Socialists, imprisoned its Deputies, flogged its noblest citizens, oppressed its Jews...'[61] Brailsford, MacDonald, Nevinson and C. P. Scott were among those who sat on the executive of the Anglo–Russian Committee. One of the most active members was Lucien Wolf, who was brought into the campaign because of his special concern with the plight of Russian Jewry. Wolf wrote a great many articles attacking Russia and, not surprisingly, he attracted a certain amount of anti-semitic comment and allegations that he was in German pay. Wolf was also rather an exception in that he did not share the more general radical assumptions of his colleagues. He had no sympathy with pacifism, unilateral disarmament or compulsory arbitration.[62] The Foreign Secretary was not very impressed by these attacks on his policy. In 1909, when attacks on the Tsar were being mounted he wrote: 'As to the Czar, the I.L.P. say there were some 800 executions in Russia last year – that is true, but they don't say that there were about 1500 murders & some thousands of terrorist outrages.' He thought that the Tsar was 'a kind moral family man, who as an English squire would be much respected in his parish. His direct control over the huge machine of Russian bureaucracy is necessarily slight – he will be remembered as the Czar under whom Russia received a Duma & a constitution.' There were, however, people in England who did not want to know the truth but to express their own emotions – 'Dram drinkers I call them for they must be in a state of emotion & when you attempt to dilute their emotions with the truth they are as angry as the drunkard whose whisky you dilute with water.' To insult the Tsar would be to play straight into the hands of the reactionaries in Russia. 'The Russian revolutionaries' he concluded, 'who wish to embroil their country with any foreign country in order to overthrow the Russian Govt. come here & find it easy to play upon the emotions of our dram drinkers – in fact supply them with the stimulant they crave for. Russia is clearly & with pain & throes working towards better things; she has progressed more in three years than seemed possible considering how slowly human affairs must move in such a vast country: Our attitude towards her internal affairs should be one of benevolent neutrality & hope.'[73] In face of such resolution, no pressure group was likely to get very far.

The campaign against the Russian agreement was closely linked with the campaign for Persia. In Persia, Brailsford wrote, 'We have been guilty of a treason against freedom, and in this treason our alliance with Tsardom has borne its natural fruit.'[64] Grey had received many petitions when the agreement had been first drawn up because of what it seemed likely to do to Persia. The most distinguished British authority on Persia, Professor E. G.

Browne of Cambridge, took a leading part in the agitation and his book on the Persian revolution impressed the younger generation of Radicals.[65] On reading the book, G. M. Trevelyan wrote 'I know the Persians are not perfect, and by European standards are asses...But if once we find ourselves engaged with the destroyers of Finland in a squabble with Germany and Turkey to defend a practical partition of Persia, we are ruined...'[66] A Persian Committee was formed with an overwhelming preponderance of M.P.s, some forty-four, on the executive. Its objectives were to focus attention on Persia, to keep in the forefront Persia's importance from a British Imperial viewpoint and therefore to maintain the country's integrity and independence. The chairman of the committee, H. F. B. Lynch, had extensive commercial connexions in Southern Persia. Large public meetings were held, both in London and Manchester, in January 1912 addressed by, amongst others, MacDonald, Professor Browne, Lynch, Ponsonby and Morel. Resolutions urging the preservation of Persian integrity and independence were enthusiastically passed. Morgan Shuster, the dismissed American adviser to the Persian Government, was given a great ceremonial welcome at a dinner in London.[67] The storm was intense, but, whatever his private feelings about Russian action, Grey refused to bow before it. He complained to Spender that he was bombarded by letters from people wanting him to break with Russia over Persia but, 'how on earth can we help Persia if we do? And it is these people who denounce partition because it would increase our responsibilities!'[68] The Persian Committee had reached its zenith and had singularly little to show for its sound and fury. Nevertheless, in the longer term, the combination of press criticism, pressure-group activity, and parliamentary debate, probably did have some effect on Grey's thinking early in 1912. Certainly, from that time on he became more sympathetic to the notion of a détente with Germany, though this was of little help to the Persians.[69]

Many of these same critics also had places on the Balkan Committee, founded after the Macedonian revolts of 1902–4. Its objectives, however, were less clear. While all agreed that Ottoman rule in the Balkans was iniquitous, they were divided as to the correct apportionment of territory after the Turks had departed. While it was necessary to keep pressure on the Government to do something about the situation in Macedonia, was that pressure to be applied on behalf of Greeks, Bulgarians, Serbs or merely Macedonians? The 'Bulgarian' supporters on the Balkan Committee tended to win, with the result that opponents dropped out and sometimes organized rival groups.[70] Nevertheless, partly as a result of the Committee's activities, Grey admitted in 1911 that it would be impossible for Britain to side with any policy in the Balkans designed to repress Bulgaria – 'any thing like Disraeli's policy of thirty-five years ago would be impossible now'.[71] But the Foreign Office was by no means enthusiastic about the activities of self-appointed 'experts' on the politics of various Balkan countries. The fact that J. D. Bourchier, the *Times* correspondent in the area, had received the honour of appearing on a Bulgarian postage stamp attired in local costume did not increase his standing in Whitehall. For their part, some of the ambassadors and ministers resented the rôle of local British newspaper correspondents. On occasion, however, the information they provided was useful and could be employed in London to offset the official reports.[72] As far as the Balkans were concerned, relations were always difficult. When, in December 1912, Noel Buxton was reported to be having talks in Sofia with the German Minister proposing the division of the Ottoman Empire, the Prime Minister minuted, with cool disdain, that Mr Buxton was 'an amiable nincompoop'[73] Of course, this feeling was returned. The Balkan Committee tended to feel that the Foreign Office was completely out of touch with the political realities. There was not a little undisguised glee in the Foreign Office when Bulgaria overreached herself in the Second Balkan War. However, with the outbreak of the World War, the supporters of the various Balkan countries again went to war on behalf of their protégés.[74] Grey himself was somewhat weary of the Balkans, and cynicism had even penetrated to members of the Balkan Committee by the end.[75]

In retrospect, Sir Edward believed that the issue which had most moved the country during his period of office was the question of the Congo. Other societies had interested themselves in the conditions in Leopold's state before E. D. Morel took up the campaign, but it was his Congo Reform Association which brought the matter to public attention.[76] Well-known sympathizers happened to gain office in the Liberal Government, and the Association appealed to a section of opinion not normally interested in the intricacies of international diplomacy.[77] Seizing on a hint that 'the Foreign Office seems to desire all the pressure from public opinion they can get', Morel developed his considerable skills as a propagandist, journalist and organizer, initially, in harmony with the Office.[78] This co-operation did not last. Morel came to regard the Foreign Office as 'tricky', since it brought into policy-making considerations which Morel, in his single-minded devotion to the Congo, thought quite extraneous.[79] For its part, the Foreign Office felt that Morel was the sort of man who would never be satisfied. Though many of his criticisms were just, they did not accept many of his solutions. Thus, from the summer of 1908, as the reform movement lost something of its popular appeal, Morel felt he was fighting a losing battle. A definite split arose between reformer and the Office.[80] From 1909 onwards, Morel became increasingly critical of the ententes and Grey's methods of diplomacy. Speaking on behalf of British public opinion, he warned the French Colonial Minister that unless the French attitude towards the Congo changed, it might weaken the entente.[81] As an organizer, Morel's skill was unrivalled, he was equally fluent with his pen. The 1911 Moroccan crisis strengthened his suspicions of France, and in his pamphlet, *Morocco in Diplomacy*, he placed the major responsibility for the crisis upon the British Foreign Office.[82]

The events of 1911 had more general consequences. A Foreign Policy Committee was set up under the presidency of Lord Courtney of Penwith, with

R. C. K. Ensor as secretary. The organizers had very ambitious plans. They wanted to try to co-ordinate the various pressure groups in order to make a strong demand for fuller parliamentary control – with the assumption that if this was achieved, many of the points of contention between the nations would be removed. But it failed to make the expected impact.[83] The outbreak of war two years later seemed to demonstrate that the old order had failed. It was then that E. D. Morel got his chance to urge the creation of an effective democratic control over foreign policy.

The members of these pressure groups all shared the assumption that their campaigns were disinterested. However, Grey, like every other statesman, had to face pressures from private traders, investors and financiers. Resolutions carried by Trade Associations, or Chambers of Commerce, letters to news-papers, pleas to government offices, inspired articles in the press and the lobbying of Members of Parliament were all forms of pressure. Possibly equally important, but inaccessible to the historians are more subtle pressures exerted through private conversation. The difficulty is to decide whether the actual initiative for a particular policy came from within or without; whether commercial, financial and official interests merely happened at some point to coincide or whether one 'caused' the other.

In the course of the nineteenth century, the Foreign Office had developed well-defined conventions governing the relationship between officials and private interests. These conventions were elaborated in the Bryce Mem-orandum of 1886, and, though it is true that individual officials, particularly at the remoter posts, might occasionally have by-passed them on their own responsibility and at the risk of a rebuke from London, the conventions remained substantially intact.[84] The Foreign Office claimed to be interested solely in preserving a 'fair field and no favour' for British traders and investors overseas. It did not intervene in the private business affairs of individual British subjects. The supply of commercial information, in the form of consular and diplomatic reports and replies to trade enquiries, was the limit of government responsibility for the promotion of trade and investment. The British Government was to have no connexion with the negotiation of contracts and concessions, or with the direction of foreign loans.

Grey was content, in normal circumstances to let these conventions stand. During his period of office, replies either to commercial or to financial pressures for further government assistance, or to requests for official inter-vention in the direction and control of British trade and finance overseas, were all governed by the rules published in the Bryce Memorandum. Yet, in a number of different areas of the world, under the growing pressure of inter-national competition, conditions had changed very radically since the 1880s. British Foreign Secretaries were finding themselves compelled, in special cases, to develop a much closer relationship with financiers and traders. In the first place, it had become a fact of international politics that banks, railways, roads, telegraphs, oil-wells – 'strategic' concessions – were used increasingly as political weapons in the rivalry between the Powers. The Imperial Bank of

Persia, after its foundation with British Government support in 1889, acted as the direct agent of British official policy in Tehran. The National Bank of Turkey, a British-Government sponsored enterprise, was established in 1909 specifically to counter French and German financial pressure on the government at Constantinople. The Bryce Memorandum itself was a recognition that if it were even to maintain the 'fair field and no favour' principle for British trade, then the British Government would have to be prepared to take positive action to safeguard British traders, concessionaries and investors from discrimination. The diplomatic pressure of rival Powers made any other course suicidal. Thus, the British Government committed itself to a policy of direct diplomatic support for the leading British interests in China – the Hong Kong and Shanghai Bank, the British and Chinese Corporation, Jardine, Matheson & Co., and the Peking Syndicate.

Therefore, like his immediate predecessors, Grey acted both in the British official tradition of non-intervention in commercial and financial affairs, and in the new, direct rule of co-operation in certain circumstances for political reasons with specific financial or commercial institutions. The earlier tradition continued to govern relationships in all such uncontroversial, if highly competitive, markets as Europe, Latin America, the United States, and the White Dominions – in which by far the greater part of British trade and investment took place. But a policy of mutual defence brought together British financiers, trade associations, and the Foreign Office in a number of difficult areas where genuine political interests were at stake, or where, alternatively, a real threat existed to the continuance of a 'fair field and no favour' for British trade and investment. In these trouble spots, Grey may, to some extent, have been responding to commercial or financial pressures. He may even have been led to exaggerate their importance by the successful propaganda of the private interests directly involved. He may have helped some men to make their fortunes, and others to lose theirs. But it is true, equally, that he was using his relationship with British financiers as an instrument in the conduct of two basic elements in traditional British policy – the defence of the Empire, and the maintenance of fair and equal conditions for the overseas trade and investment on which, as all British statesmen recognized, Britain's survival depended.

Whatever the nature of the pressure and the form of public opinion, Grey was not the man to be hastily influenced from the outside. Reflecting subsequently on his political experience, he noted that 'Government by public opinion' was no doubt an admirable formula, but it presupposed not only the existence of public opinion, 'but that on any particular question there is a public opinion ready to decide the issue. Indeed, it presupposes that the supreme statesman in democratic government is public opinion. Many of the shortcomings of democratic government are due to the fact that public opinion is not necessarily a great statesman at all.'[85]

4

Foreign policy and international law

CLIVE PARRY

LAW AND POLICY

A visitor from Mars, confronted only with the evidence yielded by the states-man's own *Twenty-Five Years*, might be pardoned if he were to assume that Grey had flourished in an era in which there was no law at all between nations, or at most a primitive code governing behaviour in war. For the references in that work to international law are confined to the following:

The British view was that there is no such thing as a 'pacific blockade' and that we could not recognize what had no existence in international law. (Vol. I, p. 13)

We decided that all copper from Swedish ports must be stopped....Whether such a measure had any precedent in international law I do not know....(Vol. II, p. 108)

Our whole transactions with neutrals were founded on the contention that vessels captured by our Navy were brought before a Prize Court and that British Courts dealt with them impartially according to international law. (Vol. II, pp. 109–10).

It is known now that in Germany, during 1916, the military and naval authori-ties pressed for unlimited submarine warfare in disregard of all considerations of international law or diplomatic expediency. (Vol. II, p. 113n.)

The status of Egypt in relation to Turkey had not, so far as international law was concerned, been affected by the British occupation. (vol. II, p. 171)

Grey indeed appeared to attribute the binding force of treaties to con-siderations of honour alone and could thus both write, concerning the week before the war, that

not once in all the arguments used to me did either the French or Russian Government or their Ambassadors in London say or imply that we were under any obligation of any kind. The appeal was made to our interest, it was never suggested that our honour or good faith was involved. (Vol. I, p. 85);

and say, in that fateful speech of 3 August:

...the Government and the country of France are involved because of their obligation of honour under a definite alliance with Russia...that obligation of honour cannot apply in the same way to us. We are not parties to the Franco–Russian Alliance. (Vol. II, p. 298)

Our Martian enquirer will learn little more of international law from Trevelyan's biography. For, apart from gathering by the way the opinion that: 'Substantially...The Hague Conference of 1907 came to nothing and marked another milestone towards Armageddon.' (*Grey of Fallodon*, p. 206) he will glean only this curious passage, regarding the annexation of Bosnia and Herzegovina:

The rebuff to Grey's policy was serious. He had tried to insist that the breach of Treaty over Bosnia should be 'regulated' by an International Conference, and found himself practically alone in the demand. The French gave him no help...It was not the last time that English effort to stand up for international legality for its own sake has been interpreted by the European Powers as a Machiavellian attempt for some concealed but no doubt selfish end. That any country could honestly regard the defence of the Law of Nations as an end in itself was inconceivable to the statesmen of Europe; but to Grey, as to other British Foreign Ministers, respect for legality has seemed the only principle by which universal war could in the end be avoided. Thus 1908 held 1914 in its arms. (*Ibid.* p. 225).

The passages quoted, with all that they imply by way of omission, must astonish the student even of international affairs. But the student of international law, if he be astonished, may perhaps keep his incredulity within bounds if he reflects upon a principle with which he has long been familiar: the principle of the intertemporal law. For it is a commonplace that events and acts of a past time are to be judged, not according to the rules and notions of law now prevailing, but rather in the light of the law as it then stood. And it is a commonplace of even wider application that men may speak prose without knowing it, or laymen conduct themselves according to an instinctive rather than an informed conception of what law calls for. Despite his fourth class in the Honour School of Jurisprudence, Grey was no lawyer; nor was Trevelyan, whose formal academic accomplishments were no doubt more notable. Yet neither was untypical of his time or viewpoint.

The institutionalization of the pattern of the international order in, first, the League, and more latterly the United Nations and the many lesser international agencies so-called, has made men aware that the system of States has a constitution of a sort and that its operation has a legal character giving expression to its phenomena in shapes and concepts long familiar within the State – in such shapes as contract or treaty, wrong or delict, and such concepts as obligation, illegality and even criminality. This awareness, however, is of very recent growth. In their apparently almost total ignorance of the legal character of the international order – or to put it bluntly, the plain fact that nations no less than men are ruled by law and are so ruled at all times – Grey and his Boswell stand nearer the figures of any other earlier period of the span of modern history than they do to our own.

In some measure no doubt the apparent divergence between the attitude towards international law of Grey and his contemporaries, as well as of all his predecessors, and that of the men of our time is a question merely of words. By the term international law today there is connoted the whole body of rules, customary or conventional, obtaining between States. Indeed there is now much that is called international law that transcends even these wide bounds, as such contemporary watchwords as 'human rights' and 'the general principles of law' sufficiently testify. As late as the early years of the century, however, in diplomatic usage 'international law' meant customary international law only, as opposed to treaty. This only semi-technical usage lingered as late as 1919 when, in the preamble to the Covenant, it was still natural to state as aims of the League both 'the firm establishment of the understandings of international law as the actual rule of conduct among Governments', and 'the maintenance of a scrupulous respect for all treaty obligations in the dealings of organized peoples with one another', as if these were different and distinct things. Furthermore, 'international law', however defined, is a relatively new term. Only a little while before Grey's birth in 1862 the framers of the Treaty of Paris were declaring Turkey 'admitted to participate in the advantages of the Public Law and System (*Concert*) of Europe', in language reminiscent of the proclamation, at Vienna in 1815, of the neutrality of Switzerland as 'part of the public law of Europe'.

It would be at least partially misleading, however, to suggest that the statesmen of Grey's time merely called what is now understood by international law by other names and made a distinction between customary law and treaty now considered unnecessary. On the contrary, they had a different attitude towards the relation of law and policy from that now apparently – it is perhaps necessary to emphasize the word apparently – prevailing, because there then obtained a different legal notion of the central problem of policy, namely war.

LAW AND WAR

Members of the Liberal Government of 1906 and their admirers have been wont to boast, not without justice, of the thoroughness and perfection of British preparation for the war of 1914. Military staff conversations with France had been begun already in 1905. The fleet had been largely turned over to oil fuel and the 15 inch gun developed in great secrecy. The celebrated War Book had been drawn up and the Territorial Army formed. As a result, when *der Tag* at length came, the German spies were laid by the heels at once, the concentrated Grand Fleet passed the Channel without lights to disappear into the northern mists, and the Expeditionary Force materialized beyond the Marne to impress Generals von Bülow and von Kluck with almost the same sense of impending doom that the sight of tripod masts behind the promontory of Port Stanley was a little later to affect the luckless Admiral Graf Spee. It is a familiar story made the more poignant by the lucky escape of the *Goeben* and *Breslau* from those who were marking them, the loss of the *Aboukir*, *Cressy* and *Hogue* to a single U-boat, and the shell shortage which so soon overtook Sir John French. If these were the accidents and unpredictabilities of war on the grand scale, what would the position have been without the preparations?

Lloyd George – rather unfairly perhaps considering his share of the responsibility – has pointed, however, to a well-nigh fatal central defect in the British planning. Despite the meticulous drawing up of military railway time-tables and the placing of guards on stores of naval cordite, it had never been decided, not only what should constitute a *casus belli*, but where to fight the predictable and known enemy and how to direct the strategy of the campaign. The result of the first of these failures in the opinion of at least some, though it is of course highly arguable, was that war came when it need not have come. Had Germany known certainly, the thesis runs, that Britain would support France, she would not have endorsed the Austrian ultimatum. The result of the second, which again is naturally disputable, was that the Expeditionary Force was inserted in the line between French armies, so that it was denied any real initiative until 1918. If instead it had gone to Antwerp the story might have been very different. And thirdly, because there was no combined General Staff. the British military effort either was, according to the taste of the particular critic, expended in futile frontal assaults in France or, as the case may be, diverted from the vital Western Front and frittered away in distant 'sideshows' such as Gallipoli.

To some extent this fatal central flaw in British preparation for war must be acknowledged. It is alluded to here not because of its intrinsic interest but because of the curious and striking parallel which is presented between it and the hideous gap which is to be perceived in the notion of the international legal order entertained at the same period. That international law was a relatively highly developed discipline at that time is not to be denied. Whether, as his reminiscences might suggest, Grey was largely oblivious of this, or whether, as his biographer might be taken to imply, he was in the forefront of the upholders and defenders of that law, does not, it must be confessed, much matter. For the fact was, or was almost universally taken to be – there being a difference here which may not be without significance – that the international law of the time condoned, even enhanced, war. This being the case, its elaborate rules upon other topics, included the precise manner of carrying on war, were inevitably prejudiced and to a degree necessarily trivial and illogical. And this being the case, the time being one of the gathering of war clouds, these rules merited little attention from those concerned with great affairs.

Again in this regard Grey is to be seen as one whose attitude, however remarkable it may seem today, does not differ noticeably from that of his forerunners. To the discerning it must be clear that war is not today a lawful institution. States may legitimately defend themselves. They may even upon occasion proceed to a 'use of force' which is not purely defensive. But they are no longer to be construed to be free, for any reason or no reason, to establish between themselves and their designated adversaries a special condition of belligerency, connoting special rights as against third parties as well as their adversaries. But it may be admitted that it is necessary to be reasonably discerning to appreciate this. The old terminology is still with us and will be with us for some time to come. It is all too easy to fall into the way of it and to continue to speak in terms of 'wars' and 'enemies' and to fail to see that such latinisms as 'hostilities' but perpetuate the error.

The end of war as a legal institution has come about by haphazard and even illogical means. The steps in the story are confused. What has been agreed upon, primarily in the Kellogg–Briand Pact (itself an engagement which, however seriously it may now be regarded, was entered into with a lack of consideration bordering upon the frivolous), is that resort to the threat or use of war is prohibited and that, as a logical consequence, the pacific settlement of all disputes is obligatory. It has further been decided by the judgment of the Nürnberg Tribunal that an individual may suffer death for engaging in the planning, preparation or waging of a war of aggression or a war in violation of treaties. There is a certain logical difficulty in relating these two propositions to each other, involving the question as to how far individuals, as distinct from States, are amenable to international law. The upshot of these and connected developments is, however, certain enough: that war has been dislodged from the position it was once taken to hold as a lawful institution, investing its participants with a special status and special privileges. As a result international law is now no longer open to the reproach that it in a manner permitted homicide and purported nevertheless to repress assault, trespass and breach of contract.

It is a tenable view that war never was in truth a legal institution and came to be considered such only as a result of the misunderstanding, if not the dereliction, of writers. Certainly no State has ever resorted to war without elaborate and often plausible explanations of the rectitude of its course, as might be expected if indeed the law gave an unrestricted right of war. While, therefore, the earlier writers may be pardoned if, acknowledging the prevalence of conflict between nations in fact, they concentrated their efforts upon designing a *jus in bello*, a code of rules directed to the mollification of some of war's worst effects, the later scholars are not to be praised, and may be seriously blamed, for assuming, and in a manner sanctifying by their authority, a *jus ad bellum*. That they did so is not to be denied.

THE LITERATURE OF THE LAW

There is no published evidence that Grey pursued his legal studies after leaving Oxford. But evidence that he never thereafter opened a book on international law is equally lacking and, despite Lloyd George's strictures upon his patrician airs, it is to be assumed that so conscientious a Foreign Secretary did in fact read in the international legal literature at least of his own country. What then is he likely to have absorbed? His formative years and his period of office coincided, as it happens, with what may be called the second generation of British monographic writers. The writings of the first generation, who provided, following Continental and American scholars, the first works to replace the malleable and classical Vattel, capable of quotation on every side in every controversy – the generation, that is, of Phillimore and Twiss – were already old books by the 1890s. But between 1888 and 1914 there appeared in England in successive editions at least four good and substantial books, offering a systematic exposition: *Westlake*'s elegant treatise appeared in two parts in 1904 and 1907; Lawrence's *Principles of International Law* was first published in 1895 and reached its fourth edition in 1910; the masterly *Hall*, first published in 1885, passed into the hands of Atlay upon its author's death ten years later, before the proofs of the fourth edition had been completely read; *Oppenheim*'s treatise, which was perhaps the least competent of the four but which was to have the good fortune of falling into the hands of distinguished subsequent editors and thus to acquire a new lease of highly influential life lasting until but a few years ago, appeared first in 1905 and in a second edition in 1912. But what could these works tell the enquiring lay statesman?

In Westlake's view:

International law did not institute war, which it found already existing, but regulated it with a view to its greater humanity...An attempt is sometimes made to determine in the name of international law the conditions on which a recourse may be had to arms, as that an offer of submitting to arbitration shall have been made, where the case is not one of those supreme ones for which it is generally considered that arbitration is unsuitable. No doubt that is the counsel of morality, and so too is that much shall be borne rather than that war shall be begun for a slight though just cause, even when there is no other recourse. But these are not rules of law for they are totally lacking in precision, the principles which they express receive nothing approaching to general observance, and the legal character of a war is the same whether they have been observed or not. The truth is that when war enters on the scene all law that was previously concerned with the dispute retires, and a new law steps in, directed only to secure fair and not too inhuman fighting (*International Law, War* (1907), pp. 3–4).

For Lawrence, the old distinctions between just and unjust wars are but

moral questions, and modern international law does not pronounce upon them. To it war is a fact that alters in a variety of ways the legal relations of all the parties concerned. Such matters [as the causes of war] are supremely important: but they belong to morality and theology, and are as much out of place in a treatise on international law as would be discussion on the ethics of marriage in a book on the law of personal status. (4th ed. 1910, pp. 333–4)

Equally, and even more explicitly, for Hall, international law

recognizes war as a permitted mode of giving effect to its decisions. Theoretically, therefore, as it professes to cover the whole field of the relations of states
which can be brought within the scope of law, it ought to determine the causes
for which war can be justly undertaken...[This] it attains to a certain degree,
though very imperfectly. It is able to declare that under certain circumstances
a clear and sufficiently serious breach of the law, or of obligations contracted
under it, takes place. But in most of the disputes which arise between states,
the grounds of quarrel, though they might probably be always brought into
connexion with the wide fundamental principles of law, are too complex to
be judged with any certainty by reference to them...International law has
no alternative but to accept war, independently of the justice of its origin, as
a relation which the parties to it may set up if they choose, and to busy itself
only in regulating the effects of the relation (*International Law*, 4th ed. pp. 63–5)

Here indeed is cold comfort for the enquiring layman. But what is
remarkable is that the makers of such statements do not, seemingly, appreciate
that, in the light of them, their supplementary pronouncements, however
elaborate and internally logical, must appear to the layman to be, if not
nonsense, then at least no law. That warfare should be conducted 'humanely',
if it be not a mere contradiction to suggest that it can, may appear desirable.
That a title to territory may be acquired by occupation or prescription or in
some other manner analogous to the processes of the law of real property
within the State may again seem a not unreasonable proposition. Similarly that
treaties, once made, should be observed, is no bad rule. But to suggest that
the State is constrained in these regards *as a matter of law* when, in the same
book if not in the same breath, it is laid down that, in Hall's words, war 'is
a relation which the parties to it may set up if they choose', that by war
territory may be wrested from an adversary, and that war may be made in
defiance of treaty is, to say the least, to tax the intelligence and the patience
of the ordinary man. To such a man it may seem that both Grey and his
biographer gave to international law in their writings as much space as it might
appear from the masters to deserve.

THE BINDING FORCE OF TREATIES

It is irrelevant to the purpose here, which is to examine how far Grey's policy
was ruled by law, to argue that the legal status of war was not then, as it is
not now, as the writers stated it. It is true that the writers are blameworthy
in no small degree. International law, as they of course rightly observed, could
not have prevented, and cannot now of itself prevent, armed conflict between
States. But it need not, and should not, and now does not, legitimate and in
a manner glorify armed conflict. For such a course, as has been pointed out,
affects not only the status of war but, by a species of reflection, every other
aspect of the relations of States. If, in short, war is lawful, and by war States

are permitted to dismember and destroy each other, it is unconvincing and illogical to characterize any other conduct of States as illicit or licit. So long as such a thesis obtains, law can have no influence upon policy save by accident or tradition, and to seek to trace any such influence, though it must be attempted, is in the last analysis unprofitable. It may or may not be the case that a particular State has, at a particular time, followed in its policies what has been stated to be the law. But that it did so is immaterial. For, if it was free to divest itself of all restraint by declaring itself a belligerent, the course it in fact followed was dictated by choice, or convenience, or interest, or by some consideration other than obligation, such as is of the essence of law.

The *jus in bello* is no exception here under a system of law which permits war for whatsoever cause; there is no true obligation to wage war in this way rather than that, by these means rather than those. For no penalty and no disability other than retaliation by the adversary can follow from disregard of whatever restraint may be conceived to exist. Equally there is no duty upon a belligerent to observe the rights of so-called neutrals. Only considerations of his own interest limit his freedom to declare neutrals to be enemies also and by so doing to abolish their rights at a stroke.

But in the present context it is worth while to examine, even upon the assumptions of the textbook writers as to the nature of the international legal system, one specific and subordinate problem. This is the question of the binding force of treaties. Grey, as has been seen, would not have been wrong if, upon a consideration of the writers, he had dismissed, as his own book might be taken to suggest, international law as largely irrelevant to the conduct of international relations. For the writers themselves, by their concession of the legality of war, largely abdicated that sovereignty they might and should have claimed for the law. It is nevertheless striking that he should appear, in contrast to the writers, to regard treaties as binding in honour only; and equally that his biographer, Trevelyan, should seem to have attributed to treaty the somewhat perfunctory role, and by implication only that role, of regularizing an irregularity. At first sight these attitudes appear to contrast, if not to conflict, with those of the textbook writers, for whom the treaty is a contract, binding under the law, and primarily creating rather than extinguishing obligations.

Here, however, it may be that the statesman and his biographer have a more correct view of things. In the textbooks a 'law of treaties' of considerable elaboration has grown up, much influenced by the notion of contract in the law within the State. Rules governing the formation, interpretation and discharge of treaties have been laid down upon the domestic analogy, and treaties are said to be binding in law as a result of the existence of a customary rule that *pacta sunt servanda*. This structure ignores several things, such as that there can obviously be no binding rules as to how treaties should be made so long as the agreement of States is the source of the law: if there were any such rules they could always be waived. It ignores, too, that *pacta sunt servanda* is an empty phrase, meaning no more than that agreements which are, or are intended to be, binding, either are, or as the case may be are intended to be, binding. But, what is more important, it ignores too both the historical role of treaties in the relations of States and the nature of those relations. States in their relations with one another, though served by legal advisers, are not lawyers but laymen. They regard their bargains as binding upon them, as does any honest man. If pressed they may admit, for what the admission is worth, that they are *legally* binding. Whilst, however, each treaty is a distinct and binding bargain in itself, it is also merely one step in a continuing relationship, one item in a running account, which relationship or account involves many other steps or items which may not be also treaties. To the diplomat or states-man a treaty is no more than a stage, albeit an important stage, in a constant process of negotiation. Very often the fact that it has, often after infinite preliminaries, been concluded is of considerably greater significance, than what it may say. Very often it may say little enough: it may not in fact say anything which can be construed to constitute the faintest shadow of a legal obligation. Thus the North Atlantic Treaty binds each party, should another be subject to attack, to do no more than take 'such action as it deems necessary'. Grey insisted that neither the military nor the naval staff conversa-tions with France bound either side to anything. Lloyd George tells us that he personally accepted this opinion, but adds that there is 'abundant evidence that both the French and the Russians regarded these military arrangements as practically tantamount to a commitment on our part'.[1] But what of the arrangement of 1912 for the concentration of the British and French fleets in the North Sea and the Mediterranean respectively? Even Grey asked concerning this, 'Had not [this], in fact, created an obligation, in spite of express stipulations that [it was] not to do so?'[2]

Treaties are indeed binding in international law just as are contracts in municipal law. But they are also essentially negotiable, just as a man who has made one contract with another may always compromise it by a further agreement. In practice, between the limited numbers of States which form the international community, one treaty becomes in the course of time very often overlaid by others, so that what, if anything, remains of the obligation, if any, it originally imposed, is very difficult indeed to determine. And since the running account between the parties remains open, it is often not worth stopping to make that determination but more profitable to proceed to the next step or next treaty. In international relations, moreover, action very often precedes argument, and is regularized rather than initiated by treaty. That 'sadly overworked instrument', the treaty, that is to say, is employed not uncommonly to set the seal upon some rearrangement following a general upheaval. Of this character are, for instance, the Treaties of Vienna, Paris, Berlin and Versailles. Yet very little of these well-known characteristics and uses of treaties is made mention of in the books of international law. In this regard the phraseology of statesmen and historians is more informative but is not to be taken as a denial of the binding legal character of treaties.

THE LEGAL ADVISERS

A Foreign Secretary is not of course obliged to take his law from elementary textbooks, but has legal advisers. Traditionally the legal advisers of all branches of government have been the Law Officers.[3] As a result of more or less of accidental circumstance which there is cause to regret, the office of the Law Officer specially learned in the law of nations, the Advocate-General, ceased to be filled after 1872, though until 1887 Dr (afterwards Sir James) Parker Deane continued in effect to discharge the duties of the office. There remained however, and still remain, the offices of Attorney- and Solicitor-General, and of Lord Chancellor, some of the holders of which have been notable international lawyers. The Liberal administration of 1905 brought in Loreburn as Lord Chancellor and Sir J. Walton and Sir W. Robson as Attorney- and Solicitor-General respectively. Loreburn had been a Law Officer briefly in 1894–5. He had been of counsel in both the British Guiana Boundary arbitration with Venezuela (1897) and the Alaska Boundary dispute (1903). He thus had considerable experience relevant to the work of the Foreign Office. He resigned in 1912 for reasons of health, to be replaced by Lord Haldane, never a Law Officer and, despite that he served occasionally as deputy for Grey, of no particular international legal experience. Haldane in fact preceded Grey in withdrawal from office, being excluded from the Coalition Government in May 1915, when he was replaced by Buckmaster, who had been Solicitor-General from 1913. Walton had no special international experience before becoming Attorney-General and gave place to his junior, Robson, already in 1908, when the latter was succeeded as Solicitor-General by Sir Samuel Evans, later to be the Prize Judge. Robson was succeeded by Rufus Isaacs in 1910. In that year Isaacs became Attorney and Simon Solicitor. Simon succeeded to the Attorneyship in 1913 with Buckmaster, as has been said, as Solicitor.

It is probably not unfair to say that markedly less international legal talent was available to Grey in the persons of the Chancellors and Law Officers of his time than had been at the service of his Conservative predecessors, Salisbury and Lansdowne, whose Chancellor had been Halsbury, under which title there was disguised Sir Hardinge Giffard, a Law Officer as early as 1875, and whose Law Officers had been Webster, Finlay and Carson. The second-named of these not only held office continuously from 1895 to 1905 but was to return as Chancellor in 1916 and to become a judge of the Permanent Court of International Justice in 1922. During the Liberal years, he had been counsel in the North Atlantic Fisheries case (1910), his greatest forensic triumph.

But the Foreign Office had come to consult the Law Officers less and less even by the mid-nineties. Many causes may be suspected to have contributed to this. One, mentioned already, was the fortuitous disappearance of the Advocate-General, the officer who was, as a Civilian practitioner, not merely specially learned in international law but by reason of the permanence of his appointment, specially experienced. Another was a certain contempt for the expert entertained by Lord Salisbury and, it would appear, inherited by Grey no less than Lansdowne. But a major cause was the acquisition by the Foreign Office of its own internal legal advisers. The first such adviser, Pauncefote, filched from the Colonial Office in 1876, developed a taste for diplomacy and soon went off into the 'lay' side of the Office, ending his career as Ambassador to the United States. He was succeeded by Davidson who, having been appointed in 1886, was still active when Grey became Secretary of State and was in fact to remain Legal Adviser until 1918. In 1902 Hurst had been brought in to assist him, principally in connexion with the drafting of legislation for the Protectorates for which the Foreign Office was still responsible. These two were joined by Malkin in 1914.

It is no doubt the fate of every legal adviser of a ministry of foreign affairs, external or internal, to discover constantly that he has never been called in when he should have been called in, or that he has been called in much too late, or that his advice, when it is sought, is either ignored or misunderstood. But the degree to which he is made use of, and to which in consequence he, and his mistress the law, will he able to influence policy, must depend upon his personality. Some legal advisers have clearly exerted a great influence upon policy – even to the extent, as in the case of Pauncefote, of exchanging the role of adviser for that of actor or policymaker. The late Sir Cecil Hurst from as early as 1919, as witness his celebrated 'Revision' of the draft of the League Covenant, was manifestly highly influential. How far his chief, Davidson, made any impact upon policy is difficult to assess. He was undoubtedly a considerable lawyer, as he was, incidentally, a considerable mountaineer. But it must be admitted that he was a somewhat narrow lawyer. As Tilley and Gaselee relate, because of his insistence that he was a lawyer and nothing more, and of his early incautious declaration that 'quoad legal adviser' he thought one thing, whereas 'quoad Davidson' he might well think another, he suffered the soubriquet of 'quoad Davidson' throughout his career.[4] It is difficult to believe that a man called 'quoad Davidson' can have had much influence upon policy.

Davidson wrote a myriad of minutes during his career – many times more, incidentally but nevertheless significantly, than either of his immediate successors, Hurst and Malkin. Many of them are of high interest and value, albeit increasingly acidulous in tone. That they are not great State papers – if indeed there were any great State papers in this period – is not necesarily Davidson's fault, even if he is to be held responsible for what would appear to be certain defects in his character. For even if his overly professional approach to matters, and perhaps a not overwarm manner, discouraged consultation with him upon issues upon which, for instance, Hurst might in his place have been consulted, it does not follow that the result would have been different.

The Foreign Office, it is well known, underwent a reorganization in 1906, just as Grey came in. Students of this metamorphosis have tended to attribute, it is thought, too great an importance to it. They aver in effect that it transformed the Office from a body of clerks who formed a species of personal secretariat of the Minister into a great policy-making organisation with a personality of its own akin to that which, rightly or wrongly, is attributed to the Department of State. A reading of the archives of the Office does not bear out the truth of this hypothesis. On the contrary, the papers of the period after the reorganization are by and large less instructive than those of the earlier period. Trevelyan, moreover, reports Grey as having laid it down that 'I did not regard anything except my own letters and official papers as deciding policy' (p. 169). In these circumstances it must follow that the degree to which his legal advisers had any influence upon him must have depended on Grey's own attitude to legal advice which, as has been suggested already, would not appear to have been marked by any degree of enthusiasm.

Davidson, whatever his limitations, was a man of courage, as his career as an Alpinist ought to make clear. He was not of the sort of departmental legal advisers who refer to the Law Officers when they are 'windy'. On the contrary, there is some evidence that he actively discouraged references beyond himself. As a result, the process of diminishing reliance upon the Law Officers, begun under the previous administration, continued under Grey's regime. There were thus fifteen references in 1906, twenty-six in 1907 (including one to the Lord Chancellor), ten (including one to the Law Officers and Lord Chancellor) in 1908, twelve in 1909, fifteen (including one to the Lord Chancellor) in 1910, ten in 1911, and twelve in 1912.

THE OTHER ADVISERS

'In this matter of international law', the First Lord of the Admiralty stated to the House of Commons on 28 June 1911, 'under the practice of the Admiralty, the expert adviser is the Director of Naval Intelligence who is always an admiral of distinction...'[5] This proposition is at first sight somewhat startling. It appears less so when it is recalled that the mother country no less than the daughter has ever lived under a government of laws rather than of men and that the whole 'Whitehall operation' is in essence a legal operation. To nobody familiar with the Foreign Office papers will it come as a surprise that the first paper in the collection[6] put together hastily when Grey came in to acquaint him with what might come up at the Hague Conference was a paper[7] on proposals for the exemption from capture at sea of private property by Sir Edward Hertslet, the veteran Librarian, compiler of the *Treaties*, of *British and Foreign State Papers*, and of the *Map of Europe* and *Map of Africa by Treaty*, author of a thousand memoranda, often wrong, often misleading, but by their continuity and mass constituting a distinct archive of immense value.

Law is not hard to pick up, especially for a Government servant, and the formal requirements of admission to the Bar of England are still not such that the omission of anyone concerned with the law to satisfy them is of much consequence. Nevertheless it will indeed come, it may not be doubted, as a surprise to students, even informed students, of international law no less than international history that the principal advisers in relation to the great international legal questions of the time were not the Chancellor or the Law Officers nor yet the Foreign Office legal staff, but men of whom they very likely never heard and whose names are for the most part not to be found in any law list – men like Sir John Ardagh, Sir George Clarke, later Lord Sydenham, and, though he indeed was in the law list, Hamilton Cuffe, Earl of Desart.

Sir John Ardagh was a sapper officer who became Director of Military Intelligence and in that capacity interested himself in international legal questions relating to war on land arising in the course of the struggle with the Boers. Any reader of his memoranda cannot fail to see that he mastered this new field of endeavour with the same skill he displayed in marshalling the base details during the Nile expedition.

Sir George Clarke is a more mysterious figure in the present context. How this professional soldier, again a sapper turned administrator, came to be the principal adviser on questions of maritime belligerent rights is clear enough. For he was Secretary to the Committee of Imperial Defence and those were the days when, as Lord Hankey's career was to prove so signally, the civil administration looked particularly to the regular services to fill positions of a politico-military flavour. It is surprising, nevertheless, that someone with greater previous experience of either the sea or the law was not called on instead.

Lord Justice Fry, selected as leader of the delegation to the Hague Conference, was of course a lawyer of distinction, though also a considerable botanist. He may be said, moreover, to have had previous experience of international relevance. He was Legal Assessor in connection with the Dogger Bank enquiry. Even before this he had been arbitrator in the Pious Funds case between the United States and Mexico (1902). He attained his 80th birthday during the Conference.

The Earl of Desart, despite that he served in the Royal Navy from his thirteenth to his sixteenth year, was presumably not designated as principal delegate to the Conference which drafted the Declaration of London on account of his naval expertise. On the contrary, he had held simultaneously the offices of King's Proctor and Director of Public Prosecutions for many years. He was in short a Government lawyer of great eminence, very much on the home side of things, though he too had had a modicum of international experience in that he had, as Treasury Solicitor, been responsible for presenting the British case in relation to the Dogger Bank incident in 1904.

THE PRINCIPAL LEGAL QUESTIONS

The prominence of these unfamiliar figures in relation to the principal international legal questions which arose in Grey's time is to be explained by the nature of these questions. For they had to do primarily with the laws of war on land and with the law of sea warfare. They arose in short from the Second Hague Conference of 1907 and its aftermath, the miscalled London Naval Conference, which drafted the Declaration of London. They were thus questions of prime interest not only to the Foreign Office but also the Service Departments. And they were therefore questions which had in the past been dealt with directly by the Admiralty and the War Office as much as by the Foreign Office. Thus if we go back to the Napoleonic Wars we shall find that the Law Officers are advising the Lords Commissioners as much and as often as the Secretary of State.[8] Similarly, the St Petersburg Conference of 1868 had been an affair of military delegates and the Brussels Conference of 1874 largely a War Office matter.

Ardagh's prominence in connection with South African war questions[9] indicates that the system had not changed by the end of the century in so far as matters affecting the laws and customs of warfare on land were concerned: such questions were War Office rather than Foreign Office questions. Grey perpetuated the system by confirming, when he came in, his predecessor's nomination of Ardagh as leader of the delegation to the Geneva Conference of 1907 for the revision of the Red Cross Convention. The Foreign Office in fact abstained from any intervention in relation to this Conference even when the delegates entered a reservation against the articles of the draft Convention designed to protect the Red Cross emblem from commercial use on the unduly technical ground that Parliament might refuse to enact the necessary implementing legislation.[10]

Sir Edward Grey, as Foreign Secretary, of course 'spoke for England', and spoke no less when he was silent. A policy is to be attributed to him notwithstanding that it was the policy of his predecessors continued unchanged or that it was pronounced by the mouth of a delegate allowed to be selected by the War Office or the Admiralty rather than the Foreign Office. It is, however, more difficult than usual to distinguish between the attitudes of the statesman and the State where there exist such practices as those alluded to. British policy in relation to the questions of maritime law raised at the Hague Conference, and current afterwards right up to the final abandonment of the Declaration of London in 1916, has appeared in retrospect to be bizarre. That policy was Grey's in the sense that he permitted it to be pursued, Grey's and the Foreign Office's. It must nevertheless be clear that it did not actually originate with Grey or with the Foreign Office, still less with the Foreign Office lawyers, but rather with officials, mostly not lawyers at all, of other Departments. It is possible that this has to some extent been overlooked in the assessment of this policy from the point of view of its effectiveness or otherwise *qua* foreign policy. It ought not to be overlooked in the consideration of the question as to how far Grey's policy was influenced by legal considerations.

THE HAGUE CONFERENCE

The Liberal Government of course in a manner inherited The Hague Conference. Count Benckendorff's letter convoking it had gone out only on 3 April 1906, sketching an agenda which included revision of the 1899 Convention on pacific settlement, the completion of the codification of the laws of land warfare, and the elaboration of a convention on the rules of maritime warfare and the adaptation to maritime warfare of the Red Cross Convention.[11] But as Davidson had minuted on 13 December 1905, 'Great Britain is pledged to join in such a conference whenever it is held',[12] and Secretary Hay had circularized American representatives abroad on the agenda already on 4 November 1904.[13] What seems to have brought the matter first of all to Grey's notice was the forwarding by the Board of Trade of communications from the Liverpool Shipowners' Association and the Manchester Chamber of Commerce urging the appointment of an expert committee 'to consider the question of national indemnity against loss from capture at sea in time of war, and the advisability of effecting an international agreement that private property be altogether exempt from capture in war'.[14] Upon this Grey himself minuted, 'My difficulty in the matter is that there is no authority (except the belligerents themselves) to enforce the application of any international agreement; and if we were at war we should never be able to entrust the great and tempting prize of British commerce to no other protection than an abstract rule of The Hague Conference.' Assuming that hindsight is correct and that the economic war, the so-called blockade, largely defeated Germany, this, it must be confessed, was about the most sensible thing to be said about the matter on the British side before war actually broke out.

For looking now to the most fateful of the four topics adverted to in Count Benckendorff's letter, the elaboration of a convention on the rules of maritime warfare, it is to be remarked that the British Government was to follow in relation to this matter a course which appears in retrospect to be wellnigh incredible. But it must also be confessed that neither Grey's initial view, nor any other expressed in the course of the formation and execution of the policy actually followed, appears to have been influenced in the least by legal considerations. The matter was looked at solely from the point of view of national advantage. It was known that the question of exempting private property from capture would be raised by the Americans as they had raised it on every possible occasion since 1856 and before. In a paper written for the Committee of Imperial Defence in 1904 Sir George Clarke had argued 'that the right of capture of neutral vessels (a) had not the value which is commonly assumed to this country as a belligerent; (b) would, if exercised in certain cases, involve risks [of embroilment with neutrals]; and (c) might inflict considerable injury on British interests; (d) might prove a serious inconvenience to our trade, and would be a danger to our peace where Great Britain is a neutral'.[15] Why the pronouncing of virtually the most authoritative word upon this subject should have been entrusted to a military engineer of whom, though probably wrongly, his superiors did not think all that much, has been explained already. But the future Lord Sydenham was not alone in advocating the concession of everything to America before that great country's hour had yet struck. For Loreburn, then still Sir Robert Reid, the ex-Attorney-General, and still for a few more weeks in opposition, had written to *The Times* on 14 October 1905, urging that 'now that the Russo-Japanese war is ended' the 'vital question of international law' involved should be taken up – and solved by the exemption of 'private property at sea from capture unless really contraband, or its place of destination be a beleagured fortress;' for no more relevant forensic reason than that 'We have more to lose by the law as it stands, and less to gain than in former days.'[16]

Two things must indeed be distinguished here: the exemption of neutral shipping from interference, whether carrying contraband, however defined, or goods of enemy origin or ownership; and the exemption of private property from capture, whether carried in neutral or enemy bottoms and with or without exceptions in case of contraband character, however defined, or of destination to a blockaded place. Clarke was advocating the former, Reid the latter, and, as Clarke was to point out in a later memorandum, penned after his own party, the Liberals, came in, the former question 'is absolutely distinct from that of the immunity of the private property of a belligerent under his flag, with which it has been most inconveniently confused, and any international agreement increasing the privileges of the neutral flag would leave the status of the merchant ships of a belligerent and of the cargoes they carry, being belligerent property, unchanged'.[17] It is perhaps unfair to the architect of the Imperial General Staff to suspect that the distinction was not quite so clear in his mind as he asserted. For certainly he was, in his later memorandum, uncompromisingly opposed to the surrender of the right to seize enemy property at sea under the enemy flag. It is odd nevertheless to read his comment that 'The advocates of the abandonment of the right of maritime capture, with some inconsistency, do not propose to abolish blockades', in the possession of knowledge that he was one of those advocates, and that 'C.I.D. paper No. 41B', to which he refers so neutrally, was his own earlier paper on the subject. To Clarke, moreover, there is to be traced the origin of the suggestion, which was to startle the Conference and which must still leave us astonished, that 'the principle of contraband' should be abolished altogether.[18]

The Interdepartmental Committee appointed to consider 'the subjects which may arise from discussion at the Second Peace Conference', presided over by Walton, the Attorney-General, and containing among others in addition to Clarke, Captain Ottley of the Admiralty, Lord Desart, and Davidson, Crowe and Hurst of the Foreign Office, would have none of the first of these heresies. For, on the question of the right of capture of private property generally, they came 'clearly and unanimously to the conclusion that our reply should be in the negative', though expressing 'with great diffidence [their] dissent from the conclusions at which an authority of the eminence of Lord Loreburn has arrived', and explaining that they had had more opportunity for investigation and discussion than he.

But, though doubting the wisdom of the policy of initiating any proposal therefor, they were 'clearly of opinion...that...a change in the Law of Nations [by] abandoning altogether the principle of contraband would be of great advantage, both to this country and in the interest of the world at large'. For here the difficulty was that 'the lists of contraband published after the outbreak of modern wars can scarcely be harmonized with any principle, or explained upon any other theory than the intention of inflicting the maximum of loss upon an enemy by restricting to the utmost extent practicable his trade with a neutral. The operation of the present system creates, in short, a breach of the spirit of the Declaration of Paris by an undue extension of the right to cripple a neutral's trade by treating as contraband articles that could not in 1856, nor can now, be properly considered to possess that character.'[19]

All this, however, is an auld sang now. The British delegation did in fact declare that its Government was, 'in order to lessen the difficulties encountered by neutral commerce in time of war...ready to abandon the principle of contraband',[20] a proposal in the light of which the same delegation's refusal to accept the motion for the abolition of the right of capture altogether paled into insignificance. But any consideration other than national self-interest behind these gestures is not to be discerned. 'Now', Clarke wrote, 'as always, this question will be viewed by each Power from the standpoint of its own advantage, and the fact that the surrender of the right of capture appears to be still the official policy of the United States does not relieve His Majesty's Government from the necessity of examining the matter in the light of purely British interests.'[21] He thus set – or perhaps caught – the general tone.

If attention be turned to other matters upon Count Benckendorff's agenda or with which the Conference concerned itself, the impression is not different. The attitude which the British delegation adopted reflected by and large no significant departure by the Liberal Government from the policies of their predecessors, in most cases nothing that could be said to originate with the Foreign Office rather than other, and notably the Service, Departments, and nothing indicative of any comprehension of the international legal system other than as a set of rules which might or might not operate for the benefit of British interests.

Thus, as the German White Book on the Conference rightly remarked, the question of the International Prize Court, though not on the Russian agenda, had 'occupied for decades public opinion and the literature of international law'.[22] British support of the proposal for such a court implied no particular or distinctive policy. The proposal by itself, moreover, reflected no great respect at least for the content of the then law. 'International law today' said Lord Justice Fry, the leader of the delegation, in extolling the Twelfth Convention by which the Court was proposed to be set up, 'is not much more than a chaos of opinions which are often contradictory, and of decisions based on national laws. We hope to see little by little formed in the future, around this Court, a system of laws truly international...'[23]

Nor if we look further do we see more. The treatment of what the Interdepartmental Committee which sat before the Conference called Minor Points – all the rest of the possible questions other than the revision of the 1899 Convention on Peaceful Settlement, some seventeen in number – was not significantly different. The make-up of the delegation was unremarkable. Fry had been a judge, but not a judge specially learned in international law, though, as has been said, not without international experience. Satow, the author of the valuable *Diplomatic Practice*, was, it is true, also a member of it (but his book was not yet written), and Hurst accompanied it. But it was not perhaps as strong a delegation as had gone to the First Conference in 1899, over which Pauncefote presided and which contained, in addition to Admiral Fisher, whose realism made everyone's blood run cold, Sir John Ardagh whose merits as an international lawyer have been considered. In some sense the British delegation played a relatively minor role in the 1907 Conference. It did not, for instance, claim the presidency of any of the Committees. But nor, it must be said, did Germany. Nor did it supply any Rapporteurs. But nor, again, did Germany.

Similarly, when it fell to be considered which of the Conventions should be ratified, neither the Foreign Office nor the lawyers appeared to play much part. For though Mr Hurst was indeed called upon to explain to the new Interdepartmental Committee the intricacies of the Tenth Convention for the adaptation of the principles of the Geneva Convention to maritime warfare, it was Admiral Ottley who expounded law and policy in relation to mines and the conversion of merchant ships into warships, and Major Cockerill, on behalf of the Army Council, who alone spoke on the subject of the laws and customs of war on land.[24]

THE DECLARATION OF LONDON

The Declaration of London still stands in retrospect as one of the most ambitious, if not the most ambitious, of attempts at the codification of rules of international law. What this epitaph really means, however, must remain uncertain so long as it remains, as it still does, an open question whether codification is for the good of international law. But the story at any rate is well enough known. When it became clear at The Hague that support for the 'revolutionary proposal'[25] of Great Britain for the abolition of contraband would not be forthcoming the way was clear for the pressing of a plan, not on the original agenda but evolved in parallel by both Britain and Germany, for an international Court of Appeal from national prize courts. The British scheme for an elaborate and permanent tribunal carried the day over the German, which envisaged an *ad hoc* assembly of admirals. The British scheme was indeed for a court of law. This, however, necessarily involved laying down what the law was. The Convention could go no further in Article 7 than direct the application in the first instance of treaties binding on the States concerned; then of generally recognized rules of international law; and failing any of these the general principles of justice and equity.

The object of the Naval Conference was to identify or state the rules of law upon the discovery of which, it became clear, the ratification of the Convention depended. The decision to sponsor the Conference was in fact recommended by a committee different from that which advised on the ratification of the remaining Conventions, over which Lord Desart presided. But Desart, as has been said, was appointed chief delegate to the Conference, and the arguments developed to meet the various criticisms of the Declaration of London advanced in the course of the debates on the Bill for its implementation flowed from his pen.[26]

The Conference was presented with a memorandum of the Government's views, based on the decisions of the British Prize Courts. This is a neutral document – 'merely a compilation of rules and dicta of British courts and British practice collected for convenience, but necessarily put compendiously'.[27] How it could have been regarded as a statement of 'generally recognised rules of international law' is unclear, and it is not surprising that its circulation led to the expression of strong doubts by both the Germans and the Russians as to whether any agreement was possible as to what was the existing law and the advocating instead of the adoption of new rules. The resulting compromise was the Declaration of London. The most important questions dealt with in it were blockade and contraband. In relation to the first of these matters the British view largely prevailed in the sense that the old continental requirements of a fixed line of blockade was abandoned.[28] But the fact that no sort of blockade was possible any longer after the development of the submarine continued to elude the experts.

As to contraband, the proposals of the Declaration so far departed from what prewar British practice was understood at least in theory to allow as to exclude the application of the doctrine of continuous voyage in relation to conditional contraband. The quaint notion of abolishing the concept of contraband altogether, although it persisted long enough to figure in the instructions to the British delegation,[29] did not of course survive. On the contrary the Declaration attempted manfully to define contraband. This attempt has been described as its crux. A notable feature of it was, so writers were to say, that food and foodstuffs were to be made incapable of being declared absolute contraband.[30]

But this again is an auld sang. What the Declaration said and what happened to it are well known. It failed to commend itself to the House of Lords, and though adopted provisionally in 1914, it was adopted in emasculated form. It was at first applied tentatively by the Prize Court, but in 1916 it was thrown overboard altogether.

Equally the explanation of the vagaries of British policy at the Hague and London Conferences is quite familiar. 'The fact of the matter was', it has been well stated, 'that Great Britain had ceased for the moment to be a Power which approached these questions exclusively from the standpoint of a potential belligerent'.[31] Such events as the deliberating of a Royal Commission on the national food supply and sundry irritations arising from the proceedings of isolated Russian ships during the Russo–Japanese war had thrown a strong light upon the obvious fact that Britain had more merchant ships than any other State and imported more food and raw materials than any other State. As a consequence it seemed good to those concerned to work for changes in the law which would favour importers of food and favour neutrals generally.

In the light of subsequent events this policy has come to be felt to have been misconceived. It has been attacked, just as the policy of acceptance in 1856 of the rule 'free ships, free goods' was attacked: as a wilful abandonment of one of Britain's chief weapons of war, this time mercifully frustrated by a benign fate. With this verdict it is naturally possible to quarrel. It can for instance be argued that, had the Declaration of London been adopted and abided by, the energy and devotion which went into the so-called blockade of Germany would simply have expressed itself in other forms of action, not necessarily less effective. Be that as it may, what is relevant to be pointed out here is simply that the question as to what the law of maritime capture was or should be was considered at all times exclusively from the standpoint of what would advantage the State most. What might be the rule most advantageous to the international community at large never came in question. It is, furthermore, doubtful whether the story would have been different had matters been exclusively in the hands of the Foreign Office or of more orthodox experts in international law than soldiers and sailors commonly are. For, once the requirements of humanity are met, the formulation of a *jus in bello* is an absurdity. As Loreburn had observed in his letter to *The Times*, 'No operation of war inflicts less suffering than the capture of unarmed vessels at sea.' If that be conceded, then its attempted regulation has no point.

ARBITRATION AND PACIFIC SETTLEMENT

When war actually came questions of the law of war, despite the concern therewith of other Departments, naturally became the prime legal concern of the Foreign Office – at least until the possibility of a postwar League of Nations came to be discussed. These matters, however, are treated of in other chapters in this volume. Of questions not having to do with the *jus in bello* arising before the war only one perhaps is worthy of special mention. This was the question of peaceful settlement of international disputes, in particular by arbitration, a question likewise on Benckendorff's agenda for the Hague Conference. Neither at the first nor at the second Conference was any true progress made towards a general system of compulsory arbitration. The advocacy of such a system was indeed official British policy. In sanguinary or complacent accounts of that policy it is not uncommonly said that Britain had, at the time of the 1907 Conference, already had a long and largely advantageous experience of arbitration and conciliation, beginning with the Jay Treaty, marked by the great Alabama arbitration, and culminating in the enquiry into the Dogger Bank incident. Possibly these accounts exaggerate the extent to which Britain can be said to have 'won' her cases, just as the apparent cynicism of such statesmen as Lord Salisbury in relation to arbitration is exaggerated. In all arbitral settlement there is an element of compromise and it is a characteristic of boundary arbitrations in particular that, if something is conceded to one side here, something else is always to be found allowed there to the other side. In all arbitral and judicial proceedings, too, whether on the international or any other plane, each side not only hopes to win but is convinced of the correctness of its arguments and the rectitude of its demands.

If this be conceded, then it may fairly be claimed that the Liberal Government and Grey confirmed and made peculiarly their own the policy of their predecessors for some decades in relation to arbitration. The Liberal years thus saw one more of the series of great Anglo–American arbitrations – the North Atlantic Fisheries case. To some extent Great Britain was, in relation to this case, simply the agent of Canada, already emerging as a distinct international person. Paradoxically, too, the case furnished the occasion for the greatest forensic triumph not of any of the Liberal Law Officers,[32] but of Finlay, the former Conservative Attorney–General and future Conservative Chancellor. Walton, however, the Liberal Attorney, led Finlay in the case and himself earned distinction. And this was not of course the only actual arbitration. In the Savarkar case with France in 1911, it is interesting to note, the presentation of the British argument was entrusted, as it emerged with eminently satisfactory results, to Eyre Crowe, the Chancellor and Law Officers merely advising in the preliminary stages, and W. F. Craies, a barrister instructed by the Treasury Solicitor, drawing the case.

In the history of international as contrasted with national law the distinction between *lex lata*, the law which actually is, and *lex ferenda*, the law which is projected or advocated, is not of absolute importance. For in retrospect it may well appear that that which is merely proposed, albeit unsuccessfully, to be adopted as treaty law, still goes, despite its failure of adoption, to form part of that practice of States which is the source of customary law. In relation to arbitration, moreover, the arbitration treaty between States is still important though no occasion for any actual arbitration arises. That only four or five arbitrations occurred during Grey's term of office, the North Atlantic Fisheries and Savarkar cases being the chief of these, is no necessary measure of the significance of British policy in this area. On the other hand, the significance of arbitration treaties is not to be exaggerated. Indeed it was a feature of all too many arbitration treaties of this period that they in fact bound the parties to nothing, requiring in most cases a further agreement before any arbitration could come about and containing further an exception from any shadow of obligation in relation to any matter which any party might deem to affect its national honour.

Not too little and not too much, then, is to be made of the British attitude to arbitration in these years. But in retrospect we may see that Great Britain emerged from the war firmly convinced that the world must be endowed with institutions for the pacific settlement of disputes, and it must be clear that the policy of the Liberal Government towards arbitration contributed to this conviction. To this extent, therefore, Trevelyan's reference to Grey's 'respect for legality' is not misplaced, and to this extent 1907 held 1919, the year of the League Covenant, in its arms. But at the same time it is even more clear that the final argument for peaceful settlement was the war itself, and it does not at all follow that, had the war not broken out, the contribution of Grey and Britain to the elimination of the right of war from the catalogue of rights international law permits to the State would have been of any decisive or particular significance. Of the Powers, Britain had perhaps, even certainly, the greatest 'respect for legality' in Trevelyan's sense. But the extent of that respect was not, by the standards of today, so very great, for in truth the then law did not merit more.

CONCLUSION

Anyone who reads in the legal archives of the Foreign Office, and more especially in the series of opinions furnished to the Foreign Office since its first establishment in 1782 by the Law Officers of the Crown, cannot indeed fail to appreciate that he is reading the story of a Department of the Government of a State which, in the conduct of its many and varied foreign affairs, has been, day by day, year by year, over a great stretch of time, consciously ruled by law. But in this regard there is nothing whatsoever to distinguish the Office during the time when Sir Edward Grey presided over it from any earlier time. Nor, by that time, had the law as yet been purged of the fatal inconsistency involved in the recognition of war as a legal institution. The picture may perhaps be distorted by an undue emphasis upon the *jus in bello* occasioned by the Hague and London Conferences. But if anything the time was one in which the legality of war was more certainly taken for granted than in any earlier time. It was nevertheless a time in which the utility of the exclusion of war by legal means was beginning to be appreciated, if but dimly. To this extent Grey was no doubt on the side of the Angells.

BEFORE THE WAR:
EUROPE AND THE NEAR EAST

5

Great Britain and France, 1905–1911

K. A. HAMILTON

The formation of the Liberal government on 10 December 1905 was not considered by Paul Cambon, the French ambassador in London, as likely to portend any radical change in Great Britain's relations with France. He assured the French foreign minister that although the traditional inclination of the Liberals was towards Germany, they were above all pacifists, and the *entente* with France had their support because it was a guarantee of peace. Such confidence in the new government was no doubt in part due to Sir Edward Grey's public endorsement of the broad lines of Lord Lansdowne's foreign policy.[1] In fact, however, during the next five years Grey displayed a greater readiness than his immediate predecessor to accept the Anglo–French understanding as a fundamental and permanent element in Britain's relations with the continental powers.

Given the prevailing international situation at the time of his appointment, it was natural that Grey's attitude towards Anglo–French relations should have differed from that of Lansdowne. The accord which the latter had concluded with the French government in April 1904 had been essentially a colonial arrangement, one result of which had been to commit Britain to giving diplomatic support to France's aspirations for a protectorate over the greater part of Morocco. When, therefore, the German emperor landed at Tangier, and his government demanded an international conference to settle Morocco's fate, this was regarded in Paris and London as a challenge to the *entente*. Lansdowne endeavoured to work in close cooperation with the French, but the resignation on 6 June 1905 of Théophile Delcassé, the French foreign minister, who was most closely associated with the English understanding, severely shook his faith in the ability of France to resist German pressure. After a good deal of squabbling, the French government conditionally accepted the idea of an international settlement, and in January 1906 Grey was confronted with the prospect of a conference at Algeciras.[2] He was well aware that upon its outcome might depend the future of the *entente*.

Grey was determined both to support France within the terms of the 1904 agreement and to defend Britain's interests in Morocco. Like Lansdowne he sought from the French government full information about their aims and intentions.[3] At the same time Paul Cambon had since May 1905 been under the mistaken impression that Lansdowne had desired discussions which would lead to an Anglo–French alliance. In a letter of 25 May 1905 Lansdowne had sought 'full and confidential discussions' between the French and British governments 'in anticipation of any complications to be apprehended'. Cambon had assumed this to be an invitation which, if accepted, would 'entrer dans la voie d'une entente général qui constituerait en réalité une alliance'.[4] He now tried to regain the opportunity which he believed his government had missed. He received some encouragement in this endeavour from King Edward, but only limited support from Maurice Rouvier, the French premier and minister of foreign affairs, who had never been enthusiastic about closer ties with Britain.[5] Moreover, although Grey on 30 December assured Colonel Repington, the military correspondent of *The Times*, that he had not 'receded from anything Lord Lansdowne said to the French', he was not cognizant of the interpretation that Cambon had put upon his predecessor's words.[6]

Grey could not, however, afford to neglect the possible eventuality of Britain and France being allies in a war with Germany. On 3 January he warned Metternich, the German ambassador in London, that if Germany forced war on France 'public feeling would be so strong that it would be impossible to be neutral'.[7] Some five days later he counselled Haldane, the secretary of state for war, that 'popular feeling' might compel the government to aid France, and that he might suddenly be asked what he could do.[8] Already during 1905 the service departments had examined the best means of assisting France in a European war. But while the Admiralty had favoured a strategy based upon naval raids upon the north German coast, senior army officers had recommended the despatch to the continent of a force of 100,000 men. The enactment of such a plan required accurate information about France's military dispositions, and for this purpose unofficial contact was made in January 1906 between Sir George Clarke, the secretary of the Committee of Imperial Defence, and the military *attaché* of the French embassy at London.[9]

Although on 9 January Grey gave his approval to those military conversations, the prime minister was not informed of this until the end of the month, and over five years were to pass before the whole cabinet were to learn of them.[10] But Grey's authorization of Clarke's action did not imply his acceptance of any commitment to intervene in a Franco–German conflict. That he made clear to Paul Cambon. Indeed, the French ambassador was anything but satisfied by Grey's reply to his enquiry on 10 January as to whether Britain would be prepared to give armed assistance to France in the event of German aggression against her. With a general election pending, and the cabinet dispersed, Grey felt unable to pledge the country to more than 'neutrality – a benevolent neutrality if such a thing existed'. Nevertheless, he went a little further than Lansdowne had done by expressing to Cambon his personal opinion that if Germany attacked France in consequence of a question arising out of the 1904 agreement, 'public opinion in England would be strongly moved in favour of France'.[11]

The provisional nature of Grey's assurances to Cambon allowed certain of his officials the opportunity to press for a firmer commitment to France. Louis Mallet, his private secretary who had for sometime favoured a French alliance, urged Sir Francis Bertie, the British ambassador at Paris, to write a 'very strong letter to Grey', and to 'prime C. Hardinge (the permanent under-secretary)', who must 'do everything he can to buck up these miserable creatures'.[12] Bertie fulfilled this request not with a personal letter, but with an official despatch of 13 January. In this he tried to dispel any fear that a pledge of military support to France would lead the French to adopt a more provocative stance. They were, he pointed out, already confident that England would for her own sake give France armed assistance in a Franco–German war. Yet if Grey could not assure them of more than continuing diplomatic support or neutrality, there would, he predicted, be a 'serious danger of a complete revulsion of feeling on the part of the French government and of public opinion in France'.

Ever since the spring of 1905 Bertie had been anxious to avoid a situation in which France might purchase German acquiescence in her Moroccan policy by making concessions which would be harmful to British interests. He warned Grey that the French might now be prepared to do this rather than risk a war without an ally.[13] Yet it is doubtful whether Bertie's argument could have carried much weight with Grey. Anxious though he was that the French should take Britain's interests in Morocco into account, he was not overwhelmingly opposed to making concessions to Germany there or elsewhere. Already on 9 January he had suggested to Campbell–Bannerman that the acquisition by Germany of a coaling station on Morocco's Atlantic coast might offer a solution to the crisis. The moment, he thought, might come when a 'timely admission that it is not a cardinal object of British policy to prevent her having such a port may be of great value'.[14]

By mid-January Grey's views were 'still in solution'. Nevertheless, he rejected the idea of giving to France a promise that would oblige Britain to participate in a continental war. That, he thought, would transform the *entente* into an alliance, and alliances were not in accordance with Britain's traditions. He did, however, assure Bertie that if war arose over the 1904 agreement, Britain would not be able to stand aside. Furthermore he indicated the terms which the British government would require if they were to offer France a pledge of military support. These were that the British government should be free to propose to the French modifications in their declarations concerning Morocco, and such concessions as might be made to Germany. The French would, he observed, have to take the British government into their confidence, and take 'no independent action in Morocco which might lead to a war with Germany without keeping us informed and hearing what we have to say'. As for a *quid pro quo*, Grey thought the French might promise at least to remain neutral and keep other powers neutral in an Anglo–German war.[15]

This may have encouraged Bertie to believe that Cambon might obtain the assurances that he desired. During a stay at Windsor he told the French ambassador that he thought it possible that Grey would agree to giving a verbal promise that Britain would not abandon France in the event of German aggression against her.[16] When, however, on 31 January Cambon again raised the matter with Grey, the latter's response was no more accommodating than that which he had given on the 10th. He told Cambon that people in England would not be prepared to risk a war to put France in possession of Morocco. If it appeared that Germany was forcing a war on France in order to break up the *entente*, then, he assured Cambon, 'public opinion would undoubtedly be very strong on the side of France'. Yet he could not give a decided opinion on whether this would be sufficient to overcome the 'great reluctance which existed amongst us now to find ourselves involved in a war.'[17]

Meanwhile at the Algeciras conference, which had commenced its work on 16 January, Franco–German differences crystallized on two issues: the future policing of the Moroccan ports, and the establishment of an international bank for Morocco. Rather than concede to France and Spain the mandate which they desired for organizing the police, von Holstein, the architect of Germany's Moroccan policy, would personally have preferred to see the conference fail. But the seemingly contradictory statements of German diplomats did not allow foreign observers to reach any simple conclusions about their policies and intentions.[18] When on 19 February Metternich informed Grey that his government had met the latest French proposal with a point blank refusal, the British foreign secretary feared that he was about to see the early termination of the conference. In a memorandum drafted on the following day he ruminated that in that event Germany might try to establish her influence in Morocco, the French would counteract them, and the Germans might make this a *casus belli*. Horrible as he admitted the prospect of Britain's involvement in a Franco–German war was, he nevertheless emphasized that if she failed to support the French in a conflict over Morocco, her honour and international standing would be seriously compromised.

It was with a view to avoiding such a situation that Grey also suggested that Britain and France should find out what compensation Germany would require for recognizing French claims in Morocco. Indeed, the only real objection that he could see to conceding to Germany a port or coaling station in Morocco was that the French might 'think it pusillanimous and a poor result of the *Entente*'. The Admiralty were prepared to acquiesce in Germany acquiring a port on Morocco's Atlantic coast, and not until Cambon had made anxious enquiries about the Foreign Office adopting this line, did Grey abandon the idea.[19]

Grey was less willing to yield to French wishes when during the following month the German delegation at the conference adopted a more conciliatory approach. After having failed either to secure the support of the majority of the neutral powers, or to open direct negotiations with the French, von Bülow, the German chancellor, authorized the Austrians to put forward a project which conceded to the French almost everything that they had asked for with regard to the police. French and Spanish officers were to have control of the police at seven of the Moroccan ports, while at Casablanca the police were to be under a superior officer or inspector who would be a national of one of the smaller powers.[20] This was regarded by the majority of the powers represented at the conference as a considerable concession on Germany's part, but it did not satisfy the Quai d'Orsay. The establishment of a police inspectorate would, in Rouvier's opinion, mean introducing into Morocco an unacceptable element of internationalization. Moreover, he had received from Berlin information which indicated that the German government would probably retreat further.[21]

The new proposals only added to the dilemma in which Grey had been placed by his desire on the one hand to support France, and on the other to make some concessions towards Germany. Besides if the conference were to break up on this issue, the result would almost certainly be blamed on France and her associates. Sir Arthur Nicolson, the British delegate at Algeciras, doubted if the Germans would be prepared to concede more, and advised his French colleague that it would be unfortunate if Britain, France and Spain were left isolated.[22] Hardinge, who found the Austrian scheme a 'complete justification of M. Delcassé's policy of resistance to Germany', suggested that Grey should repeat Nicolson's advice to Cambon. With this Grey agreed, and while he assured the French ambassador that Nicolson would continue to support their delegate, he also urged upon him the importance of France accepting a Swiss inspector at Casablanca rather than letting the conference fail.[23]

Grey's statement to Cambon elicited an immediate protest from Bertie who was worried by the effect that it might have upon opinion in France. If the French government did give way, then he feared they would make out that they had been pressed by England to do so.[24] His argument was reinforced by the uncertain state of French politics. On 7 March the French government was defeated in parliament, and although Rouvier remained at the Quai d'Orsay for another week, he was soon to be replaced there by Léon Bourgeois. In these circumstances Bertie thought that it was even less likely that the French would want to give way. Moreover, parliamentary elections were due shortly in France, and Révoil, the French delegate at Algeciras, warned Nicolson that the nationalists and others might, if Grey's warning were to transpire, declare themselves against the *entente*.[25] Grey, however, had no intention of pressing the French to accept the Austrian proposals, and on 14 March he affirmed to Bertie that if they would not give way, 'we shall of course support them'.[26]

Grey's pledge sufficed to reassure Bourgeois of Britain's continuing support. But before its delivery to the Quai d'Orsay by Bertie, the French had begun to show signs of being nervous about Britain's intentions. Reports emanating from Berlin indicated that the British and German delegates were in accord at Algeciras, and Révoil informed the Quai d'Orsay that Nicolson felt himself to be in a position to negotiate a compromise arrangement. Even Bourgeois wondered if the role being played by Nicolson was not an indication of a change of attitude on the part of England.[27]

Bourgeois's misgivings were shared by others inside the French cabinet. According to Georges Clemenceau, the Minister of the Interior, who visited Bertie on the evening of 15 March, he alone had combated the supposition that had been raised in the council of ministers that Britain had made arrangements behind the back of France and Germany.[28] Already on the previous evening at a party which Bertie had attended at the German embassy, Étienne, the minister of war and *de facto* leader of the colonial party, had practically accused the British government of intending to abandon France at Algeciras.[29] Moreover, from London, Paul Cambon warned Bourgeois that Grey would have to take into account the views of the cabinet, the majority of whose members were of a Gladstonian persuasion, and who might draw away from France if she appeared to endanger the success of the conference.[30]

Grey was indignant at the distrust which the French exhibited in Britain's intentions. Especially irritating was the fact that while at one moment Britain was being accused of urging the French on against Germany, at the next she was accused of not supporting her enough. 'A nation', he remarked to Bertie, 'which is always suspecting her friend will never be able to keep her friend'.[31] Bertie also regretted that 'Frenchmen of education and position should be found ready to believe imputations against England of bad faith'. Nevertheless, he observed to Grey,

One must take the French as they are and not as one would wish them to be. They have an instinctive dread of Germany and an hereditary distrust of England, and with these characteristics they are easily led to believe that they may be deserted by England and fallen upon by Germany.[32]

In the end the net outcome of this episode was a fresh reaffirmation by Grey of his intention to stand by France. 'Cordial co-operation with France in all parts of the world', Grey wrote to Bertie on 15 March, 'remains a cardinal point of British policy and in some respects we have carried it further than the late Government were required to do.'[33] During the remainder of the month Grey continued to back France on the police question, and on 26 March in the face of Anglo–French firmness, the Germans climbed down. By the general act of Algeciras of 7 April France and Spain secured the control of the police at all eight Moroccan ports with the proviso that those at Casablanca and Tetuan should be mixed, and a Swiss officer appointed by the sultan as inspector. It provided also for the establishment of a state bank, which would be open to the capital of all nations, but with a special concession to the French.[34]

The common experience of having stood together in the face of German pressure at Algeciras did much to strengthen the understanding between Britain and France. Moreover, despite the threat which Germany seemed to pose to the security of the British empire, the diplomatic position which Britain occupied at the conclusion of the conference was not an unfavourable one. Grey recognized that while the *entente* existed Germany had less opportunity for exploiting the differences between her neighbours, and therefore less chance of achieving the hegemony of Europe.[35] The Anglo–French understanding did not, however, represent a complete means for containing Germany's ambitions. After Algeciras the Quai d'Orsay was anything but anxious to engage in any course of action which might provoke another strong German reaction. Thus Bourgeois was reluctant to proceed with Britain and Italy towards an agreement on their respective interests in Abyssinia for fear lest it should lead to a German intervention.[36] Similarly his successor Stephen Pichon had no wish that France should appear as the principal opponent to the acquisition in December 1906 by a German firm of landing rights for a telegraphic cable in the Canaries.[37]

German diplomacy at Madrid did, however, cause some concern amongst French and British officials about the designs which Germany might harbour on Spain's possessions. Already in the previous year the idea of a bilateral accord between Britain and Spain on Gibraltar and the Spanish islands had found favour in the Foreign Office.[38] From Nicolson the French embassy at Madrid had learned of this, and on 22 December 1906 Paul Cambon suggested to Bertie that Britain, France, and Spain should conclude an agreement upon the preservation of the *status quo* in the Mediterranean and the Spanish islands in the Atlantic.[39]

Bertie was an ardent advocate of an Anglo–Spanish arrangement, which he regarded principally as a means of combating German influence at Madrid.[40] But Hardinge was interested in another aspect of such an accord. In a minute of 8 December 1906 he pointed out that although the Spanish government had promised France that they would not alienate any of the Moroccan territory designated to them by their agreement of October 1904, they had given no such undertaking to England.[41] Grey, like Lansdowne, recognized the importance of ensuring that the northern littoral of Morocco should not fall into the hands of another great power. He was, however, unenthusiastic about the multiplying Britain's treaty obligations, and he insisted that what would determine his decision was the necessity for making further provision for the security of Gibraltar.[42] That, the government's military advisers thought, could be achieved less well with specific Spanish pledges than through the maintenance of Spain's friendship.[43]

While the debate continued in England on the subject of a Spanish accord, Jules Cambon, the French ambassador at Madrid, acted. After only having discussed the possibility of such an arrangement with his British colleague, he drafted, and in January 1907 submitted to the Spanish government a project for an agreement on the maintenance of the *status quo* in the western Mediterranean and eastern Atlantic. This action was resented by Grey and his officials, who regarded it as an untimely intervention by the French.

Moreover, they were unhappy about the prospect of a tripartite treaty, which Hardinge feared would appear as a 'tightening of the net spread around German political activity'.[44] Such an arrangement could not in Grey's opinion be kept a secret, and it would, he thought, meet with difficulties in parliament if Spain gave no fresh assurances on Gibraltar.[45]

Nevertheless, Grey seems to have been convinced of the value of some kind of an accord with Spain, and for this he obtained the support of the prime minister. On 28 March Hardinge proposed that instead of engaging themselves in a treaty, the British and Spanish governments should exchange notes. He suggested that in these the two governments should assure each other of their desire to maintain the territorial *status quo* in the Mediterranean and that portion of the Atlantic which washed the shores of Europe and Africa, and promise to consult in the event of it being menaced by a third power.[46] Both the French and Spanish governments would have preferred a tripartite treaty, but in April Hardinge, who accompanied the king on an official visit to Carthagena, succeeded in overcoming Spanish objections to his proposals. At Paris Bertie was also able to persuade Clemenceau, who had in October 1906 succeeded Sarrien as French premier, to supplement France's existing agreement with Spain with a new note.[47] Grey declined to accept a similar and separate engagement between Britain and France. Instead he agreed to an exchange of verbal declarations with the French ambassador giving recognition to what Britain and France were doing with Spain, and containing assurances similar to those contained in their respective notes. This was effected when on 16 May identical notes were exchanged by the British and French governments with that in Madrid.[48]

The significance of these exchanges was enhanced when on 8 June Grey further assured Cambon that he regarded the 'spirit of the Agreement of 1904 as applying to the provisions of these Notes, and the same support would be forthcoming as we had given in connection with the 1904 agreement'. This was confirmed by Bertie, who on 22 June told Pichon that in the event of German pressure upon France in consequence of the notes exchanged with Spain, the British government would give France the same support as had been given to her at the Algeciras conference.[49]

The arrangements with Spain and the promises given by Grey and Bertie extended beyond Morocco the geographic limits within which Britain was pledged to give diplomatic support to France. Yet, after 1905 the *entente* could not be defined in terms of such formal undertakings. It was far more dependent upon the acceptance by governments and public opinion in both countries of the view that co-operation between Britain and France was in their mutual interest. For this reason Grey, with Bertie's encouragement, made every effort to avoid hurting the tender feelings of the French. Visits to Germany by the king and British statesmen and other prominent citizens were accompanied by profuse assurances to Paris of Britain's good intentions, and loyalty to the *entente*.[50] Even a suggestion from Portugal that British representatives should participate in the celebration of the centenary of England's victories in the peninsular war was frowned on by Bertie on the grounds that 'Royalist, nationalist, and German subventioned newspapers would make capital of it'.[51] Similarly in January 1909 Churchill, who was credited in France with pro-German inclinations, was advised by Grey against making a visit to Paris because it might create confusion in the minds of the French.[52]

There was good reason for Grey's caution for, as Bertie rarely failed to remind him, the *entente* was not without its critics in France. The insufficiency of the military support which Britain could render to France in the event of a war, the danger of France becoming the battlefield for an Anglo–German conflict, and the benefits to be had from political and economic co-operation with Germany, had to be weighed against the advantages France gained from her association with England. Certainly the idea of an accommodation with Germany on a variety of extra-European issues had its attractions for those who sought to consolidate France's position in North Africa and the Near and Middle East. Rouvier, who favoured co-operation between French and German business, had in May 1905 suggested to Radolin, the German ambassador at Paris, a Franco–German accord on the Baghdad railway, Morocco, and central Africa.[53] In November 1906 Eyre Crowe minuted that there was 'still observable in France, even in ministerial circles, a desire to find a "working arrangement" with Germany'. He also recalled the friendly support given by Bismarck to Ferry on colonial matters, and pointed to the menace of Germany trying to create friction between Britain and France. Such fears were discounted by Hardinge, who thought that the French experience at the hands of the Germans had been too bitter to allow any friendly understanding, and they would require 'something more than smiles'.[54] Yet, as Bertie contended, 'Germany would probably be ready to make great sacrifices to obtain French support in pursuit of her world policy and the British Empire would be the sufferer.'

The fear that in a war France might only be able to rely on receiving naval support from Britain was in Bertie's opinion another factor which induced 'many Frenchmen to think it would be wiser to come to terms with Germany'.[56] Even such a staunch defender of the *entente* as Clemenceau was worried by Britain's military inferiority. During 1907 and 1908 he persistently pressed the British government and its representatives to adopt a system of conscription, which would better enable Britain to play a continental role in any future conflict. He made few attempts, however, to extract any further promises from London of British aid to France. Indeed, Bertie thought that the French government realized the difficulties in the way of Grey giving such a pledge, and reconciled themselves to the conviction that Britain would be bound by her own interests to support France in a conflict.[56]

Clemenceau was nevertheless determined to maintain the impression in public that there were more binding ties between Britain and France than those contained in the convention of April 1904. Thus when on 20 November 1906

5

he was questioned in the senate about the existence of an Anglo–French military convention, his reply was both cryptic and evasive. He said that he had been in office a few weeks, and that he had not seen anything of that kind in the documents laid before him. There might, he contended, be occasions when a government 'conscious of its responsibilities ought not to reply to such questions', and, he added, 'it was not right that anything should be said from the Tribune which might "décourager des amitiés" or "rompre des accords"'. The implication was, as Hardinge recognized, that there might be a military convention of which Clemenceau did not know.[57]

Within the Foreign Office Clemenceau's explanations caused some consternation, especially as it was feared that it might provoke a similar question in the Commons. Grey, however, was more sympathetic towards Clemenceau's predicament than were his officials. He considered it to be an awkward question for Clemenceau to have to reply to without giving the appearance of discouraging the *entente*. If the matter were raised in parliament then Grey was determined not to contradict him.[58]

Criticism of the Anglo–French understanding in France could not, however, be contained simply by avoiding any definite statement about the true nature of the relationship. In an address given on 22 February 1907 at the *École libre des sciences politiques*, André Tardieu, the foreign editor of the *Temps*, gave clear expression of the concern felt in France about the value of Britain as a friend. He objected that though her friendship was a 'precious guarantee of peace', it would in time of war be unavailing in witholding a German invasion of France. Putting aside the violently polemical tone which he had hitherto adopted towards the Germans, he spoke of the need for France to show goodwill towards Germany, and of a possible arrangement between the two powers.[59]

Bertie was perturbed by Tardieu's language, but he was not inclined to over-exaggerate the importance of those in France who favoured the idea of an accommodation with Germany. Its chief supporters were in his estimation the German subsidized press, a limited number of office-seeking politicians, and those nationalists, and ultra-royalists, who considered Germany to be more antagonistic towards the republican system than England. 'Other patrons of such an understanding', he observed, 'are those who for financial reasons desire closer relations with a country which requires capital and where profitable business can be done.'[60] This seemed to be only too evident to Bertie in the attitude assumed by French financiers and their representatives towards the German sponsored Baghdad railway project.

Tardieu in his address outlined an arrangement whereby Germany might agree to acquiesce in France's acquisition of Morocco in return for French co-operation in the financing of the Baghdad railway. Already as the result of an agreement concluded with the Deutsche Bank in 1903 the French controlled Imperial Ottoman Bank had been allotted a 30% share in the financing of the railway. But with a view to protecting France's railway network in Syria and the interests of her Russian ally, Delcassé had persuaded his cabinet colleagues to deny a quotation for the railway securities on the Paris *bourse*.[61]

Grey, who had no desire to see the line continued to the Persian gulf without Britain's participation, sought to work in common accord with France and Russia on this issue. In this he was aided by Pichon, who assured Bertie of his readiness to restrain French bankers from participating in the scheme.[62] Bertie, however, had little faith in the adequacy of the controls that Pichon had at his disposal. Moreover, at Constantinople neither Constans, the French ambassador there, nor the agents of French finance, were inclined towards working with their British colleagues in order to thwart German ambitions.[63] Despite the efforts of Clemenceau and Pichon to ensure Anglo–French collaboration, Britain's representatives received little or no support from the French embassy when during the autumn of 1906, they attempted to apply such conditions to the granting of a 3 % rise in Turkish customs dues as would prevent any surplus revenues being employed as security for the financing of the railway.[64] A French group of financiers appeared to be acting in collusion with the Germans, and at Berlin negotiations began in March 1907 between representatives of the Ottoman Bank and the railway company.[65] During the next few months the press in France and Germany took up with vigour the idea of a Franco–German arrangement on a basis similar to that recommended by Tardieu.[66]

It appeared to Grey's officials that the Germans were bent upon extending their influence in Turkey and separating France and England. So long, however, as Clemenceau remained in office, it seemed unlikely that the Germans would succeed in this. The danger was, as Bertie suggested, that Clemenceau's government might fall and be succeeded by one out of which the Germans might be able to squeeze an agreement.[67] It was in these apparently precarious circumstances that Campbell-Bannerman made a brief, but unfortunate incursion into foreign affairs.

When on 9 April the prime minister, who had been enjoying a private visit to France, met with Clemenceau, the latter expressed his regret at the reductions which he believed the Liberals were making in the size of Britain's army. According to Clemenceau's account Campbell-Bannerman replied that he did not think that English public opinion would 'allow of British troops being employed on the Continent in Europe'. Alarmed at this, and anxious lest it should indicate some change of attitude on Britain's part, Clemenceau put it to Bertie that the effect of this on his colleagues would be disastrous. Subsequently Campbell-Bannerman denied the accuracy of Clemenceau's account, and insisted that he had only dwelt upon the reluctance of the British people to commit themselves to obligations which would involve them in a continental war. Grey too was at pains to explain that the prime minister had said nothing new, and that in the event of Britain being involved in a war her armed forces would be used in a way which they would be most effective'.[68] But, Bertie cautioned Mallet,

The danger for us to avoid will be to make the French lose confidence in our support and drive them into some arrangement with Germany, detrimental to us while not being harmful to France. At the same time we must not encourage the French to rely on our material support to the extent of encouraging them to beard the Germans.[69]

In fact Grey could hardly neglect the extent to which the idea of a Franco–German accommodation continued to find favour in influential political circles in France. An arrangement of that kind might well free France from the threat of German interference in Morocco at a time when both the French and Spanish governments were finding it increasingly necessary to resort to coercive action there. Both Clemenceau, who was anxious to avoid another quarrel over Morocco, and Étienne, an ardent exponent of a forward policy there, saw advantage in working with Germany on this question. In July 1907 Étienne travelled to Germany and had discussions with the German emperor and chancellor at Kiel. Although he rebuffed the emperor's proposal for a Franco–German alliance, he did promise to work in France for better relations with Germany. He proposed that financial co-operation, even in Morocco, might be good preparation for a political agreement. Moreover, on his return to Paris he claimed in the *Dépêche Coloniale* that France would not be able to rely on British aid in a war over Morocco, and that in an Anglo–German war France would become Germany's hostage.[70]

This did not, however, mark any new departure in France's foreign policy. Étienne was not a minister at the time, and Clemenceau and Pichon disclaimed any official support for his mission. For his part Bertie felt able to dismiss Étienne's motives as being purely pecuniary. Indeed, the apparently inconclusive results of his talks appear to have convinced the British ambassador that there was no real danger of a general Franco–German understanding. 'So long', he wrote in his annual report for 1907, 'as Alsace-Lorraine remains part of the German Empire there cannot, in my opinion, be any real political understanding of any consequence between France and Germany.'[71] Nevertheless, not all of his colleagues felt so sure about France's future policies. There remained in Hardinge's view the possibility that the French might panic if the Germans again adopted a threatening stance towards them.

To Bertie Hardinge confessed in July 1908 that he was 'always afraid that if the French became really frightened there may be a general stampede'.[72] But French conduct during that autumn lent little credence to these fears. When the intervention of a French officer in an attempt by the German consul at Casablanca to aid the escape of a group of army deserters led to a row between Berlin and Paris, the Quai d'Orsay firmly insisted on arbitration on its terms. Grey was favourably impresssed by the tone, temper, and attitude of the French government.[73] In view of the crisis in the Near East with which the affair coincided, he did not think that Germany would risk a war.[74] Nevertheless, Grey could not avoid considering it and the possibility of a

British military intervention.[75] As in 1906 he found it impossible for the government to come to a decision beforehand as to what course it would take in a conflict. There was no doubt though about where Grey's sympathies lay. If Germany fastened a war on France in connexion with Morocco, she would, he thought, say that France was being attacked because of the *entente*. In those circumstances, he told the Russian ambassador, 'for us to fold our hands and look on would not be a very respectable part'.[76]

Although the troubles in Morocco and the Balkans compelled the British and French governments to once more face the prospect of their being allies in a continental war, this did not disguise the fact that there were still very real differences between the partners in the *entente*. Already in March 1908 Bertie had proposed to Grey that since France was now so dependent on England in matters of foreign policy, 'pressure might be used to bring the French Government to show a more accommodating spirit in some of the questions in which the two countries were not entirely agreed'.[77]

Nowhere was disagreement more evident between Britain and France than in the sphere of colonial and extra-European affairs. Despite the attempt which the two powers had made in 1904 to solve the outstanding colonial difficulties which divided them, they continued to quarrel over those issues with which their convention had purported to deal, and those which Lansdowne and Delcassé had left aside. Even in Morocco old rivalries came to the fore when the German menace receded. Moreover, representatives of Britain and France in Africa and Asia, and ministries and departments of state other than the Quai d'Orsay and the Foreign Office, did not invariably endorse the spirit of co-operation which the *entente* was supposed to represent. Immediate and local interests seemed at times to be put before the wider aspects of the Anglo–French understanding.

From Paris Bertie complained that while the French accepted the British support which was ungrudgingly given to them in Morocco, they were not prepared to work in a friendly fashion with Britain in a variety of colonial issues. His views were shared by other British officials. Eyre Crowe was particularly critical of what he stigmatized as the 'well-known French method of dealing with unpleasant questions...which may be characterized as "pigeon hole and no answer"'.[78] The troubles which arose from the imprecise drafting of the convention of 1904 as it affected the Newfoundland fisheries, and the enforcement of the colonial laws and regulations, was a constant source of irritation to the Foreign Office. When in March 1908 Paul Cambon protested over the fining of a French fishing vessel, Eyre Crowe minuted that the French 'permit themselves in addressing us an attitude which borders on the impertinent'. He likened the French ambassador's communication to those which the Foreign Office used to receive 'when relations between the two countries were little removed from open hostilities'.[79] In similar terms Eldon Gorst complained persistently from Egypt about the efforts made by the French representatives and colony there to obstruct the efficient administration of the khedivate. The French, Hardinge lamented to Bertie in March 1910, 'like...to make us pay twice over for everything'.[80]

Neither with regard to the Newfoundland fisheries nor Egypt was Grey prepared to take as firm a line towards the French as his officials would have liked. His response to French complaints about the treatment of their fishing vessels was more conciliatory than Eyre Crowe would have hoped for, and he was reluctant to follow the suggestion made by Gorst in May 1908 that he should give the French a 'rap over the knuckles about their attitude'. The difficulty, he thought, about complaining to the French over their conduct in Egypt was that they had 'got such a bad bargain in Morocco that one doesn't like to set off one against the other'. He valued the *entente* too much as an asset in his European policy to want to risk it in the settlement of a colonial dispute.[81]

It was partly with a view to overcoming the rivalry which persisted between the representatives of British and French interests at Constantinople that Grey gave his blessing in January 1907 to a projected Anglo–French financial and commercial combination. The plan, which was put forward by Sir Arthur Vere, the agent there of Armstrong, Whitworth and Company, was for the establishment of separate British and French syndicates, which together, would seek out and share concessions in the Ottoman empire. If successful the relative decline in British investment in Turkey might thus be halted, and the growth in German influence over the Porte checked.

Both at London and Paris it was expected that the Ottoman Bank, which was in form an Anglo–French institution, would be prepared to participate in the combination. But the bank's support for the scheme soon proved to be more apparent than real, and the obstructive tactics employed by its committees in London and Paris during the next two years did much to hinder any progress towards the formation of the consortium. The trouble was that while co-operation with British capital might enable the bank to surmount those limita-tions on its conduct which seemed to result from France's political association with Britain, it could gain little from the emergence of a group at Constan-tinople over which it could not exercise a preponderating influence. As a result after six months of negotiations at Paris in which the British embassy played an important role, the only French syndicate which was in prospect of forma-tion was one which would be dominated by the Ottoman Bank, and what Bertie termed the 'protestant Germanophile faction'. Moreover, there was also official opposition to the scheme in France. Joseph Caillaux, the minister of finance, and Arsène Henry, the commercial director of the Quai d'Orsay, feared the effect that it might have upon Franco–German relations.

Only after Bertie had persuaded Clemenceau to intervene personally in the affair, was a French group formed in July 1907 in which the Ottoman Bank was limited to a 30% share. In London, however, the bank's English committee continued to prevaricate over the part which it would play in a British group. Despite pressure from Paris, the Foreign Office refused in February 1908 to support a syndicate formed by the bank. When in July the government finally gave its backing to a broad based British group there still remained the problem of drafting an agreement which would bring the combination into existence.

These delays proved to be fatal for what had become known to the Foreign Office as the 'Industrial Entente'. The Young Turk revolution seemed to herald a dramatic reversal in Britain's fortunes at Constantinople, and Grey and some of his senior officials thought that this would lead to a revival of British investment in Turkey. In this they hoped to find a more satisfactory basis for collaboration between British and French interests. When, however, in November a group of English financiers did begin to show a fresh interest in the Ottoman empire, they did not seek the co-operation of the French. Instead they proposed to participate along with the empire's new rulers in the establishment of a new state bank, which was to be known as the National Bank of Turkey.

Sir Ernest Cassel, on whose support Vere had counted, intended along with his associates to provide the capital for the new bank, and the Foreign Office was to be given the opportunity to share in the appointment of its directors. The venture was favoured by Grey, and Hardinge considered it a far more important undertaking than the Anglo–French consortium. Indeed, the indifference which Hardinge began to show towards the latter project led Bertie to warn his colleeagues in London that the part Britain had played 'however blameless in reality would not seem to the French quite straightforward'. He was right. At Paris the National Bank scheme was regarded as a blow to the Ottoman Bank and the influence of French finance in Turkey. To the French government it seemed as if Britain had deserted them in order to take advantage of the new situation there.

Although Bertie endeavoured to defend the Foreign Office against French critics of its conduct in this affair, his colleagues were hardly cautious in their declarations. When on 20 January 1909 Vere protested that the National Bank would be bitterly opposed by the French, Mallet replied that 'we were top dogs at Constantinople nowadays and it was more likely that the French would wish to make terms with us'. It was an attitude which was not discouraged by the tiresome difficulties to which attempts to maintain cordial economic relations with the French in Morocco and China gave rise. In a letter to Bertie of 21 January in which he criticized the activities of the French and Germans in Morocco, Hardinge concluded that it made him think that 'on the whole it is a good thing for our commercial and industrial people that we failed to get an Anglo–French group'. Even Bertie, who could not completely endorse Hardinge's views, was unhappy about the part played by a desire for financial gain in the determination of France's foreign policy. Both the French desire to effect an early withdrawal of the international force from Crete and Caillaux's efforts to limit the size of the proposed Bulgarian indemnity, were regarded by him as examples of French policy being in part decided by economic factors.

French ministers were bitter in their complaints about Britain's new role in Turkey. According to one report which reached Bertie, Caillaux was putting it about that 'les Anglais commencent à nous embêter à Constantinople'.[82] On 1 February Clemenceau exclaimed to Saunders, the *Times* correspondent in Paris, that the English wanted to 'get everything in Turkey for themselves'. His resentment was not softened by a British suggestion for bringing the Germans into a projected Anglo–French railway loan in China. Astonished at this suggestion, he warned Saunders: 'There is a cleft in the entente and care must be taken that it does not widen.' This raised doubts in the Foreign Office not only about Anglo–French co-operation in the financial and commercial sphere, but also about the whole future of the understanding.[83]

In a letter to Bertie of 3 February Tyrrell recounted that he had heard from Paris that people there believed that Britain wanted war to result from the Near Eastern crisis on the off chance that France would then become involved in a war with Germany.[84] Bertie, however, seems to have been unperturbed by either these reports or Clemenceau's outburst. He reassured Tyrell that the French premier 'must not always be taken quite literally'. 'The French', he observed, 'are not always pleasant bedfellows but we might go further (viz. Berlin) and fare worse'.

Bertie also suggested that one reason for Clemenceau's opposition to Britain bringing Germany into the railway loan project in China was that the French themselves would like to have proposed it.[85] There may have been some truth in this for on 6 February he was informed by Pichon that an agreement had been negotiated between the French and German governments on Morocco. Moreover, within the next fortnight he learned from a 'reliable source' that an agreement had been concluded between the French group which had been intended to form part of the Anglo–French combination and a German group which included the Deutsche Bank. There were also reports from Constantinople that the Ottoman Bank had again emerged in open alignment with German finance there.[86]

Grey had been warned early in January by his minister at Tangier that something might be afoot between France and Germany, but British officials had thus far only been able to speculate on what its form and content might be.[87] In fact the Franco–German declaration of 9 February 1909, and the explanatory notes exchanged by the two governments pledged German political disinterest in Morocco in return for French promises of financial and commercial co-operation. It was the sort of arrangement which had already been envisaged in the discussion which had taken place between representatives of France and Germany during 1907. But in sanctioning an agreement at a time when relations between the great powers were strained by the problems of the Near East, and when Anglo–German relations were hardly at their best, Clemenceau had been ready to risk causing some disharmony in the *entente*. He and his colleagues were probably influenced by the attitude

assumed by the British government on the question of co-operation at Constantinople. Of more importance, however, would seem to have been the
recognition by the governments in Paris and Berlin that they might be drawn
by their alliances into a Balkan conflict which was not of their making.[88]

The Franco–German accord was not regarded by Bertie as evidence of
any change in France's foreign relations. Indeed, he appears to have been far
more disturbed by Clemenceau's resignation in July 1909 and the entry into
the new government of two ministers who were reputed to be sympathetic
towards Germany.[89] In the Foreign Office the news of the agreement had a
mixed reception. Hardinge regarded it as a 'complete vindication of the
"entente"', but other officials and Grey were uneasy about whether they had
been informed by the French of everything that had been agreed. What they
feared, however, was not that some secret political understanding had been
concluded, but that some tacit agreement had been reached between Paris and
Berlin which would prove harmful to British commercial and financial
interests in Morocco.[90]

For their part the French continued to resent the part played by British
finance in the establishment of the National Bank. Nevertheless, in the following year Grey sought their collaboration in an effort to compel the Turks to
adopt a thoroughgoing reform of their financial system.[91] With this in mind,
he pressed Cassel to desist from competing for a Turkish loan contract, and
in the autumn of 1910 another fruitless attempt was made to secure a working
arrangement between British and French firms at Constantinople.[92] Neither
the Quai d'Orsay nor the Ottoman Bank wished to make any real sacrifices
for the sake of a financial *entente*, and Grey and his officials in London were
reluctant to give further offence to the French.[93] Yet in the same period the
results of the Franco–German accord on Morocco were disappointing for its
initiators. Co-operation between French and German individuals and banking
institutions did not form the basis of a durable political friendship.

When on 3 August 1909 Bertie had the opportunity to speak to Pichon about
the composition of the new government of Aristide Briand, he warned him
that at Berlin there would probably be attempts to magnify any small matters
into negotiations for a Franco–German understanding on general policy.[94] No
further progress, however, was made in this direction, and during the next
eighteen months it was French rather than British susceptibilities which were
to be ruffled by Germany's dealings with their friends.[95] Not that either Pichon,
who remained at the foreign ministry, or Paul Cambon appear to have been
unduly perturbed by Grey's efforts during 1909 and 1910 to improve Britain's
relations with Germany. Although Bertie cautioned the Foreign Office about
the use which German 'agents' in France would make of their discussions
with Berlin, he had to admit that the French would not object to an agreement
which was limited to the removal of outstanding differences.[96]

The French had little to fear. Grey was emphatic in his view that an
understanding with Germany should not imperil those which Britain already

had with France and Russia. It should not, he insisted, prevent Britain from giving to those powers the sort of support which she had given to France at Algeciras.[97]

What was worrying from the French point of view was the conduct of their Russian ally in the east. The visit in November 1910 of the Emperor Nicholas and Sazonov to Potsdam, and their conclusion with the Germans of a tacit understanding on Persia and the Baghdad railway was much resented in France. To French and British officials alike it seemed as though Germany was bent upon dividing Britain, France, and Russia.[98] Moreover, Pichon's efforts to 'gloss over' the significance of the Potsdam meeting were not aided by the press attacks which Tardieu launched against his foreign policy. Potsdam had not in Tardieu's opinion severely weakened France's foreign combinations, but it had, he thought, demonstrated the need for a concerted policy between the British, French, and Russian governments in the east. 'The Triple Alliance, which went in for action, was', he protested, 'confronted by the Triple Entente, which slumbered.'[99]

At a time when he was about to resume negotiations with the German government on a naval and political agreement Grey was well aware of the importance of preserving in public the impression that Britain and France were acting together. On 3 February 1911 he assured Paul Cambon that he wished to avoid the appearance of France having been isolated as a result of first Russia, and then Britain having done something with Germany.[100] Already on 12 January the French ambassador had informed Pichon that he did not think that the Germans would find their task as easy at London as they had done at St Petersburg.[101] Nevertheless, when Briand's government fell at the end of February, he warned Pichon that unless his successor were a man of experience who carried some weight 'la Triple Entente risque de s'effriter'.[102]

Jean Cruppi, who became foreign minister in the government of Ernest Monis, possessed neither of the qualities desired by Cambon.[103] After having only recently been initiated in the mysteries of the *entente*, he was distressed to learn that Grey had told the Commons on 30 March that the extent of Britain's commitment to France was that 'expressed or implied in the Anglo–French Convention'. This declaration had been purposely worded in order to avoid giving the impression that the accord of 1904 might not 'be construed to have larger consequences than its strict letter'. But Cruppi was unimpressed by Grey's verbal niceties. Worried by the effect that it might have upon French parliamentary opinion, he protested to Bertie that he would have preferred that there should have been some suspicion that an 'understanding did exist for possible eventualities'. But he received little comfort from the ambassador.[104] When on 5 April he took to him the text of a statement, which he proposed to make in the senate, Bertie objected to its containing the assurance that both powers would remain friendly and united in all eventualities, and would give 'le moment venu une forme précise à leur entente'.[105] As Nicolson pointed out, this would have given the impression that 'something

very serious was impending', and that the British and French governments
had come to a definite understanding.[106]

Bertie suspected that the line which Cruppi was taking in this matter was
not his own, but that of the Quai d'Orsay.[107] Already in February the
international situation had prompted Pichon and his officials to think in terms
of a tightening of their *entente* with England through a resumption of the
military conversations which had languished since 1908.[108] Moreover, on 8
April General Foch suggested to the British military *attaché* at Paris that there
was a need for both a military understanding regarding the action to be taken
by the British and French armies in a war with Germany, and a political
understanding which would state exactly what the two governments were
prepared to concede and resist in the many questions of the moment.[109] Four
days later Cruppi also put it to Bertie that in the present situation it 'behoved
the French and British Governments to carry matters further as regards
possible co-operation in certain eventualities than had hitherto been done'.

What Cruppi desired, Bertie informed Grey, was not a formal convention,
but an understanding which would define what joint action the two powers
should take in case they had to co-operate in a conflict. He had, Bertie
observed, probably not delved very deeply into the subject of the military
conversations, and had raised the question 'theoretically' rather than 'practically'. Indeed, although Grey expected to be 'asked something', and chose
this occasion to formally inform Asquith of the military conversations, over
a month passed before Cruppi on 13 May spoke to Bertie of his wish to make
the *entente* 'active and evident'. By then, however, the troubles which were
already stirring in Morocco had entered a new and disturbing phase.[110]

Two factors seem to have induced Cruppi to approach Bertie on 13 May:
the prospect of Germany seeking to exploit Franco–Spanish differences over
Morocco, and the growth of German influence in Turkey. But Bertie responded to the foreign minister's appeal for 'joint action' in Turkish affairs
by reminding him of the Ottoman Bank's opposition to Anglo–Turkish financial co-operation at Constantinople.[111] Indeed, the failure of Britain and
France to achieve this clearly demonstrated the limits of the *entente*. Nevertheless, the fractious attitude which the Quai d'Orsay at times assumed towards
Britain on extra-European questions gave neither Grey nor his senior officials
cause to doubt the value of France's friendship in Europe. When in October
1910 Cassel complained to Nicolson about the efforts of the Foreign Office to
restrain the activities of the National Bank, he was warned by the new
permanent under-secretary that the *entente* was the 'bed-rock of our policy
and could on no account be broken'.[112]

There seemed to be no attractive alternative in Grey's opinion to the
understanding with France. Without it he feared 'we should be isolated and
might have everybody against us'. Moreover, Bertie still thought it possible
that if the French did not feel confident of Britain's support, they might be
forced by Germany into a separate accord which would damage British

interests. Evidently unaware of what had been settled by the Anglo–French staff talks, he recommended to Nicolson on 14 May 1911 that 'everything military and naval ought to be arranged unofficially to meet the contingency of British and French forces *having* to act together'.[113] In fact, despite the reluctance of Britain's naval chiefs to participate in joint planning with the French, the military conversations had resulted in agreement being reached on a number of issues relating to the possible transfer of a British army to the continent.[114] It remained, however, to be seen whether these measures and Grey's continuing diplomatic support of France would be sufficient to enable the *entente* to survive a fresh crisis in Franco–German relations.

6

Great Britain and Russia, 1905 to the 1907 Convention

BERYL WILLIAMS

The Liberals took office in December 1905. On 13 December Grey assured Benckendorff, the Russian ambassador, that he was in favour of an agreement with Russia.[1] The Government of India were asked for their terms in March 1906[2] and Sir Arthur Nicolson arrived in St Petersburg as the new British ambassador on 28 May,[3] having 'talked entente in and out, up and down' with Grey, Asquith and Morley before leaving London.[4] Formal negotiations were launched on 7 June.[5]

The speed with which Grey inaugurated negotiations with the Russians, at a time when Russia was still in a turmoil of revolution and the Russo-Japanese war a recent memory, bears witness to his own convictions in this direction as well as his desire to maintain continuity of foreign policy with his predecessors.[6] The ground had been prepared by the Conservatives and tentative discussions had taken place in 1903, but although the Liberals were committed to uphold the Anglo-French entente, they were not committed to continue negotiations to extend it. However Grey had spoken in favour of an agreement with Russia as early as 1902,[7] and in his City speech in October 1905 he declared that the 'estrangement between us and Russia has...its roots not in the present but solely in the past'.[8]

The Foreign Minister saw an agreement with Russia partly as an extension of the French entente. 'We could not pursue at one and the same time a policy of agreement with France and a policy of counter alliances against Russia...an agreement with Russia was the natural complement of the agreement with France'.[9] The entente with France, however, was recent and by no means cordial between the fall of Delcassé and the Algeciras Conference. Enough was known in London of the meeting between the Tsar and the Kaiser at Bjorko for English diplomatists to be apprehensive of a possible Russo-German alliance and worried about the loyalty of France.

Grey had pledged himself to improve relations with Germany as well as with Russia,[10] but there seemed little possibility of this early in 1906 and Grey saw a need to check the growth of German power by both preserving and extending the French entente. When sanctioning the military conversations with France he argued that if Britain remained neutral in a future Franco-German war 'the French will never forgive us...Russia would not think it worth while to make a friendly arrangement with us about Asia...we should be left without a friend and without the power of making a friend and Germany would take some pleasure...in exploiting the whole situation to her advantage'. Hardinge added that 'an agreement or alliance between France, Germany and Russia in the near future' would be a 'certain' consequence.[11]

Thus re-establishing Russia as a 'factor in European politics',[12] on the side of France and England was crucial to Grey's aim of maintaining a balance of power in Europe. 'An entente between Russia, France and ourselves would be absolutely secure. If it is necessary to check Germany it could then be done.'[13] Fear of Germany – German sea power, German encroachment in the Middle East; a possible Russo-German rapprochement – was evident throughout the negotiations.[14]

Grey's attitude marked a change in emphasis from the Conservative policy of seeing Russia basically as a potential or actual menace to the Empire and especially India, to one of regarding her as a potential ally in Europe. 'If Russia accepts, cordially and wholeheartedly, our intention to preserve the peaceable possession of our existing Asiatic possessions', declared Grey before taking office, 'then I am quite sure that in this country no government will make it its business to thwart or obstruct Russia's policy in Europe. On the contrary it is urgently desirable that Russia's influence should be re-established in the Councils of Europe.'[15]

The urgency came not only from the international situation but also from the realities which were revealed to the Liberals of Britain's military and naval position. These affected both her potential role of holder of the balance of power in Europe against Germany and more immediately her ability to defend her Empire against possible Russian aggression. It was brought home to the Government that Britain was no longer able to meet all her commitments. By January 1907 the General Staff and the Admiralty had agreed that it was no longer possible to hold the Straits alone against Russia. Grey urged the necessity of keeping this information strictly secret.[16] The Anglo-Japanese alliance had been welcomed by the navy as a means of reducing the Far Eastern fleet,[17] and the Russo-Japanese war had reduced the Russian fleet, but the growth of the German navy was putting such strain on naval resources as to increase reluctance to risk a military conflict with Russia in Asia. This was bound to have political repercussions.[18]

The Liberals came to power pledged to social reform, economy and re-trenchment. Naval estimates would have to rise but Haldane at the War Office was determined to cut the army costs. Esher explained early in 1907 to the King that 'the peace requirements of India govern and cover the military requirements of the Empire in as much as a war with Russia on the North West Frontier, being the gravest military operation which Your Majesty's army could be called upon to undertake, covers by its magnitude all other conceivable operations'.[19] It was moreover in Central Asia that friction with Russia had increased in recent years to an extent that the Government of India, and parts of Whitehall, saw Russian activity as a serious threat against which the present military position was insufficient.

The last years of the Conservative Government had seen a forward policy against Russia by Curzon and Kitchener from India. Lansdowne had been unhappy about certain aspects of this policy but had encouraged a firm stand against Russia generally. The Russo-Japanese war had done little to relax tension. Both Hardinge at St Petersburg and MacDonald at Tokyo took seriously for a time the possibility of the Russians seeking renewed popularity at home and success abroad by turning against Japan's ally in India.[20] The British delayed a renewal of the Anglo-Japanese treaty until the Japanese agreed to extend its scope to cover not only India but the adjacent regions as well. Balfour defined these as 'Afghanistan, the strip of Persian territory adjoining Afghanistan and Baluchistan, or if the last be too large, then Seistan alone, or possibly Tibet.'[21]

At the same time, and only five months before Grey became Foreign Minister, the Indian chief of General Staff, Lord Kitchener, put forward proposals for increased preparations against 'the menacing advance of Russia towards our frontiers'.[22] Kitchener was convinced that 'our Northern neighbour is pushing forward her preparations for the contest in which we shall have to fight for existence. Even at this moment...the political outlook is threatening; he would be a bold man who would venture to predict that we shall not become involved in the struggle before our preparations are complete.'[23] He outlined a plan which, in its essentials, was to be put forward, both by the Government of India and by at least sections of the War Office, as an alternative to negotiations with Russia throughout 1906 and the first half of 1907.

Kitchener did not foresee an actual invasion of India in the near future, but he pointed out that for the first time the extension of the Russian railway system into Central Asia brought this within the bounds of practicality. Two railway systems now gave the Russians lines of approach through either Kandahar or Kabul,[24] and Hardinge was later to describe these as a 'sword of Damocles hanging over Britain's head'.[25]

A third Russian 'tentacle for the absorption of Afghanistan and subsequent attack on India' was the Persian route through Seistan.[26] It was this that Grey was to be chiefly concerned with in the negotiations but the Government of India was in many ways more worried about Afghanistan, having with Kitchener no doubt that Russia intended 'to establish herself in Afghanistan sooner or later'.[27]

Early in 1907 a War Office survey endorsed the view that the extension of the Russian railway system meant that 'without necessarily intending to conquer and absorb our Indian Empire she aims at eventually making her frontier and that of India conterminous', and concluded 'when that has been effected the military burdens of India and the Empire will be so enormously increased that, short of recasting our whole military system, it will become a question of practical politics whether or not it is worth our while to retain India or not'. This meant that Britain faced 'practically...the military burdens and anxieties of a Continental state'.[28]

Kitchener proposed that any Russian encroachment on Afghanistan should be met by a declaration of war. He advocated a military alliance with the Amir; firm steps against the rebellious frontier tribes and, most controversial of all, that the India railway system should be extended towards the Afghan border.[29] This policy would mean an increase in the Indian army and Kitchener claimed that there had been a Conservative promise of 100,000 men (8 divisions) as reinforcements from England during the first year of a war.[30]

When the new Viceroy, Lord Minto, was seen to support Kitchener's ideas, the whole question was discussed by the new Government at a meeting of the Committee of Imperial Defence in March 1906. The Indian proposals were badly received. Haldane insisted on regarding them as having been drawn up on the assumption of immediate danger from Russia during the Japanese war and argued that a change in the international situation and revolution in Russia had rendered them obsolete.[31] He had revealed the previous day in the House of Commons that he intended to start his army economies in India, as Russia was no longer a serious threat.[32] One problem, which Simla may not have realised, was that the army, after the military conversations with the French, was now geared strategically, as was the navy, to Europe.[33] Robertson, of the Intelligence Division of the War Office, supported the idea of an agreement with Russia as it would 'weaken Germany's military position in Europe, and therefore...strengthen our own as well as that of France'.[34] Moreover in the autumn Esher was to admit that the size of the army, which Haldane was preparing to cut, was not adequate to defend India in time of war. Denying that any pledge had been given to Kitchener, Esher said that 'the eight divisions named of infantry do not at present exist',[35] an argument with which Morley was to defend the Convention in September 1907.[36]

Grey was frankly sceptical of Russia's ability to threaten the Indian frontier at a time when she confessed herself unable to drive back some Turkish troops on the Persian border,[37] but in face of the Indian Government's refusal to consider reducing the size of the Indian army, the Cabinet was bound to take the problem seriously. A sub-committee of the C.I.D. held six meetings throughout January and February 1907. Headed by Morley it included Grey and Asquith as well as representatives of the Army, Navy and the Government of India. Its report in May 1907 accepted Kitchener's report in its main essentials including the railway lines and the eight divisions of reinforcements.[38]

Meanwhile Grey, although participating in these discussions, had been following his alternative policy of a negotiated agreement with St Petersburg. We cannot know what line he would have taken on the C.I.D. report if the negotiations had failed, but in the light of it Morley's support for Grey against Minto was obviously of great importance, as Grey himself admitted.[39] It also highlights the reality behind Sanderson's comment the month the Convention was signed; 'the process of working in constant antagonism is too expensive'.[40] Grey admitted in his memoirs that an agreement was 'the only practical alternative to the old policy of drift, with its continual complaints, bickerings and dangerous frictions'.[41] More to the point was a private minute, that it was also the only alternative to 'a certain and, as I think, intolerable increase of the military responsibilities of India and the Empire and would provoke Russia to make it her object more than ever to worry us in Asia; an object which might in time develop into a real design upon India, which I do not believe Russia has yet seriously entertained'.[42]

If Grey was unconvinced that Russia really wanted to threaten India or even occupy Afghanistan, he was well aware that the fear of this had been in the past a 'formidable diplomatic weapon' in Russian hands in gaining concessions elsewhere and described the loss of this as a great gain to Britain and 'the cardinal British object in these negotiations'.[43] He also had more faith than the Indian Government in Russia's good intentions. In this he was backed by the important figure of Hardinge, who was now Permanent Under Secretary at the Foreign Office and an old advocate of agreement, and Nicolson, who went to Russia 'personally anxious for an agreement' and who saw difficulties arising from 'simple misunderstandings of each other'.[44] Nicolson was probably even more anxious than Grey to see an agreement in order to counterbalance Germany. He had been suspicious of the Germans since his experience as British representative at Algeciras and was to urge turning the agreement into a more definite form of alliance in 1909 as an anti-German move.[45]

The Russians were far more willing to receive overtures than they had been in 1903. The appointment of Isvolsky to the Russian Foreign Ministry signified a turn from Asian adventures and a renewed interest in the Balkans and European problems. However Isvolsky was to have similar troubles with the military in Russia, and for similar reasons, as Grey had with the Government of India. Moreover the two powers had in the Middle East a limited and clear cut area of increasing friction, which was sufficiently dangerous to make an agreement worth having and sufficiently localised not to concern any other power. Although the European implications of the agreement were recognised from the start, Nicolson stressed the need for the discussions to be 'strictly businesslike, and the field in which they were to operate must be strictly defined'.[46]

The negotiations turned out to be long and difficult and were more than once on the point of breaking down completely. All three areas concerned – Persia, Afghanistan and Tibet, were interwoven during the discussions and there were long periods of quiescence. Isvolsky's nervousness about German reactions was rivalled only by Nicolson. It was not until October 1906 when a trip to Berlin, which caused considerable suspicion in London,[47] convinced Isvolsky that the German attitude was not hostile, that the negotiations got off the ground. The situation in Russia, and the British public's reaction to it, did little to help. The Foreign Office was besieged with anti-Tsarist petitions of various kinds and Campbell Bannerman's unfortunate 'vive la Douma' speech required tactful handling.[48] As Grey wrote 'there is so much in foreign affairs which attracts attention and had much better be left alone'.[49]

The negotiations opened with Tibet, which was not expected to cause difficulties of the magnitude of Persia or Afghanistan. The Government of India had been following a forward policy aiming at establishing direct British influence in Tibet to the exclusion of the Russians. The gains of the Younghusband expedition of 1904 were not as great as Curzon had hoped owing to modifications by Whitehall of the resulting Lhasa Convention. Nevertheless that document established a British Trade Agent at Gyantse, an occupation of the Chumbi valley for three years or until an indemnity was paid – both sources of potential British pressure – and excluded concessions to any other power.[50]

Minto's first task on arriving in India was to cope with an official visit by the Panchen Lama. The Dalai Lama's flight before Younghusband had made this dignitary the most important Tibetan official and Indian agents had encouraged him to expect British friendship and aid against both the Dalai Lama and his Chinese overlords. Minto, in conformity with the new Liberal policy, was discouraging.[51] Grey had come to power too late to stop the visit, but regarded it with dismay as altering the status quo in an area which he hoped to keep static while the Russian negotiations proceeded. Any move which might give rise to Russian protests was discouraged.[52] The outstanding negotiations as to Chinese adherence to the Lhasa Convention were resumed by the Liberals, and concluded in April 1906 on terms which Dr Lamb has suggested neither Curzon nor the Conservative government would have found acceptable, implying as they did that Tibet was a part of China.[53] The Chinese were allowed to pay off the Tibetan indemnity and by agreeing to this Grey sacrificed the hope of using the Lhasa Convention to strengthen British interests in Tibet. Even Minto, far from a Curzonian, began to feel that too much was being relinquished,[54] but Grey and Morley were adamant and the British impressed on Isvolsky the need to distinguish between the good intentions of both governments and the policies of local agents brought up in the spirit of the Great Game of Anglo-Russian antagonism.[55] For both sides Tibet 'provided an obvious opportunity...to demonstrate their moderation and good faith, the better to reach settlement on the really vital issues of Persia and Afghanistan'.[56]

The Indian attempts to get Tibet to carry out the Lhasa Convention had been worrying the Russians since 1905 and St Petersburg would undoubtedly have preferred a joint renunciation of all influence over Tibet.[57] The British were worried about possible Russian penetration through the Russian Buriats for whom the Dalai Lama was a spiritual leader. Pilgrimages of Russian Buddhists to Lhasa were one thing, but it was known that the Tsar had been in contact with the Dalai Lama through a certain Dorjiev for some years. Although the Russians protested that the contacts were only of a spiritual nature Minto was well aware of the difficulties of ensuring that no commercial or political matters ensued.[58] The plan for a Russian Buriat escort to take the Dalai Lama back to his capital in May 1906 was described by Grey as 'objectionable as constituting an interference in the internal affairs of the country on the part of Russia'.[59]

Nicolson's instructions in June 1906 centred round five points.[60] First, that Russia should recognise Chinese suzerainty over the country and its territorial integrity, and refrain from interfering in its internal administration. Secondly that Britain had a special geographical interest in seeing that Tibet's external relations were not 'disturbed by any other power'. The other points specified that both sides were to engage not to send a representative to Lhasa, obtain concessions or control over Tibetan revenues. The negotiations centred round point two, the others being incorporated into the final draft without much discussion.

Several separate issues were involved, one of the most important being the status of the two Lamas. Grey felt that the present Dalai Lama, who was believed to be pro-Russian, was safer remaining in exile in Mongolia, but it was obviously impossible to deny Russian Buddhists access to him. The problem was to prevent this access being used as a cover for a commercial or political agent. Grey succeeded in getting Isvolsky to agree not to demand political relations and the final agreement merely said that Buddhist subjects of both Russia and India could enter into direct relations with the Lamas on purely spiritual matters.

Both Nicolson and Grey were convinced early in the negotiations that the real Russian interest was not Tibet but Mongolia and that the importance of the Dalai Lama to the Russians lay in his influence over the Mongols rather than the Buriats.[61] Grey believed that 'what the Russian government desire is...a loose, ill-organised Mongolia on the Chinese side which will give her the opportunity for expansion later on', but he was determined to keep the two issues separate and rejected Isvolsky's proposal in January 1907 that Mongolia should be included in the Convention.[62]

The other points at issue came over regulating the direct British contacts left by the Lhasa Convention. These were kept firmly to commercial matters and all other contacts by both powers with Tibet were to be carried on via Peking. Isvolsky failed to get similar Russian rights to send trade agents into the country but obtained a considerable concession in a separate annex to the Convention. This assured the Russians that the Chumbi Valley would be evacuated by 1908 as long as the indemnity was paid and the trade marts functioning, and promised further Anglo-Russian talks if these conditions were not met.[63]

By this Grey sacrificed one of the most important potential gains of the Lhasa Convention, but he had not been aiming to consolidate in any way the position achieved for the British by Younghusband. On the contrary he merely wished to establish Tibet as a *cordon sanitaire* against Russian advance,[64] and this isolation of Tibet was strengthened by the agreement of both sides to forbid access to the country to geographical or scientific explorers for three years.

It was with Afghanistan that the Government of India was chiefly concerned, as Kitchener's memorandum indicated. Relations between Great Britain and Afghanistan were peculiar. The external relations of Afghanistan had been under British control for the last twenty-five years and Britain was pledged by treaty to safeguard the integrity of the Amir's dominions. The Amir received through India money, arms and advice, yet the actual situation belied this apparently close, protected–protector relationship. No British or Indian agent was allowed to reside in Kabul, and Simla depended on an unreliable Afghan agent who was little better than a prisoner. The British complained that they had no way of receiving reliable information about the country they were pledged to defend. The Amir refused to allow them to construct the roads, railways and telegraphs thought necessary for his defence and was not adverse to intriguing with the Russians and India's rebellious border tribes.[65]

By 1903 the Russians had acquired a long common border with Afghanistan and were demanding contact with the Amir for the settlement of border disputes which it was difficult to refuse. They were also trying to establish a commercial agent at Kabul, and India was again worried at the difficulty of separating commerce from politics. In 1905 the Dane mission was sent from India to impress the new Amir, and a new British–Afghan treaty was signed which left Afghanistan's external relations in British hands. It remained to settle the problem of Russian contacts.

Nicolson was permitted to open negotiations on Afghanistan in September 1906 but these were delayed on his request while the more pressing problem of Persia was dealt with.[66] Grey's draft proposals were finally submitted on 23 February 1907, once the Russian proposals on Persia made the prospect of agreement seem sufficiently good to warrant it.[67] Almost three months elapsed before the Russian reply. The Russian military were as concerned with Afghanistan as their British counterparts and Nicolson was increasingly worried that the Russian proposals would prove unacceptable. He expected Russia to demand some security against the possibility that India would transform Afghanistan 'from a buffer state into an avant-garde of the Indian empire'.[68]

The Russian proposals finally arrived in the middle of May and Nicolson, anxious to finish the negotiations, urged that they were a satisfactory basis from which to work. Both Grey and Hardinge disagreed. They disliked the use of the term 'buffer state', but the English objections really centred on two points. Firstly the Russian draft recognised the country as out of the Russian sphere of influence but it asked for a British guarantee not to occupy or annex any part of the country and not to interfere in Afghanistan's internal affairs.

Hardinge objected to this on the grounds that it was conceivable that the Amir would ask for British aid in developing his country and anyway the British had to have some way of making him fulfil his treaty obligations. Secondly the Russians, while not asking immediately for a commercial agent, proposed future discussions on this if trade increased.[69] Grey's problem was that he could not promise the Russians anything – like possible future commercial contacts – which depended on the Amir's consent which he could not guarantee.

Grey was also involved in 'a great struggle with the Government of India and the Technical Committee of the Indian Office', and Hardinge urged Nicolson to explain to Isvolsky that 'the difficulties which we meet from the Government of India...are not less than those made by the military party in St Petersburg'.[70] Minto in fact objected to negotiating over Afghanistan at all and openly preferred the friendship of the Amir to that of Russia.[71] The Government of India could not be persuaded to see the wider implications of the Convention and after the British counter-draft had been through their hands it so altered the Russian proposals as to constitute a fresh start.[72] Isvolsky complained that it 'made all the engagements by which Russia might benefit, such as frontier relations and trade, dependent on the consent of the Amir, while all the obligations which Russia took upon herself were to become operative immediately'.[73] He made this point too about the new British proposal to make bilateral the engagement not to occupy or annex the country. Nicolson hastened to London in July and had considerable success in persuading Grey to be more accommodating.[74] Isvolsky however was not satisfied with the exclusion of the bilateral clause. In the middle of August he came forward with a new article which provided for 'a friendly interchange of views' if the political status of Afghanistan was altered in any way.[75] Nicolson advocated acceptance,[76] and Grey seemed to be considering this as an unavoidable necessity.[77] But on this point the Government of India won their main, and indeed only, real victory during the negotiations by persuading Grey of the necessity of rejecting the Russian proposal out of hand.[78] There was some fear that this refusal would cause the Russians to abandon the entire convention, and it took Grey's letter of 27th August, referring for the first time during the negotiations to the possible non-Asiatic implications of an Anglo-Russian entente, to persuade Isvolsky to relent.[79]

The final Convention was a pacific enough looking document. The British declared that they had no intention of changing the political status of Afghanistan, and would exercise influence at Kabul in a pacific and in no way anti-Russian sense. The Anglo-Afghan treaty of 1905 was reaffirmed and Britain renounced any intention of occupying or annexing the country or of interfering in internal affairs with the saving clause; as long as Afghanistan kept her treaty commitments.

The Convention acknowledged the already existing Russo-Afghan communications over local issues by the frontier officers of both sides, and established the principle of the Russian right to equality of trading opportunities and facilities with the Indians in this region. Both these were to furnish cause for future difficulties. The possibility of providing in the future for Russian commercial agents was also envisaged, 'en égard bien entendu aux droits souverains de l'Emir'. This was the only reference to the sovereignty of Habibullah Khan.[80] The Amir was known to be likely to object to articles Three and Four and to take offence at the wording of article One. In these circumstances Grey's decision that the Convention was not to come into force until consent had been obtained to its provisions from an Amir who had not been informed or consulted about it, was an obvious seed of future trouble. It was decided, however, that to delay signature was too dangerous given the increasing fear of German activities in Persia.[81]

The English Foreign Office were well satisfied with the Afghanistan section. 'We have now, for the first time', wrote an official, 'obtained from Russia in writing and in the form of a definite treaty engagement, assurances on three points which had hitherto been only verbal and, as the Russian government stated, not binding indefinitely upon them.' These were the admission by St Petersburg that Afghanistan was outside its sphere of influence; that all Russian political relations with Afghanistan were to be conducted via Whitehall, and that Russian agents were forbidden to enter the country.[82]

Both sides regarded the Convention regarding Afghanistan as by no means the least important part of the whole entente, especially as it would be the section most noticed by the general public. Morley admitted to the Viceroy that 'the public will not trouble itself deeply about Thibet or even about Persia so long as the Gulf is kept in status quo. But any yielding about Afghanistan or even any contingent disturbance there will provoke, and rightly provoke, a fierce row.'[83] Isvolsky, in an interview with Edward VII at Marienbad shortly after the entente was signed, also remarked that it was to this area that most attention would be paid in Russia.[84]

Nevertheless all sources agree that Persia was the central part of the agreement for both the negotiating powers. It was also the part of the Convention which brought into sharp relief the fear of German expansion behind the negotiations. The discussions started amid a scare that the Persians had applied to Germany for a loan and, throughout the long-drawn-out negotiations, Nicolson urged their continuation at times of crisis or stagnation, when even Grey found him 'sanguine' about Russia's future,[85] by pointing out that the Germans would benefit both locally and in Europe if they broke down. He feared, he wrote, Persia turning into another Morocco, and urged the completion of the agreement before 'Germany has any ostensible pretext for interference, otherwise we shall have difficulties.'[86]

The loan question merely highlighted for the British the extent of Russian advance in recent years. Russia had pursued a policy of economic and political penetration in Persia far more intensively and seriously and with far greater success than in either Afghanistan or Tibet. Russian policy right up until the arrival of Isvolsky at the Foreign Ministry had been to dominate the north and eventually the whole of Persia by obtaining economic concessions without actually invading the country.[87] With regard to the northern half of Persia they had had considerable success. The establishment of a troop of Persian cossacks under Russian officers; the acquisition of concessions of various kinds, the establishment of a bank and above all loans amounting to over three million pounds to the Shah, aroused the lively apprehension of the British. Russia was also aiming at a foothold on the Persian Gulf and had acquired a commercial shipping line and a consul at Bunder Abbas by 1905. The Annual Report for Persia that year listed a long line of Russian activities despite the Far Eastern War and the revolution.[88]

In opposition to this impressive array of successes, the only real British gain had been the Imperial bank, but the British had lent only a fraction to Persia compared to the Russian loans. In 1905 Persia applied again for a loan, first to Russia and then to Britain, but both powers offered too small sums and hedged them around with unacceptable conditions.[89] When Grey first entered the Foreign Office he received within a month a memorandum from the Government of India urging that a loan to Persia should be reconsidered. Its author argued that it would put Britain in a strong bargaining position if she decided later to negotiate with Russia and added that in the eventuality of Persia breaking up it would be advisable to have secured as many concessions as possible.[90]

Grey's response to this suggestion showed that, unlike Simla, he was not thinking in terms of increasing British influence in Persia – a country of which, Benckendorff told Isvolsky, the new Foreign Secretary knew little.[91] 'It is a good argument', Grey minuted, 'if we have made up our minds that our interests require us to strengthen our hold on South Persia. I do not believe they do.'[92] He had already decided that he had no wish to prop up financially a decrepit government. It would need, he thought, more than money to do this effectively. Some form of protectorate at least over the south would be necessary and he did not feel 'that either strategy reasons (military or naval) or commercial prospects in Persia are such as to require this'.[93] He stressed to Spring Rice later in 1906 that even if the negotiations with Russia broke down, 'whatever happens I will not go in for a forward policy in Persia'.[94]

Rejecting the Indian memorandum in January 1906 he decided instead to use the loan issue to show the Russians that he was genuinely concerned to reach an agreement, and proposed a joint loan.[95] This was repeated in May when rumours of a possible German interest reached London.[96] The Russians agreed in August to act on what Isvolsky termed the 'tacit agreement of January'.[97] Grey replied that unless 'the Persian Government were likely to seek it elsewhere' he preferred to defer the loan.[98] However a week later Isvolsky informed Nicolson confidentially that he had confirmation that Persia had approached Berlin.[99]

This galvanised Grey into action. Receiving Nicolson's telegram in the country he returned immediately to London and persuaded Morley to advance half the sum. He excused himself for not consulting the Prime Minister on grounds of urgency. 'My fear was that if we refused Isvolsky's request he might, rather than let Germany lend alone, join with Germany in a loan. We should then find Germany and Russia partners against us in Persia and any chance of a future arrangement with Russia would be gone.' However he also suggested conditions, 'which will test the sincerity of Russia's intentions to make a settlement with us. If she agrees with our proposal, the lines of a division of spheres of interest between us and her in Persia will be laid down. We shall have left the north and west and the upper part of the Gulf open to her but the mouth of the Gulf, the south and Seistan will be secured as our interest.'[100]

The loan was thus seen as a first step towards a general settlement and Morley supported it as such.[101] Nicolson rejoiced at the change in Russia's attitude which even prompted Isvolsky to accept English financial aid in order to join in the loan.[102]

Grey now was in no hurry to push the negotiations. 'We have shown enough of our hand to convince the Russians that a fair agreement with us is a practical policy' he wrote, and was also in favour of keeping the advance as small as possible.[103] It was Nicolson, for ever wary of Germany, who pushed the negotiations with increasing impatience. Robertson of the War Office was also in favour of the agreement as a way of detaching Russia from Germany. It was desirable, he wrote, that we 'should have her on our side when Germany reaches the Persian Gulf – a contingency which is far less to be descried than Russia's presence there'.[104]

Thus the idea of a deal based on spheres of influence was Grey's position from the beginning of the negotiations, and indeed the idea goes back to 1903. The issue of what was meant by spheres of influence was contentious. Spring Rice pointed out, correctly, that Persia would see it as a partition[105] and there were those in Whitehall prepared to refer to it in almost these terms. Fitzpatrick, referring to a previous proposal, remarked that spheres of interest 'in the ordinary course would be certain to develop into protectorates',[106] which was the policy Grey had rejected. Morley facetiously compared it with the eighteenth-century partitions of Poland.[107] Neither Grey nor Nicolson would agree to this. In a private note Grey referred to the convention merely as 'a mutual self denying ordinance recognising Persian independence'.[108] Nicolson also wrote in a private letter to Grey 'Spring Rice seems to wish that we should limit ourselves to a railway, telegraph and sanitary convention. But this I gather is in substance what our arrangement will be – there will presumably be in the agreement no mention of the words 'sphere of influence'. We should, I presume, mutually agree in certain specific districts, not to compete for concessions and we should obtain from the Persian Government an engagement not to cede concessions to other powers in those districts. This doubtless would in fact be a recognition of spheres of influence but we should be following in some measure on the lines adopted by France and Spain at

Algeciras.'[109] He even denied this to Spring-Rice. 'We lay no obligation on Persia, we ask her for nothing and we do not infringe either on her independence or integrity.'[110]

The negotiations started slowly. Nicolson had asked in September 1906 to take Persia before Afghanistan but it was not until February that the Russian draft was received.[111] The negotiations centred round where the lines were to be drawn. Grey made no attempt to question Russia's position in the north. The Russians proposed as the limit of their sphere a line from Kasr-i-Shirin, through Isfahan and Yezd to the Afghan frontier. Grey replied that the Russian zone could not be allowed to touch Afghanistan, and by May he had succeeded in getting it to end at a point on the Persian frontier where the Russian and Afghan frontiers met, and preventing it touching Afghan territory.[112]

With regard to the line marking the English sphere Grey had more trouble with the Indian Government than with the Russians. The line started on the Afghan border and went through Birjand and Kerman to Bunder Abbas. This was by no means the whole of South Persia, and indeed not even the whole of the Gulf. It was also much smaller than the Russian sphere. Grey insisted that it was limited 'to an irreducible minimum based on strategic not commercial considerations'.[113] The main point for Grey was that it included the Seistan triangle, and thus expelled Russian influence from this crucial strategic area.[114] Grey regarded this as sufficient to meet the needs of Indian defence and both Nicolson and Hardinge saw the chief gain of the Convention as 'the exclusion of Russia from Seistan, Charbar and Bunder Abbas'.[115]

It was because of the British hope that they would achieve complete control of Seistan that the Russian seizure of the Seistan end of the telegraph line from Meshed to Seistan was opposed by Whitehall. Grey regarded the Russian take-over of the line in September 1906, which seems to have been done on the initiative of the Russian representatives in Persia, as an undesirable modification of the status quo and also as a test case of Russian good will.[116] In fact Isvolsky proved reluctant to relinquish it, arguing that by doing so he would attract undesirable attention from third powers.[117] Finally however Grey won his point that it was desirable for all Russian personnel to leave Seistan and an exchange of notes with the Convention arranged for it to be exchanged for control of the Meshed–Tehran line.[118]

The Convention recognised the independence and integrity of Persia and went on to divide the country into three spheres – Russian, British and a neutral zone between them. The two contracting powers engaged not to seek for themselves, or encourage their subjects or those of third powers to seek, concessions of a political or commercial nature in the sphere of the other.[119]

The size and extent of the British sphere involved the question of the Persian Gulf. The Lansdowne declaration of May 1903 had warned the Russians that any attempt to fortify a port on the Gulf would be 'a very grave menace to British interests and would be resisted by all means at Britain's disposal'.[120] Grey however in February 1906 could not see 'the danger of Russia having access to the Gulf' and felt that no settlement which did not give Russia such access was possible.[121] Isvolsky first raised the question when the British line was first suggested,[122] and Grey told the King that he expected to have to grant access in some form.[123] However Isvolsky did not follow up his interest and it was Grey who, under pressure from the Indian Government who were complaining about the size of the British sphere, at the last minute tried to get a clause added recognising British interest in the maintenance of the status quo in the Gulf. Grey seems to have given in to the Government of India under pressure from Edward VII, but he justified it to Nicolson on grounds of public interest in the area. Its omission, he said, 'would seriously affect the popularity of the agreement when concluded'.[124] Nicolson, who failed 'to understand the nervousness of some people as to our position in the Gulf', warned that Isvolsky would never accept this as it would affect German interests over the Bagdad Railway.[125] Grey tried several alternative phrases but Isvolsky refused to agree and finally Grey capitulated.[126] The British formally took note that Russia did not deny British interest in the status quo of the Gulf and a declaration to this effect was published with the Convention.[127] Grey privately regarded the Lansdowne declaration as too strong. 'I should' he wrote 'prefer something with less menace and more substance',[128] but the final declaration also drew attention to previous declarations of British policy in order 'to make it quite clear that the present convention is not intended to affect the position in the Gulf, and does not imply any change of policy respecting it on the part of Great Britain'.[129]

The other main area omitted from the Convention was, of course, the Straits. Benckendorff raised the question of the opening of the Straits on March 15th 1907 but, as Grey commented, 'unless she [Russia] could have it open for exit to herself, without its being open for entrance to others, she would rather the question should not be raised at all.' Grey replied that he was sure that the old policy of closing the Straits would have to be abandoned but although he wished it 'to be understood that the question was one which we were prepared to discuss', the interests of other powers made it undesirable to write it into the Convention. He also felt that it would involve Russian concessions in Egypt or about the Bagdad railway but left the initiative to Isvolsky.[130] The Russian Foreign Minister regarded this favourable reply as 'a great evolution in the relations of the two countries'.[131] Grey was careful to stipulate that he had not committed Britain to any particular proposal such as the opening of the Straits only to Russia, but he wrote privately to Nicolson that 'if Asian things are settled favourably the Russians will not have trouble with us about the entrance to the Black Sea'.[132] He seems indeed to have expected the Near East to feature in a 'complete arrangement'[133] but Isvolsky was content to leave the matter outside the Asian Convention.

That the matter of the Straits was raised shows the European implications of what purported to be merely a settlement on the Indian frontier, and Grey defended the Convention against its many critics with the argument that it was intended 'to begin an understanding with Russia which may gradually lead to good relations in European questions also'.[134] Meanwhile he believed that it had secured 'us for ever, as far as a treaty could secure us, from further Russian advances in the direction of the Indian frontier'.[135] This was ultimately a question of faith in Russia's good intentions, and on this issue Grey's apparent optimism was not shared either by Curzon or by Curzon's successor in Delhi.

7

Constantinople and Asiatic Turkey, 1905–1914

MARIAN KENT

Sir Edward Grey's policy towards Constantinople and Asiatic Turkey in the years up to the First World War had three basic aims: first, to maintain Britain's paramount influence in the Persian Gulf; second, to protect Britain's commercial interests in Asiatic Turkey, particularly in Mesopotamia; and third, to preserve as far as possible the territorial integrity of Turkey and thus the peace of Europe. British strategy, British commerce, and international balance of power considerations thus emerged as the three features providing a guiding thread. Grey saw his policy towards Turkey as an unequal relationship between, on the one hand, one of the world's greatest Imperial Powers intent on preserving her own defined world interests and upholding international peace and morality, and, on the other, apart from one brief moment of hope, a declining and decadent Empire threatened with extinction and needing guidance in its internal affairs and external relations.

The British Government's relations with the Government of Sultan Abdul Hamid II were uneasy and unsatisfactory. Grey himself wrote later of 'Abdul Hamid and his detestable camarilla'[1] and even less moralistic observers had to recognise the difficulties arising for the British from such a system. G. H. Fitzmaurice, Chief Dragoman since 1907 at the Embassy in Constantinople, described the situation succinctly in April 1908:

During the last few years our policy, if I may so call it, in Turkey has been, and for some time to come will be, to attempt the impossible task of furthering our commercial interests while pursuing a course (in Macedonia, Armenia, Turco-Persian Boundary etc.) which the Sultan interprets as pre-eminently hostile in aim and tendency. These two lines are diametrically opposed and consequently incompatible with one another. In a highly centralized theocracy like the Sultanate and Caliphate combined, with its pre-economic conceptions, every big trade etc. concession is regarded as an Imperial favour to be bestowed on the seemingly friendly, a category in which, needless to say, we are not included...any British Ambassador here must necessarily find himself in the equivocal, if not impossible position of having to goad the Sultan with the pinpricks of reform proposals while being expected to score in the commercial line successes which are dependent on the Sultan's goodwill.[2]

Not that all the Powers were equally embarrassed. Grey wrote, albeit with some exaggeration, in his *Twenty-Five Years*:

Germany at Constantinople exploited the situation steadily to her own advantage. We sacrificed our influence and material interests in Turkey; we did indeed keep our hands clean and acquit the national conscience... [but with only]... a very barren and unsatisfying result.

German policy seems to have been based upon a deliberate belief that moral scruples and altruistic motives do not count in international affairs... The highest morality, for a German Government, was the national interest: this overrode other considerations, and as such she pursued it at Constantinople. Her policy was completely successful, ours was deadlock and failure. Germany pushed her commercial interests in Turkey; the wealth of Asia Minor was passing into her hands... [3]

According to Grey, it was by fostering Germany's friendship towards his country and by playing off the Great Powers and their various interests one against the other, that Abdul Hamid was able to preserve his position. Grey's anxiety to use concerted Great Power pressure on the Sultan to implement the various reforms in Turkish administration that Britain thought essential remained, therefore, unassuaged. [4]

When the Young Turk Revolution broke out in the middle of 1908, with the proclamation of the 1876 Constitution on 23 July, the British Government immediately offered its official congratulations. [5] As Grey wrote to Sir Gerard Lowther, the new British Ambassador, who arrived in Constantinople on 30 July amid the excitement of the revolution:

The telegrams and my speech in Parliament will have explained to you my attitude. We should avoid making the Turks suspicious by attempting to take a hand where we are not wanted: but we should make them understand that, if they are really going to make a good job of their own affairs, our encouragement and support will be very firm, and that we shall deprecate any interference on the part of others. I do not mean that we should go to the length of intervention to protect them; but that our diplomatic attitude will be benevolent, and our influence used to secure a fair chance for them... we must make it clear that our quarrels have been, not with the Turkish people, but with the government of creatures against whom the Turks themselves have now protested... our course is clear: we must be ready to help the better elements, to wait upon events, and give sympathy and encouragement when required to the reform movement. [6]

Hopefulness was, nonetheless, tempered with caution. Less than a fortnight after the letter quoted above, Grey was writing to Lowther with some prescience that 'what has happened already in Turkey is so marvellous that I suppose it is not impossible that she will establish a Constitution, but it may well be that the habit of vicious and corrupt government will be too strong for reform and that animosities of race and religion will again produce violence and disorder. Or out of the present upheaval there may be evolved a strong and efficient military despotism.'[7] Lowther, who had similar misgivings, still felt, nonetheless, that 'considering the country is being run by the Committee of the League, a collection of good-intentioned children, things are going pretty well'.[8] To the British Government, the best aspect of this was, of course, the fact that Britain was now in the favoured position with the Turkish Government previously filled by the Germans.

Even after the upheaval of the abortive counter-revolution in April 1909, Grey did not despair of the Young Turks altogether. As he wrote to Lowther on 30 April:

> I see that you are becoming pessimistic. I was becoming so, on hearing that corruption was creeping into the Committee and the Young Turks. But I cannot help being impressed by the decision, purpose, discipline and strength which have characterised the leaders of the Army which is now in power... No doubt they have made plenty of mistakes. But it seems clear to me that the best elements in Turkey are on their side, and we must back up those elements and be sympathetic to them...I think that during the last three or four months we have let ourselves slide too much into a critical attitude towards the Committee [of Union and Progress] and the Young Turks.[9]

British observers gradually grew more pessimistic, however, as the evidence mounted of Young Turk rule turning into military despotism and Britain losing her favoured position. In a despatch of 30 July 1910 Lowther summed up the realities of the situation:[10] although there was still much sentiment in favour of Britain among the Turkish population, Britain had disappointed the governing régime by her attitude to Crete, Egypt, Mesopotamia and the Persian Gulf, by her support of Persia in frontier disputes, by her refusal to sell a warship to Turkey, by failing to agree to the proposed 4% customs duty increase, and by the criticism increasingly voiced by British public opinion about the arbitrary and unconstitutional acts of the Young Turk régime. Germany, by contrast, through her close connection with the Turkish army, elements of which now constituted the Turkish government, was well on the way to recovering her predominant position. This trend was to continue, culminating in the Turkish–German secret alliance of 1914 bringing Turkey into the World War in November of that year.

Discussion of British policy towards Asiatic Turkey in the years before the First World War has to be seen against the background of the negotiations over the Baghdad Railway, as the eventual negotiations and settlements closely involved so much of British policy and interests in the area. By the time of Grey's taking office Britain's share in railways in Asiatic Turkey, originally almost monopolistic, had declined to the 380-mile track of the Smyrna–Aidin Railway. Further, present and future freedom of action for Britain was governed by two recently concluded agreements. First, the Black Sea Basin Agreement of 1900 granted Russia a monopoly of railway construction in the provinces of Asiatic Turkey near to the Black Sea and the Russian border, an agreement supplemented by others extending France's railway interests beyond those she already possessed in Syria. Second was the 1903 Baghdad Railway agreement. This 99-year concession gave definite form to the 1899 convention conceding to the Anatolian Railway Company which already held rights for railway construction from Haidar Pasha to Angora and Konia, an extension from Konia to the Persian Gulf via Adana, Nissibin, Mosul, Baghdad, Kerbela, Zubeir and Basra. It also granted permission for a number of branch lines including one to Khanikin on the Persian frontier and one to the Mediterranean, and for the construction of ports at Baghdad, Basra and at the terminal point on the Persian Gulf. The Ottoman Government undertook to guarantee funds for both the construction of the railway and supply of its rolling stock, and for its working, the latter to be covered by a killometric guarantee. The company enjoyed exemption from all customs dues for essential imported materials; exemption from all taxation on its entire property and revenue for the whole period of the concession; extensive mining, quarrying, forestry and water rights along its route and various commercial concessions in addition.

Thus by 1905 German interests held a well-secured concession and it seemed likely that the railway would be completed and working within the foreseeable future. For British interests this railway constituted a far greater potential threat than any of the other railways in Anatolia.[11] It was to traverse a region where British–Indian trade had long been paramount and unrivalled; it was to pass Kerbela and Nejef, Shiah religious shrines visited annually by increasing thousands (in 1905 some 11,000) of British–Indian subjects; its mineral rights came more and more to be seen as a threat to British oil aspirations in the Mosul and Baghdad provinces; and its navigation rights on the Tigris River and its port rights at Baghdad and Basra challenged the long-held British concession of the Euphrates and Tigris Steam Navigation Company. It was likely to influence the political situation in the Persian Gulf profoundly, threatening Britain's predominant influence both on land and sea and, at the same time, by providing a more direct route to India than any yet in existence, it constituted a potent strategic threat.[12] All these factors were bound to affect Britain's prestige in Asiatic Turkey and the Middle East generally. It was not so much the railway itself that caused concern – though competition in the transport field was clearly a factor – as the side issues and the far-reaching implications. These forced it on the attention of the British Government and led to a complicated system of cross-bargaining which was finally settled only shortly before the outbreak of the First World War.

How was Grey to deal with this potential and wide-ranging threat to Britain's interests in Asiatic Turkey and the Persian Gulf? The answer first seemed to be, on advice from the Committee of Imperial Defence and other quarters, that since the line was going to be built it was better tactics to seek to control it from within than from without. In other words, the *entente* powers should participate in the project, with Britain controlling the section between

Baghdad and the Persian Gulf.[13] In 1909, however, an alternative was proposed: a British concession for a railway between Baghdad and the Gulf via
the Tigris Valley to Basra, thence possibly continuing up the Euphrates and
eventually to the Mediterranean. At the same time British was refusing her
assent to the Turks' request for a 4 % increase in her customs dues, permission
for which had to be obtained from all the Powers. She withheld her agreement
on the grounds that she could not agree to the increase if it were to be 'used,
whether directly or by liberating other revenues, to facilitate the prolongation
of a railway which must, as at present controlled, have a prejudicial effect on
established trade interests in Mesopotamia'.[14] Britain would only change her
attitude if she received either participation in the Baghdad–Gulf section of
the Baghdad Railway or received her own alternative railway concession. This
would appear to be not mere obstruction as is sometimes said[15] but rather an
attempt to produce a solution in the only feasible way, that is, by hard
bargaining using the one lever – the customs increase – that was really vital
to the Turks. Thus, blocking the progress of the Baghdad Railway was a
by-product of unsuccessful negotiations by Britain rather than a basic aim.
The preferred Persian Gulf terminus for the railway was Koweit. But here,
since her secret agreements of 23 January, 1899 and 15 October, 1907 with
the Sheikh of Koweit, Britain had secured to herself control over the Sheikh's
territory, the latter agreement specifically to protect her own Persian Gulf
interests from the Baghdad Railway.[16] More, Britain's determination not to
make any agreement over the Baghdad Railway without the full consent of
her *entente* partners caused further delays until a settlement was made more
urgent by two intervening factors. These were the conclusion of the German–
Turkish conventions of March 1911, providing revenues for completing the
building of the Baghdad Railway as far as Baghdad, and the German–Russian
Agreement of August 1911, which split the solid *entente* front Grey had been
hoping to maintain. Within a few years the Railway would be completed as
far as Baghdad and Britain's long-held sphere of influence and trade in
Mesopotamia would be penetrated by the most pushing of rivals. As Grey put
it in his confidential address to the Imperial Conference Delegates in May 1911:

We have only got two objects as regards the Baghdad Railway; one is to secure
that when that railway is made British trade shall not be at a disadvantage in
the rates which are levied on goods transported by the railway; and we should
like to have some say in the management of the line or some part of the line
[in order to ensure this]... The other object is that the situation in the
Persian Gulf – the strategic situation – should not be altered in a way which
would damage our prestige or damage our strategical situation.[17]

In July 1911, therefore, he rejected the Turkish proposal for internationalising
the Baghdad–Gulf section of the line.[18] Constructive negotiations were
undertaken between 1911 and 1913, culminating in the series of agreements
between Britain and Turkey initialled or signed in July and August 1913, in

which Britain secured her basic interests in Asiatic Turkey: the preservation of British influence and commerce in Mesopotamia and of British influence in the Persian Gulf.

The convention concerning the Baghdad Railway was initialled on 12 August 1913; signature had to await signature of a parallel agreement between Britain and Germany.[19] The British had by now decided that their interests were best protected not by a minor participation (which was all they would be allowed) in the railway south of Baghdad, but by other means. Accordingly the convention secured equality of treatment on all railways in Asiatic Turkey and the participation of two British directors, acceptable to the British Government, on the board of the Baghdad Railway Company. It was also laid down that the Railway was to terminate at Basra, and that any railway beyond Basra towards the Persian Gulf would depend on prior agreement with the British Government.

The Baghdad Railway convention was supplemented by other agreements, further securing Britain's *desiderata* in Mesopotamia and the Persian Gulf and making some concessions to Turkey.[20] More directly relevant to the Baghdad Railway were the convention of 29 July 1913 establishing in detail a navigation commission on the Shatt-el-Arab [21] and the declaration confirming and extending British navigation rights on the Tigris and Euphrates.[22] These covered water transport and other matters between the Gulf and Basra and Baghdad. Worth noting also are the agreements over the Smyrna–Aidin Railway[23] and over the Turco-Persian Frontier.

All these agreements provided many benefits for British interests. They forbade discrimination against British or Indian merchandise on all railways in Asiatic Turkey and seated two British directors on the board of the Baghdad Railway. They increased the mileage of the British Smyrna–Aidin Railway by over 50%, prolonging its concession until 1999 and avoided any competition with the Baghdad Railway, and made British consent essential for any railway enterprise beyond Basra to the Gulf. On navigation of the Tigris and Euphrates rivers where British ships had held a foreign monopoly for over 200 years a compromise was reached by securing a formal predominance for British ships, and British participation in the Ports Company for construction at Baghdad and Basra. The agreements also ensured that the Shatt-el-Arab waterway between the junction of the Tigris and Euphrates and the Persian Gulf, used in 1912 by 217 British out of a total of 240 ocean-going ships, would be maintained in a better state with British assistance, and would be open to all nations. As in all future irrigation works, in the major, Wilcocks, irrigation project British contractors would have a fair field except where they reserved prior rights to sections of the scheme for which they had already tendered and incurred expense. In the major oil-fields development, British interests received a majority share[24] under an agreement of 19 March 1914 which brought about an amalgamation of competing groups. The *status quo* was affirmed on the shores and waters of the Persian Gulf where the *Pax Britannica*

6

had for the last 100 years greatly reduced piracy, slaving and tribal feuding, and where rival foreign influence, especially German, was now limited by the termination of the Baghdad Railway nearly 100 miles upstream at Basra. Britain also secured the examination of the Turkish light dues levied upon shipping, with a view to their reduction; the submission to arbitration of a large number of pecuniary claims against Turkey, and the removal of the Turkish veto on the borrowing powers of Egypt. Further, the legal position of British-run religious, educational and medical institutions in Turkey was regularised and confirmed. As regards frontier delimitation involving Britain's interests, the Aden boundary agreement of 1905 was ratified and the limits of Ottoman territory in Southern Arabia were defined, as was the Turco-Persian frontier, parts of which had been in dispute for nearly 300 years. Particularly important in the Turco-Persian frontier settlement was the 'cession' of certain oil-bearing 'Transferred Territories' to Turkey and the upholding of the Persian-granted oil concession rights of the British concessionnaire company, the Anglo-Persian Oil Company. Britain also succeeded in persuading the Turks to recognise the special position and rights of the Sheikh of Mohammerah, who had close treaty relations with Britain, whose Persian territories bordered Turkey, and who had much *de facto* power over shipping and commerce in both Persian and Turkish areas.

For their part the Turks achieved a number of important fiscal concessions. These included British assent without any time limit to an increase of the Turkish customs duties from 11 % to 15 % *ad valorem* and to the eventual conversion of the *ad valorem* duties into a specific tariff; to the application of the 'temettu' tax (in effect an income tax) to British subjects resident in Turkey; to the creation of further sources of revenue in the form of monopolies and consumption taxes on certain commodities especially petroleum, and to the imposition of *octroi* dues to help provide funds for development works in the larger towns. Britain also agreed to the abolition of British Post Offices in Turkey. While refusing to abolish the capitulations system, Britain did agree to allow a mixed commission to examine various disputed legal points and any Turkish proposals to improve the existing judicial system relating to mixed cases.[25]

Just as British strategic and commercial interests in Asiatic Turkey were constantly at the back of the minds of Foreign Office officials, so too was their belief in the desirability of maintaining the territorial integrity of the country. Time and again this occurs in the British documentation. For example in officially presenting Britain's views in 1910 on the importance of her interests in Mesopotamia and the Persian Gulf and the threat posed by the Baghdad Railway, Grey stressed that 'The policy of Great Britain in Mesopotamia is directed towards the maintenance of the *status quo*, His Majesty's Government emphatically disclaim any designs of territorial aggrandisement in those regions, and they are prepared to furnish the Ottoman Government with the most binding assurances to this effect.'[26]

In the turmoil of 1913 Grey was at pains to reassure the Germans, perpetually afraid of a partition of Asia Minor being planned behind their backs.[27] In January, for example, he told them that he quite agreed that France, Russia, and Britain could not treat Asia Minor in the same way as Morocco, but if there was to be a partition Germany must be thoroughly involved in it and he, Grey, would not think of trying to exclude her. Britain had no political designs in Anatolia. All she wanted was security regarding the Persian Gulf and its littoral.[28] On 12 August Grey stated in the House of Commons in connection with the Balkan Wars: 'Our policy towards Turkey is that which I have stated in the House before, of consolidating and securing Turkish authority and Turkish integrity in her dominions in Asiatic Turkey... That policy which depends upon reforms in Asiatic Turkey, which depends on sound finance if it is to be successful, [aims at] the establishment of justice, order and good government in the Turkish dominions.'[29] And on 4 November Grey told the Italian Ambassador that if Italian claims in Anatolia 'did not conflict with the legitimate interests of the Smyrna–Aidin Railway we would certainly not oppose [their desire for a concession]; but this Railway was the only British Railway in Asia Minor: it is so to say our ewe lamb, and we must see that its rights were protected'.[30] 'We have no political aims in the district in question and therefore no desire to exclude other parties [from concessions]' wrote Grey to Mallet, although he 'could not agree to admit any [foreign] sphere of influence there'.[31]

The views of Grey's own personnel did not entirely reflect Grey's official hopes of Turkish consolidation, reform, and ultimate territorial integrity. In 1908 Fitzmaurice had cynically repeated Disraeli's definition of a 'process of consolidation' of the Ottoman Empire as the violent separation from it of dissident provinces.[32] In June 1913, shortly before the parliamentary speech quoted above, Lowther, Grey's retiring Ambassador in Constantinople, was suggesting that 'in view of the possible ultimate dissolution of Turkey and formation meanwhile of foreign spheres of interest it seems desirable to maintain and even increase our establishment in Mesopotamia which is the region where our stake is most large and our claims greatest...'[33] By December, his successor, Mallet, too, was writing realistically to Grey that 'All the Powers, including ourselves, are trying hard to get what they can out of Turkey. They all profess to wish the maintenance of Turkey's integrity but no one ever thinks of this in practice.' Nonetheless, as perhaps befitted a former private secretary of Grey, Mallet felt that it would still be much against Britain's interests to do anything to injure the Turkish Government or to precipitate its collapse; on the contrary, he advocated positive support.[34]

In the period between August and November 1914 Grey repeatedly offered Turkey a formal guarantee of her territorial integrity. Although Turkey's secret treaty of alliance with Germany was still unknown, the strength of the pro-German members of the Turkish Cabinet and the Army was such that Grey could hope for only, at most, Turkish neutrality, or at worst, to delay as long as possible her entry into the war and when it came to ensure it was clearly the result of unprovoked Turkish aggression. He employed both persuasion and threats, persuasion including the offer of the territorial guarantee. He insisted on inserting the offer into a telegram of 15 August that Churchill was sending Enver Pasha, Turkish Minister of War, as a personal appeal: he instructed Mallet on 22 August to join with his fellow *entente* Ambassadors in offering a written guarantee; he was backed up on 24 August by Admiral Limpus, head of the British Naval Mission to Turkey. On 5 September Mallet repeated Grey's offer to the Turkish Minister of the Interior and continued throughout the month, much to the anger and frustration of the First Lord of the Admiralty, to encourage Grey to hope that Turkey might yet accede to Britain's request.[35] In a very short time any such idea was to be proven vain.

Grey's policy on Constantinople and the Straits remained basically consistent during the years up to the outbreak of war: the maintenance of the *status quo* unless it was altered equally for all the Powers. The position had been laid down under the treaties of 1856 and 1871, which stated that the Straits were open to commercial navigation but closed to all non-Turkish warships. Such a situation suited Britain quite well, although in view of the consolidation of Britain's position in Egypt the Committee of Imperial Defence had decided in 1903 that free Rusian egress through the Straits, or even Russian occupation of the Dardanelles 'would not fundamentally alter the present strategic position in the Mediterranean'.[36] Under the existing regulations it was Russia who was at most disadvantage, for her Black Sea fleet remained bottled up, to her great inconvenience in war time such as the Russo-Japanese war. Up to that time Russia had been fairly content with the *status quo*, making occasional evasions of the Treaty obligations in peace time. Since then, however, she saw the desirability of securing an alteration in the *status quo* securing a concession for herself to be able freely to navigate the Straits with, preferably, the continued denial of such freedom to all non-riparian Powers. During the Anglo-Russian negotiations of 1906–7 the Russians raised the question. Although it became clear that while both Isvolsky and Grey were willing to discuss the matter in principle, neither would commit himself to any change in the existing regulations without the consent of the other signatory Powers.[37]

After the annexation of Bosnia in 1908 Isvolsky again raised the question in London.[38] But Grey refused to press the unwilling Turks. In any case, as Hardinge wrote privately to Nicolson:

> From a strategical point of view, there is no possible advantage in our ships being able to go into the Black Sea in time of war. It is already a settled principle of naval warfare with us that in no case would our ships enter the Straits, unless Turkey were our ally. The consideration of reciprocity, however, is a shop-window ware, since the public do not understand these strategical considerations.[39]

Grey set out Britain's views finally in a memorandum of 14 October 1908 which acquired some importance as a source of future reference for policy.[40] The British Government agreed that the opening of the Straits was 'fair and reasonable' and in principle would not oppose it, especially if the Straits were to be opened completely to all nations equally. Britain felt however, that the present crisis was a very inopportune time for seeking general assent to a plan by which Russia and the Danube riverain Powers sought exclusive if limited rights. Moreover, while agreeing in principle that 'some opening of the Straits' was reasonable, the British still felt that a purely one-sided agreement, giving the Black Sea Powers in war time the advantage of an inviolable harbour and base for quick raids would not be acceptable to Britain. A suitable arrangement must be one 'which, while giving Russia and the riverain Powers egress at all times under...[carefully] limited conditions ...and securing them from menace or the establishment of foreign naval power in the Black Sea in time of peace, would yet contain such an element of reciprocity as would in the eventuality of war place belligerents on an equal footing with regard to the passage of the Straits'. Finally, Grey stressed that Turkey's consent was 'a necessary preliminary to any proposal' and that the present moment was not the time to seek it at the risk of overthrowing the new Turkish Government. To sugar the pill and strengthen Isvolsky's difficult position at home, Grey gave him a private written assurance that although their current conversations had centered so much upon the inopportuneness of the present moment for discussing the question, his motive was certainly not a desire to keep the Straits closed. On the contrary he desired positively to see a suitable arrangement made for he considered this essential to establishing permanent good-will between Britain and Russia.[41]

Turkey's own position was very clearly stated in August 1909 by Rifaat Pasha, Turkish Minister for Foreign Affairs and former Ambassador to London. He declared that: 'neither the general opening of the Straits nor the limited opening could ever be acceptable to Turkey. If the Straits were open to Russia alone Turkey would be at her mercy while if open to all the Powers Turkey would lose her privileged geographical position.'[42] Further, a British Foreign Office memorandum of 4 October 1909 stated that, 'H.M. Government have never seriously contested the fact that the navigation of the Black Sea by any other Powers than Russia and Turkey and the Riverain States of the Danube, depends entirely upon the will of the Sultan as to allowing merchant vessels to pass through the Bosphorous'.[43]

This view was tested in the years 1911 and 1912 when Turkey was engaged in war first with Italy and then with the Balkan States. On the first occasion, when Russia asked the Turks to allow her warships passage through the Straits in return for a Russian guarantee of Constantinople, Grey observed that 'while war was going on no Power could enter into fresh political relations of an intimate kind with one of the belligerents without a breach of neutrality'.[44] As regards the possibility that the Turks might close the Straits altogether, he remarked that the Turks were 'entitled to take defensive measures providing that they did not infringe the rights which neutrals might have under the regulations governing the Straits'.[45] When, in fact, Turkey did close the Straits in early 1912 as a result of Italian bombardment of the Dardanelles, Grey could only press on the Turks the great commercial and financial distress this was causing British interests. The day following this representation, the Turks announced their reopening of the Straits. Whether or not this amounted to yielding to British pressure, or to finding it a convenient excuse to undo their rather excessive reaction to the Italian incident, the fact remains that the Turks had demonstrated their freedom and ability to close the Straits.[46]

It was a week after this, on 8 May 1912, that a Foreign Office memorandum drawn up by Crowe and revised and approved by Grey defined the strategic importance for Britain of her position in the Eastern Mediterranean, particularly its significance to 'oriental minds'. 'The influence of Great Britain at Constantinople...such as it was at any given moment,...has always rested mainly on her position as the mistress of the Mediterranean Sea.'[47] For some time the British had indeed been trying to strengthen their position in the Eastern Mediterranean by extending their influence over the Turkish Navy, through the appointments successively, since the end of 1908, of Rear Admirals Gamble, Williams and Limpus. The latter, with a staff of five officers, was appointed in May 1912 to continue the work of organising and instructing the Turkish Navy. There was no active service in war time, however, a convention that was formally written into Limpus's contract. Although this favoured British position was not happily accepted by Russia, Grey's opinion was that the Turkish Government were determined in any case to regenerate and strengthen their navy and if Britain did not help them then some other Power, possibly Germany, would readily do so.[48]

Later in 1912 the question of the Straits and Constantinople came again into diplomatic debate with the Balkan Wars. Grey unofficially pressed the Greeks not to extend their naval operations towards the Dardanelles, lest this cause Turkey to close the Straits; and at the same time he urged Turkey to close the Straits only in the direst necessity. But he could do no more for, as he repeated to the Russians, he was bound by the 1908 agreement with Isvolsky. Similarly, he felt that any conquest of Constantinople would have to be dealt with by a conference of the Powers.[49] In the negotiations among the Powers the Straits question only took the form of a debate about staging a combined naval demonstration by the Powers or sending ships to Constantinople for the purpose of defending the Embassies and European nationals in the event of a threat or occupation of Constantinople by the opposing Balkan belligerents, a plan fully sanctioned by Turkey.[50]

In 1914 the question came up again through the Greek–Turkish crisis over the Aegean Islands. Grey informed the *Entente* Ambassadors in London that if the Straits were closed for weeks or months, then if Britain intervened at all, it would only be on commercial grounds of inconvenience to British shipping. In this particular issue Grey had the additional headache that Britain was training the navies of both sides.[51]

The major diplomatic conflict concerning the Straits and Constantinople during these immediately pre-World-War years came not from the Balkan Wars but from quite a different matter. At the end of October 1913 the Foreign Office learnt that a German military mission of over forty officers and others under the command of General Liman von Sanders had been appointed to Turkey to reorganise the Turkish army, with Liman von Sanders himself appointed as Commander of the first Turkish Army Corps in Constantinople.[52] By the end of November and during December the appointment constituted an international diplomatic crisis. Russian–German relations deteriorated as Germany refused on grounds of prestige to change the appointment. On 2 December Grey sent a very serious telegram to Mallet, pointing out the difference between Liman von Sanders's role of executive command supported by a large body of German officers, and that of General von der Goltz who had headed a more limited mission at a time when German influence at Constantinople was much less.[53] Now the whole *corps diplomatique* at Constantinople would be in German power, the key of the Straits would be in German hands, and the German commander could take military action impairing the sovereignty of the Sultan. Finally, he said, the equilibrium of the Powers would be broken 'which is the guarantee of the existence of Turkey'; other Powers would make similar demands to secure their own positions and Turkey would be unable to deny them. Grey proposed that the British, French and Russian Ambassadors, should seriously warn the Turks in identic notes of these dangers, and he asked Mallet to seek exact information on von Sanders's contract. Britain, however, should not be the first to press the Turks; as Nicolson put it, 'there is a certain disinclination on our part to pull the chestnuts out of the fire for Russia'.[54] But Mallet deprecated any diplomatic pressure at all, pointing out the Turkish perturbation at any such move and that the importance of von Sanders' post depended on the character of the holder rather than the particular position; in any case a friendly settlement between Russia and Germany was clearly desirable if possible.[55] After all, Britain herself was not in a strong position to make objections demanding special compensation since already a British Admiral, Limpus, commanded the Turkish fleet, a point which was being made much of by Turks and Germans and which Mallet admitted was a good point. Further, Mallet knew that British Armstrong–Vickers interests had just secured a monopoly of dockyards and arsenals for thirty years. Nevertheless, although Mallet advised that any curtailing of Limpus's powers might severely disturb the Turkish government and damage British prestige, as a compromise he had sounded Limpus confidentially and unofficially as to whether, on the renewal of his appointment in April, he could forgo the title of commandant of the fleet while retaining the real power. As Mallet pointed out to the Foreign

Office, Limpus already had absolute command of the Turkish fleet in peace, though his contract precluded active service in time of war and could in fact 'do anything except break the law or exceed the budget'. By this time finally, enough had been found out about von Sanders's proposed powers to make both Britain and France extremely chary of pressing any protests. The First Army Corps did not conrol the Straits, and whether or not von Sanders was to be on the Turkish Military Council seemed immaterial since the Council did not wield the real power.[56]

On receiving further reports from the St Petersburg Embassy of Russia's adamant stance, therefore, the Foreign Office deemed Sazonov 'ridiculous' and 'almost incredibly jejune'.[57] Accordingly the British made their eventual representation to Turkey on 13 December as a polite verbal inquiry seeking information on the contract of von Sanders and the scope of his functions, while assuming pointedly 'that Turkey would not do anything that would impair independence of Turkish Govt'.[58] All the same, a friendly settlement between Russia and Germany was clearly desirable, and on 12 December Grey had agreed to the Russian suggestion of moving Limpus's headquarters away from Constantinople [to Ismid] if it would help solve the difficulty about the German command[59] (although Mallet subsequently pointed out that this would not be possible until the Ismid dockyards and arsenal were completed in some years time).[60] In this same letter of 14 December, Mallet reported he had reached a compromise solution with Limpus about the Admiral's title. Without relinquishing real power Limpus could be called 'Adviser' when his contract next came up for renewal and a statement inserted into the contract that his duties would comprise any service assigned to him by the Turkish Government. Limpus pointed out what the Foreign Office already knew well, that the Turkish Government was determined to have a good fleet and if Britain failed them they would apply elsewhere.

Sazonov was anything but pleased at these manoeuvrings. On 14 December he threatened in effect to withdraw from the Triple *Entente* unless the other two members showed more determination in dealing with the affair.[61] At the same time the Foreign Office was only partially satisfied by the Grand Vizier's assurances in reply to Mallet's enquiry. The Grand Vizier had replied on 15 December that although the German general would have no authority over the Straits of Bosphorous nor the Dardanelles nor would he have command of Constantinople during a state of siege, he would command the First Army Corps and would create model regiments through which officers of other regiments would pass.[62] This still seemed to be an important lever in Germany's favour, and so Grey spoke to the German Ambassador on the trouble caused by the affair and the upset it had caused to Russia. The Ambassador's response was that the question was much over-rated. Von Sanders was only going to be accompanied by 6 officers and not the 42 that Britain thought, and Germany had only unwillingly acceded to the Turkish request in the first place.[63]

As a result of this, Grey telegraphed to his Russian and Berlin Embassies on 16 December that it was quite clear that if any of the *entente* Powers went so far as to make a formal protest at Constantinople the matter would cease to be a Turkish question and become a European one.[64] The next step should be, therefore, discussions at Berlin. If the German Government would agree to modify Liman's contract then Britain was prepared to agree to Limpus's contract being modified to correspond with it.

By 21 December the Russian threats appeared to be working, for Buchanan telegraphed Grey that the Germans were giving way. The Russian Chargé d'Affaires in London confirmed and extended his information, and Mallet in Constantinople telegraphed Grey to the same effect. But the Powers were by no means out of the wood. On 29 December the Foreign Office thought it necessary to warn Russia that the question should not be allowed to become the subject of an ultimatum unless Russia were prepared to make it a *casus belli* and Grey did not think it worth that.[65] On 7 January Grey told Lichnowsky that the question of German command at Constantinople was causing him more anxiety than all other questions together, and that he hoped that as long as the German Government really wished to find a solution to the difficulty there would be no ostentatious demonstration that would make it difficult for the German Government to come to an arrangement with Russia. Lichnowsky answered that a Triple *Entente démarche* at Constantinople would make everything impossible,[66] and on the same day an Imperial proclamation officially announced Liman's promotion to the command of the First Army Corps at Constantinople. It was in vain that Russia pressed her *Entente* friends to withhold their consent to the 4% customs increase in the agreements just about to be signed by the Powers with Turkey. The Foreign Office was thinking very differently. As Nicolson minuted, Sazonov's apparent belief that France and Britain would actively cooperate in any measure the Russian Government might devise or contemplate was 'too wide an assumption'. Britain would raise no objections to any measures which Russia might think fit to adopt to establish the position and safeguard her interests, and was quite ready to use her good offices with Germany towards a satisfactory arrangement, but that was all. Grey entirely agreed with this minute, adding that as the Powers had already consented to the 4% customs increase they could not now introduce an entirely new condition.[67]

At this point, the Russians and Germans reached a compromise solution, Liman being promoted to 'Inspector General' of the Turkish Army without a direct command, and a German officer was to act as Chief of Staff. Buchanan reported from St Petersburg that the awkward position in which Britain might otherwise have found herself seemed to be avoided, for Sazonov was perfectly satisfied with this arrangement. Sazonov was in fact still unhappy that the command of the 3rd Division of Army Corps at Scutari was to be under a German officer but the German Government chose to regard the incident as closed.[68] Grey was satisfied enough: as he told Buchanan on 11 February, 'as to the German Military Command in Constantinople, I think that the intrinsic importance of it has been very much exaggerated, and the general impression produced has been that Germany has had a diplomatic setback, which the German press had to explain away as best it could. I do not see why Sazanov should not be content with that.'[69]

Can it be said that British foreign policy towards Constantinople and Asiatic Turkey was directed to any great extent by commercial motives? Were the Anglo-Turkish agreements of 1913 and 1914 really concerned with profits as opposed to power politics? Hardly so, it would seem, from all the evidence. But there are other areas in which this question of economic motivation might well be asked, particularly regarding banking and concessions.

The National Bank of Turkey was British financed and managed, and founded in 1909 with encouragement – though not initiative – from the Foreign Office. Yet very quickly it disappointed the hopes of both its founders and the Foreign Office that it would be instrumental in expanding British influence in Turkey.[70] This it was unable to achieve largely because of Britain's foreign policy, specifically her policy of *entente* with France. French financial interests were deeply entrenched in Constantinople through the Imperial Ottoman Bank, nominally Anglo-French but in reality pursuing purely French aims. Grey's aim was above all to maintain the *entente* with France and whenever this aim clashed with French financial interest, it was British banking that suffered through deficient Foreign Office support. The Foreign Office was chasing the illusion of Anglo-French financial cooperation to reinforce the political *entente*, whereas such cooperation was of no interest to the already powerful Ottoman Bank.

Turkey was chronically in deficit, surviving from loan to loan, and large international loans obviously affected the political influence in Turkey of the countries which made these loans. But the Foreign Office's attitude over the large loan of 1910 was to encourage France to obtain the issue, relying on the National Bank's loyalty – rightly as it turned out – to withdraw its own offer. When the Bank's freedom of action was eventually grudgingly restored by the Foreign Office after the French negotiations had fallen through, it was too late and a German group obtained the issue. A year later the National Bank, anxious to support British competition for Northern Anatolian railways and ports, met with anything but encouragement from the Foreign Office. The latter pointed out that Britain was bound to abide by the 1900 Black Sea Basin Agreement granting priority in those areas to Turkish and Russian interests, and complained that the Bank was so concerned with its financial operations that it was blind to the political considerations that had to guide foreign policy. When the Bank joined an international group to seek concession rights for oil location and development in Mesopotamia it again received, to its chagrin, no Foreign Office support. On the contrary, its group met strong opposition, for the Foreign Office was pledged to support a rival. Altogether the Bank became so disillusioned by its failure to obtain diplomatic support that in 1913 it announced to the Foreign Office its intention of going into liquidation. The Foreign Office was not impressed: while it would have liked a British banking institution to be operating in Turkey it felt that it could not urge the National Bank to remain if it felt its interests were better served by withdrawing. As it happened the Bank did not withdraw at that time. It lingered on, being bought up by the British Trade Corporation in 1920, and finally expired, still a subject of Foreign Office indifference, late in 1931.

If the National Bank, as a contender for the Mesopotamian oil concession received no support from the Foreign Office except, eventually, in merging its interests in an amalgamation with the Foreign-Office-supported rival – and this as part of the settling up of Anglo-German differences achieved in early 1914 – why was the Foreign Office supporting the rival?[71] This was partly because the rival, the Anglo-Persian Oil Company (later to become known as B.P.) was purely British, whereas the National Bank's group had been mixed with German and Dutch interests; but above all, because the Anglo-Persian Oil Company was the monopoly concessionaire in Central and Southern Persia. Persian oil potential was viewed with relish by the Admiralty as a suitable source of fuel in an area of purely British influence. Foreign oil interests in Mesopotamia, therefore, would not only encroach on what the Foreign Office regarded as a sphere of British commercial predominance, but would constitute a threat to established British interests in Persia. Even in this apparently economic question, therefore, the overriding interest was political and strategic.

Finally, it might be asked whether Sir Richard Crawford's appointment in 1908 to reorganise the Turkish customs administration represented a commercial or political move in British policy. Again it would seem to have been the latter. While it was undoubtedly beneficial to the international financial community and a clear example of Grey's more moralistic approach to the question of reform in Turkey it was above all the result of power politics. The French had obtained a French appointee as Financial Adviser to the Turks; and friendly as Britain was towards France in the interests of the *entente*, the increased French influence required, in Grey's eyes, a counterbalancing British appointment. Hence the appointment of a British official to the Turkish customs.[72]

Grey's foreign policy towards Constantinople and Asiatic Turkey up to 1914 has thus been examined in several major spheres: Grey's attitude towards the Turkish Government, both before and during the Young Turk régime; the Baghdad Railway negotiations and Britain's basic interests in Mesopotamia and the Persian Gulf; Grey's attitude towards Ottoman territorial integrity; Grey's attitude towards the Straits and the Liman von Sanders question; and the place of economic bases in Grey's policy towards Turkey. In each of these areas the same conclusion emerges. Commercial interest played little real part in Grey's aims. In the years of Grey's Foreign Secretaryship up to 1914 British foreign policy towards Constantinople and Asiatic Turkey was clearly based on considerations of strategy and the balance of power.

8

Relations with Austria-Hungary and the Balkan states, 1905–1908

F. R. BRIDGE

According to the *Standard* of 18 August 1905, the interests of Britain and Austria-Hungary lay so far apart that, were it not for the awe in which the British held the Emperor Franz Joseph 'the two Empires might conceivably remain indifferent to each other'.[1] Certainly, Britain's links with Austria-Hungary were not so close as they had been in the later 1880s: links with the Triple Alliance generally had been weakened by the Anglo-German estrangement; more particularly, the clearest expression of Anglo-Austrian co-operation to check Russia in the Near East, the Mediterranean Entente of 1887, had been abandoned in the mid 1890s; and a move by the British to revive it early in 1903 had been ignored by the Austrians, who preferred to put their trust in an entente with Russia. In fact, the Austro-Russian entente of 1897, like the Neo Holy Alliance and the Dreikaiserbund earlier, left the British little scope for an independent or effective Balkan policy, and Lansdowne was perhaps making a virtue of necessity when he determined to take his cue from Vienna in these questions.[2] In some respects, the British were more Austrian than the Austrians, even – breaking off relations with Serbia on the occasion of the murder of King Alexander and Queen Draga in June 1903, and hoping for an Austrian occupation of Belgrade.[3]

By 1906 the British were more reserved. Grey tended to base his Balkan policy on the concert of Europe rather than on the special connexion with Austria-Hungary. For example, the Foreign Office had always maintained the most scrupulous regard for the restrictions imposed on Bulgaria's sovereignty by the treaty of Berlin, and Grey was impressed when the Austrians pointed out that the secret Serbo-Bulgarian customs treaty of December 1905 contravened a most-favoured-nation clause of that Treaty.[4] But he made his support for the economic sanctions which Vienna proceeded to impose on Serbia conditional on the support of all the other Powers – which, needless to say, was not forthcoming.[5] Indeed, as the 'Pig War' progressed, British sympathy for Austria-Hungary declined. The British vice-consul in Belgrade had been quick to point out that British firms might take advantage of the cessation of Austro-Serbian trade, and in February 1906 the Foreign Office passed this information on to the Board of Trade for circulation.[6] In April, Grey restored diplomatic relations with Serbia, and was applauded by the British radical press.[7] It would be an exaggeration to talk of an Anglo-Serbian rapprochement: the increase in Anglo-Serbian trade was not significant – it was Germany who took the lion's share of what the Austrians lost.[8] And the British had certainly no political axe to grind in Serbia: they gave no support to the schemes of Serbian malcontents to replace King Peter by the Duke of Connaught or a Teck;[9] and not even in the Bosnian crisis did Serbia become really popular in England. Nevertheless, after 1906 the British would be, at best, disinterested spectators in Austro-Serbian disputes.

Britain's contacts with the other Balkan states in these years were slight, but whereas Anglo-Roumanian relations, such as they were, were cordial enough,[10] Anglo-Greek relations were decidedly cool. Cyprus was not the only open sore.[11] Crete had been granted an autonomous regime by the six Great Powers after the Greco-Turkish war of 1897. The Powers, through their consuls, supervised the Cretan administration and finances (notably customs rates); and their contingents in the island safeguarded the Sultan's residual sovereign rights and the Turkish flag. Not that the British were insensible to the national aspirations of the Greek majority on the island: in 1898 they had complied readily enough when at Russian instigation[12] Prince George of the Hellenes was appointed High Commissioner of Crete (whereas the indignant Germans and Austrians had withdrawn their troops and virtually washed their hands of the question); and the decision of the remaining four protecting Powers in 1906 to appoint yet another Greek, M. Zaimis, to succeed Prince George, was very much the work of Grey and the French.[13] But such gestures of sympathy were not enough for the Greeks, who would ultimately be satisfied with nothing less than the union of Crete with Greece. Their attempts to achieve this however (by riots in Crete that in 1905 had forced the unlucky protecting Powers to govern by martial law) only had the effect of pushing the protecting Powers into a position of apparent hostility to Greece. There could, after all, be no question of appeasing her at the cost of estranging Turkey. For even the Turkey of Abdul Hamid was worth far more than Greece, whose army and navy were notoriously weak. In June 1907 Grey rejected a Greek request for an alliance.[14] The situation might have changed had not the Greeks in turn rejected as insulting a Franco-British loan project of December 1907 designed to build up the Greek navy as a torpedo-boat fleet that might serve as a useful adjunct to their own Mediterranean forces.[15] As it was, Grey could only regret the Greeks' stubborn refusal to understand him; whereas the nagging complaints of King George, transmitted through his sister, Queen Alexandra, met with a markedly stronger reaction from Edward VII.[16]

Grey's attitude to all these Balkan states was overshadowed, indeed, determined, by larger considerations than their petty ambitions: namely, the future of Macedonia and of the whole Ottoman Empire. The Great Powers, much as they might disagree as to means, were all agreed that these were matters which they themselves must settle – and the Balkan states would have to come into line.

Macedonia, handed back to the Turks at the congress of Berlin, had been the scene of increasing strife since the 1890s – largely a result of Bulgarian terrorist efforts to cow the inhabitants (Bulgars, Greeks, Serbs, and Roumanian Koutzo-Vlachs) into subjection, and to provoke the Turks to commit such atrocities that the Great Powers would intervene and possibly set up an autonomous Macedonia, which might then be absorbed by Bulgaria at a convenient time. By 1903 the great power intervention had indeed been conjured up, but it was designed not to fulfil, but to thwart, the wishes of the terrorists. The Austro-Russian Vienna Note of February 1903 and the Mürzsteg Punctation of October, were designed to prolong Turkish rule in Macedonia by forcing the Turks to make life tolerable for the Christians. The Mürzsteg programme envisaged the reform by stages of the gendarmerie, finance and judiciary of Macedonia, under the supervision of Austria-Hungary and Russia, assisted in the second line by advisers from the other Powers.

All the Great Powers accepted the aim and principle of the Mürzsteg programme for, as Grey observed, behind the Macedonian question lay the Turkish question;[17] and the longer the raising of the latter could be postponed, the better. But there was still plenty of room for debate about the tempo at which the reforms should be introduced. The Germans, for example, sought only to humour the Sultan and to do very little; whereas the two Mürzsteg Powers, as most likely to be affected by an explosion in Macedonia, were determined to press ahead – but cautiously, lest Abdul Hamid lose patience, veto all reforms, and seek salvation in a wholesale massacre of his Macedonian subjects. Lansdowne, however, had seen in speedy and radical reforms the only way to save Turkey from revolution and the British Government from the propaganda of the Balkan Committee. This body, founded in 1903, consisted of humanitarian intellectuals, some, such as the Archbishop of Canterbury, of high standing. It was, thanks to the influence of Noel Buxton and J. D. Bourchier, strongly Bulgarophil in character – as was British public opinion generally – and never tired of recounting the sufferings of Christians in Macedonia. Although no atrocities campaign to compare with those of the 1870s or 1890s occurred, Lansdowne lived in terror of the Committee – hence his persistent and, by the end of 1905, successful efforts to stiffen the reform proposals of the Mürzsteg Powers and to secure more influence for British officials on the reform commissions.

When Grey replaced Lansdowne the pressure relaxed. The new foreign secretary, who could rely on Conservative votes against his own back-benchers, was in a stronger position to resist Slavophil and humanitarian pressure groups. Ironically enough, therefore, just as these groups were growing stronger and more vocal, their influence on British policy declined. From the first, Grey was at pains to assure the Mürzsteg Powers that his Balkan policy would be thoroughly conservative; Hardinge told Mensdorff, the Austro-Hungarian ambassador, that the Foreign Office would not be influenced by such cabinet ministers as Bryce, a former president of the Balkan Committee;

and Grey's parliamentary critics now rebuked him for subordinating British policy to the concert, and held up Lansdowne's last achievements as a reproach.[18]

It was not until the autumn of 1906 that Grey began to stir. The line he would take had been foreshadowed in a curiously ambiguous remark he had made in the Commons on 5 July: 'Our great object is to keep in step with the Powers, or to keep them in step with us, as the case may be.'[19] Unfortunately for Grey, his attempt to revive Lansdowne's policy of keeping the Powers in step with Britain coincided with the arrival at the Austro-Hungarian foreign office of the vigorous Aehrenthal, equally determined that the Mürzsteg Powers, not Britain, should dictate the pace of Macedonian reform. The next nine months saw a marked deterioration of Anglo-Austrian relations.

That disorder was increasing in Macedonia all were agreed. Partly this was due to the changed nature of the conflict, now fast becoming one between different national groups of Christian terrorists (whose appetites had been whetted by the unfortunate clause III of the Mürzsteg programme, envisaging an administrative division of Macedonia along 'national' lines). Whereas the 'Greek' patriarchist population of Macedonia had been very hard pressed by both Bulgarian terrorists and Turkish officials in the years following the Greco-Turkish war of 1897, an abortive exarchist rising in August 1903 had concentrated Turkish hostility on the 'Bulgarians' who wilted before a 'Greek' terrorist counter-offensive which was in full swing by 1907.[20] But the trouble was also due to the fact that the Turks had not enough money to apply the reforms efficiently: by the end of 1906, for example, the gendarmerie had not been paid for several months and were naturally demoralised.[21] Since early 1905 the Turks had been seeking permission from the Powers to raise their customs duties from 8 to 11 % in order to pay for the expensive reforms – a request which the Mürzsteg Powers found reasonable. In September 1906, however, Grey held things up at the last minute by reverting to some very strict conditions drawn up by Lansdowne in February 1905: he insisted on Customs-House reforms (to appease British traders, who would after all bear the main burden of the increase) and on a stringent control of Turkish expenditure, coming close to impinging on the Sultan's sovereign rights (in order to ensure that the Turks really spent the money on Macedonia, and not on the army, or on such obnoxious projects as the Baghdad Railway).[22] Despite incessant Austro-Russian pleadings, Grey refused to accept Turkish promises which he considered evasive,[23] and caused further delays by referring the matter to the slow-moving Board of Trade.[24] Not that this policy went unchallenged at home. If some commercial circles complained about Grey's agreeing to the customs increase even conditionally, others interested in the commercial exploitation of Turkey accused the Government of wasting chances and strengthening the position of Germany at Constantinople by its punctiliousness.[25] Hardinge for one recognised the importance of British trading interests in Turkey, and told Mensdorff that Turcophobia had no roots in Britain except among Slavophile nuisances in Parliament.[26] By the spring of 1907 the British press was beginning to realise that it was the internecine quarrels of the Christians rather than the misgovernment of the Turks that lay at the root of the Macedonian problem;[27] and in April Grey sent a sharp rebuke to Athens and Belgrade for their complicity.[28] On the other hand, as he observed to Mensdorff on 21 March, in the Orient trade could not be divorced from politics, and fears were still being voiced in the Commons that the 3% Customs increase might be spent on the Baghdad Railway.[29] Press talk of an Anglo-Turkish rapprochement,[30] therefore, came to nothing; and Grey held out stubbornly till the Turks accepted all his conditions before agreeing to the increase on 25 April. The affair may have impressed the Turks with the power of Britain;[31] it had certainly added to the tension between Britain and Austria-Hungary.

The two Powers were already at odds over the other Macedonian issue of the day – judicial reform. Aehrenthal had already convinced Izvolsky that the Mürzsteg Powers should keep the lead in their own hands by drawing up a project of control and asking the other Powers to join in applying it; and he refused to proceed with new demands on Turkey until the 3% Customs increase had been settled. In London, this secretiveness and apparent lethargy were regarded, mistakenly, as an attempt to fob the Powers off with a sham reform, and to exclude them from participation – a misunderstanding for which the British and French ambassadors at Vienna were partly responsible.[32] Grey was in any case anxious for something more vigorous than a mere control; but how any kind of judicial reform, for which he now promised his 'strenuous support', would help against the violence of the terrorists, he did not say.[33] By February 1907 he was suggesting that the gendarmerie be given extended powers to deal with this problem;[34] and he also proffered his advice to the Russian and Austro-Hungarian ambassadors at Constantinople, who were engaged in drafting the proposed judicial reform.[35] To the alarm of the Austrians, the Russian ambassador, Zinoviev, seemed not unwilling to incorporate some of the suggestions of his British colleague.[36]

The wavering of Russia in fact only made Aehrenthal the more determined not to allow the British to force the pace. Indeed, they seemed to him to be remarkably and inconveniently busy in the spring of 1907: Edward VII's visits to Cartagena and Gaeta foreshadowed perhaps new power combinations in the Mediterranean; and British plans to raise the armaments question at the Hague Conference portended yet another humiliation for an isolated Germany if Aehrenthal and Bülow could not bring Russia into line.[37] It was in an effort to check this British activity, to put Britain in a strait-jacket inside the concert, rather than to exclude her from it,[38] that Aehrenthal made his perhaps unduly notorious soundings to Paris and St Petersburg at the end of May, with a view to preventing a serious discussion of the armaments question, and to adopting a moderate tempo in Macedonia.

His timing was unfortunate. The British were already impatient at the delays over Macedonian reform: Mallet and Hardinge, although they thought British and Russian views on Macedonia still too far apart 'to admit of any real rapprochement' in the question, nevertheless suggested that a separate approach to Russia might speed things up, especially as the approaching Anglo-Russian settlement was generating so much goodwill.[39] Grey, however, decided that Britain needed a breathing space after her recent exertions over the 3 % customs increase, and decided to wait for the proposals of the Mürzsteg Powers.[40] The British felt their patience ill-rewarded, therefore, when on 17 May they received a garbled version of Aehrenthal's manoeuvres: according to the French, Aehrenthal was seeking to exclude Britain from the Balkans and, acting as a catspaw of Berlin, to break up the Anglo-French entente.[41] Goschen, a fervent believer in Aehrenthal's subservience to Berlin, and in the conspiratorial speculations of the *Times* correspondent, H. W. Steed, scented 'a Quadruple Alliance to the exclusion of Great Britain and Italy'.[42] Aehrenthal's denials gained no credence in London, especially as news of his soundings in St Petersburg trickled in. On 29 May Grey warned the Austro-Hungarian ambassador that he was on Aehrenthal's track, and could gain an easy popularity if he chose to retaliate with an independent Anglo-Italian policy in Macedonia.[43]

This did not happen. In fact, the explosion cleared the air, the Austrians made great efforts to prove their good faith and met with a conciliatory reception in London, and a spell of Anglo-Austrian co-operation occurred. Aehrenthal, for example, decided to try to restrain the British by collaborating with them,[44] and received the news of the Anglo-Franco-Spanish Mediterranean Agreements of 16 May in good part, even Grey's naïve gloss that British policy was 'practically the same as that embodied in the Agreement' of 1887.[45] He was, in turn, pleasantly surprised by British tractability at the Hague (and greatly irritated at German intransigence). A visit to London by his special emissary, Prince Kinsky, confirmed that the two Powers both wished to maintain the Ottoman Empire, and had merely disagreed about the best means of achieving this. The far-reaching plans of British Slavophils for a Christian governor and virtual autonomy for Macedonia were, Hardinge declared, quite impractical.[46]

Early in July Aehrenthal was able to oblige Grey, who was worried about an impending confrontation with the Balkan Committee, with a definite pledge that the judicial reform scheme would appear during the course of the summer; and on 9 July Grey sternly rebuked an important deputation headed by the Archbishop of Canterbury, putting the blame for the troubles in Macedonia squarely on the terrorists and the Balkan States, keeping his doubts about Turkish connivance private.[47] Aehrenthal was delighted by this reply, and even more goodwill was generated by Edward VII's visit to Franz Joseph at Ischl on 15 August. On this occasion, Hardinge and Aehrenthal agreed that the disastrous activities of the bands must be checked, and that the Balkan States implicated – especially Greece – should be reproved, and reminded that Article III of the Mürzsteg programme would not apply to areas whose national character had been changed by violence.[48] Aehrenthal promised that the judicial reform would soon be ready; and the British in turn were willing to leave the initiative with Vienna.[49] For a few weeks all was well. The Anglo-Russian convention of 31 August did not worry the Austrians, who regarded it as a purely Asian affair.[50] Izvolsky too was prolific with fair words, promising at Swinemünde and Vienna to go hand in hand with the Austrians in Macedonia. And when the joint Austro-Russian *démarches* planned at Ischl were made at the Balkan capitals in October the British hastened to lend their support.[51] The Mürzsteg system, much to the dismay of Russian nationalist opinion which wanted to see it replaced by Anglo-Russian co-operation in the Balkans,[52] seemed to be entering upon its heyday, and to be enjoying for the first time the hearty and unqualified approval of the British.

In the subsequent judicial-reform negotiations,[53] however, the Anglo-Austrian rapprochement came to grief. This was due not to any basic disagreement but to an accumulation of petty misunderstandings which built up into a deep mutual mistrust, misunderstandings resulting largely from the cumbersome diplomatic method employed, namely, conferences of ambassadors at Constantinople. Instructions to the ambassadors were often delayed – in this respect the British, after months of hectoring Vienna, were now the chief offenders: Grey, who received the judicial reform proposals of the Mürzsteg Powers on 16 August left town for a holiday and did not send instructions to O'Conor, until 27 September.[54] Thus, when instructions arrived, they had usually been overtaken by events. More serious, the ambassadors, both susceptible to pressure from the Porte and confident that they knew better than their distant masters, constantly flouted their instructions.[55] There were thus, in fact twelve rather than six parties to the negotiations, and it was hardly surprising that it was not until January 1908 that ambassadors and governments finally reached agreement. Personal factors increased the friction: Pallavicini, the Austro-Hungarian ambassador, was enraged by what he regarded as O'Conor's efforts to induce Zinoviev to stray from the strait and narrow path laid down at Mürzsteg.[56]

Aehrenthal was undoubtedly worried by signs of growing British influence over Russia; but he still wished to co-operate, both to restrain the British and to preserve at least the form of the Mürzsteg system of Austro-Russian control. A chance seemed to arise in December 1907 when Grey tried to seize the initiative. Grey now proposed that the Mürzsteg Powers deliver another rebuke to the Balkan states; and that the internationally controlled gendarmerie in Macedonia be strengthened and used against the terrorists. The Turks could afford this if they were forced to reduce their army; and as they would have to be coerced into accepting the judicial reform, Grey argued, they might at the same time be forced to agree to the gendarmerie proposal, to commercial concessions, and to another 'thorough-going scheme of reforms which would really be effective'.[57] This, Grey said, would be his last effort: if the other Powers refused to follow him, he would denounce them to Parliament and wash his hands of Macedonia. These were brave words; but in fact, Grey's attempt 'to bring the Macedonian question to a head'[58] quite misfired, and produced merely a solidification of the cautious Mürzsteg front. Aehrenthal and Izvolsky stalled for a month and then replied with cogent arguments: representations to the Balkan states lost their force by too frequent repetition; only the Turkish army could cope with the guerillas; and in any case, the Mürzsteg reforms were designed to protect the Christians from the Turks, not from each other – it would be disastrous to involve the gendarmerie in the maelstrom of Balkan rivalries.[59]

Confronted with this, there was little Grey could do. He warned the Austro-Hungarian ambassador that he would have to tell Parliament what had happened to his proposals: but at the same time he refused to take any independent initiative outside the concert, 'which I regard as a guarantee of peace in the Turkish question'.[60] Outside the Foreign Office, public opinion was becoming heated: the Balkan Committee declared that the Mürzsteg Powers, especially Austria-Hungary, had proved themselves incompetent, and that Britain should 'restore the Concert of Europe... organised public opinion is the most important diplomatic weapon... in the hands of any foreign minister'.[61] Even inside the Foreign Office there were those who made a distinction between the two Mürzsteg Powers (although their replies to the proposals had been identical). Mallet suggested that Britain might use her special ties with France and Russia to secure further reforms. But Grey still refused to act.[62]

An opportunity for action soon occurred, however, when Aehrenthal's announcement of the Sanjak railway project on 27 January produced a rift in the Mürzsteg entente. And that the British took advantage of it, changing their Macedonian policy to one of exclusive co-operation with Russia was due partly to calculation, partly to an ill-founded mistrust of Aehrenthal's sincerity. Hardinge noted that 'the struggle between Austria and Russia in the Balkans is evidently now beginning, and we shall not be bothered by Russia in Asia ...The action of Austria will make Russia lean on us more and more in the future. In my opinion this will not be a bad thing'.[63] Mallet was quick to discern German expansionist ambitions behind the railway project;[64] and Steed and Goschen, meditating on the Moroccan crisis of 1905, even concocted the story that Austria-Hungary, at Germany's instigation, was seeking to test the Anglo-Russian entente.[65] Finally, by an unfortunate coincidence, on 5 February, the day following the issue of the Turkish *irade* for the railway project, the ambassadors at Constantinople again disobeyed their instructions, and refused to present the judicial reform scheme to the Porte because they thought the Turks were not yet in a mood to accept it.[66] In their reports, the ambassadors all blamed each other for this decision, but O'Conor and Zinoviev both blamed Pallavicini, and the rage of the British, who accused the Austrians of sabotaging Macedonian reform to secure their railway scheme, was boundless.[67] They now revoked their original promise[68] to support the railway project, and Grey described the failure to proceed with the judicial reform as a first step towards breaking up the concert.[69]

His own loyalty to the concert was not above reproach, however. For although he at first talked of pressing on with the judicial reform, yet when Aehrenthal agreed (and even suggested that the Turks be urged to form mobile columns of troops to deal with the bands) Grey did not respond.[70] He listened rather to Izvolsky, who on 17 February told Nicolson that he wished 'to get out of a dual action with Austria to rally himself to...those Powers who are sincerely desirous of reforms'.[71] At least, both Grey and Hardinge approved a minute by Mallet to the effect that 'this marks a very important development of the Anglo-French and Anglo-Russian agreement policy, Russia is now asking for our co-operation in the Near East'.[72] Moreover, in his speech to the Commons on 25 February – chiefly notable for its public denunciation of Aehrenthal's supposed disloyalty to the concert, which provoked another round of recriminations between London and Vienna – Grey concealed the drift of Foreign Office thinking. Indeed, he was at some pains to reject the demands of the Balkan Committee that Britain work with Russia, bribing Germany with concessions over the Baghdad Railway, and ignoring Austria-Hungary. This, he said, would paralyse the concert, which he was about to approach with new proposals.[73]

In practice, the Foreign Office showed scant regard for the concert. (Even the Cabinet was treated with less than frankness: Hardinge and Grey amended the new proposals after the cabinet had approved them, so as to give the Turks control over the whole reform organisation if they would agree to extend it – a serious infringement of the Mürzsteg principle of European control.)[74] Even more significant, Grey at once sent a draft of his proposals to St Petersburg, but to no other capital, in the hope of provoking, not a concerted discussion, but a dialogue. As he explained to Nicolson,[75] he had in his speech

'...deliberately abstained from hinting at the possibility of our co-operating with one Power more than another inside the Concert...But this reticence on my part must not be construed as meaning that co-operation with Russia would be at all unwelcome: on the contrary, if M. Izvolsky accepts my views or suggests proposals going some way to meet them, our co-operation will certainly be forthcoming.'

On the other hand, Aehrenthal's desperate efforts in the ensuing weeks to preserve some shreds of the Mürzsteg system by keeping in step with the various Russian proposals, met with little sympathy in St Petersburg; and his notes to London – although almost identical with Izvolsky's – were scoffed at or disregarded.[76] Izvolsky was abandoning the Mürzsteg system with alacrity, suggesting, for example, on 13 March that the financial delegates of the other Powers be given a position of complete equality with the Russian and Austro-

Hungarian civil agents – 'an abandonment of the dual co-operation and the merging of Russia in the general European concert',[77] and sending his replies to London without consulting Vienna. Similarly the British, whose 'sole object', according to Hardinge, was 'to come to terms with Russia'[78] sent their drafts to St Petersburg without waiting for Aehrenthal's opinion. Indeed, there was Schadenfreude in Hardinge's remark to Edward VII on 21 March that the 'chief characteristic' of Izvolsky's counter-proposals was 'its complete break with Austria in...the Balkans, and Aehrenthal will probably be more angry than ever'. At this, the traditionalist King protested: 'it will never do to break with Austria' and Izvolsky 'must be told that we cannot agree to such a proposition – my personal regard for the Emperor of Austria is so great that I could not sanction a policy which would cause him either trouble or pain': but Hardinge 'explained' with Orwellian aplomb, that he had only meant to say that Russia was 'now working with the other Powers and especially with us'.[79] To Goschen he was pleased to announce that 'the Mürzsteg Programme is as dead as a doornail'.[80]

Its demise was at first ill-received in Vienna. In an outburst of 23 April Aehrenthal formally declared his attempts to co-operate with the British at an end, blaming London for their failure, and remarking that whether Grey intended to raise the whole Eastern Question or not, that would certainly be the result if Russia were drawn further away from the Central Powers.[81] But he soon calmed down. For by the early summer the Russians had recovered from the Sanjak railway crisis and were making the soundings at Vienna that were to culminate in Buchlau; and they seemed, moreover, to be exercising a salutary restraining influence on their British friends.

For example, although Hardinge swore on 7 May not to abate the British demands 'by one jot', Grey was more realistic – 'weak' according to Hardinge – and made some concessions: Izvolsky would have to be humoured if he were to be of use 'in getting Germany and Austria into line'.[82] As the British and Russians proceeded to work out their plans for the pacification of Macedonia (by getting the Turks to organise mobile columns of troops), they met with no opposition from the Austrians, who decided that they were after all glad to be rid of the responsibility. In fact, Russian restraint was not all that effective: the British claimed the Reval meeting, where the draft scheme was finally settled, as 'a huge success in every way' for themselves.[83] Certainly the Anglo-Russian scheme, when it finally appeared in July, went too far for Aehrenthal, who suggested handing it over for scrutiny to the conference of ambassadors at Constantinople. At this Grey, with his memories of the judicial-reform fiasco, was in turn greatly taken aback,[84] and another Anglo-Austrian wrangle was only averted when the Young Turk revolution rendered pacification unnecessary as the peoples of Macedonia laid down their arms to greet the new era.

This development was welcome to both Vienna and London: the British were particularly pleased to be rid of the 'millstone' of Macedonian reform, and to have a chance, with the disappearance of the Sultan's camarilla, to recover their position at Constantinople.[85] But although Aehrenthal wished them well, his feelings were not reciprocated in the Foreign Office. There, mistrust of Austria-Hungary had reached almost pathological proportions by the summer of 1908. For instance, although the British themselves had no interest in Balkan railway schemes, they were very indignant when Izvolsky insinuated that Vienna was intriguing against Serbian projects;[86] and very impressed by rumours, put about by the Turks to spread dissension, and encouraged by Izvolsky and the Western press, of Austrian attempts to secure a monopoly of concessions in the vilayets of Salonica and Kossovo.[87] Even Aehrenthal's gestures of goodwill towards the Young Turks – his instructing the Austro-Hungarian gendarmerie officers to take unlimited leave in the middle of August – were interpreted in London as signs of some deep machiavellian purpose.[88]

It is notable that these suspicions of Austria-Hungary persisted despite Edward VII's visit, on 12 August, to Franz Joseph at Ischl – a visit arranged in the spring, on Austrian initiative, and apparently without Foreign Office intervention.[89] On a monarchical level, the meeting was a great success; and Hardinge, who accompanied the King, had reason to be pleased. The behaviour of the Russians in Persia was worrying him at this time,[90] and he had been reconsidering relations with Austria-Hungary – 'for so many years a plank in our political platform that it is very desirable to remove any little coldness...Moreover, as difficulties with Germany are likely to grow more acute in the not far distant future, a friendly Austria will be a very convenient check on her ally'.[91] Hardinge and Aehrenthal were agreed about the need to preserve Turkey; Aehrenthal's remarks about the possibility of constitutional changes in Bosnia were of necessity vague at this stage – the plans for annexation had not yet been discussed by the council of ministers; and although he refused to put pressure on the Germans to cut down their naval programme, arguing that the question was none of his business, he was sympathetic, telling Hardinge not to worry, as German finances were by no means brilliant.[92]

The story that the Austrians had on this occasion given the British a sharp rebuff,[93] making a show of loyalty in rejecting a supposed British attempt to seduce them from the alliance with Germany, is not supported in either British or Austrian archives – although it won them much gratitude in Berlin at the time.[94] In fact, this very issue had just been thrashed out in the Foreign Office, where Sir Fairfax Cartwright, recently chosen to succeed Goschen at Vienna, had argued in a long memorandum of 1 August that Britain should seek, by encouraging Austro-Hungarian independence of Berlin, to convince the Germans that 'in spite of the Triple Alliance, Austria's fidelity could no more be depended upon in...a crisis – brought on by them – than that of Italy.'[95] This would 'force' Germany, Cartwright argued, 'to join a genuine league of peace...which would be for the benefit of the world'. The Foreign

Office, however, deemed this plan 'fraught with considerable danger. The balance of Power in Europe would be completely upset and Germany would be left without even her nominal allies.'[96] It might even provoke her to 'risk everything in defence of her honour, dragging Europe into what would be the most terrible war in all history'. Grey summed up with his wonted arguments:

An attempt to isolate Germany by setting Austria against her might precipitate a conflict. On the other hand...if Germany dominated Europe the result would also be war. We have to steer between these two dangers. At present there is a fair equilibrium and we should not try to make a breach between Germany and Austria.

The Ischl meeting, therefore, did not present any threat to the existing grouping of the Powers, and between London and Vienna things went on much as before. The Foreign Office moved in a fog of suspicion, as was shown by the contretemps over the withdrawal of the gendarmerie officers; and even more strikingly by the immediate assumption that Austria-Hungary was behind the quarrel that blew up between Turkey and Bulgaria in September, when the Turks began to emphasise the vassal status of Bulgaria in protocol matters (refusing to invite the Bulgarian representative, Gueschov, to a diplomatic banquet at Constantinople), and the Bulgarians recalled Gueschov and seized the Bulgarian section of the Orient Railway. Although no other Power apart from Britain supported the Turks in their stiffly legalistic attitude (and in the Foreign Office, some of the younger men doubted the wisdom of supporting them at all),[97] it was on the Central Powers that British suspicions concentrated – and this despite the fact that only those two Powers showed any inclination to join Britain in rebuking Sofia for her expropriation of the Orient Railway Company, whose headquarters were in Vienna.[98] For Hardinge, the mood of Ischl was a thing of the past when he wrote on 30 September, that 'the Bulgarians are being egged on in their aggressive intentions by the Austrians, who like fishing in troubled waters.'[99]

At the end of September, therefore, it was Bulgaria who the British feared might disrupt the *status quo*, possibly by declaring her independence; the fear that this would 'probably entail the annexation of Bosnia and Herzegovina by Austria' was, as it were, only an additional embarrassment.[100] After all, the British press had been speculating about the possibility of an annexation, or even of Turkey's recovering the provinces, ever since the Young Turk revolution;[101] and both the ambassador in Vienna and the vice-consul in Sarajevo reported a growing feeling in favour of annexation.[102] Clearly, the British were aware of the situation: what is surprising, in view of their outbursts after the annexation, is their complete passivity in the weeks preceding it. No doubt this was partly due to their recent habit of brooding in silence on their suspicions of Austria-Hungary. Certainly, it was not calculated to shake the ill-founded confidence that prevailed in Vienna since Ischl. To the council of ministers on 19 August Aehrenthal explained that he would have to consult Russia, Germany and Italy before proceeding to the annexation; but he did not plan to approach Britain who, he laconically observed, 'desires good relations with us'.[103]

He was of course profoundly mistaken. Indeed, ever since the Sanjak railway crisis the Foreign Office had seen in him the arch-intriguer; and the effect of the Ischl meeting had been short-lived, even on Hardinge. By late September, the British were more mistrustful than ever. The moment was hardly propitious to announce to them the imminent annexation of Bosnia. Yet, partly owing to Aehrenthal's propensity for wishful thinking; more, probably, owing to the fact that the British had never come into the open with their suspicions, the sudden confrontation with reality in the form of Grey's stand against the annexation was to strike the bemused Aehrenthal with the force of a physical blow – and to add a further element of bitterness to Anglo-Austrian relations in the ensuing crisis.

9

The Bosnian crisis

D. W. SWEET

The British government was determined from the outset not to lose the opportunity, which was presented by the Young Turk revolution of July 1908, of replacing German commercial hegemony at Constantinople with an Anglo-French hegemony. Even before the Bosnian crisis broke, therefore, it was involved in attempts to protect the Young Turk *régime* from humiliation in two related episodes, the Gueschov incident and the Bulgarian seizure of the Oriental railway, which it assumed (with some justice) to be the prelude to a proclamation of Bulgaria's independence.[1] Coming in the middle of these attempts, the news of the impending annexation of Bosnia and Herzegovina applied a 'cold *douche*' to British hopes of averting a crisis, and provoked an outburst of keen resentment against Austrian policy, on the ground that the annexation could only encourage the Bulgarians to proceed with their plans; and would also provoke several other governments to demand compensation at Turkey's expense.[2]

In the event; the declaration of Bulgaria's independence on 5 October 1908 preceded the formal annexation of Bosnia and Herzegovina by some forty-eight hours. Even so, Grey was convinced that Aehrenthal must have been a party to the designs of the Bulgarians, while as late as 4 October protesting his ignorance of them; and he complained at being treated with such bad faith.[3] Hardinge too concluded that there had been a 'deep-laid plot on the part of several Powers, which has been studiously concealed from us'; that Germany had been an 'accomplice' in the Austrian intrigue with Bulgaria; and that Russia had concurred in all but the actual date of the annexation of Bosnia.[4] (If it exaggerated the extent of German involvement, this estimate of Isvolsky's complicity was accurate enough). Although the independence of Bulgaria and the annexation of Bosnia were recognised as developments which 'sooner or later were inevitable, and...can do us no harm considered in themselves', the indignation of the British was genuine. They were disturbed by the damage that Bulgaria and Austria had done to the prestige of the new *régime* in Turkey, and much afraid that Serbia, Montenegro and Greece would all come forward with demands for compensation from Turkey, while Russia would press for modifications in the rule of the Straits.[5] They doubted if the constitutional government in Turkey could survive so many blows, and in these circumstances Asquith agreed with Grey that Britain's first concern should be to defend her position at Constantinople and in the Muslim world, by coming forward as the champion of Turkish interests.[6] The British government therefore would not recognise either Bulgarian independence or the annexation until suitable (that is, financial) compensation had been secured for Turkey. Accordingly, Grey told the Turkish ambassador, Rifaat Pasha, that Britain would not grant recognition until the other powers signatory to the Treaty of Berlin of 1878 (which governed the status of both Bulgaria and Bosnia) had been consulted, and Turkey satisfied; and he promised to support Turkish claims for compensation.[7] Aehrenthal was informed that, in accordance with the protocol of 17 January 1871 to which Austria–Hungary was a signatory, Britain would not recognise a deliberate violation of the Treaty without the assent of the contracting parties, including Turkey; while the Bulgarians were similarly advised that their proclamation of independence could not be approved or recognised until Turkey and the other powers had been consulted. This position was made public by Grey in a speech on 17 October.[8] Thus the British, taking their stand on the sanctity of treaties and appealing to the highest principles of international behaviour, moved to defend their interests at Constantinople, and at the same time increased the dependence of the Young Turks upon them.

To adopt this position did not, however, dispose of the major problem of keeping British and Russian policy in line; rather, a collision was now more likely if the Russians should insist on concessions from Turkey in the Straits question. Grey urged the Russian government to join with him in supporting Turkey, and Tcharykov, Isvolsky's deputy in St Petersburg, replied that he wished to do so; but he made it clear that the Russians wanted an international conference summoned, not only to compensate Turkey, but also to revise those stipulations in the Treaty of Berlin which were onerous to Russia and the smaller Balkan states.[9] The French, eager to emphasise the solidarity of the *entente* powers, wanted the Russian proposal for a conference to take the form of a joint initiative by Russia, France and Britain. Grey was not ill-disposed to the idea of a conference, provided his conditions were met: there must be a 'distinct understanding' that the occasion would not be used for the 'further dismemberment' of Turkey; a preliminary agreement on the compensation to be afforded to Turkey should precede the conference; and the Straits question would require 'most careful consideration' by the British government before it could be raised. He suggested to the Russians that substantial financial compensation might be arranged for Turkey in the form of a loan guaranteed by the powers, and persisted in advocating this solution until finally it was wrecked by Turkish fears of the foreign control which would be involved; while he was relieved of the embarrassment of frustrating the desire of his *entente* partners for a conference when the Turks themselves called for one.[10] But it is worth observing that he had been prepared, in the short term, to place a higher priority on the defence of Turkish interests than on pleasing the Russians and French.

This order of priorities was important, because the anticipated repercussions of the annexation were beginning to be felt. Serbia's demands included not only the 'reversion of rights relinquished by Austria–Hungary in the Sanjak', but also a territorial adjustment which would give her a common frontier with Montenegro; the latter state demanded the abolition of the restrictions on her sovereignty imposed by article 29 of the Treaty of Berlin.[11] (There was, of course, no prospect of Austria ceding territory in Bosnia to compensate Serbia; and as for the Sanjak of Novi Bazar, it was in order to keep Serbia and Montenegro separate that the Austrians had established themselves there in the first place.) A more immediate affront to Turkish prestige was the union of Crete with Greece, which was proclaimed by the Cretan assembly on 7 October. The British government refused to recognise the union (although privately Grey thought it the only long-term solution to the Cretan problem);[12] it persuaded the other protecting powers (France, Russia and Italy) to return a similar refusal, and underlined its determination to prevent Greek intervention by sending a squadron of the Mediterranean fleet to Marmaris, on the Turkish coast opposite Crete.[13] The most significant modification of the *status quo* which was being canvassed, however, was the revision of the Straits convention in favour of Russia and the minor Black Sea powers, and in this question Grey was already committed to a view sympathetic to Russian aspirations by the conditional undertakings given to Benckendorff in April 1907.[14] Tcharykov told Nicolson on 7 October that Russia would propose that 'free egress through the Straits...should be accorded to Russian, Bulgarian and Roumanian war-ships', and the British inferred (correctly) that this was part of the bargain which Isvolsky was trying to strike on his disastrous European tour.[15] They still entertained a faint hope that a Turkish loan guaranteed by the powers might enable the Young Turk *régime* to make a concession over the Straits (and over Crete as well) without compromising its prestige too much; but Grey was careful to reassure Rifaat that, while the British government had 'felt for some years that the international denial to Russia of all egress through the Straits was a thing which could not be maintained for ever', nevertheless he would not allow the question to be raised at the conference unless Turkey agreed.[16]

In spite of misgivings about his recent activities, therefore, the British awaited Isvolsky's arrival in London expectantly. They were anxious to discover his views about the conference and the questions to be raised there, and particularly to secure his assent to the 'great point' that the Straits question should not be raised.[17] The visit was on the whole a success from the British point of view. On 10 October Isvolsky made it clear that he was prepared to adopt a 'stiff' attitude towards Bulgaria, making her pay financial compensation to Turkey for the loss of the Eastern Roumelian tribute and the Oriental railway. At Grey's insistence, he agreed to abandon the demand for specifically territorial compensation for Serbia and Montenegro, and instead to propose unspecified '*avantages*' for them; and he further agreed to relegate the Cretan question to a postscript in the programme of the projected conference, reserving it for negotiation between Turkey and the protecting powers. Most important of all, he abandoned his intention of raising the Straits question at the conference.[18] Grey was then able to secure the approval of the cabinet for the proposed conference programme on 12 October, and to inform the Turks that it was acceptable.[19] When Isvolsky sought to obtain a private assurance about Britain's attitude to the Straits question, he was offered little more than the conditional promises of 1907, and the advice that he could best promote a future agreement about the Straits by a 'disinterested co-operation between Russia and England to pull Turkey through the present crisis'.[20] The objection to the Russian proposals about the Straits was not primarily strategical, and it is clear that Grey's reason for refusing to countenance a modification in the circumstances of October 1908 was that the moment was 'inopportune' for anything that would further embarrass the Young Turks. While he was anxious that Isvolsky should not carry away the impression that Britain was permanently opposed to changes at the Straits, he also made a point of telling the Turks that it was British insistence which had obliged the Russians to postpone the question.[21]

It was an undoubted success for Grey's diplomacy that he had averted a collision between his Russian and Turkish policies, by persuading Isvolsky to subordinate his aspirations at the Straits to the British policy of support for the Young Turk *régime*. He was able to accomplish this largely because Isvolsky was on weak ground when he argued that he wished to join Britain in strengthening Turkey 'as a barrier against the Austrian advance', while yet proposing an arrangement which must have the effect of weakening the Turkish government.[22] And it was all the easier for Grey to refuse unconditional support for Isvolsky's Straits policy because he knew from Nicolson that Russian opinion was in general much less concerned about the Straits than about 'general Slav interests', which Isvolsky's dealings with Aehrenthal had compromised.[23] The British correctly surmised that Isvolsky was grossly overstating his case when he claimed that the survival of the Stolypin government and the whole policy of the Anglo-Russian *entente* depended upon his being able to take back with him to St Petersburg a success in the Straits question.[24] If they were to emerge from the affair with any credit at all, the Russians could not afford to antagonise either Britain or her *protégé* Turkey. Isvolsky's stern attitude towards Bulgaria, and his readiness to follow Grey's lead over Crete, showed that he appreciated the need to support Turkey; it was pursuing the logic of this policy only a little further to oblige him to defer the Straits question as well.

Although privately Grey was still 'not at all wedded' to the idea of a conference, and was quite amenable to some other method of regularising the alterations in the Treaty of Berlin, the three *entente* governments now had an agreed programme for the conference.[25] The Italians, anxious to appear as the protectors of Montenegro, also associated themselves with the programme. As for the Germans, Grey had all along been anxious to involve them, in the hope of using their influence with Austria to promote a negotiated settlement; and to this end he kept Metternich informed about his discussions with Isvolsky. Bülow, however, made it clear that he would not abandon the Austrians, but would regulate his attitude towards the conference in accordance with theirs, a reservation which Grey regarded as reasonable enough.[26] The fate of the conference thus depended upon Austria, and it was well known that Aehrenthal would allow it merely to register the annexation, not to discuss it; while his efforts to induce the Turks to abandon the conference altogether were recognised as an attempt to avoid proposals for compensating Serbia and Montenegro.[27] The task of persuading Aehrenthal to agree to a conference was left to Isvolsky, but as relations between the two deteriorated, the prospect of an agreement about its scope and competence receded, and it became increasingly unlikely that (if it ever met at all) it would be able to do more than ratify whatever arrangements might be made directly between the governments most immediately concerned.[28] This was a further defeat for Isvolsky, but it was accepted without dismay by the British government, which actively promoted the alternative of direct negotiations: on 16 December Grey told Mensdorff that, if the powers most concerned – Austria, Turkey, Russia (for Serbia) and Italy (for Montenegro) – could reach agreement, no difficulties would be raised by Britain, France or Germany.[29]

In fact, the British were more actively involved, as advisers and protectors of Turkey, than this statement implied, and as a result they came into sharp conflict with the Austrians, who suspected that they were actively encouraging Turkey to resist Austrian offers. It was indeed true that Grey consistently advised the Turks to maintain their protest against the annexation until they received satisfactory compensation from Austria; and he refused Austrian requests to apply pressure to the Turkish government to make it more amenable, on the assumption that the Austrians, if left alone with the problem of conciliating Turkey, would have to improve their offer. On the other hand, he invariably encouraged the Turks to be realistic in their notions of satisfactory compensation, and to concentrate on securing a cash return for the loss of their theoretical rights in Bosnia.[30] Aehrenthal's irritation was increased by the prolonged Turkish boycott of Austrian goods, which he attributed partly to British encouragement.[31] Grey persisted in refusing to help him out of his difficulties with the Turks, and eventually he had to offer them financial compensation, which Grey persuaded them to accept.[32] The Austro-Turkish settlement of 11 January 1909 was welcomed in London as 'the first break in the obstacle that blocked the stream', and Grey had good reason to be satisfied; for without having to intervene formally in the negotiations he had had a decisive influence in securing financial compensation for the Turks.[33]

But in the process he had infuriated the Austrians. Aehrenthal complained bitterly that Britain's attitude towards Austria was 'at the bottom of the present troubles': not only had Grey supported the Turks, but he had also encouraged the 'pretensions' of Serbia and stiffened Isvolsky with 'evil advice'.[34] He even suspected Grey of exploiting the Balkan crisis to precipitate a European war, so that Britain could put an end to the German naval challenge.[35] At the root of these grotesque misrepresentations there was, according to Cartwright, the new British ambassador in Vienna, one substantial grievance: that the presence of the British squadron in Turkish waters had been interpreted as a warning to Austria 'to abstain from touching the new Turkish *régime*'.[36] There is nothing in the record to suggest that the reason for sending it to Marmaris in October 1908 had been anything other than that stated, to uphold Turkish sovereignty in Crete. But when he learned that the squadron had had a restraining effect upon Austrian policy, Grey made sure that it remained on hand to repeat the operation if necessary.[37] Further, when pressed by the Italians about his attitude to an Austrian attack upon Turkey, he was willing to leave open the possibility of British intervention:

I have put in a sentence which implies (though it does not commit us) that we might intervene. I think this is quite safe in the form I have given it, and as Tittoni will probably repeat everything to Austria, I think it may be wholesome.[38]

These exchanges, which were accompanied by strident press campaigns in Vienna and London,[39] were a measure of the deterioration in Anglo-Austrian relations – a deterioration which had begun, however, with the Sanjak railway affair at the beginning of the year, and which was in any case the predictable consequence of Britain's increasingly close relations with Russia.

The Anglo-Russian intimacy performed a more positive service in settling the crisis between Turkey and Bulgaria. In this crisis too the British supported the Turks, while at the same time discouraging their more fantastic notions of compensation, such as the separation of Eastern Roumelia from Bulgaria.[40] The three *entente* governments sought to mediate between Constantinople and Sofia, in the hope of strengthening the position of the Young Turks while, at the same time, detaching Bulgaria from Austria; though the British characteristically reserved their sternest warnings for the Bulgarians, and the Russians theirs for the Turks. They succeeded in persuading the two governments to avoid open provocations, and to negotiate upon the basis of financial compensation to Turkey for the loss of the Eastern Roumelian tribute and the revenues of the Oriental railway.[41] The chief problem then was to find a figure which both the Turks and the Bulgarians would accept; the Turks demanded £10,000,000, the Bulgarians offered £4,000,000, and the French, called upon to employ their 'intimate knowledge' of the finances of both states, fixed Bulgaria's liability at £5,680,000.[42] Grey was eager to secure a settlement which would avert the danger of Bulgaria making common cause with Austria against Turkey, while a Turco-Bulgarian reconciliation might form the basis of a Balkan coalition to contain further Austrian encroachment, which the Russians were keen to promote. In his anxiety to prevent a rupture, Grey progressively reduced the figure which the Turks were to accept: although £6,500,000 was in his view a fair settlement, by late January he had reduced it to less than £5,000,000, with a defensive understanding between Turkey and Bulgaria as an added inducement.[43] But these efforts failed to bridge the gap, and the Bulgarians continued to threaten war; Isvolsky, fearing that this would throw Bulgaria 'into the arms of Austria and Germany', blamed Grey for his failure to make the Turks more accommodating.[44] But since it was Russia who had most to lose from Bulgaria's adhesion to the Triple Alliance, Isvolsky was obliged to come forward with the proposal which formed the basis of the eventual settlement: that Russia should provide acceptable compensation for Turkey by renouncing part of the Turkish war indemnity of 1878, while the Bulgarians would be required to pay interest only on the £4,000,000 which they had been prepared to offer. In the end, the Russians renounced forty instalments of the war indemnity, producing for Turkey a sum which could be capitalised at £6,500,000 – the figure originally favoured by Grey.[45]

The British were naturally enchanted with Isvolsky's proposal, which provided a solution to the Turco-Bulgarian crisis at Russia's expense. Politically, of course, Russia stood to gain a good deal, and Hardinge was 'much impressed' by the cleverness of Isvolsky's plan: it would attach Bulgaria to Russia rather than Austria, satisfy popular Slav feeling in Russia, and at the same time prepare the way for a revision of the rule of the Straits by improving Russo-Turkish relations.[46] Since it also served their own interests in Constantinople, the British were adamant that it must be accepted; Turkish fears that it would turn Bulgaria into the advance guard of a new Russian drive in the Balkans, and form the prelude to renewed Russian pressure at the Straits (for which there was some justification), were swept aside as 'childish and grotesque', and under strong British pressure the Turks eventually gave way and accepted the Russian proposal.[47] The subsequent negotiations between Turkey and Bulgaria dragged on for some weeks, and were still not complete when Abdul Hamid attempted his counter-revolution in Constantinople on 13 April; joint Anglo-Russian pressure, however, dissuaded the Bulgarians from exploiting this opportunity, and formal agreement between Turkey and Bulgaria was reached on 19 April 1909.[48] The Russians (to the annoyance but hardly to the surprise of the British) had begun recognising Bulgaria's independence before this, but formal international recognition was delayed until 23 April, after the settlement with Turkey, as Grey had always insisted it should be.[49]

In this way, British diplomacy played a crucial role in promoting a settlement of the Turco-Bulgarian crisis which was favourable to Turkey, and to the mutual advantage of Britain and Russia. Without the advocacy of Grey, the Turks would not have secured so much from Russia; and without the confidence which they felt in his advice and support, the Russian proposal would hardly have been accepted in Constantinople. It would be no exaggeration to describe the Turco-Bulgarian agreement, over which Britain and Russia co-operated to impose their own solution by exploiting their influence in Constantinople and Sofia respectively, as the first European success of the Anglo-Russian *entente.*

In the Cretan crisis the British continued to defend Turkey's interests, in spite of their private recognition that in the long run Crete must be united with Greece.[50] Having prevented an immediate union, and having removed the question from the main agenda for the conference, Grey assured Rifaat that it would not come before the conference at all, unless Turkey and the four protecting powers could find an amicable solution.[51] He persuaded the other three governments to keep their troops in Crete and to maintain the *status quo* as it existed prior to 7 October, although he had some difficulty with the French, whose Philhellenism was a recurring problem for him whenever Crete was in question.[52] On 28 October, after prolonged haggling, the four protecting powers issued a declaration to the Cretan administration, in which they insisted that union with Greece could only be accomplished with their assent, and that the island must remain tranquil pending discussions with Turkey.[53] Not that Grey had any intention of allowing the Turks to be forced into a discussion until they were in a more assured position: he preferred to delay until July 1909, when the troops of the protecting powers were in any case due to be withdrawn, and the status of the island would naturally come up for reconsideration.[54]

In insisting on a line so sympathetic to Turkey, Grey risked a breach with the other protecting powers, particularly France. Clemenceau at first wished to exempt Crete from the general principle that no territorial sacrifice should be demanded from Turkey at the conference, and it was only with difficulty that Grey persuaded him that it would be 'the height of folly to throw away our influence at Constantinople for the sake of getting the good-will of Greece'.[55] Britain's differences with her *entente* partners were reflected in a curious and mischievous suggestion of theirs, that she should herself compensate Turkey for the loss of Crete by the retrocession of Cyprus. This was first proposed by Isvolsky, and then repeated by Pichon, 'non pas comme ministre mais comme ami'.[56] To some degree it resembled the sacrifice subsequently made by Isvolsky when he surrendered the Turkish war indemnity of 1878, but the British had no difficulty in finding respectable reasons for rejecting it.[57] The four protecting powers kept their troops in Crete until the following summer when, since they could not find a definitive solution acceptable to both Turkey and Greece, they agreed to maintain the theoretical status of Crete by continuing to fly the Turkish flag, under the protection of their own gunboats. This arrangement enabled them to withdraw their troops on time, despite the protests of the Turkish government.[58] Ironically enough, it was the British, who had been the most energetic champions of Turkish interests, who incurred most of the odium at Constantinople for agreeing to the withdrawal.

This was, however, symptomatic of the general tendency of Anglo-Turkish relations. In the complex of interconnected crises over the annexation, Bulgaria and Crete, the British had contributed materially to preventing war, had played an active part as mediators on Turkey's behalf, and to their own satisfaction had achieved for her terms as favourable as she could realistically have expected. But in spite of all this, by the time of the withdrawal of the troops from Crete in June 1909, the Anglo-Turkish honeymoon of the previous year was plainly over, and the British saw themselves once more losing influence at Constantinople. The financial compensation upon which they had concentrated had not been sufficient to restore the prestige of the Young Turks at home: and in suggesting, however discreetly, that they seek defensive arrangements with their Balkan neighbours, Grey had unwittingly offended Turkish national pride. Nor, although ready to provide informal naval support, would he commit himself formally to the defence of Turkey; in November 1908 he rejected tentative approaches from the Young Turks for a defensive alliance, and so denied them a psychologically important success; though of course his refusal was entirely consistent with the normal British antipathy towards continental commitments, and with the discouraging reply which he had just returned to a similar enquiry from the Russians.[59] However well-judged and indeed generous it might appear from London, British policy had not provided the constitutional *régime* in Turkey with enough benefits to avert the attempted counter-revolution of April 1909. The *régime* which followed it was increasingly nationalist and military, and increasingly pro-German; and it found the policy of the British government in such questions as the Baghdad railway and the Tigris valley concession inconvenient and annoying.[60] In spite of their pro-Turkish policy during the Bosnian crisis, the British failed to create lasting confidence in Constantinople; while, in spite of their association with Austria–Hungary, the Germans were able to begin the restoration of their former position there.

The most intractable problem created by the annexation, the question of compensation for Serbia and Montenegro, did not directly affect the Turks once it was established that compensation was not to be at Turkey's expense. Consequently, Grey at first showed little interest in the matter. Though Serbia was not directly injured by the annexation of Bosnia and Herzegovina, it was a bitter blow to the hope that those territories might one day be incorporated in a greater Serbia. But intense as was Serbian resentment at this, even more intense was the fear that the annexation was only the first stage in an Austrian drive to Salonica, which would effectively seal off Serbia from the Adriatic and, commercially at least, subject her to Austria. The Serbian government therefore sought compensation in the form of a barrier against such an advance: a common frontier with Montenegro, either in the Sanjak of Novi

Bazar or in Bosnia itself. The first alternative was vetoed by Britain, the second by Austria, and it was clear that, whatever else the conference might accomplish, diplomacy alone could not secure territorial compensation for Serbia.[61] At the end of October Grey told Milovanovitch, the Serbian foreign minister, that he would give diplomatic support to Russian efforts to secure compensation for Serbia, but would not press for more than could be obtained by peaceful means. He had in fact little sympathy with the Serbian 'clamour' for compensation, and it was only because he was anxious not to 'cold-shoulder' Russia that he was prepared to support the Russian position.[62]

The most immediate danger was that Serbia's irreconcilable attitude would provoke a punitive invasion by Austria, which would present the Russians with the dilemma of either abandoning Serbia or plunging into a hopeless war. Isvolsky therefore urged prudence upon the Serbs, and he was supported by Grey, as well as by the French and Italians. At a 'conférence intime' in the Serbian foreign ministry the representatives of the four powers were asked for their advice, and on 18 November they replied, as agreed, that the Serbian government should withdraw its troops from the Austrian frontier, and prevent the formation in Serbia of guerrilla bands destined for service in Bosnia.[63] Up to a point, the Serbs complied, and during the winter the Austro–Serbian crisis remained suspended; but this period of relaxation was recognised as temporary and precarious. At the end of January 1909 the Serbs were still demanding territorial compensation, and only Russian and British pressure prevented them from embodying this demand in a circular to the powers.[64] By the middle of February there were ominous signs that Austrian patience was wearing thin, and so alarmed was Grey at the prospect of a general war in the Balkans that he at last took the initiative, proposing that the 'neutral' powers (by which he meant Britain, Germany, France and Italy) should mediate between Vienna and Belgrade. When the King and Hardinge visited Berlin on 9 February, Bülow had spoken of his willingness to work with Britain and France in the question, and there was no doubt that his support would be indispensable in persuading the Austrians to make concessions. The British initiative was designed to test the sincerity of Bülow's protestations.[65] In return, Grey was prepared to use his influence in St Petersburg to force the Serbs to climb down, and in particular to abandon their claim to territorial compensation. If Anglo-German co-operation could be arranged, there appeared to be a real prospect of progress:

Our object is to set the ball rolling by ascertaining what are the economic concessions which Austria would be disposed to make to Servia and Montenegro. I think it quite on the cards that Aehrenthal will reply by declining to formulate the economic concessions which he is ready to make until Servia and Montenegro shall have definitely declared their renunciation of all territorial or political concessions. It will then be our turn to see what pressure we can put upon Russia, in a friendly manner, to get Servia to make this renunciation. Even the Russians know that territorial concessions are out of the question. They have got to come out into the open some time or other, and that may be a means of getting them to do so.[66]

The British initiative thus involved obtaining from the Austrians a statement of the terms which they were prepared to offer, and from the Russians a statement of the non-territorial compensation with which the Serbs would have to be contented. But Aehrenthal insisted that the former was not the concern of the powers, while Isvolsky was reluctant to consider the latter; the Germans, when it came to the point, refused to take part in collective representations in Vienna, and the Italians would not join without them.[67] All that was left of Grey's 'neutral' mediation, therefore, was an intervention by Britain and France, who could not hope to carry much weight in Vienna, and whose motives would be suspect in St Petersburg if they appeared to be urging unilateral concessions upon Russia. Nevertheless, it served its basic purpose of getting negotiations started, with the Germans as well as the British seeking a diplomatic solution to the crisis. The two governments did not, of course, differ seriously as regards this end: where they did differ was in the method by which the solution was to be achieved, for each sought to impose a procedure which would produce a settlement and advance its wider diplomatic interests at the same time.

As a counter to Grey's initiative, Kiderlen-Waechter proposed that all the great powers, including Russia, should simply issue a collective demand requiring the Serbs to moderate their attitude; and that Britain and France should use their influence in St Petersburg to induce the Russians to co-operate. Grey refused to comply unless the Germans would first press Austria to offer economic concessions to Serbia; the Germans refused to put pressure on Austria unless the British would first persuade Russia to make Serbia renounce territorial compensation.[68] In spite of this deadlock, there were points of similarity in the two schemes: both required the Serbs to renounce territorial compensation at one stage or another, and both recognised that only Russian pressure could accomplish this. But so long as the Germans refused to use their influence in Vienna, the British were reluctant to use theirs in St Petersburg, and preferred that 'somebody else' should make the necessary representation there.[69] In view of Isvolsky's suspicious reaction to the King's visit to Berlin, and his warning to Nicolson that a fiasco for Russia's policy in the Balkans might force him to reconsider the whole question of her European alignments, Grey was particularly unwilling to be identified with a German proposal which would be displeasing to the Russians.[70] When Aehrenthal followed up the Kiderlen proposal by inviting the powers to urge Serbia formally to accept the Austro-Turkish settlement, and thus in effect recognise the annexation before negotiating with Austria for compensation, Grey declined the invitation unless Aehrenthal would agree to state confidentially what concessions he proposed to offer to Serbia. He tried also to persuade the French to take a similar line because, as he had feared, their sympathetic reception of the Kiderlen proposal, together with their agreement of 9 February with Germany about Morocco, was regarded by Isvolsky as amounting almost to a denunciation of the Franco-Russian alliance.[71] But he remained perplexed as to how to induce the Russians to put pressure on Serbia, without alienating them as the French had done; and at last, on 27 February, he authorised Nicolson to broach the subject with Isvolsky.[72] Before these instructions could reach Nicolson, Isvolsky had himself decided to advise Serbia to renounce her territorial claims, and it only remained for Grey to welcome his 'statesmanlike step', and to lend it full support in Belgrade. It was by good fortune rather than by design, therefore, that he was relieved of the necessity of speaking too plainly to the Russians.[73]

The next step in the British scheme for settling the crisis was to use Isvolsky's conciliatory gesture on territorial compensation to persuade Aehrenthal to discuss with the powers the economic concessions which he was prepared to offer to Serbia. This Aehrenthal refused to do, insisting instead on direct bilateral negotiations; indeed, in spite of strong British pressure, he refused to consider economic concessions at all, even in bilateral negotiations, until the Serbs had formally announced that they completely withdrew their opposition to the annexation and renounced political compensation.[74] This seemed to Isvolsky merely to confirm that Aehrenthal intended to inflict a total humiliation on Serbia, without allowing the other powers a word. In an effort to avert this, the three *entente* governments persuaded Serbia to address a note to Austria and the other powers, formally renouncing territorial compensation and entrusting her case on economic compensation to their collective decision; but Aehrenthal remained adamant.[75] As a rupture between Austria and Serbia approached, Isvolsky lapsed into apathy and despair, observing with resignation to Nicolson on 16 March that, if Austria should attack Serbia, he hoped to be able to keep Russia out of the war.[76]

It was the virtual withdrawal of Russia from the question which finally drew Grey into the centre of the dispute in an attempt to find a formula which would avert an Austrian ultimatum to Serbia. For the next ten days he was busily engaged in trying to secure Aehrenthal's assent to the terms of a note which the powers could then oblige Serbia to present to Vienna. Aehrenthal did not like Grey's draft, which in his view let the Serbs off much too lightly. On 19 March – apparently at the prompting of Cartwright, who was acting on his own initiative – he presented a counter-draft which required Serbia not only to adopt a good-neighbourly attitude towards Austria and open direct negotiations for a commercial treaty, but also to recognise the Austro-Turkish protocol of 26 February and thereby accept the annexation.[77] This was too much for Grey to swallow, since it involved Serbia recognising the annexation in advance of its ratification by the great powers themselves. Cartwright (again acting without instructions) then asked Aehrenthal to modify his text so as to require Serbia simply to accept whatever decision the powers might take about the annexation; while the powers were to give Vienna written assurances that they would in fact recognise it at the conference. On this express condition Aehrenthal agreed; but Grey, who had no knowledge of Cartwright's proceedings and was still determined to withhold recognition until the Austro-Serbian dispute was peacefully settled, rejected what he took to be simply a further draft of Aehrenthal's. Thus by 23 March each had rejected the other's final draft, and the negotiations were deadlocked.[78]

The deadlock was broken by the German *démarche* of 22 March in St Petersburg. The refusal of Germany to take part in the collective mediation proposed by Grey on 16 February had been interpreted in London as proof that Bülow's real intention, notwithstanding his assurances to Hardinge, was to exploit the crisis to detach Russia from her western partners; and the British were convinced that, however softly the Germans might speak in London, in St Petersburg they would show themselves 'more Austrian than the Austrians'.[79] Grey did not know that the German *démarche* was a response to a plea for help from Isvolsky, but there were in any case good grounds for suspecting that it was also the culmination of a manoeuvre which was designed to forestall his own attempt at mediation and secure international recognition of the annexation before the question of compensation for Serbia had been settled. This manoeuvre took the form, initially, of a proposal to abandon the idea of a conference to ratify the solutions achieved by direct negotiation. On 16 March, in acknowledging receipt of the text of the Austro-Turkish protocol, Grey suggested that it was time to revive the conference proposal 'to deal with this question and others also, as to which it would now appear that sufficient preliminary agreement has been or is on the point of being reached'.[80] The governments of Austria and Germany proposed that the powers should instead settle each point in the conference programme by an exchange of notes as its solution was achieved: thus the Austro-Turkish protocol, the Turco-Bulgarian agreement, and the amendment of article 29 of the Treaty of Berlin (relating to Montenegro) could be dealt with at once.[81] Under this procedure, Austria would have secured ratification of the annexation before the dispute with Serbia was resolved. Grey therefore refused to accept it until his mediation had secured an acceptable solution to that dispute.[82] Isvolsky's reply to the proposal was merely evasive, and consequently on 22 March the German ambassador in St Petersburg demanded that he should accept it in 'clear and precise terms'; if he refused, Germany would leave Austria to take military action against Serbia.[83] The Russian cabinet had already ruled out the possibility of Russia going to war, and Isvolsky was therefore quick to comply with this demand. The last thing he wanted was to be exposed to a barrage of contrary advice from the British, and when Nicolson begged him to take time for consultation with Britain and France, he justified his refusal to do so with the argument that Russia had already been abandoned by them.[84]

The British were satisfied that it was Russia's military weakness rather than her isolation which had forced Isvolsky to capitulate, and in this they were fundamentally correct.[85] But it was also true, as Isvolsky observed, that Russia could not hope for material assistance from Britain and, in spite of the Franco-Russian alliance, could not expect much from France either: for the French were so anxious not to be drawn into conflict with the central powers that even their diplomatic support was less consistent than Grey's. However, Isvolsky's principal complaint against Britain was not that she denied him military assistance, but that she withdrew her diplomatic support at a critical moment: he had learnt from Vienna that Cartwright was saying that 'the question of peace or war rested in the hands of Russia', and was advising Aehrenthal to approach the powers for their assent to the annexation.[86] The account of the 'Cartwright proposal' which he had received seems (not surprisingly) to have been somewhat garbled; and even the inquest instituted by the Foreign Office into this odd little episode did not uncover the whole story.[87] There was nevertheless a kernel of truth in Isvolsky's allegation about British policy: for the suggestion advanced by Cartwright, in an attempt to facilitate Grey's mediation in Vienna, was virtually indistinguishable from the Austro-German proposal that the annexation should be recognised before Serbia had been compensated. Grey told himself that Isvolsky 'wanted an excuse for giving in to Germany and was too glad to have one to stop and enquire into its truth'.[88] But the activities of Cartwright, together with the attitude of the French, contributed to his sense of Russia's isolation. Nor could it be denied that the pacific attitude of Britain and France had encouraged the central powers:

Neither Austria nor Germany would have taken matters with such a high hand had it not been for their *knowledge* that we had informed Russia that our support would stop short of war, and their *surmise* that France would do all in her power to avoid it.[89]

The Russian capitulation cut the ground from under Grey's feet in his negotiations in Vienna, and was received in the Foreign Office with anger and contempt.[90] Having secured Russia's assent, the Germans expected that similar assurances would automatically follow from the other powers, and on 25 March Metternich asked Grey for unconditional assent to the annexation similar to that given by Isvolsky. As the German embassy had given prior notice of this request, the Foreign Office was able to prepare its answer, a crisply-worded refusal to comply until the Serbian question had been settled 'in a pacific manner'.[91] This reply led to a sharp exchange between Metternich and Grey, but it was endorsed by the cabinet; and it so heartened the French that they substituted for their initial weak answer (which was based on Isvolsky's) a much sterner one along the lines of the British memorandum.[92] Indeed, the only party other than Germany and Austria which appeared displeased with the British reply was Russia: at the very moment when Metternich was trying to soften the effect of his original *démarche* upon Grey, the first secretary of the Russian embassy was in Hardinge's room, strenuously urging that Britain should assent unconditionally to the German demand, as Russia had done.[93] But although Grey could salvage some credit by refusing to yield to German pressure, he recognised that Russia's abandonment of Serbia made it useless for him to persist in taking a stiff line with Austria, particularly when Isvolsky declared himself willing to accept the Austrian draft of the proposed Serbian note, rather than the British.[94]

When the Austrians became pressing, therefore, and set a time limit within which he was to agree to their terms, Grey had to accept the draft which previously he had found unacceptable. He also had to undertake to give his assent to the annexation, and the only reservation he was able to make was that the Austrians should promise to receive the Serbian note favourably, and to allow article 29 to be modified in Montenegro's favour.[95] This formula, which conceded virtually everything Aehrenthal had demanded, was reluctantly approved by the cabinet on 31 March. The powers presented the text of the note to the Serbian government, which dutifully addressed it to Vienna; and the Austro–Serbian crisis was over.[96] Once the Italian government, as the patron of Montenegro, had settled with Austria the amendments to article 29, the powers were ready to proceed to the abrogation of article 25, thus endorsing the annexation of Bosnia.[97] Despite his previous insistence that they should formally countersign the changes in the Treaty of Berlin, Grey was too exhausted and discouraged to propose that a conference should now be summoned. In any case, if there were no conference there would be no opportunity for Isvolsky to expose himself to further humiliations, or for the discussion of the 'tiresome' question of Crete.[98] The British government preferred that the Treaty of Berlin, which was by now a 'worthless instrument', should simply remain in its existing 'chaotic state'.[99] There was no conference.

The outcome of the Bosnian crisis was, by general consent, a diplomatic triumph for the central powers and a humiliation for Russia. It was small consolation to the British that they had saved 'what face there was to be saved' for the *entente* powers by 'giving Germany's proposal the answer it deserved'.[100] For the fact that this had to be done without, and even despite, the Russians showed how far Austro-German diplomacy had succeeded in separating Russia from Britain and France. It is true that, in the Austro-Turkish, Turco-Bulgarian, and Cretan aspects of the crisis, British policy was far from ignominious, and successfully defended the real interests of Turkey without alienating the Russians. But these successes were soon vitiated: partly by the subsequent pro-German inclination of the Young Turks, but principally by the acknowledged failure of British diplomacy in the Austro-Serbian crisis. In the aftermath of the Bosnian affair, the immediate question for British policy was what effect the success of the central powers had had upon the balance of power in Europe; and what, if anything, should be done to salvage the *entente* with Russia.[101]

10

The German background to Anglo-German relations, 1905–1914

JONATHAN STEINBERG

No examination of Anglo-German relations can ignore the facts of Germany's astonishing economic growth. Diplomacy went on against such a background, and the historian must begin with it. By the year 1906, 25 years after the founding of the Empire in 1871, the Reich's population had grown from about 41 million to 62,863,000. National income had risen from the early 1890s, when it stood at 22,638,000,000 marks, to 39,919,000,000 marks by 1906. Income per capita had advanced from 445 Mk to 635 Mk.[1] Over the first half of the decade 1900–10, national income had risen by 11.5%, not the highest growth in the history of the Empire but respectable.[2] The transformation of the German Empire from an agricultural to an industrial society was rushing ahead. In 1871 63.9% of the population had lived in rural areas; 40.0% did so in 1910. More striking was the growth of large cities. In 1871 4.8% of the German population lived in cities of more than 100,000, but by 1910 21.3% did.[3] The decade 1896 to 1906 had been a period of rising prices and increasing prosperity for the masses as well. Meat consumption per head of population, the most sensitive indicator of general well-being, rose more rapidly between 1892 and 1900 than at any period in the history of the German Empire,[4] and the income pyramid had become much broader in the middle strata. Whereas in Prussia in 1896 67.2% of the population had incomes below 900 Mk, by 1906 only 55.1% were still in the lowest category.[5] Between 1897 and 1906 hard coal extraction had risen from 91 to 136 million tons, pig iron production had doubled, and German foreign trade had risen in value from 8,455,000,000 Mk to 14,582,000,000 Mk.[6] Overseas capital investment between 1897 and 1905 amounted to 20,814,000,000 Mk.[7] Germany's industrial base and population were already larger than that of the United Kingdom and she had become a serious threat in trade and finance, activities hitherto dominated by British enterprise.

The rapid emergence of the German Empire as an economic and technological super-power upset many of the prevailing calculations in international relations. For Germans the rate of change was stupefying, for foreign observers alarming. Germany seemed to be bursting the seams of the old order in Europe, and to be expanding in every direction. Eyre Crowe of the Foreign

Office summed up these developments in his famous memorandum of 1 January 1907:

No modern German would plead guilty to a mere lust of conquest for the sake of conquest. But the vague and undefined schemes of Teutonic expansion ('die Ausbreitung des deutschen Volkstums') are but the expression of the deeply rooted feeling that Germany has by the strength and purity of her national purpose, the fervour of her patriotism, the depth of her religious feeling, the high standard of her competency, and the perspicuous honesty of her administration, the successful pursuit of every branch of public and scientific activity, and the elevated character of her philosophy, art, and ethics, established for herself the right to assert the primacy of German national ideals.[8]

In the broadest sense, Anglo-German relations from the fall of Bismarck in 1890 to the outbreak of war in 1914 had no other focus than the problem of coping with the explosive expansion of German power. Both the German and the British governments struggled to adjust to the astonishing reality of the unfolding situation. German diplomats and journalists, professors and civil servants, stirred by the spectacle of industrial growth, naturally called for a place for Germany in the affairs of the world to match her economic achievements. This was what *Weltpolitik* really meant or what Crowe dismissed as 'vague and undefined schemes of Teutonic expansion'. In Britain, men, perhaps inevitably, saw such German claims as a challenge. Whether the challenge was 'real' or the product of certain Edwardian illusions about Empire, manliness and force, is a tantalizing subject for speculation, but not crucial. The German claims were seen as a challenge in Britain, and frequently announced as such in Germany. This was, after all, still the old Europe. The Great War had not yet shattered the social structure nor crushed its antique values. Gentlemen still had codes of behaviour. One met one's challenges squarely.

The difficulty was that the German challenge was at once very concrete and very abstract. Great Britain had quarrels with states of every shape and size, but most of these concerned definable material interests. Such conflicts could be resolved, at a price, by doing deals about strips of territory, trading concessions, railway consortia or spheres of influence. How could one negotiate on what Crowe called the 'primacy of German national ideals'? What was the price, let alone the definition, of *Weltmacht, Weltgeltung* and all the other cloudy terms in which Germans put their demands? At the other extreme the Imperial German Government seemed to be perpetually threatening war over issues such as Samoa or Morocco, where German interests were scarcely worth mentioning. The obvious explanation that the Germans did not know what they wanted was rejected by the experts as too simple.

To the Germans the situation was perfectly clear. As early as 1896, Albrecht von Stosch, former head of the Admiralty in Germany, wrote to his brightest pupil, Alfred Tirpitz:

The rage of the English against us, which broke out as a result of the Krüger Dispatch, finds its explanation in the competition of Germany in world markets. Since foreign policy in England is directed exclusively by commercial interests, we have to reckon with the hostility of the island people.[9]

Writing in 1909, General Count Schlieffen, retired Chief of the Great General Staff, put the case more strongly:

The powerful expansion of Germany's industry and trade earned her another implacable enemy, England. This hatred of a formerly despised rival can neither be tempered by assurances of sincere friendship and cordiality nor aggravated by provocative language. It is not the emotions but questions of debit and credit which determine the level of resentment.[10]

Such views, which were widely held in Germany, compounded conservative distaste for democracy with a certain aristocratic contempt for the small tradesmen in Britain, who, unlike a Krupp or a Freiherr von Stumm, had not been civilized by contact with aristocracy. In German eyes, the British were often seen as a nation of hypocritical shopkeepers, men with one hand on the Bible and the other on the accounts ledger. Their aristocracy was corrupted by intermarriage with the children of grocers and mechanics. The seeping of social Darwinian ideas into German thought completed the image of the British, a people at once timid and rapacious, whose democracy contained both the dusty pieties of the nonconformist hypocrites and a struggle among mining kings and steel barons, the commercial and financial beasts of the jungle. As German commerce expanded, such a people were bound to envy it. '*Handels-neid*' or trade envy must grow. The future could only bring struggle, as Hans Delbrück, historian of note and editor of Prussia's most respectable monthly, put it in 1899:

We want to be a world power and pursue colonial politics in the grand style. That is certain. Here there can be no step backward. The whole future of our people among the great nations depends upon it. But we can pursue this policy either with or against England. With England means in peace; against England means through war.[11]

As long as many Germans saw the world powers locked in an inevitable struggle for survival, and as long as the British could only see in German expansion a direct threat, Anglo-German relations were unlikely to improve beyond a certain point.

As the German Ambassador, Count Metternich, rightly observed in a dispatch, 'it is always difficult to characterize the relations between two peoples in a word'.[12] In early 1906 Anglo-German relations were being altered by activities which had not yet become public issues. Of these the most important were developments within the *Reichsmarineamt* (the Imperial Naval Office) in Berlin. Since 1889, the German Navy had been organized, after the model of the Prussian Army, in two main divisions,[13] the *Reichsmarineamt* which, like the Prussian *Kriegsministerium*, was responsible for administration, finance and

relations with parliament, and an *Admiralstab,* or Admiralty Staff, which served
as planning, command and nerve centre for the fleet. This division between
operations and supply was complicated by Prussian military tradition and by
the role of the Kaiser as Supreme War Lord. Commanding Generals and
Admirals had the right to request direct audiences of their Sovereign as
Commander-in-Chief and were rarely refused. The Kaiser retained all his
inherited powers over military and naval appointments and the Palace's naval
secretariat, which dealt with naval personnel, the *Marinekabinett,* became an
office of great influence. Given the personality of Kaiser Wilhelm II, and the
proximity of the *Kabinett* to the Sovereign, the chief of the *Marinekabinett,*
in spite of his rank, could often control events. Admiral von Tirpitz
observed:

One had to speak to the Kaiser alone, because if a third party was present,
his own real judgement would easily be distorted by the need to appear in
the eyes of the other person as 'The Kaiser' on every issue. The cabinet chief
attended all the official audiences of each responsible officer, and it was
natural that when that officer had gone, the Kaiser would discuss the affairs
raised. The cabinet chief had only to wait for the right moment and to tune
into the temperament and phantasy of the Monarch to get his own way.[14]

From 1897 onward, the largest branch of this complex and unwieldy naval
administration, the *Reichsmarineamt,* was under the firm control of Alfred von
Tirpitz, a fluent, polished but strong-willed personality. Tirpitz took office in
June of 1897 firmly convinced that the German Empire needed naval power
as a 'political power factor against England'.[15] In 1898 and 1900 he introduced
two substantial Navy Laws, which laid down, and hence bound the *Reichstag*
to accept, a fixed establishment for the German fleet. These Navy Laws or
Flottengesetze merely established the legal framework for naval expansion by
settling the number of warships to be constructed in each class. The establishment by law of the size of the German fleet liberated the naval administration
from an annual battle over the estimates, a peculiarly uninviting prospect in
a *Reichstag* without stable majorities. Tirpitz, whose feel for political tactics was
remarkable in a career naval officer, understood this from the start. He had
called the *Flottengesetz* of 1898 a *lex imperfecta* because it merely settled the
numbers of ships to be built and the annual rate at which they were to be laid
down or replaced.[16] The appropriation of the individual vessels and their
design specifications went into the annual naval estimates. If the *Flottengesetz*
provided that two battleships and one heavy cruiser were to be laid down in,
say, 1906, the *Reichstag* could hardly refuse the supplies necessary to carry it
out. As Tirpitz put it in his memoirs,

By tying itself legally to carry out the fleet plan, it had bound itself morally
not to make any difficulties about money...lest it wished to be accused of
building inferior ships.[17]

During the years between 1898 and 1906, the Imperial Navy expanded steadily at the annual rate of two battleships, one heavy cruiser, two light cruisers and two torpedo-boat divisions, but much of the planned expansion was still on paper and some of the existing vessels had been launched in the mid 1890s.[18] Gradually the British responded to this new threat in the North Sea and in 1904 regrouped the Royal Navy so that its main fighting strength lay in home waters.[19] This reinforced the conviction in the German navy and government that the British were preparing to launch a surprise attack on the German fleet in the manner of the attack on Copenhagen in 1807. However implausible this fear might have been, it grew out of the aspirations which underlay the so-called 'Risk Theory' of Admiral von Tirpitz.[20] In the simplest formulation of the theory, Tirpitz argued that Great Britain was uniquely vulnerable to naval attack. Her sea-borne Empire rested on naval supremacy, a supremacy which had to be as global as the Empire itself. Hence Great Britain could never concentrate all her forces in home waters and a relatively small German fleet could exercise political pressure or leverage out of all proportion to its size. Building such a German fleet brought with it certain dangers. He saw that between the point at which Germany had no fleet to speak of and the point at which she had a fleet large enough to deter any potential British aggression there would be what he called a 'danger zone'. Within that zone the Royal Navy could easily 'Copenhagen' the German fleet or engage it in battle without running the risk of losing command of the seas.[21] Germany could best traverse the 'danger zone' by keeping calm and pursuing a pacific foreign policy, until such time as her growing naval strength began to force Great Britain to accede to German demands. In the event, the Germans lost their nerve before the British and by the winter of 1904–5 a war scare spread through the German government. In December of 1904, an emergency meeting was held at the *Reichsmarineamt* to consider the naval position if war should suddenly break out,[22] and Captain August von Heeringen, Tirpitz's most trusted disciple, expressed deep misgivings about his chief's policy. 'In every measure we take', he argued, 'we must ask ourselves not what will happen in some distant future but what real increase in power it brings us in the immediate period ahead of us.'[23]

Tirpitz replied that the navy could not have done more:

Since 1898 we have done our utmost to drive the fleet programme forward: the navy laws, the highest possible navy estimates, postponement of coastal fortifications, curtailment of our overseas service, limitation on the number of gunnery practice ships, torpedo, training and experimental ships, etc., etc., all prove this. The concentration of our resources on one purpose has been fought through against the resistance of the entire navy. That the programme is not finished can only be used against us in a war if it can be shown that in the years 1898 to 1904 more could have been achieved...the idea that we must subordinate 'tomorrow' to 'today' is correct only with the greatest reservations. The danger zone for Germany is not just there today, but will in all probability also be there tomorrow, and we must reckon with these facts in the development of our navy.[24]

Tirpitz and Heeringen found themselves tied up in the coils of what we now see as the classical dilemma of the arms race. No matter how fast Germany built, as long as Great Britain remained resolute, the gap between the powers stayed the same, or in Tirpitz's terminology, the 'danger zone' became infinite. By implication the German fleet could never meet the threat for which it had been designed, nor grow rapidly enough to make that threat less ominous.

When Tirpitz first developed the 'Risk Theory' in the middle of the 1890s, Great Britain was diplomatically isolated. He had assumed that all the secondary naval powers had a common interest with Germany in assailing Britain's naval monopoly, which in her isolation Britain could hardly hope to maintain against all comers. The German fleet must increase Germany's '*Bündnisfähigkeit*', that is the German ability to make alliances and her desirability as an ally.[25] The Anglo-Japanese Alliance of 1902 and the Anglo-French *entente* had reversed the maritime power equations while the Russo-Japanese War and the revolution of 1905 had virtually eliminated the Russians as a potential ally. Even the Italians could no longer be counted as reliable allies. Hence by 1905 the Imperial German Navy had now to reckon with the possibility of war without the aid of a major naval power, a war for which the 'Risk Theory' had made no provision. On 2 February Mr Arthur Lee, Civil Lord of the Admiralty, virtually assured the Germans that their worst fears of a 'Copenhagen' were justified by promising in a speech that the British public would, if war broke out against Germany, be able to read of the destruction of the German fleet on the morning of the first day.[26] Later in 1905 German tensions focused on France and at several points during the spring and summer war with France over Morocco seemed possible.

The threatening diplomatic situation of the *Reich* put Tirpitz under considerable pressure. The *Flottenverein*, the German Navy League, grew in numbers and belligerence. The Kaiser sent Tirpitz bellicose memoranda, and admirals afloat intrigued against him. By the autumn of 1905 he was compelled to offer the *Reichstag* some new naval legislation. He chose the modest course of demanding six additional heavy cruisers and argued that this demand merely restored the original number of cruisers in the *Flottengesetz* of 1900, since the *Reichstag* had stricken six from that law during its passage.[27] On October 1905, at an audience in the Kaiser's hunting lodge at Rominten, he extracted an agreement from the Kaiser to approve this demand, although Wilhelm II wanted much more.[28] Tirpitz believed that the risk of a British attack was too great to permit the Germans to expand the navy more rapidly. His bill merely restored the original design of 1900 and was thus not a genuine expansion of the fleet. The leaders of the Navy League furiously condemned this proposal as inadequate and in an interview in the *Reichsmarineamt* on 7 November 'declared war on the naval administration'.[29] They pressed hard and had useful aristocratic connections. Prince Bülow began to waver and asked the Admiral for an opinion on whether, in fact, it might not be a good moment to demand a squadron of battleships. Tirpitz's reply set the limits within which the naval administration had to operate:

Against such a bill there are two grave objections, the first in the field of foreign policy, the second in domestic policy... The fact that in the next four years Germany would lay down 16 capital ships of 18,000 tons and in addition the awareness that in future England would have to reckon with 50 to 60 first-class German capital ships involves such a shift in *real power factors* that even a calm and reasonable English policy *must* come to the decision to crush such an opponent before it reaches a military strength too dangerous for England's position as a world power...

Domestic policy: A bill like the one sketched above alters the *character* of our naval policy completely and explicitly. According to the present conceptions the German fleet should be made so strong that England dare not attack us since possible success is not proportional to the probable risk. For such a task there is in the nation and the *Reichstag* a solid majority. If the government now introduce a bill from which one may conclude – and not without reason – that they intend to have a fleet equal to the English, the government will not find a majority in *this* parliament. It is very doubtful that a dissolution will bring a better one.[30]

The amendment to the Navy Law of 1900, the *Novelle*, was introduced to the *Reichstag* on 27 November 1905, accompanied by an economic white paper giving figures of the spectacular growth of foreign trade over the years since 1897.[31] The bill went into Committee in December and had its third reading from 7 to 13 March 1906. Hans Delbrück, unaware of the bitter fight within the hydra-headed naval administration, scarcely thought its passage worthy of comment. 'There is no need', he wrote in May, 'to talk about the navy bills any more. They go by themselves.'[32]

Delbrück saw results, but Tirpitz saw the effort which had gone into the bill. On 4 April 1906, he submitted his resignation on the grounds that his health could no longer stand the strains of his office.[33] This was not the first resignation he had tendered. During his first eighteen months in office he had offered to resign four times in the struggle to steer the first *Flottengesetz* through and to establish his authority against the swarms of courtiers, cabinet chiefs, admirals afloat and royal favourites. The Kaiser, in whose close entourage such independence of character was virtually unknown, burst out in disgust: 'Tirpitz is neurasthenic and doesn't know how to obey'.[34] Yet it was hard to obey a monarch who could order specifications for warships from foreign builders and then comment to his naval cabinet chief:

After I received the photos from Ansaldo last night, I spent the whole evening and this morning chuckling so hard at the thought of Tirpitz's face when he sees them that my wife began to wonder if there was something wrong with me.[35]

Although the 1906 resignation crisis, as had all the others, ended with Tirpitz still in office, the grounds for Tirpitz's dissatisfaction remained. Throughout his career he was obsessed by the need to make his navy laws automatic and self-operating. Only if the expansion of the fleet could go ahead each year by legally fixed amounts, could he be safe from intrigue from above and interference from below. To make the *Flottengesetz* 'eternal', as he put it, the active life of capital ships had to be so fixed that the right number of warships reached replacement time every year, ensuring that the new ships to be laid down and the old ships to be replaced yielded a constant sum. The fixity of the navy laws had for Tirpitz an importance so central that if it were endangered he would have to go. Contemporary critics refused to understand this point. Tirpitz seemed stubborn and inflexible, relentlessly pushing his *Flottengesetz* and closed to any thought of compromise. The British frequently demanded that Tirpitz slow down his rate of construction, or, in his words, 'the building tempo', but for Tirpitz the demand was unreal. The 'tempo' built into the law its dynamic element and could not be altered without opening the whole issue of the fleet again. Again and again Tirpitz tried to make this point clear to the British. In an interview with Captain Heath, the British naval attaché in Berlin, in 1909, at the height of the acceleration panic, he tried again:

I want to explain to you the essence and significance of the Navy Law...It would certainly be better – and I have thought about it a great deal – to build regularly three ships a year. But that would have broken the law at one point. The *Reichstag* would say: if you don't replace this ship or that one, you can perfectly well wait a little longer. A battle about shipbuilding would begin which I want to avoid at all costs. Given the doctrinaire character of the Germans, that would have the most appalling consequences. Hence I have to cling to the law under all circumstances. *I stick to the law.* [English in the original][36]

In the spring of 1906, Tirpitz had not yet reached the point at which the *Flottengesetz* could be made 'eternal', in his words an *Aeternat*, and hence safe from the 'doctrinaire character of the Germans'. But he was getting close. In May of 1906, Rear-Admiral Eduard Capelle, an original member of his 1897 'brains trust' and now, as head of the Budget Section, the principal parliamentary tactician of the *Reichsmarineamt*, submitted a scheme:

Following the general directives of your Excellency the *next* goal of further development will be the attainment of a twenty-year replacement period for battle ships and the stabilization of the 'three tempo' so that a fleet of 60 great capital ships results with a building tempo of three ships per year...This memorandum assumes that 1910 will be the time to introduce a new bill, since from 1911 on the previous building tempo of 2 battle ships and 1 cruiser will diminish. A demand for two additional battle ships will be necessary in order to raise the present total of 58 to the number necessary to stabilize a 'three tempo':

$$\frac{40+20}{20} = 2+1 \text{ per annum.}[37]$$

Tirpitz and Capelle knew that they had no choice but to face the unsavoury prospect of another amendment in the not too distant future. According to section II, paragraph 1 of the *Flottengesetz* of 10 April 1898, battleships and coastal armoured vessels were to be replaced after 25 years, heavy cruisers after 20, and light cruisers after 15.[38] Capelle's scheme to 'eternalize' the building programme at 3 capital ships per year required a *Novelle*, an amendment to alter the life of battleships from 25 to 20 years. The building programme as amended by the *Novelle* of 1906 looked like this:[39]

	1900 Navy Law	Novelle 1906
1903	3	—
1904	3	—
1905	3	—
1906	2	3
1907	2	3
1908	2	3
1909	2	3
1910	2	3
1911	2	3
1912	2	3
1913	3	2
1914	2	2
1915	2	2
1916	2	2
1917	2	2

The *Novelle* of 1906 had bought time. By adding six heavy cruisers to the establishment, it assured that a steady flow of contracts for capital ships would continue until 1912 and that the fleet would grow by three capital ships each year. Yet the building programme in the right-hand column was still inconsistent, 'imperfect' by Tirpitz's criteria, because it lacked that regularity which could alone assure the automatic growth and replacement of the German battle fleet and the equally permanent exclusion of the *Reichstag* from interfering in that growth.

An even more pressing problem had been posed by the launching on 10 February 1906 of H.M.S. *Dreadnought*. The *Dreadnought* was a revolutionary development. She had a speed of 21 knots, 2 knots faster than any battleship afloat or building, a main battery of ten 12-inch (30.5 cm) guns, turbine engines and no secondary armament.[40] Shortly thereafter the keel-plate was laid for H.M.S. *Invincible*, a startling new type of battle-cruiser. The *Invincible* displaced 17,200 tons, had all-big-gun armaments and was designed for 25 knots.[41] These developments were particularly unpleasant for Tirpitz because ships of such displacement could not navigate the Kiel Canal, and hence, were Germany to follow the British lead, the canal must be widened. Tirpitz disliked following 'fashions'. In his initial audience in June 1897 he had argued:

If we were to take existing ships of foreign nations as the standard for design of our own and to try always to match their performance, we should be compelled constantly to change our designs. We should never arrive at a development of consistent designs, uninfluenced by the fashions of the day, and we should impair the maximum performance of our fleet.[42]

The *Dreadnought* 'fashion' had to be followed, and Tirpitz always harboured a special bitterness for Sir John Fisher, who had 'forced' the '*Dreadnought-Sprung*' on him.[43] The *Dreadnought* was an escalation not only of the arms race with Britain but also of domestic conflicts within the *Reich* itself. The peculiar structure of Bismarckian federalism left the Imperial Government utterly dependent on indirect, and hence regressive taxation, of consumer goods, on tariffs and on a complicated system of subsidy from state governments to the *Reich* called *Matrikularbeiträge*. In theory the Imperial government (or to use the contemporary term 'The Associated Governments') had the power under Article 70 of the Constitution to introduce direct taxation, but the power both of the conservatively controlled federal states and the unwillingness of the *beati possidentes* made such a move difficult to achieve.[44] The navy was becoming expensive. During the nine years of his administration of the *Reichsmarineamt* Tirpitz had seen the annual naval estimates rise from 117 million to 252 million marks, the number of personnel grow from 23,302 officers and men to 43,474. The estimate for shipbuilding and armaments in 1906, 109 million marks, was itself nearly as large as the total budget for 1897.[45] Price changes in the economy had also taken their toll. If 1913 is 100, then the index of prices had risen from 80.2 in the first years of the 1890s to 92.5 for the period 1906–10.[46] Wages had risen during 1905 by about 10% and the working day was steadily shortening to a 9-hour average.[47] These hard economic facts pressed on Tirpitz, not only because the *Reichsmarineamt* operated two large nationalized dockyards at Wilhelmshaven and Kiel, but, much more important, because the mounting expense of the navy was beginning to alienate its best friends in the *Reichstag*. It was not a Socialist but Richard Müller of Fulda, a leading Catholic Centre deputy and navalist, who, on 20 February 1906, warned 'those circles who continually push the Reich into ever greater expenditure, because they don't have to pay for them' that the Centre might begin to demand a *Reich* income tax.[48] Unfortunately for the Imperial Naval Office, the 1906–7 estimates showed that the first generation of German Dreadnoughts, the *Nassau* class, cost 36,500,000 marks each, a 50% increase over the pre-Dreadnought *Schlesien* class.[49] To the rising cost was added an awkward delay in naval expansion. The specifications for pre-Dreadnoughts had to be thrown away, and work began in a hurry on the new class of battleships. Final designs were not completed until July 1906, nine months late, and the plans for the 1907 cruiser *Blücher* were not completed for nearly fourteen months, as the Construction Department explained, 'because the completion of design specifications for the *Blücher* had to take second place to those of the *Nassau* class'.[50]

Tirpitz and the *Reichsmarineamt* had little choice but to accept the challenge thrown at them by Sir John Fisher, but the full significance of the challenge only became obvious with the keel-laying of H.M.S. *Invincible*. Its specifications were closely guarded, but Captain Coerper, the naval attaché in London, understood reliably that it would displace 20,000 tons and have 12-inch guns. The cruiser estimates must now go up along with the battleships, and Tirpitz baulked. The Chief of the Central Department, Captain von Trotha, replied bluntly:

It is clear that your Excellency must give in, if at all possible, to the movement for large heavy cruisers and in such a way that it does not look like compulsion but like a free choice. If not, we shall live through a situation in which your Excellency has to step down only to see your successor having to do it anyway.[51]

On 18 July 1906 Tirpitz, who was at his summer home in the Black Forest, conceded defeat to the expansionists. In a general order, he authorized the *Reichsmarineamt* to plan for an immediate escalation in the armaments of both Dreadnoughts and battle cruisers. In violation of one of his strictest principles, the principle that all the units of a class should be comparably armed, he demanded that the third and fourth Dreadnoughts of the *Nassau* class, the 1908 Dreadnoughts (the future *Posen* and *Rheinland*) be armed with 12-inch instead of the 11-inch guns which he had considered adequate for the *Nassau* and the *Westfalen*. The battle cruiser for 1908, the future *von der Tann*, was to be armed with eight 12-inch guns as well.[52] The Construction and Weapons Departments of the *Reichsmarineamt* began to work furiously. Within a week it was clear that the new designs would cost 44 million for the battleships and nearly as much for the cruisers.[53] Highly coloured, often conflicting reports on the specifications of the *Invincible* kept arriving from Coerper, and Tirpitz, knowing only too well their effect on the Kaiser's temperament, exploded at Coerper's 'utter frivolity' in writing such stuff.[54] By September 1906 Coerper had to report that the British battle-cruiser was going to be nothing like the monster he had predicted and, much relieved, Tirpitz ordered a reduction in the dimensions and armaments of the German equivalent.[55] Toward the end of September 1906 Tirpitz travelled to Rominten for his annual audience at the Kaiser's hunting lodge, that audience in the year which he most hated. The combination of the unbusinesslike surroundings, the irresponsible entourage and the importance of the Kaiser's approval of the programme for the forthcoming session of the *Reichstag* always made the Admiral uneasy and upset his stomach and disposition for weeks before.[56] The Kaiser had been excited by Coerper's reports and needed much attention before he would accept that the German battle-cruisers would be adequate if armed with 28 cm (11-inch) guns instead of 30.5 cm (12-inch). The Kaiser was not impressed by the fact that even the reduced designs would cost 37 million marks, more than the *Nassau* class, the first generation of Dreadnoughts. The increase in cost for the future *von der Tann* battle-cruiser meant that plans for changes in the navy law discussed earlier in the year would have to wait. Above all, Tirpitz urged the Kaiser to consider the international implications of the new construction programme:

At first our move will call forth stronger agitation on the part of the Conservatives against the Liberals. The English now realise that they made a mistake in going ahead with the *Dreadnought* against Germany and are peeved about it. This irritation will grow when they see that we are following their lead in battle cruisers at once, all the more so, since our battle cruiser will in fact be somewhat larger than *Invincible*. It will be very important either to deny or to conceal this fact...His Majesty agreed in particular that for the next two to three years we should hold back on new engagements until the time for the *Novelle*.[57]

As the navy prepared the details of the estimates, the *Reichstag* began its work in an angry mood. On 14 November 1906 Ernst Basserman, the leader of the National Liberals, the most consistent friend of the navy in the House and an advocate of a forward foreign policy, delivered a slashing attack on Prince Bülow's diplomacy:

Today the Triple Alliance has no further practical use. The Italian Press and population lean more and more toward France. Austria has been overly praised for her role of 'brilliant second', which she herself declined. The Franco-Russian Alliance remains intact, and the disposition of France toward us is less friendly than formerly. The declarations at Cronberg between the English and German Sovereigns will not prevent England from pursuing her old policy of isolating us. We are living in an era of alliances between other nations...Our policy lacks calm and consistency, and we see brutal hands derange well prepared plans.[58]

Foreign policy was not the only difficulty facing the *Reich* government. The colonial rebellion in Southwest Africa would not subside. Stories of atrocities and scandals in colonial administration inflamed opinion. In addition, Hermann von Stengel, the *Reich* Minister of Finance, had appalled the Chancellor and State Secretaries with alarming news of a monster deficit for fiscal year 1907.[59] The Catholic Centre Party under the leadership of its youngest and most radical deputy, Matthias Erzberger, had now joined the Social Democrats in a concerted attack on the government, not least on the mounting cost of *Weltpolitik*. When on 12 December the *Reichstag* refused to vote a supplementary credit for the war in Southwest Africa, Bülow dissolved it. At a meeting of the Prussian *Staatsministerium* a few days earlier Bülow had disclosed his plans but met with only token opposition.[60] It was not that Bülow feared defeat over the relatively small supplementary estimate, for the Chancellor was responsible to the Kaiser, not the *Reichstag*. It was rather that Bülow, whose foreign and domestic policies lay in ruins, saw an elegant way to extricate himself from his financial, naval and diplomatic difficulties.[61] In 1887 Bismarck had used a patriotic issue to produce a 'National', that is, a pro-Bismarckian, majority in the *Reichstag*, the so-called *Kartell*. Bülow hoped to repeat the trick with his 'bloc', an alliance of all the bourgeois parties from the Radical People's Party on the left to the Conservatives on the right. The foe was the Catholic Centre, the party which Bismarck had furiously condemned as 'an enemy of the Reich'. The results of the elections on 25 January 1907, and the run-off ballot a week later, were unexpected. All the heavy guns of Protestant fanaticism and the *Kulturkampf* had been dusted off and fired, but the Centre Party had come through the 'Hottentot Elections' unharmed.[62] They were still the largest party in the *Reichstag* with 105 deputies and had even gained a few new seats. When the smoke cleared, the Social Democrats had been hit instead, unseated in traditional bastions like Gotha, Braunschweig, Breslau, Königsberg and Magdeburg and forced into the second, or run-off, ballot in safe seats such as Stettin, Bremen and Frankfurt/Main.[63] Hans Delbrück was ecstatic:

The dice have been thrown and the wildest hopes have been fulfilled...The first and most important task falls to the Radicals. What that task is must be plain – the creation of a national democratic party...Any pacts with the Social Democrats will ruin the party morally in the eyes of nationally minded persons...[64]

The defeat of the Social Democrats had been utterly astonishing. They returned to the *Reichstag* with only 43 members left of the 81 who had gone into the campaign. There were now fewer S.P.D. members in the *Reichstag* than at any time since the elections of 1893.[65] The socialists' debacle gave Bülow the victory he wanted over the Centre as well, although in an unexpected way. The power of the Centre had rested indirectly on the strength of the Social Democrats. As long as the Centre and S.P.D. together made up a majority of the 397 members of the *Reichstag*, a potential 'Black–Red' coalition threatened the Government. As Ludwig Windhorst, the Centre's leader, had said on being invited to a Bismarck *Bierabend* for the first time, '*extra centrum nulla salus*'. The Centre's potential veto was its most powerful weapon, and it had now been broken.

Tirpitz had always been unusually solicitous of the Centre without which there was no *salus* for the navy either. On the passage of the *Flottengesetz* of 1898, he had sent the then leader of the Centre, Dr Ernst Lieber, an autographed picture of himself together with a letter:

The passage of the Navy Law marks the end of the dogma that the Centre is an internal enemy. A new future opens before our people and nation... The country cannot get along without you.[66]

Certainly the navy could not. Tirpitz took care to reward Lieber and Richard Müller, the Deputy from Fulda, who was now warning the government aloud, for their services in helping the 1900 *Flottengesetz* to safe harbour. Such an attitude made Tirpitz unpopular among the taut Prussian conservatives at court and in government circles. His request for decorations for both Lieber and Müller was turned down flat, because the Kaiser would not reward Catholic politicians, no matter how worthy.[67] By 1907 Tirpitz's reputation as a 'Black' was almost equalled by his notoriety, especially at court, as a 'Red'. His relative liberality in dealing with trades unions at the Imperial dockyards and his courtesy to the Social Democratic press made him a dangerous 1..dical to conservative critics. He had dared to express the view that there were 'many honourable Social Democrats and radicals who are true to the Fatherland and understand its necessities'.[68] To Prussian tories an honourable Social Democrat was a contradiction in terms.

The sudden lurch to the right caught Tirpitz off balance. Although for the first time since 1887 a 'national', that is, a Protestant, bourgeois majority existed in the *Reichstag*, Tirpitz had doubts about its usefulness. He was unwilling to abandon the good will painfully gathered during eight years of close co-operation with the Catholic party for the uncertain enthusiasms of the *Bloc*. The Radicals worried him most. Fiercely anti-Catholic, and divided into three different parties, they supported the *Bloc* at some risk. As Hans Delbrück saw it:

Tactically their task is a very difficult one. On the one hand they have to win a good relationship with an agrarian, protectionist government while on the other they cannot do without the support of the Social Democrats against those who push up the cost of living.[69]

The Radicals shared some of the characteristics of those 'strangers' who swarmed into the House of Commons in January 1906. They inherited the free-trading, Gladstonian traditions of European liberalism and shared the same profound suspicion of the military establishment as their nonconformist opposite numbers in the Palace of Westminster. Tirpitz had good reason to fear them. Their former leader, Eugen Richter, had been the finest parliamentary performer of his generation. His death in 1906 took from the *Reichstag* a man whose biting wit caused more anxiety at the *Bundesrath* table than any other opposition speaker. Richter's line had been simple: first give us responsible parliamentary government and then we shall vote military and naval supplies. He had no intention of voting one *Pfennig* for a regime in which, as he put it,

ministers are plucked like flowers from the field, and when the wind from above blows over them, their petals are wafted away and in a few weeks nobody speaks of them any more...(Prolonged laughter).[70]

Rear-admiral Capelle was more adventurous. His analysis of the new parliament suggested that there would be a stable majority for naval expansion.

On 18 February 1907 he proposed to Tirpitz that a *Novelle* be introduced in the autumn which would lower the life of battleships to twenty years but would leave the legally established number of battleships at 38, that is, two short of the 40 which would make the system 'eternal'. Capelle estimated that the cost of converting to larger ships and 12-inch guns might add 700 or 800 millions over the coming decade and hence it would be prudent to have a *Novelle* which would 'look very meagre and small'.[71] Tirpitz gradually accepted this view. On 9 March he reported to the Kaiser that there would be a small *Novelle* in the autumn of 1907, and that the 1908 battleships would have 12-inch guns, thus costing about 25% more than the first generation of Dreadnoughts. His notes for the audience make the strategy clear:

The occasion must be used to shorten the active lives of the battleships by five years. More would be impractical. A large estimate and a small change in the law. Politically unavoidable, because we cannot outbid England. The *Novelle* now planned will stir up enough dust...If the fourth *Novelle* passes, the fleet will be 'eternalized' at 3 tempo with a slight irregularity, which in fact may turn out to be an advantage. His Majesty the Emperor has approved this programme with in addition the authorization to declare, if necessary, that we do not intend to depart from the 3 tempo.[72]

By the end of May 1907 the details of the *Novelle* had been agreed with the Chancellor, Prince Bülow,[73] and the *Reichsmarineamt* began the delicate process of lobbying the Radicals without losing the Centre. In July, Captain Dähnhardt of the Naval Office had a secret meeting with Dr Ernst Müller, whom Dähnhardt called 'the recognized leader of the young Radicals'. Müller was, Dähnhardt continued, 'thoroughly sympathetic to the bill but ...also a raving, almost fanatical foe of the Centre...He would be willing to make great sacrifices to prevent the Centre from getting back its old dominant position'.[74] Dr Peter Spahn, Deputy from Cologne and leader of the Centre, was next on Dähnhardt's list, and the *Reichsmarineamt*, against Capelle's protests, who thought it 'most unwise', treated Spahn to a gala cruise at the navy's expense.[75] Bülow used his extensive contacts to lobby prominent politicians on behalf of the *Novelle* and made suggestions for further approaches to radicals who were 'socially susceptible to flattering attentions'.[76]

Tirpitz began to find himself in an uncomfortable position. The real reason for the *Novelle* could not be revealed: the creation of an *Aeternat*, a self-replacing fleet beyond parliamentary interference. A *Novelle* just to change the active life of ships looked indeed 'meagre and small', given the political situation, but also illogical, especially since, if it were passed, the entire *Siegfried* class would be made obsolete at a stroke and eight replacement battleships could in theory be started in 1909 and 1910.[77] The international consequences might be serious. On 11 August, Spahn delivered a major speech in Rheinbach and demanded both an additional 40 million marks for the naval estimates and the construction of 20,000 ton warships.[78] Tirpitz was much relieved by Spahn's gesture. As he explained to the Chancellor a few days later:

the most knowledgeable and hence most dangerous analysts of the true significance of the Navy Law sit in the Centre Party. At the moment, most politicians and politicizers do not fully understand it. I have framed the *Novelle* as your Highness wished it, so that internationally and domestically it looks as small and harmless as possible... The final figures which we cannot entirely conceal speak, alas, their own language.[79]

Tirpitz knew that he had to placate the Centre, even at the risk, as Capelle warned, of again being 'branded as the Centre's man'.[80] He also knew that a financial crisis of the first order was now ahead. The 1907 budget had been delayed several months by the elections and covered in the end only by drawing on the contributions (*Matrikularbeiträge*) of the Federal states to the sum of 82 million marks, of which 63 was left uncollected.[81] Early in August, Capelle had written to say that the 1908 budget was likely to be worse and only to be balanced, assuming that no reforms or new taxes were enacted, by more fiscal juggling.[82] A demand for new taxes would in turn certainly split the *Bloc*. The political situation had become unusually delicate, since the Centre Party could simply not be ignored. Its leaders were making friendly speeches and demanding large sums for the navy, because, Capelle believed, they were 'afraid of being pushed back into anti-national isolation'.[83] In the summer of 1907 Bülow sounded the leaders of the *Bloc* about possible new taxes, and in September the Treasury's assessment of the probable deficit for fiscal 1908 surpassed by 60 million marks the most pessimistic projections of the previous May. Tirpitz faced a situation which looked favourable for the moment, i.e. the competition in naval enthusiasm between Centre and Radicals, but which was bound to end if he asked too little and waited too long. On 18 September he decided to act. He sent a cable to Bülow at his summer home in Norderney to say that 'an urgent matter' made it vital for him to see him at once.[84] According to his note for the meeting, he told Bülow that he had to see him before the annual audience of the Kaiser on the coming year's programme at Rominten, because 'several considerations are different'. He reviewed the naval agitation within Germany, the party situation, the newspaper comments, the results of the trips taken by his naval emissaries and then the foreign situation. His notes continue:

Foreign political situation now not dangerous. Acceleration, therefore, to use the military and political advantage of the moment. This possible through an apparently small alteration which must be presented as purely technical-legal, that is, 4 capital ships.[85]

This small alteration became the *Novelle* of 1908. The entire text of the *Novelle*, or, to give the bill its full name, 'A law to amend Paragraph 2 of the Law concerning the German Fleet of 14 June 1900' amounted to the following paragraph:

With the exception of ships destroyed, battleships and cruisers shall be replaced after 20 years. Active life extends from the year of appropriation of the first instalment on the ship to be replaced to the appropriation of the first instalment of the replacement ship. For the period 1908–1917, construction of replacement ships will follow the plan in 'Appendix B'.[86]

This apparently insignificant piece of legislation in reality meant a sharp escalation of the Anglo-German arms race, undoing in 60 words the entire improvement in relations since 1906. The *Novelle* was a genuine 'acceleration' in every sense of the word and a sharp break with Tirpitz's practice in the preceding ten years. In March of 1907 he had told the Kaiser that an annual building rate of 3 capital ships per year would be adequate. In September he jumped to 4. The difference was partly the expression of improved Anglo-German relations and partly the result of Tirpitz's domestic difficulties. The alteration in the active service of battleships from 25 to 20 years would have occurred in either version of the *Novelle*. Both made the eight armoured coastal defence vessels of the *Siegfried* class obsolete by a stroke of the pen. These 4,000 ton vessels had been approved by the *Reichstag* in 1888 and 1889, and by an adroit calculation, for which he now earned the dividend, had been included by Tirpitz in the 1898 *Flottengesetz*, as battleships. They could, therefore, be replaced by battleships, in fact by Dreadnoughts of the *Ostfriesland* class. This second generation of German Dreadnoughts, planned for the 1908 estimates, were to have 12-inch guns and 22,800 tons displacement. The *Siegfrieds* had been appropriated in lots of two and six, so that in theory Germany could build four Dreadnoughts in 1908–9 (two new and two replacements for the *Siegfrieds*) plus a battle cruiser, and eight in 1909–10 (two new plus six replacements for the *Siegfrieds*), and a battle-cruiser. The German shipbuilding industry simply could not have coped with such a feast, and the plan which Tirpitz subsequently presented to the Kaiser involved building an additional Dreadnought for each of the four years from 1908/9, the famous '4 tempo'. As he explained to the Kaiser, according to his notes,

1 Political situation compared to the Spring much more favourable. No danger in foreign affairs as opposed to two years ago. Domestically chances for the bill good.
2 Hence propose to go further than hitherto suggested to Your Majesty. Reich Chancellor agrees.
3 Going forward consists of moving up to 4 tempo for four years in the first instance...
4 In 6 years a double squadron...possibility of topping up in 1913 made easier. Navy Law not endangered because no complete gap created.[87]

This sharp, sudden escalation was a gamble, and Tirpitz knew it. By nature, he preferred steady, unspectacular advance to the brilliant dash forward, but he could not let the unique constellation of elements disperse. He thought he had to move quickly and he very nearly got away with it.[88] The *Novelle* was published on 19 November 1907, very much overshadowed by the news of the

Kaiser's visit to Windsor, which came to a successful end on the same day. The bill moved easily through the *Reichstag*, where very few deputies understood its significance. Tirpitz in a speech from the *Bundesrath* table called the *Novelle* 'a purely technical rather than a military or political matter'.[89] It passed without a roll call on 27 March 1908.

In the autumn of 1907 another chain of circumstances began, which had a direct, if unforeseen, impact on Anglo-German relations. The prolonged boom in trade which marked the years 1904 to 1907 faltered. At the beginning of August 1907 the United States Steel Corporation announced a 25 % contraction of the demand for steel and prices for metals dropped sharply, giving rise in American business circles to 'rumours and rumours and rumours'.[90] On 22 October 1907 the Knickerbocker Trust Company collapsed, followed by Westinghouse Electric on the following day. A stock exchange panic hit Wall Street and a wave of bank failures swept across the U.S.A.[91] During the previous hectic expansion, Wall Street had borrowed heavily in London against securities, and nearly £5,000,000 of gold had been shipped to America in the month of September 1906 alone.[92] When the panic's shock waves hit Europe, German banking, heavily committed to industrial investment, began to totter. Even before 22 October, a famous old firm in Hamburg, Haller Soehle and Co., had closed its doors, and a sudden liquidity crisis forced bank rates to shoot up all over Europe. Early in November the Bank of England took the 'extraordinary step' of jumping to 7 % Bank Rate, which the *Reichsbank* soon topped by going to 7½ %.[93] The impact of the financial panic on domestic industry in both Germany and Britain was sharp and immediate; as Arthur Gwinner of the Deutsche Bank put it, 'it was the worst crisis in peacetime the world had ever seen'.[94] The industrial production index in Britain shows that production fell from 81.6 in 1907 to 77.1 in 1908, while imports dropped from £646,000,000 in 1907 to £593,000,000 in the following year and exports declined from £426,000,000 to £377,000,000.[95] In Germany pig-iron production fell from 13.05 million tons to 11.8, and general activity declined more sharply than in any other business cycle before 1914.[96] By November 1908 industrial production in Germany was 16.3 % below the level of November 1907.[97]

In both countries the measures to counter the liquidity crisis were unusually effective. The Bank of England attracted gold from twenty-four countries during the 1907–8 panic and was able to reduce its rate by nearly 2 % in the month of January 1908.[98] The British trade recession which ensued was less severe than the German, but shipbuilding in both countries was hard hit. The number of steamships completed in German dockyards fell from 435 in 1907 to 305 in 1908, a drop in total tonnage of more than one third.[99]

In both countries the depression of 1907–8 was a rude shock. Shipbuilders and industrialists, trade unionists and financiers, put pressure on governments to assist by placing orders in those industrial areas hardest hit by the recession. In Britain the recession weakened the anti-armaments bloc within the Liberal

Party and during the 1909 crisis over armaments, even Labour found its phalanx crumbling, as MPs from shipbuilding constituencies voted with the Government for larger naval estimates.[100] In Germany the shipbuilders tried to influence the *Reichsmarineamt*, and in this were largely successful. Tirpitz, who had a strongly developed commercial sense, knew that the private ship-building industry played a vital role in his naval programme. Not the least of his reasons for wanting the naval orders to be steady was his concern for the employment, investment and profitability of these firms.

At the same time, he had the good liberal's fear of trusts. There were only six major dockyards in Germany, and only one major producer of armour-plating, the perfect situation for a price ring or *Kartell*.[101] He always tried hard to keep his distance from the great entrepreneurs[102] and suffered from what he called a '*cauchemar der Werftkoalitionen*', the nightmare that one day he would face a solid front of shipbuilders offering him fixed prices. In order to prevent ganging-up, Tirpitz always spread shipbuilding orders evenly between the Imperial dockyards and the private sector. The acceleration to a building rate of four capital ships a year posed new problems. The state enterprises could only handle one large vessel at a time, and construction occupied the facilities for two years. This meant that three large capital ships a year must go to the private sector, and the shipyard owners knew it. The 1908 vessels were no problem. Tirpitz put out one of the battleships to the Imperial dockyard at Wilhelmshaven. The battle cruiser went to Blohm and Voess in Hamburg who were expected to specialize in this type and thus keep costs down. The other two contracts for Dreadnoughts went to the two lowest tenders, Howaldtswerke in Kiel and Weser AG in Bremen.[103] The distribution of orders was more remarkable than it sounds, for Howaldt and Weser were notoriously unstable enterprises. Neither had paid a dividend for years and Howaldt had never before been trusted to tender for a large capital ship.[104] Tirpitz had now run out of stratagems. Two of the 1909 battleships would have to be put out to tender among the three big private shipbuilding concerns. With three companies bidding for two contracts, the conditions for a price ring were ideal.

In the meantime the trade depression in Germany deepened. In June 1908 the managing director of Schichau of Danzig begged the *Reichsmarineamt* for a contract on a 1909 battleship, even though the estimates for 1909 would not go before the *Reichstag* until the following year. If the request were refused, the managing director painted a dark picture of mass unemployment in Danzig and the permanent loss of skilled, irreplaceable craftsmen and fitters. The future of the navy as well as of the port would be jeopardized. Tirpitz knew that he could squeeze a low bid from Schichau and agreed to place one of the 1909 battleships, the future *Oldenburg*, with the company, subject to eventual approval by the *Reichstag* and at the company's risk. The completion date, Spring 1912, remained what it would have been under normal circum-stances for 1909 contracts.[105]

In October of 1908 the new British naval attaché in Berlin, Captain H. L. Heath, got wind of the arrangements and reported to the Admiralty that the Germans were accelerating their building programme.[106] By January of 1909, the Sea Lords had convinced themselves that this must be so and calculated that by the Spring of 1912 the German fleet would have seventeen Dreadnoughts as 'a practical certainty'.[107] In fact Germany had eleven by that date, including the *Blücher* which was a battle cruiser only by courtesy. While the British were accusing Tirpitz of building in secret too rapidly, the Kaiser was accusing him of building too slowly, and in 1910 the *Reichsmarineamt* had to defend itself by providing the Kaiser with exact figures on every Dreadnought.[108] Tirpitz denied the British accusations in the *Reichstag*, but his word was not accepted. In March of 1909 he called Captain Heath to the *Leipzigerplatz*, the site of the *Reichsmarineamt*, to discuss the matter privately:

ATTACHÉ: But in the newspapers in October of the previous year it was stated that the contracts for the 1909 ships had already been completed.
STATE SECRETARY: That was false! In any case it concerned two ships at the most. I did it for business reasons and business reasons alone. If I had waited until the 1st of April, I should have had all four dockyards against me and would have had to pay what they asked...The building period begins from the 1st of April, that is, from the day on which the Reichstag approves the money. The contract is for three years building time. It is, therefore, nonsense to say that we shall have 17 ships in 1912. Any even moderately close acquaintance with our affairs must lead to that conclusion. That Mr McKenna refuses to believe our repeated explanations has angered me as a naval officer...and I must say to you as one naval officer to another how deeply offended I am.[109]

The 'acceleration panic' was a red herring. In their sudden discovery of secret building the Sea Lords ignored the public acceleration involved in the *Novelle* itself. Tirpitz's anger, though perfectly genuine, has a certain ironic timbre. His account of the *Oldenburg* fits the evidence, although it is more dramatic than accurate. He could not have faced all four private shipyards on 1 April 1909, as he claimed. Howaldt and Weser were fully engaged until 1910 and hence could not have bid for 1909 vessels. Blohm and Voess bid for battle cruisers only, and he still had a berth at the Imperial dockyard in Kiel, where the future *Kaiser* of the 1909 estimates was eventually constructed. Had he not offered Schichau an advance contract, he would at worst have faced three private concerns bidding for two contracts. On the other hand, Tirpitz was right when he denied that there had been 'secret' acceleration in McKenna's sense of the term. The offending warship, S.M.S. *Oldenburg*, completed her trials and joined the High Seas Fleet no earlier than the others of her class, the contracts for which had been placed in the ordinary way. An unfortunate combination of commercial caution and the trade cycle led to the advanced placement of one contract, and hysteria did the rest.

In a broader sense, the 'acceleration panic' reflected the emergence of trends now very familiar. By developing the *Dreadnought*, Sir John Fisher thought that Britain had won the arms race. The opposite was true. He had devalued all other British warships or, more accurately, naval experts began to believe that he had done so. Britain and Germany seemed to be in a brand-new competition. The experts reached for their pencils and began to count number of Dreadnoughts afloat or building. Politicians seized these figures and reduced them to the currency of campaign slogans. An obsession grew in both Britain and Germany that naval power could be measured by simple arithmetic. The *Dreadnought*, grandparent of all subsequent superweapons, generated an illusion about security in amounts of 'hardware', a sinister feature of modern, technologically based, arms races. In reality power cannot be so measured. When the World War broke out in August 1914, Germany had 13 Dreadnoughts and 4 battle cruisers to 22 and 9 in the Royal Navy, but nobody on either side had any idea whether that margin was too great or too small. The very absurdity of the question suggests that sea power, as all other forms of military power, rests on many considerations: geography, strategy, tactics, will, related technologies and so on. It is arguable that the modern arms race owes its viciousness at least as much to the character of mass politics as it does to technology. As the issues of modern government become more technical, politicians work harder to simplify, the press to publicize, the bureaucrats to control, developments which are less and less susceptible to such handling. Fisher's Dreadnoughts had weaknesses and Tirpitz's virtues which had nothing to do with the size of their guns, but only experts ever suspected it. Numbers became the game and even men who instinctively knew better played it.

After 1907 this game became obsessive and men did their Dreadnought sums more frequently. German warships took 36 months to build from appropriation to launching. The Navy Laws were public documents. It was easy to figure that by 1911 the Imperial Navy must have in commission at least six Dreadnoughts (*Nassau, Westfalen, Rheinland, Posen, Helgoland* and *Ostfriesland*) and two battle cruisers (*Von der Tann* and *Moltke*). The 'Cawdor Programme', as amended by the Liberal Government, meant that in all probability the Royal Navy would have no more than eight Dreadnoughts and three or four battle cruisers. Such calculations were complicated both by the fact that British estimates were set annually and also by the assumption that Germany would not follow the British example as rapidly and efficiently as she did. Defending himself against Conservative criticism, Edmund Robertson, Parliamentary Secretary at the Admiralty, told the House of Commons on 5 March 1907 'I am here on the part of the Admiralty to say that, in their opinion, the Two-Power standard will be adequately maintained with the programme of shipbuilding which we are bringing forward today.' He went on to argue that in the Spring of 1909 Great Britain would have completed four Dreadnoughts and three battle cruisers of the 'Invincible' type, while Germany would have nothing at sea equal to them.[110] While this statement was strictly correct, it was misleading. The *Nassau* class, although approved in April of 1906, had been delayed at the planning stage for nine months, from 4 October 1905, when pre-Dreadnought sketches had been completed, to July 1906, when the modified plans were approved. Contracts for the *Nassau* and *Westfalen* had been awarded on 31 May 1906 and 31 October 1906.[111] Both warships were completed in the autumn of 1909 and in commission by early 1910. The British monopoly would last for less than a year. The gap between the two fleets would then narrow steadily.

These considerations reinforced the treadmill of the modern arms race, embittered relations between the two powers and provided a sort of counterpoint to the endeavours of diplomats to master them. Six decades and succeeding disasters have not made Anglo-German relations before 1914 any easier to understand. As long as the German leaders clung to a massive, relentless building programme, the British would feel threatened, and hence would increase their own programme. As long as the Germans believed that the British intended to isolate and then crush them, they would insist on building at any cost. Yet the Germans were not entirely honest in protesting that their programme had no anti-English bias. Tirpitz from his first day in office had built his fleet 'against England', not as a means to war but as a diplomatic lever, by which to compel the British to be more forthcoming in international bargaining. He had taken the first genuine improvement in Anglo-German relations for several years as the opportunity to 'accelerate' the Navy Laws. In short, the laws were fixed when the talk was of arms limitation but flexible when increases were required. German diplomacy became tied to the policy of a defence establishment rather than tying defence to the conditions of diplomacy. What ought to have been the means had become the end.

The rest of this section will examine the part played by diplomats and statesmen in these events, that is, the area of effective action open to the men of that time. It will ask the question: could British statesmen have done better than they did in dealing with the German problem? The answers will vary not only with the opinions of the historians but also with the period discussed, since British diplomacy may be thought to have been more effective at some times than at others. Yet the biggest question of all, the one that men at the time and historians after them have worried and prodded incessantly, cannot really be answered: was there a chance of a genuine settlement on the German side? Was the Prusso-German military state capable of de-escalation? Was the social order there so threatened by the rise of new masses and classes that it could only survive by exporting its tensions?[112] Or were German military men increasingly able to dominate the administrative machine to the exclusion of civilian considerations?[113] Or was it miscalculation or governmental incompetence which made Germany's international behaviour erratic and incomprehensible? Or, most plausibly of all, was it a combination of these and many other complex historical developments which explain German intransigence and truculence, aggression and anxiety, febrile diplomacy and menacing aspect?[114] Whatever answer the subsequent chapters may offer to some or all of these questions, the reader must always bear the melancholy possibility in mind that there was no fulfilment to Germany's aspiration short of war. Just before the First World War, and in many subtle ways wonderfully representative of that era, Friedrich Meinecke published a memorable book, *Radowitz und die deutsche Revolution*. In more than 500 pages Meinecke examines one of the nineteenth century's more interesting failures, Joseph Maria von Radowitz, friend and adviser to Frederick William IV and the man who tried to unify Germany 'from above' by a free association of the German princes. He failed at Olmütz in 1850 and left the job to Bismarck to do in 'blood and iron'. Yet for Meinecke, Radowitz failed in an attempt that had to be made:

So war die Niederlage, die er erlitt, von vornherein wohl sicher, und wir wissen, dass er mit der Ahnung der Niederlage in den Kampf ging. Aber es gibt Kämpfe in der Geschichte, welche unausweichlich gekämpft werden müssen, auch wenn die Niederlage vor Augen steht.[115]

(So the defeat he suffered was probably certain from the beginning, and we know that he went into the struggle with a premonition of defeat. Yet there are battles in history which have to be fought out quite unavoidably even if defeat stares you in the eye.)

Was Meinecke right that there are battles that must be inevitably fought out even if defeat is certain? For the purposes of this volume it may be enough if the reader remembers that a great many Germans in 1913 thought so. That itself would be enough to set limits to the achievements of British diplomacy in its relations with the German Empire.

11

Great Britain and Germany, 1905–1911

D. W. SWEET

In the important speech on foreign affairs which he made in the City a few weeks before taking office as foreign secretary, Grey included among the foreign-policy objectives of the incoming Liberal administration an improvement in relations not only with Russia, but also with Germany: so long as such an improvement was not exploited 'in any way to impair our existing good relations with France'.[1] This speech was carefully calculated to reassure those in Britain (and in Europe) who feared that the Liberals would abandon the connection with France, while at the same time encouraging those who hoped for a better understanding with Germany. But there is good reason for thinking that Grey was genuinely, if cautiously, favourable to the policy of improved relations with Germany, and certainly he was well aware of the advantages which would follow in domestic politics if an understanding could be achieved which would allow the government to reduce the burden of expenditure on naval armaments. The Liberal programme contained the customary commitment to retrenchment in military and naval expenditure, and this commitment acquired increasing urgency as the cabinet faced the growing problem of financing its large programme of social reform without excessive increases in taxation. Although he was less sanguine about its prospects than Campbell-Bannerman, the prime minister, Grey accepted the case for an internationally agreed limitation of naval armaments, and recognised that the assent of the German government was essential to any agreement.

In the circumstances of the unresolved Moroccan crisis in which the new government took office, however, it seemed to Grey more important for the moment that it should emphasise its attachment to France than that it should seek to conciliate Germany; and the suspicion that the Germans had precipitated the crisis in a deliberate attempt to break up the developing Anglo-French *entente* continued thereafter to sour his attitude towards them.[2] Compelled by events to contemplate the possibility of British involvement in a continental war, he made a point (as his predecessor Lord Lansdowne had done) of warning the German ambassador, Count Metternich, that Britain would not stand aside if Germany were to force a war upon France.[3] On the other hand, he tried to prepare the ground for a subsequent improvement in Anglo-

German relations by promising Metternich that, if the German government pursued a conciliatory policy at the Algeciras Conference, there would be an immediate response from Britain; and privately he was willing (as Lansdowne had not been) to allow Germany a port on the Atlantic coast of Morocco, if that would promote a peaceful solution to the crisis.[4] He was even able to persuade the Admiralty that such a concession would not be fatal to Britain's strategic interests, and only abandoned the idea when it became clear that the French were not merely opposed to it, but regarded it as evidence that British support could not be relied upon.[5] Forced by French intransigence at Algeciras to choose between a policy of unqualified support for the French position, and a policy of conciliation towards Germany, he opted for the French, even when he thought their demands unreasonable.[6] As a result, the German government was deprived of the consolation even of the Austrian compromise proposal (which the British privately favoured), and was obliged to acquiesce in a French diplomatic victory, rather than allow the Conference to break down.

With the successful conclusion of the Algeciras Conference on 7 April 1906, the way was clear for the improvement in Anglo-German relations which Grey had promised Metternich, and which his colleagues wished him to promote. During May and June, the more radical of them sedulously patronised a series of public demonstrations of Anglo-German friendship. Haldane, who as secretary for war had been responsible with Grey for authorising the Anglo-French military conversations, was also the most effective exponent of the pro-German policy in the cabinet, and he made strenuous efforts to convince the German embassy of British goodwill.[7] In August the King, attended by the permanent under-secretary at the Foreign Office, Sir Charles Hardinge, met the Kaiser at Cronberg. The meeting was cordial, but Hardinge was at pains to emphasise the official view of Anglo-German relations, which Grey had already put to Metternich, and which was markedly more temperate than the enthusiasm of Haldane and the radicals: that relations had indeed improved, and were now 'normal'; that there was nothing in the Anglo-French *entente*, nor in Grey's negotiations with Russia about Persia and central Asia, which need disturb them; and that there was no reason why they should not continue to improve alongside Britain's other relationships.[8] Hardinge left Cronberg with the impression that the Germans now recognised that 'friendly relations with us cannot be at the expense of our *entente* with France'.[9] But it was precisely because they were known to be exploiting these demonstrations of cordiality to convince the French that an Anglo-German *entente* inconsistent with the Anglo-French *entente* was being established, that Grey remained cool towards them.[10] For the same reason, he was anxious that Haldane's attendance at the German military celebrations on 1 September would impose too great a strain on French confidence, and did what he could to minimise its significance.[11] It is clear that he was sceptical about German motives in seeking a closer understanding, and reluctant to enter into it, unless indeed it led to some real progress in the naval question.

During 1906 there were strong pressures within the cabinet for a reduction in the Cawdor programme of naval construction, which required that four capital ships be laid down in 1907–8. Asquith, the chancellor of the exchequer, proposed to reduce this to two, and was supported by the radicals, who on this issue commanded a majority in the cabinet. The Russian government's proposal for a second Peace Conference at the Hague provided the opportunity both for a compromise (which was suggested by Haldane), and for raising the question of a limitation of armaments with the other powers: the cabinet was able to agree to reduce its programme for 1907–8 to three capital ships, of which moreover one was to be held in suspense, and proceeded with only if the Conference failed to secure a naval agreement; and it was then able to present this compromise to the other governments as an earnest of its desire for a general reduction in naval construction.[12] Grey recognised that the success of the British initiative depended above all on a favourable German response, and he was inclined to regard the issue as a useful test of the sincerity of the German government's desire for better Anglo-German relations.[13] Thus from the outset he adopted the position that a naval agreement was the *sine qua non* of any improvement in those relations, and that any *rapprochement* would be hollow and meaningless if it did not produce a reduction in the burden of naval expenditure. British approaches to Germany on the question were, however, met with an indifference which soon became open hostility, because it was assumed that they were merely a cover behind which Britain's naval supremacy could be maintained without effort.[14] Campbell-Bannerman and Grey persisted into the spring of 1907 in their efforts to promote an agreement, and it was not until 30 April that their hopes were finally extinguished by Bülow's formal declaration in the Reichstag, which ruled out any prospect of Germany participating in discussions about the limitation of naval armaments at the Hague.[15] The failure of the Peace Conference to make any progress in the question was therefore entirely predictable: on 17 August 1907 it adopted unanimously a vacuous declaration that it was 'hautement désirable' that the subject should receive further 'étude sérieuse'.[16] The Liberals then had no alternative but to proceed with the third Dreadnought of the 1907 programme, and thus ended their first attempt to achieve a naval understanding with Germany.

These discussions were the context in which Eyre Crowe's 'Memorandum on the Present State of British Relations with France and Germany' (1 January 1907) was received by the government. This cogently argued paper was to become the classic exposition of the views of the anti-German group within the Foreign Office, but at the time it had a more limited purpose, to issue a warning against the temptations of an ill-considered and unequal agreement with Germany.[17] Grey attached to it a minute cautiously commending its contents to the attention of his colleagues, and circulated it to Campbell-Bannerman, Ripon, Asquith, Morley and Haldane: without exaggerating the significance of Crowe's memorandum, it may be inferred from Grey's decision to circulate it that he wished to communicate some of its reservations about Germany to those members of the cabinet most closely in touch with foreign affairs (and it may be added that the memorandum written by Lord Sanderson in an attempt to modify some of its implications was *not* similarly circulated). Nevertheless, Grey's view of the German question remained more flexible than that of Crowe, and he remained fully aware of the advantages which a limited agreement with Germany, which did not undermine the *entente* with France, might produce. During 1907 the British government continued to make gestures of good-will towards Germany, for instance by assisting in the suppression of a native rebellion led by Morenga in German South-West Africa.[18] This episode, and the exchange of royal, official and unofficial visits and courtesies during the summer, helped to create an apparent climate of public *détente*, although the underlying realities of the naval competition and Germany's ambitious diplomacy continued to exercise the more sceptical minds in the Foreign Office.[19] There were also apprehensions that German policy towards France in Morocco, which was on the surface most conciliatory, was designed to draw France into an *entente* with Germany, and Grey observed that the attempt to separate France from Britain in this manner was 'the one and only barrier which prevents Germany from being on satisfactory terms with both of us'.[20] There was, then, always a residual anxiety that any movement towards a *rapprochement* with Germany would be misrepresented and used by the Germans to accomplish by insinuation what they had failed to accomplish by menace in the Moroccan crisis, the rupture of the Anglo-French *entente*.

This anxiety explains the extraordinary sensitivity shown by Grey and Hardinge over the proposed visit by the band of the Coldstream Guards to Mainz. In September Grey declined to sanction the band's excursion, on the ground that enough Anglo-German courtesies had already taken place that year, and that the Army Council had refused a similar request for a military band to visit France in June.[21] When the question was re-opened at the beginning of October between the German embassy, the War Office and Edward VII, without the Foreign Office being informed until permission had already been given, Hardinge and Grey reacted with such force that, reluctantly, Haldane and the King had to concede the point; the latter remarking (with some justice) that the Anglo-French *entente* must indeed be a fragile connection if it could be ruptured 'on such a trumpery point'.[22] But quite apart from the intrinsic merits of the case, Hardinge and Grey reacted so violently because they had been kept in ignorance of an arrangement which had political implications, and which they had already vetoed.[23] When Grey insisted that, unless such communications went through the Foreign Office, he could not be 'responsible for foreign policy', he was not so much threatening resignation as asserting the rights of his office.[24] The fact remains that his initial refusal was based upon the assumption that too much Anglo-German cordiality would make the French nervous about Britain's commitment to the *entente*.

A similar assumption underlay his handling of the Kaiser's visit to Windsor, which was planned for November 1907. Such a visit was overdue, and had in fact been postponed in 1906 because of the Moroccan crisis. In the summer of 1907 Grey and Hardinge were optimistic that it could be useful in improving Anglo-German relations without disturbing the understanding with France.[25] But they were determined that it should not be turned into a political demonstration, as was the habit of the Kaiser, or given undue importance by the presence of a major political figure such as Bülow.[26] Although they failed to dissuade the German government from sending two ministers with the Kaiser, they did at least succeed in preventing Bülow from coming; this was accomplished by a blunt conversation between Hardinge and Metternich.[27] On the other hand, when the Kaiser, suffering from nervous prostration as a result of the Eulenburg scandal, announced that he was unable to carry out the visit, the British cordially exerted themselves to stiffen his resolve, lest its cancellation be ascribed to 'evil causes'.[28] For, although Grey was anxious that the visit should not assume undue political significance, he was equally anxious that an accidental cancellation should not itself become a matter of political significance, and disturb the appearance of normality in Anglo-German relations which he wished to maintain.

In a climate of such nervousness, only a German concession on some major issue could effect any real improvement in Anglo-German relations. The attitude of the Germans before and during the Hague Conference had demonstrated emphatically that their naval programme was not negotiable, an emphasis which was further underlined by the publication in Berlin on 18 November, the very day the Windsor visit formally ended, of an amended and extended Navy Law. The only alternative subject of sufficient importance was the Bagdad railway, and it was in fact this which the Kaiser chose for his initiative: a choice which the British government had anticipated, and prepared its position accordingly.[29] The Bagdad railway was to be the backbone of a future German domination of Asiatic Turkey; from the British point of view, it was the chief instrument of a developing challenge to Britain's commercial and strategic position at the head of the Persian Gulf. The British government, taking the view that the railway would be constructed eventually with or without British assistance, was chiefly concerned to secure British participation on the terms most favourable to its own interests; it also wished to concert its policy with the French (who for financial and commercial reasons wished to participate) and with the Russians (who, fearing the intrusion of Turkish and German influence towards the Caucasus and northern Persia, did not). When he took office, Grey was prepared to promote the participation of all three in a railway all sections of which should be under full international control.[30] But during the spring of 1907, under departmental pressure, this position was reversed, and at the end of May the cabinet decided that Britain should stipulate for control of the southern section 'from a point north of Bagdad to the Persian Gulf'.[31] Since this stipulation was not acceptable to the French or the Russians, it was not possible to achieve an agreed negotiating position in time for the Windsor visit, but the British were quite ready to insist that the interests of France and Russia should be safeguarded in any negotiations.[32] As for Britain's control of the likely terminus of the railway at the head of the Persian Gulf, that was to some extent safeguarded by her treaty relations with the Sheikh of Koweit.[33] So the British could afford to wait for the Germans to make proposals.

After a fruitless conversation with Grey at Windsor on 12 November, the Kaiser turned to Haldane, who was recognised by the Germans as a Germanophil, and who, after his experiences of the previous year, saw the reconciliation of Britain and Germany as his personal mission.[34] Haldane explained that what Britain required was a 'gate' to protect the strategic out-works of the Indian defence system from troop movements down the Bagdad railway; the same point was put by Morley, the secretary-of-state for India, in a conversation with Metternich.[35] The Kaiser undertook to concede the gate, thus meeting the principal British condition for participation, and at the same time tacitly inviting the British to abandon the French and the Russians, and settle bilaterally with Germany. Grey therefore insisted that the negotiations could not proceed further *à deux*, but must continue *à quatre* with France and Russia, a position which the British maintained even when von Schoen, the German foreign minister, revealed that he had already had negotiations *à deux* with the Russians about the Bagdad railway. After some hesitation, the Kaiser agreed to negotiations *à quatre*.[36] But the absence of Bülow proved disastrous for Haldane's success with the Kaiser, for Bülow had no intention of conceding the Gulf section to exclusive British control, or of negotiating from a minority position with the three *entente* governments together. On 26 November Metternich indicated that the German government was having second thoughts.[37] Nothing further was heard on the subject of the Bagdad railway until June 1908, when the Germans finally ruled out any prospect of negotiations *à quatre*.[38] Meanwhile the British had begun to pursue alternative schemes, such as an Anglo-Russian railway through Persia, as a means of putting pressure on the Germans to be more accommodating over the Bagdad railway.

Whatever cordiality had been generated by the efforts of the Kaiser and Haldane at Windsor, therefore, proved to be both superficial and ephemeral. Immediately after the visit, the cabinet had to determine Britain's naval programme for 1908–9, in the light of the German supplementary naval bill. The Admiralty's proposals, which Grey was confident would be adequate to meet the immediate situation, were moderate; they included the construction of only one Dreadnought, but even so required an increase in expenditure over the 1907 programme, whereas the cabinet would have liked to make further economies.[39] Consequently, by the end of January 1908 a cabinet crisis had developed, which set the pattern for subsequent controversies over naval expenditure. The dispute was not over the role of the naval competition in

Anglo-German relations, but over the proportion of armaments expenditure in the government's total budget; there was no argument about whether Britain's naval supremacy should or should not be defended, but only about the level of expenditure required to maintain that supremacy, while at the same time releasing revenue for social reform, and satisfying the government's supporters in Parliament.[40] In so far as the controversy affected foreign policy, it did so by increasing the disposition of the radicals in particular, and the cabinet as a whole, in favour of an understanding with Germany which would enable the government to cut expenditure without endangering Britain's naval superiority; Grey sympathised with this disposition, while insisting that a naval understanding would not be possible until the Germans had been convinced of Britain's determination to maintain that superiority. The 'economy' party in the cabinet (notably Lloyd George, Harcourt, McKenna and Burns) at one point went so far as to threaten to resign if the estimates were not reduced, while Tweedmouth and the Board of Admiralty threatened to resign if there were any cuts in the construction programme.[41] Ultimately, a compromise was achieved which avoided resignations, and conceded the substance of the Admiralty's requirements: on 17 February the cabinet approved estimates which pared down the increase over 1907 to less than a million pounds, while leaving the construction programme intact.[42]

This cabinet crisis took place while a major press campaign was being conducted, with the object of forcing the government to embark upon a large naval programme based on comparisons with the German programme.[43] The body of opinion associated with Eyre Crowe was entirely in sympathy with this object, and although there is no evidence to connect members of the Foreign Office with the agitation, it has been made abundantly clear that Fisher, the First Sea Lord, was the source of much of the material which appeared in *The Observer*.[44] The press storm so incensed the Kaiser that he first complained to Lascelles about the British disposition to blame the requirements of the British naval programme upon Germany, and then wrote directly to Tweedmouth to object to a particularly provocative contribution to the agitation, which Lord Esher had published in *The Times*.[45] In reply, the British government insisted that, while every power had the right to determine its own naval programme without interference from abroad, the growth of the German fleet was of necessity an important factor which it must take into account in deciding its own rate of construction. As a conciliatory gesture, however, Grey (who had on 13 February renewed in the House of Commons the offer, first made at the Hague Conference, to exchange information privately about the number of warships to be laid down each year) allowed Tweedmouth to communicate to the Kaiser the British estimates for 1908, before they had been laid before Parliament; thus compounding the Kaiser's constitutional impropriety with one of his own.[46] In the debate on the estimates on 9 March, Asquith announced the government's determination to make whatever provision might be necessary in future years to maintain Britain's lead over

Germany in Dreadnought construction, and he reaffirmed its attachment to the 'two-power standard' as a basis for calculating naval requirements.[47] This was by no means the first occasion on which the Liberals had indicated their acceptance of the policy implied by the two-power standard, but the statement helped to calm the press agitation, and at the same time advanced the policy favoured by Grey and Hardinge, of making a vigorous display of British determination in order to persuade the Germans to moderate their programme.[48]

This policy was pressed a stage further in July, and significantly it was done by Lloyd George, who had become Chancellor of the Exchequer in Asquith's reconstruction of the government at the beginning of April, and who was eager to achieve a relaxation in the naval competition before the estimates for 1909–10 had to be settled. By arrangement with Grey, he twice met Metternich, to impress upon him the importance of finding some arrangement whereby a major increase in the construction programme could be avoided; this need not necessarily be a formal arrangement, for any visible reduction in the German programme, even if undeclared, would enable the British government to justify keeping its own programme to modest proportions. Lloyd George assured Metternich that, in the absence of such an arrangement, he would make whatever financial arrangements were necessary to maintain Britain's superiority.[49] In the Foreign Office, preparations were made to raise the question when the King, with Hardinge in attendance, met the Kaiser at Cronberg in August. The King preferred not to embark upon the sensitive topic of the German naval programme with his touchy nephew, so it was left to Hardinge to do so: his suggestion of a 'friendly discussion' between the two governments was rejected by the Kaiser as being 'contrary to the national dignity', and his alternative proposal of a slackening in the pace of German construction, without a written or even a verbal agreement, did not elicit a favourable reply.[50] Thus the Germans, having at the Hague rejected the idea of a general limitation of naval armaments, had at Cronberg refused bilateral discussions leading to a naval understanding, however informal and unofficial it might be. Grey concluded that the only resort left to the British government was to increase its own programme.[51] And although he and Asquith had to call Lloyd George and Churchill to order for publicly advocating an Anglo-German naval agreement, he was able to carry the cabinet with him in his conviction that, following the Cronberg meeting, further allusions to the question would serve only to embitter Anglo-German relations; and by creating the impression that Britain was trying to dictate to Germany the size of her fleet, would actually make it more difficult for the German government to moderate its programme.[52] Thus all shades of opinion in the cabinet were reconciled to a larger construction programme for the coming year, although how much larger remained to be settled. On 12 November in the House of Commons, Asquith once again insisted upon the government's determination to maintain the two-power standard, which he defined as a preponderance of ten per cent over the combined strength of the next two naval powers.[53] Although a month later Bülow declared that an agreement to limit naval armaments was out of the question, there is clear evidence that he recognised that the British desire for a naval understanding was such that it could be used to promote a more general Anglo-German *entente*.[54] The signs of this change of attitude were interpreted by Hardinge as being a success for the government's 'repeated and categorical statements' on the subject of the two-power standard.[55]

The tension over the naval question inevitably affected Grey's attitude to lesser questions during 1908. On the one hand, for strategic reasons the British felt obliged to resist German attempts to secure a coaling station in the Canary islands, and also to obtain control of Walfisch Bay as a port for South-West Africa.[56] On the other hand, Grey was well aware that the Germans were disposed to regard all such checks as evidence of Britain's rooted hostility towards them, just as they interpreted royal visits such as that paid by Edward VII to the Tsar at Reval in June as confirmation of their fear of encirclement, a fear which was articulated by the Kaiser in his address to a military review at Döberitz.[57] In the past, when he had discouraged the idea of making the French *entente* into a more formal commitment, Grey had argued that it was important not to create even the impression that Germany was being encircled; although he regarded the Kaiser's apprehensions as extravagant, therefore, he also understood them.[58] Recognising that the conclusion of agreements from which they were excluded tended to increase the Germans' sense of isolation, he sought where possible to promote arrangements which included them. So for example, in urging upon the Russian government the advantages of an arrangement *à quatre* about the Bagdad railway, he observed that it would prove to the Germans that 'no ring was being made' against them.[59] Similarly, he pressed his colleagues in the cabinet (as well as the French government) to approve the conclusion of agreements guaranteeing the *status quo* in the Baltic and North Seas:

I am not sure that Germany has any motive except to show that she is not isolated; she may have intended to separate us from France, but if so that is over, for she has now put the North Sea proposal before France... If Germany is set upon appearing before the world arm in arm with us and France, it will not do to affront her by refusing... If we did, Germany would have some pretext for saying that we aimed at her isolation.[60]

The agreements, signed on 23 April 1908, performed a dual function: they neutralised a potentially damaging Russo-German *rapprochement* in the Baltic, and they served to associate Germany in an innocuous arrangement with the three *entente* powers which, it was hoped, would lessen international tension and improve the existing climate of mutual suspicion.[61]

With the same motives, Grey consistently attempted, without compromising his relations with France, to prevent the minor crises which periodically arose in relations with Germany from reaching the point at which the German government might be tempted into a belligerent policy. In December 1907 he urged the French not to press their resentment over the covert Russo-German Baltic agreement too hard, lest they alienate the Russians or bring about a rupture with Germany.[62] At the end of October 1908, when the crisis over the annexation of Bosnia was further exacerbated by a Franco-German dispute over Morocco (concerning German deserters from the French foreign legion at Casablanca), and by a minor storm in Anglo-German relations (following the publication in the *Daily Telegraph* of a characteristically indiscreet interview given by the Kaiser), Grey exerted himself to prevent the situation from becoming too inflamed. While making covert preparations to give the French naval support if necessary, he urged upon them the advantages of a cool response to German threats, and upon the Germans the desirability of submitting the dispute to international arbitration.[63] At the same time, partly to soothe German feelings and promote a peaceful solution to the Casablanca affair, he and Asquith treated the *Daily Telegraph* interview with studied calm; and when it appeared that the storm might be renewed by the publication of a second and even more indiscreet interview with the Kaiser (the Hale interview), the Foreign Office let it be known that Grey would 'strongly deprecate' publication.[64]

In this episode Grey's policy was intended to combine conciliation on inessentials with firmness on essentials, and he was gratified that the French had taken the same line; in particular, he was determined that the Germans should be given no reason for complaining that they were being 'cold-shouldered, isolated, or squeezed', and consequently for attempting some ambitious stroke to restore their position.[65] It was in this spirit that he welcomed the Franco-German agreement of February 1909 about Morocco, which he believed would eliminate one of the persistent obstacles to better Anglo-German relations; though he also warned the French of the importance of maintaining the *entente* in full vigour.[66] He allowed the King's visit to Berlin on 9 February to go ahead as planned, in spite of German support for Austria in the Bosnian crisis, as the best way of demolishing the German belief that the King's foreign excursions were dedicated to the encirclement of Germany.[67] But he would not accompany the royal party himself, although the cabinet insisted that a responsible minister should go, lest his presence should suggest that the visit possessed particular political significance, and imply a 'special co-operation' which would have the unwelcome effect of altering the 'present grouping of the Powers'.[68] All through the Bosnian crisis he would have liked to secure the co-operation of Germany in settling it, and at Berlin Bülow assured Hardinge that he was ready to work with Britain for a peaceful solution; the *communiqué* issued at the end of the visit referred to the two governments' identity of view about the crisis.[69] When the German position was tested by Grey's initiative in the Austro-Serbian dispute, however, it soon became apparent that the German idea was to promote a solution which

would embarrass the British in their relations with the Russians; and indeed
the chief consequence of the *communiqué* was to make Isvolsky uncertain of
Britain's loyalty to Russia.[70] There was no Anglo-German co-operation in
resolving the crisis; on the contrary, the solution imposed by Germany upon
Russia was deeply resented by the British, and regarded by them as a German
victory over the governments of all three *entente* powers: just the kind of brutal
stroke which Grey had hoped to avoid.[71]

Conclusive evidence that Grey's policy towards Germany was not one of
encirclement is provided by his response to the suggestion which was made
from time to time (notably by the French) that efforts should be made to detach
one or other of Germany's partners from the Triple Alliance. He always
rejected the idea summarily, on the ground that the only effect of such an
attempt would be to confirm the worst fears of the Germans, and drive them
to precipitate the general conflict which above all he desired to avoid:

Real isolation of Germany would mean war: so would the domination of
Germany in Europe. There is a fairly wide course between the two extremes
in which European politics should steer. Italy is best left as she is – an ally of
Germany by Treaty, with a strong leaning to friendship with us and France.[72]

In essence his policy was directed towards the maintenance of a balance of
power in Europe, as the mechanism best calculated to deter aggression and
preserve the peace; he was remarkably consistent in the optimistic belief that
this policy could be made to succeed, and consequently was not primarily
concerned with the building of precautionary defences against Germany in
preparation for war. For domestic reasons peculiar to the Liberal party, he
could not openly avow the power-political character of his policy, but in
private conversation with foreign diplomats – including the German ambassador – he could be frank enough about it.[73] In his view the balance of power
depended upon the continuing independence of France, which was primarily
guaranteed by the Franco-Russian alliance, with some reinforcement from
Britain which would be adjusted as circumstances dictated, but which stoppped
short of the obligations of an alliance. It was this preoccupation with the
balance of power which made him so uneasy about German efforts to loosen
the ties between the three *entente* powers either by force or conciliation.
British policy was not committed to the creation of a 'triple *entente*' in any
formal sense, for such a creation would inevitably be viewed by the Germans
as being indistinguishable from an alliance; but the term became increasingly
current during the period of the Bosnian crisis, so current indeed that Grey
instructed British ambassadors to avoid its use in their official correspondence,
lest it should be assumed by the Germans to indicate an arrangement more
definite than in fact existed.[74] One reason why Grey and Hardinge were
unwilling to make their commitment to Russia more formal or binding, even
though they feared that otherwise Russia might be drawn into a German
orientation, was that such an extension would be interpreted as a further stage

in the process of encirclement, and would lead to a general war precipitated by Germany in order to destroy the ring.[75]

All the efforts made on both sides to give Anglo-German relations a less nervous and more normal character were thus unavailing; mutual suspicion still lay close to the surface, and there remained the questions of the German naval programme and the Bagdad railway to stimulate it. The British had at first hoped that the Young Turk revolution of July 1908 would solve the problem of the Bagdad railway for them, and they were quite ready to use their influence with the new *régime* to prevent its completion as an exclusively German undertaking.[76] Early in 1909 it became clear that the Young Turks were not prepared to offend the Germans by making difficulties over the railway, and the British government therefore adopted the policy of putting pressure on the Turks as a means of obliging the Germans to negotiate: it refused to agree to an increase of four per cent in the Turkish customs, for which the Turks applied to the powers in May 1909, unless they could guarantee that the revenues would not be used to finance the Bagdad railway, or until conversations *à quatre* had made progress towards participation by the *entente* powers; and it applied to the Turks for the concession for a railway along the valley of the Tigris from the head of the Persian Gulf to Bagdad, which would in effect pre-empt the construction of the German railway south of Bagdad.[77] When these pressures forced the Turks to ask the Germans to renounce the proceeds of the customs increase as a source of revenue for kilometric guarantees, the British insisted that German assurances on this point should be conveyed to them directly, not through the Turks.[78] This demand was calculated to force the Germans to the realisation that they could not any longer delay an accommodation with Britain, if they wished to proceed with the railway. The proposals which Dr Gwinner of the Deutsche Bank put forward in November 1909 were regarded by the British as a vindication of the policy which they had been pursuing since 1907: the policy of creating for themselves so strong a negotiating position that the Germans would be forced to admit Britain (together with France and Russia) to the project on terms which would safeguard her strategic interests in the Persian Gulf.[79]

In the naval question British policy was fundamentally the same: a determination not to be outstripped in the construction race, coupled with a willingness to negotiate. In the winter of 1908–9 the Admiralty gathered information, which it regarded as conclusive, that the Germans were contriving covertly to accelerate their building programme by placing contracts and accumulating materials and equipment for their battleships in advance of their official starting date.[80] The Admiralty's programme for 1909–10 therefore had to be based upon Germany's ship-building capacity rather than upon her stated programme; it included six Dreadnoughts, with estimates increased by three million pounds over the previous year, and precipitated another cabinet crisis in January and February 1909. Four of the Dreadnoughts were generally agreed to be necessary, and it was only the additional two which were in question, until in February the Admiralty increased its proposal to eight. McKenna, as First Lord of the Admiralty, was now the leading exponent of the navalist arguments; his most vehement critics in cabinet were Churchill, Harcourt, Burns and Morley, while his most consistent supporter was undoubtedly Grey. Lloyd George was prepared for any compromise which would enable him to spread the burden of expenditure over more than one year, and on 24 February the cabinet agreed to a solution whereby the 1909 programme was to consist of only four Dreadnoughts, while the government was to take powers by act of Parliament to lay down a further four in the same year if the progress of German construction showed them to be necessary.[81] Grey took a leading part in reconciling McKenna and the Admiralty to this solution, and it was only assurances from him and Asquith that the cabinet's decision in practice amounted to a commitment to undertake all eight Dreadnoughts which satisfied Fisher.[82] In the debate on the naval estimates in the House of Commons on 16 and 17 March, the government justified its programme by reference to its calculations about the potential as well as the announced rate of German construction, and Asquith silenced radical criticism by explaining that British proposals for an Anglo-German understanding to limit naval expenditure had been rejected.[83] The revelation of the apparently narrow margin of superiority on which the government was relying converted the press campaign which was then in progress into a major naval scare, which was fed by such influential figures as Esher and Fisher so as to force the government to proceed with all eight Dreadnoughts in 1909.[84] In reply to a Conservative motion of censure on the government's inadequate construction programme, Grey gave the most emphatic assurances of its determination to defend Britain's naval superiority.[85] On 26 July McKenna announced that the four contingent Dreadnoughts were to be laid down, without prejudice to the programme for 1910–11, justifying this decision by reference to information recently received (which suddenly made the two-power standard particularly relevant) that the Austrian government was beginning the construction of Dreadnoughts.[86] In this way, the government once again demonstrated that it would go to any lengths necessary to maintain its lead in Dreadnought construction.

The controversy over the suspected acceleration of the German programme not unnaturally irritated German opinion and strained diplomatic relations, but it also led to the first serious suggestions from the German side for a naval understanding; and Grey was always careful to emphasise his readiness to negotiate. From January to March 1909 he conducted a series of interviews with Metternich, in which he tried to elicit a clear statement, which could be used in cabinet and Parliament, of the extent to which the German programme was being anticipated; under pressure, Metternich acknowledged some degree of anticipation, though not as much as the Admiralty suspected. Since they both found themselves ill-equipped to deal with the technical questions involved, Grey seized the opportunity to renew his previous proposal for an exchange of technical information through the naval *attachés*.[87] On 17 March Tirpitz publicly denied Asquith's claim that Germany had rejected proposals for a naval understanding; Grey's desire to refute Tirpitz by publishing the record of his conversations with Metternich was frustrated by the latter's refusal, but on 23 March von Schoen admitted in the Reichstag that the British had indicated their willingness to enter into an understanding.[88] In his speech in the Commons on 29 March on the Conservative motion of censure, Grey reiterated the government's desire for an understanding which would put an end to the naval competition, and explained his proposal for an exchange of information.[89] These indications convinced Bülow that, since the British were so insistent about the naval question, an agreement which enabled them to limit their construction programme would be so attractive that they would be prepared to enter into a far-reaching political understanding to secure it. Between late March and the resignation of Bülow in the middle of July, Kiderlen-Waechter, von Schoen and von Stumm all indicated that the German government was now thinking in terms of a resolution of the naval competition as part of a comprehensive political understanding between Britain and Germany.[90] No definite proposals were made until Bethmann-Hollweg had succeeded Bülow as Chancellor: then, after preliminary soundings conducted through Albert Ballin of the Hamburg–Amerika shipping line and the British financier Sir Ernest Cassel, Bethmann-Hollweg launched a major diplomatic initiative in which he proposed a naval arrangement as part of a 'scheme for a good general understanding'.[91]

This proposal was, in a real sense, the point to which British policy had been seeking to lead Germany since the failure of the Hague Conference in 1907. Having reached it, the British hesitated. Opinion in the Foreign Office (including Hardinge as well as the Eyre Crowe school) believed that the real purpose of German policy was to divide Britain from France and Russia.[92] Even Grey, who had the most pressing political reasons for pursuing a naval understanding, feared that the German advances were 'an invitation to help Germany make a European combination which can be directed against us when it suited her so to use it'.[93] When Grey accepted Bethmann-Hollweg's invitation to negotiate, a new phase was opened in Britain's foreign policy, in which the brief hope of an agreement with Germany was combined with anxiety about its possible repercussions upon the French and Russians. Because of this, Grey was careful to keep them informed about the negotiations; and he sought to include them in any political arrangement which might be concluded, so that there could be no mistaking his commitment to maintaining the *ententes*.[94] On 1 September he explained the Bethmann-Hollweg initiative to the cabinet, which approved a statement of the British position for communication to the Germans:

.... while we must have regard to our existing relations and friendships with other Powers, we should receive with the greatest sympathy any proposition on the part of Germany for an 'understanding' which was not inconsistent with the preservation of those relations and friendships.[95]

Thus the anxiety of Grey and the Foreign Office that the *ententes* should not be imperilled was reconciled with the eagerness of the radicals to take up the German offer.

The German proposals, as outlined in detail by Bethmann-Hollweg and von Schoen on 14 October, were that the British, in return for a naval understanding, should enter into a political arrangement which would give Germany security in Europe, and also eliminate friction in extra-European questions, such as the Bagdad railway. In accordance with his instructions Sir Edward Goschen, the British amabassador in Berlin, pointed out that Britain could not go further in declarations of friendship with Germany than she had with France and Russia, though of course there would be no objection to an exchange of pacific assurances, or a statement that the *ententes* were not directed against Germany. On the key question of the naval concession which Bethmann was offering, Goschen soon elicited the admission that the Germans were not prepared to reduce their programme, and would promise no more than a 'relaxation of the tempo' of construction over the next three years.[96] Grey insisted that a general understanding, far from soothing public opinion in Britain, would only inflame it further unless it were accompanied by a real reduction in naval expenditure. And when on 4 November Bethmann gave a sketch of the political formula he envisaged, it became clear that the gap between the German and British positions was wide indeed: for it included not merely a statement that neither party harboured aggressive designs against the other, but also an undertaking that, if either were at war with a third power or powers, the other would remain neutral.[97] This was in effect the formula which Kiderlen had proposed in March, and on that occasion Grey and Asquith had endorsed a vigorous criticism of it by Hardinge.[98] The restatement of these objections now was all the more decisive, in that the naval concession was so slight:

...no naval agreement can be of any permanent usefulness to restore friendly relations between Germany and England unless it contains some provision for the modification of the present German naval programme. No political agreement between the two Powers would be acceptable on the lines suggested by the German Chancellor, which are so far-reaching as to be likely to disturb the political equilibrium of Europe.[99]

Nothing which the German government subsequently offered was adequate to resolve the incompatibility between the German and British positions; in the middle of April 1910 Grey explained the inadmissibility of the German proposals in language very similar to that of Hardinge:

We cannot enter into a political understanding with Germany which would separate us from Russia and France, and leave us isolated while the rest of Europe would be obliged to look to Germany. No understanding with

Germany would be appreciated here unless it meant an arrest of the increase of naval expenditure.[100]

These formulations may be regarded as definitive for the whole period of Anglo-German negotiations which followed the Bethmann-Hollweg initiative. Less than three months after the brief spurt of optimism which it engendered, Grey had concluded that, unless the Germans changed their position significantly, there would be no naval agreement worth having, while the political formula offered was far too comprehensive and binding to be acceptable; it was therefore with some relief that he felt able to suspend the negotiations on 17 November, on the ground that the questions raised were too grave to be considered by the cabinet until after the elections in January 1910.[101]

Meanwhile, discussions proceeded about the Bagdad railway, the major point of extra-European friction which the Germans wished to include in the general understanding, and which they were prepared to use as a further inducement to persuade the British to agree to the political formula. Gwinner's proposal was that, in return for Britain ending her opposition to the railway and agreeing to the Turkish customs increase, the Gulf section should be handed over to a new company, in which Britain should have a 50 per cent share. Cassel, who conducted the negotiations with Gwinner, was confident that he could be persuaded to agree to rather more favourable terms which would assure Britain absolute control of the Gulf section, and so enable the government to accept the proposed settlement.[102] Grey was not prepared to abandon altogether the condition that France and Russia must also be satisfied, but he was now willing to negotiate *à deux* a preliminary accord of the kind adumbrated by Gwinner and Cassel, postponing the stage of negotiations *à quatre* until the French and Russians had arranged the terms on which they would participate.[103] The German government, however, was not interested in settling the Bagdad railway question except as part of the general understanding which it was pursuing; and it argued that, as it would be making a considerable surrender in admitting Britain to the project, it would have to be paid with some concession in addition to British agreement to the customs increase.[104] To the British, it was now clear that the Bagdad railway, like the German naval programme, was being used as a lever to force them into Bethmann's general understanding.[105] At the end of March 1910 Grey suggested that the question might be settled by an agreement covering Persia as well as the Bagdad railway, a proposal which was designed to serve several purposes. The Germans, who wanted to be in a position to construct branch lines of the railway into Persia, had for some time been applying pressure against the Anglo-Russian hegemony there, and an agreement covering both questions would satisfy them without endangering the stategic interests of Britain and Russia; it could also be represented as the kind of additional concession which the Germans were demanding; and by extending the negotiations to Persia, it would necessarily bring the Russians into them, and oblige the Germans to come to terms with them about the Bagdad railway as well: negotiations *à trois*, if not *à quatre*.[106] Bethmann, however, replied that the Persian question should certainly be included in the general understanding, but that like the Bagdad railway its settlement would only be possible if accompanied by a political formula of the kind he had already outlined.[107]

The British government therefore concluded that an agreement on the Bagdad railway was, for the time being, out of the question, and consequently it reverted to its alternative policy of resisting the customs increase and demanding for itself the concession for the Tigris valley railway.[108] The Germans continued their pressure upon the Anglo–Russian position in Persia, and at Potsdam in November 1910 they succeeded in concluding a bilateral agreement with the Russians (although it was not actually signed until 19 August 1911). Under this agreement the Germans agreed to respect Russia's special position in northern Persia, while the Russians undertook to construct a branch of the Bagdad railway in Persia, from Khanikin to Tehran.[109] The British were angry and disappointed with the Russians for settling with Germany before their own conditions about the Gulf section had been met, and they regarded the Potsdam agreement as a characteristic German manoeuvre to loosen the bonds between the *entente* powers.[110] There was no doubt that their negotiating position was weakened by Germany's success with Russia. Although their pressure on Turkey over the Tigris valley railway forced the Turks to resume negotiations about the construction and control of the Gulf section of the Bagdad railway, the terms which they were offered on 1 March 1911 were less favourable than those proposed by Gwinner, and were not regarded as being acceptable; in any case, it was recognised that no agreement with Turkey could become effective without the approval of Germany.[111]

For all practical purposes, therefore, by April 1910 the negotiations about the Bagdad railway had reached the same state of deadlock as the naval conversations; and although the Anglo-German negotiations continued intermittently until they were interrupted by the second Moroccan crisis in July 1911, no real progress was made. Without the prospect of a naval agreement, the British government continued with the large construction programme advocated by Grey and McKenna, accompanied as always by dissension in the cabinet, criticism in Parliament, and agitation in the press. After the eight of 1909, the estimates for 1910–11 and 1911–12 provided for five Dreadnoughts to be laid down in each year.[112] The radical assault, led in cabinet by Churchill, was turned aside by an agreement between McKenna and Lloyd George that the naval estimates, which by 1911 stood at over forty-four million pounds, should by 1913 show a reduction to forty millions.[113] In July 1910 Asquith explained in the House of Commons that the high level of expenditure was necessary because the German government had declined to reduce its programme as established by law; but he expressed the hope that 'the very top of the wave' had now been reached.[114] On 13 March 1911 Grey also suggested that naval expenditure had reached its peak and would, if the existing German Navy Law were not extended, soon start to decline, and he held out the hope of an agreement which would ensure that Germany did not increase her programme, while a 'frank exchange of information between the two Governments through their Naval *attachés*, would guard against surprise'.[115] This speech, which was regarded by the Germans as something of a surrender to the inexorable pressure of their naval programme, did indeed indicate that British policy had moved somewhat from the position adopted in 1909, that no agreement would be accepted which did not include a reduction in the German programme.[116]

When Metternich attempted on 22 March 1910 to resume the negotiations which had been suspended for the elections, Grey repeated that there was no prospect of an understanding, without the diminution of naval expenditure; and he then diverted attention to his proposals about the Bagdad railway and Persia.[117] Asquith's speech on the naval estimates in July led the German government to revive the question; and at the end of the month the British cabinet, at the instance of Lord Loreburn, decided that Grey (who was evidently reluctant) should resume discussions for an understanding without insisting on an actual reduction of the German programme, and to that end gave unusually close scrutiny to a memorandum which Goschen was to communicate to Bethmann-Hollweg.[118] This memorandum contained the proposition that an Anglo-German understanding might be based upon an agreement that the German programme would not be increased, backed up by an exchange of technical information between the two admiralties. On 12 October the Germans accepted the proposal for the exchange of information, but insisted that they would require a *quid pro quo* for any undertaking about their naval programme, and that only a political formula could meet that requirement.[119] Thus they responded to what was, after all, a softening of the British position with a restatement of their own hard line; and this reply was accompanied by a catalogue of grievances against British policy, which occasioned an unedifying but indicative exchange of recriminations.[120] Grey was once again relieved that he could suspend the negotiations on the major question until the elections of December 1910 were over, but he welcomed Metternich's announcement that the Germans were prepared to continue with the minor question of the exchange of information, without making it dependent upon a political formula.[121] It therefore appeared that the initiative ordered by the cabinet in July had at least promoted an agreement to exchange details of naval construction, which Grey had been advocating for the past three years.

Even this small success proved ultimately to be illusory. When Grey and Goschen tried to pin the Germans down to a precise agreement, it quickly transpired that Tirpitz wished to attach conditions which went far beyond Grey's intentions, and in effect bound each government to abide by the programme it had announced to the other. Grey would not agree to limit his government's freedom to determine its naval programme by reference to the German programme, and would not go further than an undertaking that subsequent variations would be notified in the same way as the original programme. For political reasons, Bethmann-Hollweg accepted this modification on 27 June 1911.[122] In principle, therefore, agreement on the exchange of information appeared to be complete; it was held in suspense during the Agadir crisis and the consequent deterioration in Anglo-German relations, but it was the subject of further discussion at the end of the year. However, it was eventually lost in the disappointment which followed the failure of the Haldane mission of February 1912, and it never came into practical operation.[123]

The larger question of a naval agreement linked to a political understanding was referred to the cabinet committee on foreign affairs which was set up in January 1911 as part of a general reorganisation of the cabinet's conduct of business.[124] Foreign Office opinion was concerned that this committee would be unduly favourable to the German view that the political understanding should take precedence over the naval agreement, and certainly the reply to Bethmann-Hollweg which was approved by the committee, and then scrutinised and amended 'sentence by sentence' in full cabinet, was markedly cordial in tone.[125] The extent of the surrender to the German position should not, however, be exaggerated. There was no explicit statement that the British still required an actual reduction in the German naval programme, but on the other hand no admission that they would be satisfied with less; there was no insistence that the naval agreement should precede the general understanding, but this omission was not as novel as is sometimes suggested; and there remained a clear insistence that the two should at least be concluded simultaneously. Finally, there was a categorical restatement of the importance to Britain of maintaining unimpaired her *ententes* with France and Russia; and Grey did not hesitate to inform them that the negotiations had been resumed, and to tell Bethmann-Hollweg that he had done so.[126] Thus the British position still combined a willingness to negotiate with a continued insistence upon certain minimum requirements. Consequently its terms appeared inadequate to Bethmann, who complained that Grey's idea of a political understanding appeared to be no more than a settlement of the Persian and Bagdad railway questions, in return for which he expected an agreement to reduce naval expenditure. Bethmann replied formally on 9 May that the time when he could offer a reduction in the tempo of naval construction was now past, and that consequently he did not know what the basis of a naval agreement could be, and would have to await Grey's suggestions; as to the general understanding, all agreements would be meaningless if they did not incorporate a formula which excluded 'all possibility of an attack by one party on the other'.[127]

This reply extinguished any prospect of an agreement which would permit a reduction in naval construction; the best that could be hoped for was something which would restrain its further increase. Grey therefore reported to the cabinet that, while there was still room for further negotiations, on the central question of naval expenditure Bethmann-Hollweg's communication was 'of an unsatisfactory and discouraging character'.[128] The British government had to consider whether, in return for such a limited agreement, it was prepared to countenance a political formula which was so extensive and comprehensive that it amounted to a declaration of neutrality, which was what the Germans were still demanding, and if there was one point on which the British position had been consistent throughout the negotiations, it was that nothing must be accepted which would endanger its relations with France and Russia. This was the point which the attempt to reach an understanding between Britain and Germany had reached when the Agadir crisis intervened, and suspended for the time being any further discussion. The question of how far Britain would go towards the neutrality formula desired by the Germans remained unresolved, but the incompatibility between their respective positions was already manifest.

12

Great Britain and Russia, 1907–1914

D. W. SWEET AND R. T. B. LANGHORNE

Whereas for Russia the policy of the Convention would be a success only if it promoted a grand design in Europe, for England it would be a success if it did no more than stabilise Anglo-Russian rivalries in central Asia and Persia; while there would be an additional benefit for British policy if it also steadied the wavering Russian commitment to the Franco-Russian alliance. From the British point of view, therefore, the operation of the Convention in the areas to which it specifically referred, Persia, Afghanistan and Tibet, was of cardinal importance to Anglo-Russian relations in general. With respect to Tibet, the British government carried out punctiliously its undertaking to abstain from intervention in internal Tibetan affairs, and to withdraw its forces from the Chumbi valley which had been occupied since the Younghusband expedition of 1903. Under the terms of the Lhasa Convention of 1904, the evacuation of the Chumbi was dependent upon the conclusion of satisfactory arrangements for trade between India and Tibet, but at the India Office Morley insisted on pressing ahead with the evacuation before the trade regulations were complete, in spite of objections from India; to do otherwise, he argued, would make the Russians suspicious and so 'stultify our Asiatic policy at the beginning'.[1] The withdrawal was complete by the middle of February 1908, and thereafter Morley and Grey consistently rejected Indian proposals for the resumption of the forward policy in Tibet. Thus Benckendorff was able to assure Isvolsky that no-one in London had 'aucune intention d'éluder la convention', and Morley had the satisfaction of overruling what he called the 'Empire of Swagger'.[2] During the negotiation of the Anglo-Russian agreement he had shown himself fully capable of controlling the Viceroy and the government of India, and of insisting that Indian frontier policy must be made to conform to overall imperial policy; and so long as he was at the India Office the government's policy of disengagement in central Asia was safe. Not even the assertion of Chinese sovereignty over Tibet by military force in 1909 and 1910 could induce Grey and Morley to embroil Britain once more with Russia by adopting an interventionist policy in Tibet.[3]

The policy of the Russian government with regard to Afghanistan was equally conciliatory, although it was the Afghan part of the general agreement which Isvolsky had had the greatest difficulty in persuading military and reactionary opinion in Russia to accept.[4] The Afghan convention did not technically come into force until it had been ratified by the Amir, and his assent the British were quite unable to secure, the only response they ever succeeded in eliciting from him on the subject being indefinite but unquestionably hostile to the convention.[5] If the British government had to declare itself unable to obtain the assent of the Amir, the Russian adherents of the forward policy might take the opportunity to engineer a Russian repudiation of the agreement; if on the other hand a punitive expedition was sent to Kabul to coerce the Amir, the whole object for which the agreement had been concluded would be defeated, and the Russians would be able to argue that the *status quo* in Afghanistan had been so altered that the whole question must be re-opened. British frontier expeditions in the spring of 1908 against the hill tribes on the north-west frontier caused the Russian government some uneasiness, in spite of Morley's insistence that they should be kept to minor proportions, and Benckendorff's efforts to reassure Isvolsky about their purpose.[6] In order to dissuade the British from intervening extensively in Afghanistan and so exposing him to criticism in St Petersburg, Isvolsky gave a warning that intervention might 'oblige the Imperial Government to re-open the question', and at the same time he offered 'absolutely to observe the spirit' of the agreement in spite of Britain's failure to secure its ratification by the Amir; when he came to London in October 1908, he and Grey agreed that they would continue to work together in the spirit of the Afghan convention, in spite of the Amir's refusal to give it his unambiguous assent.[7] Isvolsky's conciliatory attitude was the result of his anxiety to secure Grey's consent to the modification of the Straits rule, and the diplomatic support of the British government in the Balkan crisis precipitated by the Austrian annexation of Bosnia and Herzegovina, but it was none the less welcome to Grey and Morley, who were determined not to be drawn into intervention in Afghanistan.[8] They were able to accept as satisfactory evidence of Isvolsky's good faith the studiously correct policy which his government pursued in the incident of July 1908 on the Russo-Afghan frontier north of Herat, an incident which had all the characteristics initially of those episodes by which the Russians had in the past pursued their forward policy in central Asia, but in which on this occasion they were careful 'loyally' to observe the stipulation in the convention that they must abstain from direct political relations with the Afghans, and conducted their negotiations with Kabul (and even with Herat) through the British.[9] Thus the Afghan convention operated in practice quite successfully without the formal assent of the Amir.

The area in which it proved most difficult to implement the policy of the Anglo-Russian Convention was Persia, for it was there that the two powers had the most important economic interests, and there that their representatives, right down to the conclusion of the Persian arrangement, were engaged more or less openly on opposing sides in the Persian constitutional struggle.[10] Given the extent of their commercial, financial and political involvement, it was in practice impossible for them to retreat to a policy of total non-intervention even had they wanted to, but there were two considerations which made for a degree of co-operation: if the policy of *détente* were not applied in Persia, the two governments would eventually be faced with the uncomfortable choice between an open confrontation and a formal partition; if they continued to compete rather than to co-operate, it would be impossible to concert their action in defence of their mutual interests against the intrusion of third parties, of whom the one specifically envisaged was Germany.[11] Thus the situation in Tehran and the wider policy of the Convention both required a substantial revision of established attitudes, to enable the two governments to agree on a common policy towards both sides in the constitutional struggle. Inevitably such a policy was difficult and painful to achieve, and the first success for Anglo-Russian co-operation in Persia was not so much political as financial: the appointment by the Persian government of a French financial adviser named Bizot, forestalling the attempt of the German legation in Tehran to secure the post for its own nominee, and placing the reform of Persia's financial administration in the hands of an official whose instructions ensured that he would be favourably disposed towards the predominance of Britain and Russia.[12]

Mohammed Ali Shah, with the active encouragement of the Russian minister in Tehran, N. G. Hartwig, remained determined to overthrow the constitution conceded by his father Muzaffar ed-Din during the revolutionary upheavals of 1906. On 15 December 1907 he attempted his first *coup* against the national assembly (*majlis*) and the nationalist government, arresting a group of envoys sent by the *majlis* to negotiate with him, and sending into exile the liberal and Anglophile prime minister, Naser ul-Mulk; the Persian Cossack brigade, which was commanded by Russian officers, allowed a reactionary mob recruited for the occasion to occupy the centre of Tehran. The nationalists, however, refused to be drawn into a violent confrontation, and the Shah, cheated of the pretext he had been seeking, failed to complete the *coup* by dispersing the *majlis* and arresting the nationalist leaders.[13] Hartwig attempted to associate the British *chargé d'affaires*, Charles Marling, in his support for the Shah's actions, and Grey was obliged to suspend all joint Anglo-Russian action in Tehran until Hartwig received fresh instructions from Isvolsky, and resumed at least the appearance of an agreed policy. The two representatives then extracted from the Shah an assurance that he would in future abide by the constitution, which they communicated to the *majlis* in an attempt to restore confidence between it and the Shah.[14] In return for this concession by Isvolsky to the British view, Grey agreed to withdraw British protection from the Shah's uncle, Zill es-Sultan, who had been a British *protégé* since the 1880s, and who had been seeking to advance his own ambitions to the throne by associating himself with the nationalist cause.[15] Further, the British government agreed to offer the Shah joint protection with the Russians, if he should be forced to seek asylum with either legation, and to guarantee his safety if he should be obliged to abdicate and go into exile.[16] The result of the Anglo-Russian declarations was that the crisis passed with the Shah still on his throne, while somewhat to the chagrin of the British the German legation took over Britain's traditional role as patron of the nationalist cause.[17]

During the early months of 1908 the appearance of Anglo-Russian co-operation in Tehran was maintained, though the British made more concessions than did the Russians to achieve this appearance. In March 1908 the Russians exploited a series of incidents on the Russo-Persian frontier to send a punitive expedition into Persia and so embarrass the nationalist *régime*; when the Persian foreign minister appealed to Britain for help, Marling merely advised him to accede to all the Russian demands, and rely on the Russian government to deal generously with Persia – advice which was realistic as well as cynical, for there was no prospect of Britain exercising influence upon events in northern Persia, and further intransigence on the part of the nationalists would only have provoked a larger Russian expedition, the suppression of the constitution, and the restoration of the autocracy under Russian protection.[18] As it was, the Russian action precipitated the second major confrontation between Mohammed Ali and the nationalists. At the beginning of June the cabinet resigned and the nationalist political clubs (*anjumans*) proclaimed the deposition of the Shah and invited Zill es-Sultan to assume the regency.[19] When Grey refused to do more than repeat his previous assurance about affording the Shah the joint protection of the two governments, Isvolsky complained that British and Russian policies in Persia were still diametrically opposed, and that the British 'desired to follow a line of policy of which the result would be the accession to power of the Zill es-Sultan, whose sympathies were British'.[20] To reassure him, Grey then agreed that the two legations should jointly warn the Zill that he must abandon all pretensions to the throne.[21] But the success of the Shah's forces encouraged Hartwig to abandon any pretence of Anglo-Russian co-operation. After fighting between the nationalists and the Shah's Cossack brigade, the Cossacks surrounded the *majlis* and shelled it; large numbers of nationalists then took refuge (*bast*) in the British legation, and to prevent this the commander of the Cossack brigade, Colonel Liakhov, who was appointed military governor of Tehran on 22 June, surrounded the legation compound with Cossack guards. Martial law was proclaimed throughout every city in Persia, and Marling characterised the situation as being 'scarcely distinguishable from intervention by Russia'.[22] In spite of repeated protests, the Cossacks continued to invest the legation, and Hartwig, well satisfied with the intolerable situation which he and Liakhov had created for the British, refused Marling's requests for joint action to secure their withdrawal.[23] It was only when Grey, with the approval of the cabinet, threatened to occupy the Persian Gulf port of Bushire with British troops that Isvolsky was induced to reassert his authority over Hartwig.[24] The resumption of Russian support for the British demands secured the withdrawal of the Cossacks, a satisfactory apology from the Shah, and guarantees for the safety of those taking *bast* in the British legation which enabled them to leave.[25] But in spite of this face-saving outcome for the British, the *coup* of June 1908 had undoubtedly succeeded in its main objectives: the Shah's power had been reasserted, the constitution suppressed, and the *majlis* dispersed, all with the active encouragement of the Russian legation; while it was Zill es-Sultan and not the Shah who, under strong British pressure, was forced to go into exile.[26]

Nationalist opinion in Persia and liberal opinion in Britain were both equally critical of Grey for having abandoned the Persian constitution for the sake of maintaining the Anglo-Russian Convention.[27] But Grey was adamant that it was the physical realities of the Persian situation and not the Convention which rendered British policy impotent:

Had Tehran been in the south of Persia, and had we been willing to intervene to the extent of supporting the Popular Party against the Shah, we might have kept the Constitution on its legs afterwards, but even so we could not have made a good job of it without becoming not only its sponsors but its guardians. With Tehran, the central seat of Government, situated in the north we should not, even if willing to attempt this, have been able to carry it through.[28]

The best hope therefore for the Persian constitution as well as for British policy was that Grey should continue the Anglo-Russian co-operation and try to moderate Russian policy by private diplomatic pressure. When Isvolsky arrived in London in October to seek British support for a modification of the Straits rule, Grey and Morley read him a stern lecture on the 'unfavourable effect' produced on British public opinion by the 'action of Russian officers in Persia in suppressing the Constitution'.[29] Since he urgently needed British support not only in the Straits question, but also and more immediately in the whole Balkan question, Isvolsky was forced to recognise that the success of Hartwig's Persian policy was endangering his own European policies and that it must therefore be moderated. Grey was thus given an opportunity, by exploiting the weakness of Isvolsky's diplomatic position in Europe, to force a reversal of Hartwig's policy of sustaining the Shah, and to secure the recall of Hartwig himself from Tehran. A new British minister, Sir George Barclay, had arrived in Tehran on 1 October to attempt to restore the British position there; in mid-November Hartwig left Persia, leaving behind as *chargé d'affaires* Sabline, who was much more amenable to British pressure.[30] The annexation of Bosnia was thus followed by a period in which the Russians were induced by repeated British representations to abstain from intervention in the later stages of the Persian revolution, and ultimately to acquiesce in the deposition of the Shah. It was this period which corresponded most closely to the British interpretation of the Anglo-Russian Convention.

The *coup* of June 1908 in Tehran was followed by revolts of the *anjumans* in the provinces and the rapid disintegration of the authority of the central government. At Tabriz, the principal city of Persian Azerbaijan, which was the province in which Russia's economic and strategic interests were greatest, the seizure of the city by a large force of nationalists was followed by its investment and bombardment by royalist forces.[31] The Russian government was preparing to send troops to restore order in Azerbaijan, when it was dissuaded by a virtual ultimatum from Grey warning it that such intervention would make it impossible for him to continue supporting Russian policy in Europe.[32] The Russian expeditionary force was therefore halted at the frontier town of Julfa, and the Russian officers who had accompanied the Persian Cossacks to Tabriz were ordered to return to Tehran.[33] The two legations in Tehran then began a long process of persuasion to induce the Shah to restore the constitution, and make his peace with the nationalists by holding elections for a new *majlis*.[34] In the face of his obduracy, between January and April 1909 the British and Russian governments worked out between them an agreed programme of reforms which they were to impose on the Shah by joint pressure, thus resolving the constitutional struggle.[35] But when Barclay and Sabline presented the programme to him on 21 April, the Shah's response was discouraging, for he was confident that after a siege of over seven months Tabriz was about to fall to his forces. In order to relieve Tabriz, put an end to royalist outrages in Azerbaijan, and impose the reform programme on the Shah, Grey agreed at last to support the despatch of the Russian force from Julfa to Tabriz, and on 23 April Russian troops entered Persia, thus cheating the Shah of his expected victory over the nationalists.[36] This was the beginning of Russia's military occupation of northern Persia which proceeded from pretext to pretext down to and beyond the outbreak of the war in Europe, and which was uninfluenced by Grey's repeated and urgent requests for a reduction or withdrawal of the troops.[37] On the other hand, the Russians yielded to British insistence that they should not intervene militarily in support of the Shah, or use their troops to prevent the advance of the nationalist forces upon Tehran; and their abstention made it possible for Grey to defend their policy, and the continuing Anglo-Russian co-operation in Persia, both in cabinet and in the House of Commons.[38] Under pressure from the Russian action at Tabriz and the nationalist advance upon the capital from both north and south, the Shah hastily accepted the Anglo-Russian reform programme and agreed to restore the *majlis*.[39] But the nationalists were in no mood for a compromise, particularly one associated with the Russian legation, and they refused to heed the joint representations of the British and Russian ministers.[40] On 13 July the nationalist forces entered Tehran; they were not opposed by the Cossack brigade, and were permitted to depose the Shah and replace him with his twelve-year-old son Ahmed Mirza, who was recognised as Shah by the British and Russian governments on 21 July. A nationalist government was formed, and Liakhov agreed to place the Russian officers of the Cossack brigade under its command. On 15 November 1909 the seal was set upon the Persian revolution when the young Shah opened the newly-elected *majlis*.[41]

Even supposing that the British government had concluded the Convention with Russia in order to defend the Persian constitution, the record of its policy was not wholly ignominious, for it succeeded in averting Russian intervention in support of the Shah, and thus enabled the revolution to succeed. But its true purpose was different, to secure the British position in south-east Persia without an extension of military and imperial commitments, and to that purpose the form of government in Tehran was irrelevant, so long as it was not a government so subservient to Russia that British interests were jeopardised. Clearly the nationalist *régime* was far from subservient to Russia, and Grey was satisfied that it was the Convention which had allowed that *régime* to come to power, while at the same time 'preventing a break-up of Persia' and its consequent partition between Russia and Britain.[42] Quite apart from any considerations relating to the balance of power in Europe, the British government regarded the Russian understanding as both necessary and advantageous: in January 1909 Hardinge argued that 'our whole future in Asia is bound up with the necessity of maintaining the best and most friendly relations with Russia'; and in April 1909, in an important memorandum which was endorsed by Grey, Asquith and the King, he suggested that even a pro-German orientation on the part of Russia in Europe need not and should not lead to the collapse of the Anglo-Russian understanding in Asia, since that understanding was in the interest of both parties.[43] The policy of the Convention in Asia, difficult though it was to maintain and embarrassing to defend in public, was the best available for the defence of British interests.

The Anglo-Russian connection first entered European affairs by way of those areas in which Isvolsky's revisionist diplomacy was at its most active, the Baltic and the Balkans. The British government was prepared to go some way to humour the Russians (though not far enough wholly to satisfy them), in order to persuade them that there were solid gains to be made from loyalty to their existing diplomatic arrangements, and that there was nothing to be gained by abandoning their French alliance for a pro-German orientation. In the Baltic question, Isvolsky intended to exploit the dissolution of the Swedish-Norwegian union in 1905 to increase Russian influence in Scandinavia, to destroy the guarantee system under which France and Britain had since 1855 been committed to defending Sweden against Russian encroachment, and to secure the abrogation of the convention, appended to the Treaty of Paris of 1856, which precluded Russia from using the strategically-situated Åland islands as a military or naval base.[44] At the meeting of the Kaiser and the Tsar at Swinemünde in August 1907, he proposed to Bülow a secret Russo-German understanding, into which Sweden was also to be drawn, which envisaged 'l'exclusion complète des affaires de la mer Baltique de toute influence politique étrangère'.[45] At the same time, he was engaged in discussions with the Germans about the Bagdad railway and the Russian position in northern Persia, of which the British remained in ignorance until they were enlightened by a calculated German indiscretion during the Windsor visit in November.[46] In spite of mounting evidence that the purpose of the projected Baltic arrangement was to exclude British naval power from that sea, Grey and Hardinge were reluctant to recognise the full extent of Isvolsky's duplicity, and paradoxically they were able to form a remarkably accurate estimate of the actual terms upon which the Russians and the Germans agreed in the secret protocol of 29 October, namely the maintenance of the *status quo* in the Baltic, qualified only by the abrogation of the Åland islands convention.[47] It was therefore left to the French to protest in St Petersburg against Isvolsky's clandestine negotiations. This protest caused a temporary estrangement between Russia and France which was a source of anxiety to Grey, but it also produced an uncovenanted benefit in the form of an increasing Anglo-Russian intimacy, for Isvolsky was disposed to contrast the 'disagreeable' and 'sympathetic' attitudes of France and Britain respectively; at the same time, he was becoming disillusioned with his attempt at co-operation with Germany.[48] British satisfaction with these developments did not, however, lead to any concession to Isvolsky's wishes, but instead Grey used Russia's growing dependence upon Britain to control and moderate them. He resisted pressure from the Admiralty to sacrifice Swedish interests, and the Åland islands convention, to the need to build Russia up as a naval counterpoise to Germany in the Baltic; instead, he advised the Russians that he would not abrogate the 1856 convention without the assent of Sweden, and conveyed to them a warning that the question should not be pressed, or the developing Anglo-Russian intimacy would be endangered.[49] This pressure forced Isvolsky to concede the point, since he was receiving no support in the question from Germany either, and in the final outcome all that he secured from his Baltic manoeuvre was an innocuous international declaration whereby Denmark, Germany, Russia and Sweden undertook to respect and maintain the territorial *status quo* in the area.[50]

These developments in the Baltic and the progress made in Macedonia,[51] when added to the tensions between Russia and Germany resulting from Schön's indiscretion at Windsor about the Bagdad railway discussions, and from German intrigues with the Persian nationalists during the abortive *coup* of December 1907, seemed to the advocates of close Anglo-Russian co-operation to indicate the evolution of a general understanding; Nicolson and Hardinge in particular were exultant at this evolution.[52] Grey, however, looked more realistically at the real prospects of an Anglo-Russian understanding leading to progress in Near Eastern affairs, and his cautious and limited appraisal was less strident than their reaction, and more characteristic of the tone of British policy towards Russia in European questions:

We must go carefully in the Macedonian question. I am quite pleased, from the point of view of general policy, that events are bringing Russia and us together. But a combination of Britain, Russia and France in the Concert must for the present be a weak one . . . Russia is weak after the war, and her internal affairs are anything but secure. Ten years hence, a combination of Britain, Russia and France may be able to dominate Near Eastern policy; and within that time events will probably make it more and more clear that it is to the interest of Russia and us to work together: but we must go slowly.[53]

In this context, it is clear that the allusion to the 'concert' does not refer to general European questions, but specifically to Turkey and the Balkans, the last area in which the nineteenth-century notion of the 'concert of Europe' still applied, in rhetoric if not in fact.[54] In any case, both the enthusiastic reaction of Nicolson and Hardinge and the more temperate one of Grey ignored an important element in the Anglo-Russian relationship, namely the real objects of Russian diplomacy, and specifically the price Isvolsky would demand in the form of a concession to his ambitions at the Straits. Nor could either view indicate how the diplomatic co-operation of Britain and Russia would directly advance the reconstruction of Russia as a military factor on the side of France in the European balance, which for the British had been the main European object of the Anglo-Russian *rapprochement*.

During 1907 and 1908, Clemenceau repeatedly urged the British government to increase substantially the size of the military force which it had available for operations on the continent.[55] Grey's response to these importunities was always the same, that he had no intention of retreating from the position he had adopted at the time of the first Moroccan crisis, but that Britain's primary concern must be to maintain command of the seas, and that the proper 'counterpoise' to Germany's military power was not an enlarged British army, but the Russian army.[56] The obvious flaw in this argument was the continuing weakness in the military condition of the Russian counterpoise, in spite of the repeated representations of the French general staff.[57] In April 1908 consternation was caused in London as well as Paris by the news that the Russians, instead of concentrating on increasing their military strength on their western frontier, intended to build up their naval strength in the Baltic and the Black Sea, and to resume railway construction in the Far East; and Mallet proposed that Isvolsky should be privately warned how unwelcome this news was to the British and French governments.[58] This was the context in which the British prepared for the meeting of the King and the Tsar at Reval on 9 and 10 June. The original purpose of the meeting was to 'cement' the Anglo-Russian relationship in general, and in particular to put the finishing touches to the Anglo-Russian programme of Macedonian reforms; and this purpose was well served by the conversations between Isvolsky and Hardinge, by the general air of cordiality in which the celebrations took place, and by incidents such as the King's impulsive gesture of appointing the Tsar an honorary Admiral of the Fleet which, as Hardinge well knew, was constitutionally improper but highly effective.[59] But Hardinge went further, and sought to impress on Isvolsky the importance of Russia concentrating her resources on her military position, urging upon him that Russia, 'if strong in Europe, might be the arbiter of peace, and have much more influence in securing the peace of the world than at any Hague Conference'. This was the hint which Mallet had wished to be conveyed to Isvolsky; and Hardinge went on to suggest that Britain and Russia should maintain the same cordial relations as existed between Britain and France.[60] In this part of his conversation, he unquestionably came close to advocating something very like a triple *entente*, and although this was the underlying purpose of the pro-Russian group in the Foreign Office, it was not the policy of the cabinet. Since he had no formal written instructions, it is not possible to conclude that he had exceeded them, but it was Hardinge's record of the entire meeting, and not merely the King's impropriety in appointing the Tsar an Admiral of the Fleet, which led Asquith to suggest to Grey that on such occasions in future the King should be attended by a responsible minister.[61] In any case, Hardinge failed to impress upon Isvolsky the one point which was of vital importance to Britain, that Russia should concentrate her strength on her western frontier, for Isvolsky left the meeting with the impression that the British government wanted Russia to be as strong as possible at sea as well as on land, and the Russian government decided to proceed with its railway construction in the Far East.[62]

There is no support in the accounts of either Hardinge or Isvolsky for the allegation found in other Russian sources, that at Reval the British gave the Russians an undertaking to support a revision of the Straits rule in Russia's favour.[63] But the conditional undertaking given by Grey in 1907 was sufficient to encourage Isvolsky to expect British support, when a convenient moment for raising the question should arise.[64] After the *débâcle* of his Baltic venture, Isvolsky was eager to proceed to a success at the Straits, and to this end set about securing the assent of the other interested governments, a policy which led him to his compromising agreement with Aehrenthal at Buchlau, and consequently to the humiliations of the Bosnian annexation crisis. One government he made no attempt to conciliate was the Turkish, expecting that the Turks would be obliged to accept whatever the great powers pressed upon them. But the Young Turk revolution of July 1908, offering the British a real prospect of reversing the relative positions of Britain and Germany at Constantinople, and hence of materially advancing British commercial interests, completely altered the British government's attitude towards Turkey. In so doing it presented the first serious challenge to Britain's nascent *entente* with Russia, a challenge which crystallised around the question of the Straits, in which Britain could not defend the interests of Turkey without opposing the ambitions of Russia. The danger inherent in such a clash of interests was immediately apparent to Grey:

The delicate point will presently be Russia – we cannot revert to the old policy of Lord Beaconsfield; we have now to be pro-Turkish without giving rise to any suspicion that we are anti-Russian.[65]

And he remarked upon the importance of avoiding giving the Russians any ground for suspecting that Britain was reverting to the 'old policy of supporting Turkey as a barrier' against them.[66]

By the time Isvolsky reached London, however, to canvass a revision of the Straits rule, it was so necessary for him to secure Grey's support in the more immediate problems following Austria's annexation of Bosnia that he was obliged to agree that the Straits should be excluded from international discussion, until the situation of the Turkish government was more secure.[67] But he made strenuous efforts to influence opinion in London in favour of an eventual revision in Russia's favour, as the only way to save his own position, to ensure the survival of the Stolypin government, to advance the cause of liberal reform in Russia, and to salvage the policy of the Anglo-Russian *entente*.[68] There was in fact considerable sympathy for Isvolsky's proposals, and no disposition to overestimate the strategic value to Britain of maintaining the closure of the Straits; and at the instance of Asquith, Grey, McKenna and Haldane the cabinet agreed on 14 October that Britain would support a modification of the Straits rule, on the basis of reciprocal rights for belligerents in time of war.[69] Grey was then able to inform Isvolsky that if Russia helped Turkey through the present crisis, and the Turkish government gave its consent to such a revision, the British government would support it; and privately he promised that he would urge the Turks to accept it when a more favourable opportunity occurred.[70] This reply, which constituted a commitment only slightly more definite than the conditional assurances of 1907, was the limit of Grey's concession to Isvolsky in the question of the Straits; but although it did not give Isvolsky the success for which he had hoped, it did give him a renewed incentive to work with Grey in support of Turkish interests and to promote, for instance, the solution to the Turco-Bulgarian crisis which was a major success for the Anglo-Russian connection in Europe.[71] In this way, the potential collision between Grey's Russian and Turkish policies was for the moment averted; and the Russian government was not to raise the Straits question again until (in October 1911) the Anglo-Turkish honeymoon which followed the Young Turk revolution was long since over.

The Bosnian crisis was thus the occasion of substantial Anglo-Russian diplomatic co-operation, but it was also the crucial episode in determining the limits beyond which that co-operation would not be carried. From the outset Grey made it plain that he would not give more than diplomatic support to the Russian position, and when on 10 November 1908 Benckendorff asked him directly whether Russia could hope for British military support in the event of her being involved in war with Austria and Germany, he refused to answer the hypothetical question.[72] His severely discouraging reply to Benckendorff may be compared with the reply he gave to Cambon in parallel circumstances in January 1906, when he gave the French as much reason as he legitimately could to expect British assistance in the event of a Franco-German war.[73] And in the same conversation in which he gave Benckendorff such a discouraging answer, Grey went out of his way to tell him that he had just been considering the likelihood of Britain giving armed support to France in a possible Franco-German conflict over the Casablanca incident. There could hardly have been a more pointed juxtaposition. Without the prospect of military support, the diplomatic support of Britain was powerless to save Russia from the humiliation of March 1909, and in the aftermath of Isvolsky's *débâcle* it seemed likely that, if the British did not protect him by offering a virtual Anglo-Russian alliance, he would be driven from office under German pressure as Delcassé had been in 1905; in that event, it was expected that a reactionary successor such as Goremykin would demand an alliance, and when it was refused would denounce the Convention and adopt a pro-German orientation.[74] At Grey's request, to answer Nicolson and the advocates of a Russian alliance in the Foreign Office, Hardinge drew up a considered policy memorandum which was endorsed by Grey and Asquith, and which may be regarded as a definitive statement of the government's position on the question of extending the Anglo-Russian understanding, and formalising it as a binding European commitment; it is all the more impressive in that it emanated from the man who was the principal architect of the Convention of 1907 and a strong advocate of Anglo-Russian co-operation. Hardinge argued that Britain need not and should not enter into any more binding arrangement with Russia: such an engagement would be superfluous, since the Russians would in any case maintain the understanding with Britain in Asia; it would be impossible from the point of view of public opinion, which would not tolerate an alliance with an autocratic Russian *régime*; and it would be unnecessary, since even if Britain should become isolated in Europe following the desertion of Russia (and consequently of France) to the German camp, her security was assured by the maintenance of her naval supremacy. It is perfectly plain from this memorandum that, if the price of maintaining Russia's loyalty to her western partners was a British commitment to her defence, that price was too high.[75] In European affairs, the Anglo-Russian connection was in the last resort expendable. British policy therefore reverted to the position defined by Grey, attempting simply to 'keep an *entente* with Russia, in the sense of keeping in touch so that our diplomatic action may be in accord and in mutual support'.[76] The Tsar was cordially urged to maintain Isvolsky in office, and replied that it was his 'firm intention' to maintain the understanding with Britain.[77] At the beginning of August 1909 he and Isvolsky were received at Cowes, and without pressing for any closer definition of the *entente*, they expressed their keen appreciation of the identity of view which the two governments enjoyed.[78] It was clear that the Anglo-Russian connection had survived the pressure applied to it by the German *démarche* in St Petersburg, without in the process being transformed into anything more definite or binding.

The two years between the conclusion of the Anglo-Russian Convention in August 1907 and the visit of the Tsar and Isvolsky to Cowes in August 1909 were the critical period for the definition of the scope and content of the Russian connection in Britain's Asian and European policies. Thereafter British policy did not significantly depart from the attitude towards Russia which had been worked out under the pressure of events during those years: in Europe the British government would welcome diplomatic co-operation with Russia in matters of common interest and would seek to promote Russian loyalty to France, but it was not prepared to give Russian wishes precedence over other considerations, nor to regard the Russian position in eastern Europe as an issue over which Britain would in any circumstances go to war; in Asia it would seek to maintain the convention for the relative security which it conferred upon the Indian frontier, and although in Persia it would attempt to moderate Russian policy by private diplomatic representations, in the last resort it was prepared to recognise the reality of Russian preponderance in the north. The Bethmann-Hollweg initiative of 21 August 1909 opened a new phase in British policy in which the central issue was the relation of Britain to Germany in Europe and the Middle East, and in which the Russian connection was of less immediate interest: in this phase the British could do no more than seek to maintain their Russian *entente* as already defined. On their side the Russians, following their disappointment over the Åland islands and the Straits, and their humiliation in the Bosnian crisis, nevertheless continued to look for advantages through bilateral understandings with whatever government seemed able to offer them, without any undue concern for consistency or for the kind of loyalty to the western powers which the British still seemed to expect. In the questions which arose during the next years, this opportunist policy did nothing to advance the intimacy of the Anglo-Russian *entente*, and the kind of co-operation which had seemed so promising in the Balkans during 1908 and 1909 was not repeated, particularly as the British government was determined to preserve its detachment from Balkan affairs, and regarded a renewed Austro-Russian understanding as the best hope for stability in the area.[79]

Isvolsky's first move towards reconstructing his diplomatic position in the Balkans, and at the same time promoting a future revision of the Straits rule, was to reach an agreement with the Italians at Racconigi in October 1909, in which each undertook to regard sympathetically the ambitions of the other at the Straits and in Tripoli respectively.[80] This agreement was not communicated either to the French or to the British, and the Foreign Office was left with the impression that nothing more had been discussed than the maintenance of the *status quo* in the Balkans.[81] In September 1910 Isvolsky was at last eased out of the foreign ministry in St Petersburg and took up the embassy in Paris, and it was from there that he attempted to exploit the opportunity presented by Italy's invasion of Tripoli in October 1911 to revive the Straits question. He demanded French support for a revision of the Straits rule, while in Constantinople Tcharykov sought to make a revision palatable to the Turks by offering a Russian guarantee of Turkey in Europe as a *quid pro quo*. The French, however, would not support the Russian proposal without Grey's agreement, and the Turks would not acquiesce without the prospect of a British alliance to back up the Russian guarantee; the British cabinet of course would not even consider an alliance with Turkey, and Grey declined to go further on the Straits question than the undertaking he had given Isvolsky in October 1908. Consequently when Sazonov (Isvolsky's successor as foreign minister, who had been convalescing in Switzerland) arrived in Paris to find the Straits proposal once again blocked by Turkish intransigence and British temporising, he had no alternative but to repudiate the initiative of Isvolsky and Tcharykov.[82]

Another source of coolness in the *entente* was the divergence of British and Russian policies towards the Bagdad railway. The Anglo-German negotiations which followed the Bethmann-Hollweg initiative inevitably alarmed the Russians, in spite of British efforts to reassure them, for as they well knew one of the major elements in the projected Anglo-German arrangement was a settlement of the Bagdad railway question. The Russians disliked the railway as a threat to their commercial and political ascendancy in northern Persia. In 1907 they had attempted to secure themselves against its worst effects by a direct understanding with Germany, and were induced to abandon this attempt only because Grey's proposal that Britain, France and Russia should only negotiate collectively on the question with Germany (which was intended to secure their admission to the project on the most favourable terms possible) seemed to them to hold out hopes of blocking the project altogether.[83] Thus both the British and Russian governments regarded co-operation in the question as a useful way of advancing their interests, and during 1908 they jointly examined a range of alternative railway routes in Persia, and agreed to co-operate in securing the concessions for them from the Persian government, so as to forestall any attempt by the Germans to secure them as branch lines for the Bagdad railway.[84] But as soon as he was informed about the Gwinner–Cassel discussions in November 1909, Isvolsky took fright, assuming that Grey was about to settle bilaterally with Germany and thus abandon his commitment to collective negotiations; Nicolson was alarmed at the prospect of the Anglo-German negotiations beginning the dissolution of the Anglo-Russian *entente*.[85] Grey tried to convince Isvolsky that an agreement between Britain and Germany about the southern section of the railway would merely be a preliminary to collective negotiations, and suggested to him that a parallel Russian preliminary might be achieved by reviving the idea of a Russo-German bargain over the Khanikin branch line and northern Persia.[86] When Sazonov succeeded Isvolsky as foreign minister, he at once took up the project, and at Potsdam in November 1910 he and Bethmann-Hollweg adumbrated an agreement which in effect completed the negotiations which had been broken off in 1907, and provided for the construction of a branch line of the Bagdad railway to Khanikin (on the Persian frontier), where it would connect with a Russian railway to Tehran.[87] Thus the Russian government was

HBF

the first to reach a bilateral agreement with Germany over the Bagdad railway, an agreement which was far from welcome to the British, who found themselves unable to prevent Sazonov from surrendering Russia's position to Germany before they themselves had obtained satisfactory terms for the southern section of the railway. Although it was partly the result of their own bilateral negotiations with Germany, the British were very resentful at Sazonov's abandonment of the principle of collective negotiations.[88]

It was, however, in Persia itself that Russian policy subjected the Convention to its severest strains, and here the British government, while trying to moderate the actions of the Russians, felt constrained in the last resort to acquiesce in them since the available alternatives were even less palatable. It was no accident that Russia's military intervention in northern Persia began at the end of April 1909, only a month after Isvolsky's ignominious capitulation to the German *démarche* relieved him of the need to retain British support in the Bosnian crisis. Thereafter the Russians looked upon northern Persia as an area in which they could secure compensation without interference, for they were confident that the British would not dare to oppose them there, because of their preoccupation with the balance of power in Europe.[89] And it is true that Grey was prepared to accept this policy of compensation, so long as it was confined to the Russian zone in Persia, and to use it to persuade them of the continuing utility of their association with Britain whenever they appeared to be drifting into a German orientation: in September 1909 he warned the Persians that they should not expect the Russians to 'accept quietly a less influential position in northern Persia than that which they had occupied prior to the fall of Mohammed Ali', and a year later he advised Barclay that it was 'absolutely essential, on European and not merely on local grounds, that the solidarity of action of the two Powers in Persia should be maintained'.[90] On numerous occasions, Barclay was instructed to support demands intended to sustain Russia's preponderance in the north; and when, for instance, the Persian government applied to the two powers for a loan the British, who would have liked to help set the nationalist *régime* on its feet, allowed the Russian government to attach so many conditions to the loan that the nationalists were bound to refuse it.[91]

When in February 1911 the Persian government appointed an American customs expert, W. Morgan Shuster, as Treasurer General of Persia, Grey welcomed the prospect of an improvement in Persia's financial position; when Shuster began to organise a Treasury *gendarmerie* to protect the collection of taxes in the anarchic state of Persia, and appointed as its commander the British military *attaché* in Tehran, Major Stokes, Grey recognised that the Russians would be suspicious and antagonistic, though at first he hoped to induce them to acquiesce in the appointment.[92] But under Russian pressure he acknowledged that the employment of a British officer in a military capacity in northern Persia would be 'a breach of the spirit of the Anglo-Russian Convention', and refused to allow Stokes to take up the appointment.[93] One reason for Russian objections to the appointment was the important part played by Shuster's organisation in supplying the nationalist forces which were raised to resist an attempt by the ex-Shah to recover his throne with the connivance of the Russians. The Russian government, which in 1909 had agreed not to intervene to prevent the deposition of the Shah, now declined to intervene to prevent his return; many of its local officials in Persia gave him practical assistance, but early in September 1911 his forces were defeated by the nationalists.[94] After Mohammed Ali's failure, the Russians announced that the increasing chaos in northern Persia, and the hostility to Russian interests which under Shuster's influence the nationalist *régime* had developed, would oblige them to take 'measures of extreme vigour'; on 10 November 1911 they issued an ultimatum to the Persian government, and made ready to send troops to Kasvin (a key position on the road to Tehran). It was to prevent Russian troops being sent to occupy Tehran that Grey agreed to support the Russian demands.[95] At the same time, perturbed at the violent antipathy which Russian policy had provoked in Britain, he urged the Russian government not to take any more extreme measures lest the 'whole question of [the] foreign policy of both governments' should be raised.[96] The Russian forces did not go to Tehran, for after a major political crisis between the government and the *majlis*, the ultimatum was accepted and Shuster dismissed.[97] Barclay was left to lament in Tehran the departure of a man whose work had temporarily promised genuine reform for Persia, but in London Grey remained as convinced as ever that there was no realistic alternative to the policy of co-operation with Russia.[98] The Russians, he believed, wished to maintain the policy of the Convention, in spite of the 'untoward events' in Persia:

And of course if the Agreement were to go, everything would be worse both for us and for Persia. So I stake everything upon pulling the Agreement through all difficulties.[99]

But the difficulties were to get rather worse. Apart from the Balkan Wars, which are dealt with elsewhere, Persia, Afghanistan and Tibet continued to pose serious problems, and, of these, Persia was undoubtedly the worst. The behaviour of Russian officials in the northern zone continued to falsify the Convention, the Persian government shewed little sign of improvement, and the ability of the British to make the best of a bad job in the southern zone was greatly impaired by disagreements between the Foreign Office, the India Office and the government of India. The visit of the Russian foreign minister, Sazonov, to Balmoral in September 1912, while it undoubtedly strengthened the Anglo-Russian entente, did nothing to help the Persian situation. Sir Edward Grey seems to have obtained assurances from Sazonov that he would do what he could to ease matters, and to have pointed out that the pressure of British public opinion was real and dangerous. He also said that if Russia further extended her interference in the North, the British would have to introduce at least a British officered force into the South.[100] This last the government of India was determined not to do, and subsequent negotiations suggested that it could only be an empty threat.

So complicated did the question become, that an argument developed within the Foreign Office during 1913 as to whether Russia could or should be seriously taken to task about the conduct of her agents in Persia. In this, the position of Persia itself – apart from the quite acute degree of Parliamentary embarrassment it caused – was accidental: any quarrel with Russia must have produced the same reflections. In brief, the argument turned upon particular interpretations of Russia's regained strength: had it gone so far as to put Russia beyond the need for a British agreement; if so, any humiliation in Persia must be swallowed, since the entente had become more necessary to Britain than to Russia. In any case, this might mean that Russia would gradually turn towards the more congenial Germany, and abandon both the French alliance and the 1907 Convention. But, if the regained strength of Russia had in fact provided an additional counterpoise to Germany in Europe, then the need for a coherent triple entente was less urgent, and England would be able to speak both firmly and safely to the Russians. Such a policy would certainly find favour among the government's most bitter critics in the House of Commons.

Then the Balkan Wars intervened and the 'value of Russian support in preserving the peace of Europe (had) gained recognition even in quarters which had freely criticised Russian policy in Persia'.[101] As the Balkan Crisis settled down, however, it began to seem very desirable to negotiate a revised convention with Russia over Asiatic questions. Not only Sir William Tyrell, who was the foremost domestic advocate of speaking more firmly to the Russian government, but also Buchanan, the more cautious ambassador at St Petersburg, recommended making such an attempt.[102] Moreover, they felt that better progress would be made if the problems involved could be brought directly to the Tsar. Internal opposition, particularly from Sir Arthur Nicolson, was very strong,[103] but despite this a firm line was taken with Russia over the coercion of Turkey in July 1913.[104]

From this time until just before the outbreak of war in 1914 a continuous and at times acrimonious discussion developed in the Foreign Office, and between the governments in London and Delhi, about the desirability of trying to revise the 1907 Convention. Three attitudes primarily affected this argument: first, those who believed that Russia could and should be made to honour her obligations in Northern Persia hoped that a revision of the convention accompanied by a forward British policy in Southern Persia would accomplish their aim. Second, those who believed, with Arthur Nicolson, that Russia was now so strong as to be able to make an agreement with Germany, felt that a revised and preferably more binding convention – they recognised that an alliance was not possible under a liberal government[105] – would help to preserve the Anglo-Russian convention. Third, the government of India, which during 1913–14 made a new convention with China and Tibet, wanted a revision of the 1907 Convention to iron out contradictions which had come to exist between the two.[106] They, too, greatly wanted the agreement with Russia to survive for the sake of Indian security, but were reluctant to make any forward movement in Southern Persia, even though it was generally recognised that no change would be obtained from the Russians unless British activities in the South had come to represent an obvious counter-weight.[107] For most of the time, therefore, the Viceroy threw the weight of the government of India behind the arguments of Sir Arthur Nicolson.

After Sir Eyre Crowe took over the Eastern Department in September 1913, the pressure in favour of trying to restrain the Russians in Northern Persia, and in favour of trying to negotiate a more manageable convention, became much stronger. Crowe's slightly acerbic discussion of the problem gradually became an insistent counter voice to the constant warnings that Nicolson was apt to utter about the grave dangers of offending the Russians in any way, until, just before the war, he got his way. Crowe believed that there was no danger of Russia falling into the arms of Germany, and, indeed, the theoretical nature of Nicolson's fear was daily demonstrated as Germany and Russia indulged in a ferocious propaganda war against each other. He also believed primarily in the existence of a paramount threat from Germany – against which a Russian agreement was a desirable counter poise, but not so utterly necessary as to forbid plain speech. As the full scale of Russia's failure to observe the 1907 Convention in Persia dawned on him in late 1913, his protests grew more strident until in June 1914, he composed a memorandum of such striking effect that it marked the beginning of a deliberate attempt to renegotiate the Convention. He began by acknowledging the local facts, emphasising the effective loss of the five northern provinces to Russia. He then asserted that the continuance of Russian policy must eventually involve their taking also the neutral zone, and thus bringing about the circumstance specifically prevented by the original convention – a common frontier between India and Russia 'and the consequent obligation to face the political and military responsibilities resulting therefrom'. The only way now to secure British interests in the neutral zone and to end a situation in which there 'is under treaties and conventions, an appeal to us against the injustice and shamelessness of Russian proceedings', was to begin upon a new policy.

What seemingly is required, is
1. The establishment, support, and maintenance in power of effective and efficient local authorities. To this end:
2. A reliable police force under the only really competent officers: British;
3. The immediate opening up of the country, and the development of its trade, by the construction of roads and railways connecting the coast districts with the interior.
These three things hang together. They all cost money, and therefore the further requirement is

4. The acceptance of definite financial responsibilities. I am aware of the difficulties and objections to be urged, and do not underrate them. But I feel confident that

(a) the sacrifices involved cannot in the long run be avoided or evaded, and that, moreover,

(b) to postpone them will mean to increase them.

Above all, I see in the suggested change of policy the only possible way of maintaining our general understanding with Russia, which I consider essential to our interests as an Empire. Under the conditions which now prevail in Persia, and which involve our sharing before the world the responsibility for Russia's unscrupulous proceedings in that country, the understanding will break down. No British officials can actively cooperate with Russian officials: the difference of methods and of standards of conduct is practically unbridgeable. Nor is it likely to become otherwise within reasonable time. In order to be able to work with Russia it is, I think, necessary, to have a clear and definite geographical line of division between us beyond which we may refrain from troubling as to what Russia does, and how she does it. So long as there is under treaties and conventions, an appeal to us against the injustice and shamelessness of Russian proceedings, there will be a growing tendency to quarrel, and a growing estrangement between the two governments. To my mind this most serious difficulty can only be overcome by definitely cutting away the ground on which such an appeal can technically be made. To this necessity we must sacrifice the fiction of an independent and united Persia. I do not think we are in any way morally bound to shrink from such a sacrifice. It is not perhaps an heroic course, but it is not open to blame and it is the only one that will preserve us from grave political and national peril.[108]

Almost immediately after this memorandum appeared, Crowe protested to the Russian chargé d'affaires in a new and firm tone, which the Foreign Secretary warmly endorsed in a similar interview shortly afterwards.[109] At the same time, the question of leasing from the Persian government some islands in the Persian Gulf arose. It would involve a more or less permanent control of their administration and was a part of the policy of extending British influence in the Gulf both by arrangements with Turkey and the Trucial Chiefs, and by agreement with Germany about the latter end of the Baghdad railway. Crowe was strongly in favour of obtaining such a lease and obtained Sir Edward Grey's consent. It is interesting to observe that his chief argument for so doing was that the British government had now accepted that Northern Persia had passed to Russia, and that therefore that part of the 1907 Convention which bound the parties to respect the integrity of Persia was practically a dead letter.[110] Two days later, a long and highly critical memorandum was sent to the Ambassador at St Petersburg for communication to the Russian government. It was chiefly the work of Sir Edward Grey himself,[111] and it was the first move towards renegotiation. The reply from Russia came almost exactly one month later, and was in Buchanan's view 'weak' and 'childish';[112] but the discussions continued and by 20 July even Nicolson was optimistic about their result.[113]

Three days later the Austrians sent their ultimatum to Serbia, and the war quickly followed. The immediate effect was to bring about an alliance between Britain and Russia, which removed any grounds for supposing that an attempt to be firm about Persia would lead to a breakdown in Anglo-Russian relations. In the autumn of 1914 and spring of 1915 British protests about Russian policy in Persia grew louder. In March 1915 a new settlement was at last achieved. Russian influence in the North was accepted by the British in return for the cession of the neutral zone to them, which was in turn accepted by the Russians in return for the eventual possession of Constantinople. Both powers were to have 'complete liberty of action'. Effective partition had come at last.

While Grey was gradually moving towards the idea of confronting the Russians directly with the Persian question and thus embarking on a probable renegotiation of the Convention, a new element briefly entered into Anglo-Russian relations. The Russians felt, as Arthur Nicolson had constantly and rightly recognised, that they would be much more prepared to meet English anxieties about Persia in the context of a firm alliance rather than a loose understanding. The Tsar and Sazonov, however, had certainly come to understand that no alliance would be given by England, but in April 1914 they began to prospect for a naval agreement, as an additional safeguard in place of the unobtainable alliance. They moved the French to raise the idea with Grey when he accompanied the King and Queen to Paris in early May 1914. Grey, who had been previously warned both by Buchanan in St Petersburg and by the French, had already decided that the Russians could be told how matters stood militarily with the French; and that they could be offered similar discussions. On 19 May 1914 Benckendorff and Cambon saw Grey together at the Foreign Office and such an arrangement was approved. Strategic considerations meant that Anglo-Russian naval conversations could never have the significance of the Anglo-French exchanges, but conversations evidently did take place, if unprofitably,[114] and their progress was regarded as important by the Russians – to the point where it was possible for Buchanan to report on 25 June 1914 that discussion of Persian and Tibetan questions might be affected by them.[115] In the event, both naval discussions and the Persian situation were soon swept into the general maelstrom caused by the outbreak of war.

13

The Balkans, 1909–1914

R. J. CRAMPTON

The two years after the settlement of the Annexation crisis were, for the Balkans, a period of relative calm. The Young Turks, preoccupied with the consolidation of their power, had not yet revealed the true implications and dangers of their 'Ottomanizing' policies, whilst the mutual jealousies of the Balkan states held each one in check. Furthermore the Annexation crisis had diminished Russia's prestige and authority in the peninsula, leaving Austria the dominant Power, and an exaggerated fear of Austrian expansionist aims was a further rein upon adventurous spirits in the Balkan capitals.

In the Great Power capitals adventurous spirits were few. With the dawn of the constitutional era at Constantinople and the temporary disappearance of the Macedonian question the Powers had been glad to extricate themselves from the maelstrom of Macedonian reform. Grey himself, perhaps chastened by his experiences in the Bosnian crisis, gradually dissociated himself from Balkan affairs altogether, and was content to advocate an alliance between Turkey and the Balkan states as the best means of maintaining a Balance of Power in the area.[1] In particular he favoured an alliance between Turkey and Bulgaria, whom he regarded as the strongest of the Balkan states, even ordering the new Minister in Sofia, Lindlay, actively to press this policy on the Bulgarians.[2] The latter, however, wanted British help in securing concessions from the Porte whereas Grey shrank from anything so reminiscent of the Macedonian imbroglio,[3] and began to wonder whether any alliance whatever on the Balkan peninsula might not be regarded as a provocation by the Austrians, who were now behaving with commendable restraint.[4] Moreover as it became clear that such an alliance could not be achieved without direct Great Power involvement, Grey decided that the price was too high.

Until the Balkan wars, therefore, he concerned himself only with routine affairs in the Near East, and only rarely consulted the other Powers. In the autumn of 1909 he assured the Bulgarians that 'His Majesty's Government would view the existence of closer relations between Bulgaria and England with the greatest satisfaction',[5] but little came of these overtures beyond Britain's consenting to the abolition of the Capitulations in Bulgaria.[6] The other Balkan states occupied even less of Grey's time. A Montenegrin offer of an Adriatic harbour was brushed aside as 'no agreement with the Prince of Montenegro is worth the disturbance which the knowledge of it would create amongst the Powers'.[7] The Foreign Office made little effort to strengthen its loose relations with either Belgrade or Bucharest – even though in 1909 and 1910 the Serbians began actively to advocate an alliance with Bulgaria.[8] In 1910 Grey was willing to send a mission to reform the Greek navy,[9] but only because he could not refuse the Greeks a favour he had already extended to their rivals the Turks,[10] and because he did not regard it as involving any political commitment.

Abstention from the Balkans was a policy whose attractions grew with time as it freed Britain from the embarrassment of having to put pressure on the Porte in an area in which she was not vitally interested. When in 1911, the Greeks asked the Powers to make the Porte end its boycott of Greek goods and shipping, Grey held back not wanting 'to be pushed into the forefront in this matter. We must keep that for the Persian Gulf etc.'[11] In the Albanian revolts of 1910 and 1911, which revealed the long-term results of young Turk policies, he left the initiative to the three most interested Powers, especially Austria, and 'not once did he revert to the tactics of 1908, of seeking agreement with Russia in the hope of compelling the others to follow suit'.[12] By the end of 1911 he was completely passive:

It would be a mistake for us to take an initiative in opposing Austria in the Balkans: it is for Russia to make up her mind as to what she wants and approach us if she wishes to do so. If we take an initiative in proposing a Balkan policy to Russia we shall be committed more deeply than it is necessary or wise for us to be committed in Balkan affairs.[13]

From the Cretan question, however, Britain could not escape; and here Grey was uneasy as long as only four (and after the outbreak of the Italo-Turkish war, three) of the Great Powers remained responsible for the island. Grey had no sympathy for either the Greek Cretans or for the kingdom in which they wished to be included,[14] and involvement in their affairs meant unpopularity both in Greece and Turkey. If Austria and Germany could be brought back into the affair they would carry their share of this unpopularity and if Grey could persuade the two absentee Powers to rejoin the Concert he would limit their chances of making political capital out of the Cretan question: those two Powers 'would do far less mischief inside a conference than out of it'.[15] Thus in July 1910 Grey declared that the Greco-Turkish dispute encompassed not only Crete but both the Turkish boycott of Greek goods and shipping, and Macedonia, and was therefore a matter of concern for all Powers. But Berlin and Vienna would not be drawn and Grey had to give up, testily declaring that though he for his part would remain faithful to his Cretan obligations he would do nothing if a Balkan war developed from the affair.[16] But as long as the Great Powers themselves seemed unlikely to be involved in such a war Grey could remain aloof.

When Italy declared war on Turkey in September 1911, however, the situation was radically altered. Italy had promised Austria–Hungary not to extend the war to the Balkans[17] but there was always the danger that the Balkan states or even a Great Power might take advantage of the war.[18] Complete abstention from Near Eastern affairs was no longer possible for if changes in that area were under consideration Britain had weighty interests to guard, though it was not in isolated action by the Entente that Grey saw his shield. When in February 1912 Sazonov proposed Franco-Russian diplomatic pressure at Sofia and Constantinople, and the French replied that they could not act without Britain,[19] Grey, in turn, refused to act without Germany and Austria. He felt that Austria and Russia should formulate a common policy, but if they could not agree then the five Powers should act in unison for 'if Russia fell out with Austria, we, and I supposed the French also, would have to consider the lengths to which we would be prepared to go in support of Russia'.[20] Anglo-French discussions on the Balkans had already taken place, and Grey had told Paris of Britain's extreme reluctance to face European complications for the sake of Russia's Balkan ambitions. Also he did not share the French fears that Austro-Russian co-operation would lead eventually to a Russo-German *rapprochement* to the detriment of the ties between Russia and France. Such co-operation, he pointed out, had not previously impaired the solidarity of the Franco-Russian Alliance, and the danger of 'upsetting the present grouping of the Powers would be far greater if Russia became involved in a war with Austria than if she came to a working agreement with that country'. Moreover, such an agreement might make Austria 'more independent of Germany than she now is'. [21] Although he did not press the point further, deciding at this stage that Austro-Russian co-operation was more probable 'if we do not mix ourselves in the matter',[22] he had adumbrated the policy he was to pursue when the Balkans erupted into war in the autumn of that year.

In the meantime there were signs that the situation in the Balkans was growing more dangerous. In March the British Minister in Sofia, Sir Henry Bax-Ironside, hastened to inform the Foreign Office of the signature of the Serbo-Bulgarian treaty that was to form the cornerstone of the Balkan League,[23] but his account was incomplete. By April the British had learned that the treaty was as much an offensive weapon against Turkey as a defensive mechanism against Austria,[24] and they became even more critical than the French of the wisdom of Russian policy. Grey saw that the creation of the Balkan League, by removing the restraint which mutual jealousy had placed on its members, added a new threat to the already precarious Near Eastern peace. He was equally painfully aware of Britain's embarrassing position:

We shall have to keep out of this and what I fear is that Russia may resent our doing so: the fact that the trouble is all of her own making won't prevent her from expecting help if the trouble turns out to be more than she bargained for. On the other hand Russia would resent still more our attempting to restrain her now in a matter that she would at this stage say did not concern us.[25]

The spring and summer of 1912 witnessed developments in the Balkans which were to justify the worst anxieties of those who feared that the Balkan League would precipitate the end of Turkish rule in Europe. The vilayets of Scutari, Kossovo, and Janina where the Turks were trying to enforce unprecedented restrictions of native Albanian law and custom remained the most disaffected areas and the rebellion of 1911 revived with greater intensity; the Albanians, noting Turkish setbacks in Tripoli and the increasing danger from the Balkan states, began to doubt Turkey's ability to protect them from their traditional Slav and Greek enemies, and demanded autonomy.[26] In July they forced the resignation of the Young Turk government in favour of a more conciliatory cabinet with Ghazi Moukhtar as Grand Vizier.[27] In the same month a radical government under Pašić took office in Belgrade[28] presaging a more active foreign policy by Serbia, and in Bulgaria the pacific Minister President, Gueshov, was under increasing pressure from a belligerent public.[29] A spate of incidents along the Turkish–Montenegrin border, which had been in dispute since 1878,[30] and the alarming rate of war preparations throughout the Near East,[31] increased the fears of the Powers that the Balkan allies were seeking an excuse to attack Turkey.[32] Only Italy, still at war with Turkey, regarded the situation without apprehension.[33]

Count Berchtold was the first to come forward with suggestions for diplomatic pressure in Constantinople and the Balkan capitals.[34] Grey viewed the Austrian proposals with mixed feelings, above all because he did not wish to do anything which might offend or upset the new liberal government in Constantinople.[35] He hoped the new regime would introduce meaningful reforms, to 'defuse' the situation, and he therefore preferred gentle advice to Turkish ambassadors in Europe to the more formal and weighty devices of notes and démarches.[36] This quieter approach would also reassure both the never-quiescent lobby at home which, with the Indian Moslems in mind, insisted on the need to treat the Sultan with respect, and those who feared that Turkey might, if displeased with Britain, make difficulties over the Persian Gulf.[37]

British interests in the Ottoman Empire would have been best served by abstaining from diplomatic activity at the Porte but the situation was too dangerous for any one Power to adopt an individual approach. After Berchtold's first proposal Grey participated fully in every move made by the Concert of Europe,[38] always stressing his desire to maintain the Concert and to prevent a disagreement between Austria and Russia which might plunge Europe into war. In September he rejected a plan of Poincaré's not only because he thought that in mentioning a naval demonstration it went too far, but also because it involved the three Entente Powers taking the initiative. This would have emphasized the division of Europe into two camps, a division which he wanted to ignore as far as possible.[39] For the sake of the Concert, and especially because Austria and Russia were for once agreed, he accepted the text of the Austro-Russian note presented to the Porte on 8 October much as he disliked its wording.[40]

But these efforts were in vain. On the very day that the Austro-Russian note was presented in Constantinople Montenegro declared war on Turkey and ten days later the other allies followed suit. The war was unexpectedly brief. By the end of October Turkish military power in the Balkans had been virtually destroyed and when an armistice was signed on 4 December, the Turks held only the three besieged garrisons of Janina, Adrianople, and Scutari; at sea the allies enjoyed complete supremacy.[41]

Throughout the hostilities Grey was concerned to maintain the unity of the Powers. By early November it was widely accepted that the allies could not be deprived of all the fruits of victory, but Grey still insisted that the Great Powers themselves were bound by the pledge contained in the Austro-Russian note to abjure individual gain, for if one Power received any benefit the others would demand compensation and the Concert would be completely disrupted. Thus the Foreign Office were uncomfortable when the Admiralty showed signs of being ready to make naval capital in the eastern Mediterranean,[42] and Grey rejected Kitchener's suggestion that the Balkan war provided an opportunity 'to come to some arrangement about the future of Egypt'.[43] On 5 November Grey was afraid that the Bulgarians might enter Constantinople, and sounded the Russians on the possibility of making it a free city, though as regards the Straits, 'we should, of course, agree to what was arranged with M. Isvolsky in London in 1908'.[44] Happily his alarm proved to be exaggerated and the Powers were saved from dealing with these most difficult questions. But it was significant that here Grey had approached the Russians secretly and separately, departing from what had been his normal practice since the outbreak of the Balkan war – close co-operation with Berlin.

In the summer of 1912 the Germans had suggested that a better atmosphere might be created for a general improvement in Anglo-German relations by co-operation on minor issues;[45] and when Bethmann Hollweg returned to this theme shortly after the outbreak of war Granville thought 'these Balkan troubles might be of some use in that respect.'[46] By the end of October Grey and Kühlmann had agreed to exchange opinions on, and to act together in, the Balkan crisis.[47] Nicolson was deeply suspicious of Germany's motives,[48] and in November he urged Grey to be careful: 'I may be old-fashioned in diplomatic methods but I view with apprehension a helter-skelter way such as Germany proposes.'[49] But if he was afraid that Austria and Russia might be excluded from discussions upon the Balkans, both Grey and Bethmann were determined that these two most interested Powers should actually lead the Concert,[50] and Nicolson's fears proved exaggerated. Anglo-German co-operation provided a useful means for exchanging ideas between the Alliance and Entente on such potentially explosive issues as Serbia's claim to an Adriatic port,[51] and in late November when the Powers decided that the moment had come to consider what territorial changes they would tolerate, it was Anglo-German exchanges that prepared the way for an exchange between the six Powers. On 27 November, when Kiderlen proposed that the Powers state their particular reservations and then attempt to formulate a peace settlement,[52] Grey suggested that the easiest way to do this was for the ambassadors in one of the capitals to hold informal discussions.[53]

The advantages of this *modus procendi* were considerable. The normal channels of diplomacy would be too slow and cumbersome to deal effectively with a situation where war could break out again at any moment, and in a tense atmosphere the exchange of messages between individual governments could give rise to dangerous misunderstandings. Moreover, ambassadors' meetings would also avoid the excessive formality of a conference. Grey disliked conferences generally, and his reasons for refusing one in 1908[54] remained valid in 1912: unless the agenda were well prepared a formal conference was as likely to produce difficulties as to solve them; 'if the settlement is easy', wrote Grey, 'it can be arranged without a Conference; if it is difficult, a Conference might make it worse.'[55] When he had secured German support, Grey came forward to propose an informal meeting of ambassadors, possibly in Paris. The ambassadors' task would be to determine how far the belligerents should be allowed to change the map of the Balkans; to decide which points the Powers themselves must settle; and to find a settlement on these latter issues acceptable to all powers.[56] Grey's proposals were accepted by all the Powers with the substitution of London for Paris as the venue,[57] and after brief and amicable discussions on procedure[58] the ambassadors' conference[59] began its work on 17 December. On the previous day peace negotiations between Turkey and the Balkan allies had begun in St James's Palace.[60]

When they had agreed to the discussions, the Powers had also agreed that the main items for consideration would be Albania, with the attendant problem of Serbian access to the Adriatic, and the Aegean Islands.[61] Austria had insisted on the creation of an independent or autonomous Albania and to the general relief Russia agreed in principle to this demand in the first *réunion.*[62]

This was a significant achievement, but the determination of the boundaries of the new state was to prove a much more exacting task, with Austria demanding an Albania large enough to be viable, and with Russia trying to secure as much territory as possible for her protégés, Montenegro and Serbia. Grey had anticipated these difficulties[63] and he realized that a great deal of responsibility rested upon his shoulders as host to the ambassadors' conference. His handling of the meetings was to be a remarkable exercise in patient statesmanship.

The object of British policy in the first half of 1913 remained the prevention of an Austro-Russian clash by keeping these two Powers within the Concert. The first requirement was that no Power should seek any advantage, territorial or diplomatic, from the Balkan settlement. This did not prevent Grey from striving to safeguard British financial and commercial interests in the Near East;[64] but in political matters he maintained the strictest disinterest, insisting that other Powers did likewise and that 'the terms of peace must not contain any condition that would be specifically injurious to the interests of any one of the Powers: otherwise the unity of the Powers could not be preserved.'[65]

The maintenance of the Concert also dictated that the division of Europe into two diplomatic camps should not be emphasized. Thus Grey was re-strained in his support for Russia in Albania[66] where the main difficulty was Scutari, a Catholic, Albanian city which the Austrians insisted was essential to Albania, and which the Russians wished to be given to its Montenegrin assailants. Grey's initial reaction had been to support St Petersburg's claims on the grounds that, as Austria had had her way over the creation of an independent Albania and the exclusion of Serbia from the Adriatic, it was for her to make concessions;[67] but when it became obvious that Berchtold was adamant for an Albanian Scutari, Grey began to seek 'some means...of satisfying Montenegro respecting Scutari without actually ceding it to her'.[68] At this stage Russia's interests and prestige seemed to him less important than the unity of the Powers.

This unity was preserved within the ambassadors' conference by Grey's skilful guidance. Throughout Grey insisted that no problem should be dis-cussed in a *réunion* until there was hope of reaching or making progress towards an agreement.[69] The assessment of the likelihood of such progress could be left to normal diplomatic exchanges, as the situation was now less tense. In these exchanges Grey was not unmindful of the dividends which co-operation with Germany had paid in the autumn of 1912. He took the line that Germany should preach moderation in Vienna whilst Britain would do all she could to temper Russia's demands;[70] and he readily lent his support to German proposals – provided always that Britain and Germany worked together within the Concert. For example, when, in January 1913, Turkey's refusal to cede Adrianople to Bulgaria raised the danger of a resumption of the Balkan war, and the Kaiser, terrified that in this eventuality Russia would intervene, proposed that Germany and Britain , as the least interested Powers, should exert 'gentle but firm pressure' at Constantinople in favour of a 'more accommodating tone and less dilatory methods',[71] Grey insisted on passing the proposal on to the ambassadors. He was wary of an isolated Anglo-German action for should it prove futile the British government, as host to the London conferences, would be embarrassed. Similarly German suggestions that Berlin and London tackle a dispute between Bulgaria and Roumania[72] were, at Grey's insistence, referred to an ambassadorial conference in St Petersburg.[73] The Foreign Office had been reluctant to involve itself in this dispute[74] but in the interest of the Concert its objections were overcome. The Alliance powers strove to secure for Roumania territorial concessions at the expense of Bul-garia who was to take Salonika as compensation. Britain joined France and

Russia in unflinching opposition to this plan, fearing that a Bulgarian Salonika could become an Austrian outpost on the Aegean, and when the conference ended with the St Petersburg Protocol of 8 May 1913 Roumania received territorial gains and Bulgaria merely 'the appreciation of the Powers' for its accommodating attitude.[75]

Meanwhile, the ambassadors in London had agreed on the text of a collective note urging the Turks to cede Adrianople, and even began to consider backing it up with a naval demonstration. Grey had no enthusiasm for this idea, but again for the sake of the unity of the Concert he was willing to participate.[76] Not that the Concert could solve this problem; the Turks refused to budge and on 3 February the Balkan War was renewed. This at least rescued Grey from one dilemma, for it was generally agreed that a naval demonstration now would constitute a breach of neutrality. But the renewed hostilities were to create more difficulties than they solved.

In March Russia gave up her insistence that Scutari go to Montenegro in return for the Austrian concession that Serbia have Djakova,[77] and the Powers had apparently solved the problem of the northern and north-eastern boundary of Albania. But the Montenegrins would not admit this, and continued their efforts to take Scutari, threatening to destroy the Powers' settlement, which was to Grey 'the anchor by which we must hold to preserve peace'.[78] There now arose the danger that Austria and Italy, or Austria alone, would take separate action to enforce the Powers' decision,[79] and Grey welcomed a Russian suggestion that an international fleet be sent to the Adriatic to convince the Montenegrins that the Powers really were determined that Scutari would go to Albania.[80] There were difficulties in organizing the demonstration: Russia did not have a ship available and the French were dubious.[81] The Cabinet therefore agreed that if the demonstration did not have a fully international character Britain would not feel herself bound to participate but, for the sake of the Concert, she would not 'oppose any steps taken by any other Power or Powers, which may be reasonably required to make the agreement as to Albania effective.'[82] The French at last agreed to take part in the demonstration after Russia, with encouragement from Britain,[83] had publicly consented to her doing so.[84] But the presence of an international squadron in the Adriatic did not solve the question for on 23 April the commander of the Turkish garrison, Essad Pasha, sold[85] Scutari to the Montenegrins.

This was the most dangerous moment in the Balkan crisis of 1912–13. The Cabinet agreed that the first essential was to maintain the unity of the Powers and that the fall of Scutari did not alter the decision to include the city in Albania,[86] but despite strong pressure, especially from Berlin,[87] for the use of force, they forbad the landing of marines from the international squadron for fear that this would lead to embarrassment and difficulties with Russia.[88] On 30 April they agreed that Grey should make clear that whilst Britain was determined the Powers' decision should stand, she believed that the 'question of time is...of less importance than the paramount urgency of preserving the Concert of Europe.'[89] Britain could afford to urge restraint upon the Powers, for on that very morning the Foreign Office had received from a city financial concern information that Montenegro would be ready to cede Scutari for two million francs.[90] Grey informed the company that no money must be given to Montenegro whilst she continued to occupy Scutari but 'should she submit to the will of the Powers and evacuate Scutari there would be no political objection whatever to supplying her with funds...'[91] On 4 May King Nicholas announced his intention to evacuate Scutari and ten days later detachments from the international squadron took control of the city.[92] The danger of Austrian intervention and the destruction of the Concert had passed.[93]

Yet this danger had been real and had led Grey to clarify his priorities. On 1 May he wrote of the dangers of acting 'against the wishes of Russia and of separating ourselves from France *at a moment when it seems most necessary that we should keep in close touch with her and Russia*'.[94] Indeed before the *réunion* of 28 April, Grey had taken the unusual step of seeing the French and Russian ambassadors to co-ordinate Entente policy.[95] In the last analysis, Grey considered the unity of the Entente even more important than the unity of the Concert, but he still hoped to avoid having to choose between the two. After the shock of the Scutari crisis he was anxious to end discussions on the Balkan peace settlement lest similar crises wreck the unity of the Powers. In the end he submitted a draft treaty to the St James's Conference and on 27 May ordered the delegates to sign it or leave. Three days later the Treaty of London was signed.[96] At the same time he strove to conclude the ambassadors' meetings. He feared that

there was a growing disposition on the part of the Foreign Ministries of Europe to throw upon the shoulders of the Ambassadors' Conference in London the burden of settling each new question as it arises (for example the future of Asiatic Turkey),[97]

and he therefore proposed 'to wind up the proceedings of the conference' by submitting to it the two questions still outstanding amongst those it had agreed to discuss: the organization of Albania and the future of the Aegean Islands.[98]

Before these questions could be settled, however, war broke out again when, on 29–30 June, Bulgaria attacked her former Greek and Serbian allies. Roumania and Turkey joined in against Bulgaria who was forced at the ensuing treaty of Bucharest (10 August) to yield many of her recent gains. The inter-allied conflict had not been unexpected[99] and in the weeks preceding it the British had hoped that if war broke out between the allies the Powers would stand aside and let them settle their differences between themselves.[100] Grey was not unduly worried by the outbreak of the Second Balkan war,[101] and continued to enjoin complete non-interference upon the ambassadors' conference,[102] a policy he maintained with relative ease until the Turks recaptured Adrianople on 21 July. At this Sazonov demanded that Turkey be made to observe the Treaty of London, and the Powers faced the danger of unilateral Russian intervention.

Grey's attitude was determined by Britain's interests in Asiatic Turkey rather than in the Balkans. The greatest danger was that Russia would invade Turkish Armenia precipitating a scramble for territory in Asia Minor that would plunge Europe into war. Even if a general war were avoided Britain would be greatly embarrassed, for in the Cyprus Convention of 1878 she had assumed vague obligations to defend Asiatic Turkey against Russian encroachment.[103] Grey therefore suggested that 'a possible alternative might be a naval demonstration and a landing near Constantinople'.[104] Nothing came of this, however, and the danger of Russian intervention remained. True, Sazonov was now thinking in terms of an Entente rather than a purely Russian action, but this Grey deemed 'the worst conceivable course',[105] and he also refused to apply the financial pressure at the Porte which Russia proposed.[106] He did not wish to disturb the delicate Anglo–Turkish negotiations on the Bagdad Railway and the Persian Gulf then in progress in London:[107] the Constantinople embassy which had suggested economic pressure on Turkey was told that Britain would not suspend her negotiations with Turkey for the sake of Adrianople, 'as to do so would merely cause offence and damage our own material interests without any assured advantages'.[108] Grey had never shown great enthusiasm for the Bulgarian cause in Adrianople[109] but the determining factor in his policy remained his fear of disturbing the situation in Asiatic Turkey, over which negotiations with both Germany and Turkey had been going well.[110] It was with this in mind too, that the Foreign Office refused once again[111] to consider a Turkish offer of an alliance with Britain on the grounds that a rapprochement between Britain and Turkey would cause too much suspicion abroad, especially in Berlin.[112]

The difficulties over Adrianople (which the Turks retained) had of course done nothing to shake Grey's conviction that the ambassadors should end their meetings. He impressed upon them that the holidays were rapidly approaching and that if the conference were not to be discredited he must be able to tell Parliament that agreement had been reached on the future of Albania and the Aegean Islands.[113] Some progress was made in that it was agreed to establish commissions to delimit southern Albania[114] and to administer the new state until a Prince acceptable to all Powers could be found.[115] But, as in December 1912, an agreement in principle left plenty of difficulties over details.

The Islands question had plagued the Powers for over a year. In April and May 1912 the Italians, in an effort to force a conclusion to the Tripoli war, had occupied a number of islands in the Southern Sporades, including Rhodes and Stampalia.[116] Despite indications that the Italian occupation might be more than temporary[117] Grey decided he could not interfere until the end of the war, although he did ask the Admiralty about the effect on Britain's naval position if Italy established herself permanently in the Aegean.[118] In the Admiralty's view, British strategy in the eastern Mediterranean was based upon the assumption that any hostile fleet would have to operate from ports at least a thousand miles distant and could therefore be observed and controlled by ships based on Gibraltar or Malta. Should a naval Power be established in the Aegean Britain's trading interests in the Levant and the Black Sea would be endangered and her position in Egypt threatened to 'an unprecedented degree'.[119] Moreover, as all the Powers were interested in trade passing through the Straits, the fate of the Aegean Islands (whence the Straits could be threatened) should be determined by all the Powers together.[120] The Admiralty memorandum determined British policy throughout discussions on the Islands.

The Treaty of Lausanne appeared to have eliminated the problem, providing for the return of the occupied islands to Turkey when all Ottoman forces had left Cyrenaica, and guaranteeing there would be no reprisals against the islanders when reversion took place.[121] (This obviated one of Grey's fears, namely that Turkish repression might provoke rebellions amongst the Christian populations and present the Powers with a 'number of new Cretes'.)[122] It was not long, however, before fresh difficulties arose. The predominantly Greek population of the Islands made them a natural objective of Greek attack in the Balkan war and, as Italy still held the southern Sporades, this attack was directed against the more northerly islands including those near the Straits.[123]

Grey remained committed to the doctrine of non-intervention in the Balkan war but the possibility of a second closure of the Straits placed him in an extremely embarrassing position. He had been greatly angered in April when an Italian attack on the Dardanelles had forced the Turks to close the Straits[124] and a closure in the autumn would be even more disastrous, 'the grain trade being especially important at this time of the year'.[125] Despite his urgent desire to avoid any departure from the strict neutrality he had declared at the beginning of the Balkan war, he admitted, therefore, that 'we may have to interfere if the Dardanelles are closed'.[126] Luckily, they remained open and the fate of the islands in Greek occupation did not need to be considered until the armistice of December 1912. Yet the problem remained. Strong rumours were current that Italy wished to take advantage of Turkey's difficulties to secure permanent possession of at least one island,[127] and the Admiralty wished to be ready to seize adequate compensation should this happen. The Foreign Office too, were alarmed by what Nicolson called 'the Churchill project as to Corfu'[128] and although the Admiralty denied it had ever raised the question of Britain occupying an island Grey admitted 'it is true that it had not been raised officially between the Departments but it had in conversation with me, and it certainly would be raised officially if any Great Naval Power acquired or kept an Aegean Island...'[129] Further embarrassment was saved only by the decision to put the Aegean Islands on the agenda of the forthcoming ambassadors' conference.

Whilst the Balkan wars continued the Ambassadors paid little attention to the Islands. Although Britain would have preferred to see them ceded to Greece to avoid future 'Cretes',[130] a German proposal to neutralize them was accepted, not least because too great an increase in Greek naval power was a disconcerting prospect.[131] But after the signing of the Treaty of London Grey re-opened the question. He was still convinced that 'to get Italy out of the Islands and to put them into the hands of Greece is a great thing for us as well as for Greece'.[132] He had resolutely resisted suggestions from the Triple Alliance that those islands near the coast of Asia Minor should revert to Turkey, lest in Greek hands they become bases for a political agitation amongst the Greeks of the mainland which could disrupt the *status quo* in Asiatic Turkey.[133] Grey's argument was that the islanders would not tolerate renewed subjection to the Porte, and that even if given autonomy they would still declare for union with Greece, and in either event only intervention by the Powers would save the peace. Unless the Powers were willing to commit themselves to this, which he doubted, 'to offer Turkey the retention of the Islands would not be an honest offer'.[134] To lessen the Alliance Powers' objections to the cession of the Islands to Greece, Grey proposed that the Aegean question be settled jointly with that of the Greco-Albanian frontier.

Austria and Italy had been adamant that this frontier be so drawn as to include the Corfu channel (whence a naval Power could control the Straits of Otranto) in neutral Albania.[135] This Grey was willing to concede if the Austrians and Italians would in turn make concessions to Greece in the Aegean sufficient to enable Venizelos to effect the exceedingly unpopular evacuation of Northern Epirus (Southern Albania).[136] He hoped that Italy, in order to see the Corfu channel neutralized, would agree to evacuate the Aegean islands she was occupying. No Great Power would then have secured any territorial advantage in the Near East and the Concert would be maintained.

He was to be disappointed. In Albania the International Control Commission and the commission for the delimitation of the southern frontier met with many difficulties from Greek irregulars operating in Northern Epirus. Serbian troops meanwhile had been forced to withdraw from Northern Albania by an Austrian ultimatum of 18 October, and this the Powers had accepted as Serbia was contravening a decision already taken by the Concert.[137] However, a separate Austro-Italian démarche in Athens (30 October) insisting upon the evacuation of Greek forces from Southern Albania by 31 December,[138] caused great indignation in Entente circles, as Austria and Italy had acted without reference to the other Powers in a matter upon which the Concert was still deliberating. On 12 December, therefore, Grey made an effort to re-emphasize the Concert and proposed a joint and immediate settlement of the Epirote and Aegean problems; Greece was to be told to evacuate Epirus by a given date and would in return receive a guarantee from the Powers that she would keep those islands she already occupied (except Tenedos and Imbros);[139] the islands in Italian occupation would be granted autonomy under Turkish suzerainty.[140]

The British Circular of 12 December was a distinct concession by Grey in response to increasing tension in the Near East: the Greco-Turkish peace treaty of November 1913 had left the question of the Islands unsolved;[141] Italy was patently intriguing for economic concessions in Asia Minor as compensation for her expenses in occupying the southern Sporades;[142] and the Triple Alliance Powers were hinting that despite Grey's insistence[143] they did not consider the problems of Epirus and the Aegean were inseparable.[144] The final straw was a telegram from Athens in which Venizelos threatened to resign unless the Powers could compensate Greece in the Islands in return for her leaving Albania.[145] The Foreign Office knew that Venizelos was the only Greek politician capable of persuading the Greek public to accept the loss of Epirus, and to keep him in office Grey was anxious to secure confirmation of the principle that the Aegean and southern Albanian questions were interdependent.

He failed however, to restore vitality to the Concert. Despite his warnings that a failure to settle the Islands question would reopen that of the Albanian frontier[146] the Triple Alliance reply of 31 December ignored the Aegean completely.[147] When the Alliance Powers did finally present their views on the Islands on 14 January[148] Grey set about planning collective démarches in Athens and Constantinople. Certainly the Triple Alliance Powers had ignored his proposals regarding the Italian-held islands and merely reiterated their old view that the settlement of these islands was a matter between Rome and Constantinople, but, undaunted, Grey concentrated on securing agreement on the texts of the projected démarches. Moreover, in the Foreign Office's view, the Powers could not urge a settlement upon Greece and Turkey without agreeing to enforce it:

If the Powers are not in accord on this point, then neither litigant would regard the 'decision' as more than mere 'recommendations', and it would not be consistent with the dignity of the Powers nor conducive to peace for such an interpretation to prevail.[149]

The Triplice, however, refused even to contemplate the use of force[150] and although the démarches were made, the Concert had been emasculated. The final blow to any hopes that it was still an effective working organization came on 8 March, when Italy and Austria, without consulting the other Powers, again made a separate démarche in Athens, the representatives of the Entente only learning of it from an announcement of the Greek Foreign Minister in parliament.[151]

In Albania, meanwhile, Grey had made every effort to maintain the Concert. He had always regarded Austria and Italy as the most interested Powers and had allowed them their way whenever this did not infringe the principle or impair the practice of an international settlement. Thus Vienna and Rome had secured the Albanian throne for Prince William of Wied[152] and had determined who should represent Albania on the International Control Commission.[153] Grey had, however, resisted Austrian and Italian plans to achieve a privileged position in Albania. He had refused to accept the Austro-Italian banking monopoly which the Provisional Government in Valona had granted, insisting that if there were to be a bank in Albania, it must be an international one.[154]

The independence of Austro-Italian diplomacy in the spring of 1914, however, made Grey reconsider his position. Even as early as October 1913, when the French Chargé in London had suggested that his government's impatience with Albania might lead it to follow the example set by Germany and Austria in Crete and withdraw, Grey had admitted that his thoughts were 'tending in much the same direction'.[155] In December Crowe too urged withdrawal, noting the long term advantages this course had to offer: if the Triple Alliance was left alone in Albania, Italy and Austria would soon fall out and Germany would have to choose between her allies.[156] Grey would have accepted Crowe's recommendations immediately 'if France and Russia had not to be consulted',[157] but Russia believed that for the Entente to leave Albania would be too great a loss of prestige.[158] By May when the principality was being destroyed by its own centrifugal forces Grey's lack of interest was obvious and he refused to ask Parliament or the Cabinet for permission to commit British forces for the protection of the state and throne the Powers had created:[159] he was 'disposed to leave Austria and Italy to find their own way out of the difficulties that are mainly due to their own intrigues...'[160] As Crowe noted, no doubt with the Irish crisis in mind,

this is not the time or occasion for a Quixotic crusade on our part on behalf of a conglomeration of noble bandits struggling to remain free. The general political situation counsels us to keep out of entanglements that might embarrass us when we were least able to afford such a luxury.[161]

By May 1914, therefore, with Albania dissolving into anarchy; with war threatening between Greece and Turkey over the Islands; and Italy remaining defiantly in possession of the southern Sporades, the Concert of Europe was discredited – and this only a few months before the Sarajevo crisis.

Whilst the Concert of Europe was exhausting itself with the legacies of the Italo-Turkish and the Balkan wars, Grey faced another problem in the Near East: the maintenance of the Russian Entente. Although the Russo-German tension arising from the Liman von Sanders mission[162] has received more attention from historians (perhaps as a result of developments in 1914), it should not be forgotten that Britain's comparable effort to strengthen Turkey's naval forces was subjecting Anglo-Russian relations to considerable strain. A British naval mission had been in Constantinople advising the Turkish Ministry of Marine since 1909, but the Balkan wars, and the quarrel with

Greece over the Islands convinced Turkey of the need to strengthen her fleet, and she turned to Britain for help. In October 1913 a concession for the construction and maintenance of all Turkish dockyards was granted to a British consortium.[163] and with the concession came definite agreement on the delivery of two British-built dreadnoughts and orders for two light cruisers, six destroyers and two submarines.[164] In December the Turkish Ministry of Marine requested more British officers and petty officers to help train men for the new ships; and the Foreign Office was willing to help, although some difficulty was experienced in finding volunteers to go to Turkey.[165] The Russians were furious.

Even at the height of the crisis with Germany in December 1913 Sazonov had expressed some anxiety at the prospect of Turkey's purchasing British-built dreadnoughts:

the Turkish fleet might, with the assistance of a British Admiral and with the Dockyards and Arsenals about to be built by British firms, be for a time at any rate a menace to Russia, whose Dreadnoughts now under construction in the Black Sea would not be completed till 1916 at the earliest.[166]

His anxieties increased and persisted long after the settlement of the Liman dispute until in May he warned the British that if Turkey's naval strength continued to increase at the current rate he would have to raise the question of the Straits.[167] The Foreign Office recognized that Russia wished to be able to move capital ships from the Baltic to the Black Sea, but this was the first occasion since 1908 that St Petersburg had talked so boldly of the Straits, and Nicolson noted that 'the questions raised are so important that they cannot be debated in departmental minutes'.[168]

No incident could have been more illustrative of the complexities of the Near Eastern situation. Britain had established and maintained a Naval Mission in Constantinople in order to keep out the Germans;[169] the Dock Concession had helped to consolidate her position at the Porte in the face of increasing German influence, and she had sold Turkey dreadnoughts partly to avoid offending her and forcing her into Germany's arms. This policy had back-fired and was threatening to drive a wedge into the Entente. Serious differences between Britain and Russia in the Near East were prevented only by the final breakdown of the Concert and the outbreak of war.

14

British policy during the Agadir Crisis of 1911

M. L. DOCKRILL

Early in 1911 a serious revolt broke out amongst the tribes in Morocco against the Sultan, Mulai Hafid. By early April 1911 the monarch was besieged in his capital, and the French began to prepare a military expedition, whose stated purpose was to be the protection of the lives and property of Europeans in Fez, but which was, in reality, intended to save the sultan from the consequences of his incompetence and chronic maladministration.[1]

Neither Grey nor his officials welcomed the prospect of a renewed crisis over Morocco which might follow the advance of a French army to Fez. There were two dangers. The Germans might claim that the Act of Algeciras had been breached and would, as a result, be provided with an opportunity to demand a new settlement of the question. The other danger was that Spain might occupy her sphere of Tetuan and Laraiche as a counter to a French occupation of Fez. The foreign office feared that Germany might be only too willing to encourage independent action by Spain in Morocco as a further means of reopening the question. Furthermore, Grey's officials were concerned that, if France persisted in ignoring Spanish interests in Morocco, Spain would turn to Berlin for support in the future. Thus, during the Spring and early summer, Grey attempted to restrain France from adopting over-hasty measures in Morocco and to persuade her to withdraw her troops from the Moorish capital. At the same time he pressed France to negotiate a settlement with Spain.

In both cases his efforts failed. The French despatched a flying column to Fez at the end of April, while Spain began to assemble troops for a descent on Laraiche and Alcazar. In attempting to restrain France Grey's hands were tied both by Britain's obligations under the 1904 convention and by his insistence that the entente must be maintained at all costs. Thus he minuted in April that 'what the French contemplate doing is not wise, but we cannot under our agreement interfere', while Nicolson insisted that whatever happened Britain would adhere to the position she had adopted in 1906.[2] Further than this, however, Grey would not go. He rejected French suggestions that he intimate at Berlin that Great Britain fully supported French action in Morocco, and French pressure for more active Anglo-French military cooperation.[3]

The French had good reason to be concerned about the possible reactions of Berlin to their move. Kiderlen was already dissatisfied by the 1909 convention,[4] which had not reaped the dividends that the Germans had originally anticipated, in the shape of greater Franco-German cooperation and a much increased German commercial and financial stake in Morocco. The French had no intention of endangering their political preponderance in the country by encouraging the Germans to secure a stranglehold on Morocco's economic resources. The two countries were already engaged in a bitter quarrel about joint participation in railway, mining and other concessions there.[5]

The German Foreign Office looked upon the advance of the French military expedition on Fez with gloomy satisfaction. A French occupation of Fez was bound to strengthen French political influence in Morocco, and provide Germany with an opportunity to secure concessions at France's expense. Nevertheless Kiderlen decided to await developments before acting.[6] When the French insisted that their action was compatible with the 1909 agreement, Kiderlen and the chancellor denied the contention, and at the same time indicated that they doubted that the lives of Europeans in Fez were in danger. The Germans were of course merely safeguarding their position, for Kiderlen gave a grudging approval to the occupation of Fez on 21 May, although he insisted that it should be of temporary duration, and at the same time reserved his right to demand an exchange of views with the French should the necessity arise.[7]

The British suspected, as did Kiderlen, that the French would be unable to withdraw from Fez once they had restored order there, and the British foreign office became increasingly alarmed about likely German reactions in this event. Many of Grey's officials feared that France might give way to German pressure and agree to a tripartite division of Morocco (with Spain), with Germany securing a Moroccan port and other concessions affecting Britain's strategic and economic interests. They feared that the refusal of Asquith and Grey to make any gesture designed to reassure France that Britain's support would be forthcoming in the event of a new crisis, coupled with the cabinet's willingness to continue the fruitless political and naval negotiations with Germany, would lead both Germany and France to assume that Britain would not intervene in the event of a new Moroccan crisis.[8]

By June, despite frequent French promises to evacuate Fez, their troops looked like remaining in the capital. On 5 June, Spain, after the collapse of Franco-Spanish negotiations, occupied Laraiche and Alcazar and refused to withdraw, despite further British pressure.[9] It had now become apparent in London that France and Spain had become so closely involved in Morocco that they would be unable to withdraw their forces. Given these circumstances, Grey began to contemplate the eventual partition of the country between France and Spain, with Germany receiving compensation, although he hoped that this would not be in Morocco.[10]

Foreign Office fears that Germany would intervene in Morocco were at last realised when, on 1 July 1911, the German gunboat the 'Panther', moored at Agadir. This startling gesture provided her critics in London with further evidence that her foreign policy was both unpredictable and malevolent. On this occasion British assumptions about the motives for Germany's action were to some extent justified. Kiderlen knew that the French were prepared to offer Germany unspecified concessions in return for German agreement to a free hand for France in Morocco.[11] Towards the end of June Wilhelmstrasse optimism in this respect was enhanced when Joseph Caillaux formed a new government in Paris, with the inexperienced de Selves as Foreign Minister, as Caillaux was an advocate of a Franco-German rapprochement by means of a fairly generous settlement in Germany's favour of outstanding colonial differences.[12]

Kiderlen's motive in despatching the 'Panther' to Agadir, taken after discussions with Bethmann and the German Emperor, was to demonstrate both to France and her friends that Germany had as much right to compensation in the event of the alteration of the status quo in Morocco as had Britain, Spain and Italy. The chief calculation in Kiderlen's mind was that Germany's action would bludgeon those in the French Ministry who might oppose compensation for Germany, and at the same time strengthen the hands of those who, like Caillaux, were anxious to treat German claims in a magnanimous spirit. As usual with German diplomacy in these years, the very opposite took place: in the long run the 'Panther' stiffened French resistance, provoked French patriotic and chauvinist sentiments, and eventually drove Great Britain to the support of her entente partner. What Kiderlen wanted was not concessions in Morocco (although some of his associates wanted these), but a substantial territorial gain in the French Congo which was to form the basis for a large German empire in Central Africa.[13] If, as a by-product of this policy, British support for France in the ensuing bargaining was only lukewarm, and, as a result, the entente collapsed, this, from the German point of view, would have been all to the good.[14]

It was this aspect of Germany's strategy which inevitably caused Britain the most concern, for while Grey was not opposed to German expansion in Central Africa,[15] he was determined to uphold the entente against Germany's attempts to wreck it. The French, well primed by Bertie, were well aware of his fears and, by playing on them, endeavoured to secure British support to reduce the concessions that they were forced to make to the Germans to the narrowest limits. Throughout the early part of the crisis a cautious and troubled Grey was under strong pressure from his officials, and from the French, to adopt a much more determined stand in favour of France than he thought desirable or than the cabinet or liberal opinion would in any case accept.

Part of the trouble was that Kiderlen could hardly reveal his motives to the British. As a result Metternich could only offer confusing explanations for the conduct of his government, or remain silent, which merely increased British suspicions of German policy. German efforts to exclude Britain from what she regarded as her legal right to be consulted about possible changes in Morocco were, naturally enough, resented in British official circles, and as a result exaggerated rumours about Germany's ambitions quickly gained currency. Hence, at the outset, Crowe assumed that Germany contemplated a division of Morocco between France, Spain and herself, with the ultimate aim of ousting the other two altogether from the country. Both he and Nicolson urged Grey to take a leading part in the dispute, as the future of the Mediterranean and Atlantic coasts was of the utmost strategic importance to Great Britain. Nicolson, in dwelling on the need for British military and naval precautions, demanded at the very least the despatch of a British warship to Morocco as a clear warning to Germany that Britain was determined to uphold her interests there. At the back of the Foreign Office pressure lay the continuing fear that, if Britain did not come out in support of France, Germany would be able to bully her into an agreement affecting British interests.[16]

While both Grey and Asquith were irritated by Germany's precipitate move – the Prime Minister described it as 'an interesting illustration of Realpolitik' – neither favoured over-reacting to the German move at this stage. Grey merely commented to Metternich on 3 July about the 'abrupt' nature of Germany's action, and insisted that Britain must participate in any discussions about the future of Morocco, thus reflecting fears that Britain might be excluded from any subsequent negotiations. Asquith, for instance, considered that the German action was designed to provoke 'a new diplomatic settlement of Morocco' between Spain, France and Germany, 'on the basis of the Bismarckian doctrine: "beati possidentes"'. Grey would say no more to the German Ambassador until the cabinet had discussed the question on 4 July.[17]

At this meeting the cabinet concentrated on how British interests could best be protected and the Ministers wasted little sympathy on France, whose actions, many believed, had been responsible for the crisis. It was decided that a British warship was not to be sent to Agadir and that the German Ambassador should be informed that 'any discussions or negotiations which take place must be not à trois but à quatre'. The cabinet also agreed that Grey should tell Paul Cambon that the British Government would honour its obligations to France under the 1904 convention and that France must make proposals for the settlement of the dispute. The Cabinet resolution suggested that the powers might 'have to give a more definite recognition than before to German interests in Morocco'. Finally, it insisted that three British interests must be safeguarded in any future Moroccan settlement:

(1) No German port on the Mediterranean shore.

(2) No new fortified port anywhere on the Moroccan (Atlantic) coast.

(3) The 'open door' for British trade in Morocco must be maintained.

The cabinet thus adopted a cautious policy and there is no evidence that Grey differed at this stage from the decisions that had been reached.[18] He relayed the gist of the cabinet's resolution to Paul Cambon on the same day, informing him that, if France offered Germany compensation in Morocco or elsewhere in return for her recognition of France's special position in Morocco, Great Britain for her part, would have to decide what 'conditions' she would require from Germany. He informed Metternich that the British Government would not recognise any Moroccan settlement about which it had not been consulted.[19]

Inevitably Grey's officials were extremely disappointed by what they regarded as the weak response of the cabinet towards Germany's provocative diplomacy. As Cambon put it, referring to Grey's refusal to send a British gunboat to Agadir, 'mais obtenir une mesure quelconque du Cabinet libéral anglais est impossible. Il en a toujours été ainsi, et du temps de Gladstone c'était exactement la même chose.' The foreign office evidently hoped that France would put up a determined resistance to any German claim for compensation in Morocco, and somehow drag the British along with her. Certainly Caillaux was anxious that no hint of the British cabinet's attitude on this question should reach Germany's ears, while Bertie, equally hostile to the policy adopted by his government, encouraged French resistance to Germany's demands. Thus, he claimed that before 11 July he had been in ignorance of the cabinet's decision not to oppose a German Atlantic port, and had been supporting French opposition to a permanent German presence in Morocco.[20]

Grey firmly resisted the efforts of his officials to associate Britain with an intransigent French attitude towards what he regarded as Germany's legitimate right to some compensation should changes be made in the Moroccan status quo. While his officials continued to fulminate against what they regarded as his timorous policy, and to press for firm British support for France, lest she be thrown 'into the Teuton embrace',[21] Grey exhibited his anxiety for a pacific settlement of the dispute. He agreed, on 11 July, to the holding of separate Franco-German discussions between Jules Cambon and Kiderlen at Berlin, on the basis that the German government 'will be content with a new delimitation of the French Congo in favour of Germany, and withdraw any territorial or strategical claims in Morocco'.[22] As far as Grey was concerned, a settlement on these lines would be entirely satisfactory. France promised to keep both Britain and Spain (who, to her chagrin, was excluded from participation in the Berlin talks) informed of their progress, although Crowe cautioned Grey against placing too much reliance on French veracity.[23] At the same time Grey rejected further French suggestions for joint action to secure the removal of the German gunboat from Agadir on the grounds that it would only cause further difficulties.[24]

The Franco-German negotiations seemed likely to collapse almost as soon as they had been begun. On 15 July Kiderlen revealed that his country would expect practically the whole of the French Congo in return for German agreement to forgo her political interests in Morocco and hinted that Germany might be prepared to cede the north Cameroon and Togoland to France. De Selves, complaining of 'des prétentions excessives', believed that it would be fruitless to continue the negotiations.[25] As far as the British foreign office was concerned, Germany's demand was the final proof, if such were required, that Germany sought to humiliate France and wreck the entente. Grey was accordingly deluged with exhortations from his permanent officials who maintained that this would be the outcome if Britain did not declare her determination to fight alongside France, if necessary, to resist this latest German onslaught on the balance of power. The prime minister, describing Germany's demand as a 'choice specimen of what the Germans call "diplomacy"', ordered a cabinet meeting for 19 July.[26]

At this meeting Grey exhibited considerable anxiety about Germany's intentions. He suggested that he propose to Berlin that a conference be held on Morocco, and that, if Germany refused, it should be intimated to her that 'we should take steps to assert and protect British interests'. Lord Loreburn, the Lord Chancellor, one of Grey's most persistent critics during the crisis, 'strenuously resisted' this proposal. He felt it was unnecessary since Great Britain's direct interest in Morocco 'was insignificant, and that as a result of such a communication, we might soon find ourselves drifting into war'. 'A long and animated discussion' followed. The cabinet evidently could not reach agreement on what to tell the Germans, for it decided to defer any communication to Berlin until its next meeting on 21 July. Meanwhile, since the German proposals were unacceptable, France was to be advised to submit her counter-proposals to Germany on the subject of compensation in the French Congo. She was also to be asked whether she was prepared to resist '*à outrance* the admission of Germany, under ANY conditions, into Morocco'. The cabinet here entered a *caveat* that France was to be informed 'that under proper conditions such admission would not be regarded as fatal to British interests, and could not be treated by us as a *casus belli*'. However, Grey was authorised to tell France that, if all else failed, 'we shall suggest a Conference, in which it will be our aim to work in concert with French diplomacy'.[27]

This somewhat indecisive resolution was conveyed to Paris in the form of a note of 20 July, which requested the definite views of the French Government on the subject before the cabinet meeting of Friday 21 July.[28] It was hardly calculated to reassure the French as to the steadfastness of the British government's support for the entente. Crowe expressed the general dejection when he wrote to Bertie on the 20th that he 'was sorry beyond words at the line we are taking up in this Morocco business. It seems to me that our Cabinet are all on the run, and the strong hints we are giving to France that she must let Germany into Morocco makes me ashamed as well as angry.' Bertie was equally depressed.[29]

Grey now shared, to some extent, the fears of his officials. The cabinet resolution had not been entirely a setback for him, for in his note of 20 July to the French, he stated that the British Government reserved its right to propose a conference, and that it would inform Berlin that, in the event of a German refusal to attend, Britain 'will be obliged to take action to protect

British interests'.[30] Nevertheless Grey felt that Germany, as well as France, should be informed of the British view. He wrote to Asquith after the cabinet meeting of the 19th to point out that Germany had still not responded to his statement to Metternich on 4 July. He feared that if Britain continued to remain silent, Germany would conclude that she would not intervene, and would, as a result, further increase her demands on France. He suggested that if Germany had not replied by 21 July, he should be authorised to remind her that Great Britain must participate in any further discussions on Morocco, should the current Franco-German negotiations collapse.[31]

Nevertheless, he still refused to adopt the hard line advocated by his officials. He wrote to Bertie on 20 July to repeat his view, that Great Britain could not be expected to go to war either to put France in possession of Morocco, or to turn Germany out of Agadir. British intervention in a continental war could only be justified, he insisted, by a direct threat to her vital interests, and he instanced a deliberate German effort to humiliate France. After all, he added, France had turned Morocco into a virtual protectorate, and Germany had every right to compensation if it was decided to recognise this fact. If Germany's demands on France became excessive, the most he could do would be to propose an international conference to discuss the whole question.[32] In a telegram on the same day to the ambassador, Grey expressed his opinion that Great Britain did not want 'to acquire more tropical territory on any extensive scale and prefer to concentrate on [the] development of what we have'. On the draft of this telegram, Grey deleted an additional paragraph he had written which stated that 'if Germany is very unreasonable our own interests may require us to take a foremost front position in the controversy ...and go to extremes if need be, but we cannot move without knowing what is the object that France wishes to attain, and having a clear understanding with her'.[33]

The French, in their reply to the British note, re-emphasised their opposition to a German presence in Morocco.[34] Their alarm at developments was further increased by another angry conversation between Jules Cambon and Kiderlen on 20 July, during the course of which Kiderlen repeated his demand for the French Congo, and complained bitterly that details of their previous discussions had been published in the Paris press on the 19th.[35] The cabinet met on the morning of 21 July to discuss British policy in the light of this steadily deteriorating atmosphere. The prospects for a calm assessment of the situation were not improved by the knowledge that Germany's demands on France had been published in *The Times* on the previous day, and had resulted in much press comment, mostly unfavourable to Germany.[36] To the international tension was added mounting industrial unrest, the angry debates about the Parliament Bill, and a phenomenal heat wave. Asquith reported to the King that:

Sir E. Grey gave a full account of the communications which have passed during the last few days between the Foreign Office and the French Government on the subject of the Franco-German negotiations. It appears from them that France is about to make counter-proposals to Germany in regard to the Congo frontiers. Otherwise matters remain much where they were. After some discussions it was agreed that Sir E. Grey should point out to Count Metternich, whom he is to see in the afternoon, that 17 days had elapsed without any notice being taken by Germany of the British statement of our position; that while we wished well to the negotiations for any arrangement in the Congo or elsewhere in West Africa, which would be satisfactory to Germany and France, and put an end, for the time at any rate, to any question of compensation for Germany in Morocco, yet if that proved impossible it must be clearly understood that we should recognise no settlement in Morocco in which we had not a voice.[37]

Grey's statement to Metternich after this meeting,[38] and Lloyd George's speech at the Mansion House in the evening, were both in line with this cabinet resolution, although there is no record that Lloyd George's speech was discussed in the cabinet. It appears to have originated as an independent initiative by the chancellor of the exchequer, who presumably felt that it would look odd if he did not make some allusion to the Moroccan crisis in his speech.[39]

There is no evidence to support the contention that the chancellor's words were addressed as much to Caillaux and the French as to the Germans.[40] All the clues in fact point the other way. The French had been reminded several times what Great Britain's position was, and, according to Asquith, the cabinet met on 21 July solely to decide what Germany should be told. Grey's officials no longer believed that France might engage in some shabby back-stairs intrigue with Germany. They now feared that, bullied by Germany and unsure of British support, she would be forced to give way entirely to Germany's demands. Few at the time regarded the speech as in any way addressed to France (except in so far as it put fresh heart into her),[41] least of all Germany as her angry reaction demonstrated. From Grey's point of view, the defection of the supposedly 'pro-German' Lloyd George from the 'anti-German entente' camp had two beneficial effects – the chancellor's speech had more influence on the Germans than any comparable effort by Grey would have done, and it left the other 'pro-Germans' in the cabinet rather helpless.[42]

As a result of the speech relations with Germany took a sharp turn for the worse. There were no doubts in German minds as to whom the speech was directed. Grey had a stormy interview with Metternich on 24 July, when the ambassador complained that Lloyd George's speech had a tone of provocation; that, instead of using the normal diplomatic channels, the British Government had made public declarations which had encouraged the chauvinism of the French and British press, and had been widely interpreted as a threat to Germany. The resulting poisoned atmosphere would interrupt the Franco-German negotiations and could even lead to war. Grey retorted that the speech was intended to assert Great Britain's right to be treated as a great power, and it would not have occasioned such surprise in Germany unless there had been a tendency there to think that Great Britain might be so disregarded.[43]

The foreign office staff were delighted by the turn of events which had brought those former 'pro-Germans', Lloyd George and Churchill, who also sided with the chancellor, to accept their views on the hostile nature of German policy. On 27 July Nicolson wrote that 'the attitude of the Cabinet is exceptionally good. They are firm and fully realise the objects towards which Germany is in reality working'.[34] If Grey and the foreign office were pleased, other were not. Loreburn and Morley were extremely alarmed. Both ministers complained to Grey and Asquith on 27 July about the provocative nature of the speech and expressed their fears that, unless the British Government made some statement designed to efface its unfortunate effects on German opinion, war might ensue.[45] Grey continued to deny that the speech was provocative. He told C. P. Scott on 25 July that the warning to Germany on the 21st was intended to prevent her from committing herself so far in her demands on France that she could not subsequently withdraw. He emphasised that his policy was intended to prevent France from falling under German influence which would lead to the collapse of the triple entente and to Germany's complete ascendancy in Europe.[46]

Nevertheless Grey remained acutely suspicious of, and anxious about, Germany's intentions, and his anxiety increased when Kiderlen, alleging that Lloyd George's speech and subsequent Anglo-French press comment made it difficult for him to compromise, refused for a time to modify his demands on France. Nor would he allow Grey to inform Parliament of Metternich's belated assurance of the 23 July that Germany did not seek an outlet on the Moroccan coast. Grey had already written to McKenna on 24 July to urge that naval precautions ought to be taken, since relations with Germany might become strained at any moment, and 'we are dealing with a people who recognise no law except that of force between nations'.[47]

Asquith did not mention, in his report to the king on the 26th, that there had been any protests in the cabinet meeting of the previous day about Lloyd George's speech. He merely noted that, after Grey had reported on recent developments and on 'his very grave interview' with Metternich, 'no decision was called for'.[48] On the 27th, as if to reinforce the advice of Loreburn and Morley, Metternich came to the foreign office with a communication from his government which expressed the hope that Grey would tell Parliament that the Franco-German negotiations did not touch British interests, and that the British government would welcome a settlement. The ambassador felt that this would have a calming influence on public opinion in the three countries. Grey was willing to seize the opportunity to lower the temperature, and Asquith incorporated some soothing words into his speech to the Commons that afternoon, which both Goschen and Jules Cambon reported had an excellent effect on German opinion.[49]

With this welcome improvement in the atmosphere, Grey began to contemplate further steps he might take to ease the passage of the negotiations. Despite Kiderlen's anger with Lloyd George's speech, he continued his talks with Jules Cambon. After meeting the German Emperor at Swinemünde at the end of July, Kiderlen announced that he was prepared to modify his demands for the whole of the Congo, and proposed instead that France cede the line of the Alima to the south, with access to the Congo and the sea. He also withdrew his offer of the Togoland, on the grounds that German public opinion would not accept the loss of this colony. The French still considered the German demands excessive, particularly if they were not to get the Togoland as part of the bargain.[50] Since both sides dug in their heels, the August meetings were not very productive.

Grey endeavoured to persuade the French to make more generous counter-offers in the French Congo, and insisted that de Selves should not be the first to break off negotiations on this issue. Crowe thought that 'anything we can do to make the French keep a cool head, will be useful'.[51] Grey's officials were well aware of the need for Germany to be the first to put herself in the wrong in the eyes of British public opinion.[52] Nor would Grey yield to French pressure to further define British policy in the event of a breakdown of the negotiations. He did agree, after prompting by Paul Cambon at the end of July, to obtain the cabinet's formal approval to call a conference of the powers on Morocco, if necessary, but further than this he would not go. The French, naturally enough wanted to know what steps the British would take if the conference collapsed, or if Germany refused to attend, but Grey would not commit himself. He told Cambon that, in this event, he would have to consult his colleagues, but he did not think that the time had yet come to consider such hypothetical contingencies. He suggested that the signatory powers of Algeciras might be asked for their views.[53] There was little in all this to give the French much comfort, nor were they any more satisfied by the British foreign secretary's negative responses to their repeated requests during July and August for an Anglo-French initiative to compel the Germans to withdraw their warship from Agadir.

Grey clung to the line he had already adopted on this issue. He told Cambon that if the Germans landed troops at Agadir, he would propose a return to the status quo of the Algeciras Act. However, while the German warship remained peacefully at anchor outside the port, he would certainly take no steps to dislodge it – to despatch Anglo-French warships to Morocco would merely exacerbate the situation and could only be regarded as the first step in a war.[54] Grey had no intention of giving the French any encouragement to adopt an obstructive or provocative attitude in their dealings with Germany. Indeed, he told the cabinet on 17 August that the Berlin talks 'seem to be assuming a more hopeful form'. As a result the cabinet agreed 'that there was no present necessity for sending a ship to Agadir', a step which Grey had, of course, already ruled out, except as a last resort. Asquith evidently made no mention of a forthcoming meeting of the Committee of Imperial Defence either then, or at subsequent cabinet meetings in August.[55] Morley and the other dissenters, Loreburn, Harcourt and Burns, were not invited, an omission that enraged Morley and the others later when they found out. Indeed, it appeared that foreign and military policy during the late summer and early autumn had fallen into the hands of a small clique consisting of Asquith, Grey, Haldane, Lloyd George and Churchill, with Henry Wilson, the Director of Military Operations at the War Office, acting as their military adviser.[56]

The Committee of Imperial Defence met on 23 August, in order to consider, in Asquith's words, 'action to be taken in the event of intervention' in a Franco-German war. Asquith, Grey, Haldane, Churchill, Lloyd George, McKenna and the service chiefs were present. Both General Wilson and Sir William Nicholson, the C.I.G.S., outlined the plans of the general staff, which envisaged the despatch of 160,000 troops to France immediately on the outbreak of war. The committee was informed that tactical and organisational problems had already been carefully worked out. Against the army's confident plans the admiralty put up a badly argued case. The first sea lord, Admiral A. K. Wilson, claimed that the navy's other tasks would not leave it with enough ships to protect the passage of the expeditionary force across the Channel. He even thought that the plan to send the army to France had been abandoned. He defined the navy's strategy as one of protecting the shores of Great Britain from invasion, blockading the North German coast and launching a succession of lightning military-naval operations against German ports, islands and signal stations, which the admiralty believed would tie up at least ten German divisions.

The feeling of the meeting was entirely against the admiralty. Haldane, Churchill and the army leaders were especially critical of the plans for naval raids, which Nicholson described as 'madness'. Grey supported the war office. He believed that the land struggle in France would be decisive. McKenna attacked the plans of the war office root and branch, protesting that the French army was quite large enough to deal with the German army without British support, and he warned the meeting that a pledge of British assistance might make France less inclined to accept reasonable German terms for a Moroccan settlement. Possibly in response to pressure by McKenna, the prime minister reiterated that the final decision about questions of war and peace rested with the cabinet. Nevertheless, the majority of those present accepted the plans of the war office, rather than the somewhat confused admiralty schemes, as the basis for British strategy in war-time.[57]

Three days after this meeting, Grey received a further protest from Loreburn about the direction of British foreign policy. Loreburn complained that France had not been straightforward in her dealings with Great Britain, since he had heard rumours of secret Franco-German negotiations which had taken place before the despatch of the 'Panther' to Morocco. The Lord Chancellor thought that, as a result of this lack of frankness on the part of the French, the cabinet was not in possession of all the information necessary to determine

British policy. He pressed Grey to make a frank statement to Germany that Great Britain was not opposed to German colonial expansion, that she genuinely desired Anglo-German friendship and that she would welcome a Franco-German settlement. He believed that otherwise war might ensue, with France confident of active British support, and he demanded that the foreign secretary should remove this impression. He warned Grey that neither Parliament nor the country would sanction British intervention. Under the circumstances, he urged Grey to tell the French that they could rely only on British diplomatic support.[58]

Grey presumably felt confident about the strength of his position in the cabinet and of Loreburn's isolation there.[59] Loreburn received scant, although courteous, satisfaction to his enquiries. Grey once again denied that he was opposed to German expansion, and he insisted that it would not help to maintain peace if he gave assurances to France and Germany that Great Britain would remain neutral in the event of war; indeed, he reminded Loreburn that any such statement would require prior cabinet approval. He added that he did not believe that there had been Franco-German talks before Agadir – 'obvious romance' – and that, in any case, to raise the matter now would only make mischief.[60]

Grey had little to fear from the querulous Loreburn while he had the staunch support of those erstwhile 'pro-Germans' Lloyd George and Churchill. Indeed, there is some evidence that these two wanted to go further in the matter of military and naval preparedness than Grey deemed prudent.[61] Shortly after the C.I.D. meeting Lloyd George wrote to Churchill that 'the thunderclouds are growing' and that in his view Great Britain was taking 'it all too carelessly'. He feared that the pressure of German public opinion might soon force the German Government to go to war with France, and he wanted to know if the entente had taken any steps to help Belgium resist a German invasion.[62] Churchill forwarded this letter to Grey and urged him to enter into a triple alliance with Russia and France to protect the independence of Belgium, Holland and Denmark. The home secretary was also concerned that British intervention in a war should be based on larger grounds than a squabble over Morocco, He suggested to Grey that, if France decided to send ships to Morocco, Great Britain should move her main fleet to north Scotland, thus demonstrating to Germany and to the world that British interests were European and not Moroccan, and, as he told Lloyd George,

Where it wd be at once the most effective & least provocative support to France & a real security to this country. It is not for Morocco, nor indeed for Belgium, that I wd take part in this terrible business. One cause alone cd justify our participation – to prevent France from being trampled down and looted by the Prussian junkers – a disaster ruinous to the world and swiftly fatal to our country.[63]

This resulted in the despatch of another letter from Lloyd George to Grey on 1 September warning the foreign secretary that war was 'by no means inevitable but it is becoming an increasing probability'. He pressed him to take every step 'which would render the issue of war more favourable'.[64] Grey was thus faced with a campaign by Lloyd George and Churchill to persuade him to tighten the bonds between Great Britain, France and Russia, and to promise support to the Low Countries – measures which would certainly come to Germany's knowledge and thereby increase the likelihood of war.

From Berlin there came pressure of a different kind. Sir Edward Goschen reported that Jules Cambon wanted Grey to persuade de Selves to make more 'generous' colonial offers to Germany. The French ambassador believed that this was the only way by which France could secure a free hand in Morocco and ensure that the affair was settled peacefully.[65] Grey was quite willing to follow this advice. He still did not think that France was offering enough. He told Bertie and Paul Cambon on 4 and 5 September that he thought that France should give way and concede the line of the Alima to Germany. He warned the French that the extent to which British support would be forthcoming if trouble arose in the future would depend upon its being clear that France had 'no reasonable and honourable way of avoiding it'.[66] He telegraphed Bertie on 5 September, 'if [the] French Gov[ernment] can be induced to make [a] really acceptable offer, it would strengthen the hands of H.M. Gov[ernment] both as regards public opinion in England and in any subsequent conversations with [the] German Govt'. He reiterated that both he and Asquith were willing to propose a conference in case of need, but he continued to refuse to discuss possible contingencies which might excite public opinion.[67]

At the same time Grey made efforts to restrain Churchill's ardour. He had dinner with the home secretary on the 4th and outlined his policy should the Franco-German negotiations collapse. He would, he said, at once propose a conference. If however this was rejected he might evoke the arbitration of President Taft. On the following day he wrote to the chancellor of the exchequer telling him of his efforts to persuade France to enlarge her offer in the French Congo and stating his opinion that Germany did not want war at present.[68]

Grey was also having difficulties with Asquith, who was becoming concerned about the reports of the Anglo-French military conversations that were reaching him. They 'seem to me rather dangerous', he wrote to Grey, especially references 'to possible British assistance. The French ought not to be encouraged in present circumstances to make their plans on any assumption of this kind.'[69] Although Grey was willing to press the French to make territorial concessions, he was not prepared to upset them by forbidding the military talks at this stage. He replied that, while he realised that the conversations and speeches had given the French some expectation of British support, he could not see how this could be 'helped'. It 'would create consternation' in France if he forbade the talks now.[70]

Grey told Asquith that he was now more hopeful about the prospects for the Franco-German talks.[71] His optimism was dispelled to some extent on 10 September when he learnt that Kiderlen had, on 7 September handed Jules Cambon new German counter-proposals demanding economic concessions for Germany in Morocco, and a portion of south Morocco as her special economic sphere, demands which, according to the French, would give Germany a large measure of political control of Morocco.[72] Bertie and Nicolson were already becoming anxious about Grey's willingness to press the French to make large colonial concessions as they feared that this might be misconstrued in France and strain the entente. They used the latest German proposals to underline the dangers of not supporting France firmly. Nicolson told the French chargé that these proposals were unacceptable, since Great Britain wanted France to have a free hand in Morocco and opposed special economic concessions to Germany there. At the same time the permanent under secretary wrote to Grey that 'prospects do not look hopeful'. He trusted that no further pressure would be exerted on France to be more generous towards Germany regarding colonial compensation. He believed that if Great Britain and Russia 'hold firmly to France' the Germans would soon give way and would accept an arrangement allowing France a free hand in Morocco. 'Our combination is a very strong one and Germany would not care to face it.'[73]

Grey agreed that 'no more is to be said at Paris by us at present about increasing the offers in the French Congo'. But he would not allow Nicolson to repeat his objections to the French about the latest German proposals, since he thought that it would create more ill-will if Germany discovered that Great Britain was 'instigating and stimulating' French objections. He would acquiesce in French objections to unreasonable German demands but would not prompt them. He repeated that it was important that France should not break off the negotiations since, if war broke out, it must be absolutely clear to British public opinion that Germany had caused it. Once more Grey insisted that he would call a conference if the negotiations failed. If Germany refused to participate she would place herself in the wrong in British eyes.[74]

Haldane was also alarmed by Germany's obstructiveness. He wrote to Grey on 11 September that 'things do not look happy', and 'things may in consequence get out of control'. For that reason he cancelled the cavalry manoeuvres that had been scheduled for September.[75] Churchill told Lloyd George that the latest German proposals were unsatisfactory, and warned the chancellor that he could find nothing in the print which could justify expectations that Germany would give way. The home secretary kept in close touch with Grey, visiting Fallodon on 16 September, and on the previous day Grey instructed Nicolson to keep Lloyd George informed about the progress of the negotiations.[76]

However, the situation improved again on 19 September when the French reported that Germany, influenced by a financial crisis in Berlin, had withdrawn her demand for a special commercial position in Morocco.[77] Gradually, the Franco-German difficulties over Morocco moved towards a solution. At the end of September Grey agreed that various military and naval precautions, which had been taken earlier in the crisis, could be relaxed.[78] Nevertheless Goschen remained concerned because the French were still making difficulties about compensation in the Congo. Accordingly on 6 October Grey warned Cambon that the worst possible impression would be created in Great Britain if France, having secured a virtual protectorate over Morocco, refused to give Germany a considerable concession in the Congo.[79]

By 10 October the final draft of the Moroccan convention was drawn up. Nevertheless Grey was becoming increasingly alarmed about the mounting xenophobia in the French press, and he feared that the French Chamber might refuse to ratify the settlement, which would have disastrous effects on British public opinion.[80] However, the Franco-German negotiations were all but concluded on 22 October when Kiderlen and Jules Cambon at last settled the main boundaries of the French Congo. Grey summarised the situation in his report to the first cabinet of the new session on 25 October. 'Grey [was] very good, calm, lucid, decisive', wrote John Burns, 'trouble over Morocco has terminated and war now impossible between France and Germany'.[81] The Franco-German convention on Morocco was signed at Berlin on 4 November.[82]

That the Agadir incident was solved without war had been partly a result of Grey's efforts. He had steered a narrow course between the pressure of the faint-hearted in the cabinet, like Loreburn, who wanted Great Britain to have as little to do with the dispute as possible, and the fire-eaters in the foreign office, and later Lloyd George and Churchill who pressed Grey to go further in support of France and in opposition to Germany than he thought wise. Grey was determined to go to war to support France if Germany tried to humiliate or force war on her. But he insisted that all means must be exhausted before Europe was plunged into war. He wanted Great Britain to take all possible precautions in case Germany went to war, while, at the same time, supporting, from the sidelines, efforts to achieve a reasonable settlement of the dispute. Hence his occasional pressure on France, despite Nicolson's opposition, to accept reasonable German proposals and to make generous colonial offers to the Germans, and his efforts to dissuade France from taking steps likely to cause the breakdown of her negotiations with Germany.

Germany's angry reaction to the Mansion House speech convinced Grey that it had discouraged her from going too far. He told Asquith that the Germans were annoyed by the speech because they had assumed that Great Britain could be left out of account. At the same time both the foreign secretary and the chief whip were delighted that the speech had demonstrated to 'people in this country' that the cabinet was united over foreign policy.[83] Thereafter Grey reverted to his strategy of leaving it to France and Germany to pursue their negotiations, making plans to intervene only if the talks broke down.

Although the future of Morocco was settled by the Franco-German agreement in November, Grey now found himself at the centre of an angry debate within the Liberal Party about foreign affairs which threatened to undermine the foundations of his foreign policy, and, indeed, to drive him from office. To some extent British Liberal criticisms of his foreign policy were provoked by bitter German attacks on the role Great Britain had adopted during the Agadir crisis. During the autumn relations between Great Britain and Germany became more strained than ever before as German newspapers and politicians asserted that Britain's interference in the dispute had needlessly prolonged and envenomed the Franco-German negotiations. Incidents like the Cartwright interview, and subsequent revelations of Britain's special defensive measures, agitated German opinion, which was already dangerously overheated.[84] The radicals in Great Britain soon took up the cry claiming that Grey's pro-French policy had nearly involved Great Britain in a war for the sake of French interests. The vociferous attacks on the pro-French orientation of his policy soon developed into a campaign for his removal from office and his replacement by a minister who would dedicate himself to the task of securing an Anglo-German détente.[85]

He attempted to counter the attacks of his British and German critics in his speech to the House of Commons on 27 November 1911. During the course of his long exposition, the foreign secretary described his exchanges with Metternich during July, insisted that Lloyd George's Mansion House speech had not been intended as a threat to Germany, and appealed to British public opinion to keep 'calm and sober'. He denied rumours that Great Britain had reached agreement with France to come to her assistance in the event of war. He described his policy as seeking to maintain Britain's friendship with France and Russia, which was the best guarantee that neither would follow a provocative policy towards Germany, and he deplored talk of a return to 'splendid isolation'. He maintained that he sought a rapprochement with Germany, although he insisted that this must not be at the expense of the ententes. He suggested that, with the settlement of the Moroccan crisis, the way was now open for a relaxation of Anglo-German tension.[86]

His speech failed to conciliate his critics either in England or Germany, and he now began to consider more tangible means of demonstrating both to the British radicals and to the Germans that he sought an Anglo-German détente. Thus on 20 December he discussed with Metternich the possibility of a revision of the Anglo-German agreement on the Portuguese colonies.[87] Harcourt too had been discussing an Anglo-German colonial agreement with Kühlmann of the German Embassy during the autumn.[88] By the end of 1911 Grey was converted to a cautious policy of improved relations with Germany. Undoubtedly he had been alarmed by the way in which the two countries had so nearly drifted into war in 1911. Furthermore he calculated that better relations between the two countries would help to reduce tension in Europe in the future.

The Agadir crisis can be seen in retrospect as an interlude in the struggle in British official circles between those who wanted a substantial improvement in relations with Germany, and those who feared that any approaches to Germany would estrange France and Russia and lead eventually to British isolation on the continent. The struggle was resumed with greater intensity in 1912. The Haldane mission and the Harcourt–Kühlmann talks for that year together with Grey's more flexible approach towards Germany, provided the former group with an opportunity of achieving their aims.[89]

15

Great Britain and Germany, 1911–1914

R. T. B. LANGHORNE

THE NAVAL QUESTION

In both England and Germany the Agadir Crisis gave urgency and point to the arguments of those who wished to force their governments to adopt a friendlier attitude towards each other before a catastrophe supervened. There were for example in England three groups at least who were determined to achieve a *détente*: those on the left of the Liberal party or in the Labour party who believed passionately in internationalism; those who could sense a coming disaster and feared its economic consequences – Sir Ernest Cassel was among them – and those who were pacifists. F. W. Fox, for example, Chairman of the Anglo-German Friendship Society and a Quaker, thought that he personally had brought about the Haldane Mission in 1912.[1] This sanguine view is illustrative of the kind of pressure such men brought to bear and gained for them – particularly under the description 'pro-German' – an unenviable reputation in the Foreign Office. In Germany similar pressures existed, particularly in the group of big-business men who saw economic ruin in a conflict with England. Of these, Albert Ballin was among the foremost. The negotiations over the Portuguese colonies were one by-product of this atmosphere, but, more important, it provoked what was to be the last genuine discussion of the real issues between England and Germany: the naval arms race, and a formula of political agreement. The two were connected in that the Germans always hoped to obtain a declaration of neutrality from England in return for minimal naval concessions, while Britain hoped for a substantial reduction in naval armaments in return for minor political concessions – preferably in Africa. This disagreement was fundamental, and shewn to be so, after the failure of the Haldane mission.

The inception of the mission remains an historical mystery, although the appearance of Professor Lamar Cecil's work on Albert Ballin[2] has made a reconstruction possible if not certainly accurate.[3] The point is important because each side felt that the other had initiated the discussions and had then deserted its first position – thus bearing responsibility for the eventual failure. Elucidation is the more difficult, because the first moves were made by men who were not officially connected with either Foreign Office: Albert Ballin, chairman of the *Hamburg–Amerika Linie*, associate of the Kaiser, and Sir Ernest

Cassel, banker, expatriate German and friend of Edward VII.[4] Sir Harold Nicolson thought that Cassel turned originally to Ballin,[5] and this view was given by Churchill in an oversimplified account in the *World Crisis*.[6] The editors of the *Grosse Politik*, however, suggest the reverse:

As a matter of fact the proposal was apparently first made for a fresh Anglo-German discussion by Albert Ballin, the Chairman of H.A.P.A.G.[7]

Their view is supported by two letters of Churchill and by a remark made by Ballin in Berlin.[8]

Grey himself, at the time, consistently took the view that the suggestion had come from the Kaiser; thus he wrote to Goschen in this sense on 2 February, and later told the Russians, who suspected the opposite, that 'the first communication of those [advances]...came to us from Berlin...'.[9] But this was evidently an assumed confidence, for in *Twenty-five Years* he was to write:

The intimation had come to us through an unofficial channel: it had not come to me, but had reached members of the Cabinet who were most likely to be favourable to it. The information was very vague. I did not feel at all confident that the Emperor had taken any initiative in the matter. I never really knew whether the suggestion had emanated from a British or a German source.[10]

The evidence will not permit a final conclusion, except that the operations of Ballin and Cassel gave to the Kaiser the impression that the British government would like to send a minister to Berlin; and to Winston Churchill the impression that the Kaiser would like the British government to send such a minister for discussions.[11] Nevertheless, it seems most likely that the first approach came from Ballin. If the most recent discussion of this problem has to admit that a crucial letter from Ballin to Cassel is missing,[12] the same discussion provides a convincing reconstruction of its contents from two other sources.[13] Even if this were not the case, the position that men such as Ballin occupied in Imperial Germany as powerful independent operators on the edge of the government, whose actions might or might not enmesh themselves in political action, makes it extremely likely that Ballin did approach Cassel. His responsibilities as Chairman of H.A.P.A.G. often made him wish to share his consequent worries as to the state of Anglo-German relations with the sympathetic Cassel: there was nothing untypical in this case. What is odd about the result was that Cassel could present such an exchange, and in the circumstances of the time quite rightly, as a political fact. And Churchill, in reply, refused an invitation to go with Cassel to Germany to talk to Ballin, because it would have been too much a political fact, requiring extensive formalisation, perhaps by means of a royal visit.[14] If all had gone well, no one would have been concerned that negotiations had been begun in the political twilight wherein powerful German businessmen operated. As it was, the German government retreated behind the undeniable fact that Ballin's vast political influence was not official and recognised only that official British response when it emerged, and the British remained convinced, rightly, that they had responded to something much more official than Ballin's worries.

Although Churchill refused, he did so pleasantly enough, and the Germans then invited Grey himself. What exactly happened at this point is not easy to decide. Churchill did not inform Grey for some days of what had passed: a delay which is strange in view of Grey's office, but less so, given that he described himself as not being among those in the Cabinet who would be favourable to a new dialogue with Germany. The German Chancellor, in a memorandum of 29 January indicated that Cassel was then sent to Berlin with a memorandum drafted by Churchill, Lloyd George and Asquith. It envisaged recognition of British naval superiority and the retardation or reduction of Germany's present naval programme. There was to be English assistance for Germany's colonial aspirations and a political formula, debarring either power from joining aggressive combinations against the other.

Grey was quite clear that he would not himself go, as his presence in Berlin would raise great hopes and correspondingly great disappointment if nothing was achieved. In a conversation with Metternich, he politely declined.[15] On 3 February, despite the ominous demand from Berlin that naval estimates for 1912 must be included in Germany's present naval strength, Grey brought the matter before the Cabinet, and his proposal that Haldane should go to Berlin was accepted.[16] The German Chancellor evidently heard of this rapidly through the same unofficial sources that had carried the first intimations of a new approach, and telegraphed revealingly to Metternich.

I consider it impossible that Sr. E. Grey will be prepared to negotiate on this basis. We cannot judge from here whether a liberal cabinet would agree to it, if the Foreign Secretary were no longer a member of it. We, however, have shown the greatest accommodation in the naval question in the hope of making just such a result possible, whilst at the same time justifying ourselves before public opinion.[17]

Whether he gleaned his hints at the possibility of shaking Grey from Cassel or from Metternich, it is difficult to decide. It could well have been both.[18] Meanwhile Grey sent for and saw Goschen,[19] comforted the Russians and the French and explained to Metternich how much better it was that Haldane should go to Berlin than himself, while warily refusing to discuss any of the unofficial pourparlers that had already taken place.[20] He also wrote to Bertie in Paris and his letter contains a private *resumé* of events up to that point:

Last month a communication reached one of my Colleagues from the German Emperor through Ballin and Cassel. It was brought to me, and some further communications passed through the same channel. The Emperor expressed a strong wish that I should go to Berlin, and he sent me an invitation...It happens to be convenient for Haldane to go to Berlin about the business of a University Committee...He is to see Bethmann-Hollweg, and have a very frank exchange of views about naval expenditure...and what they want in return.

I have discussed the whole ground thoroughly with him and with Goschen. The question is not very easy. The Germans are very vague about what is possible as regards naval expenditure; and, though we are quite prepared to satisfy them that we have no intention of attacking them or supporting aggressive policy against them, we must keep our hands free to continue the relations which we already have with France.[21]

Haldane arrived in Berlin at 7.30 a.m. on Thursday 8 February and after a preliminary meeting with Goschen at the Embassy[22] lunched there with the Imperial Chancellor, before the first round of discussions. This conversation was arranged by Goschen on the telephone, as it appeared that Haldane might not understand the importance of now conducting the operation on an entirely official basis. The misunderstanding about who had started the ball rolling had already taken place.[23] He began by saying that although he had come with official approval, he intended only to talk over the ground, not to commit himself or the German government to any 'propositions'. The Chancellor wanted and obtained an assurance that England did not have secret agreements which would preclude a new agreement with Germany. Haldane dismissed the Chancellor's concern over the warlike posture adopted by England during the preceding August, but pointed out firmly that England would never be able to stand by and watch France being overwhelmed.

Bethmann then brought up the question of a political formula and produced a draft version. Haldane, whose primary task was to obtain a reduction in naval armaments, applauded the spirit of this somewhat naïve document[24] and then asked whether Germany would be satisfied with

mutual undertakings against aggressive or unprovoked attacks and against all combinations, military and naval agreements, and plans directed to the purpose of aggression or unprovoked attack. He said it was very difficult to define what was meant by aggression or unprovoked attack. I replied that you could not define the number of grains which it took to make a heap, but one knew a heap when one saw one.

Bethmann seemed encouraged by this, although he must have known quite well that this was inadequate for the purpose of his colleagues whatever he may have felt himself. Haldane now raised the problem of the German Fleet. He spoke forcefully against the proposed German additions, admitting her perfect right to do what she liked, but pointing out that it would lead to additional British construction – even at the cost of an extra shilling on the income tax. He forecast the possibility of a naval reorganisation, as did eventually occur in September 1912, whereby British ships would be brought back from the Mediterranean by agreement with France. Bethmann was finally convinced of the strength of British feeling, and sighed over the difficulties that he experienced with Admirals. A third squadron there must be, and a few ships must therefore be built. Could Haldane suggest a way out of the difficulty? He could, but he should not have done; he suggested retarding the tempo of construction, over 'twelve years if he could not do better'. They then briefly discussed territorial questions, but postponed them until a later meeting, and then retired jointly satisfied with their lengthy conversation.[25] Haldane recorded:

The Chancellor recognised that we desired to preserve to the fullest degree the existing relations with France and Russia; and Germany also had analogous obligations which we would not desire to interfere with. I had said that I could not commit anybody in what I had said and he on his part wished to say that he could commit nobody...

I have reason to think that he went immediately to see the Emperor. There is no saying what difficulties may not crop up. It is evident to me that, as regards other than the Emperor, the Chancellor has not an easy task before him, but I was impressed with what appeared to me to be his absolute sincerity and goodwill...

The next day was less easy going. Haldane lunched with the Kaiser and Tirpitz.[26] The naval question was immediately brought up, as the Germans claimed that their increase was justified and a great deal less than it might have been. Haldane said that to make an agreement the first result of which was a considerable strengthening of the German fleet would be impossible to explain to the British public. He insisted that fundamental modification was essential. The Kaiser was perturbed by Haldane's uncompromising account of how German additions would provoke new British construction proportionately, and, like Bethmann on the previous day, he asked Haldane for suggestions. He proposed that since they evidently would not drop the new naval law, they should drop one ship. Tirpitz reacted violently against this suggestion, so much so that Haldane was moved to retreat still further and proposed slowing the tempo of construction. On this basis, agreement was reached on a programme which involved new keels in 1913, 1916 and 1919. Tirpitz then made complaints about the two-power standard which Haldane rebutted.[27] Then perhaps as a friendly gesture, without understanding its full implications, Haldane made a serious error:

The idea occurred to all of us...that we should try to avoid defining a standard proportion in the agreement, and that, indeed, we should say nothing at all about ship-building in the agreement, but that if the political agreement was concluded the Emperor should at once announce to the German public that this entirely new fact modified his desire for the Fleet Law as originally conceived, and that it should be delayed and spread out to the extent we had discussed.

So the two-power standard was to be ignored; naval retardation was not to be mentioned; in short, a political agreement was, as the Germans had always intended, to precede naval concessions. This was a marked advantage for the Germans, in return for a small concession. The Kaiser was justifiably pleased, but, unjustifiably, ignored Haldane's statement that he would report back and await the judgement of his colleagues. The Kaiser's certainty, although typically headstrong, was evidently not entirely without foundation. That same evening, Haldane himself began to have doubts about the afternoon's proceedings. He dined with the Chancellor and dilated gloomily on the paucity of the German naval reductions and foresaw difficulties with his colleagues. The Chancellor was disappointed and spoke emotionally about the 'destiny' which would befall them if a *détente* failed to materialise. Haldane was unmoved:

But how would our agreement look if it were followed by more ship-building? And that this was to be so arose from, I did not for a moment say the fault, but the initiative of Germany. He looked depressed.

The extent of the Chancellor's alarm became apparent the next day – 10 February. At lunch, von Stumm, Counsellor at the German Foreign Office, told Haldane that Bethmann did not intend to allow intransigence on the part of Admiral Tirpitz to bring the negotiation to nothing and that it would, therefore, help him if Haldane could take a strong line to the effect that there must be more naval concessions.

I took the hint...I began by saying that continued reflection had made me even more unhappy than I was after leaving the Emperor's Palace on the previous day. English public opinion would not improbably be unmanageable and, I thought, with reason...But keep the two-power standard we must, and our people would resent the increasing burden Germany proposed to put on us. It might be fatal to the much-desired *Verständigung*. The Chancellor said he would try.

They then turned to territorial questions, involving a swap by which England would obtain a controlling interest in the southern section of the Baghdad Railway in return for surrendering a piece of Angola hitherto reserved for her in the 1898 agreement, and Zanzibar and Pemba. These discussions were really pre-empted by other negotiations on the future of the Portuguese colonies, although either Haldane was misconstrued or made a mistake in apparently offering Zanzibar and Pemba without adequate counter concession. The island of Timor, which was also mentioned, was in a sense non-negotiable through being already the subject of a treaty giving the Dutch a right of prior purchase. Neither side seemed to know this.[28]

The main feature of this meeting was the presentation of Bethmann's 'Sketch of a Conceivable Formula'. It ran thus:

The high contracting Powers assure each other mutually of their desire for peace and friendship.

2. They will not either of them, make any unprovoked attack upon the other or join in any combination or design against the other for purpose of aggression, or become party to any plan or naval or military combination alone or in conjunction with any Power directed to such an end.

3. If either of the high contracting parties becomes entangled in a war in which it cannot be said to be the aggressor, the other will at least observe towards the Power so entangled a benevolent neutrality, and use its utmost endeavour for the localisation of the conflict.

4. The duty of neutrality which arises from the preceding article has no

application in so far as it may not be reconcilable with existing agreements which the high contracting parties have already made. The making of new agreements which render it impossible for either of the high contracting parties to observe neutrality towards the other beyond what is provided by the preceding limitation is excluded in conformity with the provision contained in article 2.

5. The high contracting parties declare that they will do all in their power to prevent differences and misunderstanding between either of them and other Powers.[29]

In the light of what the Germans were later to claim that Haldane had said and done, it was a pity that he accepted any sort of formula; even a form of words described as no more than a 'sketch', outlining an arrangement felt merely to be 'conceivable'. For in truth it was far more than a sketch: it was, from the point of view of those who were anxious for the safety of the *ententes*, far too explicit. It spoke of 'benevolent neutrality', which was a phrase not 'conceivable' in any agreement acceptable to England.

At the time, however, Bethmann appears to have understood the situation pretty well. Whatever was to be claimed by Germans who ignored Haldane's warnings as to the informality of the proceedings, the Chancellor could write thus to Metternich on the day after Haldane departed:

He [Haldane] described our formula of neutrality as going too far and he proposed a formula really only guaranteeing neutrality in the event of an unprovoked attack by a third party. In Lord Haldane's opinion the British cabinet will not be satisfied with our offer to postpone construction.[30]

As a result Metternich was to emphasise that the degree to which the Germans would give way on the naval question would depend on the character of the political agreement.

Except for the general air of congratulation surrounding Haldane on his return,[31] the atmosphere in London soon seemed as gloomy as in Berlin it had seemed hopeful.[32] The text of the new German Navy Law, which Haldane had brought, unread, from Berlin was being studied at the Admiralty, while in the Foreign Office, Crowe and Nicolson began to dissect Lord Haldane's reports before the whole, with the agreed formula enclosed, had arrived.[33] This fact makes for an interesting comparison. Having dismissed formulae as necessarily vague, Crowe rejected a naval understanding because, by engineering a political crisis at home, the German government could be forced to abandon the agreement they had made. Therefore there remained only the question of territorial adjustments, and this he proceeded to discuss without knowledge of what Haldane, if provisionally, had thought reasonable. The two versions do not compare. Where, asked Crowe, was a great enough counter-concession for Germany to give to Great Britain?

This has always been the difficulty in our previous understandings with Germany. It was generally solved by England making the concessions, and Germany replying by an assurance of general friendship. The result was invariably found to be disappointing...Germany made the experience and saw it repeatedly confirmed that the policy of first getting up great public excitement against England and then offering more friendly relations in return for some tangible token of British good will, in the shape of a definite concession, invariably led to her getting a good deal, if not all of what she wanted.

He then listed possible concessions which Germany might make,[34] and included in them that she refrain entirely from activity in the British and neutral zones of Persia. 'The essential thing is' he concluded,

that if we are to have no naval agreement, and a political is nevertheless decided upon, then there should be an overwhelming advantage to us in any merely political agreement.

Nicolson, while less devastating in his language, suggested a complete recasting of a sketch for a formula. He objected to the second part of article 2, on the ground that it would preclude England from making arrangements which, while defensive in policy, were offensive in strategical terms. The third article he wanted omitted altogether. 'Benevolent' neutrality had never been allowed in the policy of England, because the mere fact of benevolence violated the neutrality. It was difficult to decide who was the aggressor: 'A country, and history furnishes many examples, may be forced by the political action of her adversary to assume the rôle of an apparent aggressor.' Moreover, 'localisation' might well involve belligerent action. Article 4, being dependent on article 3, should also be dropped: it was open to the further objection that it bound Britain while leaving the Triple Alliance free. 'No. 5 could remain' he concluded. 'The formula would then consist of No. 1, part of No. 2 and No. 5. It is true it would be then a brief document – but it is even then going further than anything we have signed hitherto, our Japanese Alliance of course excepted.'[35]

Goschen wrote to Nicolson on 10 February, echoing remarkably what the latter had been minuting – though in different terms.

What does it amount to? That if what has been suggested is carried out the Germans get what, under Grey's instructions, I have been opposing for two years, namely a political understanding without a naval agreement...I told Haldane that in my opinion they were getting, more or less, their hearts' desire at a cheaper price than we had fixed before. And I think this is a pity as recent events have shewn that our position, unhampered by a political understanding, is a strong one, and our price should therefore have been raised not lowered.[36]

But all this was as nothing compared with the effect that was to be produced by the Admiralty's reaction to the proposed German Fleet Law.[37] The Admiralty memorandum was handed to Metternich at a meeting on 28 February, and its general tenor may be deduced from the following extract:

These increases [the contents of the new German law had been examined] go far beyond the standard of Naval strength prescribed by the 1900 Fleet

Law and its subsequent amendments. They are more than is necessary either to provide for the increased complements of modern ships or for the institution of such a Training Squadron as would be adapted to relieving the 1st and 2nd squadron of the High Sea Fleet from their present burden of training recruits during the winter months which, it appears, the formation of a 3rd Active Squadron is to effect.

The memorandum ended by saying

£18,500,000 spread over the next six years, together with a certain further concentration of the Fleet in Home Waters would be the additional bill and consequence of the *Novelle*. It is difficult to understand how public opinion in both countries could be brought to regard these serious measures and counter-measures as appropriate to the coincident re-establishment of cordial relations.[38]

This highly critical view of the new law went to Germany after a meeting that had begun badly in any case.[39] and predictably it changed the whole atmosphere of the negotiations. The Kaiser was provoked to some extravagant minutes, concluding that any objection to the proposed fleet increases constituted an encroachment on the functions of the Supreme War Lord, and

Grey must confess frankly...that Haldane is disavowed, and that the points which he agreed with me, have been dropped.[40]

A reply came on 6 March, and was couched in distinctly aggrieved tones.[41] The German government set out a considerably simplified view of the Berlin discussions, and claimed that Haldane had committed himself to their results. These were:

1. to conclude a general political agreement with the German government which should preclude an aggressive policy directed by England or Germany against each other;
2. to support such plans for the acquisition of the Portuguese colony of Angola, as well as parts of the Congo State, as it may eventually be the policy of Germany to entertain;
3. to cede Zanzibar and Pemba to Germany.

Lord Haldane on his part demanded:

(a) a retardation of the rate of construction as regards the three battle ships provided for in the German Navy Bill;

(b) the renunciation of German claims to Timor arising under the treaty with the British government of 1898.

(c) due consideration of the wishes of the British government respecting the Bagdad Railway.

The Imperial government have accepted Lord Haldane's offers.

It is difficult to reconcile with these declarations and it amounts to a shifting of the basis on which the negotiations have so far been conducted, that the British government should now criticise the increases in personnel provided for in the Navy Bill and the additional vote for submarines.[42]

They spoke harshly of British reservations as to the cession of Zanzibar and of the minimising of German concessions over Timor and the Baghdad Railway.[43] It was quite clear that they regarded the conclusion of a neutrality agreement as the first objective without which no agreement on naval construction could be arrived at. But the British were offered a new concession.

The Imperial government...are ready to restrict their demand for new battleships under the Navy Bill to the years 1913 and 1916, that is a third of a ship for each year, and altogether to refrain from indicating at present any year for the construction of the third ship.

They concluded with a veiled threat that if the British government did not now come forward with a proposal on the neutrality question, the negotiations would not be continued.

Metternich read this memorandum to Grey and Haldane at a meeting in the Foreign Office, where the Ambassador added an expression of the Chancellor's disappointment at the progress of the negotiations. Grey, who had always been sceptical about the willingness of Germany to come to an agreement expressed no surprise, but merely said that if no public agreement came out of these negotiations, he hoped they could at least retain the better atmosphere created by Lord Haldane's visit.[44]

Crowe was less calm. It was, he considered, the worst bargain offered yet and that the German position was arrived at by 'distorting Lord Haldane's proceedings and the attitude of HMG'.[45] On 11 March a memorandum from Haldane arrived in the Foreign Office. He emphasised the *ad referendum* character of his discusssions, and denied that he could have accepted a new naval bill while ignorant of its contents.[46]

That the memorandum of 6 March from Berlin was not solely the product of German irritation at the British reaction to the *Novelle* became apparent when, on 12 March, there came a *volte-face* in the German attitude.[47] It had been clear to some that the Chancellor had no hand in the German reply and this development seemed to argue his revived authority.[48] Late that evening Haldane received an urgent message from Metternich, asking to see him as soon as possible. He went round to the German Embassy at once where the Ambassador told him that he had gathered from Berlin that:

if the British Government would offer a suitable political formula the proposed Fleet Law as it stood would be withdrawn

and another much reduced version would take its place. The British government were not to be then forced into accepting such naval reductions as Germany saw fit to make. She was to be quite free to withdraw a formula, and such a formula need not go beyond a 'disclaimer of aggressive intentions and combinations'.

I asked whether he wished this communication to be treated as merely between him and me. He said no, he was officially instructed, but he wanted to see me in the first place to say that time pressed, as a statement would have to be made almost at once in the Reichstag about the Fleet Law, and the Chancellor wished to be provided with the offer of a formula from us as a reason for not proceeding with the original proposals.[49]

Discussions began at once to find a formula to submit to a Cabinet on 14 March. Grey was deeply involved in the Coal Strike Conference and unable to assist greatly; but Haldane spent some hours at the Foreign Office, drawing up a draft with Nicolson, which they finished by the end of 14 March.[50] After the Cabinet, Metternich called on Grey and informed him officially of the new position,[51] and in return was handed a copy of the formula just agreed to by the Cabinet.[52]

England will make no unprovoked attack on Germany and pursue no aggressive policy towards her. Aggression upon Germany is not the subject, and forms no part of, any treaty, understanding or combination, to which England is a party, nor will she become a party to anything that has such an object.

But it was all to no avail: despite Metternich's assurances to Haldane neutrality still had to be mentioned. The Ambassador replied at once

Dear Sir Edward,
    I am afraid that the political formula you left with me to-day will not be found sufficient at home, as no mention is made of neutrality. Neutrality formed the most important part of the draft Haldane made in Berlin with the Chancellor.[53]

Grey replied

Dear Ct. Metternich,
    I shall be glad to see you at the F.O. at 5 o'c this afternoon.
    I should have to submit to the Cabinet any proposed addition to the formula and if this has to be done, I think it should be after the formula has been considered by the Chancellor. I hope therefore you will meanwhile send it to him as it stands.
                                                        Yours sincerely,
                                                        E. Grey[54]

Metternich answered. When they met on the following day, the Ambassador almost desperately tried to persuade him to agree to some such addition as 'England will therefore as a matter of course remain neutral if a war is forced upon Germany.'[55] He pleaded that English intention to remain neutral might be inferred from her own formula. To this Grey agreed, but was provoked into giving a straightforward warning. The growing might of Germany, he said, had given rise to suspicions in England,

That a day might come when a German Government might desire to crush France. If such a contingency arose, though our hands were quite free, as they were now, we might not be able to sit still: for we should feel that, if we did sit still, and allowed France to be crushed, we should have to fight later on.[56]

The Ambassador's urgings had their effect, however. On 16 March a Cabinet was held to discuss what additional formula could be produced, and amid some extra anodyne, it was agreed to 'amplify the present words by saying "England shall neither make *nor join in* any unprovoked attack upon Germany."'[57] The Ambassador replied that he feared, 'that unless the word "neutrality" was used it would be impossible to secure a reduction in the Novelle'.[58] This proved to be the case. The Chancellor telegraphed to Metternich on 18 March, rejecting the new formula as 'worthless to our purpose'[59] or, as Metternich put it to Grey, 'so elastic as to be valueless'. And when Grey said that what the Chancellor wanted now was a declaration of absolute neutrality, the Ambassador agreed that this was in effect the case.[60] Grey than bade farewell to the chance of a political agreement based on a reduction in the *Novelle,* saying that he hoped something might be negotiated after public opinion had recovered from the shock of its appearance. He promised to continue the territorial discussions that were going on with Harcourt.[61] In general he was as dry about this *dénouement* as he later claimed in *Twenty-Five Years* that he had been about the proposition. His statement to the Japanese ambassador was typical:

I told him that Germany was not content with our draft formula. She had asked for a declaration of neutrality on our part in the event of her being at war with another Power. I had said that if another Power, France for instance, made an unprovoked attack upon Germany, we would not join in it; and I had offered to insert in our formula the words 'not join in any unprovoked attack'. But we had not been able to promise neutrality in the form which Germany asked, and Germany had decided that the formula which we offered was not sufficient to justify her in reducing naval expenditure. For the moment, therefore, the question of a formula had dropped.[62]

Nor did Haldane's own reply to the German memorandum of 6 March alter the situation at all. He insisted that he had only gone to Berlin *ad referendum*:

On this footing the conversations, which were very free and unrestrained, and were conducted in the most agreeable spirit, proceeded. Nothing was excluded.

Over the question of the Navy, he could not have objected to provisions in a Bill of which he was ignorant. He had made no territorial offers.

Lord Haldane no more regarded the Imperial Goverment as making formal offers, or as actually negotiating a Treaty, than he so regarded himself. Both were in his view on a voyage of discovery...

The British government therefore hoped that, in the light of what has been above stated, the Imperial German Government will see that there has been no desire to shift the basis on which the conversations were conducted at Berlin. They take the opportunity of repeating their assurance of good feeling.[63]

Discussions dragged on for a month or so, in desultory fashion with Germany, and more urgently with France, who, almost at the moment when the question of a genuine Anglo-German *détente* became academic, began to be alarmed about her own position.[64] The formula that the Cabinet had finally been prepared to offer made French alarm far from academic, however, and although French anxiety was misplaced, it was not surprising: but the German reaction most certainly was. On 29 March Goschen had a long conversation with the German Chancellor and inquired about the formula.

I asked what he thought of our formula. He said that it didn't go half far enough; he would simply be laughed at if he produced such a meagre little formula as a reason for reducing the demands of the Naval Party, or as the basis of an understanding. We must furnish something fuller [*etwas mehr rund*] than that 'Make no unprovoked attack' – why it is nothing! I said that Sir Edward Grey's last suggestion was 'will neither make nor join in any unprovoked attack'. He said he had not heard of that suggestion, but that it did not make much difference; he wanted something more comprehensive.[65]

That the Chancellor should have thought that the unaltered formula was 'meagre', 'nothing', shows him either to be unintelligent or else much less reasonable than he was very concerned to show that he was. That he could think the amended formula so unimportant, even if he had not heard of it before, is well nigh incredible. It is perfectly possible that the Chancellor was not speaking with due care; nevertheless such a reaction could be interpreted in an even less favourable sense. For it might seem to show that even Bethmann-Hollweg regarded what was offered as safe anyway. He never expected an unprovoked attack from England; he never expected her to join in such an attack by another party. Therefore only something more was useful to Germany, something that would guard her wholly from the consequences of aggression: among these consequences the possibility of English opposition was foremost.

There may also be a more technical reason for this reaction, which would explain as well the extraordinary and immediate rejection of the British offer. Only if the German government was actually expecting as well as hoping for something much more, can their rejection of what was a great – even fatal – concession be accounted for. There is evidence to suggest that they *were* expecting much more.

When the negotiations were held up because of the British Admiralty's shocked reaction to the draft *Novelle*, Bethmann begged Ballin, who reappears at this point,[66] to do something to keep the negotiation alive.[67] Ballin sent Hüldermann to Marseilles to talk to Cassel, who was on holiday there, and Cassel was persuaded to return to England, whither Ballin himself also arrived on about 12 March. He spoke with Metternich, Haldane and Churchill and, in particular, had a long discussion with Churchill on 14–15 March. In view of the very recent *volte face* on the part of the German government, Churchill was naturally sounding optimistic, and, moreover, optimistic about a political agreement. Ballin took this to mean, which Metternich had specifically excluded in speaking to Haldane,[68] that Britain might make a declaration of neutrality as a first gesture towards an agreement.[69] Ballin was correspondingly elated and, declining an invitation to dine with Asquith and Grey, he returned post haste to Germany on 17 March. He went straight to Berlin and Admiral von Müller recorded:

Ballin back from England where he spoke and ate with Haldane and Churchill. At 11 a.m. report at the Palace in the presence of Valentini and myself. Ballin entered the Star Chamber with the words; 'Your Majesty, I bring the alliance with England'. Ballin apparently very taken in by the diplomats. Navy and especially Tirpitz disturbers of peace, 'want war'. Decision of English Cabinet on our neutrality proposal on its way; will arrive in the afternoon. Envisions already a defensive and offensive alliance in development.[70]

He also said that a message from England would arrive in the course of the afternoon. It did. In such an atmosphere, the formula so painfully worked out at the English cabinet meeting on 16 March seemed small and inadequate; taken as proof that they were right by the anti-English party, and a disastrous disappointment to the embattled supporters of the *détente*.

While this was going on, the French began to exhibit signs of alarm. At first Paul Cambon, who was told what was passing on his return from Paris on 22 March, seemed unperturbed.[71] Three days later, however, he was less serene; Nicolson 'told him that I believed you had not yet formally submitted Ct. Metternich's proposal to the Cabinet and had not yet given reply to the latter. M. Cambon seemed a little disappointed. I told him I did not think he need be unhappy.' Grey agreed with this, though pointing out that what he had not yet put to the Cabinet – 'though it goes without saying that this must be declined' – was the absolute neutrality demand.[72] But he was much exceeded in his anxieties by those of the British Ambassador at Paris. Bertie, always a man of explosive temperament, had fulminated privately against the Mission, and continuing discussion about formulae was more than he could bear. On 27 March he went to see Poincaré and, having divested himself of his ambassadorial status, proceeded to say things that were improper however informally put. The burden of his conversation was that the attitude of the British government needed stiffening and that the French government must instruct Cambon to exercise pressure.

Sir F. Bertie me déclare qu'il veut me parler 'comme s'il n'était pas ambassadeur'. Sir Ed. Grey a écrit que M. Cambon avait été très satisfait de ce qu'il lui avait expliqué au sujet du projet de déclaration anglo-allemande. 'J'en suis', me dit-il, 'fort surpris, car, si cette déclaration est écartée pour le moment, elle n'est pas définitivement repoussée. L'Allemagne voulait obtenir une assurance de neutralité et même de neutralité bienvaillante, ce qui est absurde car une neutralité bienvaillante n'est plus une neutralité.' Sir Ed. Grey a refusé, mais il est actuellement très affaibli et du reste entouré de partisans d'un rapprochement avec l'Allemagne. Je ne comprends pas sa politique et je suis inquiet. Il faut empêcher que cette déclaration soit échangée et elle peut l'être d'ici à quelque temps, si l'Allemagne revient à la charge. Nous nous trouverons ainsi liés. On nous demander de nous engager à rester neutres si l'Allemagne est attaquée; or qui peut garantir la France, provoquée ou menacée par une mobilisation, ne sera pas forcée de prendre l'offensive? Il est indispensable que Cambon n'ait pas l'air satisfait. Si vous-même vous parlez à Londres avec un peu de fermeté, on hésitera à commettre la faute que je redoute.[73]

[Sir Francis Bertie said that he wished to speak to me 'as if he were not the Ambassador'. Sir E. Grey has written that M. Cambon had been very satisfied with his explanation of the projected Anglo-German declaration. 'I am extremely surprised at it,' he said to me, 'for while this declaration may be set aside at the moment, that does not mean it is definitely rejected. Germany would want to obtain an assurance of neutrality, even benevolent neutrality – in itself a contradiction.' Sir E. Grey has refused this, but he is very much weakened at the moment and moreover surrounded by supporters of a rapprochement with Germany. I do not understand his policy and I am anxious. It is essential to prevent the possibility of any change in the declaration, which could happen at any time, should Germany return to the charge. Thus we would find outselves committed. It is asked that we should guarantee to remain neutral if Germany is attacked; but who can guarantee that France, provoked or menaced by a mobilisation, would not be forced to take the offensive? It is vital that Cambon shows no sign of satisfaction. If you yourselves take a firmer line in London, there would be some hesitation before the error which I dread is committed.]

The next day he wrote to Nicolson on the same subject[74] and discussed the difficulty that arose over discovering the true aggressor where a Power had been provoked into action. Should this happen to France, and England give her the only aid that would be any use – immediate – Germany could say that England had joined an aggressor. While Poincaré was acting on Bertie's hints, Metternich was driving another nail into the coffin. He admitted to Grey informally that it was felt in some quarters in Germany that she should exchange a naval agreement only for an alliance similar to that with Japan – an alliance which contained pledges absent from the ententes with France and Russia. He also asked Grey to believe only what he was told formally.[75]

Thus when Cambon called at the Foreign Office on 29 March, spurred on by Poincaré's account of his interview with Bertie, he found Grey able to reassure him with the news that the Cabinet had rejected the demand for neutrality.[76] On 1 April Nicolson replied to Goschen's account of his interview with the Chancellor and put the Foreign Office view quite succinctly.

Your conversation with the Chancellor was most interesting and illuminating, and it is perfectly clear to me that they are endeavouring to entangle us in some engagement which would absolutely prevent us from having full liberty of action in case of certain eventualities. That we should get anything in return from them is quite out of the question, and so it would be really a very one-sided arrangement, and it would moreover certainly impair and weaken our relations with France and Russia, which we have only quite recently assured those two countries we have no intention whatever of doing. It is equally clear to me that so long as we remain free to act as circumstances may require, there is a very good chance of peace being maintained; while on the other hand, if the Germans were certain that we would not intervene, I could not give many months for peace being maintained. However, I do not think – in fact I am almost sure – that the Cabinet would go so far as the Chancellor would like us, though as you know there are many elements in the Cabinet who would do anything to obtain the so-called goodwill of Germany.[77]

Nevertheless, exchanges with France continued. Bertie wrote on 6 April that the French were seriously worried and uttered a stern, if unnecessary warning,[78] postulating a threat from French opponents of the *entente*. This despatch provoked an enormous minute from Crowe which, as it is not written on sheets attached to the text, together with the further comments by Crowe and Nicolson, is unlikely to have been seen by Grey. Nicolson read it, however, before writing his own. It was accurate and uncomfortable. Why had the government apparently changed their priorities from a naval agreement to any agreement? If it was in order to improve Anglo-German relations, had their present poor condition been analysed? Everything depended upon a correct appreciation of German policy; did the Cabinet understand what that policy was? Before any further negotiations were undertaken, it would be well to investigate these questions, since if poor relations were the consequences of a policy which was unlikely to be changed by such exercises as Lord Haldane's mission, British efforts could only be pointless and possibly dangerous.[79]

Nicolson was equally firm, but more concerned with France, concluding 'I see no reason for any new departure.' Not surprisingly Grey could not wholly agree:

All this [he wrote] is true and not to be disregarded but on the other hand it has to be borne in mind that Russia and France both deal separately with Germany and that it is not reasonable that tension should be permanently greater between England and Germany than between Germany and France or Germany and Russia.[80]

On 14 April Fleuriau, the French chargé d'affaires, delivered to Nicolson a letter from Cambon which revealed that both he and Poincaré were most worried on two counts: what might be the meaning of the words 'without provocation'; and, if such a declaration were published, what effect would it have on the Entente Cordiale? He posted it at once to Grey, with his own sombre comments.[81]

By now Grey was beginning to take the French situation seriously, and telegraphed private reassurances to Bertie in Paris,

There is no new development about the formula and nothing more to be said, unless the Germans make a new suggestion. I refused to put in the word neutrality because it would give the impression that our hands were tied. If

Germany attacked and forced war upon an ally or friend of ours it would be provocation to us and therefore formula as we proposed it would not tie our hands. I shall see French Ambassador on his return and be ready to consider anything he has to say.[82]

He evidently also consulted the Prime Minister. Asquith's reply showed that Nicolson need not have worried about his attitude at least:

My Dear Grey

I agree that the French are somewhat unduly nervous. But I confess I am becoming more and more doubtful as to the wisdom of prolonging these discussions with Germany about a formula. Nothing I believe will meet her purpose which falls short of a promise on our part of neutrality: a promise we cannot give.

And she makes no firm or solid offer, even in exchange for that.

        Yours ever
        H.H.A.[83]

The German government, however, ended all these speculations in the most definite possible way by announcing on 10 April that the *Novelle* was to be proceeded with.[84] By 15 April Nicolson was demonstrably happier.[85]

There was to be one more rumble as the storm died away, and it came when Metternich was succeeded by Baron Marschall von Bieberstein in June of 1912. Bertie was immediately anxious at the appointment of such a famous and able diplomat,[86] but all he did at first was to raise the formula question, and allow himself to be politely headed off by Grey, who pointed to the negotiations about the Portuguese colonies.[87]

Before turning to other issues, it would perhaps be right to attempt a judgement of Lord Haldane's part and that of the German government. It certainly does seem as though Haldane did not represent British interests as efficiently as he might have done. He should not have permitted the formula to be called 'conceivable'; for it certainly was not.[88] He made two errors over Zanzibar and Timor. Zanzibar particularly would only have been surrendered in exchange for impressive reductions in the German naval programme. He appears to have been less firm at his meeting with the Kaiser and Tirpitz than his knowledge, even as it then stood, of the main features of further German naval expansion would have warranted: later he was to take a stronger line with the Chancellor. It was also unfortunate that Haldane should have suggested retardation when retardation unaccompanied by any reduction whatever was almost certain to be rejected in London. On both occasions when this happened Haldane's own record shows clearly that he was outmanoeuvred into making suggestions when it was really the turn of the Germans to do so.

Where he cannot be criticised is over the suggestion, made by the Germans in the memorandum of 6 March, that he went to Berlin and *concluded an agreement*. This he certainly did not do, and Bethmann at least, was perfectly aware of the fact. It was deliberate misrepresentation on the part of the Germans who drafted the paper to ignore Haldane's frequent warnings that he had come only *pour tâter le terrain, ad referendum.* This was a highly dishonest mode of approach, made easier no doubt by the split in the German government, demonstrated by their wavering in March, but it should not be allowed to obscure completely Haldane's own sins. Minor though these were, they did give to the German government a small degree of justification for their claim that the British had shifted the basis of the negotiations.

It becomes easier to understand why the Germans took this line when it is realised that there was a fundamental cleavage in the attitude adopted in Berlin and London towards Lord Haldane's mission. The Germans never understood *how* tentative the mission really was. In the same way as they misunderstood the British monarch's position in foreign affairs, they were unable to conceive how a senior minister sent out with the authority of the King and Cabinet could arrange anything which the government would not later agree to in all but secondary detail. They would be unlikely to see such a visit, as Bertie incorrectly did, as a manoeuvre of the Grey-must-go wing of the Liberal party, or to realise quite how opposed the Foreign Office was to the whole operation. Bethmann-Hollweg showed some knowledge of English affairs, possibly because he believed – unlike others round the Kaiser – what Metternich reported from London; but neither he nor others could grasp a further significant fact.

It was always extremely difficult to identify the source of responsibility within the German government, and it has already been pointed out how Ballin's position made for an additional blurring of the lines.[89] The conduct of policy by changing cliques had attained the quality of a tradition in Berlin, but on this occasion it was paralleled in London. Cassel dealt first with Churchill, who, as Grey later pointed out,[90] only told his friends. It looks strongly as though Lloyd George and Churchill kept the early stages of the negotiations from Grey – or clearly omitted to inform him – for at least a week and even then the professional diplomatists did not become involved. Thus, at the start, clique was speaking to clique through private channels. It is not surprising that Eyre Crowe questioned the efficacy of such proceedings with something more than his usual fervour for administrative tidiness.[91] Not until 3 February, more than a month after the first moves had been made, was the matter discussed at a full Cabinet and a formal decision taken that Haldane should go to Berlin.

The naval question rumbled on for some time yet however. Chiefly, it took the form of confused, though illuminating, exchanges at several levels, about the presentation of naval estimates. In March 1912 Churchill began this phase by introducing in his estimates a new proposal.

Any retardation or reduction in German construction will, within certain limits, be promptly followed here...by large and fully proportioned reductions. For instance, if Germany elected to drop out any one, or even any two, of these annual quotas...we will at once, in the absence of any dangerous development elsewhere not now foreseen, blot out our corresponding quota, and the slowing down by Germany will be accompanied naturally on our larger

scale by us. Take as an instance...the year 1913. In that year...Germany will
build three capital ships, and it will be necessary for us to build five in
consequence. Supposing we were both to take a holiday for that year...The
three ships that she did not build would therefore automatically wipe out no
fewer than five British potential super-Dreadnoughts, and that is more than
I expect them to hope to do in a brilliant naval action.[92]

The Kaiser responded that such an arrangement would only be possible
between allies and privately insisted that 'it does not matter what measures
England takes'. Nothing ensued, and during 1912 and early 1913 nothing
whatever was said about the naval question. There was however a mildly
surprising exception. In December 1912 Prince Henry of Prussia visited the
King at Sandringham and there raised with him the question of neutrality.

He asked me point blank, whether in the event of Germany and Austria going
to war with Russia and France, England would come to the assistance of the
two latter Powers. I answered undoubtedly yes under certain circumstances.
He professed surprise and regret but did not ask what the certain circumstances were. He said he would tell the Emperor what I had told him. Of
course Germany must know that we could not allow either of our friends
to be crippled.

Although Grey must have doubted whether he could have got such a statement
past the Cabinet, he applauded it on the royal lips:

Sir Edward Grey thinks that it would be dangerous and misleading to let the
German Government be under the impression that under no circumstances
would England come to the assistance of France and Russia, if Germany and
Austria went to war with them, and he thinks it very fortunate that Your
Majesty was able to give an answer to Prince Henry that will prevent him from
giving this impression at Berlin.[93]

So successful was this silence that one distinguished Foreign Office official, Eyre
Crowe, thought that Anglo-German relations were actually improved by
making no attempt to solve the serious problems and that any effort to come
to a settlement would make matters worse again.

I am firmly convinced that one of the main reasons why Anglo-German
relations are now more cordial (– I do not overlook the obvious other
reasons –) is that we have entirely ceased to discuss the question of a limitation
of armaments. I feel equally certain that any resumption of that discussion
will have the inevitable effect of making relations worse again.[94]

Such a stalemate is interesting in itself for general reasons; but as far as the
navies were concerned, Crowe's judgement was remarkably confirmed in
March 1913, when Churchill repeated his offer. He did so because in presenting the German estimates, Admiral Tirpitz, subsequently supported by the
German foreign secretary, had been deliberately conciliatory. The reason for
this, as Grey remarked, was not 'the love of our beautiful eyes, but the extra
50 millions required for the German army'.[95] This letter is such a clear

exposition of Grey's views on the naval question as it presented itself at this point that it is worth giving the major part of the text.

For seven years some of the Pan-Germans in Germany have been working upon Pro-Germans in this country. The Pan-Germans are chauvinists; our Pro-Germans are pacifists; but the latter are nevertheless very subject to the influence of the former. It came to my knowledge that Professor Schiemann, one of the Pan-Germans aforesaid, had written to one of the Pro-Germans here after Tirpitz's speech, emphasizing the friendly nature of the statement, and saying that everything would depend upon whether we responded to it.

I had no intention of responding by proposing a naval agreement. In the first place, I had been given to understand, indirectly, that when Lichnowsky came here he hoped that I would not raise the question of naval expenditure with him.

In the second place, if I were to do so, the naval Press Bureau in Germany would, if it suited it, construe my action as an attempt to put pressure on Germany to reduce her naval expenditure; and Tirpitz might, at some future time, say that his moderate statement had been abused for this purpose, and that therefore he could not say anything again of which similar advantage might be taken.

In the third place, I do not wish to enter upon a discussion of a proportion of 16 to 10, because we never intended Colonial ships to be included in that, and we do not wish to enter into explanations.

Had it simply been a question of exchanging anodyne comment in the two Parliament houses, the matter would have been relatively simple. But while the Germans made public their wish to be conciliatory, they privately informed the British, through their new ambassador, Lichnowsky, that any response would be resented.[96] Their reluctance to receive proposals was evidently the more accurate description of their position, since when Churchill called their bluff by repeating his holiday proposal in the 1913 estimates speech, it produced nothing but odium on the other side of the North Sea.[97] Once again, the Germans made it clear that they would resent proposals about naval matters coming from England, while publicly saying that they awaited them.[98] Churchill forthrightly said to Grey that if no further reference to the naval holiday was to be made, then the British government ought to announce that they had been asked to refrain from putting proposals.

The German government cannot expect to enjoy the advantages of saying in public that they 'await proposals' and of saying confidentially that they will resent it if they are made. If therefore it is decided that no further reference to a 'naval holiday' should be made at the present time, I ought to be at liberty to state that we have received representations from the German Government to the effect that they do not desire to discuss any such proposals.[99]

This Grey did not want to risk; and Churchill in October 1913 again tried to float his proposition, with the consequence that the German press staged something like an uproar.[100] Unabashed, Admiral Tirpitz again said in February 1914, when presenting his estimates to the Reichstag, that he was awaiting proposals from England, which, if they came would be examined with 'good will'. Grey's reaction to this neatly sums up the position

The sole reason why positive proposals from us have not reached Germany is that private intimation reaching us from high German sources gave us to understand that such proposals would be unwelcome and impair good relations between Germany and ourselves...We desire not to make any proposal that would be unwelcome, but being quite ready ourselves to make proposals, if they would be welcome, we must either make them or give some explanation in Parliament why after Admiral Tirpitz's statement as reported we do not do so.[101]

Inevitably there was no result, except, oddly, that Churchill was invited to the German fleet review at Kiel as the official guest of the Kaiser. He was greatly enthusiastic at the prospect. But, at last, Grey had had enough: he wrote to Churchill

...hitherto all efforts on our part to get naval expenditure discussed have been resented by Tirpitz even when welcomed by Bethmann Hollweg. When Lichnowsky arrived an intimation was conveyed to me on his behalf that it was hoped in the interest of good relations between the two countries that I should not mention naval expenditure to him. I think therefore that a visit to Germany with the intention of raising with Tirpitz the points in the memorandum may not only be futile but may cause resentment.[102]

This was the last to be heard of the naval question until the battle of Jutland.

THE FUTURE OF THE PORTUGUESE COLONIES

Like the negotiations about the naval question, the discussions about the Portuguese colonies were begun late in 1911, in response to a desire in both countries to ease the atmosphere after the Agadir Crisis.[103] In this case, however, the episode is interesting not so much for its content but for its character. The Portuguese colonies were not a vital issue. Indeed, as will be seen, it was precisely because the issue was relatively minor that discussions about it seemed to offer a chance of success. It was important to be having discussions, to be able to refer to the fact, and to be able to reach agreement without thereby upsetting international arrangements already made by both Powers. For these purposes, the future partition of the Portuguese colonies was an entirely suitable question.

Like the naval question too, the problems of Portugal's empire had already played a part in Anglo-German relations. This had led, on another level, to the desirability of a new discussion, since the previous arrangements had become unsatisfactory to both parties. They were unsatisfactory to Germany because they had not resulted in a quick and substantial addition to her African empire at the expense of the Portuguese: for this, they believed that

English bad faith was to blame.[104] They were unsatisfactory to England, because circumstances had forced her to make agreements with Germany and Portugal that were contradictory, even, as Grey told the Cabinet, 'inherently false'.[105]

The situation in 1911 was governed by secret agreements made with Germany in 1898[106] and with Portugal in 1899.[107] The former regulated the partition of the Portuguese colonies in the event of the demise of Portugal; and the latter, which was a reaffirmation of England's ancient treaties with Portugal,[108] committed her to the defence of Portuguese territories, including her colonies. Both treaties were connected with the Boer crisis in southern Africa. In the first case, the British had for some time been trying to push the Portuguese into giving support against the Boers in exchange for an English loan, but had encountered some suspicion at Lisbon, where the regime was in any case being opposed by armed insurgents. The financial position of Portugal was clearly parlous,[109] and when, in 1897, the Germans seized Kiao-Chow the lesson was not lost on any of the smaller European colonial Empires. The Portuguese asked for help from London, and were told that they could have it in exchange for at least passive assistance in southern Africa.[110] The Germans, who already possessed territory in the area, were anxious to gain more, and also anxious to exploit British difficulties to this end. They therefore threatened Salisbury quite openly that unless they were brought into arrangements that might be made with Portugal about southern Africa, the much flaunted German neutrality over the Boer War would be converted into active assistance against England.[111] The Secret Agreement of 1898 followed from this, and stated what should happen if Portugal needed to raise a loan. Such a loan would now have to be joint, and if the further consequence was to be the mortgaging, or even sale, of her Empire, the territory was to be divided between Britain and Germany, in roughly equal shares.[112]

Fortunately for British policy, this division never came to be made, because even through revolution and near bankruptcy, Portugal managed to survive without having to raise money on the security of her empire. It was not only fortunate for the British, because they did not want the Portuguese empire to collapse – or at least the Germans to gain thereby – but because on 14 October 1899 the exigencies of the Boer War forced Salisbury to make a new agreement with the Portuguese. This took the form of a reaffirmation of the ancient treaties, and it included a guarantee by Britain of all the Portuguese territories. In return, Portugal rendered assistance against the Boers and promised not to declare herself neutral. This treaty remained secret for longer than most, and even in 1913–14 the Germans seemed only to have had a inkling of it. In the summer of 1912 the Councillor of the German Embassy asked Sir William Tyrell – Grey's secretary – if he could

kindly let me know, if apart from this Arbitration Treaty of 1904 any Treaty or Convention confirming the old Alliance Treaty was signed between England and Portugal *after* the publication in 1898.

The minutes showed how embarrassed the Foreign Office was made by this enquiry. They concluded that it was improper and therefore need not be answered. The effect on Kühlmann was naturally bad and he clearly communicated his work to the Ambassador, Baron Marschall, who made a fuss about the point in his next conversation with Grey one week later.[113]

For Sir Edward Grey, who was opposed to secrecy, it was uncomfortable to be the inheritor of two secret treaties which moreover would be contradictory unless the British view of the 1898 Convention was adhered to. In any event, they entailed the stressing of one attitude to Germany and another to Portugal. Thus there was another reason why the British government might wish to try to appease Germany through the agency of the Portuguese colonies in such a way as to remove the contradictions inherent in the British position. The consequence of this desire was to produce the conflict which eventually ruined the success of the negotiations: for Britain, the results must be published, otherwise she would merely have added a third to her existing embarrassments; for Germany, however, it was essential that the results should not be published, otherwise the Portuguese government would have an opportunity to try to prevent Germany from entering upon her inheritance.

There was one further reason why at least the British government might wish to come to some arrangement with Germany about Portuguese Africa. While it was true that no British foreign secretary was in a position to assist the Portuguese in divesting themselves of their empire, any Liberal minister, and certainly Sir Edward Grey, might well find himself wishing that Portugal would slip over the brink into irretrievable bankruptcy. In such a case, even if Portugal did not surrender her sovereignty over the colonies, she would be in no position to resist the advice of her creditors – Britain and Germany – as to their governance. The manner in which Portugal had governed her territories had been a matter of the gravest censure amongst all European liberals. Grey felt strongly that such misrule should be brought to an end, preferably by persuasion, but, ultimately, should Portugal actually collapse, by the operation of the 1898 Convention – or its successor.[114]

The question of the renegotiation of the Anglo-German agreements on the future of the Portuguese colonies falls into three distinct phases. First the period during which it was gradually decided to attempt to negotiate a new agreement. This stage is much complicated by the fact that two separate agencies were involved, having different objectives. The first discussions seem to have taken place between Richard von Kühlmann and Lewis Harcourt on a private basis during the autumn of 1911. Harcourt told the Cabinet in March 1912 that

I ought to say that on the evening before I met Count Metternich and Sir E. Grey, I had a conversation with Herr von Kuehlmann who had been my *confidant* in the autumn, in which I told him that I was distressed and disturbed at the German answer about the Fleet Law...and that I began to despair of that accord which I knew both he and I so much desired.[115]

The unpleasant atmosphere following the Agadir crisis was principally responsible for these discussions and a general amelioration of Anglo-German relations their principal object. By December, Grey himself had become involved

As to the future, it is clear to me from what Metternich has already said that the Germans would like a division of the Portuguese Colonies to take place as soon as possible. So should I. These colonies are worse than derelict so long as Portugal has them; they are sinks of iniquity...the Union of South Africa will never rest so long as she [Portugal] has Delagoa Bay: on every ground, material, moral and even Portuguese, it would be better that Portugal should at once sell her colonies. *But* how can we of all people put pressure on Portugal to sell: we who are bound by an alliance to protect and preserve her colonies for Portugal – an alliance renewed secretly for value received during the Boer War? And Portugal won't part with her colonies...for when nations have gone downhill until they are at their last gasp, their pride remains undiminished if indeed it is not increased. It clings to them as Tacitus says the love of dissimulation clung to Tiberius at his last gasp.

However, I am to meet Harcourt next month and study the map with him in a pro-German spirit: then the Cabinet will review the situation. For a real bargain about naval expenditure in which Germany gave up the attempt to challenge our naval superiority we might give something substantial, but the difficulty is that cession of territory can hardly from the German point of view be *in pari materia* with a naval arrangement.[116]

and by February the matter had become official.[117] It is perhaps typical of the character of these negotiations that Harcourt, Kühlmann, and even Grey, wanted to use the issue at an emotional level in order to improve Anglo-German relations, while the Foreign Office had been spurred into discussing the problem by practical problems involving the directing of British business interests.[118]

The conjoining of these two strands of discussion produced the first round of official and thoroughgoing territorial negotiations, leading in May 1912 to the formal proposal of a draft revision by the German side.[119] Further debate both with the German government and within the British ministry eventually led to the initialling of a new convention in October 1913.[120]

At this point the question entered upon its third and final stage: disagreement over the possibility of publishing the new arrangements. Crowe had already laid down the lines of this argument

The demand now is for a fresh bargain: On one side England is to have the privilege of publishing the convention that so clearly illustrates her goodwill towards Germany. Germany, on her part, is to be left free to despoil Portugal of her colonies definitely and in advance of any such financial difficulties in Portugal as the agreement contemplates...It would not be a fair bargain because for England to sully her good name by abandoning her ally...would ...be ill compensated by the permission to publish a convention which she concluded most reluctantly at German dictation in 1898 and has now revised to Germany's further advantage... Nothing could be more calculated to place us in a false position than the publication simultaneously of the fact that in 1899 we solemnly reaffirmed our obligation to defend Portugal's colonial possessions against foreign aggression – in return, too, for a special consideration, namely Portugal's undertaking not to declare neutrality during the South African war –; and yet that in 1898 we had made an agreement with Germany affecting the Portuguese colonies in S. Africa, to which we now declared that the alliance did not apply. It would be an impossible position...

In face of this dilemma the safest and wisest course would be that we should refuse altogether to sign any new convention unless it is agreed to publish it. The reasons for publicity are so strong, and the advantages to Germany under the revised convention so obvious, that she may be counted upon with some degree of assurance, not, finally, to reject our conditions, which should be: full publicity, and no tampering with the Anglo-Portuguese alliance in connection with the arrangement of 1898.[121]

This disagreement is by far the most important aspect of the whole question. The territorial discussions have an interest as showing how relatively uncontroversial the purely 'colonial' aspect turned out to be. It is almost as if the same influences which had made possible the Anglo-French entente and the Anglo-Russian convention were operating similarly in this case. But the publication of an Anglo-German agreement would automatically have given the settlement a significance far beyond Angola and Mozambique. In the end, Grey himself recorded the basis of his attitude absolutely clearly: 'It is, I think, only fair to the German government to give this assurance.'[122] For the Germans the matter was simpler. They felt that the publication of all the arrangements that existed – including the Anglo-Portuguese declaration of 1899 – would make the new agreement seem insufficiently advantageous to Germany in the eyes of the German public. More specifically, Kiderlen-Waechter had written to Lichnowsky:

whereupon the fate of the Treaty will be sealed, probably for ever. We have no inducement...to risk our expectation of inheriting Portugal's colonial possessions merely out of consideration for Sir E. Grey's sentimental scruples...

We shall only be able to agree to communication of the Treaty to the Portuguese government and its publication, if it is to be carried into effect at the same time.[123]

Despite the exchanges of 1914, this remained the basic German attitude. On 27 July 1914 Jagow responded to an attempt by Lichnowsky, the German Ambassador in London, to make new progress by saying

It was feared that a fresh start would be used to present us with alternatives: unconditional immediate signature and publication or giving up the whole convention. In that case we should have to choose the latter. We have sacrificed enough to Grey's obstinacy...[124]

This was precisely what Crowe was recommending. Grey himself had carefully avoided presenting the Germans with such a choice, but Crowe had advocated that:

we should not allow the offer of the revised convention to remain open indefinitely. If the latter is not signed within reasonable time, it should be clearly understood that this chapter is closed. It would be most inconvenient and not equitable if Germany were left free to come down at any time it may suit her in future years, to demand the signature of the new agreement. She ought to be put to the choice of (a) signature and publication, or (b) abandonment of the convention.[125]

There is no reason to suppose that he would have changed his mind about the dependence of signature on publication. How long Grey would wait, leaving the agreement merely initialled, was the subject of speculation by Lichnowsky and Jagow alike, a speculation which was rudely answered by events.

In this case, as in the case of the naval question, there is evidence to refute the assertion sometimes made that between 1911 and 1914 Anglo-German relations improved.[126] The negotiations over the Portuguese colonies certainly revealed a willingness on the part of both governments to talk – and talk successfully – about extra-European territory. But goodwill and good intentions on the ground in Africa could not be translated into an international agreement. The initialled agreement had to be dropped because discussions about publication became so acrimonious that such progress as had been made was jeopardised. The value of the question as being an area of Anglo-German friendly discussion to which public reference could be made was destroyed.

As has been seen, the naval question is even less susceptible of being interpreted as evidence for a détente. In the widest possible sphere, it was the symbol for some Germans of one aspect of their struggle for world-power status. It was at the very core of their belief that England stood in their way. For others, it was a more subtle means of pressure whereby England might be induced to abandon her opposition to German continental ambitions. It was this aspect that was prominent between 1912 and 1914. The navy was to be used to extract a pledge of neutrality from England, since circumstances precluded the building-up of the Fleet into a genuine threat. But England could not permit an attempt to divide her from her friends, so that she might be dealt with separately later, nor allow her food supplies to be menaced. No bargain was possible on the basis of a naval détente – even for one year's holiday – and a political agreement: there was no common ground between the two ideas.

Nor was it purely as an issue in international politics that the naval question was important. There was an emotional need behind the expansion of the German navy which did not derive solely from the desire to possess the proper accoutrements of a Great Power. The navy was the vehicle for the technological advances of the late nineteenth century and technological prowess was one of Germany's chief means of power. She would, like her ruler, have concealed a withered arm if she had not deployed that prowess on the water. Moreover, in a dangerously disunited country, which was the victim of serious social malaise, the navy was national rather than separatist, and, if not classless, at least middle-class. It was, in addition, the chief hobby of Kaiser Wilhelm II.

To discover that this institution had become so painful a point that England saw little future in raising the issue, and Germany declined to discuss it after March 1912, brings a forcible realisation of the deadlock that had come into existence. No negotiations over the future of the Portuguese colonies – although these, too, had broken down in June 1914 – could be a substitute for serious discussion of the major issue; not even the passing co-operation between Berlin and London during the Balkan Wars – particularly not when it is learnt that the Germans had decided that these were not the issue nor was 1912–13 the time when they wished to go to war.[127] The Kaiser may have believed that the naval race was bringing England to him: in fact he was watching his other country substitute a rigid policy where she had once shown flexibility, and a determination not to be drawn where she had once wished to negotiate.

16

Grey and the Tripoli War, 1911–1912

C. J. LOWE

Sir Edward Grey's attitude towards the Tripoli War was that it was dangerous. There were two principal considerations. The complexities of the Italian position straddling the Triple Alliance–Triple Entente confrontation were such that any sudden shock might upset the delicate European equilibrium and bring war. Equally, the longer the war dragged on the greater the temptation to the Balkan states to utilise this opportunity to deal Turkey a death blow, with incalculable consequences in view of Austro-Russian interests. Hence Grey's conviction that it was essential to refrain from any temptation to exploit this situation to bring either Italy or Turkey into the Entente camp, lest the cure prove worse than the disease. This was compounded by a well-founded belief that any Power which intervened in this struggle with positive proposals would, in all probability, get its fingers burnt. If there was to be any intervention it had to be by the Five Powers acting together in the name of Europe, an idea to which Grey gave some support as the dangers of allowing the war to drag on became more apparent; but any question of isolated British pressure upon one or the other of the combatants he completely ruled out. In retrospect it is possible to criticise this attitude: for example a Turkish alliance could have been obtained for the asking in 1911, an omission which was to prove expensive in 1915. But at the time Grey thought the safest course lay in strict neutrality and all the various proposals made to use the war to bring either Turkey or Italy over to the Entente broke on this rock.

British interest in Tripoli *per se* was negligible and since 1878 successive Foreign Secretaries in London had made no secret of this. Since at least 1890 it had been earmarked as part of the Italian heritage: Lansdowne in March 1902 went so far as to assure Rome not only that Britain had 'no aggressive or ambitious designs in regard to Tripoli', but also that 'if at any time an alteration of the status quo should take place, it would be their object that ...such alterations should be in conformity with Italian interests'. Although British trade with Tripoli was greater than that of Italy it was still insignificant. Nor was there any strategic objection to Lansdowne's offer: Cairo and the Admiralty saw in this 'nothing detrimental to British interests in the Mediterranean', despite their recognition that in Tobruk was a first-class port.[1] The key to this vicarious generosity lay of course in European international politics: the Franco-Italian rapprochement, and Lansdowne's desire to insure against any Italian commitments to France of a nature inimical to British interests in the Mediterranean.

But even if this agreement of 1902 marked a further step for Italy away from the Triple Alliance towards an alignment with Britain and France, what has been termed the 'sistema Visconti-Venosta',[2] there is no suggestion that Lansdowne had any similar intentions. For him, the basic objection to any form of alliance with Italy was that in the event of war, 'it might be of less importance to us to save Italian ships and ports than to concentrate our ships at those points where we were most threatened'.[3] Similarly Currie maintained that any Franco-Italian rapprochement 'is a distinct gain to us', precisely because it lessened the chances of incurring the liability of having to support Italy: 'we should have found Italy a very broken reed to lean upon either in negotiation or war'.[4] Once the negotiations for an Anglo-French agreement proved successful, this only reinforced previous conclusions. Rome, caught between the rival power-alignments, looked increasingly to London, but there was no reciprocal incentive for British policy-makers.

Whilst therefore events between 1905 and 1911 – the Moroccan Conference and Bosnian Crisis – seemed to some to widen the gap between Italy and her allies, 'so that her foreign policy has tended to become more and more associated with that of England, France and Russia',[5] there is no reason to suppose that Grey wanted to draw Italy out of the Triple Alliance. Barrère and Rodd, from Rome, periodically urged making Italy a fourth partner in the Triple Entente but neither Paris nor London showed much interest in this.[6] Grey even went out of his way to assure Imperiali in February 1911 that 'we had really no difficulties with Germany which strained our relations'[7] – a curious action if he had any ambitions to draw Italy out of her German orbit. Visconti-Venosta's dictum of 1902, that 'as far as England is concerned there are no difficulties but you may say there are also no relations'[8] was still fundamentally true on the eve of the Tripoli War.

Certainly, there is nothing to suggest that Grey encouraged Italian ambitions in Tripoli to create problems for the Triple Alliance, and German suspicions on this score were completely unfounded. His remarks to Imperiali and to Lowther at Constantinople expressing sympathy with Italian complaints 'if it really was the case that Italians were receiving unfair and adverse economic treatment in Tripoli',[9] should not be taken out of their context. Up to that point he had received no indication either from Rodd or Imperiali that Rome contemplated war: San Giuliano was still talking in terms of negotiations with Turkey on 31 July, the strongest phrase he used being that 'it was unfortunately not altogether impossible that some change of policy might be forced upon the Italian Government'.[10] Grey was thinking in terms of supporting Italy diplomatically at Constantinople to prevent war, as Germany was doing, not encouraging her to embark on an attack. Though Rodd had reported on 3 July that San Giuliano's reaction to the French procedure in Morocco was to talk in terms of compensation for Italy,[11] it was not until September that he concluded that Italy would go for Tripoli. Even then his conclusions were tentative and derived from the press rather than from San Giuliano or Giolitti, who were maintaining a conspiracy of silence.[12] As he explained to Grey on 4 September, he had to rely on the 'somewhat vague evidence open to me. Rome is a desert as usual in this season.' Privately he was more positive, remarking that 'we must be prepared for the eventuality of a move in Tripoli',[13] but this was the first real indication that Grey received that Italy was likely to go to war to achieve her compensation.

Moreover, in Rodd's view, an Italo-Turkish war would pose a serious problem for Britain:

The direction in which her [Italy's] sympathies will thereafter incline, with its important bearing on Mediterranean questions, will depend on the attitudes which the two groups of powers adopt towards her action. With Egypt on the one side and Tunis on the other the goodwill of Great Britain and France will be of paramount importance to her. The bidding for Italian friendship at the international auction may have to be rapid.[14]

At the time this was fully realised by Grey. Though no advocate of drawing Italy out of the Triple Alliance, and viewing her ambitions in Tripoli as 'tiresome', he nevertheless recognised the accuracy of Rodd's analysis – especially at a time when a general European war over the Moroccan question still seemed a possibility. If the Turks were attacked and appealed for British assistance, he told Nicolson on 19 September, they should be referred to Germany and Austria – 'It is most important that neither we nor France should side against Italy now.'[15]

Nevertheless, when war actually broke out Grey made a strong protest to Imperiali on 29 September against Italy's aggression as 'very embarrassing to the Powers'. The explanation for this lies, in all probability, in the strength of the public reaction in Britain. The press from Left to Right was uniform in its denunciation of the Italian action, stressing both its immorality and its likely repercussions in the Muslim world.[16] In view of the strength of radical criticism of Grey's policy in Morocco and Persia,[17] this strong press reaction against Italy was certainly sufficient to prevent Grey's openly declaring his sympathy for her. His efforts to 'induce some of the less unreasonable editors to maintain a decent neutrality' in the next few days, though mainly directed at preventing a deterioration in Anglo-Italian relations,[18] may well have had as a secondary consideration the protection of his own position and that of the Foreign Office.

Hence, while from July to September Grey's neutrality had shown a strong pro-Italian bias, from October onwards his policy of non-intervention was genuine. The Office view in the early stages of the war was to avoid any expression of sympathy towards Turkey lest it prolong and extend the fighting,[19] but as the war dragged on with no signs of any conclusion this became increasingly difficult. With the renewal of press attacks on Italy after the Tripoli 'massacre' of 23–6 October and House of Commons feeling openly pro-Turk – or pro-Muslim – in the debates of 2–6 November, it was impossible to ignore popular feeling.[20] Though Grey personally never became pro-Turk, this popular feeling, plus a growing irritation with Italy for having re-opened the 'Eastern Question', was sufficient to kill any prospect of an Anglo-Italian understanding whilst the war lasted.

Even so, *most* British diplomats and Foreign Office officials favoured a pro-Italian orientation to British policy. Fitzmaurice deprecated the traditional policy 'that Italy should remain in the enemy's camp...one can't help wondering whether it would not be safer to have her in the Anglo-French camp'. By February of 1912, alarmed at the results of the Carthage and Manouba incidents and of 'the anti-Italian tone in the British press in October and November last' he urged some form of reconciliation.[21] Louis Mallet, who was of some importance in view of his reputation as a special protégé of Grey, continually argued in a pro-Italian sense. When Kitchener, alarmed by the dangers of arousing the hostility of the Muslim world, advocated a pro-Turk orientation, Mallet minuted vigorously against this: 'I do not believe in the bugbear of Moslem resentment against us and consider that Italy is doing us a service in her attack on the Turkish Empire.'[22] When Granville, from Berlin, pointed to the danger of Italy's acquiring Tobruk and advocated British mediation, Mallet preferred leaving this thorny task to Germany: 'So long as we maintain our naval supremacy, the possession of Tripoli must weaken Italy.'[23] Nicolson was openly pro-Italian: it was 'exceedingly foolish that we should displease a country with whom we have always been on the most friendly terms and whose friendship to us is of very great value, in order to keep well with Turkey, who has been a source of great annoyance to us and whose Government is one of the worst that can well be imagined'.[24] He was infuriated with the British press as 'most short-sighted and one-sided – but this is a very British characteristic',[25] and took the lead in trying to muzzle it for the sake of Anglo-Italian relations. Cambon, who approached him on 28 October to take up the Barrère–Rodd suggestions for an understanding with Rome, found him generally favourable, but reluctant to proceed until Italy had resigned herself to accepting continued Turkish suzerainty over Tripoli.[26] All hopes of this were dashed when Italy proclaimed the annexation of Tripoli in full sovereignty on 5 November.

Not that this deterred Rodd. In a series of private letters in October and November[27] he sought to interest Grey in promoting an arrangement whereby Italy would contract out of the Triple Alliance as far as any war with Britain was concerned. Though aware of the lukewarm interest in Italy shown by the Foreign Office in the past, he emphasised that 'when she stands astride across the narrowest segment of the open waters...her friendship may be valuable in the Mediterranean in the next phase'. Above all, he urged, Grey should keep out of any arbitration schemes: this would be fatal at a time when Germany was working hard at Rome to stress her support for her alliance partner. As an inducement to Italy he proposed offering her a guarantee of Tripoli, since this acquisition 'will add greatly to her vulnerability, as well as contribute to her acceptance as a Mediterranean power'. Reflecting no doubt the origin of this scheme in the 'subtle mind' of Barrère, it was in fact to be a new Triple Entente:

An agreement between the three Powers most interested in the Mediterranean and the North African coast – though nominally for Mediterranean purposes only – would take all the sting out of the Triple Alliance, as far as Italy is concerned...

Though recognising that it might be difficult to convert San Giuliano, he thought Giolitti and the king were open to persuasion.[28]

But Grey was immovable. True, he shared Rodd's views on arbitration, instructing Cartwright on 26 October 'not to say anything that may be used to misrepresent us as having suggested bringing pressure to bear at Rome'.[29] But to make an actual agreement with Italy at this moment was impossible. In the first place public feeling in Britain was utterly hostile 'and the feeling being what it is, I should not be justified in making overtures to Italy for any political understanding'. Secondly, Rodd's scheme of guaranteeing the Italian position in Tripoli meant in practice supporting her in the war against the Turks, and this would be incompatible with British neutrality. Grey's irritation with Italian tactics was now apparent: they had been 'very foolish in putting out their foot so far in this Tripoli business'.[30] After the decree of annexation the war seemed likely to drag on indefinitely and, whereas in the initial stages there had seemed a chance of a speedy settlement if the Powers did not show too much sympathy for Turkey, a long-drawn-out affair threatened so many British interests that Grey could not possibly side with Italy. Though he rejected an alliance proposal from the Turks at this time, he was increasingly careful not to alienate them – especially in view of Tcharykov's feelers at Constantinople: as he told Benckendorff, 'one of the reasons why we had made our reply so civil was that we did not wish to discourage the overtures that Russia might be making for a better understanding with Turkey'.[31]

Even so, Grey was at best only lukewarm towards Tcharykov's proposals for promoting an understanding between Turkey and Russia as a solution to the Straits problem. If at the end of 1911 Grey's primary concern had been to avoid obstructing Russian diplomacy at Constantinople, as 1912 wore on this changed to a desperate anxiety to avoid war. To this end he fully endorsed Sazonov's five power peace plan, or even an Austro-Russian understanding, but resolutely refused to contemplate mediation by the Triple Entente.[32] Moreover, as the war spread from Tripoli to the eastern Mediterranean the complexity of British interests involved made any alignment with Italy as a prelude to enticing her from the Triple Alliance increasingly unlikely.[33] The Italian bombardment of Beirut in February and the Turkish closure of the Straits not only interfered with British trade[34] but also increased the danger that the conflict would spread to the Balkans, and that an Austro-Russian clash would produce a general war on an issue on which public opinion would not allow Britain to support Russia.[35] As Italy refused to compromise, and extended the war by attacking the Dardanelles and occupying the Dodecanese, British sympathy with Italy faded away completely. On 30 April Grey sought assurances from Rome that there would be no further attacks and on 6 August bluntly warned San Giuliano against annexing the Dodecanese. By March 1912 Mensdorff in London noted that a more friendly feeling prevailed there towards Turkey than of late and even the King, never a Turcophile, had to admit the need to consider Muslim feeling in India.[36]

Behind this increasing Foreign Office concern with developments in the Eastern Mediterranean lay also the Admiralty decision to concentrate the Mediterranean fleet in home waters. This decision, according to Crowe and Nicolson, would not only remove Britain's main means of influencing Turkey and tempt her to renew her ambitions to regain Egypt, but leaving Italy alone to face the entire French fleet would 'throw her completely into the arms of the Central Powers and place her in a position of definite hostility to France and Great Britain'. With both Turkey and Italy hostile, the British hold upon Egypt and means of communication with India would become increasingly precarious. Hence Crowe's suggestion of a naval agreement with France, whereby she concentrated in the Mediterranean and Britain in the North Sea: this would be in Nicolson's view 'the cheapest, simplest and safest solution'.[37]

Crowe's idea, enthusiastically endorsed by the C.I.D. conference at Malta,[38] eventually bore fruit in the exchange of letters between Grey and Cambon on 22–3 November 1912. But meanwhile it revived the project for a Mediterranean understanding with Italy. Rodd, who had vainly aired the idea once or twice earlier in the year,[39] reverted to it when on leave in London early in May, suggesting 'some mutual engagement between France, Italy and G[rea]t Britain that each country would respect and maintain the integrity of the possessions of the others'.[40] The point of this manoeuvre was that although Poincaré wanted an agreement with Italy to safeguard the transportation of troops from Algeria to France in the event of a European war, which operation had been made precarious by the British withdrawal from the Mediterranean, French relations with Italy were so bad after the Carthage and Manouba incidents that the initiative would have to come from London.[41]

In May Grey stalled on the familiar ground that any negotiation would have to await the end of the war;[42] but he had a nagging fear that Italy might conclude that the Anglo-French naval arrangements under discussion were directed against her[43] and once peace was signed between Italy and Turkey on 15 October, he hastened to open negotiations with Rome.

In a series of conversations at the Foreign Office between Imperiali, Grey and Nicolson, and in Rome between Rodd and San Giuliano,[44] it emerged that

Grey was anxious to conclude some sort of North African agreement with Italy, but that San Giuliano was in no hurry. Each, in fact, wished to push the other into taking the initiative of producing a draft.[45] On 23 November Rodd, on his own initiative, took the plunge, proposing to San Giuliano a far-ranging Anglo-Italian arrangement providing for the neutralisation of Tripoli and Egypt; but this idea found no favour in either Rome or London.[46] Nevertheless, though it was severely criticised by Crowe and Nicolson and dismissed by Grey on the practical grounds that 'if we did go to war with Italy the area could not be artificially limited by Treaty', it at least forced the Foreign Office to clarify its ideas.

These, when tabulated by Crowe on 6 December, revealed all too clearly the basic flaws in the whole concept. It had originated in Barrère's desire to use the issue of Tripoli to draw Italy further away from the Triple Alliance, but in fact events had already drawn Italy back towards that Alliance. The incidents with France during the war and French naval concentration in the Mediterranean had hardened Italian policy against closer relations with Paris. In fact San Giuliano not only renewed the Triple Alliance at this time, but also permitted extensive Italo-German military conversations. Hence, for Italy, if there were to be any new 'North Africa' agreement, it would have to be between Italy and England, not Italy and the Entente: whilst Germany would accept the former – indeed according to Kühlmann would welcome it – she would not accept the latter.[47]

In London this was regarded as useless. As Crowe's memorandum declared, an agreement including France would be 'businesslike', amounting to 'recognition that the 3 Powers accept the division of Northern Africa among themselves as a necessary and beneficient arrangement which they agree not to disturb', but a purely Anglo-Italian arrangement 'amounts to very little and is almost superfluous'.[48] Finally, anything more than this – so much for Barrère's visions – was dangerous: it would be fatal to give the impression in Berlin and Vienna of trying to detach Italy from the Triple Alliance.[49]

This appreciation of the difficulties involved and San Giuliano's own preference for the Triple Alliance[50] killed the negotiations: on 13 February 1913 Rodd was given permission to use Crowe's draft only if San Giuliano referred to the question, which he never did.[51] With a similar hiatus in Franco-Italian relations as Barrère got no support from Paris, there was no incentive to rush what was clearly a delicate subject. As Grey observed to Cambon in March, the Italians 'might wish to mix the question of the Aegean Islands, and perhaps the coast of Asia Minor, with any designation of a "status quo" that should be respected'.[52] It was best to leave Italy to take the initiative.

Grey's suspicions on this score were fully justified when, in October 1913, San Giuliano finally opened his mind. As part of a general Mediterranean understanding Italy was certainly to keep the Dodecanese and preferably obtain concessions from Turkey in Asia Minor in addition. This attitude posed serious problems for it was not only a question of moral outrage – real enough on Grey's part – but also of strategic objections from the Admiralty. In June 1912 they announced that

possession by Italy of Naval bases in the Aegean Sea would imperil our position in Egypt, would cause us to lose our control over our Black Sea and Levant trade at its source, and would expose in war our route to the East via the Suez Canal to the operation of Italy and her allies.

To make matters worse, the Office suspected – quite correctly – that the Triple[53] Alliance would shortly pool their naval resources in the Mediterranean, creating a much more formidable opponent than the feeble Italy.[54]

Hence Grey's objective was to eject Italy from the Dodecanese, not confirm her possession; but obtaining this was difficult without risking an open breach. It may well be true, as has recently been argued,[55] that temperamentally Grey was no Salisbury, that he lacked the nerve to tell the 'sturdy beggars' bluntly where they stood in the European hierarchy. But Grey had a much more delicate situation to cope with than Salisbury had enjoyed in the nineties. Consequently, Rome's continual stream of excuses – that occupation was but temporary, would cease when Turkey paid Italy her expenses, when Turkish officers were withdrawn from Libya, or when Greece was ejected from Albania – were given some credence; though even the gentle Grey snapped at one stage to Imperiali that Italy's demands were equivalent to a 999 year lease.[56] At no stage would he agree to Italy retaining the Dodecanese or become involved in San Giuliano's schemes for trading this off against concessions in Asia Minor. 'We cannot encourage that', he minuted in October 1913, 'we must oppose Italian projects in the Islands.' Instead, Italy was to be reminded of her 'repeated and solemn assurances' of evacuation.[57]

Obviously this attitude prevented an agreement but it may be doubted whether Grey would have obtained anything more concrete if he had succumbed to San Giuliano's blandishments. For when, in October 1913, the Sicilian opened his diplomatic offensive in London with talk of a Mediterranean understanding, it is clear that he did so for quite other reasons. His objective was to pressure his allies into concessions to Italy in Asia Minor and Trieste by frightening them with the spectre of an Italo-French-British understanding.[58] Grey, by pushing the ball back into the Italian half of the court and leaving San Giuliano to make concrete proposals, effectively defeated the Sicilian's manoeuvre.[59] True, an agreement on a minor issue, a share for Italian concessionaires in the British project for a Smyrna–Aidin railway, was initialled in March 1914, but this had little to do with the real question. For Grey this remained the evacuation of the Dodecanese and San Giuliano's shiftiness on this issue was the major cause of a deepening distrust which lasted until the latter's death in October 1914.[60] Only the necessities of war in the Spring of 1915 led Grey to swallow Italian annexation of the Aegean islands, submerged in the vaster distortions of the Treaty of London.

The net result, therefore, of Grey's diplomacy during the Tripoli war was, if anything, to confirm Italy's position in the Triple Alliance. Alienated by the France of Poincaré, distrusted by Grey, San Giuliano not only renewed the Triple Alliance but revived the military and naval conventions dormant since 1902. His approaches to London and Paris for a Mediterranean understanding were not meant seriously, an indifference that was largely reciprocated in the Entente capitals. Indeed, it is clear that much of the futile discussions on this project originated with Barrère's schemes, swallowed whole by the gullible Rodd. The basic problem of Italy's position in Europe was in fact insoluble, as Crowe noted succinctly in May 1914:

Italy wants to square the circle: without exposing herself to a change of faith she wants to remain in the Triple Alliance and yet not go to war with France in accordance with its stipulations. No Anglo-Italian "formula" can solve this ethical problem.[61]

17

Great Britain and France, 1911–1914

K. A. HAMILTON

The appearance on 31 January 1911 of an article in the Parisian newspaper, *Le Temps*, which contrasted the virility of the triple alliance with the inactivity of the triple *entente*, led Eyre Crowe to comment:

The fundamental fact of course is that the Entente is not an alliance. For purposes of ultimate emergencies it may be found to have no substance at all. For an Entente is nothing more than a frame of mind, a view of general policy which is shared by the governments of two countries, but which may be, or become, so vague as to lose all content.[1]

The development of the Anglo-French relationship during the summer and autumn of 1911 bore out the justice of this observation. Though Britain and France appeared to withstand successfully the German challenge at Agadir, friction over the future of Morocco, and criticism of the *entente* by prominent politicians on both sides of the Channel served to emphasize the degree to which it was dependent upon personalities rather than diplomatic instruments. During the next two and a half years efforts were made to define and clarify the extent to which each power was committed to the other in the European context. British and French military authorities continued to plan together for a war which they might have to fight as allies, and conversations on possible naval cooperation were placed upon a firmer footing. But the French still had to base their hopes for British aid in a possible war with Germany on what they believed to be Britain's interest in maintaining the independence and integrity of France. In the same period the governments in both countries still found reason to grouse at each other's conduct in matters relating to their respective rights and interests in Africa and Asia.

A dispute over an extra-European issue in the immediate aftermath of the Agadir crisis threatened to undermine the whole basis of the Anglo-French understanding. Both Grey and Caillaux expressed doubts about the future of the *entente* when differences arose between the two countries over the extent to which the Franco-Spanish agreement of 1904 might be modified so as to compensate France in Morocco for her losses in the Congo. Angered by Grey's defence of Spanish rights and British interests, Caillaux complained to Bertie on 4 November that had it not been for the understanding with England,

'France might long ago have come to terms with Germany'.[2] Moreover, during the next fortnight he also succeeded in quarrelling with Bertie, whom he openly accused of having intrigued against him.[3] Although under pressure from his colleagues and in the face of mounting opposition to his policies, Caillaux subsequently retreated from his more extreme demands, the language which he had used and reports of his dealings with Berlin were sufficient to worry even the most stalwart supporters of the *entente* in London.[4]

Bertie was probably correct in thinking that Caillaux was *au fond* for the *entente*. He was not noted for his caution, and may simply have over-reacted to the ambassador's protests over France's treatment of Spain.[5] Moreover, Caillaux's proposals were essentially those of that section of the Quai d'Orsay which was concerned with Morocco, and the collapse of his government in January 1912 still left Bertie apprehensive as to what France's intentions were. His successor, Raymond Poincaré, had had little experience in dealing with foreign affairs, and his decision to act as both premier and foreign minister caused doubts to be expressed in the British embassy in Paris about whether he would continue to be influenced by the same officials who had encouraged Caillaux.[6] Poincaré, however, showed himself to be only too willing to dissipate any anxieties which might have been caused by the 'wild words' of his predecessor, and to assure the British government of his goodwill and desire for 'intimate and confidential relations'.[7]

Grey responded to Poincaré with expressions of a similar sentiment, but the course which he adopted during the next few months was anything but reassuring to the new government in France.[8] Already during November 1911 Grey had been compelled to defend his diplomacy in the cabinet and parliament. The secret military conversations with France were called into question by his colleagues, and, while their continuation was accepted, Grey had to agree to a formula which formally stated that they were non-binding and required cabinet sanction. He had also to reckon with considerable criticism from those amongst his fellow Liberals who considered that Britain had adopted an unduly provocative stance towards Germany during the preceding crisis. It was partly in order to satisfy these critics that Grey found it necessary to try once more to improve relations between Great Britain and Germany.[9]

As the *entente*'s survival was to a considerable extent the result of the distrust felt in Britain and France of Germany's ambitions, the relationship was always sensitive to any attempt by either power to seek an accommodation with the latter. Grey's decision therefore to try and place Anglo-German relations on a 'less unfavourable basis', and his dispatching of Lord Haldane to Berlin, raised the fears of protagonists of the *entente* in both countries.[10] Bertie, who was critical on grounds of general policy of an approach to Germany on naval and imperial matters, feared that it would cause suspicion in France of Britain's intentions.[11] In London his anxiety was reciprocated by Nicolson and Paul Cambon, although the French ambassador was at first more worried by the possible effects on Britain of undue criticism in France than by Grey's attitude towards Germany.[12] For his part, Grey certainly had no qualms of conscience about discussions with the Germans. Both the French and Russians, he explained to Nicolson, had dealt separately with them, and 'it was not reasonable that tension should be permanently greater between England and Germany' than between Germany and the other two.[13] What he desired, he subsequently told Goschen, was that all three powers should be 'on the best of terms with Germany without losing touch with each other or impairing the confidence which exists between us'.[14] This involved, as he was well aware, promising nothing to Germany which would prejudice Britain's freedom to go to France's aid in time of crisis. For this reason any reference to British 'neutrality' was strictly avoided in any of the proposals for an Anglo-German agreement.[15]

Any formula designed to satisfy German fears of British intentions was almost certain to meet with objections from the defenders of the understanding with France. Even Grey's seemingly harmless proposal of 14 March for a declaration which stated that Britain would neither pursue an aggressive policy towards Germany, nor join in an unprovoked attack upon her, could, as Bertie contended, be so construed as to hamper Anglo-French cooperation. France might, Bertie thought, strike the first blow against Germany if troop movements and other measures led her to suspect an impending attack. In that case France would not necessarily be the real aggressor, but Germany would be able to pose as a victim of aggression. He was opposed to any agreement which would tie Britain's hands by a neutrality promise, for if, as he considered unlikely, France or Russia were to launch an unprovoked attack upon Germany, 'the crushing of France', he believed, 'would still be a great danger to England'.[16] Yet despite vigorous protests from Bertie, and the rejection by the German government of his formula, Grey was still unwilling to abandon his discussions with Germany.[17]

Equally disturbing to Bertie was the acquiescence shown by the French government and its representatives to the Anglo-German *pourparlers*. This was due partly to a desire not to antagonise the British government over discussions which seemed to present no great danger to the *entente*, and which Paul Cambon believed to have little chance of success. Besides the French also misunderstood both the exact state and nature of the discussions. Poincaré had been led to believe that all Grey had intended by his formula was a verbal declaration to Germany, and Paul Cambon had thought that the German refusal of the formula had brought the discussions to an end.[18] Convinced that Grey's policy was due to the influence of those cabinet members who favoured a rapprochement with Germany, Bertie attempted to make the French more keenly aware of its dangers, and thereby to bring additional pressure to bear on the British government. On 27 March he explained his fears to Poincaré and urged him that if he were to speak to London 'avec un peu de fermeté, on hésitera à commettre la faute que je redoute'.[19] A fortnight later on 10 April, he appealed to Poincaré to speak with energy and to arm Grey against his colleagues by enabling him to demonstrate that it was not worth the risk of compromising the *entente* for the sake of an illusory and deceitful agreement.[20] In so far as he rejuvenated latent French fears of Britain being entrammelled by German policy, he was entirely successful. His concern lest, in the event of a Franco-German conflict, the British cabinet should equivocate on the basis of Grey's formula was soon shared by Fallières and Poincaré.[21] To Paul Cambon the latter wrote that the proposed declaration would be interpreted in France as a voluntary abandonment by Britain of the policy pursued since 1904.[22]

Warnings by Bertie and Paul Cambon as to the possible ill effects of an Anglo-German agreement on public opinion in France, and of the encouragement that it would give to the opponents of the *entente* there, seem to have convinced Nicolson that Britain was arriving at a 'very critical moment' in her relations with France. He urged Grey to drop his formula for it would be disastrous were Britain for the sake of it to risk alienating France and consequently Russia.[23] Neither French pleas nor Bertie's arguments could, however, alter Grey's desire to improve relations with Germany, or his conviction that his formula would not inhibit Britain in aiding France in time of conflict. If war were forced upon a friend or ally, that, he informed Bertie, would be regarded as provocation.[24] 'So long', he observed, 'as France is kept informed of anything of importance that takes place, and we do nothing with Germany which is really of detriment to France and we do not change our general policy, the French must not complain'.[25] The ultimate failure of the negotiations with Germany was due not to the effects of French objections but to the refusal of Grey to go beyond his offer of a non-aggression formula to the Germans. Indeed the continuing Anglo-German dialogue on colonial matters and the appointment of Baron Marschall von Bieberstein as German ambassador to London, was sufficient to set off a fresh wave of speculation in France and the Foreign Office about a political agreement with Germany.[26] A draft proposed by Nicolson assuring Poincaré 'that all questions of any political formulas had been definitely and finally abandoned', was considerably modified, and Grey would go no further than to instruct Bertie on 31 May to inform Poincaré that the British government were 'fully determined...not to adopt any line of policy which would in any way impair the intimate and friendly relations which they desire to maintain with France'. They had, he concluded, 'no intention of entering into any political engagement with Germany which would have this effect'.[27]

The Anglo-German negotiations high-lighted for the French government the nebulous nature of their *entente* with England. Despite the evident goodwill which prevailed between Britain and France, Grey had been prepared in the face of French opposition to continue his search for an accommodation with Berlin.[28] Already uneasy about the state of Germany's military preparations and plans, the French were given reason to fear that they might soon lose an effective deterrent against German aggression. Indeed, in Cambon's opinion, the efforts of the Wilhelmstrasse to assure Britain's neutrality had indicated that Britain was regarded as the power which 'held largely the balance for or against peace'.[29] At the same time, however, a relationship which was based solely upon a community of interest and reciprocal confidence, was, as Cambon asserted, always open to criticism from those who were opposed to England and who claimed that the *entente* offered no security to France. With these factors in mind, Cambon and Poincaré appear to have decided that the time had come to reinforce their relationship with Britain either by securing some fresh assurance of British support, or by at least giving some precision to the existing understanding.

Relieved at the apparent failure of the British and German governments to agree upon a formula, Cambon, with Poincaré's approval, sought to profit from the situation by raising with Nicolson on 15 April the whole issue of Britain's future support for France. He asked if they could not seek a formula with which to reassure 'les esprits inquiets et incrédules'. While he said nothing precise as to what assurances might be given, he referred to Lansdowne's willingness in 1905 to 'strengthen and extend' the understanding with France, and he suggested that declarations might be exchanged in the form of notes. Nicolson might personally have welcomed the suggestion, but in the circumstances he could only advise Cambon to leave matters as they were. The cabinet, he thought, would not be prepared to bind themselves to act in any contingency, and an attempt at reshaping the *entente* might be taken as offering 'umbrage and a challenge' to Germany.[30]

If the response to Cambon's initiative was disappointing for the French, the naval question which had proved to be one of the main obstacles to closer Anglo-German relations was ironically to provide them with the opportunity for a renewed attempt to extract from Britain a more formal definition of the *entente*. The Admiralty's concern with the development of the German navy had already led them by December 1907 to concentrate the preponderant might of the Royal Navy in home waters. But in the spring of 1912 they were faced with the prospect of a further increase in German naval strength, and the development by Italy and Austria–Hungary of a force of dreadnoughts which would soon render obsolete the British fleet in the Mediterranean, and place it in a very precarious position in the event of a war with the triple alliance.[31] To meet this challenge the Admiralty proposed a reorganisation of the fleets, the essence of which was outlined by Churchill to the commons on 18 March.[32] This involved the withdrawal from Malta of the six pre-dreadnoughts then stationed there, and the formation of a new battle quadron which would be based at Gibraltar and be able to reinforce other squadrons in the North sea and the Atlantic, or re-enter the Mediterranean if circumstances so dictated. As Churchill subsequently reasoned, Britain's peace-time dispositions would thus approximate to those which it had been intended to assume in time of conflict.[33]

In planning for a future war neither Churchill and his advisers, nor their predecessors, had neglected the part which France and the *entente* might play. The British war plans of 1907 and 1908 had reckoned with the possibility of obtaining aid from France in the Mediterranean. Moreover, although Churchill always insisted that in the absence of either an agreement with Germany or a substantial increase in British naval expenditure, the new dispositions were the best that the navy could adopt, he also recognised that without French assistance, British interests in the Mediterranean would be dangerously exposed in time of conflict. When on 29 April Asquith instructed the Committee of Imperial Defence to inquire into the effects of the projected naval changes upon the strategic situation in the Mediterranean and elsewhere, he also requested that they should examine the 'degree too of reliance to be placed on the cooperation of the French fleet'.[34] Nevertheless, before the Agadir crisis there had been no conversations between the British and French naval authorities of a kind similar to those which had proceeded between their military staffs.

In 1906 Fisher had been reluctant to discuss naval war plans with the French, and only in December 1908 did he indicate to the French naval attaché in London that in a war in which France was allied with Britain she should concentrate her naval forces in the Mediterranean. Since, however, the French had already decided in 1907 to shift the greater part of their naval strength to the Mediterranean, Fisher's remarks complemented rather than determined the deployment of their fleets. Even when tentative discussions did begin in the summer of 1911 between the First Sea Lord, Sir Arthur Wilson, and representatives of the French navy, the net result was only a verbal agreement which included provisions for possible cooperation in the Mediterranean.[35]

The attention of the Foreign Office was first drawn to the progress of these conversations by Paul Cambon, who on 4 May 1912 suggested to Nicolson that they should be resumed, and that Britain might join France and Russia in a naval convention. He said that what his government desired was that the British government should look after the Channel and France's northern coasts, while the French should undertake the care of the Mediterranean.[36] Both Grey and Churchill were insistent that any such talks should await the completion of the government's consideration of the Admiralty's proposals, but Nicolson was surprised and irritated by Cambon's reference to conversations about the extent and nature of which he knew nothing. Indeed he and his colleagues might well have been excused for assuming that the projected naval moves were not unconnected with such talks.[37]

Grey's officials were far from happy about the Admiralty's proposals which appeared in their view to denude Britain's interests in the Mediterranean of sufficient naval protection.[38] Eyre Crowe contended that the British 'withdrawal' from the Mediterranean would lead to a diminution of Britain's influence there and alter the whole power structure of the area to her disadvantage. But most of these difficulties, he argued, might be avoided if French cooperation were assured, and their fleet were in a position to beat those of Italy, Austria and Turkey combined.[39] Yet neither Nicolson nor Bertie believed that France's help could be secured without Britain first undertaking some fresh obligations towards her. Discounting the possibility of an increase in the naval budget, or an alliance with Germany, Nicolson recommended that the only other alternative was an understanding with France which would have 'very much the character of a defensive alliance'. While he doubted if the cabinet would approve this, he thought that it offered the 'cheapest, simplest, and safest solution'. An ardent exponent of a 'free hand' where relations with Germany were concerned, Nicolson protested to Bertie, 'we can hardly continue sitting on the fence very much longer and continue to give evasive and uncertain answers.'[40]

Bertie was more cautious than Nicolson. He admitted that the French could hardly be expected not to make some use of Britain's 'desertion' of the Mediterranean 'as a lever to extract someting tangible from us', but he did not believe that the government would have to go as far as an alliance in order to secure their assistance. In a private letter to Nicolson on 9 May he suggested that the French might be satisfied with an exchange of notes between the two governments which would define generally their respective and joint interests, and state that in the event of these being endangered they would consult together. The French, Bertie assumed, would be prepared to accept that the question of an alliance should be settled when hostilities seemed near, but they desired, he thought, to have arranged exactly what military assistance Britain could give them, and what mutual naval support there should be. Britain would have to do something like this, he concluded, 'unless we prefer to run the risk of being stranded in splendid isolation'.[41]

Neither the Admiralty's proposed redeployment of the navy, nor the idea of a closer relationship with France were generally regarded in London as the best solution to Britain's difficulties. In part this was because the former project was wrongly felt to be dependent upon the latter. The War Office, the Board of Trade, and the Colonial Office were all worried by the way in which Britain's Mediterranean communications might be exposed to possible enemy attack. Within the cabinet McKenna, Harcourt, and Morley opposed the naval redeployment, which they feared would lead to a closer association with France, and Grey would have preferred an increase in naval expenditure to a split with his colleagues. Churchill's advisers also favoured this alternative to an alliance with a 'country of unstable politics with no particular sympathy towards British interests except in so far as they represent French interests as well'. Moreover, while the Conservative press were prepared to subscribe to the idea of an alliance with France, both it and the Liberal newspapers were critical of the idea of relying on a foreign power to defend British interests.[42]

Some modifications were made in the Admiralty's plans as the result of consultations which had taken place on Malta at the end of May between

Asquith, Churchill, and Kitchener. The latter's preoccupation with the defence of Egypt led Churchill eventually to agree to maintain a force of two or three battle cruisers and a cruiser squadron at Malta, and to seek an agreement with France. In a memorandum of 15 June, in which he defended the new dispositions, Churchill argued that an Anglo-French combination in a war would be able to keep full control of the Mediterranean and afford all necessary protection to British and French interests there.[43] Yet McKenna, who had preceded Churchill at the Admiralty, and who was the most adept of his critics, was quite incorrect in his assertion that an alliance with France was an 'essential feature' of the new strategy.[44] Churchill clearly stated in his memorandum of the 15th that the Admiralty's measures stood by themselves. What he desired was not an alliance, but a 'defensive naval arrangement which would come into force only if the two powers were at any time allies in a war'.

Despite his insistence upon the sufficiency and autonomous nature of the Admiralty's provisions, Churchill still failed to overcome the opposition of his colleagues in the cabinet. After a lengthy meeting of the defence committee on 4 July he was compelled to abandon the scheme, and accept their resolution that subject to the provision of a 'reasonable margin of superior strength' in home waters, the Admiralty

...ought to maintain available for Mediterranean purposes and based on a Mediterranean port a battle fleet equal to a one-Power Mediterranean standard excluding France.[45]

This decision did not mean the abandonment of the idea of a naval arrangement with France. Implicit in it was the assumption that Britain would find herself opposed by both Austria and Italy only in the event of a conflict in which France would also be involved. Moreover, Churchill's defeat was more apparent than real. Given Britain's existing naval strength it would not be possible for her to secure battleship parity with Austria in the Mediterranean before 1915, and Churchill's opponents in the cabinet were not prepared to sanction the necessary expenditure to achieve even this.[46]

Such information as the Quai d'Orsay were able to obtain about the Admiralty's future plans, and the public discussion of a possible alliance with France, encouraged the French to think in terms of a tighter relationship with Britain.[47] Moreover in July Delcassé, the French minister of marine, finally gave approval for his war staff proposals to move their remaining battleship squadron at Brest to Toulon. This, de Saint-Seine, the French naval attaché in London, told Admiral Bridgman on 10 July, would make France stronger in the Mediterranean than a combination of the Austrian and Italian fleets.[48]

The resumption of talks between the French naval attaché and the Admiralty, and the possibility that plans might be arranged for co-operation in the Mediterranean, raised the whole question of Britain's liberty of action. On 16 July the cabinet resolved that it should be made plain to the French that conversations between military and naval experts would not prejudice the freedom of decision of either government in the event of war.[49] The danger, was, however, that the French might claim that since their naval dispositions were dependent upon an arrangement with Britain, she was morally obliged to defend their northern coasts against attack. To avoid involvement in such a commitment Churchill endeavoured to have it explicitly stated in any arrangement between the naval authorities of Britain and France that the deployment of their respective fleets was independent of any conversations between them. Thus while he recommended to de Saint-Seine that France should keep in the Mediterranean a fleet equal to that of Austria and Italy combined, he also insisted that the new dispositions which the Admiralty proposed were made in 'our own interests, and adequate in our opinion to the full protection of British trade and possessions in the Medit(erranea)n'.[50]

Bertie, who met Grey on 17 July, had doubts about whether the cabinet's decision would be palatable to the French. He warned the foreign secretary that they would require a *quid pro quo* for looking after the Mediterranean, and he repeated to him the proposal for an exchange of notes which had been made to Nicolson on 9 May. But Grey showed no enthusiasm for what seemed to him to be 'something like an alliance', and on 23 July Bertie was informed that the cabinet had rejected it.[51] On the same day the French naval attaché received from the Admiralty a draft agreement outlining a plan for Anglo-French naval cooperation in the Mediterranean and the straits of Dover.

At Churchill's instigation the details of this project were preceded by a declaration to the effect that the agreement would relate solely to the case where Britain and France were allies in a war, and that it would not affect the political freedom of either power with regard to embarking on such a conflict. It also stated:

It is understood that France has disposed almost the whole of her battle fleet in the Mediterranean leaving her Atlantic seaboard in the care of Flotillas.

Great Britain on the other hand has concentrated her battle fleets in home-waters, leaving in the Medit(erranea)n a strong containing force of battle and armoured cruisers and torpedo craft. These dispositions have been made independently because they are the best which the separate interests of each country suggests, having regard to all circumstances and probabilities and they do not arise from any naval agreement or convention.[52]

As Bertie had predicted, the French were anything but satisfied with Churchill's draft agreement. Paul Cambon wrongly assumed that the achievement of the dispositions to which Churchill referred was the object rather than the basis of the proposed accord. On 24 July he protested to Nicolson that the project entailed a deployment of the French navy in such a way as would leave France's northern coasts unprotected while 'England was free to aid France or not as she liked, and be under no obligation to do so'. It was possible, he concluded, that the French naval authorities would require first to have assurances that British naval aid would be forthcoming for the Channel and Atlantic ports of France. Churchill's explanation to the French naval attaché that these dispositions were to be arrived at quite independently by each navy was rejected by Cambon. France, he insisted to Grey, had concentrated her fleet in the Mediterranean as the result of naval conversations begun with Fisher in 1907.[53]

Cambon's claim, which had no factual basis, appears to have perplexed Churchill. Nevertheless, while he admitted that he had not been aware of the extent to which the Admiralty had been committed by his predecessor, he still considered the non-committal proviso to be 'desirable and perfectly fair'. The present dispositions, he observed, 'represented the best arrangements either power could make independently', and it was not true that the French were occupying the Mediterranean to oblige Britain.[54]

Although Bertie continued to work for an exchange of notes, by the end of the month, he, Nicolson, and Tyrrell all accepted Churchill's thesis. There was therefore, Bertie noted, 'no question of a *quid pro quo* being due to France in the shape of a protection for her Atlantic and Channel coasts by the British fleet'.[55] Having been advised by Bertie not to press his views upon the British government, Poincaré also abandoned his argument about the interdependence of the naval moves. Instead he raised the whole question of the meaning of the *entente*.

On 30 July Poincaré frankly admitted to Bertie that the decision of the French government with regard to the deployment of ther fleet was 'quite spontaneous', but he asserted that it 'would not have been taken if they could not suppose that in the event of Germany making a descent on the Channel or Atlantic ports of France, England would not come to the assistance of France'. The object of the *entente*, he contended, was for the 'maintenance of each other and their defence against attack – unprovoked attack and the balance of power'. If the *entente* did not mean that England would come to France's aid in the event of a German attack on her ports, then, he observed, 'its value to France is not great'. Ostensibly Poincaré's chief objection to Churchill's draft arrangement was the technical one that a political resolution should not form part of an agreement which was strictly between experts. His object, however, seems to have been to avoid any explicit Anglo-French declaration denying the connexion between the naval arrangement and the *entente*, and to bring the British government to redefine their position *vis-à-vis* France.[56]

Grey had already rejected a suggestion put to him by Cambon on 26 July that if Churchill's proviso were to remain at the head of the proposed naval agreement, there should be an exchange of notes between the two governments which would provide for joint consultation in the event of peace being menaced.[57] But Grey's verbal assurance to Cambon that as matters were the two governments would consult together in time of crisis did little to assuage French aspirations. On 30 July Poincaré indicated to Bertie his desire for some form of declaration, which would entail conversations taking place between the two governments the moment that their interests appeared to be endangered so that they might decide at once whether the arrangements arrived at by their experts should be put into effect.[58]

From Paris Bertie gave his support to Poincaré's proposal, and on 13 August he reiterated to Grey his belief that what the French wanted was an exchange of notes defining British and French interests, and providing for consultations. Were this impossible, then he thought that they might accept an exchange of declarations stipulating that, notwithstanding any arrangements signed by experts, the two governments remained entirely free to determine, whenever circumstances arose, whether they would give each other armed support. The French accepted the autonomous nature of the new naval dispositions, but Bertie argued, it was their contention that they would not have been made if each power had not been confident of the assistance of the other in the area from which they were withdrawing. In fact Poincaré had attributed to the Anglo-French understanding a meaning and definition which implicitly involved a British moral obligation to defend the interests of France.[59]

Fully aware of the dangers of accepting Poincaré's views and Bertie's interpretations of them, Churchill warned Asquith on 23 August: 'Everyone must feel who knows the facts that we have all the obligations of an alliance without its advantages and above all without its precise definitions.' Nevertheless he was quite prepared to abandon his draft declaration. He informed the prime minister that he was not particular as to how his views should be given effect to, and made 'no avail' as to the document in which they were set forth.[60] Asquith agreed that this was a matter of form on which they might give way 'if Bertie could suggest some manner of affording this agreement of not too formal a character'.[61] But in abandoning Churchill's original preamble, and in accepting the separation of this from the proposed naval agreement, the government left itself open to the conclusion of an arrangement whose non-committal provisions were less precise, and on which could be placed very different interpretations.

Before any new formula was found with which to replace Churchill's declaration, Cambon returned again to the subject of a consultative agreement. Evidently he still hoped to use the redeployment of the French navy as a bargaining counter in negotiations with Grey for on 19 September he warned him that the concentration of the French fleet in the Mediterranean would not be definitive until they knew where they stood with England. The two governments, he proposed, should agree that in the event of either of them apprehending aggression by a third power or complications menacing to peace, they should discuss the situation, and 'rechercheraient les moyens d'assurer de concert le maintien de la paix et d'écarter toute tentative d'agression'.[62] As Grey recognised, this statement simply expressed what would happen under the existing circumstances. Indeed, it was as Asquith described it 'almost a platitude'.[63] For Cambon, however, the important point was to have something of this nature in writing.

Grey seems to have had no personal objection to offering Cambon the assurance which he requested, but he had doubts as to the form in which it should be given. The publication of an exchange of notes, he feared, would have a 'very exciting effect in Europe', and both he and Asquith were at first reluctant to accept anything which could not be communicated in parliament. Cambon, however, persisted in pressing for some written understanding, and in agreement with the prime minister, Grey finally consented to an exchange of private letters with the ambassador if this were sanctioned by the cabinet.[64]

As the cabinet had already rejected Bertie's earlier suggestion for an exchange of letters, their simple approval of Cambon's proposal might have seemed unlikely. Such an arrangement did however provide both an opportunity for them to obtain an explicit statement on the non-committal nature of the naval and military conversations, and a substitute for Churchill's projected preamble. Thus on 30 October Grey was able, with the consent of his cabinet colleagues, to propose to Cambon that three points be recognised in an exchange of letters: that conversations between experts had taken place; that these did not bind their governments to action; and that in the event of a threatening situation the two governments would consult with one another.[65] These were to form the basis of the notes exchanged on 22 and 23 November by Grey and Paul Cambon.[66]

The only explicit reference in the exchange of notes to the dispositions recently assumed by the British and French fleets was the assertion by Grey that they were not 'based upon an engagement to cooperate in war'. But in January and February 1913 three agreements were concluded between the British and French naval authorities providing for cooperation in the straits of Dover, the English Channel, and the Mediterranean. Each of these contained the provision that they were to become effective in the event of the two powers being allies in a war with Germany or the triple alliance.[67]

In itself the exchange of notes between Grey and Cambon did little to extend the existing relationship between the two countries. It simply committed to paper in a precise form the nature of the *entente* as it related to a possible European conflict, and the terms upon which Britain and France would continue to cooperate with each other. Unlike, however, the declaration which Churchill had proposed in August, neither the notes nor the non-committal provisos of the agreement of February, affirmed the autonomous nature of the dispositions assumed by the British and French navies. They merely stated that they were not the result of an alliance. Indeed since the arrangements worked out in February 1913 were dependent upon the maintenance of the new dispositions, it might be contended that Britain had thereby incurred a moral obligation to defend the northern coasts of France in the event of a continental war. Certainly nothing was contained in the notes which could be held to refute the claims made by Cambon on 1 August 1914 that at Britain's request, France had moved her fleets to the Mediterranean.[68] By then, however, circumstances had changed. Faced by a cabinet which was as yet undecided as to the course which it would pursue in the even of a Franco-

German war, Cambon's appeal seemed to Nicolson like a 'happy inspiration'.[69] Even Churchill who had disclaimed any such obligation during 1912, was prepared to endorse Grey's contention that Britain must defend the northern shores of France.[70]

Between November 1912 and July 1914 the French made only one more attempt to extend their understanding with England, and even that went no further than a fresh proposal on a consultative arrangement. Had they endeavoured to achieve more it seems unlikely that they would have been successful. For Britain to go beyond the assurances which had already been given to France would, in Grey's opinion, have involved splitting the cabinet, and he displayed no enthusiasm for that. Indeed, he was very reluctant either to make any new declaration on the *entente* or to attempt any fresh definition of its meaning. On the other hand, he could see but little advantage in a radical change of course. Neither isolation in Europe, which he found abhorrent, nor alignment with one of the continental groupings, were in his view practicable alternatives.[71]

Grey's letter to Cambon on 22 November 1912 still left open the question of what attitude Britain would adopt in the event of war involving France, and Grey continued to insist that this would depend on the circumstances in which war broke out, and the reaction of public opinion. In two cases, however, he was reasonably certain as to Britain's position. As he told Sazonov, the Russian foreign minister on 24 September 1912, public opinion 'would not support any aggressive war for *revanche*, or to hem Germany in'. On the other hand, if Germany 'were led by her great . . . unprecedented strength to attempt to crush France', he did not think that Britain would stand by and look on.[72]

The chances of France launching a preventive war or a war for the recovery of her lost provinces were always fairly remote. Nevertheless Grey could not ignore the possibility of this, and the chauvinistic press campaign which accompanied the pressure in France for the adoption of a three year military service law and the elevation of Poincaré to the presidency, could not but disturb the British government. Even Bertie, who was inclined to stress the pacific desires of the French, warned Grey on 3 March 1913 of his fear that in the 'present temper of the French people any incident with Germany might lead to war'.[73] An over-confident France could be a menace to the European peace, and, as Bertie later observed to Grey, one reason for not offering her an alliance was that it 'might encourage the French to be too defiant to Germany'.[74] From Bertie's point of view, the advantage of the *entente* was that while it made the French more confident in their power to resist German aggression or threats, the uncertainty as to Britain's military aid acted as 'a restraint on the French government in the way of making them very prudent in controversies with the German government in order not to appear as aggressors or provokers'.[75]

Grey's dilemma was that France might be involved in a continental war in whose cause Britain had no interest, and over which public opinion and the majority of the cabinet were unprepared to fight. Yet the outcome of such a conflict might be German hegemony in Europe, and the isolation of Great Britain. The crises in the Balkans and the danger they presented of France being drawn by her Russian alliance into a war between Russia and Austria exemplified this problem. In such an event, Grey told the King, 'it might be necessary for England to fight...for the defence of her position in Europe and the protection of her own future and security'.[76] However, he could tell Paul Cambon no more than that the public would be probably more ready to fight if the war arose from Austrian aggression than Serbian provocation.[77]

It was Bertie's contention that the French appreciated the 'parliamentary difficulties' which stood in their way of achieving an English alliance, and that they anyway believed that interests alone would compel Britain to aid them in a war brought on by Germany. Nevertheless, he thought that they would like to have something that would assure them the 'immediate material aid of England' in such a conflict. In his view the essential point remained that of assuring speedy assistance to France, and to that end he continued to advocate that kind of accord which he had outlined to Nicolson on 9 May 1912.[78]

On 23 June 1913, on the eve of the state visit to London of Poincaré and Pichon, Bertie warned Grey that he thought the French might attempt to obtain some fresh assurances as to Britain and France consulting each other if their interests were menaced. The French might be satisfied, he believed, by 'an exchange of notes of a less vague character than the private letter to M. Cambon'. Grey, however, did not think that the cabinet would consent to anything further being said, and in the event neither of the French statesmen raised the subject during their stay.[79] A second favourable opportunity for extracting from Grey some new pledge on the *entente* was presented to Bertie the following year by the Russian desire to tighten the bonds of the Triple Entente, and the determination of the French to raise this subject during Grey's visit to Paris in April.[80] He suggested to Paul Cambon that notes should be exchanged between France, England and Russia, 'setting forth their common interests'. In the event of any these interests being in the opinion of one of the powers in danger, they would undertake to confer together immediately as to what should be done to protect them, and if they should decide to proceed to extreme measures, then the plans already agreed to by their military and naval authorities should be carried out at once.

Both Poincaré and Doumergue, the French premier, considered Bertie's suggestion a good one, and they agreed to put it to Grey. For his part, Bertie, who thought his proposal would have more chance of success if it came from the French than if it came directly from himself, absented himself from Grey's interview with Doumergue. Not however, until towards the end of his discussions with Grey on 24 April, did the French foreign minister raise the question of an exchange of notes and even then, he omitted to mention Bertie's proposal for recording their respective interests. What he suggested was that Britain, France and Russia should agree in an exchange of notes that if one of the three powers should subsequently find itself menaced, and the general situation made it necessary, there should be immediate conversations. But the proposal was overshadowed by the French desire to bring the British government to agree to the opening of conversations on naval cooperation with the Russians. Bertie had wanted to give more precision to the Entente, but the proposal made by Doumergue appeared simply as an attempt to extend to Russia the arrangements of November 1912. While Grey did not reject the idea of a new exchange of notes, the idea seems to have made little impression upon him. and in his own record of his conversation he made no mention of it.[81]

The initial impetus for the French seeking some more formal definition of their understanding with Britain had been in part provided by the increased flexibility which Grey had displayed in his approach to relations with Germany. Indeed any shift towards an accommodation with Berlin seemed bound to arouse the suspicions of those of Grey's officials who feared giving offence to France. Bertie reminded Grey in October 1913 of the ill-effects that might be produced in France by allowing the French to suspect that he was prepared to agree with Germany on a matter affecting general policy. His assertion however, that the French were desirous of obviating the chances of their being drawn into an Anglo-German conflict, and would therefore be prepared to accept a *rapprochement* between Britain and Germany based on the removal of outstanding difficulties, was only a half-truth.[82] A reference, for instance, by Tirpitz in a Reichstag declaration to a possible naval accord with Britain was sufficient to cause Jonnart, Poincaré's successor at the Quai d'Orsay, to warn Bertie on 10 February of the nervousness thereby engendered in French parliamentary circles.[83] Moreover cooperation between the British and German governments in the affairs of the Balkans, and their efforts to reach agreements on the future of Portugal's colonies and the Baghdad railways, tended to produce friction between France and Britain.

Where the Balkans were concerned, Anglo-French relations were complicated by France's alliance with Russia. Bertie insisted that the French desired Britain to moderate their ally's 'Balkanic zeal', but no French government in this period had any wish to appear to have separated themselves from Russia. This was made painfully clear to the Foreign Office by Pichon's reluctance in April 1913 to engage a French warship in the naval demonstration before Antivari.[84] Under the impression that the Germans were making every effort to draw Britain away from her friends, Nicolson pressed Grey to support as far as possible the wishes of France and Russia.[85] Yet, Nicolson's influence over the making of foreign policy was in decline. Grey was more inclined to listen to the advice of Tyrrell, who, while he did not advocate a break with the *entente*, cared less for French susceptibilities and was prepared to recommend a favourable response to German overtures.[86]

The visit of Poincaré and Pichon to London in June 1913 did little to check the drift towards closer relations with Germany, and in contrast with earlier periods when every overt sign of friendship towards her had been preceded by numerous assurances to France, Nicolson now noticed a 'desire to assume an almost apologetic tone to Berlin for the civilities which we accorded to the French president'.[87] Harcourt, the colonial secretary, who favoured a friendlier understanding with Germany, even took the opportunity to demonstrate his views by refusing to be presented to Poincaré.[88] More disturbing to the French than this demonstration, however, was the apparent neglect of France's rights and interests by Britain in negotiating the revision of their secret convention of 1898 with Germany on the future of Portugal's colonies.[89]

The chief French objection to what they understood to be the new Anglo-German arrangement was based on the attribution to Germany of the reversion of Cabinda and Loanda, which, if effected, would have led to a further extension of German influence in the Congo basin, and the near encirclement of France's colony there.[90] Moreover, since the original agreement provided that the two signatories should support each other in the exclusion of third parties from the territories to which they laid claim, the British government would be bound to support Germany against France if the latter should attempt to establish political or economic interests in Angola.

Paul Cambon recognised that to press Grey to alter the terms of the 1898 agreement in order to preclude Germany from obtaining Cabinda would involve Britain in complex questions of compensation. In order to mitigate any danger to the *entente* or to the development of their interests in Africa, the French therefore concentrated upon trying to prevent the publication of the Anglo-German agreement. Great emphasis was laid by Cambon, Poincaré and the new French premier, Doumergue, upon the ill-effects which news of the new agreement would have upon opinion in France.[91] Poincaré complained to Bertie on 11 February 1914 that Britain had not kept France fully informed of the course of her negotiations with Germany and that for her to disinterest herself in the islands of San Thomé and Principé was not in the interest of France. If the agreement were published, he threatened that this would necessitate a protest by the French government on the basis of the Franco-German convention of 4 November 1911, which had stated that in the event of a territorial change in the Congo basin, the signatories of the Berlin Act would confer together.[92] A week later Cambon warned Grey that although the original treaty with Germany had been concluded in 1898, this would be counteracted in France by the reflection that Britain had, by reviving it, confirmed it in the present day.[93]

Fearing that when the arrangement with Germany was published there would be a 'great outcry in the French parliament and in the French press', Bertie wrote to Grey on 12 February pleading that this should be avoided.[94]

Even the King, who was planning a state visit to Paris in April, told Bertie that he hoped that the negotiations would fall through and that he was determined that there should be no publication before his visit for he would 'not run the risk of the resulting hisses in the streets of Paris'. But French pleas, and especially Poincaré's warning to Bertie of 11 February, caused Grey to modify his attitude. German objections to the publication of Britain's previous assurances to Portugal would, he hoped, lead to the abandonment of the project, and he was doubtless relieved when on 3 March Lichnowsky suggested that the matter should be dropped.[95]

Paradoxically in a period when both the British and French governments were finding it easier to cooperate with Germany in extra-European affairs, their relations with each other continued to be marred by long-standing and unsettled imperial disputes. These included differences over the future of the Egyptian capitulations, the British transit trade through French possessions in north Africa, the position of British missionaries in Madagascar, and the problems raised by the Anglo-French condominium in the New Hebrides. An attempt by Britain in June 1912 to halt the arms trade conducted by French merchants in the Persian gulf also led to an acrimonious quarrel between the two governments over France's commercial rights in Muscat.[96] Moreover, despite the conclusion in November 1912 of a Franco-Spanish convention on Morocco, Grey continued to withhold British recognition of the French protectorate there until a satisfactory arrangement was arrived at on the international administration of Tangier.[97] An exchange of notes between London and Paris in March 1914 settled their differences over Muscat, but the future of Tangier remained unsettled at the outbreak of the war.

French conduct with regard to both Muscat and Morocco was viewed with a mixture of suspicion and annoyance by British officials who were otherwise supporters of the *entente*. While Eyre Crowe complained of the French trying 'to ride roughshod over Britain's treaty rights in Morocco', a suggestion that France might abrogate her rights in Muscat in return for the cession of the Gambia led Bertie to observe that the French were 'almost invariably blackmailers in such matters'.[98] In turn Britain's attitude towards Morocco served to increase suspicion in French parliamentary circles of British connivance with Germany behind the back of the French government.[99] Yet neither of these disputes nor the difficulties encountered elsewhere were of such importance as to seriously menace the existence of the *entente*. Indeed Grey rarely put such problems before the situation in Europe. Just as he was unwilling to separate Britain openly from France during the Balkan wars, so he was reluctant to reveal any breach over a non-European issue. Faced in October 1912 with the prospect of the French sending a warship to Muscat, he warned Bertie that it would be 'very undesirable that we should each send a big cruiser to stare at each other, especially at this juncture in Europe'.[100] Even a suggestion made by Villers in February 1913 that Britain might approach France with a number of her complaints was opposed by Eyre Crowe on the grounds that the time was not propitious for a 'frank general talk'.[101]

So long as there was a government in London which believed that the maintenance of the European balance of power might require it to intervene in a continental war on France's side, squabbles in north Africa and Asia remained essentially peripheral issues. But the continuing friendship of Britain and France was not entirely the product of European politics. The very fact that their interests clashed in so many corners of the world was in itself a reason for the *entente*. Nicolson, for whom the difficulties encountered with France and Russia were 'merely family troubles which must be borne and dealt with in a friendly manner', thought that 'an unfriendly France and Russia would give us infinite trouble, especially the former, in localities where we should find it extremely difficult to maintain our own'. [102] After 1911 it seemed unlikely that Britain would have to reckon in the near future with a continental coalition, but a potentially hostile France could severely handicap her freedom of manoeuvre. By 1914 the French were still too weak in Europe, and too dangerous elsewhere, to make the abandonment of the *entente* an attractive proposition.

18

Great Britain and the Triple Entente on the eve of the Sarajevo Crisis

MICHAEL G. EKSTEIN

From the British Government's point of view the Anglo-French and Anglo-Russian ententes had come into being to serve two ends, to ease the burdens of imperial defence and to secure the friendship of European Powers as a balance against Germany. By 1914 the Franco-Russian alliance was much stronger than it had been in 1907, the danger of German domination of the continent had receded and Anglo-German relations had improved. The anti-German aspect of the Triple Entente was, therefore, becoming an increasing embarrassment to Grey. It remained, however, of vital importance to maintain the ententes for the sake of global security. In this situation how to secure the understandings with France and Russia without upsetting Germany was the central dilemma of British foreign policy.

In 1913 and 1914 all the chancellories of Europe were noting the growth of Russian military power. Russia's collapse in 1905 had been swift; but like France after 1871 and Germany after 1919, she soon re-established her place among the Powers. Industrialisation went forward apace, finances were put in sound order, her army and navy were being enlarged and, or so it appeared, made more efficient.[1] The British Foreign Office observed and exaggerated Russia's revival. Fashionable geopolitical and social Darwinist theories magnified the natural inclination to be over-impressed by emerging power. Grey, for instance, was convinced that Germany could not inflict a decisive military defeat on Russia. No matter what initial setbacks the Russians suffered, they would be able to retire into their continental heartland, where they would be able to marshal their resources.[2] He was also aware that Russia, in constructing new strategic railways up to her German frontier, was imitating the methods of rapid mobilisation and concentration of forces that the more compact states to her west looked to for their very survival.[3] Tsarist autocracy seemed to provide a good political base from which to conduct strong foreign policy. Darwinists like Arthur Nicolson were convinced that the subordination of the individual to the state was a necessary tendency in a competitive world;[4] while liberals forgot the weaknesses of a creaking bureaucracy when they reflected on the Russian menace.[5]

Russia's expanding might was the major development in international relations in the year or so before the outbreak of war. British diplomats believed that she would shortly overtake Germany as Europe's leading military Power. From St Petersburg Buchanan sent back a stream of reports on the Russian army and navy, predicting that 'unless Germany is prepared to make still further financial sacrifices for military purposes, the days of her hegemony in Europe will be numbered'. His despatches were digested by the Foreign Office, and his theme was taken up enthusiastically by the Permanent Under-Secretary. Grey himself recognised that a profound, disturbing change was about to take place in relations between Germany and Russia. On the basis of reports of German reactions to Russia, he anticipated the possibility of her further expanding her army or even mounting a preventive war against Russia. Other members of the Cabinet were also aware of the problems Russia was creating for Germany. Morley told C. P. Scott that Russia was 'rapidly becoming a menace to Europe with her vast and rapidly increasing population and her rapidly increasing prosperity'.[6]

The implications of Russia's new-found strength were still more significant when set against other developments. Well-informed British observers felt Germany to be near the limit of the resources which she could devote to defence. Signs of strain were unmistakable; with loans floated by the Imperial and Prussian Governments in 1913 failing and a capital tax newly introduced to finance further military expenditure. In contrast, Russia's long-term position appeared healthy – she was a developing country and, as Buchanan explained, had 'more staying powers than Germany'. Austria-Hungary's weakness aggravated the problems of the Central Powers. It was common surmise that the Habsburg Empire would soon disintegrate. If Germany's principal partner was growing weaker, France was passing through a period of military and spiritual revitalisation. And as France revived her foreign policy became more truculent. Grey found her ungenerous and unhelpful; and sensed that she was using the shift in international power to assert her own position against England and Germany.[7]

The changing military and political balance in Europe coincided with the Anglo-German détente. Together the two developments were modifying Great Britain's interest in the ententes with France and Russia. The real value of the understandings now lay in securing interests in the Mediterranean, the Middle East and Central Asia, where Great Britain could not afford to incur French and Russian hostility.[8] The European advantages of the Triple Entente had become more questionable. The need to contain Germany was giving way to the problem of preventing France and Russia leading Great Britain into quarrels in which she had no interests directly engaged. Russia in particular was insisting on British support against Germany and Austria as the price of friendship – a demand which would have inevitably involved Grey in taking sides in Balkan disputes and in quarrels with Germany. Balancing the need for Russian goodwill against the risk of renewed German antagonism preoccupied British foreign policy on the eve of war. In April 1914 the ambassador at Berlin wrote:

But all such matters seem to dwindle down into unimportance when compared with the great question as to whether our understanding with Russian should be solidified into a defensive alliance or not. I suppose that the real question to be decided is whether the advantages of being intimate friends of Russia is greater in the inverse ratio than the disadvantage of being on our former cold terms with Germany. I doubt, no! I am sure we cannot have it both ways: i.e. form a defensive alliance with France and Russia and at the same time be on cordial terms with Germany.[9]

Most of the senior career diplomats favoured a closer relationship with Russia for the sake of the world position. Buchanan was convinced that, if Great Britain did not consolidate her friendship with Russia, relations would soon deteriorate. In the Foreign Office Nicolson was very pro-Russian and persistently advocated an alliance, his argument being that the future lay with Russia and that, if she were alienated, interests in Persia and on the Indian frontier would be in grave danger. Crowe, who saw Germany as being as menacing as ever, agreed. Goschen (at Berlin) and Bertie (at Paris) also wanted closer ties with the Franco-Russian alliance.[10]

Grey recognised the force of the case for remaining on good terms with St Petersburg. Yet he had to think of opinion within the Liberal Party – its ideological hostility towards Russia, its suspicion of continental commitments, its desire to see a further improvement in Anglo-German relations. These views, which had many advocates in the Cabinet, could not be squared with anything approaching a Russian alliance.[11] Quite apart from these considerations, Grey had personal reservations. Tsarist autocracy, unchecked by democratic process, was all too often fickle and unprincipled in its foreign policy. Even Nicolson was prepared to admit that it was an 'autocratic and, if you like, somewhat unscrupulous Government'.[12] No less important were German sensibilities. Co-operation during the Balkan Wars; the apparently pacific attitude of Bethmann-Hollweg, Jagow and Lichnowsky; progress with the negotiations over Portuguese colonies and the Baghdad Railway – these developments pointed to the possibility of a real end to Anglo-German tensions, and the Foreign Secretary had no desire to throw the opportunity away. Grey's priorities had support from Tyrrell and some of the younger officials at the Foreign Office, several of whom were moving in a more pro-German and anti-Russian direction.[13]

Russo-German tensions, however, could not be avoided. The sending of the German military mission of General Liman von Sanders to Constantinople and the ensuing crisis of the winter of 1913–14 set in motion the final spiral of Russo-German antagonism. Each Power now tried to wrest Great Britain from the sway of the other, but Grey's hope was to maintain good relations with both. The drift of his policy was to placate Berlin without precipitating a breach with St Petersburg. But it was a course that was increasingly difficult to steer. Russia believed that Germany, through the establishment of her military mission at Constantinople, had gained controlling influence there; and that she would be able to block her access to the Mediterranean and strangle the trade of southern Russia. The Foreign Secretary was grudgingly driven to support Russia. He attempted to explain his predicament to the German Government.

I do not believe that the whole thing is worth all the fuss that Sazanov makes about it; but so long as he does make a fuss it will be important and embarrassing to us for we cannot turn our backs on Russia.[14]

The Liman von Sanders crisis served to strengthen the Russian desire to consolidate the Triple Entente and convert the understanding with England into an alliance. In March 1914 Buchanan warned that the future of the Anglo-Russian entente would hang on the support Great Britain would give to Russia in future confrontations with Germany. At about the same time as the ambassador was saying this, Sazonov began his bid for an English alliance with an appeal for joint military and naval planning. Most of the senior permanent officials at the Foreign Office welcomed this opportunity to make sure of Russian goodwill. Grey, fearful of domestic reaction and wary of French and Russian motives, wanted to put off discussions.[15] It was not, however, an easy gambit to decline. In late April he was to accompany King George on the State Visit to France to mark the tenth anniversary of the *entente cordiale*. The French were hand in glove with the Russians; and a few days before Grey's departure the French embassy gave notice that Anglo-Russian military talks would be a subject of discussion with him in Paris. When the matter was raised, Grey said he thought naval talks would be possible providing that they in no way bound his country to go to war in advance. He further explained that he could not make the decision personally and would have to consult the Prime Minister and the Cabinet.[16]

In the course of negotiations over closer relations with Russia, Grey spoke on several occasions of the differences he saw between the nature of the Anglo-French and Anglo-Russian ententes. The former was practically a defensive alliance. The latter was a more limited understanding. There was a basic community of interest between the two democratic Powers in the west of Europe. Great Britain could not be expected to involve herself in Russian problems in eastern and central Europe. British public opinion was sympathetic towards France. It was an obstacle to very friendly relations with Russia. Anglo-French military and naval arrangements committed neither side to go to war, but the closeness of Anglo-French understanding made it likely that they would be implemented. Parallel arrangements with Russia would be much more academic.[17] It was a sign of Grey's feelings towards Russia that, when Bertie had suggested privately to the Quai d'Orsay a way of getting round British hesitations about closer ties with Russia – the Entente Powers should exchange notes, indicating their intention to work together in various areas of outstanding tension[18] – he carefully sidestepped the idea.[19]

On returning to London, Grey consulted with Asquith and on 14 May the Cabinet on the subject of Anglo-Russian naval talks. The Cabinet agreed to talks. But with conditions: they were to be conducted on the strict basis of the Gray–Cambon letters; the arrangements were to come into force only if and when the two Governments agreed to go to war; they were to exclude the Mediterranean until such time as the Russo-German conflict at Constantinople had been resolved.[20]

A secretary at the Russian embassy in London, De Siebert, was a German spy and provided Berlin with copies of documents relating to the naval talks.[21] This gloomy news from London heightened German anxieties about the future and renewed fears of encirclement. Bethmann-Hollweg took the view – probably correct – that Grey's policy during the Liman von Sanders crisis and his agreement to naval talks meant that Great Britain would be less and less able to follow a German policy independent of Russia.[22] In order to raise the question of Anglo-Russian naval talks without compromising De Siebert, the German Foreign Office persuaded Theodor Wolff, editor of the *Berliner Tageblatt*, to publish information about what was afoot. Concealing his connection with the Wilhelmstrasse by naming a Paris source, Wolff appealed to English Liberals to check the move towards Russia.[23]

Crowe correctly saw that the *Tageblatt* disclosures had the ulterior purpose of causing trouble between England and Russia. Grey was less perceptive, and was mainly concerned to repair any damage that the leakage of information might be doing to Anglo-German relations.[24] When a question about the rumoured talks with Russia was tabled in the Commons, the Foreign Secretary used the opportunity to quieten his domestic critics and allay German suspicions. 'There were', he maintained, 'no unpublished agreements which would restrict or hamper the freedom of the Government or of Parliament to decide whether or not Great Britain should participate in a war.'[25] Berlin remained unconvinced and resentful. Indeed, right up to the end of July the Foreign Secretary was having to deny to the German Government that there was anything to fear.[26]

If the repercussions of naval talks caused Grey to be more sympathetic towards Germany, they also left him disenchanted with France and Russia. On 25 June, Bertie found him 'much exercised at the leakage which has occurred somewhere in regard to what had been represented to the German Government to be a Naval Convention or alliance between Britain and Russia ...he...is inclined to suspect Iswolsky or Poincaré'. Bertie then put it to him that the incident might not be such a bad thing because 'it was the fear of British naval intervention that prevented Germany from going to war with France about Morocco'. The Foreign Secretary countered with remarks that reveal how far he had moved from the idea of the Triple Entente as an anti-German 'bloc'. In the first place, he held that 'we are on good terms with Germany now and desire to avoid a revival of friction with her, and wish to discourage France from provoking Germany'. And he went on to say that

Germany was dangerously frightened of Russia and that, therefore, the very power of the Triple Entente was creating problems.

The truth is that whereas formerly the German Government had aggressive intentions...they are now genuinely alarmed at the military preparation in Russia, the prospective increase in her military forces and particularly at the intended construction at the instance of the French Government and with French money of strategic railways to converge on the German frontier.[27]

The actual naval talks with Russia made little progress before they were overtaken by the war itself. In a manner characteristic of the period, Grey thought preparations for war were the preserve of military men, and the negotiations were left entirely to the Admiralty. St Petersburg wanted to press on as quickly as possible, and one or two meetings took place with the Russian naval attaché in London, Captain Volkoff. But Churchill eventually decided that Volkoff was not senior enough. It was agreed that Battenberg, the First Sea Lord, would handle the negotiations when he visited his relations, the Russian Royal Family, in late August.[28]

The crisis of July 1914 broke, then, at a difficult moment for British foreign policy. There existed within the British Government and among its advisers a wide spectrum of opinion as to what the Triple Entente was and what it ought to be. At one extreme there was Harcourt, the Germanophil Colonial Secretary, insisting that the very expression 'the Triple Entente' should not be used in diplomatic correspondence because it gave the misleading impression of a bloc similar and opposed to the Triple Alliance.[29] At the other extreme, Nicolson at the Foreign Office was writing that offending Russia was 'such a nightmare that I would at almost any cost keep Russia's friendship'.[30] Grey tried to balance and reconcile these conflicting points of view. He recognised that their contradictions had their roots not in personalities, nor in ideology, but rather in the impossible complexities raised by Great Britain's over-extended position in the world. He was trying to satisfy all interests, while probably inwardly knowing that the fundamental problem was beyond resolution.

In the short term, the Foreign Secretary was disturbed by the way France and Russia were asserting themselves. In Europe their relations with Germany and Austria were troubling; elsewhere their lack of good faith and goodwill was a source of anxiety. Russia's forward policy in Persia was especially galling, while France was maddeningly niggling over many small colonial disputes.[31] Yet Grey's policy never really reflected this frustration with his entente partners. Over the Liman von Sanders affair and naval talks with Russia he had yielded to St Petersburg. In late June 1914 Sazonov suggested an Anglo-Russian–Japanese agreement to guarantee each other's Asiatic possessions. The war intervened before anything was agreed upon; but the fragmentary evidence shows that Grey would not have let the proposal drop.[32] Berlin may well have been right in believing that improved Anglo-German relations would eventually have been sacrificed on the altar of the Russian entente. Nonetheless Grey was still striving to be on good terms with both Germany and Russia.

On the eve of war Great Britain's international situation *looked* better than at any time since the turn of the century. The policy of being friendly with Germany *and* the Franco-Russian alliance appeared to have paid off – the Anglo-German detente seemed to be a reality; the ententes remained intact. But pragmatic compromise had bought success at a price. In seeking friendship with both European power blocs, Grey was putting himself in a position where he was reluctant to fall out with either; and so in July 1914 he lacked a capacity for decisive action. It was left to other more committed nations to take the lead.

BEFORE THE WAR:
THE FAR EAST AND THE NEW WORLD

19

Great Britain and China, 1905–1911

E. W. EDWARDS

Grey's arrival at the Foreign Office coincided with a relaxation of tension in the far east which, for ten years previously, had been the storm centre of international relations. The defeat of Russia by Japan removed, at least for a time, the most dangerous threat to China itself and to British interests, which were bound up with the maintenance of China's territorial integrity and independence. Whatever its consequences elsewhere, in the far east the war had eased the British position by exhausting the two powers combining territorial ambitions in China with the capacity to exert serious military pressure there. At the same time, it had encouraged confidence and self-assertion among the Chinese. China, Grey was warned, 'has become conscious that she is a nation', and she had discovered in the boycott an effective means of bringing pressure upon foreign powers.[1] The appointment of a new minister, J. N. Jordan, to the Peking legation in the summer of 1906 gave opportunity for a redefinition of British policy to meet the changed conditions. Jordan's instructions emphasised that, while the British government would continue to insist on observance by China of undertakings and engagements already made, a conciliatory attitude, sympathetic to China's dignity as a sovereign and independent state and helpful towards the reforms she was attempting, was henceforth to be shown in relations with her.[2]

Of the major issues involved in British relations with China one, opium, was essentially if not exclusively an Anglo-Chinese matter.[3] The opium question was a long-standing issue in which moral principles were in conflict with material interests, for the export of opium to China was an important element in the revenues of India and in the economy of the producing areas there. The inauguration in September 1906 of the campaign for the eradication of the cultivation and use of opium in China, the most successful of the Manchu reforms, brought difficulties for British policy. Public opinion in the United Kingdom, strongly represented in the Liberal party, was warmly sympathetic to the campaign as were ministers who, however, could not ignore the effect on India if cessation of the export of opium to China, a necessary complement to the internal campaign, was too abrupt. The fact that the trade had been declining for some time past tended to ease the acceptance in India of its now clearly impending end, but in the negotiations which now opened with China

Grey, and Morley at the India Office, insisted, in face of pressure from their own supporters and from China, that gradualism in its termination was essential. This principle was embodied in an Anglo-Chinese agreement, January 1908, providing for curtailment over ten years subject to a satisfactory progress in eradication by China during an initial period of three years. A subsequent agreement, 8 May 1911, in which, under pressure from China and from American and British anti-opium groups, Indian interests were sacrificed, provided for complete cessation of cultivation in China and of the export trade from India by 1917 and even before this in face of clear proof that cultivation had ended in China.

Tibet, over which China claimed authority, and which occupied a strategic position of significance for the security of India was a problem of a different order because the interests of another great power, Russia, were concerned. In the Tibetan question the new policy of conciliation had been applied before Jordan took up his post. Grey's moderation had resulted in an Anglo-Chinese convention of 27 April 1906 which, to the dismay of Indian officials, went far to meet the Chinese claim that Tibet was a part of China. The issue, however, remained active throughout Grey's period. Though the Anglo-Russian settlement of 1907 acknowledged Chinese suzerainty in Tibet, Chinese efforts to establish domination there continued up to 1911 to the growing disquiet of the government of India which, by that time, feared an extension of the well-established Chinese power in Eastern Tibet to further areas on the Indian frontier.[4]

The focal point of international relations in China was after as before 1905, the railway question, but with the significant difference, reflecting the new situation, that political motives were now giving way, except in Manchuria, to the more purely commercial attitude which had always been dominant in British policy. Railway concessions of the old type, conferring wide powers of control and management upon foreign companies and occasionally foreign governments who sometimes saw in them means to territorial encroachment, were no longer acceptable to Chinese opinion which objected to agreements with foreign interests even on a commercial basis, claiming that Chinese railways should be financed by Chinese capital and constructed under Chinese provincial control, and demanding the redemption of concessions already granted. The Chinese government, well aware of the economic and strategic necessity of a centrally organised railway system, understood that without European capital little progress could be made, but could not ignore the temper of the provinces and was itself determined to reduce, as far as possible, the degree of control exercised by foreign lenders. It was thus obvious, as a condition of any advance that the conciliatory attitude which, in general, Grey proposed to show to China, must be carried into railway policy. It was the view of Francis Campbell, Grey's chief adviser on far eastern affairs, that the development of a railway system in China, with equal rights for all was, because of the impetus it would give to trade, a major British interest superior to exclusive British control of the financing and contruction of particular lines. Jordan was instructed that, while the terms of existing undertakings must be observed, Britain would welcome a change which would give China a larger share in her railways, provided that new agreements allowed equal opportunity for the traffic of all nations.[5]

It was also recognised by Campbell that compromise and co-operation with other interested powers might well be necessary to facilitate construction otherwise likely to be impeded by Chinese obstruction, international rivalries and the disinclination of the British public to invest in Chinese railway loans. His advice had contributed to a significant development before Grey took office. This had brought together, in October 1905, British and French interests, for long bitter rivals in China, in a partnership for railway business north of the Yangtse through French participation in a British company, Chinese Central Railways.[6] The company had been formed in 1904, with Foreign Office encouragement, by the two major British concerns engaged in railway enterprise in China, the British and Chinese Corporation (essentially an association between the Hongkong and Shanghai Bank and Jardine, Matheson and Company) and the Peking Syndicate, originally to thwart French competition for the concession for the proposed Hankow–Szechwan railway. When Grey came in he found that the French had contrived to extend the partnership south of the Yangtse so as to obtain a share in the contingent rights acquired by the British in September 1905 for the financing and construction of the Hankow–Canton line and other railways in the provinces of Hupei and Hunan. This extension, opposed by the men on the spot, Satow and the Governor of Hong Kong, and unwanted by the Foreign Office, had become virtually a fait accompli which Grey had no choice but to approve save at the risk of angering the French.[7] There is, however, no reason to believe that, had he been free to do so, he would have made any other decision. Indeed, though he was to show a close concern with far eastern questions, his attitude towards issues involving conflict of interests among the powers there was, for the most part, decided by determination to maintain the bases upon which his general policy rested, the Anglo-French entente, the Anglo-Japanese alliance and from 1907 the rapprochement with Russia, and he was consequently predisposed to conciliation and co-operation. In these circumstances a slow retreat in China in face of the continuing pressure of competition was the inevitable result; the task of British diplomacy was to minimise infiltration into British preserves as much as possible.

The immediate aim of British railway policy was to secure implementation of the contingent rights which would enable them to finance and construct the Hankow–Canton line, a railway particularly important for British interests because it would greatly enhance the trade of Hong Kong, through the connecting line from Canton to Kowloon, and open new opportunities for British trade in the Yangtse valley. When in December 1906 Chang Chih-tung, the governor-general of Hupei and Hunan, sceptical of the prospects of the company which the Chinese in this area had set up to build the railway, agreed to open negotiations for a loan, it soon became evident that the association with France was to be a hindrance not a help to British prospects. Chang, markedly anti-French since the Tongking war, and faced now with the Anglo-French partnership refused to deal with it, maintaining, justly, that his pledge had been made to the British alone.[8] When it appeared in June 1907 that the Canton governor-general was prepared to borrow from the French, a solution seemed possible to the British and French banking groups and to the Foreign Office on the basis of the effacement of the British from the negotiation of the Canton loan, which would cover the construction of the southern position of the line, in return for a similar withdrawal by the French from the Hupei loan. This compromise was not acceptable to the French government which insisted that the French element should enjoy the appearance as well as the reality of participation in the Hupei loan. Moreover, France now claimed what had not been envisaged by the British side when it had accepted partnership for the Hankow–Canton scheme – equality not only in financial participation but also in construction rights. It was made clear to Grey that the matter was seen in Paris as one of prestige and as a test of the solidarity of the Anglo-French financial entente.[9] At the same time, the Colonial Office, which from the first had disliked the association with the French, sharply criticised the proposal that they should finance and construct the southern section of the line. 'The Hong Kong government', it pointed out, 'could not view with equanimity the prospect of the line from Canton northwards being controlled even partially by French engineers.'

In the ensuing exchange of views between the departments, the Foreign Office, while undertaking to combat in detail the French claims, insisted that the principle of equal French participation and control, having been agreed to, could not now be invaded.[10] For some time no progress was made either in the loan or in adjustment of the problems within the Anglo-French group and British attention was concentrated on negotiations for loans for the Tientsin–Pukow and Soochow–Ningpo lines.[11] In February 1908, however, an agreement between C. S. Addis, London Manager of the Hong Kong Bank. as representative of the British group, and Stanislas Simon, Director of the Banque de l'Indo-Chine, for the French side, following a meeting with Caillaux, now minister of finance in the Clemenceau government, seemed to promise an equitable settlement. The agreement set off British pre-eminence in negotiation of the Hankow–Canton loan and construction rights for the whole of the railway against a similar pre-eminence and construction rights for France in the loan to be negotiated for the redemption by China of the Peking–Hankow railway. Each group was to have a half-share participation in both loans.[12]

Friction did not entirely disappear but by October, Jordan, who earlier had been critical of 'the disposition amongst the Powers to utilize these alliances and ententes to secure our assistance in the industrial exploitation of China', and who held that 'if we had stood alone' the Canton–Hankow business would have gone through, was favourably impressed by the French attitude over the Peking–Hankow redemption scheme. 'The French' he observed 'seem to me to have behaved very well throughout, better than we should have done had we seen a British railway losing its character.' He was now optimistic as to the future. 'I think we have turned the corner in railway matters' he reported to Campbell; 'The prejudice against borrowing foreign capital is gradually disappearing and with decent luck we should soon see further developments.'[13] The Foreign Office had to meet a further barrage of criticism from Hong Kong where Lugard, who was now governor, reiterated the complaints and apprehensions of the colony. These were, in some instances, unjustified or outdated, but in any case Grey made it clear that the partnership with France would be maintained. 'China', the Colonial Office was informed 'cannot be ruled out' of the sphere of the entente with France.[14]

Jordan's optimism was ill-founded, for serious difficulties lay ahead from foreign competitors. The interest of Japan, politically linked with Britain and France, was more in co-operation than competitition. Chang Chih-tung had secured for them a participation in the supply of engineers for the Hankow–Canton scheme and the first suggestion that this should be extended, which came from France at the end of 1906, was evidently designed as a means whereby, through Japanese association with the British and French groups, greater pressure could be brought on China to carry through railway agreements. Grey accepted the suggestion in principle, but nothing came of it since by April 1907 the French had lost their earlier enthusiasm.[15] Soon after, though the British group was ready to co-operate, an independent Japanese initiative also came to nothing because the Japanese were not prepared to raise any part of the proposed loan in Japan. The Japanese seem to have shown no resentment.[16] It was clear that Japanese presence and ambitions in the Yangtse valley were growing,[17] but lack of capital restrained their activity and capital was the first need of China if the necessary railways were to be built. Here, now that the Chinese government seemed to be ready despite provincial intransigence to raise foreign loans, there were to be more dangerous competitors in the field, Germany and the United States.

Germany, after a period of unpopularity in China was now recovering her standing, assisted by the very fact of her isolation from other powers. The Chinese were persistently suspicious of powers working in groups, and, in particular, of the aims of the French and Japanese. This influenced Chinese attitudes towards Britain, the ally of one and the associate of the other.[18] Jordan had given warning early in 1908 that stiff competition was to be expected from the Germans for the Hankow–Canton loan.[19] Now they were ready to move for, after a period of stress, the German money market had abundant funds for investment and Cordes, the agent of the Deutsch-Asiatische Bank, had ingratiated himself with the Chinese by accepting markedly lenient terms for the Tientsin–Pukow loan.[20] In January 1909 the Deutsch-Asiatische Bank let it be known to the British group that the Chinese government had approached it for a loan 'for railway purposes' which was evidently intended to finance the Hankow–Canton line and made it clear that, if its right to participate in the loan was not admitted by the British group under agreements of 1895 and 1898, it would go its own way.[21] German penetration into the Yangtse basin would be a blow to British prestige but reaction in London to the prospect of German financial participation, at least on the part of the Foreign Office and of the British group, was not unfavourable. The Hong Kong Bank possibly saw in association a means of protection against competition not only from foreign interests but also from other British banks. As for the Foreign Office and the Colonial Office, which concurred in agreeing in principle to the admission of the Germans, the major factor was the desire to get the Hankow–Canton line built. There was determination to maintain the right to provide engineers and material included in Chang's pledge of 9 September 1905, but recognition too that opposition to German entry might mean loss of the loan and therefore of construction rights as well.[22]

The British view was accepted by the French group but met sharp opposition from the French government. Caillaux rejected any ad hoc agreement for admission of German interests to the Hankow–Canton loan, but was prepared for an 'entente generale' for all financial business to cover the whole of China and possibly extend elsewhere.[23] This, in respect of railway loans to China, was what eventually came about but hard bargaining was necessary before final agreement. The British group and the Foreign Office were ready to co-operate in railway loans, recognising that competition between lending groups, which must result from failure to agree with the Germans, would enable the Chinese to obtain loans on their own terms. By 1 March agreement was achieved in principle between the British, French and German groups for a general entente on all railway loan business in China on terms highly satisfactory to the British and French. It was agreed that the Hankow–Canton loan should be negotiated on 'Canton–Kowloon' rather than on 'Tientsin–Pukow' conditions and the way was left open for the British to retain the preferential rights promised them under the agreement with Chang.[24]

Satisfaction soon disappeared because Cordes maintained contact with Chang, and when, on 6 March, Bland, on instructions from Addis, rejected Tientsin–Pukow terms, Cordes signed next day a preliminary agreement on that basis for a loan for the Hupei and Hunan sections of the Hankow–Canton line. This was morally, if not technically, a breach of faith with the British and French groups but the Germans, even if shamefacedly, used the advantage they now held to press for better terms than they had accepted in the preliminary inter-group agreement of 1 March. They now wanted, in return for admitting the British and French to their Hankow–Canton loan, not only the general agreement on railway loans but a further triple agreement to cover all loans to China. This was close to Caillaux's proposal but was not all for the Germans now claimed to share in the Hankow–Szechwan (Hupei section) loan and, of course, the associated constructional advantages.[25] The German claim constituted a threat to the British position in the Yangtse valley and counter-action was rapidly mounted. A sharp protest was made to the Chinese against the ignoring of the 1905 agreement, and in Berlin the British and French ambassadors pointed out to Schoen the inadvisability of making loans to China on terms so lacking in proper control as those agreed upon by the German group for their Hankow–Canton loan.[26]

This démarche had no result but Grey held firm when the French group wavered and it appeared that the Chinese would ignore the British protest. He rejected a proposal that the German group, in return for withdrawal from the Hankow–Canton loan, should take over completely the Hankow–Szechwan business. 'The Germans', he declared, 'cannot be left in exclusive possession of the Hankow–Szechwan line; such an abandonment of the line would be out of the question.'[27] However, as Jordan had anticipated, the Chinese did give way sufficiently to allow a compromise on the supervision of loan funds for the Hankow–Canton line, and the way was thus open for the British and French groups to participate in the loan and meet German claims on the Hankow–Szechwan line.

As negotiations now got under way there was some conflict on the British side between the determination of Jordan to safeguard British interests and the desire of the Hong Kong Bank not to push definition of the respective construction rights of the three groups on the Hankow–Szechwan line so far as to upset the compromise necessary to get the general financial entente which promised lucrative business.[28] Grey accepted Jordan's view that the question of the division of construction rights along the whole length of the line must be settled as part of a general agreement between the three groups. Addis, who was to represent the British group, was so instructed and an agreed division formed part of the settlement reached in Berlin on 14 May. Addis felt that a settlement 'on terms so favourable to British interests' was a matter for congratulation,[29] and on a short term view he was justified, certainly so in respect of the interests of the Hong Kong Bank, linked in a powerful association with good prospects of being able to press the Chinese government to accept satisfactory conditions for loans. Grey, too, could find satisfaction in having maintained the British interest in the Hankow–Canton line, though the Germans were to have a share in the supply of materials. Yet from a wider standpoint the agreement marked a further retreat by the British in the Yangtse valley, for Germany as well as France was now admitted to share in the influence and material advantage to be drawn from railway finance and construction in the area which was the centre of British trade. The German penetration, unlike the French in 1905–6, was in no way a response to the pressures of ententes and alliances in Europe. What had made it possible was the new spirit in China and the determination of the Chinese not to be 'cornered' by the Anglo-French association. In fact, Chinese manoeuvering had had limited success, for the general entente envisaged by the financial groups was designed to remove competition and to enable them to face the Chinese with a united front. But any hope among its members, and particularly the British and French who had made concessions, that the way was now open for successful operations was almost immediately thwarted by the re-emergence of the United States as an active element in the politics of the far east.

A hint of reviving American interest in Chinese railways had come in December 1908,[30] but the official indication in June 1909 that the Americans who, hitherto, had shown no interest in the rights they possessed jointly with the British to finance the Hankow–Szechwan line, now proposed to take up these rights came as an unwelcome surprise to the Foreign Office.[31] American intervention threatened the whole basis on which the proposed arrangement between the three financial groups rested and raised the danger that the already diminished British interest would have to suffer further reduction. The first British reply, reflecting the resentment felt, recalled the abortive enquiries made in 1905 as to American intentions and declined to interfere with arrangements so arduously come to.[32] Yet the need for caution was recognised for these inter-group arrangements would have significance only when China decided to proceed with what was now termed the Hukuang loan, and American pressure in Peking might well deter the timorous Chinese authorities. Moreover, there was doubt about the attitude of France and Germany.

The German group was opposed to American entry but it soon appeared that the German government, with obvious political motive, was very ready to accommodate the United States and to manoeuvre to present Britain as the obstacle.[33] In Paris, Pichon, the foreign minister, had initially taken the same line as Grey – acceptance of American participation in future loans but resistance to their attempt to enter the present business which would probably result in breaking the whole matter off. But signs of a shift in attitude were soon evident. The French, made aware that Russia would press for a place in the financial entente, saw at once the difficulty of refusing Russia participation while granting it to the Americans. Hence the French group moved to oppose American entry into the triple-group entente while accepting their financial participation in the Hankow–Szechwan loan. In view of this Alston advised that Grey should follow suit but Campbell believed that 'it will not be practicable to keep the Americans out of future business unless the Anglo-French–German consortium are prepared to face formidable competition'.[34] As it became clear that the United States would, at the least, insist on participation in the Hankow–Szechwan loan, British opinion moved to acceptance. Grey clearly hoped, in view of what was known to be the essentially political motive of Taft's policy, that the Americans would be more concerned with an arrangement for future business than with insisting upon their full bond in the Hankow–Szechwan scheme, but he was to be disappointed.[35]

The acquiescence of the European powers in American participation in the

Hankow-Szechwan loan was followed by a conference of the four financial groups in London in July 1909. The share claimed by America appeared excessive to the European groups but, though American financiers seemed ready to compromise, the State Department stood firm and the conference adjourned indefinitely.[36] The Americans also met resistance from Chang Chih-tung, but this was overborne by Taft's unprecedented communication to the Prince Regent and by recognition on the part of the Chinese government that in America they had their sole supporter against the aggression of the Japanese in Manchuria. In this situation, unless the European governments were prepared to protect the triple agreement or see the whole project collapse, acceptance in principle of the American demand was the only course, though this could clearly bring a great accession of prestige to the United States in China.[37] No one was prepared to stand out, Germany, indeed, being ostentatiously sympathetic to the Americans, while for Britain and France, aware of the danger of a German-American entente, the matter was not sufficiently important to risk a break with the United States. Grey now emphasised to Reid, the United States ambassador in London, his goodwill towards American participation. It was, he explained, American intervention at the last moment when arrangements had already been made, which had placed him in a difficult position.[38]

Difficulties continued after the principle of American participation in all respects had been conceded, for the wrangle over the division of shares was inevitably resumed. The British aim was to confine discussion to the Hankow-Szechwan line so as to retain in full the position secured for the Hankow-Canton route under the triple group agreement. Grey was resolved not to give way and resisted all pressures to agree to a German or French participation as part of a general settlement.[39] Various solutions were offered as one party or the other refused to yield. When, in November 1909, agreement seemed in sight following a concession by Germany, the French government, though not the French group, felt that the French share was inadequate and demanded as compensation that a French sub-engineer be appointed for the Hankow-Canton line. Pichon let it be known in London that unless settlement was reached on the basis of complete equality, he would prefer rupture with all its consequences, namely a blow at the entente cordiale.[40] Grey stood firm to the particular resentment of the United States. In face of the American challenge to the British claim to a special position on the Hankow-Canton line, he considered breaking off the whole negotiation but the French withdrew their demand thus making final settlement possible.[41] On 23 and 24 May 1910 agreement between the four groups provided for a loan to cover the Hupei sections of the Hankow-Canton and Hankow-Szechwan lines and for division of sections on the latter line. Full engineering rights on the whole Hankow-Canton line were expressly preserved for the British, justifying Campbell's view that 'we came out of it fairly well'. Grey's tenacity had kept British concessions to a minimum though overall, as compared with the prospect in

1905, the Anglo-French group had suffered a check to their hopes and the British, in particular, had had to abandon all prospect of controlling the railway communications of the Yangtse valley.[42]

The future of the scheme, once agreement was reached between the governments (for it was they rather than the financiers who had been intransigent) now depended upon the readiness of the Chinese authorities to accept the extension beyond Ichang of the Szechwan line, which was an essential aspect of the intergroup agreement, and indeed to ratify the loan agreement itself. Clearly, in view of the attitude of provincial opinion in China, united and consistent pressure by the powers upon the Chinese government would be required. To the surprise of the British, the United States now seemed disposed to mark time. It was suspected, with some reason, that this was partly the result of resentment at the British attitude over the Chinchow–Aigun scheme; but it was also a consequence of the diversion of American interest to another project, the currency-reform loan. Reform of the chaotic Chinese currency was a long-standing aim of all the trading powers but two aspects of the scheme, that a small proportion of the loan be devoted to industrial development in Manchuria and that an American financial adviser should supervise the reform, disturbed Grey. The Manchurian proposals plainly constituted another American–Chinese challenge to Russia and Japan in Manchuria, and the proposal for an American adviser would place the United States in a position of advantage. The British attitude was shared by France, and to the satisfaction of the Foreign Office, France, Russia, and Japan made objections thus enabling the British to avoid appearing again as a major obstacle to American policy.[43]

In railway matters in China proper, however, the future looked brighter by the spring of 1911. The Chinese government, despite provincial clamour, determined to assert central control over railway construction. An imperial decree of 9 May 1911 made a scathing indictment of provincial inefficiency and corruption and proposed that all trunk railways should be declared imperial lines, provincial activity to be limited to the construction of branch lines. The British government, eager in the general interest of British trade to see progress made with the main lines and especially the Hankow–Canton route, welcomed the decree. A few days later, on 10 May 1911, the Chinese at last signed the Hukuang loan agreement. The four major financial powers were 'working together in perfect harmony' on railway policy.[44] Their association promised not only to encourage efficient development of China's economy but also to reinforce stability in international relations in the far east. These were prime British objectives, but international co-operation had come about not so much in consequence of a clearly conceived British policy as in response to changing circumstances. Each stage, from the association with France, had been a re-adjustment to an evolving situation. The British financial group had been more readily disposed to association than official opinion in general, but the initiative had come from other powers who had more to gain. The British had fallen in, conceding potentially significant railway positions in the process, but contributing to a development which seemed to be to the advantage of British interests in general.

That judicious concession had brought a highly satisfactory result seems evident from the attitude of Jordan, for long unsympathetic to and sceptical of financial co-operation, who was now won over to the course which Campbell had long advocated and encouraged. In June 1911 Jordan radiated optimism. 'Railway matters', he wrote 'are progressing splendidly and I feel in a very triumphant mood.' He had every confidence in the ability of the Chinese government to deal with opposition to the decree of 9 May. 'It has boldly faced the issue and faced it in a way which either compels acquiescence or invites rebellion. It is not difficult to predict the result. The provinces will doubtless indulge in noisy remonstrances, but they will soon realise the necessity of yielding to firmness.'[45] A few months were to show how ill-founded was this judgment.

20

Great Britain, Japan and North-East Asia, 1905–1911

I. H. NISH

Grey accepted the Anglo-Japanese alliance as the backbone of his policy in east Asia. In August 1905, before the Liberal cabinet came to power, the alliance had been revised. Grey announced his acceptance of it while he was in opposition and remained steadfast to it during his term of office. It was under his auspices that the military-naval talks of 1907 with Japan, which had been envisaged in the alliance treaty, were arranged, though they proved to be unfruitful in the main. When Grey and the Japanese entered into agreements with Russia in 1907, the original anti-Russian character of the Japanese alliance disappeared. But Grey tried to convince the Japanese that these changes only 'made the objects of our alliance more secure'.[1] It is likely that there was a large element of wishful thinking in this view; but the Russians and Japanese certainly developed close cooperation. Grey in his speech to the dominion prime ministers in 1911 took a very favourable view of the alliance, claiming that the Japanese had been good allies.[2] His views were not entirely shared by other Liberal ministers, especially John Morley, but Grey's policy was accepted by the cabinet as a whole.

The alliance was the subject of criticism in quarters abroad to which the British government had to be sensitive. From the time the San Francisco school question arose in December 1906, the administration of Theodore Roosevelt had a succession of immigration disputes with Japan and sought to enlist the support of Britain, whose dominions in Canada, Australia and New Zealand were in a position analogous to California. Grey's policy was not to confuse the immigration issue with the alliance. He therefore avoided approaching Japan in a common front with the Americans but encouraged the dominions to reach their own settlements with the Japanese. It took some time for the Lemieux agreement of 1908, by which the Canadians agreed on a quota system with the Japanese, to regulate immigration effectively, but the Canadian prime minister at the Imperial conference in 1911 agreed that it was working satisfactorily. Grey told the same assembly that he was convinced that it was Japan's policy 'to concentrate her people in Korea and Manchuria and the parts neighbouring to herself in the Far East. and she does not want to encourage them to go abroad, though she has some difficulty in preventing them'.[3] This seems to reflect Grey's over-all attitude to Japanese emigration:

if the problem was to be avoided in British dominions, Japan had to be allowed some latitude for commercial expansion in Korea, Manchuria and even in China.

But the Americans were not inclined to accept any such view and in the decade following the Russo-Japanese war there was frequent talk of an American–Japanese confrontation. Had this reached the proportions of a war, it would have placed Britain in a delicate position: she was required under the alliance to go to Japan's aid in the event of attack by one power but was in general trying to cultivate good relations with the United States. In practice, Grey discounted most of this war talk, because neither side was likely to engage in war with the other:

The Americans talk angrily but they have no means of getting at the Japanese, unless they build a much larger fleet. It is true that Japan cannot materially hurt the Americans, except in the Philippines which would be no great loss, but unless America could bring Japan to her knees, she would lose prestige and Japan would gain it.[4]

Though this was an optimistic forecast, it was a perceptive assessment of the balance of forces in the area; and Grey was confident that Britain was not likely to become involved in a clash between two powers whose friendship he was anxious to retain at all costs. Fortunately his forecast proved to be accurate, and the governments managed to patch up their differences in the Root–Takahira note of November 1908, despite occasional outbursts of hostile feeling on both sides.[5]

Apart from these trans-Pacific problems, Grey was faced with the intractable problem of Manchuria, where the question most at issue was the maintenance of the Open Door. By their development of the South Manchurian railway the Japanese had made clear their determination to dominate the commerce of Manchuria. A joint Anglo-American remonstrance in March 1906, asked for Open Door principles, to which the Japanese were committed, to be observed at the ports and on the railway; and certain concessions were made by Japan. But the Chinese were endeavouring with foreign help to break the growing Japanese monopoly. In November 1907 China made arrangements with the British railway contractors, Pauling & Co., to construct 50 miles of railway from Hsinmintung to Fakumen. Japan protested that it was a violation of undertakings China had given her in 1905. Grey, faced with the choice of defending the British contractor or upholding Japan's rights, came to the conclusion that the company could only have his support if it proved that the line would not compete with the Japanese. Since this could not be claimed, he declined to promote the enterprise.[6] Grey was not prepared to be a party to any Chinese schemes with political overtones 'which would depreciate the value of the Japanese section of the Railway, the only asset of commercial value which the Japanese gained by their war with Russia'.[7]

The American government which unofficially supported these Chinese

plans in Manchuria, became more active there in 1909 under the new administration of President Taft. The issue came to a head when an American
consortium secured from the Chinese in October an agreement to build the
Chinchow–Aigun railway, which would span the whole of Manchuria and
challenge the railway interests of both Russia and Japan.[8] Britain was involved
because the construction work was again to be undertaken by the British firm
of Pauling & Co. Grey again showed himself to be sensitive to the position
of Japan whose railway rights he had acknowledged in 1907 and of Russia with
whom Britain had concluded an agreement in 1899, promising not to interfere
with Russia's railway building north of the Great Wall. Grey therefore took
the stand that the issue was one between China and the two interested powers
and that no useful purpose would be served by his active intervention.

In November Secretary of State Knox proposed to Britain that Manchurian
railways should be owned by China and financed and operated by an international commission in the interest of the Open Door policy. Britain, realizing
that these neutralization proposals would also not be favoured by Russia and
Japan, was studiously lukewarm.[9] When the scheme was referred to Russia
and Japan, they affirmed their position as interested powers in the area and
in July 1910 signed a treaty extending the 1907 agreement over Manchuria.
Knox blamed Britain for the failure of his initiative on the ground that she
had failed to support the Open Door in Manchuria. Grey denied this,
expressing regret that 'the ill-timed proposals for the internationalization of
railways in Manchuria – a proposal which moreover totally disregarded the
legitimate interests of both Russia and Japan as expressly confirmed by the
Treaty of Portsmouth – should have indirectly had the result of rendering the
task of keeping the door open in Manchuria increasingly difficult'.[10] They had
misfired by consolidating the opposition of those powers who already had
railway rights in Manchuria. Grey who had in 1907 sacrificed the rights of a
British company, now rebuffed the American initiative for a common front
of Open Door powers on the ground that this was not the time to use the
railway issue to secure political benefits for China in Manchuria. He had no
serious doubts about the legality of the Russian and Japanese position there
and was not inclined to sacrifice his diplomatic relations with these two powers
over an area where Britain herself had few interests. Dearly as Grey wished
to improve Britain's relations with the Americans, he was highly suspicious
of the American syndicate's actions over railways and the Hukuang loan and
the influence it enjoyed in the State Department.[11]

If Grey was considerate towards the Japanese, British public opinion was
critical of them on a number of issues, including the re-negotiation of the
Anglo-Japanese commercial treaty where Japan was seeking complete tariff
autonomy. The initial Japanese approach was made in March 1910 but negotiations were deadlocked and did not get under way until the autumn.
Chambers of commerce became very heated over the tariff proposals and
conducted a public campaign against them throughout 1910. The new treaty

which was eventually signed on 3 April 1911 incorporated a conventional tariff acceptable to Britain and the public outcry quickly subsided.

Another issue which attracted public criticism was Japan's annexation of Korea which took place in August 1910. In 1905 Britain had acquiesced in the imposition of a Japanese protectorate over Korea but was not committed to approving the annexation of the peninsula. Britain was given an assurance in December 1909 that 'the status quo would be maintained in Corea' and it was only in May 1910 that the Japanese divulged that their cabinet had agreed in principle on the need for annexation but had not fixed any date. Both in Tokyo and London, Britain argued that the moment was inopportune and tried to discourage Japan from taking action.[12] The Japanese enquired in July whether Britain would approve annexation if her existing commercial privileges were upheld; and Grey accepted the principle of annexation provided that the old Korean tariff remained in force for another ten years.[13] Shortly after Britain's economic demands had been met, Japan went ahead with the annexation. Contrary to a widespread belief,[14] Britain did not have much advance warning of the annexation. The Foreign Office files indicate that, while Britain would have preferred no change, she made only half-hearted attempts to dissuade Japan from converting the protectorate into a colony.

The United States was inclined to blame the Anglo-Japanese alliance for this neglect of the Open Door in Manchuria and Korea and for her failure to secure Britain's cooperation there. But Grey was anxious not to imperil Anglo-American relations in other parts of the world because of the far east.[15] When, therefore, feelers were put out in the summer by Andrew Carnegie, the millionaire industrialist, in favour of an Anglo-American agreement for extended arbitration, Grey indicated that overtures from America would be favourably received.[16]

Late in September Grey, believing that some arbitration proposals might come from the United States government, suggested to Japan that, if the Americans were to offer Britain a new arbitration treaty, Britain could either propose in reply the inclusion of Japan within the treaty or take steps to ensure that the terms of the treaty did not conflict with the current alliance. The Japanese were asked to consider their reaction.[17] The arbitration negotiations took a long time to get under way. Grey was determined to leave the initiative to Washington because it was important that President Taft should formulate his own proposals in the way best suited to secure their acceptance by the Senate. The lack of initiative from Grey's side does not indicate that he was indifferent to an improved arbitration treaty with the United States. In January 1911 Japan rejected the proposal to become a party to such an arbitration agreement but confirmed that she had no objection to the conclusion of an Anglo-American arbitration treaty, provided the provisions of the alliance were excepted from it. While Japan offered to use the occasion to make some minor amendments to the alliance, Grey did not wish to get involved in revising the alliance until it was clear how the arbitration proposals would fare.[18]

Early in 1911 the British cabinet was examining the alliance from the angle
of defence where it greatly assisted Britain's policy of naval concentration in
home waters. An Imperial Conference was due to be held in the summer; and
it was expected that there might be a move by those dominions who were
disaffected towards Japan to advocate ending the existing alliance when it was
due to lapse in 1915. The Committee of Imperial Defence made it clear that

From the Defence point of view, it is extremely desirable to know a few years
beforehand what are the probabilities of the Alliance being renewed or not.
At present we maintain only a small naval force in the Far East relying on
our alliance with Japan...One may well imagine too that the reinforcement
of our China Fleet to anything commensurate with the strength of the
Japanese Navy would imply an important increase to our building programme.[19]

The Foreign Office itself took the view that

the maintenance of the Alliance is of such vital Imperial interest that its
prolongation or otherwise should not be dependent on the view of the
Dominions, [though] it might be desirable to explain the value of the
Alliance.[20]

The needs of Imperial defence dictated that the alliance should be renewed
in 1915 because the cabinet, with a heavy programme of shipbuilding for
European waters, could not assume further obligations for the Pacific area.

On 27 March, Grey was told again that Japan wished not merely to continue
the alliance but also to strengthen and improve it. He put the issue to the
cabinet two days later; and it was agreed in principle to revise the alliance
alongside the arbitration treaty and to extend its term. He informed Japan
that it would be difficult to know how to amend it until after the American
draft arrived.[21] The initiative had come from Japan; but Grey was not yet ready
for even the small-scale revision that Japan proposed. Indeed, Grey was
advised by his Tokyo embassy against extending the alliance so far in advance
of its termination. But Grey had to consider Britain's world-wide commitments, both naval and political, and an arbitration agreement and a continuation of the alliance were vital for Britain's imperial defence needs. The
Japanese terms were passed over to Grey on 13 April. Apart from the
extension by 10 years which was their prime purpose, the Japanese proposed
to delete the clause relating to Korea from the 1905 alliance and tried unsuccessfully to get Britain to recognize Japan's special rights beyond the Korean
frontier, that is, in Manchuria.[22]

The dominion prime ministers, assembled in London for the Conference,
attended a special session of the Committee of Imperial Defence on 26 May,
to discuss foreign policy. In the course of a long speech Grey argued for the
alliance to be maintained and received the approval of the dominions for its
continuation by 10 years.[23] Grey therefore concluded that 'as the Dominion
Representatives had agreed so cordially to the extension of the Alliance, we

had better proceed with it, even if the Arbitration negotiations with the United States hung fire'.[24] Since the draft of the arbitration treaty eventually arrived on 29 May, it was possible to conduct the alliance and arbitration negotiations simultaneously. Though last-minute difficulties were encountered over the alliance clause dealing with arbitration, the revised alliance was signed on 13 July.

The Japanese government claimed the prime credit for extending the alliance and modifying its terms, and was justified in doing so. Britain's main wish was to ensure that the alliance did not run counter to the forthcoming American arbitration treaty. Once she had received Japan's consent to this, she was agreeable to meeting Japan's demands by extending the alliance – which in any case suited her naval plans – and acknowledging the annexation of Korea. The clause in the 1905 alliance on Indian defence was dropped. The arbitration clause was rather distasteful to the Japanese but their leaders realized from the start that there was little likelihood of Britain ever assisting Japan in war against the United States; so Japan's concession on this point was a minor one, though her press was not inclined to admit it.

Article IV of the new treaty excluded from its purview any third power which had an arbitration treaty with either ally. The American arbitration treaty which was the mainspring of the new alliance was signed in Washington on 3 August and passed to the Senate for ratification. The Foreign Relations Committee struck out an important part of the treaty; and the Senate adjourned without taking any decision. Despite the endeavours of President Taft, the treaty was ratified by the Senate on 7 March 1912 with reservations which frustrated the objects of the British and American administrations. An Anglo-American treaty was signed at Washington on 15 September 1914 whereby all disputes were to be placed before a special investigation commission. Britain informed Japan that it considered that this treaty was equivalent to one of general arbitration, and that article IV of the alliance therefore came into force. But this was a unilateral assertion which was never accepted by Japan.[25]

21

China and Japan, 1911–1914

E. W. EDWARDS

British policy in the Far East between 1911 and 1914 was dominated by the revolution in China. The rapid expansion of the rising at Wuchang on 10 October 1911 into a formidable movement extending over the greater part of southern and central China brought immediate problems for all powers with a stake in the country. British interests and British citizens, scattered throughout China, were particularly concentrated in the Yangtse valley and in the south, where the revolutionaries were soon in control. Not only did the revolution threaten property and personal security; it brought too, if it were to be prolonged, a danger of foreign intervention. On all counts, its speedy termination and the restoration of stability, either by quick victory for one side or by compromise, were the major British interests. The four power banking consortium, established in 1910, marked the substitution of co-operation for competition in financial and economic policy and promised to facilitate common action on the part of the major financial powers. Intervention to exploit the divisions in China was most likely to come from Russia and Japan, the two powers 'strong enough to put through any policy they please',[1] but their action would be determined by the development of the internal struggle.

The immediate issue for Britain was to decide its attitude to the two sides in China. Was the Peking government to be supported in its efforts to crush the revolution or was Grey to maintain, and persuade other powers to maintain, a policy of neutrality? The issue was quickly raised by a request from the government to the consortium agents in Peking for a loan to meet its immediate and urgent needs. Jordan hesitated at first and then advised in favour of the loan on conditions which included supervision by foreign members of the customs staff over the spending departments and the establishment of a reformed government at Peking with capable men at its head including Duke Tsai-tse and Yuan Shih-k'ai.[2] Grey's attitude was cautious. In the Foreign Office Campbell was opposed to a loan which would lead China into an accumulation of debt and bring a financial crisis. He thought, 'taking a broad view it is doubtful policy on our part... to bolster up this corrupt and rotten Manchu government. I can hardly help feeling that, putting aside present convenience, it might be the best thing for China in the long run if the rebellion were successful'.[3] Moreover, there was the important fact of the vast British stake in the area controlled by the rebels who had so far shown remarkable consideration for foreigners and foreign interests. Any action by Britain which might be represented as support for the Peking authorities could provoke serious counter-measures. Grey sounded the other consortium powers, emphasising the desirability of agreement and the need to take time to consider the implications of a loan, and found that they agreed on prudence.[4]

Similar caution marked policy towards the rebels. Consular representatives at Hankow, the centre of the movement, entered into essential relations with the rebel authorities with the approval of the diplomatic body in Peking, but appeals from British residents there for military protection were rejected.[5] At the same time, it was agreed that Sun Yat-sen, who arrived in London from the United States, was to be allowed an unimpeded passage through Singapore and Hong Kong on his journey to China. Sun was given clear indication that Grey, though not concealing his regard for the merits of Yuan Shih-k'ai, was concerned less with the nature of the regime which might emerge in China than with its efficiency. 'We wished to see', Grey had remarked to Sun's intermediary, 'a strong Chinese government that would keep the door open for trade. It was indifferent to us by whom this Government was constituted'.[6]

By now a clear agreement on neutrality had been arrived at between the governments of the four consortium powers, to which Japan and Russia also adhered. The bank agents in Peking, anxious to carry on with their normal business, were uneasy at the danger that competitors might establish themselves in the Chinese loan market, but the governments fell in line with British views and insisted that there should be no loan, direct or indirect, until responsible administration emerged in China, a decision which the four groups acknowledged in Paris on 8 November.[7] The British attitude did not change when, early in December, further requests came from Peking for temporary assistance in order to pay troops and prevent anarchy. Jordan, who had in November moved to the Foreign Office view that there should be no loan, was ready to support the request on the unlikely condition that the rebels, with whom an armistice had been arranged, should acquiesce. The French and German governments and the majority of the foreign representatives in Peking were prepared to agree to a loan whatever the rebel attitude. The United States was opposed unless the rebels acquiesced, and so was Grey, despite the fact that Yuan Shih-k'ai, regarded by British official opinion as the one man who could bring order and strong government, was now in authority in Peking. Financial stringency, Grey held, was likely to influence the two sides to agreement – and there was always the compelling fact for him of the British lives and interests 'more or less at the mercy of the rebels'.[8]

It was comparatively easy for the four powers to prevent money reaching the Peking government. Their efforts, especially those of Britain and France, succeeded by December in blocking a loan from a minor Anglo-Franco-Belgian group and now, with the situation of the government increasingly unstable, there was no greater eagerness on the part of banks outside the consortium to lend in Peking. It emerged in January 1912, however, that loans were being arranged in the south, ostensibly for commercial purposes, but, in fact, with the consequence that a portion of the funds made available went to the rebel cause, thus threatening to prevent what Grey hoped would be for both sides the pacifying influence of empty treasuries. The first information of these operations, communicated by the United States government, was of loans negotiated by Japanese concerns, which, it appeared, were part of a scheme for Japanese capital to secure a controlling interest in important commercial and industrial enterprises in the Yangtse valley.[9] Japan had adhered to the policy of neutrality adopted by the powers and Grey made representations in Tokyo. He was embarrassed by evidence that the Shanghai branch of the Hong Kong Bank had also been engaged in transactions which had resulted in money passing to the rebels. This, which drew sharp criticism from France, was certainly without Grey's knowledge and resulted from the bank's wish both to insure itself against the possible triumph of the rebels and to carry on its normal business of assisting commerce to function.[10]

The Japanese loans, too, had a precautionary motive, as the Foreign Office perceived, but they did not reflect a well-thought out policy. The revolution had come as a surprise to the Japanese government and its reactions were confused and uncertain. Opinion in Japan was divided as to the course to be followed, but it was quickly recognised that there was opportunity for extension of influence in China and Manchuria. Officially Japan aligned herself with the other powers in the policy of neutrality, but there was support among conservatives for the retention of the Manchu regime; elsewhere, and notably in the army and public opinion, sympathies were with the rebels in whose ranks were numerous Japanese advisers.[11]

Signs that Japan intended to strengthen her position in Manchuria had not been long delayed. On 31 October Jordan, concerned for the maintenance of communications between Peking and the sea, suggested consideration of joint military protection by the powers of the Peking–Shanhaikwan section of the Peking–Mukden railway.[12] The Japanese, seeing an opportunity to test the British attitude, proposed that the remainder of the line, from Shanhaikwan to Mukden, should be put under their protection. Grey agreed in principle, though deprecating any action until actual threat appeared, a reply which Japan rightly regarded as an acknowledgment of her special position in south Manchuria.[13] Then followed, on 1 December, a proposal from Japan for concerted action with Britain to bring intervention by the powers in China, possibly by force, to restore order under a constitutional monarchy preserving nominal sovereignty for the Manchu dynasty. This initiative was not well received in London where doubts about Japanese intentions were rising. Grey's reply, after consultation with Jordan, indicated willingness to join with Japan in giving Yuan assistance in securing the retirement of the Prince Regent but suggested that, for the moment, it would be as well to await the result of the conference of the two sides which was to follow the armistice arranged on 1 December.[14]

News of the armistice and the conference had come as a surprise in Tokyo where there was disquiet because the British consul-general at Hankow had played some part in the armistice negotiations. Japan feared that the British had stolen a march and did not hide her suspicion. In fact the consul-general had acted on authority from Jordan not from the Foreign Office, which was not quite clear as to how he had got involved.[15] It was, however, deemed advisable to soothe the disturbed Japanese. Jordan's suggestion that they be invited to co-operate with Britain in assisting negotiations between Yuan and the rebels was adopted and he was instructed to keep in touch with Ijuin, the Japanese minister at Peking.[16] But Grey was not prepared to take the active and leading role which the Japanese, also pro-Yuan, wanted him to share with them. He felt that action should be confined to mediation; the nature of the future regime was one for the Chinese people. Any departure from this position should be taken in common by the major powers. The Japanese accepted this view.[17]

British efforts during the Shanghai negotiations and the confused period following their collapse were all directed to encouraging agreement between the two sides. Though the preference of Grey's advisers was for a constitutional monarchy, the overriding aim of British policy was to keep the country together irrespective of the nature of the regime though with very clear indication that, whatever form it might take, Britain wanted to see Yuan Shih-k'ai as its effective head.[18] Attempts by the Nanking regime to obtain recognition were rejected by all the powers while Yuan manoeuvred with skill and ruthlessness. The boy emperor abdicated on 12 February 1912 and a republic with Yuan as its provisional president emerged as successor, its authority, nominally at least, extending over all the dominions of the former Manchu empire.

Two issues now confronted the powers, recognition of the republic and measures to meet its acute financial problems. The first was raised by Japan in a memorandum of 22 February, in the first instance to the British, Russian and United States governments, which pointed to the necessity for consideration of the terms on which recognition should be accorded and proposed as a condition such guarantees from China as would fully safeguard the common rights and interests of the powers. It was the stated wish of Japan that the principle of joint action should be extended to the question of recognition so that, in this as in other action in the meanwhile, the powers should act in concert;[19] but plainly Japan, in taking the lead, intended to assert a special position. Grey, who had earlier shown his intention of keeping in close touch with the United States on the Chinese situation, enquired as to American reaction, which was favourable in principle, before making his own reply in similar terms.[20] Russia, too, accepted the proposal subject to agreement to her freedom to take necessary measures of protection for her rights in north Manchuria, Mongolia and west China. The recognition question, however, lapsed because of the evident weakness of the new regime and its inability to enforce any guarantees it might give. Much more urgent was the matter of its finances and it was this which dominated China's relations with the powers for the next twelve months.

The question of temporary advances, raised in mid-February by the bank groups' agents in Peking, required urgent decision, not only to block Japanese loans to the Nanking government but also because of the direct British interest in preventing financial chaos which would be disastrous to trade. Two matters of policy were involved for Grey, a domestic issue as to the constitution of the British banking group, at present confined to one institution, the Hong Kong and Shanghai Bank, and the question of the widening of the consortium to include Russia and Japan. On this point, Grey's view was clear. Loans were now highly political and it would not do to advance money, even on a temporary basis, without inviting the two powers to participate.[21] No doubt he saw in the linking of Russian and Japan to the consortium by precise engagements, as did the French, a means of fettering dangerous competitors and of preventing isolated action such as that by Japan which had already caused alarm. He agreed to Poincaré's proposal that the political entente of the six powers should be extended to finance in order to maintain the unity of China, and agreed also to act with France to influence Russia. But aware of the suspiciousness of his ally, he took care to inform Japan, simultaneously with Russia, of the desirability of adhesion.[22]

The urgency of the situation led to the first temporary advance while the question of Russian and Japanese participation was still unresolved, but it was soon plain that difficulties would be made within the consortium by Germany, who judged the interests of the two powers as essentially political, and by Russia, determined to secure extended recognition of her interests and fundamentally opposed to the emergence of a strong China. Japan agreed, on 18 March, to participate provided that loans made by the consortium would not conflict with her special rights and interests in south Manchuria, but Russia was determined to delay decision as long as possible, partly in order to arrange a direct loan to China outside the consortium.[23] This scheme, the Anglo-Belgian loan, was thwarted by British, French and German official action and Grey and Poincaré urged on Sazonov that Russia, within the consortium, would be in a better position to defend her interests. They promised to oppose the introduction into the terms of the proposed consortium loan of any conditions prejudicial to Russia's treaty rights north of the Great Wall or of those rights and interests deriving from her special economic position and her secret conventions with Japan. As the French noted, there was no enthusiasm on the British side for Russian entry; it was accepted as a not particularly agreeable necessity. On 6 April Russia decided to participate but difficulties continued as to the extent of the guarantees to be given.

Deadlock was reached early in June when Germany and the United States refused to sign any agreement in which Russian and Japanese special interests were not specifically limited to those defined by treaty. The French government let it be known that if Russia was not prepared to accept this reservation France would leave the consortium. Japan indicated that she would follow suit.[24]

This threatened chaos in China but Grey, even so, refused to press Poincaré to dissociate France from Russia in the matter.[25] China was less important for Britain than the maintenance of the links with France and Russia. The crisis was resolved by agreement that Russia and Japan would be entitled to withdraw from the consortium if any business contrary to their interests was considered. Grey was very satisfied, for the unity of the powers was maintained. As he told the Japanese ambassador, he 'was much more anxious to see the groups kept together than to see them in a hurry to make large advances. If the groups split up, some of them might lend while others abstained, and political difficulties between the Powers would be added to confusion in China'.[26] There was now what there had not been hitherto, the prospect of a common policy by the powers towards China and therefore of a restraint which was very much in British interests, and what was equally important, with Russia and Japan in the consortium, the danger of conflict between British interests in the Far East and the needs of general policy seemed to be diminished.

Grey was no doubt equally satisfied by the decision of the Paris meeting that the business of the organisation of the loan should be centred in the Hong Kong Bank in London. This meant that direction would be in the hands of an institution in close relations with the Foreign Office, where the ability of the Bank's London manager, Charles Addis, was well recognised. Yet the special position of the Hong Kong Bank as the sole British institution in the consortium was a source of concern. The degree of official support which the Bank and its affiliates had received in China had drawn protests in the past from rivals. Now, with the apparent stabilising of the situation there and the consequent prospects of a rich field for financial operations, animosity to the Bank grew rapidly. It had been early manifested in February 1912 with Sazonov's attempt to outflank the consortium by arranging a direct loan with the Chinese government. The Russian scheme had involved the formation of an international syndicate, the Anglo-Belgian group, which included leading British banks as well as the Russo-Asiatic bank. When in March the Chinese, anxious to escape from dependence on the consortium and the conditions it imposed, contracted a loan with the Anglo-Belgian group, the consortium immediately suspended advances, as well as negotiations on the large re-organisation loan, possibly for £60 million, which was intended to put Chinese finances upon a secure basis. The governments were asked to prevent the syndicate raising funds on their markets. Germany and France took immediate action and Russia, as she moved closer to entering the consortium, warned off the Russo-Asiatic Bank. Grey, however, was in a more difficult position.

Chinese action in contracting the loan was in breach of the understanding on which the consortium banks, on the uncertain security of Chinese treasury bonds, had agreed to make temporary advances and it threatened a return to the old policy of unprofitable competition which would make the market unfavourable for flotation of the reorganisation loan and therefore end the opportunity of the reform of China's financial structure which was so much to be desired in the interests of trade. Yet Grey did not have the power to prevent British banks from lending abroad.[27] He could, and did, refuse support to the British element in the Anglo-Belgian group which in return criticised the alleged monopoly of official support enjoyed by the Hong Kong Bank. This was a well-founded charge, all the more significant in that the consortium powers had agreed that Yuan Shih-k'ai be requested to undertake not to negotiate any loan which might conflict with or weaken the security of the large reorganisation loan if he looked to the consortium banks to co-operate in this. It was not surprising, therefore, that Grey, in pledging on 14 March exclusive support to the Hong Kong Bank in respect of the temporary advances and the reorganisation loan, should have urged the formation of a British group similar to those representing France and Germany, and the participation of competing British houses in the issue of any share of the loan which might fall to British capital.[28] Having undertaken to give exclusive support Grey was not, for the time, moved from it. His motives were plain: not merely recognition of the contribution of the Hong Kong Bank to the creation of the consortium but determination in the general interest of the British position in China to keep the consortium in being and understanding that this depended to a considerable extent upon the close links between Addis and his Continental and American counterparts. Some British members of the Anglo-Belgian group, the Eastern Bank and Schröders, found partial solace with Russia's entry into the consortium, for the group now constituted the Russian group in the consortium.

Hardly had this internecine conflict subsided on one front than it broke out in even more embarrassing form on another. The determination of the consortium governments that their banks should enforce strict foreign supervision of Chinese finances and administration of the security, the salt gabelle, as a condition of the reorganization loan, was resented by the Chinese who argued that such conditions were completely unacceptable to public opinion in China. Even more than this, the inclusion of Russia and Japan in the consortium had alarmed Yuan and his government, who feared that it had now become a means for the dismemberment of China.[29] They therefore again turned elsewhere, and from the end of May, as relations with the consortium moved to deadlock, were secretly in negotiation with a British financier, C. Birch Crisp. On 23 August Crisp informed the Foreign Office that his syndicate which, he claimed, included leading British banks, was negotiating a loan for

£10 million with China on the same security as was intended for the reorganisation loan, the salt gabelle. The consortium governments on 9 July had
announced their intention of instructing the banking groups to suspend all
advances to China pending acceptance of their terms, and of preventing her
borrowing elsewhere until arrangements were reached with the consortium
for the repayment of advances already made. In conformity with this policy
Crisp was told that Grey could not approve a loan outside the consortium
while these arrangements were still unmade. The new development, however,
presaged an awkward situation.

The consortium was under attack from radical opinion in Britain because
it was alleged to be exploiting the needs of China, and G. E. Morrison, who
had resigned as *The Times* correspondent in Peking to become adviser to the
Chinese government, was in London directing a campaign against it and in
favour of allowing China freedom to borrow, a campaign which gained
strength from the recent improvement in China's credit.[30] In these circumstances, with the Crisp loan impending and the consortium negotiations
making no progress, Grey's commitment to exclusive support to the Hong
Kong Bank seemed likely to become a major political incubus. A change in
British policy was therefore suggested by J. D. Gregory, who was now coming
to the front in the Far Eastern department. If, Gregory argued, the consortium
failed in a new attempt to reach agreement with the Chinese government this
should be regarded as final; exclusive support could no longer be maintained,
the consortium would dissolve and Grey be free to consider on its merits any
application for support from a respectable British group. Conditions could
be imposed on such a group which would go some way to meet the British
political aim of bringing into being an efficient Chinese regime, but there
would no longer be the obligation to give exclusive support to any group.[31]

Jordan criticised these proposals as being likely in practice to encourage the
competition and produce the financial confusion which the policy of the
consortium was designed to avert. It was preferable to keep the consortium
in being but this depended upon the willingness of the six powers to relax
their terms.[32] His advice was accepted and British policy was directed to secure
relaxation. Addis pressed the case with some success among the banking
groups who were anxious to secure the business but Grey met resistance from
the governments who pointed to the structure of the British group as the real
cause of difficulty. Their groups all controlled their respective markets and
could block opposition; the Hong Kong Bank was not in this position and the
necessary reform was not to relax conditions for China but to widen
membership of the British group on the continental model. Grey was well
aware of the weakness of the British position in this respect and Addis, now
under renewed pressure from the Foreign Office, was able in December to
announce that Baring Bros., the London County and Westminster Bank,
Parr's Bank and J. H. Schroeder and Co., had come into the group.

By this time Grey's warning to the powers that unless the conditions required of China were relaxed Britain might leave the consortium[33] had brought the desired result and negotiations between the consortium and China were resumed on 5 November. Difficulties continued because France, always eager to establish direct control over Chinese finances, put forward demands for six financial advisers to be nominated from the nationals of the consortium powers. These were rejected by the Chinese and this split the consortium. France was supported by Russia, but Grey, at one point, was again ready to leave the consortium and informed Addis that, if the groups did not reach agreement, he was at liberty to proceed with those who assented to the best terms he could arrange.[34] This pointed to an Anglo-German partnership and was perhaps intended as a means of pressure on France and Russia. At all events, a compromise was arrived at which satisfied Grey since, while reducing the number of advisers to four, it gave the major post, that of chief salt-inspector, to the British. The Chinese, however, still insisted on advisers from neutral countries. As matters dragged on, with Yuan anxious for the loan but afraid of public reaction if he yielded, the sudden decision of the new Wilson administration to withdraw the United States from the consortium and the terms in which it was publicly announced threatened a new disruption. The financial significance of the American withdrawal was not of much consequence and the five remaining members were resolved to carry on, but Wilson's statement of justification was damaging. Nevertheless, the deteriorating relations between Yuan and the Kuomintang made his need for money paramount if he was to crush the dissidents. In spite of the warnings of Sun Yat-sen to the groups, and the protests of the National Assembly, the loan agreement, for a sum of £25 million, was signed on 27 April.[35]

In the breach now opening between North and South in China, British sympathies were firmly with Yuan Shih-k'ai, who confided to Jordan his intention to deal with Sun and his associates by force if necessary. There was no overt departure from neutrality but, where possible, steps were taken to ease Yuan's path. Immediately following Sun's warnings against the loan, Grey urged the other consortium governments to sign the agreement, and Jordan took measures to restrict export of arms from Hong Kong to south China and promised that Britain would not sanction any loan to the southern provinces unless it was approved by the central government.[36]

The speedy suppression of the rebellion was followed by recognition of the Chinese republic by the majority of powers. Movement towards this step, long resisted by the consortium powers, where the lead of Japan had been accepted, was well under way before the rebellion broke out. Unilateral American action was the catalyst. The United States government, before the change of administration had, in the summer of 1912, under pressure of public opinion, urged recognition but had agreed to keep in line with its partners, none of whom was eager to renounce prematurely a useful bargaining weapon. Grey was aware that, with recognition conceded, China could well become more difficult in relation to foreign rights and privileges generally. There was, further, the particular issue of Tibet where the Chinese republic was determined to reassert the authority established by the imperial government in its closing period but lost in the chaos following the revolution, whereas what the British wanted was a situation in which Tibet 'even if Chinese in name, must be a region where actual Chinese power was nominal'.[37] President Wilson's decision in April 1913 to recognise the republic, put into effect on 2 May, moved Japan to action. The first Japanese reaction to the American move was to conclude that in view of the internal situation in China it was premature and would be tantamount to granting assistance to Yuan against Sun and his party, but within a few days this attitude was reversed and by 9 April Grey was informed that Japan intended to proceed to recognition at an early date.[38] Grey, while reiterating the desire, shared by the Japanese, for acceptance by China of treaty obligations and for the powers to proceed in concert, felt it necessary to follow Japan. When Germany indicated intention to accord recognition if Yuan were formally elected president by a considerable majority, the Japanese, anxious to keep the powers together, moved rapidly. Yuan, approached by Jordan at the request of Ijuin, secretly agreed on 31 May to make a declaration, judged satisfactory by the Japanese, promising observance of treaty undertakings entered into by the former Manchu and provisional regimes with foreign governments and individuals, and all rights and privileges enjoyed by foreigners under international engagements, national enactments and established usages on record.[39] Japanese haste had to be tempered by caution because of the strong sympathies for Sun in Japan, and the rebellion itself delayed matters. With the acceptance in September by the consortium powers of the form of declaration Yuan had agreed to make (with the omission of the words 'on record')[40] and with his election as president on 6 October, recognition was accorded.

Common action over recognition was achieved despite the emergence of sharp economic rivalries involving Britain with France and Japan, which had brought about by the end of 1913 a situation in many respects resembling the scramble for concessions in 1897–8. This was in large measure the consequence of the expansionist plans of the Chinese government and its desire to encourage participation of foreign enterprise, but was also contributed to by a deliberate British policy designed to restore freedom of competition in industrial loans to the consortium powers. Two motives influenced Grey. Though the expansion of the British group at the end of 1912 had to some extent freed him from supporting a monopoly, there remained the narrow base of the railway loan element consisting of affiliates of the Hong Kong Bank, to which he was also committed to give exclusive support.[41] If industrial loans directed to specific economic objects were removed from the consortium agreements, leaving its authority confined to financial loans for state and provincial administration, Grey would be freed of the embarrassment involved in exclusive support. Reinforcing this argument was the growing belief, strongly held by the summer of 1913, that the agreements binding the consortium groups to share all industrial loans and material advantages were a handicap to British enterprise. There was also the danger that non-members would secure business at the expense of the consortium. That this was serious had been demonstrated in October 1912 when a Belgian group, behind which, it seemed, were French and Russian interests, negotiated an important railway loan. There was reason to believe that the consortium governments, as Grey later put it, would be unable to control their nationals.[42] The solution on all counts appeared to be free competition for industrial loans.

Britain was alone in taking this view but met with little opposition,[43] obtaining agreement in January 1913 for the relaxation of the veto on industrial loans which were still to be subject to conditions, and then in June, in the changed conditions resulting from American withdrawal, on unconditional freedom of action. Though France immediately implemented this agreement Grey still felt bound by his pledge to the British group until 31 March 1914. By August 1913, in the face of mounting evidence of the activity of competitors, this situation seemed intolerable and it was decided 'in the higher interests of the British commercial and industrial position in China as a whole' to secure immediate termination (by agreement, not unilaterally) of the undertakings of 1909 and 1910 which bound the groups.[44] This was achieved on 26 September, and thus, apart from the restrictions still remaining on financial loans, the whole structure of international economic co-operation seemed to have disappeared. It was the British who had taken the lead in dismantling a system which they had done much to build up. Jordan, who was optimistic of the chances for British enterprise under free competition, welcomed the change in policy, as did Alston and Gregory who saw it as a clearing of the decks to meet what had become very determined attempts by French and Japanese interests to expand in the Yangtse valley.[45]

Signs had multiplied from the beginning of 1913 that France was intent upon a considerable economic expansion in China. The Belgian loan was followed in March by the emergence of the Banque industrielle de Chine which had among its directors the brother of Philippe Berthelot, formerly head of the Asiatic department at the French Foreign Office and now Chef de Cabinet to Pichon, the foreign minister. It was recognised in London that the Banque industrielle was intended to spearhead French economic advance, but because of its constitution as a Chinese institution, it was not possible to find ground for protest even though, at the time, the prohibition on industrial loans still held good.[46] An additional complication, in which the British were at fault, developed with the conclusion in May 1913 of the Pukow–Sinyang railway loan agreement. French interests, through participation in the Anglo-French company, Chinese Central Railways, had rights to share in the loan and the supply of materials, but these, though admitted, were not supported by their British partners. French resentment was marked and probably gave impetus to, if it did not inspire, a counter-stroke through the Banque industrielle which secured a loan contract for harbour works at Pukow in the heart of British interests in the Yangtse.[47] This operation made the British the victims of their own policy, for it was not possible to prevent the French from pushing an industrial loan once the consortium agreement had been amended.[48]

At the same time as the French economic offensive was mounting, anxiety had been growing about the intentions of Japan. Apart from momentary indications in the early stages of the revolution of a desire to exploit the situation, Japan had been a stabilising element working in close co-operation with Britain and had shown 'conspicuous loyalty' in the negotiations for the reorganisation loan.[49] In the summer of 1913, however, it became clear that Japan intended to extend her interests in the Yangtse. Initially the Japanese looked to co-operation with British railway interests; they lacked the capital to proceed alone but no doubt feared, with the freeing of industrial loans, that inactivity on their part would mean missed opportunities. No doubt also there was, as came to be felt in London, the calculation that they could exploit the alliance to their commercial advantage.[50] Unofficial Japanese approaches early in 1913 were not regarded unfavourably. Though Jordan was opposed, Langley remarked 'Our policy in the Far East is founded on the Japanese alliance and anything that makes for a greater solidarity of the interests of the two countries in China is to our advantage'.[51] Alston too, from Peking, recognised that in view of the interests acquired by Japan in Kiangsi and the Yangtse 'it seems difficult to ignore their offer of co-operation'. But the British attitude changed sharply in consequence of the rebellion in the South. Evidence of growing Japanese preparations for economic advance there had mounted during the summer and their involvement in the rebellion and apparent intention to exploit incidents to secure political advantage were reported with great emphasis by Alston. Despite the scepticism of Greene, the ambassador in Tokyo, Alston's despatches, coupled with evidence of Japanese activity in India and Tibet, made a sharp impression.[52] In September, after Alston's warning that Japanese policy, if followed to its logical conclusion, would lead to the disintegration of China and was at variance both with the declared policy of Britain and with the spirit of the Anglo-Japanese alliance, the attention of Japan was called to her obligation under the alliance to consult Britain if she contemplated action in China which might disturb the status quo.[53] The immediate tension subsided, but there was now a considerable element of suspicion in the British attitude to Japan.

As the end of the year approached the position of the British in China was ironic – in sharp conflict with Japan and France but on good terms with Germany.[54] An Anglo-German association to maintain the 'open door' and to preserve the territorial integrity of China, if attractive in the limited perspective of Chinese affairs, was politically impossible and could not be contemplated. What was decided upon was a direct approach to France and Japan for agreement which would limit encroachment upon the areas in which British trade was mainly concentrated. The early months of 1914, therefore, saw a very marked assertion, in terms which even in the Foreign Office were regarded as 'somewhat high-handed', of British interests in the Yangtse valley against these rivals.

The position taken approached very closely to a proposal for definition of spheres of influence though the term itself was carefully avoided. A claim was made to traditional and acknowledged, though undefined, fields for British enterprise. Tactics were adapted to meet particular situations. The Japanese were informed that, in return for reciprocity in south Manchuria, they would be admitted to the participation they desired in the railway proposed from Nanking to Hsiangtan; to the French, with whom Grey was looking for 'a purely informal agreement', it was pointed out that 'harmony between the Powers can only be maintained by each Power discouraging its nationals from embarking on enterprises in areas where another Power has, by long association, acquired special interests'.[55] When the French, while accepting the principle put forward by Grey, refused to withdraw the Banque industrielle from the Pukow harbour scheme, Grey, rejecting their suggestion for joint enterprise at Pukow, raised a claim under the Anglo-French agreement of 1896 for participation in the Yunnan–Chungking railway. The Anglo-French conflict subsided by July 1914 because the Banque industrielle ran into difficulties which made it dependent on the London money-market and seemed to open the way for the Pukow contract to pass into British hands. Together with this came a French proposal that the 1896 agreement in respect of Yunnan and Szechwan should be regarded as obsolete, which was acceptable to Grey because it freed him to support a British application for a railway from Yunnan to the Burma frontier which would balance the French Yunnan line.[56]

The Japanese gave more trouble. As anticipated, they were not prepared to accord reciprocity in south Manchuria and withdrew their claim to participate in the Nanking–Hsiangtan line, but then requested British support for a line from Foochow to Hankow which would penetrate to the centre of British interests and carry dangerous military possibilities. This could not be tolerated and Japan was informed that any extension of their line beyond Nanchang to Hankow must be under British enterprise. British resolve to assert against all powers their claims to a privileged position in that part of the Yangtse where their interest were predominant was emphasised in Tokyo.[57] In face of the unconcealed ambitions of Japan all thoughts of commercial co-operation with her were now abandoned and suggestions from Tokyo that the alliance should be commercial and industrial as well as political, with its field of action in China, were turned aside. Japan, it was felt, in view of recent developments in Russian policy, needed the alliance as much as Britain did. It was not necessary to make industrial concessions to her on the Yangtse.[58]

Organisation of defensive machinery, however, ran into difficulties in face of the markedly commercial attitude of British finance. To the dismay of Jordan, who had long called for a British group on continental lines, which would be essentially a political weapon in the service of the higher interests of British trade, the bankers were reluctant to co-operate. They would not put up money for political objects on inadequate security and pressed for a new reorganisation loan. Moreover the Foreign Office itself was uneasy about the implications of encouraging investment abroad and ill-equipped to organise an industrial investment group.[59]

In the spring of 1914 the British could feel that the Yangtse position had been successfully defended.[60] Moreover the territorial integrity of China had been in the main preserved despite the upheaval of the revolution. Yet the general outlook was not comforting. Russia and Japan had strengthened themselves in the outlying territories but Grey had failed to get the settlement he desired in Tibet. Britain still dominated the China trade but the hope of maintaining a vast preserve in the Yangtse valley was unreal. Stability had not come to China's finances and with the Chinese refusing to accept strict conditions, in particular currency reform for a new loan, the situation in respect of financial loans resembled that of the autumn of 1912. Indeed the Chinese government, desperate for money and refused short term advances by the consortium, was once more in touch with Crisp.[61] Moreover relations between the powers had deteriorated. The Consortium remained but much limited in its authority and weakened by the ending of co-operation in industrial finance. Foreign Office encouragement of this development had rested upon an unjustified optimism as to the energy and capacity of British enterprise in China.[62] The Japanese alliance was obviously under strain and little remained of the harmony of interests which had brought it into being. Japan was clearly determined to establish herself in southern China. For the moment she was restrained by financial weakness in face of stronger competitors and by need to pay some respect to the interests of her ally. With the outbreak of war in Europe her opportunity in China had come.

22

Great Britain and the New World, 1905–1914

P. A. R. CALVERT

In *Twenty-five Years*, Sir Edward Grey remarked that he was unable to recall any important problems that had troubled relations between Britain and the United States between 1906 and 1912.[1] Apart from Mexico, those of Latin America were not mentioned at all. Yet this period was one of important diplomatic realignments for both the continental countries of South America and for the maritime system of the Caribbean. British businessmen, merchants and strategists had a significant interest in both areas. Each of those interests was disturbed in some degree by the events of the period. The question is, therefore, how far those interests were actually subordinated to questions of world policy in Grey's diplomacy, or how far does this apparent lack of interest reflect the overwhelming importance in retrospect of the World War that followed?

The key to the problem clearly lies in the position of the United States. When Grey left office for the first time in 1894 the United States, like Britain, was a country diplomatically isolated. Intensely concerned with its own economic crisis, the Cleveland administration was reluctant to come to terms with the fact that as a rapidly industrialising country, America's strength was still potential rather than actual. In the *Baltimore* incident with Chile in 1892 its predecessor had taken a belligerent line which had little or no relevance to its capacity to enforce it. Three years later, Cleveland's Secretary of State, Richard Olney, took much the same sort of line with Britain itself over the question of the boundaries of Venezuela and British Guiana. But both incidents were formal rather than actual. The realities of economic interdependence were better demonstrated by Cleveland's determination to stick to the Gold Standard, and the railing of the Populists against the domination of the Western States by the 'money power' of Wall Street and, behind it, Lombard Street.

In 1905 Britain had moved from its isolation. It was now linked to Japan by the Anglo-Japanese Treaty of 1902, and encouraged by the successful appearance of the Entente. Meanwhile the United States had undertaken a successful war with Spain, acquiring by this and by the annexation of Hawaii, a small but noticeable imperial holding. The new Liberal Government, with its mildly imperialist tendency, felt a certain sympathy for the reluctance of the United States as much as for its resolution. And in Theodore Roosevelt, entirely American but at the same time sympathetic towards England, the United States had a vigorous and outspoken President whose commitment to internal reform and human well-being was very congenial.

For the first thing that was of importance in British relations with the United States was that here, alone in the world, the Foreign Office dealt with an English-speaking power. It was this, as much as the sharing of a common cultural tradition and the emergence of certain common interests, that made friendship between individuals in both countries possible. It is unlikely that, to take but the most obvious example, Roosevelt's friendship with Grey would have developed so easily had they not shared a common interest in English birds and been able to talk about them together.[2] More immediately important was the special ease and facility that British Ambassadors in Washington enjoyed in early intelligence about domestic political moves and events there, though this advantage was to some extent offset by the informality of American decision-making, which made the effects of such moves difficult to translate in terms of possible diplomatic initiatives.

As an authority on American Government, James Bryce (ambassador 1906–13) was in an especially favourable position both to carry out his formal duties and to make friends. Not only was he accorded the respect many Americans felt for an Ulsterman who had made, they believed, the first really serious attempt in Britain to understand their system of government and way of life, but also the friendship felt for a person who was indefatigable in maintaining his contacts with others, whether in person or by correspondence.[3] His successor, Sir Cecil Spring-Rice, it appears, was no less successful in making friends, for at the time of his appointment the very fact that most of his friends were Republicans was thought to form a potential source of embarrassment in his relations with the Wilson administration.[4] He was, however, more in the classic 'English' mould, and his temperament and frequent illness (most of which we would now recognise as stemming from allergies), made him less effective as a representative than he might otherwise have been. In a sense his best days came after the onset of war overwhelmed the traditional methods of pacific diplomacy in favour of direct communications and links through special agents.

Secondly, perhaps because of the recognition of common tradition, United States imperialism was not seen as an unpredictable threat, but instead as a predictable stage of development of a power stemming from British origins. Thus benignly regarded, it was accommodated by British governments with a certain sense of paternal pride. This accommodation allowed for a concurrent development of a concept of sharing in imperial responsibilities, which was already established by 1904 at the time of the Roosevelt Corollary. The Liberals were keen to reduce the burden of Imperial defence, which strained their intra-party divisions perhaps more than any other issue. Informal association with United States interests came, therefore, to be regarded as a possible partial solution, at least in the Caribbean area.

Thirdly, the one possible major area of conflict with the United States had already been eliminated. With the delimitation of the Alaskan Boundary – though in circumstances regarded with great hostility by Canadians – the existence of Canada as an independent entity, with a three thousand mile undefended frontier, was effectively assured. By 1908 the entire Canadian boundary was defined by treaty. As such, Canada ceased to be an issue in the Foreign Office, and became a question for the Canadians themselves.[5] Their vote for Laurier in 1911 destroyed the Taft administration's proposals for trade reciprocity, but it was not a cause for war. Two other questions that did arise were settled by entirely pacific methods. The question of the restriction of sealing in the Behring Straits was resolved (to the dissatisfaction of all parties, but to none more so than to the seals themselves) by negotiation, and the conflict between the Newfoundlanders and the fishermen of New England over fishing rights was sent to arbitration at the Hague.

Times were therefore propitious for a productive and harmonious relationship between Britain and the United States. There was, moreover, a general climate in the world for peace, reflected in the appearance of international conferences and treaties designed to avoid war. Two were of particular significance: the Conference of 1908 which resulted in the Declaration of London restricting the use of search in naval warfare, and the negotiation by the Taft administration of the series of treaties of arbitration with friendly countries. That with Great Britain was signed in 1911 but in the political climate of the day failed of ratification by the United States Senate. It is of particular interest because it led to a decision which was to have momentous consequences.

It was an irony that the first and most significant of Britain's treaty obligations should have been concluded with the one country in the world with which United States relations were difficult. The reasons for this were internal and peculiar to the United States. After the relaxation of travel outside Japan, an increasing number of emigrants had been travelling to the West-Coast states, where by 1900 they formed a substantial community. Though they were mostly engaged in truck-farming in California, their hard work and community spirit made them appear a considerable threat to the immigrant Irish and Scandinavians who had preceded them. In 1905 the San Francisco School Board under pressure, announced measures to segregate Japanese children. Intense irritation was aroused in Japan. However worse was to follow, for it speedily became apparent that the move was only part of a much wider drive for 'Asian Exclusion', the form it took in San Francisco owing perhaps most to the irritating aplomb with which the Japanese had received and surmounted the crisis of the great earthquake.

Negotiating in secret, Roosevelt obtained from the Japanese government a so-called 'Gentleman's Agreement' to restrict emigration to the United

States at source. On the whole this was effective.[6] But, being secret, it did not check the rumours of war that filled the newspapers of both countries, which were watched by the British Foreign Office with more than a little anxiety. The revision of the Anglo-Japanese Treaty of 1905 was thought to be fool-proof, since it bound Britain to aid Japan only in the event of an 'unprovoked attack' by another Power. It has not occurred to the Foreign Office that the United States might mount such an attack, and yet the irrational pressure for some belligerent move was certainly there.

Roosevelt, however, acted with caution and decision. On the one hand he intervened to prevent the California Legislature passing an Act to deprive Japanese settlers of the right to own land. On the other, he sent the United States Fleet on a dramatic world tour to advertise American preparedness. The crisis passed. Yet during the Taft administration the agitation did continue, together with periodic scares that the Japanese were trying to acquire naval bases in Central America. The one of these referring to a fishing concession in the Magdalena Bay of Lower California was taken so seriously that it became the basis for the so-called 'Lodge Corollary' of 1912.

In 1911 the revision of the original Anglo-Japanese Treaty fell due. Taking advantage of the Taft Administration's initiative for a General Arbitration Treaty with Great Britain, the Foreign Office obtained Japanese consent for the insertion of a clause excluding the possibility of war with any state with which such a treaty existed. The treaty, as we have seen, was not ratified, but the Japanese were encouraged to conclude that if they did have a quarrel with the United States, they were not likely to be able effectively to call on British support. Accordingly when in 1913 the California Legislature finally passed the Alien Land Act, British involvement was confined to friendly exhortations to both sides in the dispute to settle it by pacific means. What was not settled was the bitter feeling of many Japanese that they were still second class citizens of the world. But their attempts to redress that situation were to be a problem for a later Roosevelt and for a Churchill who was no longer a Liberal First Lord of the Admiralty.[7]

With this exception, however, the years 1905-14 saw British relations with the United States as being entirely unaffected by the disputes of either with other major powers. The main area of their interaction, therefore, fell where their interests overlapped, and this, above all, was in Latin America.

SOUTH AMERICA: THE BALANCE OF POWER

The great states of South America had by 1905 already begun to make their appearance on the world stage. Geography, distance and the poorness of communications, however, denied to them the substantial role in world politics, to which their size and strength might seem to have entitled them. Politically, South America formed a largely independent sub-system of diplomacy, and this was reflected in the staffing of British diplomatic posts there and in the specialisation of members of the Foreign Office in London. This had two contradictory aspects.

On the one hand, British diplomacy with Argentina, Chile, Brazil, Peru and Uruguay at least was accorded importance fitting to the extent of British trade with, and investment in those countries. Historical ties dating back to British naval support in the Wars of Independence, were still strong. There were large British colonies there, many of whose members intermarried with local families, but who still preserved traditional loyalties and worked to preserve them. British diplomatists posted to South America felt at home there, and many of them showed strong sympathy with the countries of their posting.[8] But once there, they tended to find themselves off the main diplomatic circuit, and it was rare for promotion to lead them back to a major Embassy in Europe.

As distinct from British diplomatists, therefore, British policy makers seldom had the opportunity to develop close ties with South American rulers or officials. In any case, something of the 'Black Legend' still clung in their minds to Spain, and Hispanic culture was not part of the general equipment of the educated Briton. In keeping with the minimal commitment of the Foreign Office to problems of no immediate urgency, therefore, British policy towards South America tended to be one of observation and mediation. The consular side, involving the extensive dealings of merchants and investors there, seldom impinged on this. It operated almost independently, on the general principle of facilitating within the vary narrow limits of capacity then current, the work of British subjects overseas. And those British subjects seldom spoke with any degree of enthusiasm about the amount of help they had actually received from His Majesty's Government.[9]

To safeguard, not to extend, British interests: that was official policy. Diplomatically, the sole threat to them in 1905 – a generation after the War of the Pacific – lay in the possibility that the balance of power might again be upset. As it was, it was always difficult for any power to maintain good relations simultaneously with any two countries having so many situations of potential conflict. Already, however, negotiations for the settlement of the most important – the boundary dispute between Argentina and Chile in the southern territories – were well on the way, and came to a satisfactory conclusion at Rio de Janeiro in 1906.[10] Furthermore, the conclusion of peace between Chile and Bolivia in 1904 left only the status of Tacna and Arica to be settled between Chile and Peru, and this was to drag on until the plebiscite of 1924. Continued fears that other powers might back Peru in the dispute led Chile into a close understanding with Brazil, with which, alone of the Spanish-speaking states, she had no common frontier.

Brazil was then at the apogee of its power in South America. Between 1900 and 1912 its foreign policy was controlled absolutely by one man, the Barão de Rio-Branco.[11] Rio-Branco's life work was to establish the boundaries of Brazil and so secure its national territory. In the process he added more than 342,000 square miles to it, highlights being treaties with Bolivia 1903, Ecuador

1904, Venezuela 1905, the Netherlands 1906 and Peru 1909, and an under-standing with Columbia 1907. The boundary with British Guiana was referred in 1901 to the arbitration of the King of Italy, who in 1904 awarded the area in dispute to the United Kingdom, but so great was Rio-Branco's past success that in 1909 he deliberately negotiated, without opposition, a treaty with Uruguay which gained nothing but good will by giving that country access to the Jaguarão River.

British relations with Brazil under Rio-Branco, however, were correct rather than cordial. Partly the reason was personal: Rio-Branco had spent almost his entire active diplomatic career as Brazilian consul in Liverpool, and, besides, he had an intense personal antipathy for the British Minister, Sir William Haggard. Partly it was nationalistic: Rio-Branco wished to obtain the first Embassy in South America, and did so in 1905 (in the same year that he obtained a Cardinal's hat for the Archbishop of Rio). But he obtained it from the United States, which shortly afterwards accorded a similar recognition to Mexico, while Britain did not follow suit until 1918. But this stemmed from conservatism rather than any diminution of British interests which still lay far ahead of those of all other countries. The fact was that the Foreign Office – always conscious of the rigid economies enforced by the Treasury – simply saw no reason to alter a policy that had hitherto served them well. Only in 1911, with the collapse of the Amazon rubber industry in face of the plantation methods of South-East Asia, were some Brazilians bitterly reminded of the instability of fortune, and inclined to remember none too kindly the theft of the rubber seeds from their country by an Englishman.

The rubber industry of the Amazon did, nevertheless, lead to a diplomatic initiative on Grey's part which was unique in South America, though it had a contemporary parallel in Mexico. This was the disclosure by a young American in 1909 of the existence of a system of virtual slavery in the disputed Peruvian territory of the Putumayo River, where thousands of rubber-gatherers were shot, clubbed or beaten to death by their local overlords.[12] Intervention was called for, since not only were many of the gatherers Barbadian inden-tured workers, but the company which handled the rubber, the Peruvian Amazon Company, was registered in London. Unwilling to act without evi-dence, Grey dispatched Roger Casement, the former British Consul-General at Rio,[13] as a volunteer, to investigate. The rumours themselves were so scarifying that public pressure for action was great. But Casement's report disclosed that the facts were infinitely worse. Diplomatic representations to Peru having had little or no effect, the decision was taken to publish the report as a Blue Book, whereupon the Peruvian Amazon Company was wound up. The system itself, though, was not ended and did not end until the collapse of the rubber boom, though the scandal did have an important by-product in the establishment of the Brazilian Indian Service (1911). Policing the 'inland sea' was beyond the capacity of any British government, and in this case at least, British intervention was based purely on humanitarian grounds.

Despite the Brazilian initiative, United States influence in continental South America was not materially increased. A pointer to the future, however, was the 1906 tour of Secretary of State Elihu Root to the major South American capitals, which established as basis for closer relations and had a material influence on the subsequent growth of the Pan-American movement and the conferences that accompanied it.[14] With this, at this stage, British diplomacy had little to do.

THE ISTHMUS: STABILITY AND DEFENCE

In the Caribbean the situation was very different. Since 1898 the United States had held Puerto Rico and exerted a virtual protectorate over Cuba, commanding the northern access to the basin.[15] Its strategic interests, with the heightened consciousness of naval power generated by Admiral Mahan, called for a canal to link the Atlantic and Pacific. Until the secession of Panama (1903) however there was no certainty where that canal would be located, and by that time it was already apparent that the question of the defence and protection of the canal was no less important than the link itself.

In the nineteenth century Britain had obtained by treaty with the United States certain rights in the building of such a canal, and the establishment of a rail link across the Isthmus of Tehuantepec in 1895 by British–Mexican interests gave it additional bargaining strength. The surrender of these rights to the United States in the Hay–Pauncefote Treaty (1901) therefore carried the agreement that British ships would be allowed to pass freely through the canal at the lowest rates.

Otherwise there were apparently few points of conflict. British interests, whether in Central America or in Haiti and Santo Domingo, were minimal. Where they existed, they took the form of investment in government securities rather than in trade or commercial enterprise. British possession of its own island territories was not in dispute, while that of British Honduras was much mitigated by the fact that at that period Mexico still exercised considerable opposition to the claims of Guatemala. The low priority accorded in the Foreign Office to Central America was reflected in the low status of its representation there, the four northern states being accredited a single Minister-Resident who lived in Guatemala. Between 1905 and 1913 this representative was Lionel Carden.

The protection of the interests of British bondholders was intimately bound up with the stability of Caribbean governments. But the governments of the islands were notoriously unstable, and the collapse of a government was normally accompanied by the repudiation of its debt. It happened that the early years of the century in Central America had been a time of peaceful negotiation for the reformation of the old Central American Republic. When these negotiations broke up, acrimony was intense, and each state attempted to pursue its own ends in its own way. When this resulted in open war in 1907 the United States intervened diplomatically to enforce a settlement involving the arbitration of future disputes in a Central American Court.[16]

The significance of this lay in the outcome of the crisis in Venezuela in 1902. Venezuela, though a large main land state, bordered the Caribbean, and its ports were of major significance in commanding the southern access. The dispute itself resulted from the customary default on the national debt, which became the occasion for one of the largest European naval interventions by a combined fleet of ships from Germany, Great Britain and Italy. This brought home the potential risk of such defaults to Roosevelt's administration, and, following diplomatic negotiations, in 1904 Roosevelt announced his 'Corollary' to the Monroe Doctrine, that in future his country would take over responsibility for policing the area.[17]

It was assumed in Britain that the principle of the 'open door' – long advocated by the United States in China – would be maintained, and public opinion on the whole greeted the announcement with relief. But there were two problems. Roosevelt himself had difficulty coercing the Venezuelan government and eventually in 1907 had to resort to a second blockade of the mouth of the Orinoco. And other European powers continued to intervene, highlights being the German punitive expedition in Brazil in 1906 and their assistance in the fall of a Haitian government in 1911. Meanwhile the debts of Nicaragua, Honduras and Guatemala remained.

The efficacy of the new hegemony, therefore, had yet to be proved when the Taft administration came to power (1909). Pacific in sentiment, the new Secretary of State, Philander C. Knox, characteristically opened his term with a tour devoted to Central rather than to South America. He was not entirely reluctant to use stern diplomacy, as his unnecessarily rough handling of the Alsop Co. claims in Chile in the same year showed.[18] But he saw the remedy for European intervention in the Caribbean as lying in the introduction of United States finance rather than in the use of military force, and set to work to achieve this. It was a logical policy, but not one necessarily likely to appeal to British interests. Its weakness, however, lay in the inefficiency and carelessness of its execution rather than in its inherent disadvantages.

Knox's immediate problem was the instability generated by the ambitions of José Santos Zelaya of Nicaragua, which had been a prime cause of the Central American War. His resentment towards the United States was manifest, but in 1909 he went too far in furnishing a pretext for intervention in the execution of two United States subjects, a further intervention in 1910 aiding the formation of a government friendly to the United States and prepared to accept its financial control. Grey's attitude towards this development was summed up by him in the following words:

These small Republics will never establish decent government themselves – they must succumb to some greater and bettter influence and it can only be that of the U.S.A. We cannot compete with that and must obtain the best terms we can as occasion offers for vested British interests and commercial opportunities. The more we can support the U.S. contention for the open door in other parts of the world the stronger our position will be morally in contending at Washington for the open door in Central America. A strong position morally is not everything but it is not without some value.[19]

The type of financial protectorate established in Nicaragua, of course, had its antecedent in Cuba. In fact it was not achieved until after the fall of the Taft administration in 1913. But meanwhile negotiations were opened by the State Department for a similar convention with Honduras, and there negotiations went more quickly, being concluded in January 1911.[20] Part of the bargain was the refunding of the national debt of that country, and here it rested on a settlement (1909) which it was felt in England neglected the interests of the bondholders, despite State Department promises to the contrary. A noticeable shift in British policy followed.

This time the debate arose in Guatemala, which had defaulted in 1899 and was now the last country (apart from the United States itself) with which British bondholders needed a settlement. Politically their position was precarious. Unlike Zelaya, Estrada Cabrera, constitutional dictator of Guatemala, had never failed to realise that survival in the new Caribbean depended on the good will of the United States. He had maintained his financial position by short-term loans and tax farming through an American syndicate, and he had the good will of the United Fruit Company, then just starting its operations in that area. Above all, he had hypothecated the revenues attached to the British debt to a new loan in the United States.[21] But the bondholders demanded, and were entitled to demand, a full settlement. When, late in 1910, the British Government anticipated further United States action by indicating its support for the case of the bondholders, Estrada Cabrera therefore took full advantage of every opportunity for procrastination.

In 1912 the revenue alienated to the American loan fell vacant. Carden was immediately instructed to press for full restitution.[22] At first his work was handicapped by sudden doubts by the bondholders' representatives, who were inclined to accept a new compromise they had been offered by the American interests. Then a further delay was incurred to avoid injecting an untimely issue into the American Presidential elections.[23] But at all times the objectives of the British government remained limited to the task in hand. As Grey put it:

The weak point in our position is that we (at any rate I am) are reluctant to use force to collect debt. People who invest in bonds of these faithless republics must do so at their own risk. I propose to reserve the use of force for some case such as the ill treatment of a British subject.[24]

Much of the effect of the initiative therefore rested with Carden himself. As instructed, he presented an ultimatum early in 1913 threatening the ending of diplomatic relations if a settlement were not reached. Estrada Cabrera let the ultimatum run to the limit, but, lacking the clear support of the transitional

United States government, he gave way.[25] The initiative, accordingly, was a triumphant success, for which Carden duly received a knighthood. There were on the other hand to be certain unfortunate consequences, arising from the alienation of United States sympathy.

As 1913 opened, Britain needed administration support to counter the decision made by Congress in 1912 to charge a lower rate for shipping in the Panama Canal in its own vessels. This was in apparent violation of the Hay–Pauncefote Treaty, but Britain had only moral pressure to enforce its claims. And her moral position had momentarily been seriously weakened by a flurry of events in Mexico.

MEXICO

In Mexico in 1910 British interests were very large indeed, probably equal to those of the United States.[26] This situation stemmed from three causes: the proximity of Mexico to the United States, and its past history, which made Mexicans anxious to seek a counterpoise in Europe; the long rule of Porfirio Díaz (1877–80, 1884–1911); and the friendship between Díaz and the British entrepreneur and engineer, Weetman Pearson, subsequently Lord Cowdray. It was Cowdray's firm that had built the Tehuantepec Railway and finally completed the Grand Canal, but after 1901, in the face of strong American opposition, he had climaxed his work in Mexico by the discovery and astonishingly rapid development of the enormously productive oil fields.

In the later years of Díaz, therefore, Mexican relations with Britain were excellent, and its strength and stability such that Mexico as we have seen resumed its earlier interest in its southern neighbours. It was easy to forget that the strength of Mexico rested on the personal and political survival of Díaz himself. For in the early years of the century, as Díaz himself entered his seventies, the weaknesses of his regime began to become apparent. His economic progress rested on privilege, his diplomacy on the assumption of the disinterest of the United States, and his power in the indefinite suppression of the aspirations of nine-tenths of the population. By 1910 all these were in disarray and in the same year revolution broke out, eventually to topple him in 1911.

Significantly, in the same year, there broke out in the United States the furore which followed the revelation of a system of debt slavery on the sisal plantations of Yucatán. Though holding a confirmatory report on the system from its (unpaid) Consul at Progreso, for his sake and because British subjects were not involved the British Government was not able to act on it as it had in the Peruvian case.[27] However United States government withdrawal of confidence did not rest on the disclosures in Yucatán, and its continued disenchantment with the government of the revolutionary leader, Francisco I. Madero (1911–13), arose from doubts as to its stability and power, as well as willingness, to protect American interests.

In 1913 Madero was overthrown in the course of a barrack revolt, and replaced by his Commander-in-Chief, Victoriano Huerta (1913–14). Subsequently Madero and his Vice-President were murdered in circumstances that suggested Huerta's complicity. Anxious for the safety of British interests which Huerta's government had obliquely suggested might otherwise be endangered, the Foreign Office departed from its usual custom and extended formal recognition to the new government once it was satisfied that it had been constitutionally endorsed by the Mexican Congress. The United States government of President Taft hoped to make the occasion a pretext to settle outstanding claims, and United States recognition was, therefore, not accorded before he went out of office.

Some months went by while the new administration of Woodrow Wilson (1913–21) went through the laborious process of transition and replacement of Republican officials. During this period the Admiralty in London announced its accelerated plan of converting its ships to oil fuel. It was clear that in the event of war one of Britain's major sources of supply was expected to be the Mexican oil fields. When, therefore, reports reached the Wilson administration of the circumstances of Huerta's rise to power, its members were inclined to believe that his dictatorial regime, to which a considerable armed revolutionary opposition had already developed, was sustained by the British government. Both Wilson and his Secretary of State, William Jennings Bryan, were devoted to the eradication of the power of financial interests in their own country. In the tradition already established by Roosevelt, they were anxious to secure better government in the Caribbean, but they brought to this task a sense of moral commitment which made it difficult for them to accept compromise.

First, therefore, Wilson announced in a public address at Mobile that his administration proposed to regard European financial penetration in the area as being a handicap to its political development. This was, in effect, a new corollary to the Monroe Doctrine, but its terms were so vague that it failed of much of its intended effect. Next he proceeded to exercise diplomatic pressure to force Huerta to give way to a new candidate at the Mexican Presidential elections. Huerta sidestepped this by arranging for the elections to be invalid, so that he remained in office. It was at this point that, by an unfortunate coincidence, a new British Minister arrived in Mexico to present his credentials, and that Minister was Sir Lionel Carden (1913–14).

There ensued a major diplomatic confrontation between Britain and the United States: the most serious, in fact, to disturb the peace of the two countries during the period. Both Bryan and (to a lesser extent) Wilson believed that British policy was being dictated by Lord Cowdray. Their belief received some apparent support from the fact that at the same time an agent of Cowdray's firm was active in Colombia, Ecuador and Costa Rica negotiating oil concessions. Seen as being in dangerous proximity to the Panama Canal, the United States government, which momentarily was even inclined to accept the extraordinary delusion that the British were planning a rival canal, intervened to check them. In the most important case – that of Colombia – this was done by offering an indemnity for the United States role in the secession of Panama ten years before.[28]

In fact, however, Huerta's government did not depend for support on Lord Cowdray or any other source of outside finance, but on the military. With them his position was only strengthened by the evidence of United States hostility. Grey had not only no intention of opposing United States policy; he was still less prepared to take the risks inherent in mediating, as the United States desired. As he put it to the American Ambassador in London, '...if we urged Huerta to get out of the way when there was nothing to succeed him, and worse disorder followed, in the course of which British lives were sacrificed, we might in a sense be held responsible'.[29]

While the situation lasted, much of the tension was due to the failure of diplomatic communications between the two countries, owing to the disorganisation of the State Department and the illness of Spring Rice. To put this right, Grey's Private Secretary, Sir William Tyrrell visited Wilson in November 1913, made clear the British position and established that his government was acting as reasonably as it could and not under any external financial influence. With the public restatement of the British position by Asquith, the dispute substantially came to an end. Further efforts by the United States to have Carden removed from Mexico were checked, though, when news of the negotiations was leaked to the press.

Meanwhile Wilson had already turned to negotiating with the revolutionary opposition to Huerta, the Constitutionalists. He was willing to allow them free importation of arms if he was satisfied that out of them a truly constitutional government could be devised. Here the problem lay in the fact that there were many factions among them, one of the most powerful being the army led by Francisco ('Pancho') Villa, which had a well-merited reputation in Europe for indiscriminate atrocities. In February 1914 the eventuality that Grey had feared came to pass when Villa personally shot a British subject, William Benton. Benton was not, perhaps, an attractive personality, and his own belligerence was probably the cause of his death. But the public outcry in Britain was at the time considerable, and protests and representations through Washington proved of no avail in face of the continued optimism of the President that his policy would bear fruit.[30]

Finally in April 1914 an incident involving the crew of an American whaleboat at Tampico gave Wilson a pretext for intervening.[31] He chose to order a landing at Vera Cruz, in order to intercept a cargo of arms from Germany that were reported to be on their way to Huerta. After Mexican casualties had been incurred, there existed in effect a state of war between Mexico and the United States. Still Huerta's government did not fall. As a graceful way out, Wilson accepted the offer of mediation from the governments of Argentina, Chile and Brazil; an act for which the two former governments shortly received the ambassadorial representation already accorded the last. Ironically, it was British influence and the advice of the much maligned Carden that brought Huerta's representatives to the conference table.[32] The conference itself settled little. It did, however, avert further war, and by the time that Huerta eventually resigned in July, the European situation was already too black for events in Mexico to have much significance. If the events of the past two years had proved anything, they had proved that whatever the shifts and turns of power in Mexico, the oil would continue to flow from the wells at Tampico into the waiting tankers as long as there was anyone around to collect the dues.

Meanwhile, in February 1914 Wilson had gone before Congress and requested the repeal of the Panama Canal Tolls Act of 1912 as a point of honour for the United States. Congress, not unmindful of the Mexican situation, gave him his wish. When the canal was opened to traffic, eleven days after the outbreak of the World War, the first ship to pass through was Colombian; but the second was British.

To conclude, therefore, Grey's policy towards the Western Hemisphere was above all characterised by recognition of the status of the United States as a Great Power, and by the cultivation of its friendship. Such friendship, to be real, had to carry reciprocal obligations. Grey therefore felt free to pursue as far as was convenient the traditional policy of maintaining British interests, and equal opportunity for them with others. Though personally disinclined to make use of force, he was prepared to use it in circumstances which seemed to require it, though in practice this meant only the use of comparable force on the body of a British subject.

In his hope for a 'better influence' in the smaller Latin American states he was not so far removed from the Wilsonian position as sometimes appeared. But he was a shrewd and practical man with a very real understanding of the limitations of physical power in a world of quarrelling states. Moreover he was well aware of the extent and significance of the extension of United States power in the Caribbean during his term of office. The growth of United States influence in South America during his term is much harder to assess, since it was not (apart from the Alsop case, which was inconclusive) tested by any overt conflict. It is hard to say, therefore, whether he recognised the growth of anything so insubstantial. It was in fact in just these years that British investments in Argentina and Uruguay reached their zenith, while for all its undoubted advances, Brazil had still a long way to go before achieving that status in South America to which she then aspired.

Finally, it would be fair to judge that United States friendship was sought primarily for its own sake. Secondarily it was valued for its convenience in regulating the affairs of the Caribbean, and relieving the strain on Britain's commitments there, but only so long as it appeared to be acting favourably. Before 1914, only indirectly was it seen as an important adjunct to British policy in other parts of the globe.

THE OUTBREAK OF THE WAR
AND THE WAR YEARS

23

The Sarajevo Crisis

MICHAEL G. EKSTEIN and ZARA STEINER

British policy in the Sarajevo crisis falls into two unequal parts. The first centred on Grey's attempts to find a peaceful solution. He had been aware of the danger of war from 6 July. He tried to co-operate with Germany to hold Austria in check. By 29 July it was evident that a general war on the Continent was virtually inevitable. Events moved into their second stage, when the main problem was whether to enter the war and the focus of decision-making was the Cabinet Room at Downing Street rather than the Foreign Office.

Since the Balkan Wars it had been plain that tension between the Habsburg Monarchy and its Slav neighbours could lead to a war involving all the European Powers. Grey, reflecting public opinion, wanted to avoid being drawn into disputes in the Near East in which Britain had no important interests directly engaged.[1] Yet he was obliged to recognize the wider implications of the power struggle in the Balkans – the risk of general war and the possibility that, in denying Russia diplomatic support, he would damage the Anglo-Russian entente.[2] During 1912 and 1913 both these dangers had been avoided by working together with Germany, thereby securing the restraint of Austria.[3] Grey looked upon this success as a blueprint for future Balkan troubles. In May 1914 he had explained to Buchanan that he would be looking to Berlin in the event of new emergencies in the Near East, because 'it seemed to me that in essential matters of policy that were really important Germany sometimes restrained Austria and Italy, particularly the former, and allowed them only to go to a certain point'. Three days before the murders at Sarajevo he spoke in similar terms to the British ambassador at Paris.[4]

The Berlin embassy was not convinced of the soundness of the Foreign Secretary's faith in the German Government. He seemed to exaggerate Bethmann Hollweg's influence, ignoring too much the sway of Tirpitz and the Kaiser's Military Cabinet. In the Foreign Office too there were sceptical voices. Eyre Crowe, the leading German expert, maintained that the Wilhelm-strasse played-up the pacific role of civilian elements as a means of securing diplomatic advantage.[5] Grey, who wished to avoid entanglement with Russia as much as possible and to develop the détente with Germany, ignored this advice.

On 28 June 1914 at Sarajevo in Bosnia, a Pan-Serb terrorist, Gavrillo Princip, shot and killed the heir apparent to the Austrian throne and his wife. The Archduke Franz Ferdinand had been widely regarded as a disruptive influence and reactions to his death, inside as well as outside the Habsburg Empire, hardly concealed a sense of relief that he had been removed from the scene. Initially, therefore, there was little reason for Whitehall to anticipate serious trouble.[6] The assassination, however, raised larger issues than the dead Archduke. For Vienna it burst open the question of whether a strong, independent Serbia was compatible with the continued existence of Austria–Hungary as a Great Power. Franz Joseph, Conrad and Berchtold now decided that it was not. Whether they would be able to bring Serbia to book depended on Berlin.

In the late spring of 1914, Germany was disturbed by a deteriorating international position: a rapid growth of Russian military power, signs of closer Anglo-Russian ties, the weakness of Austria, the easing away of Roumania from the Triple Alliance seemed to demand some *coup* in foreign policy to retrieve the situation. The German Government decided to back Austria in taking strong action against Serbia.[7] Lichnowsky, who was home for a short holiday at this time, writing shortly after the outbreak of war, described the situation.

Herr von Bethmann-Hollweg did not share my optimism [about Anglo-German relations] and complained about Russian armaments...I went to see Dr. Zimmermann, who was acting for Herr von Jagow, who told me Russia was about to raise 900,000 additional troops. His language betrayed unmistakable annoyance with Russia, which was 'everywhere in our way'. There were also difficulties in economic policy. Of course I was not told that General von Moltke was pressing for war; but I learnt that Herr von Tschirsky [the German ambassador at Vienna] had been reprimanded because he reported that he had counselled moderation towards Serbia in Vienna. On my return from Silesia to London I stopped only a few hours in Berlin, where I heard that Austria intended to take steps against Serbia in order to put an end to an impossible situation.[8]

Lichnowsky was nervous, and on arriving back in London went to see Haldane[9] and (on Monday 6 July) Grey at the Foreign Office. The ambassador spoke freely, though privately, to the Foreign Secretary about the 'anxiety and pessimism he had found at Berlin'. Anglo-Russian naval talks and Russian armaments had created a feeling that 'trouble was bound to come and therefore it would be better not to restrain Austria and let trouble come now rather than later'. Bethmann Hollweg himself was 'pessimistic'. Could Grey do anything, the ambassador asked, to save the situation?

The interview left Grey filled with foreboding.[10] But the Cabinet did not want to be caught up in Balkan affairs at a moment when the Ulster crisis was coming to a head.[11] Grey did not intend to act decisively; the Cabinet's pre-occupations left him with a relatively free hand. The Foreign Secretary hoped to coax Germany back into a mood where she would be willing to restrain Austria. When he saw Lichnowsky again on 9 July, he began by making reassuring statements about the Anglo-Russian naval talks and Russo-German relations, and went on to the possible repercussions of Sarajevo.

I would continue the same policy as I had pursued through the Balkan crisis [co-operation with Germany]...the greater the risk of war the more closely would I adhere to this policy.[12]

At the same time Grey asked Cambon and Benckendorff that everything possible be done to quieten German apprehensions. He also indicated to them that he anticipated grave difficulties arising between Vienna and Belgrade. Not wishing to provoke embarrassing entente demands for diplomatic support, he explained these apprehensions by referring not to Lichnowsky's revelations but to overheated public reactions at Vienna.[13] Quite different analyses of the popular mood at Vienna were reaching Paris and St Petersburg from the Austrian capital. Equally unfortunate, Cambon, who knew Grey was given to gloom, went down to see Nicolson for further information. The Permanent Under-Secretary suspected the Germans of inventing problems to strain Anglo-Russian relations and was dismayed by the naive attention which Grey seemed to pay to their complaints. He assured Cambon that Grey was being over-anxious.[14]

Berlin and Vienna, having made their crucial decisions in the first week of July, tried to move British opinion in a pro-Austrian direction. Their embassies dined journalists; their ambassadors worked on eminent public men, including Rosebery and Lansdowne; Albert Ballin was sent by the Wilhelmstrasse to London to see his friend Haldane and excite pro-German opinion in the Liberal Party. They had some successes – on 17 July the *Westminster Gazette*, the newspaper closest to Grey, ran a leader sympathetic to Austria; Ballin found Haldane and Grey well-disposed towards Germany. But the Central Powers were being over-optimistic if they believed that such subtle methods would survive the reaction to excessive Austrian demands.[15]

Although the German and Austrian Governments went about their business as if everything was normal, London became increasingly uneasy. The diplomats of the Central Powers were conspicuously nervous.[16] From Berlin Rumbold wrote that Lichnowsky's confidences probably amounted to a correct reading of the situation.[17] De Bunsen reported from Vienna that he had it from a reliable source,

a kind of indictment is being prepared against the Servian Government for alleged complicity in the conspiracy which led to the assassination...the Servian Government will be required to adopt certain measures in restraint of nationalist and anarchist propaganda, and the Austrian Government are in no mood to parley with Servia, but will insist on immediate and unconditional compliance, failing which force will be used.

He went on to report that this procedure was one with which Germany was in 'complete agreement'.[18] When Bertie saw the Foreign Secretary on 16 July, he noted how disturbed Grey was by the sudden turn for the worse in Russo-German relations, indeed Grey had gone so far as to speak of Germany mounting a preventive war against her eastern neighbour.[19] The same day, Benckendorff, following up an earlier description of Grey's fears with regard to the Serbian problem, wrote:

Grey told me yesterday that he had received no further news from Berlin and Vienna during the last few days. Nevertheless, he did not seem very reassured ...he says we can no longer count on Germany being the peacemaker under all circumstances.[20]

Disquieting reports continued to build up. Particularly alarming, the semi-official press in Germany grew markedly anti-Serb, and on 22 July Jagow told Rumbold that Germany was not counselling restraint at Vienna.[21] By now Grey had to face, at least for the time being, the breakdown of attempts to persuade Berlin to work together with him. What was to be done?

Grey advised the Russian and Austrian Governments to discuss the Serbian crisis between themselves.[22] The proposal was received in St Petersburg while Poincaré was there on his state visit. With the Russian capital ringing with affirmations of entente solidarity, it was not a good moment to suggest that Russia negotiate alone. Poincaré disliked the idea of talks à deux. He and Sazonov countered that the entente Powers should jointly caution Vienna.[23] Even the most pro-entente elements of the Foreign Office recognized that this would inflame Austrian opinion. For several reasons Grey himself was reluctant to agree: Austria's terms were as yet unknown; he did not want to increase German fears; he was suspicious of Poincaré; he sought to avoid direct involvement so long as the matter remained one between Austria and Serbia.[24]

Mensdorff gave Grey a general assessment of the ultimatum of 23 July, and on the following morning the Austrian embassy provided the Foreign Office with a copy of the text delivered to the Serbian Government on the previous evening. Grey categorized the ultimatum as 'the most formidable document I have ever seen addressed by one state to another that was independent' and strongly disapproved of the forty-eight hour time limit.[25]

It was not until the afternoon of 24 July, at the close of a discussion on Ulster that the Foreign Secretary brought the international crisis – 'the gravest for many years past in European politics (Asquith)' – before the Cabinet. He was still thinking in terms of an Austro-Russian solution, though now oiled by good offices of the four less interested Powers – Great Britain, France, Germany and Italy. His colleagues agreed with this approach.[26] After the Cabinet Grey saw Paul Cambon. Partly out of a wish to see Britain move closer to France and Russia, partly from a wish to help, the ambassador emphasized the inevitableness of general war once Austria had marched against Serbia. When Grey saw Lichnowsky later in the afternoon, he took up Cambon's point, stressing the need for an immediate holding back of Austria as a first step in four Power mediation.[27]

The next day saw an unexpected break in the clouds. The news came that Belgrade was accepting nearly all Austrian demands. Vansittart remembered going home from the Foreign Office on that Saturday evening thinking that 'another crisis had been surmounted'. It had not. Vienna was dissatisfied. The last fragments of blue sky had covered over.[28]

Nicolson was in charge of the Foreign Office on Sunday 26 July. Faced with the prospect of imminent war, he seized on a hint of Sazonov – if the Serbs agreed, Russia would stand aside and allow four-Power mediation. Nicolson proposed a four-Power conference of ambassadors at London. The Foreign Secretary was at his cottage in Hampshire, where Nicolson's telegram arrived the same afternoon. Grey approved and invitations were sent off to Paris, Berlin and Rome.[29] In fact, Nicolson had little confidence in the conference idea and would have preferred a very different solution of the crisis. Since coming back from St Petersburg to head the Foreign Office, he had been haunted by the prospect of a breakdown in the understanding with Russia. The dreadful moment now appeared to be at hand. Sazonov was making ever more pressing demands for support. 'For us', warned Buchanan, 'the position is a perilous one and we shall have to choose between giving Russia our active support and renouncing her friendship.' In these circumstances Nicolson wanted to back Russia.[30] He and Crowe believed the case for so-doing was no less persuasive when argued on the basis of what was happening at Berlin. They maintained that Germany was looking for a triumph, if necessary by war, to establish her hegemony in Europe. Only by throwing her weight on the side of France and Russia could Britain hope to dissuade Germany from her reckless course.[31]

Grey made some concessions to the Crowe-Nicolson viewpoint. On his return to London on Sunday evening, he was informed by Churchill that the Fleet had been kept together after the naval review at Spithead. He favoured publicizing the Admiralty's step as a way of steadying the Central Powers and soothing Paris and St Petersburg.[32] Yet fundamentally he did not agree with his permanent officials. He knew he could not rely on official or public support for a bold line and this made him susceptible to arguments against it.[33] Was it morally right or politically feasible to commit the nation while the dispute was confined to Austria and Serbia? Would France and Russia use a pledge of support to provoke Germany? Thus, on 29 July Samuel wrote that the Cabinet agreed it would be better to maintain an equivocal position because 'if both sides do not know what we shall do, both will be less willing to run risks'.[34] Grey preferred to go back to a policy of persuading Germany to restrain Austria: the peaceful civilian elements at Berlin might still save the situation. J. A. Spender, a regular visitor to the Foreign Office in those tense days, noted that Grey had told him he trusted Jagow when he said he was working for peace.[35] On 29 July, Samuel indicated that the Cabinet still believed the 'doves' at Berlin would use their influence in favour of peace.

It remains to be seen whether or not Germany regarding war as inevitable will then strike at France. There is still some hope that under the influence of the Emperor and Bethmann Hollweg, the Chancellor, she may not.[36]

Even on 30 July, after the German Government had virtually given notice of its intention to attack France through Belgium, Grey was still reassuring Germany about the future in the hope of securing her goodwill and co-operation.[37] Recalling the events of this crisis many years later Crewe wrote to G. M. Trevelyan:

All through the month, we attempted to exercise a mediating influence; probably the whole government, including Grey, were a little over-flattered by the success of the Balkan Conference the year before. On this occasion such a statement [about Belgian neutrality], almost a threat, would have been considered like the action of somebody sitting down to play a round game and saying to the party 'I suppose we may assume that nobody is going to cheat this evening.'[38]

One attempt after another was made to turn hoped-for German co-operation into an achieved fact. Each failed. The request that Germany advise Austria not to make war on Serbia was passed on to Vienna without comment. On 27 July Berlin rejected the four-Power conference proposal on the grounds that it would be a tribunal judging Austria. Bethmann Hollweg and Jagow, however, hoping for British neutrality, claimed to favour mediation in principle. Grey refrained from immediately taking them up on this point because direct Austro-Russian talks had at last begun at St Petersburg and he wanted to avoid a confusion of peace efforts.[39] Not that he had to hold his hand for long. On 28 July Austria declared war on Serbia and the Austro-Russian dialogue collapsed. He now informed the German Government that, as it had said it was in favour of mediation, let it propose the form of mediation desired.[40] The very fact that such diplomatic finessing was necessary was an indication that Grey was losing confidence in his own assessment of the situation at Berlin.

By 29 July the Foreign Secretary had edged closer to the position of Crowe and Nicolson. At the Cabinet meeting at mid-day, he asked for some decision on the question of whether or not to enter the war. When this was not forthcoming, he gave a private warning to Lichnowsky that Germany should not rely on British neutrality.[41] For despite Lichnowsky's earlier communications to Berlin, the German Government had been hoping that England would stay out, at least in the early stages of the war. Grey's statement came as a shattering blow, and in the small hours of 30 July Bethmann Hollweg tried to reverse the wheels of German policy. Vienna was advised to carry the war no further than Belgrade. London was assured that every effort was being made to persuade the Austrians to accept Grey's mediation proposals.[42] Grey picked up these threads in his last attempts to find a peaceful solution. On 30 and 31 July he backed the 'halt at Belgrade' proposal at St Petersburg, and suggested once more four-Power mediation in support of Austro-Russian talks that had recommenced at Vienna.[43]

It was too late; military developments in Russia and Germany were running away with events. The war that military bureaucracies had planned for generations was upon them. General Staffs pressed for the implementation of mobilization schemes that, once in motion, were difficult to stop short of war, and which created a new range of threats and pressures. Belgrade was shelled on 29 July. Russia mobilized her southern armies. On 30 July Berlin demanded this order be revoked. On 31 July Russia, Germany and Austria ordered general mobilization. The problem now was whether to join the war rather than try to prevent it.[44]

Grey believed his policy had failed because the military in Germany had imposed their will on the civilian leadership. This image of a struggle between civilian 'doves' and military 'hawks' was not something newly invented. Friction between the two elements had impressed Haldane during his mission to Berlin in 1912;[45] the Berlin embassy had also commented on it[46] and just prior to the final crisis, Bethmann Hollweg had been complaining to Grey that Anglo-Russian naval talks would make it almost impossible to resist pressure from 'militarists'.[47] In late July Grey believed that the civilians had been defeated. 'Jagow did nothing. Bethmann-Hollweg trifled and the military intended war and forced it', wrote Grey in March 1915.[48] Most of the Cabinet agreed with him. The editor of the *Manchester Guardian* made notes of a conversation he had with Simon and Lloyd George on 3 August.

He [Simon] began at once by saying he had been entirely deceived about Germany and that I ought to know that the evidence was overwhelming that the party which had gained control of the direction of affairs throughout the crisis had deliberately played for and provoked war. The Emperor was away on his yacht and in his absence the Crown Prince and the war Party – Tirpitz and the rest – had brought things to a point at which they were beyond control . . . He [Lloyd George] confirmed also the secrecy and deliberation with which the war had been prepared by the military camarilla.[49]

For the Foreign Secretary Great Britain faced a bid on the part of one power for domination in Europe, such as France had presented a century earlier and as Germany had already attempted in 1905 and 1911. Britain could not allow Germany to dominate Europe, especially the west of Europe, and use it as a base from which to threaten the British Isles. As he explained to the Committee of Imperial Defence on 26 May 1912:

There is no danger, no appreciable danger, of our being involved in any considerable trouble unless there is some Power, or group of Powers, in Europe, which has the ambition of achieving what I would call the Napoleonic policy.[50]

Britain's global interests also required that she enter the war, for, if she did not stand by France and Russia, then she would be in an impossible position after the war ended. This consideration weighed heavily with many senior diplomats. 'I only pray', wrote Buchanan, 'that England will prove true to herself and to her friends, as if she deserts them in their hour of need she will find herself isolated after the war, and the hours of our Empire will be numbered.'[51]

At a preliminary Cabinet discussion on intervention on 27 July it was agreed to examine the question of the neutrality of Belgium at the next meeting.[52] By the time the Cabinet met again – 11.30 to 2.00 on 29 July – the international situation had gravely deteriorated. Discussion broadened into a debate on whether to go to war or stand aside, Grey advocated supporting France. At this stage he was probably thinking as much in terms of having a stronger bargaining position against both blocs as of actually entering the war. It would be much easier to restrain France and Russia and threaten Germany if he knew exactly where he stood. Churchill backed him, as did the Liberal Imperialists Haldane and Crewe. Asquith too was on the Foreign Secretary's side, although uppermost in his mind in the short term was the need to hold the Cabinet together.[53] The rest baulked at war. Simon and Morley disliked fighting alongside Tsarist Russia: others, notably the Colonial Secretary, were sympathetic towards Germany. All were moved by a horror of war. Grey did not get his own way. As the Prime Minister wrote to the King:

After much discussion it was agreed that Sir Edward Grey should be authorised to inform the French and German ambassadors that at this stage we were unable to pledge ourselves in advance either under all circumstances to stand aside or in any condition to go in.

On the neutrality of Belgium, the Cabinet came to the same conclusion as had Gladstone's Government in 1870. Obligation to uphold the 1839 Treaty fell collectively rather than individually on the five signatory Powers – France, Great Britain, Prussia (Germany), Austria and Russia – and, therefore, 'the matter if it arises will be rather one of policy than of legal obligation'.[54] Burn's laconic diary entry for 29 July summarises the Cabinet's discussion very adequately: 'critical Cabinet at 11.30. The discussion ensued. Situation seriously reviewed from all points of view. It was decided not to decide.'[55] The Cabinet resolved on 30 July to make up its mind the next day. But 31 July saw no decision. Further procrastination was preferred to an immediate split.[56]

Developments in the east were now casting their shadow in the west. On 29 July the German Chancellor made a clumsy bid for British neutrality. If Britain stayed out, Germany would 'in the event of a victorious war' aim at 'no territorial acquisitions at the expense of France'. When Goschen asked whether self denial would extend to French colonial possessions, Bethmann-Hollweg could give no similar undertaking. But he did pledge that the integrity of Belgium would be respected in the peace settlement. It amounted to an admission that war in the west would soon be inevitable.[57] 'Deciding not to decide' was becoming an impossible position for those who wanted to go to war.

Churchill busied himself preparing the Royal Navy. On 26 July the Admiralty had on its own initiative kept together the Fleet after the Spithead review. Three days later the Cabinet agreed to Churchill's request for a preliminary mobilization of the Fleet. On the evening of 29 July the First Lord asked the Prime Minister for permission to send the Fleet to war stations. Churchill described the scene in an essay on Asquith: the Prime Minister 'Looked at me with a hard stare and gave a sort of grunt. I did not require anything else.' On 1 August Churchill, against the expressed wishes of the Cabinet, although he had obtained the tacit approval of the Prime Minister, mobilized the Fleet.[58] Lt. General Sir Henry Wilson, the Director of Military Operations, was equally eager to prepare for an early despatch of the expeditionary force to France. Since the end of 1905 it had been the contention of protagonists of military co-operation with France that the British army could have a decisive influence on the great battles in the north-west of France which would occur at the outset of a Franco-German war. Wilson watched with mounting dismay and rage the Cabinet's fumbling. An Ulster Protestant, he hated 'Squiff and his filthy Cabinet' and had no qualms about intriguing against it. Wilson paid repeated visits to the Foreign Office where he saw both Nicolson and Crowe. He was in close touch with the French embassy and went so far as to warn the leaders of the Opposition of the disastrous implications of the Cabinet's delay in sending the B.E.F.[59]

The Unionist leadership had been kept well-informed of diplomatic developments by the Foreign Office.[60] Bonar Law, Lansdowne and Austen Chamberlain maintained that there was an obligation to defend France against German aggression, and if this duty were not fulfilled England would 'incur indelible disgrace and lasting danger and insecurity'. Up to 31 July they believed that the Government shared their views.[61] Then through a number of channels came reports of the Cabinet's hesitation. Winston Churchill, anticipating a break up of the Cabinet, was putting out feelers for a coalition through his friend F. E. Smith. There were Henry Wilson's alarums as well as information from the French embassy through George Lloyd, Maxse and Amery. Those not in London hurried back and on the morning of 2 August met in Lansdowne House in Berkeley Square. From there Lansdowne and Bonar Law wrote to Asquith:

it would be fatal to the honour and security of the United Kingdom to hesitate in supporting France and Russia at this juncture; and we offer our unconditional support to the Government in any measures they may consider necessary for this object.

As yet they were not thinking seriously in terms of a coalition in the event of one half of the Cabinet refusing to go to war, rather they hoped to strengthen the hand of those in the Cabinet who agreed with them.[62]

The Cabinet would not offer a promise of support to France. Paris grew anxious. On 30 July Poincaré was unable to extract from Bertie a declaration of solidarity.[63] The following day the President of the Republic made a personal appeal to George V. The King reluctantly replied in terms that reflected his Government's indecision.[64] Worse news lay ahead. Grey informed Cambon on 31 July that the crisis was quite different from the Moroccan crisis three years earlier when France's own interests had been challenged; now she was only involved because of her alliance with Russia. In these circumstances Britain could not undertake a definite pledge to intervene in the war.[65] After the Cabinet of the morning of 1 August, the Foreign Secretary reiterated this point and told the distraught ambassador that the Cabinet would not be discussing the question again.[66] Cambon refused to communicate this message to his Government. The Cabinet's stand appalled Crowe and Nicolson, who both insisted that there was a moral obligation to defend France. Harsh words were exchanged between the Permanent Under-Secretary and his chief. In September 1914 Nicolson wrote in disgust to Hardinge: 'I may tell you *quite privately* I passed an anxious forty hours at one moment. The Cabinet was not prepared to stand by France.'[67]

Crowe and Nicolson paid scant regard to the pressures against war that the Cabinet had to face.[68] Before 3 August the Liberal press – the *Manchester Guardian*, the *Daily News* and the *Westminster Gazette* – were for keeping out of the war. Many Liberal M.P.s voiced their opposition to war. The Liberal Foreign Affairs Committee, a group of about 70 M.P.s which regarded itself as a watch committee on Grey's foreign policy, threatened revolt. Arthur Ponsonby, one of their leaders, wrote to Asquith that 'any decision in favour of participation in the European conflict' would meet with their 'actual withdrawal of support for the Government'.[69] Ministers also had to take account of the City's strong opposition to war. Even more important, the financial chaos in late July was such that even Grey was thinking that Britain might have to stay out as 'the only means of preventing a complete collapse of European credit'.[70]

Other, as it turned out, dominating issues were coming into focus. In October 1911 Churchill had written: 'Belgium is a factor of prime importance. Violation of Belgian neutrality will put Germany in the wrong more plainly than any other step.'[71] Keeping a strong military Power out of the Low Countries was an axiom of British foreign policy, cherished by public opinion as an historic doctrine and formalized in the Treaty of London of 1839. It was known to the British Government that the German armies would march through Belgium to turn the flank of the Franch army. The only lingering doubts that persisted after Bethmann Hollweg's statements to Goschen on 29 July concerned whether Germany would violate all or only the southern tip of Belgium.[72] On 31 July the German and French Governments were asked whether they would undertake to respect the neutrality of Belgium.[73] The French agreed but the German reply, evasive and hedged with complaints against the Belgians, was tantamount to a refusal.[74] When Germany declared war on Russia on 1 August it was clear that the Cabinet could not long delay defining their position with regard to Belgium. On the morning of 2 August it was decided that a substantial violation of the neutrality of that land would constitute a *casus belli*.[75] Wartime propaganda was to represent this policy as expressing Britain's interest in defending the rights of small peoples. At the beginning of August 1914 very different considerations had been at issue. Then the Belgians had been at pains to lean neither towards France and Britain nor towards Germany, lest in so doing they should bring down an aggressive attack on their own heads. When the Cabinet resolved to go to war in the event of a German violation of Belgian neutrality it did not know what the Belgians would do. In fact, in the late afternoon of 2 August Grey told the French ambassador that even if the Belgians threw in their lot with the Germans (which seemed a distinct possibility), Belgian neutrality would still be regarded as a *casus belli*.[76] The Liberal Government, for all its high-minded pacifism, was prepared to go to war only in defence of narrow national self-interest.

A second *casus belli* arose. The Anglo-French naval arrangements of 1912 had left the western Mediterranean to the French and the Channel to the Royal Navy. On 1 August Cambon, in despair about the British refusal to stand by France, brought to the Foreign Secretary's attention that his country's northern shores were undefended. Grey agreed to bring the matter to the attention of the Cabinet on the following morning.[77] It was characteristic of politicians in this era that they should have given little thought to the political implications of strategic plans and military agreements. Only when the Cabinet looked closely at naval relations with France was it realized how far it had committed itself. Most members of the Cabinet saw that there was an obligation to protect the Channel coast of France from German naval attack. It was also generally felt that it was a British interest not to have the Germans operating freely in the Channel. Four ministers – Beauchamp, Burns, Morley and Simon – resigned rather than agree to what they considered a provocative policy toward Germany. Beauchamp and Simon, however, were eventually persuaded to stay on. The decision was communicated to the French Government in the afternoon.[78] Willingness to uphold the naval agreements with France is important in showing that the Cabinet were prepared to accept war for the sake of the security of the British Isles. In this respect, the upholding of the neutrality of Belgium, keeping the German navy out of the Channel and protecting the French coast hung together. But the Anglo-French fleet arrangements were not the decisive factors in bringing Britain into the war for the Germans were to undertake not to send their warships into the Channel.[79]

Grey spent much of the night of 2–3 August drafting his statement to the Commons. In the morning the Cabinet gave its approval.[80] Considering the Foreign Secretary had been subjected to terrible strains, it was a well-articulated statement. On a quiet note, Grey unemotionally piled up the case for intervention. His own simple style was more effective than any chauvinistic appeal to arms could ever have been. When he had gone to the House, he had expected half of his own Party to come out against him. By the end of his speech it was clear that the Conservatives, nearly all Liberals and half the I.L.P. had been won over.

The push to war continued. In the early hours of 3 August came news that Berlin was demanding from the Belgians freedom to march their troops across Belgian territory. The Belgians refused and the King of the Belgians appealed to Great Britain.[81] On the morning of 4 August the Cabinet agreed that if Germany did not reverse her policy with regard to Belgium, Britain and Germany would be at war 'by tonight'. Grey sent a succession of protests to Berlin about the German ultimatum to Belgium. In the early afternoon he prepared to send a further telegram. His drafts show his mind moving between another strong protest and an ultimatum, coming down eventually in favour of the latter. If the German Government did not agree to respect Belgian neutrality by twelve o'clock (German time) that night, Goschen was to ask for his passports and say: 'His Majesty's Government feel bound to take all steps in their power to uphold the neutrality of Belgium and observance of a Treaty to which Germany is as much a party as ourselves.'[82]

The collapse of the opposition to war in the Cabinet requires explanation. One consideration was a shift in public opinion as perceived by the Cabinet in the attitude of the press and the Bank Holiday crowds in the streets. By 3 August Ministers believed war was popular.[83] Yet the problem goes deeper. There was really never any doubt that, given the German intention to come through Belgium, Britain would have to go to war. No serious disagreement took place in the Cabinet on the need to protect the security of the British Isles. If this is so there should have been no ambiguity about a decision to intervene. Even though the sequence of events from an Austro-Serb war to a German march through Belgium was predictable, the members of the Cabinet were unwilling to follow this train of events to its logical conclusion. Churchill described this mental attitude in *The World Crisis*:

The Cabinet was overwhelmingly pacific. At least three-quarters of its members were determined not to be drawn into a European quarrel, unless Great Britain were herself attacked, which was not likely. Those who were in this mood were inclined to believe first of all Austria and Serbia would not come to blows: secondly, that if they did, Russia would not intervene; thirdly, if Russia intervened, Germany would not strike; fourthly, they hoped that if Germany struck at Russia, it ought to be possible for France and Germany to neutralise each other without fighting. They did not believe that if Germany attacked France, she would attack her through Belgium and if she did the Belgians would forcibly resist...[84]

This liberal view of international relations made for loose thinking. Idealistic, pacifist and underpinned by assumptions of natural law, it encouraged the attitude that pessimistic reasoning was cynicism. Lloyd George also illustrates the general point very well. He was the only figure in the Cabinet of sufficient stature to have led an effective anti-war party and both sides of the Cabinet knew this. He had highly developed political instincts and an extraordinary intuitive feeling for the psychological tensions and intellectual framework of those around him. He could see more clearly than most the nature of the debate in the Cabinet. War was hateful but the German move against France made it inevitable, and Belgium would make participation acceptable to Liberals and preserve the unity of the party. When the Germans marched through Belgium, they shattered the naive world of most of the Liberal Cabinet and relieved the arch-realist Lloyd George of the burden of having to pretend that it existed.[85]

What can now be said of Grey's policy in July 1914? His ideas on how to manage a Balkan crisis had been worked out before the Sarajevo murders. For most of July he hoped that there was a civilian peace party at Berlin that would restrain Austria. Accordingly he tried to give the Germans time to act. The severity of Austrian demands seriously weakened his own position at St Petersburg, and in the days that followed his actions were further inhibited by the Cabinet. His diplomatic initiatives were checked by Berlin. The Germans did not co-operate and, fatally, they mistook Grey's willingness to work with them as a sign that Britain would remain neutral. In the end warnings to Germany came too late. The question now was whether to go to war. The Cabinet would not undertake to do so to defend France, and the matter was only finally decided when the Germans marched through Belgium.

Grey made his own policy during these July days. At the start he did not consult his officials; as the crisis developed, he often disregarded their advice. The later battles took place in the Cabinet. It has been said that Grey should have warned the Russians that it was better to accept diplomatic defeat in the Balkans than to risk a European war. Such action would have implied a reversal of the entente policy and a rejection of the assumptions on which it rested. Grey has been condemned for failing to warn the Germans earlier that Britain would not be neutral. In his defence it can be said that it would have been difficult to have made such a statement given the Cabinet's indecision, and a warning would have made little difference in Berlin. But, as his own private caution to Lichnowsky on 29 July shows, it was not impossible. Grey was guilty of an error of judgment. In fact, he did not want to bring pressure to bear on the Germans because, until the very last days, he was relying on their goodwill. He had fully grasped that the mounting tensions between Russia and Germany could lead Germany into war, and wanted to reassure Berlin. The basic problems facing Grey and the fundamental cause of the weakness of Britain's influence in the Sarajevo crisis lay in the diversity of the international pressures he was trying to satisfy. He had to reconcile too many opposing forces: a Liberal Cabinet and Tsarist Russia; pacifism in his own party with entente demands for solidarity; a need for a strong European policy with a reluctance to offend a friendly Germany; a desire to limit commitments in Europe with a pattern of alliances in which all local conflicts could assume Europen dimensions.

In the last resort, Grey's policies were over-ambitious. He believed Britain could act as a mediator while supporting France and Russia against Germany. While Grey led the Cabinet into war, he more than anyone had a horror of war and forebodings about its consequences. Britain's entry into war was both a victory and a defeat.

24

Italy and the Balkans, 1914–1915

C. J. LOWE

The major difficulty that faced Grey in the first two years of the war was that foreign policy was now completely dependent upon factors outside his control. Neutral powers, inevitably, were mainly influenced by the ebb and flow of the tides of war, and for the Entente 1914–15 was mostly ebb. 'A diplomacy which was suitable when the Allied armies were having a success', Grey wrote, 'was hopelessly unsuitable when Germany seemed to be winning.' As the course of war was largely unpredictable this made the pursuit of any grand design on the part of the Foreign Office largely a waste of time, a fact which helps to explain the increasing frustration within its portals and the rapid collapse of its pre-war mystique and prestige outside. All that could be done, in Grey's view, was to remind themselves that 'if diplomacy could do little in Europe to win the war, it happily could do little to lose it'.[1]

In retrospect this seems reasonably obvious, but that Grey, writing in the twenties, was constrained to make this defence of his conduct of British diplomacy in wartime reflects the fact that some thought otherwise. The leading element amongst his critics in the Cabinet, Lloyd George, held that the office under Grey was unimaginative, clinging to both the 'old diplomacy' and the old diplomats. If instead the 'new' technique of sending out roving missions with plenipotentiary powers had been followed, he claimed, much better results could have been achieved in 1915 and in particular Bulgaria need never have have been lost.

Whether or not this was true, it is clear that Bulgaria's decision to join the Central Powers in October 1915 was the starting point of a general recrudescence of radical criticism of Grey's handling of foreign affairs, provoking violent debates in the House of Commons and an attempted vote of censure in November and December 1915. It was, in all probability, a vast over-estimation of the importance of Bulgaria's contribution to the European conflict, but to appreciate this obsession it is necessary to bear in mind the vast hopes pinned on the Dardanelles campaign in 1915 as the only sure way of finishing the war quickly. Whether this would have been a success with better planning or more enterprising naval and military commanders has remained a matter of dispute ever since 1915 and it is not proposed to enter upon a discussion of its merits here. But to understand the sudden importance of the Balkans in British diplomacy in 1915 this background of the Dardanelles must be remembered.[2]

This operation, originating in the Cabinet's desire to find some means of breaking the deadlock on the western front, was rapidly built-up into the strategic counterstroke of the war. If the fleet, or later the army, could only break through to Constantinople this would, the Cabinet were told, bring Italy and the Balkan states tumbling over each other to join the Allies. This in turn could 'close the circle', somehow redressing the deadlock in the west and the patent inability of Russia to deliver the death blow in the east. In the initial stages at least the Dardanelles operation was not conceived in terms of opening up a supply route to Russia; rather it was to knock out the weakest German ally, Turkey, and mop up all the Balkan neutrals by the sheer attraction of a dazzling success.[3]

But as Gallipoli expanded from a simple naval exercise to a military operation of some magnitude, rapidly it became part of a vicious circle. It was impossible to call it off once the initial bombardment had taken place without a bad – Kitchener thought disastrous – effect upon British prestige in the East.[4] But it was equally difficult to achieve a victory. The standard formula for this in 1915 was more troops. But none could be spared from the western front, or at least Kitchener said they could not, which was the same thing. Nor could the Russians, who initially promised an army corps, in fact produce them once the Germans opened their spring offensive with the shattering victory at Gorlice.

British military weakness in 1914–15 was greatly magnified by Kitchener's concept of what constituted a fighting force. Since he was sceptical of the value of Haldane's Territorials – the week-end soldiers – as fighting troops, a scepticism which extended to the Anzacs, this meant in his view that there were no troops available:[5] what few Regular forces still remained had to be reserved for France. Though not as manic as Sir John French, Robertson and Haig in his devotion to the Western Front, Kitchener held that any serious effort elsewhere must await the development of his New Army, which was to be built up and preserved under his special care to be used only when and where he thought fit. Misusing his position as Minister of War, he not only concentrated all power in his own hands but kept all information in his head, releasing such driblets to his colleagues as he thought fit, making criticism of his ideas on technical grounds extremely difficult. In any case, until the munitions crisis of 1915, Loos, and the Dardanelles disasters made it apparent that even Kitchener was fallible, Asquith, Grey, Lloyd George and the Cabinet collectively worshipped their new demigod as avidly as the public: Kitchener was War Lord.[6] It was only the cumulative effect of these setbacks and the strong pressure of the growing Lloyd George–Bonar Law–Carson alliance that finally nerved Asquith to take advantage of Kitchener's temporary absence at the Dardanelles to create an alternative source of military authority in Sir William Robertson.[7] 'Wully', if as contemptuous of the 'bloody politicians' as the demoted Kitchener, had at least the merit that he was a systematic administrator who believed in Staff planning and provided the Cabinet with the technical information to form a basis for intelligent decisions.

The effect of this situation was then that for most of 1915 the Cabinet, War Council, Dardanelles Committee and War Committee[8] accepted the War Minister's advice as to what was technically possible without any real knowledge of whether this had any factual basis, a condition which foredoomed schemes such as those propounded by Lloyd George for a major British military expedition to Salonica in order to force the Balkan States over to the Entente. In the War Council in January and February 1915 Lloyd George and Churchill, convinced that the Western Front was a mincing machine, pushed their case vigorously, pressing that they should 'send an army to the Balkans in order to bring all the Balkan States into the war on our side and settle Austria'. But it came up against the rock-like obstinacy of Kitchener who, though not opposed in principle to sending an army corps to Salonica, was 'not quite sure that the right moment had arrived'. Joffre, he said, would object strongly if they did not send all their men to France and, though Churchill was all for ignoring Joffre, the general feeling was, as Balfour put it, that 'we had to keep on friendly relations with the French'.[9] Not even Lloyd George's wire pulling in Paris to interest the French Cabinet[10] in his project, could overcome Poincaré's support for Joffre. It was not until he became eager to get rid of Sarrail in July 1915 that Joffre wavered from his devotion to the Western front, and even then it took three months to actually produce the troops for Salonica.[11]

The failure to appreciate the complete change in emphasis in German strategy in 1915 had catastrophic results. Falkenhayn, adamant that Germany could not stand the addition of the Balkan States and Italy to her enemies, concentrated on an offensive in the East, first breaking the Russians at Gorlice in May then turning on Serbia in October: a concentration of power which effectively supported German diplomacy in the Balkans.[12] In London, by contrast, the Foreign Office was powerless since Asquith's Cabinet, blocked by Poincaré and Joffre, hesitated to overrule Kitchener, and embarked instead on the disastrous Gallipoli campaign whose main attraction – or so it was thought – was that it would swing Italy and the Balkan states without the necessity of finding troops.[13] Not until this had been tried and written off did the Cabinet again seriously consider the Salonica expedition, by which time of course it was six months too late.

Initially planned as a means of persuading the wavering neutrals to join the Allies, now they could only achieve success at the Dardanelles if the neutrals joined in the attack. But most of the potential allies awaited a success before they would join. To the Great Powers, fully convinced of the nobility of their own motives for fighting, this seemed a sordid preoccupation with material gain rather than sheer common sense, but the effect upon Allied diplomacy was obvious enough. As Grey later reflected:

in war words count only so far as they are backed by force and victories. Up to the end of 1916...Allied diplomacy had little enough of this backing.[14]

If the necessity to wait upon military success was the major stumbling block, the next critical factor was that British diplomacy was but part of a greater whole. The treaty of 4 September 1914 bound the three allied powers to continue the war together until a satisfactory peace could be obtained. This had the effect that negotiations with anyone else had to be conducted on a tripartite basis, since Grey at least took the view that the all important thing was to avoid 'the fatal danger of falling apart'.[15] Nor was this an idle consideration. After the enormous Russian losses by the first winter of the war and the basic internal divisions, Britain and France had to concentrate on keeping those favourable to them in power in Petrograd. Sazonov undoubtedly exploited this in the Spring of 1915 and it is quite evident that it had a powerful effect in the negotiations which led to Constantinople being decreed a Russian inheritance, completely contrary to British and French interests. The vital point of this, as of most of the secret treaties of 1915 which afterwards came in for such heavy criticism, was quite simply, as Grey explained, that 'they were, in fact, done solely because they were essential to prevent Allied disruption'.[16]

If these two points – military events and keeping the Allies together – were the primary influences upon British foreign policy in the first two years of the war, there was yet a third. Inevitably some thought had to be given to what the Allies were fighting for. As far as Britain is concerned there is no evidence that the initial entry into the war was directed by any distant political objectives. Beyond the immediate considerations of assisting Belgium and France there were, it is true, the concept of the balance of power, the idea that if Russia were abandoned it would only lead to Germany hegemony and endless trouble for Anglo-Russian relations in the future. But these considerations were too nebulous to constitute a political objective. It was only with the entry of Turkey into the war and the prospect that this opened up of a division of the Ottoman Empire that the idea of British compensation for her war effort began to gain ground.

Inevitably this was sharpened by negotiation with the allies and potential allies in the course of 1915 as they too began to demand their pound of flesh. This seems to have come as something of a surprise to the British War Council who, initially, thought in terms of reserving all territorial settlements until the end of the war. First they must beat the Germans was Grey's somewhat naive view. It was only, for example, Russian insistence on a hard and fast agreement giving them Constantinople as their price for consent to the Dardanelles operations, that forced the Cabinet to think of what they themselves wanted in the Middle East.[17]

The discussion that emerged from this in March 1915 proved so far ranging that it produced for the first time a general review of what Britain wanted from the war. Even so it is evident that no real thought was given to this and the best they could do in the Constantinople Agreement was to reserve their own position. Grey was still afraid that if they began to bargain seriously about the post-war world before they had won the war the most probable result would be to split the allies and lose the war. Nevertheless, the hard fact remained that Russia, Italy and the Balkan states all had clear political objectives, often competing, and in this way the negotiations for the secret treaties of 1915 forced the Cabinet to formulate their own too.

Oddly enough the Dardanelles expedition had a more favourable effect upon Italy than upon the Balkan states. From August 1914 until March 1915, successive Italian foreign ministers had played a waiting game. This had a variety of origins: military unpreparedness, the difficulties of fighting a winter campaign, fear that war would bring social unrest, but most of all political indecision. As the weakest of the great powers it was essential for Italy that she should join the winning side. Moreover, her interests were by no means clear cut. If, on the one hand, she feared Austro-German preponderance in Europe as the death knell of her irredentist aspirations in the Trentino and the Adriatic, on the other she was equally apprehensive of a Slav colossus in the Balkans directed by a vastly expanded Russia. This apart from fear of France. In fact what Di San Giuliano had hoped for in August 1914 had been a combination of British neutrality, German defeat of France and Russian defeat of Austria-Hungary.[18]

Consequently, although Di San Giuliano sent London a list of Italy's terms for joining the Entente as early as 12 August 1914, this did not mean much: two days earlier he had suggested rejoining the Triple Alliance after the war. Grey in any case rejected what he termed 'hypothetical' negotiations, first Italy must decide, then they could discuss terms: a view he repeated at intervals until late February 1915. In fact from October onwards, as the clash between Italian aspirations in Dalmatia and Russian claims to protect Slav interests became more obvious, there was a marked cooling off within the Foreign Office. Nicolson, for one, was afraid lest 'we will have a southern Slav question with Italy in place of Austria'.[19]

In these circumstances Salandra's decision on 30 September to wait until the Spring before reaching a decision meant that there could be no further meaningful negotiations with London. Nor was this solely Grey's distrust of Di San Giuliano: Sidney Sonnino, who went to the *Consulta* on 7 November, found Grey equally adamant.[20] It would be wrong therefore to assume that it was Sonnino's desire to negotiate with both sides that delayed the conclusion of what became the Treaty of London. At no stage until the last minute *volte face* by Burian on 6 May did Sonnino believe anything worthwhile would emerge from the long-drawn-out haggle with Vienna, a view shared by the pro-Austrian ambassador, Avarna. It was simply that with Grey unwilling to discuss terms in advance of an Italian commitment, Sonnino might as well – if only for internal purposes – spend the winter in probing Austrian intentions.[21]

In these circumstances the opening bombardments at the Dardanelles had an electrifying effect. On 26 February Sonnino urged upon Salandra that they should open negotiations at London, a proposal which the premier accepted on 3 March, obviously influenced by the rumour that Greece was about to join the Entente.[22] If there were a Balkan landslide the last man in would obtain least, a pre-occupation which probably explains Sonnino's deliberate failure to inform Roumania of his intentions until the last minute.[23]

Even in February 1915 there was a lack of any feeling of urgency on the part of the Entente in their negotiations with Rome. Sazonov was distinctly hostile. He told Buchanan that in the Russian view Italian naval and military co-operation 'had lost much of its value', that if approaches were made they should 'evade giving a definite answer': certainly there was to be no question of taking the initiative. Grey agreed and he told the War Council on 1 March that he was prepared to sit back and wait for Sonnino.

As Foreign Office prophecies appeared to come true in the first days of March when both Greece and Bulgaria showed clear signs of joining the Entente, correspondingly Sonnino could afford to wait no longer lest the Italian currency should depreciate too far. On 4 March Imperiali, on instructions, told Grey of the Italian intention to intervene and read him her 16 conditions, reiterating in scarcely veiled terms their insistence on insuring against too great Slav success.[24]

Grey, although observing that some of the terms seemed excessive from the general point of view, had no objection to them as far as British interests were concerned. Now that Sonnino had abandoned his hypothetical stance there was everything to be gained from bringing in Italy, especially as the earlier expectations of Greek co-operation in a march on Constantinople faded in the face of Russian obstinacy. Italian adhesion might turn the scale after all in deciding the Balkan waverers, especially as there was reason to believe that Italy and Roumania had an understanding of sorts. As he told Delcassé and Sazonov at this juncture, their common object was to finish the war as quickly as possible on satisfactory terms:

The participation on our side of Italy and the Balkan States would enormously facilitate this object; it probably would, in a comparatively short time, effect the collapse of German and Austro-Hungarian resistance.[25]

The argument that now developed with Sazonov over Italian participation finally settled the fate of Constantinople, as conceding it to Russia was the major lever in removing Sazonov's suspicions and objections to Greek and Italian participation. The recognition of Russian claims in the *aide-mémoire* of 12 March had some effect.

With Delcassé supporting Grey,[26] Sazonov began to come round. Though still insistent that neither Italy nor Greece should take part in any operations in the Straits, he was not opposed, he claimed, to their joining in the war and he was prepared 'to accept any arrangement on which France and Great

Britain were agreed that would secure this'. But what Sazonov gave with one hand he took away with the other. On the argument that her intervention was not worth as much as in August 1914, he added that 'he would not consent to Italy taking any of the Dalmatian coast south of Spalato (Split)'.[27]

The ban on Italian action at the Straits presented no problem as this had never been envisaged in London: Italian intervention was valued chiefly for the effect it would have upon the Balkan States. It was the Greek aspect that was more worrying in this context.[28] Nor did the bulk of the Italian claim, for the Trentino, Trieste and Istria as far as Volosca present any problems. Supilo and the Yugoslav Committee might protest at the handing over of this predominantly Slav population in Istria to Italian rule, but neither Pašić nor Sazonov were disturbed. Preoccupied only with a Greater Serbia, the fate of Croats and Slovenes was not worth prolonging the war for 'half a day', in Sazonov's happy phrase.[29]

But what did give rise to concern and occasioned all the difficulties in the negotiations over the next six weeks was the contrast between Sazonov's attitude and the Italian demand for the whole of Dalmatia down to the Narenta, together with the offshore islands and the Sabbioncello peninsula. This Sazonov had opposed since October 1914, an opposition which in the past had met with every sympathy in the Foreign Office: even in March 1915 the Cabinet 'agreed that these were very sweeping claims'.[30]

Why then did the British government now become ardent advocates of ceding Dalmatia to Italy? Certainly there were no illusions about self-determination. Sonnino never attempted to justify his case on these grounds and in conversation with Rodd on 20 March admitted as much. Italy's entire object was 'safety for future years'. Her whole Adriatic coast, Sonnino claimed, was 'the most vulnerable in the world'. Lacking a defensible port from Venice to Brindisi, the only way to guard against exchanging the incubus of Austria for that of Russia was to occupy as much of the opposite coastline as possible and to fortify the islands.

Italy would enter into the struggle in practical alliance with peoples who had certain rival interests, and therefore it was necessary to reassure her that she would not be fighting for a cause which might eventually prove to her disadvantage.[31]

It was not an enlarged Serbia that Sonnino feared but Russia, who, 'if she obtains control at Constantinople may become in future the leading naval power in the Mediterranean'.[32] If this was *sacro egoismo* it was also sound common sense. Sazonov's heavy heart at having 'to sacrifice...to the Italian alliance the interest of the Serbian people' was presumably not unconnected with the view of the Grand Duke Nicholas that 'Cattaro is very important as a harbour, where our Fleet may lie and on which it may be based'.[33]

Although there is no positive evidence, there are indications to suggest that Sonnino's line of argument had some appeal in London. During the War

Council discussions of 1 and 10 March at which the somewhat reluctant decision was taken to cede Constantinople and control of the Straits to Russia forthwith, there were dissentient voices. Balfour, an influential figure in view of his long-standing membership of the Committee of Imperial Defence, was 'not very anxious that Russia should be able to control the outlet from the Black Sea' and thought it 'injurious to our interests to allow Russia to occupy a position on the flank of our route to India'. Kitchener and the naval authorities, whilst raising no objection to Russian having Constantinople, were adamant that Britain should take Alexandretta as an equipoise, as 'it was essential we should retain command of the sea in the Mediterranean'.[34]

Similarly, Churchill and Haldane consoled themselves with the thought that once German naval power was shattered 'we ought to be able to build a Mediterranean fleet against France and Russia'. Fisher, unperturbed by diplomatic protests from Grey, thought the solution simple: all they had to do was to hang on to Lemnos as this would 'enable us to control the exit from the Black Sea'.[35] In other words the War Council though accepting the overriding necessity of the immediate cession of Constantinople, were far from reconciled to the emergence of Russia as a strong Mediterranean naval power. This would help to explain the ease with which the Cabinet accepted Italy's 'very strong strategic case' for Dalmatia:[36] if nothing else it kept it out of Russian hands.

But, if this feeling had some effect, the main reason for the ardent British advocacy of Italian claims at Petrograd lay elsewhere. If one of the original major objects of the Dardanelles adventure had been to impress the waverers and bring in Italy and the Balkan states,[37] by mid-March this had become a vicious circle, which steadily got worse as the failure of the navy was followed by that of the army. Increasingly the only way to snatch victory from defeat was to obtain Balkan support, especially that of Greece and Bulgaria. Yet this was blocked by Russia, just when Greece had shown favourable signs of responding. This was doubly exasperating when, as Grey pointed out, the 'direct fruits of these operations will, if the war is successful, be gathered entirely by Russia'.[38]

Hence two moves. First, ceding Constantinople to Russia to remove Russian suspicion so that 'Russia should not now raise objection to the co-operation of any Power which offers its help as an ally on reasonable conditions'. Second, insistence on accepting Italian terms on the grounds that her intervention 'will be the turning point in the war'.[39] Italian action would decide that of Roumania and jointly this would tip the scale in the Balkans, enabling the Allies to take Gallipoli and Constantinople. No wonder that the Cabinet decided that the 'importance of bringing in Italy without delay appeared to be so great that it was agreed to give general consent to what she asks and to press on Russia to do the same'.[40]

Grey himself initially, had shown signs of mild opposition to Sonnino's sweeping demands in Dalmatia on the grounds that 'we did not want to dishearten Serbia',[41] but this faded rapidly after the disastrous news from the Dardanelles on 19 March. Now appeals from Supilo, then in Petrograd, to the 'protection of England for [the] principle of nationality' found a strange lack of response in Liberal hearts. As Clerk minuted vigorously with an unusual dose of Realpolitik, 'the answer, if one ever has to be given, is that we cannot strain the principle of nationality to the point of risking success in war'.[42] Once the Cabinet endorsed this view on 24 March, Grey simply turned Sonnino's 16 points into a draft agreement and sent it to Petrograd.[43]

Sazonov, of course, did not share the British government's eagerness to buy Italian intervention with concessions at Slav expense but, in the long run, he dared not prejudice his chance of Constantinople. Fortified by the Russian capture of Przemysl on 22 March, he began by putting up a fight, adopting the line that an agreement 'is no less important for Italy than it is for us'. The utmost he would concede to Italy, he told Grey on 25 March, was the coast from Zara [Zadar] to Cape Planka: any idea of neutralising the Montenegrin coast he rejected utterly.[44]

Though it took another month to achieve it, the essence of the final agreement was put forward by Grey the same day. The principle he thought essential, was that the Slavs should have 'full commercial access to the Adriatic ...National unity and commercial liberty and opportunity was what I would claim for them.'[45]

For this reason he suggested that Sonnino should abandon his claim to Spalato [Split], since, although the original Italian proposal left Ragusa [Dubrovnik] to the Slavs, this, lacking any means of inland communication, could not function as a commercial outlet. Italian strategic interests, he thought, could be covered by taking the offshore islands and imposing the neutralisation of the Slav coastline. 'That', he told Imperiali, 'would be a solution that I could really press against Russian objections.'[46]

Basically Sonnino accepted Grey's proposal of 25 March. On 29 March Imperiali announced that Italy would leave to Serbia the coast from Cape Planka to the Voyusa, including Spalato and the five neighbouring islands, provided that all this was neutralised and that Italy obtained all the other islands and the peninsula of Sabbioncello.[47]

But what Grey thought of as a compromise Sazonov rejected as pure concession to Italy. The utmost he would concede by 31 March was that the entire coast from Zara to the Narenta, Sabbioncello and Cattaro should be neutralised, together with the islands, of which Italy could have four. The rest of the islands and Sabbioncello should go to Serbia, with no obligation to neutralise them or the coast south of the Narenta apart from the exceptions above. This, he insisted, was as far as he would go and he began to complain of the 'downright pressure from Grey' to which he was being subjected, not at all what he had expected when consenting that the negotiations should be conducted in London.[48]

Although equally bitter at Sazonov's insistence that they should prolong the

war 'solely in order to secure Serbia another limited coastal strip',[49] Grey was
sufficiently impressed to translate the latest Russian terms into an Allied *aide-
mémoire* on 1 April and present them to Imperiali as 'the utmost that they can
concede'. Simultaneously Rodd was instructed to work on Sonnino along the
lines that Italian prospective gains in the Trentino, Istria and northern
Dalmatia were so enormous that by comparison minor issues like the Curzolari
islands dwindled into insignificance. Wistfully, Grey added, the full Italian
terms would 'not only involve a sacrifice of that principle of nationality...
but would permanently disturb the relations between Italy and her new
neighbours'.[50]

Sonnino's reply was brutally realistic, worthy of Bismarck. If these were the
final Allied terms, 'he would have to advise that the negotiations should close'.
The Italian objective 'in taking the hazard of war would be to make the
Adriatic her naval base'. Italian naval experts insisted on the Curzolari group
as the key to this sea, without which Italy could not hope to contain the
expansion of Russian naval power after the war. Reckoning on Slav hostility
as a certainty whatever happened, Sonnino saw no point in assisting their
expansion to the sea whilst Italian naval bases remained confined to the north
'and [the] majority of [the] Italian coast would have no additional guarantee
of security than at present'.[51]

In Rodd's judgement this really was Sonnino's final word[52] and, since he
was the 'dominant personality', Salandra was unlikely to think otherwise. The
point was that the Italian Government 'must be able to show that the sacrifice
is worth its while' if they were to overcome basic inertia and neutralism.
Though sympathetic to Dalmatian feeling, Rodd considered that 'we must look
to our own interests first. It is not as if...we were considering ideal
arrangements...this is a case of Reipublicae salus suprema lex'. He had no
doubt that if Italian terms were not fully met they would not get her support,
'which at the present moment would be invaluable, and on which probably
depends the decision of Roumania and perhaps of the other Balkan states'.[53]

Even before this information came through, Grey and Asquith had been
active at Petrograd. Parallel with his action at Rome, Grey, as a parting shot
before going off to Howick to rest his failing sight, sent Sazonov an *aide-
mémoire* expressing his bitter disappointment with the latter's obstructive
tactics over Dalmatia, 'which will have highly unfortunate consequences for
us'.[54] Consequently, informed of the gist of Sonnino's 'final view' on 1 April,
Sazonov made a concession: the Italian share of the Dalmatian coastline need
not be neutralised, nor her four islands as long as nothing was said publicly
about this.[55]

The next breach in the Russian dyke was made by Delcassé. Since 4 March
he had left the negotiations to Grey and Sazonov, prepared to accept anything
they could agree upon. But faced with deadlock he intervened, since, he told
Bertie, 'he would be ready to pay almost any price for Italian co-operation
as he thinks it would bring to us Roumania and Greece and Bulgaria'. Nor

had he any fear of Italian expansion in the Adriatic: 'he does not believe the Italians to be as they themselves think the modern ancient Romans'.[56] Hence, to solve the deadlock, he proposed an exchange of the outstanding issues: Italy should let Serbia have a neutralised Sabbioncello; Sazonov should concede Italy the Curzolari group free of restrictions.[57]

Delcassé's initiative fortunately coincided with a change in Russian interests. The diplomatic tug of war between London and Petrograd since 4 March had been conducted on the premise that whereas Grey actively needed Italian aid for its effects in the Balkans, Sazonov not only doubted its military value[58] but feared its consequences. With the Carpathian offensive going well he did not want Italy or Roumania in the war with the embarrassments that this entailed in Dalmatia, the Banat and the Bukovina. But as the offensive ground to its inevitable halt on 6 April, Grand Duke Nicholas informed Sazonov that Italian intervention 'would be of particular importance': the Tsar now authorised his minister to cede even Sabbioncello if necessary.[59]

Now that Russia needed Italy and Roumania the negotiations speeded up overnight. On 7 April Sazonov accepted Delcassé's compromise and, more significantly, 'in order not to delay negotiations by a detailed discussion of questions which are, after all, secondary', he referred the whole question of neutralisation to Asquith, agreeing to accept whatever he decided. Nothing gave a better indication of Sazonov's new-found urgency than this and his insistence that for the agreement to be valid Italy must enter the war by the end of April.[60]

Given this free hand two days later Asquith produced the settlement which had eluded Grey. It contained four points and was a model of ingenuity. (1) Italy was to have the coast from Zara to Cape Planka, with no restrictions. (2) Serbia was to receive from Cape Planka to Cattaro, including Sabbioncello, neutralised except as under (4) below. (3) The Curzolari group and Sazonov's original four islands were to go to Italy without restriction. (4) The coast from Sabbioncello to Castelnuovo was to be unrestricted.[61]

This contained something for everyone and was difficult to fault for this reason. With the minor alteration that 'a point 10 miles south of Ragusa' was substituted for Castelnuovo in (4), on Sonnino's insistence that the latter was too near the dreaded Bocche di Cattaro for comfort,[62] this was accepted in Rome on 14 April. That it took another twelve days to sign what became the Treaty of London was due to a new difficulty introduced by Sonnino, his insistence on a month's delay between signature and the Italian declaration of war.

Sazonov protested vehemently at this since his willingness to make concessions had been based on his desperate necessity. Now his earlier delaying tactics recoiled upon his own head and, since Sonnino could not be budged, Sazonov finally gave in on 20 April. In view of the difficulties Sonnino and Salandra experienced in actually manoeuvring the Italian parliament into war their caution was fully explicable: at the moment of signature, on 26 April, the majority of the Chamber of Deputies were still strongly opposed to intervention.[63]

In fact therefore by the time Italy declared war on 26 May the Allies had lost the initiative. The Russian armies had abandoned Lemberg (Lvov) and were streaming eastwards; the landings at Gallipoli, whilst not a complete disaster, had achieved none of the high promise of February. It was difficult in these circumstances to persuade the Balkan states that the addition of Italy was going to be the vital factor in the defeat of the Central Powers: in the summer of 1915 it was, as Grey discovered, considered not safe to join the Allies. The major difficulty was quite simple: 'The attraction of a promise is not its size, but the prospect of its being fulfilled.'[64]

25

Russia, Constantinople and the Straits, 1914–1915

MICHAEL G. EKSTEIN

The agreement of March 1915 whereby Great Britain and France agreed that Russia would receive control of the Straits and Constantinople at the end of the war has been variously interpreted. For the radical left at the time it was another example of the cynicism of secret diplomacy. When news of the arrangement seeped out, E. D. Morel, the Secretary to the Union of Democratic Control, wrote bitterly that the Allies were fighting to crush Germany and 'to make Russia mistress of the N[ear] E[ast], to give her Constantinople, and to extend her territory in Europe. That is what our sons are being conscripted for.'[1]

Grey maintained that his hand had been forced by Russian demands and the need to hold together the Entente, and for a long time this view was to represent the weight of historical orthodoxy.[2] Recently, however, some scholars have been arguing that Britain's role was more complicated: Grey tried to divert Russian ambitions towards Turkey, either as a means of preserving a European equilibrium after the war by substituting aspirations there for war aims in Central and Eastern Europe, or out of a mixture of motives – securing Russian co-operation in the conduct of the war, safeguarding British interests in Persia, finding Russia compensation elsewhere once it became clear that she was unlikely to get anything in Europe.[3] It is perhaps best not to try to resolve these differences of opinion, but rather to begin by setting the particular issue within the general framework of the conduct of foreign policy at the beginning of the First World War.

The crisis of July 1914 unfolded with bewildering speed. For Grey in particular the week and a half after the Austrian ultimatum was a shattering experience, a nightmare of decision and moral burden that marked him deeply. In the winter his friend and Under-Secretary Arthur Acland observed that 'the war had changed him, but that was only to be expected'.[4] Not only Grey was left dazed by the scale and pace of events. As level-headed a colleague as Crewe wrote on 6 August:

The development of events has been so amazingly rapid that we all feel as though we were living through a novel by Wells, and in no real world.[5]

There had been little time to reflect on what war would mean to the conduct of foreign policy, nor was there, as there was a quarter of a century later, a comparable struggle to look back to for enlightenment. In as much as Grey imagined anything, he saw Britain's position being like that she had enjoyed during the Napoleonic Wars. As he told the Commons on 3 August:

For us, with a powerful fleet, which we believe able to protect our commerce, to protect our shores, and to protect our interests, if we engaged in war, we shall suffer little more than we shall suffer even if we stand aside.[6]

But it was soon evident that a methodical conduct of war in the terms that Grey was thinking of would be impossible. British foreign policy had somehow to dovetail complex, far-flung interests with the overriding need to defeat the enemy and the inevitable crises of the struggle. War brought with it no agreement between the Entente Powers as to how it was to be conducted, no moratorium in their rivalries or common view of the shape of the post-war settlement. How to reconcile the egocentric pre-war structure of national interests with the insatiable demands of victory and allied unity? This was the central problem that the war posed British foreign policy. Grey personified the dilemma. As a Foreign Secretary of Whig background and temperament who believed in weighing pressures, balancing issues, and trying to maintain orderly procedures of international behaviour and change, the subordination of every objective to achieve one end did not to him come easily. As a Liberal, the suspension of judgement on a whole range of moral equations because of the ultimate good of a single objective was painful to the point of being grotesque. As an individual, he instinctively held back from the implications of the daemonic momentum of war: his only memorable phrase – 'The lamps are going out' – encapsulated his horror. Yet the gulf between Grey's conception of foreign policy and the demands that war was to make did not appear at once, and in the early months of the conflict he strove to find some path that would allow him to preserve pre-war objectives in their complexity.

It was symptomatic of the Foreign Secretary's attitude and nervous temperament that at the outset he hoped to organise events so that the war would be fought in a way and at a pace that would suit Great Britain's narrow national self-interest. He came out against sending the army to France in case British preoccupations with events on the Continent were to be the occasion for disorder in Egypt or in India.[7] So that Russia would not be drawn by further Balkan complications to divert forces from her German front, he backed (on 10 August) Venizelos's scheme for a reconstitution of the Balkan League that would bring all the Balkan States in on the side of the Entente Powers.[8] He, the India Office, the Government of India and Kitchener wanted to keep Turkey out of the war in case conflict with the Porte provoke unrest amongst the Muslim subjects of the Empire.[9] Inside the Foreign Office there were officials who criticised this attempt to put the Near and Middle East into cold storage as impractical and lacking energy.[10] In truth, Grey's policy ran into difficulties from the very beginning.

The final crisis had, after all, grown out of a dispute in the Balkans. Several British Cabinet Ministers, including Morley, Simon and Lloyd George, felt that the real cause of the conflagration there lay not in Vienna or Berlin but at St Petersburg. Russian intrigues in the Balkans and her rocketing level of armaments expenditure had driven the Central Powers to pre-empt inevitable catastrophe. On 16 July Grey himself had privately explained that:

She [Germany] is now really frightened of the growing strength of the Russian army and may...bring on a conflict with Russia at any early date before increases in the Russian army have their full effect and the completion of Russian strategic railways.[11]

Behind particular complaints lay pervasive distrust of Russian methods, Tsarist autocracy and imperialism. Even in the Foreign Office, for the most part free of Liberal squeamishness about the Anglo-Russian entente, there were continual complaints. In February 1914 Bertie found the Foreign Secretary:

very much preoccupied at the internal situation in Russia and the vacillating policy of the Russian Government in foreign affairs, the result of contending factions at court and the weariness of the Emperor and want of concord in the Russian Cabinet.[12]

Recrimination was for some a matter of moral outrage, for others an expression of the political disagreements that were bedevilling the Anglo-Russian understanding. Russia's forward policy in Persia had brought her into direct conflict with British interests there, while her Balkan quarrels threatened dangerous European complications from which Great Britain had nothing to gain. Political and ideological differences had been at the root of the Liberal Government's refusal to turn the entente into an alliance. During the Liman von Sanders crisis, Grey had tried to avoid involvement in the Russo-German struggle at Constantinople. When, the following spring, the Cabinet reluctantly agreed to Anglo-Russian naval talks, the Mediterranean was excluded as an area of co-operation until the situation at the Porte had resolved itself. As it turned out, the war came before any naval arrangements were concluded, so in August 1914 there was not even a structure of military co-ordination to set against the residue of mistrust.

Problems with Russia in the Near and Middle East did not end with the outbreak of war, they just became more secret. While Great Britain was declaring war on Germany, Sazonov, the Russian Minister for Foreign Affairs, without any prior consultation with his 'allies', began negotiation at Bucharest with a view to bringing Roumania into the war.[13] At the same time St Petersburg sent out alarums about the situation in Turkey – now, that the Porte was the creature of the German embassy and would shortly declare war on the side of the Central Powers; now, that the Austrian fleet, possibly aided by German and Turkish vessels, would attack Russia in the Black Sea; now, that the Entente Powers deliver a joint warning at Constantinople that an act of war against one would be considered as an act of war against all.[14] On 14 August Sazonov dismissed the Balkan League scheme as a 'chimera', and asked what Great Britain would do were Serbia attacked by Bulgaria and/or Turkey, and Greece came to her aid.[15] Meanwhile news was coming in that Russian troops were being sent south to her Turkish frontier.[16]

A Russo-Turkish war seemed imminent. George Russell Clerk, the Foreign Office's Near Eastern expert, minuted on 14 August that:

M. Sazanov's view as here reported, and what we are told of Russia's attitude towards Turkey shows a dangerous tendency.[17]

The previous evening Nicolson had told Benckendorff, the Russian Ambassador, that Russia should not try to extend the war to Turkey for 'it would be unfortunate if efforts to this end (defeating Germany) were diverted to side issues'. Grey warmly approved of his Permanent Under-Secretary's language, and Russian assurances that troops were not being held back from the German front did little to allay his fears.[18] On 15 August he himself saw the Russian Ambassador. Great Britain, he explained, did not want 'to fasten any quarrel on Turkey during the present war as long as she remained neutral'. The war would be decided in the forthcoming battles in the North-West of Europe, and all allied efforts should be directed towards winning them. It would moreover, he went on to argue, 'be very embarrassing for us, both in India and Egypt, if Turkey came out against us'.[19]

The Foreign Secretary was prepared to barter promises about the settlement in Asia Minor for Russian goodwill. On 13 August the Russians were assured that should Turkey attack any successes would be 'wiped out in [the] terms of peace'.[20] Two days later he told Benckendorff:

If Turkey sided with Germany and Austria, and they were defeated, then we could not answer for what might be taken from Turkey in Asia minor.[21]

On 16 August the warning that Great Britain would not try to maintain Turkish integrity were she to throw in her lot with Germany and Austria was repeated to Constantinople:

You [Mallet, the Ambassador] should make it quite clear that neutrality does mean security for Turkey, but that if Turkey sides against us there are no limits to the loss that she may incur.[22]

These statements may not have amounted to a clear promise to deliver Constantinople and the Straits to Russia in the event of a Russo-Turkish war, but they went a long way towards it. Sazonov was later to say that he had believed that even before Turkey entered the war Russian aspirations had been agreed to by Great Britain.[23]

When Russia formally demanded Constantinople and the Straits in March 1915 Grey told the War Council that if refused:

Russia might claim that the sacrifices she had made in East...in the early days of the war had saved the Allies from defeat.[24]

The promises of August 1914 were more a matter of continuing pre-war trends in foreign policy and strategic doctrine than a dramatic reversal of tradition. During the nineteenth century the belief had indeed grown up that it was an axiom of British foreign policy to protect the routes to India by excluding Russia from the Mediterranean, by upholding the integrity of the Ottoman Empire and by closing the Straits to Russian warships. By the 1890s, however, the doctrine was far from sacrosanct. On the one hand acquisition of Cyprus and Egypt had strengthened Great Britain's own military position in the Eastern Mediterranean; on the other, it was increasingly clear to Salisbury and his military and naval advisers that Great Britain could not in fact defend Constantinople against Russian attack even if she wanted to.[25] In 1903, a sub-committee of the Committee of Imperial Defence unanimously decided that Russian possession of Constantinople would not 'fundamentally alter the present strategic situation in the Mediterranean' and 'maintenance of the *status quo* as regards Constantinople is not one of the primary interest of this country'.[26] These were findings with which the War Office and the Admiralty agreed.[27] So too did the succeeding Liberal Government. During the Bosnian crisis of 1908 Asquith wrote to Balfour:

I attach very little strategic value – so far as I am concerned – to the maintenance of existing restrictions (with regard to the Straits) and this is the opinion of our military and naval advisers.[28]

The conclusion of the Anglo-Russian entente brought a new political flexibility towards Russian claims for secure outlet to the Mediterranean. From the outset Grey considered that a relaxation of existing restrictions was a price worth paying for an improvement in Anglo-Russian relations.[29] During the Bosnian crisis the Cabinet agreed in principle to Isvolsky's demand for an opening of the Straits as compensation for the Austrian annexation of Bosnia. It baulked at immediate implementation, however, for fear of public opinion at home.[30] Yet the pledge to review the matter in a sympathetic spirit at a later date was neither empty nor forgotten. In December 1914 Grey was to say that 'we must carry out our promises of 1908'.[31] The undertaking given in August 1914 was not then a capitulation of traditional interests at a moment of acute crisis. In fact, rather the reverse: it was an attempt by Grey to uphold Britain's position in the Middle East, to secure the British line on Entente policy with regard to war in the Balkans, while still meeting the emergency of the hour.

The respite was short-lived. Early September saw skirmishing between Russian and Turkish detachments near Azerbaijan in Northern Persia.[32] Larger clashes followed and, against the background of ever shriller demands from Tehran that foreign troops leave her soil, a build-up of troops on both sides.[33] By mid-October the stage was set for a full-scale Russo-Turkish war in Persia. On 30 October a Turkish flotilla, which had left Constantinople under the cover of night, bombarded Russian Black Sea ports.

The development of events could hardly have been less welcome. To the

considerations which had caused such anxiety in mid-August – the diversion
of the Russian war effort from her European fronts, the offence that would
be given to Muslim opinion in Egypt and India – was added a still more
pressing concern, the independence of Persia and the security of Great
Britain's position there. All at once pre-war wounds about Russian expansion
in Persia were torn open. It has been suggested that Grey's purpose in making
further promises to Russia in November was to buy Russia out of Eastern and
Central Europe in order to maintain a 'balance of power' after the war.[34] But
there is no evidence that he opposed Russian war aims in Central and Eastern
Europe and it is plain from the Foreign Office's Persian files that the concern
for Persia was the mainspring of Grey's diplomacy. Moreover, although the
Foreign Office continued to use arguments about public opinion in England
and Muslim opinion in Egypt and India when asking Russia to keep her hands
off Persia, this was a tactful disguise for its own fears of Russian expansion.
As Clerk minuted, 'we should use the argument of opinion here and in India
as sparingly as possible, it makes the Russians suspicious, and if we always
bring it out it loses weight'.[35] But Grey did often use it.

Earnestly impress upon [the] M[inister] [for] F[oreign] A[ffairs] that the
inevitable war with Turkey may be a strain on Mohammedan opinion in India
and Egypt. It is therefore essential that the Russian Government should do
all in their power to ease [the] strain and help us conciliate Mussulman
opinion by being most friendly to Persia and avoid all harshness there...
M.F.A. should realise the necessity of impressing on all Russian personnel
in Persia that a conciliatory and friendly attitude there is essential. There may
be no limit to the embarrassment and weakening of our hands that may be
caused unless the war with Turkey is set off by [a] benevolent attitude in
Persia.[36]

Yet Russia gave no signs of drawing back. In London on 2 November
Benckendorff informed the Foreign Office that his Government was being
obliged to strengthen its forces in Persia.[37] On the same day in St Petersburg
Sazonov explained to Buchanan:

Turkey would almost certainly attack Russia on the flank through Azerbaijan,
and in protecting herself on that side she would also be protecting Persia from
aggression.

The ambassador was so alarmed by this statement that he replied that Russia
should not try to dismember Persia.[38] A warning Grey shortly afterwards
reiterated to Benckendorff.[39] On 12 November, having consulted with the
Secretary of State for War, the Foreign Secretary frankly told the Russians
that if they did carry the war into Persia, then Great Britain would defend
her own interests by strengthening her garrisons in the Middle East.[40]

The pleas and warnings flying between London and St Petersburg were,
as in August, accompanied by the assurance that if Russia fell in with British
wishes, her aspirations in Asia Minor would not be opposed. On 1 November
Grey promised the Russians that:

Turkey has shown herself incorrigible and impossible, and deserves and should receive no consideration...we give up all plea for consideration as far as Turkey is concerned.[41]

The following morning the Cabinet reviewed the Turkish question and the situation in Persia. In the Foreign Office and the Cabinet there had been serious doubts over the course of the previous three months about the policy of appeasing Turkey. Churchill had wanted to bring the Balkan States into the war with the offer of Turkish territory.[42] Lord Crewe representing the India Office was thinking that Mesopotamia might be annexed to the Empire.[43] Kitchener had his own schemes for a British land route from the Mediterranean to the Persian Gulf.[44] Negotiations with the Arabs were in hand to obtain their support in a conflict with their Ottoman masters. Beneath particular threads lay a pent-up fury with Turkey's diplomatic manoeuvring and the final treacherous attack on Russia. It was decided, as Asquith wrote in his letter to the King,

henceforward Great Britain must finally abandon the formula of 'Ottoman Integrity' whether in Europe or Asia.[45]

The way was now open for further concessions, and on 12 November, at the same time as the Russians were being informed that incursions into Persia would lead to a strengthening of British garrisons in the Middle East, Grey made a further appeal. Any movement of Allied forces away from the main European fronts would be unfortunate and

I shall like the M.F.A. to know that however much we may assume a defensive attitude in the war with Turkey...we regard the conduct of the Turkish Government as having made a complete settlement of the Turkish question including that of the Straits and Constantinople in agreement with Russia inevitable. It will of course be effected after Germany is defeated and whether or not Turkish rule is overthrown in the course of present hostilities.[46]

On 13 November King George told Benckendorff that Russia must have Constantinople at the end of the war.[47]

The promises of November 1914, like those of August, amounted to an attempt on Grey's part to reconcile underlying British interests with the demands of fighting a war in global coalition. Others – Crowe at the Foreign Office and Churchill – who had accepted from the first a need to subordinate pre-war interests to the high aim of victory, would have lanced the Turkish boil earlier and let political complexities sort themselves out later. Grey's caution had led him along a more tortuous path. This conflict between the demands of war and the Foreign Secretary's inner desire not to let it run away with all pre-war norms or to embark on policies the coherence of which he could not understand took on more general form in the winter of 1914–15.

Grey was never very hopeful about the outcome of the war, and by December 1914 his vague apprehensions were crystallising into pessimism.[48] Kitchener and French left no doubt as to the difficulties there would be in pushing the

Germans out of France and Belgium.[49] Discouraged by the prospects on the
Western Front, Churchill and Lloyd George began to cast around for an
Eastern strategy to break the military deadlock.[50] Hankey, the influential and
sober Secretary to the Committee of Imperial Defence, wrote to Grey that to
believe the German armies could be driven back to their own frontiers would
be to live in a 'fool's paradise'.[51] These assessments preyed on Grey's mind.
As early as 4 December he was writing:

We will, of course, make every effort to prevent the war from being a long
one and are training men and developing equipment as fast as we can. What
we fear is lest the war must be a long one in order to be conclusive and lest
France weary of the strain.[52]

Things were no better in the East, where the Russians, who had been
terribly mauled in their initial drive into East Prussia, were now thrown back
on the defensive.[53] While in the Balkans the Serbs, after initial successes, had
drawn perilously close to disaster.

In these gloomy circumstances what sort of peace settlement was possible?
No peace would have been acceptable to Great Britain which did not involve
the evacuation and compensation of Belgium and some military victory which
would discredit the Prussian military who, Grey believed, had launched the
war.[54] No peace would have been acceptable to France that did not at least
bring the restoration of the Lost Provinces. But what would happen in the
East if, as seemed likely, no outright defeat of the Central Powers was
possible? Grey began to think in terms of giving Russia Constantinople as the
totality of her compensation for her sacrifices in the war. At the end of
December 1914 there were rumours that Germany might be willing to make
peace. Chandler P. Anderson, a Secretary at the United States Embassy about
to return to Washington, was called to the Foreign Office and given a verbal
message with regard to the terms of peace the Entente Powers would want
– the evacuation and compensation of Belgium, the return of Alsace-Lorraine,
and Russian possession of Constantinople and the Straits.[55] In February 1915,
when Colonel House was in London discussing possible terms of peace with
Grey, he found the Foreign Secretary:

thought Russia might be satisfied with Constantinople and we [House and
Grey] discussed that in some detail.[56]

The Russians were not informed of the terms Grey had in mind. Grey's
reticence in this matter is not hard to explain. From conversations Buchanan
had with Sazonov in September and with the Tsar in November he knew that
Russia had grandiose ambitions in Central and Eastern Europe. Her
aspirations in Asia Minor, in contrast, were ill-defined. Sazonov had only:

alluded vaguely to the necessity of regulating the question of the Straits in a
manner satisfactory to Russia and Roumania.[57]

For his part, the Tsar had asked for no more than an internationalisation of Constantinople. It is possible that Grey believed Russia wanted more than she was asking for,[58] but whether this is so or not he plainly preferred her to expand at the expense of Turkey than try to continue the war to wrest territory from Germany and Austria. It is also clear that after December 1914 he was actively encouraging Russian territorial expansion in Asia Minor. In January 1915 it seemed that the Government of Enver Pasha would be overthrown by a pro-Entente faction. Grey, far from making any attempt to prepare the ground for a negotiated settlement with the new regime, instructed Buchanan:

there are rumours of trouble at Constantinople which may result in the overthrow of Enver and pro-German policy. This is much to be desired, but whatever changes take place there or whatever happens during the war all that I said to M.F.A. about Constantinople and the Straits holds good as far as we are concerned.[59]

Shortly before the Fleet began its bombardment of the Dardanelles' forts in February 1915, the Commander of the 1st Turkish Army Corps at Constantinople started negotiations with the British Goverment through Greek intermediaries. He offered to stage a *coup d'état* the moment the bombardment began on condition that the Entente Powers recognised his regime and Turkey suffered 'no discrimination or penalty'.[60] Nicolson felt the offer should not be passed over because the liquidation of the Ottoman Empire would prove a 'strenuous task'.[61] Grey, however, informed the Russians:

I should not propose to negotiate any conditions which impair or qualify what I said to M.F.A. about the Straits and Constantinople after Turkey attacked Russia in October.[62]

Grey's encouragement of Russian aims in Turkey at a time when he was studiously avoiding saying anything about her claims in Central and Eastern Europe raises questions about a political motivation for the Dardanelles operation. There is no doubt that the main impulse was strategic; even the desire for a military victory to bring the Balkan states into the war was a decision of grand strategy rather than Near Eastern policy. Yet it does seem probable that the Foreign Secretary's plan for the shape of the peace settlement was a subsidiary motivation for the attack on the Straits. The evidence is fragmentary. It was not a subtlety that the politicians of the time would have referred to in their memoirs – nor did they. On the other hand all those at the top concerned with planning the operation in January and February knew that Russia was to receive Constantinople and the Straits.[63] What is more, there is in the report of the Dardanelles Commission, the official wartime inquiry into the debacle, a revealing section: the operation, if successful, 'would have gone far to settle a question which has been a constant source of trouble for centuries past.'[64]

It would be pleasant to conclude from this that Grey was far-sighted, that had the military operations been better executed or even blessed with good

fortune he would have secured a reasonable settlement. But this would be to
trivialise the issues. If he did hope for a settlement, to talk of it was so fraught
with danger for allied unity that the Foreign Secretary never even reached
the point where he dared explain to the Russians what was on his mind. Even
if he had, even if the Dardanelles campaign had gone well, even if the war
on the Western Front had gone well, what chance was there that the
Governments at Berlin, Belgrade, Vienna and St Petersburg, driven by demands for security no less urgent than those of the Western Powers and facing
public opinion no less nationalist, would had been able to accept the *status quo
ante bellum* settlement Grey envisaged? Nor had Great Britain the power to
enforce Grey's ideas. He had, as he had intended, retained a coherent view
of events and a plan for the future, and it was to his moral credit that he should
have done so. But he had kept both at the expense of realism. Nothing
illustrates this quite so forcefully as what actually happened in March 1915.

In January and February 1915 opinion in the Duma had begun to run
strongly in favour of Russian acquisition of Constantinople and the Straits,
and in a speech on February 9 Sazonov made reference to solving the
problems of Russian access to the Mediterranean. The Foreign Minister's
statement was reported by *The Times* and a question was tabled in the
Commons about it.[65]

Grey thought it would be a good opportunity to prepare public opinion for
the changes he planned for the peace settlement in Asia Minor.[66] After
consulting with Benckendorff and Asquith,[67] he told the Commons:

This aspiration [he was referring to Sasonov's statement] is an aspiration with
which we are in entire sympathy. The precise form in which it will be realised
will no doubt be settled in the terms of peace.[68]

This statement was so misquoted in the Russian press as to give the impression that Grey opposed Russian ambitions. At the same time the Fleet began
its bombardment of the Dardanelles fortifications. All the old Russian fears
about traditional British policy with regard to blocking her access to the
Mediterranean welled up. The Foreign Secretary was asked to give a further
public statement indicating positive sympathy and support for Russian
claims.[69] Public opinion at home, however, was not yet ready to accept a
complete reversal of what many still saw as a vital national interest. As
Nicolson minuted when he heard of the Russian demand:

we know very well Russia will have Constantinople...the Government will no
doubt decide whether public opinion in this country is ripe for so categorical
a statement as M. Sazonov asks.[70]

Asquith thought it was not.[71] Grey hoped to ride out the storm by soothing
the Russians: Buchanan was instructed to reassure Sazonov,[72] while Grey
himself wrote to Benckendorff

I am more disappointed than I can express to hear from Sazanow that my
statement in the House of Commons about the Straits has been unfavourably

received in Russia. I wish I had said nothing at all. I have telegraphed to Buchanan to explain that I cannot be more Russian than the Russian Government in my public utterances. I have not told Buchanan that I had shown you the answer before I gave it, but I should be very pleased if you could telegraph something to Sazanow to explain how the answer came to be given and what I said to you about my desire to say in public what I said to Sazanov in private; and if you could explain this to the Emperor it would be very useful, for I hear he is upset.[73]

But the situation was already beyond Grey's control. On 2 March the Foreign Office was informed by the Russian embassy that Russia claimed access to the Mediterranean and a guarantee of the southern shore of the Sea of Marmara.[74] These demands were immediately circulated to the Cabinet and Bertie was instructed to ascertain the views of the French Government.[75] No sooner had these steps been taken, however, than St Petersburg was coming forward with a new set of proposals. On 4 March the Russians dropped their request for a public statement and asked instead for a secret agreement that the question of Constantinople and Straits would be settled in accordance with their traditional aspirations. Russia would receive Constantinople, the western shore of the Bosphorus, the Dardanelles, the Sea of Marmara, Southern Thrace as far as the Enos–Midia Line, and certain extensions of territory necessary for the protection of these areas. The British and French Governments could then in their own time and their own way educate their publics to the new realities. In return the special interests of Great Britain and France at Constantinople would be scrupulously respected, and their claims for expansion at the expense of Turkey-in-Asia would be sympathetically received.[76]

The permanent officials at the Foreign Office were in favour of accepting Russian demands while doing everything possible to secure Great Britain's financial and trading interests at Constantinople and free navigation of the Straits.[77] Their wish to comply was encouraged by the suspicion that the French were trying to manoeuvre them into a position where it would seem to the Russians that London was being difficult; in this way the Quai d'Orsay would obtain the withdrawal of Russian claims and shift the odium onto the British. In consequence there was no British attempt to work out a common policy with the French.[78]

If we had opposed Russia [wrote Grey later in the month] the French would have laid upon us at Petrograd the responsibility for opposition, as it is they lay upon us at Paris the responsibility for concession. The latter is preferable.[79]

On 9 March the matter went before the Cabinet. Kitchener, Churchill and Hankey raised no strategic objections, and Asquith noted: 'Russia's claim irresistible – no English or French interest against.' The larger part of discussion was taken up not with the question of whether to accept but with the Russian offer to consider favourably Britain's claims in Asiatic Turkey. As agreement was to constitute a binding pledge and ran counter to long-cherished ideas in the country at large, Asquith thought it wise to consult the leaders of the opposition.[80]

Bonar Law, Lansdowne and Balfour (who had a regular seat) were all present at the War Council on the following day. Grey led off the discussion, addressing the meeting in his usual straightforward, undramatic though nonetheless impressive way. He went over the negotiations since the beginning of the war, tripping rather lightly over the promises of August and November, and emphasised the dangers of Russia leaving the war unless some gesture was made to keep up her morale and interest in the struggle. The War Council agreed to Russian demands on certain conditions – Constantinople was to be a trade entrepot; free navigation of the Straits for all commercial vessels; Russia was to consider favourably British claims that might be formulated with regard to the Ottoman Empire; Russian aims were only to be realised after the war had been brought to a satisfactory conclusion.[81] By the time Grey had returned to the Foreign Office he had added counter demands of his own – Russia was to renegotiate the Anglo-Persian agreement and Great Britain was to have the neutral zone; Petrograd was to be more co-operative in negotiations to bring Bulgaria into the war – and these he incorporated in his telegraphic replies.[82]

British desiderata in Turkey-in-Asia were examined in the spring of 1915 by an inter-departmental committee under the chairmanship of Sir Maurice de Bunsen, the former ambassador at Vienna.[83] Renegotiation of the Anglo-Russian Asiatic agreements was debated at some length between the various departments concerned, but in the hectic pace of the war officials seem to have had insufficient time for a thorough investigation of the issue.[84] Indeed the whole question of British ambitions in the Middle East and Central Asia was in a constant state of flux throughout the war, changing with the course of military campaigns and the stresses of inter-allied diplomacy. In contrast, the more limited issue of safeguards for British rights at Constantinople was promptly considered and precisely defined. No stipulation was to be made as to the fortification of the Straits; there was to be free passage for shipping; free pilotage; no duties or dues on lights, dock wharfs and other facilities; Constantinople was to be a free port; only a small tariff on imports was to be levied in the area taken over by Russia.[85]

In conclusion it can be said that the archives do suggest a need to modify generally accepted interpretations of the Straits Agreement of March 1915. It did not mark a dramatic *volte face* in British policy with regard to the Straits and Constantinople, which, in fact, had been in the process of modification from the mid-1890s onwards. Nor was it forced on Great Britain by the Russians. In August and November 1914 Grey had used the promise of Constantinople and the Straits to obtain Russian co-operation. Thereafter he preferred Russia to expand at the expense of Turkey so that, on the one hand, she would have some prize to keep up her interest in the war, and, on the other, the Western Powers would not have to continue the struggle to realise Russian ambitions against Germany and Austria.

There is a second, no less important point, that emerges. In his Rhodes Lectures at Oxford in 1929 Elie Halévy said that modern wars are revolutions – their causes have roots deep in changes in national societies and, when they come, they have all the daemonic momentum of revolutions. The efforts of politicians like Grey to hold back events he dismissed – 'Pills to cure an earthquake'.[86] Grey, as his bouts of diffident detachment and dark forebodings indicate, intuitively understood this situation. But obviously, as the Foreign Minister of a satisfied Power, he wished to limit the damage that the dislocating effects of war would do to British interests. He tried to keep pre-war interests in good repair and prevent a too open-ended commitment to the war. The thread that runs through the negotiations over Constantinople was the one of caution. In August and November 1914 he sought to channel the war in directions that would not threaten British interests in the Middle East and keep Russian eyes focused on Europe. Later he hoped for a peace settlement in which Russia would have Constantinople as a way out of military deadlock and possibly endless war. That in the end Russia did not receive Constantinople and Grey's image of the peace settlement bore no resemblance to what emerged was not accident, but was a reflection of what in his heart Grey knew and what Halévy stated a decade and a half later – modern wars are revolutions and the direction in which they will lead events is unpredictable.

26

Asiatic Turkey, 1914–1916

MARIAN KENT

Strategy and politics were to remain paramount in the two years between the outbreak of war and the end of Grey's Foreign Secretaryship in 1916, and yet Britain's position and policy towards Constantinople and Asiatic Turkey was to change dramatically. By the end of Grey's term of office in the middle of the Great War, Turkey was an enemy belligerent. Most British commercial interests in Turkey were seized or unable to operate. The Straits were closed and Britain suffered humiliating defeat by the Turks in her effort to breach the Dardanelles defences. Imperial troops were attempting to defend British interests in Southern Persia and Mesopotamia, battling their way up the rivers from the Persian Gulf. All the carefully made 1913–14 agreements remained in abeyance never to be ratified since Turkey as an enemy had taken such unilateral action as she liked, including abrogating the capitulations. Britain was deeply involved in schemes to partition Asiatic Turkey and had promised to give Russia Constantinople and the Straits and to exclude Germany from any post war participation in her former interests in the area. And finally by 1916 we see the intrusion of the service departments and the War Council into foreign policy, for war policy is foreign policy.

For Britain and her interests in Asiatic Turkey, the war meant four things. First, British personnel and interests within the area must be protected, so far as possible. Second, communications must be kept open between the Mediterranean and the East, via the Suez Canal and the Red Sea, and a hostile presence must be kept from the Persian Gulf and its hinterland. Both of these meant that any effort by the Turks to stir up Moslem opinion against the British both in these areas and in India either by a Jihad or Holy War, or by some other means, must be averted or nullified. Finally, military operations in Mesopotamia came increasingly to be seen as desirable in the interests of the above three points and also as operations to divert Turkish troops, Arab opinion and save British face in contrast to the stalemate and disasters of the Western front and the Dardanelles.

The pattern of British war-time policy in this region during 1914–16 can be seen in both military and political aspects. On the one hand there was the military campaign in Mesopotamia. On the other hand were the political features. These included the promises made to the Arabs in return for an Arab uprising to support the British, embodied in the Hussein–McMahon correspondence. Simultaneously Britain was having to examine its own territorial desiderata in the area, in the light of the requirements of these promises and of her allies. Resulting from the definition of desiderata was the agreement of 1916 between Britain and France, adhered to by Russia, known as the Sykes–Picot agreement. What needs to be investigated, therefore, is the extent to which Grey as Foreign Secretary initiated, approved, directed, or perhaps only blindly followed suggested policy on all these matters.

Although after the outbreak of war with Germany, Turkey remained neutral yet the strength of the pro-German element in the Turkish cabinet, the increased presence of German officers in Constantinople and the series of aggressive acts by Turkey showed Britain that the neutrality was a mere façade while Turkish war preparations increased and that sooner or later Turkey was likely to enter the war on the German side. Grey's efforts to persuade Turkey to remain neutral for as long as possible have already been described.[1] These efforts demonstrate a degree of passivity by Grey and his colleagues comprehensible only in terms of letting sleeping dogs lie while Britain got on with the war elsewhere, and an initial hope that Turkey would surely not risk the break-up of her Empire by foolish intervention in the war on the 'wrong' side. Though this hope increasingly faded Grey still did little to avert what can be seen in retrospect as a virtually inevitable conflict with Turkey. This inactivity bears out the claim in his memoirs that: 'We did not know at the time that Turkey already had a secret treaty binding her to join Germany...'[2] although that claim, in view of the evidence to the contrary reaching the Foreign Office from very early in August, merely demonstrates an attitude of short-sightedness inexcusable in the circumstances.[3]

Grey had agreed at the end of July 1914 to Admiralty insistence that the two Turkish battleships (the Reshadieh and the Sultan Osman I) built in Britain and paid for by Turkish public subscriptions should be retained in Britain for the British war effort against Germany and Turkey be repaid their cost.[4] This action, if again understandable, was at the least provocative and humiliating for the Turks. The subsequent action of the two German warships, the Goeben and the Breslau in evading British naval pursuit, entering the Dardanelles, and undergoing the formality of transfer of ownership to Turkey all in less than a fortnight after Britain's seizure of the two Turkish ships was a further clear indication of the closeness of Turkish–German ties. Even more so was the start of mobilising the Turkish army on 11 August, the proclamation of martial law and the seizure of British property. Yet Grey still took only the strictly legalistically correct action of requiring satisfaction that first, the transfer of the ships was genuine and second, that the German officers and crews of the ships were returned to Germany, which, in fact, was never done.[5] In view of the non-likelihood at this stage of Russian support in any action against the Turks Grey continued to hope despite the mounting evidence to the contrary that Turkey might yet be persuaded to remain neutral. To this end, following the advice of Mallet in Constantinople, he refused Churchill's request that Admiral Limpus, head of the now virtually ousted British Naval Mission in Constantinople, should be allowed the command of the Eastern Mediterranean forces, as this would be seen by the Turks as a provocative step.[6] He quite agreed with Churchill that 'Turkey is behaving so disgracefully that she ought to be informed we shall not forget it after the war is over', though he added that she 'should be punished' but 'I could not say definitely how this is to be done'.[7] At the cabinet meeting on 23 September Grey's proposals prevailed and it was decided that Mallet should inform the Porte that 'while not contemplating for the moment hostile measures, we are grievously dissatisfied with the recent action of the Turkish Government, which has resulted in placing Constantinople under German and no longer under Turkish control. Unless the "peace party" soon succeeds in getting the upper hand we shall be compelled to adopt an attitude of hostility and to take measures accordingly'.[8] By the end of October, however, after further Turkish transgressions, including the mining of the Straits in September (thus cutting off supplies and egress to Russia), and the bombardment by the Goeben and the Breslau of the Russian Black Sea ports on 29 October, war with Turkey was clearly imminent and Grey could no longer believe in Turkish neutrality. This to him, was the unprecedented, 'wanton, gratuitous and unprovoked attack' which he used subsequently to provide the justification for abandoning the formula of 'Ottoman territorial integrity'.[9] Grey informed Turkey on 29 October that unless immediate reparation were made to Russia war was unavoidable and on 30 October he sent an ultimatum demanding within twelve hours the removal of all German personnel from the Goeben and Breslau and dismissal of the German Naval and Military Missions. If this failed, Mallet was instructed that he and the Embassy should ask for their passports and leave Constantinople.[10] Later that day he and the Russian and French Ambassadors did ask for their passports and next day, 31 October, Grey instructed Mallet to leave.[11] That day the British Consul at Basra and several British subjects had been arrested by the Turks and late that night the Foreign Office issued a Press announcement that 'the British Government must take whatever action is required to protect British interests, British territory, and also Egypt from attacks that have been made and are threatened'.[12] British naval actions followed, including the preliminary bombardment of the Dardanelles on 3 November. On 4 November the Turkish Ambassador in London called on Grey and asked for his passport. That day also the cabinet decided a formal declaration of war against Turkey could no longer be postponed and on 5 November war was declared on Turkey.[13] On 6 November the Expeditionary Force 'D' landed at the Turkish port of Fao at the head of the Persian Gulf,[14] having been decided on as early as 20 September, despatched from Bombay on 16 October and been waiting off Bahrein under sealed orders until ordered to proceed to the Shatt-el-Arab on the outbreak of war with Turkey.

At only the last minute therefore, had Grey come round to facing up to the inevitability of war with Turkey. But there was one area in which he approved attempts to make positive provision for such a war. This came in Indian efforts to shore up Britain's position in her areas of special interest, Mesopotamia, the Persian Gulf and Arabia, by strengthening Britain's ties with local chieftains already disaffected towards Turkish rule. On 18 August Grey had asked the Viceroy to consider, in view of possible conflict with Turkey, what political and other measures could be taken in the Persian Gulf areas to create a diversion and help secure British interests. The Viceroy replied that Britain had already received offers of loyal cooperation from the Sheikhs of Koweit and Mohammerah, and other Arab chiefs could also probably be relied on.[15] During August and September 1914 the Government of India prepared collective assurances to the Gulf Chiefs and individual assurances to the Sheikhs of Koweit, Mohammerah and, later, Qatar, and the Amir of Nejd, Ibn Saud, and the Idrisi. The individual assurances mostly built on already existing treaties and understandings, some of which dated back to the middle of the previous century.[16] Most of them were issued on 3 November 1914, timed to coincide with the outbreak of war.[17] Ibn Saud and the Sheikhs of Koweit and Mohammerah were promised, in return for cooperation with Britain in the capture of Basra, that Basra would never again be allowed to be subject to Turkish authority, and Britain promised to safeguard them, so far as she could, against any encroachment on their rights or any unprovoked attack by a foreign power. Koweit would be 'recognised as an independent principality under British protection' while the British would 'do our best to maintain Mohammerah in its present state of local autonomy'. The Sheikh of Qatar was not effectively independent, however, and would not, it was recognised, be able to evict the isolated and relatively innocuous Turkish garrison without British help. Consequently it was not until 3 November two years later that Britain signed a treaty with him, in which he undertook to have no relations or correspondence with any other power without British consent and in return obtained a British undertaking of naval protection against aggression by sea, and an intentionally vague assurance of British good offices in the event of unprovoked aggression by land.

It was also on 2–3 November 1914 that the Government of India issued proclamations containing general assurances for the Gulf Sheikhs. They were assured that Britain would do its utmost to preserve their liberty and religion. More specifically, Britain committed herself to preserving from British or Indian molestation the Moslem Holy Places of Mecca and Medina and those in Mesopotamia, and the port of Jeddah, provided that there was no serious interference with Indian pilgrims to those Holy Places. It was these assurances which fundamentally underlay the subsequent correspondence with the Sherif Hussein of Mecca.

War with Turkey, once embarked upon, was beyond the responsibility of a merely civilian Foreign Office. The Mesopotamian and Dardanelles campaigns were therefore largely a matter of Admiralty, War Office and India

Office concern, supervised or sanctioned by the War Cabinet. Grey had a voice, varying in significance at different times, in these joint councils, but once the tide was running there was little he could do to stem or control it – had he wanted to. As far as the Dardanelles expedition was concerned Grey supported the initial naval bombardment, expecting that its success would bring the collapse of Turkey, panic in Constantinople provoking a coup d'état and a new government favourable to the Entente. The Turks would be 'paralysed with fear' and a successful attack would 'settle the attitude of Bulgaria and the whole of the Balkans'. It would also provide both material and moral strength to Russia, already seen by Grey as an uncertain ally.[18] As far as Mesopotamia was concerned, Grey's involvement was deeper, although he had to direct his attention largely to the implications of the conduct of the war on Britain's present and future commitments in the region – in itself, as it turned out, a major aspect of affairs.

Although the Expeditionary Force which landed at the Persian Gulf port of Fao acquired in time strategic importance as the other claw of the pincer when the Dardanelles campaign was faring badly, it had initially largely political objectives. These objectives were embodied in telegrams, between London and India, drawn up either at or resulting from, conferences of War Office, Admiralty, India Office and Foreign Office representatives.[19] They included redress of Turkish provocation in Basra, and of frightening the Turks with a show of British strength, which could also cover the landing of reinforcements if necessary, while encouraging Indian Moslems and assuring the local Arab populations of British support against Turkey – the last reason generally considered the most important. One of the instructions the force received was to defend the oil installations and pipeline in Southern Persia and Abadan Island, although it was well recognised in London and India that the troops initially despatched could not possibly give any real protection to the long pipeline.[20] Continued Admiralty insistence that these installations be defended meant, in fact, an opposite drain of men and material away from an advance up the Tigris and Euphrates.

The Expeditionary Force 'D' quickly occupied Abadan and, within three weeks, Basra. This provoked considerable debate among London and Indian Government departments and individuals concerned, for Basra was undoubtedly a key strategic city for both Mesopotamia and the Persian Gulf. India wanted Basra retained permanently as part of the Empire, and this was recognised in the subsequent political discussions concerning the future of Mesopotamia, although even Indian opinion was not united over the form in which it was to be retained.[21] The chance of retaining Basra was, indeed, the one thing that made the Viceroy change his mind about the wisdom of the British government having bought a majority shareholding in the Anglo-Persian Oil Company, with its installations in Central-South Persia, its hundreds-of-miles-long pipeline, and its refinery installations on Abadan Island in the Shatt-el-Arab. Now he could write to Nicolson of his change of mind, since the large British stake meant that Basra, the key to the Gulf and to the trade of Mesopotamia, would have to be retained, indeed, he hoped, made 'into a second Egypt'.[22] Annexation was not yet in the Foreign Office's mind, however. A protectorate or even a lease was as far as Foreign Office opinion would go and it was concerned to prevent Indian ambitions from getting out of hand.[23] On 16 December 1914 the Viceroy was formally telegraphed that His Majesty's Government desired that 'no declaration of permanent annexation should be made, as it would arouse French and Russian suspicions and would be contrary to principle that occupation of conquered territories by allies is provisional pending final settlement at close of war'.[24]

The continuing advance up the Tigris and Euphrates obviously contained implications for Britain's political interests in the regions and these will be examined later in the context of the political discussions of 1915 and 1916. Basically, however, the advance was at first more a wartime combination of reply to Turkish counter action and continued momentum resulting from success, although as the Government of India was directing the operations until February 1916, and Hardinge was Viceroy of India there was the annexationist element also. In October 1915 he commented jauntily, if prematurely, in a letter to the King's Private Secretary, that 'My little show in Mesopotamia is still going strong and I hope that Baghdad will soon be comprised within the British Empire.'[25] Later, after the setback at Kut-el-Amara, the War Office took over general direction of military operations in February and control of administration of the Mesopotamian Force in July 1916.[26] By the end of that year advance to Baghdad became a military necessity, partly to forestall any likely Russian advance there from the North and partly to raise British prestige in the eyes of the Moslem world after the setback in Mesopotamia and the catastrophe of the Dardanelles.

Grey's attitude towards an advance to Baghdad varied, from caution, when it was first discussed at the end of 1914, to enthusiasm when it was discussed again a year later. In November 1914 the official British government view was that it was 'premature to take action, which appears to oblige consideration both by Allies and by Arabs of ultimate settlement regarding Mesopotamia and other parts of the Turkish Empire. It will be a most complicated matter, and we are not at present able to do more than assert, as we have, our paramount claims and powers at the head of the Persian Gulf.'[27] By October 1915, however, when continued successes of the Expeditionary Force made the short remaining distance to Baghdad seem relatively easy, and an interdepartmental committee and the cabinet both favoured an advance, Grey supported them.[28] From the political point of view advance 'was of the very greatest importance, particularly in view of the present critical situation in Persia and even in Afghanistan'.[29] A further reason was that as the Baghdad province contained Moslem shrines, Indian Moslems might feel that by the capture of the city they were deriving some return from the war. Grey was also strongly influenced by the need for Britain to regain prestige somewhere

15

in the East, even if only temporarily, and an advance to Baghdad would achieve this – a view supported by Nicolson.[30] He pursued this idea at the meeting of the War Committee on 21 October, stressing the current approaches of the Sherif of Mecca and suggesting that British forces enter Baghdad as part of Britain's support for the Arab movement and be willing eventually to make Baghdad over to the Arabs. 'It was necessary', as he explained afterwards to Hankey, 'to gain strength by eating *now*, even if it involved indigestion later on.'[31] Indigestion certainly followed, though not yet for Grey. After the effective failure of the advance with the retreat to Kut-el-Amara, the War Committee had painfully to reassess the importance of the Mesopotamian theatre. Grey and Balfour's desire to send reinforcements to permit a renewed advance and successful capture of Baghdad was defeated and the mission of the Mesopotamian force now defined as purely defensive.[32] From now on until late 1916 the Mesopotamian campaign remained relatively quiescent and the fall of Baghdad did not come about until March 1917. Foreign policy regarding Asiatic Turkey had therefore during 1916 to seek other avenues of expression. The failure of this stage of the Mesopotamian campaign on top of the failure of the Dardanelles campaign make understandable Foreign Office restlessness over the continued delay in the outbreak of the Arab revolt and its pursuit of the French and Russian negotiations involved in the Sykes–Picot agreement – both of which facets of policy are discussed later.

Away from the scene of the military operations, the British Government meanwhile, between March 1915 and July 1916, had been examining its own territorial desiderata. Discussions revolved, basically, around how large an area of Mesopotamia was to become British and in what form this was to occur. It is often stated that a major determining factor for Britain in both military operations and political partition schemes was oil. This view however, is quite erroneous,[33] for although certain individuals participating in the discussions from time to time mentioned or pressed for Mesopotamia's oil potential to be an important reason for occupation or annexation, the fact remains that the documentation of the stages by which the British sphere became defined paid scant attention to oil.

First discussions concerned the occupying and retaining of the port and hinterland of Alexandretta, on the Syrian coast.[34] This was one of the possible bases for mounting a diversionary land attack against Turkey which were examined early in 1915 and ended in the decision to conduct the Dardanelles operation. But any British intentions and activity in Syria required consideration of French susceptibilities, for France had long had interests in Syria as had Britain in Mesopotamia, and French economic influence, in particular, could command great political leverage in Paris. More, France's delay in agreeing to Russia's claims to Constantinople and the Straits appears to have been substantially influenced by consideration of how to secure her own position in Syria. Although Grey dates French 'initiative' in seeking to partition

Asiatic Turkey to a conversation he had with the French Ambassador in London, M. Paul Cambon, on 23 March 1915,[35] it is evident that French determination to ensure her Syrian paramountcy was known in the British government well before that date as it is an accepted factor in the discussions of the War Council on 10 March 1915.

At this meeting, and at a subsequent one on 19 March, held at a time when Britain also had to commit itself one way or the other to Russia's claims to Constantinople and the Straits, the question of Alexandretta was discussed, bringing with it almost inevitably the question of British and French spheres of influence.[36] Alexandretta was seen by Kitchener and by the Admiralty (but not by Balfour) chiefly as the means of facilitating rapid communication between the Mediterranean, Mesopotamia and India, although Indian opinion did not agree. Churchill urged British claims to Alexandretta, the best port on the Syrian coast, in terms of upholding Britain's position against French claims to Syria and Russian claims to Constantinople and the Straits, and pressed British claims to the whole of Mesopotamia. He and Grey agreed, however, that consideration of the question of Alexandretta was premature until Britain made up its mind about Mesopotamia. Grey felt, after all, that Britain already had as much territory as it could hold and he was most reluctant to involve Britain in further territorial complications. But this, as was pointed out by the Prime Minister (who had a short time before privately described Grey as 'tired out and hysterical'),[37] was just not possible. If France and Russia were to 'scramble' for Turkey, Britain's government must 'do its duty' and join in. It was decided, therefore, to temporise and tell Russia that it was indeed premature to discuss the partition of Turkey but meanwhile the questions of Arabia and of an independent Moslem political entity must be discussed. Russia was, accordingly, so informed on 19 March and Grey spoke with Cambon, on 23 March.[38] Britain and France should henceforth discuss their respective desiderata in Asia Minor 'unofficially'.

Britain had now to ascertain more clearly her own desiderata in Asiatic Turkey. To that end an inter-departmental committee, the Committee on Asiatic Turkey, was set up by the Prime Minister on 8 April 1915, under the chairmanship of the Rt Hon Sir Maurice de Bunsen, and it presented its report on 30 June.[39] The committee's aim was 'a final settlement, without the handicaps imposed upon us by the conditions under which Hakki Pasha was able to negotiate'.[40] Nine desiderata were determined, including 'final recognition and consolidation of our position in the Persian Gulf' (i), 'maintainance of our strategic position in the Eastern Mediterranean and in the Persian Gulf, and security of our communications, with the minimum increase of naval and military expenditure and responsibility' (vi), 'fulfilment of pledges given, or under consideration to the Gulf and Arabian Sheikhs', and, 'generally, ... of assurances given to the Sherif of Mecca and the Arabs' (iii), prevention of discrimination in trade and commercial enterprises and maintenance of existing markets (ii), and security for development undertakings such as oil production, river navigation, and irrigation construction work, and other matters. Above all, however, the committee pointed out how 'the Persian Gulf and the growth of our position there dominate our policy, and compel us for good or ill to claim our share in the disintegrating Turkish Empire...we have to face the fact that now is an opportunity of settling once for all our position in the Persian Gulf...'[41]

Of the various types of schemes examined for partitioning the Ottoman Empire, the committee decided that the best was Ottoman federal decentralisation with certain detached areas. Basra was to be British and the area to the North as far as Zakho and Amadia in the East and Acre in the West was to be under British influence. This area included Haifa as the Mediterranean replacement for Alexandretta as a harbour and railhead, and also Mosul. This latter inclusion was chiefly to provide a defensible frontier for the British sphere, although other reasons, such as being the head area for irrigation and water supply, and its commercial and oil potential were also given.

Ensuring that Arabia and the Moslem Holy Places remained under independent Moslem rule and providing a satisfactory solution to the Caliphate question were also recognised in the Report as important British aims (desideratum vii). All the schemes considered did designate the area below a convex line from Aquaba to above Koweit as 'Independent Arabs', although the committee recognised that details had to await separate discussion with the other Powers. But the report did at least define British desiderata in that area.[42] Britain must fulfil her undertakings with such of the Arab Sheikhs as responded to her advances; there should be peace in the Persian Gulf and that required friendship with the Power or Powers in the Arabian hinterland; the Red Sea thoroughfare must be kept open, and that required no potentially hostile Power being able to acquire a Naval Base on the Arabian coast or islands; the arms traffic had to be stopped; and Koweit and the British area of interest in Mesopotamia needed to be secured against infringement from Central Arabia.

Britain had thus, only a few months after the outbreak of war with Turkey, completely changed its views on the desirability of maintaining Ottoman territorial integrity. Considerable areas of Asiatic Turkey were to be completely detached from Turkish rule and the rest retained only under stringent terms. Even Grey accepted the inevitability of the dissection, however reluctantly and however long he might prefer to delay it. So far, by mid-1915, he had accommodated Russian claims over Constantinople and the Straits, he was in the process of accommodating French claims to Syria and defining British claims in Mesopotamia. Now, later in 1915, he was to become even more enmeshed, with the need to accommodate Arab claims. This, in turn, brought a need for closer alignment of French and British claims, producing in 1916 the Sykes–Picot agreement for partition of the Ottoman Empire.

The Hussein–McMahon correspondence of July 1915 to June 1916 concerned the terms by which the Arabs in Asiatic Turkey were to revolt under the authority of Sherif Hussein of Mecca against their political and spiritual head, the Sultan–Caliph in Constantinople.[43] The revolt was intended to aid the British war effort by creating a diversionary action against the Turks over a wide area of Syria and Arabia. In return the British promised Hussein and the Arabs independence of Turkish rule and also an Arab Caliphate.

At the outbreak of the war with Turkey Britain was committed formally to the Arabs in this region only to the extent of the Government of India proclamations of 2–3 November 1914 and the individual agreements with the Persian Gulf Sheikhs. During the first half of 1915 political control over the region of Western Arabia, formerly in the hands of the Government of India, was resumed increasingly by the British government, to be run by its representative in Cairo. This area included the Hedjaz. When, therefore, the negotiations with Sherif Hussein of Mecca were undertaken, they were conducted by the British High Commissioner in Cairo, Sir Henry McMahon, assisted by his Cairo and Soudan advisers (later incorporated into the Arab Bureau), and authorised by the Foreign Office in London. The degree of Foreign Office authorisation and Cairo responsibility has become an important facet of both contemporary and subsequent disputation about the negotiations, as also the associated problems of the exact meaning of the type of 'independence' offered the Arabs and the geographical area over which it was to extend.[44]

What has to be said is that had the documentation been available sooner and all the sources closely examined, the long controversy associated with the content and meaning of the Hussein–McMahon negotiations could have been avoided. The 'independence' promised by Britain to the Arabs was clearly independence of Turkish domination and the political forms that this would take in the different Arab regions were to be determined after the war in conjunction with the Powers which were to uphold their special interests in particular areas, and also in the context of the circumstances of ending the war and making the peace.[45] This was repeated time and again by Grey to his British colleagues, his French and Russian allies, to McMahon, and by McMahon to the Sherif.[46]

Grey's attitude towards the negotiations appears from the evidence to have developed from one of initial caution, to commitment, to a cynical fatalism. Initially, as expressed to McMahon on 14 April 1915, he sought as small and as vague a commitment as possible. This was that Britain would make it an essential condition in the terms of peace that (without territorial exactitude) the Arabian peninsula and its Moslem Holy Places should remain in the hands of an independent sovereign state, while the question of the Caliphate should be settled independently by the Moslems themselves. A proclamation embodying this policy was distributed in Arabia, Egypt, and the Soudan in late June that year. But Grey was pushed to a more precise commitment by pressure and 'evidence' (subsequently proved false[47]) from the Sherif and his associates that if Britain did not promise the Arabs independence over an area bounded by Persia, the Indian Ocean (excluding Aden), the Red Sea, and the Mediterranean up to a line from Mersina to Adana at latitude 37°, then they would have no alternative but to succumb to German blandishments and join the war on their side. More precise commitment was also strongly urged on Grey by authorities in Cairo – McMahon, Brigadier-General Sir Gilbert Clayton (Director of Military Intelligence, Egyptian Army) and by the General Officer Commanding in Egypt, General Sir John Maxwell.[48] Under the weight of such authorities and arguments Grey did not object to allowing a more precise British commitment, and authorised McMahon 'to give cordial assurances' along the lines he proposed, 'unless something more precise is required, and in that case you may give it...'. He did, however, continue to urge circumspection.[49] The fact that the arguments used to secure this commitment have only recently been shown to be false cannot reflect on McMahon. McMahon's resulting letter of 24 October 1915 to Hussein in which he gave detailed application to Grey's broad if reluctant permission to give a more substantial undertaking to the Sherif still contained many provisos. Although he declared Britain's willingness to recognise and support Arab independence in the area sought, he did exclude some areas of Western Syria including portions 'lying to the West of the districts of Damascus, Homs, Hama, and Aleppo' which, he said, were not purely Arab. He also stressed the sanctity of Britain's existing treaties with Arab chiefs, and Britain's freedom to negotiate only where this could be done without prejudicing French interests (an intentionally vague phrase since, as he wrote to Grey, he did not know the extent of French claims), and he allowed for British advice, guidance and officials in forms of government to be devised to take account of Britain's special interests and need for administrative control. McMahon's further letter to Hussein of mid-December 1915 (authorised in detail by Grey) specifically spoke of Arab 'independence from Turkish domination' and of the essential condition of a successful Arab revolt.[50] And these were the terms which Hussein declared on 1 January 1916 that he fully 'understood' and was 'greatly satisfied by',[51] although he pointed out that he would seek re-negotiation after the war of the areas left to France.[52] The promises to the Arabs were at no stage considered to be other than conditional on a widespread Arab revolt; this revolt took a long time to come about, and when it did finally break out in June 1916 it was purely local and of limited duration and effectiveness. Moreover, whatever success it had was due to British help with arms, money and manpower.

On the question of whether or not McMahon exceeded his authority it has to be concluded that although his letter of 24 October committed Britain so much more in detail, this alarmed the Foreign Office only because it was now being obliged to honour its undertakings and not because these were in any way being misinterpreted. At no other stage did McMahon do other than communicate to the Sherif anything more than that for which he had expressly requested – and received – Foreign Office authority. Crewe claimed on 17

December 1915 that McMahon's negotiations were 'carried on . . . without great wisdom'. Although intended as a general condemnation of the whole proceedings, this can only be attached to the letter of 24 October, and even then it mainly only shows up the grossly unfair attempts at diverting blame evident in the Foreign Office correspondence at a time when criticism by India and suspicion by France were adding to Foreign Office disquiet.[53]

McMahon's 'fault', that also of his highly responsible and respected fellow British representatives in Cairo – Wingate (Governor General of the Soudan and Sirdar of the Egyptian Army), Clayton and Maxwell – was to assume that the Arab revolt was potentially a far more serious and useful prospect than it actually turned out to be. It was, after all, on this opinion that the Foreign Office, despite its own misgivings, was obliged to act.[54] But the Foreign Office was in a difficult situation in any case because of the claims of its allies, France and Russia, and the partition discussions and agreement which these led to. It was those very misgivings about Arab potential which made the Foreign Office regard the projected revolt with more cynicism than seriousness, thus to some extent compensating for Cairo's over-confidence.[55] In any case McMahon was not informed of the Sykes–Picot negotiations until generally and unofficially in March 1916 and officially at the end of April 1916. Cairo's military opinion of the arrangements was that 'from a political point of view, quite apart from obvious military objections, they made the action on the lines proposed by the Sharif difficult'.[56]

In the last resort the Foreign Office and its chief, Grey, and to a lesser extent, its permanent, non-political chief, Nicolson, have to bear the responsibility for the policy carried out in their name. And the conclusion that has to be drawn is that on this issue the leadership was poor. Grey let himself be swayed, against his better judgement, and to be carried along by events which he made little effort to dominate or modify. He was, as the discussions of the War Committee on 23 March 1916 show, no less than his colleagues cynical of the arrangements his department had let itself become committed to negotiating.[57] And, what was worse, he did not even properly understand them, as his minute of June 1916 admits, commenting on British undertakings in Mesopotamia about which he did not 'have a clear head'.[58] This combined cynicism and confusion allowed promises and arrangements to be made which, when they did come to fruition, would become a source of long-standing embarrassment to his country.

These arrangements – and the criticism of them – included the negotiation of the Sykes–Picot agreement. This had been undertaken as an integral part of the investigations into Britain's territorial desiderata in Asiatic Turkey, essential for defining the limits of the areas of Arab 'independence'. McMahon had recognised even in his early letters that although the extent of French claims in Syria was not known, the French would still defend them vociferously, hence his intentional vagueness over those parts of his letters. The Foreign Office, too, was well aware of this problem, and, following on McMahon's letter of 24 October, it undertook discussions inter-departmentally and with a French government representative, Georges Picot, and invited British Arabist, Lt.-Col. Sir Mark Sykes, throughout November and December 1915, to try to ascertain the irreducible minimum of French claims.[59] Against opposition from the Admiralty and from the Director of Military Intelligence, Brigadier-General G. M. W. Macdonogh, who pressed the need of urgency in securing Arab support and decried detailed territorial examination, the committee decided to delegate detailed investigation to Sykes and Picot.[60] This could have been partly due to the fact that its chairman, Nicolson, pessimistic, even initially destructive about the proceedings, and writing to Hardinge, that 'we are endeavouring now to water down...the proposals which McMahon originally made to the Grand Sherif', now thought the best way to deal with the problem was to smother it under detail.[61] But Sykes and Picot thrashed out the details during December 1915 and January 1916 and in the proposals they worked out, submitted first in early January and then later in an amended version, were set out the territorial scheme later to become embodied in the 'Sykes–Picot agreement'.[62]

The 'Arab Proposals' finely delineated French and British interests and spheres in Asiatic Turkey, in many ways going far beyond what had ever been envisaged either in the de Bunsen recommendations or when the Hussein–McMahon negotiations had been started. Basic criteria which they attempted to meet in compromise were stated to be: for France, compensation for inconvenience and loss attendant upon the disruption of the Ottoman Empire, which would safeguard her historic, traditional and economic interests and aspirations in the Near East and especially Syria; for the Arabs, recognition of their nationality, protection from alien oppression and 'an opportunity of re-establishing their position as a contributing factor in the world's progress'; for Britain, assurance of her position in the Persian Gulf and commercial and military land communication between the Gulf and the Mediterranean, and regarding religious beliefs, proper account to be taken of 'the conscientious desires of Christianity, Judaism and Mahommedanism in regard to the status of Jerusalem and the neighbouring shrines'.[63]

Working from these criteria the amended version of the Arab Proposals divided the Arab populated areas of Asiatic Turkey into several types, though under the general description of 'an Arab State or a Confederation of Arab States'. Based on their traditional spheres of interest France and Britain each had an area (marked on the map in blue for France and red for Britain) in which they could exercise direct or indirect administrative control, plus an area in which each had economic priority. The British areas extended roughly from Gaza diagonally to the Persian frontier above Kirkuk in the North to a Southern boundary running from Aquaba to the South of Basra province, and the French areas lay above the British area with a Northern boundary from East of the Gulf of Adalia over to the Persian frontier via Bitlis. A further area, Palestine (marked brown on the map), was to be under international control, while the Arabian peninsula and the Hejaz contained no such spheres of influence, excluding, of course, Aden. Other proposals included Britain receiving the ports of Haifa and Acre, Alexandretta becoming a free port for British Empire trade as Haifa was to be for France, and Britain having the right to build, own and operate a railway connecting Haifa with her own Mesopotamian area. Neither the French nor the British, 'as protectors of the Arab State', were to cede any of their rights except to the Arab State or States, nor would they allow any third power to acquire territory or construct naval bases in the Arabian peninsula. The significance of the proposals for the Arab Movement was, as Nicolson pointed out to Grey, that the four town of Homs, Hama, Aleppo and Damascus will be included in the Arab State or Confederation, though in the area where the French will have priority of enterprise, etc.'[64] Britain also lost Mosul to the French sphere, which the India Office considered 'a serious sacrifice for us', although it recognised the fact that in these proposals Sykes had succeeded in cutting down French claims considerably.[65]

The committee met again on 17 January, and discussed the draft proposals, noting their dependence on the Arab uprising, and, despite Nicolson's continued private pessimism, a further inter-departmental discussion on 4 February decided to accept the scheme.[66] It had to be pointed out to the French government, however, that this would 'entail the abdication of considerable British interests [i.e. control of Mosul, especially], but provided that the co-operation of the Arabs is secured, and that the Arabs fulfil the conditions and obtain the towns of Homs, Hama, Damascus and Aleppo...' then Britain would make the sacrifice. But since French claims extended so far Eastwards and affected Russian interests it was essential to obtain Russia's consent before proceeding further.

The French government agreed to this on 9 February and so Picot and Sykes now proceeded to Petrograd, the former as French government negotiator, the latter as informed assistant to the British Ambassador, Sir George Buchanan, though especially, as Nicolson put it to Grey, 'to keep an eye on the French discussion'.[67] Buchanan was instructed to make it absolutely clear to the Russians that the Anglo–French proposals were dependent both on Russian consent (which was not to be dependent on any unwilling Russian concessions) and on Arab cooperation, and further, that all was dependent upon the general arrangements concerning Asiatic Turkey to be made at the end of the war. Because of the frank relations between Buchanan and the Russian Foreign Minister, Sazonov, Picot's attempts to bluff the Russians into accepting the French claims were able to be squashed.[68] He had threatened to stir up the Lebanon Maronites to oppose the Arab movement and had pretended that France's Eastwards claims were due to a British desire for a buffer between her own and Russian territory. The Russians insisted on the French taking less in the East – in other words nothing East of a line from Zakho to Bitlis – and allowing them in compensation more in the North, or a triangle covering roughly Kharput–Sivas–Kaiseriyah.[69]

At the meeting of the War Committee on 23 March 1916 Grey explained the negotiations with France and Russia.[70] Here his views are most clearly demonstrated. Against Balfour's arguments that allowing Russia the Eastern area would open up the way for Russia to the Persian Gulf, the precise reason why Russia did not want France there, Grey's reponse was, firstly, that it was a question to be settled between France and Russia. But, significantly, he made clear his own belief that nothing would ever come anyway of either the territorial arrangements or the Arab rising on which they depended. The meeting thereupon followed his suggestion and approved the Russian change. Grey's attitude towards the Arab revolt has already been discussed, but this, surely, demonstrates a degree of either supineness or cynicism which is difficult to credit in a man of his personal integrity. That after so many months spent in investigation and discussion and, by now, considerable Government financial investment in an Arab uprising, Grey could either (an unlikely reason) try to pull the wool over his colleagues' eyes or (most likely) show such complete indifference to the outcome of these negotiations and their important strategic implications, shows a lack of, at the very least, the expected qualities of political leadership of a Foreign Secretary and one, moreover, operating in a time of war.

The Arab revolt had still not broken out. Nonetheless the correspondence which was in effect to transform the Sykes–Picot 'Arab proposals' into the 'Sykes–Picot agreement' was in train. This comprised letters written over the period 13 April to 23 October 1916, between the Russian Foreign Minister, Sazonov, the French Ambassador in Petrograd, M. Paléologue, Grey (and, in August, Crewe), the French Ambassador in London, M. Cambon, and the Russian Ambassador in London, Count Benckendorff, agreeing to and slightly further defining the Sykes–Picot proposals already discussed in London, and Petrograd.[71] By mid-May, however, in the so-called 'Grey–Cambon correspondence', the Anglo-French agreement was already settled. The tail was, therefore, already in April 1916 beginning to wag the dog. The Foreign Office might fulminate privately over the Arab situation, and Grey stress over and over again to his allied diplomats that 'the arrangement was entirely conditional upon action taken by the Arabs', but the fact is that no real effort was ever made to undo it.[72] As Sykes pointed out clearly in June 1916 in his War Cabinet memorandum on 'The Problem of the Near East', 'the fact is that all moves or events taking place in the Turkish and Arabian areas are assumed to be ancillary or subordinate to two main factors of the war as a whole: (1) the military factor of the Western Front being the decisive theatre of war, and (2) the main political factor that the solidity of the alliance must take precedence over any other political considerations'.[73] Similar reasons were adduced by Hirtzel in May, when he concluded: 'The only completely and finally satisfactory settlement of Asiatic Turkey is one that involves either partition or division into spheres of influence on lines such as those which have actually been adopted in the recent Russo-Franco-British agreements.'[74]

These, then, were the dilemmas facing the Foreign Office and help explain its attitude of reluctant fatalism. That attitude, in turn, helps settle the historical controversy over alleged discrepancies, in content or intention between the British promises to Hussein and the situation provided for in the Sykes–Picot agreement. No discrepancies were intended and the step-by-step analysis undertaken of the defining of British aims in Asiatic Turkey to the making of the Sykes–Picot agreement shows clearly the intentions of its makers and the attempts made at accommodation of different interests. Analysis of the Hussein–McMahon correspondence, in turn, shows that there were in fact no real discrepancies at the time between promises made to the Arabs and the provisions of the Sykes–Picot agreement except in terms of openly-stated Arab dislike of France, and attempts were made to meet this by the use of spheres of less formal influence in addition to those of more formal control. Controversy arose subsequently in the context of Arab ambitions at the peace and the unavailability of the documentation to check the record. In retrospect it is easy to see that the Sykes–Picot agreement should never have been made, if for no other reason than the immediate post-war bitterness it gave rise to between Britain and France and between the Arabs and these two. But then it was never intended by the Foreign Office to be anything other than a temporary solution to a difficult war-time situation. It was due to Foreign Office ineptitude that it became anything else. Grey himself wrote subsequently in his *Twenty-five Years*: 'I was not very anxious to carve up Asia Minor in advance: if we won the war, spheres of interest would have to be defined; but the thing seemed rather premature: what we needed first was to concentrate on winning the war...I never regarded this Treaty as entailing any obligation on us except to fulfil a promise to give the Arabs independence. There was no obligation on us to occupy or administer Mesopotamia, but it was desirable to make sure that other European Powers would not push into Mesopotamia and down to the Persian Gulf.'[75]

The war-time conduct of Britain's foreign policy towards Asiatic Turkey provides a sad political epitaph for a man imbued with the highest personal ideals and probity. But it also shows that this man, Grey, in this arena at least, was not the right man for the job. His policy was traditional, cautious, and short-sighted, producing lack of incisiveness, of understanding and of effectiveness. War ended Grey's world, and the man who could pursue traditional policy reasonably successfully in pre-war Asiatic Turkey presented a very different picture by the end of 1916.

27

Japan and China, 1914–1916

I. H. NISH

The first few weeks of war in the far east were weeks of confused diplomacy. Britain underestimated the eagerness with which Japan would enter a war which seemed to be rooted in European causes. British naval circles had neglected the strength of Germany's far eastern fleet and the threat which this would present to British trade routes in event of war. Accordingly they had underestimated the extent of Britain's naval dependence upon Japan, which was one of the essential underlying features of the alliance between them. These two factors were brought forcibly to Britain's attention in the first week of the war. This led to confusion and contradiction in Grey's policy towards Japan and China; but this confusion was not confined to the far eastern region and only confirmed that Britain was unprepared for war.

Britain's initial reaction was to keep the far east out of the war if at all possible. On 1 August Grey told Japan that 'if we did intervene, it would be on the side of France and Russia, and I therefore did not see that we were likely to have to apply to Japan under our alliance'.[1] This view was based on the traditional view of the alliance whereby Russia was the 'enemy contemplated' and on the conviction that in the circumstances the alliance would not come into play. The Foreign Office was convinced that there was no immediate threat to Britain's special interests in east Asia or India. Still, Grey thought it wise to put the formal legal position before Japan: he explained that 'if hostilities spread to the Far East, and an attack on Hong Kong or Wei-hai Wei were to take place, we should rely on their support'.[2] This was Japan's obligation under the alliance treaty of 1911. When Japan replied that she would maintain a strict neutrality towards a European war but would be ready to support Britain if called upon, Grey told the Japanese ambassador that he would avoid, if he could, drawing Japan into any trouble: 'but, should a case arise in which we needed her help, we would gladly ask for it and be grateful for it'.[3] From this it would appear that Britain was relieved that the far east would remain outside the zone of hostilities and would not entail all the problems which an additional war-front would present.

On 5 August Grey set the Far Eastern department to study German naval strength in far eastern waters. The conclusion reached was that British and German strength was roughly equal and that Japanese naval help would be required if British trade was not to be seriously affected. The study was undoubtedly coloured by indications which had been received from the Japanese that they were more willing to take part in the war than earlier messages had suggested and that their cruiser squadrons were ready for action. Grey then discussed the Foreign Office conclusions with the First Lord of the Admiralty and authorized the despatch of a request which seemed to alter Britain's position:

As our warships will require some time to locate and destroy the German warships in Chinese waters it is essential that the Japanese should hunt out and destroy German armed merchant cruisers who are attacking our commerce now...It means of course an act of war against Germany, but we do not see how this is to be avoided.[4]

The Japanese replied that they could not be limited to action against armed merchantmen and would prefer to settle the matter by an attack on the German position at Kiaochow.[5]

The implications of Japan's reply caused grave misgivings in some quarters. The distinguished British minister in China, Sir John Jordan, reported his concern that China would stand to suffer most from Japan's active participation in the war. Secondly, the dominions of Australia and New Zealand did not view the prospect of Japan's naval presence in the south Pacific with any relish. Thirdly, the United States was apprehensive about the possible occupation by Japan of the strategically placed group of German islands in the Pacific.

In this dilemma, Grey concentrated for the next fortnight on getting Japan to limit her activities and to limit the sphere of her operations. On 10 August he told Japan that acts of war in the far east should be restricted to the sea alone and that he would not invoke action by Japan under the alliance. Obviously he wanted to avoid any Japanese attack upon Kiaochow. Japan, however, replied that, to prevent anxiety in any quarter, the two powers should give China assurances that she could rely on them for the maintenance and protection of peace and order there. By 12 August Grey considered that there was little he could do to keep Japan neutral: while Britain's special interests in east Asia were not so seriously menaced for him to appeal for Japanese help under the alliance, he recognized 'that Japan has also interests to be considered and that she alone has the right to judge what action is required'. He agreed that Britain and Japan should issue a statement that they 'considered it is necessary for each to take action for the protection of *the general interests contemplated by the Alliance*' (my italics), but insisted that it should therein be stated 'that the Japanese action will not extend beyond the China Seas to the Pacific Ocean, nor beyond Asiatic waters westward of the China Seas, nor to any territory on the Continent in Eastern Asia which is in the occupation of Germany'.[6] Thus Grey withdrew his appeal to Japan under the alliance but conceded that Japan might wish to intervene in the war in her own national self-interest. He also tried to circumscribe Japan's action to a very narrow sphere in accordance with Britain's own needs. The Japanese Foreign Minister, Baron Katō, disregarding the snub implied in Grey's message, replied that it seemed to offer the Japanese a free hand and that he would prepare a statement, omitting the suggestions regarding limitations. Grey made one last attempt to urge on Japan the need for a declaration specifying the geographical limits of her action and added, as a sop, that if she would accept these limitations, British cooperation would be complete.[7]

On 15 August Japan issued her ultimatum to Germany. She asked for the immediate withdrawal of German warships from Chinese waters and the delivery to Japan within a month without condition or compensation of the entire leased territory of Kiaochow, with a view to its eventual restoration to China. While the last phrase was something of a reassurance to the world, it did imply that, if there was no favourable reply from Germany, she would start an attack on Kiaochow, which was quite contrary to Grey's original intentions. No reply came from Germany within the eight days' time-limit stated in the ultimatum; and on 23 August Japan declared war on Germany.

The issue of Japan's ultimatum did not end Grey's diplomatic offensive to get Japan to announce publicly the limits of the action she contemplated. The only card he could play was the threat that, if Japan did not do so, he himself would make a public statement on lines which would reassure the United States and the self-governing dominions. Under this threat the long-awaited public statement was made by Premier Okuma on 18 August: 'Japan harbours no design for territorial aggrandisement and entertains no desire to promote any other selfish ends. Japan's warlike operations will not, therefore extend beyond the limits necessary for the attainment of that object and for the defence of her own legitimate interests.' This slightly ambiguous statement did not reach the Foreign Office in time to forestall the issue of a more far-reaching statement in the London press on the following morning:

It is understood that the action of Japan will not extend to the Pacific Ocean beyond the China Seas except in so far as it may be necessary to protect Japanese shipping lines in the Pacific nor beyond Asiatic waters westward of the China Seas, nor to any foreign territory except territory in German occupation on the Continent of Eastern Asia.[8]

To issue a unilateral statement about the intentions of another power was a questionable tactic. Grey had to admit that it was only a British version of what was understood to be Japan's intentions. In retrospect Grey's attitude was tinged with regret. In *Twenty-five years* he wrote: 'to explain to an Ally that her help will be welcome, but that you hope it will not be made inconvenient, is a proceeding that is neither agreeable nor gracious'.[9] However the press notice was explained to Japan, it was highly offensive. When Japan entered the war, she was very much out of step with her ally.

The month of August had revealed serious weaknesses within the Anglo-Japanese alliance. Firstly there was the desire to keep Japan neutral. As one official wrote, 'the Japanese may perhaps have taken some offence at the desire which was certainly felt here at first to avoid additional complications in the Far East. We did not at first realise how keen they were to come in'.[10] Then, there was the serious step of inviting Japanese assistance and withdrawing the invitation, to which the Japanese were understandably sensitive. Finally there was the attempt to confine Japanese actions within limits which were not acceptable to her and, to compound the offence, the release of a press announcement prescribing these limits. Though these issues arose in the context of the war, they were in fact a reflection of deep-seated differences – differences over China, over the British dominions, and over the United States which were brought to the surface by the world crisis. In dealing with these problems, Japan could no longer be browbeaten by Britain. Japan had adopted a policy and she had the power to follow it through, despite British opposition and suspicions.

It is in this context that the cold response given to the repeated requests of France and Russia in August and September for their inclusion within the Anglo-Japanese alliance should be understood. Great Britain and Japan recognized that their alliance was in the doldrums and needed to be steered carefully if it was not to be entirely wrecked. They were both intent on leaving the alliance as it stood without complicating matters by taking in other members of the Entente.[11]

There were good reasons why Grey should exercise extreme caution to nurse relations with Japan back to normal after the slights offered her in August. The war had hardly been going a month when it was discovered that Japan's assistance was needed in the Indian Ocean and beyond. Britain put out feelers in September for Japanese troops to be sent to Europe but the Japanese government was resolutely opposed. There was more hope of naval support. In September Britain asked for the Japanese battle fleet to be sent to the Mediterranean and, in November, for a squadron to be sent to the Dardanelles.[12] But the Japanese decided not to put at risk their comparatively small fleet in waters so far away from their own shores and for purposes with which they were only marginally identified; Japan was not inclined to mobilize her fleet indefinitely or to bear the heavy financial cost which would necessarily be involved. Grey foresaw that these requests were likely to be repeated as the war developed and contrived to avoid undue criticism of Japan's policy, especially in China, even when he disapproved of it.

China, who had even less interest in the European issues behind the war than Japan, adopted a policy of strict neutrality. But when Japan announced her intention of taking part, China grew alarmed. She first put out feelers as to whether Germany would return the leased territory of Kiaochow to her direct; and Germany evidently made a definite offer. At this point Premier Okuma made his statement that Japan had no designs on China and sought no territorial aggrandisement. Grey passed on to China assurances that Japan would ultimately return Kiaochow to her. Although the Chinese were sceptical about this and said 'save us from our friends' they did not proceed with negotiations with Germany.[13]

After Japan's ultimatum it was clear that a military operation would be launched to wrest Kiaochow from Germany. But it was not immediately clear what form it would take. China seems to have offered to join any operations by land but was not taken seriously because of her parlous financial position.[14] France and Russia too proposed that they should join in the operations; but Japan would not countenance this and only agreed with reluctance to her ally, Britain, sending a contingent. Britain, while not pressing for a role for her European associates, was ready to take part, even if on a small scale, in the hope of playing a moderating influence with the Japanese military. There was, thus, suspicion rather than friendship underlying the joint Anglo-Japanese expedition which emerged.

Grey tried to persuade the Japanese to join him in presenting a declaration of intent to the Chinese before invading their territory. It appears that he and his minister in Peking, Sir John Jordan, both believed that Japan had told China that she 'entertains no idea whatever of territorial aggrandisement and she will without fail restore Kiaochow to China'.[15] Jordan tried to convince the Chinese to treat the Japanese assurances with complete confidence. But the Chinese were looking beyond diplomatic assurances to the expansionist newspaper reports in the Japanese press and took the most serious view. In the end the joint declaration was scrapped, and China was dissuaded from making a protest on the ground that the operation would be for her benefit in the long run.

After this unhappy diplomatic introduction began the unhappy military-naval expedition against Kiaochow. It was part of the Japanese strategy to attack the Germans from the rear by landing at Lungkow, which was well outside the Kiaochow leased territory and was thus a violation of Chinese neutrality. Nonetheless Japan's armies persisted in this operation. The British troops who did not take part until 24 September, were explicitly instructed by Grey 'not to arrange cooperation with Japan involving violation of Chinese territory'.[16] The modest British force from Tientsin consisted of one battalion of British infantry and one company of Sikhs, together with a naval force of the cruiser *Triumph* and the destroyer *Usk*. It was a token force whose object was to give the operation a representative character and to meet the wishes of China that she should not be left to the sole mercies of the Japanese. It landed at Laoshan bay within the former German territory, long after the Japanese had secured the beaches. On 7 November the Japanese captured the stronghold of Tsingtao to which the Germans and Austrians had retreated.

The Japanese, having violated China's territory to start with, proceeded to take over the German-owned railway which ran from the leased territory of

Kiaochow into the Chinese hinterland of Shantung. They occupied the railway towns early in October and were in complete control of the railway by the time Tsingtao had fallen. The Chinese requested the British, whose troops had taken no part in this aspect of the operation, to prevent this violation of her territorial rights. But the Foreign Office declined, on the ground that continued German control of the railway was impossible and Japanese action was necessary and justified.[17]

It may have been a political necessity for Britain to share in this expedition but it yielded few results. By fighting alongside the Japanese armies, Britain appeared to be condoning their acts. This disposed the rank and file of Chinese against Britain during the war. China's leaders probably took a longer view and saw Britain's presence as a moderating influence on Japan. They felt some disappointment in November when Britain announced the withdrawal of her troops from Kiaochow for it seemed to destroy one shred of hope that the German territory would be restored to them.[18] Nor did the presence of a British force have a favourable effect on Japan. It added to the tactical difficulties of the Japanese officers and led to a number of incidents. Nor did it give Britain any say in the ultimate settlement for the territory.

Turning to the war in the Pacific, the first task for Britain was to clear the German fleet from the ocean. The German cruisers – *Gneisenau, Scharnhorst, Nürnberg* and *Leipzig* – inflicted considerable damage before they were sunk in various actions leading up to the battle of the Falkland islands in December. The light cruiser *Emden* escaped to the Indian Ocean and sank many merchant ships before it was destroyed at the battle of Cocos islands (9 November). Thus throughout the autumn the Pacific and Indian oceans were unsafe and the Royal Navy was dependent on Japanese help in chasing these raiders, in patrolling and in convoy duty.

Britain's next problem was to deal with the German Pacific islands, whose main significance was as radio stations. New Zealand had occupied Samoa late in August, Australia had taken New Guinea in September. By October the Japanese fleet took the Marshall, Caroline and Mariana groups, chains of islands lying north of the equator. This created a serious diplomatic crisis for Grey. For the Japanese to occupy permanently a girdle of islands stretching across the centre of the west Pacific pleased neither the Americans nor the Australians. At the same time, it was scarcely feasible for Britain, who was so dependent on the Japanese, to drive them out by force or to request them to leave.

On 12 October Japan informed Grey that Japanese opinion was calling for some return for the help Japan was giving the allies and asked Britain not to request that any islands which Japan occupied be transferred (say) to the Australians. This seemed to contradict the assurances which had been given by Premier Okuma on 18 August. Nonetheless the British ambassador in Tokyo recommended that it would be at once politic and graceful if we offered them some signal mark of our confidence which would vindicate their policy in the eyes of the nation and would assure us their further assistance, should we require it.

This object, he claimed, could be attained, without alarming American and Australian sentiment, by refraining from requesting at the present juncture the transfer to Britain of any islands which Japan might occupy.[19] Grey had already discussed with Harcourt, the Colonial Secretary, the future of the island of Yap and had agreed that for political reasons it was desirable that it should be taken over by an Australian expedition. The Japanese accepted this suggestion amicably enough and promised to remain in occupation until the arrival of the Australians.[20]

A crisis developed on 22 November when the Australians announced their expedition to 'relieve the Japanese occupying Yap and other islands north of the Equator'. Two days later the Colonial Office asked that the expedition should not proceed to islands north of the equator. To allow the political questions to be resolved, the expedition was temporarily held up. On 1 December the Japanese foreign minister intervened to demand that the Australian expedition should not visit any of the islands in the Caroline, Marshall, Mariana and Pellew groups which were all in the possession of the Japanese navy. He added confidentially that Japan would naturally insist on retaining permanently all German islands lying north of the equator and asked for British support for this proposal.[21] This was to hold a pistol to Britain's head; and Britain, relying on Japanese naval support, could not afford to appear unsympathetic. Grey replied that it was not British policy to commit herself to recognizing Japan's permanent retention of the islands in question; but 'we are ready to proceed to the end of the war on the understanding that all occupation of German territory will be without prejudice to the final arrangements'. He further assured Japan that the Australians were being asked not to send their expedition north of the equator.[22] On 3 December the Colonial Office to the great disappointment of Australia announced that it was most convenient for strategic reasons to allow the islands (including Yap) to remain in Japanese occupation until the end of the war. Meanwhile Grey told Japan that the only basis for dealing with territories occupied during the war was that it should be without prejudice to the final arrangements to be made in the terms of peace at the end of the war.[23]

Active hostilities in the far east ceased by the end of 1914. Britain's position had been shown to be much more vulnerable there than was thought when the war broke out. Japan had made a considerable contribution to the cause of the Entente and was already in occupation of substantial areas as a result. It was to be Grey's major headache to avoid commitments about these territories as Japan continued to press for her right to retain them.

There now arose the greatest crisis in the far east between the Russo-Japanese war and the Manchurian crisis of 1931–2. On 18 January 1915 Minister Hioki presented President Yuan of China with a memorandum containing twenty-one demands. Since Tsingtao had fallen on 7 November, it was inevitable that some sort of arrangement should be reached between Chinese and Japanese over the administration of the former German territory. But the Japanese demands went far beyond this to take in demands covering all parts of China. Japan passed on the substance of the demands to Grey confidentially on 22 January. The other powers were not so notified, because Japan claimed to be disclosing them as required by the alliance. Because of leaks, the Japanese on 10 February revealed to Grey that, in addition to the demands, they had informed China of certain 'wishes' in what came subsequently to be known as 'Group V'.

Though not invited to comment, Grey on 20 February offered some general observations. He asked Japan to 'refrain from advancing any demands which could reasonably be considered to impair the integrity or independence of China' as it would be difficult 'to reconcile such demands with the terms of the Alliance'. Where the terms seemed to impinge on Britain's interest in China, Grey asked that they should be freely discussed with him.[24] On 9 March, when no satisfactory reply had been received, Grey asked for an assurance that 'there is nothing in Japanese action which conflicts with the Anglo-Japanese Alliance' and promised, if he received it, to justify Japanese action in parliament. He conceded that 'there must be an expansion of Japanese interests and influence in China as there has been in the case of other Powers, and that Japan naturally expects to see this increased'.[25] Grey evidently wanted to avoid any wartime rupture with Japan, while he did not want to see any armed conflict develop between Japan and China.

Realizing the weakness of Britain's position, the Foreign Office studied the various options open. Grey agreed that 'our right policy is to efface ourselves over the demands, as far as is consistent with any actual British rights which they may affect, and bide our time in China till the war is over and trust to being then able to repair the damage'.[26] Britain was understandably slow to commit herself until the United States had shown her hand and in her note of 13 March the latter did not take a strong stand. Late in April she was inclined to propose a common front against Japan; but Britain held that the moment for effective international action had already passed.[27]

Negotiations between Japan and China had ended unfruitfully on 16 April; and Japan presented a set of demands which were no relaxation of her former terms. Japanese armies were made ready in Manchuria and Shantung; and an armed conflict seemed imminent. On 3 May Grey told Japan that the only outstanding question was really Group V and asked her not to press these points.[28] This message was unexpectedly well-timed for it arrived just as the Elder Statesmen were assembling to review the cabinet's policy over China. It was they who insisted on Group V being dropped in the final ultimatum which was passed to China on 7 May. But so seriously did Grey view the situation that he referred the question to the cabinet on 6 May and, with its sanction, asked Japan not to 'shut the door upon the possibility of agreement with China without consulting with us and giving us an opportunity of promoting a friendly settlement'.[29] There is no doubt that Britain took the most pessimistic view of the emergency before she made her offer of mediation. In the end, her mediation was not taken up because the Chinese accepted the Japanese ultimatum on 9 May and the treaties were signed on 25 May. Sir John Jordan had on his own initiative advised the Chinese to make concessions since he thought that it was futile to resist the Japanese; but this advice was probably not crucial because President Yuan knew full well that his armies were no match for the Japanese.

At this critical point in the history of the far east, Britain's voice had carried little weight, less perhaps than it had carried for a century. Through the Japanese alliance, Grey had brought a certain amount of moral pressure to bear on Japan. But this was a modest achievement and it would have been unwise for Grey to have pushed this too far since Britain's power was in practice minimal in the area and her bluff might have been called by Japan. This crisis forced Grey to recognize that Britain's role in the far east during the war years would have to be an insignificant one. His ambassador in Tokyo recommended that Britain should 'mark time'[30] and avoid being drawn into discussions with Japan over China which could only reflect the gulf between British and Japanese policies there. In fact this came close to the policy of 'effacement' to which Grey had given his blessing when future policy was under discussion in March.

Since the German collapse at Tsingtao in November Japan had taken a more relaxed attitude towards the war than the other Entente powers. She had refused to send an army to the western front; she had shown reluctance to extend her naval commitment; she was hesitant to extend her effort while the Germans kept the fighting on enemy territory. In the interest of the war effort, it was Grey's object to induce Japan to make a greater contribution. First, there was the serious Russian shortage of arms and ammunition. Strong pressure was put on Japan in August 1915 to supply Russian requirements urgently along the Trans-Siberian railway. The Japanese were able to show that, unknown to Britain, they had already supplied formidable amounts of arms. But they proceeded to put their arsenals on 24-hour working and encouraged private enterprise to set up armament factories. Secondly, it was desirable to tighten Japan's relationship with the Entente. Since the beginning of the war, France and Russia had sought to achieve this end by themselves joining the Anglo-Japanese alliance; but this solution had not commended itself to Japan. Instead they pressed for Japan to join the treaty of London of September 1914. It was not until the resignation of Katō as foreign minister in August that this was favourably entertained. Japan finally adhered to the treaty on 19 October and thereby undertook not to make a separate peace with Germany.

The situation in China was no more encouraging for Grey. The Germans in China were deeply involved in anti-British intrigues and propaganda. Moreover there were numerous Chinese arsenals which seemed ripe for reorganization and conversion to supplying the armament needs of the Russians. Grey's problem was that the more he tried to involve China in the war, the more he upset Japan who had become intolerant of interference by other powers there. Grey was prepared to follow a 'policy of effacement' in China; but, while he accepted the fact that he must consult Japan before making important approaches to China, the need for mobilizing the resources of neutral countries had to take priority.

By the autumn of 1915 President Yuan Shih-k'ai was ready to restore the monarchy in China and claim the throne for himself. The Japanese, who regarded Yuan as their enemy, told Britain that they were completely opposed to a restoration of the monarchy and rallied the powers against the scheme. Grey agreed that Britain should be associated in the joint protest made to Yuan on 28 October. Yuan replied that there would not be undue haste but permitted the scheme to mature regardless. A further warning was given on 15 December but Yuan announced his enthronement on New Year's day, 1916. Grey told China that he neither opposed the monarchy nor the emperorship of Yuan but felt the project should be postponed because it would be resisted in south China and lead to civil war. Grey wrote that it was most foolish of Yuan to disturb the status quo: 'my real apprehension was that rebellion in China might result in a war between North and South China and assume the most formidable proportions'. This could only prejudice British interests at a time when she was unable to safeguard them.[31]

Soon after the first protest against his monarchical ambitions, Yuan tried to win the confidence of the European powers by offering to join the Entente. On 6 November China proposed to Britain an arrangement whereby her arsenals would borrow substantial sums from British and Russian banks in return for which their total manufacture would be sold to the banks for use by the Entente; it was better 'to throw off the mask and deal with the question of supplying arms and ammunition on a regular footing', even if it forced Germany to declare war on her.[32] Refusing to act without Japan's concurrence, Grey put the proposal before Japan on 12 November as his own initiative and combined it with the notion that China should expel German nationals, even if this shattered the pretence of Chinese neutrality. Ten days later strong representations were made in Tokyo by Britain, France and Russia.

The Japanese saw in this approach a move against themselves and were not deceived by Grey's pretence that the initiative was British. It coincided with reports in the Japanese press that an Anglo-Chinese alliance was being negotiated. The furore which this aroused reached such proportions that Grey had to issue an abject *démenti*: 'no such thing has been contemplated and we have no intention of entering upon political negotiations with China except in consultation with Japan'.[33] While the air was cleared, the Japanese reply on 6 December was categorically opposed to the Entente proposal: Japan would not permit the development of China's arsenals by Entente help; nor would she associate herself with measures for expulsion of Germans if this would lead China into the war.[34] This was a diplomatic snub to the European powers, unexampled in the recent history of the far east.

Grey gave up the arsenal scheme without delay; and, while the powers pretended to cooperate in the elimination of German intrigues for some months, that too petered out by the spring of 1916. Japan had shown her claws; and Grey was anxious to avoid making her 'more resolved than ever on preventing a rupture between China and Germany'.[35]

In face of Japanese suspicions and harsh attacks on Britain in the press, Grey had to move warily because of the calls he had to make for naval assistance. On 1 February 1916 the Admiralty asked Grey to approach Japan for a flotilla of destroyers to be sent to the Mediterranean or to British home waters. Feeling that this was pitching his demands too high, Grey confined his formal request to a cruiser squadron for the Indian Ocean with a small force of destroyers to patrol the Malacca Strait. Japan agreed to offer four cruisers and four destroyers if Britain could ensure that Australia and Canada would adhere to the Anglo-Japanese commercial treaty of 1911 and if a Japanese scheme for recognition of Japanese doctors in the Straits Settlements were approved.[36] On neither point did the Japanese completely receive the concessions which they had sought. But the ships were sent and worked amicably with the Royal Navy.

Grey continued to depend on Japan as a supplier of arms for the Russian war effort. In January 1916 the Grand Duke George Michaelovich visited Japan with a goodwill mission which laid the foundations for a Russo-Japanese alliance, finally concluded in July. The negotiations began in February; and Japan who was in a strong bargaining position, presented a strong statement of desiderata. Foreign Minister Sazonov referred to Grey for guidance throughout. He thought that the negotiations would offer a good pretext for getting Japan's agreement to China's entry into the war. Grey advised him not to confuse the issue; it would be disastrous if the negotiations reached deadlock.[37] For military reasons Grey wanted closer relations between Japan and Russia and discounted the rumours that Britain was an opponent of a Russo-Japanese rapprochement. Late in June the text of the treaties was passed to Grey in advance of signature and he expressed himself fully satisfied: it would reinforce the Anglo-Japanese alliance and supplement it. It is sometimes argued that the Japanese replaced the British alliance by a Russian alliance. There is no evidence that this is how Grey regarded the new treaties: there was nothing antithetical in them. Indeed, they served British objects: they tied Japan more securely to the Entente and prevented her from being swayed by German overtures.

While the Russian negotiations were under way, Germany was making unofficial overtures to Japan. There had been conversations in China during 1915; but the most significant were those held at Stockholm between March and May 1916. On 1 April the Japanese minister was told by the German minister that Germany hoped Japan would make a separate peace and assist in getting Russia to make peace. This intelligence was passed to Grey on 5 April with the minimum of delay. Grey replied on 27 April that Japan should consult France and Russia so that a common decision could be arrived at. Two further secret parleys were held in Stockholm; and these two were communicated to the Entente powers. After the overture had been discussed by the British cabinet, it was decided to suggest to Japan that there was no indication that Germany would agree to any terms which would be tolerable to the allies. This was conveyed to Japan on 11 May and the Japanese duly replied to the German minister in Stockholm that they were not in a position to conclude a separate peace but would be ready to pass any German proposals to their allies.

There is evidence that Grey was worried early in 1916 that Japan would listen to German peace overtures and felt that her government required concessions which could be shown to its critics who claimed that she was getting nothing out of the war. Over the Stockholm talks Japan seems to have acted properly and loyally to her obligations to the Entente by communicating the terms to her allies. There were in Britain widespread suspicions that Japan was not 'playing the game' but, since she was continuing her negotiations with Russia all the while, it must be assumed that she was not genuinely interested in the German approach. There is reason to believe that Grey's view is well expressed by his successor as foreign secretary when he stressed in March 1917 that suspicions of Japan were not well placed and he did not view Japan's likely actions with the least apprehension.[38]

If Japan's relations with the Entente had improved by the end of Grey's ministry, Japan's policy to China did not become any more acceptable to Britain. Japan, through her military agents and her continental expansionists, was very much associated with the anti-Yuan forces in China. Yuan's monarchical scheme had attracted wide opposition; and these opponents rallied a wide range of discontented elements. In the early months of 1916 fighting between rebels in the south and Yuan's forces was intense and the rebels had the upper hand. Faced with a spread of the rebellion, Yuan withdrew his acceptance of the imperial throne on 23 March. The rebels called for his resignation. Britain, who had throughout been Yuan's supporter – though not an uncritical one – tried to convince Japan that the retirement of China's 'strong man' would lead to a crisis of serious dimensions. But Japan declined to intervene in the interest of Yuan's survival. Yuan became ill and died on 6 June. This removed from the scene one of the elements which divided Britain from Japan. The crisis of civil war in China had passed without Grey seriously alienating either Japan or China; but it had been a delicate balancing act.

Yuan's successor as president was General Li Yuan-hung. Many members of Li's government had been educated in Japan and were assumed to be pro-Japanese. Grey, who was necessarily mindful of the low state of the Entente, felt that the Japanese might now be more amenable to dealing with the problem of German activities in China. In September an opportunity arose to revert to this topic. He told Japan that he had in fact decided not to raise this question again nor to encourage it being raised unless he was sure that the Japanese had changed their views on the subject. He would however be ready again to discuss the project at any time if the Japanese Government cared to take the initiative.[39] Such was Britain's war-time position in the far east that she could only raise issues guardedly and hesitantly, in the hope that they would commend themselves to Japan. As it happened, Japan was in the throes of a cabinet crisis, the government resigned on 6 October, and China policy was thrown open for re-examination. It was not until March 1917 that China, on the invitation of the United States, broke off relations with Germany. Since this action was approved by Japan, she finally entered the war on the Entente side in August.

During his period at the Foreign Office, Grey had seen Britain's position in the far east decline from one of strength – even if illusory strength – to one of comparative impotence. As one of his officials wrote in 1916, Britain was 'most clearly powerless to pursue any policy but one of absolute non-interference'.[40] British sympathies lay with China but there was little that Grey could do to support her while he had to conciliate Japan and keep her on the Entente side. Britain's attitude towards Japan was defensive, cooperating with her for the sake of the war effort but bitterly critical of her conduct in China. The state of the Anglo-Japanese alliance was at its nadir. The war years had been years of uninterrupted criticism of Britain in the Japanese press and, while this probably did not reflect the feeling of the Japanese government, it was a warning to Grey to act circumspectly.

If Grey's sympathy for Japan declined after 1914, his policy was still animated by a remarkable understanding of Japan's desire for expansion in China and by a readiness to make allowances for it. Balfour, his successor as foreign secretary, reported that Grey 'held the view that if you are going to keep Japan out of North America, out of Canada, out of the United States, out of Australia, out of New Zealand, you could not forbid her to expand in China: a nation of that sort must have a safety valve somewhere'.[41] This was indeed the position which Grey expressed on countless occasions. Balfour went on to say that he thought that 'Grey carried his doctrine to excess'. Certainly Grey and his officials took a profoundly pessimistic view of Britain's power to influence events in the far east and to guide the actions of Japan during the war. After the presentation of the twenty-one demands, he followed a policy of marking time and avoided arguments with Japan which could only throw into relief the divergences between British and Japanese policies in China. After the snub of December 1915, he moved with even greater caution. At the same time, Grey sometimes expressed surprise that Japan, who had the ball at her feet, did not make greater demands than she did; he had expected Japan in 1915 to demand further concessions in the Yangtse region, Britain's traditional sphere of influence, but she had not done so.[42]

It might be thought that Grey with many claims on his attention in war-torn Europe would have had little time to devote to far eastern affairs and would have been forced to accept the policies worked out for him by senior officials. The evidence is otherwise: he seems to have studied far eastern files, often contributed long minutes and regularly wrote telegrams himself. He enjoyed a cordial relationship with officials of the Far Eastern Department but he was by no means their puppet. He had views of his own on Sino-Japanese problems and had a sure grasp of the limited role which Britain could play in resolving them.

28

Anglo-American Relations: Mediation and 'Permanent Peace'

C. M. MASON

By virtue of her geographical position and economic development, Britain held a key position in the complicated wartime relations between the Allies and the United States. America's industrial and financial capabilities made her potentially the arsenal of both sides in the war, but British command of the Atlantic largely denied these resources to the Central Powers while London became the centre for the organisation of the supply of money and materials to the Allies. The blockade violated some neutral rights and harmed sections of American industry, but the business of supplying the Allies brought compensations to the American economy. These economic disruptions, together with the German submarine campaigns and other, more emotional pressures stemming from the war in Europe, set up conflicts within American society which President Wilson had to take into account in determining how far he should go in resisting Allied encroachments on neutral rights and in permitting the provision of supplies to the Allies; and Grey had to take cognisance of the pressures within the United States as well as of the demands of his colleagues and the Allies for the vigorous prosecution of the war. The legal, economic and political questions that arose between London and Washington had to be resolved as far as possible in their own terms, but both governments took it as a guiding principle that it would be disastrous for either of them to come into unqualified conflict with the other. In this respect, the extent to which each was able to sympathise with the other's understanding of the causes and objects of the war, was of great importance, for it affected the degree to which each was ready to accommodate the interests of the other.

There was from the start an underlying tension between the Allies' determination to fight on until they could impose their terms on Germany and President Wilson's need for the war to end as soon as possible. Wilson sought a negotiated peace as the quickest way to finish the fighting; but he was not in fact indifferent to the issues at stake in the war, nor did he make peace at any price his objective. He suspected the selfishness of Allied intentions, but he thought that immediate responsibility for the outbreak of war lay with Germany's military leaders, and he had no desire that the war should end in a way that could be represented as a vindication of militarism. He did not expect an Allied victory that produced an upsurge of Russian militarism to bring much benefit to the world or America, but he saw Britain as the diplomatic leader of the Entente and judged Grey to be a statesman whose devotion to peace was almost equal to his own. He accordingly thought Grey might be persuaded to work for an early peace of lasting value. Furthermore, he was reluctant to make an offer of mediation that did not have Grey's approval.

Grey hoped for a lasting peace but he saw little prospect of an early one. He did not expect Germany to accept voluntarily any terms that were evidence of failure on the part of her military leaders or to give up easily the extensive territories that would be demanded by the Allies. He accordingly sought to fend off any offer of mediation that could result in a premature peace conference through which the Germans might avoid defeat and where dangerous divisions might be opened up between the Allies. He never failed to warn the President that neither side showed any readiness for a mediated peace and that all German hints to the contrary were insincere. There was, however, a risk that this line would lead the President to conclude that it was only Allied intransigence and desire for conquests that stood in the way of peace. The danger could be contained to some extent by laying emphasis on the good and unselfish ends that made the defeat of Germany indispensable, such as the restoration of Belgium and the vindication of the rights of small nations and the sanctity of treaties. Grey added to these, in private correspondence with the United States as well as in public statements, the idea of the establishment after the war of some permanent arrangement between the Powers to deter aggression and to give security in equal measure to all. When Wilson offered mediation with the avowed object of securing lasting peace and the elimination of militarism, Grey asked him whether the United States would be prepared to propose such a permanent arrangement and become a party to it. Wilson and Colonel House, his personal adviser on foreign affairs, understood Grey to mean that unless the United States accepted this suggestion, there could be no question of American mediation. For a time they believed, as Grey may have intended, that America's 'unwritten law' of shunning involvement in European affairs placed a limit on their right to press the Allies to accept mediation; but by the end of 1915 the pressures of the war were so acute that the President was persuaded by House that he would have to try to overcome this obstacle and he began to adopt the idea of a League of Nations as his own, as a ticket which conferred on him the right to mediate.

The germ of the British commitment to a League of Nations can be seen in the earliest days of the war. The immediate British war aims were the restoration of Belgium and such a defeat of the German armed forces as would destroy the political influence of the German military establishment and so secure the Empire and Western Europe against German expansionist ambitions. It was neither difficult nor far-fetched to express these national objectives in terms of universal significance, as Asquith did in September and

October 1914. He declared in Dublin on 25 September that the Empire was fighting for 'the enthronement of public right as the governing idea of European politics', for the right of small nations to independence and free development, and for 'a real European partnership based on the recognition of equal right and established and enforced by common will'. He had said earlier (in the House of Commons on 6 August) that if Germany had agreed to Grey's proposal of a conference to resolve the European crisis, Britain would have been prepared to consider 'some arrangement to which Germany could be a party, by which she would be assured that no aggression or hostile policy would be pursued against her or her allies by France, Russia or ourselves...' But with the war two months old, Asquith proclaimed that the creation of a better system of international relations to replace the pre-war condition of a precarious equipoise based on force and the clash of competing ambitions, would require a definite repudiation of militarism. A firm link was thus established between the waging of unremitting war against Germany and the achievement of a lasting peace, and this not only helped to cement British public opinion to the Entente but also weighed in the balance of liberal opinion in Britain and America against the more self-interested aspects of Entente war aims.[1]

These general notions about lasting peace became of diplomatic importance in early September 1914 when Bryan, the U.S. Secretary of State, took precipitate action on rumours in Washington that the Germans would welcome American mediation. Sir Cecil Spring-Rice, the British Ambassador, suspected that the Germans expected a long war (the Allies had just concluded the Pact of London) and so were putting it about that they would make peace without demanding new territory, in the hope of turning American public opinion against the Allies as the powers intent upon continuing the war for the sake of conquest. Spring-Rice suggested that this strategem might be turned back upon its authors if the Allies were to welcome the idea of mediation, but make the condition that the ensuing peace was 'not only to end this war, but all wars, by a thoroughly satisfactory settlement' including guarantees of permanency.[2] Grey's reply to Bryan, which partially accepted this advice, laid down the fundamental line of British policy on a negotiated peace. It was for Germany to declare the terms on which she wished to make peace and nothing could be achieved by the United States without ascertaining what these were. The German terms would be considered by the Allies in common (as laid down in the Pact of London). For her part, Britain would insist on compensation for Belgium, and could not again have a great military power forcing war upon Europe. He added that 'if the United States could devise anything that would bring this war to an end and prevent such another being forced on Europe', he would welcome the proposal.[3]

Bryan's enterprise collapsed on 16 September when the Germans told him that they did not desire mediation but were ready to receive their enemies' application for peace. The Administration might have been put off by this rebuff; but Colonel House thought it was due to the ineptness of Bryan's methods. He privately sent Grey through Spring-Rice his personal assurance that the Germans might accept a peace based on an end to militarism, the establishment of permanent peace, and the evacuation and compensation of Belgium. House thought that Britain should be prepared to accept such terms, since to refuse them would be to put the Entente in the wrong, and he argued that even an Allied victory would only replace Prussian with Russian militarism. There was nothing in this that Grey could have taken up with his Allies, nor, indeed, any indication that the United States might make a contribution to keeping the peace. It seemed, furthermore, to bear out Spring-Rice's suspicions that the peace game as played in Washington would be used to turn American public opinion against the Allies and to sow mistrust between them. Grey accordingly saw no advantage in encouraging House to act the part of peace-broker and merely repeated that if Germany desired peace she should communicate her terms through the President to all the Allies.[4]

House did not see this message as a rebuff – perhaps because Spring-Rice passed it to him in an allusive and obscure personal letter[5] – and in early October again urged Grey to take heed of the dangers to peace that would be posed by a victory for Russian militarism. Only a negotiated peace could discredit all militarism. In answer to the question that Grey had earlier put to Bryan, House thought that the United States might be able to suggest as a guarantee of permanent peace a settlement by which: (1) every nation in Europe should guarantee the territorial integrity of every other; (2) there should be government control of arms manufacture and a scheme of mutual inspection of armaments factories; and (3) 'sources of national irritation should be removed before they become malignant'. It is interesting that House selected three ideas that were later supposed to be cardinal features of the League system – territorial guarantee, arms control, and the principle of nationality – but his message was of no practical importance because, it seems, his chosen intermediary, Walter Page, the American ambassador at London, omitted to deliver it.[6]

House's letter would probably not in any case have made a good impression on Grey, with its reiterated attack on Britain's Russian ally. Furthermore, Grey was well aware of the extent to which France and Russia were hostile to the idea of American mediation. The French ambassador at Washington had been instructed in September to prevent any attempt at mediation[7] and all three Allied ambassadors thought then that House was simply being used by the Germans to weaken the Allies' trust in each other.[8] In November the Tsar was to enunciate a concise policy for peace-making: '...the general conditions of peace will have to be imposed on Germany and Austria–Hungary; no congress and no mediation'.[9] Even Asquith, in September, had suggested to Grey that as a precondition for considering any enemy overtures, the Allies should insist on the Central Powers' making a military and naval submission that would have been not much less abject that that eventually inflicted on them in 1918.[10] It would thus have been extraordinarily difficult for Grey to have persuaded his Allies, and perhaps his colleagues, to look favourably on an American endeavour to mediate that went beyond the mere passing of messages.

The rumours of peace which flowed out of Washington made little impression in London until December 1914, when Spring-Rice reported that the German and Austrian ambassadors were asking Wilson to send a peace mission to Europe, saying that they believed their governments would be willing to pledge themselves before negotiations began to evacuate Belgium and grant her compensation. House thought this development important and was ready to advise the President to take action as soon as the Allies agreed. Spring Rice suspected that the Germans' objective was to create a favourable climate for a loan they were about to float.[11]

Grey's initial response was cautious: he did not want 'to discourage any advance towards peace that is sincere' and would consider his full reply. Unfortunately Spring-Rice decided to garnish this simple message with a little lecture to House on the Allies' obligations to each other to make peace in common, the wisdom of the President's acceptance of the Allies' aims with regard to Belgium and militarism, and the untrustworthiness of the German and Austrian ambassadors. House quite missed the point of the ambassador's remarks and understood him to say that it was Grey's personal attitude that 'it would not be a good thing for the Allies to stand out against a proposal which embraced indemnity to Belgium and a satisfactory plan for disarmament'. He made up his mind to set out for Europe forthwith.[12]

Grey's substantive reply, which he stressed was his personal attitude, in fact came close to confirming House's impression of his views. In that respect it drifted dangerously far from the line laid down by the French and Russian Governments. He thought that the barrier to peace discussions would be removed if Germany agreed in advance to the full restoration of Belgium. There would then have to be a durable peace that would secure the Allies from future aggression. Grey obliquely met House's point about Russian militarism by acknowledging that in the long run the crushing of Germany would be as impracticable a way of securing permanent peace as was Germany's attempt to dominate Western Europe. To make Germany a democracy would be a step in the right direction, but it could not be enforced from the outside. A possible solution might be a general agreement for mutual security and preservation of peace. Germany could benefit from it equally with the Allies and it might work 'if the United States would become a party to it and was prepared to join in repressing by force whoever broke the Treaty'.[13]

Spring-Rice and House gave differing accounts of the conversation in which this message was delivered, but there were three salient points in the ambassador's report that came out equally clearly in House's diary. First, House had given renewed assurances that the German and Austrian ambassadors had been speaking on instructions about Belgium and security against renewed aggression. Second, House had turned down flat any idea that the United States could join in the sort of agreement that Grey had proposed. Finally, Spring-Rice had done his best to dissuade House from going to Europe, saying that Grey's personal views did not commit the Allies and that a peace mission might be in vain: but without success; House wished Grey to consult the Allies on whether they would consider terms while hostilities continued, and he would go to Europe, if negotiations seemed possible, as soon as Grey gave the word.[14]

Grey now found himself in a considerable difficulty. It must have occurred to him that the German Government would hardly bind itself, as a precondition of negotiations, to the restoration of Belgium, unless the military and naval leaders had lost control in Berlin, and that this in itself would be a marked defeat for German militarism. On the other hand he cannot have thought that negotiations could succeed on the sort of terms that France and Russia had in mind. French and Russian demands were likely to go far beyond Alsace-Lorraine and Constantinople and the Straits. The Tsar, at the same time as he had rejected all idea of mediation, had envisaged a settlement that would have broken up both the German Empire and the Dual Monarchy. Prussia would have been reduced in effect to the dynastic territories of the Hohenzollerns in the east and the Habsburgs would have been confined to their German lands. The German colonies would have been shared by France and Britain and Russia would have acquired Thrace and Armenia. Permanent peace was to be ensured by a permanent alliance between the victors. Grey thought such talk 'academic' or worse, and heartily approved Buchanan's remark to the Russian Foreign Minister that these were not the sort of objectives that Asquith had set before the British people.[15] He may have thought that following a German defeat he would be able to moderate Allied demands; but if he had found himself in early 1915 in a premature conference with both sides fit for further fighting, he would have been faced with an impossible choice between supporting his allies' extreme demands and thereby losing American sympathy, and pursuing a moderate line that would have undermined Allied trust in British loyalty. Either way, the conference would probably have broken down and the eventual outcome might well have been a German victory.

Grey therefore had to put a stop to House's peace mission. He did so with a clear conscience because he did not in fact believe that the Germans had any intention of making peace on the terms being put about by their ambassador. He told House this, but gave more prominence to the point that, if the United States could not come into any peace-pact, he did not see how permanent peace could come except by the exhaustion of one side or the other. He asked whether House had any idea how, with Germany undefeated, a durable peace and reduction of armaments could be achieved, 'unless there were some League for preservation of Peace, to which United States were a party and which could effectively discourage an aggressive policy or breach of treaties by anybody'.[16]

By January 1915, however, the President was determined that House should go to London, Paris and Berlin. He thought that House might be able to discover in Europe foundations for peace which were not visible in America, but he was more concerned that his friend should make a personal investigation of the difficulties that were coming upon the United States on account of the opposing blockades. House arrived in London on 6 February.[17]

Throughout January, House had continued to talk vaguely about a scheme of permanent peace that the President might bless, though the United States would not actually support it. When he met Grey, however, it appeared that his ideas were not concerned so much with the prevention of future wars as with ensuring that they were not waged in such a way as to endanger neutral commerce. He reminded the Foreign Secretary that it was 'the unwritten law [and] fixed policy' of his country not to become involved in European affairs, and this was understood to rule out not only American membership of a league of peace but also active participation in peace-making. He then suggested that the United States might 'join all nations in setting forth clearly the rights of belligerents in the future and agreeing upon rules of warfare that would take away much of the horror of war'. This 'second convention', as House began to call it, meaning that it would be separate from the peace treaty, would have been a considerable extension of the work begun at the pre-war Hague and London Conferences, covering such matters as the prohibition of attacks on non-combatants from the air, guarantee of neutral territory, and the establishment of certain lanes of safety at sea where all commercial shipping, whether belligerent or neutral, would be free from attack. House did not say how these rules would be enforced; nor did he say how they would be compatible with American isolationism if the practical implication of his suggestions about neutral territory was that France and Germany would only be able to 'get at one another by sea' (he had suggested that Alsace and Lorraine might be neutralised if they were returned to France).[18]

House was surprised to find that Grey did not oppose the idea of 'lanes of safety at sea'. He was told by Tyrrell (Grey's Private Secretary) that the Foreign Secretary might go further than that: 'if an agreement should be made between all the Powers, neutral and belligerent, to establish rules governing future warfare, Great Britain would consent to the absolute freedom of merchantmen of all nations to sail the seas in time of war unmolested'. Such a policy might protect Britain against the submarine better than an overwhelming navy.[19]

Grey was speaking personally, but House seems to have thought that the Foreign Secretary's views would prevail in Government without too much difficulty. House was also impressed by the flattering attention paid to him, as the President's friend, by other British ministers whom he met. He saw nothing ironical, for example, in Balfour's careful observation that his schemes were 'unique and practicable as far as he could see at the moment'. He began to believe that the British could be brought to see the establishment of 'the freedom of the seas' as a national interest, and then considered whether this new British interest might not be the ground for peace that he had been despatched from Washington to seek.

While he waited in London for a peace sign from Berlin, House conceived the notion that the Germans might be willing to concede the restoration of Belgium if the British relinquished their claim to the right to impose a general blockade against a continental enemy. He would not, of course, tell the Germans that Grey believed the freedom of the seas might work to Britain's advantage. On 27 March he was able to report to the President (having gone to Berlin without too much encouragement from the Germans) that he had put it to Bethmann-Hollweg that 'through the good offices of the United States, England might be brought to concede at the final settlement the Freedom of the Seas [and] the United States would be justified in bringing pressure upon England in this direction, for our people had a common interest with Germany in that question'. This would enable the German Government to assent to the restoration of Belgium, for it could say to its people 'that Belgium was no longer needed as a base for German naval activity, since England was being brought to terms'.[20]

House was greatly abusing Grey's confidence and, moreover, handing to the Germans a marvellous opportunity to play havoc with Anglo-American relations (they had only to make his proposals public and identify the President's friend as their author); and by proposing a way in which the war could end with a success for Germany, he was also drifting away from his own avowed objective of giving a check to militarism. But it seems clear that his intention was to find a path round the Belgian question as the obstacle to peace talks and so to lure the Germans into a conference where an American–British settlement could be imposed on the world. He wrote to Grey from Paris on 12 April to explain his plan (omitting the part about the freedom of the seas being a *quid pro quo* for the restoration of Belgium);[21] but it was rendered obsolete almost at once when the Germans began to use House's idea, without ascription, in an American propaganda campaign. Dr Dernburg announced that only English navalism stood in the way of the liberation of Belgium and that if England refused to grant the Freedom of the Seas, Germany would establish a permanent fortified base on the English Channel.[22] Grey at once told House that he would have nothing to do with any 'freedom of the seas' that was not securely linked with 'some League of Nations' that provided guarantees against war and provision for reduction of armaments. Germany might be a member of it, but she could not be free to make war upon other nations at will on land while guaranteed against naval blockade. In June he added the further condition that if Britain agreed to 'the freedom of the seas' the United States would have to be pledged to uphold that freedom by force.[23]

The *Lusitania* incident killed peace-talk for a few months, but by September

16

1915 the President was again subject to intolerable pressures that stemmed from the impact on neutral commerce of the war at sea. Grey received a warning from House that the President might be compelled to issue 'some colourless declaration in favour of peace' but that he 'would never be a party to any terms not including the liberation of Belgium and France and the end of Militarism'. This was followed by a letter asking whether the President could make peace proposals 'upon the broad basis of the elimination of militarism and a return, as nearly as possible, to the status quo'.[24]

Disregarding House's abortive efforts in March, this was the first time that Grey had received a suggestion that American mediation should go beyond the office of intermediary and include a definite suggestion of terms. Grey did not hurry over his reply, which, dated 22 September, was handed to House by Spring-Rice on 13 October. He first reminded House that Britain was bound to make peace only in concert with her Allies; he did not think that they or the enemy were ready for peace, and he could not in any case consult them without knowing the details of the proposed initiative. As for a return to the status quo, Britain wished to see France win back Alsace and Lorraine and Russia obtain an outlet to the sea (Grey could not reveal the secret bargain made with Italy). The great objective, however, was security against future aggression. Grey had kept before House throughout the summer the idea of a League of Nations. He now asked again how much the United States would do for permanent peace: 'would the President propose that there should be a League of Nations binding themselves to side against any Power which broke a Treaty; which broke certain rules of warfare on sea or land...; or which refused, in case of dispute, to adopt some other method of settlement than that of war?' Only such a system could offer the hope of disarmament, which was what he had understood House to mean by the elimination of militarism and navalism; and only the United States Government was in a position to make such a proposal.[25]

This letter should have made it clear to House that if the President was to have any hope of making an intervention acceptable to the Allies, he would have to put forward terms that took account of territorial questions as well as a general peace-keeping arrangement. Perhaps House realised this, and thought such a course politically impossible. In his reply he passed over the issue with the same vague reference to militarism and navalism and an allusion to 'the lines that you and I have so often discussed', but offered instead of terms that the President should make his peace initiative in a manner that would be bound to work to Germany's disadvantage. House's plan was that when Grey considered the moment 'propitious', House would confer with him in London and then go to Berlin and tell the Germans 'that it was the President's purpose to intervene and stop this destructive war, provided the weight of the United States thrown on the side that accepted our proposal could do it'. The 'proposal' would be for a peace conference. If the Germans did not accept it when made privately it would be repeated publicly. 'If the

Central Powers were still obstinate, it would probably be necessary for us to join the Allies and force the issue.' The key to the scheme was to be to let the Germans think that a proposal which in fact would have been concerted with Grey, would be unwelcome to the Allies and rejected by them.[26]

Grey's first response to this far from colourless suggestion was to ask by telegram whether the proposal for the elimination of militarism and navalism was the same as the proposal for a League of Nations contained in his letter of 22 September.[27] House realised that the answer would have to be that it was. He told Wilson that 'we must throw the influence of this nation in behalf of a plan...by which the peace of the world may be maintained...This is the part I think you are destined to play...it is the noblest part that has ever come to a son of man. This country will follow you...'[28] Wilson agreed. House's reply was sent by telegram on 11 November 1915, but the same day Grey wrote to House that the state of opinion in all the belligerent countries was such that House would do well to drop his intervention plan.[29]

Now that Wilson had signalled his acceptance of some sort of American participation in a league of nations, Grey was forced to recognise that it did not make a lot of difference from the Allied point of view to the practicability or desirability of a negotiated peace. Indeed, it is almost certain that he had made up his mind to discourage House and had drafted his letter before he saw House's telegram. It may have occurred to him that House's proposal clearly implied an intention to deceive both Germany and the American people and that he himself might be involved in some deception of his Allies. It would certainly have been an enormously difficult task to bring the Allies into line without any hint of the President's true intentions reaching Germany or his political opponents in America; and Grey would have had to persuade his colleagues and the Allies that House's plan offered them more real advantages than they could hope to achieve by military means.

When House received Grey's rebuff, on 25 November, he was surprised and angered that an offer which was 'practically to insure victory to the Allies', had been refused. He complained in his diary that 'the British are in many ways dull', and made up his mind that, since he could not rely on Spring Rice or Page to argue his case, he would have to go to Europe himself. Wilson agreed, and House left for Falmouth on 28 December.[30]

House had prepared the ground for his mission by sending Grey several messages to the effect that his mind was *not* running upon peace, that the President was determined to do all that public opinion allowed to see the Allies through, and that the United States was very close to a breach with the Central Powers. His private conviction that his country could not allow 'a military autocracy to dominate the world' if American strength could prevent it, led him, however, to exaggerate to himself, as well as to the British, the extent to which the President was prepared to commit himself to the Allied cause. Wilson doubted whether the United States could help the Allies to defeat Germany if they could not do it on their own and he was also anxious that House should press the British hard for relief for legitimate American commerce with Germany. He told House that America had 'nothing to do with local settlements' but was concerned 'only in the future peace of the world and the guarantee to be given for that'. These guarantees were to be disarmament and 'a league of nations to secure each nation against aggression and maintain absolute freedom of the seas'. He was prepared to use his 'utmost moral force' to oblige the belligerents to negotiate peace on such a basis; but if either side refused, the only sanction he envisaged was the disapproval of world public opinion.

All this was vague enough, but there was also a reluctance, perhaps deliberate, on Wilson's part to get to grips with House's plan. When House asked for instructions, Wilson replied: 'you do not need any. Your own letters... exactly echo my own views and purposes'; and he complimented House on his dealings with the German ambassador, in which the two men had discussed the possibility of a peace based on general disarmament. House had told Bernstorff that the President would not be concerned with the details of peace, but he had also assured the President that the Allies could be relied on to 'take care of the territorial and indemnity questions'. House had thus already begun to offer the same general terms of peace to both sides, and although he told the President that he did not want to get involved too soon with the Allies in controversies on territorial and indemnity questions, he was acting as though he already had a secret understanding with Grey on how matters were to be managed to the Allies' advantage. Wilson sought no detailed information on how this complicated business was to be carried through, or even on the risk that it entailed, of being drawn into the war.[31]

House spent two periods in London (6–20 January and 9–25 February 1916) and visited Paris and Berlin in the interval. His discussions with British Ministers culminated in agreement (on 22 February) on the 'House–Grey Memorandum'. He had told the press when he left America that he had no peace mission but his delight in being elaborately secretive was well-known, and Grey can hardly have been surprised at their first meeting when House gave him a full exposition of his peace plan.[32]

The course of House's talks in London reflected the concerns of the British side rather than the President's belief that the United States should leave alone the details of peace and stick to the general principles. Little was said about a League of Nations after the first meeting, when House 'intimated' that the United States would join a League of democracies 'based upon a demand for the freedom of the seas and the curtailment of militarism'. (There was an unfortunate implication here that there might not be room for Russia or the Triple Alliance powers in a league of democracies, but Grey did not pursue it.) There was more discussion of the territorial terms that the Allies might demand at a peace conference, and of their likely acceptability to the President. In conversation with Asquith, Grey, Lloyd George, Balfour and Reading on 14 February, House was sympathetic to the British position, but in the

Memorandum he expressed support only for the Allied position on Belgium, Alsace-Lorraine and the Russian 'outlet to the sea' (Constantinople) and qualified this with a reference to the need to give Germany compensation outside Europe.

The British were mainly anxious to know how the President might make his intervention. House was more definite about what the President did not want to do than about his actual intentions: he did not want to break with Germany on the submarine issue. House told Balfour and Grey that Wilson wished 'when the opportunity comes to cooperate in a policy seeking to bring about and maintain permanent peace among civilized nations'. By this he meant a policy based on disarmament and the freedom of the seas. He rejected the idea that the President might lead his country into an involvement in European politics and resented Balfour's attempts to draw him with '*supposititious* cases' into a discussion of how the President's principles might be applied in European affairs.

The essence of House's plan as it finally emerged was that the President would not publicly set any conditions for peace, but merely demand that war cease, and a conference be called. He would do this when Britain sent him a secret signal that the time had come for him to make the proposal to all the belligerents as though he was acting entirely on his own initiative. Wilson would not of course be able to make such an intervention if it appeared that Germany was about to win a decisive victory. If Germany refused the offer of a conference, or refused to agree to a peace which both the Allies and the President regarded as reasonable, the United States would probably join in the war against Germany; but it was unlikely that the President would agree with the Allies before the conference on a minimum programme for a reasonable peace.

House returned to Washington convinced that Grey was personally enthusiastic about the scheme and that it was only a matter of time before the call came for the President to act. The Foreign Secretary had, however, considerable reservations about mediation by Wilson and the fact that he had let House go away without making him understand this was to contribute to the feelings of frustration, and even betrayal, which the President and his friend experienced when they learnt that the British would not take up the offer.

On the one hand, Grey had a high personal opinion of Wilson's envoy. Although Grey had told Paul Cambon, when giving him a copy of the Memorandum, that House was a naive electoral broker,[33] when Bertie wrote to him disparaging the 'sheep-faced but fox-minded gentleman...out on an electioneering mission for the President', the Foreign Secretary told him sharply that he regarded the Colonel as a trusted friend. He was not blind to the degree to which House's diplomacy was aimed at coping with Wilson's immediate domestic political problems and creating favourable conditions for the Presidential and Congressional elections in November, but he did not see why this alone should prevent American mediation from working to the Allies' advantage. He considered the House plan might be a possible means of helping the Allies in certain circumstances to make a tolerable peace; but he saw no need to take it up so long as there was a reasonable chance of the Allies doing the job on their own. He explained his position succinctly to Bertie: 'As long as the Military and Naval Authorities of the Allies say they can beat the Germans there need be no talk of mediation: but if the war gets to a stalemate the question to be asked will be not whether mediation is good electioneering for President Wilson, but whether it will secure better terms for the Allies than can be secured without it.'[34]

Grey did not think that that situation had yet been reached. He had kept the French generally informed about House's proposals and had let them have a copy of the Memorandum; but when he put the matter to the War Committee on 21 March 1916, he did not urge his colleagues to make use of House's offer, but rather sought to share responsibility for leaving it alone and for not taking it further with the French unless they wished to pursue it.[35] He put it to the Committee that 'if, in the next six months, the Allies were likely to be able to dictate their own terms [to] Germany, or to improve considerably their military position, it was certain that [they] would get better terms then, with or without the intervention of the United States than could be obtained now, and it would be better not to consider President Wilson's proposals'. But if there was likely to be deadlock at the end of six months, when their financial and economic position would be weaker, or if there was any prospect of one of the allies, such as Russia, being defeated in that time, they should consult the French at once on the expediency of taking up Wilson's suggestion. Grey warned that though the offer could be taken up at a later date, it might not be repeated indefinitely.

No one present thought that things had come to such a pass that they had to have recourse to Wilson. Law spoke of the impending battle on the Somme as the big push that would end the war and though Kitchener and Lloyd George expressed doubts about the value of the planned Russian offensive, they thought the Russians would hold up through the summer. Grey himself said that he did not think the French would want Wilson's intervention.

The War Committee might have examined the Allies' prospects in the war more carefully if they had been more attracted by the role that Wilson was likely to play in a peace conference. But Grey had warned them that the President would undertake only to conduct the negotiations 'in a manner generally sympathetic to the Allies' and that this sympathy might not go much beyond the Belgian question. Law spoke for the Committee when he said that peace could only be made at the moment on the basis of the *status quo* before the war, and that public opinion would not accept that. The War Committee were not put off the idea of a mediated peace by the prospect of a League of Nations – they did not discuss this question – but rather by the risk that a Wilsonian peace would not satisfy the Allies' territorial claims and might even have the result of vindicating German militarism.

Finally, there were doubts about the Americans' good faith. House had made a bad impression on some Ministers by appearing too anxious to persuade them that the Allies might never be able to defeat the Central Powers. Asquith affected to regard House's mission as 'humbug and a mere manoeuvre of American politics',[36] and so did Balfour. The Prime Minister had had a long talk on 18 March with Edwin Montague, who, while acknowledging that Wilson's electoral purposes might indeed be best served if he could bring about a pro-Ally peace, had objected to House's scheme because 'the whole proposal is not really an honest one as presented to us'. House had come to London as a neutral and offered to engage in a subterfuge against Germany. He had also visited Berlin: the British had no means of knowing that he had not made a similar offer there. Montague's second point had been that if Wilson's initiative resulted in a peace conference, and the President proved not to be generally sympathetic to the Allies, it would be very difficult for them to appeal to a secret bargain.[37] At the War Committee Asquith spoke firmly against the House scheme, saying that he doubted Wilson's capacity to carry through his policy. His doubts may have been reinforced by the fact that Wilson had added 'probably' to the House–Grey Memorandum where it said that the United States would come into the war if Germany proved obstinate.[38]

Grey had presented House's plan only as a way of ending the war in case of stalemate. He paid no attention to the possibility of encouraging the President to call a conference, in the hope that it would fail and thus work as a means of involving America in the war, although he had no doubt that Germany would not agree even to a *status quo* peace, let alone one on lines acceptable to Wilson. If his colleagues gave any thought to this aspect of House's proposal, they can only have thought it too fantastic to merit discussion.

Although it was minuted that the War Committee had decided that no action should be taken on House's proposal 'at present', the plain fact was that British Ministers, including Grey, did not want American mediation at all if they could finish the war without it. Grey was rather more open than others to the suggestion that it might be necessary one day, but he was very afraid of the consequences of opening the subject too early with the French and of giving them the idea that Britain was getting tired of the struggle. He feared that if he did this, the French reaction would be, not to agree to American mediation but to seek a separate peace with Germany.[39] The cordiality of his personal relations with House and the degree to which he had let House believe in London that he saw a league of nations as the main prize to be won through the war, made it hard, however, for him to tell House frankly that Britain preferred outright victory to American mediation. So he told House that the Government felt unable to take the initiative in proposing a conference to France, who had borne the brunt of the war and was not yet ready to stop.

For a while in April it seemed that America might come into the war on the U-boat issue (a possibility that the War Committee had not discussed) and

House tried to get the Allies to take up his offer in time to avert that, but Grey replied that it might be difficult for the President to persuade the Germans to accept him as a mediator in the middle of a German–American crisis. That crisis was resolved, pressure increased on the President to take firm action against British infringements of neutral rights, and again House begged Grey to act on his proposal. He told him that the President was contemplating a public declaration in favour of a league of nations, which would be followed by a summons to a peace conference, and urged him not to miss this opportunity to bring about a lasting peace. Grey welcomed the prospect of the public declaration, but refused to take action with the French on mediation, now stressing what House had forgotten, that in the London talks House had said that the President could make no commitment before a conference as to terms: he feared that such an offer of mediation would be construed by the Allies as a pro-German move. House pointed to the dangers of the Allies losing sympathy in the United States, and of plans for world peace being lost from sight in a division of spoils between victors, but without avail. House's last plea was that Grey should see the President's offer as a means, not of mediation, but of bringing America into the war to fight for permanent peace: if Britain and France were to accept the offer of a conference, Germany would either have to abandon her claim to a peace based on the existing military position or face war with America. Grey continued to ignore this prospect, and repeated that he could not ask France to make peace while the battle raged round Verdun. House made a last approach direct to the French, who had already told him in Paris that they did not favour his plan, and then gave up.[40]

Wilson and House felt that the British were throwing away an opportunity to make a satisfactory peace. House also felt that he had been entitled to expect a positive response from Grey. He complained in his diary that for two years the Foreign Secretary had been telling him 'that the solution of the international well-being depended upon the United States being willing to take her part in world affairs...'[41] In particular there had been Grey's seemingly significant question in November, whether the President was offering a League of Nations. Wilson had made the commitment which Grey had appeared to be seeking, and now it transpired that the Allies would not accept it as a solution to their problem. House was too much under Grey's spell to accuse him of deception, but he was bitter about the lack of coherence in British government and the difficulty, as he found it, of telling whether a minister's views accorded with those of his colleagues. In fact, House had not been thwarted by any 'lack of coherence' on the British side so much as misled by his own preference for secretive diplomacy, his distrust of established diplomatic institutions and his exaggeration of the importance of personal expressions of opinion. Grey had never disguised from him that the thrust of British and Allied policy was to secure a military decision.[42]

Wilson was still anxious to intervene to stop the war, but he was now much less concerned to secure prior Allied approval for his diplomacy. Anglo-

American relations deteriorated in the aftermath of the Easter Rebellion in Ireland and with the increasing friction over blockade issues; the atmosphere of irritation was intensified by the clear determination of the Allies to refuse mediation and by the feeling in France and England that Wilson did not really understand what was at stake in the war. This feeling was strengthened by Wilson's first move in his new peace diplomacy, his address on 27 May to the American League to Enforce Peace. (This body was thought wrongly in England to be a 'stop the war' movement: in fact it was exclusively concerned with promoting a post-war league of nations and its membership was decidedly pro-Ally.) This speech intimated Wilson's belief that the United States should play some part after the war in upholding a system of peace and law, and many of its ideas were taken from Grey's correspondence with House. But its language was both high flown and vague, it left the exact role of the United States in doubt, it gave prominence to the undefined 'freedom of the seas', and it proclaimed the President's 'indifference' to the causes and objects of the war; all in all it made a bad impression on allied opinion and on Grey.[43]

From May 1916 until he left office, the league idea was not much used in Grey's diplomacy, although it was deployed more in Ministers' public utterances about allied war aims. These followed well-established lines.

Grey's ideas on a league of nations were scattered through his correspondence and public statements and he made no attempt, while in office, to gather them into a systematic exposition.[44] His approach to the subject of permanent peace was essentially backward-looking, born of his anguished reflections on what more he might have done to avert the outbreak of war. He convinced himself that he had done all that he could within the limits of his power: but that the war might have been avoided if only there had been some greater power which, by the mere threat of unconquerable force, had been able to compel Germany to accept a conference or to deter the attack through Belgium. This 'if only' approach led him to the idea that the United States had such power and that it must be harnessed to prevent future wars. American participation in world affairs would have to be organised through some general arrangement, a league of nations, and the league would have to be bound by obligations which made it an impartial instrument. Grey continually added to his idea of what these obligations might be: to uphold the sanctity of treaties; to compel the reference of disputes to means of peaceful settlement; to enforce the law of war and maintain 'the freedom of the seas'; to promote disarmament. His suggestions were similar to those advanced in the schemes of the Bryce Group, the (British) League of Nations Society and the (American) League to Enforce Peace, all showing the legal bias of the liberal irenicist tradition.[45] Grey's proposals, however, were not part of a consistent scheme for world peace through world law, so much as by-products of his endeavours to relate the salient issues of the day to a system of international order that would command the allegiance of the United States. The essential feature of this system would be that, freed from the rigidities imposed by inflexible and competing alliances, it would automatically provide a preponderance of power to check whoever might challenge the *status quo* with force.

Grey took no steps beyond his American diplomacy and his speeches to prepare the ground with the Allies for the establishment of a league of nations. Although he made agreements on territorial war aims that he deemed essential to keep his Allies in the war and to extend the military capabilities of the grand alliance, he discouraged discussion of war aims that was not relevant to some immediate military purpose. He lacked confidence in Britain's ability to impose her views on the Allies, and a general discussion on how to maintain permanent peace would have been as likely to produce dissension as agreement. When urging Wilson to take the initiative on a league, Grey had not foreseen that the President might make his move before the United States were ready to enter the war or the Allies to end it. From May 1916 until the end of American neutrality, there was a danger that if the British showed too much enthusiasm for laying plans for a league of nations, it would have been understood by their Allies as indicating a readiness to accept American mediation. In any case, in Grey's view, a league of nations was academic until Germany had been defeated.

In April 1915, Haldane had thought that Britain should not be afraid to take an initiative on this subject. In a paper entitled 'Future Relations of the Great Powers', the Lord Chancellor questioned by implication the wisdom in the long term of the enticements that were being offered to Italy and the Balkan States to bring them into the war. He warned that after the war the Empire would inevitably be threatened by a resurgent Germany that was unable to accept defeat as the the final verdict on her ambition to be the Great Power of Europe. The new Germany would add to her energy and organising ability a wiser diplomacy and 'would prepare to strike at England, her most formidable foe, having taken care first to isolate her'. Developments in submarine and aerial warfare might make it impossible for Britain to survive against such an attack. Haldane drew two conclusions. To guard against isolation, Britain should take the initiative in promoting a definite agreement between the Allies and the other Great Powers with the general objective of making it 'perilous for any Great Power to develop unduly the means of aggressive action'. Drawing on the same intellectual tradition as Grey, Haldane suggested that this would be achieved by making recourse to force unlawful except in cases where methods of peaceful settlement had been given a chance; the parties to the agreement would be bound to exert pressure, by force if necessary, on any state which broke this moratorium. This suggestion differed from the Foreign Secretary's approach in that Haldane advocated a direct British initiative and did not think that his scheme would be rendered ineffective if the United States were not committed to use force in all cases of breach of the treaty. Haldane's second conclusion, which implied that the British initiative should be taken before the end of the war, was that the Allies should not develop such extravagant war aims that they quarrelled among themselves at the peace conference or discouraged neutrals from joining an association to maintain the settlement.[46]

If Haldane had hoped to provoke a systematic discussion of war policy, he was disappointed. The only reaction came from Kitchener who, although he dismissed as unreal the idea of an association devoted to upholding impartially the rights of all nations, agreed with Haldane to the extent of urging his colleagues to avoid at all costs the addition of further territory to an Empire whose frontiers were already too long for purposes of defence. (Kitchener was afraid of a militarist Russia, checked in the west by a continental alliance between Germany, France and Italy and turned against an isolated British Empire in the east.)[47] Other ministers were prepared to grumble in private about the Government's drift into supporting annexationist plans, but the Prime Minister and his senior colleagues were incapable of reaching a collective view on the questions raised by these papers, just as they were unable to relate the conduct of the war in practical terms to any objective more precise than the defeat of Germany.

The early months of 1916 produced a number of statements by British ministers, affirming the link between the idea of a league of peace and the Allied cause.[48] Their common theme was that peace should be maintained after Germany's defeat by the combined force of those countries, including the United States, who avowed an interest in upholding it. Bonar Law spoke of a 'League of Peace...whose duty it would be to keep the world in order'; Grey, of 'a League of nations that would be united, quick and instant, to prevent, and if need be, to punish violations of international treaties...' Exactly how this league would work was less than clear and certain officials, notably Hankey, were alarmed that without a thorough examination of this question, the Government might find itself committed to an idea that was wholly impracticable.

To Hankey, the essence of the league idea was that each nation was to rely for its security upon the assurance that if it were attacked, it would receive the assistance of a lot of states who were not concerned with the immediate issues in dispute, but who would nevertheless go to war in defence of a principle of moratorium or of peaceful settlement. In other words, a league of nations was to be a 'League of Neutrals'. It was asserted that relying upon the League, states would be able to reduce their armaments. Those, like Britain, who took the new system seriously, would indeed relax their defences, with the result that they would lay themselves open to despoliation by unrepentantly militarist countries such as Germany and Russia who, while avowing their loyalty to the League, would make military preparations in secret. When they were ready, an incident would be manufactured; half the 'League of Neutrals' would run away and the other half would take sides on the merits of the dispute. Such a system, far from discouraging the hardiest aggressor, would give him every reason to hope for success.

Hankey's argument was that nations could not be expected to learn new rules of behaviour overnight. It gained its effect by taking simplistic promises about an entirely new system of international relations, to the point of absurdity. It was hardly an answer to his case to expostulate, as Drummond did, that nations would have to adopt these new rules if the world was to be saved, that therefore they must do so, and that 'some war must be the last war...it is possible that this war may be, and worth while attempting to ensure that it shall be'.[49]

The best case for a league to enforce a moratorium was made by Crowe in October 1916, in a commentary on a draft paper by Cecil entitled 'Proposals for the Maintenance of Future Peace'.[50] Cecil's proposals were for a territorial guarantee between all the Great Powers to safeguard the peace settlement, a review conference after five years to rectify the mistakes made at the peace conference and a system of conferences to deal periodically with other problems as they arose. Crowe demonstrated that, leaving aside all questions of good or bad intentions, a conference system would be incapable of resolving every dispute that involved urgent questions of vital national interest, and that it could not on its own be relied on to assure the security of every state. His conclusion, however, was that the true value of conference was that it facilitated conciliation and compromise if only by making more time for it: 'the more it can be a rule that, before appealing to the sword, nations should bring their quarrels before a conference in which all are heard and none are coerced, the better will be the prospect of rival claims being peacefully adjusted, and the stronger will grow the feeling that any Power embarking on war without previously pleading its cause before a parliament of nations commits an offence against the Community of States, for which the penalty may be a general combination against the offender'. Cecil did not claim substantially more than this, and retitled his paper 'Proposals for Diminishing the Occasion of Future Wars'.

The Cecil and Crowe papers marked the start of the systematic examination in Whitehall of the possible workings of a league of nations. They provided the basis for a generally favourable report on the subject by the Milner Committee of the Imperial War Cabinet (IWC) in April 1917, and for the work of the Phillimore Committee, which was set up by Balfour on Cecil's advice in November 1917. The Phillimore scheme translated Crowe's description of how the international system might become more peaceful, into the language of treaty obligations; its substance was incorporated into the Covenant. Crowe's paper also demonstrated to Cecil's satisfaction – and to that of the majority of the IWC – the impracticability for a very long time to come of a general scheme of disarmament. Cecil and Crowe became the exponents of a Foreign Office view that the league should have definite but limited functions. Lloyd George, however, remained an enthusiast for disarmament and, under the influence of Hankey and Philip Kerr, developed a quite different and more ambitious conception of a league that would be a development of the Supreme War Council, a league to keep the world in order.[51]

At the end of August 1916 the War Committee decided that they must examine their war aims as a whole, in case Germany or President Wilson or both came forward with a peace initiative. Although no final decision was reached on a set of terms (the Committee was diverted by Lansdowne to considering whether they were right to assume that they would be able to inflict a crushing defeat on Germany) the papers produced by Balfour and the Foreign Office provided a basis for the British response to Wilson's December peace note.[52]

Balfour argued that, the principal object in the war being 'a durable peace', the best way of attaining it was by 'the double method of diminishing the area from which the Central Powers can draw the men and money required for a policy of aggression, while at the same time rendering a policy of aggression less attractive by rearranging the map of Europe in closer agreement with what we rather vaguely call "the principle of nationality"'. The idea of pacifying Europe by giving 'full scope to national aspirations as far as possible' had also been prominent in the Foreign Office paper. As Balfour observed, one of the great attractions of the principle was that, if applied by the Allies, it supplied a justification for breaking up the territories of their enemies. In so far as the principle reflected badly on the British and Russian Empires, the Foreign Office suggested that it should be modified by taking account of the requirements of economic development, of pledges given to Allies and of the importance of not pushing it so far 'as unduly to strengthen any State which is likely to be a cause of danger to European peace in the future'.

To a large extent the principle of nationality was taken up because it offered a rationalisation of what the Allies wanted to do in any case. Balfour used it to justify both depriving Germany and Austria–Hungary of territories which could be claimed on ethnic grounds to be French, Danish, Slav or Italian, and permitting the German peoples to come together in one realm. The General Staff, who advanced the apparently different principle of the balance of power as the basis of the peace settlement, nevertheless reached the same conclusions as Balfour on the territorial arrangements: Germany and Austria might be formed into one state as a counterweight to Russia, but the new state would be deprived of certain territories to limit its power and gratify the Allies.[53] It is worth noting that after two years of war, it was generally accepted that even a 'crushed' Germany would be a considerable force in international relations and unlikely to be reconciled to its defeat.

The Foreign Office paper dealt briefly with the prospects for a league of nations. It had been drafted in part by Tyrrell, Grey's former Private Secretary, and showed the same tendency as had been remarked in his successor, Drummond, to treat the problem as one which turned upon the degree to which states could be expected to be governed by good intentions. The Foreign Office had no doubt that a durable peace could not be expected without a satisfactory territorial settlement. The prospects of permanent peace would, however, be greatly enhanced by an end to the arms race. This in turn would be facilitated if arbitration were an entirely reliable instrument for settling disputes, but this degree of reliability could not be expected unless all states pledged themselves in all sincerity to use it in preference to force. Such a pledge was not to be expected from Germany for some time. A 'less effective' safeguard in the meantime would be a league of nations that was prepared to use force against any state that tried to break away from its obligations under international law. Even the league would not be really effective until nations had learnt 'to subordinate their personal and individual ambitions and dreams for the benefit of the community of nations'. This process had occurred over a long period in the development of civil society and it could not be expected to come at a faster pace in international society. This section of the paper concluded with Grey's long-held view that United States adherence to the league would add greatly to 'the weight and influence' of its decisions.

The fall of Asquith's government made no real difference to the reply the British made to Wilson's call to the belligerents to publish the terms on which they would make peace. The pressures that had governed British diplomacy since the start of the war still ran strong and the new government had little choice but to follow Grey's practice by working to ensure both that the Allies acted in concert and that the joint reply was as conciliatory as possible to the President even though it gave nothing away to the Central Powers. Their full reply compared favourably with the Germans', which seemed evasively brief, and the principle of nationality – not entirely new to Allied propaganda, since it extended the scope of the Allies' original claim to be fighting for small nation-states to include small nations that had not yet achieved statehood – served a useful purpose in so far as it helped the President to accept many Allied territorial claims as liberations rather than as conquests. It was also in line with Grey's policy that Balfour sent Wilson a separate British note to remind him that durable peace required that 'the aggressive aims and unscrupulous methods of the Central Powers should fall into disrepute among their own peoples' and that 'behind all the treaty arrangements for preventing and limiting hostilities some form of international sanction should be devised which would give pause to the hardiest aggressor'.[54]

Grey's most personal contribution to official British thinking about 'permanent peace' was his conviction that it depended on Anglo-American cooperation. This had profound effects. It started the process by which the British Government sought to focus attention on President Wilson as the leader of the League of Nations movement, despite the misgivings of those, such as Spring Rice, who never believed that the American people would do all that their President promised. Grey's correspondence with House had also, of course, started the process by which Wilson came to believe that he was uniquely qualified to save mankind.[55] Grey had been looking for an American initiative that would lead to an Anglo-American partnership. The treatment accorded to House–Grey Memorandum plan had, however, persuaded Wilson that the British were not entirely sound on the question of permanent peace and he made up his mind that the league of nations should not turn out to be a device to harness American power to British purposes. Throughout 1917 and 1918 Cecil tried in vain to get Wilson's agreement for an Anglo-American commission to draw up a scheme for a league.[56] Wilson would not give way on this until the opening of the Peace Conference made cooperation on this subject inescapable.

29

The Blockade

ARTHUR MARSDEN

'All the evidence available tends to show that, with some minor exceptions, practically no goods coming from overseas are getting through to Germany.'[1] This rather complacent assessment of the consequence of economic pressure on Germany, written shortly after Grey had laid down the seals of office, would not have been at all justified in the early stages of the war. It is not that the government had made no preparations in this field to meet the contingency of a clash with the central powers. Indeed, the secretary of the Committee of Imperial Defence went so far as to say, later, that 'from the King to the printer everyone knew what he had to do',[2] and for some two years before 1914 the economic objectives laid down in the War Plan had been to drive the German mercantile marine from the seas and to confiscate all contraband on its way to the enemy.[3] Detailed orders and proclamations in a so-called 'war book' were ready and duly issued to control all shipping belonging to the enemy and to proscribe all British trade with him. From the very beginning to the end of hostilities his vessels found the highways of international commerce closed to them.[4] But in spite of all this, it proved impossible for the British Government to make full and immediate use of its naval power to deny the enemy the supplies of raw materials and food he was by now accustomed to import by sea.[5]

Much of the difficulty in the way of effective action can be traced to inconsistent pre-war policies. While, on the one hand, there had been preparations to meet the possibility of involvement in a major war with Germany, the Foreign Office, on the other hand, had simultaneously been seeking general acceptance for rules of war advantageous to Britain only if she remained neutral in such a war. Indeed, at the Second Hague Conference, Grey had proposed the abolition of the very right that was to be Britain's principal economic weapon seven years later, the right to capture contraband of war.[6] Though the suspicions of other powers had killed this idea, he had been more successful in getting agreement for another drastic innovation, designed to safeguard neutral commerce from undue interference by belligerents, the establishment of an International Prize Court to serve as a court of appeal from decisions of the prize court of any belligerent. In addition, British initiative had been responsible for the London Naval Conference

(1908–9), which met for the purpose of concerting an acceptable code of law to be administered by the court.[7]

This policy, which had been endorsed by expert naval opinion, aimed at safeguarding the interests of Britain in war, whether she were an offensive belligerent, a defensive belligerent or a neutral. At the time it was the last two categories which seemed the most important in the light of recent experience, particularly that in the Russo-Japanese war, when Russian contraband policy had given much cause for concern. After all, Britain was herself potentially more vulnerable than Germany, being the possessor of half the merchant shipping of the world, importer of three quarters of her food and long standing defender of the doctrine that civilian food supplies should have immunity from capture.[8] For most of the decade before the war, therefore, what the Admiralty had been concerned to preserve had been the traditional right to blockade an enemy's ports and coasts, under the belief that the attempt to seize contraband by traditional search at sea had become too difficult and would now cause so much irritation to neutrals that it would outweigh any advantage gained. In any case it was thought that an enemy's trade would automatically find new and secure channels to avoid capture. Only in May 1912, after the creation of a naval staff, was it fully and frankly acknowledged that the development of the submarine and the mine had made the close blockade of Germany impossibly dangerous. To subject an enemy to economic pressure Britain would, after all, have to rely on the previously little esteemed right to capture contraband.[9] By that time, of course, the damage had been done. Grey, who had personally promoted the policy on contraband and had, with unusual warmth, told the cabinet in 1911 that criticisms of it were 'ignorant or perverse',[10] reasserted in parliament – as late as March 1914 – that he was still ready to consider abolishing the right of capture if it would help to reduce armaments. Two months before hostilities commenced he was still actively trying to secure the ratification of the rules agreed at the London Conference, which, if observed, would have rendered the navy relatively useless as a means of bringing economic pressure to bear on the central powers.[11] Five days before hostilities commenced, he was pressing for the immediate introduction of the Naval Prize Procedure Bill which was complementary to those rules.[12]

When, therefore, Britain was involved in war, she was ostensibly bound absolutely by a code of international law fashioned for a bygone age, and bound morally to observe the rules agreed at London. Traditional practice had been formalised and to a certain extent modified in the Declaration of Paris of 1856, and it was understood that, with the exception of contraband (a term not defined), a belligerent could not seize enemy goods in a neutral ship or neutral goods in an enemy ship. Even more fundamental was the fact that a blockade, to be binding, had to be formally declared, effective and confined to the enemy's coasts and ports.[13] The existence, in addition, of the unratified and sometimes badly drafted Declaration of London was bound to cause some confusion. There was nothing new in its adaptation of three categories, 'as old as Grotius', for contraband – with 'absolute' contraband signifying goods primarily for military usage, 'conditional' contraband signifying goods capable of either military or peaceful usage, and a 'free' list signifying goods exclusively for peaceful purposes, which could not be declared contraband in any circumstances. However an attempt to indicate the class of commodity included in each category showed an abysmal lack of realism as well as continuing concern for the interests of neutrals rather than belligerents. Goods, such as cotton, copper, nickel, rubber, hides or iron-ore, which were to prove indispensable to the German munitions industries, were classified as 'free'. Conditional contraband, which included foodstuffs, fodder, coal and bullion, could only be confiscated if its proven destination were a hostile force or government, and not even then if consigned by way of a neutral port.[14] It was all very well for someone like the redoubtable Admiral Fisher to say, 'You can no more tame war than you can tame hell', and that unrealistic agreements would crumble as soon as hostilities commenced.[15] The British government was still faced with the embarrassment, which could not be resolved overnight, that both neutral and enemy expected that she would observe a certain code of conduct acknowledged by her to conform with recognised principles of international law and would be disposed to resent and resist each and every departure from it, however inevitable it might seem in London.[16] In consequence an informed French writer has gone as far as to say that the actual conduct of economic warfare 'was marked for two years by infirmity of purpose born of the fear of offending the neutrals'.[17]

It was clear that no legal blockade of the central powers could ever be established during the war. The essential requirement that it should be 'effective' could not be met owing especially to naval inability to operate freely in the Baltic. Nor could such a blockade of enemy coasts have served much purpose when it is remembered that Germany had long been accustomed to import substantial quantities of food and raw materials via what were now neutral countries, particularly (under the Convention of Mannheim, 1868) by way of the Rhine.[18] This question had soon to be urgently considered. Immediate naval operations, and measures taken in support, had much the effect of a technical blockade, though in theory, of course, Germany could have continued to import necessary supplies through her own ports by using neutral vessels. In fact, very few neutral ships were at her disposal. In the nature of the case, the steamship tonnage of Britain, France, Russia, Belgium and Japan, 67 per cent of the world total, was not available, and much of what remained preferred the lesser risk of supplying the intensified British demand for sea transport or was deterred by reputed mine-laying or by the liability to search, detention and possible condemnation following on the promulgation of an extensive list of contraband on 4 August.[19] Deprived of the use of her own ports and shipping, Germany quickly made every effort to channel her overseas trade through neighbouring neutral countries. Grey and his colleagues in London were therefore faced with the problem of deciding whether to implement the unratified Declaration of London, which would have sanctioned most of those imports, or to develop a policy of economic warfare involving serious interference with the trade and assumed rights of a number of neutral states, some of whom were in a position to retaliate.

What made that decision the more urgent was a proposal from the leading neutral, the United States, followed by one from Britain's ally, France, that acknowledged law as stated in the declaration should be put unaltered into force. Pressure on London was all the greater because the Germans naturally showed themselves in favour and because the navy itself was working to rules unknown to Britain's Prize Courts.[20] At a high level conference which met to resolve the issue,[21] there was probably no one apart from its chairman, Grey, and the Attorney General with many doubts as to which line to take. The conference approved an Order in Council, promulgated on 20 August, by which the British Government (supported later by the French and Russians) proclaimed an intention to act as if the declaration had been ratified – but with modifications which transformed it completely. The most important of these was the stipulation which revived the doctrine of 'continuous voyage' for conditional contraband (article 5), the destination of which could now be inferred from 'any sufficient evidence' (article 3). Thus was Germany deprived of the gain in the Declaration of London she prized most.[22] One further point on which there was agreement at the conference was that all possible steps should be taken to prevent foodstuffs in particular reaching Germany. As British economic pressure on Germany was later to be stigmatised as a 'hunger blockade'[23] it may be useful to examine this aspect of the question briefly and note which sectors of the German economy were most vulnerable to such pressure. First, however, it needs to be said that Grey does not seem to have had much to do personally with the pre-war contingency planning for economic warfare. His role, once war had broken out, also, was to deal with such problems only when they led to 'international complications', and he made little attempt to familiarise himself with 'executive details'.[24] Indeed, if Cambon is to be believed, he even thought, on 4 August, that a declaration of war would be followed by a British blockade of German ports. He seems too to have shared the somewhat exaggerated expectation that the economies of belligerents would be speedily devastated in war, which had led the Prime Minister's sub-committee on the military needs of the empire to leave open the question as to whether to rely on economic pressure as the *only* means for defeating Germany.[25]

One particular reason why the question of food imports featured large in the discussion of the August conference was because of mistaken Admiralty reports that the German government had taken control of all food supplies, thus apparently constituting them contraband and liable to capture.[26] Moreover the Committee of Imperial Defence had convinced itself early in the war, and indeed long before, that food supply was Germany's 'Achilles heel' to be 'attacked systematically', and why this should be so is not easy to see. As the nation hitherto better fed than any other belligerent, Germany – even allowing for considerable amounts of imported fertilisers and concentrated foodstuffs – normally produced 85 per cent of her food within her own borders. There was no fundamental reason, as the second world war was to show, why her food should be specially vulnerable, particularly since some additional supplies could be expected from neighbouring neutrals. There was no reason either to anticipate as yet the domestic difficulties the Germans were to experience in extracting food from reluctant farmers and distributing it equitably; the indiscriminate priority to be given to supplies for military use; the diversion of most ammonia and nitrates produced (so essential for central European soil) to the manufacture of explosives; the retention of too high a proportion of food-consuming livestock; or the unwise conscription of experienced labour.[27] It should, however, also be noted that Germany had to import 20 per cent of even her pre-war requirement of fats and the quantities now needed were not available from contiguous neutral countries. Fats and oils were of course important not only because they were an essential food but because they were convertible into glycerine for the manufacture of munitions.[28] Along with fat, certain supplies for German industry were both vital and vulnerable in war, and these included copper, nickel, tin, rubber, mercury, cotton and hardening agents for steel. The flow of coal, iron-ore and zinc became sufficient only because of the occupation of Belgium and Northern France.[29] Some of Germany's most indispensable imports were, therefore, on the 'free list' of the Declaration of London, and it is not surprising that a British proclamation should deal a second body-blow to the declaration on 21 September 1914 by classifying as conditional contraband some of these commodities – copper, rubber, iron-ore, hides and skins.[30] Britain was now, it might seem, well placed to exert telling pressure on Germany's essential overseas trade; but this was not yet to be.

In the first place the mechanisms being evolved were in their infancy and were not yet capable of such pressure. Organisations hastily assembled or developed from pre-war planning committees operated from the Foreign Office, the Admiralty, the Board of Trade and the Treasury, without a superabundance of co-ordination or good temper. Large numbers of ships belonging to irritated neutrals were being searched in designated ports rather than, in the traditional way, at sea, but few cargoes were seized. For all such seizures had to be justified before Britain's Prize Court – which administered *international* law – or risk liability for heavy damages, and evidence sufficient to secure conviction was often more than difficult to secure. It was to remedy this deficiency that Churchill formed the restriction of enemy supplies committee, which proceeded from the first weeks of the war to establish a network of agents at neutral (and British) ports where information from the consular service on the movement of foodstuffs and raw materials was inadequate. What was also to become eventually the 'great executive organ of the blockade', the contraband committee, was no more, until November, than an *ad hoc* group of Foreign Office and Admiralty officials striving to achieve a measure of collaboration.[31]

Yet there was an even more severe restriction on Allied freedom to damage the economy of the central powers – the attitude of the most powerful neutral, the United States, whose lead in defence of neutral rights would obviously influence the actions of the lesser neutrals. Hopes in London that a speedy defeat of the German navy would leave Britain in a strong position to deal with enemy supplies from overseas were dashed by the Kaiser's reluctance to risk his big ships in battle.[32] The question now for Britain was to decide how far it was possible to prosecute economic warfare without reaching the point where the disadvantages of antagonising the United States outweighed the advantages to be gained by disrupting the German economy. As even Grey came soon to see it, opposition to British policy was formulated on grounds of international law, but arose, as far as American commercial interests were concerned, from a desire to trade uninterruptedly with Germany (as well as the allied powers) irrespective of the fact that a war was in progress. However much this might oversimplify the rich variety of personality and interest that interacted to create American policy, he had summed up crudely the essence of the British problem. But appreciating the problem did little to indicate a precise solution. There was not much doubt what Grey himself would advocate. It was a policy involving no risk. To antagonise Washington, especially in view of British dependence on the increasing flow of munitions and other supplies from the new world, was to him tantamount to losing the war. Rather than that he would give up all attempts to intercept German imports.[33] In this he was supported by the prime minister, who was 'more anxious than many of his colleagues' to conciliate American opinion; but there were others, like Churchill and Runciman (President of the Board of Trade), who were all for 'brinkmanship' before giving way.[34] The time for decision came five weeks after the Order in Council of 20 August, when the American president suddenly initiated conversations about it by expressing informally his government's 'great concern' and 'conviction of the extreme gravity of the situation'.[35] There were other factors also to be considered. France, already incensed at British failure to consult her before important economic decisions were taken and sure that the Americans could be won round, thought it 'supreme folly and quite unnecessary weakness' not to cut off German supplies of foodstuffs and cotton. On top of this the Russians proposed a limited food blockade. However, Grey preferred friction with France to friction with America and his views carried the day against allies and colleagues. They were told that to impede trade in grain, meat and cotton in particular, would incur the risk of war with the United States[36] and Grey still continued to honour the unreal distinction between foodstuffs for civilians and soldiers. The result was that, in slightly confused discussions with Washington, Britain limited her future programme of economic warfare in the interests of avoiding adverse side effects on sectors of the American economy which were in danger of recession. Though the State Department finally dropped its menacing insistence on British ratification of the Declaration of London after four attempts had been resisted, an Order in Council was promulgated on 29 October designed to pacify the Americans, which gave immunity to conditional contraband delivered to a named consignee in a neutral country. Neutrals bordering Germany, it was hoped, would agree to prohibit the re-export of such goods, for it had proved impossible to convince the Prize Court that the intention of a subsequent neutral owner to send them to an enemy country justified seizure. This, in addition to the inadequacies of the machinery for contraband control and the limitations on action in deference to American opinion, had the result that Britain now concentrated her efforts on simply preventing petroleum, rubber and especially copper from reaching the enemy. These and other military requirements were therefore declared absolute contraband.[37] What Grey's conciliation of the United States meant was that, for the time being, hardly any consignment of conditional contraband could be detained and no attempt could be made to prevent numerous cargoes for Germany, especially of cotton and food, passing unmolested.[38]

Yet, in spite of all this vigorous appeasement, there were still American complaints. It is true that the State Department, though displeased, did not add to the chorus of neutral protests when the Admiralty, without consulting Grey, declared the North Sea a 'military area' on 2 November (with the object not merely of retaliating against German mine-laying but of inducing Dutch and Scandinavian shipping to pass by way of the Channel and the Straits of Dover, where apprehension and search was easier).[39] However, at a time when the Allies were facing military disasters, the Americans were quite ready to deny Britain belligerent rights which they had claimed for themselves in the past, especially during the Civil War. In November they challenged the, to Britain, indispensable right to detain ships bound for neutral ports, as well as the right of search at a British port, instead of at sea. They made it more difficult to intercept contraband by forbidding publication of a ship's manifest until a month after sailing. They condemned British demands for guarantees from neutrals against the re-export of contraband cargoes. The President himself vigorously sponsored a dubiously neutral proposition to purchase German merchant ships immobilised in American ports. No wonder that the even tempered Eyre Crowe himself lost all belief in the possibility of fair treatment from President or State Department, or that the Foreign Office preferred to negotiate in London with the more understanding and reliable American Ambassador, Walter Hines Page, and with individual traders and agents.[40] Grey even took pro-German demands by some American politicians for an embargo on supplies to all belligerents seriously enough to remind Spring-Rice of Britain's ability to retaliate if necessary – by withholding supplies of rubber, manganese, plumbago, wool, bauxite, and molybdenum, of which the Allies had a near monopoly.[41]

In the circumstances, even to concentrate on stopping contraband in no more than three commodities still meant antagonising powerful American interests, with resultant complaints to Grey from the insecure and susceptible Wilson cabinet. Evidence too was steadily reaching London that abnormal amounts of copper were being dispatched to the neutrals bordering Germany. This particular problem was virtually answered in December by agreement with the copper producers, but the basic dilemma for the London cabinet was how to 'cripple Krupps' without damaging American commerce or provoking more American awkwardness.[42] A solution which seemed worth trying was to cut the supply line to Germany in Europe rather than in the Western hemisphere and one of the attractions of this policy was that Washington itself had suggested an arrangement with the border neutrals. The principal countries concerned, therefore, Holland, Denmark, Norway and Sweden, each received a memorandum on 3 November suggesting a bargain by which they would be able to import contraband, with little more interference than the verification of ships' papers, in exchange for guarantees that neither the imports themselves nor equivalent stocks would be re-exported.[43] For Grey intended to rely on such neutral prohibitions, which he sought to make as extensive as possible, despite the fact that trade between the neutrals concerned would render prohibitions useless unless all proscribed the same commodities.

Each of the 'northern neutrals' too[44] posed a different and usually difficult problem. In the case of the Netherlands in particular, the danger arising from the existence of the Rhine Convention was self-evident. For the Dutch had long played a prominent part in the German import and distributive trades, and fear of Germany, allied to eagerness to take advantage of high German war prices, was a powerful incentive to continue that role. Churchill observed that, from a purely technical point of view, war with Holland would be preferable to peace. Indeed Dutch prohibitions of export were obviously useless, since goods could be declared in transit to Germany the moment they arrived in a Dutch port. Soon it was learned that enormous quantities of petroleum, copper and rubber were making their way up the Rhine and considerable irritation was caused in London when the Germans – over two years – received almost the whole of Holland's surplus agricultural produce, a large part of which had hitherto come to Britain.[45] Simultaneous pleas that Holland, normally an exporter of meat, had to import large quantities of meat, lard, maize and other foodstuffs for the native population, left an enduring impression in London of Dutch deceit. The French demanded a concerted allied protest and action to stop enemy supplies travelling through Holland; but, given Grey's general policy, there were few economic weapons to hand. Any determined hold-up of cargoes for Holland soon brought American protests, and any machinery created to intimidate the Dutch by withholding allied produce could be countered by similar German pressure on supplies of coal, fertilisers and potash.[46] Caught between the Allies and the Central

Powers, the Dutch government introduced prohibitions of export in August 1914 simply to safeguard domestic stocks. In September, for the same reason, it had all imports of cereals, copper, and petroleum consigned to itself and, after declining British requests to guarantee home consumption of imported contraband, set up a committee of businessmen to deal with suspicious transactions between Dutch merchants and the subjects of belligerent powers. It was this committee which, alarmed at the possibility that Holland might be treated as a base of supplies for the German army under article 2 of the October Order in Council, took up a suggestion of the flamboyant British commercial attaché, Sir Francis Oppenheimer, and set up an independent organisation, the Netherlands Overseas Trust (N.O.T.), which would receive and guarantee against exportation all contraband received in the Netherlands and not consigned to the government. It was in fact under the threat – or perhaps bluff – that article 2 would be invoked that the Dutch ministers gave their approval to this arrangement on 26 December 1914.[47] Two days later, as if to illustrate how narrow the scope for British manoeuvre was, Page handed Grey the first American note of protest against interference with cargoes proceeding to neutral ports.[48]

For Britain something important had been achieved. A step had been taken towards devising a system 'within the recognized comity of nations' by which to bring economic pressure to bear on Germany without depriving neutrals of their right to trade. Its object, of course, was still the limited one of preventing the passage of contraband through Holland. Preventing the passage of contraband through Denmark, however, had, by November 1914, become even more important, and the free harbour of Copenhagen – swarming with German buyers, American suppliers and pseudo-American suppliers – had become the main source of German imports from overseas, as the restriction of enemy supplies committee suddenly discovered. It was known that meat imports had trebled, that unprecedented quantities of foodstuffs, rubber, copper, oil and especially lard were flooding into the country, and that surplus domestic produce, tinned meat and horses were being sold for the astronomic prices offered by the Germans. Denmark was, of course, strategically vulnerable as no other country, even Holland, to attack by her powerful neighbour, and was desperately concerned to avoid giving mortal offence to either belligerent party, but above all the Germans. The government even saw to it that Britain received her customary quota of agricultural produce which would have fetched ten million pounds more on the German market, while, simultaneously, in deference to the Germans, refusing to extend Danish prohibitions of export to cover all contraband, refusing to discontinue exemptions from prohibitions and refusing to retain prohibitions when stocks were surplus to requirements. Soon Denmark, her fears receding, expected to be able to trade normally and resented Allied interference, while the extensive involvement of American nationals in the swollen import trade was an additional complication.[49]

The first British move to meet this situation came even before the N.O.T. agreement was signed, when, in November, the United Steamship company agreed to carry contraband for Scandinavians only and under guarantee. Then, shortly afterwards, the alarmed Danish government itself appealed to Britain to prevent goods, in amounts tempting to Berlin, reaching a country already choked with supplies. Grey was by now persuaded that he would have to invoke article 2 of the October Order in Council so as to apply the doctrine of continuous voyage to conditional contraband going to Denmark. However, negotiation continued, though the Danish government still rejected the sort of arrangement which the Dutch had, according to Grey, proposed 'of their own accord'. Finally, on 9 January, there was agreement on a 'master guarantee', which included the important provision that the existing Danish prohibitions of export would not be rescinded. Denmark would also be able to export home-produced meat, provided imports were normal, and to export contraband to Scandinavian countries, provided re-export was prohibited there. To achieve this useful though limited understanding, Grey had declined advice to apply article 2, ostensibly to preserve Danish food supplies for Britain, but no doubt also not to compromise simultaneous negotiations with other neutrals, or to stimulate concerted opposition from the Scandinavian monarchs.[50] The policy towards Denmark thus begun, sympathetic to her problems rather than harsh, was not to be unsuccessful.

Much less success, however, attended allied policies towards Sweden, easily the most intractable of the European neutrals with whom Britain had to deal. The royalist government was not only conservative, pro-German and intensely anti-Russian, but less susceptible to allied pressure. Sweden's overseas imports included much food, oil and petrol, while almost all her coal came from Britain. But she also produced a good deal of food herself, had to allow for German not British primacy in the Baltic, and was in a position to intimidate Russia – by halting the flow of supplies on the easiest route from the west and by denying specialised engineering plant on which the Russians depended. Moreover, evidence of Scandinavian collaboration soon made it clear that Sweden was not without influence on the policies of her weaker neighbour, Norway, who, though more sympathetic towards Britain, dreaded the possibility of an attempt to avenge the secession of 1905.[51] On the outbreak of war Sweden introduced prohibitions of export to safeguard domestic stocks, which had, however, loopholes enabling the transhipment of supplies for the central powers. Nevertheless, the foreign minister, Wallenberg, was not ostensibly as unfriendly as the court, and, in October, these loopholes were stopped up at Britain's request, though with the proviso that 'regular through traffic' would not be affected. Thus the important overland transit trade to Russia would not be jeopardised.[52] Detentions of shipping however, caused great indignation and, when the North Sea was declared a military area, Sweden initiated joint Scandinavian protest notes on 13 November, though no further action was taken when the notes went unanswered.[53] Ironically, it was the Swedish foreign minister who gave the apparently least unfriendly welcome to the Anglo-French memorandum of November 3, suggesting that, if neutrals were to prohibit the export of contraband, Britain should not intercept it provided the consignee were named. However, he insisted on the right to grant exemptions to such embargoes and to export contraband to Sweden's Scandinavian associates. Against its better judgement, the Foreign Office was persuaded to agree, in the face of urgent representations by the ambassador at Stockholm, Sir Esme Howard, on the need to conciliate the Swedes and avert possible intervention in the war. An Anglo-French memorandum embodying the agreement was signed on 8 December.[54] Far from improving relations, however, with Sweden it exacerbated them. 'Smart tactics' by Wallenberg in granting copper exemptions for considerable stocks before export prohibitions became effective, gave Whitehall the impression that Howard had been duped. On the Swedish side, an angry Wallenberg suspected Britain of bad faith when she failed to honour the agreement immediately, since the unfortunate Howard had reported its signature by very slow diplomatic bag, not telegraph. The wording of the memorandum, too, was such that Sweden could, and did, object when Britain detained any cargo, the re-export of which was prohibited. Seizure of copper in particular, though its export prohibition was ineffective in practice, was taken as a reflection on the honesty of the Swedish government. All British attempts at conciliation failed and, on 13 January 1915, a Swedish decree dealt the Russians a body blow by prohibiting transit traffic in arms and war material through Sweden. By March, the Swedes were using their bargaining position to initiate their 'compensation system', under which licences were demanded for export to Germany of quantities of goods equal to amounts passing to Russia. Export prohibitions were now extensively evaded and large-scale exemptions, as Wallenberg admitted, were granted, especially for lard and even after shipments had been passed by Britain on the understanding that there would be no re-export.[55]

In contrast to the position in Sweden, public opinion in Norway was overwhelmingly sympathetic towards Britain. There were, however, still awkward problems, for the country was inferior to Sweden in population and resources, feared possible action by Swedes and Germans, and consequently co-operated with Sweden and went further than it wished in resistance to Britain's economic war measures. Yet, as possessor of 2,500,000 tons of shipping using the North Sea, as an importer of corn and other necessities by sea, and as purchaser of essential coal supplies from Britain, Norway was open to allied pressure. Understandably the Norwegians protested vigorously in November 1914 against the North Sea being declared a military area and joined with Sweden and Denmark in their protest to all belligerents. When, however, the Norwegian government did agree to prohibitions of export at Britain's request, the prohibitions were made remarkably effective. What it did insist on was the right to grant exemptions and the right to trade in contraband with other Scandinavian countries (as decided at Malmö). Britain did not really contest the exemptions as full details were given, but the trade with Sweden and particularly Denmark caused anxiety – and for a long period – owing to the weak enforcement of export prohibitions in those countries. Moreover, the Norwegians would not consider an embargo on their metallic ores, especially copper, which were mined in Norway and refined in Sweden, and curiously enough, the Foreign Office made no energetic bid to purchase all the Norwegian copper and so thwart the desires of Germany, which also continued to receive the accustomed supplies of fish, pyrites and nickel. However, by the end of the year, Norway's prohibitions were sufficiently comprehensive for Britain to stop pressing for a general agreement. After all, Norway, with its long coastline and its unco-ordinated and scattered commercial community was not like Holland, with its two main ports and highly concentrated business fraternity.[56]

Supplies of contraband were also reaching the central powers by way of Italy and Switzerland, the combating of which involved considerations of no small complexity. Imperfect though the British information services still were, nothing could hide the fact that the port of Genoa was working to capacity to import foodstuffs and raw materials, much from America, for the Italians, the Swiss, the Germans and the Austrians. At the beginning of the war German high prices denuded Italy of vital stocks, particularly of rubber, copper and wool, so that fresh supplies had soon to be imported, while German purchasing agents were as active as ever in sending home essential war material by way of Switzerland. Well organised smuggling was tolerated when Britain and France attempted counter measures. But Italy was in no position to risk a break with the allied powers. Though she normally traded equally with both belligerent groups, she was so dependent on overseas imports, especially coal from Britain, that a conflict with the allies would have been completely disastrous – so much so that even restricted imports could mean industrial unemployment. Grey also had to tread warily and endeavour to restrain impolitic French and Russian commercial pressure. For he felt it unwise to discourage Italian ministers who were secretly talking of possible participation in the war on Britain's side or to provoke excessively the Americans and their copper trade. In the event, the Italian government, faced with the British memorandum of 3 November, the detention of copper consignments at Gibraltar and a hint that coal too might not arrive in future, issued a royal decree that no goods could be declared 'in transit' to a foreign country after arrival in Italy and if for Switzerland or Germany had now to be so marked. Though there was no formal Anglo-Italian agreement and the Italians still retained the right to grant exemptions, these were stringently controlled and the traffic in contraband going directly to Germany withered away.[57]

There remained, of course, the problem of supplies ostensibly for Swiss use. A landlocked, small, industrial country, bordering on neutral Italy on one side and belligerent states on all others, Switzerland presented a difficult and unique problem for the blockade policy-makers. For both the warring alliances could have strangled Switzerland economically with ease. Many of the most important firms were under French or German influence, and many an industrial process involved trans-shipment across the border, possibly several times, to a parent or associate company. This was not all. On the one hand Germany normally supplied most of the Swiss requirements in steel (70%), other metals and coal, and anticipated allied economic measures by devising an elaborate system by which these essentials were bartered for Swiss manufactures. On the other hand, Switzerland imported most of her cereals (80%) and much raw material along sea and land routes dominated by Britain and France. When those nations forbade the use of the Rhine waterway, Swiss imports were virtually obliged to use the increasingly congested ports and railways of a suspicious and none too co-operative France (under an agreement of February 1914) or the choked up port of Genoa and the Italian railways. If Switzerland were not to be completely ruined, she would have to trade to some extent with both central powers and allies. Realisation of this slowly dawned on London, where the suspicion persisted into the spring of 1915, because of inadequate information, that the Swiss might be conniving at passing contraband (especially copper) to Germany. But even before that, Grey had decided to rely on Swiss prohibitions of export and reiterated assurances, despite anxiety over the determined retention of the right to grant unlimited exemptions – and possible smuggling. Yet neither party could feel satisfied with so 'hit or miss' an arrangement for long, as cargoes were detained at Gibraltar or Genoa and evidence of Swiss shortages accumulated. Grey's advisers also began to appreciate Switzerland's potential as a source of manufactures valuable to the war effort and working arrangements with reliable traders commenced. Finally in April 1915, Oppenheimer was despatched to Berne to negotiate formation of a syndicate of importers analogous to the N.O.T.[58]

The first eight months of the war, therefore, gave the British government an appreciation of the difficulties in the way of curbing German trade. The limited progress made to this end could, even at this stage, have been appreciably greater but for appeasement of the Americans (as by the Order-in-Council of 29 October to meet their complaints) and Grey's consequent determination to rely mainly on neutral prohibitions of export in Europe to prevent contraband reaching Germany. He was obviously hurt in January that the United States government's 'one act on record' was a protest singling out Britain as the only belligerent whose conduct deserved censure, and Spring-Rice too was rather shocked that this 'very moral state should only protest where its grossly material interests are affected'. But public opinion was roused and, in the view of the carnage and stalemate in France, demanded a more energetic use of the economic weapon.[59] The situation was further exacerbated by two apparently provocative American 'test case' actions. The first was when German-Americans purchased a German ship, the *Dacia*, for the export of cotton to Rotterdam, with support from Wilson's government; and the second when German agents attempted to send an American ship, the *Wilhelmina*, loaded with food for civilians, directly to Hamburg – again with government assistance. The *Dacia* was tactfully intercepted by a French patrol, since American anti-blockade feeling was anti-British rather than anti-French, and the *Wilhelmina* detained as a vessel bound for a base for enemy forces. However courteous the diplomatic language of the American government, therefore, it had challenged Britain's right to detain contraband going to neutrals which had no prohibition of re-export to Germany, and it had sought to widen the channel along which tens of thousands of tons of vital cotton and foodstuffs were already flowing through British naval cordons directly to Britain's enemies. Then the Germans, on 4 February 1915, as a reprisal against alleged British violations of the Declaration of London and international law, announced an unrestricted submarine campaign against hostile merchant vessels in waters round the United Kingdom, with a grim warning to neutrals that the British trick (ruse de guerre) of having its merchantmen fly neutral flags made mistakes unavoidable. The Americans protested strongly to the Germans, and Bryan, the Secretary of State, with a curious 'neutral' logic that made it necessary to criticise German torpedo and British Prize Court as equally reprehensible, used severe language to the British Ambassador on his country's 'disregard of the law of nations'.[60]

The German action created an almost irresistible demand in Britain for stronger economic measures, provided simultaneously the excuse for such measures and blunted neutral opposition to them. Moreover it seemed now reasonably clear, through conversations between Grey and the 'President's friend', Colonel House, that even if Washington might bark at British reprisals, it was not likely to bite. The premium that Grey had insisted on to insure against American hostility, non-interference with much of the trans-Atlantic trade with Germany, was now obviously higher than necessary. Exports from the United States to the central powers and the neutrals supplying them, in Norway, Sweden, Denmark, Holland and Italy, totalled 66,200,000 dollars in January 1915 compared with 57,500,000 the previous January; imports into the United States from these countries were 22,600,000 dollars in place of 26,900,000. The failure, in deference to American wishes, to place cotton – so important in the manufacture of explosives – on the contraband list, meant that American exports to Scandinavia and Holland were approximately seventeen times above normal in the first five months of 1915, and those from Britain about fifteen times above normal.[61] Sterner action than hitherto could and would obviously now be taken against German trade and Churchill said as much in the House of Commons on 15 February. But the cabinet were not of one mind as to what that action should be. Asquith, Grey and Crewe were still fearful of alienating neutral, especially American, opinion, despite a pronounced reaction in the United States against the German submarine campaign. Indeed Grey went as far as to indulge in a dangerous speculative discussion on future rules of war with Colonel House, saying he thought

Britain would agree to immunity for the merchant shipping of all nations, which shows that the foreign secretary was still thinking of defence against the submarine rather than appreciating the offensive possibilities of economic warfare. However, when Wilson, encouraged by this, proposed a scheme (under prompting from the German ambassador) whereby Germany would cease to employ mines and submarines against merchant vessels in return for non-interference by Britain with American food supplies for German civilians and no deceptive flying of neutral flags, Grey found that his voice was no longer decisive. Opinion in the Foreign Office thought that the proposal would simply prolong the war 'to purchase the safety of a few tramp steamers'; a powerful Committee of Imperial Defence memorandum claimed that food supplies were the only weakness yet shown by Germany; and Asquith himself gave no support for the 'freedom of the seas'.[62]

Though the French were reluctant to risk American opposition by a reprisals policy, the outcome was the Order-in-Council (and corresponding French decree) of 11 March, which, justified as reprisals against the Germans, cut at last the Gordian knot of legal entanglements in which the allies were enmeshed. All cargoes of presumed enemy destination, origin or ownership were now to be detained. 'The British fleet,' wrote Grey, 'has instituted a blockade, effectively controlling by cruiser "cordon" all passage to and from Germany by sea'. There followed what the French minister in London called a 'war of notes' with the United States, an intermittent and rather sterile series of exchanges between London and Washington, unnecessarily complicated by the popular, misleading and unwise British use of the word 'blockade' (not mentioned in the Order) to describe the new measures, and designed, on the British side, to counter what Page himself obliquely characterised as his country's 'lawyers' disquisitions out of textbooks'. The object was to avoid provoking any American resort to unfriendly action.[63] However, the practical consequences of the Order were that Britain now claimed, not the traditional right of seizure and confiscation, but simply to detain non-contraband as well as contraband goods going to Germany and to stop the exports which earned Germany the foreign currency needed to pay for essential imports.

With the doctrine of continuous voyage re-asserted despite the near impossibility of distinguishing adequately between neutral and enemy imports, the development of a comprehensive system to attack enemy trade was now possible. The Americans, of course, protested. They claimed that the so-called 'long distance blockade' was illegal, firstly because German trade with border neutrals and Baltic countries made it ineffective; secondly, because it could not be applied equally to all nations; thirdly, because it took in *neutral* ports, and finally, because it was retaliatory. Later they questioned Britain's right to stop German exports through neutral ports. Foreign Office replies relied heavily on American precedent, especially that dating from the Civil War period, but Britain's real answer, more perhaps than in soothing words, was in conciliatory behaviour towards American interests in applying the blockade.[64] American reactions, however, were never quite predictable. For on the one hand, powerful interests, the meat packers and the cotton and oil trades in particular, wanted to do business with Germany and were vigorously supported by Irish and German organisations and the influence of much of the Catholic church and the Jewish community. On the other hand, the recipients of increasingly heavy orders from the allied powers were no less anxious for those orders to continue. In the event Americans at large took the Order in Council very calmly, no doubt because of the general prosperity of the economy, especially the steadily increasing prices of copper and cotton, and the way Britain alleviated the implementation of the Order in individual cases. A deterioration of American relations with Germany, not unwelcome to Grey, also followed the sinking of the *Lusitania* in May.

Yet the American protests had their effect in London. While those like Crowe fulminated against the 'malevolent pressure by Americans officially and unofficially,' exclusively directed against Britain, Spring-Rice argued that 'some blackmail' would have to be paid, and Grey was ready to drop the whole reprisals policy in order to avoid trouble with the United States. But he was now, according to Hankey, 'a rather pathetic figure, suffering in general health and with his eyesight menaced'. Even however when convalescing, he urged the cabinet through his deputy, Lord Crewe, to end the prohibition on all food-stuffs for Germany and to re-consider a deal, which he had secretly encouraged the Americans to propose, in exchange for the ending of German submarine and gas warfare. In July, he submitted to the cabinet 'with some diffidence' four general policy alternatives on the American trade controversy – to adhere to the Order in Council with the prospect of an increasingly disagreeable deadlock; to argue the unfairness of the American demand for a reversal of British policy while Germany continued to sink British and neutral shipping; to abandon the Order, including all restraint on German exports via neutral countries, by which – he thought – Britain would 'lose very little'; or finally, after telling the Americans 'the truth' that their legalist demands for Britain to give up all economic pressure simply covered a selfish desire to continue trading with Germany, to come to an agreement, before abandoning the Order, as to the particular measures Britain could lawfully employ.[65]

Grey's efforts to emasculate the blockade policy came to nothing. When he asked for the views of the French, who had initially opposed reprisals, he found the Paris Government irritated at the perfunctory consultation of France in blockade matters, and opposed to a *volte-face* under pressure at a time of military reverses on the Russian front. At home Hankey deplored any relaxation of the blockade, especially regarding foodstuffs, and Foreign Office officials urged retention of the Order along with further practical measures to appease the Americans. Moreover loud newspaper demands for an intensification of economic warfare were echoed in the cabinet after political crisis in May had resulted in a coalition government with the Tories. An ailing Grey was obviously uncertain of himself, almost simultaneously arguing that the Order should be dropped and supporting the view that the blockade could still be justified even if the Germans did abandon their submarine campaign. He even seems to have considered declaring a formal blockade, which Lord Robert Cecil told him would be illegal under international law.[66] What may be said to have ended Grey's chances of revising policy was the fact that German cotton imports were under discussion at the same time. All concerned appeared agreed that this was the most serious issue in dispute with the Americans and it was this issue that had most aroused the British public, unaware, it would seem, that cargoes known to be for Germany had been detained since March and that a quarter of a million bales, forwarded under existing contracts, had been seized and purchased by the Board of Trade. Alarmist reports, predicting the possible cessation of American supplies for Britain, came from the panicky Spring-Rice, with details of protests by disgruntled (albeit prospering) meat and oil, as well as cotton interests, and recommendations for their pacification 'even at great sacrifice'. When Grey brought the matter before the cabinet, the whole question of relations with the Americans seemed to hinge on allied treatment of cotton. 'Cotton', wrote a Foreign Office pen, 'is the real crux, and if we can assure the grower his market, the trouble is met'. From Paris Delcassé inveighed against any jettisoning of measures just beginning to prove effective, while Cecil, Eustace Percy and even Page supported the contention that all cotton for Germany should be declared contraband. Grey was obliged to deny any departure from the Order in Council of 11 March and, on 20 August, cotton was declared absolute contraband. This was after an agreement (approved by President Wilson) with the United States federal reserve board, for Britain to purchase cotton at eight cents a pound whenever prices were low. The only consequence was that cotton for Germany could now be confiscated, not just detained, but the potentially troublesome agitation of the American cotton trade withered away.[67]

It was not that all ostensible danger was past. For Wilson seemed to think that a 'concession' from one belligerent should be balanced by a concession extracted from the other. He had warned in the spring that he would move hard against Britain if he could get the Germans to surrender in the sour negotiations taking place over the submarine campaign and, in September, they did agree to stop such warfare against merchant ships in the channel and off the west coasts of Britain. On 5 November, therefore, a trenchant note reached Grey on the subject of economic warfare, reiterating American objections, which, if acceded to, would – as Grey said – have 'struck the weapon of sea-power' from British hands. Attitudes to the United States in London were, however, changing. Complaints of 'damage' to American trade with Europe, which had increased fifty per cent, were received with increasing scepticism and resentment. When Spring-Rice suggested giving up the prohibition on German exports to satisfy American purchasers, the reaction was simply one of irritation. Even Grey, in an uncharacteristic outburst on a minor point, declaimed against the 'moral failure' of the United States, saying, 'They have murdered international law and prolonged the war, and the talk of the President makes me sick.' American diplomats had been hinting, moreover, that their note was only a 'safety valve' and the issue would not be pressed further, while Page and House did not hide from Grey their belief that an American rupture with Germany was eventually inevitable. Renewed American–German tension towards the end of the year over intriguing German and Austrian embassy officials and submarine warfare, could only add to determination in London not to give way. Of course, not only Grey but others involved in decision making like Lord Robert Cecil acknowledged that active opposition by the United States would mean ending the blockade, and possible defeat.[68] But what German policy had done was to blunt American criticism of Britain sufficiently for the Order in Council of 11 March and the construction of a complicated and effective blockade machine to become politically possible, and by the end of 1915 a great deal had been accomplished.

The organisations that sprang up in that year to implement the blockade policy were not devised under any comprehensive and well considered plan, but were an *ad hoc* growth within several ministries in response to the pressure of circumstances – though increasingly effective for all that. Once the Order in Council of 11 March had been promulgated, a list of commodities, including foodstuffs, was drawn up which the Restriction of Enemy Supplies Committee was determined Germany should not get. Severe treatment of German exports by the Enemy Exports Committee soon led to refusal of further consignments by neutral lines. Detentions by the Contraband Committee of vessels with cargoes possibly for Germany multiplied. The Coal Export Committee exploited the dependence of several neutral countries on British coal, while Britain's world wide bunkering facilities were denied to ships whose owners refused to co-operate. Military censorship of neutral mails, and later cables, passing through British hands was extended to yield commercial information invaluable to the efficiency of the blockade and German attempts to use the parcel post to transport vital goods were frustrated. An advisory body of bankers, the Cornhill Committee, strove to prevent the use of banking facilities by the enemy and his agents.[69] Naturally, one of the tasks that fell to the Foreign Office was to counter neutral dissatisfaction with such measures, but it was also beginning to negotiate a most elaborate network of agreements with neutral countries, shipping lines, trading associations and firms, which did much to enhance the effectiveness of the blockade. For the extremely difficult problem still remained of how to ensure that the European neutrals imported from overseas only such quantities of essential commodities as required for their own consumption, when every subterfuge was being employed to disguise the destination of goods for the central powers and prize court condemnations required positive evidence. A solution was made no easier by the determination of the Board of Trade that British traders should share in supplying the inflated requirements of the European neutrals and the resultant generous issue of export licences. Two linked allied objectives began to emerge – for a trusted organisation, such as the N.O.T., to assume responsibility in each country that imported goods or their equivalent would not be re-exported, and for a system of rationing based on the normal consumption of the countries concerned to be introduced.

At allied conferences in Paris and London in June and August, the French pressed hard for the rationing of neutrals contiguous to the central powers, but, though the British representatives were prevailed upon to agree in principle, a decision of the prize court in the following month, in the 'Kim' case, was unsettling. It showed that, as the law stood, statistical evidence of imports by a neutral far in excess of domestic requirements was not enough in itself to secure condemnation of a particular cargo. Common prudence therefore dictated that no attempt should be made to impose rationing on neutrals as a whole, and that the government should instead bring every possible pressure to bear so that voluntary rationing would be accepted by bodies representing the whole or important sectors of the foreign trade of each neutral concerned.[70] Indeed, in the prickly negotiations already under way with the Swiss Federal Council, Oppenheimer was successful in the same month (September) in achieving these objects. Since Italy was now in the war, resistance by Switzerland was more than ever hopeless and commercial pressure was deliberately brought to bear by the allies to make her more amenable. Of course the Swiss used to the full their bargaining power as suppliers to the allies of vital dyestuffs, condensed milk and specialised war materials, and the discussions were further complicated by German threats to cut Swiss coal supplies and by the determination of the British, French and Italian governments not to see their respective country's trade taken over by the other two. Despite the geographical proximity to Switzerland of the two Latin allies, it was the policy of the better organised British contraband apparatus which predominated and, following Oppenheimer's basic idea for a two tier trust, the *Societé Suisse de Surveillance Économique* (or S.S.S.), was finally created. Ostensibly an independent organisation for foreign trade, with subordinate syndicates for individual trades, such as the Metals Syndicate, it was really (unlike the N.O.T.) sponsored and initially financed by the government, which exercised a clandestine control. The agreement was almost certainly as satisfactory a one as could have been made and such drawbacks as it had were inevitable in the circumstances. Some Swiss trading with Germany and Austria had to be agreed to, if only because some manufactures required part processing in those countries and because Germany demanded goods in exchange for exports vital to Switzerland. Moreover attempts to reduce Swiss dependence on Germany by arrangements to provide coal from allied sources came to nothing and the trust agreement was to prove inadequate to prevent Italian fruit and silk seeping through to Germany.

However, a committee to ration Switzerland was set up in Paris with representatives of the governments of Britain, France, Italy and, because Britain feared being outvoted, Russia. It was hoped that the committee might be the nerve centre of a general rationing scheme for concurring neutrals, but disagreements between the allies and the fall of events decreed otherwise.[71] Apart from anything else, Lord Crewe's new and influential War Trade Advisory Committee rejected compulsion and held up the development of a full rationing policy for months under the belief that successful prize court decisions were essential. Nevertheless some rationing by agreement was possible in 1915 and, in negotiations with the northern neutrals, British hands were much more free from Latin interference than in Switzerland.

The original N.O.T. agreement had, of course, simply aimed at preventing the passage of contraband through Holland, and the reprisals policy, which elicited only a formal Dutch protest, led inevitably to new arrangements. Evidence of increasing Dutch imports and of even English goods going through to Germany led, after severe treatment of Dutch commerce, to explanations in May which re-established British confidence in the 'reliability and straightforwardness' of the trust itself, and especially of its chairman, M. van Vollenhoven. A parliamentary act then ordered all United Kingdom exports for Holland to be consigned to the N.O.T., but the position was clearly still not satisfactory. Fines imposed by the trust were not heavy enough to overcome all the attraction of the lucrative German market; goods once distributed to retailers in small quantities could be re-exported as 'coming from stocks' and imports of, for example, meats often served to set free for export similar Dutch products. Further discussions resulted in an agreement, on 19 July 1915, consolidating all arrangements with the trust, which also consented to endeavour to restrict imports to amounts required for home consumption. 'Rations' were then negotiated at intervals to cover the more important imports that might find their way to Germany, and Britain's allies were induced to adhere to the N.O.T. agreement.[72]

The Order in Council of 11 March also made the January agreement with Denmark obsolescent, and it was proving an impossible burden for the United Steamship company to obtain satisfactory guarantees for goods carried. Heavy shipments of lard, meat products and hides seemed obviously intended for the central powers and American exporters were not at all deterred by the 'Kim' verdict. Contraband from overseas also passed by way of Denmark to Sweden and thence through lax Swedish embargo controls to Germany. Since the Danish Government rejected an official trust, long negotiations took place with the Merchants' Guild of Copenhagen (the *Grosserer Societat*) and the Chamber of Manufactures (the *Industriraad*) during which the Danes used to the full their inability to prevent German arms seizing their agricultural riches at will and the importance of their bacon and meat exports to Britain. Grey and his colleagues were pleased, however, with an agreement made on 19 November, by which the two associations gave guarantees against re-export even to Norway and Sweden. Danes would police Danes and special exemptions would preserve Copenhagen as *entrepôt* for the Scandinavian trade, while vital 'exchanges' with Germany would continue. Subsidiary rationing agreements were negotiated separately. Indeed, cotton was already rationed, but British detentions and embargoes continued until a wide-ranging list of commodities received Danish assent on 29 February 1916. In London, arrangements with Denmark seemed for a time quite satisfactory and Britain's allies were once again induced to signify approval.[73]

Negotiations for a general agreement with Norway on imports and rationing never came, however, to fruition. Geography, of course, made a trust like the N.O.T. more difficult to construct there than in the Netherlands. But a trust was what the Foreign Office favoured, after information was received that prohibited goods were going in large amounts via Norway to the enemy.[74] Numbers of vessels were detained and, under this pressure, the unwilling Norwegians sent delegates from two associations to negotiate in London. These, however, turned out to be pro-German and hopeful that imports allowed to a trust would facilitate exports to Germany. Nevertheless, by September, a draft agreement had been drawn up, and, after ten weeks' cogitation, the Norwegians' Union of Merchants and Manufacturers inclined towards acceptance, only to find that the British government now rejected the idea of a Norwegian trust. Its probable leaders seemed more than suspicious and British objectives, it was thought, would be attained at least as well by the existing policy of separate agreements with various interests, the course preferred by Findlay, the ambassador at Christiania. Even more decisive, perhaps, was the feeling that public criticism of the recent Danish agreement made another politically unwise. Grey dutifully 'rubber stamped' each variation of policy by his blockade experts and the negotiation of commercial agreements, therefore, continued apace. Indeed, in the end, there were to be no less than sixty-nine, including fourteen shipping agreements and twenty-one oil and margarine agreements, while the legation itself exercised a detailed regulation of coal and bunkering. These so-called 'branch agreements' gradually consolidated British control and, when rations of raw material imports had been fixed, Norwegian groups or associations assumed responsibility that their members used supplies according to promises given.[75]

No such agreements were possible with the intractable Swedes, whose attitude was so Germanophil as to be 'non-belligerent' rather than neutral. In the British view, Sweden seemed to claim the right not merely to make itself the principal base of German supplies, but to draw those supplies from overseas on the pretence that they were for home consumption, while concealing all statistical information which would have revealed violation of Swedish undertakings and embargoes. Sweden's one-sided interpretation of neutrality also insisted that goods going through Swedish territory to Russia should be balanced by equivalent goods to Germany (with which country Sweden had a secret understanding). This was despite the fact that the transit trade to

Russia involved only a redeployment of allied resources, not normally preventable by Germany, while goods for Germany via Sweden involved a clear addition to German resources that had crossed the seas only with allied permission. The Swedes held the March Order in Council to be illegal and vigorous British detention of vessels and withholding of supplies, especially of coal, copper and oil, together with the interception of Swedish iron ore intended for Germany, caused much hostility. In 1915, of course, it was still conceivable that Sweden might intervene in the war, and Grey was, therefore, all caution. One solitary rationing agreement proved possible in June, with the Swedish Cotton Spinners Association, but the Swedish government actively discouraged other agreements with private bodies, though some were made with international traders supplying Sweden.

It soon became clear that the Swedes would never accept an import trust, or indeed any foreign control, not even investigation of the efficiency of Swedish embargoes, though import figures for the six months ending in August showed a rise in almost every commodity to which Britain attached importance. Conversations were kept going, however, during which some transit traffic vital to Russia was permitted, and by August, an agreement was actually negotiated, though never ratified. In these discussions Britain's main preoccupation was that Sweden should have no pretext for hostilities during a period of Russian disaster. Gradually the evidence emerged, however, that British reliance on Swedish exports was less than Swedish dependence on imports from Britain and, in October, when Russia's position had improved somewhat, the conversations terminated.[76] Though no formal rationing agreement was possible during the period that Grey was in office, the circumstances of 1916 enabled a substantial measure of informal control. Horror at the carnage of war and a greater awareness of the economic consequences of participation considerably reduced Swedish belligerency. Hammarskjöld could still secure passage of a War Trade Law to prohibit private agreements with warring states, but the pressure of bunker control as well as navicerting, a system of 'commercial passports' for cargoes, effectively reduced Swedish imports. No neutral, it has been claimed, was so severely treated. As a contraband department official succinctly summed up the position in November:

We are already rationing Sweden by means of embargoes imposed on the advice of the Rationing Committee in the case of all important commodities. By refusal of export licences and navicerts we are able to stop the shipment altogether of large quantities of goods thus embargoed. Goods which do get shipped are unloaded and put in Prize Court in the hope that it may be possible to defer the hearing until the rationing system again permits import of the particular commodity into Sweden.

This system has worked surprisingly well when one considers that it is – at present – devoid of all legal sanction and is largely built up on bluff.[77]

Though still hampered by the inability of the Ministry of Munitions to free itself from dependence on Swedish ball bearings, steel, pig and bar iron, scrap and perchlorate of ammonia, Britain could, therefore, now continue quite well without a general agreement, but even the proud Swedes were obliged at least to begin negotiations in the Autumn.

This pressure on Sweden in 1916 was one of the results of general changes in blockade administration and policy. There had been complaints regarding the efficiency of what Findlay called 'the chaotic mess of committees and departments' and their lack of co-ordination[78] and a less well informed, but vigorous, public clamour for an intensification of the economic campaign was not without its effect. In February, Lord Robert Cecil, while retaining his position as under-secretary at the Foreign Office, entered the cabinet as Minister of Blockade. Since he now controlled virtually all committees and departments (in the various ministries) concerned with economic warfare, there was hardly any question that the Foreign Office – rather than the Admiralty – would now invariably have the final word in policy making and, within his own ministry, the influence of Grey in blockade matters was naturally even further attenuated. The Contraband Department of the Foreign Office, which had increased five-fold in size in twelve months, now became the central executive body for the blockade, directing and advising policy towards neutrals, and the influential War Trade Advisory Committee henceforward reported to Cecil, not to the cabinet. More detailed and accurate information from the War Trade Statistics Department and the War Trade Intelligence Department made for greater efficiency, especially in rationing, the fundamental element in 1916 policy.[79]

The new minister favoured an uncompromising economic policy and viewed with distaste the gaps in the patchwork of rationing agreements. Already a reluctant Grey had been talked by his colleagues into conceding that 'forcible rationing', based on estimates of a neutral's normal requirements, had to be attempted, and Cecil, stating that statistics were henceforth to be the basis of the blockade, gave instructions that the shipping of countries without agreements should be subjected to 'every legitimate delay and difficulty'. On 13 April, to settle the rations for neutral imports not covered by an agreement, he set up a Rationing Committee, which completed its task between August and December, by which time statistics, modified by political considerations, were found adequate. The list of contraband lengthened and one of Cecil's first acts was to draft two Orders in Council. The first, promulgated on 30 March, was to practically abolish the distinction between absolute and conditional contraband. The second, promulgated on 7 July only after overcoming French legal objections, repealed all parts still in force of the Declaration of London (which Cecil had, incidentally, opposed in 1909). On 13 April, moreover, the awkward and unscrupulous Chicago meat packers accepted control of their exports in an agreement so favourable to them as almost to amount to payment of Danegeld, but the steep rise in their consignments to

Sweden and Denmark thereafter fell to below normal. Another innovation was the system of 'navicerts', or documents assuring uninterrupted passage for certified goods, which began on 16 March. Originally proposed by the American consul-general in London to facilitate American commerce, it was adapted as a powerful British instrument for the coercion of shipping. A further turn of the screw on enemy supplies was provided by extending the use of the 'Black Lists' of firms that had traded with the central powers, and, on 29 February, Cecil began publishing a 'statutory' list of companies against which evidence was irrefutable, so that they could be ostracised by allied traders and shipping.[80]

In the nature of the case, appreciably harsher treatment of the European neutrals was only possible as long as the Americans, however disapproving, remained inactive. A less accommodating attitude towards the United States now shown by Cecil was in line with the hardening temper of opinion inside and outside the government, which even had some effect on Grey. Besides, the trusted 'expert opinion' of Lord Eustace Percy gave comforting assurance of the desired American passivity in a presidential election year:

> ...the fundamental common interests of the two countries cover so wide a field that serious conflict between them is a possibility so remote as to be negligible. Americans do not love us...but as a matter of fact they want us to win...If the above is anything like correct, it follows, I think, that we need not be deterred in our blockade policy by the fear of an embargo, or other hostile action by the United States.[81]

An unwilling, hesitant and increasingly irate Wilson came to something like the same assessment. The logic of the situation was that the material interests of the United States forbad effective measures, let alone hostilities, against the allied powers. However, as the second half of 1916 showed, logic would not necessarily determine policy when national feeling was aroused. While, in the spring, Grey was ineffectually discussing with House the possibility of peace through co-operation with the United States and the intensification of German submarine warfare led to two months of acid German–American controversy over the sinking of the *Sussex*, Washington was unlikely to make any strong show of hostility. However, the scepticism of Asquith and others about American mediation, and the improvement of American relations with Germany following the surrender (with reservations) of the latter in May on the question of submarine warfare, produced a new situation, in which Wilsonian exasperation with Britain was exacerbated by Cecil's policies and their general lack of appeasement. Significantly it was not the severe measures to ration half the European continent which roused most ire. The March Order in Council was characterised as 'intentionally discourteous'; that of July 'at variance with the law and practice of nations', and American rights were reserved. But what really irritated was the 'insulting' inclusion without warning of American firms in July's published Black List, the refusal of bunkering facilities to others and the censoring of American mail on its way to various neutral countries, all matters affecting *amour propre* rather than fundamental material interests. The irony in American fury over the black listing and bunkering regulations was that all they did was forbid the use of 'British coal, British ships and British money' to help Britain's enemy. But then the decisions on which firms were to be ostracised were also British. Retaliatory legislation in September gave the president power to deny clearance to vessels discriminating for or against American citizens and to ban exports to countries with a prohibition on American imports. Yet despite the fact that Wilson could now ostensibly impede and obstruct the blockade by any retaliation short of war, the Foreign Office was not particularly impressed, believing the act to have been only a Congressional manoeuvre. Spring-Rice as ever deplored the refusal of substantial concessions and urged London to pay the price of dependence on the United States. But the fuming president made no irrevocable move in the face of incontestable evidence – some conveniently supplied by Britain – that allied counter-retaliation could inflict considerably more damage on the American economy than the blockade itself. Much American trade was carried in British ships; £121,000,000 of essential imports came from the British Empire, and those same blockade measures that restricted trade with European neutrals also transmitted safely 259,000,000 dollars' worth of American goods.[82] The policy makers of the blockade were, therefore, right to believe that the United States would tolerate the stringencies of 1916, but they were straining American forbearance a little more than they realised, and an untoward incident could have had illogically severe repercussions.

. 'The mere statement of what is being done in the way of restriction', wrote Spring-Rice in July 1916, 'would astonish the world, and it is being done without raising any special difficulties'. The relatively moderate friction caused by the rationing policy was partly the result of favourable circumstances, but even more because the machinery for enforcement was complete. Indeed, British policy towards the European neutrals went beyond the simple rationing of imports and much effort was made to prevent the export to the enemy of even the domestic produce of those countries and to divert it to allied consumers. As the Danes in particular were sending an increasing proportion of their exports to Germany, a vigorous effort was made by the Contraband Department to get back Britain's normal share. When the Danes, caught between British and German menaces, temporised, drastic action to deprive them of coal, foodstuffs, forage and margarine imports was considered, but rejected as liable to lead to a German seizure of Danish produce and its complete loss to Britain. The Foreign Office was satisfied, therefore, with a modest gain in deliveries of bacon, eggs, and butter. However, an attempt to prevent fish being sold to Germany by depriving Danish trawlers of oil failed when the Germans made up the deficiencies with supplies from the newly conquered Rumanian fields. There was no difficulty in securing an option on all the exportable produce of Iceland, which acknowledged the Danish crown.[83]

As for Norway, the system, as Findlay called it, worked 'with wonderfully little friction', and not a single breach of agreement was recorded on the part of any association concerned. Motivated, on the other hand, by fear of the Germans, by pressure from the Swedes and by irritation with blockade-induced shortages, the Norwegian government itself resisted every British innovation, and it was not easy to check the flow of Norwegian fish, pyrites and nickel to the central powers. In the case of fish, Britain first, at Norwegian prompting, bought most of the spring catch at an exorbitant price, but was able on 18 August to secure an option on all future landings with exception of an amount of up to fifteen per cent for Germany. Arrangements with the Americans had also given Britain control over most of the world supply of copper and this was used to compel the Norwegians to agree not to export copper or pyrites to a belligerent except against equivalent imports, though nickel exports could only be reduced to a moderate level by very substantial payments. In spite of some fish and pyrites reaching the Germans illegally, they reacted sharply to the Anglo-Norwegian agreements with a submarine campaign against Norwegian shipping so violent as to amount to a challenge to the whole blockade system as such, and, on top of this, the unfortunate Norwegians had their coal supplies from Britain cut, to 'encourage' them to resist the pressure being exerted on them. Luckily for Britain, the Norwegians neither yielded to the German demands which might have had the disastrous consequence of other neutrals following suit, nor did they, by their policy, provoke a German attack on their country.[84]

The Dutch, who felt themselves capable of some resistance to the Germans, had nevertheless irritated the blockade ministry by sending nearly all their surplus agricultural produce, some forty per cent of the total, to Germany and exports to that country were even increasing in the early months of 1916. Dutch trawlers returning home laden with fish possibly for Germany added to British sensitivity. In view, however, of the lack of legal sanction for any interference with such trade, London was cautious, but an agreement in June on the question of agricultural produce failed to work, something not very surprising. For, when the Foreign Office reluctantly agreed to what it thought would be the seizure of a few obviously guilty trawlers, the Admiralty, in the euphoria of its 'victory' at Jutland, rounded up sixty-five. Fortunately the owners preferred negotiation to the prize court proceedings they would certainly have won, and Britain was able to make an agreement by which she got half Holland's surplus fish and effective control over eighty per cent of herring landed. In the circumstances a new and satisfactory agricultural agreement was only concluded after British threats to bring Holland's trade to a standstill by depriving her of foodstuffs, fertilisers, jute, lubricants and the use of bunkering and cable facilities. However, to avoid subjecting the Netherlands to German retaliation, the Foreign Office settled for no more than the approximate quantity of Dutch agricultural imports received before the war. Ironically, one of the greatest obstacles, in the difficult negotiations, was

Britain's inability to guarantee protection for the vessels bringing the produce to British ports.[85]

The complexities of the Swiss problem also were not easily handled by the committee of four bickering allies in Paris. The direct control of the blockade was, of course, in Italian, but more particularly French hands. While few imported goods, with the exception of Italian fruit and some silk, were re-exported, attempts to limit Swiss trade with Germany and Austria caused considerable difficulties, and not only because of peremptory German demands on the federal government for valuable goods in exchange for absolutely essential supplies like coal. Much criticised and in a shaky condition for some time after its creation, the S.S.S. had to face severe French restrictions on Swiss trade. These took the form of black-listing and refusal of adequate transport facilities, above all for 'competitive' goods from Britain, and were imposed by various French authorities, sometimes contrary to the wishes of the French blockade ministry. Britain, whose policy was to do all possible to avert the collapse of the S.S.S., prevailed on the French to moderate their attitude by threatening to treat French commerce with other neutrals in a similar manner. A further complication arose when the Swiss warded off danger from Germany by an agreement in September which gave the central powers the sort of guarantee against re-export the allies themselves usually exacted. Britain and France protested vigorously, mainly because the Germans would receive a large number of surplus Swiss cattle under the agreement. Rather extreme demands insisted on by the French to restore 'equality of treatment' for the allies were reduced to a more reasonable proposition agreed by both parties in January 1917, by which intricate adjustments were made in the regulations controlling Swiss imports and exports. Cecil still did not regard the position as satisfactory, but, beyond increasing the scope of rationing, he felt there was nothing more that could be done.[86]

By the end of 1916, therefore, the machinery of the blockade, a product of evolution rather than scientific organisation and functioning harmoniously only with the advent of the Ministry of Blockade in the spring, had been exerting its maximum pressure on the enemy powers for about six months. As complex an operation as putting four national armies in the field and much better co-ordinated than the military war effort, if only because British domination of allied policy (except towards Switzerland) gave it greater cohesion, its importance has only tardily been fully recognised. However much lacking the seductive appeal of military exploits, it may be said to have constituted the most devastating, offensive use of sea power devised in the war. In the circumstances peculiar to the first world war, it is difficult to imagine any more sensitive and effective machine. The main objective had been achieved. 'All the evidence tends to show', said Cecil to the cabinet in January, 'that, with some minor exceptions, practically no goods coming from overseas are getting through to Germany.' Going even further than this, the allies had begun to make inroads into the freedom of European neutrals to sell their own produce across their own borders to Britain's enemies. Policies towards each European neutral had been so calculated that it seemed likely that any severe increase in pressure would mean more loss to the allies than gain. With the amount of shipping for commerce already in decline, neutrals, even the Swedes, Dutch and Americans, were the more disposed to tolerate restrictions, some – like navicerts – without the support of positive law, which did guarantee that their cargoes would escape Britain's increasing interference. Nor were reports of the effects of the blockade on the enemy countries discouraging. True, the German armies in particular seemed still well enough supplied with food and equipment, and some of the shortages arising from the blockade, like the exhaustion of manganese stocks, had been overcome by new manufacturing processes or by the use of substitutes. But all was being sacrificed to military needs and there were fifty-six food riots in German cities in 1916. Lack of labour in the fields, the use of fats for making explosives, a disastrous failure of crops, especially potatoes, and an equally disastrous inability to get all available food from disgruntled farmers or arrange equitable distribution – all served to make the 'turnip-winter' of 1916–17 the worst period of the war. As a detailed investigation was to show, the weight of the average German fell rapidly and he was kept alive at that time only by his own fat tissue. It was surely a little ironic that someone like Lloyd George should opine at an allied conference in November that the Germans were never in less danger of starving. Others equally out of touch with the blockade machine thought that supplies to be expected from conquered Rumania had ended all hopes of coercing the central powers by means of economic war. Grey summed up the impact of Britain's blockade policy far more accurately shortly before he left office for good, when he wrote:

All our information points to the fact that this policy is pressing more and more severely on German economic and industrial life and that its effect in the war is of the greatest importance.[87]

30

The Foreign Office and the War

ZARA STEINER

The outbreak of war had an immediate impact on the Foreign Office. Within twenty-four hours, the department had become a central post office for the service ministries. Over four hundred telegrams arrived daily and the Parliamentary department which handled ciphering and deciphering was put on a three-shift basis to handle the flood of correspondence. Visiting diplomats, even the near-sighted Spring Rice who could only type with one finger, were pressed into temporary service and permanent staff were asked to work on Saturdays. Arthur Nicolson agreed to remain on as permanent under-secretary and Francis Bertie, whom he was to replace at Paris, stayed in the French capital. It was Eyre Crowe who first realised that the office would have to be reorganised. On 7 August he suggested to Nicolson that the Western and Eastern departments be amalgamated to create a single War Department under George Clerk. Crowe, assisted by a private secretary (Lord Drogheda), was to be sent all papers of importance connected with the war 'so as to preserve unity of direction'. The Treaty Department was to be strengthened, the Commercial department given new responsibilities and the remaining political departments reduced in size to a bare minimum.[1]

During the first three months of the war, Crowe and Clerk seem to have been omnipresent; even minor matters were referred to them. William Tyrrell, too, was in constant attendance as he did his best to relieve Grey from as much pressure as possible. Nicolson, though forced to work a full six-day week, responded well to the challenge and reported that he was enjoying unusually good health.[2] The pace was somewhat frantic as the office not only had immediate political problems to solve but continued to act as an information outpost for the War Office and Admiralty. These first months were dominated by the search for allies in the East; much of the activity took place in Constantinople and in the various Balkan capitals. Telegrams went back and forth for not only did the various British ministers have to be consulted but St Petersburg and even Paris. As in the period leading up to the war, Grey dominated this scene and was responsible for all the major diplomatic moves. He supported Louis Mallet's efforts to maintain Turkish neutrality until the ambassador was forced to concede defeat. Sometimes in opposition to his own officials, Grey determined which course was to be followed at Sofia, Bucharest,

Athens and Rome though his freedom of action was curtailed by Balkan rivalries, Russian suspicions and above all the military situation. The Foreign Secretary even found time to keep a firm grip over American and Far Eastern affairs. Almost from the start of the war, Grey was more concerned than his colleagues with the need to conciliate Washington and made every effort to maintain his links with Wilson through the friendly American ambassador, Walter Page. Though experienced officials outlined the possible alternatives, it was Grey who adopted and shaped the policy of 'marking time' in the Far East.

In his own house, then, Grey remained the master but there were from the summer of 1914 important differences from the pre-July period. Foremost, Grey believed that, in wartime, the diplomats served the interests of the service chiefs and diplomacy was the handmaiden of the service ministries. The Foreign Secretary went further. Conscious of his lack of expertise in military matters, he believed he was in no position to question or influence the judgments and priorities of the generals. He therefore willingly accepted a subordinate role in the cabinet and deferred to Lord Kitchener even on those rare occasions when he had doubts about the wisdom of a proposed course of action. With disastrous consequences, he failed to recognise the integral connection between strategy and diplomacy and never understood how one could assist the other if properly coordinated. Grey's disinterest weakened both the cabinet and his department for isolated diplomatic planning in wartime was almost doomed to failure.

There was yet another factor to explain why even before the collapse of the Asquith government, the Foreign Office suffered a loss of power. Grey had been exhausted by the July crisis; he could not recover from the shock of war and was constantly pursued by the thought that he might have done more to prevent it. In sharp contrast to Churchill, he was horrified by the actual events of the war and did his best to uphold the crumbling structure of pre-war morality and international law. When Churchill was dismissed at the end of 1915, Grey wrote commiserating, '...it adds to my hatred of the war – I shall look back upon it if I survive it, as a time of horrible memory. I hated it beforehand & I hate it now, though I do not see how it could have been avoided.'[3] The stalemate on the Western front and the defeats in the East brought out that pessimistic streak in Grey's character and made him a 'despondent and dolorous' ministerial companion. Even a rest at Christmas 1914 when Haldane substituted for him at the Foreign Office did not suffice to revive his spirits. The Foreign Secretary's deteriorating eyesight and premature ageing were in part physical manifestations of an inner turmoil which left him depressed and exhausted. A department without a strong head is rarely a powerful one and the Foreign Office was particularly vulnerable in this respect.

Others beside Grey felt the strains of war. Crowe, in particular, was driven to distraction by the government's inability to marshal its resources. He believed that the Germans were far better organised and that the well-prepared German army was backed by a fully mobilised civilian population. He was particularly annoyed by certain hesitations in the period subsequent to the declaration of war. He was irritated by the ambiguity over the position of Austria-Hungary. He found the bargaining at Constantinople fruitless and dangerous. He considered the careful policy being pursued towards Japan inexplicable in view of the driving need to crush the German fleet in Far Eastern waters.[4] 'In a war of this kind and magnitude', he argued on more than one occasion, 'there is one supreme and overriding consideration: to smash the enemy definitely, rapidly and with the employment of every legitimate means.'[5] Crowe was far less concerned than Grey with the niceties of international law or the possible consequences of present actions on future international relations. Crowe had a healthy respect for German strength and never underestimated the price which would have to be paid for victory.

In the autumn of 1914 there was some kind of clash between Grey and Crowe. Bertie, not always the most reliable of reporters, recorded that 'Crowe had completely lost his head. His Prussian blood came out and he was insubordinate and insolent to Grey, who had decided that his appointment to succeed Nicolson is impossible.'[6] There were others, such as Nicolson, who were somewhat disturbed by the vigour with which the under-secretary pressed his views. Even Tyrrell, Crowe's good friend, was apparently quarrelling with him and reported to Grey that Crowe was unduly pessimistic about the future course of the war.[7] Before the end of the year, Crowe, already removed from the War Department, was made head of a newly created Contraband department which, along with an inter-departmental Contraband Committee constituted at the same time, was authorised to negotiate contraband agreements with neutrals. The transfer may well have been a convenient way of solving a difficult internal situation but was considered a serious setback to Crowe's career. The moment was an unfortunate one: Crowe became the victim of an anti-German campaign which singled out Foreign Office officials with German relatives and contacts. This ludicrous attack almost drove Crowe to resign in the autumn of 1915.[8]

William Tyrrell, not the strongest of men, found it even more difficult than Crowe to keep his balance. Though he seems to have played a central role in the autumn of 1914 ('everything in the way of initiative seems to centre in Willie Tyrrell', Chirol reported) the effort proved too great.[9] In the spring, Tyrrell had a complete breakdown precipitated by the death of his son at the front. He left the Foreign Office and did not return until the summer of 1916 when he was asked to work on the formulation of Britain's post-war goals. He was replaced by Eric Drummond, Asquith's private secretary and an extremely able official who was soon a major influence at the top echelons of the Office.

Crowe's transfer and Tyrrell's collapse placed a heavy burden on Nicolson who had never been particularly talented for administration. He was forced to take on the War Department and for a brief time was Grey's major adviser on Balkan and Russian problems. Nicolson, even more than Grey, believed that only battles mattered in wartime and that a policy of inaction in the Balkans would bring the best results. It was only after Turkey entered the war and the hope of a Balkan alliance began to fade that Grey switched to a more active line. Nicolson continued to argue that no amount of bribery would bring Bulgaria in on the Allied side without a major military victory to swing the balance. He strongly disapproved of the various efforts made to tempt the Bulgarians and during the spring of 1915 withdrew from any real share in Grey's Balkan activities.[10]

It was not long before the permanent under-secretary realised that it was going to be a long and difficult war.[11] His early enthusiasm and spurt of energy vanished though he remained convinced of eventual victory and would neither consider the possibility of a conditional peace nor countenance a discussion of war aims until the British were in a position to dictate the terms. Despite the erratic course of the Russian campaign, Nicolson refused to lose faith in 'his beloved Russians' who remained for him Britain's most valuable asset and ally. He thought she would emerge from the war much strengthened though being a bureaucratic rather than a militaristic nation she would not pose a threat to the European balance of power. More sympathetic to the Austrians than Crowe, Nicolson wanted to see the Empire preserved and Russian ambitions directed elsewhere. Yet he was uncertain as to the possibility of dividing Turkey's non-European territories. Never a strong believer in nationalist movements, Nicolson showed little initial enthusiasm for the projected Arabian revolt and feared that a division of these Turkish spoils with Russia and France would result in dangerous quarrelling. Nevertheless, as the negotiations with Hussain and the French proceeded during 1915, Nicolson became converted to partition (as were most of his colleagues) and welcomed Russian gains in northeast Turkey.[12]

Though he handled a mass of routine work which left him physically exhausted, Nicolson realised he was playing a relatively unimportant role at the Foreign Office. His correspondence became more sporadic and he appeared to be somewhat bewildered by the tone and problems raised by war-time practices. In April 1916 he used the excuse of Hardinge's projected return from India as the occasion to offer his resignation to Grey. On 20 June 1916, a frail, bent and yet authoritative figure left the Foreign Office for good.

During Nicolson's last year, the focus of activity changed from the search for allies (the Treaty of London was signed in April 1915, Rumania came in during the summer of 1915, the troublesome Greeks continued to equivocate until 1917) to a discussion of peace terms and post-war settlements.[13] George Clerk who remained head of the War department gained in prestige throughout these months. He was intimate with Hankey, and at critical moments – before the Salonika landings, for instance – was one of the few men at Whitehall with any link to the military authorities.[14] Still hopeful in early 1917 of a decisive military victory, Clerk favoured a punitive peace which would end the German threat of world domination: the Clerk–Tyrrel–Mallet memorandum of January 1917, one of the earliest definitions of British aims, reflected the optimism of the writers.[15]

The War Department over which Clerk presided was a small one, never numbering more than six clerks but it was the centre of political activity throughout this period. The Assistant, Lancelot Oliphant, the Eastern and Persian expert in the office, became one of the chief supporters of the Arab War which he hoped would restore British prestige in the Middle East. He also participated in the discussions over the division of Turkey's Asiatic possessions with the French and on one occasion managed to save for the British a strip of land in the Camerouns amounting to over 34,000 square miles, a vast area which Grey would have yielded to the French to secure their good will.[16] The members of the Third Room, Rowland Sterling, Lord Eustace Percy, C. H. Smith and Harold Nicolson were engaged in a wide variety of diplomatic negotiations ranging from Greek and Italian affairs to more long range post-war settlements. Laurence Collier who subsequently joined the department wrote, 'We juniors had the chance of our lives, and some of us had some really bright ideas, particularly Nicolson [Harold] whose fertile brain turned out a prodigious mass of minutes and memoranda. He had learned how to dictate and virtually monopolised the services of our one typist.[17]

Apart from the War Department, it was the Contraband department which became the vital nerve centre of the Foreign Office. This had begun with a small nucleus of clerks, attachés and even a consular official, under Crowe's direction. With the intensification of the campaign against neutral shipping, the department expanded rapidly. By the end of 1915, some fifty officials were involved in its operations with their own clerical staff and registry system created by Alwyn Parker. The department was divided into sections dealing with commodities or with individual neutral countries. Some of the ablest junior men were to serve here – Craigie, O'Malley, Percy, Waterlow, and Carr – though it was generally agreed that the sensitive but extraordinarily capable Francis Oppenheimer, previously Consul-General in Germany, was the real brain behind such ingenious schemes as the Netherlands Overseas Trust which controlled the vital Netherlands trade. There was also a Foreign Office representative on the Contraband Committee which both initiated the activities of the various departments (particularly the Admiralty and Foreign Office) working on blockade questions and coordinated them.

In this early period, 1914–15, blockade policy was hammered out on an *ad hoc* basis, for the British were pursuing a line of action against the neutral states (for whom the United States became the chief spokesman) which, in the days of peace, the Foreign Office had declared contrary to international law. From the start, commercial and political questions were intricately linked and in the work of the Contraband department no clear line was drawn. During 1915, the department began to negotiate a whole range of contraband agreements with shipping lines, insurance companies, trading firms and even private individuals which would cut Germany off from essential imports but would satisfy the basic home requirements of each country. Each neutral state and commodity turned out to be a special case and men who had never dealt with such matters rapidly became technical experts. Grey found these operations, so far removed from the normal currents of political businss, 'nauseous' and apart from the major political decisions (particularly with regard to the United States) left the daily work in Crowe's capable hands.[18] Crowe found this an important and creative outlet for his many talents and his juniors were given an equally unique opportunity to work out problems on their own initiative. 'I was quite a junior clerk at the time', O'Malley recalled, 'I can remember well all the types I was in close touch with – natives and foreigners – and the endless memoranda and despatches and letters to other government departments I wrote, and most of it I did without ever referring to the head of the department. I can remember when we took the whole of the Norwegian mercantile marine in charter – a million and a half tons deadweight at seventy shillings a ton deadweight per month for an indefinite period. No bloody nonsense about having been at Radley and Magdalen about that I can assure you. I and Waterlow and Craigie and Tom Fisher, R.N., from the Admiralty, were up to the neck in all that day after day, and up to the neck with practically all the foreigners who were having their cargoes vetted by the Xth Cruiser Squadron and the coal merchants who were bunkering their ships all over the world and the underwriters who were insuring all ships and goods at sea. And we were good at picking up all the necessary knowledge as we went along and at getting ourselves trusted by all the odds and sods of the business world just because we had been at Radley or Eton, at Oxford or Cambridge...and because it came naturally to us to take quick and independent decisions without fear or favour.'[19]

There can be little doubt that despite the long hours and detailed negotiations, men such as O'Malley enjoyed the challenge which confronted them. It is equally apparent that the Foreign Office experience with blockade problems alerted Crowe, Percy and others to the important role which economic policy was going to play in the post-war world. This new experience explains, in part, why an internal committee headed by Crowe in 1916 strongly recommended an extensive post-war expansion in the Office's responsibilities for overseas trade.[20] The committee's recommendations (which were not fully understood by either Grey or Hardinge) led to a sharp conflict with the Board of Trade. The result was the compromise Department of Overseas Trade, created in 1917, which suited neither of the parent departments. At the same time, it was agreed to strengthen the economic side of the Foreign Office by having a special economic specialist in each of the political departments and asking embassies to make similar arrangements abroad.[21] Some of these changes took place in the immediate post-war period.

Though the Contraband department itself rapidly extended its competence in this new field of activity, the development of an effective blockade policy was attended by a number of unresolved difficulties.[22] In the first place, there was no single authority responsible for the direction of these first attempts to define and stop contraband materials from reaching the Central Powers. There were misunderstandings betwen the Foreign Office, Admiralty and Board of Trade. The first was repeatedly accused of ordering the release of cargoes seized by the Navy and of upholding neutral rights at the expense of British war interests. It was after all the Foreign Office which had agreed to the abortive but now embarrassing Declaration of London. More important, Grey's appeasement of the United States delayed the elaboration of an effective blockade policy. Particularly during the first eight months of the war, Grey and his advisers were unwilling to undertake any measure which might threaten Anglo-American relations. Britain's dependence on American war supplies as well as Grey's general wish to abide by pre-war distinctions between war and non-war goods explain the Foreign Secretary's sensitivity towards the United States. But the failure to achieve a major naval victory and the rapidly developing military stalemate created pressures which even Grey could not resist. Despite all his efforts to find some other solution, the promulgation of the Order-in-Council of 11 March 1915 marked a new stage in the evolution of an aggressive economic campaign. Even then, the Foreign Secretary dragged his feet, always concerned about neutral opinions and American complaints. In the summer of 1915, there was a major crisis over the inclusion of cotton on the absolute contraband list. Robert Cecil, who had entered the Foreign Office in May 1915 as parliamentary Under-Secretary with special responsibilities for blockade affairs, defended his much criticised chief and the Contraband department in the Commons. In fact, Cecil like other members of that department, had been converted to a harsher line and, despite Grey's doubts, cotton was declared absolute contraband after an ingenious financial agreement with the cotton exporters and a firmer tone was taken with all subsequent American objections.[23]

These new measures led to the development of numerous *ad hoc* bodies within the many departments involved in blockade work and also greatly increased the work of the Contraband department which had to handle the resulting complaints from the neutral powers.[24] The lack of coordination amongst these committees was an obvious block to the successful prosecution of the economic campaign. The War Trade Advisory Committee, created in October 1915 under Lord Crewe, failed to impose any control over these various groups and Grey's general directions became increasingly perfunctory as his objections to a more aggressive line were overruled and his eyesight continued to deteriorate. In response to pressure from Cecil and Crowe as well as from the public at large, Grey suggested to Asquith that a separate department be created under a Minister connected with the Foreign Office but with his own Cabinet seat.[25] Cecil was the obvious choice. His appointment in February 1916 led to a further diminution in Grey's power not only over blockade questions but over general political issues as well.

There were other if less important changes at the Foreign Office.[26] The Passport Office, for instance, which in 1914 consisted of one second division clerk and a door keeper had by 1916 a staff of forty-four (including twelve women) and had to be moved to Victoria Street from where it controlled all exit and entry permits. In early 1915, a News Department (the only wartime creation which survived the war) was established to collect information from the foreign press, supply copy to the domestic press, control censorship (a responsibility abolished on 20 December 1916) and to act as a liaison office with the newly established War Propaganda Bureau under John Masterman.[27] A Prize Court Department and a Foreign Claims Office, both connected with the blockade, and in November 1916, a Prisoner of War Department under Lord Newton and Robert Vansittart (who could hardly have welcomed his transfer from the Contraband Department) all had to be housed outside the Foreign Office. The only contraction of staff took place in the American and Far Eastern departments. Much of the work of the American department was done in the Contraband Department; the supervising under-secretary, Ralph Paget, was sent as minister to Copenhagen in 1916. Walter Langley, the experienced and realistic observer of the Far Eastern scene continued to oversee Far Eastern affairs. Beilby Alston and Sir Ronald Macleay, the former Counsellor at Peking who became head of the department in September 1916, actually had first-hand knowledge of the area with which they were dealing. Grey was, therefore backed by an extremely powerful team in London not to speak of John Jordan and Conyngham Greene in the field. The reduction of junior staff had little effect on the quality of the advice he received.

Lord Hardinge hardly recognised his old office when he returned in the summer of 1916: '...there are about 500 people working here instead of the usual 150', he reported to Lord Errington, 'and every day there were about 300 telegrams'.[28] The number of temporary staff soared; women came in to take over positions formerly occupied by second division clerks and the number of typists rose from eleven in 1914 to forty-one in 1916.[29] There was an acute shortage of space; rooms had to be divided and sub-divided as hundreds of people were crowded into a building designed for a small staff. The Contraband Department, despite its expansion, remained within the Foreign Office; the big reception room at the top of the stairs (now known as the Locarno Room) became its Third Room 'roaring with typewriters and full of people rushing about in a very undiplomatic state of hurry'.[30] All the other blockade departments were located elsewhere: despatches were sent from one building to another and some duplication of staff and function could not be avoided. The whole operation would have been cheaper and more efficient if it could have been organised from the start as a single department under one roof. As it was, Alwyn Parker, the first senior clerk of the Contraband Department, imposed what administrative order there was.

The changes were not just physical. Hardinge had already been warned by Bertie that the Foreign Office was 'in great part a "pass-on department", viz. it issues instructions at the instance of other offices often without considering whether such instructions are advisable or feasible and sometimes in ignorance seemingly of what has already been said and done by some other Department of the Foreign Office'.[31] Though the new permanent under-secretary attempted to re-establish his old relationship with Grey, he must have been struck by the physical deterioration of his chief. The Foreign Secretary's eyes were so weak and he, himself, so tired, that he was forced to make an arrangement by which Crewe relieved him at regular intervals. Soon after Hardinge returned, Grey left for a six-week break. The failure of the Somme offensive in the months which followed was almost the final blow to Grey's sinking morale. Bertie may have been unduly suspicious of Grey's willingness to consider a negotiated peace but his warning that Grey was 'au fond' a pacifist who felt acutely the Boche accusation that he could have prevented the war struck near to the truth.[32] Quite apart from Grey, Hardinge thought the coalition cabinet 'unbelievably weak and ineffective. Asquith is always waiting to see and is being forced all the time by all sorts of outside influences.'[33] Deeply conservative though he was, Hardinge recognised soon after his arrival that only Lloyd George could provide the leadership so obviously missing at Downing Street.

There were also complications within the office. 'It is curious also having a department working in the Foreign Office using the name of the Secretary of State for Foreign Affairs and yet having an independent Secretary of State, i.e. Bob Cecil at its head. It has one great advantage for me in that it absolves me from all responsibility for contraband questions which are very numerous and highly technical but it presents some difficulties since undoubtedly at times it overlaps the political side of the question. Bob Cecil does it very well...'[34] Hardinge respected Cecil's abilities and indeed feared that his colleague might be forced out of office because of disagreements over Lloyd George's Irish policies. When, however, Grey was replaced by Balfour, Cecil's position within the Foreign Office hierarchy, quite apart from purely contraband questions, was considerably strengthened. Differences between Hardinge and Cecil shattered their earlier partnership; it was Cecil who most frequently emerged the victor and became Balfour's *alter ego*.[35]

It should also be remembered that Hardinge had been considerably changed by his years in India. He had been much shaken by the attempt on his life in 1912 and by the sudden loss of his wife in 1914 followed by the death of his son in the war. He was constantly worried about his second son who was also serving on the western front. Coming back from the Viceroyalty to London required a considerable psychological adjustment difficult for a man of Hardinge's temperament. He had always tended to be imperious; his Indian years exaggerated this tendency. His record in India was not an unblemished one. A Commission of Enquiry into the Mesopotamian campaign had been appointed in July 1916 and Hardinge spent a good deal of his free time preparing a lengthy statement for the Commissioners defending his advice and action. The Commission's report and the War Cabinet's subsequent demand for his resignation although rejected by Balfour left a lasting mark on Hardinge's relationship with the Lloyd George government.

At first there were hopes that Hardinge might restore the morale of the office which, on the political side, had been much shaken by the diplomatic defeats of the first years of war. Hardinge was far more active and aggressive than Nicolson. Although he did not become a member of the War Cabinet, the real centre of action, he was asked to attend daily in an advisory capacity.[36] During the summer of 1916, he convinced Grey to recall Ronald Graham, an old friend serving in Egypt, who returned to the department to serve as assistant under-secretary in charge of the War Department. Hardinge was anxious to have a loyal understudy who could deputise for him and relieve him of some of the routine work which Nicolson had found so onerous. Hardinge had further ambitions for Graham whom he hoped would succeed him as permanent under-secretary when Hardinge went to his promised posting in Paris. These plans were partly dictated by Hardinge's dislike of Crowe whom he did not wish to see returned to the mainstream of political business.[37] Graham proved to be an excellent choice. When Hardinge was at the cabinet or was receiving foreign visitors, Graham easily substituted for him and within a few months of his arrival was offering advice and taking decisions. Hardinge's future ambitions for his younger colleagues were to later bring him into direct clash with Cecil who continued to champion Crowe.

Hardinge was surprised to find that very little had been done in the way of defining British war aims. One of the reasons he wanted Grey to bring Graham back was to prepare the latter for his post-war responsibilities. During the summer of 1916, Hardinge confidently expected that the Somme offensive would break the German line and he shared the generals' optimistic views that peace was within sight. He feared that the French had already laid out their peacetime goals and that the British would be at a disadvantage in any subsequent peace negotiations.[38] If Grey were less sanguine about the possibilities of an early victory, pressure from President Wilson made some kind of discussion imperative and in August 1916 an internal Foreign Office committee (Mallet, Tyrrell and Paget were among the members) was created. Hardinge's own views were in a state of flux. He was insistent that no peace should be made with the Hohenzollerns, a view he strongly pressed on Grey whom he sometimes feared might yield to American pressure for a negotiated peace.[39] He thought that Britain's allies would remain loyal despite the influence of the pro-Germans on the Tsar and the replacement of Sazonov by Stürmer in the summer of 1916. Like Nicolson, he was extremely close to George Buchanan, the British ambassador in Russia, whose confidence in the Russians had not yet been shaken. Hardinge, therefore, had no doubt that the tide would change in Britain's favour during 1917.

Though Hardinge was insistent that British desiderata in south-east Europe and Asiatic Turkey required careful consideration, he tended to be less decisive when handling the specific daily problems of the department. First he pressed strongly for the entry of Rumania on the allied side though he later acknowledged that this had been a mistake. He thought the Greeks had been ill-used by the French, but rightly believed that the Greek court and its army and navy were too pro-German to be of any real use to the Allies. Like others at the Foreign Office, Hardinge reverted to the idea of detaching Bulgaria from the side of the Central Powers but he had few concrete suggestions to make this fruitless proposal a reality. Hardinge did state that "We have no desire to dismember Austria–Hungary but we would like to see the Austrian Empire composed of autonomous states in personal union with the Emperor."[40] By this date, April 1917, the possibility of a separate peace with Vienna was being actively discussed.

More strangely, perhaps, as Hardinge was an expert in Middle Eastern affairs, was the permanent under-secretary's uncertainties about what should be done with Turkey's Asiatic possessions. He was never enthusiastic about the Arab revolt but when Kitchener threw his weight behind Hussain and the revolt became a reality, Hardinge was anxious to see it succeed lest British prestige in the Middle East be shattered and her interests in Mesopotamia, Persia and along the Indian frontier adversely affected. Hardinge was more adamant than usual in his opposition to the military chiefs, who when Hussain got into difficulties, did not want to despatch troops to this 'side-show'. There were others at the Foreign Office who deferred to General Robertson and Grey did not speak with a very clear voice. Though Hardinge was loath to increase British responsibilities, he clearly did not wish either the Italians or the French to make major gains in Asia Minor. He found the Italians unbelievably greedy and a rather petulant note runs through some of his letters to Rodd, the strongly pro-Italian British ambassador. The Sykes–Picot agreement had been concluded before Hardinge returned; he did not disguise his dislike of the arrangement and his distrust of Mark Sykes who 'inundates the War Cabinet with a terrible lot of rubbish' and whose 'combination of a swollen head, bluster and incompetence is...not conducive to harmony'.[41] Hardinge probably had a better grasp of the realities of the Middle Eastern situation than did Grey but had as little influence on the decisions taken in this area as his chief.

If Hardinge was less dynamic than in earlier years, he was an experienced administrator determined to strengthen the power of his office. He regretted Grey's retirement but welcomed Balfour's appointment and clearly anticipated having a major share in the new foreign secretary's deliberations. If he had his doubts about the new War Cabinet and Lord Curzon's propensity to look into the affairs of individual departments, he admired Lloyd George's dynamism and acknowledged his firm hand on the war machine. Despite the appalling losses on the Western front and the German submarine offensive Hardinge somehow remained highly optimistic about the future and scornfully rejected both the German peace note and the American intervention-bid in December 1916. Hardinge had some grounds for thinking that by the end of 1916, the Foreign Office was geared for a war-time role if only the politicians permitted it to act. Robert Cecil's appointment had been fully justified by the results. He brought new direction and unity to the numerous departments and committees involved in blockade procedures and proved to be an able departmental advocate at the cabinet level. Even before Grey left office the Germans were beginning to feel the adverse effects of a more stringent economic policy. Cecil was extremely accurate when at the end of 1916 he reported that 'with some minor exceptions, practically no goods coming from overseas are getting through to Germany'.[42]

Eric Drummond stayed on as Balfour's private secretary and participated in efforts to break up the unity of the Central Powers and to map out what should be Britain's post-war claims. He proved to be a popular figure within the private secretary's office, a definite asset at a time when diplomatic nerves were frayed by shortages of staff and soaring living costs abroad. William Tyrrell had come back to work on an *ad hoc* basis. Until his appointment as head of the Political Intelligence Department in 1918, he did a variety of jobs which made full use of his tact, intelligence and flexibility. Hardinge could well argue that at the next level too the clerks serving in the administrative and political departments were becoming increasingly expert as assignments became more specific and regular staff was in increasingly short supply. The Foreign Office had always had area 'experts', now it had clerks equally expert operating in entirely new realms of diplomacy. The members of the News Department were handling press correspondents and independent agents who were collecting and disseminating information abroad. C. H. Montgomery, for instance, became one of the chief contact men, first with Masterman and then with John Buchan who even before the establishment of the Department of Information in early 1917 was given a room at the Foreign Office to coordinate propaganda activities. In the Contraband Department, which under Cecil became the chief executive organ of the Blockade, junior clerks were becoming commodity specialists in oil and fats, coal, jute and copper, and were making a whole range of new contacts in commercial and service circles. The days of departmental isolation were over.

Yet this picture of a department successfully mobilised for war cannot obscure the fact that the Foreign Office had lost its pre-war place. The balance sheet was not a healthy one – the disaster at Constantinople and in the Balkans, hesitations in the Middle East, and the repeated difficulties with the United States weighed far more heavily than the adhesion of Italy and Rumania to the Allies and the solidarity of the Allied powers. The defeats in the Balkans convinced Grey's most vocal critics that the Foreign Office had not only failed to preserve the peace but was unable to contribute to victory in war. The public, it is true, did not realise how dependent wartime diplomacy was on military power but there was considerable substance to the charge that the Foreign Office had too easily abdicated its share of the responsibility to the service chiefs. Grey, for instance, did not press his diplomatic objections to the Dardanelles campaign and though the decision to send troops to Salonika was dictated by diplomatic motives he made little effort to enquire whether sufficient troops were available to carry out such a campaign. George Clerk was too junior to provide the necessary liaison: Crowe who by interest and temperament might have filled the gap had been removed from the War Department. There were some who were fully conscious of the cause for the debacle in this area. When Lord Eustace Percy came to write up the story of British diplomacy in the Balkans in 1915, he bitterly complained to Eric Drummond: 'I am in absolute despair. The present situation is the abdication of the Foreign Office, and if it is to continue, for Heaven's sake let us juniors all go and fight and leave foreign policy to the D.I.D.'s and the D.M.O.'s wandering agents.'[43]

In the Middle East, too the Foreign Office was plagued by indecision and the initiative was left to others. In the case of the Arab revolt, there was a tendency to follow the advice and accept the decisions of the local men, McMahon, the High Commissioner in Egypt, Ronald Storrs and Wingate.[44] One has the distinct impression that Grey felt totally out of his depth and no one at the Foreign Office seemed very clear as to the extent of the promises made to the Sherif or the responsibilities acquired in Mesopotamia. Even the discussions with France were conducted not by a Foreign Office man but by Mark Sykes, a young orientalist on Kitchener's staff who seems to have worked almost entirely on his own. Whether in its wavering support for Hussain or in its non-annexationist approach to the Anglo-French and Anglo-Italian negotiations, the Foreign Office failed to give a forceful lead. In these early years of the war, commitments were made which severely limited Britain's future freedom of action so that the Arabs would take the field against Turkey. But when Hussain launched his revolt, he needed military support and neither General Robertson nor, indeed, the Foreign Secretary, were willing to despatch troops to save the Arabs forces from defeat. Months were wasted in futile debate at the cabinet table. The muddle in the middle east involved the War Office, the India Office and the Foreign Office not to speak of the authorities in Egypt and India. The subsequent expansion of British interests in this area created diplomatic and administrative chaos which the Foreign Office could not cut through because of the many overlapping jurisdictions.

Finally, though it is perfectly true that by the end of 1916 a consistent blockade policy had been developed, the stages of its evolution were marked by hesitancy and confusion. It was only after the creation of a separate Ministry that the last vestiges of the Declaration of London were jettisoned and that the measures introduced earlier were welded into a coherent and effective programme. Much of the delay could not have been avoided, for the difficulties were real and solutions had to be hammered out gradually with each neutral power. Nevertheless, many of the most positive steps were taken despite Grey's opposition and hindsight suggests that the Foreign Secretary and his chief advisers were too sensitive to American complaints and excessively fearful about the consequences of reversing peacetime procedures. Even after Cecil's appointment, Grey continued to raise objections but these were generally disregarded or overruled. Despite the turning tide in the economic struggle, the new Department did not escape criticism. There were critics who claimed that as long as the direction of blockade policy remained in Foreign Office hands it could not be pursued with the vigour and singleness of purpose necessary for success. Few outside the ministry realised how unjust this charge was.

It was not surprising that throughout this period the Foreign Office was under continuous public attack. The generals still stood high in public estimation but Grey, his officials and diplomats, were more vulnerable targets. The Editor of *The Times*, whose clash with the Foreign Office over Mallet's policy at Constantinople had led to a six month estrangement in 1915, echoed common opinion when he wrote 'I become more and more convinced every day that our diplomacy, our hesitations, our want of policy, our choice of agents have often been quite inexcusable. My own impression is that Sir Edward is thoroughly stale and tired.'[45] The refrain that Grey was one of the great failures of the war was taken up by Grey's friends as well as his enemies. Munro Ferguson wrote to Grey's cousin, 'E.G. was never intended for the service of Mars.'[46]

The Balkan debacle gave the newly-created Union of Democratic Control fresh ammunition and its members renewed their individual pre-war demands that the whole method of conducting diplomacy should be altered so that parliament and hence the people would have more control over foreign policy.[47] In the summer and autumn of 1915, Morel, Ponsonby and Trevelyan pressed the case for a negotiated peace and at the same time called for a sweeping reform of the Foreign Office and Diplomatic Service, an end to its aristocratic bias and the shattering of the control exercised by a small clique of professional advisers far removed from public control. Grey, as well as other members of the Foreign Office, particularly those connected with blockade policy such as Crowe and Oppenheimer, was also the victim of numerous rumours about a pro-German conspiracy in the Foreign Office which supposedly accounted for his lukewarm prosecution of the war.[48] Pacifists, radicals, and rabid anti-Germans were united in their identification of the Foreign Office as the chief villain.

The failure, during the first year of the war, to adequately develop Britain's economic weapons against Germany added to the chorus of criticism about Grey's Turkish and Balkan diplomacy. *The Times* led the attack during the summer of 1915 when it critically reviewed the tragic record of the War Committee and the Foreign Office. In January 1916, in four separate leaders, it repeated its charge that the blockade was ineffective and that the Foreign Office was largely at fault because of its adhesion to principles no longer, in a wartime situation, applicable. This was followed by statistical reports in the *Morning Post* and *Daily Mail* proving that the neutral countries were importing more raw materials, including foodstuffs, than they had required in peace-time. Though Grey and Crewe contested these conclusions, the controversy only confirmed the public impression that the Foreign Office had failed in yet another field of activity. In March 1916, despite the creation of the Department of Blockade, the record of the Foreign Office was described in the Commons as 'deplorable' and the old charges of élitism, economic incompetence and consular weakness were again revived. The Association of Chambers of Commerce took up the latter point and added its voice to those demanding a more aggressive economic stand not only during the war but in the post-war period.[49]

Given the rising wave of anti-American feelings, few observers gave Grey any credit for his careful handling of Anglo-American relations and Spring Rice's seeming inactivity and decision not to propagandise the British case came under sharp attack. Even in the Foreign Office, there was considerable feeling that more could be done in Washington and that the British ambassador did not have the ear of either Wilson or the American public. The denunciations in the Northcliffe press, the use of William Wiseman (an intelligence agent) as the channel of communication to Wilson and House and the sending of the Balfour mission were some of the steps leading up to Lloyd George's much more direct assault on Spring Rice and on the general authority of the Foreign Office. The sending of Northcliffe in the summer of 1917 was almost the symbol of a clash between two kinds of diplomacy in which the traditional methods and machinery were clearly, if temporarily, abandoned.[50]

The members of the Foreign Office were fully aware of the charges being made and the increasingly hostile atmosphere in which they operated. Most officials were so involved in their daily concerns that they had little time to consider the long-range implications of this changed climate of opinion. Men such as Nicolson and Hardinge undoubtedly believed that in wartime naval and military operations determined foreign policy and that when the war was won the Foreign Office could once again re-establish its control over external affairs. It was, after all, the failure of Britain's military policies which was the decisive factor in the years 1914–16. There were other men, for example Cecil, Drummond, Crowe and more junior officials, who clearly realised that the very dimensions of diplomacy were being expanded and that the Foreign Office would have to develop new competencies if it were to re-establish its primacy in the post-war world. If the official hierarchy were annoyed by Ponsonby's repeated denunciations of its power and isolation, it could not easily dismiss the more detailed and constructive recommendations of the MacDonnell Commission which completed its investigation of the Foreign Office, diplomatic and consular services just before the outbreak of war. Already in 1916, an inter-departmental committee had been created to consider what changes could be made to meet the Commission's criticisms. A broader entrance procedure, the amalgamation of the Foreign Office and diplomatic service, an improved salary scale were all questions which were considered though no major changes were made while the war lasted.[51] There were many in the Foreign Office who were fully aware of the need to change and modernise and who rightly feared that those departments actively intervening in foreign affairs during wartime would not easily accept a return to the *status quo ante*. It would be impossible to met this challenge without a radical reconstruction. Above all, there were the politicians who, responsive to the critique of the 'old diplomacy', were determined to create an alternative system. When Grey left the Foreign Office in December 1916, none could have predicted what shape this 'new diplomacy' would take but the initiative clearly lay with the new Prime Minister.

The immediate needs of war dictated Grey's diplomacy in almost every section of the globe. The Foreign Secretary's decision that in war-time military considerations determined his actions obviously restricted the role of the Foreign Office from the start. The shock of war and a certain physical deterioration further weakened Grey's reactions to some of the crises which confronted him during the first two years of hostilities. One has the impression of a statesman overwhelmed by the conditions of war. The contrast between the man who entered the Foreign Office at forty-three and the aged figure who left it ten years later is a sharp one. To a lesser degree, there was a similar decline in the status of the Foreign Office which neither talent nor industry could arrest. The public know little about those areas in which the Foreign Office was successfully meeting the challenge of war; its defeats were common knowledge. Under Grey's leadership, the Foreign Office played a secondary role in the early years of the war. Lloyd George gave it no opportunity to recover the initiative.

31

Foreign policy, Government structure and public opinion

K. G. ROBBINS

While the Foreign Secretary had lived throughout his period of office under the constant possibility of war, its actual outbreak was a shocking and distasteful event. Grey was now a man of peace whose policy had failed. His one memorable phrase, 'the lamps are going out all over Europe...', reflected his consciousness of failure. The world, his world, would never be the same again, and the streak of anarchism in his make-up made him feel that the judgement was just.[1] From the outbreak of the war, the position of the Foreign Secreatry was changed, and Grey himself was a different man. Others might have struggled to retain the status which the Foreign Secretary had in peacetime. Sir Edward, however, took perhaps an unnecessarily restricted view of the rôle of the Foreign Secretary in wartime. He believed that he had no qualities which would establish him as an amateur strategist; and even if he had possessed them, he hoped that he would have been strong enough to resist the temptation to use them. As he himself expressed it, 'the position of a civilian in a war council, who feels that, from a lack of military knowledge and training, this limitation is imposed upon him, is not glorious. He knows that credit is not due to him for successful strategy, and yet he must feel some responsibility for mistakes in which he has acquiesced.'[2] Nor was this the only difficulty. Grey did not find it easy to adjust his style of diplomacy to what many believed to be the exigencies of the hour. The careful, patient and lengthy search for an acceptable compromise had perhaps been replaced by the need for unilateral action. In this changed context for diplomatic operations, it was suggested that Grey was not sufficiently ruthless and remained a strickler for formal correctness of dealing. The problems of the Foreign Secretary were further complicated by the fact that many of the traditional boundaries between government departments were being questioned, though, at the outset, few grasped the full administrative and political implications of the war.

At first, it seemed possible that 'Business as usual' could even apply to the management of the war at the very highest level. Little attempt was made to discipline the organization of the Cabinet. There was still to be time for the leisurely expression of opinion, and there was still no provision for the recording of decisions. The Cabinet of 1914 contained nineteen members – which hardly made for swift decision-making, if everyone, at least in theory, was to be allowed to speak. But in practice, as had happened before 1914, the Prime Minister relied on a smaller number of intimates, though this arrangement was never formally regularized. Thus the Cabinet as a whole did not approve the final text of the ultimatum to Germany. After it had been sent, Asquith asked Haldane to call a Council of War and himself select those who should attend. On 5 August, Asquith, Grey, Haldane and Churchill, together with all the leading soldiers, went over the plans for the despatch of the British Expeditionary Force to France. The Cabinet met the following day and agreed with the recommendation that four divisions should be sent at once and a fifth to follow. By then, they were already on their way. The military authorities ignored the Cabinet's wish that the troops should land at Amiens.[3]

The appointment of Kitchener as Secretary of State for War meant, initially, that the direction of affairs was left largely in his hands, with some assistance from Churchill. Kitchener brought to the Government 'a great asset of public confidence'.[4] Subsequently, however, Grey was to wonder whether a civilian Secretary of State, backed by an effective General Staff, might have not been a better proposition. The Committee of Imperial Defence faded away, though several of its sub-committees continued to examine specific questions. The Cabinet was working overtime, meeting almost daily throughout August, and almost as frequently throughout September and October. But under Asquith's direction, it did not really seek to exercise mastery over the war. Substantially, it merely received reports from Kitchener and Churchill, both of whom had to work closely together. When specific decisions had to be taken quickly, hasty conferences took place to authorize action. These meetings were composed of anyone who could be quickly contacted. Asquith, McKenna, Pease and Lloyd George authorized Kitchener to pay an admonitory visit to France early in September. Grey, Kitchener and Churchill hastily conferred on the night of 2 October and agreed that Churchill might go to Antwerp. The Prime Minister was out of town. As usual, Grey felt incompetent to pass a military judgment, but nevertheless acquiesced in the plan when Kitchener agreed to it. The situation was now confused. Opinions differed as to whether the full Cabinet, either in theory or practice, was fully responsible for naval and military decisions, or whether, at any rate in practice, this unofficial ring was really responsible.[5]

Asquith summoned a meeting of this inner group on 25 November, and announced his intention of giving it the official designation of the War Council. Grey, Kitchener, Churchill and Lloyd George attended, together with Balfour (there in a personal rather than official capacity) with a couple of experts. The idea was to range broadly over the war, and to discuss possible new departures of policy or strategic operations. Other members of the Cabinet could be summoned if their departments were particularly involved. The Cabinet was to remain in being and be informed of the Council's proceedings. No 'decisive action' was to be taken without it being consulted.

Such was the theory. The practice is more difficult to disentangle. The War Council lasted until June 1915 when, re-formed and re-shaped, it emerged as the Dardanelles Committee. Altogether, it had eighteen meetings, and ranged over many different aspects of the conflict. The fact that by March 1915, Crewe, Haldane, McKenna, Harcourt and Admiral Wilson had joined, clearly increased the Council's importance at the expense of the Cabinet.[6] Those members of the Cabinet who were not on the Council do not seem to have been too ardent in their pursuit of detailed information, although Asquith did report on its conclusions. Even within the Council, it seems to have been the case that Kitchener and Churchill, backed by the Prime Minister, were the directing triumvirate, with the others only occasionally intervening. The project of a naval attack on the Dardanelles was discussed at three meetings in the middle of January, but the decision was not revealed to the Cabinet until a few days before the first bombardment. But the War Council did not become an executive body for the Dardanelles operation, nor is it properly described as an inner Cabinet. It did not meet between 19 March and 14 May, during critical stages of the expedition. Asquith gave as an explanation that the Cabinet had met and discussed the Dardanelles on eleven occasions in those weeks. The basic question, of course, was really that of Asquith's own leadership. It mattered little whether the plans of the War Office and the Admiralty were harmonized in the War Council or the Cabinet, so long as they were harmonized. But this did not happen. Effective co-ordination of the Dardanelles operation would not have removed the differences of opinion, but it might have overcome them.

The fact that the reconstructed War Council was renamed the Dardanelles Committee after the formation of the coalition government in May 1915 is evidence that it was not thought to constitute a permanent addition to the structure of government. The new Cabinet grew to twenty-two members, and there was obviously a need for a smaller body, but the fact of coalition made the composition of such a committee more difficult. When Carson was added to the Committee in August, a Unionist majority was in fact created, since the other members were Asquith, Lansdowne, Curzon, Kitchener, Balfour, Bonar Law, Grey, Crewe, Lloyd George, Churchill and Selborne. It was also no longer the case that the Cabinet accepted the deliberations of the Committee without serious questioning. Both bodies, however, were oppressed by failure in the Dardanelles and disagreement about the respective claims of the Western Front, Gallipoli, and the new candidate, Salonika. In September, both in order to appease critics and co-ordinate activity, Asquith proposed the creation of a smaller War Council, although Lloyd George made plain his view that nothing would improve whilst Kitchener remained at the War Office. In the following month, Carson resigned in protest against the muddle and confusion.

A few days later, the Cabinet (chaired by Crewe in the absence through illness of the Prime Minister) made it clear that the prevailing system of government was inadequate. 'All were agreed that the body should be quite small, and so far as can be, non-departmental.' In a private letter to Crewe, Grey endorsed this judgement.[7] In an attempt to stave off criticism just before Carson's speech in the Commons, Asquith announced a further attempt to create a War Committee of not less than three and not more than five. But still the ambiguity was not resolved. In the Commons, Asquith stated that such a Committee ought to have power to take decisions and act upon them. On the other hand, he was very jealous of the maintenance of 'collective Cabinet responsibility for large changes and new departures in policy; but I believe that in practice it will be found perfectly capable of working out two things together'.[8] Carson replied that all experience hitherto cast doubt on that proposition. What was necessary was a small Cabinet endowed with full powers. He was proved right insofar as the membership slowly increased to seven – Asquith, Balfour, Lloyd George, Bonar Law, McKenna, Kitchener and Grey – and experts and other Cabinet members appeared from time to time.[9]

The ineffectiveness of the new arrangement was demonstrated without delay. While 'Asquith's month' at the War Office had seen striking changes – most notably Robertson's appointment as C.I.G.S. with direct access to the Cabinet – the fatal flaw remained. Kitchener, who was in Gallipoli while these changes were going on, telegraphed back suggesting the evacuation of Suvla Bay and Anzac Cove, but the retention of Helles. The War Committee on 23 December accepted this report (although it wished to evacuate Helles as well), but when this decision went to the Cabinet on the following day, it was rejected. Curzon launched himself against the proposal, and at this, and the following Cabinet, gained enough support to cause a delay. But when it became clear that the French could not be coerced into withdrawing from Salonika (the alternative), the Cabinet, just in time, authorized total withdrawal. The paradox was that the Committee was composed of departmental ministers, while those without such responsibilities were forced to exercise their talents in the Cabinet. It was not surprising that Bonar Law circulated a memorandum that 'the war cannot be carried to a successful issue by methods such as these'.[10]

Asquith had now made a number of attempts to strengthen the administrative structure of his Government. For another six months, the situation drifted on, with some improvement but without any strong political leadership. In effect, Asquith, Grey, Crewe, Bonar Law and McKenna were content to let the soldiers try conclusions on the Western Front. The loss of Kitchener at sea in June 1916 removed the necessity of replacing him. Lloyd George, as his successor, had to preside over the slaughter of the Somme. He was also depressed by Russia and Roumania, by the failure to establish an Air Board, and other matters. Faced with disagreements which he could not resolve, the Prime Minister had a habit of 'turning round to the mantelpiece to see whether any temporary relief from his perplexities was indicated by the position of the hands of the clock'.[11] Once again, after discussions with Carson,

Beaverbrook and Bonar Law, Lloyd George raised the issue of the War Committee. It should be reduced to three members and the Prime Minister was not to be Chairman. The inference was obvious. The crisis had begun which was to end the Asquith Government and make Lloyd George Prime Minister.

From this analysis of the structure of government, one thing is quite clear: the Foreign Secretary had declined in importance long before Lloyd George formed his Government. The reasons for this are complex. In the first place, they are personal. For long, Grey had complained of the oppression of office – but for all his private complaints, could not resist retaining it. Office in wartime was even worse. But to have resigned at the outbreak of war would have had a very bad effect on national morale. The strain on his eyes became steadily greater. The critics who surrounded him were more ebullient, if little younger, men. His dislike of city life was such that there was no question of hanging on to power for its own sake. He stayed for the sake of others – chiefly for Asquith who, however, found him 'dolorous and despondent on occasion'.[12] He was sustained in office for the first six months by the commonplace hope that the war would not last very long. In March 1915, while not seeing how the war could be brought to an end, he was '...certain that the war cannot last more than a few months longer. England could go on for a long time, but the Continent cannot; and particularly Germany cannot...'[13] Once these ideas were recognized for the mirages they were, the prospect of the long haul had little appeal for him.

The Foreign Secretary seems to have played little part in the moves that led to the formation of the first Coalition. Details of the manoeuvres can easily be found elsewhere. Despite their old political friendship and unusually smooth co-operation as Prime Minister and Foreign Secretary, Asquith told Grey nothing of what was going on. Asquith's willingness to exclude Haldane in response to Tory pressure shocked the Foreign Secretary. Grey tried to get the decision reversed and, failing, asked Asquith to accept his resignation.[14] At this point, it seems likely that the Prime Minister told Grey how much he needed him at a difficult time; together they could hold the Liberal ship steady. Grey yielded and agreed to carry on. Haldane was Grey's closest political friend, and it is hardly likely that his feelings for Asquith were unaltered by the affair. Yet whatever his own feelings, his political future was now closely linked with that of the Prime Minister. And Asquith having secured his objective, took remarkably little notice of Grey. Sir Edward's standing was, therefore, somewhat paradoxical. The murmurings against him in the early months of 1915 had come to nothing. On the other hand, the status of Lloyd George, his severest critic, had been advanced. Some Liberals, rather dazed by Asquith's action, now professed to see Grey as a potential Prime Minister. Lloyd George recognized that the Foreign Secretary still retained considerable prestige, but dismissed the possibility. His eyesight was bad, but more importantly, Grey had 'even less push and drive than the present Prime

Minister'.[15] After this crisis, Grey associated himself closely with Runciman and McKenna. There was little improvement in his relations with Lloyd George. Yet, at the same time, he was by no means devoted to Asquith. In the conscription crisis in the latter months of 1915, he shared the views of Runciman and McKenna. They had no objection to conscription in principle, but felt that it would result in grave undermanning of domestic industries. In December, on the assumption that they were going to resign, he again offered his own resignation. He had always felt that he should have gone in May, and the reasons of public policy which had restrained him then no longer applied. In reply, Asquith said that he had not in fact received any other resignations, and the letter filled him with despair. 'If I am to be deserted in this time of stress by all my oldest and best friends, it is clear that I must reconsider my own position.'[16] As a final argument he added that the resignation would be universally interpreted as a German triumph. A compromise on the immediate issue was reached and once again Asquith's moral blackmail had succeeded.

Although Grey remained in office, both friends and critics observed privately that he seemed stale and weary.[17] They suspected that he would willingly have resigned. His health did not improve. In the spring of 1916, an oculist told him that if he could have a rest from work for a year or more, then he might preserve his sight, but if not, his chances were poor. In order to relieve the pressure on him, Lord Crewe took over the Foreign Office for some ten days in every six weeks. Because of this indispensable arrangement there must have been many matters over which Grey no longer exerted the influence which had once been his. He made at least one further attempt to resign. Asquith, however, could not afford to let him go and, instead, successfully offered him a peerage in July 1916. When the final break-up of the Government came, he accepted the situation with remarkably little animosity. He did not join in the recriminations, believing, unfortunately, that 'The real causes of the break-up of the Government are too private to be written about. They are not to be found in any correspondence between Asquith and Lloyd George or in Lloyd George's account of the matter. The ostensible causes in such cases are not the real causes.'[18] While there were 'very many unpleasant circumstances in the way the Asquith Government was displaced' and he had unpleasant things said about him, 'so far as I was concerned I was at one time very much overpraised and I was really always miserable and out of place in public life'.[19] These personal aspects of the decline of the Foreign Secretary should not be underestimated, but on the other hand, fit or unfit, ailing or active, Grey's presupposition about the supremacy of military factors and the necessity of military men interpreting their significance was bound to lead to a loss of influence.

The eclipse of Grey also undermined the position of the Foreign Office. The department was slow to reorganize itself to met the new problems created by war. Nicolson remained as permanent under-secretary until 1916; the breach with Grey healed under the stresses of war. For a brief time he took a lead in shaping British diplomacy, particularly in the Balkans, but the lack of success forced Grey to look to others for fresh ideas. Increasingly preoccupied with routine matters, which he intensely disliked. Nicolson's headship did little to improve the efficiency of the office. 'Under his rule', Bertie, a not unprejudiced observer reported, 'the office is in a state of chaos. There is no discipline and the tail waggles the dog.'[20] In this situation, the real burden of work fell on Eyre Crowe and William Tyrrell. The former, in the weeks after the war broke out, attempted to see all diplomatic correspondence relating directly to the war. In August, Crowe suggested that the work of the Western and Eastern departments be combined under a single head, George Clerk, a Foreign Office specialist in middle eastern affairs, and that this War Department deal with all political, naval and military issues arising out of the war, including such matters as censorship, neutrality and blockade. The suggestion was adopted, and Crowe was made supervising under-secretary with Clerk to assist him. In this position, Crowe seems to have supplied what unity of direction there was within the Foreign Office. Crowe was infuriated by Grey's indecisiveness and the inability of the Cabinet to prosecute the war with any sense of urgency. He seems to have lost his temper and quarrelled bitterly with Grey who, in turn, decided not to promote him to the permanent under-secretaryship when Nicolson retired.[21] Apart from Crowe, it was William Tyrrell who bore the major brunt of the transition from peace to war. Unfortunately, however, the strain of the new conditions proved too much for him. Overworked and overwrought, stunned by the death of his younger son in France, Tyrrell had a complete nervous breakdown in the spring of 1915 and was forced to leave the Foreign Office.[22] Grey felt this blow severely, as he had come to rely on Tyrrell. He in turn was further depressed. The return of Hardinge from India in the summer of 1916 to take Nicolson's place failed to restore the morale of the Foreign Office. He, too had suffered personal loss and was too conservative to carry through the changes being demanded by reformers both within and outside the Foreign Office.[23]

Since the substantial issues of foreign policy during the war are discussed in detail elsewhere, they will only be mentioned in what follows insofar as they provide illustrations of these personal, political and bureaucratic complications. The Balkan question, for example, exemplified all the differences between Grey and his critics as regards method. Sir Edward accepted it as axiomatic that what would determine the allegiance of the undecided Balkan states was their estimate of the likely ultimate victor. There was a certain limited amount which diplomacy could do, but in his opinion, no amount of talk about the pro-Entente sympathies of the Bulgarian people (even supposing this assertion to be well-founded) could disguise the fact that the King of Bulgaria was waiting and seeing. If the military and naval men had not miscalculated in the Dardanelles, then it would have been possible to have worked on these states to achieve the desired result. Military failure now made this impossible. His critics reversed the order. If Grey's diplomacy had achieved a Balkan federation, then military success would have been assured. Churchill circulated a memorandum to the Cabinet to this effect, placing the blame on the Foreign Office for failing to gain Bulgarian adherence. Grey scrawled on the Prime Minister's copy that the War Council had originally only agreed to the whole enterprise on the 'understanding that the Navy would do it alone, and that if the Navy failed the whole thing would be treated as a demonstration and give up & that no troops would be required. It appears however from this paper signed W. S. C. that the failure for the Dardanelles operation is due to Lord Kitchener and myself, though neither of us have been at the Admiralty.'[24]

Grey also saw little cause to depart from his accustomed diplomatic procedures. He would not make special trips to make special bargains by special means. In particular, he refused to go on any such assignment to the Balkans, an area whose problems were already very familiar to him over many years. He had distrusted the claims and plans of the Buxton brothers in 1912–13 and saw no reason to entrust them with special responsibilities. He refused to believe that the British Minister in Sofia was the stumbling block in the way of a settlement as was alleged. Churchill and Lloyd George, on the other hand, supported the Buxton brothers in their forays. Lloyd George subsequently wrote the scathing comment on this period that Grey 'mistook correctitude for rectitude'. Not in danger of making that mistake himself, Lloyd George, in conjunction with Noel Buxton, was trying to fix a settlement of the difficult boundary questions with the Bulgarian Minister in London, purporting to be making his offers with Cabinet authority. Grey was very angry. He told the Minister that while the Chancellor's remarks could be reported back to Sofia, he wished to see them first if they claimed to be with the authority of the Cabinet. In any case, fundamentally, Grey was a 'westerner' with a dislike of 'side-shows'.[25]

There was one issue, however, on which Grey was not prepared to accept the subordination of diplomacy to possible military advantage. He was not prepared to jeopardize the relations with the United States. Early in September 1914, he wrote to Spring-Rice in Washington that 'we wish in all our conduct of the war to do nothing which will be a cause of complaint or dispute as regards the United States Government; such a dispute would indeed be a crowning calamity...'[26] In this determination he was supported by Asquith and some, though not all, of his colleagues. On the other hand, he was not prepared to accept the American demand that Britain should abide by the Declaration of London in its entirety. He stood firm, on the other hand, against the French demands that cotton should be put on the contraband list.[27] Runciman, the President of the Board of Trade, supported Grey – 'My own wish would be to impede Germany in every way possible and *effective* short of a quarrel with American opinion. Ineffective expedients are worse than useless...'[28] But against this success, Grey gave in to the military fait accompli of a mine-war zone, though fortunately this did not lead to friction with the United States. Throughout this period, therefore, the Foreign Secretary was under attack from his more ruthless colleagues and from the Americans. The American Ambassador, Page, gives a good picture of the position: 'I fight Sir Edward about stopping cargoes, literally fight. He yields and promises this or that. This or that doesn't happen or only half happens. I know why. The military ministers balk him. I inquire through the back door and hear that the Admiralty and the War Office of course value American good-will, but they'll take their chances of a quarrel with the United States rather than let copper get to Germany.'[29] As the months passed, however, and his own position weakened, Grey was increasingly unable to resist military demands for an intensified economic warfare, whatever the consequences on American policy-makers. All of these problems were not to Grey's taste. 'The F.O. is nauseous in war time', he wrote to Rosebery, 'a mass of questions of contra-band & kindred subjects that don't exist in time of peace and are a disagree-able brood spawned by war.'[30]

The extension of the blockade policy naturally came to involve the Foreign Office more closely in the problems of neutral trade. The aim was to reach agreement with the neutral states based on mutual self-interest. In the process, the Foreign Office became more deeply involved with commercial agreements, indeed with business men themselves, than ever before. The Board of Trade was supposed to be in charge of the direction of British exports and it was anomalous, to say the least, that it seemed to encourage exports to new markets at a time when the Foreign Office wished to restrict imports into neutral countries. The writer of the Official History comments: 'Our fault was therefore one of omission rather than of deliberate intention: the government had neither co-ordinated the divergent policies of the two departments of state, nor established a central authority with the necessary powers.'[31] The Foreign Office had established a Contraband Department as part of the War Department. In 1915 Crowe was appointed its head. As the work expanded, it was later subdivided into a Foreign Trade Department, a War Trade Intelligence Department, a War Trade Statistical Department and a Restric-tion of Enemy Supplies Department.[32]

A Cabinet order of November 1914 established the Contraband Committee, which became the executive organ of the blockade. It was chaired by a common lawyer and was composed of representatives of the Foreign Office, the Board of Trade and the Admiralty.[33] The Order in Council of March 1915 led to a big increase in the volume of blockade work, and Lord Robert Cecil was appointed as Under-Secretary for Foreign Affairs with special reponsibility for blockade on the formation of the new Government in May 1915. In September, the War Trade Advisory Committee was formed under Lord Crewe, composed of the chairmen of all committees engaged in contraband work. But there was still much overlapping and friction. In February 1916, Grey told Asquith that 'there ought to be control by some Minister in touch with the Foreign Office'.[34] It was then agreed that Cecil should undertake this work, retaining his existing office, but becoming a member of the Cabinet. In effect, therefore, there was a dual command at the Foreign Office, and it was Cecil's empire that seemed to be growing. Similarly, the Contraband Department seemed to be expanding at the expense of the Foreign Office proper. Friction between the Foreign Office and the Board of Trade was not removed by this appointment. At the end of August 1916 Grey protested to Runciman about a proposal which would leave the Foreign Office, that is the Embassies and Legations, with such diplomatic work as could be disentangled from the commercial which would be taken over by the Board of Trade. He was most anxious that 'the F.O. should not be abolished without a hearing'.[35] With the fall of the Asquith Government, Cecil was given direct access to the War Cabinet, not, as before, through the Foreign Office. It seemed to represent a further demotion. It is difficult, however, to be certain about the exact significance of these administrative changes, and it may be that the Foreign Office contrived to exert more influence than these developments would suggest.

The pressures on the Foreign Office did not simply come from changes in the political and administrative structure consequent upon the war. They also came, to an extent, from outside critics. As has been seen elsewhere, despite predictions to the contrary, the number of those in July 1914 who were resolutely opposed to war was very small. The great bulk of opinion was in favour of going to war. Nevertheless, even amongst supporters of the war there was a feeling that the Foreign Office was somehow discredited by what had happened. The 'pacifists' seized on this feeling in their propaganda. Although disappointed by the amount of support for the war, the dissenting minorities began to organize themselves against the day when, if the war should be prolonged, their voice might again become important. The intellectuals, Hobson, Angell, Brailsford and Dickinson were all horrified by the war, but somewhat uncertain what they should do about it. Lowes Dickinson, in particular, wanted to see a gradual campaign develop so that 'instead of terms imposed by victors or vanquished, a general congress including the neutral powers, and, of course, in particular, the United States' should assemble.[36] But he was not in favour of a public campaign. A small group should work privately to formulate plans in anticipation of peace whenever it should occur.[37] One public organization, however, was to hand. Charles Trevelyan, with financial assistance from Arnold Rowntree and Philip Morrell, persuaded E. D. Morel to accept the secretaryship of a new body which was to be called the Union of Democratic Control. The title emphasized the continuity with the pre-war campaign against secrecy in the conduct of foreign affairs. Some distinguished figures, like Gilbert Murray, C. P. Scott and Lord Bryce, who might have been expected to be sympathetic, refused to associate with it publicly.[38] They were now convinced that the war ought to be won and Grey supported. Trevelyan thought it was the duty of advanced men 'to prepare for the day when doubts begin to arise', for he feared that the Liberal Ministers 'can't stand the unpopularity which would be poured on them by the Tories and the more violent anti-Germans. They will take the irreconcilable line...my firm convinction is that we are in for a war *à outrance* unless English opinion can be made to change.'[39] Here was the supreme paradox of the U.D.C. position. On the one hand it was necessary to ensure that public opinion would be in a position to ensure that Governments made a satisfactory and just peace. Yet at the same time the U.D.C. had to conduct a campaign to educate public opinion into seeing the need for such a peace.

Trevelyan was right in supposing that, at the outset, the difficulties of a Liberal Government would not come from his group but from that other public opinion which was more concerned to see the war won, or at least not lost, than to produce the principles or details of an ultimate settlement. In the first place, many Tories were convinced that there was something infinitely curious about the war being conducted by a Liberal Government. Discontent on the Tory back benches began to show itself. In 1914, it seemed as though the most effective contribution parliament could make to the war was not to meet. It assembled from 25 August to 17 September to deal with Home Rule, and then adjourned until 11 November. By then, the expectation that the war might soon be over no longer seemed feasible. The Government, however, had already developed the habit of keeping information to itself. In any case, members of parliament were inhibited in their questioning by the desire not to lower public morale or themselves appear unpatriotic. It was unlikely, however, that energetic opposition back benchers were going to accept this supine rôle permanently. For example, many of them did not share Grey's attitude towards the United States and the blockade.[40] A Unionist Business Committee was set up in January 1915, partly as a result of discontent on this subject. Conservatives also began to mount a campaign in favour of conscription. Their anger, however, was as much directed against the supposed passivity of their own leadership as against the Government. The resignation of Fisher and the 'Shell shortage' brought matters to a head. Although there was much subsequent criticism of the part played by the Harmsworth Press in the crisis, it was a fact that in the absence of parliamentary information and activity, it was inevitable that the Press should assume this rôle. When writing to French, Northcliffe was only exaggerating in his claim that 'In the absence of some strong statement from you the Government have your friends at their mercy, because they are able to get their newspapers to say that any agitation for less secrecy is unpatriotic and playing the enemy's game.'[41]

The power of the Press was not, however, unlimited. For example, at Northcliffe's behest, the *Daily Mail* launched strong attacks on Kitchener, the 'people's idol' he had helped to create. Paradoxically, Northcliffe's outspoken attacks saved the Secretary of State. 'Patriotic opinion', which the *Mail* claimed to represent, reacted very strongly against the attacks, burning copies of the offending paper in public places.⁴² 'Public opinion' did not wish its views to be disturbed. Similarly, a later plan to leave Kitchener in the Middle East as Commander-in-Chief was prematurely disclosed, and the adverse reaction to the suggestion caused the Government to shelve it. In fact, as the final result of the crisis that led to the first Coalition demonstrated, the leading politicians on both sides were determined to play their own hands and not be moulded either by the Press, though they might on occasion try to use it, or their own back benches. Despite the attacks of his back benchers, Bonar Law, acting with Austen Chamberlain and Lansdowne, had no wish to destroy the Government. He might have been able to win a General Election and form a Unionist Government, but from a wider perspective, there was much to be said, in a dangerous situation, for Liberal men being manoeuvred into passing Tory measures in order to survive.

As one would expect, the official relations between Press and Government were rather delicate. At the outbreak of the war, a Press Bureau was established to restrict and guide news for publication, In theory, these restrictions were supposed to be very limited 'because of the underlying principles upon which popular government in this country must repose'.⁴³ The work was done by a News Department in the Foreign Office which started after the war began. There was considerable press irritation at this system. Because no blank spaces were left in newspapers, there was no means of judging what had been excluded. The bureau was to be the means by which '*all* information relating to the war which *any* of the Departments of State think right to issue is communicated to the Press'. In this way, it was supposed to prevent one department from issuing information which another would have preferred to have been kept secret. In addition, the journalists at the front were severely circumscribed, being in Lord Burnham's words, 'treated as if they were criminals let loose; war correspondents were locked up in stalls by a corporal's guard'.⁴⁴ Because of the irritation which the system caused, it was abolished in December 1915, and newspapers had to take their own responsibility for the publication of despatches concerned with foreign affairs. Apart from the general friction which was, to a degree, inevitable, it was quite possible for relations between the Foreign Office and one particular newspaper to be bad. *The Times* in 1914–15 was a classic instance. Grey had been offended by the attacks made in the newspaper concerning his policy at Constantinople just before the outbreak of war with Turkey. He was especially irritated at the way the British Ambassador, Sir Louis Mallet, was singled out. As a result, relations with *The Times* were severed through the winter of 1914 and not patched up until after the signing of the Treaty of London in April 1915.

As far as public opinion in a wider sense was concerned, the most significant event in the politics of the war was the formation of the Coalition Government. It could be looked upon as a sign of national unity. The willingness of Arthur Henderson to serve in the Government seemed to symbolize the support of Labour for the war. Nevertheless, in a curious way, the formation of a coalition sharpened some differences of opinion. Henderson's appointment, for example, accentuated the split in Labour's ranks. Philip Snowden castigated the Labour Party for accepting office. 'As an independent force it might have rendered powerful help in shaping the peace terms. It has chosen so completely to identify itself with the late government, with the present government, and with any government that may be formed, that it has lost its claim to represent any distinct phase of democratic thought and action in Great Britain.'[45] A considerable number of Liberals also felt that the Coalition would do little to preserve the essence of Liberalism. Charles Hobhouse wrote to Walter Runciman that 'Nothing will persuade me that this is not the end of the Liberal Party as we have known it.'[46] He and other ex-Ministers foresaw a steady increase in the campaign for conscription until Britain became almost indistinguishable from Germany in respect of 'militarism'. The Coalition also meant that the U.D.C. and its supporters further emphasized their claim to represent the real alternative. It seemed obvious, they claimed, that the war was going to end in stalemate, so it was better to recognize that fact sooner rather than later. The trouble was that 'the men fighting don't talk or think, and the people left at home are savage, irrational, and often, in France at least, reactionary'.[47] At the end of 1915, the great difficulty for the 'pacifists' was to get any propaganda for a 'reasonable' settlement and a negotiated peace under way. 'Everybody, and especially everybody with a reputation to lose, feels that "the time is not ripe".'[48]

Propaganda of another kind was not so difficult to mount. The operation of the blockade was still a subject for anxious and blatant press comment on the Tory side. Grey's weakened political position, and his absence from his post, allowed a campaign for more ruthless enforcement to make headway. The *Daily Mail* (and other Tory papers) wanted to see cotton added to the contraband list, declaring 'Every bale of cotton which reaches Germany means either an Allied cripple or a corpse'. When cotton was finally added, the *Mail* believed that 'the Foreign Office has at last confessed to the Cotton Crime ...13 months too late'.[49] Cotton was soon replaced as the subject of criticism by attacks on Grey's Balkan diplomacy, culminating in despair and anger when, in the middle of October 1915, Bulgaria joined the Central Powers. The criticism might possibly have been modified if the complexity of the situation had been made more apparent. But there was no Commons debate following Grey's short announcement on the subject. In December 1915, the American Ambassador even felt that Grey's scalp was not safe because of his alleged desire for leniency.[50] When Colonel House was in London in February 1916, Grey informed him that he could not publicly support a proposal that the President of the United States should summon a peace conference for fear of British public opinion. House noted in his diary, 'Grey believes they would even go so far as to smash his windows.'[51] Attacks of this kind continued until the end of Grey's career, though he claimed that they did not distress him. 'The only papers I see', he wrote to a friend, 'are the Times, Daily Tel: &

Westminster Gazette; I have seen in these one outrageous untrue attack upon me quoted from the Daily Mail... The attacks upon the diplomacy of the Allies are very ill informed, and to hold me personally responsible for the whole of that policy is ludicrous.'[52] He wrote to the editor of the *Spectator* that the attacks of the *Morning Post* and the *National Review* were disgraceful. If they were really 'typical of British thought, opinion, and temperament, many of us who are devoted to the country would despair of its success in this war and of its future.'[53]

The Foreign Secretary was therefore under attack from both Right and Left. The U.D.C. was equally critical from the opposite vantage point. Before the war, Grey had been able to rely on the solid Liberal centre to see him through: now it no longer existed. Free Trade, financial orthodoxy, opposition to government control were all crumbling. Asquith, having delayed as long as possible, finally agreed to the introduction of conscription in 1916. Whether rightly or wrongly, public opinion had now come to feel that conscription was a necessary sign of determination to win the war. Only one Minister, Simon, resigned, and only some fifty Liberals voted against the Military Service Bill.[54] But the cleavage was in reality much greater. Liberal members were now beginning openly to divide. An unofficial War Committee was formed in January to press yet again for more efficient government and, although some of its members were by no means out-and-out Lloyd Georgeites, others felt that salvation lay in only one direction. Other Liberals simply felt saddened and dispirited by Asquith's behaviour. It would only be a matter of time before the demand was raised for the conscription of married men. *The Nation* lamented that there was a type of Liberal 'whose idea of patriotic duty during war consists in throwing to the wolves one after another of his Liberal principles... Free Speech, Free Press, Habeas Corpus, Voluntary Service, Free Trade – let them all go in this war for Liberty!... But it has become so automatic and indiscriminate as to threaten the safety and sanity of the nation.'[55] If this description fitted Asquith, it fitted his successor even more aptly. Conscription, of course, brought all sorts of additional problems with it. Asquith had succeeded in preserving the right of conscientious objection. Until 1916, opponents of the war had never had to be counted. Now, the number of those who were prepared to become conscientious objectors could be assessed – though there were a very great number of reasons, political, religious and philosophical, for objecting to military service. A new body, the No Conscription Fellowship, was formed; but the threatened mass labour unrest if conscription were introduced failed to materialize.[56]

The triumph of Lloyd George meant, in foreign policy, the victory of a man who, at a time when some of his colleagues, in both parties, were contemplating the possibility of peace, was determined to strike the knock-out blow. Grey had written to him doubting the wisdom of such remarks. Lloyd George was not worried by such criticism. As far as government structure was concerned, the new Prime Minister was determined to set up that effective War Council which had been meditated for so long. He prided himself on his disregard of custom or institution if he considered either an impediment to action. He would show no tender regard for the preserves of the Foreign Secretary and shared a certain Radical contempt for the ways of the Foreign Office. At the end of 1916, the bulk of public opinion supported him. On the other hand, if, instead of victory, another costly stalemate ensued, individuals and organizations were at work which would turn public opinion from an asset into a serious difficulty for the Government.

Notes

1. THE FOREIGN SECRETARY, THE CABINET, PARLIAMENT AND THE PARTIES

1 A. V. Dicey, *The Law of the Constitution* (London, 1897), pp. 393–5.
2 F. Gosses, *The Management of British Foreign Policy before the First World War* (Leiden, 1948), pp. 89–90, citing the works of contemporary constitutional writers.
3 P. G. Richards, *Parliament and Foreign Affairs* (London, 1967), has a brief historical introduction, though the bulk of the work is concerned with the contemporary situation.
4 A great many accounts of this episode now exist. See R. Jenkins, *Asquith* (London, 1967), pp. 167–76. T. Boyle, 'The formation of Campbell-Bannerman's Goverment in December 1905', *Bulletin of the Institute of Historical Research*, XLV, no. 112, November 1972.
5 J. E. Tyler, 'Campbell-Bannerman and the Liberal Imperialists, 1906–8', *History*, xxiii, 1938. H. C. G. Matthew, *The Liberal Imperialists* (Oxford, 1973), K. G. Robbins, 'Sir Edward Grey and the British Empire', *Journal of Imperial and Commonwealth History*, i, no. 2, January, 1973.
6 R. Hyam, *Elgin and Churchill at the Colonial Office, 1905–08* (London, 1968), p. 47.
7 G. Monger, *The End of Isolation* (London, 1963), pp. 257–9 seems to overstate the position.
8 Grey to Campbell-Bannerman, 22 January 1906, Campbell-Bannerman MS. 52514; J. Wilson, *A Life of Sir Henry Campbell-Bannerman* (London, 1973), pp. 528–34.
9 See the discussion in S. R. Williamson, *The Politics of Grand Strategy* (Cambridge, Mass., 1969), p. 83.
10 Campbell-Bannerman to Ripon, 2 February 1906 in J. A. Spender, *Life of Sir Henry Campbell-Bannerman* (London, 1923), ii. p. 257.
11 Monger, *End of Isolation*, p. 256.
12 Sir S. Lee, *King Edward VII* (London, 1927), ii, pp. 445–6.
13 In his speech of 3 August 1914, Grey stated that Asquith had been informed, and he repeated this view after the war – for example, in conversation with G. P. Gooch – G. P. Gooch, *Under Six Reigns* (London, 1958), pp. 227–30. Lloyd George also states that Asquith knew and was unhappy. D. Lloyd George, *War Memoirs* (London, 1938), i, p. 30. There is no evidence from the Asquith side that he knew.
14 Grey to Haldane, 3 September 1906. For the background and details of Haldane's visit see Monger, *End of Isolation*, pp. 303–6. Haldane MS. 5907.
15 Rosebery to Haldane, 11 August 1916, Haldane MS. 5913.
16 P. Knaplund, ed., *Speeches on Foreign Affairs, 1904–14, by Sir Edward Grey* (London, 1931), pp. 26–32. Grey wrote to J. A. Spender of the *Westminster Gazette* asking him to give the speech emphasis if he agreed with it. 'I am afraid the impression has been spread with some success by those interested in spreading it, that a Liberal

Government would unsettle the understanding with France in order to make it up to Germany. I want to do what I can to combat this...I think we are running a real risk of losing France and not gaining Germany, who won't want us, if she can detach France from us.' Grey to Spender, 19 October 1905. Spender MS., Add. MS. 46389.

17 Grey to Ripon, 27 July 1906, Ripon MS., Add. MS. 43640.
18 Lloyd George, *War Memoirs*, I, p. 28: Monger, *End of Isolation*, pp. 307–8.
19 Beryl J. Williams, 'The Strategic Background to the Anglo-Russian Entente of August 1907', *The Historical Journal*, IX, 3 (1960).
20 Grey to Campbell-Bannerman, 31 August 1907, Campbell-Bannerman MS. 52514. The Prime Minister also congratulated Grey on the agreement.
21 Morley to Minto, 6 February 1908, Morley MSS. Eur. d/573/3: D. A. Hamer, *John Morley* (Oxford, 1968), p. 351.
22 Parliamentary Debates, Series 4, clxxxiii.
23 D. Judd, *Balfour and the British Empire* (London, 1968), p. 80.
24 P. Magnus, *King Edward the Seventh* (London, 1964), pp. 405–6. The agitation was repeated in the following year when the question of a return visit was raised. The King met the Tsar at Cowes and the visitor did not venture near the capital.
25 R. Blatchford, *My Eighty Years* (London, 1931), pp. 200–1 and 224–5. W. Kendall, *The Revolutionary Movement in Britain, 1900–21* (London, 1969), Ch. 3.
26 A. J. Marder, *From the Dreadnought to Scapa Flow* (London, 1961), I, pp. 135–8.
27 Memorandum by Grey, 23 July 1908, Grey MS. F.O. 800/91.
28 Hardinge to Grey, 15 August 1908, B.D. vi, 110: Memorandum by Hardinge, 16 August 1908, B.D. vi, 117.
29 Speech by Lloyd George, reported in the *Daily News*, 28 July 1908.
30 Grey to Bertie, 26 August 1908, F.O. 800/101: Lloyd George to Asquith, 21 August 1908, F.O. 800/101; Grey to Asquith, 22 August 1908, F.O. 800/100: Asquith to Grey, 24 August 1908, Asquith MS. 23.
31 Grey to Lord Sanderson, 12 September 1908, F.O. 800/111.
32 E. Marsh to H. Montgomery, 11 December 1908: W. Tyrrell to E. Marsh, 22 December 1908: W. S. Churchill to Grey, 24 December 1908: Grey to Churchill, 26 December 1908, F.O. 800/89. Churchill was, of course regarded as 'pro-German' at that time.
33 R. S. Churchill, *Winston S. Churchill* (London, 1967), II, pp. 514–17.
34 Cabinet Letter, 15 February 1909, Asquith MS.
35 Cabinet Letter, 24 February 1909, Asquith MS.
36 R. McKenna to W. Runciman, 28 March 1910, Runciman MS.
37 Jenkins, *Asquith*, p. 216.
38 Asquith to Grey, 19 March 1909, cited in G. M. Trevelyan, *Grey of Fallodon*, p. 213.
39 A. Tilney Basset, *Life of John Edward Ellis* (London, 1914), p. 253.
40 J. A. Spender and C. Asquith, *Life of Lord Oxford and Asquith* (London, 1932), I, p. 254.
41 L. Masterman, *C. F. G. Masterman* (London, 1939), p. 125.
42 Knaplund, ed., *Grey's speeches*, pp. 123–44.
43 Grey himself wrote to Sir Henry Newbolt: '...I understand your anxiety about the Navy: there is plenty in the press to make people anxious – plenty which ought never to be there, for the attempt to fix the Navy estimates by press controversy, in which each side inspires its own journalists, is not dignified'. Grey to Newbolt, 10 February 1909, Newbolt MS.
44 A. J. Marder ed., *Fear God and Dread Nought, The correspondence of Lord Fisher of Kilverstone* (London, 1956), II, pp. 227–8.
45 G. P. Gooch to the *Westminster Gazette*, 28 July 1909. I owe this reference to Mr A. Cowpe.

46 Minute by Grey on Goschen to Grey, 21 August 1909, B.D. vi, 187.

47 Goschen to Grey, 4 November 1909, B.D. vi, 204: Grey to Bryce, 12 December 1909, Bryce MS., f. 28: Goschen to Grey, 11 April 1910, B.D. vi, 344: Grey minute on the same: Grey to Goschen, 5 May 1910, B.D. vi, 361.

48 Loreburn's own views on the origins of the war can be found in *How the war came* (London, 1919). See also the chapter on Loreburn in R. F. V. Heuston, *Lives of the Lord Chancellors, 1885–1940* (Oxford, 1964). Cabinet Letter, 20 July 1910, Asquith MS.

49 Cabinet Letter, 29 July 1910, Asquith MS.

50 Cabinet Letter, 20 July 1910, Asquith MS.: Asquith to Lloyd George, 24 September 1910, Lloyd George MS., C/6/11/7.

51 Haldane to Grey, 26 December 1910, F.O. 800/102.

52 Lloyd George had again been complaining of being left in the dark about essential features of foreign policy. Diary of Arthur Murray, 27 January 1911, Murray MS. 8814: Asquith to the King, 20 January 1911, Asquith MS.: Asquith to Grey, 25 January 1911, F.O. 800/100.

53 Cabinet Letter, 9 March 1911, Asquith MS.

54 Cabinet Letters, 4 and 19 July 1911, Asquith MS.

55 Grey to Asquith, 19 July 1911, F.O. 800/100.

56 Cabinet Letter, 22 July 1911, Asquith MS. Loreburn and Morley continued to be unhappy at the possibility of war. Loreburn to Grey, 27 July 1911, F.O. 800/99: Morley to Asquith, 27 July 1911, Asquith MS.

57 Lloyd George insisted that the initiative for the speech had been his own. See R. A. Cosgrove, 'A Note on Lloyd George's Speech at the Mansion House, 21 July 1911', *The Historical Journal*, XII, 4, 1969. K. Wilson, 'The Agadir Crisis, The Mansion House speech and the double-edgedness of agreements', *The Historical Journal*, xv, 3 September 1972.

58 J. L. Hammond, *C. P. Scott of the Manchester Guardian* (London, 1934), pp. 152–7.

59 T. P. Conwell-Evans, *Foreign Policy from a Back Bench, 1904–18* (London, 1932), is based on Buxton's papers. Ponsonby was formerly a member of the Diplomatic Service from which he resigned, becoming subsequently private secretary to Campbell-Bannerman and succeeding to his parliamentary seat. M. Anderson, *Noel Buxton: A Life* (London, 1952), pp. 50–1.

60 Williamson, *Politics of Grand Strategy*, p. 140.

61 Jenkins, *Asquith*, p. 270.

62 Minutes of the 114th Meeting of the C.I.D., 23 August 1911, Asquith MS.

63 W. Runciman to L. Harcourt, 24 August 1911, Runciman MS.

64 L. Harcourt to W. Runciman, 26 August 1911, Runciman MS.

65 R. S. Churchill, *Churchill*, II, pp. 529–35.

66 Grey of Fallodon, *Twenty Five Years* (London, 1925), I, p. 94.

67 Cabinet Letter, 2 November 1911.

68 Sir Henry Wilson recorded that 'Morley, Crewe, Harcourt and some of the small fry were mad that they were not present on August 23.' C. E. Callwell, *Sir Henry Wilson* (London, 1927), I, p. 99.

69 Diary of John Burns, 2 November 1911, Burns MS. 46333.

70 Cabinet Letter, 16 November 1911, Asquith MS. J. P. Mackintosh, *The British Cabinet* (London, 1968), p. 342, shrewdly comments: 'The history of the military conversations with France shows that to the development of levels of power within the Cabinet must be added the further possibility of withholding information on the early stages of policy-making from the Cabinet. Indeed, the two are interconnected, for the only sanction behind the convention that the Cabinet must be consulted on all important questions was fear of the consequences – a crisis and the disintegration of the ministry. All the factors which gave the Premier a strong

position and increased the politician's desire for office also made ministers less likely to force showdowns or resign in large numbers on the grounds that they had not been fully informed, albeit on some very important issues.'

71 Hammond, *Scott*, p. 144.
72 When Grey informed him of the decision to publish, Lansdowne replied: 'We shall at any rate hear no more of the confident statements which are still being made to the effect that we had bound ourselves by these articles to afford one another material assistance of a definite kind in certain eventualities.' Lansdowne to Grey, 22 November 1911, F.O. 800/108.
73 P.D., vol. xxxii, cols. 43–65; K. G. Robbins, *Sir Edward Grey* (London, 1971), pp. 246–54.
74 P.D., vol. xxxii, cols. 66 and 70. Shortly before the debate, H. A. Gwynne of the *Morning Post* reported that he had had a conversation with Grey's private secretary, Tyrrell, who intimated his willingness to see Bonar Law. Gwynne offered to make the introduction – 'of course he is a vigorous defender of Grey but I imagine we all are, especially as the extreme left are going for him like pickpockets...' H. A. Gwynne to Bonar Law, 20 November 1911, Bonar Law MS. 24/6/63. Tyrrell did see Bonar Law and Grey himself passed over an outline of his intended speech. Grey to Bonar Law, 25 November 1911, Bonar Law MS. 24/4/80.
75 P.D., vol. xxxii, cols. 80–95; F. S. L. Lyons, *John Dillon* (London, 1968), p. 321.
76 P.D., vol. xxxii, col. 125.
77 P.D., vol. xxxii, cols. 74–80.
78 P.D., vol. xxxii, cols. 2617–20. J. King, a late speaker in the debate, made the point that up to that time, there had been nineteen speeches of which only five were made by Unionists and two made by Irish members.
79 For the development of Ponsonby's critique see Z. Steiner, *The Foreign Office and Foreign Policy, 1898–1914* (Cambridge, 1969), Appendix 4.
80 Gosses, *British Foreign Policy*, pp. 85–8.
81 See, for example, S. Low, *The Governance of England* (London, 1914), pp. 299–300: P. Morrell, 'The control of foreign affairs', *The Contemporary Review*, 1912, pp. 659–72.
82 A. Ponsonby, *Democracy and Diplomacy* (London, 1915), pp. 121–7 for the evidence.
83 Cabinet Letter, 3 February 1912, Asquith MS.
84 Haldane to this mother, 23 January 1912, Haldane MS. 5987: Grey to Churchill, 29 January 1912, Lloyd George MS., CI/3/15/14: Diary of Lord Haldane's visit to Berlin, 10 February 1912, B.D. vi, 506.
85 Grey to Bertie, 13 February 1912, B.D. vi, 514: Memorandum, 16 and 19 February 1912, Bertie MS. F.O. 800/171.
86 Memorandum by Lord Haldane of a conversation with Count Metternich, 12 March 1912, B.D. vi, 533.
87 Cabinet Letter, 14 March 1912, Asquith MS.
88 'Interview with Haldane and Grey 11–12.15 p.m.', Notes by Harcourt, 14 March 1912, Harcourt MS. Box 14.
89 Cabinet Letter, 30 March 1912, Asquith MS.
90 Asquith to Grey, 10 April 1912, F.O. 800/100.
91 L. Harcourt to Sir John Anderson, 23 December 1911, Harcourt MS.
92 W. R. Louis, *Germany's Lost Colonies, 1914–19* (Oxford, 1967), pp. 33–4.
93 Memorandum of 23 February 1914, Bertie MS. F.O. 800/176: Grey to Bertie, 4 March 1914, F.O. 800/176.
94 L. Harcourt to E. Grey, 8 January 1914: E. Grey to L. Harcourt, 10 & 11 January 1914, F.O. 800/91.
95 R. S. Churchill, *Churchill*, ii, pp. 598–600. The Radicals were disturbed by the further acceleration, but only 28 Liberals went into the lobby against the Government following Churchill's speech on 22 July.

96 Minutes of the 118th Meeting of the C.I.D., 11 July 1912, Asquith MS. Foreign Office Memorandum, 8 May 1912, B.D. x (ii), 386.

97 'Memorandum by the Secretary of State for War on the effect of the Loss of Sea Power in the Mediterranean on British Military Power', 9 May 1912, CAB 37/110/68.

98 'Memorandum on the naval situation by Reginald McKenna', 24 June 1912, CAB 37/111/79: 'Memorandum by Reginald McKenna', 3 July 1912, CAB 37/111/86; Morley to McKenna, 3 July 1912, McKenna MS.

99 Minutes of the 117th Meeting of the C.I.D., 4 July 1912, Asquith MS.

100 Cabinet Letters, 5, 12, 15 and 16 July 1912, Asquith MS.

101 Churchill to Grey, 27 July 1912, F.O. 800/105: Churchill, *Churchill*, ii, p. 596.

102 Memorandum by Bertie, 25 and 27 July 1912, Bertie MS. F.O. 800/165.

103 Cabinet Letter, 20 and 21 November 1912; Grey *Twenty Five Years*, i, pp. 97–8.

104 Lloyd George, *War Memoirs*, i, p. 28.

105 Cabinet Letter, 9 January 1913, Asquith MS.

106 Cabinet Letters, 20 December 1913, 29 January 1914 and 11 February 1914, Asquith MS.

107 Grey to Lloyd George, 23 January 1914: Lloyd George to Grey, 26 January 1914, Lloyd George MS. C/4/14/12.

108 Churchill, *Churchill*, ii, pp. 681–2.

109 Memorandum by Bertie, 27 June 1914, Bertie MS. F.O. 800/171.

110 Grey to Lloyd George, 20 June 1913, Lloyd George MS. C/4/14/9.

2. THE FOREIGN OFFICE UNDER SIR EDWARD GREY

1 R. Jones, *The Nineteenth Century Foreign Office* (London, 1971), pp. 124–35.

2 Public Record Office, *The Records of the Foreign Office* (London, 1969), p. 63.

3 *Ibid.* pp. 4, 9, 63.

4 Z. Steiner, *The Foreign Office and Foreign Policy, 1898–1914* (Cambridge, 1969), pp. 70–6. G. W. Monger, *The End of Isolation* (London, 1963), pp. 101–3.

5 Z. Steiner, 'Grey, Hardinge and the Foreign Office, 1906–1910', *The Historical Journal*, x, 4 (1967), p. 431.

6 N. d'Ombrain, *War Machinery and High Policy* (Oxford, 1973), p. 6. It seems clear, however, that Hardinge never examined the full implications of such talks and that his role on the C.I.D. sub-committee was of limited importance.

7 For an exception, see K. Robbins, *Sir Edward Grey* (London, 1971), p. 177.

8 Hardinge had some doubts about Grey's ability to stand up against Lloyd George and Churchill. In a letter to Knollys at the height of the naval estimate debate, he wrote: 'I always told you that Grey is a weak man. I thought that success had given him confidence and even strength but as regards the latter characteristic I was mistaken...' Quoted from Royal Archive W55/8 in K. Robbins, *Sir Edward Grey*, p. 199. Compare this with his letter to Villiers quoted in Steiner, *op. cit.* p. 92 for a different view.

9 S. Gwynn, *The Letters and Friendships of Sir Cecil Spring Rice* (London, 1929), vol. I, p. 400.

10 Hardinge MSS. vol. 17, Hardinge to Bryce, 4 June 1909.

11 K. Robbins, *op. cit.* pp. 199–200.

12 F.O. 800/193A, Hardinge to Lowther, 30 April, 18 May 1909.

13 F.O. 800/92, Hardinge to Nicolson, 29 March 1911.

14 Hardinge MSS. vol. 17, Hardinge to Nicolson, 26 March 1909.

15 B.D. v, no. 195.

16 F.O. 800/341, Hardinge to Nicolson, 28 October 1908.

17 M. B. Cooper, 'British Policy in the Balkans 1908–9', *The Historical Journal* VII (1964–5), pp. 258–79.

18 Bertie MSS. F.O. 800/180, Hardinge to Bertie, 30 July 1908.

19 F.O. 800/193, Hardinge to Lowther, 1 December 1908.

20 F.O. 800/342, Tyrrell to Nicolson, 17 February 1909.

21 B.D. v, Appendix III, Memorandum by Hardinge, 4 May 1909.

22 F.O. 800/342, Hardinge to Nicolson, 12 May 1909.

23 It is ironic that Stead's attack was made just at the time when Hardinge was complaining of his inability to influence Grey. Robbins, *Grey*, p. 200.

24 Monger, *op. cit.* pp. 189–92.

25 I am grateful to E. W. Edwards for much of the following information.

26 D. C. M. Platt, *The Cinderella Service* (London, 1971), p. 59.

27 For an excellent assessment of Crowe's influence, see R. Cosgrove, 'The Career of Eyre Crowe: A Reassessment', *Albion*, vol. 4, no. 4 (Winter, 1972), pp. 193–200.

28 B.D. III, Appendix A.

29 *Ibid.* Appendix B.

30 F.O. 371/457, Lascelles to Grey, 9 January 1908, minute by Crowe.

31 For a further extension of this argument see Steiner, *The Foreign Office and Foreign Policy*, pp. 109–18.

32 Lascelles to Fitzmaurice, 21 September 1906, Lascelles MSS. vol. III, pt (1).

33 The King, Prime Minister and Foreign Secretary all had a voice in ambassadorial appointments though the permanent under-secretary and private secretary were not without influence.

34 For Tyrrell's contacts with August Bebel, see R. Crampton, 'August Bebel and the British Foreign Office', *History*, vol. LVIII (June, 1973), pp. 218–32.

35 F.O. 800/241, Tyrrell to Spring Rice, 10 December 1907, 15 April 1908.

36 F.O. 800/93, Tyrrell to Grey, 27 and 28 August 1909.

37 F.O. 800/342, Tyrrell to Nicolson, 17 February 1909.

38 F.O. 371/900, minute by G. S. Spicer, 12 January 1910.

39 Monger, *op. cit.* pp. 300, 304, 316; F.O. 371/460, Cartwright to Grey, 16 June 1908. Minute by Villiers.

40 Platt, *op. cit.* p. 59.

41 Monger, *op. cit.* pp. 315–16.

42 F. R. Bridge, *Great Britain and Austria-Hungary, 1906–1914* (London, 1972), pp. 18–19.

43 *Ibid.* pp. 133–5.

44 Ian Nish, *Alliance in Decline* (London, 1972), pp. 8–9.

45 H. Nicolson, *Lord Carnock*, p. 334.

46 F.O. 8000/355, Nicolson to Goschen, 22 April 1913.

47 Hardinge MSS. vol. 92, Hardinge to Chirol, 5 April 1911.

48 B.D. VI, no. 462.

49 F.O. 800/349, Nicolson to Goschen, 24 July 1911.

50 B.D. VII, no. 392, minute by Crowe.

51 F.O. 800/160, Crowe to Bertie, 20 July 1911.

52 Hardinge MSS. vol. 69, Tyrrell to Hardinge, 21 July 1911.

53 F.O. 800/351, Nicolson to Goschen, 12 September 1911.

54 *Ibid.*

55 Balfour MSS. no. 49767, Sanders to Balfour, 17 September 1911.

56 F.O. 800/181, Nicolson to Bertie, 21 September 1911.

57 B.D. VII, nos. 533, 534, F.O. 800/93, Nicolson to Grey, 5 September 1911.

58 Crowe was wrong about Caillaux.

59 B.D. VII, Appendix III.

60 For details see P. Halpern, *The Mediterranean Naval Situation 1908–1914* (Cambridge, Mass., 1971), particularly chapters 1 and 4 and S. R. Williamson, *The Politics of Grand Strategy: Britain and France prepare for War 1904–114* (Cambridge, Mass., 1969).

61 *Ibid.* p. 383.
62 Halpern, *op. cit.* p. 92.
63 Nicolson, *Lord Carnock*, pp. 402–3.
64 F.O. 371/1400, Rennie to Grey, 22 October 1912, minute by Crowe.
65 Robbins, *op. cit.* p. 254.
66 F.O. 371/1372, Captain Watson to Goschen, 8 February 1912, minute by Crowe.
67 F.O. 800/171, Nicolson to Bertie, 6 April 1912.
68 B.D. VI, nos. 527, 529, minutes by Crowe.
69 F.O. 371/1373, Goschen to Grey, 18 June 1912, minute by Nicolson.
70 B.D. VI, no. 564, undated minute by Nicolson.
71 B.D. VI, no. 579; Hardinge MSS. vol. 70, Chirol to Hardinge, 7 June 1912.
72 B.D. VI, no. 562.
73 P. H. S. Hatton, 'Harcourt and Solf, The Search for an Anglo-German Understanding through Africa, 1913–14', *European Studies Review*, I, no. 2 (1971), p. 128.
74 For details see R. Langhorne, 'Anglo-German Negotiations concerning the future of the Portuguese Colonies, 1911–1914', *The Historical Journal*, XVI, (1973).
75 F.O. 800/111, Grey to J. A. Spender, 24 September 1911.
76 F.O. 800/193A, Nicolson to Lowther, 21 August 1911.
77 For information on Nicolson's policy towards Italy, see R. Bosworth, 'Great Britain and Italy's Acquisition of the Dodecanese, 1912–1915', *The Historical Journal*, XIII (1970), pp. 683–706.
78 F.O. 600/131, Nicolson to Grey, 18 October 1911.
79 F.O. 800/193, Nicolson to Lowther, 14 October 1912.
80 Hardinge MSS. vol. 71, Chirol to Hardinge, 10 April 1913.
81 F.O. 800/365, Nicolson to Goschen, 11 February 1914; Nicolson, *Lord Carnock*, p. 402.
82 Bridge, *Great Britain and Austria–Hungary, 1906–1914*, pp. 199–202.
83 D.D.F. 3 ser, II, no. 363,Cambon to Poincaré, 18 April 1912; Taylor, *Struggle for Mastery in Europe*, p. 479. B.D. VI, no. 576, minute by Nicolson, 15 April 1912.
84 Hardinge MSS, vol. 93, Chirol to Hardinge, 22 May 1914.
85 Robbins, *op. cit.* p. 268.
86 Steiner, *op. cit.* p. 148.
87 F.O. 800/176, Tyrrell to Bertie, 5 February 1912.
88 F.O. 800/355, Tyrrell to Grey, 2 April 1912; Hatton, 'Harcourt and Solf...', *European Studies Review*, pp. 127–8.
89 D.G.P. 33, 12284–12287; Nicolson, *Lord Carnock*, pp. 384–6.
90 D.G.P. 33, 12285, 12295; B.D. IX, ii, no. 62.
91 Hardinge MSS. vol. 93, Chirol to Hardinge, 10 April 1913.
92 F.O. 800/105, Tyrrell to Chirol, 3 January 1912.
93 Steiner, *op. cit.* p. 149.
94 Hardinge MSS. vol. 93, Hardinge to Chirol, 30 April 1913.
95 *Ibid.* 71, Chirol to Hardinge, 23 May 1913.
96 F.O. 800/373, Nicolson to Buchanan, 7 April 1914.
97 B.D. x (ii), Nicolson to Buchanan, no. 540, 27 April 1914.
98 F.O. 800/373, Nicolson to Buchanan, 21 April 1914.
99 B.D. XI (ii), no. 535.
100 B.D. x (ii), Appendix I.
101 B.D. x (i), no. 542, minutes by Nicolson and Mallet, 7 July 1913.
102 B.D. x (i), no. 379, minute by Nicolson.
103 B.D. x (i), no. 393.
104 B.D. x (ii), no. 540.
105 For an estimate of the effects of these disclosures on German thinking see E. Zechlin, 'Deutschland zwischen Kabinettskrieg und Wirtschaftskrieg', *Historische Zeitschrift*, 199 (1964), pp. 347–458.

106 Hardinge MSS. vol. 93, 15 January 1914.
107 Balfour MSS. no. 49747, Mallet to Short, 4 May 1912.
108 B.D. x (i), pp. 901–2.
109 *Ibid.* no. 507, minute by Mallet, no. 535, minute by Mallet, 3 July 1913.
110 For a detailed treatment of this dispute see Peter Calvert, *The Mexican Revolution, 1910–1912* (Cambridge, 1968).
111 Calvert, *op. cit.* pp. 157–8, 162.
112 Hardinge MSS. vol. 93, Mallet to Hardinge, 19 August 1913, quoted in full, Steiner, *op. cit.* p. 106.
113 Hardinge MSS. vol. 93, Hardinge to A. Parker, 18 August 1913.
114 B.D. x (ii), no. 123.
115 *Ibid.* no. 567.
116 B.D. x (i), nos. 412, 452.
117 B.D. x (ii), nos. 547, 561.
118 *Ibid.* no. 537.
119 Quoted in Hatton, *op. cit.* p. 141.
120 Details may be found in P. Lowe, *Great Britain and Japan, 1911–13* (London, 1969).
121 Lowe, *op. cit.* pp. 155–7, 160.
122 F.O. 800/372, Grey to Nicolson, 9 January 1914.
123 B.D. x (i), minute by Parker, no. 664, 31 January 1911.
124 Hardinge MSS. vol. 70, Parker to Hardinge, 9 July 1912.
125 B.D. x (ii), nos. 140, 146, 148.
126 *Ibid.* no. 139.
127 Hardinge MSS. vol. 93, Oliphant to Hardinge, 23 February 1914.
128 F.O. 800/188, Austin Lee to Bertie, 14 April 1914.
129 There were six political (African, American, Eastern, Far Eastern, Western and Consular) and six non-political (Parliamentary, Commercial and Sanitary, Financial, Library, Treaty and Registry) departments in 1905 when Grey took office. In 1914 there were five political departments the African department having been disbanded and its remaining work distributed between the Western and American departments. In 1912 a Controller of Commercial and Consular Affairs was appointed to relieve the pressure on the three assistant under-secretaries.
130 For details of the dispute which produced this petition see Steiner, *op. cit.* pp. 154–5. For further information on the Royal Commission see pp. 167–70.
131 See Z. Steiner and M. Dockrill, 'The Foreign Office Reforms, 1919–1921', *Historical Journal*, vol. 17, 1 (1974), pp. 150–1.
132 F.O. 800/338, Grey to Nicolson, 3 October 1908.
133 D. C. M. Platt, *Finance, Trade and Politics in British Foreign Policy, 1815–1914* (Oxford, 1968), *The Cinderella Service* (London, 1971).

3. PUBLIC OPINION, THE PRESS AND PRESSURE GROUPS

1 B.D. II, pp. 68–9.
2 G.P. xx, ii, no. 6860.
3 It is interesting to note that the Official Secrets Act was passed at the time of the Moroccan crisis.
4 The only editor with whom he was on terms of friendship was J. A. Spender. See W. Harris, *J. A. Spender* (London, 1946).
5 See J. R. M. Butler, *Lord Lothian* (London, 1960), pp. 35–60.
6 A Council for the study of International Relations existed in the early years of the First World War, but I am not able to say when it was founded.
7 For a discussion see J. Frankel, *National Interest* (London, 1970).

8 H. Pelling, *Popular Politics and Society in Late Victorian Britain* (London, 1968), p. 82; R. Price, *An Imperial War and the British Working Class* (London, 1972).

9 R. S. Churchill, *W. S. Churchill*, II (London, 1967), p. 85.

10 Pelling, *Popular Politics*, p. 86; K. O. Morgan, *Wales in British Politics, 1868–1922* (Cardiff, 1963), pp. 178 ff. and Pelling's rejoinder, p. 93 n.

11 See, for example, the debate in the House of Commons on 12 and 13 March 1912. P.D., xxxv; Sir I. Hamilton, *Compulsory Service* (London, 1911); D. James, *Lord Roberts* (London, 1954). I owe some of this information to Mr J. Rosenbloom.

12 Robbins, *Grey*, p. 231 and pp. 248–9.

13 Sir R. Harrod, *Life of John Maynard Keynes* (London, 1951), p. 214: Letters from L. Woolf, D. Garnett, J. Strachey and D. Grant to J. M. Rae cited in his London Ph.D. thesis, 1965, 'The development of official treatment of conscientious objectors to military service, 1916–45', p. 128. J. M. Rae, *Conscience and Politics* (Oxford, 1970).

14 B. Kidd, *Social Evolution* (London, 1894); K. Pearson, *National Life from the standpoint of Science* (London, 1901), and other writings. H. W. Koch, 'Die Rolle des Sozialdarwinismus als Faktor im Zeitalter des Neuen Imperialismus um die Jahrhundertwende', *Zeitschrift für Politik*, 1970.

15 D. C. Watt, *Personalities and Policies* (London, 1965), pp. 22–4, notes that W. T. Stead's notion of *Anglo-Saxonia contra mundum* was far stronger in Britain than in America. Some believed it fitting that Stead should have been drowned in mid-Atlantic. There were those, for example, much attracted by the ideal of Russia presented in the writings of Stephen Graham, for example his *The Way of Martha and the Way of Mary* (London, 1915). S. Hynes, *The Edwardian Turn of Mind* (Princeton, 1968).

16 J. A. Hobson, *Imperialism* (London, 1902), pp. 66–7 and 253–4. The literature on Hobson and his critics is now very great. For an excellent survey see B. Porter, *Critics of Empire* (London, 1968).

17 H. N. Brailsford, *The War of Steel and Gold* (London, 1914), p. 61; cf. D. C. M. Platt, *Finance, Trade and Politics in British Foreign Policy, 1815–1914* (Oxford, 1968), pp. 217–18, 'Whether it was in trade, contracts, mining concessions or communications, the British Government in Turkey was prepared to protect but not to lead.'

18 R. Lane (Norman Angell), *Patriotism under Three Flags* (London, 1903), p. 24.

19 R. Macdonald to N. Angell, 11 June 1912; N. Angell to R. Macdonald, 13 June 1912; Angell MS. N. Angell, *After All* (London, 1951), pp. 110 f.

20 N. Angell, *Europe's Optical Illusion* (London, 1908), pp. 22–3 and 26–7.

21 For a selection see *Germany on the Brain, Gleanings from the National Review* (London, 1915).

22 N. Angell, *Europe's Optical Illusion*, pp. 105–6.

23 The Angellite journal, *War and Peace* appeared first in October 1913: see Esher's lecture, *Modern War and Peace* (Cambridge, 1912). Grey's comments, at Manchester in February 1914, in P. Knaplund, ed., *Speeches on Foreign Affairs, 1904–14 by Sir Edward Grey* (London, 1931), p. 235.

24 F. Williams, *Dangerous Estate* (London, 1957), pp. 144–5.

25 Williams, *Dangerous Estate*, p. 143.

26 Viscount Camrose, *British Newspapers and their controllers* (London, 1947), p. 39; A. J. P. Taylor, *Beaverbrook* (London, 1972).

27 Williams, *Dangerous Estate*, pp. 157–8.

28 A. G. Gardiner, *Life of George Cadbury* (London, n.d.), pp. 219–20; S. E. Koss, *Fleet Street Radical: A. G. Gardiner and the Daily News* (London, 1973).

29 Camrose, *British Newspapers*, pp. 6–8.

30 *The History of The Times, 1884–1912* (London, 1947), Chapters 14 and 16.

31 R. Pound and G. Harmsworth, *Northcliffe* (London, 1959), pp. 291 and 414.

32 R. C. K. Ensor, *England 1870–1914* (Oxford, 1952), p. 532.

33 J. L. Hammond, *C. P. Scott of the Manchester Guardian* (London, 1934), p. 97.

34 G. Lansbury, *Miracle of Fleet St.* (London, 1925).

35 A. S. Wallace *et al.*, *C. P. Scott: The Making of the Manchester Guardian* (London, 1946), p. 77; D. Ayerst, *Guardian, Biography of a Newspaper* (London, 1971); P. F. Clarke, *Lancashire and the New Liberalism* (Cambridge, 1971).

36 H. J. Massingham ed., *H. W. M.: A Selection from the writings of H. W. Massingham*, London, 1925, p. 131.

37 Sir W. Beach Thomas, *The Story of the Spectator* (London, 1928).

38 Ensor, *England*, p. 536; E. Hyams, *The New Statesman, 1913–63* (London, 1963), pp. 15–18; W. Martin, *The New Age under Orage* (Manchester, 1967), p. 10.

39 For example, O. J. Hale, *Publicity and Diplomacy with special reference to England and Germany, 1890–1914* (New York, 1940). See also *The Times, 1884–1912*, pp. 806–9.

40 The Conservative press was, however, divided in its attitude towards Fisher.

41 A. M. Gollin, *The Observer and J. L. Garvin, 1908–14* (London, 1960), pp. 77–82.

42 *The Economist*, 24 July 1909: G. J. Marcus, 'The Naval Crisis of 1909 and the Croydon By-Election', *Journal of the Royal United Services Institute*, November 1958. Grey was also capable of using the naval question to further his own diplomatic purpose: 'With regard to any misunderstanding with Germany, the attention of public opinion here is concentrated on the mutual arrest or decrease of naval expenditure as *the* test of whether an understanding is worth anything...', Grey to Goschen, 5 May 1910, B.D. VI, pp. 478–9.

43 Kennedy Jones, perhaps with some exaggeration, has described the reception a journalist might expect: '...He was ushered into a chilly waiting room by a still more chilly attendant, and after having declared his business was left to his own reflections for an indefinite time. Then the attendant would return...and with a lofty air would announce: "The Foreign Office has no communication to make, but it may issue a statement later,"' Kennedy Jones, *Fleet St. and Downing St.* (London, 1920).

44 Grey did, however, on occasion, see editors who were critical of his policy, in an attempt to convince them of its justice. See, for example, Hammond, *Scott*, pp. 158–61. Grey's correspondence with St L. Strachey is in the Beaverbrook Library, London.

45 J. A. Spender, *Life, Journalism and Politics* (London, 1927), I, p. 171.

46 H. Spender, *The Fire of Life* (London, 1926), p. 154.

47 Tyrrell to Spring Rice, 16 July 1908, F.O. 800/241.

48 B.D. x (1), no. 256.

49 Hammond, *Scott*, pp. 150–1.

50 *Daily News*, 16 November 1911.

51 See J. A. Murray, 'Sir Edward Grey and his Critics, 1911–12', pp. 147–50 in L. P. Wallace and W. C. Askew, ed., *Power, Public Opinion and Diplomacy* (Durham, N.C., 1956).

52 Grey to Mrs L. Creighton, 4 February, Creighton MS.

53 Ed., A. Grant Duff, *The Life-Work of Lord Avebury* (London, 1924), pp. 61–2.

54 *The Peacemaker*, July 1911.

55 *The Peacemaker*, February 1912 and December 1912. See also the monthly circulars of the National Peace Council.

56 E. B. and P. J. Noel Baker, *J. Allen Baker, M.P. A Memoir* (London, 1927). Also very active was another Liberal M.P., Sir Willoughby Dickinson; H. C. White, *Willoughby Hyett Dickinson* (Gloucester, 1956). Grey to J. Allen Baker, 21 December 1912, F.O. 800/105.

57 *The Peacemaker*, June 1914.

58 Sir T. Barclay, *Thirty Years. Anglo-French Reminiscences* (London, 1914), pp. 289–93.

59 Hale, *Publicity and Diplomacy*, p. 300.

60 Spence Watson of the National Liberal Federation had been among those who had taken the Russian cause under their wing. I am indebted to an unpublished paper by the late Dr B. Hollingsworth for information on this subject.

61 H. N. Brailsford, *The Fruits of our Russian Alliance* (London, 1912), pp. 59–63.

62 M. Beloff, *Lucien Wolf and the Anglo-Russian Entente, 1907–14* (London, 1951).

63 Grey to Lady K. Lyttelton, 28 June 1909, Lyttelton MS.

64 Brailsford, *Russian Alliance*, p. 58.

65 E. G. Browne, *The Persian Revolution of 1905–9* (Cambridge, 1910).

66 G. M. Trevelyan to W. Runciman, 24 October 1910, Runciman MS.

67 H. F. B. Lynch for the Persian Committee, *Sir Edward Grey on Persia* (London, 1912); Murray, 'Grey and his Critics', p. 163.

68 Grey to J. A. Spender, 24 September 1912, F.O. 800/111. The original signature of the Russian agreement had, of course, been denounced in like manner. F. Kazemzadeh, *Russia and Britain in Persia, 1864–1914* (Yale U.P., New Haven, Conn., 1968), pp. 504–5.

69 The details of the Cabinet's reaction can be found in Chapter 12.

70 For the activities of the Balkan Committee see M. Anderson, *Noel Buxton. A Life* (London, 1952); Lady Grogan, *Life of J. D. Bourchier* (London, n.d.); H. N. Brailsford, *Macedonia: its Races and their Future* (London, 1906); D. Dakin, *The Greek Struggle in Macedonia, 1897–1913* (Thessalonika, 1966); H. N. Fieldhouse, 'Noel Buxton and A. J. P. Taylor's "The Troublemakers"' in M. Gilbert ed., *A Century of Violence, Essays to A. J. P. Taylor* (London, 1966).

71 Grey to Cartwright, 3 February, 1911, F.O. 800/40.

72 It seems that Steed's reports from Vienna were read with care and his view that the Austrians followed the Berlin was used to counter reports to the contrary being sent from the Embassy in Vienna. The older men in the Diplomatic Service often resented the role of the local newspaper correspondents. Bertie to Grey, 21 February 1909, Bertie MS. F.O. 800/171.

73 Minute by Asquith on H. Bax-Ironside to W. Tyrrell, 8 December 1912, F.O. 800/43.

74 K. G. Robbins, 'British Diplomacy and Bulgaria, 1914–15', *Slavonic and East European Review*, vol. XLIX, no. 117, October 1971.

75 G. P. Gooch, *Under Six Reigns* (London, 1958), p. 160.

76 W. R. Louis and J. Stengers, eds., *E. D. Morel's History of the Congo Reform Movement* (Oxford, 1968).

77 S. J. S. Cookey, *Britain and the Congo Question, 1885–1913* (London, 1968), p. 150; R. Slade, 'English Missionaries and the beginning of the anti-Congolese campaign in England', *Revue Belge de philologie et d'histoire*, XXXIII, 1955 points out, however, that English missionaries were at first reluctant to join in the campaign.

78 C. A. Cline, 'E. D. Morel and the Crusade against the Foreign Office' in *Journal of Modern History*, June 1967.

79 In particular, Morel had little regard for the Foreign Office anxiety not to alienate Belgium.

80 Louis and Stengers, *E. D. Morel's History*, pp. 200–8.

81 Cline, 'E. D. Morel and the Crusade...'.

82 E. D. Morel, *Morocco in Diplomacy* (London, 1912).

83 A. J. P. Taylor, *The Troublemakers* (London, 1957), pp. 118–19.

84 I am indebted to Professor D. C. M. Platt for the following paragraphs on commercial policy. Further information on the Bryce Memorandum can be found in his book, already cited.

85 Viscount Grey of Fallodon, *Fallodon Papers* (London, 1926), p. 93.

4. FOREIGN POLICY AND INTERNATIONAL LAW

1 *War Memoirs*, vol. I, p. 29.
2 *Twenty-Five Years*, vol. II, p. 3.
3 For a general account of the system of provision of external legal advice to the Foreign Office, see *British Digest of International Law* (London, 1965), vol. 7, pp. 242–81.
4 *The Foreign Office*, p. 118.
5 Quoted by Lauterpacht and Jennings in *Cambridge History of the British Empire*, vol. III, p. 709.
6 *Selected Papers and Correspondence respecting Capture of Private Property at Sea in Time of War, Part I, 1854–1906* (Conf. 8672).
7 Memorandum on the Declaration of Paris and the Proposed Exemption of Private Property at Sea from Capture by a Belligerent, Sir E. Hertslet, 9 February 1893: *Ibid.* Annexe I.
8 See generally McNair, *International Law Opinions* (Cambridge, 1956). And see *Law Officers' Opinions to the Foreign Office* (facsimile ed. by Parry) (Farnborough, Hants, 1970).
9 For some memoranda by Ardagh on these questions see *British Digest of International Law* (London, 1965), vol. 6, pp. 209–30.
10 *Correspondence respecting a Conference at Geneva for the Revision of the Red Cross Convention, 1904–7* (Conf. 9056).
11 *Correspondence respecting the Second Peace Conference held at The Hague in 1907* (Cd. 3857).
12 *Selected Papers etc.* (Conf. 8672), minute on no. 11.
13 *Ibid.* no. 6.
14 *Ibid.* no. 11, Inclosures. These communications, incidentally, seem to have been provoked by Reid's letter to *The Times*, referred to below.
15 *The Value to Great Britain of the Right of Capture of Neutral Vessels*, C.I.D. Paper no. 41B, 12 December 1904 (Conf. 9328*, § 14).
16 Reid had a great interest in the topic and even wrote a monograph entitled *Capture at Sea* (London, 1913). This seems to have been an entirely individual interest, unaffected by political affiliations.
17 *The Capture of the Private Property of Belligerents at Sea*. C.I.D. Paper no. 71B, 14 May 1906 (Conf. 9328*, § 15).
18 *Memorandum on the Law of Contraband. Report of the Inter-Departmental Committee appointed to consider the Subjects which might arise for Discussion at the Second Peace Conference*, 21 March 1907 (Conf. 9041*), Appendix 10.
19 *Report etc.* (Conf. 9041*).
20 *La Deuxième Conférence Internationale de la Paix, Actes et Documents*, tom. iii, p. 1156, annexe 27.
21 *The Capture of the Private Property of Belligerents at Sea*, C.I.D. Paper no. 71B (Conf. 9328*, §15).
22 *Memorandum on the Second International Peace Conference*, translated from the German White Book no. 537 (Conf. 9325*, § P).
23 Quoted by Pearce Higgins, *The Hague Peace Conferences* (Cambridge, 1909), p. 520.
24 *Inter-Departmental Committee*, Minutes (Conf. 9325*).
25 Lauterpacht and Jennings in *Cambridge History of the British Empire*, vol. III, p. 700.
26 See his various Notes and Memoranda: Conf. 10500*, 10501*, 10502*, etc.
27 *Correspondence respecting the London Conference on International Maritime Law, 1908–9* (Conf. 9668), Inclosure in no. 40.
28 Lauterpacht and Jennings in *Cambridge History of the British Empire*, vol. III, p. 707.
29 *Correspondence etc.* (Conf. 9668), no. 124.

30 See *Notes by the Earl of Desart: Declaration of London* (Conf. 10500§). For details on the importance of the Declaration of London during the 1914–18 war, see chap. 24.
31 Lauterpacht and Jennings in *Cambridge History of the British Empire*, vol. III, p. 704.
32 See the section on 'The legal advisers', pp. 98–100.

5. GREAT BRITAIN AND FRANCE, 1905–1911

1 *Documents diplomatiques français* (hereafter cited as D.D.F.), 2nd ser., VIII, 79 and 219. G. M. Trevelyan, *Grey of Fallodon* (London, 1937), p. 92.
2 G. Monger, *The End of Isolation* (London, 1963), chapter 8; C. Andrew, *Théophile Delcassé and the Making of the Entente Cordiale* (London, 1968), chapter 14. See also E. W. Anderson, *The First Moroccan Crisis* (Chicago, 1930).
3 *British Documents on the Origins of the War* (hereafter cited as B.D.), III, 200. Grey to Bertie, 21 December 1905, Bertie MSS., A, F.O. 800/164.
4 D.D.F., 2nd ser., V, 465.
5 D.D.F., 2nd ser., VIII, 262 and 265. On Rouvier's attitude towards France's foreign relations during 1905 see P. Muret, 'La politique personelle de Rouvier et la chute de Delcassé', *Revue de l'histoire de la Guerre Mondiale*, 17 (1939), pp. 209–31, and 305–52.
6 Grey to A Court Repington, 30 December 1905, Grey MSS. F.O. 800/160.
7 B.D. III, 229.
8 F. Maurice, *Haldane: 1856–1928* (London, 1937–9), I, pp. 172–3.
9 The opening of the Anglo-French military conversation is treated fully in S. R. Williamson, *The Politics of Grand Strategy* (Cambridge, Mass., 1969), chaper III.
10 *Ibid.* K. Robbins, *Sir Edward Grey* (London, 1971), pp. 142–50.
11 B.D. III, 210.
12 Mallet to Bertie, 11 January 1906, Bertie MSS., A, F.O. 800/164.
13 B.D. III, 213.
14 Lord Grey, *Twenty-five Years* (London, 1925), I, pp. 117–18.
15 B.D. III, 216.
16 D.D.F., 2nd ser., IX, pt 1, 55.
17 B.D. III, 219.
18 N. Rich, *Friedrich von Holstein* (Cambridge, 1965), II, pp. 734–6. Bertie to Grey, 4 February 1906, Bertie MSS., A, F.O. 800/170. D.D.F. 2nd ser., IX, pt I, 120, and pt II, pp. 991–3.
19 B.D. III, 299. *D.D.F.*, 2nd ser., IX, pt I, 313.
20 S. L. Mayer, 'Anglo-German Rivalry at the Algeçiras conference', in *Britain and Germany in Afirca*, edited by P. Gifford and W. R. Louis (Yale, 1967), pp. 236–7. B.D. III, 331.
21 D.D.F., 2nd ser., XI, pt II, 392 and 407. B.D. III, 337 and 338. Mallet to Bertie, 9 March 1906, Bertie MSS., A, F.O. 800/160.
22 B.D. III, 352. *D.D.F.*, 2nd ser., IX, pt II, 422 and 931–6.
23 B.D. III, 333, 335 and 344.
24 Bertie to Grey, 12 March 1906, Bertie MSS., A, F.O. 800/160.
25 B.D. III, 340 and 342. Bertie to Grey, no. 16, 10 March 1906, F.O. 371/71.
26 B.D. III, 350 and 352.
27 B.D. III, 358. *D.D.F.*, 2nd ser., IX, pt. II, 437 and 440.
28 Bertie to Grey, 15 March 1906. Bertie MSS., A, F.O. 800/160.
29 B.D. III, 355 and 356. Bertie to King Edward VII, 16 March 1906, Bertie MSS., A, F.O. 800/164.
30 D.D.F., 2nd ser., IX, pt II, 449.
31 B.D. III, 357.
32 Bertie to Grey, 17 March 1906, Bertie MSS., A, F.O. 800/164.

33 B.D. III, 357 and 358.
34 S. L. Mayer, pp. 238–41.
35 G. M. Trevelyan, *Grey of Fallodon*, pp. 114–15. Grey to Bertie, no. 620, 8 November 1906, F.O. 371/74.
36 Bertie to Grey, 28 and 29 May 1906, Bertie MSS., A, F.O. 800/160.
37 D.D.F., 2nd ser., x, 380.
38 B.D. VII, 1 and 2.
39 Nicolson to Lansdowne, nos. 46 and 49, 4 July 1905, F.O. Spain 2211. B.D. VII, 7.
40 B.D. VII, 6 and 8.
41 B.D. VII, 3.
42 B.D. VII, 4. Minute by Grey, 12 December 1906, *Spain, Morocco and Gibraltar*, 44C, CAB. 38/12/58.
43 B.D. VII, 5. Note by Sir George Clarke, 28 December 1906; Minutes of the 9th meeting of the C.I.D., 20 December 1906, CAB. 38/12/59 and 62.
44 B.D. VII, 9, 10 and 19. *D.D.F.*, 2nd ser., x, 384 and 412. Bertie to Hardinge, 19 January 1907; Tyrrell to Bertie, 17 January 1907; Bertie MSS., A, F.O. 800/179.
45 B.D. VII, 23.
46 Grey to Campbell-Bannerman, 11 January 1907, Campbell-Bannerman MSS. 52514. Campbell-Bannerman to Grey, 14 January 1907, Grey MSS. F.O. 800/61. B.D. VII, 20 and 21.
47 B.D. VII, 24, 25, 26 and 28. *D.D.F.*, 2nd ser., x, 458. Hardinge to Bertie, 10 April 1907, Bertie MSS., A, F.O. 800/179. Bertie to Grey, 18 April 1907, Grey MSS. F.O. 800/49.
48 B.D. VII, 39, 40, 41, 42, 43 and 44. Hardinge to Bertie, 30 April 1907, Bertie MSS., B, F.O. 800/193.
49 D.D.F., 2nd ser., x, pp. 805–7. B.D. VII, 50. Grey to Bertie, 14 June 1907, Grey MSS. F.O. 800/49. Bertie to Grey, no. 320, 22 June 1907, F.O. 371/364.
50 Memorandum by Grey, 20 June 1906, Grey MSS. F.O. 800/49. B.D. III, 442.
51 Lister to Grey, no. 221, 21 May 1906, F.O. 371/72. Grey to Bertie, no. 620, 6 November 1906, F.O. 371/74. Bertie to Grey, 13 September 1908, F.O. 371/510. Campbell to Bertie, 31 August 1908, Bertie MSS., A, F.O. 800/176.
52 Tyrrell to Bertie, 18 December 1908; Bertie to Tyrrell, 19 December 1908; Bertie to Grey, 19 December 1908, Bertie MSS. F.O. 800/165. Marsh to Montgomery, 15 December 1908; Tyrrell to Marsh, 22 December 1908; Churchill to Grey, 24 December 1908; Grey to Churchill, 26 December 1908; Grey MSS. F.O. 800/89. Montgomery to Grey, 25 December 1908, Grey MSS. F.O. 800/92.
53 Prince Radolin, the German ambassador at Paris, had been informed of this by a confidant of Rouvier. *Die grosse Politik der Europäische Kabinette*, xx, ii, 6645.
54 Minutes by Eyre Crowe and Hardinge on Bertie to Grey, no. 453, F.O. 371/255.
55 *General Report for the year 1906*, F.O. 371/255.
56 Bertie to Grey, 2 January 1906, Bertie MSS., A, F.O. 800/164. Memorandum by Grey, in Tyrrell to Bertie, 1 May 1908, Bertie MSS., A, F.O. 800/170. Bertie to Grey, 10 September 1906, Grey MSS. F.O. 800/49. Memorandum by Grey, 28 April 1908, Grey MSS. F.O. 800/92. Bertie to Grey, 25 December 1907, Bertie MSS., B, F.O. 800/193. King Edward VII to Hardinge, 25 August 1908, Hardinge MSS., 12; Hardinge to Kind Edward VII, Hardinge MSS., 14. H. Wickham Steed, *Through Thirty Years* (London, 1924), I, pp. 284–7.
57 B.D. III, 443.
58 B.D. III, 444.
59 Bertie to Grey, no. 146, 22 March 1906, F.O. 371/253.
60 Pichon informed Bertie on 30 March 1907 that £300,000 had been placed at the German ambassador's disposal for the purpose of founding a French newspaper

to advocate a Franco-German understanding. B.D. VII, 22. *Annual Report for 1907*, F.O. 371/456.

61 A. S. J. Baster, *The International Banks* (London, 1935), pp. 97–106. W. I. Shorrock, 'The Origin of the French Mandate in Syria and the Lebanon: the Railroad Question, 1901–1914', *International Journal of Middle Eastern Studies*, vol. I, no. 2 (April 1970), pp. 133–6. B.D. V, 147.

62 Grey to Goschen, 31 December 1909, Grey MSS. F.O. 800/61. Bertie to Mallet, 10, 11 and 21 November 1906; Bertie to Hardinge, 2 December 1906, Bertie MSS., A, F.O. 800/174. D.D.F., 2nd ser., x, 231.

63 *Annual Report for 1910*. F.O. 371/1119. Block to Hardinge, 24 January and 14 May 1907, *private*, F.O. 371/344. Hardinge to Goschen, 9 March 1908; Hardinge to Nicolson, 1 April 1908, Hardinge MSS. 13.

64 J. B. Wolf, *The Diplomatic History of the Baghdad Railway* (Columbia, Mo., 1936), p. 34. B.D. V, p. 169. Block to Hardinge, 20 October 1906, *private*, F.O. 371/155.

65 Block to Hardinge, *private*, 15 October 1906; *Memorandum communicated to M. Cambon*, 24 October 1906; F.O. 371/155. Mallet to Bertie, 18 November 1906; Bertie to Mallet, 24 November 1906, Bertie MSS., A, F.O. 800/174. Bertie to Hardinge, 10 January 1907, Bertie MSS., A, F.O. 800/180. Bertie to Grey, no. 46, 23 January 1907, F.O. 371/340. D.D.F., 2nd ser., x, 354, 358 and 361.

66 Bertie to Grey, no. 165, 20 March 1907; no. 176, 5 April 1907; no. 180, 7 April 1907; no. 183, 8 April 1907; no. 192, 12 April 1907; Lascelles to Grey, no. 139, 10 April 1907; no. 182, 17 April 1907; F.O. 371/253. R. Poidevin, *Les rélations économiques et financières entre la France et l'Allemagne de 1898 à 1914* (Paris, 1969), pp. 413–46.

67 B.D. VII, 22. Bertie to Grey, 11 February, 31 March, 3 April 1907, Bertie MSS., A, F.O. 800/164. Bertie to Grey, 18 April 1907, Grey MSS. F.O. 800/49.

68 J. Wilson, *A life of Sir Henry Campbell-Bannerman* (London, 1973), pp. 540–4.

69 Bertie to Mallet, 15 April 1907, Bertie MSS., A, F.O. 800/164.

70 R. Poidevin, *Les rélations économiques*, pp. 413–57. Bertie to Grey, no. 311, 19 June 1907, F.O. 371/255. B.D. VII, 35 and 36.

71 According to an account given by Clemenceau to Bertie, the talks between the emperor and Étienne had broken down when the latter had said that for a Franco-German understanding 'it would be necessary to settle the territorial question'. Bertie to Grey, 9 July 1907; Memorandum by Grey enclosed in Tyrrell to Bertie, 1 May 1908; Bertie MSS., A, F.O. 800/170. *Annual Report for 1907*, F.O. 371/456.

72 Hardinge to Bertie, 8 July 1908, Bertie MSS.., A, F.O. 800/170.

73 B.D. VI, 106. But Hardinge was still worried by the prospect of the French collapsing under strong German pressure. He wrote to Villiers: 'I have always felt about the French that it would not be difficult for Germany to stampede them.' Hardinge to Villiers, 1 April 1909, Hardinge MSS., 1909, vol. III.

74 B.D. VII, 134.

75 B.D. VII, 132.

76 B.D. VII, 129. Grey to Nicolson, 10 November 1908; Hardinge to Nicolson, 11 November 1908; Nicolson MSS. F.O. 800/341.

77 *Annual Report for 1907*, F.O. 371/456.

78 Minute by Eyre Crowe on a communication from the French embassy, 16 January 1908, F.O. 371/454.

79 Memorandum by Eyre Crowe, 5 January 1908, F.O. 371/453.

80 Gorst to Grey, 17 May 1908, Grey MSS. F.O. 800/47. Hardinge to Bertie, 3 March 1910, Bertie MSS., A, F.O. 800/152.

81 Grey to Gorst, 25 May 1908, Grey MSS. F.O. 800/47.

82 These efforts to achieve co-operation between British and French firms are treated in detail in K. A. Hamilton 'An attempt to form an Anglo-French "Industrial Entente"', *Middle Eastern Studies*, vol. XI (1975), . 47–73.

83 B.D. VII, 148.

84 Tyrrell to Bertie, 3 February 1909, Bertie MSS., A, F.O. 800/155.

85 Bertie to Tyrrell, 5 February 1909, Bertie MSS., F.O. 800/155.

86 B.D. VII, 149. B.D. V, 579. Block to Hardinge, 2 March 1909, F.O. 371/762.

87 B.D. VII, 146, 147 and 148. Goschen to Hardinge, 26 January 1909, Hardinge MSS., 1909, vol. I.

88 E. W. Edwards, 'The Franco-German Agreement on Morocco, 1909', *English Historical Review*, vol. 79 (1963), pp. 483–513. D. R. Watson, 'The Making of French foreign policy during the first Clemenceau ministry, 1906–1909', *English Historical Review*, vol. 86 (1971), pp. 774–82. Poidevin, *Les rélations économiques*, pp. 483–513.

89 Bertie to Grey, no. 296, 26 July 1909, F.O. 371/668.

90 B.D. VII, 152 and 153. Minute by Villiers on de Bunsen to Grey, no. 5, 9 February 1909, F.O. 371/695. Hardinge to Lister, 9 December 1909; Hardinge to Villiers, 29 April 1909; Hardinge MSS., 1909, iii. Bertie to Grey, 20 April 1909, Grey MSS. F.O. 800/51. Hardinge to Bertie, 18 Feburary 1909, Bertie MSS., A, F.O. 800/171.

91 Pichon to Daeschner, 19 September 1910, in papers communicated by A. J. Barry to the Foreign Office, 29 September 1910; Bertie to Grey, 4 May 1910, and no. 349, 14 September 1910; F.O. 371/993. B.D. VI, 358.

92 Hardinge to Cassel, *private*, 19 September 1910, F.O. 371/993.

93 Babington Smith to Nicholson, *private*, 7 October 1910, F.O. 371/993. Lowther to Nicolson, 11 October 1910, Nicolson MSS. F.O. 800/334.

94 Bertie to Grey, 3 August 1908, Grey MSS. F.O. 800/51. Bertie to Grey, no. 316, 4 August 1909, F.O. 371/669.

95 A Court Repington to Grey, 23 November 1909, Grey MSS. F.O. 800/110.

96 *Annual Report for 1909*, F.O. 371/898 and *Annual Report for 1910*, F.O. 371/1119.

97 Grey to Goschen, 1 September 1909, Grey MSS. F.O. 800/61. Hardinge to Goschen, 26 April 1910, Hardinge MSS., 21. B.D. VI, 361.

98 D.D.F., 2nd ser., XIII, 31, 121, 122 and 124. Nicolson to Hardinge, 12 January 1911; Bertie to Hardinge, 16 March 1911, Hardinge MSS., 92.

99 Bertie to Grey, no. 34, 19 January 1911, F.O. 371/1213. Bertie to Grey, 31 January 1911, F.O. 371/1117.

100 B.D. VI, 429.

101 D.D.F., 2nd ser., XIII, 116.

102 H. Cambon (ed.), *Correspondance* (Paris, 1940), vol. II, p. 318.

103 Cruppi's only previous ministerial experience was as minister of commerce.

104 B.D. VII, 197, 205 and 206.

105 B.D. VII, 200 and 201. Bertie to Grey, 6 April 1911, Grey MSS. F.O. 800/52.

106 B.D. VII, 202.

107 B.D. VII, 200.

108 D.D.F., 2nd ser., XIII, 152.

109 B.D. VI, 460.

110 B.D. VII, 207 and 269. Bertie to Grey, 15 April 1911. Bertie MSS., A, F.O. 800/165. *Lord Grey*, vol. I, p. 94.

111 Bertie to Grey, no. 214, 14 May 1911, F.O. 371/1240.

112 Memorandum by Nicolson, 4 October 1910, F.O. 371/993. Nicolson to Bertie, 5 October 1910, Nicolson MSS. F.O. 800/344.

113 B.D. VII, 269.

114 S. R. Williamson, *Politics of Grand Strategy*, pp. 89–115.

6. GREAT BRITAIN AND RUSSIA, 1905 TO THE 1907 CONVENTION

1 B.D. IV, no. 204.
2 Morley to Minto, 23 March 1906, Morley MSS., vol. I.
3 Sir H. Nicolson, *Lord Carnock* (London, 1930), p. 204.
4 Morley to Minto, 25 April 1906, Morley MSS., vol. I.
5 B.D. IV, no. 224.
6 G. W. Monger, *The End of Isolation* (London, 1963), p. 260.
7 B. Semmel, *Imperialism and Social Reform* (London, 1960), p. 75; G. Trevelyan, *Grey of Fallodon* (London, 1937), pp. 82–3.
8 Trevelyan, *op. cit.* pp. 90–2.
9 Grey of Fallodon, *Twenty-five Years* (London, 1925), I, 152–3.
10 Trevelyan, *op. cit.* p. 92.
11 B.D. III, no. 299; Grey MSS., vol. 53, Hardinge's minute on Grey's memo 20 February 1906 is dated 23 February.
12 Grey to Spring Rice, 19 February 1906. Grey MSS., vol. 33.
13 B.D. III, no. 299.
14 Monger, *op. cit.* p. 293.
15 Trevelyan, *op. cit.* pp. 90–2.
16 Cab. O. 4.2 and 2.2/1.
17 Z. Steiner, 'G.B. and the Creation of the Anglo-Japanese Alliance', *Journal of Modern History*, March 1959.
18 Spring Rice commented in 1904, 'If we are at war with Russia, Germany would either take Russia's side or exact very hard terms from us for her neutrality. The German fleet has really revolutionised politics.'; S. Gwynn (ed.), *Letters and Friendships of Sir C. Spring Rice* (London, 1929), I, 422–3.
19 M. V. Brett (ed.), *Journals and Letters of Viscount Esher* (London, 1934), II, 218.
20 B.D. IV, nos. 26, 117.
21 Balfour to Lansdowne, 30 June 1905, Balfour MSS., B.M. Add. MSS. 49729.
22 Lord Kitchener, *A Note on the Military Policy of India*, Kitchener MSS., P.R.O. 30/57.30; Sir A. Arthur, *Life of Lord Kitchener* (London, 1920), II, 151–9.
23 Arthur, *op. cit.* II, 206.
24 Kitchener MSS. P.R.O. 30/57.30.
25 Quoted in Cambon to Pichon, 27 October 1910, no. 401, M. des A.E., N.S. (Eur.), 28.
26 *The Military Resources of the Russian Empire* (London, 1907). W.O. 33/419, p. 286.
27 Kitchener MSS. P.R.O. 30/57.30.
28 W.O. 33/419.
29 Kitchener MSS. P.R.O. 30/57.30.
30 Cab. O. 6/1; 2/1. See Monger, *op. cit.* pp. 95–6.
31 Cab. O. 2.2/1.
32 *Parliamentary Debates*, 4th ser., vol. 153, p. 675.
33 J. P. MacKintosh, 'The Committee of Imperial Defence before 1914', *English Historical Review*, July, 1962.
34 Memo. by Robertson, 20 March 1906. Grey MSS., vol. 53.
35 Brett, *op. cit.* II, 188. Thus the commitment to defend the integrity of Afghanistan could not be carried out in practice.
36 Morley to Minto, 19 September 1907. Morley MSS., Eur. d/573/2.
37 C.I.D. Minute, 25 May 1906, P.R.O. Cab. O. 2.2/1.
38 Morley MSS., Eur. D/573/37g; Cab. O. 6/3.
39 Grey to Ripon, 8 September 1907. Ripon MSS., B.M. Add. MSS. 43640.
40 Sanderson to Spring Rice, 6 August 1907. Spring Rice MSS., vol. I.

41 Grey, *op. cit.* I, 153.
42 Grey minute on Spring Rice to Grey, 16 July 1907, no. 155, F.O. 371/371.
43 Grey, *op. cit.* I, 159.
44 Sir A. Nicolson, *Diplomatic Narrative* (unpublished), I, 63.
45 Sir H. Nicolson, *op. cit.* p. 305.
46 *Ibid.* p. 207.
47 Grey told Nicolson that he would expect frank statements and progress in the negotiations when Isvolsky returned as proof that the Germans 'are not putting spokes in the wheel'. B.D. IV, no. 235.
48 Grey, *op. cit.* p. 155.
49 Grey to Nicolson, 3 October 1906, Grey MSS., vol. 33.
50 A. Lamb, *The McMahon Line* (London, 1966), pp. 12–13.
51 India Office, Political External File 1908/22. Minto to Morley, 16 January 1906.
52 Lamb, *op. cit.* p. 26.
53 *Ibid.* p. 51.
54 Minto to Morley, 15 February 1906. Morley MSS., Eur. D. 573/7.
55 Sir A. Nicolson, *Diplomatic Narative*, p. 117.
56 Lamb, *op. cit.* p. 77.
57 B.D. IV, no. 306.
58 Minto to Morley, 13 July 1906, F.O. 371/177.
59 B.D. IV, no. 308.
60 For details of the negotiations see Lamb, *op. cit.* ch. VI.
61 Nicolson to Grey, 5 July 1906. Nicolson MSS., s.v.
62 Minute on Nicolson to Grey, 6 January 1907, no. 19. F.O. 371/382.
63 Lamb, *op. cit.* p. 94.
64 Sir H. Nicolson, *op. cit.* p. 234.
65 W.O. 33/419.
66 Nicholson to Grey, 2 August 1906, Nicolson MSS., s.v.
67 B.D. IV, no. 472.
68 B.D. IV, no. 473.
69 B.D. IV, no. 478.
70 Hardinge to Nicolson, 12 June 1907, Nicolson MSS., 1907, vol. I.
71 Minto to Morley, 12 June 1906, Morley MSS., Eur. D. 573/8.
72 R. P. Churchill, *The Anglo-Russian Convention of 1907.* (Cedar Rapids, Iowa, 1939), p. 291. B.D. IV, no. 479–84.
73 B.D. IV, no. 486.
74 A trip which, he wrote to Spring Rice, would 'determine the fate of the Convention'. Nicolson to Spring Rice, 17 July 1907. Spring Rice MSS., vol. I.
75 B.D. IV, no. 494.
76 B.D. IV, no. 495.
77 B.D. IV, no. 496.
78 Viceroy to I.O., 20 August 1907. F.O. 371/120.
79 Churchill, *op. cit.* pp. 302–3; B.D. IV, no. 507.
80 B.D. IV, p. 619.
81 Nicolson to Hardinge, 16 May 1907. Nicolson MSS., s.v.; *Diplomatic Narrative*, I, 126.
82 B.D. IV, no. 549.
83 Morley to Minto, 18 July 1907. Morley MSS., Eur. D. 573/2.
84 Memo. by Edward VII, 8 September 1907. Hardinge MSS., vol. 9.
85 Grey minute on Nicolson to Grey, 17 June 1906, no. 325, F.O. 371/124.
86 Nicolson to Hardinge, 29 July 1906, Nicolson MSS., s.v.
87 *Krasnyi Arkhiv*, 4 (53), 1932, p. 14.
88 Grant Duff to Grey, 27 February 1906, no. 53. F.O. 371/106.
89 *Ibid.*

90 Memorandum. Sir Hugh Barnes, 8 January 1906, F.O. 371/169.
91 A. Isvolsky, *Au Service de la Russie* (Paris, 1937), I, 339–40.
92 Sir Hugh Barnes, *op. cit.*
93 Grey MSS., vol. 53.
94 Grey to Spring Rice, 30 November 1906, Spring Rice MSS., vol. I.
95 B.D. IV, no. 326.
96 B.D. IV, no. 329.
97 B.D. IV, no. 336.
98 B.D. IV, no, 340.
99 Nicolson to Grey, 12 September 1906. Nicolson MSS., s.v.
100 Grey to Campbell Bannerman, 13 September 1906, Campbell-Bannerman MSS., B.M. Add. MSS. 41218, vol. 13. The loan was to be for £200,000 immediately and a similar sum later.
101 Morley to Grey, 4 September 1906. Grey MSS., I.O. 1905–16, vol. 59.
102 Nicolson to Grey, 26 September 1906. Nicolson MSS., s.v. The loan was never accepted by Persia.
103 Grey to Nicolson, October 1906. Nicolson MSS., 1906 vol. Grey wrote that he just hoped that the negotiations wouldn't 'go to sleep'. B.D. IV, no. 370.
104 Memorandum. Robertson, 20 March 1906. Grey MSS., vol. 53.
105 Gwynn, *op. cit.* p. 86.
106 Minute on Grey memo., 18 December 1905. Grey MSS., vol. 53.
107 Morley to Grey, 21 November 1906. Grey MSS., I.O. 1905–16, vol. 59.
108 Grey minute on Spring Rice to Grey, 26 April 1907. Grey MSS., vol. 31 (Persia).
109 Nicolson to Grey, 24 October 1906. Nicolson MSS., s.v.
110 Nicolson to Spring Rice, 20 May 1907. Spring Rice MSS., vol. I.
111 B.D. IV, no. 389.
112 B.D. IV, no. 395.
113 Ritchie Draft for Government reply to Curzon's criticism of Convention in House of Lords. Morley to Ripon, 8 February 1908. Ripon MSS., B.M. Add. MSS. 43541.
114 B.D. IV, no. 350.
115 Nicolson to Hardinge, 8 May 1907, Nicolson MSS., s.v.
116 G. of I. to Morley, 3 September 1906. T. no. 274. F.O. 371/110. Grey's minute.
117 Nicolson to Hardinge, 19 June 1907. Nicolson MSS., s.v.
118 Nicolson to Grey, 31 August 1907, no. 444. F.O. 371/372.
119 B.D. IV, p. 618–19.
120 Described by Lord Ripon later as 'unusually threatening language for a diplomatist to use'. Ripon to Fitzmaurice, 3 July 1907. Ripon MSS., B.M. Add. MSS. 43543.
121 Minute by Grey, I.O. to F.O., 14 February 1906. F.O. 371/169.
122 B.D. IV, no. 347.
123 B.D. IV, no. 350.
124 B.D. IV, no. 417; Grey to Nicolson, 6 June 1907. Nicolson MSS., vol. 1907.
125 Nicolson to Hardinge, 19 June 1907, Nicolson MSS., s.v.
126 B.D. IV, nos. 434, 435, 438.
127 B.D. IV, no. 455.
128 Minute on B.D. IV, no. 444.
129 B.D. IV, no. 455. There was nothing in the Convention to deny Russia commercial or rail access.
130 B.D. IV, nos. 257, 258.
131 B.D. IV, no. 259.
132 Grey to Nicolson, 1 April 1907, Nicolson MSS., 1907 vol.
133 Grey to Nicolson, 6 November 1906. Nicolson MSS., 1906 vol.
134 Minute on Spring Rice to Grey, 16 July 1907, no. 155, F.O. 371/371.
135 Grey, *op. cit.* I, 159.

7. CONSTANTINOPLE AND ASIATIC TURKEY, 1905–1914

1 Grey, *Twenty-Five Years*, I, p. 174, and see his speech at Scarborough of 19 November 1908 quoted in *The Times* of 20 November.

2 Fitzmaurice to Tyrrell, private, 12 April 1908, B.D. V, no. 196. See also Grey to O'Conor, private, 17 December 1907, *ibid.* V, no. 174, and Annual Reports for 1907 and 1908, *ibid.* V, esp. pp. 43, 260.

3 *Twenty-Five Years, op. cit.* I, pp. 133, 172–4.

4 *Ibid.* I, pp. 172–3, 211–12, 257–60.

5 Annual Report for Turkey for 1908, B.D. V, p. 251.

6 Grey to Lowther, private, 31 July 1908, *ibid.* V, no. 204. This policy was expanded in Grey to Lowther, private, 23 August 1908, *ibid.* V, no. 208.

7 Grey to Lowther, private, 11 August 1908, *ibid.* V, no. 207.

8 Lowther to Grey, private, 4 and 25 August 1908, *ibid.* V, nos. 205 and 209. See also views of Fitzmaurice and Nicolson, *ibid.* V, nos. 210 Ed. Add., and 215.

9 *Ibid.* V, no. 219.

10 Lowther to Grey, no. 521 confidential, 30 July 1910, *ibid.* IX(1), no. 161.

11 See esp. Grey to Lowther, no. 107, secret, 28 April 1910, *ibid.* VI, no. 352. Further detailed information is to be found in J. B. Kelly, 'The Legal and Historical Basis of the British Position in the Persian Gulf', in *St Antony's Papers*, no. IV, Middle East Affairs no. I (Oxford, 1958) and in *Britain and the Persian Gulf 1785–1880* (Oxford, 1968).

12 See, e.g., 'Note of a Private Conversation between Sir Edward Grey and Mr Haldane on November 14, 1907', of which a copy was given to the German Emperor, B.D. VI, no. 62.

13 *Ibid.* VI, chs. XLVI and XLVII *passim*. The best detailed published account of these matters is in M. K. Chapman, *Great Britain and the Baghdad Railway 1888–1914*, Smith College Studies in History, vol. XXXI (Northampton, Mass., 1948), esp. chs. IV, V, VI, VII, IX, X.

14 Repeatedly stated by Grey to Lowther and to the Turkish Ambassador, see B.D. VI, nos. 292, 340, 350, 388.

15 Chapman, *op. cit.* ch. V ff. argues this, but relies heavily on the documentation in *Die Grosse Politik*, which, not surprisingly, supports such a view.

16 For text of 1899 Agreement see B.D. X(2), p. 107; see also Marling to Grey, no. 14 secret, 4 January 1911, *ibid.* no. 6; Foreign Office Memorandum of 12 February 1908, Confid. Print, F.O. 881/9161 and C.I.D. Sub-Committee Report, 26 January 1909, Cab. 16/10. For a documented account of Koweit and Anglo-Turkish relations 1905–14, see B. C. Busch, *Britain and the Persian Gulf 1894–1914* (Berkeley, Calif., 1967), ch. X.

17 B.D. VI, App. V, pp. 786–7.

18 *Ibid.* X(2), ch. XCI, and Chapman, *op. cit.* ch. IX.

19 For the Anglo-Turkish negotiations from 1913–14, see B.D. X(2), chs. XCII, XCIII and XCIV. The railway agreement is no. 133, and the other agreements no. 124.

20 Apart from B.D. X(2), and Chapman, *op. cit.* useful detail on all these negotiations is contained in the 1914 draft Foreign Office despatch to Sir Louis Mallet, F.O. 371/2125 no. 33655.

21 B.D. X(2), no. 124, encl. 1.

22 For the concession as finally signed on 12 December 1913, *ibid.* X(2), no. 188.

23 Agreement initialled 28 March 1914 and annexed as 'Heads of Proposed Agreement' to the Anglo-German convention initialled on 15 June 1914, *ibid.* X(2), pp. 404–6.

24 For details see Marian Kent, *Oil and Empire. British Policy and Mesopotamian Oil, 1900–1920* (London School of Economics/Macmillan 1976), *passim*.

25 Turco-Persian Frontier Declaration concerning the Sheikh of Mohammerah, 29 July 1913, B.D. x(2), doc. 3 of no. 124. See also para. 9 of Report by Mallet and Hirtzel, 'The Negotiations with Hakki Pasha', 3 May 1913, *ibid.* p. 114, and explanation in Grey to Buchanan, 26 August 1913, *ibid.* no. 142. The Turco-Persian Frontier Protocol was signed on 17 November 1913. See also F.O. 371/1431–2, file 52, F.O. 371/1713–5, file 261, and F.O. 371/2062–3, file 601; and Marian Kent, *Oil and Empire, op. cit.* App. IV, 'The Transferred Territories'.

26 Grey to Lowther, no. 107 secret, 20 April 1910, *ibid.* VI, no. 352. On similar views expressed in 1909 see *ibid.* IX(1), minutes on no. 58, and Grey to Sir B. Whitehead, no. 51, 23 October 1909, *ibid.* IX(1), no. 69.

27 E.g. *ibid.* IX(2), nos. 503 and 1018; X(1), nos. 168, 476–7, 499; X(2), nos. 454–5. The question of Armenian reforms is dealt with in vol. X(1), ch. LXXXVIII, pp. 424–548. See also Asquith MSS., Cabinet letters to the King 1913–14, vol. 7, meeting of 9 July 1913.

28 Grey to Rodd, private, 13 January 1913, B.D. x(2), no. 455.

29 P.D. 5th ser., LVI, 2281–2296. Quoted in Knaplund, *op. cit.* p. 218.

30 Reported in Grey to Dering, no. 269, 4 November 1913, B.D. x(2), no. 157.

31 Grey to Mallet, telegram no. 551, 22 November 1913, *ibid.* x(2), no. 167, and Grey to Bertie, no. 11, 6 January 1914, *ibid.* x(1), no. 194.

32 Fitzmaurice to Tyrrell, private, 12 April 1908, B.D. V, no. 196.

33 Lowther to Grey, telegram no. 301, 25 June 1913, *ibid.* x(2).

34 Mallet to Grey, private, 17 December 1913, B.D. x(1), no. 174. See also Memorandum by Sir L. Mallet, 19 June 1913 and Grey's minutes on it, *ibid.* x(1), App. pp. 901–2. For opinions on Lowther's Ambassadorship, see Hardinge MSS. 93/I/35, 93/II/25, 93/II/26, and on Mallet's Ambassadorship, 93/II/42, 93/II/48, 93/I/65, 93/I/68.

35 See *Twenty-Five Years, op. cit.* II, pp. 164–6, 167, 174–7, and documentation from the Churchill MSS. quoted in Martin Gilbert, *Winston S. Churchill, III, 1914–1916* (London, 1971), nos. 21/36 and 13/45, pp. 194–5 and 828–9, and p. 198; also text pp. 207–10 and p. 216.

36 See B.D. IV, pp. 58–60, Ed. Note containing Sir Charles Hardinge's 'Memorandum respecting the passage of Russian War Vessels through the Dardanelles and Bosphorus', 16 November 1906, including extracts from the relevant C.I.D. papers of 1903.

37 The negotiations can be followed in *ibid.* IV, no. 210, and pp. 254–96, *passim.* See also J. T. Shotwell and F. Deak, *Turkey at the Straits* (New York, 1940), pp. 73–7.

38 Lowther to Grey, telegram no. 317, 12 October 1908, B.D. V, no. 362; Grey to Nicolson, no. 317, 12 October 1908, *ibid.* no. 364; and Grey to Lowther, telegram no. 348, 13 October 1908, *ibid.* no. 370.

39 Hardinge to Nicolson, private, 13 November 1908, *ibid.* V, no. 372.

40 B.D. V, no. 377; only mentioned in *Twenty-Five Years, op. cit.* I, p. 186. This was in fact no departure from the tradition laid down by Lord Salisbury in 1891. See B.D. XI(1), no. 304 and App. II, pp. 774–6.

41 Grey to Isvolsky, private and confidential, 15 October 1908, *ibid.* V, no. 382. See also Grey to Nicolson, private, 26 October, *ibid.* encl. (b) in no. 409.

42 Lowther to Grey, no. 681 confidential, 21 August 1909, *ibid.* IX(1), no. 46.

43 'Memorandum respecting the Passage of Merchant Vessels through the Dardanelles and Bosphorus', initialled by Alwyn Parker, 4 October 1909, *ibid.* IX(1), no. 65.

44 Grey to Goschen, no. 262, 6 November 1911, *ibid.* IX(1), no. 304.

45 Grey to Cartwright, no. 77, 22 November 1911, *ibid.* IX(1), no. 317.

46 *Ibid.* IX(1), Ed. Note and no. 370, p. 368. See also nos. 376, 393, 394, 395, 399, 402 and 403.

47 'Memorandum on the effect of a British Evacuation of the Mediterranean on questions of Foreign Policy', 8 May 1912, *ibid.* x(2), no. 386. The Foreign Office views held in this memorandum were upheld in an Admiralty memorandum of 20 July 1912, *ibid.* IX(1), encl. in no. 430.

48 *Ibid.* v, no. 197, and IX(1), Ed. Note, p. 282, and nos. 177, 184 and 379.

49 Grey to Buchanan, private, 7 April 1913, *ibid.* IX(2), no. 815.

50 On whole paragraph, see *ibid.* IX(2), Ed. Note, no. 63, and nos. 56, 62, 70, 91, 92, 142, 196, 250, 783, 789, 803, 817, 830, 1198 and 1218. Also x(2), Ed. Note p. 779, and no. 537.

51 See correspondence in *ibid.* x(1), nos. 277, 282 and 370. See also Ed. Note p. 337.

52 The documentation for this section comes from *ibid.* x(1), ch. LXXXVII.

53 Grey to Mallet, telegram no. 557, 2 December 1913, and private letter of same date, *ibid.* x(1), nos. 387 and 392.

54 Nicolson to O'Beirne, private, 2 December 1913, *ibid.* x(1), no. 393.

55 See correspondence from Mallet to Grey, 5–11 December 1913, and Foreign Office minutes, *ibid.* x(1), nos. 403, 405, 407, 414 and 416, and Foreign Office minutes in *ibid.* x(1), no. 403.

56 Mallet to Grey, telegram no. 602, 4 December 1913, *ibid.* x(1), no. 400, and reports from Military Attachés in Berlin and Constantinople, received 9 and 15 December, encl. in *ibid.* x(1), nos. 402 and 427.

57 O'Beirne to Grey, telegram no. 404, 7 December 1913 and despatch of 9 December, *ibid.* x(1), nos. 406 and 412.

58 Grey to Mallet, telegram no. 570, 9 December 1913, and Mallet to Grey, telegram no. 621, 13 December 1913, *ibid.* x(1), nos. 408 and 426.

59 Grey to O'Beirne, telegram no. 789, 11 December 1913, *ibid.* x(1), no. 417; Grey to Mallet, telegram no. 577, 12 December 1913, *ibid.* x(1), no. 420; and O'Beirne to Grey, telegram no. 411, 13 December 1913, *ibid.* x(1), no. 425.

60 Mallet to Grey, telegram no. 623 confidential, 14 December 1913, *ibid.* x(1), no. 428.

61 O'Beirne to Grey, telegram no. 413, 14 December 1913, *ibid.* x(1), no. 429. See also long despatch no. 384 from O'Beirne to Grey, 18 December 1913, no. 439.

62 Mallet to Grey, telegram no. 628, 15 December 1913, and Foreign Office minute, *ibid.* x(1), no. 430; given more fully in Mallet to Grey, no. 1010, 15 December 1913, *ibid.* x(1), no. 433. See also Mallet to Grey, telegram no. 630, 16 December 1913, *ibid.* x(1), no. 435.

63 Grey to Goschen, no. 366, 15 December 1913, *ibid.* x(1), no. 431.

64 Grey to O'Beirne (repeated to Berlin), telegram no. 803, 16 December 1913, *ibid.* x(1), no. 434.

65 Minute by Sir Eyre Crowe, 29 December 1913, and accompanying minute by Grey, *ibid.* x(1), no. 452; see also *ibid.* x(1), nos. 443, 444 and 446.

66 Grey to Goschen, telegram no. 4, 7 January 1914, *ibid.* x(1), no. 461.

67 Mallet to Grey, telegram no. 15, and Buchanan to Grey, telegram no. 6, 8 January 1914, and Foreign Office minutes, *ibid.* x(1), nos. 464 and 465.

68 Grey to Mallet, no. 51, 26 January 1914, *ibid.* x(1), no. 471, and Buchanan to Grey, no. 22, 20 January 1914, and to Nicolson, private, 21 January 1914, *ibid.* x(1), nos. 468 and 469. Such a solution had in fact been presaged by the British Ambassador in Berlin as early as 1 January 1914, see Goschen to Grey, telegram no. 1, *ibid.* x(1), no. 456.

69 Grey to Buchanan, private, 11 February 1914, *ibid.* x(1), no. 474.

70 For details of the Bank and its activities, see Marian Kent, 'Agent of Empire? The National Bank of Turkey and British Foreign Policy', *The Historical Journal*, vol. XVIII, no. 2, pp. 367–89, June 1975.

71 See Marian Kent, *Oil and Empire, op. cit.* and Marian Jack (Kent), 'The purchase of the British Government's Shares in the British Petroleum Company, 1912–1914', in *Past and Present*, no. 39, April 1968, pp. 139–68.

72 Lowther to Hardinge, private telegram, 30 August 1908, and private letter, 31 August, and Grey to Lowther, private telegram no. 190 P., 2 September 1908; F.O. 371/546, no. 30181. See also, F.O. 371/549, nos. 31452, 31548, 34124, 38400, 39579, 41016, 41449, 42603 and 44967.

8. RELATIONS WITH AUSTRIA–HUNGARY AND THE BALKAN STATES, 1905–1908

1 *Standard*, 18 August 1905.
2 F.O. 120/780, Lansdowne to Plunkett, d. 38, 12 March 1902.
3 *The Times*, 16 June 1903.
4 F.O. 368/3, Memorandum, 15 January 1906 and minutes.
5 *Ibid.*
6 F.O. 368/3, Thesiger to Grey, 25 January 1906; F.O. to Board of Trade, 20 February 1906.
7 *Tribune*, 24 April 1906.
8 F. Fischer, 'Weltpolitik, Weltmachtstreben und deutsche Kriegsziele', *Historische Zeitschrift*, 199, p. 304.
9 [H.H.S.A.] P.A. VIII/136, Schönburg to Goluchowski, t. 4, 1 February 1906.
10 B. Zwerger, 'The diplomatic relations between Great Britain and Roumania 1913–14' (London, M.A. thesis, 1971), pp. 1, 9.
11 E. Driault and M. Lhéritier, *Histoire diplomatique de la Grèce* (Paris, 1925–6), t. iv, p. 18ff.; P.A. XII/193 v. Macchio to Aehrenthal, 20C, 30 May 1908.
12 Of all the powers, the Russians were the most inclined to connive at Greek designs on Crete. They were planning, in the event of the collapse of Turkey, to buy Greece off with Crete, and secure the Macedonian heritage for their Bulgarian protégés. D. Dakin, *The Greek Struggle in Macedonia* (London, 1968), p. 298.
13 D. Dakin, 'The Greek proposals for an alliance with France and Great Britain, June–July 1907'. *Balkan studies*, Thessaloniki, 3, 1962.
14 *Ibid.*
15 *Ibid.*
16 P.A. XII/294, Mensdorff to Aehrenthal, no. 46, 25 June 1909.
17 Speech at Berwick, *The Times*, 20 December 1907, p. 8.
18 P.A. VIII/136, Schönburg to Goluchowski, 15B, 27 February 1906; Mensdorff to Goluchowski, 12B, 22 February 1906; e.g. *The Times* 10 April 1906, p. 14, Balkan Committee to Grey.
19 Hansard VI, 160, c. 325.
20 D. Dakin, *The Greek Struggle in Macedonia* (London, 1968), p. 306ff.
21 P.A. XII/334, Aehrenthal to Mensdorff, d. 102, 25 January 1907.
22 F.O. 120/829, Memorandum for the Cabinet, 19 September 1906.
23 P.A. XII/334, Mensdorff to Aehrenthal, d. 68A, 14 December 1906.
24 *Ibid.* d. 6A, 29 January 1907.
25 P.A. VIII/137, Szilassy to Aehrenthal, d. 10C, 20 February 1907.
26 *Ibid.* Mensdorff to Aehrenthal, d. 19A, 27 March 1907.
27 E.g. *Daily Telegraph*, 30 March 1907.
28 P.A. VIII/137, Mensdorff to Aehrenthal, d. 21B, 5 April 1907.
29 P.A. VIII/137, Mensdorff to Aehrenthal, d. 16B, 21 March 1907; Hansard IV, 171, c. 226.
30 E.g. *Daily Mail*, March 1907; P.A. VIII/137, Mensdorff to Aehrenthal, d. 16B, 21 March 1907.

31 P.A. xii/338, Pallavicini to Aehrenthal, d. 24A, 22 April 1907.
32 D.D.F. x(2), no. 341; B.D. v, no. 150.
33 F.O. 120/829, Grey to Goschen, d. 143, 10 December 1906.
34 P.A. xii/334, Mensdorff to Aehrenthal, d. 7A, 8 February 1907.
35 Grey MSS., Turkey, Grey to O'Conor, private, 6 February 1907.
36 P.A. xii/338, Pallavicini to Aehrenthal, 23E, 17 April 1907.
37 F. R. Bridge, *Great Britain and Austria-Hungary 1906–14* (London, 1972), pp. 49 ff. Apart from a few remarks to Goschen, the British ambassador, about the folly of discussing such a contentious and unmanageable issue, Aehrenthal did not pursue the matter with the British (D.D.F., 2nd series, x, 485). He concentrated on bringing Russia and Germany to agree on evasive tactics. Goschen reported quite wrongly that Aehrenthal's views on the armaments question were merely an echo of German views: it was, rather, the other way round. Grey MSS., Austria, Goschen to Grey, private, 7 April 1907.
38 Cf. E. Walters, 'Aehrenthal's attempt in 1907 to re-group the European Powers'. *Slavonic Review*, 30.
39 F.O. 371/377, Goschen to Grey, d. 56, 9 May 1907 and minutes.
40 *Ibid.*
41 Hardinge MSS. x, Memorandum, 27 May 1907.
42 *Ibid.* Goschen to Hardinge, private, 23 May 1907.
43 B.D. v, 157.
44 F.O. 120/839, Grey to Goschen, d. 48, secret, 6 June 1907; F.O. 371/364, Goschen to Grey, t. 8, 16 June 1907; Hardinge MSS., Goschen to Hardinge, private, 28 June 1907.
45 F. R. Bridge, *From Sadowa to Sarajevo* (London, 1972), p. 294.
46 Hardinge MSS. x, Goschen to Hardinge, private, 28 June 1907; P.A. viii/138, Mensdorff to Aehrenthal, d. 36C, 17 June 1907.
47 F.O. 371/377, Balkan Committee to Grey, 3 July 1907; B.D. v, 162.
48 B.D. v, 165; P.A. 1/484, Aehrenthal to Bülow private, 21 August 1907.
49 B.D. v, 165, Botschaftsarchiv Petersburg, Aehrenthal to Berchtold, t. 91, 17 August 1907.
50 H. Hantsch, *Berchtold* (Cologne–Graz–Vienna, 1963), i, p. 83.
51 A. & P., vol. 125.
52 [H.H.S.A.] Botschaftsarchiv Petersburg, Fürstenburg to Aehrenthal, 38E, 39D, 5, 19 October 1907.
53 F. R. Bridge, *Great Britain and Austria-Hungary 1906–14*, pp. 67–71.
54 P.A. xii/339, Mensdorff to Aehrenthal, d. 49C, 5 September 1907.
55 For example, in the conference of 21 September, all ambassadors preferred a Turkish to the Austro-Russian project; and on 19 October O'Conor ignored his instructions and threw the whole scheme into the melting-pot.
56 W. M. Carlgren, *Iswolsky und Aehrenthal vor der bosnischen Annexionskrise* (Uppsala, 1955), pp. 199–200.
57 B.D. v, 174.
58 *Ibid.*
59 P.A. xii/327, Aehrenthal to Pallavicini, 30 December 1907, d. 1858. (It was Izvolsky who rejected Grey's proposal for demarches: P.A. xii/327; Berchtold to Aehrenthal, t. 10, 18 January 1908.) Aehrenthal to Mensdorff, dd. 91 and 93, 24 January 1908. F.O. 371/581: Files 3240, 3241, Memoranda, 28 January 1908.
60 F.O. 120/848, Grey to Goschen, dd. 10 and 13, 28 January 1908.
61 F.O. 371/581, Moore to the editor of the *Morning Post*, cutting and minutes.
62 *Ibid.*
63 F.O. 371/581, Nicolson to Grey, d. 59, 30 January 1908 and minutes.
64 *Ibid.*

65 Hardinge MSS. XI, Goschen to Hardinge, private, 21 February 1908.

66 B.D. v, 181; D.D.F. XI(2), 271, 320; G.P. XXII, 7732; P.A. XII/339, Pallavicini to Aehrenthal, private, 5 February 1908 (blaming O'Conor).

67 B.D. v, 180, 184.

68 P.A. XII/344, Mensdorff to Aehrenthal, d. 2B, 24 January 1908.

69 P.A. XII/345, Mensdorff to Aehrenthal, t. 7, 10 February 1908; F.O. 120/848, Grey to Goschen, d. 18, 10 February 1908.

70 P.A. XII/339, Note from British Embassy, 12 February 1908; Aehrenthal to Mensdorff, t. 11, 15 February 1908; F.O. 120/848, Grey to Goschen, d. 22, 19 February 1908.

71 F.O. 371/581, Nicolson to Grey, private, 17 February 1908 and minutes.

72 *Ibid.*

73 Hansard, VI, 184, cc. 1692–1708.

74 F.O. 371/581, Memorandum for the Cabinet, 26 February 1908, with amendments.

75 *Ibid.* Grey to Nicolson, private, 26 February 1908.

76 Hardinge MSS. XIII, Hardinge to Goschen, private, 7 April 1908.

77 F.O. 371/582, Nicolson to Grey, private, 13 March 1908.

78 Hardinge MSS. XIII, Hardinge to Goschen, private, 7 April 1908.

79 Hardinge MSS. XIV, Hardinge to Edward VII, 21 and 28 March 1908; Edward VII to Hardinge, 24 March 1908.

80 Hardinge MSS. XIII, Hardinge to Goschen, private, 7 April 1907.

81 P.A. XII/346, Aehrenthal to Mensdorff, d. 502, 23 April 1908.

82 Hardinge MSS. XIII, Hardinge to Barclay, private, 7 May 1908; to Goschen, private, 19 May 1908; F.O. 371/583, Barclay to Grey, t. 104, 5 May 1908.

83 B.D. v, 195; Hardinge MSS. XIII, Hardinge to Goschen, private, 16 June 1908.

84 F.O. 120/849, Grey to Goschen, d. 85, 31 July 1908.

85 Hardinge MSS. XII, Hardinge to Block, private, 31 July 1908; F.O. 371/585, De Salis to Grey, d. 330, 28 July 1908 minute.

86 B.D. v, 240, 244, 254; F.O. 371/583, Nicolson to Grey, private, 24 April 1908, minute.

87 W. M. Carlgren, *Iswolsky und Aehrenthal*, pp. 244–5; Hardinge MSS. XIII, Hardinge to Barclay, private, 7 May 1908; F.O. 371/584, O'Beirne to Grey, d. 317, 10 July 1908.

88 F.O. 371/585, Lowther to Grey, d. 236, 22 August 1908; Erskine to Grey, d. 129, 23 August 1908 and minute.

89 Hardinge MSS. XI, Goschen to Hardinge, private, 17 April 1908; Mensdorff MSS., Diary, 28 June, 8 July 1908.

90 Hardinge MSS. XIII, Hardinge to Goschen, private [letter], 28 July 1908.

91 Hardinge MSS. XIII, Hardinge to Goschen, private, 28 July 1908.

92 Mensdorff MSS., Diary, 15 August 1908; B.D. v, pp. 827–30. P.A. III/167, Schlagworte für eine Unterredung mit [...] Hardinge.

93 G.P. XXIV, 8230 and note; 8242.

94 P.A. VIII/142, Note, of 15 June 1920, reports that searches in the archives in 1917 concerning the so-called 'Apage Satanas' of Franz Joseph to Edward VII had proved completely negative.

95 F.O. 371/399, Cartwright to Grey, d. 86, 1 August 1908.

96 *Ibid.* minutes.

97 F.O. 371/550, Lowther to Grey, d. 559, 13 September 1908, minute.

98 B.D. v, 268; F.O. 371/550, Buchanan to Grey, t. 21, 24 September 1908, minute.

99 3. Hardinge MSS. XIII, Hardinge to Nicolson, private, 30 September 1908.

100 F.O. 371/550, Lowther to Grey, d. 585, 17 September 1908, minute.

101 E.g. *Morning Post*, 12 and 13 August; *Daily News*, 13 August 1908.

102 F.O. 371/399, Goschen to Grey, d. 111, 21 August 1908; d. 119, 10 September 1908, and minute.

103 F. Conrad von Hötzendorf, *Aus meiner Dienstzeit* (Vienna, 1921), I, p. 104.

9. THE BOSNIAN CRISIS

1 See chapter 8, p. 176.

2 Hardinge to Grey, 3 October 1908: Grey MSS. F.O. 800, vol. 91; B.D. v, no. 287.

3 B.D. v, no. 299.

4 Hardinge to Bertie, 5 October 1908; to Buchanan, 6 October 1908: Hardinge MSS., vol. 13, fols. 90– , 12– ; minute by Hardinge on Lowther to Grey, tel. no. 292, 5 October 1908; and on Bertie to Grey, no. 380, 4 October 1908, received 6 October: F.O. 371, vol. 550.

5 Hardinge to Bertie, 5 October 1908: Hardinge MSS. 13, fol. 90– ; Fitzmaurice to Grey, 6 October 1908: Grey MSS. F.O. 800/91.

6 Grey to Asquith, 5 October 1908; Asquith to Grey, tel., 6 October 1908: Grey MSS. F.O. 800/99.

7 Hardinge to Bertie, 5 October 1908: Hardinge MSS. 13, fol. 90– ; B.D. v, nos. 296, 317. The Treaty of Berlin is printed in E. Hertslet, *The Map of Europe by Treaty*, vol. IV (London, 1891), pp. 2764–98.

8 B.D. v, nos. 302, 318–20; Memorandum by Parker, 29 July 1909: F.O.C.P., vol. 9512, pp. 6–7. For the 1871 protocol, see Hertslet, *Map of Europe by Treaty*, vol. III (London, 1875), p. 1904.

9 B.D. v, nos. 301, 303.

10 B.D. v, nos. 303, 311, 312, 314, 321, 360; F.O.C.P. 9456, nos. 257, 395, 404.

11 B.D. v, nos. 328, 356, 374; F.O.C.P. 9456, no. 263. Article 29 is printed in B.D. v, p. 412.

12 Grey to Howard, 3 April 1906: Grey MSS. F.O. 800/107.

13 F.O.C.P. 9456, no. 97; F.O.C.P. 9490, nos. 105, 106, 108–12, 117, 118, 125, 147.

14 B.D. IV, nos. 258, 268, 276; *Alexandre Isvolsky: au service de la Russie: Correspondance diplomatique 1906–1911*, ed. Hélène Isvolsky and Georges Chklaver (Paris, 1937–9), vol. II, pp. 23–4, 26–7. See chapter 6, p. 146.

15 Nicolson to Grey, tel. no. 192, 7 October 1908: F.O.C.P. 9456, no. 255; minute by Hardinge on Bertie to Grey, no. 389, 7 October 1908: F.O. 371/551.

16 B.D. v, nos. 338, 349.

17 Minute by Mallet on Bertie to Grey, no. 389, 7 October 1908: F.O. 371/551.

18 B.D. v, nos. 363, 379; F.O.C.P. 9456, no. 367. Whereas the renunciation of Austrian rights in the Sanjak was the only compensation Aehrenthal had intended to afford Turkey for the annexation, the programme proposed by Isvolsky and Grey provided opportunites for further compensation by abrogating articles in the Treaty of Berlin which were offensive to her.

19 Cabinet letter, Asquith to Edward VII, 12 October 1908: Asquith MSS., box 5, fol. 50– ; B.D. v, nos. 361, 390.

20 B.D. v, nos. 364, 387.

21 B.D. v, nos. 383, 394, 409(b). For further discussion of the Straits question in Anglo-Russian relations, see chapter 12, pp. 245–6.

22 B.D. v, no. 379; also B.D. v, nos. 364, 387.

23 B.D. v, nos. 366, 391; also Nicolson to Hardinge, 21 October 1908; Hardinge MSS. 12, fol. 77– ; V. N. Kokovtsov, *Out of my Past: the Memoirs of Count Kokovtsov* (Stanford, Calif., 1935), pp. 214–18; and N. V. Tcharykov, *Glimpses of High Politics, through War and Peace 1855–1929* (London, 1931), pp. 269–70.

24 B.D. v, nos. 372, 414.

25 B.D. v, no. 409(b).

26 F.O.C.P. 9456, no. 469; B.D. v, nos. 350, 373, 376, 386, 401, 410, 411.

27 B.D. v, nos. 351, 369; minute by Grey on Lowther to Grey, tel. no. 347, 21 October 1908: F.O. 371/553.

28 B.D. v, nos. 369, 453, 488, 491, 495; F.O.C.P. 9492, no. 526.

29 Minute by Hardinge on Lowther to Grey, no. 768, 13 November 1908, received 18 November: F.O. 371/556; Hardinge to Lowther, 1 December 1908: Hardinge MSS. 13, fol. 224– ; Grey to Cartwright, no. 153, 16 December 1908: F.O.C.P. 9492, no. 439.

30 B.D. v, nos. 384, 402, 407; F.O.C.P. 9456, nos. 480, 549, 580, 585, 641.

31 Bittner *et al.* (eds), *Oesterreich-Ungarns Aussenpolitik* (Vienna, 1930), vol. I, nos. 681, 695, 768; B.D. v, nos. 475, 485.

32 B.D. v, nos. 483, 510; F.O.C.P. 9503, nos. 67, 120. For the text of the Austro-Turkish protocol, signed 26 February 1909, see B.D. v, no. 622.

33 Grey to Hardinge, 13 January 1909: Hardinge MSS. 18, fol. 60– .

34 B.D. v, no. 483; Cartwright to Grey, 19 December 1908: Grey MSS. F.O. 800/39.

35 Cartwright to Grey, tel. no. 104, 21 December 1908: F.O.C.P. 9492, no. 475.

36 Cartwright to Grey, tel. no. 105, 21 December 1908: F.O. 371/558.

37 'It may be very desirable that some ships should cruise in the Aegean, say about the beginning of March. If Near Eastern affairs go badly this may have a good moral effect, as the presence of the squadron at Marmarice had lately.' (Minute by Grey, 7 January 1909: F.O. 371/747.) See also minutes by Hardinge and Grey on Cartwright to Grey, tel. no. 105, 21 December 1908: F.O. 371/558; and Skinner to Tyrrell, 12 January 1909: Grey MSS. F.O. 800/86.

38 Grey to Asquith, 13 December 1908, with minute by Asquith approving Grey's draft: Grey MSS. F.O. 800/99. For the text of the reply, see B.D. v, no. 509.

39 F. R. Bridge, *Great Britain and Austria-Hungary 1906–1914* (London, 1972), pp. 117–21.

40 B.D. v, nos. 362, 370, 388.

41 F.O.C.P. 9456, nos. 454*, 459, 462, 465–7, 475, 485, 530, 538, 581, 616, 629, 658, 660; F.O.C.P. 9492, nos. 39, 52.

42 B.D. v, no. 442; F.O.C.P. 9492, nos. 64, 157, 415, 438.

43 Hardinge to Buchanan, 1 December 1908; and to Lowther, 1 December 1908: Hardinge MSS. 13, fols. 21– , 224– ; F.O.C.P. 9492, nos. 293, 309, 323, 325, 351; F.O.C.P. 9503, nos. 6, 63, 123, 124, 219; also B.D. v, ed. note p. 563, and nos. 499, 515.

44 B.D. v, nos. 436, 494, 529, 542; F.O.C.P. 9503, no. 279.

45 B.D. v, nos. 535, 536, 539, 541, 542, 696 and note; Isvolsky, *Correspondance diplomatique*, II, pp. 195–7, 201–5.

46 Hardinge to Nicolson, 2 February 1909: Hardinge MSS. 17, fol. 326– .

47 Hardinge to Lowther, 6 February 1909: Hardinge MSS. 17, fol. 269– ; B.D. v, nos. 548, 551, 552, 561; F.O.C.P. 9503, nos. 347, 357, 369, 377; F.O.C.P. 9531, nos. 63, 77.

48 F.O.C.P. 9531, nos. 641, 645, 649, 658, 681, 720.

49 B.D. v, nos. 584, 850, 851; F.O.C.P. 9503, nos. 535, 591.

50 Hardinge to Bryce, 23 October 1908: Hardinge MSS. 13, fol. 33– .

51 B.D. v, nos. 373, 390; Grey to Lowther, no. 441, 20 October 1908: F.O.C.P. 9490, no. 175.

52 F.O.C.P. 9490, nos. 171, 173, 183, 199.

53 F.O.C.P. 9490, nos. 225, 240.

54 Grey to Lowther, no. 381, 19 October 1908; to Elliot, no. 93, 29 October 1908: F.O.C.P. 9490, nos. 172, 209.

55 Grey to Bertie, 7 December 1908: Grey MSS. F.O. 800/49; also F.O.C.P. 9490, nos. 152, 253.

56 Hardinge to Nicolson, 28 October 1908: Hardinge MSS. 13, fol. 273– ; Grey to Bertie, 29 October 1908: Grey MSS. F.O. 800/49; and F.O.C.P. 9490, no. 219.

57 'The fact that there are already three Greeks to every Mussulman in Cyprus is a very good reason for not giving the island back to Turkey, and thereby creating another Cretan question.' (Hardinge to Nicolson, 28 October 1908: Hardinge MSS. 13, fol. 273– .) See also Grey to Bertie no. 566, 7 December 1908: F.O.C.P. 9490, no. 288.

58 F.O.C.P. 9534, nos. 205, 209, 214, 237, 239, 240, 242, 272.

59 Grey to Lowther, 13 November 1908; and minute by Grey on Chirol to Tyrrell, 26 November 1908: Grey MSS. F.O. 800/78. For Grey's reply to Benckendorff on 10 November, see chapter 12, pp. 246–7.

60 Lepsius *et al.* (eds), *Die Grosse Politik* (Berlin, 1922–7), vol. XXVII. i, nos. 9798–9802; vol. XXVII. ii, nos. 9963, 9964; B.D. v, nos. 218, 219. For British policy in the Bagdad railway and Tigris valley questions, see chapter 11, pp. 227, 231–2.

61 F.O.C.P. 9456, nos. 288, 442; B.D. v, nos. 379, 405, 411; *Grosse Politik*, XXVI. i, nos. 9091, 9096; *OUA*, I, no. 180 and ff.

62 Grey to Whitehead, no. 53, 28 October 1908: F.O.C.P. 9456, no. 643; minute by Grey on Nicolson to Grey, no. 580, 11 December 1908, received 21 December: F.O. 371/558; also B.D. v, nos. 411, 412.

63 B.D. v, nos. 420, 431, 437, 448.

64 F.O.C.P. 9503, nos. 163, 402.

65 Hardinge to Nicolson, 16 February 1909: Hardinge MSS. 17, fol. 328– ; B.D. v, ed. note pp. 608–9. and no. 574.

66 Hardinge to Cartwright, 23 February 1909: Hardinge MSS. 17, fol. 91– .

67 B.D. v, nos. 573, 583, 585, 593, 602, 603; F.O.C.P. 9503, nos. 483, 525.

68 B.D. v, nos. 598, 616; F.O.C.P. 9503, nos. 564, 577.

69 Minute by Hardinge on Nicolson to Grey, tel. no. 97, 24 February 1909: F.O. 371/751.

70 B.D. v, nos. 567, 568, 571, 572.

71 B.D. v, nos. 601, 604, 606, 611, 612, 617.

72 B.D. v, no. 621.

73 B.D. v, nos. 619, 626, 627, 641; von Siebert (ed.), *Graf Benckendorffs diplomatischer Schriftwechsel* (Berlin, 1928), vol. I, nos. 22, 23. Neither the official nor the private papers contain any indication on the British side of overt pressure on Isvolsky to instruct the Serbs to renounce territorial compensation. The Russians did, of course, know that Britain would not support demands which went beyond what could be obtained by diplomatic means; Nicolson more than once pointed out to Isvolsky (with Grey's approval) that territorial compensation would be impossible to obtain without war; and Benckendorff reported that this was the view generally held in London. (B.D. v, nos. 613, 621; *Benckendorffs diplomatischer Schriftwechsel*, I, no. 21; Bernadotte E. Schmitt, *The Annexation of Bosnia 1908–1909* (Cambridge, 1937), pp. 161–4.)

74 B.D. v, nos. 638, 643, 652, 655, 659; F.O.C.P. 9531, nos. 62, 86, 87.

75 B.D. v, nos. 654, 656, 658, 666–8, 674, 682.

76 B.D. v, no. 693.

77 B.D. v, nos. 699, 702, 704, 713; F.O.C.P. 9531, nos. 251, 280.

78 B.D. v, nos. 721, 725, 732, 737, 739, 747, 750, 767. For Grey's attempt at mediation between Austria and Serbia, see A. F. Pribram, *Austria-Hungary and Great Britain 1908–1914* (London, 1951), pp. 131–8; and Bridge, *Great Britain and Austria-Hungary 1906–1914*, pp. 131–2.

79 Minute by Mallet on Goschen to Grey, no. 76, 3 March 1909, received 8 March, F.O. 371/752; also Hardinge to Edward VII, 17 March 1909, Hardinge MSS. 18, fol. 23– .

80 B.D. v, no. 692.

81 B.D. v, no. 700; G.P. xxvi. ii, nos. 9515, 9517; O.U.A. ii, no. 1259.

82 B.D. v, nos. 700, 714.

83 B.D. v, nos. 722, 753; F.O.C.P. 9531, no. 284; G.P. xxvi. ii, no. 9460.

84 B.D. v, nos. 753, 764; Baron Michael de Taube, *La politique russe d'avant-guerre et la fin de l'Empire des Tsars 1904–1914* (Paris, 1928), p. 228; Serge Sazonov, *Fateful Years 1909–1916* (London, 1928), pp. 18–20.

85 B.D. v, nos. 748, 761, 764; Goschen to Grey, 26 March 1909: Hardinge MSS. 15, fol. 276– ; Cabinet letter, Asquith to Edward VII, 26 March 1909: Asquith MSS. 5, fol. 98– .

86 Nicolson to Grey, no. 206, 31 March 1909, F.O. 371/756; also B.D. v, nos. 441, 764; and F.O.C.P. 9503, nos. 161, 471.

87 Memorandum by Hardinge, 28 March 1909, F.O. 371/757; Cartwright to Grey, private tel., 1 April 1909, Grey MSS., F.O. 800/40; Hardinge to Cartwright, 2 April 1909, Hardinge MSS. 17, fol. 95– ; see also B.D. v, nos. 732, 735, 820; and Bridge, *Great Britain and Austria-Hungary*, pp. 133–4.

88 Minute by Grey on Nicolson to Grey, no. 206, 31 March 1909, received 13 April, F.O. 371/756.

89 Goschen to Hardinge, 2 April 1909: Hardinge MSS. 15, fol. 283– .

90 Minute by Hardinge on Nicolson to Grey, tel. no. 168, 24 March 1909, F.O. 371/755; Goschen to Grey, 26 March 1909, Hardinge MSS. 15, fol. 276– ; Hardinge to Edward VII, 31 March 1909, Hardinge MSS. 18, fol. 33– ; also B.D. v, no. 764.

91 B.D. v, no. 768; Hardinge to Goschen, 30 March 1909, Hardinge MSS. 17, fol. 179– .

92 G.P. xxvi. ii, no. 9476; Cabinet letter, Asquith to Edward VII, 26 March 1909, Asquith MSS. 5, fol. 98– ; Hardinge to Edward VII, 26 March 1909, and 31 March 1909, Hardinge MSS. 18, fols. 26– , 33– ; B.D. v, nos. 769, 783.

93 B.D. v, nos. 775, 787; G.P. xxvi. ii, no. 9475; Hardinge to Edward VII, 31 March 1909, Hardinge MSS. 18, fol. 33– .

94 B.D. v, nos. 757, 758, 773.

95 Hardinge to Edward VII, 26 March 1909, Hardinge MSS. 18, fol. 26– ; B.D. v, nos. 771, 781, 785, 786, 789.

96 Cabinet letter, Asquith to Edward VII, 31 March 1909, Asquith MSS. 5, fol. 100– ; B.D. v, nos. 805, 808, 809, 819.

97 F.O.C.P. 9531, nos. 500, 608, 845B.

98 Minute by Grey on Rodd to Grey, no. 78, 27 March 1909, received 30 March, F.O. 371/755; also B.D. v, nos. 816, 859, 860.

99 Hardinge to Cartwright, 15 June 1909: Hardinge MSS. 17, fol. 107– .

100 Goschen to Hardinge, 2 April 1909, Hardinge MSS. 15, fol. 283– .

101 For a discussion of the effect of the Bosnian crisis on Anglo-Russian relations, see chapter 12, pp. 246–7.

10. THE GERMAN BACKGROUND TO ANGLO-GERMAN RELATIONS, 1905–1914

1 W. H. Hoffman, J. H. Müller *et al.*, *Das deutsche Volkseinkommen, 1851–1957* (Tübingen, 1959), p. 14. Two very important collections of essays should be mentioned here as background to an understanding of the explosive qualities of Wilhelmine Germany: M. Stürmer (ed.), *Das Kaiserliche Deutschland. Politik und Gesellschaft 1870–1918* (Düsseldorf, 1970) and Herbert Schottelius and Wilhelm Deist (eds), *Marine und Marinepolitik 1871–1914*, published by the Militärgeschichtliches Forschungsamt (Düsseldorf, 1972). The latter is abbreviated below as 'Schottelius and Deist, *Marine*'.

2 P. Jostock, 'The Long-term Growth of National Income in Germany' in S. Kuznets (ed.), *Income and Wealth*, Series v (Cambridge, 1955), Table 2, p. 91.

3 *Ibid.* Table 4, p. 97.

4 Jürgen Kuczynski, *Studien zur Geschichte des Kapitalismus* (Berlin-East, 1957), pp. 171–76.

5 Klara Perls, *Die Einkommenentwicklung in Preussen seit 1896* (Berlin, 1911), Table IIId, p. 69.

6 Dr Karl Schürman, 'Arbeitslohn und Teuerung', *Preussische Jahrbücher*, Bd. 129, Heft II (August, 1907), pp. 205 ff.

7 Paul Bücher, 'Deutschlands Handelsbilanz', *ibid.*, Bd. 126, Heft III (December 1906), pp. 492 ff.

8 Eyre Crowe, Memorandum, F.O. 371/257, 'On the Present State of British Relations with France and Germany', 1 January 1907, in *British Documents on the Origins of the War 1898–1914*, ed. G. P. Gooch and Harold Temperley, 11 vols. (London, 1928–36), (abbreviated hereafter as B.D.), III, Appendix A, p. 406.

9 Stosch to Tirpitz, 12 February 1896, in A. von Tirpitz, *Erinnerungen* (Leipzig, 1920), pp. 53–4.

10 Alfred Graf von Schlieffen, 'Der Krieg in der Gegenwart', *Deutsche Revue* (Stuttgart/Leipzig, 1909), pp. 13 ff.

11 Hans Delbrück, 'Politische Korrespondenz', *Preussische Jahrbücher*, Bd. 98, Heft III (December, 1899), p. 588.

12 Metternich to Bülow, 4 May 1906, in Lepsius *et al.* (eds), *Die Grosse Politik der europäischen Kabinette 1871–1914* (Berlin, 1922–7), Sammlung der diplomatischen Akten des Auswärtigen Amtes, ed. Johannes Lepsius, Friedrich Thimme, Albrecht Mendelssohn-Bartholdy (Berlin, 1922 and after) (abbreviated below as G.P.), vol. XXI, i, no. 7180, p. 425.

13 Kaiser Wilhelm II to the Reichskanzler, 30 March 1889, in Walther Hubatsch, *Der Admiralstab und die obersten Marine-Behörden in Deutschland, 1848–1945* (Frankfurt/Main, 1958), Document 13, p. 236; for a discussion of the new organisation, pp. 149 ff.

14 Tirpitz, *op. cit.*, p. 135.

15 Tirpitz, '*Allgemeine Gesichtspunkte bei der Feststellung unserer Flotte nach Schiffsklassen und Schiffstypen*', June 1897, in J. Steinberg, *Yesterday's Deterrent. Tirpitz and the Birth of the German Battle Fleet* (London, 1965), p. 217. Two brilliant analyses of Tirpitz's strategy from a maritime-military point of view are Paul M. Kennedy 'Maritime Strategieprobleme der deutsch-englischen Flottenrivalität' and Vizeadmiral a.D. Edward Wegener, 'Die Tirpitzsche Seestrategie', both in Schottelius and Deist, *Marine*, pp. 178–210 and 236–64 respectively.

16 J. Steinberg, *Yesterday's Deterrent*, pp. 145–6.

17 Tirpitz, *op. cit.*, p. 109.

18 A. von Tirpitz, *Politische Dokumente*, vol. I. *Der Aufbau der deutschen Weltmacht* (Stuttgart/Berlin, 1924), pp. 13 ff., and Appendix with tables of construction.

19 A. J. Marder, *From Dreadnought to Scapa Flow. The Royal Navy in the Fisher Era* (Oxford, 1961), vol. I, p. 42.

20 Dr Volker Berghahn offers an alternative synthesis. He argues in a brilliant, work that the Navy must be seen primarily as a device to maintain the domestic status quo. Its national appeal, commercial and industrial relations and monarchical apex made it an ideal vehicle for integrating what he sees as a dangerously divided society. Cf. V. R. Berghahn, *Der Tirpitz-Plan. Genesis und Verfall einer innenpolitischen Krisenstrategie unter Wilhelm II* (Düsseldorf, 1971); also V. R. Berghahn 'Flottenrüstung und Machtgefüge' in M. Stürmer (ed.), *Das Kaiserliche Deutschland*, pp. 378–96, and idem., 'Zu den Zielen des deutschen Flottenbaus unter Wilhelm II', *Historische Zeitschrift*, Heft 210/11, February 1970, pp. 34–100, both of which contain

summarized statements of the general argument. In English, there is a summary to be found in my review of Dr Berghahn's *Der Tirpitz-Plan*, J. Steinberg, 'The Tirpitz Plan', *The Historical Journal*, vol. XVI, no. 1, March 1973, pp. 196 ff.

21 J. Steinberg, 'The Copenhagen Complex', *The Journal of Contemporary History* (1966), vol. I, no. 3, pp. 23 ff.; also J. Steinberg, 'Germany and the Russo-Japanese War', *American Historical Review* (December, 1970), vol. LXXV, no. 1, pp. 1965–86.

22 Protokoll über die Sitzung am 8 Dezember 1904, Berlin, German Naval Archives in Militärgeschichtliches Forschungsamt, Dokumentenzentrale, Freiburg im Breisgau (abbreviated below as MGFA-DZ): F. 2046, PG 66086, RMA1.3, 1–13.

23 Kapitän z.S. von Heeringen, '*Schlussvotum des Vorsitzenden der R. Kommission*', *ganz geheim*, 14 December 1904, MGFA-DZ: F. 2044, PG 66077, RMA XVII.

24 Tirpitz, minute, 20 December 1904, *ibid.*

25 Steinberg, *Yesterday's Deterrent*, pp. 84 and 206.

26 Mr Lee's speech can be found in Eugene Anderson, *The First Moroccan Crisis, 1904–1906* (Chicago, 1930), p. 181; on reading it, the Kaiser wrote to Tirpitz, 4 February 1904:

> Dear Maestro, You will have read in Wolff the astounding speech of the Civil Lord of the Admirality with its open threat of war against us. I have just had Lascelles here and made it clear to him in unambiguous terms that this revenge-breathing corsair must be disavowed and rectified by his government by morning. Otherwise there will break out such a storm in our press that it can only be met through the speedy introduction of a colossal new building programme forced on us by 'public opinion'. [English in original]

MGFA-DZ: F. 2044, PG 66077 reprinted in Tirpitz, *Politische Dokumente*, i, p. 17.

27 Berghahn, *Der Tirpitz-Plan*, Tables 17–19, pp. 612–13; and Hansgeorg Fernis, *Die Flottennovellen im Reichstag, 1906–1912* (Stuttgart, 1934), pp. 5ff.; Tirpitz, *Politische Dokumente*, i, pp. 15–20.

28 Tirpitz, *Vortrag*, Rominten, 4 October 1905, MGFA-DZ: F. 2044, PG 66079, '*Reichsmarineamt – Zentralabteilung*'.

29 Tirpitz, *Politische Dokumente*, I, p. 22. I have had occasion to compare the printed versions in the *Politische Dokumente* with the original documents and have found them to be accurate and complete. Historians have understandably avoided using the Tirpitz papers, because they could not be verified, but they stand comparison with any published collection of the 1920s.

30 'Denkschrift für den Reichskanzler', Berlin, 13 November 1905, Tirpitz MS. 'Entwicklung der Marine. Novelle 1905–6'. (I am profoundly indebted to the late Korv.-Kapt. a.D. Dr Wolfgang von Tirpitz for permission to use the Tirpitz MS. in the family home at Irschenhausen, Germany.)

31 Fernis, *op. cit.* p. 14.

32 Delbrück, *Preussische Jahrbücher*, 27 May 1906, Bd. 124, Heft III, p. 578.

33 Tirpitz to Wilhelm II, 4 April 1906, MGFA-DZ: F. 2045, PG 66079, '*Reichsmarineamt XIX*'.

34 Diary Entry, 6 October 1898, Fürst Chlodwig zu Hohenlohe-Schillingsfürst, *Denkwürdigkeiten der Reichskanzlerzeit*, ed. K. A. von Müller (Stuttgart/Berlin, 1931), p. 463. Prince Heinrich of Prussia, the Kaiser's brother, was also dismayed by Tirpitz's behaviour. 'I find this repeated threatening to resign not entirely loyal. In any case, a Monarch who had the courage to let Prince Bismarck go will not hesitate to accept the resignation of a Tirpitz.' Prince Heinrich to Senden, 25 July 1898, in Steinberg, *Yesterday's Deterrent*, p. 52, n. 59.

35 Pencil minute, January 1904, Freiherr von Senden Bibran, 'Nachlass Senden', Bundesarchiv, Koblenz, K-08-7, vol. 1.

36 Conversation of State Secretary with English naval attaché Captain Heath, 28 March 1909, Document II, 'Die Verständigung mit England', *Süddeutsche Monatshefte*, Bd.

23, Heft 2 (November 1925), p. 99. Dr Berghahn's interpretation of Tirpitz's intentions places greater emphasis on the anti-parliamentary aspect of an *Aeternat.* The fixed Navy Law was, he believes, part of a strategy to bolster absolute government.

37 '*Denkschrift über die weitere Entwicklung der Marine*' (signed) Capelle. Tirpitz MS. '*Privat 1906–7*', *ganz geheim.*

38 Tirpitz, *Politische Dokumente*, I, Appendix for full texts of all the Navy Laws.

39 Table II, Fernis, *op. cit.* p. 155.

40 Marder, *op. cit.* I, p. 43.

41 *Ibid.* p. 44.

42 Cited in Steinberg, *Yesterday's Deterrent*, p. 217.

43 Tirpitz, *Erinnerungen*, p. 174.

44 Dr Peter-Christian Witt has opened an entirely new area of research in these matters with his pioneer study of the finances of the Reich, cf. *Die Finanzpolitik des Deutschen Reiches von 1903 bis 1913*, Historische Studien, Heft 415 (Lübeck and Hamburg, 1970). A sketch of his views as they apply to naval matters can be found in Peter-Christian Witt, 'Reichsfinanzen und Rüstungspolitik 1898–1914' in Schottelius and Deist, *Marine und Marinepolitik*, pp. 146–177.

45 '*Vergleich der Etats 1897 und 1906*', Tirpitz MS.

46 Hoffmann, Müller, *et al., op cit.* p. 15.

47 Schürmann, *op. cit.* pp. 208ff.

48 Peter-Christian Witt, 'Reichsfinanzen und Rüstungspolitik' in Schottelius and Deist, *Marine und Marinepolitik*, p. 158.

49 'The German Naval Estimates, 1906–7', reprinted in *Empire Review*, XI, 66 (July 1906), pp. 515–31.

50 'Denkschrift zum Immediatvortrag, betreffend Kiellegung der Schiffe', Konstruktionsabteilung I. 16233, Berlin, 20 October 1910, pp. 9–10, with table, MGFA-DZ: PG 93993.

51 Kapt. z. See von Trotha to Tirpitz, 7 June 1906, Tirpitz MS.

52 'If the plans of the English to enlarge the displacement and armaments of their 1906 battleships and cruisers, which have recently come to my attention, should be confirmed, it will become necessary on our side to go ahead with further enlargement of our designs even for the estimates for 1907. I therefore order the Construction Department, in cooperation with the Military Department, to prepare for the audience at Rominten suitable sketches and to lay them before me as soon as possible. The following are the types:

    1 Battleship 12×30.5 cm (12 inch)
                   12×15 cm (5.9 inch)
                   Turbines
    2 Cruiser   8×30.5 cm
                   8×15 cm (possible double turret)
                   Turbines

This order is to be treated as very secret. All persons entrusted with the preparations are to be especially informed of the obligation to maintain strict security.' Tirpitz, *Notiz, ganz geheim*, St Blasien, 18 July 1906, Tirpitz MS.

53 Tirpitz to Capelle, 21 July 1906; Capelle to Tirpitz, 24 July 1906; Tirpitz MS.

54 Tirpitz to Capelle, 29 July 1906; Tirpitz to Scheer, 12 August 1906; Scheer to Tirpitz, 14 August 1906, Tirpitz MS.

55 Tirpitz, *Notiz an K., A. und W.*, 7 September 1906, Tirpitz MS.

56 Personal communication to the author from Korv.-Kapt. a.D. Dr Wolfgang von Tirpitz.

57 Tirpitz, *Vortrag*, Rominten, 28 September 1906, Tirpitz MS.

58 Ernst Basserman (Nat. Lib.), 14 November 1906, *Stenographische Berichte der Verhandlungen des deutschen Reichstags*, Bd. 232, XII. Legislaturperiode, I Session, p. 4238.
59 Berghahn, *Der Tirpitz-Plan*, pp. 526–8, and G. D. Crothers, *The German Elections of 1907* (New York, 1941), pp. 21 and 74ff.
60 *Ibid.* pp. 88–9, and Berghahn, *Der Tirpitz-Plan*, pp. 523–4.
61 Berghahn, *Der Tirpitz-Plan*, p. 529.
62 E. R. Hüber, *Dokumente zur deutschen Verfassungsgeschichte*, II (Stuttgart, 1964), no. 392, 'Ergebnisse der Reichstagswahlen 1871–1912', p. 539.
63 Robert Jaffe, 'Die letzten Reichstagswahlen und die Zukunft der Sozialdemokratie', *Preussische Jahrbücher*, Bd. 128, Heft II (May 1907), pp. 303–4.
64 Hans Delbrück, *ibid.* Bd. 127, Heft II.
65 Quellen zur Geschichte des Parlamentarismus und der politischen Parteien, erste Reihe, Bd. 3/1. *Die Reichstagsfraktion der deutschen Sozialdemokratie*. Bearbeitet von Erich Matthias und E. Pikart (Düsseldorf, 1966). Social Democratic Party's Election Results:

Year	Seats won l. ballot	Second in no. of seats	Run-off seats won	Success rate	Totals
1898	32	98	24	24%	56
1903	56	118	25	21%	81
1907	29	90	14	16% (p. xxiii)	43

66 Tirpitz to Lieber, 23 April 1898, MGFA-DZ: F. 2050, PG 66105.
67 Freiherr von Wilmowski to Tirpitz, 14 December 1900, Tirpitz MS.
68 Tirpitz, *Erinnerungen*, p. 230.
69 Hans Delbrück, *op. cit.* Bd. 127, Heft II (February 1907), p. 379.
70 *Stenographische Berichte der Verhandlungen des deutschen Reichstags*, 9. Legislaturperiode, V. Session, 5. Sitzung, 7 December 1907, p. 78.
71 Capelle, *Vortrag*, Berlin, 18 February 1907, *ganz geheim*, Tirpitz MS., and also Ktr. Admiral von Heeringen, *Denkschrift* A.V.a. 43, 23 February 1907, *ganz geheim*, Tirpitz MS.
72 Tirpitz, *Zum Immediatvortrag* (pencil notes), 9 March 1907, *ganz geheim, ibid.*
73 Tirpitz, *Notiz: Novelle, ganz geheim*, 27 May 1907, *ibid.*
74 Dähnhardt to Tirpitz, 23 July 1907, *ibid.*
75 Capelle to Tirpitz, 4 August 1907, *ibid.*
76 Bülow to Tirpitz, 10 August 1907, *ibid.*
77 Berghahn, *Der Tirpitz-Plan*, pp. 581–5.
78 *Schulthess' Europäischer Geschichtskalender*, XXXIII (1907) (Munich, 1908), p. 34.
79 Tirpitz to Bülow, 14 August 1907, *ganz geheim*, Tirpitz MS.
80 Capelle to Tirpitz, 17 August 1904, *ibid.*
81 P.-C. Witt, *Die Finanzpolitik des Deutschen Reiches*, pp. 170–1.
82 Capelle to Tirpitz, 4 August 1907, in Berghahn, *Der Tirpitz-Plan*, pp. 586–7.
83 Capelle to Tirpitz, 17 August 1907, *ganz geheim*, Tirpitz MS.
84 Tirpitz to Bülow (telegramme), 18 September 1907, in Berghahn, *Der Tirpitz-Plan*, p. 583, n. 97.
85 'Vortrag beim Kanzler: Nordeney', September 1907, *ganz geheim*, Tirpitz MS.
86 *Stenographische Berichte der Verhandlungen des deutschen Reichstags*, Bd. 232, XIII. Legislaturperiode, I. Session, 132. Sitzung, p. 436.
87 'Stichworte zum Vortrag in Rominten', 29 September 1907, *ganz geheim*, Tirpitz MS.

88 Much less obvious is the position of the Chancellor. The Kaiser was clearly delighted and, in part, Tirpitz hoped to prevent yet another Imperial ukase by accelerating first. But Bülow? Dr Berghahn argues (*Der Tirpitz-Plan*, pp. 587–8) that Bülow saw a naval bill as, perhaps, the last hope of getting a tax increase through the disintegrating Bloc-dominated Reichstag. Naval euphoria might help to carry an otherwise unpopular measure with it. This interpretation directly grounded on evidence from Bülow's own hand, certainly seems plausible.

89 *Stenographische Berichte der Verhandlungen des Deutschen Reichstags*, Bd. 232, XII. Legislaturperiode, I. Session, 60. Sitzung, 28 November 1907.

90 J. H. Chapham, *An Economic History of Modern Britain*, vol. III. *Machines and National Rivalries (1887–1914)* (Cambridge, 1938), p. 55.

91 'The Panic of 1907', *Concise Dictionary of American History*, ed. T. C. Cochran (New York, 1962), p. 710.

92 Clapham, *op. cit.* p. 54.

93 *Ibid.* p. 57.

94 Gwinner to Bülow, 20 November 1908, in Peter-Christian Witt, *Die Finanzpolitik des Deutschen Reiches*, p. 193.

95 David Butler and Jennie Freeman, *British Political Facts, 1900–67* (London, 1968), ch. IX, 'The Economy', pp. 222–7.

96 G. Haberler, *Prosperity and Depression. A Theoretical Analysis of Cyclical Movements*, 3rd Edition (New York, 1946), 'General Indices of Cyclical Movements in Various Countries', pp. 266–7. Pig iron figures in Fritz Fischer, *Krieg der Illusionen. Deutsche Politik von 1911 bis 1914* (Düsseldorf, 1969), p. 19.

97 Peter-Christian Witt, *Die Finanzpolitik*, p. 193, n. 222.

98 R. S. Sayers, *Central Banking after Bagehot* (Oxford, 1957), pp. 60–2.

99 Wolfgang von Tirpitz, *Wie hat sich der Staatsbetrieb beim Aufbau der Flotte bewahrt?* (Leipzig, 1923), p. 101, Table 4, columns 1–4.

100 Howard Weinroth, 'Left-wing Opposition to Naval Armaments in pre-1914 Britain', *Journal of Contemporary History*, vol. 6, no. 4, 1971, pp. 114–16.

101 Cf. P.-C. Witt, *Die Finanzpolitik des Deutschen Reiches*, pp. 140–1, for estimates of the monopoly costs and profit.

102 There is a fascinating exchange of letters between Tirpitz and Gustav Krupp von Bohlen und Halbach (Tirpitz MS.), in which Tirpitz refused an invitation to hunt on Krupp's estates (Tirpitz to Krupp, 9 August 1910). Krupp wrote again (Krupp to Tirpitz, 17 December 1910) much regretting that Tirpitz had been unable to join him and hoping that some day he might have the pleasure of the Admiral's company in Essen. The tone of both letters suggests that Tirpitz was keeping his distance socially from Krupp.

103 Wolfgang von Tirpitz, *op. cit.* pp. 98–9, Table 1.

104 *Ibid.* p. 101, Table 3, Column 9.

105 *Ibid.* pp. 81–2.

106 Captain Heath to Board of Admiralty, 20 and 21 October 1908, in E. L. Woodward, *Great Britain and the German Navy* (Oxford, 1935), pp. 489–90.

107 Memorandum, signed by the four Sea Lords, January 1909, *The Jellicoe Papers*, edited by A. Temple Patterson, I (Navy Records Society, 1966), no. 6, p. 16. Also Marder, *op. cit.* pp. 152–3, and Woodward, *op. cit.* Appendix VI, pp. 480–93.

108 Kaiser's marginal comments on memorandum, cited in n. 50 above.

109 Cf. note 36 above, *ibid.* pp. 98–9.

110 Quoted in A. J. Marder, *From Dreadnought to Scapa Flow*, I, pp. 129–30.

111 Cf. note 50.

112 Dr Berghahn closes his analysis of these events with a letter of late November 1907, in which Tirpitz complains that the *Flottenverein* have not understood 'that the Kaiser has a powerful interest in removing the existence of the fleet permanently

from the parliamentary might of unstable majorities'. (*Der Tirpitz-Plan*, p. 590.) Dr Berghahn sees this attitude as part of the grand domestic crisis strategy of the ruling classes, an alternative to an anti-parliamentary *coup d'état* or the attempt to do away with universal suffrage. My own view is that one only need look at the appalling condition of the French navy in these years to explain Tirpitz's desire to remove the fleet from the power of parliament. Cf. Volkmar Bueb, *Die 'Junge Schule' der französischen Marine. Strategie und Politik 1875–1900*, Wehrwissenschaftliche Forschungen, no. 12 (Boppard am Rhein, 1971); for the later period, Paul Halpern, *The Mediterranean Naval Situation, 1908–1914*, Harvard Historical Studies, vol. LXXXVI (Cambridge, Mass., 1971). For those who want to find the latest general statement by Dr Berghahn of the theoretical framework on which his work rests, there is his *Rüstung und Machtpolitik. Zur Anatomie des 'kalten Krieges' vor 1914* (Düsseldorf, 1973). In this work, Dr Berghahn begins to apply the techniques of recent work in the sociology of war and peace to the period under review here.

113 Adolf Gasser, 'Der deutsche Hegemonialkrieg von 1914' in *Deutschland in der Weltpolitik des 19 und 20 Jahrhunderts: Fritz Fischer zum 65. Geburtstag*. I. Geiss and J. Wendt (eds) (Düsseldorf, 1972).

114 For a discussion of some of these issues, see my review of Berghahn, *op. cit. Historical Journal*, p. 196.

115 Friedrich Meinecke, *Radowitz und die deutsche Revolution* (Berlin, 1913), p. 522.

11. GREAT BRITAIN AND GERMANY, 1905–1911

1 G. M. Trevelyan, *Grey of Fallodon* (London, 1937), pp. 90–2; see also Keith Robbins, *Sir Edward Grey* (London, 1971), pp. 132–5.

2 Grey to Lascelles, 1 January 1906, and 8 January 1906, Grey MSS., Foreign Office series 800, vol. 60. For Liberal policy and the Moroccan crisis, see above, Chapter 5; and G. W. Monger, *The End of Isolation: British Foreign Policy 1900–1907* (London, 1963), pp. 257–80.

3 Gooch and Temperley (eds.), *British Documents on the Origins of the War 1898–1914*, vol. III, nos. 229, 296; *Die Grosse Politik der europäischen Kabinette 1871–1914*, vol. XXI.i, nos. 6923, 7018.

4 Grey to Lascelles, 1 January 1906, Grey MSS. F.O. 800/60; *British Documents*, vol. III, nos. 229, 299, 348; Viscount Grey of Fallodon, *Twenty-Five Years 1892–1916* (London, 1925), vol. I, pp. 117–18.

5 Monger, *End of Isolation*, pp. 275–6.

6 B.D. III, nos. 193, 200, 333, 339, 342, 350–7; Monger, *End of Isolation*, pp. 276–80.

7 *Grosse Politik*, vol. XXI.ii, nos. 7180, 7181, 7185, 7191.

8 B.D. III, nos. 422, 425.

9 B.D. III, no. 425.

10 B.D. III, nos. 413, 416, 418–20; *Documents diplomatiques français*, 2nd series, vol. X, nos. 120, 144; Monger, *End of Isolation*, pp. 299–302.

11 B.D. III, nos. 428–434; Grey to Haldane, 3 September 1906, Haldane MSS., vol. 5907.

12 Monger, *End of Isolation*, pp. 310–12; *Hansard*, 4th series, vol. CLXII, cols. 69–72.

13 B.D. III, no. 435; VI, no. 4; VIII, nos. 162, 168–70, 175, 184, 197. The selection of documents on the Anglo-German naval question printed by the editors of the *British Documents*, in particular in vol. VI, *The Anglo-German Tension 1907–1912* (London, 1930), presents a full and accurate record of British policy in this question, which has not been altered in any essential by resort to the full manuscript archives. The account by E. L. Woodward, *Great Britain and the German Navy* (Oxford, 1935), which is based on the printed British, German and French documents, remains the definitive account of the subject, at least down to the Haldane

mission of 1912. See also A. J. Marder, *From the Dreadnought to Scapa Flow*, vol. I: *The Road to War 1904–1914* (London, 1961).

14 B.D. VIII, nos. 163, 174, 175, 179; G.P. XXIII. i, nos. 7815, 7841, 7927.

15 B.D. VIII, nos. 194, 195.

16 G.P. XXIII. ii, no. 7984; B.D. VIII, no. 240.

17 B.D. III, Appendix A. For discussions of the memorandum, see Oswald Hauser, *Deutschland und der englisch-russische Gegensatz 1900–1914* (Göttingen, 1958), pp. 30–2; Immanuel Geiss, *July 1914* (London, 1967), pp. 28–32; Monger, *End of Isolation*, pp. 313–15; Zara S. Steiner, *The Foreign Office and Foreign Policy 1898–1914* (Cambridge, 1969), pp. 68–9, 111–15; Ludwig Dehio, *Germany and World Politics in the Twentieth Century* (London, 1959), p. 81.

18 B.D. VI, no. 25; Foreign Office Confidential Print, vol. 9217, nos. 8–13, 17, 27, 28; Edward VII to Wilhelm II, private telegram, 18 August 1907, Grey MSS. F.O. 800/39.

19 Cartwright to Grey, no. 58, 8 June 1907, with minute by Hardinge, Foreign Office series 371, vol. 260; B.D. VI, nos. 35, 37, 39.

20 Minute by Grey on Cartwright to Grey, no. 79, 21 August 1907, F.O. 371/253; also *Documents diplomatiques français*, (2) XI, nos. 77, 79–81; and B.D. VI, nos. 22, 33, 35.

21 Minutes by Grey and Spicer on von Stumm to Grey, 13 September 1907, F.O. 371/262; Grey to Knollys, 6 October 1907, Haldane MSS. vol. 5907, fol. 216– .

22 Sir Sidney Lee, *King Edward VII* (London, 1925–7), vol. II, p. 552; Knollys to Grey, 5 October, 6 October, and 8 October 1907, Grey MSS. F.O. 800/102.

23 Hardinge to Grey, 7 October 1907: Grey MSS. F.O. 800/91.

24 Grey to Knollys, 6 October 1907, Haldane MSS. 5907, fol. 216– .

25 B.D. VI, nos. 44, 45.

26 Grey to Haldane, 4 September 1907, Haldane MSS. 5907, fol. 188– .

27 Memorandum by Hardinge, 7 October 1907, with minute by Grey: Hardinge MSS., vol. 10, fol. 46– ; also B.D. VI, nos. 47–51.

28 Campbell-Bannerman to Grey, 4 November 1907, Grey MSS. F.O. 800/99; also B.D. VI, nos. 56–8.

29 B.D. VI, no. 59. On the Baghdad railway, see *inter alia* E. M. Earle, *Turkey, the Great Powers and the Baghdad Railway* (New York, 1923); Herbert Feis, *Europe, the World's Banker 1870–1914* (New Haven, Conn., 1930), pp. 342–60; J. B. Wolf, 'The Diplomatic History of the Baghdad Railroad', *University of Missouri Studies*, XI, 1936; M. K. Chapman, *Great Britain and the Baghdad Railway 1885–1914* (Northampton, Mass., 1948); Oswald Hauser, *Deutschland und der englisch-russische Gegensatz 1900–1914* (Göttingen, 1958), pp. 41–5, 127–36; Jens B. Plass, *England zwischen Deutschland und Russland: der Persische Golf in der britischen Vorkriegspolitik 1899–1907* (Hamburg, 1966), pp. 99–106, 441–51; R. Kumar, 'The Records of the Government of India on the Berlin–Baghdad Railway Question', *Historical Journal* v, (1962); D. C. M. Platt, *Finance, Trade and Politics in British Foreign Policy 1815–1914* (Oxford, 1968), pp. 207–17.

30 B.D. VI, nos. 222, 224, 230, 246.

31 Memorandum by Grey, 31 May 1907; also Memorandum by Hardinge, 7 April 1907, F.O. 371/340.

32 B.D. VI, no. 59.

33 J. B. Kelly, 'Salisbury, Curzon and the Kuwait Agreement of 1899', in *Studies in International History: Essays presented to W. N. Medlicott*, K. Bourne and D. C. Watt (eds) (London, 1967); A. Parker, 'Memorandum respecting British Interests in the Persian Gulf', 12 February 1908, F.O.C.P. 9161, especially pp. 4–5, 64; also F.O.C.P. 9056*, nos. 1, 3, 8, 16 and *passim*.

34 B.D. VI, no. 60; G.P. XXIV, no. 8171; Haldane to his mother, 12 November 1907, Haldane MSS. 5978, fol. 137– . On the Windsor visit, see M. V. Brett and Oliver

Viscount Esher (eds.), *Reginald Viscount Esher, Journals and Letters* (London, 1934–8), vol. II, pp. 254–7; Sir Sidney Lee, *Edward VII* (London, 1925–7), vol. II, pp. 557–63; Richard Viscount Haldane, *Before the War* (London, 1920), pp. 47–51; Haldane, *An Autobiography* (London, 1929), pp. 219–21; Dudley Sommer, *Haldane of Cloan: his Life and Times 1856–1928* (London, 1960), pp. 196–200; John Viscount Morley, *Recollections* (London, 1917), vol. II, pp. 237–8; Wilhelm von Schoen, *Memoirs of an Ambassador* (London, 1922), pp. 59–63; G. P. Gooch, *Before the War: Studies in Diplomacy* (London, 1936–8), vol. II, pp. 40–2.

35 B.D. VI, no. 65; G.P. XXV.i, no. 8670.

36 B.D. VI, nos. 62, 63; G.P. XXV.i, nos. 8668, 8669.

37 B.D. VI, Appendix VIII; G.P. XXV.i, no. 8673.

38 Foreign Office Memorandum, 3 July 1908, F.O.C.P. 9473, no. 34.

39 B.D. VI, no. 73; Asquith, 'Memorandum on Naval and Military Expenditure', 18 November 1907, Asquith MSS., box 97, fol. 155–.

40 Haldane to his sister, 5 February 1908, Haldane MSS. 6011, fol. 42–; compare with Churchill's very similar arguments in his letter to Grey during the cabinet crisis of February 1909, in Randolph S. Churchill, *Winston S. Churchill*, Companion to vol. II (London, 1969), part 2: *1907–1911*, pp. 954–5.

41 Esher, *Journals and Letters*, II, pp. 280–4; Burns, diary entry for 28 January 1908: Burns MSS., B.M. Add. MSS., vol. 46325; Tweedmouth to Campbell-Bannerman, 11 February 1908, Campbell-Bannerman MSS., B.M. Add. MSS., vol. 41231, fol. 175–.

42 Cabinet letter, Asquith to Edward VII, 17 February 1908, Asquith MSS. 5, fol. 1–.

43 *The History of The Times*, vol. III: *The Twentieth Century Test 1884–1912* (London, 1947), pp. 602–3; Alfred M. Gollin, *The Observer and J. L. Garvin: a Study in a Great editorship* (London, 1960), pp. 28–32, 35–55; Oron J. Hale, *Publicity and Diplomacy, with Special Reference to England and Germany 1890–1914* (Gloucester, Mass., 1964), pp. 304–7; G.P. XXIV, nos. 8173–9.

44 Gollin, *The Observer and J. L. Garvin*, pp. 35–50. For a sample of Foreign Office opinion, see minutes by Spicer and Hardinge on de Salis to Grey, no. 529, 4 December 1907, F.O. 371/262; Bertie to Grey, 25 November 1907, Grey MSS. F.O. 800/49; Cartwright to Grey, no. 3, 8 January 1908, with minutes by Crowe, Langley and Grey, F.O. 371/457 [the minutes are printed without the despatch in B.D. VI, Ed. note p. 108]; and B.D. VI, nos. 78, 80.

45 B.D. VI, no. 78; Wilhelm II to Tweedmouth, 14 February 1908, Grey MSS. F.O. 800/86; G.P. XXIV, no. 8181; Esher, *Journals and Letters*, II, pp. 285–98.

46 B.D. VI, nos. 82–4; *Hansard*, 4th series, CLXXXIV, 202; G.P. XXIV, no. 8182; Tweedmouth to Wilhelm II, 20 February 1908, Grey MSS. F.O. 800/86.

47 *Hansard*, 4, CLXXXV, 1336–8.

48 Hardinge to Edward VII, 14 March 1908, Hardinge MSS. 14, fol. 63–; Memorandum by Grey, 28 April 1908, Grey MSS. F.O. 800/91; also *Churchill*, Companion to vol. II, part 2, *1907–1911*, pp. 931–2. For the Parliamentary history of the two-power standard, see Woodward, *Great Britain and the German Navy*, Appendix II.

49 G.P. XXIV, nos. 8217, 8219; B.D. VI, no. 99, and Appendix III; Esher, *Journals and Letters*, II, pp. 329–30.

50 B.D. VI, Appendix III and nos. 111, 116, 117.

51 Minute by Grey on Lascelles to Grey, no. 350, 14 August 1908, F.O. 371/461.

52 Asquith to Lloyd George, tel., 20 August 1908; Lloyd George to Asquith, tel., 21 August 1908, Asquith MSS. 11, fols. 174–, 176–; Esher, *Journals and Letters*, II, pp. 332–3; *Churchill*, Companion to vol. II, part 2, p. 836; minute by Grey circulated to the cabinet, 22 August 1908, Grey MSS. F.O. 800/91.

53 *Hansard*, 4, CXCVI, 560.

54 G.P. XXIV, nos. 8216, 8217, 8219, 8220, 8225, 8226, 8229, 8239, 8244, 8248; G.P. XXVIII, nos. 10234, 10235, 10238, 10240, 10241, 10243, 10244; B.D. VI, nos. 108, 110.

55 Hardinge to de Salis, 29 December 1908, Hardinge MSS. 13, fol. 335– .

56 F.O.C.P. 9405, nos. 65, 71; F.O.C.P. 9415, nos. 10, 27, 57, 66; F.O.C.P. 9440, nos. 22, 60. On Walfisch Bay, F.O.C.P. 9455, nos. 1, 3, 4, 6, 8, 16, 19, 21. It was not the policy of the British government to refuse the Germans facilities for a commercial outlet at Walfisch Bay: the objections to that came from the South African governments; but equally there was no intention of allowing the Germans a strategic foothold there. See Grey to Crewe, 17 June 1908; also 23 June 1908, and 12 August 1908, Crewe MSS., box C/17.

57 Prince Bernhard von Bülow, *Memoirs* (London, 1931–2), vol. II, p. 308; Erich Eyck, *Das persönliche Regiment Wilhelms II* (Erlenbach–Zürich, 1948), p. 478; Hale, *Publicity and Diplomacy*, pp. 310–11; see also B.D. VI, no. 96, and F.O.C.P. 9405, no. 92.

58 B.D. III, no. 439; minute by Grey on Cartwright to Grey, 19 June 1908: F.O. 371/460.

59 Grey to Nicolson, no. 230, 6 June 1907, F.O. 371/340.

60 Grey to Ripon, 13 December 1907, quoted Grey, *Twenty-five Years*, I, p. 149; also Memorandum by Grey circulated to the cabinet, 16 January 1908, Cabinet papers, Cab. 37, vol. 91, no. 4; and B.D. VIII, no. 136.

61 D. W. Sweet, 'The Baltic in British Diplomacy before the First World War', *Historical Journal*, XIII (1970), especially pp. 457–77.

62 Lister to Hardinge, 12 December 1907, Bertie MSS. F.O. 800/177, Rus. 07/7; Grey to Lister, 16 December 1907; Grey to Bertie, 30 December 1907, F.O. 371/527; B.D. VIII, no. 136.

63 D.D.F. (2) XI, nos. 497, 518, 520, 538, 544, 545, 558; B.D. VII, nos. 128–32, 134, 136; Esher, *Journals and Letters*, II, pp. 355–60.

64 Tyrrell to Grey, 20 November 1908, Grey MSS. F.O. 800/91; B.D. VI, nos. 130, 131, 142. For the *Daily Telegraph* and Hale interviews, see Hale, *Publicity and Diplomacy*, pp. 313–24.

65 B.D. VI, nos. 135, 142; D.D.F. (2) XI, no. 566.

66 B.D. VII, nos. 152, 153, 155, 157, 158; G.P. XXIV, nos. 8485, 8490–2.

67 Grey to Bertie, 24 November 1908, Grey MSS. F.O. 800/49.

68 B.D. VI, no. 143.

69 B.D. V, nos. 350, 373, 386, 410, 411; ed. note pp. 608–9; and no. 567; Hardinge to Springe-Rice, 26 February 1909, Hardinge MSS. 17, fol. 423– .

70 B.D. V, nos. 567, 568, 571–3, 583, 593, 598, 701, 753. See Chapter 9, pp. 187–91.

71 Minutes by Mallet and Hardinge on Nicolson to Grey, tel. no. 168, 24 March 1909, F.O. 371/755; Goschen to Grey, 26 March 1909, Hardinge MSS. 15, fol. 276– ; Hardinge to Edward VII, 26 March 1909, Hardinge MSS. 18, fol. 26– ; Hardinge to Villiers, 1 April 1909; and to Goschen, 6 April 1909, Hardinge MSS. 17, fols. 440– , 182– .

72 Minute by Grey on Rodd to Grey, no. 47, 10 February 1909, F.O. 371/599. See also minute by Grey on Cartwright to Grey, no. 86, 1 August 1908, F.O. 371/399; Hardinge to Bax-Ironside, 28 October 1909, Hardinge MSS. 17, fol. 25– ; and D.D.F. (2) XI, no. 577.

73 B.D. VI, no. 182; H. S. Weinroth, 'The British Radicals and the Balance of Power 1902–1914', *Historical Journal*, XIII (1970).

74 B.D, IX.i, no. 7; Hardinge to Lowther, 18 May 1909, Hardinge MSS. 17, fol. 283– .

75 Hardinge to Nicolson, 25 May 1909, Hardinge MSS. 17, fol. 345– .

76 Hardinge to Bertie, 30 July 1908; to Lowther, 21 September 1908, Hardinge MSS. 13, fols. 88– , 214– ; minute by Hardinge on Memorandum by Parker, 19 September 1908, F.O. 371/538.

77 B.D. VI, nos. 270–2, and ed. note pp. 373–4; Memorandum by Hardinge, 28 May 1909, F.O. 371/762; minute by Mallet on Lowther to Grey, tel. no. 321, 13 September 1909, F.O. 371/764.

78 G.P. XXVII. ii, nos. 9964, 9969, 9972, 9978; B.D. VI, Appendix VI; Grey to Hardinge, 13 August 1909; Hardinge to Goschen, 15 August 1909; Goschen to Grey, 23 August 1909, F.O. 371/763.

79 B.D. VI, nos. 279, 282, and Appendix VII; minute by Hardinge on Marling to Grey, tel. no. 351, 5 November 1909; and minute by Mallet on Goschen to Grey, no. 372, 5 November 1909, F.O. 371/764.

80 McKenna to Asquith, 3 January 1909, Asquith MSS. 21, fol. 22– . On the acceleration crisis, see Woodward, *Great Britain and the German Navy*, pp. 203–64; Marder, *From the Dreadnought to Scapa Flow*, vol. I, pp. 151–75; Gollin, *The Observer and J. L. Garvin*, pp. 64–91; Hale, *Publicity and Diplomacy*, pp. 341–65; Friedrich Haselmayr, *Zehn Jahre Grossflottenbau und seine Auswirkung 1900–1909* (*Diplomatische Geschichte des zweiten Reichs 1871–1918*, vol. V, Munich, 1962), pp. 424–51; Eyck, *Das Persönliche Regiment Wilhelms II*, pp. 519–24.

81 Cabinet letters, Asquith to Edward VII, 19 December 1908; 2 February 1909; 15 February 1909; 24 February 1909; 5 March 1909, Asquith MSS. 5, fols. 75– , 79– , 83– , 86– , 88– ; Lloyd George to Asquith, 2 February 1909; 8 February 1909, Asquith MSS. 21, fol. 61– ; 12, fol. 23– .

82 McKenna to Asquith, 4 March 1909; Grey to Asquith, 4 March 1909, Asquith MSS. 21, fols. 161– , 157– ; A. J. Marder (ed.), *Fear God and Dread Nought: the Correspondence of Lord Fisher of Kilverstone* (London, 1952–9), vol. II, nos. 165–7.

83 *Hansard*, 5th series, II, 930–44, 955–64.

84 Esher, *Journals and Letters*, II, p. 378 and ff.; Gollin, *The Observer and Garvin*, pp. 68–83.

85 *Hansard* (5) III, 52–70; Marder (ed.), *Fear God and Dread Nought*, II, no. 175.

86 *Hansard* (5) VIII, 855–9.

87 B.D. VI, nos. 151–6; G.P. XXVIII, nos. 10249, 10266, 10269, 10271, 10273.

88 B.D. VI, nos. 156, 159; G.P. XXVIII, no. 10275.

89 *Hansard* (5) III, 52–70.

90 Goschen to Hardinge, 25 March 1909; 8 May 1909, Hardinge MSS. 15, fols. 270– , 306; B.D. VI, nos. 174, 179, 183; G.P. XXVIII, nos. 10302–4. 10302–4.

91 B.D. VI, no. 186; G.P. XXVIII, nos. 10323, 10330; also Hardinge to Goschen, 27 July 1909, Hardinge MSS. 17, fol. 202– .

92 Minutes by Spicer and Crowe on Goschen to Grey, no. 131, 8 April 1909, F.O. 371/673; Hardinge to Edward VII, May 1909, Hardinge MSS. 18, fol. 51– ; Hardinge to Goschen, 30 May 1909, Hardinge MSS. 17, fol. 178– .

93 B.D. VI, no. 174.

94 O'Beirne to Grey, tel., 31 August 1909, Grey MSS. F.O. 800/72; Bertie to Grey, private, 7 October 1909, F.O. 371/675; B.D. VI, nos. 186, 187, 190, 191, 193–5, 198, 206.

95 Cabinet letter, Asquith to Edward VII, 1 September 1909, Asquith MSS. 5, fol. 148– . For Grey's telegram and letter transmitting these instructions to Goschen, see B.D. VI, nos. 194, 195.

96 B.D. VI, nos. 200, 201; G.P. XXVIII, no. 10347. The documents on these negotiations printed by the editors of the *British Documents*, vol. VI, chapters XLV–XLVIII, are a full selection to which there is little of substance to be added.

97 B.D. VI, nos. 202, 204; G.P. XXVIII, no. 10355.

98 B.D. V, Appendix III; with minutes by Grey and Asquith, F.O. 371/733; and B.D. VI, pp. 311–12.

99 B.D. VI, no. 204.

100 B.D. VI, no. 344.

101 B.D. VI, nos. 204, 207; Grey to Bryce, 12 December 1909, Grey MSS. F.O. 800/81; and minute by Hardinge on Foreign Office Memorandum, 12 January 1910, F.O. 371/900.

102 B.D. VI, nos. 278, 279, 282; Appendix VII; no. 309; G.P. XXVII.ii, nos. 9985, 9986.

31 December 1909, F.O. 371/765.

104 B.D. VI, nos. 308, 317, 343; G.P. XXVII.ii, nos. 9990, 9993.

105 B.D. VI, nos. 308, 317, 343, 348.

106 B.D. VI, nos. 337, 338.

107 B.D. VI, nos. 324, 342–4, 348; G.P. XXVII.ii, nos. 9995, 9997.

108 B.D. VI, nos. 344, 351, 352, 355, 357, 377, 384, 388; minutes by Parker, Hardinge and Grey on Llewellyn Smith to Hardinge, 4 March 1910; memorandum by Parker, 14 March 1910, F.O. 371/991.

109 G.P. XXVII.ii, nos. 10152, 10155, 10156, 10219, 10223; B.D. X.i, nos. 605, 608, 618, 740, 741.

110 B.D. X.i, nos. 608, 616, 618; minute by Mallet on Buchanan to Grey, tel. no. 332, 10 December 1910, F.O. 371/1016.

111 B.D. X.ii, nos. 14, 15, 22, 26, 30, 34.

112 Memoranda by McKenna, 14 February 1910, and 16 February 1911, Cab. 37/102, no. 2, and Cab. 37/105, no. 12; Cabinet letters, Asquith to Edward VII, 17 February 1910, and Asquith to George V, 1 March 1911, Asquith MSS. 5, fol. 186– , and 6, fol. 13– ; Marder, *Dreadnought to Scapa Flow*, I, pp. 214–21.

113 Cabinet memoranda, 15 July 1910; 17 October 1910; 3 February 1911, Cab. 37/103, nos. 32, 51, and Cab. 37/105, no. 7; Cabinet letter, Asquith to George V, 1 March 1911, Asquith MSS. 6, fol. 13– .

114 *Hansard* (5) XIX, 644–5.

115 *Hansard* (5) XXII, 1977–91.

116 G.P. XXVIII, nos. 10434, 10435.

117 B.D. VI, nos. 336, 337; G.P. XXVIII, nos. 10379, 10382; also Hardinge to Goschen, 26 April 1910, Hardinge MSS. 21, fol. 113; minute by Hardinge on Goschen to Grey, no. 203, 17 July 1910, F.O. 371/900; and B.D. VI, no. 361.

118 Cabinet letters, Asquith to George V, 20 July 1910; 30 July 1910, Asquith MSS. 5, fols. 238– , 240– ; Memorandum circulated to cabinet, 2 August 1910, F.O. 371/900; B.D. VI, nos. 387, 391, 392.

119 B.D. VI, nos. 399–402; G.P. XXVIII, nos. 10416, 10417.

120 B.D. VI, nos. 400, 402, 404, 406, 407, 414, 417, 419–21, 424.

121 B.D. VI, no. 425; G.P. XXVIII, no. 10427.

122 B.D. VI, nos. 427, 428, 431, 433, 436, 449, 454, 455, 457; G.P. XXVIII, no. 10452.

123 Woodward, *Great Britain and the German Navy*, pp. 305–7; Marder, *Dreadnought to Scapa Flow*, I, pp. 230–2.

124 Cabinet letters, Asquith to George V, 20 January 1911; 23 February 1911, Asquith MSS. 6, fols. 1– , 10– ; B.D. VI, nos. 434, 440.

125 Cabinet letter, Asquith to George V, 4 March 1911, Asquith MSS. 6, fol. 15– ; Cabinet memorandum, 4 March 1911, Cab. 37/105, no. 20; with note by Grey, F.O. 371/1123; B.D. VI, nos. 444, 461.

126 B.D. VI, nos. 447, 448, 454.

127 B.D. VI, nos. 454, 462, 464, 466; G.P. XXVIII, no. 10442.

128 Cabinet letter, Asquith to George V, 17 May 1911, Asquith MSS. 6, fol. 37– ; also B.D. VI, no. 468.

12. GREAT BRITAIN AND RUSSIA, 1907–1914

1 S. A. Wolpert, *Morley and India 1906–1910* (Berkeley and Los Angeles, 1967), p. 92; also Morley to Grey, 2 January 1908: Grey MSS. F.O. 800/97. For the Lhasa Convention and the Anglo-Chinese Convention of 1906, see B.D. IV, nos. 298, 305; and Alastair Lamb, *The McMahon Line: a Study in the Relations between India, China and Tibet 1904–1914* (London, 1966), vol, I, pp. 3–15, 32–55.

2 Isvolsky, *Correspondance diplomatique*, II, p. 97; Stephen E. Koss, *John Morley at the India Office 1905–1910* (New Haven, Conn., 1969), pp. 114–17; Wolpert, *Morley and India*, pp. 91–3; Lamb, *The McMahon Line*, vol. I, pp. 141–57; Foreign Office Confidential Print, vol. 9468, nos. 101, 113, 116, 118.

3 Wolpert, *Morley and India*, p. 93; Lamb, *The McMahon Line*, I, pp. 181–225; Ira Klein, 'The Anglo-Russian Convention and the Problem of Central Asia 1907–1914', *Journal of British Studies*, XI, 1971, pp. 133–6.

4 B.D. IV, nos. 473, 476; B. H. Sumner, 'Tsardom and Imperialism in the Far East and Middle East 1880–1914', *Proceedings of the British Academy*, XXVII, 1941, pp. 61–2; R. P. Churchill, *The Anglo-Russian Convention of 1907* (Cedar Rapids, Iowa, 1939), pp. 301–4.

5 Grey to Nicolson, tel., 18 September 1908: Grey MSS. F.O. 800/72.

6 B.D. IV, nos. 514, 515; Isvolsky, *Correspondance diplomatique*, II, p. 162; Koss, *Morley at the India Office*, pp. 114–17; C. Collin Davies, *The Problem of the North-West Frontier 1890–1908* (Cambridge, 1932), pp. 145–52.

7 B.D. IV, no. 515; Grey to Nicolson, tel. no. 497, 14 October 1908: Foreign Office Confidential Print 9465 (F.O.C.P.) no. 40.

8 Minute by Grey on India Office to Foreign Office, 26 August 1908: F.O. 371/516; Wolpert, *Morley and India*, p. 90.

9 F.O.C.P. 9494 nos. 23, 31, 32, 43, 53, 59, 63, 71, 72, 74, 77; F.O.C.P 9629 nos. 16, 27, 36, 72; Nicolson to Hardinge, 9 September 1908; Hardinge to Nicolson, 30 September 1908: Hardinge MSS. vol. 12 fol. 58–, vol. 13 fol. 264–.

10 On British and Russian policy in Persia down to the Convention of August 1907, see R. L. Greaves, 'British Policy in Persia 1892–1903', *Bulletin of the School of Oriental and African Studies*, XXVIII, 1965; Nikki R. Keddie, 'British Policy and the Iranian Opposition 1901–1907', *Journal of Modern History*, XXXIX, 1967; A. K. S. Lambton, 'Secret Societies and the Persian Revolution of 1905–1906', *St Antony's Papers*, IV (London, 1958); Firuz Kazemzadeh, *Russia and Britain in Persia 1864–1914: a Study in Imperialism* (New Haven, Conn., 1968), *passim*, especially pp. 448–501. E. G. Browne, *The Persian Revolution of 1905–1909* (Cambridge, 1910), remains the indispensable account of its subject.

On Anglo-Russian relations in Persia between the Convention and the Shuster affair of 1911, the editors of the *British Documents* have printed very little, presumably because of the extensive coverage in Blue Books (Cd. 4581, 4733, 5120, 5656, 6104, etc.). There is a brief account based on the printed sources, and particularly helpful on German and Russian policy, in Oswald Hauser, *Deutschland und der englisch-russische Gegensatz 1900–1914* (Göttingen, 1958), pp. 111–27; on Russian policy, see also B. H. Sumner, 'Tsardom and Imperialism in the Far East and Middle East 1880–1914', *Proceedings of the British Academy*, XXVII, 1941, pp. 53, 57–65. A fuller account, which makes some use of the fragmentary Russian sources in the *Krasnyi Arkhiv* and occasional use of the F.O. 371 series as well as the Blue Books, is in Kazemzadeh, *Russian and Britain in Persia*, pp. 510–80; A. K. S. Lambton, 'Persian Political Societies 1906–1911', *St Antony's Papers*, XVI (London, 1963), provides an account of British policy derived largely from the Blue Books, which has been criticised by Ira Klein, 'British Intervention in the Persian Revolution 1905–1909', *Historical Journal*, XV, 1972.

11 B. G. Martin, *German–Persian Diplomatic Relations 1873–1912* (The Hague, 1959), pp. 107, 111, 120, 154–8; G. W. Monger, *The End of Isolation: British Foreign Policy 1900–1907* (London, 1963), pp. 288–9, 292–3; Hauser, *Deutschland und der englisch-russische Gegensatz*, pp. 120–3; Jens B. Plass, *England zwischen Deutschland und Russland: der Persische Golf in der britischen Vorkriegspolitik 1899–1907* (Hamburg, 1966), pp. 395–441; Eugene Staley, 'Business and Politics in the Persian Gulf: the Story of the Wönckhaus Firm', *Political Science Quarterly*, XLVIII, 1933; Lamar Cecil, *Albert Ballin: Business and Politics in Imperial Germany 1880–1918* (Princeton, 1967), pp. 79–86; Isvolsky, *Correspondance diplomatique*, II, pp. 104–5; F.O.C.P. 9299 nos. 127, 148, 407, 430, 481, 497, 503.

12 F.O.C.P. 9296 no. 447; F.O.C.P. 9299 nos. 20, 127, 148, 175, 187, 429, 458, 462; F.O.C.P. 9302 nos. 50, 136, 276; *Documents diplomatiques français*, series 2, vol. XI, nos. 151, 280.

13 F.O.C.P. 9299 nos. 380, 382, 383, 399, 406.

14 F.O.C.P. 9299 nos. 410, 424, 425, 427, 428.

15 Lambton, 'Persian Political Societies', *St Antony's Papers*, XVI, p. 61; Isvolsky, *Correspondance diplomatique*, II, pp. 100–1; F.O.C.P. 9299 nos. 430*, 449.

16 F.O.C.P. 9299 nos. 460, 461, 478, 498.

17 F.O.C.P. 9299 nos. 407, 430, 481; minute by Mallet on Marling to Grey, tel. no. 409, 23 December 1907: FO 371/374; Marling to Hardinge, 3 January 1908: Hardinge MSS. II, fol. 285–.

18 F.O.C.P. 9307 no. 88*; B.D. V, no. 195; *Benckendorffs diplomatischer Schriftwechsel*, I, no. 3.

19 F.O.C.P. 9307 nos. 225, 232, 240, 260.

20 O'Beirne to Grey, tel. no. 95, 13 June 1908; F.O.C.P. 9307 no. 280; also F.O.C.P. 9307 no. 273, and Lambton, 'Persian Political Societies', *St Antony's Papers*, XVI, pp. 64–5.

21 F.O.C.P. 9307 nos. 285, 305, 308; Hardinge to O'Beirne, 24 June 1908; Hardinge MSS. 13 fol. 296–; Isvolsky, *Correspondance diplomatique*, II, pp. 166–7.

22 Marling to Grey, tel. no. 159, 27 June 1908: F.O.C.P. 9307 no. 351.

23 F.O.C.P. 9307 nos. 363, 364, 366; Isvolsky, *Correspondance diplomatique*, II, pp. 166–71.

24 F.O.C.P. 9307 no. 371; F.O.C.P. 9416 nos. 12, 13, 24; Cabinet letter, Asquith to Edward VII, 1 July 1908: Asquith MSS., box 5, fol. 40–; O'Beirne to Hardinge, 1 July 1908: Hardinge MSS. 12 fol. 145–.

25 F.O.C.P. 9416 nos. 87, 120, 175.

26 F.O.C.P. 9307 no. 348; F.O.C.P. 9416 no. 466.

27 *Hansard*, 4th series, vol. CXC, 184–5; vol. CXCI, 87–9, 954, 956–7, 1460; vol. CXCII, 63–6, 606–7, 1085–6, 1711–12; vol. CXCIII, 951–4, 976–8, 1755–6; vol. CXCIV, 467–8; Browne, *Persian Revolution*, pp. 251–3; H. S. Weinroth, 'The British Radicals and the Balance of Power 1902–1914', *Historical Journal*, XIII, 1970, pp. 668–70. Hardinge was extremely frank about the embarrassment Grey was caused by having to defend Russian actions in the House of Commons: 'I think we may justly say that the attitude of their *employés* there has been excessively trying to our patience and has rendered extremely difficult the maintenance and justification of our agreement in Parliament and elsewhere. Grey has constantly, during the past year, had to appear in the House of Commons as the advocate of the Russian Government. We have had to suppress the truth, and resort to subterfuge at times, to meet hostile public opinion. This is entirely owing to their lack of control over their officials.' (Hardinge to Nicolson, 28 October 1908: Hardinge MSS. 13 fol. 273–.)

28 Minute by Grey on Marling to Grey, no. 188, 17 July 1908, received 4 August: F.O. 371/577.

29 B.D. V, nos. 364, 372.

30 Isvolsky, *Correspondance diplomatique*, II, pp. 183–5, 188; F.O.C.P. 9465 no. 54.

31 F.O.C.P. 9416 nos. 256, 438, 569; F.O.C.P. 9465 no. 4.

32 Grey to Nicolson, tel. no. 521, 19 October 1908: F.O.C.P. 9465 no. 54; also F.O.C.P. 9465 nos. 38, 47, 48, 50.

33 F.O.C.P. 9465 nos. 55, 69.

34 Minute by Grey on Nicolson to Grey, tel. no. 251, 12 November 1908: F.O. 371/578; and F.O.C.P. 9465 nos. 163, 224, 255, 261.

35 F.O.C.P. 9535 nos. 116, 231, 291, 302, 319, 344, 442*; F.O.C.P. 9540 no. 135; Nicolson to Hardinge, 11 February 1909: Hardinge MSS. 16 fol. 73–; minute by Grey on Nicolson to Grey, tel. no. 113, 3 March 1909: F.O. 371/804; Isvolsky, *Correspondance diplomatique*, II, pp. 197–200, 210–12.

The six points of the programme were: (1) Resignation of the Shah's reactionary advisers; (2) Reintroduction of constitutional government in the following manner: (3) A cabinet to be formed from a list of names acceptable to and supplied by the two legations [which included the pro-Russian Saad ed-Dowleh and the pro-British Naser ul-Mulk]; a council of 'enlightened persons' from different parties to be formed to draft a new electoral law: (4) A general amnesty for all political offences: (5) The date for elections and for the summoning of the *majlis* to be announced immediately: (6) Russia to advance £100,000 to the Persian government as soon as the Shah had complied with points (1) to (5); Britain to make a similar loan once the *majlis* had met and approved it. (F.O.C.P. 9540 no. 161.)

36 F.O.C.P. 9540 nos. 230, 242, 324, 326.

37 For example, F.O.C.P. 9540 nos. 450, 456, 557, 566, 579, 624, 807; Isvolsky, *Correspondance diplomatique*, II, pp. 233–4, 235–6; *Benckendorffs diplomatischer Schriftwechsel*, I, no. 81.

38 Cabinet letter, Asquith to Edward VII, 30 June 1909: Asquith MSS. 5 fol. 128–, and ff.; *Hansard*, 5th series, vol. VI, 447, 804, 806–7, 1523; vol. VII, 1010–12, 1827–39; vol. VIII, 251–3, 1948–9; Grey to O'Beirne, tel. no. 932, 19 July 1909: F.O.C.P. 9552 no. 243.

39 F.O.C.P. 9540 nos. 353, 364, 385, 405, 746.

40 F.O.C.P. 9540 no. 775; F.O.C.P. 9552 nos. 36, 67, 87.

41 F.O.C.P. 9552 nos. 135, 190, 196, 218, 266, 312, 337, 367, 412, 413, 458, 540, 590; F.O.C.P. 9633 no. 146.

42 B.D. IX . i, no. 34.

43 B.D. v, ed. note, pp. 549–50; and B.D. v, Appendix III. For the minutes by Grey and Asquith on Hardinge's memorandum, see the copy dated 4 May 1909 in F.O. 371/733; for the approval of the King, Hardinge MSS. 18 fol. 72–.

Hardinge was under no illusions about the policy Russia was likely to pursue in Persia if, as was feared, Isvolsky should be driven from office and be replaced by a reactionary such as Goremykin, for he assumed that in that event Hartwig would become assistant foreign minister and would promote an active and forward policy. Even so, it is clear that Hardinge thought it would still be in Britain's interest to maintain the understanding in Persia rather than terminate it.

44 On the Swedish–Norwegian guarantee question, the Åland islands, and the *status quo* in the Baltic, see for the French documents *Documents diplomatiques français*, series 2, vol. XI, nos. 23, 42, 45 and ff.; for the German documents *Die Grosse Politik der europäischen Kabinette*, vol. XXIII . ii, nos. 8024–8159; for the British documents, *British Documents on the Origins of the War*, vol. VIII, no. 81 and ff.; and for Russian policy, Taube, *La politique russe d'avant-guerre*, pp. 123–71; and Bompard, *Mon Ambassade en Russie*, pp. 281–3. For a full account of the question, see F. A. Lindberg, *Scandinavia in Great Power Politics 1905–1908* (Stockholm, 1958); and D. W. Sweet, 'The Baltic in British Diplomacy before the First World War', *Historical Journal*, XIII, (1970).

45 G.P. XXIII . ii, no. 8083.

46 B.D. VI, no. 63.

47 G.P. XXIII.ii, no. 8095; Hardinge to Grey, 23 November 1907: Grey MSS. F.O. 800/91; and Grey to Bertie, 29 November 1907: Grey MSS. F.O. 800/49.

48 B.D. VIII, nos. 121, 124, 132, 136, 138; D.D.F. (2) XI, nos. 222, 227, 228; Bompard, *Mon ambassade en Russie*, pp. 282–3; F.O.C.P. 9284 no. 175; Lister to Hardinge, 12 December 1907: Bertie MSS. F.O. 800/177, Rus 07/7 (this letter is the unidentified original referred to in B.D. VIII, no. 134, note 2); Grey to Lister, 16 December 1907; F.O. 371/527; and Grey to Nicolson, 25 December 1907: Grey MSS. F.O. 800/71.

49 A. J. Marder (ed.), *Fear God and Dread Nought: the Correspondence of Lord Fisher of Kilverstone* (London, 1952–9), vol. II, no. 118; B.D. VIII, no. 143; Minute by Hardinge on Vaughan to Grey, tel. no. 7, 4 February 1908: F.O. 371/528; Nicolson to Hardinge, 25 February 1908: Hardinge MSS. 12 fol. 29–.

50 B.D. VIII, nos. 146, 148, 156; F.O.C.P. 9282 no. 203.

51 See Chapter 8, 'Relations with Austria-Hungary and the Balkan States 1905–1908'.

52 Nicolson wrote privately to Hardinge: 'The stars in their courses are drawing him nearer and nearer to us. He sees, I think, clearly that German policy in the Middle East will not work to the advantage of Russian interests, and as he is, for the moment, a little hipped with France, who has been unduly sensitive as to his Baltic and Bagdad Railway *causeries*, he is disposed to lean more on us, and it will be well to encourage him.' (B.D. VIII, appendix II; and also Nicolson to Grey, 12 February 1908: Grey MSS. F.O. 800/72. For Hardinge's response to Nicolson, see B.D. VIII, nos. 137, 139.)

53 B.D. IV, no. 550.

54 See for instance Nicolson to Grey, tel., 18 February 1908: F.O. 371/531: 'He [Isvolsky] desires gradually and without any *éclat* to merge himself in the European Concert, and abandon the special position with Austria.... He is anxious to work with us, France, and if possible Italy; and he thinks this combination, with the Sultan's good will, would be able to accomplish much.' Also Grey's exposition of the concert in Parliament on 25 February 1908 in *Hansard*, 4th series, vol. CLXXXIV, 1692–1708.

55 B.D. VI, nos. 9, 10, 11, 100; B.D. VII, no. 50; B.D. VIII, no. 134; D.D.F. (2) X, no. 472; D.D.F. (2) XI, nos. 17, 44, 372, 434; Lister to Hardinge, 28 May 1908: F.O. 371/455; H. Wickham Steed, *Through Thirty Years 1892–1922* (London, 1924), vol. I, pp. 283–8; Lee, *King Edward VII*, II, pp. 628–31.

56 Grey to Bertie, 30 December 1907: F.O. 371/527; Memorandum by Grey, 28 April 1908, printed in Viscount Grey of Fallodon, *Twenty-five Years 1892–1916* (London, 1925), vol. II, appendix C; Asquith to Grey, 7 September 1908: Grey MSS. F.O. 800/99.

57 D.D.F. (2) X, no. 310; D.D.F. (2) XI, nos. 116, 455.

58 F.O.C.P. 9317 nos. 58, 74; V. N. Kokovtsov, *Out of my Past: the Memoirs of Count Kokovtsov* (Stanford, Calif., 1935), pp. 209–12; minutes by Mallet and Hardinge on O'Beirne to Grey, no. 213, 2 May 1908, received 11 May: F.O. 371/516.

59 B.D. V, nos. 194, 195; *Benckendorffs diplomatischer Schriftwechsel*, I, no. 3; Taube, *La politique russe d'avant-guerre*, pp. 182–7; Lee, *Edward VII*, pp. 590–4.

60 B.D. V, no. 195.

61 Asquith to Grey, 17 June 1908: Grey MSS. F.O. 800/99.

62 *Benckendorffs diplomatischer Schriftwechsel*, I, no. 3; Kokovtsov, *Out of my Past*, pp. 211–12.

63 Taube, *La politique russe d'avant-guerre*, pp. 182–7, quoting also from the journal of A. Polovzev in the *Krasnyi Arkhiv*.

64 B.D. IV, nos. 258, 268, 276; Taube, *La politique russe d'avant-guerre*, p. 140.

65 Minute by Grey on Lowther to Grey, tel no. 218, 7 August 1908: F.O. 371/545.

66 B.D. V, no. 207 Ed. Add.

67 For British policy in the Bosnian crisis, see above Ch. 9, especially pp. 179–81.

68 B.D. v, nos. 372, 379; Hardinge to Bertie, 12 October 1908: Hardinge MSS. 13 fol. 93– ; Balfour to Asquith, 14 October 1908: Asquith MSS. 11 fol. 215– ; Memorandum by J. A. Spender, October 1908: Spender MSS., British Museum Add. MSS. vol. 46391 fol. 278– .

69 Hardinge to Nicolson, 13 October 1908: Hardinge MSS. 13 fol. 269– ; B.D. v, nos. 364, 372; Edward VII to Asquith, 13 October 1908; Knollys to Asquith, 14 October 1908: Asquith MSS. 1 fols. 52– , 54– ; Knollys to Grey, 14 October 1908: Grey MSS. F.O. 800/102; Cabinet letter, Asquith to Edward VII, 14 October 1908: Asquith MSS. 5 fol. 52– ; minute by Hardinge on MacDonald to Grey, tel. no. 76, 21 October 1908: F.O. 371/560.

70 B.D. v, nos. 377, 387.

71 See above, pp. 183–5.

72 B.D. v, no. 441.

73 B.D. III, nos. 210(a), 212, 219, 220; D.D.F. (2) VIII, no. 385; D.D.F. (2) IX.i no. 106. See above, pp. 114–15.

74 B.D. v, nos. 701, 753, 764; B.D. IX.i, no. 6; *Benckendorffs diplomatischer Schriftwechsel*, I, nos. 61–3; Isvolsky, *Correspondance diplomatique*, II, pp. 209, 214–17, 221–5; minute by Mallet on Nicolson to Grey, tel. no. 168, 24 March 1909: F.O. 371/755; Hardinge to Spring-Rice, 25 March 1909; to Villiers, 1 April 1909: Hardinge MSS. 17 fols. 426– , 440– ; Nicolson to Grey, tels., 7 April 1909 and 8 April 1909: Grey MSS. F.O. 800/72; Nicolson to Hardinge, tel., 9 April 1909: F.O. 371/729.

75 B.D. v, Appendix III; with minutes by Grey and Asquith, F.O. 371/733.

76 B.D. v, no. 823.

77 Hardinge to Nicolson, tel., 8 April 1909: F.O. 371/729; B.D. v, nos. 835, 836, 842.

78 B.D. IX.i, nos. 29, 32, 33, 37; *Benckendorffs diplomatischer Schriftwechsel*, I, no. 95.

79 B.D. IX. i, nos. 64, 528; Nicolson to Findlay, 18 October 1910: Nicolson MSS. F.O. 800/344.

80 René Marchand (ed.), *Un livre noir: diplomatie d'avant-guerre d'après les archives russes, Novembre 1910–Juillet 1914* (Paris, 1922–3), vol. I, pp. 357–8; Albertini, *Origins of the War of 1914*, I, pp. 306–11.

81 B.D. IX.i, nos. 70, 73, 74, 109, 112, 116, 131, 136.

82 D.D.F. (3) I, nos. 18, 54, 94, 106, 114, 326; B.D. IX.i, nos. 289, 347, 348, and Appendix IV. IV.

83 Isvolsky, *Correspondance diplomatique*, II, pp. 92–3; *Benckendorffs diplomatischer Schriftwechsel*, I, no. 2; J. B. Wolf, 'The Diplomatic History of the Bagdad Railroad', *University of Missouri Studies*, XI, 1936, pp. 72–4.

84 B.D. v, nos. 192, 195; B.D. VI, nos. 254, 259; *Benckendorffs diplomatischer Schriftwechsel*, I, nos. 4, 5.

85 *Benckendorffs diplomatischer Schriftwechsel*, I, nos. 121, 124; B.D. VI, nos. 288, 290, 292, 294, 301, 302.

86 *Benckendorffs diplomatischer Schriftwechsel*, I, nos. 129, 141; B.D. VI, nos. 297, 298, 310.

87 G.P. XXVII.ii, nos. 10152, 10155, 10156 and ff.; *Un livre noir*, II, pp. 331–4; *Benckendorffs diplomatischer Schriftwechsel*, I, nos. 308, 312, 315, 316; B.D. X.i, nos. 605, 607, 608; Wolf, 'Diplomatic History of the Bagdad Railroad', *University of Missouri Studies*, XI, pp. 84–7.

88 B.D. X.i, nos. 596, 597, 599, 601, 603, 604, 605, 606, 617, 618, 629.

89 G.P. XXVII.ii, no. 10141; *Benckendorffs diplomatischer Schriftwechsel*, I, no. 294.

90 Grey to Barclay, tel. no. 453, 1 September 1909: F.O.C.P. 9552 no. 554; Grey to Barclay no. 283, 28 September 1910: F.O. 371/964.

91 B.D. IX.i, no. 34; F.O.C.P. 9552 nos. 496, 507, 622; F.O.C.P. 9633 nos. 47, 148, 162, 248 and ff.; Marling to Grey, no. 117, 4 July 1910: F.O. 371/962; Grey to Barclay, no. 174, 15 October 1910: F.O. 371/964; Kazemzadeh, *Russia and Britain in Persia*, p. 551 ff.

92 B.D. x.i, nos. 771, 775, 777, 778, 791. For the Shuster and Stokes episodes, see W. Morgan Shuster, *The Strangling of Persia: a Personal Narrative* (New York, 1912); and Kazemzadeh, *Russia and Britain in Persia*, pp. 581–645.

93 B.D. x.i, nos. 802, 808, 815, 824.

94 B.D. x.i, nos. 785–9, 792–7, 806, 823–5.

95 B.D. x.i, nos. 828, 833, 842, 846, 849, 851, 854, 856, 860, 862, 865, 868, 871.

96 B.D. x.i, nos. 885, 887, 898, 901.

97 B.D. x.i, nos. 890, 908.

98 For Barclay's lament, see Harold Nicolson, *Sir Arthur Nicolson, Bart., First Lord Carnock: a Study in the Old Diplomacy* (London, 1930), p. 356. Grey summarised the position as follows: 'It was no part of the Anglo-Russian agreement to destroy Russian influence or to extend our responsibilities to protect Persia. I would never have been a party to committing this country to extension of responsibility in that direction...For us to have supported the Persians against the Russians would have been contrary to the whole spirit of the Anglo-Russian agreement and would have been perfectly futile unless we had been prepared to make war upon Russia in Europe...Since the Anglo-Russian agreement was made (it does not apply only to Persia) the Russians have scrupulously abstained from doing anything prejudicial to the security of our Indian frontier. If the agreement is to be declared at an end we must prepare to put the defence of our Indian frontier on a war footing and sooner or later there must be war between Russia and ourselves over these Asiatic questions.' (B.D. x.i, no. 914.)

99 Grey to Hardinge, 28 January 1912: Grey MSS. F.O. 800/93.

100 See Memoranda 1, 2 and 3 by Sir Edward Grey, 24/25 September 1912, printed as no. 538 in F.O.C.P. 10167, Affairs of Persia, Part XXXI, July–September 1912.

101 Sir Valentine Chirol to Hardinge, 23 May 1912, Hardinge Papers, vol. 71, 187.

102 'But, with the end of the Balkan Crisis it was very desirable that a fresh start under more satisfactory conditions should be made in regard to those Asiatic questions which demanded cooperation between GB and Russia.' Sir William Tyrell, as reported by Sir Valentine Chirol, Chirol to Hardinge, 23 May 1913, Hardinge Papers, vol. 71, 187. Memorandum by Buchanan, 19 May 1913, F.O. 371/1745/24413.

103 Nicolson to Hardinge, 2 July 1912, Hardinge Papers, vol. 71, 148. Chirol to Hardinge, 4 July 1913, Hardinge Papers, vol. 71, 157.

104 Tyrell to Spring-Rice, 30 July 1913, F.O. 800, 241, p. 350.

105 See, for example, Nicolson to Goschen, 10 February 1914, F.O. 800, 372, p. 174.

106 Buchanan to Nicolson, 21 January 1914, F.O. 800, 372, p. 20. Hardinge to Nicolson, 5 February 1914, F.O. 800, 372, p. 214.

107 Nicolson to Buchanan, 24 March 1914, F.O. 800, 373, p. 31. Minute by Crowe, 21 March 1914, on Townley to Grey, 20 March 1914, F.O. 371/2066/12446.

108 Minute by Crowe, 2 June 1914, on Townley to Grey, 13 May 1914, F.O. 371/2059/24443.

109 Memorandum by Crowe, 3 June 1914, and Minute by Grey, 5 June 1914, F.O. 371/2076/25918.

110 Minute by Crowe, 8 June 1914, on India Office inquiry, 5 June 1914, F.O. 371/2060/25231.

111 Grey to Buchanan, 10 June 1914, B.D. x, ii, 547, and note 4, p. 798.

112 Buchanan to Grey, 11 July 1914, B.D. x, ii, 561.

113 Nicolson to de Bunsen, 20 July 1914, F.O. 800, 375, p. 118.

114 Churchill to Grey, 7 July 1914, B.D. x, ii, 559.

115 Buchanan to Grey, 25 June 1914, B.D. x, ii, 556. The evidence for this burst of naval negotiations is in B.D. x, ii, nos. 537–43.

13. THE BALKANS, 1909–1914

1 M. B. Cooper, 'British Policy in the Balkans, 1908–1909', *The Historical Journal*, vol. 7, no. 2, 1964, pp. 258–79, see pp. 275–7.

2 See Lindlay to Grey, 90 confidential, 27 September 1909, F.O. 371/606.

3 See Lindlay to Grey, 89 Confidential, 28 September 1909, *ibid.*

4 F. R. Bridge, *Great Britain and Austria-Hungary 1906–1914. A Diplomatic History* (London, 1972), p. 146.

5 Grey to Lindlay, tel. 130, 15 October 1909, F.O. 371/606. Hardinge's draft had merely said, 'the development of business relations between the two countries would be regarded with great satisfaction by H.M.G.'.

6 See file 17250, F.O. 371/605.

7 Minute by Grey on document 45468, from the file of the same number, F.O. 371/694.

8 In 1909 the Foreign Office still refused to believe there was any military agreement between Austria and Rumania. See minute by Mallet on document 38382 from file of the same number, F.O. 371/724.

9 See file 40639, F.O. 371/913 and for 1911 file 1928, F.O. 371/1129.

10 See Annual Report for 1909, Turkey, p. 25.

11 Minute by Grey on Cartwright to Grey, tel. 36, 3 May 1911, F.O. 371/1130.

12 Bridge, *op. cit.* pp. 1–4, 170–2.

13 Minute by Grey on Cartwright to Grey, 205 confidential, 5 December 1911, F.O. 371/1054.

14 See Grey to Elliot, Private, 7 June 1910, Grey MSS. F.O. 800/63.

15 Grey to Bertie, Private, 17 June 1910, Grey MSS. F.O. 800/52.

16 See Bridge, *op. cit.* p. 156.

17 Luigi Albertini, *The Origins of the War of 1914*, vol. I, p. 342.

18 Montenegro had already offered Italy aid at the outbreak of hostilities (E. C. Helmreich, 'Montenegro and the Foundation of the Balkan League', *The Slavonic and East European Review*, vol. 15, pp. 426–34, see p. 429). In Paris Isvolsky was certainly intriguing with the Serbian and Bulgarian representatives, both of whom were influential in their capitals. See F. Stieve (Ed.), *Im Dunkel der europäischen Geheimdiplomatie* (Berlin 1926), pp. 171–5.

19 B.D. IX, i, 547, p. 540.

20 Grey to Bertie, 53 confidential, 3 February 1912, F.O. 371/1490.

31 B.D. IX, i, 537, pp. 527–8. Grey consistently over-estimated the dependence of Vienna upon Berlin.

22 *Ibid.*

23 For the text of the Serbo-Bulgarian treaty, see B.D. IX, i, pp. 781–2. For the formation of the Balkan League see, E. C. Thaden, *Russia and the Balkan Alliance of 1912* (Pennsylvania State University Press, 1965); I. E. Geshev, *The Balkan league* (London 1915); E. C. Helmreich, *The Diplomacy of the Balkan Wars 1912–13* (Cambridge, Mass., 1938), chapters 1 to 4; Otto Bickel, *Russland und die Entstehung des Balkanbundes 1912* (Berlin and Königsberg, 1933). For the part played in the *of the Times*, vol. III (London, 1947), pp. 610–13, and Lady Ellinor Grogan, *Life of J. D. Bourchier* (London, n.d.), chapter 12. Another intriguer appears to have been the United States Minister in Athens, Mr Moses; see Quadt to Auswärtiges Amt, tel. 238, 25 June 1913, G.F.M. 6/103.

24 Bax-Ironside had reported that 'the two contracting parties should jointly resist any advance of a third power into the territories at present under the dominion of Turkey' whereas Benckendorff revealed that the two Balkan states had 'engaged to come to the aid of each other if either were attacked by a third power', a much more vague and dangerous wording when border incidents between these states and Turkey were a frequent occurrence. (See Nicolson to Grey, very confidential,

6 April 1912, B.D. IX, ii, appendix II.) Little more than a week later French sources informed London that the treaty provided for a division of Macedonia, a fact which the Foreign Office had not realised (Minute by Nicolson on above document).

25 Minute by Grey, 15 April 1912, F.O. 371/1493.

26 For the Albanian revolt see, Stavro Skendi, *The Albanian National Awakening, 1878–1912* (Princeton, 1967), pp. 428–31; J. Swire, *Albania, the Rise of a Kingdom* (London, 1929), pp. 100–26; M. Edith Durham, *The Struggle for Scutari* (London, 1914), pp. 122–58.

27 Feroz Ahmad, *The Young Turks; the Committee of Union and Progress in Turkish Politics, 1908–1914* (Oxford, 1969), pp. 106–9. Bernard Lewis, *The Emergence of Modern Turkey* (London, 1968), pp. 223–4.

28 Slobodan Jovanović, *Moji Savremenitsi* (Windsor, Ontario, 1962), p. 161.

29 B.D. IX, i, 585, pp. 582–3; 589, pp. 585–7.

30 The history of the Turkish–Montenegrin frontier dispute is outlined in a report of the British Minister in Cettinje, Count de Salis, to Grey, 29, 10 August 1912., F.O. 371/1497.

31 Serbia and Turkey bought horses in Hungary, the Skupshtina voted extra supplies and the Bulgarians fished for a loan in Paris. See 'A Diplomatist' (George Young) *Nationalism and the War in the Near East* (Oxford, 1915), p. 185. In September Lloyds Bank were approached by the Serbian government with a request for help in the immediate purchase of 75,000,000 cartridges (Minute by C. W. Lister, 16 September 1912, F.O. 371/1472).

32 See Barclay to Grey, tel. 32 confidential, 30 August 1912, *ibid.* It was known in Berlin that the King of Montenegro was urging this course of action upon his allies, see G.P. 33, 12107.

33 Bertie reported that he saw the Italian Ambassador in Paris, Tittoni, 'grinning and chattering with the Greek Minister like a barrel organ monkey delighted at the prospect of coming trouble helping the lame Italians over the stile'. Bertie to Grey, private, 3 October 1912, Grey MSS. F.O. 800/53. Until the signing of the Treaty of Lausanne on 17 October Italy remained outside the Concert.

34 On 13 August Berchtold suggested the Powers advise the Porte to continue its decentralising policy in Albania and urge the Balkan states to afford the Turkish Cabinet the peace and time it needed to work out and apply this policy. (Bittner *et al.* (eds), *Österreich-Ungarns Aussenpolitik von der Bosnischen Krise 1908 bis zum Kriegsausbruch 1914*, IV, 3687.) A second Austrian proposal was put forward on 29 August suggesting that the Powers request the Porte to allow the Christian races of the Empire full and fair participation in the forthcoming elections. *Ibid.* 3744.

35 Fears that diplomatic pressure might disturb the Ottoman Cabinet were legitimate. Ghazi's government was not secure against the extreme nationalists and should he show signs of bending to the dictates of the Powers the Young Turks could easily mobilise these elements against the regime.

36 B.D. IX, i, 641, pp. 629–30, and minute by Grey on 660, p. 645.

37 '...if we join in pressing Turkey...our negotiation regarding the Persian Gulf will be jeopardised' Parker noted, *Ibid.* 671, p. 655.

38 These moves were plentiful but ineffective. On 17 September Sazonov proposed urging the Turks to institute real reforms; Poincaré's '*Projet d'Accord*' put forward on 22 September, was a more substantial scheme, even mentioning a naval demonstration; finally a joint Austro-Russian note was presented, on behalf of all the Powers, to the Porte and the Balkan states on 8 October, insisting that no changes in the territorial *status quo* could be tolerated. For details see B.D. IX, i, chapter 77.

39 *Ibid.* 741, pp. 748–9; 745, p. 714.

40 *Ibid.* 781, p. 734. See also Nicolson to Granville, 250, 9 October 1912, F.O. 244/781.

41 For the military events see Colonel Reginald Rankin, *The Inner History of the Balkan*

War (New York, n.d.), and A. Toshev, *Balkanskite Voini*, 2 vols. (Sofia, 1929 and 1931).

42 The Admiralty wished to be ready to counter any gains Italy might make in the region. See below, pp. 265–6.

43 Kitchener to Grey, private, 3 November 1912, Grey MSS. F.O. 800/48. For Grey's reply see *ibid.*, letter of 4 November.

44 Grey to Buchanan, tel. 1176 secret, 5 November 1912, F.O. 371/1504.

45 See Grey to Goschen, 187 secret, 8 August 1912, F.O. 371/1377, and Goschen to Grey, 388, 30 August 1912, F.O. 371/1378.

46 Granville to Grey, 454, very confidential, 19 October 1912, F.O. 371/1371.

47 The first approach seems to have come from London if it can be assumed that Tyrrell's famous conversation with Kühlmann on 7 October (G.P. 33, 12284) was instigated by Grey, and although the record is silent on this point the evidence available suggests that Grey did know of Tyrrell's intentions. Important meetings between Grey and Kühlmann followed later in the month; on 25 October they exchanged views and information upon the Balkan crisis and Kühlmann carried out instructions to express a readiness 'pari-passu mit England in der Balkanfrage vorzugehen'. (*Ibid.* 12285.) Grey was ready to co-operate and accepted the German conditions that all conversations be held in secret and that only when agreement had been reached an approach be made to the other Powers. (*Ibid.* 12295, B.D. IX, ii, 62, pp. 49–51.)

48 See his private letter to Hardinge, 21 November 1912, Hardinge MSS. vol. 70.

49 Nicolson to Grey, private, 30 November 1912, Grey MSS. F.O. 800/94.

50 Grey insisted that he had 'stuck to this as a text'. B.D. IX, ii, 82, p. 69.

51 For details of discussions on this point see B.D. IX, ii, documents listed in index under heading 'Servian aims and ambitions', p. 1175.

52 *Ibid.* 251, p. 187.

53 *Ibid.* 297, p. 222; G.P. 33, 12247. Grey's suggestions were made to Lichnowsky and the extent of the improvement in Anglo-German relations may be gauged from Grey's assurance to the German Ambassador that he would not press his suggestion for ambassadorial meetings unless he could be sure of German support. *Ibid.*

54 See M. B. Cooper, *op. cit.* p. 268.

55 Grey to Bax-Ironside, private, 7 November 1912, Grey MSS. F.O. 800/43.

56 B.D. IX, ii, 297, p. 222.

57 Although he could not himself suggest London Grey was unwise to mention Paris. As he should have foreseen, especially as Germany had recently complained bitterly about the activities of Isvolsky in Paris and Hartvig in Belgrade, Germany and Austria refused to contemplate discussions in which Isvolsky presented the Russian case. *Ibid.* 175, pp. 131–2; G.P. 33, 12343.

58 Discussions were to be informal and secret, without the keeping of minutes. Statements were to be issued to the press when agreement on specific issues had been reached. B.D. IX, ii, 387, p. 290.

59 Though technically incorrect the term 'conference' has been found convenient by most commentators and historians; it will be used here with the appropriate qualifying adjective 'ambassadorial' or 'ambassadors''.

60 On 3 December the Bulgarians and Serbs had signed an armistice with the Turks; the Montenegrins also ceased military operations but the Greeks, though they took part in the peace negotiations, did not sign as they wished to continue the siege of Janina and the blockade of the Ottoman coast. The protocols of the St James Conference are published in B.D. IX, ii, pp. 1026–63.

61 *Ibid.* 297, p. 222; 307, p. 230; 310, pp. 231–2.

62 *Ibid.* 391, pp. 292–3. Albania, it was agreed, was to be autonomous under the sovereignty or suzerainty of the Sultan; it was to be neutral and under the guarantee of the Powers. No decision was reached with regard to its future government and

all that could be agreed about its frontiers was that the new state should adjoin Montenegro in the North and Greece in the South. The latter agreement disposed of the once vexed question of a Serbian port, though it was decided that commercial access to the Adriatic should be afforded by the construction of an international railway to a free and neutral port.

63 *Ibid.* 176, pp. 133–6; 312, p. 233; 407, pp. 308–9.
64 Grey hoped that 'something in the nature of a satisfactory commercial treaty' could be secured in return for Britain's agreement to the abolition of the Capitulations in territory to be ceded by Turkey (Grey to Goschen, 31, 24 January 1913, F.O. 371/1758) and he admitted a desire 'to minimise the barriers to trade that may be raised by the transfer of territory from low tariff Turkey to potentially high tariff states...' (Grey to Goschen, private, 25 December 1912, Grey MSS. F.O. 800/62. For details of the financial discussions, which were eventually transferred to an abortive conference in Paris, see file 249 in F.O. 371/1774.)
65 Grey to Goschen, 57, 10 February 1913, F.O. 371/1758.
66 B.D. IX, ii, 429, p. 326.
67 *Ibid.* 395, p. 296; 399, p. 299; 414, p. 315.
68 *Ibid.* 443, p. 348.
69 *Ibid.* 426, pp. 322–4.
70 With encouragement from London, the Wilhelmstrasse had, for example, persuaded Berchtold to agree to the inclusion of Dibra in Serbia. (*Ibid.* 633, p. 513; G.P. 34, i, 12862.)
71 Goschen to Grey, tel. 2, 2 January 1913, F.O. 371/1757.
72 The Rumanians had remained neutral in the Balkan war and felt that as this policy had followed from the Powers' original insistance that the *status quo* was not to be disturbed, her good conduct had earned some reward, a reward which would also compensate for the increase in territory the war was bringing to her neighbours. Her demands, which the Sofia government resisted, centred upon a rectification of the Bulgaro-Rumanian border along a line from Silistria to Baltchik. See Helmreich, *op. cit.* pp. 269–78, 300–7.
73 *Ibid.* p. 301; G.P. 34, I, 12810. Grey to Goschen, 40, 27 January 1913, F.O. 371/1767.
74 See minutes on Grey to Goschen, tel. 31 confidential, 9 Februrary 1913, *ibid.*
75 See Helmreich, *op. cit.* 300–7. For the St Petersburg Protocol, see B.D. IX, ii, 970, pp. 787–8.
76 B.D. IX, ii, 470, pp. 375–6.
77 Buchanan to Grey, tel. 104, 20 March 1913, F.O. 371/1770.
78 Grey to Goschen, 120, 12 April 1913, *ibid.*
79 Rumours as to impending military operations by Austria had been numerous, though never fully substantiated. See, for example, Asquith's brief note to Grey on 14 March: 'Harry Lawson has just been here to tell me that he hears from the German Embassy that the Austrian army is under orders to start by signal tomorrow.' Grey MSS. F.O. 800/100.
80 See B.D. IX, ii, 735, footnote 4, p. 603.
81 Grey told the Cabinet that the 'present attitude of France is difficult to understand and still more difficult to defend'. CAB 41/31, paper 12, 3 April 1913.
82 *Ibid.*
83 See Grey to Bertie, private and confidential, 4 April 1913, Grey MSS. F.O. 800/54. The French had suggested that the policing of Montenegro be left to Britain and Austria alone, a suggestion which Grey thought 'deplorable'. (*Ibid.* For the French suggestion see Bertie to Grey, private and very confidential, 2 April 1913.)
84 B.D. IX, ii, 946, pp. 765–6.
85 On 8 April the Montenegrin delegate to the St James Conference, Popović, had informed Nicolson that the siege was continuing only because Cettinje could not find the money Essad was asking for its surrender. When questioned if Essad had

himself asked to be bribed, 'Popović said not quite so crudely – but he had said he had left a valise with £80,000 in it behind him before he had entered Scutari, and it would be to the advantage of everyone if it could be found and restored to him.' Memorandum by Nicolson, 8 April 1913, F.O. 371/1770.

86 CAB 41/34, paper 15, 23 April 1913.

87 G.P. 34, II, 13206.

88 CAB 41/34, paper 15, 23 April 1913. Nicolson to Grey, private, 23 April 1913, Grey MSS. F.O. 800/94.

89 CAB 41/34, paper 16, 30 April 1913.

90 The correspondence between the Foreign Office and Boulton Bros of Old Broad St is in F.O. 371/1810.

91 *Ibid.* for Grey's letter to Boulton Bros, 30 April 1913.

92 Helmreich, *op. cit.* pp. 324–5.

93 Even on 3 May Grey had feared that action by Austria was imminent. See his private letter to Bertie of that date, Grey MSS. F.O. 800/54.

94 This document appears as B.D. IX. ii, 920, pp. 745–6, but the passage in italics was excluded from the final draft and was not printed by Gooch and Temperley.

95 Grey to Bertie, 292, 28 April 1913, F.O. 371/1771.

96 Helmreich, *op. cit.* pp. 330–2.

97 CAB 41/34, paper 18, 4 June 1913.

98 *Ibid.*

99 Even before the opening of the St James conference Venizelos, the Greek Premier, had admitted that his main purpose in coming to London was to seek an agreement with Bulgaria rather than with Turkey. Elliot to Grey, tel. 126, 7 December 1912, F.O. 371/1516.

100 Nicolson to Grey, 18 April 1913, Grey MSS. F.O. 800/94.

101 Grey told the Cabinet 'there is every hope that the Great Powers will continue to act in harmony'. CAB 41/34, paper 24, 2 July 1913.

102 *Ibid.* paper 25, 9 July 1913.

103 See Nicolson's agitated minute on Carnegie to Mallet, private, 3 July 1913, F.O. 371/1837. Britain's obligations were vague in that an integral part of the Convention required Turkey to introduce reforms into her Asiatic provinces, and this she had failed to do.

104 B.D. IX, ii, 1175, pp. 933–4. Grey's intention was that Germany should propose this alternative to Russia.

105 Grey to Bertie, private, 31 July 1913, Grey MSS. F.O. 800/54.

106 For the Russian suggestion see, F. Stieve (Ed.), *Schriftwechsel Iswolskis* (Berlin, 1928–31), vol. III, nos. 1000, 1017.

107 For these negotiations see chapter 7, pp. 152–6.

108 Grey to Marling, tel. 409, 18 August 1913, F.O. 371/1837; for Marling's suggestion see his tel. 407 to Grey, 15 August 1913, *ibid.*

109 On 31 July he had written privately to Bertie that he was 'not very sanguine of getting the Turks out of Adrianople by bargaining and diplomatic pressure' and beyond these means he was not prepared to go. Grey MSS. F.O. 800/54. On 15 August he noted: 'We have said enough for the moment and may wait to see what someone else proposes.' Minute on Granville to Grey, tel. 134, F.O. 371/1837.

110 See chapter 7, pp. 162–4.

111 The Turks had made the same offer in 1911, see chapter 16, p. 315. For details of the 1913 offer see file 27117, F.O. 371/1826.

112 Undated memorandum by Mallet, paper 28098, misfiled by Foreign Office, see F.O. 371/1827. Asquith had no faith in the durability of the Ottoman Empire, but accepted its preservation as a short-term policy. CAB 41/31 Paper 25, 9 July 1913.

113 B.D. IX, ii, 1206, pp. 958–9; 1207, p. 959. For Grey's eventual statement to the Commons see Hansard, 5th series, vol. LVI, 2282 et seq., 12 August 1913.

114 B.D. IX, ii, 1206, pp. 958–9. A commission had already been set up to determine the details of the northern frontier. *Ibid.* 1002, pp. 814–16; 1120, pp. 892–4.

115 *Ibid.* 1186, pp. 941–3.

116 See chapter 00, pp. 000–00. The details of the Italian occupation are in a report from the British Military Attaché in Rome, Colonel Granet, see Dering to Grey, 127, 26 May 1912, F.O. 371/1383.

117 For example the customs were being collected by Italian officials and the Turkish regie had been replaced by the Italian tobacco monopoly. Lowther to Grey, tel. 177, 27 May 1912, F.O. 371/1535.

118 See correspondence between the Foreign Office and the Admiralty, *ibid.*

119 Memorandum from Admiralty to Foreign Office, B.D. IX, i, 430, pp. 413–16.

120 *Ibid.*

121 *Ibid.* 466, pp. 438–442.

122 *Ibid.* 439, pp. 420–1.

123 For details of the Greek campaign in the Aegean see F.O. 371/1521 for 1912, and F.O. 371/1759 for 1913.

124 For details see F.O. 371/1531 and 1532. See chapter 00, pp. 000–00.

125 Grey to Elliot, 65, 18 October 1912, F.O. 371/1502. The Board of Trade writing to the Foreign Office on 22 October estimated that a second closure of the Straits would involve British firms in the loss of between five and six million pounds. *Ibid.*

126 See minute on Bax-Ironside to Grey, tel. 86 very confidential, 19 October 1912, F.O. 371/1501.

127 See memorandum by Nicolson, 14 November 1912, F.O. 371/1521.

128 Nicolson to Grey, private, 27 October 1912, Grey MSS. F.O. 800/94.

129 Minute by Grey on Admiralty to Foreign Office, 11 December 1912, F.O. 371/1508.

130 B.D. IX, ii, 207, p. 158.

131 See minute by Nicolson on Elliot to Grey, 216, 25 December 1912. F.O. 371/1381. Nicolson was also anxious lest Turkey take offence at Britain's support for Greece in the Aegean, see Nicolson to Lowther, private, 8 January 1913, Lowther MSS. F.O. 800/193A. On 18 December the ambassadors had agreed that all the Islands should be neutralised. B.D. IX, ii, 394, pp. 295–6.

132 Grey to Bertie, private, 29 May 1913, Grey MSS. F.O. 800/54.

133 See Rodd to Grey, private, 20 January 1913, Grey MSS. F.O. 800/64.

134 B.D. IX, ii, 465, pp. 372–3.

135 *Ibid.* 966, pp. 780–2; 974, p. 791; 976, p. 794.

136 *Ibid.* 963, pp. 778–9.

137 See B.D. X, i, chapter 84, part 1.

138 *Ibid.* ed. note, p. 66. When the Powers had agreed to establish a southern boundary commission Austria had insisted that its work be finished by 30 November, and that all Greek troops leave areas assigned to Albania one month later. (B.D. IX, ii, 1226, pp. 975–7.) By late October it was obvious that the commission's task would not be completed by 30 November, but the Austro-Italian démarche indicated that the two Powers would still insist upon a Greek withdrawal by the last day of 1913.

139 It had always been accepted that these two islands near the mouth of the Dardanelles would revert to Turkey.

140 The full text of the note is in B.D. X, i, 91, pp. 76–7.

141 Elliot to Grey, tel. 197, 14 November 1913, F.O. 371/1848.

142 B.D. X, i, 151, pp. 136–7; 152, pp. 138–9; 168, p. 153. See also Giovanni Giolitti, *Memoirs of my Life* (London, 1923), pp. 374–5.

143 Grey to Nicolson, private, Fallodon, 7 October 1913, F.O. 371/1764.

144 Granville to Nicolson, private, 3 October 1913, *ibid.*

145 B.D. X, i, 81, p. 67.

146 *Ibid.* 102, p. 86.

147 *Ibid.*

148 *Ibid.* 103, pp. 87–8.
149 Minute by Nicolson, *ibid.* 223, pp. 211–13.
150 *Ibid.* 133, pp. 116–17.
151 *Ibid.* 123, pp. 108–10; 124, pp. 110–11.
152 *Ibid.* 76, p. 64. Also F.O. 371/1807.
153 B.D. x, i, 73, pp. 61–2. The point was not insignificant, for the appointment to the Commission of Mufid Bey, Foreign Minister in the Albanian Provisional Government established at Valona in 1912, implied that the Powers recognised this government although its authority did not extend beyond the Valona region, and this antagonised the other local leaders who were not consulted. G.P. 36, 1, 14059, 14060.
154 Grey to Kühlmann, 15 December 1913, F.O. 371/1845. For details of the long discussions on the Albanian bank, see F.O. 371/1885, 1886, and, for useful detail, G.F.M. 14/3.
155 He would not do anything, however, before full consultation with the Entente and 'fair warning to the other Powers'. Memorandum by Crowe, 27 October 1913, F.O. 371/1832.
156 B.D. x, i, 100, pp. 84–5, minute by Crowe.
157 *Ibid.* minute by Grey.
158 *Ibid.* 260, pp. 241–2.
159 Minute by Grey, Lamb (British delegate to the Commission of Control), to Grey, tel. 107, 25 May 1914, F.O. 371/1894.
160 Minute by Grey on note by Crowe, 29 May 1914, F.O. 371/1895.
161 Minute by Crowe, *ibid.*
162 See chapter oo, pp. ooo–oo.
163 Armstrong and Vickers made up the consortium. For details see file 48901, F.O. 371/1846.
164 Djemal Pasha, *Memoirs of a Turkish Statesman* (London, 1922), p. 95.
165 Foreign Office memorandum, dated 7 March 1914, F.O. 371/2123.
166 Buchanan to the King, 25 December 1913, copy in F.O. 371/2111. The danger from the Russian point of view was that the vessels purchased by Turkey had been built for other governments who could not meet the bill or did not wish to take delivery of the ships, which would thus be available in late 1914 and early 1915 respectively. Djemal Pasha, *loc. cit.*
167 Benckendorff to the Foreign Office, secret, 21 May 1914, F.O. 371/2114. See also, William A. Renzi, 'Great Britain, Russia and the Straits 1914–1915', *The Journal of Modern History*, 42, no. 1 (March 1970), pp. 1–20.
168 Minute by Nicolson, on Benckendorff to Foreign Office, secret, 21 May 1914, F.O. 371/2114.
169 See the debate on the possible ending of the mission in 1912, files 1330 and 3870, F.O. 371/1487.

14. BRITISH POLICY DURING THE AGADIR CRISIS OF 1911

1 I. C. Barlow, *The Agadir Crisis* (Durham, N.C., 1942), pp. 168–171, 178–9.
2 Minute by Grey on Nicolson to Grey, 4 April 1911, F.O. 371/1154, Nicolson to Buchanan, 26 April 1911, Nicolson MSS. F.O. 800/348.
3 *British Documents on the Origins of the War, 1898–1914*, Ed. by G. P. Gooch and H. Temperley, vol. VII, nos. 269 and 275 (hereafter B.D.), minute by Grey on Bertie to Grey, tel. 55, 7 May 1911, F.O. 371/1159. He did, however, remind Metternich on 18 May of British obligations to France in Morocco.
4 See E. W. Edwards, 'The Franco-German Agreement on Morocco, 1909', *The English Historical Review*, July 1963, pp. 483–513.
5 See Barlow, pp. 104–67 for a full account of these developments.
6 Jacques Willequet, 'Anglo-German Rivalry in Belgian and Portuguese Africa', in

Britain and Germany in Africa, edited by Prosser Gifford and W. R. Louis (New Haven, Conn., 1967), p. 257.

7 Joanne Stafford Mortimer, 'Commercial Interests and German diplomacy in the Agadir Crisis', *The Historical Journal*, x, 4 (1967), pp. 441–5.

8 Bertie to Nicolson, 21 June 1911, Bertie MSS. F.O. 800/179.

9 Barlow, *The Agadir Crisis*, pp. 203–5.

10 B.D. VII, 277 and 314.

11 *Documents Diplomatiques Français* (hereafter D.D.F.), 2e serie, vol. XIII, no. 364.

12 Barlow, *op. cit.* pp. 214–16.

13 *Ibid.* 220–225; 230–231; J. C. G. Röhl, 'Admiral von Müller and the Approach of War 1911–1914', *Historical Journal*, XII, 4 (1969), p. 652; Mortimer, *op. cit.* pp. 447–9, 450.

14 Fritz Fischer, *Germany's Aims in the First World War* (London, 1967), p. 24.

15 Willequet, *op. cit.* p. 258.

16 Minute by Crowe, 1 July 1911, F.O. 371/1163. B.D. VII, 343 and 344.

17 Asquith to the King, 4 July 1911, Cabinet MSS. CAB 41/33/20. B.D. VII, 347.

18 Grey told Cambon on 3 July that he was 'considering' whether or not to send a ship to Agadir. Lady Helen Ferguson heard that he had decided against it, which had upset Nicolson. Lloyd George claimed the credit later for stopping Grey from sending a ship, but there is little evidence that the latter was at any time eager to do so. B.D. VII, 351; Lady Helen Ferguson to Hardinge, 12 July 1911, Hardinge MSS. vol. I, part I, 1911; Memorandum by C. P. Scott, 22 July 1911, Scott MSS. no. 50901.

19 B.D. VII, 355. Both Grey and Asquith mentioned Tangier later as possible compensation for Great Britain if Germany secured a foothold in Morocco. B.D. VII, 434; Memorandum by C. P. Scott, 22 July 1911, Scott MSS. no. 50901.

20 Nicolson to Grey, 5 July 1911, Grey MSS. F.O. 800/93; B.D. VII, 372; Nicolson to Bertie, 10 July 1911, Bertie MSS. F.O. 800/171; D.D.F. (2), XIV, nos. 22 and 28; B.D. VII, 376.

21 B.D. VII, 376.

22 Barlow, p. 254; B.D. VII, 367; Asquith to the King, 11 July 1911, Cabinet MSS. CAB 41/38/2.

23 D.D.F. (2)XIV, 51: B.D. VII, 383.

24 D.D.F. (2)XIV, 48.

25 B.D. VII, 392; D.D.F. (2)XIV, 71 and 74.

26 B.D. VII, 392; Asquith to Grey, 18 July 1911, Grey MSS. F.O. 800/100.

27 Asquith to the King, 19 July 1911, Cabinet MSS. CAB 41/33/22.

28 D.D.F. (2)XIV, 87.

29 Eyre Crowe to Bertie; Bertie to Crowe, 20 and 21 July 1911, Bertie MSS. F.O. 800/160 and 171.

30 'Note of the British Ambassador', 20 July 1911, D.D.F. (2)XIV, 87.

31 B.D. VII, 399.

32 B.D. VII, 405.

33 B.D. VII, 402; draft in Grey MSS. F.O. 800/52. Bertie was not satisfied with Grey's exposition of British policy and Grey summoned him to London to discuss the situation. 'Memorandum taken to the F.O. for my interview...with Grey, Asquith, and Lloyd George on July 25', Bertie MSS. F.O. 800/160.

34 D.D.F. (2)XIV, 88.

35 D.D.F. (2)XIV, 90.

36 *The History of the Times* suggests that this information may have been leaked by someone at the Foreign Office. But it might equally have been leaked by the French, or reproduced from French press sources. The *History of the Times*, 4 vols. (London, 1952), III, 700.

37 Asquith to the King, 22 July 1911, Cabinet Papers, CAB 41/38/3.
38 B.D. VII, 411. Grey's lack of interest in colonial questions was demonstrated by his statement to Metternich on 21st that he would not object if Germany purchased the Belgian Congo or Portugal's colonies. Grey to Goschen, desp. 184, 1 August 1911, F.O. 371/1163/25641.
39 For details see M. L. Dockrill, 'David Lloyd George and Foreign Policy before 1914', in *Lloyd George: Twelve Essays*, ed. by A. J. P. Taylor (London, 1971), pp. 16–17 and Note A, p. 31.
40 Cf. A. J. P. Taylor, *The Struggle for Mastery in Europe, 1848–1918* (Oxford, 1954), p. 471. See Dockrill, 16–17.
41 See Dockrill, 16–18. Nicolson to Hardinge, 27 July 1911, Nicolson MSS. F.O. 800/349, 'It produced a most admirable effect on France'. See also Richard A. Cosgrove 'A note on Lloyd George's Speech at the Mansion House, 21 July 1911', *The Historical Journal*, XII, 4 (1969), pp. 698–701 and Keith Wilson, 'The Agadir Crisis, the Mansion House Speech and the Double-Edgedness of Agreements', *The Historical Journal*, XV, 3 (1972), pp. 513–32.
42 In Cambon's words, 'M. Lloyd George était jadis germanophile et pacifiste...ces paroles présentent une grande importance, car il me revient qu'elles représentent le sentiment du Cabinet.' D.D.F. (2)XIV, 94.
43 B.D. VII, 419.
44 Nicolson to Hardinge, 27 July 1911, Nicolson MSS. F.O. 800/349.
45 Loreburn to Grey, 27 July 1911, Grey MSS. F.O. 800/99; Morley to Asquith 27 July 1911, Asquith MSS. vol. 13.
46 J. L. Hammond, *C. P. Scott of the Manchester Guardian* (London, 1934), 158–62.
47 B.D. VII, 637. For the German side see Mortimer, *op. cit.* 450–1.
48 Asquith to the King, 26 July 1911, Cabinet MSS. CAB 41/38/4.
49 B.D. VII, 430 and 431; D.D.F. (2)XIV, 122.
50 D.D.F. (2)XIV, nos. 97, 120, 134, 154, 177, 186, 254.
51 B.D. VII, 433, 434, 440. D.D.F. (2)XIV, no. 124.
52 D.D.F. (2)XIV, no. 129.
53 B.D. VII, 444 and 446, Asquith to the King, 1 August 1911, Cabinet MSS. CAB 41/33/23. D.D.F. (2)XIV, no. 118.
54 B.D. VII, 433, 441. D.D.F. (2)XIV, 184, 206.
55 Asquith to the King, 17 August 1911, Cabinet MSS. CAB 41/33/24. The reports of the Franco-German negotiations were not circulated to the cabinet as Grey feared leaks. B.D. VII, p. 362.
56 For details of Wilson's activities and the ensuing controversy over military and naval plans see S. R. Williamson, *The Politics of Grand Strategy, France and Britain Prepare for War, 1904–1914* (Cambridge, Mass., 1969), pp. 167–204; also C. J. Lowe and M. L. Dockrill, *The Mirage of Power, British Foreign Policy, 1902–1922* (3 vols. London, 1972), vol. I, pp. 37–46.
57 Committee of Imperial Defence, Minutes of 114th Meeting, 23 August 1911, C.I.D. MSS. CAB 38/19/49; Callwell, *op. cit.* I, 98–101. See also Williamson *op. cit.* pp. 187–93.
58 Loreburn to Grey, 26 August 1911, Grey MSS. F.O. 800/99.
59 Earlier Lloyd George had described the Lord Chancellor as 'petulant' 'unreasonable' and 'always rubbing Grey the wrong way'. Hammond, *op. cit.* p. 152.
60 Grey to Loreburn, 30 August 1911, Grey MSS. F.O. 800/99.
61 See Dockrill, p. 19, on Lloyd George's role.
62 Lloyd George to Churchill, 25 August 1911, Lloyd George MSS. C/3/15/6.
63 Churchill to Grey, 30 August 1911, Churchill to Lloyd George, 31 August 1911 in Randolph Churchill, II, 529–531, and companion volume part II, pp. 1116–19.
64 Lloyd George to Grey, 1 September 1911, Grey MSS. F.O. 800/101.

65 Goschen to Nicolson, 1 September 1911, Nicolson MSS. F.O. 800/350; B.D. VII, no. 526.
66 B.D. VII, nos. 531 and 532.
67 Grey to Bertie, private tel., 5 September 1911, Bertie MSS. F.O. 800/171.
68 Grey to Lloyd George, Lloyd George MSS. C/4/14/5. Whether or not as a result of Grey's pressure, Lloyd George wrote to Churchill on 5 September opposing his scheme for a triple alliance to protect the Low Countries as 'much too risky', R. Churchill, *op. cit.* II, 2, p. 1121.
69 Asquith to Grey, 5 September 1911, Grey MSS. F.O. 800/100.
70 Grey to Asquith, 8 September 1911, Grey MSS. F.O. 800/100. While Asquith accepted Grey's arguments, the foreign secretary also became alarmed later in the month by reports of increasing French belligerence. Grey to Nicolson, private, 13 September 1911, Nicolson MSS. F.O. 800/350.
71 'To me it looks as if the negotiations were going to enter upon exceedingly tedious, but not dangerous ground', Grey to Asquith, 8 September 1911, F.O. 800/100. Asquith to Grey, 9 September 1911, Grey MSS. F.O. 800/100.
72 B.D. VII, no. 545, D.D.F. (2)XIV, 277.
73 Nicolson to Grey, 10 September 1911, Grey MSS. F.O. 800/93; Nicolson to Bertie, 11 September 1911, Nicolson MSS. F.O. 800/350.
74 Grey to Nicolson, 11, 12, 13 September 1911, Nicolson MSS. F.O. 800/350; B.D. VII, 540.
75 Haldane to Grey, 11 September 1911, Grey MSS. F.O. 800/102.
76 E. Marsh, Home Office to Lloyd George, 13 September 1911, Lloyd George MSS. C/3/15/10; Churchill to Lloyd George, 14 September 1911, C/13/15/11; Grey to Nicolson, 15 September 1911, Nicolson MSS. F.O. 800/350.
77 B.D. VII, 556, Barlow, pp. 363–8.
78 Nicolson to Grey, 26 September 1911, Nicolson MSS. F.O. 800/350.
79 B.D. VII, 570 and 580, Barlow, pp. 370–3.
80 B.D. VII, 586; Grey to Bertie, 14 October 1911, Bertie MSS. F.O. 800/165. 'Our people would say they couldn't fight for such folly.'
81 B.D. VII, 599; Asquith to the King, 25 October 1911, Cabinet Papers, CAB 41/33/27; Diary of John Burns, 25 October 1911, Burns MSS. 46333.
82 For text see B.D. VII, 626. France secured her coveted protectorate over Morocco, while Germany got two sections of the French Congo, one to the South of the Cameroons which gave her a coastal outlet in the north of Libreville, and the second section in the east on the Congo River. Grey recognised the agreement on 15 November, Barlow 374.
83 Grey to Asquith, undated, probably 29 July 1911, Grey MSS. F.O. 800/100, Minute by Grey, undated, probably end July 1911, Grey MSS. F.O. 800/93.
84 Barlow, *op. cit.* pp. 316–22.
85 See John A. Murray, 'Foreign Policy Debated: Sir Edward Grey and his Critics, 1911–1912' in, *Power, Public Opinion and Diplomacy: Essays in Honor of E. Malcolm Carroll*, eds. L. P. Wallace and W. C. Askew (Durham, N.C., 1959), p. 141; Mosa Anderson, *Noel Buxton, A Life* (London, 1952), p. 50; G. P. Gooch, *Life of Lord Courtney* (London, 1920), pp. 66–8. For a comprehensive account of the liberal opposition to Grey during this period see A. J. Dorey, *Radical Liberal Criticism of British Foreign Policy, 1906–1914* (D.Phil. thesis, Oxford, 1964).
86 Parliamentary Debates (House of Commons), XXXII, 1911, 27 November 1911, 43–63.
87 B.D. VII, 480.
88 Memorandum by Lewis Harcourt, 13 March 1912, Harcourt MSS. Box 14.
89 On the strategic consequences see Williamson, *op. cit.* p. 204.

15. GREAT BRITAIN AND GERMANY, 1911–1914

1 Fox to Grey, 20 January 1912, F.O. 371/1372/12. Cf. also J. E. C. Montmorency, *Francis William Fox: a Biography* (London, 1923).

2 L. Cecil, *Albert Ballin: Business and Politics in Imperial Germany, 1888–1918* (London, 1967).

3 The bibliography is quite large and reflects the importance which has been attached to this point: Sir Ernest Woodward, *Great Britain and the German Navy* (Oxford, 1935); B. D. E. Kraft, *Lord Haldane's Zending naar Berlin in 1912: de duitsch-Engelsche Onderhandelingen over de Vlootquaestie, 1905–1912* (Utrecht, n.d.); Bernadotte Schmitt in Louis Paetow, ed., *The Crusades and other Historical Essays Presented to Dana C. Munro*...(New York, 1928), pp. 245–88; E. C. Helmrich, 'Die Haldane Mission', *Berliner Monatshefte*, 12, Jg. no. 2, February, 1934, 112–43; Emile Bourgeois, 'La Mission de Lord Haldane à Berlin, Février 1912', *Revue des deux Mondes*, XXXV, 15 October 1926, 881–910; Walther Hubatsch, 'Der Kulminationspunkt der deutschen Marinepolitik im Jahre 1912', *Historische Zeitschrift*, CLXXVI, no. 2, October 1953, 291–322; F. Uppleger, *Die englische Flottenpolitik vor dem Weltkrieg* (Berlin, 1930), B.D. VI, Chap. XLIX, and in G.P. XXXI, chap. CCXLIII; Tirpitz' *Politische Dokumente*, 2 vols. (Stuttgart, etc., 1924–6, and *Erinnerungen* (Leipzig, 1919); Walter Gorlitz, ed., *Der Kaiser...: Aufzeichnungen des Chefs de Marinekabinetts Admiral Georg Alexander v. Müller über die Ära Wilhelms II* (Berlin, 1965); Wilhelm Widenmann, *Marine-Attaché an der Kaiserliche-deutschen Botschaft in London 1907–1912* (Göttingen, 1952); Beth-mann's *Betrachtungen zum Weltkrieg*, 2 vols (Berlin, 1919–21); Richard B. Haldane, *Before the War* (London, etc., 1920), and *An Autobiography* (London, 1929); Hüld-ermann's biography of Ballin; General Sir Frederick Maurice, *Haldane: the Life of Viscount Haldane of Cloan*..., 2 vols (London, 1937–9); Dudley Sommer, *Haldane of Cloan: his Life and Times, 1856–1928* (London, 1960); L. Cecil, *Albert Ballin: Business and Politics in Imperial Germany, 1888–1918* (London, 1967).

4 Both Ballin and Cassel were members of the highly successful Jewish group of international financiers – particularly obvious in Germany – which was becoming such a feature of pre-1914 economic life. For example: 'Speyer and some of his racial kinsfolk were discussing the prospects of European war, when one said to the other "It will be a terrible thing if we English go to war with us Germans"', 2 December 1912, A. Fitzroy, *Memoirs*, II, 499 (London, 1923).

5 H. Nicolson, *Lord Carnock* (London, 1934), p. 362.

6 W. S. Churchill, *The World Crisis* (NEL, 1968), pp. 73–4.

7 G.P. XXXI, 97. Their view is based on Hüldermann's Life of Ballin, where the evidence is insufficient to support such a definite statement.

8 Churchill to Grey, 20 January 1912, Grey Papers, F.O. 800/48; Churchill to Cassel, 7 January 1912, Grey Papers, F.O. 800/48; Goschen to Nicolson, 10 February 1912, B.D. VI, 504, The Kaiser had intimated to Ballin that 'his task was now over and that he could go...'

9 Grey to Buchanan, 10 February 1912, B.D. VI, 503; Nicolson to Hardinge, 1 February 1912, Hardinge Papers, 92, I, 204, 'Grey is determined that we will enter into no serious conversation with Germany until she is prepared to give...an undertaking to cease the naval armament race.' At that time there was only an unofficial hint of a naval arrangement.

10 E. Grey, *Twenty-Five Years* (London, 1928), II, pp. 74–5.

11 Nicolson, *Lord Carnock*, p. 362.

12 Cecil, *op. cit.*, p. 182, note 18.

13 Cecil, *op. cit.*, pp. 182–3; Cassel to Ballin, 9 January 1912, Hüldermann, *op. cit.*, pp. 246–7; Ballin to Admiral von Müller, 13 January 1912, AA, Marine-Kabinetts, XXXI.b, vol. 2, reel 18/00136/7.

14 Churchill to Cassel, 7 January 1912, B.D. VI, 492.
15 Memorandum by Bethmann-Hollweg, 29 January 1912. G.P. XXXI, 97. Grey to Goschen, 7 February 1912, B.D. VI, 497; Grey to Bertie, 7 February 1912, B.D. VI, 498.
16 Asquith to H.M. The King, 3 February 1912, Cabinet letter, Asquith MSS. 6, 91. 'Haldane, who has occasion to go to Berlin in his character as chairman of the London University Committee for Scientific Education to obtain first hand knowledge of German methods of clinical teaching, might be commissioned to see the Emperor and Chancellor.'
17 Bethmann-Hollweg to Metternich, 4 January 1912, G.P. XXXI, 105.
18 e.g. Chirol to Hardinge, 16 January 1912, Hardinge Papers, 92, II, 211. 'Cassel has never made any secret of his dislike for the Anglo-French Entente and least of all since we stopped, at the insistence of the French, his proposed loan to Turkey two years ago.'
   There are at this time references to attempts to force Grey's resignation. Morley to Hardinge, 26 January 1912, Hardinge Papers, 92, I, 202. 'The Radical Ultras are making something of an effort to hound Grey out of the F.O.' Likewise, Sanderson to Hardinge, 26 January 1912, Hardinge Papers, 92, I, 201. 'There is a considerable amount of discontent against Grey in the liberal party. A good deal of it is the inevitable result of that enthusiastic philanthropy which insists on messing about in other people's affairs, which it does not understand.'
19 It is impossible to discover what passed at this meeting, except for this cryptic remark of Paul Cambon: Cambon to Poincaré, 7 February 1912, D.D.F. Ser. 3, I, 628: 'On lui a fait verbalement connaître le véritable but de la visite de Lord Haldane sur laquelle on entend garder un secret absolu.'
20 Grey to Bertie, 7 February 1912, B.D. VI, 498; Grey to Buchanan, 7 February 1912, B.D. VI, 495; Grey to Goschen, 7 February 1912, Grey Papers, F.O. 800/23.
21 Grey to Bertie, 7 February 1912, B.D. VI, 499.
22 Haldane's journey was encumbered by some Ruritanian precautions, e.g. a false beard and slipping from one train to another across the tracks at Calais Maritime; precautions which quite failed to confuse the press. Bertie to Nicolson, 11 February 1912, Carnock MSS. I, 1912; J. Cambon to Poincaré, 9 February 1912, D.D.F. ser. 3, II, 1912, 16.
23 Goschen to Nicolson, 9 February 1912, B.D. VI, 502. All references to the negotiations are taken from Haldane's Diary which Goschen sent to Grey in instalments as the discussions proceeded. The whole was printed in F.O.C.P. 10575/64, and in B.D. VI, 506. Haldane said that he had written up his account within an hour of the conversation concerned, except for the final section which he did in the train on his return journey.
24 The main provision was that the two powers would agree not to enter into aggressive combinations against one another. Haldane at once pointed out with some bluntness that this had dangers. What would happen if Germany proceeded to the dismemberment of France, or England were to descend upon Denmark? 'He answered that these cases were not at all likely, but he admitted that they were fatal to his formula.'
25 Goschen wrote to Nicolson on the following day 'the Chancellor also told me that it had caused him the greatest satisfaction, and that he hoped it was the beginning of a real step forward in the direction of good relations...' Goschen to Nicolson, 9 February 1912, Carnock MSS. vol. I, 1912.
26 Haldane lunched with the Imperial family, and the three men retired to the Imperial study, where, as Haldane reported, 'I found relations excellent and the atmosphere genial.' The Kaiser, interestingly and typically, later told Bethmann that he had been in some trepidation as to the effect of a confrontation between

Haldane and Tirpitz. Kaiser to Bethmann-Hollweg, 9 February 1912, G.P. XXXI, 192.

27 'I said it was not a matter for admission. Germany must be free and we must be free, and we should probably lay down two keels to their one. In this case the initiative was not with us but with them.'

28 Lord Haldane, as Valentine Chirol observed in a letter to Hardinge (Hardinge Papers 92, II, 214, 22 February 1912), prided himself on his knowledge of German, which, as he reported, he had used during the Mission to prevent misunderstanding. 'Some mischievous spirits in the FO', continued Chirol, 'have taken a wicked delight in pointing out howlers in the remarks which, according to his memorandum, he appears to have made in German...' Sir V. Chirol was correctly informed. On the typewritten original of Haldane's Diary there appear exclamation marks beside the passages where Haldane made mistakes, but against the passage 'in return, she would give us what the Chancellor defined as *eine sonderbare Stelle* [a special position], and the replied '*nicht nur eine sonderbare Stelle, aber eine kontrolierende Stelle*', a clerk noted that *sonderbare* meant 'special' in the sense of odd or peculiar. But it can be seen that this was apparently the Chancellor's word, and even if Haldane had mistakenly employed it, he was doing so only to reject it.

29 B.D. VI, 506, Appendix I.

30 Bethmann-Hollweg to Metternich, 12 February 1912, G.P. XXXI, 120.

31 Haldane to his mother, 13 February 1912, Haldane MSS. 5987; Grey to Goschen, 12 February 1912, B.D. VI, 510; Metternich to Bethmann-Hollweg, 12 February 1912, G.P. XXXI, 121.

32 It is an interesting comment on the relationship between Haldane's rather independent mission and the Foreign Office that on the same day as Haldane reported joyfully to his mother, Paul Cambon telegraphed reassuringly to Poincaré (P. Cambon to Poincaré, 13 February 1912, D.D.F. ser. 3, II, 30). 'Sir Arthur Nicolson qui s'est toujours élevé contre le projet de visite à Berlin par la raison que, s'il en souhait un arrangement, ce serait au détriment de l'Angleterre et que, s'il n'en souhait rien, la tension serait pire qu'avant, m'a dit qu'il augerait mal de ces pourparlers et que sur aucun point il ne voyait une possibilité d'accord.'

33 Crowe's attitude had been foreshadowed in a minute on a naval report from the attaché in Berlin, Captain Watson (F.O. 371/1372/6060, 8 February 1912).

34 A larger share of Mozambique; direct access to eastern and western seaboard for Rhodesia and, possibly, later, Katanga; Timor to fall to England; Germany to accept everything England desired in the Baghdad Railway, and recognise exclusive British influence in the Persian Gulf. Haldane's proceedings over the first three were made almost irrelevant by the parallel negotiations in progress on the subject of the Portuguese Colonies. But, for a controlling interest in the Baghdad Railway's southern trace, he had offered a counter-concession – Zanzibar and Pemba. For recognition of British interest in the Persian Gulf, Haldane had not demurred when presented by the Chancellor with a written proposal that in exchange Germany should participate in railway construction projected for the British zone of Persia. B.D. VI, 506, Minute by Crowe.

35 Note by Sir A. Nicolson, B.D. VI, 507.

36 Goschen to Nicolson, 10 February 1912, B.D. VI, 504, also in H. Nicolson, *Lord Carnock*, p. 364.

37 Grey, Haldane and Metternich met at the house which the two British ministers shared in Queen Anne's Gate on 22 February, and there the Ambassador asked for precise information on the British view of the naval discussion Haldane had had in Berlin and on the *Novelle*. It was this request that led to the production of the Admiralty memorandum. Memorandum by Sir E. Grey, 22 February 1912, B.D. VI, 523.

38 Grey to Goschen, 24 February 1912, B.D. VI, 524, enclosure.

39 It had become apparent that the British government wished to retreat on the question of territorial adjustments. Grey said that the Cabinet felt that they had better first deal with the problems of naval expenditure and a formula. 'Time was required for the consideration of their full bearing. We had spoken of a cession of Zanzibar and Pemba and a strip across Angola. These were considerable assets, and would require compensation *in pari materiâ.*' Grey to Goschen, 24 February 1912, B.D. VI, 524. Metternich's own report agrees with this except that this record shows Grey as having agreed that the Cabinet were divided on the proposals. G.P. XXXI, 135, Metternich to Bethmann-Hollweg, 24 February 1912. Asquith did not mention such a discussion in a Cabinet letter to the King.

40 Minute on Metternich to Bethmann-Hollweg, 24 February 1912, G.P. XXXI, 135.

41 The tone of this piece led Goschen to believe that he saw in it the hand of Kiderlen Waechter, the hitherto silent Foreign Secretary. Goschen to Nicolson, 15 March 1912, B.D. VI, 541. Haldane was sure for his part that it had not been written by the Chancellor. Observations by Lord Haldane, 11 March 1912, B.D. VI, 532. Also, Haldane to his sister, 8 March 1912, Haldane MSS. 6011/195.

42 The text of the Treaty mentioned in (b) is printed B.D. I, 90, 91, 92. Balfour to Lascelles, 31 August 1898.

43 The Germans do not seem to have been entirely wrong on the possible cession of Zanzibar. Haldane letter denied that 'I made [an] offer of Zanzibar and Pemba: I merely stated that these were places which might well come into a general bargain.' (Observations by Lord Haldane, 11 March 1912, B.D. VI, 532.) Later he stated that the Chancellor might have gained a wrong impression through misunderstanding his English. (Note by Lord Haldane, 10 April 1912, Grey Papers, F.O. 800/61.) Haldane's own record does not make this point clear; but he was not always as careful as he might have been, and the Chancellor's later statement that he was sure Haldane had offered Zanzibar and Pemba because he was so surprised when the offer was made has a ring of truth about it. Also for what it was worth, the Kaiser corroborated this. Goschen to Nicolson, 29 March 1912, B.D. VI, 560. They were correspondingly annoyed when the offer was withdrawn. Kaiser's minute on Metternich to Bethmann-Hollweg, 24 March 1912, G.P. XXXI, 135.

44 Grey to Goschen, 6 March 1912, B.D. VI, 530.

45 Minute by Crowe on Memorandum communicated by Metternich, 6 March 1912, B.D. VI, 529.

46 Memorandum by Lord Haldane, 11 March 1912, B.D. VI, 532.

47 Nicolson to Goschen, 13 March 1912, B.D. VI, 534. Also Grey to Nicolson, 13 March 1912, B.D. VI, 535.

48 This is an illustration of that uncertainty of authority experienced sooner or later by those who had to deal with the Berlin government. In this case, as the attempt of the Chancellor to obtain an understanding with England had run into difficulties, it was hijacked by advisers close to the Kaiser, who, for military considerations, wished to show that such an agreement was impossible. Some extracts from the *Daily Mail* of 6 March 1912 (F.O. 371/1371/10334) indicate a resumption of the anti-English press campaign, which was very probably inspired by the German naval press bureaux, precisely coincident with the arrival of the tough memorandum. The connections which the press bureaux had with more strongly nationalist groups had for some time made them, under the sleepless watch of Crowe, most unpopular in the Foreign Office. e.g. Minutes by Crowe on F.O. 371/1375/18644, F.O. 371/1990/23239, F.O. 371/1988/10304, particularly since a notable outbreak of mis-representation in 1911, against which Sir Edward Grey had had to make a direct protest. Grey evidently took the view that the Chancellor was temporarily eclipsed and then recovered his position. For he wrote to Goschen: 'My impression is that

Tirpitz and the Navy people in Germany are determined to prevent any arrangement with us that would interfere with their naval increase; and that it is they and Kiderlen who have given this turn to the negotiations.' (Grey to Goschen, 11 March 1912, F.O. 800/61, Grey Papers.) To the Cabinet on 14 March, however, after the request for a new formula, he spoke of the Chancellor having 'got the better of Admiral Tirpitz'. (Asquith to H.M. the King, 14 March 1912, Cabinet Letter, Asquith MSS. 6, 117.) A week later, in conversation with Metternich, he inquired whether it was really the case that the Chancellor's position would be affected by British willingness or the reverse to agree to a formula. 'Ct. Metternich replied that the Chancellor wished besides having good relations with us to meet us on the naval question. If he could not do this Ct. Metternich feared that his position might be affected: the question being really whether the Chancellor or Admiral v. Tirpitz was to have the upper hand' (Grey to Goschen, 22 March 1912, Grey Papers F.O. 800/61).

49 Memorandum by Lord Haldane, 12 March 1912, B.D. VI, 533.

50 It is an illustration of the unhappy state of British industrial relations at the time that at such a moment of urgency during these negotiations, Grey was attempting to settle a very serious coal strike. If it seems odd that at such a juncture the Foreign Secretary was absent, it is worth bearing in mind not only the general mistrust prevalent, but also that Grey possessed remarkable powers of conciliation.

51 Grey to Goschen, 14 March 1912, B.D. VI, 537.

52 Asquith to H.M. the King, Asquith MSS. 6, 117, Cabinet Letter, 14 March 1912.

53 Metternich to Grey, 14 March 1912, B.D. VI, 538.

54 Grey to Metternich, and Metternich to Grey, 15 March 1912, F.O. 800/61.

55 Grey to Goschen, 15 March 1912, B.D. VI, 539.

56 Grey to Goschen, 15 March 1912, B.D. VI, 539.

57 Asquith to H.M. the King, Cabinet Letter, 16 March 1912, Asquith MSS. 6, 119.

58 Grey to Goschen, 16 March 1912, B.D. VI, 544.

59 Bethmann to Metternich, 18 March 1912, G.P. XXXI, 188.

60 Grey to Goschen, 22 March 1912, B.D. VI, 548.

61 'In any case, I was ready to continue to discuss from a friendly point of view all the questions which arose between the two Governments; and I saw no reason why this readiness should not be reciprocated by the German government.' Grey to Goschen, 19 March 1912, B.D. VI, 545.

62 Grey to MacDonald, 20 March 1912, B.D. VI, 546.

63 Grey to Goschen, 21 March 1912, B.D. VI, 547, enc.

64 See above, p. 301 and notes 71 and 72.

65 Goschen to Nicolson, 29 March 1912, B.D. VI, 560.

66 *Vide* note 4, p. 8.

67 'Through discreet private support.' Bethmann-Hollweg to Ballin, 8 March 1912, Hüldermann, *op. cit.*, p. 258.

68 *Vide* notes 42/43, pp. 23/24 *supra*.

69 'Great Britain would be willing to grant the *unconditional* neutrality agreement desired by Germany and, moreover, to do so *before* the technical points regarding ships and personnel were settled.' Cecil, *op. cit.*, p. 194.

70 Admiral von Müller, quoted in Cecil, *ibid.*, p. 195, from Hubatsch, *Kulminationspunkt*, pp. 315–16.

71 The Germans had found the formula insufficient, 'and for the time being the matter was in suspense...M. Cambon appeared quite satisfied with the information.' Grey to Bertie, 22 March 1912, B.D. VI, 550.

72 Minutes by Nicolson and Grey, 25 March 1912, B.D. VI, 553.

73 Note de M. Poincaré, D.D.F. III, ii, 266, 27 March 1912.

74 He mentioned that Cambon had seemed to Grey to be satisfied on two occasions: 'I very much doubt M. Cambon's satisfaction at the formula but no doubt he was pleased at the German Government having knocked it on the head, at all events for the time being. . . .' Bertie to Nicolson, 28 March 1912, B.D. VI, 556.

75 Memorandum by Sir Edward Grey, B.D. VI, 555, 26 March 1912.

76 Grey to Bertie, 29 March 1912, B.D. VI, 559. He also said that another more far reaching proposal had been made, which would have to be laid before the Cabinet, but it 'seemed to me still more difficult for us to accept'.

77 Nicolson to Goschen, 1 April 1912, B.D. VI, 562.

78 Bertie to Grey, 3 April 1912, B.D. VI, 564.

79 Minute by Crowe, 6 April 1912, B.D. VI, 564.

80 Undated minutes by Nicolson and Grey, B.D. VI, 564 (see editorial note, B.D. VI, p. 739).

81 Nicolson to Grey, 6 April 1912, F.O. 800/55, enc. Cambon to Fleuriau, 3 April 1912, text in Carnock MSS. III, 1912.

82 Grey to Bertie, Private tel. 9 April 1912, B.D. VI, 569.

83 Asquith to Grey, 10 April 1912, F.O. 800/61.

84 Grey to Goschen, 10 April 1912, B.D. VI, 573.

85 'I am glad to tell you that since I wrote you Metternich came here and said that as the two Governments were apparently unable to [agree]. . .the Chancellor intended to proceed with the Naval *Novelle*. . .I trust that it means that the formula question has been definitely buried and that we shall hear no more about it.' Nicolson to Goschen, 15 April 1912, B.D. VI, 575.

86 Bertie reported that the French had been made very uneasy by the news of Marschall's appointment, thinking him a past master at 'brutal methods'. Bertie to Grey, F.O. 800/14, 16 May 1912. Grey replied that he did not agree, but that 'if Marschall tries brutal methods, he will make our policy very simple and easy, but I imagine him to be much too clever to do this'. Grey to Bertie, 18 May 1912, F.O. 800/14.

87 Grey to Goschen, 4 July 1912, B.D. VI, 593.

88 Haldane was not without a warning either. Just before he left for Berlin he received a Note from the German Chancellor and a letter from Ballin. The Chancellor's note was vague. Cassel evidently felt that it was 'evasive' and, on receiving it, Ballin added a letter of his own, before sending both to England by the HAPAG General Secretary (and his own future biographer) Bernard Hüldermann. Hüldermann reprinted the text of Ballin's letter, which contained a firm warning about the need for England to agree to a 'strongly worded neutrality agreement', without which Germany would not reduce her naval programme. It is typical of Ballin, who wanted so much to reduce tension with England, but was convinced in his less sanguine moments that negotiations would break down. Hüldermann, *op. cit.*, p. 250.

89 *Vide* p. 3.

90 Grey, *op. cit.*, I, 250 ff.

91 Minute by Crowe, B.D. VI, 564, 6 April 1912.

92 *Hansard*, Parliamentary Debates, Fifth Series, vol. XXXIV, cols. 1340–1 and vol. XXXV, col. 35. For a more extensive treatment of this phase see my article, *The Historical Journal*, XIV, 2 (1971), pp. 359–70.

93 H.M. the King to Grey, 8 December 1912, B.D. X, ii, 452. Grey to H.M. the King, 9 December 1912, B.D. X, ii, 453.

94 Minute by Crowe on Goschen to Grey, 10 February 1913, B.D. X, ii, 457.

95 Grey to Goschen, 5 March 1913, B.D. X, ii, 465.

96 Nicolson to Hardinge, 29 April 1913, Hardinge Papers, 93, I, 104. See also note 95.

97 Goschen to Grey, 28 and 29 March 1913, B.D. X, ii, 468 and 469.

98 Goschen to Grey, 3 July 1913, B.D. x, ii, 480.

99 Memorandum by Mr Churchill, 8 July 1913, B.D. x, ii, 481.

100 Goschen to Nicolson, 24 December 1913, B.D. x, ii, 486.

101 Grey to Goschen, 5 February 1914, B.D. x, ii, 498.

102 Memorandum by Sir Edward Grey, 25 May 1914, B.D. x, ii, 512.

103 For a complete discussion of this question, see P. H. S. Hatton, 'Harcourt and Solf: the Search for an Anglo-German Understanding through Africa, 1912–14', *European Studies Review*, I, no. 2 (1971); and R. Langhorne, 'Anglo-German Negotiations concerning the Future of the Portuguese Colonies, 1911–1914', *The Historical Journal*, xvi, 2 (1973), pp. 361–87.

104 Jagow to Lichnowsky, 14 March 1913, G.P. xxxvii, 33: 'The general feeling in Germany is that in 1898 we were duped by England, and done out of price for which we stipulated in return for our attitude to England during the Boer War...' Grey to Goschen, 13 June 1913, B.D. x, ii, 337: 'He [Lichnowsky] said...that the position I seemed to assume was that of medical adviser to the Portuguese Colonies, while what Germany contemplated was that of being the heir.'

105 Minute by Grey, 17 July 1912, sent to a Cabinet on 24 July 1912. See also ed. note in B.D. x, ii, p. 485.

106 Balfour to Lascelles, 31 August 1898, B.D. I, 90, 91, 92. The whole agreement comprised a convention, a secret convention and a secret note.

107 Anglo-Portuguese secret declaration, 14 September 1899, B.D. I, 118.

108 1373, 1661, 1703 and 1710.

109 Portugal often seemed to be on the verge of insolvency, and in 1897 this appeared to be particularly likely. A dispute with private firms, whose contract to build the Mozambique Railway had been abruptly terminated in 1889, now led to the establishment of a Tribunal sitting at Berne. Its award was confidently expected, and as confidently expected to go against Portugal.

110 Memorandum by Francis Bertie on England and Portugal in Africa, 1 May 1898, B.D. I, i, 65.

111 Salisbury to Gough, 23 June 1898, B.D. I, 70.

112 Balfour to Lascelles, 31 August 1898, B.D. I, 92.

113 Kühlmann to Tyrell, 10 July 1912, ed. note B.D. x, ii, pp. 483–4. Grey to Granville, 17 July 1912, B.D. x, ii, 315.

114 Grey to Goschen, 29 December 1911, F.O. 800–61. There is a shortened version in B.D. x, ii, 266.

115 Memorandum by Harcourt, read to cabinet 13 March 1912, Harcourt Papers, Box 14.

116 Grey to Goschen, 29 December 1911, Grey Papers, F.O. 800–61. The version in B.D. x, ii, 266 is, as the Editors explained, cut short for reasons of international courtesy.

117 Nicolson to Hardinge, 1 February 1912, Hardinge Papers, 92, i, 204; Harcourt to Grey, 21 Februrary 1912, Grey Papers, F.O. 800–90.

118 Memorandum by Crowe, 26 January 1912, B.D. x, ii, 270.

119 See R. Langhorne, 'Anglo-German Negotiations concerning the Future of the Portuguese Colonies, 1911–1914', *The Historical Journal*, xvi, 2 (1973), p. 375.

120 Grey to Granville, 13 August 1913, B.D. x, ii, 342. Initialling in both languages had to wait until 20 October: the original text is to be found in the Treaty Series, Germany 74. Also see map in A. J. P. Taylor, *The Struggle for Mastery in Europe, 1848–1918*, p. 503.

121 Minutes by Crowe, dated 17 January 1913, on Grey to Goschen, 11 January 1913, B.D. x, ii, 323.

122 Grey to Goschen, 7 April 1914, B.D. x, ii, 373.

123 Kiderlen to Lichnowsky, 8 December 1912, G.P. xxxvii, 13.

124 Jagow to Lichnowsky, 27 July 1914, G.P. xxxvii, 137.

125 Minute by Crowe on Bertie to Grey, 11 February 1914, B.D. x, ii, 361.
126 See for example, E. Brandenburg, *From Bismark to the World War* (London, 1938), pp. 465–7; G. Lowes Dickinson, *The International Anarchy, 1904–14* (London, 1926), pp. 346–8; S. B. Fay, *The Origins of the World War* (New York, 1934), p. 359; B. E. Schmitt, *The Coming of the First World War* (New York, 1966), 1, 73; A. J. P. Taylor, *The Struggle for Mastery in Europe* (London, 1954), pp. 502–4; I. Geiss, *July 1914* (London, 1967), p. 44; for a more suspicious view, see Fritz Fischer, *Germany's aims in the First World War* (London, 1967), pp. 38–9; P. Renouvin, 'L'Afrique centrale dans les relations anglo-allemandes en 1912–1914', *Mélanges Charles-André Julien* (Paris, 1964); J. Willequet, 'Anglo-German Rivalry in Belgian and Portuguese Africa?', pp. 245–73 in P. Gifford and W. R. Louis (eds), *Britain and Germany in Africa* (New Haven, Conn., 1971); A. Springborn, *Englands Stellung zur Deutschen Welt und Kolonialpolitik in den Jahren 1911–1914* (Würzburg, 1939); P. Dubois, 'Les negociations anglo-allemandes relatives aux colonies portugaises 1912–1914' in *Revue d'histoire de la guerre mondiale*, 1939; P. H. S. Hatton, 'Harcourt and Solf: the Search for an Anglo-German Understanding through Africa, 1912–1914' in *European Studies Review*, 1, no. 2 (1971).
127 Woodward, *op. cit.*, chap. xxii.

16. GREY AND THE TRIPOLI WAR, 1911–1912

1 *British Documents on the Origins of the War*, vol. 1, p. 360: E. Serra, *L'Intesa Mediterranea del 1902* (Milan, 1957), pp. 180–1. Salisbury had given similar private assurances to Rome in 1890: see C. J. Lowe, *Salisbury and the Mediterranean* (London, 1965), p. 68.
2 Serra, *op. cit.*, p. 186. 'What the King of Italy and the present Government would like would be a working understanding with England and France...' Bertie to Lansdowne, undated (?March 1904), F.O. 800/133/134. But see E. Decleva, *Da Adua a Sarajevo* (Bari, 1971), pp. 170–6.
3 Lansdowne to Currie, 12 December 1900. F.O. 800/132/28.
4 Currie to Lansdowne, 24 December 1901. *Ibid.*
5 Rodd to Grey, 23 August 1909. F.O. 800/64.
6 G. André, *L'Italia e il Mediterraneo* (Milan, 1967), p. 124, Decleva, pp. 218–19. 'I have up to now always understood that you and a series of your predecessors at the Foreign Office have, on the whole, regarded the participation of Italy in the Triple Alliance as rather desirable than not from the point of view of the peace of Europe.' Rodd to Grey, 5 February 1912. F.O. 800/64.
7 Grey to Rodd, 20 Februrary 1911, F.O. 800/64.
8 Rodd to Lansdowne, 29 July 1902, F.O. 800/132/113.
9 B.D. ix, nos. 221 and 222, editorial note.
10 *Ibid.* no. 222. Rodd to Grey, 31 July 1902.
11 F.O. 371/27882/11/22, Rodd to Grey, 3 July 1902.
12 B.D. ix, no. 224.
13 Rodd to Grey, 4 September, F.O. 800/64. It was not until 27 September that Giolitti admitted that 'Italy would be forced to take action, as soon as French Protectorate in Morocco was definitely decided upon.' B.D. ix, no. 241.
14 Rodd to Grey, 4 September, F.O. 800/64.
15 B.D. ix, no. 231. Churchill also took this view at this time: 'clearly we must prefer Italy to Turkey on all grounds – moral and immoral.' *Ibid.* no. 240.
16 W. C. Askew, *Europe and Italy's Acquisition of Libya* (Durham, N.C., 1939), pp. 67–9. Leo Maxse of the *National Review*, however, called this 'scandalous and hysterical twaddle'. He advocated bringing Italy over to the Entente. To Mrs Joseph Chamberlain, 20 November 1911. Austen Chamberlain Papers 4/11/185.

17 See John A. Murray, 'Grey and His Critics, 1911–12', in *Power, Public Opinion and Diplomacy*, ed. L. P. Wallace and W. C. Askew (Durham, N.C., 1959).

18 See B.D. IX, pp. 288, 291, 297, 298.

19 Minutes on B.D. IX, no. 256.

20 Askew, pp. 100–105. Churchill maintained 'all the strongest elements in Liberal opinion' were anti-Italian. Now that Armageddon (over Morocco) had receded, he advocated a Turkish alliance: 'In fixing our eyes upon the Belgian frontier and the North Sea we must not forget that we are the greatest Mahomedan power in the world...Have we not more to gain from Turkish friendship than from Italian...?' To Grey, 4 November 1911, F.O. 800/86.

21 Fitzmaurice to Tyrrell, 9 February 1911, 12 February 1912, F.O. 800/356. On 16 and 18 January 1912 the Italians intercepted and removed Turkish passengers from two French ships, the *Carthage* and the *Manouba*. The incidents led to a press war of serious dimensions. André, *op. cit.*, pp. 20–5.

22 Kitchener to Grey, 2 October 1911, minute by Louis Mallet, F.O. 371/1252.

23 Granville to Grey, nos. 323, 328; 15 and 20 October 1911. F.O. 371/1254, Minute by Mallet.

24 B.D. IX, no. 267.

25 Minute on Rodd, no. 189 of 10 October 1911, F.O. 371/1254.

26 André, *op. cit.*, pp. 10–11.

27 Rodd to Grey, 10, 16 and 25 October, 6 November 1911, F.O. 800/64. The last three are printed in B.D. IX, nos. 286, 296, 302.

28 Rodd, 25 October, *ibid.* no. 296. André, *op. cit.*, p. 5, argues convincingly that Barrère lay behind these approaches.

29 B.D. IX, no. 297.

30 Grey to Rodd, 14 November, no. 308. As André points out (p. 13) this letter was penned at the height of the parliamentary attacks on Grey over Persia.

31 Grey to O'Beirne, 3 November 1911, B.D. IX, p. 781, Appendix IV.

32 Askew, *op. cit.*, pp. 165–76.

33 For example, see Drummond's minute, endorsed by Grey, on Rodd to Grey, 12 December 1911: 'It seems to me to be preferable that she should continue as a somewhat doubtful factor in the alliance than that she should be in open opposition to Austria and Germany.' B.D. IX, no. 349.

34 British shipowners were losing £9,000 a day whilst the Straits remained closed: B.D. IX, no. 399. The difficulty of protesting too much was that 'we do not want to use language when we are neutral which might be quoted as entitling neutrals to hamper our action when we are a belligerent'. Grey to Morley, 4 March 1912, F.O. 800/99.

35 See Minutes by Grey and Mallet, *ibid.* pp. 356–8.

36 *Ibid.* pp. 186, 206–13. Mensdorff to Berchtold, 19C, 29 March 1912, S.A.W. XII, 375/xxxx/4.

37 Nicolson to Grey, 6 May enclosing Crowe Memorandum of same date, B.D. X(ii), nos. 385, 386.

38 With the proviso that a very reduced British battle squadron should also be retained at Malta: Kitchener to Grey, 2 June, *ibid.* no. 392.

39 On 5 Februrary and 13 April, B.D. XI(1), no. 368, X(2), no. 419.

40 *Ibid.* no. 391. See Andre, *op. cit.*, pp. 52–3.

41 'France cannot become our substitute in this respect, and she now commands no confidence in that public opinion which here directs the orientation of politicians.' Rodd, 24 June, *ibid.* no. 396.

42 Supra no. 391: Nicolson repeated this to Imperiali on 12 July (André, *op. cit.*, p. 71), and Grey again on 21 September (Askew, *op. cit.*, p. 231).

43 Both Grey and Bonar Law were at pains to assure Imperiali on 30 July after the House of Commons debate that there was no such intention: André, *op. cit.*, p. 49.

44 14, 17, 20, 30 October, B.D. x (2), pp. 622–3; See Rodd to Grey 21 October, F.O. 800/64; André, *op. cit.*, pp. 98–99.

45 Nicolson promised Imperiali 'a brief memorandum' on 17 October. In fact it was written by Crowe on 6 December and only reached Rodd on 29 December. He was then instructed not to show it to San Giuliano without further instructions, which were never sent. See B.D. x (2), pp. 628–36.

46 B.D. x (2), no. 427 and minutes.

47 André, *op. cit.*, pp. 100–1: B.D. x (2), no. 429: 'H(is) M(ajesty) said France could never accept Italy as one of the great powers and always treated her as an inferior.' Rodd, 29 January 1913, F.O. 800/64.

48 Crowe Memo 6 December 1912, B.D. x (2), p. 630. Asquith minuted, 'I am very sceptical as to its value.' (p. 632).

49 *Ibid.*

50 'Alla Consulta...prevaleva ormai l'idea di seguire una politica rigidamente triplicista.' André, p. 101. 'At present it is almost difficult to tell which is the Italian Minister for Foreign Affairs and which is the Austrian Ambassador.' Rodd to Grey, 26 May 1913, F.O. 800/64.

51 B.D. x (2), no. 435.

52 *Ibid.* nos. 436, 438.

53 Admiralty Memo. 20 June 1912, CAB/37/111/27.

54 Nicolson to Bertie, 23 May 1912, F.O. 800/356. See M. Gabriele, 'Le origine della convenzione navale italo-austro-germanica del 1912' in *Rassegna storica del Risorgimento*, July–December 1965.

55 Bosworth, *op. cit.*, p. 689.

56 Grey to Rodd, 31 July 1913, B.D. ix (2), 1190.

57 Grey minute on Dering to Grey, 15 October 1913; Grey to Rodd, 11 December 1913, quoted in Bosworth, *op. cit.*, p. 699.

58 Decleva, *op. cit.*, p. 445.

59 Rodd to Grey, 8 December, Grey to Rodd, 17 December 1913, F.O. 800/64.

60 See C. J. Lowe, 'Britain and Italian Intervention 1914–15' in the *Historical Journal*, 1968. Crowe was at least as hostile as Grey: on 11 January 1914 he minuted, 'one thing stands out quite clear, that the words and professions of Italian governments are not to be trusted'. Quoted in Bosworth, *op. cit.*, p. 701.

61 Crowe Memo. 17 May 1914, B.D. x (2), no. 449.

17. GREAT BRITAIN AND FRANCE, 1911–1914

1 Minute by Eyre Crowe on Bertie to Grey, 31 January 1911, F.O. 371/1117.

2 Bertie to Grey, 19 October, 21 October 1911, 2 November 1911, 3 November 1911, 5 November 1911; Grey to de Bunsen, 25 October 1911; Grey to Carnegie, 30 October 1911; Grey to Bertie, 5 November 1911; *British Documents on the Origins of War* (Hereafter cited as B.D.), vol. vii, nos. 593, 598, 605, 611, 614, 618, 627 and 631. Bertie to Grey, 2 November 1911, and 3 November 1911, Bertie MSS. A, F.O. 800/179. Bertie to Grey, 4 November 1911, Grey MSS. F.O. 800/52.

3 Bertie to Grey, 19 November 1911, Bertie MSS. A., F.O. 800/179. Joseph Caillaux, *Mes Mémoires* (Paris, 1942–7), vol. ii, pp. 192–3; Raymond Poincaré, *Au Service de la France* (Paris, 1926), vol. i, pp. 146–52.

4 'Memorandum by Sir Eyre Crowe respecting Franco-German Negotiations', 14 January 1912, B.D. vii, Appendix iii. Bertie to Grey, 26 November 1911, Bertie MSS. A., F.O. 800/160. Nicolson to Goschen, 15 January 1912, Nicolson MSS. F.O. 800/383. De Lalaing to Davignon, 15 January 1912, *Belgische Aktenstücke, 1905–1914*, no. 87.

5 Bertie to Grey, 22 January 1912, Bertie MSS. A., F.O. 800/166.

6 Bertie to Nicolson, 26 January 1912 and 1 Februrary 1912, Bertie MSS. F.O. 800/166. Grahame to Tyrrell, 23 January 1912, Grey MSS. F.O. 800/53.

7 Bertie to Grey, 22 January 1912; Bertie to Nicolson, 1 February 1912; Bertie MSS. A., F.O. 800/166. Poincaré to Grey, 23 January 1912, Grey MSS. F.O. 800/53.

8 Grey to Poincaré, 28 January 1912, Grey MSS. F.O. 800/53.

9 Keith Robbins, *Sir Edward Grey* (Cassell, London, 1971), pp. 344–57.

10 *Ibid.* Grey to Buchanan, 7 February 1912; Grey to Bertie, 7 February 1912, B.D. VII, 495 and 499.

11 Bertie to Grey, 21 December 1911 and 12 December 1911, B.D. X/11, 265 and 268. Bertie to Nicolson, 11 February 1912, B.D. VI, 509. Memoranda by Bertie of 16 February 1912, and 19 February 1912, Bertie MSS. A., F.O. 800/171.

12 Nicolson to Bertie, 8 February 1912, Bertie MSS. A., F.O. 800/171. P. Cambon to Poincaré, 7 February 1912, *Documents Diplomatiques Français* (Hereafter cited as D.D.F.), 3e sér. I, 629.

13 Minute by Grey on Bertie to Grey, 3 April 1912, B.D. VI, 364.

14 Grey to Goschen, 13 May 1912, B.D. VI, 584.

15 Grey to Bertie, 13 February 1912, B.D. VI, 514. P. Cambon to Poincaré, 13 February 1912, D.D.F., 3e sér., II, 30.

16 *Draft Formula*, 14 March 1912; Bertie to Nicolson, 28 March 1912 and 1 April 1912, B.D. VI, 537, 556, and 563.

17 Grey to Goschen, 29 March 1912, B.D. VI, 557.

18 P. Cambon to Poincaré, 15 March 1912 and 22 March 1912; Poincaré to P. Cambon, 30 March 1912, D.D.F., 3e sér., II, 205, 244, and 276.

19 *Note to Poincaré*, 27 March 1912, D.D.F., 3e sér., II, 266. Poincaré *op. cit.*, pp. 170–2.

20 Poincaré to Pateologue, 10 April 1912, D.D.F., 3e sér., II, 319.

21 Poincaré to Paul Cambon, 30 March 1912; P. Cambon to de Fleuriau, 3 April 1912; D.D.F., 3e sér., II, 276 and 295.

22 Poincaré to P. Cambon, 11 April 1912, D.D.F., 3e sér., II, 329.

23 Minute by Nicolson on Bertie to Grey, 3 April 1912; Minute by Nicolson, 4 April 1912; Nicolson to Grey, 6 April 1912, B.D. VI, 564, 566 and 567.

24 Grey to Bertie, 9 April 1912, B.D. VI, 569.

25 Grey to Goschen, 13 May 1912, B.D. VI, 584.

26 Grey to Bertie, 3 May 1912; Bertie to Grey, 16 May 1912; B.D. VI, 582 and 585. Bertie to Mallet, 12 May 1912; Bertie to Grey, 16 May 1912, Bertie MSS. A., F.O. 800/171. Nicolson to O'Beirne, 8 May 1912, Nicolson MSS. F.O. 800/355.

27 Nicolson to Bertie, 28 May 1912, Bertie MSS. A., F.O. 800/171. Grey to Bertie, 31 May 1912, B.D. VI, 589.

28 Poincaré commented on the *entente* that it was not consecrated by any diplomatic act and rested solely on the military conversations between the two general staffs. 'Tout qui déconcerterait le sentiment public', he observed, 'serait donc de nature à la détruire.' Poincaré to P. Cambon, 11 April 1912, D.D.F., 3e sér., II, 329.

29 Minute by Nicolson, 15 April 1912, B.D. VI, 576.

30 P. Cambon to Poincaré, 18 April 1912, D.D.F., 3e sér., II, 363. Nicolson to Bertie, 22 April 1912, Bertie MSS. A., F.O. 800/166.

31 The subject of British and French naval planning, and the arrangements made for the cooperation between their fleets is discussed in considerable detail in. S. R. Williamson, *The Politics of Grand Strategy* (Cambridge, Mass., 1969), and P. G. Halpern, *The Mediterranean Naval Situation 1908–1914* (Cambridge, Mass., 1971), pp. 1–150.

32 *Parliamentary Debates: Commons*, 5th ser., 35, 18 March 1912, 1564.

33 W. Churchill to Haldane, 6 May 1912, R. S. Churchill, *Winston S. Churchill*, Companion Volume, II, part 3, 1911–1914 (London, 1969), pp. 1548–1549.

34 Enclosures in Hankey to Grey, 29 April 1912, in E. W. R. Lumby (ed.), *Policy and Operations in the Mediterranean, 1912–1914* (The Navy Records Society, 1970), pp. 23–31.
35 *Op. cit.* Williamson and Halpern.
36 Nicolson to Grey, 4 April 1912, B.D. x/II, 383.
37 *Ibid.* minute by Churchill. Grey to Churchill, 11 May 1912, B.D. x/II, 389.
38 Nicolson to Bertie, 6 May 1912, B.D. x/II, 384. Nicolson to Goschen, 7 May 1912, Nicolson MSS. F.O. 800/355.
39 F.O. Memorandum, 8 May 1912, B.D. x/II, 386.
40 Nicolson to Bertie, 6 May 1912; Nicolson to Grey, 6 May 1912; Bertie to Nicolson, 9 May 1912; B.D. x/II, 384, 385 and 388.
41 *Ibid.*
42 A. J. Marder, *From Dreadnought to Scapa Flow*, vol. I, *The Road to War* (London, 1961), pp. 288–91.
43 Naval Situation in the Mediterranean, enclosed in note by Churchill, 15 June 1912; 'Note of Draft Arrangement connected with Lord Kitchener'; Lumby, pp. 23–31.
44 Memoranda by McKenna and Churchill, Lumby, pp. 37–42, 44–50, and 55–7.
45 *Op. cit.* Lumby, pp. 23–31.
46 Committee of Imperial Defence, minutes of the 117th meeting, 4 July 1912; Lumby, pp. 60–83.
47 De Fleuriau, the French *chargé d'affaires* in London, pointed out to Poincaré in a despatch of 30 May, 'Les Anglais commencent à reconnaitre l'inexactitude des principes qui guidaient leur politique étrangère, mais ils commencent seulement et leur opinion n'est pas encore fermement établie.' Meanwhile, Geoffray, the French ambassador to Spain, learned from his British colleague that at the discussions on Malta 'le principe d'une entente complète avec la France avait dominé toutes les discussions'. De Fleuriau to Poincaré, 30 May 1912; and Geoffray to Poincaré, 14 June 1912; D.D.F., 3e sér., III, 56 and 102.
48 De Saint-Seine to Delcassé, 10 July 1912, D.D.F., 3e sér., III, 189.
49 Asquith to the King, 16 July 1912, Asquith MSS, vol. VI.
50 Memorandum by Churchill, 17 July 1912, B.D. x/II, 399.
51 Memorandum by Bertie, 25 July 1912, Bertie MSS. A., F.O. 800/166.
52 Grey to Carnegie, 22 July 1912, B.D. x/II, 400.
53 Memorandum by Bertie, 25 July 1912 and 27 December 1912, Bertie MSS. A., F.O. 800/166. Minute by Nicolson, 24 July 1912; Grey to Carnegie, 26 July 1912, B.D. x/II, 401 and 402.
54 Note by Churchill, 29 July 1912, B.D. x/II, 403.
55 Memorandum by Bertie, 26 July 1912, Bertie MSS. A., F.O. 800/166.
56 Bertie to Grey, 30 July 1912, B.D. x/II, 404 and 405.
57 Grey to Carnegie, 26 July 1912, B.D. x/II, 402.
58 *Op. cit.* Bertie to Grey, 30 July 1912.
59 Bertie to Grey, 17 August 1912, B.D. x/II, 409.
60 W. S. Churchill, *The World Crisis* (London, 1923), pp. 112–13. Churchill to Grey, and Asquith, R. S. Churchill, *op. cit.*, pp. 1638–9.
61 Mallet to Grey, 23 August 1912, Grey MSS. F.O. 800/94.
62 Instructions for the movement of the French squadron based at Brest to Toulon were prematurely leaked to the press on 10 September. Cambon evidently believed that he was about to lose his best bargaining counter for on 17 September he explained to Nicolson that the move was only a temporary manoeuvre. There could, he said be no permanent move without 'une garantie sérieuse de l'Angleterre'. Poincaré, *op. cit.*, pp. 217–18. P. Cambon to Poincaré, 13 September 1912, D.D.F., sér., III, 431. Grey to Bertie, 19 September 1912, B.D. x/II, 410.

63 Asquith to Grey, 11 October 1912, B.D. x/11, 412.

64 Grey to Bertie, 16 October 1912, Bertie MSS. A., F.O. 800/166.

65 Asquith to George V, 1 October 1912, Asquith MSS. vol. vi. Grey to Bertie, 30 October 1912, B.D. x/11, 413.

66 Grey to P. Cambon, 22 November 1912; P. Cambon to Grey, 23 November 1912; B.D. x/11, 416 and 417.

67 De Saint-Seine to Aubert, 14 February 1913, D.D.F., 3e sér., v, 597 (and Annexes).

68 Nicolson to Grey, 1 August 1914, published in H. Nicolson, *Sir Arthur Nicolson, Bart.* (London, 1930), p. 420. P. Cambon to Viviani, 1 August 1914, D.D.F., 3e sér., xi, 532. Grey to Bertie, 1 August 1914, B.D. xi, 426 and 447.

69 Nicolson tc Hardinge, 5 September 1914, Hardinge MSS. 93.

70 W. S. Churchill, *op. cit.*, pp. 201–2.

71 On 23 July 1912 Grey assured Bertie that he 'would not remain in the Cabinet if there were any question of abandoning the policy of the Entente with France'. In response to Bertie's protest that it was the 'Dissenting Ministers who would have to drop out', Grey said he did not wish to break up the cabinet. Memorandum by Bertie, 25 July 1912, Bertie MSS. A., F.O. 800/166. Grey to Harcourt, 10 January 1914, Grey MSS. F.O. 800/91.

72 Memorandum by Grey, 24 September 1912, B.D. x/1, 805.

73 For a recent study of French nationalism in this period see, E. Weber, *The Nationalist Revival in France* (Berkeley and Los Angeles, 1968). Grahame to Tyrrell, 26 January 1913, Grey MSS. F.O. 800/54. Bertie to Grey, 19 February 1913, B.D. x/11, 461. Bertie to Grey, 3 March 1913; Grey to Bertie, 4 March 1913, Bertie MSS. A., F.O. 800/166. Nicolson to Goschen, 11 March 1913, Nicolson MSS.

74 Memorandum to Bertie, 26 March 1913, Bertie MSS. A., F.O. 800/166.

75 Memorandum by Bertie, 8 March 1914, enclosed in Bertie to Tyrrell, 9 March 1914, Bertie MSS. A., F.O. 800/176.

76 Grey to George V, 9 December 1912, B.D. x/11, 453.

77 Grey to Bertie, 4 December 1912, B.D. ix/11, 228.

78 Memorandum by Bertie, 23 June 1913, Bertie MSS. A., F.O. 800/166. *Annual Report for France, 1912.* Bertie to Grey, 1 August 1912, 407, F.O. 371/1646.

79 Memorandum by Bertie, 3 July 1913, Bertie MSS. A., F.O. 800/54. Bertie to Grey, 25 July 1913, Grey MSS. F.O. 800/54.

80 Buchanan to Grey, 18 February 1914, Grey MSS. F.O. 800/74. Nicolson to Buchanan, 7 April 1914 and 21 April 1914. Nicolson MSS. F.O. 800/373.

81 Memoranda by Bertie, 24 April 1914 and 27 April 1914, Bertie MSS. A., F.O. 800/166. 'Note du Ministre', 24 April 1914, D.D.F., 3e sér., x, 155. Poincaré, *op. cit.*, vol. iv, pp. 96–113. P. Cambon, *Correspondence, 1870–1914* (Paris, 1946), vol. iii, pp. 64–6.

82 *Annual Report for France, 1912*, Bertie to Grey, 1 August 1913, F.O. 371/1646.

83 Bertie to Grey, 11 February 1913, 76, F.O. 371/1683.

84 Bertie observed to Grey on 7 November 1912: 'Poincaré does not at all like being dragged along by Sazonow and Isvolsky and relies on you to put the skid on the Russian coach', Bertie to Grey, 7 November 1912, B.D. ix/11, 156. Grahame to Tyrrell, 2 April 1913, Grey MSS. F.O. 800/54. Grey to Buchanan, 7 April 1913, Grey MSS. F.O. 800/74.

85 Nicolson to Hardinge, 9 January 1913; Nicolson to Goschen, 14 January 1913, Nicolson MSS. F.O. 800/362.

86 Chirol to Hardinge, 10 April 1913, 18 April 1913, 8 May 1913, 22 May 1914; Hardinge to Chirol, 30 April 1913, 8 May 1913, 11 June 1914; Hardinge MSS. 93.

87 Nicolson would anyway have preferred to see the *entente* converted into alliances. Nicolson to Hardinge, 2 July 1913, Hardinge MSS. 93. Nicolson to Hardinge, 15 January 1914; Nicolson to Mallet, 2 March 1914; Nicolson MSS. F.O. 800/372. Nicolson to de Bunsen, 27 April 1914, Nicolson MSS. F.O. 800/373.

88 Paleologue, *op. cit.*, p. 159.

89 The French government were ill-informed about these negotiations. Indeed on 24 October 1913, three days after the initialling of the Anglo-German accord, the French *chargé d'affaires* in London expressed his disbelief in the reports, current in the British press about the negotiations. Only on 28 October did the Quai d'Orsay learn from their embassy at Berlin of a statement by Zimmermann, the German under-secretary of state, that an agreement was to be signed on the Portuguese colonies. Even then, it was not until Paul Cambon approached Grey on the subject on 29 October that they received any satisfactory explanation of what was afoot. De Fleuriau to Picton, 24 October 1913; de Manneville to Pichon, 28 October 1913. P. Cambon to Pichon 29 October 1913; D.D.F., 3e sér., VIII, 378, 391 and 397. Grey to Bertie, 29 October 1913, B.D. X/II, 345.

90 Initially the French were confused about the exact provisions of the Anglo-German accord. Though Grey claimed that he had informed Cambon on 28 November that the reversion of Cabinda had been allotted to Germany in 1898, the French ambassador seems not be have understood this until 6 January 1914. Grey to Granville, 28 November 1913; Grey to Bertie, 6 January 1914; B.D. X/II, 348 and 357. P. Cambon to Doumergue, 10 December 1915, D.D.F., 3e sér., VIII, 607. P. Cambon to Doumergue, 8 January 1914, D.D.F., 3e sér., VIII, 607. P. Cambon to Doumergue, 8 January 1914, D.D.F., 3e sér., IX, 35.

91 Doumergue to de Fleuriau, 18 December 1913; de Fleuriau to Doumergue, 24 December 1913; D.D.F., 3e sér., VIII, 640 and 668. P. Cambon to Doumergue, 8 January 1914 and 27 January 1914; Doumergue to P. Cambon, 20 January 1914, 26 January 1914, 10 February 1914, and 18 February 1914; D.D.F., 3e sér., IX, 35, 92, 116, 171, 256 and 326. Minutes by Nicolson and Grey, 8 January 1914; Bertie to Grey, 11 February 1914; B.D. X/II, 359 and 361.

92 Bertie to Grey, 11 February 1914, B.D. X/II, 361. Poincaré, *op. cit.*, vol. IV, pp. 56–8.

93 Nicolson to Hardinge, 25 February 1914, Hardinge MSS. 93.

94 Bertie to Grey, 12 February 1914, B.D. X/II, 362.

95 Memorandum by Bertie, 16–20 February 1914, Bertie MSS. B., F.O. 800/188. Memorandum by Bertie, 25 February 1914, Bertie MSS. A., F.O. 800/176. P. Cambon to Doumergue, 19 February 1914, D.D.F., 3e sér., IX, 333. Grey to Bertie, 18 February 1914 and 4 March 1914, B.D. X/II, 364 and 368. Poincaré, *op. cit.*, vol. IV, pp. 69–70.

96 B. C. Busch, *Britain and the Persian Gulf, 1894–1914* (Berkeley and Los Angeles, 1967), pp. 270–304.

97 G. H. Stuart, *The International City of Tangier* (Stanford, Calif., 1955), Chapter IV.

98 Memorandum by Eyre Crowe, 16 January 1915, F.O. 371/1683. Bertie to Nicolson, 16 September 1912, Nicolson MSS. F.O. 800/358.

99 Bertie to Grey, 11 February 1913, 76, F.O. 371/1683.

100 Grey to Bertie, 16 October 1912, Bertie MSS. B, F.O. 800/174.

101 Minutes by Villiers and Eyre Crowe on Bertie to Grey, 10 February 1913, tel. 24, F.O. 371/1684.

102 Nicolson to Cartwright, 19 February 1913, Nicolson MSS. F.O. 800/363.

18. GREAT BRITAIN AND THE TRIPLE ENTENTE ON THE EVE OF THE SARAJEVO CRISIS

1 For contemporary British comment on these developments, Bodleian Library, Asquith Papers, Box 24, O'Bierne to Grey, 12 June 1912, Battenberg to Asquith, 28 June 1912; British Museum, Scott Papers, Add. 50901, Memorandum by Scott, 30 June 1914; B.D. x (ii) 528, 529, 537 for the views of the British ambassador at St Petersburg; for the views of Gen. Sir Henry Wilson, D.M.O., Egmont Zechlin, 'Cabinet versus Economic Warfare in Germany', in H. W. Koch (ed.), *The Origins of the First World War. Great Power Rivalry and War Aims* (London, 1972), p. 150.

2 B.D. x (ii), 541; F.O. 800/110, Grey to Roosevelt, 10 September 1914.

3 F.O. 800/171, Memorandum by Bertie, 27 June 1914; F.O. 800/161, Memorandum by Bertie 16 July 1914.

4 Harold Nicolson, *Sir Arthur Nicolson Bart. First Lord Carnock* (London, 1930), p. x.

5 British Museum, Scott Papers, Add. 50901, Memorandum by Scott, 30 June 1914.

6 For Buchanan's views, B.D. x (ii), 528, 529; for Nicolson's views his correspondence is important, F.O. 800/373-375: on Morley, British Museum, Scott Papers, Add. 50901, Memorandum by Scott, 30 June 1914 and the present writer's 'Some Notes on Sir Edward Grey's Policy in July 1914', *Historical Journal*, xv 2 (1972), pp. 321-4; on Grey, F.O. 800/171, Memorandum by Bertie, 27 June 1914.

7 On Germany's problems, Bodleian Library, Asquith Papers, Box 25, Memorandum by Oppenheimer, 19 June 1913; B.D. x (ii), 528, 529; F.O. 800/171, Memorandum by Bertie, 27 June 1914; F.O. 800/161, Memorandum by Bertie, 16 July 1914: for observations on Austria-Hungary, B.D. x (i), 316; B.D. x (ii), 530, 536; F.O. 800/374, Nicolson to Hardinge, 11 June 1914: for Grey's suspicions of France, B.D. x (ii), 539, F.O. 800/171, Memorandum by Bertie, 27 June 1914.

8 B.D. x (i), 431 and 457 give insights into Grey's views; F.O. 800/374, Nicolson to Goschen, 18 May 1914.

9 F.O. 800/374, Goschen to Nicolson, 24 April 1914.

10 On Buchanan, B.D. x (ii), 528, 529 and his correspondence with Nicolson, F.O. 800/373-375; on Nicolson, F.O. 800/373-375, B.D. xi, 66; on Crowe, see the present writer's, 'Sir Edward Grey and Imperial Germany in 1914', *Journal of Contemporary History*, 3 (1971); on Goschen, F.O. 800/373, Goschen to Nicolson, 23 May 1914; on Bertie, F.O. 800/171, Memorandum by Bertie, 27 June 1914.

11 B. von Siebert, *Entente Diplomacy and the World. Matrix of the History of Europe, 1909-1914* (London, 1921), edited, arranged and annoted by G. A. Schreiner, document 846.

12 On Grey's distrust of Russia, F.O. 800/188, Memorandum by Bertie, 16 February 1914; F.O. 800/374, Nicolson to Hardinge, 11 June 1914.

13 For Grey's attitude towards Germany, see the two articles by the present writer, cited above: on the attitude of Tyrrell, F.O. 800/188, Lee to Bertie, 14 April 1914: on the younger officials, Public Record Office, G(erman) F(oreign) M(inistry) 10/199, Kühlmann to Bethmann-Hollweg, 22 May 1916.

14 B.D. x (i), 431.

15 On Russian policy, I. V. Bestuzhev, 'Russian Foreign Policy February-June 1914', *Journal of Contemporary History* 1, 3 (1966); Buchanan's warning, B.D. x (ii), 528; on the attitude of Grey and his officials, B.D. x (ii), 537 and 539.

16 On Franco-Russian co-operation, Siebert, *Entente Diplomacy and the World*, documents 842, 843: on French preliminary approaches to the Foreign Office, B.D. x (ii), 539; B.D. x (ii), 541; *Documents Diplomatiques Français (1871-1914)*, Series 3, x, p. 269; Siebert, *Entente Diplomacy and the World*, documents 844, 845.

17 D.D.F. Series 3, x, p. 269; Siebert, *Entente Diplomacy and the World*, document 844; F.O. 800/74, Grey to Buchanan, 7 May 1914.

18 F.O. 800/166, Memorandum by Bertie, 24 April 1914.

19 D.D.F. Series 3, x, p. 271.

20 Siebert, *Entente Diplomacy and the World*, documents 844, 846, 847; CAB. 41/35 Asquith to King George V, 14 May 1914.

21 The same De Siebert as the author of *Entente Diplomacy and the World*.

22 Pius Dirr (ed.), *Bayerische Dokumente zum Kriegsausbruch und zum Versailler Schuldspruch* (Munich and Berlin, 1922), Lerchenfeld to the President of the Ministerial Council, 4 June 1914, p. 111.

23 On German reaction to Anglo-Russian naval talks, see Zechlin's article, cited above; T. Wolff, *On the Eve of 1914* (New York, 1936), pp. 379–80.

24 F.O. 371/2092/25526, minute by Crowe, 9 June 1914; B.D. x (ii), 545; F.O. 800/171, Memorandum by Bertie, 27 June 1914; F.O. 800/375, minutes by Nicolson and Grey, 7 July 1914.

25 *Parliamentary Debates*, 5th Series (House of Commons), vol. 63, pp. 457–8; for the draft Foreign Office replies, F.O. 371/2092/26663.

26 See Chapter 23 on the Sarajevo crisis.

27 F.O. 800/171, Memorandum by Bertie, 27 June 1914.

28 Siebert, *Entente Diplomacy and the World*, documents 850, 851, 852, 856; F.O. 800/374, Battenberg to Nicolson, 23 May 1914, minutes by Nicolson and Grey, 25 May 1914; B.D. x (ii), 556, 559.

29 F.O. 800/91, Harcourt to Grey, 8 January 1914, Harcourt to Grey, 9 January 1914.

30 B.D. x (ii), 540.

31 F.O. 800/171, Memorandum by Bertie, 27 June 1914.

32 Siebert, *Entente Diplomacy and the World*, document 856; B.D. x (ii), Appendix I; B.D. xi, pp. x–xi.

19. GREAT BRITAIN AND CHINA, 1905–1911

1 F.O. 800/44, Satow (Minister to China) to Grey, 31 March 1906.

2 F.O. 371/35, Grey to Jordan, 31 August 1906.

3 D. Owen, *British Opium Policy in India and China* (New Haven, Conn., 1934); M. J. B. C. Lim, *Britain and the Termination of the India-China Opium Trade* (London Ph.D. thesis, 1969).

4 See A. Lamb, *The McMahon Line* (2 vols., London, 1966).

5 F.O. 371/35, Satow to Grey, 16 April 1906, with minutes by Grey, Hardinge and Campbell; Grey to Jordan, 7 August 1906. E-Tu Zen Sun, *Chinese Railways and British Interests 1898–1911* (New York, 1954), pp. 21–6.

6 J. V. A. MacMurray, *Treaties and Agreements with and concerning China 1894–1919* (2 vols., New York, 1921), i, 534.

7 F.O. 405/165, Grey to Satow, 12 January 1906: P.R.O. 30/33/7/5. Campbell to Satow, private, 12 and 26 January 1906. The Chinese pledge had been made in return for a British loan on favourable terms to assist the repurchase of the Hankow–Canton railway concession from American interests. By it, if China found it necessary to borrow abroad for the construction of the railway, British interests were to have the first option, provided tenders were not less favourable than others. With the loan would go preference for machinery and materials. See MacMurray, i, 530–1.

8 F.O. 371/214, Jordan to Grey, 23 December 1906. F.O. 405/180, British and Chinese Corporation to F.O. 18 March 1907, with enclosure. Responsibility for this situation rested with J. O. P. Bland, agent for the Corporation, who, disregarding the advice of Jordan, yielded to French insistence upon joint representation. In June 1907 Chang again refused to admit the French, F.O. 405/180, Jordan to Grey, 17 June 1907.

9 F.O. 405/180, Jordan to Grey, 22 June 1907, P. Cambon to Grey, 26 June 1907.

10 F.O. 371/214, Colonial Office to F.O. 10 and 30 July, 24 August, 13 September 1907, F.O. to Colonial Office, 25 July, 17 August, 9 September 1907.

11 Preliminary agreements for these railways had been made in 1898. The Soochow–Ningpo was a purely British scheme, the Tientsin–Pukow an Anglo-German project. Negotiations were impeded by provincial agitation against foreign railway agreements.

12 F.O. 405/188, Addis to F.O. 25 February 1908. Caillaux, before taking office, had been a member of the French Committee of Chinese Central Railways Ltd.

13 F.O. 305/5, Jordan to Campbell, private, 9 July, 1 and 15 October 1908.

14 F.O. 405/189, Lugard to Crewe encl. with Colonial Office to F.O., 23 July 1908; F.O. to Colonial Office, 5 August 1908.

15 F.O. 405/168, Grey to Bertie, 23 November 1906; F.O. 371/41, Jordan to Grey, 7 December 1906; F.O. 405/180, Grey to Bertie, 3 April 1907.

16 F.O. 405/180, Jordan to Grey, 7, 11, 15, 30 May 1907; Grey to Jordan, 6 June 1907; Lowther to Grey, 10 June 1907. Jordan thought 'it would be politic' that Japan should be allowed to participate. The Japanese government, on learning of Chang Chih-tung's pledge of September 1905, directed the Yokohama Specie Bank to retire from the affair.

17 F.O. 405/181, Jordan to Grey, 25 July 1907, with enclosure; F.O. 305/5, Jordan to Campbell, private, 3 and 31 October 1907.

18 F.O. 405/175, Jordan to Grey, 21 August 1907. Jordan noted that the Franco-Japanese agreement of June 1907 had caused serious misgivings in China.

19 F.O. 405/188, Jordan to Grey, 15 February 1908; F.O. 305/5, Jordan to Campbell, private, 5 March 1908.

20 F.O. 371/622, Memorandum by Addis, 30 January 1909. On the Tientsin–Pukow negotiation see E-tu Zen Sun, *op. cit.*, pp. 129–37. The final stages were conducted by Cordes alone as Bland had returned to London. Jordan had suspected that the Germans, to ingratiate themselves with the Chinese, would give easy terms F.O. 405/81, Jordan to Grey, 6 August 1907.

21 F.O. 371/622, Grey to Jordan, 13 and 19 January 1909.

22 F.O. 371/622, Minute by Campbell on Jordan to Grey, 21 January 1909, and on memorandum from Cambon, 25 January 1909; F.O. to Colonial Office, 27 January 1909; Campbell to Baron d'Erlanger, 28 January 1909.

23 F.O. 371/622, Memorandum by Addis, 30 January 1909; Memorandum from Cambon, 2 February 1909. For Clemenceau's irritation with British policy see B.D., VII, no. 148. For the Chinese side see E-Tu Zen Sun, pp. 98–108.

24 Bland, in negotiating the Canton–Kowloon railway loan agreement, signed 7 March 1907, had insisted on strict conditions, E-tu Zen Sun, p. 88.

25 F.O. 371/622, Memorandum by Campbell, 12 March 1909; F.O. 371/623, Addis to F.O. 22 March 1909.

26 F.O. 371/623, Grey to Bertie, 30 March 1909; to Goschen, 1 April 1909; to Jordan, 3 April 1909; Goschen to Grey, 7 April 1909. Memorandum for Chinese Minister, 8 April 1909.

27 F.O. 371/623, Addis to F.O. 1 May; Grey to Jordan, 3 May 1909.

28 F.O. 371/624, Jordan to Grey, 7 and 9 May, 1909; Grey to Jordan, 7 May 1909.

29 F.O. 371/624, Grey to Jordan, 11 May 1909; Addis to F.O., 17 May 1909. The agreement for the Hankow–Canton (Hupei and Hunan section) and the Hankow–Szechwan (Hupei section) was signed between the three banking groups and the Chinese government on 6 June 1909; McMurray, *op. cit.*, I, 880.

30 F.O. 371/435, Jordan to Grey, 12 December 1908, reporting that the United States minister, Rockhill, had told him that he had been instructed, with special reference to the Hankow–Canton line, to compete with other foreign legations in securing to American financiers equality of opportunity.

31 F.O. 371/624, Reid to Grey, 3 June 1909.

32 F.O. 371/624. Memorandum to Reid, 7 June 1909; Grey to Reid, 23 June 1909.

33 F.O. 371/624, Addis to F.O., 17 and 21 June 1909, with enclosures; Goschen to Grey, 24 June 1909. Campbell was aware of the danger. 'It will not do for us to be more anti-American than the French and Germans...' Memorandum of conversation with Addis, 16 June 1909.

34 F.O. 371/624, Addis to F.O., 15 June, encl. French F.O. memorandum, and 18 June 1909, with minutes by Alston and Campbell.

35 F.O. 371/625, Bryce to Grey, 21 June 1909, with minute by Grey.

36 F.O. 371/625, Grey to Bryce, 12 July 1909. The Americans, in compensation for accepting a 25% share in the Hankow–Szechwan line in place of the 50% share they claimed, demanded 25% also of the loan for the Hupei section of the Hankow–Canton line. The European groups, to strengthen their position signed, 6 July 1909, the general agreements for co-operation in railway and financial loans agreed upon in principle in May 1909.

37 F.O. 371/625, Jordan to Grey, 22 July 1909, with minutes by Campbell and Grey; Addis to F.O., 9 August 1909 with enclosure.

38 F.O. 371/625, Grey to Bryce, 27 July 1909.

39 F.O. 371/625, minute by Grey on memorandum from Metternich, 9 November 1909. Grey was under pressure not to give way to the Germans through a campaign mounted by Chirol in *The Times* against the alleged pro-German tendencies of the Hong Kong Bank, Chirol to Grey, 6 September 1909.

40 F.O. 371/626, Addis to F.O., 21 December 1909, with enclosure.

41 F.O. 371/851, Reid to Grey, 7 March and 2 April 1910, with minute by Grey; Addis to F.O., 12 and 14 May 1910.

42 F.O. 371/851, Bertie to Grey, 24 May 1910, with minutes by Alston and Campbell. For the text of the agreements see MacMurray, *op. cit.*, I, 886–7.

43 F.O. 371/851, Max Müller to Grey, 14 July 1910, with minute by Grey; F.O. 371/1068, Jordan to Grey, 16 December 1910; Grey to Jordan, 7 January 1911; Minute by Langley on Bertie to Grey, 14 February 1911.

44 F.O. 350/7, Jordan to Campbell, private, 24 May 1911.

45 F.O. 350/7, Jordan to Campbell, private, 24 June 1911.

20. GREAT BRITAIN, JAPAN AND NORTH-EAST ASIA, 1905–1911

1 B.D. VIII, no. 350. For a more detailed discussion of these issues, Nish, *The Anglo-Japanese Alliance* (London, 1966), Ch. 17.

2 B.D. VI, pp. 789–90.

3 B.D. VI, p. 790; CAB. 38/18/40, C.I.D., 111th meeting, 26 May 1911; B.D. VIII, nos. 353–4.

4 F.O. 371/270 [26176], Grey's minute on MacDonald–Grey, 10 July 1907.

5 B.D. VIII, no. 362.

6 B.D. VIII, nos. 349–50. Grey's action was widely criticized, vide C. Pearl, *Morrison of Peking* (Harmondsworth, 1971), p. 214.

7 Grey papers [F.O. 800/43], Grey to Jordan, 13 August 1909.

8 For detailed accounts, see J. O. P. Bland, *Recent events and present policies in China* (London, 1912), pp. 309–33, and E. W. Edwards, 'Great Britain and the Manchurian Railway question, 1909–10', *English Historical Review*, 321 (1966), 740–69.

9 F.O. 371/636, Reid to Grey, 9 November 1909.

10 F.O. 371/920 [32420], Grey to Bryce, 22 September 1910. Grey minuted: 'interference with railways has been the wrong tack altogether'.

11 Cf. Grey papers [F.O. 800/83], Grey to Bryce, 7 January 1911.

12 B.D. VIII, nos. 390–1.

13 B.D. VIII, nos. 392–9.
14 E.g. C. I. Eugene Kim and Han-Kyo Kim, *Korea and the Politics of Imperialism, 1876–1910* (Berkeley, Calif., 1967), p. 213.
15 F.O. 371/920 [32420], Grey to Bryce, 22 September 1910.
16 F.O. 371/1023 [26234], Grey to Carnegie, 29 July 1910.
17 B.D. VIII, p. 542 and no. 405.
18 B.D. VIII, nos. 406–7.
19 F.O. 371/1140, Ottley–Nicolson, 15 January 1911.
20 CAB 17/74/321, Nicolson–Ottley, 18 January 1911.
21 B.D. VIII, nos. 414–15. For a detailed treatment, P. C. Lowe, *British policy in the Far East, 1911–15* (London, 1969).
22 B.D. VIII, nos. 417–20.
23 This topic is covered in more detail in Nish, 'Australia and the Anglo-Japanese Alliance, 1901–1911', *Aust. J. Pol. Hist.*, 9 (1963). CAB. 38/18/40, C.I.D. 111th meeting, 26 May 1911.
24 B.D. VIII, no. 427.
25 Cf. B.D. VIII, fn. p. 531.

21. CHINA AND JAPAN, 1911–1914

1 F.O. 371/1310, minute by Lindley on MacDonald to Grey, 16 December 1911.
2 F.O. 371/1093, Jordan to Grey, 18 and 21 October 1911.
3 F.O. 350/1, Campbell to Jordan, private, 20 October 1911.
4 F.O. 371/1093, Grey to British representatives in Berlin, Paris and Washington, 23 October 1911.
5 F.O. 371/1095, Jordan to Grey, 20 November 1911. F.O. 371/1096, China Association to F.O., 23 November 1911. Jordan's objections were removed by Russia's decision to send troops to Hankow, Jordan to Grey, 30 November 1911; F.O. 371/1097, Jordan to Grey, 23 November 1911.
6 F.O. 371/1095, Grey to Jordan, 14 and 17 November 1911; Jordan to Grey, 20 November 1911. Sun's intermediary was Sir Trevor Dawson of Vickers, Maxim. Grey declined to approve a loan for the revolutionary leaders.
7 F.O. 371/1094, Townsend (Hong Kong and Shanghai Bank, London) to F.O. 3 November 1911, with minutes by Grey, Campbell and Max Müller; F.O. 371/1095, Grey to Jordan, 11 November 1911.
8 F.O. 371/1096, Jordan to Grey, 6 December 1911; Bertie and Goschen to Grey, 9 December 1911; F.O. 371/1097, Jordan to Grey and Grey to Jordan, 16 December 1911.
9 F.O. 371/1312, Grey to Bryce, 7 February 1912; Jordan to Grey, 9 February 1912. Peter Lowe, *Great Britain and Japan, 1911–1915* (London, 1969), p. 84, notes that the Japanese government tacitly approved of the loan negotiations.
10 F.O. 371/1311, MacDonald to Grey, 26 January 1912; F.O. 371/1312, MacDonald to Grey, 8 February 1912; minute by Langley on Jordan to Grey, 21 February 1912.
11 M. B. Jansen, *The Japanese and Sun Yat-Sen* (Cambridge, Mass., 1954), pp. 131–5; M. Ikei, 'Japan's response to the Chinese Revolution of 1911', *Journal of Asian Studies*, xxv.
12 F.O. 371/1094, Jordan to Grey, 31 October 1911.
13 F.O. 371/1094, Memorandum from Yamaza, 6 November 1911; F.O. 371/1095, Memorandum from Yamaza 9 November; aide-mémoire for Yamaza, 9 November 1911. In reply to Grey's warning that Russia would take similar action, the Japanese indicated that if action were decided on, Russia would be consulted fully.

14 F.O. 371/1096, communication from the Japanese government, 1 December 1911; Jordan to Grey, 3 December 1911. Memorandum for Yamaza, 5 December 1911; F.O. 350/1, Campbell to Jordan, private, 2 December 1911.

15 F.O. 350/1, Campbell to Jordan, private, 8 December 1911. Grey approved of Jordan's action in assisting the making of the armistice, F.O. 371/1096, Jordan to Grey, 1 December 1911, with minutes. At Jordan's request he was authorised to join with ministers of the major powers in a simultaneous communication to the conference urging settlement as soon as possible, F.O. 371/1097, Jordan to Grey, 15 December 1911; Grey to Jordan, 16 December 1911.

16 F.O. 371/1096, Jordan to Grey, 8 December 1911; Grey to Jordan and MacDonald, 8 December 1911; to MacDonald, 4 January 1912.

17 F.O. 371/1098, memorandum from Yamaza, 24 December 1911; minute by Grey, 25 December 1911. The Japanese memorandum was a further statement of the case for a constitutional monarchy.

18 Kit Ching Lau, *Sir John Jordan and the Affairs of China, 1906–1916* (London Ph.D. thesis, 1968), pp. 189–90, takes the view that the Foreign Office, unlike Jordan, was unwilling to give its support exclusively to Yuan at this time. Among factors impelling caution in the uncertain period since October was the very strong support for the republican cause in Hong Kong and among the Chinese population in Singapore. Agreement was reached secretly at the Shanghai conference that the Manchu regime should be replaced by a republic and that its presidency should go to the personage who secured the abdication of the emperor. Yuan, who privately accepted this agreement, was the obvious figure. E. P. Young, 'Yuan Shih-k'ai's Rise to the Presidency' in M. C. Wright (ed.), *China in Revolution: The First Phase 1900–1913* (London, 1968), pp. 419–43, points out that this fact was recognised by the southern republicans. 'The republicans were not tricked into giving Yuan the presidency...insofar as it could be determined, he was the "people's choice".' In the view of the revolutionaries Yuan was 'the one man who could achieve the dynasty's abdication and at the same time retain national unity and keep the foreign powers at bay'. The essential condition for them was that he should accept republicanism. Sun Yat-sen, when elected on 2 January 1912 president of a separate southern government centred on Nanking, announced that he would resign in Yuan's favour when the emperor had abdicated and the republic was proclaimed. He duly did so in April 1912 having in the meantime vainly endeavoured to get the capital of the new regime established in Nanking in place of Peking, a scheme opposed by the powers and by majority opinion in China.

19 F.O. 371/1313, Memorandum from Yamaza, 22 February 1912.

20 F.O. 371/1313, Bryce to Grey, 28 February 1912.

21 F.O. 371/1313, Addis to F.O., 17 February 1912, with minute by Grey; F.O. 350/1, Langley to Jordan, private, 29 February 1912.

22 F.O. 371/1313, memorandum from Cambon, 27 February 1912, with minute by Langley; F.O. 371/1314, MacDonald to Grey, 5 March 1912 with minute by Grey.

23 F.O. 371/1314, Granville to Grey, 1 March 1912; de Fleuriau to F.O., 3 March 1912; memorandum by Langley with minute by Grey, 6 March 1912. F.O. 371/1315, minute by Langley on Russian aide-mémoire, 13 March 1912; Buchanan to Grey, 16 March 1912; MacDonald to Grey, 18 March 1912.

24 F.O. 405/208, Buchanan to Grey, 6 April 1912; F.O. 371/1317, memorandum for Benckendorff, 6 May 1912; F.O. 371/1319, Bertie to Grey, 7, 8 and 19 June 1912; *Documents Diplomatiques Français 1871–1914*, IIIᵉ série, ii, no. 334, note rélative aux emprunts chinois, 12 April 1912.

25 F.O. 371/1319, Grey to Bertie, 19 June 1912.

26 F.O. 371/1319. Addis to F.O., 22 June 1912; Grey to MacDonald, 26 June 1912.

27 F.O. 371/1319, note from Cambon, 2 May 1912; memorandum to Cambon, 9 May 1912.

28 F.O. 371/1315, F.O. to Addis, 14 March 1912; China no. 2, 1912, *Correspondence respecting Chinese Loan Negotiations 1912* (Cd. 6446).

29 F.O. 371/1322, memorandum by Gregory, 2 September 1912, on interview with G. E. Morrison.

30 F.O. 405/209, Grey to Jordan, 23 August 1912; memorandum by Gregory, 2 September 1912; F.O. 371/1322, Jordan to Gregory, 12 September 1912.

31 F.O. 371/1321, minute by Gregory, 26 August 1912; Grey to Jordan, 30 August 1912.

32 F.O. 371/1322, Jordan to Grey, 3 September 1912.

33 F.O. 371/1322, Grey to British representatives to the consortium governments, 27 September 1912, threatening the withdrawal of exclusive support; F.O. 405/209, Grey to Rumbold, 2 November 1912. China eventually cancelled the Crisp loan but Crisp secured compensation for surrender of his rights.

34 F.O. 405/211, Jordan to Grey, 20 January 1913; Grey to Jordan, 1 February 1913.

35 F.O. 405/209, Addis to F.O., 25 March 1913; F.O. 405/211, Hong Kong Bank to F.O., 26 April; Jordan to Grey, 27 and 28 April 1913. The loan was floated very successfully, the issue being largely oversubscribed; F.O. 371/1594, Addis to F.O., 21 May 1913.

36 F.O. 371/1624, Jordan to Grey, 5 June, 1913. Grey was careful not to take any measure which the southern leaders might regard as unfriendly interference and which might therefore endanger foreign lives. Grey to Greene 20 July, to Alston, 23 July 1913.

37 A. Lamb, *The McMahon Line* (2 vols, London, 1966), II, 433–4.

38 F.O. 371/1622, memoranda from Koiké, 5 and 9 April 1913. Grey observed that if the Japanese considered recognition desirable at any moment now, 'it will not do for us to be left behind', F.O. 405/211, Grey to Jordan, 14 April 1913.

39 F.O. 371/1622, Jordan to Grey, 16 and 31 May 1913.

40 F.O. 405/212, Alston to Grey, 27 September 1913. The Tibet question was left unresolved to be the subject of separate negotiations, Lamb, *op. cit.*, II, 469–77.

41 F.O. 350/11, Langley to Jordan, private, 10 January 1913, 'The pressure at this end has made Sir E. Grey thoroughly weary of the monopoly, at any rate in regard to industrial loans.'

42 F.O. 405/209, Jordan to Grey, 25 December 1912; F.O. 371/1594, minute by Grey on Alston to Grey, 19 August 1913. With industrial loans tied to the consortium, Britain could hope only for one-sixth share, yet the bulk of money lent to China came from Britain and would thus be used to finance competitors. If the loans were free a much larger proportion, it was felt, would be taken up in London, Lowe, *op. cit.*, pp. 137–8.

43 Japan and Russia were opposed. F.O. 371/1590, Grey to Rumbold, 3 January 1913; F.O. 371/1594, Benckendorff to Nicolson, 30 June 1913.

44 F.O. 371/1594, memorandum by Gregory, 19 August 1913; Jordan to Gregory, 26 August 1913; F.O. to Hong Kong Bank, 3 September 1913. The immediate occasion for action was a report by Alston, 19 August, that a German firm was pressing industrial loans upon the Yunnan government.

45 F.O. 371/1590, Jordan to Grey, 6 January 1913; F.O. 405/212, Hong Kong Bank to F.O., 26 September 1913. Jordan's optimism, not shared by Addis, was illustrative of an attitude widespread in Britain about the competitive nature of British trade overseas, D. C. M. Platt, *Finance, Trade, and Politics: British Foreign Policy 1815–1914* (Oxford, 1968), p. 104.

46 F.O. 371/1623, Bertie to Grey, 29 March 1913. Addis to Langley, 7 April 1913. It soon emerged that the Banque industrielle was sponsored by the French F.O., Grey to Jordan, 7 April 1913; Bertie to Grey, 28 April 1913. France had taken a more

independent line from the end of 1912. M. Bastid, 'La Diplomatie Française et la Révolution Chinoise de 1911' *Revue d'Histoire moderne et contemporaine*, XVI, 221–45, shows that in the months following October 1911 the dominating aim of France, concerned above all with European issues, was to preserve unity among the powers. French policy, though complicated by the attitude of Russia had then followed the British lead.

47 F.O. 405/213, Alston to Grey, 16 June 1913; Cambon to Grey, 18 July 1913; Alston to Grey, 15 November 1913.

48 371/1623, minute by Gregory on Alston to Grey, 7 November 1913.

49 F.O. 405/209, Jordan to Grey, 12 November 1912; F.O. 405/211, Jordan to Grey, 7 February 1913.

50 M. B. Jansen, *The Japanese and Sun Yat-Sen* (Stanford, Calif., 1970), p. 154 and T. E. Lafargue, *China and the World War* (Stanford, Calif., 1937), pp. 31–2, point out that Japan had fallen behind the other powers in the new scramble for railway concessions. Langley considered that Japan would not be a very formidable competitor, F.O. 371/1624, minute on Greene to Grey, 28 June 1913.

51 F.O. 371/1621, memorandum by Mayers (agent in China of the British and Chinese Corporation and of Chinese Central Railways Ltd), 7 April 1913, on his conversation with the Japanese financier, Odagiri, in January 1913; minute by Langley on Jordan to Grey, 11 April 1913; Alston to Grey, 15 August 1913. Russia also proposed co-operation of Russian and British capital in industrial enterprise in China, F.O. 405/213; Buchanan to Grey, 22 March 1913, but this was turned aside.

52 F.O. 371/1621, Alston to Grey, 15 August and 20 September 1913, with minutes; Greene to Grey, 12 and 30 September 1913. Lowe, *op. cit.*, p. 115, thinks that Alston's reports contributed significantly to the creation of an atmosphere of distrust in Anglo-Japanese relations. The Japanese government maintained a correct attitude during the rebellion.

53 F.O. 371/1625, Alston to Grey, 26 September 1913, with minutes; Grey to Greene, 27 September 1913.

54 F.O. 371/1625, minutes on Granville to Grey, 1 October 1913.

55 F.O. 371/1621, Minute by Gregory on Jordan to Grey, 13 December 1913; memorandum to Japanese ambassador, 31 December 1913; memorandum to French embassy, 1 January 1914. The reciprocity argument had been put to the Japanese in October, Grey to Alston, 11 October 1913. Conflict with France at least enabled the F.O. to escape the charge that British opposition was exclusively against Japan.

56 F.O. 371/1935, memoranda from French embassy, 5 March and 6 April 1914; memoranda for French embassy, 17 March and 6 July 1914.

57 F.O. 371/1941, Greene to Grey, 16 February 1914, Grey to Greene, 21 February 1914. Yuan Shih-k'ai was pleased by British opposition to Japanese pressure into the Yangtse valley. Minute by Gregory, 5 March, on conversation with Barton, Chinese Secretary at the Peking Legation.

58 F.O. 371/1621, Jordan to Grey, 13 December 1913; Greene to Grey, 14 December 1913. Greene to Grey, 4 January 1914. F.O. 800/31, Greene to Langley. The attitude of Langley who had earlier been inclined to co-operation with Japan is indicative. He minuted Greene to Grey, 17 May 1914, which recorded further Japanese proposals, '...it is a political alliance and we want no industrial partnership'.

59 F.O. 371/1941, minute by Gregory on Jordan to Grey, 15 March 1914; minute by Langley on Hong Kong Bank to F.O., 19 March. F.O. 371/1933, Grey to Jordan, 30 March 1914.

60 In April Jordan had felt some confidence. 'We have now a British railway from Canton to Ningpo and have drawn a big cordon of British railways round the whole district in which Shanghai is situated', F.O. 350/12, Jordan to Langley, private, 6 April 1914.

61 F.O. 371/1938, Grey to Jordan, 27 July 1914. By July Jordan was pessimistic. F.O. 350/12, Jordan to Langley, private, 27 July, '...the Tibet question is a severe handicap in obtaining concessions. This and the distracted state of home politics are telling against us just now in China and not since the dark days of the South African war has our task been more difficult in the Far East.'

62 Jordan, who had welcomed the freeing of industrial loans, was soon lamenting British ineffectiveness in face of competition; F.O. 350/12, Jordan to Langley, private, 8 March 1914.

22. GREAT BRITAIN AND THE NEW WORLD, 1905–1914

1 Edward, First Viscount Grey of Fallodon, *Twenty-Five Years, 1892–1916* (New York, 1925), II, p. 88.

2 *Ibid.*, pp. 90–6. The broader basis of Anglo-American understanding is dealt with by Bradford Perkins, *The Great Rapprochement: England and the United States, 1895–1914* (New York, 1968), chapter 6.

3 H. A. L. Fisher, *James Bryce (Viscount Bryce of Dechmont, O.M.)* (London, 1927); Edmund Ions, *James Bryce and American Democracy, 1870–1922* (London, 1968); see also James Bryce, *South America, observations and impressions* (New York, 1912).

4 Stephen Gwynn, ed., *The Letters and Friendships of Sir Cecil Spring-Rice, a record* (London, 1920).

5 H. C. Allen, *Great Britain and the United States; a History of Anglo-American Relations, 1783–1952* (London, 1954), pp. 613–14.

6 Thomas A. Bailey, *Theodore Roosevelt and the Japanese–American Crises* (Stanford, Calif., 1934).

7 There is no recent overall study of this issue. Important references are: Sidney Louis Gulick, *American Democracy and Asiatic Citizenship* (New York, 1918); Alfred Whitney Griswold, *The Far Eastern Policy of the United States* (New York, 1938), esp. pp. 339 ff.; United States, Department of State, *Japanese Emigration and Immigration to American Territory*, part II (Washington, D.C., United States Government Printing Office, 1909); *American–Japanese Discussions relating to Land Tenure Law of California* (Washington D.C., United States Government Printing Office, 1914).

8 Important memoirs of British representatives in Latin America in this period are confined to two: Ernest Hambloch, *British Consul; Memories of Thirty Years Service in Europe and Brazil* (London, 1938) and Sir Thomas Beaumont Hohler, *Diplomatic Petrel* (London, 1942)

9 Their troubles, it should be said, were often their own fault, cf. Alan K. Manchester, *British Preeminence in Brazil, its Rise and Decline* (Chapel Hill, N.C., 1933), pp. 339–42. See also D. C. M. Platt, *Finance, Trade and Politics. British Foreign Policy 1815–1914* (Oxford, 1968), p. 352.

10 That in the northern territories had been arbitrated successfully by King Edward VII in 1902.

11 E. Bradford Burns, *The Unwritten Alliance; Rio-Branco and Brazilian–American Relations* (New York, 1966), esp. pp. 194–7.

12 Well discussed in René MacColl, *Roger Casement* (London, 1956), pp. 80–103.

13 Or, as he habitually put it, the *Irish* Consul-General – Hambloch, p. 75.

14 Gordon Connell-Smith, *The Inter-American System* (London, 1966), p. 47–55.

15 See especially Allan Reed Millet, *The Politics of Intervention; the military occupation of Cuba 1906–1909* (Columbus, Ohio, 1968).

16 Dana Gardner Munro, *Intervention and Dollar Diplomacy in the Carribbean 1900–21* (Princeton, N.J., 1964), pp. 141–159.

17 D. C. M. Platt, 'The Allied Coercion of Venezuela, 1902–3 – A Reassessment', *Inter-American Economic Affairs*, xv, no. 4, Spring 1962, p. 2.

18 Frederick B. Pike, *Chile and the United States, 1880–1962; The Emergence of Chile's Social Crisis and the Challenge to United States Diplomacy* (Notre Dame, Ind., 1963), pp. 139–41.

19 Minute on Reginald Thomas Tower – Grey, 23 August 1910, no. 11. Foreign Office Papers, Political, Public Record Office, London (hereafter cited as FO) 371/928, file 32395.

20 Munro, pp. 217–35.

21 Lionel Carden – Grey, 29 January 1912. FO 371/1305, file 247/7385. For a detailed treatment of the Guatemalan affair, see Peter Calvert, 'The Last Occasion on which Britain used Coercion to Settle a Dispute with a Non-Colonial Territory in the Caribbean: Guatemala and the Powers, 1909–1913', *Inter-American Economic Affairs*, xxv, no. 3, Winter 1971.

22 Carden–Grey, Telegram no. 1, received 3 January 1912. FO 371/1305, file 247/403.

23 Council of Foreign Bondholders–Grey, 19 January 1912; Grey–James Bryce, 17 October 1912, Telegram no. 183, Confidential and reply. FO 371/1305, file 247/2777, 40249, 44237.

24 Minute on Bryce–Grey, 5 December 1912, no. 243. FO 371/1305, file 247/53530.

25 The incident is amusingly described from the American side in Hugh Wilson, *The Education of a Diplomat* (London, 1938), pp. 59–60. Instructions in Grey–Carden, 11 February 1913, no. 15. FO 371/1583, file 1266/1394.

26 Except where otherwise cited, material on Mexico from Peter Calvert, *The Mexican Revolution, 1910–1914; the diplomacy of Anglo-American conflict* (Cambridge, 1968).

27 Correspondence in FO 371/927.

28 For the Colombian negotiations and their significance see Peter A. R. Calvert, 'The Murray Contract; An Episode in International Finance and Diplomacy', *Pacific Historical Review*, xxxv, no. 2, May 1966, p. 203; and for a brief account of the Costa Rican negotiations, Munro, *op cit.*, pp. 430–2.

29 Grey–Sir Cecil Spring-Rice, 13 November 1913, no. 656. FO 371/1678, file 6269/51579.

30 Kenneth J. Grieb, *The United States and Huerta* (Lincoln, Nebraska, 1969), pp. 139–41. See also Berta Ulloa, *La Revolución intervenida: Relaciones diplomaticas entre México y Estados Unidos (1910–1914)*. Mexico, El Colegio de México, 1971.

31 Robert E. Quirk, *An Affair of Honor: Woodrow Wilson and the Occupation of Vera Cruz* (New York, 1964).

32 Grieb, *op. cit.*, p. 159.

23. THE SARAJEVO CRISIS

1 B.D. xi, 112.

2 See Chapter 18 on 'Great Britain and the Triple Entente on the Eve of the War'. For Grey's awareness of the risks involved in Austro-Serbian conflict see, for example, B.D. xi, 4.

3 See Chapter 9 on The Balkan Wars.

4 P.R.O. Grey Papers, F.O. 800/74, Grey to Buchanan, 7 May 1914; Bertie Papers, F.O. 800/171, Memorandum by Bertie, 27 June 1914.

5 B.D. vii, 352; B.D. ix (ii), 449, 556. B.D. x (i) 223, 424, 441, 455; F.O. 371/2092/11537, 11538, 11628, Minutes by Crowe.

6 L. Albertini, *The Origins of the War of 1914* (3 vols., London, 1953), translated and Edited by Isabella M. Massey, ii, 7–11, 115–19. B.D. xi, 36, 49.

7 I. Geiss (ed.), *July 1914* (London, 1967), pp. 102–31.

8 Prince Lichnowsky, *My Mission to London* (London, 1918), 31–2.

9 Major-General Sir Frederick Maurice, *Haldane 1856–1915* (2 vols., London, 1937–9), i, 348.

10 B.D. XI, 32; For Lichnowsky's eliptical account, see *Outbreak of War, German Documents* collected by Karl Kautsky and edited by Max Montgelas and Walter Schücking, translated by the Carnegie Endowment for International Peace Division of International Law (New York, 1924), 20. For an assessment of Grey's reaction, see Michael Ekstein. 'Some Notes on Sir Edward Grey's Policy in July 1914', *Historical Journal* (1972), pp. 321–4.

11 Prince Lichnowsky, *Heading for the Abyss* (London, 1928), p. 9.

12 B.D. XI, 41; Kautsky, *German Documents*, 30.

13 B.D. XI, 38 and 39; D.D.F., Series 3, x, 483.

14 D.D.F., Series 3, x, 483 and footnote 2, 484; B.D. XI, 40. For the background to Nicolson's attitude, P.R.O., Nicolson Papers, F.O. 800/375, Minute by Nicolson, 7 July 1914, printed in H. Nicolson, *Lord Carnock* (London, 1930), 407–8. B. de Siebert, edited, arranged and annotated by George Abel Schreiner, 858, *Entente Diplomacy and the World. Matrix of the History of Europe, 1909–1914* (London, 1921).

15 L. Cecil, *Albert Ballin. Business and Politics in Imperial German 1888–1918* (Princeton, N.J., 1967), 203–13. D. C. Watt, 'British Press Reactions to the Assassination at Sarajevo', *European Studies Review* (1971), I, 233–47.

16 R. Vansittart, *The Mist Procession* (London, 1958), 122. B.D. XI, 63, 74, 177, 239, D.D.F., Series 3, XI, 23.

17 B.D. XI, 44.

18 B.D. XI, 50, 56.

19 P.R.O., Bertie Papers, F.O. 800/161, Memorandum by Bertie, 16 July 1914.

20 De Siebert, *Entente Diplomacy and the World*, 858.

21 B.D. XI, 50, 68, 73, 77.

22 B.D. XI, 67, 79, 88.

23 H. Poincaré, *Au Service de la France* (Paris, 1927), IV, 252–3; B.D. XI, 76.

24 B.D. XI, 76; For Grey's wish not to excite Germany and his distrust of Poincaré, P.R.O. Bertie Papers, F.O. 800/171, Memorandum by Bertie, 27 June 1914, F.O. 800/161, Memorandum by Bertie, 16 July 1914. For his desire to avoid direct involvement, B.D. XI, 112.

25 B.D. XI, 86, 91 and Appendix A, p. 364.

26 C.A.B. 41/35, Asquith to King George V, 24 July 1914; B.D. XI, 98.

27 B.D. XI, 98; Kautsky, *German Documents*, 157.

28 B.D. XI, 111, 114; For an assessment of the Foreign Office mood on the evening of 25 July, Vansittart, *The Mist Procession*, 124 and *I Documenti Diplomatici Italiani*, Series 4, XII, 528.

29 B.D. XI, 139a, 139b, 140.

30 On Nicolson's scepticism about the conference proposal, B.D. XI, 144; On his fear of breaking with Russia, B.D. XI, 66, 239; For Buchanan's warning, B.D. XI, 125.

31 B.D. XI, 77 and 101.

32 Winston S. Churchill, *The World Crisis 1911–1914* (London, 1923), 198.

33 B.D. XI, 112.

34 Public Record Office of the House of Lords, Samuel Papers, File A/157, Samuel to Beatrice Samuel, 29 July 1914.

35 British Museum, Spender Papers, Add. 46312, Memorandum by Spender, August 1914.

36 Public Record Office of the House of Lords, Samuel Papers, File A/157, Samuel to Beatrice Samuel, 29 July 1914.

37 B.D. XI, 303.

38 Cambridge University Library, Crewe Papers, Box C50, Crewe to Trevelyan, 2 May 1936.

39 B.D. XI, 170, 179, 199, 233.

40 B.D. XI, 215, 223.

41 Lord Morley, *Memorandum on Resignation August 1914* (London, 1928), 1–3, states Grey first asked the Cabinet to make up its mind on the question of war and peace 'on or about July 24–27'. This evidence does not altogether match other reports. In the absence of Cabinet minutes there will always be room for differences of interpretation. It seems most likely, however, that Morley's account of the Cabinet of 27 July confuses, at least in emphasis, that meeting with the Cabinet of 29 July. Morley's account of the Cabinet of 27 July corresponds with other accounts of 29 July and fits together with Grey's private warnings to Lichnowsky that afternoon. With reference to Morley's accuracy, Samuel wrote to his wife on 2 August, 'Morley...is now so old that the views he expressed are sadly inconsequent and inconsistent.' (Public Record Office of the House of Lords, File A/157.) For Grey's warnings to Lichnowsky, B.D. XI, 286 and Kautsky, *German Documents*, 368.

42 Kautsky, *German Documents*, 395, 396, 409, B.D. XI, 329, 337.

43 B.D. XI, 340, 411, 417, 418.

44 C. F. Turner, *The Origins of the First World War* (London, 1970), 56–9, 91–6.

45 This is a central theme of Haldane's *Before the War* (London, 1920). Also B.D. VI, 506, 'Diary of Lord Haldane's Visit to Berlin'.

46 B.D. XI (ii), 424, 441, 455.

47 Kautsky, *German Documents*, 3. P.R.O. Bertie Papers F.O. 800/171, Memorandum by Bertie, 27 June 1914.

48 P.R.O. Grey Papers, F.O. 800/65, Grey to Rodd, 6 March 1915. For additional information see Michael Ekstein, 'Sir Edward Grey and Imperial Germany in 1914', *Journal of Contemporary History* (1971), VI, 3.

49 British Museum, Scott Papers, Add. 50901, Memorandum by Scott, 3 August 1914.

50 B.D. VI, Appendix 5.

51 B.D. XI, 665. For views of Crowe and Nicolson, B.D. XI, 66, 101, 239, Nicolson, *Lord Carnock*.

52 P.R.O. CAB. 41/35, Asquith to King George V, 28 July 1914.

53 P.R.O. CAB. 41/35, Asquith to King George V, 29 July 1914; Public Record Office of the House of Lords, Samuel Papers, File A/157, Samuel to Beatrice Samuel, 29 July 1914. The details of what passed at Cabinet meetings and which ministers took up what positions at which times needs to be reconstructed from a wealth of primary and memoir material which requires interpretation at a level that notes (unless very cumbersome) cannot reproduce. The most complete account is Cameron Hazelhurst's *Politicians at War July 1914–May 1915* (London, 1971). There are the Prime Ministers' letters to the King (CAB./41). The Spender Papers (British Museum), Add. 56383 contain much information from Cabinet Ministers which Spender gathered for his biography of Asquith. Samuel's contemporary letters to his wife, in the Samuel Papers in the Public Record Office of the House of Lords are also a helpful source. There are some notes made in the Cabinet in the Lloyd George Papers (Beaverbrook Library). The memoirs of Churchill, Grey, Haldane, Morley, Samuel and Simon all contain additional information.

54 P.R.O. CAB. 41/35, Asquith to King George V, 29 July 1914.

55 British Museum, Burns Papers, Add. 46336, Burns Appointment Diary, 29 July 1914.

56 Public Record Office of the House of Lords, Samuel Papers, Samuel to Beatrice Samuel, 30 and 31 July 1914; British Museum, Spender Papers, Add. 56386, Lord Crewe's answer to questionnaire by Spender and Professor Temperley.

57 B.D. XI, 293.

58 W. S. Churchill, *The World Crisis*, 217; M. Hankey, *The Supreme Command* (2 vols., London, 1961), I, 155–7; P.R.O., CAB. 41/35, Asquith to King George V, 30 July, 1914; Winston S. Churchill, *Great Contemporaries* (London, 1952), 109; University of

Birmingham, Austen Chamberlain Papers, AC/14/2/2, memorandum by Austen Chamberlain, on the July Crisis, written early August 1914.

59 On British military planning for war, Niel W. Summerton, 'The Development of British Military Planning for a War against Germany, 1904–1914' (unpublished Ph.D. thesis, London University), Samuel R. Williamson Jr, *The Politics of Grand Strategy* (Cambridge, Mass., 1970). On Wilson, Major-General Sir C. E. Callwell, *Field Marshall Sir Henry Wilson Bart., His Life and Diaries* (London, 1927), 151–8, and H. Nicolson, *Lord Carnock*, 419; University of Birmingham Library, Austen Chamberlain Papers, AC/14/2/2, memorandum by Austen Chamberlain on the July Crisis, written early August 1914.

60 Robert Blake, *The Unknown Prime Minister. The Life and Times of Andrew Bonar Law* (London, 1955), p. 221.

61 Birmingham University Library, Austen Chamberlain Papers, AC/14/2/2, Memorandum by Austen Chamberlain on the July Crisis, written early August 1914.

62 Lord Newton, *Lord Lansdowne, A Biography* (London, 1929), 439–42. C. F. Adam, *Life of Lord Lloyd* (London, 1948), 58–60. Robert Blake, *The Unknown Prime Minister*, 321–4. Lord Beaverbrook, *Politicians and the War 1914–1916* (London, 1928), 22–39. Birmingham University Library, Austen Chamberlain Papers, AC/14/2/2, Memorandum by Austen Chamberlain on the July Crisis, written early August 1914; AC/14/2/3 has drafts of the Unionist letter to Asquith; AC/14/2/7, George Lloyd to A. Chamberlain, 31 July 1914.

63 B.D. XI, 373.

64 New University of Ulster, Headlam Morley Papers, Memorandum by Headlam Morley on conversation with Lord Carnock, 1924; D.D.F., Series 3, XI, 457.

65 B.D. XI, 352, 367; D.D.F., Series 3, XI, 459.

66 B.D. XI, 426. New University of Ulster, Headlam Morley Papers, Memorandum by Headlam Morley on conversation with Lord Carnock, 1924.

67 New University of Ulster, Headlam Morley Papers, Memorandum by Headlam Morley on conversation with Lord Carnock, 1924, P.R.O. Carnock Papers, F.O. 800/375, Nicolson to Hardinge, 5 September 1914, Harold Nicolson, *Lord Carnock*, 419: B.D. XI, 369.

68 P.R.O. Carnock Papers, F.O. 800/375, a draft minute by Nicolson, 1 August 1914, dismisses the anti-war pressures. But in the final draft – B.D. XI, 446 – Nicolson edited his abrasive remarks.

69 Shulbrede Priory, Arthur Ponsonby Papers, Memorandum by Ponsonby, 25 July 1914, Ponsonby to Grey, 29 July 1914, Ponsonby to Asquith, 30 July 1914.

70 B.D. XI, 367

71 P.R.O. Adm. 116/3437, Memorandum by Churchill, 16 October 1911.

72 British Museum, C. P. Scott Papers, add 50981, memorandum by Scott, 4 August 1914.

73 B.D. XI, 348.

74 B.D. XI, 382, 383, 448, 476.

75 Public Record Office of the House of Lords, Samuel Papers, File A/157, Samuel to Beatrice Samuel, 2 August 1914.

76 Jonathan E. Helmreich, 'Belgian concern over Neutrality and British Intentions, 1906–1914', *Journal of Modern History* (1964), XXXVI, 4. B.D. XI, 395; D.D.F., Series 3, XI, 612.

77 B.D. XI, 426, D.D.F., Series 3, XI, 532. P.R.O., Carnock Papers, Nicolson to Hardinge, 5 September 1914.

78 Public Record Office of House of Lords, Samuel Papers, File A/157, Samuel to Beatrice Samuel, 2 August 1914. B.D. XI, 487, D.D.F., Series 3, XI, 612.

79 B.D. XI, 531.

80 Cab., 41/35, Asquith to King George V, 3 August 1914.

81 B.D. XI, 514, 515.

82 Public Record Office of the House, Samuel Papers, File A/157, Samuel to Beatrice Samuel, 4 August 1914. B.D. XI, 573, 594, the original draft is in P.R.O., F.O. 371/2162/35798.
83 David Lloyd George, *War Memoirs* (6 vols., London 1933–6), I, 67–70.
84 Winston S. Churchill, *The World Crisis 1911–1914* (London, 1923), 199.
85 For a detailed analysis of Lloyd George's position, see Hazelhurst, *Politicans at War*, 54–65.

24. ITALY AND THE BALKANS, 1914–1915

1 Grey of Fallodon, *Twenty Five Years* (1928 ed., III, 106).
2 E.g. Grey, *op. cit.*, III, 140, 'Nothing so distorted perspective, disturbed judgment, and impaired the sense of strategic values as the operations of Gallipoli.'
3 P. Guinn, *British Strategy & Politics, 1914–18* (Oxford, 1965), pp. 50–4. In the discussion of this project in the War Council the object of re-opening the Straits was to enable Russia to export wheat, thus reducing the price. Lord Hankey, *The Supreme Command, 1914–18* (London, 1961), I, 248–9, 254, 262, 271.
4 War Council discussion of 3 March 1915, Cab. 42/2/3: 'there would be a danger of a rising in the Moslem world.'
5 There were in fact over 7 divisions – 200,000 men – available; see P. Guinn, *British Strategy & Politics 1914–18* (Oxford, 1965), pp. 59–60.
6 Amongst the wealth of testimony to this effect see: R. Jenkins, *Asquith* (London, 1963), pp. 349–78; P. Magnus, *Kitchener: Portrait of an Imperialist* (London, 1958), pp. 279–88, 367–70; Murray, C.I.G.S. under Kitchener, wrote to General Sir Ian Hamilton, in command at Gallipoli, '. . . you cannot know as well as I do the awful state it [the War Office] was in during the latter years under that past master of disorganisation, Lord Kitchener. . . He seldom told the Cabinet the truth and the whole truth'. V. Bonham-Carter, *Soldier True* (London, 1963), pp. 132–3.
7 Appointed C.I.G.S. 23 December 1915: see Magnus, *op. cit.* pp. 369–70. Files D/16 and D/17 in the Lloyd George Papers, Beaverbrook Library, London make it quite clear that this triumvirate lay behind Kitchener's demotion: in particular Bonar Law to Lloyd George, 1 November 1915, supporting his view that 'nothing but disaster lay ahead of us as long as Lord K was War Secretary'. D/17/8/9. By contrast, on 7 February, Lloyd George had written Grey, 'No General except Kitchener made quite the same impression on my mind as Robertson did yesterday. . .' E/2/15/4.
8 For the relationship between these Committees and the Cabinet see the lucid exposition in *List of Cabinet Papers 1915 and 1916* (H.M.S.O., 1955), pp. vii–x or, at greater length, Hankey, *The Supreme Command 1914–1918* (London, 1961), vol. I, pp. 165–424. In practice they formulated policy which the Cabinet ratified.
9 Cab(inet Papers, Public Record Office, London, Series) 42/1/27. Series 42 are the papers of the War Council etc., Series 37 are the papers of the Cabinet itself including, from 1 January 1915, reports from the P.M. to the King. Before this date they are to be found in Series 41. The papers of the War Cabinet from 9 December 1916 are in Series 23. See *List of Cabinet Papers*, supra.
10 According to Lloyd George the French Cabinet were 'perfectly unanimously in favour of the principle of an expeditionary force of two Divisions being sent to Salonika at the earliest possible moment. . . It is now a question of persuading Joffre'. . .To Grey, 7 February 1915, Lloyd George Papers, E/2/15/4.
11 J. C. King, *Generals and Politicians* (Berkeley, Calif., 1951), pp. 72–3; Hankey, *op cit.*, I, 254; Guinn, *op. cit.*, pp. 96–7.
12 F. Fischer, *Germany's Aims in the First World War* (London, 1967), pp. 195–8; Gerard E. Silberstein, 'The Serbian Campaign of 1915', in *American Historical Review*, vol. 73 (1967), pp. 51–69.

13 Cab. 41/1/33,35, War Council Minutes, 9, 16 February 1915.
14 Grey, *op. cit.*, III, 115.
14 *Ibid.* 109.
16 *Ibid.* 116.
17 See War Council minutes, 10 March 1915, Cab.42/2/5.
18 For detailed analysis of Italian objectives see C. J. Lowe & F. Marzari, *Italian Foreign Policy 1870–1940* (London, 1974), Ch. VII, 'Neutrality and War 1914–15'; W. Rienzi, 'Italy and the Great War' in *American Historical Review*, 1968; L. Valiani, *The End of Austria-Hungary* (London, 1973).
19 Nicolson minute on Buchanan to Grey, 7 October 1914, F.O. 371/2008/57095.
20 This despite Rodd's determined advocacy. According to the British embassy Sonnino was completely reliable, 'A man of direct and straightforward character'. To Grey, 7 November 1914, F.O. 800/65.
21 See Ferdinando Martini, *Diario 1914–1918* (Milan, 1966), entry for 5 December 1914.
22 *Ibid.* 3 March 1915.
23 For Italo-Roumanian relations see Glenn E. Torrey, 'Rumania and the Belligerents', *Journal of Contemporary History*, 1 (1966).
24 Sonnino to Salandra, 1 March, A. Monticone, 'Salandra e Sonnino verso la decisione dell'intervento' in *Revista di Studi Politici Internazionali*, XXIV (1957), p. 68.
25 Grey to Bertie, 4 March, to Buchanan, 5 March, F.O. 371/2375/23560.
26 'French Government recognise...essential thing is to conquer as soon as possible.' Bertie to Grey, 4 March, F.O. 371/2375/25017.
27 Buchanan to Grey, 5 March, no. 26334.
28 Clerk minute on above.
29 A. Dallin, and others, *Russian Diplomacy and Eastern Europe 1914–17* (New York, 1963), pp. 172, 177–8.
30 Asquith to the King, 24 March, Cab. 37/126/21.
31 Rodd to Grey, 20 March, F.O. 800/65.
32 *Ibid.* 2 April, Cab. 37/127/11.
33 W. W. Gottlieb, *Studies in Secret Diplomacy* (London, 1957), pp. 331, 334.
34 Cab. 42/2/1, 5.
35 *Ibid.*
36 Asquith to the King, 24 March, Cab. 37/126/21.
37 See Hankey, *op. cit.*, I, 271; Cab. 42/2/1; Cab. 37/126/3.
38 Grey to Buchanan, 11 March, *ibid.*: Hankey, *op. cit.*, I, 287.
39 Grey to Buchanan, 22 March, Trevelyan, *Grey of Fallodon*, pp. 296–7.
40 Asquith to the King, 24 March, Cab. 37/126/21.
41 Grey, *op. cit.*, III, 181.
42 Minute on Buchanan, to Grey, 31 March, F.O. 371/2376/37639.
43 Gottlieb, *op cit.*, p. 336.
44 *Ibid.* p. 337.
45 Grey to Rodd, 25 March, Cab. 37/126/30.
46 *Ibid.*
47 Gottlieb, *op. cit.*, p. 339.
48 *Ibid.* pp. 341–3.
49 Trevelyan, *op. cit.*, p. 297.
50 Grey to Rodd, 1 April, Cab. 37/127/4.
51 Rodd to Grey, 2 April, Cab. 37/127/11.
52 'I do not think Sonnino is merely bargaining to get the most he can.' Rodd to Asquith, 2 April, F.O. 800/65.
53 *Ibid.*
54 Gottlieb, *op. cit.*, pp. 343–4.
55 Buchanan to Grey, 1 April, Cab. 37/127/3.

56 Bertie to Asquith, 5 April, F.O. 800/57.
57 Gottlieb, *op. cit.*, p. 347.
58 'he did not place [the] fighting qualities of the Italian army very high': Buchanan to Grey, 4 April, Cab. 37/127/12.
59 Gottlieb, *op. cit.*, p. 348.
60 Buchanan to Grey, 7 April, Cab. 37/127/15.
61 Asquith to Bertie, 9 April, Cab. 37/127/19.
62 Grey to Bertie, 14 April, Cab. 37/127/27.
63 'Salandra al momento della firm del patto di Londra era pienamente consciente di operare contro la grande maggioranze degli italiani.' Monticone, *op. cit.*, p. 88.
64 Grey, *op. cit.*, III, 166.

25. RUSSIA, CONSTANTINOPLE AND THE STRAITS, 1914–1915

1 London School of Economics, Morel Papers, Box F. 8, Morel to Ponsonby, undated, c. December 1916.
2 Grey of Fallodon, *Twenty-Five Years* (2 vols., London, 1925), II, pp. 179–83. See, for instance, R. J. Kerner, 'Russia, the Straits and Constantinople', *Journal of Modern History* (1929), I, no. 3.
3 C. J. Smith, 'Great Britain and the 1914–1915 Straits Agreement with Russia: The Promises of November 1914', *American Historical Review* (1964), CXXX, no. 4. The present writer's 'The Development of British War Aims, August 1914–March 1915', University of London Ph.D. dissertation (1969), Chapter 5.
4 University of Birmingham Library, Austen Chamberlain Papers, AC 13/1/14, Acland to Austen Chamberlain, December 1914.
5 Cambridge University Library, Crewe Papers, Crewe–Hardinge Correspondence, vol. II, Crewe to Hardinge, 6 August 1914.
6 Quoted in Grey, *Twenty-Five Years*, cited above, II, p. 306.
7 D.D.F., Series 3, XI, 612. Public Record Office, CAB. 22/1, Minutes of the War Council, 5 August 1914.
8 Public Record Office, F.O. 371/2164/17861 and F.O. 371/1900/41470, Minute by Clerk, 21 August 1914.
9 Public Record Office, CAB. 41/35, Asquith to George V, 17 August 1914. F.O. 371/1970/36711, Minute by Grey, undated, c. 22 August 1914.
10 For instance, F.O. 371/2970/36711, Minute by Crewe, 22 August 1914. F.O. 371/1900/41470, Minute by Clerk, 21 August 1914.
11 Bertie Papers, F.O. 800/161, Memorandum by Bertie, 16 July 1914. For evidence of Lloyd George, Simon and Morley, blaming Russia for the war, see Michael Ekstein, 'Some notes on Sir Edward Grey's policy in July 1914', *Historical Journal*, XV, 2 (1972), pp. 321–4.
12 Bertie Papers, F.O. 800/188. Memorandum by Bertie, 16 February 1914.
13 F.O. 371/6212/36298 and 36451. The Entente Powers were technically allies only after the agreement of 5 September 1914, when they agreed not to conclude peace separately.
14 O. Hoetzsch (ed.), *Die Internationalen Beziehungen im Zeitalter des Imperialismus*, Series II, VI, 13 and 18.
15 F.O. 371/1980/31986.
16 Public Record Office, F.O. 371/1900/31986, Minute by Clerk, 14 August 1914.
17 F.O. 371/2171/38796.
18 F.O. 371/2171/39446 and 39214.
19 F.O. 371/2138/40438, Grey to Buchanan, 15 August 1914, telegram.
20 F.O. 371/2171/38796, Grey to Buchanan, 13 August 1914, telegram.
21 F.O. 371/2138/40438, Grey to Buchanan, 15 August 1914, telegram.

22 F.O. 371/2172/40069, Grey to Mallet, 16 August 1914, telegram.

23 Sergei Sazonov, *Fateful Years* (New York, 1928), p. 252.

24 CAB. 22/1, Minutes of the War Council, 10 March 1915.

25 The most complete recent study based on the archives is David R. Facey Crowther, 'British Military Policy and the Defence of Egypt, 1882–1914', University of London Ph.D. dissertation (1969).

26 CAB. 4/1/RIb, 'Report of Conclusions arrived at 11 February 1903, in reference to Russia and Constantinople', by A. J. Balfour, 14 February 1903.

27 CAB. 4/1/RIb, Memorandum by W. G. Nicholson, Director General of Mobilization and Military Intelligence, 23 February 1903; Admiralty Memorandum, February 1903.

28 British Museum, Balfour Papers, Add. Mss. 49692, Asquith to Balfour, 15 October 1908.

29 Carnock Papers, F.O. 800/338, Grey to Nicholson, 6 November 1906.

30 B.D., v, 337 and 338.

31 Bertie Papers, F.O. 800/166, Memorandum by Bertie, 18 December 1914.

32 F.O. 371/2080/46559.

33 F.O. 371/2080/56209 and 57458.

34 C. J. Smith, 'Great Britain and the 1914–15 Straits Agreement with Russia: The Promises of November 1914,' *American Historical Review* (1964), cxxx, no. 4.

35 F.O. 371/2080/74916, Minute by Clerk, 25 November 1914.

36 F.O. 371/2080/6515, Grey to Buchanan, 1 November 1914, telegram.

37 F.O. 371/2080/66390.

38 F.O. 371/2080/66330, Buchanan to Grey, 2 November 1914, telegram.

39 F.O. 371/2080/69647, Grey to Buchanan, 10 November 1914, telegram.

40 F.O. 371/2080/70280, Grey to Buchanan, 12 November 1914, telegram.

41 F.O. 371/2080/65815, Grey to Buchanan, 1 November 1914, telegram.

42 Grey Papers, F.O. 800/88, Churchill to Grey, 23 September 1914.

43 F.O. 371/2080/49001, India Office to Foreign Office, 12 September 1914.

44 Jukka Nevakiva, 'Lord Kitchener and the Partition of the Ottoman Empire 1915–16', in K. Bourne and D. C. Watt (eds.), *Studies in International History* (London, 1967), pp. 316–329. CAB. 24/1/G-13, 'Alexandretta and Mesopotamia', by Kitchener.

45 CAB. 41/35, Asquith to George V, 3 November 1914.

46 F.O. 371/2080/70280, Grey to Buchanan, 12 November 1914, telegram.

47 *Die Internationalen Beziehungen im Zeitalter des Imperialismus*, Series II, VI, 506.

48 Viscount Haldane, *Autobiography* (London, 1929), p. 281.

49 Bertie Papers, F.O. 800/166. Memorandum by Bertie, 18 December 1914. Bertie Papers, F.O. 800/167, Memorandum by Bertie, 21 January 1915. CAB. 1/11, 'Remarks on the Chancellor of the Exchequer's Memorandum on the Conduct of the War', by Kitchener, 25 February 1915.

50 Bodleian Library, Asquith Papers, MS. 13, Churchill to Asquith, 29 December 1914. Public Record Office, CAB. 24/1/G-2, 'Suggestions as to the Military Position', by Lloyd George, 1 January 1915.

51 Grey Papers, F.O. 800/90, Hankey to Grey, 21 January 1915.

52 Grey Papers, F.O. 800/56(a), Grey to Bertie, 4 December 1914.

53 For pessimistic British assessment of the situation on the Eastern Front, see Public Record Office, Bertie Papers, F.O. 800/166, Memorandum by Bertie, 21 December 1914. Bertie Papers, F.O. 800/167, Memorandum by Bertie, 21 January 1915.

54 Michael Ekstein, 'Sir Edward Grey and Imperial Germany in 1914', *Journal of Contemporary History* (1971), vol. 6, no. 3.

55 Arthur Link, *Wilson: The Struggle for Neutrality* (Princeton, N.J., 1960), pp. 212–13.

56 *The Intimate Papers of Colonel House* (4 vols., London, 1926), arranged by G. Seymour, I, p. 369, House to Wilson, 9 February 1915.

57 Carnock Papers, F.O. 800/375, Buchanan to Nicolson, 13 September 1914. F.O. 371/2174/74460, Buchanan to Grey, 23 November 1914. F.O. 371/2174/71988, telegram from Bordeaux, 2 December 1914.

58 These matters are almost impossible to guage precisely, but there is some evidence that points in this direction, for instance, F.O. 371/1900/41470, Minute by Clerk, 21 August 1914.

59 F.O. 371/2506/4867, Grey to Buchanan, 14 January 1915, telegram.

60 F.O. 371/2479/14967 and 15471.

61 F.O. 371/2479/14967, Minute by Nicolson, 9 February 1915.

62 F.O. 371/2479/14967, Grey to Buchanan, 16 February 1915, telegram. This telegram was drafted by Nicolson, and Grey specifically altered the sense of Nicolson's draft to include the paragraph quoted.

63 This is deducible from the circulation list of Foreign Office files, e.g. Public Record Office, F.O. 371/2080/70280, and F.O. 371/2506/7274.

64 *Dardanelles Commission*, First Report, p. 19.

65 F.O. 371/2479/24058.

66 Grey Papers, F.O. 800/75, Grey to Benckendorff, 2 March 1915.

67 F.O. 371/2479/24021, Asquith's initials on Grey's draft statement, c. 24 February 1915.

68 Grey Papers, F.O. 800/75, Grey to Benckendorff, 2 March 1915.

69 F.O. 371/2479/24058, Buchanan to Grey, 1 March 1915, telegram.

70 F.O. 371/2479/24058, Minute by Nicholson, 2 March 1915.

71 CAB. 22/1, Minutes of the War Council, 10 March 1915.

72 F.O. 371/2479/24858, Grey to Buchanan, 2 March 1915, telegram.

73 Grey Papers, F.O. 800/75, Grey to Benckendorff, 2 March 1915.

74 F.O. 371/2449/25014.

75 F.O. 371/2499/2479/24058, Minute by Grey, 2 March 1915. F.O. 371/2479/24602, Grey to Bertie, 3 March 1915, telegram.

76 F.O. 371/2479/25969, Buchanan to Grey, 4 March 1915, telegram.

77 F.O. 371/2479/26072, Minute by Clerk, 5 March 1915, Minute by Nicholson, 6 March 1915.

78 Grey Papers, F.O. 800/57, Minute by Clerk, 14 March 1915. Bertie Papers, F.O. 800/167, Memorandum by Bertie, 16 March 1915. F.O. 371/2479/24659 and 27177.

79 Grey Papers, F.O. 800/57, Minute by Grey, undated, c. 28 March 1915, on the bottom of Bertie to Grey, 25 March 1915.

80 CAB. 41/35, Asquith to George V, 9 March 1915. British Museum, Balfour Papers, MSS. Add. 49703, Hankey to Balfour, 10 March 1915. Bodleian Library, Asquith Papers, MS. 114. Notes by Asquith, undated, but plainly either made during the Cabinet of 9 March 1915 or the War Council Meeting the next day.

81 CAB. 22/1, Minutes of the War Counil, 10 March 1915.

82 F.O. 371/2449/28770, Grey to Buchanan, 10 March 1915, telegram. F.O. 371/2479/25969, Grey to Buchanan, 10 March 1915, telegram.

83 CAB. 27/1, British Desiderata in Turkey-in-Asia. Report, proceedings and Appendices of a committee appointed by the P.M.

84 F.O. 371/2449/34054 and 83731.

85 F.O. 371/2449/28770. F.O. 371/2479/28931, Foreign Office to Board of Trade, 17 March 1915. F.O. 371/2479/36173, 'Minutes of the Board of Trade on Economic Safeguards for Russian Possession of Constantinople and the Straits'.

86 Élie Halévy, *The World Crisis of 1914–1918, an Interpretation. Being the Rhodes Memorial Lectures delivered in 1929* (London, 1930), p. 5.

26. ASIATIC TURKEY, 1914–1916

1 See above pp. 155–6. See also Cd. 7628 Misc. no. 13 (1914), 'Correspondence respecting Events leading to the Rupture of Relations with Turkey'.

2 Grey, *Twenty-Five Years, op. cit.*, II, p. 164.

3 Ulrich Trumpener, 'The Escape of the Goeben and Breslau: A Reassessment', *Canadian Journal of History*, VI, 1971, pp. 171–87. See also Sir Llewellyn Woodward, *Great Britain and the War of 1914–1918* (London, 1967), p. 60. Trumpener's assessment of 'rather fumbling conduct of business at the Foreign Office' over Turkish affairs appears well justified.

4 Tels. from Grey to Beaumont, 3 & 4 August 1914, Cd. 7628, nos. 2 & 4. See also Martin Gilbert, *Winston S. Churchill*, III, *1914–1916* (London, 1971), pp. 190–5, and Arthur J. Marder, *From the Dreadnought to Scapa Flow*, II (Oxford, 1965), pp. 20–41. The ships were renamed H.M.S. Erin and H.M.S. Agincourt.

5 Tels. from Grey to Beaumont, 11 & 12 August 1914, Cd. 7628, nos. 8 & 11. See also Trumpener, *op. cit.*, p. 185 and Gilbert, *op. cit.*, p. 197, and *Twenty-Five Years, op. cit.*, II, pp. 166–8. The ships were renamed the *Jawuz Sultan Selim* and the *Midilli*.

6 Gilbert, *op. cit.*, pp. 205–8.

7 Note by Grey, n.d., on letter from Churchill to Grey, 16 September 1914, Grey [MSS.], F.O. 800/87. This is ascribed to Kitchener in Gilbert, *op. cit.*, p. 211.

8 Asquith [MSS.], vol. 8, Cabinet letters to the King 1915–16, letter of 23 September 1916.

9 *Twenty-Five Years, op. cit.*, II, pp. 168–9.

10 Tels. between Grey and Mallet, 30 October 1914, Cd. 7628, no. 179.

11 Gilbert, *op. cit.*, p. 216.

12 *The Times*, 1 November 1914.

13 Tels. from Grey to Sir George Buchanan, Sir Francis Bertie and Sir C. Greene, 4 November 1914, Cd. 7628, no. 184; and Asquith, vol. 7, Cabinet letters to the King 1913–14.

14 Not on November 7 as in Gilbert, *op. cit.*, p. 221. For details of the decision to despatch the force see Brig-Gen. F. J. Moberly's official history of *The Campaign in Mesopotamia 1914–1918*, 4 vols. (H.M.S.O., London, 1923–7), vol. I, pp. 89–106.

15 See Moberly, *op. cit.*, I, pp. 78–9, and private letter from Hardinge to Grey, 4 September 1914, Grey, F.O. 800/97.

16 See F.O. 'Memorandum respecting British Interests in the Persian Gulf', 12 February, 1908, F.O. 881/9161, and draft despatch from F.O. to Mallet, August 1914, F.O. 371/2125, no. 33655.

17 Private letter from Hardinge to Grey, 4 September 1914, Grey, F.O. 800/97; and 'Memorandum on British Commitments (During the War), to the Gulf Chiefs', Political Intelligence Department, F.O., Confidential Print 11794*, n.d.; 'British Commitments to Ibn Saud', memo. by Political Intelligence Department, F.O., 16 November 1918, Cab. 27/70, G.T.–6314. These documents are the basis for the following section.

18 *Twenty-Five Years, op. cit.*, II, pp. 75–7, 180–3; Paul Guinn, *British Strategy and Politics 1914 to 1918* (Oxford, 1965), p. 56; J. T. Shotwell and F. Deak, *Turkey at the Straits* (New York, 1940), pp. 98–102, and War Council discussions, 19 February and 3 March 1915, Cab. 42/1 and 2.

19 Moberly, *op. cit.*, I, pp. 92–5; also Asquith 117–20, Secret, 'Précis of correspondence regarding the Mesopotamian Expedition...', I, also F.O. 370/215, no. 3248 and Cab. 22 and Cab. 24.

20 Moberly, *op. cit.*, I, pp. 94–5, and letters between Viceroy and Secretary of State for India, 7 & 8 October 1914, Asquith, 'Précis...', I.

21 See, e.g., telegrams between Sir Percy Cox and the Government of India, nos. 68B

(P. 408), and DS 13P, 27 November 1914 and 3 January 1915, F.O. 371/2482, no. 14120; and Asquith 125/23, 'Précis...', II, and Moberly, *op. cit.*, I, pp. 133–6, and 'Persian Gulf Operations', Minute on the situation by the Military Secretary, I.O. (General Barrow), 27 November 1914, Asquith, 'Précis...', II, and Moberly, I, pp. 136–7; Capt. A. T. Wilson to Col. Yate M.P., 28 November 1914, encl. in letter from Yate to Grey, 28 January 1915, F.O. 371/2482, nos. 12124 and 19342.

22 Private letters from Hardinge to Sir Valentine Chirol and to Nicolson, 2 and 10 December 1914 and 6 January and 4 February 1915, Hardinge [MSS.], 93/II/263, 266 and 290.

23 See private letter from Curzon to Hardinge, 12 January 1915, Hardinge, 93/I/347; and F.O. minutes on correspondence in F.O. 371/2482, nos. 12124 and 19342.

24 Telegram from Secretary of State to Viceroy, Secret, 16 December 1914, Asquith, 'Précis...', II; mentioned but not quoted in Moberly, I, p. 140. Grey's minute, n.d., on which this telegram was based was on telegram from Viceroy to Crewe, 5 December 1914, F.O. 371/2144.

25 Letter from Hardinge to the Rt. Hon. Lord Stamfordham, Hardinge, 105/II/115.

26 See Cab. 24/2, G.-51 and 52, and Moberly, *op. cit.*, II, pp. 287–9 and App. XVIII.

27 Private telegram from Secretary of State for India (Crewe), to Viceroy, 30 November 1914, Asquith, Précis...', II, and cited in Moberly, *op. cit.*, I, p. 137.

28 Note from Asquith to I.O., W.O., Adm. and F.O., 4 October 1915, and report of Cabinet meeting, 4 October 1915, Asquith, 46/120 and Cab. letters to the King 1915–16, vol. 8; 'Report of an Inter-Departmental Committee on the Strategical Situation in Mesopotamia', 16 October 1915, Asquith, Précis...', IV, fol. 187, Cab. 42/4/7 and Cab. 24/1, G.-28. For War Council discussions on the Report, 14 and 21 October 1915, see Cab. 42/4. See also telegram from Secretary of State to Viceroy, Private and Urgent, 8 October 1915, and Minute for P.M. from Hankey, 22 October 1915, Asquith, fols. 74 and 231. See also Moberly, *op. cit.*, II, pp. 14–19, 23–4.

29 Memorandum by the F.O., 7 October 1915, Cab. 42/4 and Cab. 24/1, G.-28 App. VII; and Asquith, fol. 187. This opinion was also followed by the Viceroy, see his private letter to Nicolson, 14 October 1915, Nic[olson MSS.], 1915, IV, F.O. 800/380. See also an additional memo. by Mallet, Cab. 24/1, G.-28 App. VII.

30 Letters from Nicolson to Hardinge, 7 and 14 October 1915, Nic., 1915, IV, F.O. 800/380.

31 Minute for the P.M. by Hankey, 22 October 1915, Asquith, fol. 231–4. The meeting considered a detailed paper of 19 October drawn up by the General Staff on the advisability of an advance, Cab. 42/6/4; Asquith, fol. 180; Moberly, *op. cit.*, II, App. VIII and pp. 24–6.

32 Minutes of War Committee meeting, 28 December 1915, Cab. 42/6/14; private tel. from Chamberlain (now Secretary of State for India) to Hardinge, quoted in Moberly, *op. cit.*, II, pp. 155–6. Guinn, *op. cit.*, pp. 109–10, comments on the 'regrettable exclusion of Grey from the smaller War Committee announced by Asquith on 11 November 1915.' But Cabinet records show that Grey was indeed present at this important meeting.

33 See Marian Kent, *Oil and Empire* (London, 1976).

34 On the Alexandretta question see also Y. Nevakivi, *Britain, France, and the Arab Middle East 1914–1920* (London, 1969), Ch. 2, and his article, 'Lord Kitchener and the Partition of the Ottoman Empire 1915–1916', in K. Bourne and D. C. Watt (eds.), *Studies in International History* (London, 1967), Gilbert, *op. cit.*, pp. 331–56, and Guinn, *op. cit.*, Chs. 2 and 3.

35 *Twenty-Five Years, op. cit.*, II, p. 230.

36 Minutes of War Council meetings, 10 and 19 March 1915, Cab. 42/2/5 and Cab. 22/1/2, and Asquith 132/256 and 114/261. See also C.I.D. papers, secret: 'The War: Alexandretta and Mesopotamia', Memorandum by Kitchener, 16 March 1915,

'Remarks on the Importance of Alexandretta as a future base', by Admiral Sir Henry Jackson, 15 March 1915, and 'Alexandretta and Mesopotamia. Memorandum by the Admiralty' (drafted by Sir Julian Corbett and approved by Fisher and Hankey), 17 March 1915, 'Note by the Secretary, Political and Secret Department, I.O.' (Hirtzel), 14 March 1915, accompanied by 'Note by General Sir Edmund Barrow on the Defence of Mesopotamia', and Hirtzel's 'Comments on Sir Edmund Barrow's Note', 17 March 1915; Cab. 24/1, G.12, 15 and 13, Asquith 114/241, 250, 244 and 226–234, Corbett MSS., Box 7 (with drafts and correspondence).

37 Gilbert, *op. cit.*, p. 330.

38 Letter from Grey to Bertie, 23 March 1915, *Twenty-Five Years, op. cit.* II, p. 230.

39 Report of the Committee on Asiatic Turkey, 30 June 1915, C.I.D. paper no. 220-B, Cab. 4/6/1 and Cab. 42/3/12. Some discussion in Nevakivi, *op. cit.*, pp. 18–25, and on the oil implications in Kent, *Oil and Empire, op. cit.* Other members of the committee were G. R. Clerk, (F.O.), T. W. Holderness (I.O.), H. B. Jackson (Adm.), C. E. Callwell (W.O.), H. Llewellyn Smith (Bd. of Trade), and Mark Sykes, with Hankey as Secretary.

40 Report, p. 3. See also above, pp. 152–4.

41 Report, pp. 3, 21.

42 Report, p. 25.

43 The correspondence was published in 1938 as Cmd. 5957, Correspondence between Sir Henry McMahon and the Sharif of Mecca. It is also printed, together with considerable other correspondence in F.O. Confidential Print, No. 10812*, January 1921. References to this source are, for brevity, simply cited hereafter as 'Print'.

44 An excellent, analytical account is given in the article by Isaiah Friedman, 'The Hussein–McMahon Correspondence and the Question of Palestine', in the *Journal of Contemporary History*, v, 2, 1970, and in the comments by A. J. Toynbee, and Friedman's reply, *ibid.*, v, 4, 1970.

45 The problem of Palestine was at this stage only an extension of this principle; the additional problem of the 'Jewish homeland' arose with the Balfour Declaration of November 1917, but even in the war-time discussions during Grey's tenure of office, it was always clearly recognised that this was an area of multi-religious complexity and could not be left to be run as a purely Arab and Moslem area.

46 See, e.g., telegram no. 173 from Grey to McMahon, 14 April 1915, Print, p. 11 and in Ronald Storrs, *Orientations* ('definitive ed.', London, 1945), p. 152; letter from McMahon to Hussein, 30 August 1915, Print, p. 15; desp. no. 36 from Grey to Buchanan, 23 February 1916, desp. no. 350 from Grey to Bertie, 11 May 1916 and dft. desp. ditto of 19 May 1916, F.O. 371/2767, no. 35529 and F.O. 371/2768, nos. 92354 and 97562.

47 See Friedman, *op. cit.*, pp. 89–92.

48 See correspondence 12–20 October 1915, in F.O. 371/2486, no. 34982, also Print, pp. 17–18.

49 Telegram from Grey to McMahon, 20 October 1915, *ibid.* See also note by Hankey 21 October 1915, Asquith, fol. 224.

50 See Grey's telegram to McMahon, 10 December 1915, Print, pp. 34–5.

51 Print, pp. 38–9.

52 See also desps nos. 16 and 26 from McMahon to Grey, 24 January and 7 February 1916.

53 On Indian attitudes see: Private letters from Hardinge to Nicolson, 25 May and 15 November 1915, Nic. 1915, II and IV, F.O. 800/378, 380; personal telegram from Viceroy to Chamberlain, 4 November 1915, F.O. 371/2486 no. 34982 and Print, p. 26; telegram from Chamberlain (via F.O.) to McMahon, 11 November 1915, Print, p. 27, and his private letter to Grey, 29 December 1915, Secret, Grey, F.O. 800/97;

Private letter from Crewe (F.O.) to Bertie, 17 December 1915, Cab. 42/6; 'Secret' letter from Chamberlain to Grey, 29 December 1915, Grey, F.O. 800/97.

54 Telegram no. 813 from Wingate to McMahon, 14 November 1915 and letter from Wingate to Clayton, 15 November 1915, and personal telegram no. 2030E from Maxwell to Kitchener, 16 October 1915; telegram no. 736 from McMahon to Grey, 30 November 1915; Memo. by Clayton, 11 October 1915; telegram no. 299 from Clayton to Wingate, 22 April 1916; Print, pp. 27–9, 30–4, 53–4. See also Friedman, *op. cit.*, pp. 96–8. Of Clayton Storrs wrote, 'His balanced advice could no more be hustled by a crisis than could his beautiful, deliberate handwriting...the "Bertie" of Khartoum, of Cairo, of Palestine, of Mesopotamia', *Orientations, op. cit.*, p. 148.

55 Letters from Nicolson to Hardinge, 16 December 1915 and 16 February 1916, Nic. 1915, IV and 1916, I, F.O. 800/380, 381; telegram from Grey to McMahon, 10 December 1915, Print, pp. 34–5.

56 Letter from Nicolson to McMahon, 8 March 1916, Nic. 1916, I, F.O. 800/381; telegram no. 339D from Grey to McMahon, 27 April 1916, F.O. 371/2768, no. 76954; and Print, p. 55.

57 Cab. 42/11. For discussion see below, p. 450.

58 F.O. 371/2774, no. 137276.

59 C.I.D. paper G.-46 Secret, War Committee Meeting, 16 December 1915, 'Evidence of Lt.-Col. Sir Mark Sykes, Bart., M.P., on the Arab Question', 17 December 1915, Cab. 42/6/9,10 and Cab. 24/1. See also Sykes's telegrams to the W.O., nos. 707 and 709, 20 and 21 November 1915, Print, pp. 35–7.

60 Letter from Macdonogh to Nicolson, 6 January 1916; Memo. by Capt. W. R. Hall ('concurred in by the First Sea Lord'), Admiralty, 12 January 1916; Memo. by Commander Hall (D.I.D.), F.O. 371/2767 nos. 3851, 8116 and 2989, and Cab. 42/11.

61 Letter from Nicolson to Hardinge, 16 December 1915, Nic., 1915, IV, F.O. 800/380.

62 'Arab Proposals. Amended Version' (by Sykes and Picot), n.d., F.O. 371/2767, no. 14106, and in Cab. 42/11. See also Yukka Nevakivi, *op. cit.*, pp. 25–44.

63 'Memorandum' by Sykes, received at the F.O., 5 January 1916, F.O. 371/2767, no. 2522, or Cab. 42/11.

64 'Arab Question'. Note from Nicolson to Grey, 2 February 1916, F.O. 371/2767, no. 23579 and Cab. 42/11.

65 Note by Sir Arthur Hirtzel for Sir Thomas Holderness (Permanent Under-Secretary, I.O.), 10 January 1916, encl. in letter from Holderness to Nicolson, 13 January 1916, F.O. 371/2767, no. 8117, or Cab. 42/11.

66 Memorandum by Sykes, Minutes of Committee Meetings, 17 January and 4 February 1916, and letter from Nicolson to Grey, 4 February 1916, F.O. 371/2767, nos. 11844, 14106, 15352, 26444 and 23579; and letter from Nicolson to Hardinge, 16 February 1916, Nic. 1916, I, F.O. 800/381.

67 Letter from Nicolson to Grey, 9 February, telegrams no. 377D from Grey to Buchanan, 9 February and no. 237 from Buchanan to Grey, 10 February 1916, Note from Nicolson to Grey, 16 February and desp. no. 36 from Grey to Buchanan, 23 February 1916, F.O. 371/2767, nos. 28324, 26444, 26744 and 35529.

68 Telelgram no. 377 from Sykes (via Buchanan) to F.O., 16 March 1916, and telegrams nos. 351, 357, 575 and 580, between Buchanan and F.O., 11, 12 and 13 March 1916, F.O. 371/2767, nos. 51288, 47088, 47950 and 48551; 'Arab Question. Note by the Secretary' (Hankey), 20 March 1916, Cab. 42/11.

69 Telegram no. 370 from Buchanan to F.O., 15 March 1916, F.O. 371/2767 no. 50225, and referred to in Hankey's 'Note' above. See also Minutes and draft conclusions of War Committee meeting, 23 March 1916, Cab. 42/11.

70 See previous note.

71 These are set out in E. L. Woodward and R. Butler (eds), *Documents on British*

Foreign Policy 1919–1939, First Series, vol. IV (London, H.M.S.O., 1952), pp. 241–51. See also F.O. 371/2768, nos. 81330, 87247, and 93696.

72 See, e.g., desp. no. 350, from Grey to Bertie, 11 May, and dft. desp. ditto of 19 May 1916, F.O. 371/2768, nos. 92354 and 97562.

73 War Cabinet memo. G.73, 20 June 1916, Cab. 24/2 and Cab. 42/16.

74 I.O. Political Dept. memo. by Hirtzel, Secret, 'The War with Turkey', 25 May 1916, Cab. 42/16. See also further 'Note on The War with Turkey', by the Under-Secretary, I.O. (Holderness), 13 June 1916, Cab. 42/16.

75 *Twenty-Five Years, op. cit.*, II, pp. 230–1.

27. JAPAN AND CHINA, 1914–1916

1 B.D. XI, no. 436.
2 B.D. XI, nos. 534 and 549.
3 B.D. XI, no. 641.
4 B.D. X, part 2, p. 823, Grey to Greene, 6 August 1914.
5 B.D. X, part 2, p. 823, Greene to Grey, 7 August 1914.
6 F.O. 410/63, Grey to Greene, 11 August 1914.
7 F.O. 410/63, Grey to Greene, 13 August 1914.
8 *The Times*, 18 August 1914.
9 Grey, *Twenty-five years*, II, 100.
10 F.O. 350/11, Langley to Jordan, 13 August 1914.
11 This topic is dealt with in detail in I. H. Nish, *Alliance in Decline* (London, 1972), pp. 147–9.
12 Cab. 41/35, Asquith to the King, 2 and 5 September; F.O. 800/68, Greene to Grey, 5 December 1914.
13 F.O. 350/12, Jordan to Langley, 4 September 1914.
14 C. Pearl, *Morrison of Peking* (Harmondsworth, 1971), p. 304. This is based on material from the Morrison archives, which I have been unable to trace elsewhere.
15 F.O. 410/63, Jordan to Grey, 1 September 1914.
16 F.O. 410/63, Grey to Jordan, 18 August 1914.
17 F.O. 350/12, Jordan to Langley, 2 October 1914.
18 F.O. 350/12, Jordan to Langley, 24 November 1914.
19 F.O. 371/2017, Greene to Grey [58696], 12 October 1914.
20 F.O. 371/2017, Greene to Grey [59527], 14 October 1914.
21 F.O. 800/68, Greene to Grey, 5 December 1914.
22 F.O. 410/63, Grey to Greene, 3 December 1914.
23 F.O. 410/63, Grey to Greene, 21 December 1914.
24 F.O. 371/2322, Grey to Greene, 20 February 1915.
25 F.O. 371/2322, Grey to Greene, 9 March 1915.
26 F.O. 350/14, Alston to Jordan, 19 March 1915.
27 F.R.U.S. 1915, Reinsch to Bryan, 24 April 1915.
28 F.O. 371/2324, Grey to Greene [54503], 3 May 1915.
29 F.O. 371/2324, Grey to Greene [56360], 6 May 1915.
30 F.O. 800/68, Greene to Grey, 8 January 1916.
31 Cab. 37/144/67, Grey to Spring Rice, 23 March 1916.
32 F.O. 371/2341, Jordan to Grey [183325], 6 November 1915.
33 F.O. 371/2341, Grey to Greene [178314], 26 November 1915.
34 F.O. 371/2341, Greene to Grey [186241], 6 December 1915.
35 F.O. 371/2338, Grey to Bertie [196071], 22 December 1915.
36 F.O. 410/65, Grey to Greene [36950], 21 February 1916.
37 F.O. 410/65, Grey to Buchanan, 3 and 5 March 1916. When Sazonov asked whether information about Japanese designs in China which he had obtained from inter-

cepts, should interfere with the negotiations, Grey hoped it would not. Grey thought that 'as Japan was always excluded from every other part of the world, it would be natural for her to expect opportunities of commercial expansion in China', F.O. 405/220, Grey to Buchanan, 16 March 1916.

38 Austen Chamberlain papers 20/77, Balfour's statement to Imperial War Cabinet, 22 March 1917. See also note 37 above.

39 F.O. 405/220, Grey to Greene [187336], 23 September 1916.

40 Cab. 37/148/12, memorandum by J. D. Gregory, 19 May 1916.

41 Austen Chamberlain papers 20/77, Balfour's statement to Imperial War Cabinet, 22 March 1917. See also note above.

42 E.g. Cab. 37/144/67, Grey to Spring-Rice [57229], 23 March 1916.

28. ANGLO-AMERICAN RELATIONS

1 The speeches quoted were published in pamphlet form: H. H. Asquith, *The War, Its causes and its message* (London, 1914).

2 Public Record Office (P.R.O.), F.O./800/84, Private telegrams from Sir C. Spring-Rice, 6, 7 and 8 September 1914. For the circumstances of Bryan's initiative, see A. S. Link, *Wilson: The Struggle for Neutrality 1914–1915* (Princeton, N.J., 1960), 196–200.

3 Despatch to Spring-Rice, 9 September 1914, reporting a conversation with Ambassador Page, as printed in Grey of Fallodon, *Twenty-Five Years* (London, 1925), II, 115–16.

4 P.R.O., F.O./800/84, private telegrams from Spring-Rice, 20 September 1914, and from Grey to Spring-Rice, 23 September. Cf. Link, *op. cit.*, 203–4.

5 C. Seymour (ed.), *The Intimate Papers of Colonel House* (London, 1926–8), I, 337: Spring-Rice to House, 24 September 1914.

6 B. J. Hendrick, *The Life and Letters of Walter H. Page* (London, 1922 and 1925), I, 412–15: House to Page, 3 October 1914. Cf. Link, *op. cit.*, 205–6.

7 P.R.O., F.O./371/2174, telegram from French Minister of Foreign Affairs (M.F.A.) to French Ambassador at Washington, communicated to the F.O., 10 September 1914.

8 P.R.O., F.O./800/84, private telegram from Spring-Rice, 22 September 1914.

9 P.R.O., F.O./371/2174, telegram no. 691 from Sir G. Buchanan, 23 November 1914 and telegram from French Ambassador at Petrograd to M.F.A., communicated to the F.O., 4 December 1914.

10 P.R.O., F.O./800/84, pencilled notes in Asquith's hand on Spring-Rice's telegram of 20 September 1914 (see note 4). Asquith thought that before enemy overtures could be considered by the Allies, Germany and Austria-Hungary would have to: (1) evacuate *all* the territory which they had invaded in Belgium, France, Russia and Serbia; (2) agree to give full compensation to all their enemies 'for all injury done to any of them'; and (3) surrender to Great Britain all their warships presently on the high seas or in Turkish ports.

11 P.R.O., F.O./800/84, private telegram from Spring-Rice, 18 December 1914. Cf. Link, *op. cit.*, 210–12.

12 P.R.O., F.O./800/84, personal telegram to Spring-Rice, 20 December 1914, and private telegram from Spring-Rice, received 21 December. For House's account, see Seymour, *op. cit.*, I, 347.

13 P.R.O., F.O./800/84, personal telegram to Spring-Rice, 22 December 1914; printed in G. M. Trevelyan, *Grey of Fallodon* (London, 1937), 314–15.

14 P.R.O., F.O./800/84, personal telegram from Spring-Rice, 23 December 1914, and Seymour, *op. cit.*, I, 347–9. The confusion arose because Spring-Rice would not let House have a copy of Grey's message in case it came into the hands of the State Department who might leak it to the Germans.

15 Telegrams cited in note 9; P.R.O., F.O./371/2174, unnumbered telegram, 16 November 1914, and telegram no. 1098, 25 November, both to Buchanan.

16 P.R.O., F.O./800/85, personal telegram to Spring-Rice, 2 January 1915; printed in Trevelyan, *op. cit.*, 315–16.

17 Seymour, *op. cit.*, I, 349–50; Link, *op. cit.*, 214–16.

18 Seymour, *op. cit.*, I, 369–77; Link, *op. cit.*, 218–22.

19 Seymour, *op. cit.*, I, 376; we have only House's account of this conversation.

20 Seymour, *op. cit.*, I, 386–9 and 414–15, House to Wilson, 23 February and 27 March 1915. Cf. Link, *op. cit.*, 225–7.

21 Seymour, *op. cit.*, I, 427.

22 *Ibid.* I, 415.

23 *Ibid.* I, 428–9, Grey to House, 24 April 1915. An extended version of this letter was sent to Spring-Rice in June; see Trevelyan, *op. cit.*, 319.

24 P.R.O., F.O./800/85, private telegram from Spring-Rice, 10 September 1915; A. S. Link, *Wilson: Confusions and Crises 1915–1916* (Princeton, N.J., 1964), 102, House to Grey, 3 September 1915. Grey received House's letter c. 20 September. Link's suggestion that House wrote in response to a letter from Grey dated 26 August (printed in Seymour, *op. cit.*, II, 87–88), must be wrong, as House was complaining that Grey's letters were taking a month to reach him (Link, *op. cit.*, 105).

25 Seymour, *op. cit.*, II, 89–90.

26 Link, *op. cit.*, 104–5, House to Grey, 17 October 1915, received early November.

27 *Ibid.*, 106.

28 Seymour, *op. cit.*, II, 91–2, House to Wilson, 10 November 1915.

29 Link, *op. cit.*, 106.

30 Seymour, *op. cit.*, II, 98 cf. Link, *op. cit.*, 108–9.

31 Seymour, *op. cit.*, II, 106–8; cf. Link, *op. cit.*, 111–14.

32 Link, *op. cit.*, chapter IV, gives a full account of House's conversations with British Ministers. The Memorandum is printed on pp. 134–5.

33 Link, *op. cit.*, 139.

34 Hardinge Papers (Cambridge University Library), vol. 23, ff. 9, 13–17, 224, 226–7: correspondence between Hardinge and Bertie in July 1916 which includes copies of letters from Bertie to Grey, 29 February and 2 March 1916, and Grey to Bertie, 5 March.

35 P.R.O., Cab. 22/13, Hankey's manuscript, amended by Grey, of a 'specially secret' discussion before the regular session of the War Committee on 21 March 1916. The meeting was attended by the members of the War Committee and by Grey, Runciman and Hankey. Hankey's record was sealed on 24 March and not opened again until 1922.

36 Lord Hankey, *The Supreme Command 1914–1918* (London, 1961), II, 480 (Hankey's diary, 16 March).

37 Asquith Papers (Bodleian Library, Oxford), ff. 95–106, E.S.M. to H.H.A., 18 March 1916.

38 Link rightly dismisses Lloyd George's disingenuous *canard* that Grey dropped the Memorandum because of Wilson's insertion of this 'probably' (*War Memoirs* (New Edition, 1938), I, 412). On the other hand, it is not improbable that some ministers, including Lloyd George, had their doubts reinforced by this insertion, which Hankey noted in his diary on 15 March (*op. cit.*, II, 479–80). It may also be worth remarking that in January 1916 British Naval Intelligence had broken the cypher that House used in cable communications with the President. If ministers were receiving reports of House's self-congratulatory messages to his friend – and it should not be assumed that they were given access to such sensitive material – it cannot have increased their confidence in American diplomacy. Stephen Roskill, *Hankey: Man of Secrets* (London, 1970), I, 247.

39 Trevelyan, *op. cit.*, 318. Grey had warned his colleagues on 18 February 1916 that Germany 'has taken care to make it known to our Allies that...at any rate France and Russia, could have peace tomorrow on comparatively favourable terms, if they would separate themselves from us...'.

40 Seymour, *op. cit.*, 271–92.

41 *Ibid.*, 283.

42 Link, *op. cit.*, 141, rightly criticises the extent to which House deluded himself and the President on the prospects for mediation. House had a habit of hearing only what he was listening for, but if there is any truth at all in his accounts of his conversations with Grey (Seymour, *op. cit.*, II, chapters V and VII), Grey did not do nearly enough to dampen House's enthusiasms, even if he did not seek consciously to encourage them 'on a personal basis'.

43 On the development of Wilson's policy of an independent intervention for peace, see Link, *op. cit.*, chapter V and his *Wilson: Campaigns for Progressivism and Peace 1916–1917* (Princeton, N.J., 1965), chapters I and V.

44 Grey's letters were published in his autobiography and in Trevelyan, *op. cit.* and Seymour, *op. cit.* See also an interview, 'A Fight for Freedom' given to the Chicago *Daily News* (reprinted, London, *The Times*, 15 May 1916).

45 For the first two see H. R. Winkler, *The League of Nations Movement in Great Britain 1914–1919* (New Brunswick, N.J., 1952), for the third, J. H. Latane (ed.), *Development of the League of Nations Idea: Documents and Correspondence of Theodore Marburg* (New York, 1932).

46 P.R.O., Cab. 37/127/17, Haldane, 'Future Relations of the Great Powers', 8 April 1915; published in part in Sir Frederick Maurice, *Haldane* (London, 1939), II, 15–16. The paper drew a distinction between justiciable and non-justiciable disputes (as did the schemes of the private groups); the proposals for arbitration were based on the Convention for Pacific Settlement of International Disputes (1908); those for conciliation, on the Anglo-American Peace Commission (1914). Haldane was the only minister, apart from Cecil, to get to grips with the technical aspects of the League of Nations question.

47 P.R.O., Cab. 37/127/34, Kitchener, 'Observations on the Lord Chancellor's Note', 21 April 1915.

48 Statements reported in the London *Times* on 21 February (Bonar Law), 11 April (Asquith), 15 May (Grey), 18 May (Balfour). *The Times* itself had an article on 'The Empire and Foreign Policy: Way to Lasting Peace' in its Empire Day supplement.

49 Hankey's criticisms of the league idea are in a C.I.D. memorandum on the Freedom of the Seas, 11 June 1915 (F.O./800/95) and a letter to Balfour on compulsory arbitration, 25 May 1916 (Balfour Papers, British Museum, Add. Mss. 49704). Hankey also circulated to the Cabinet a paper by J. S. Corbett, 'Schemes for Securing Perpetual Peace', 18 June 1916 (Cab. 17/161). The quotation from Drummond is from a memorandum on the Freedom of the Seas, 11 June 1915 (F.O./800/95).

50 Cecil's paper was written in response to the War Committee's call for papers on war aims (see below). The first draft is in the Cecil Papers, British Museum, Add. Mss. 51102. The revised version was issued as a Cabinet paper (Cab. 24, G.T. 484), in October 1916, re-issued for the Imperial War Cabinet in May 1917 (Cab. 29, P. 18) and published as an appendix in Cecil of Chelwood, *A Great Experiment* (London 1941). Crowe's 'Notes' were issued as G.T. 484a and P. 19 and published in part in Lloyd George's *War Memoirs*, I, 1062–1065.

51 C. M. Mason, 'British Policy on the Establishment of a League of Nations, 1914–1919' (Dissertation, Cambridge University Library, 1971).

52 The papers were issued in the P Series (Cab. 29) for the information of the Imperial War Cabinet. Lloyd George published most of them in his *War Memoirs*,

chapter XXXI, but in the wrong order so as to give the impression that the whole question of war aims had been got up by Lansdowne and Grey in a bid to stop the war.

53 P.R.O., Cab. 42/18. *General Staff Memorandum submitted in accordance with the Prime Minister's Instructions,* 31 August 1916.

54 Sterling Kernek. 'The British Government's Reactions to President Wilson's "Peace" Note of December 1916', *The Historical Journal,* 1970.

55 Cf. Edward H. Buehrig, *Woodrow Wilson and the Balance of Power* (Bloomington, Ind. 1955), 174: '...it must be emphasised that the intitial identification of the League with American policy was owing not to the writings of publicists but to the diplomatic process itself'.

56 Mason, *op. cit.,* chapters 4 and 5.

29. THE BLOCKADE

1 Cab. 1, 22, Memo. in regard to the present position of the blockade, by Lord Robert Cecil, 1 January 1917. N.B. Transcripts of Crown Copyright material from Foreign Office and Cabinet Office records appear by permission of the Keeper of the Public Record Office.

2 Lord Hankey, *The Supreme Command* (London, 1961), I, 139. However, Jean Gout stresses the unpreparedness of the allies for an organised offensive against the economic power of the enemy; in Denys Cochin, *Les Organisations de Blocus en France pendant la Guerre (1914–18),* p. 1.

3 A. C. Bell, *The Blockade of the Central Empires, 1914–1918* (London, 1937, confidential until 1961), p. 31; H. W. C. Davis, *History of the Blockade. Emergency Departments* (London, 1921), p. 4. Plans were also made to deprive the enemy of British goods together with insurance and banking facilities.

4 Cab. 1, 11, Notes by Sir M. Hankey, undated (? Jan. 1915); Davis, *op. cit.,* pp. 5–6. One example of detailed preparation was the Order in Council on the treatment of enemy ships in British ports on the outbreak of war, issued in August 1914, which had been drafted in 1910 after eight months detailed investigation. Among other subjects similarly dealt with were censorship, control of cables and radio, war risk insurance and prohibitions on trading with the enemy. See also Hankey, *op. cit.,* I, 87–8. As early as 1909 Asquith felt the whole ground covered by a possible war with Germany had been investigated; H. H. Asquith, *The Genesis of the War* (London, 1923), p. 116, quoted, F. A. Johnson, *Defence by Committee* (London, 1960), pp. 97–8.

5 The value of German imports in 1913 were £525,900,000 and exports £495,600,000; Comparative figures for Britain were £659,400,000 and £525,500,000; *Accounts and Papers,* 1914, no. 218, quoted M. Balfour, *The Kaiser and his Times* (London, 1964), p. 442.

6 B.D. VIII, nos. 193, 206, 207. For British policy at the Hague Conference see Chapter 4.

7 B.D. VIII, nos. 249, 263; L. Oppenheim, *International Law* (London, 1961–2), II, 876–9; C. J. Colombos, *A Treatise on the Law of Prize,* chap. 11; H. Lauterpacht, 'International Law and Colonial Questions, 1870–1914', *Cambridge History of the British Empire,* III, 702–7. After a year of actual war, a Foreign Office legal adviser, C. J. B. Hurst, regarded it as 'a special dispensation of Providence' that the British proposal had not been accepted in 1907; F.O. 382, 465, Pr., Plunkett to Grey, 30 August 1915, min. For British policy at the London Naval Conference see Chapter 4.

8 Cab. 37, 105, Memo., Declaration of London from the Point of View of the Belligerent Rights of Great Britain, 1 February 1911. Despite the temptation to put economic pressure on the Boers, Lord Salisbury had declared, in 1900, 'Foodstuffs, with a hostile destination can be considered contraband of war only if they are

supplies for the enemy forces. It is not sufficient that they are capable of being so used; it must be shown that this was in fact their destination at the time of seizure'; W. Beveridge, *Blockade and the Civilian Population* (Oxford, 1939), p. 13; *Foreign Relations of the United States, 1914, Supplement*, p. 374. See also F.O. 800, 171, Pr., Grey to Bertie, 27 October 1914; W. E. Arnold-Forster, *The Blockade 1914–19* (Oxford, 1939), p. 8, *The Economic Blockade* (London, 1920), p. 174; Bell, *op. cit.*, p. 9.

9 Cab. 1, 15, F.O. Memo., 28 December 1915; Bell, *op. cit.*, pp. 9–30. M. R. Pitt, in the best recent study of belligerent rights, has shown that the Admiralty had inclined by 1908 towards an 'observational' or distant blockade, involving patrolling lines drawn from a point in the North Sea parallel with Newcastle to Southern Norway and the Dutch coast. Sir Arthur Wilson, however, as First Sea Lord in 1911, reverted to the close blockade; *Great Britain and Belligerent Maritime Rights from the Declaration of Paris, 1856, to the Declaration of London, 1909* (Pitt, unpublished thesis: University of London: 1964), pp. 350–62. There was, incidentally, no inconsistency with the 1907 policy in the fact that the abolition of contraband did not feature in the British proposals at the London Naval Conference of 1908–9. The Hague Peace Conference was dealing in 1907 with the question as to what ought to be the law on the subject, whereas the 1908 conference in London was dealing with the question as to what was the existing rule of international law and endeavouring to harmonise the conflicting views of the great powers.

10 Cab. 37, 105, note by Grey, 1 February 1911.

11 As Germany was understandably in favour, Grey was prepared to press ratification in Parliament if the other signatories, together with the War Office and Admiralty, concurred. F.O. 372, 588, 65 Tr., Rumbold to Grey, 30 June 1914; *ibid.*, Prince Borghese to Grey, 2 February 1914; *ibid.*, Parliamentary Question by Mr Barnes and reply, 5 March 1914; Lord Grey of Fallodon, *Twenty-Five Years* (London, 1925), II, 101–2; Hankey, *op. cit.*, I, 99–100. A. J. Marder concentrates on naval opposition to any suggestion of immunity for private property at sea and still seems to endorse the optimism of the Admiralty that strangling Germany's sea-borne trade would be what would seriously damage the German economy, ignoring the flood of goods that could reach Germany by way of neutral territory and shipping; *From Dreadnought to Scapa Flow*, I, 377–83. A thorough enquiry in the years 1908–9 by the consuls at Hamburg, Antwerp, Amsterdam and Frankfort led them to contradict this admiralty view absolutely; Bell, *op. cit.*, pp. 25–7.

12 F.O. 372, 588, Crowe to Green, 30 July 1914. The Declaration of London had, in fact, been incorporated virtually unchanged in the naval prize manual. The French navy had done likewise; L. Guichard, *The Naval Blockade* (London, 1930), p. 21.

13 The declaration, for which there were no provisions for denunciation, stated that, '(1) Privateering is, and remains abolished; (2) The neutral flag covers enemy's goods, (3) Neutral goods, with the exception of contraband of war, are not liable to capture under an enemy's flag; (4) Blockades, in order to be binding, must be effective, that is to say maintained by a force sufficient to prevent ready access to the coast of the enemy.' See Oppenheim, *op. cit.*, I. 460–1, 768–82; W. N. Medlicott, *The Economic Blockade* (London, 1952–9), I, 3, 'Economic Warfare', *Chambers Encyclopaedia*, p. 776. M. R. Pitt makes the point that the declaration itself and the practice of other powers permitted British policy, in practice, considerable flexibility; *op. cit.*, Chapters 1–3.

14 Lauterpacht, *op. cit.*, III, pp. 707–9; Oppenheim, *op. cit.*, II, 800–13; Hankey, *op. cit.*, I, pp. 96–9; Medlicott, *The Economic Blockade*, I, 5–6. Other questions covered by the declaration were blockade, unneutral service, destruction of enemy prizes, transfers to the neutral flag, and the right of convoy.

15 Hankey, *op. cit.*, I, 100–1.

16 Inside the government the Attorney General, Sir John Simon, objected to any 'line of blockade' across the North Sea and Channel and to the idea of treating certain foodstuffs on their way to Rotterdam as conditional contraband. Under the Declaration of London it was illegal to bar access to neutral ports or coasts. As for cargoes for Rotterdam in neutral vessels they could only be seized if contraband. If conditional contraband, they could not be seized at all: F.O. 800, 89, Memo., 14 August 1914. On the limitation of Britain's legal commitment see W. E. Arnold-Forster, *The Economic Blockade*, p. 25, n. 2.

17 L. Guichard, *The Naval Blockade, 1914–1918*, p. 310.

18 H. W. C. Davis, *op. cit.*, p. 5; Accounts and Papers, LIII (1919), Report on Food Conditions in Germany, 927–81. See also n. 5. The French never used the term 'blockade' loosely, as Britain did, to describe the various measures developed later to put economic pressure on Germany; e.g. F.O. 382, 12, min. by Craigie, 19 November 1915. It is not surprising that the German delegate at the London Naval Conference had jumped at the chance to insist on abolishing the application to conditional contraband of the doctrine of 'continuous voyage' – under which it was the final destination of goods that mattered; Pitt, *op. cit.*, pp. 386–7.

19 Cab. 1, 11, Notes by Sir M. Hankey, January 1915; C. E. Fayle, *History of the Great War: Seaborne Trade* (London, 1920–4), I, chap. 1; Guichard, *op. cit.*, p. 9. British shipping was deterred from taking cargoes to suspect waters by the withholding of Government War Insurance. Other devices were soon resorted to, such as the chartering by the government of the only available ships or attempts to corner stocks.

20 F.O. 372, 588, Page to Grey, 7 August 1914; *ibid.*, 69Tr., Bertie to Grey, 11 August 1914; *ibid.*, Memo. by Hurst, 10 August 1914, *Foreign Relations, Suppl.*, 1914, 216.

21 Present were E. Grey, Haldane, McKenna, Churchill, Runciman, Sir John Simon, Prince Louis of Battenberg, Sir F. C. D. Sturdee, Sir E. J. W. Slade, Sir Graham Greene and C. J. R. Hurst; F.O. 372, 588, Minutes of Conference, 19 August 1914; Bell, *op. cit.*, p. 39. The Admiralty had already pronounced against ratification of the agreement; *ibid.*, Greene to F.O., 11 August 1914.

22 F.O. 372, 588, communication by Cambon, 24 August 1914; *ibid.*, Chief Censor to Sperling, 20 August 1914; *ibid.*, 79Tr., Bertie to Grey, 20 August 1914. *British and Foreign State Papers*, CVIII, 1914, Part 2, 100–2; Bell, *op. cit.*, p. 712; W. E. Arnold-Forster, *The Economic Blockade*, p. 176. Article 35 of the Declaration of London stated that, 'Conditional contraband is not liable to capture, except when found on board a vessel bound for territory belonging to or occupied by the enemy, or for the armed forces of the enemy, and when it is not to be discharged in an intervening neutral port.'

23 For example part of Bell's work (*cit.*) was pirated during World War II and published in an edition edited by V. Böhmert under the propaganda title, *Die englische Hungerblockade im Weltkrieg, 1914–1915* (Essen, 1943). See M. C. Siney, *The Allied Blockade of Germany, 1914–1916* (Ann Arbor. Mich.), p. 284; E. R. May, *The World War and American Isolation, 1914–1917* (Cambridge, Mass.), p. 440. Foodstuffs had been declared conditional contraband on 4 August; Bell, *op. cit.*, p. 722.

24 Grey, *Twenty-Five Years*, II, 109; Hankey, *op. cit.* I, 142 *et seq.* G. M. Trevelyan, *Grey of Fallodon*, p. 309.

25 F.O. 800, 90, Sec., Hankey to Drummond, 25 February 1915; D.D.F., 3, II, 754; Hankey, *op. cit.*, I, 366; Bell, *op. cit.*, pp. 24–6; Grey, *op. cit.*, II, 20; G. P. Gooch, *Recent Revelations of European Diplomacy* (London, 1940), p. 295.

26 F.O. 372, 588, Grey to Page, 22 August 1914; Cab. 1, 10, Hankey, Mins. of Meeting of Co-ordinating Committee held on 27 August, 1 September 1914; F.O. 800, 88, Grey to Churchill, 24 August 1914. By the end of September Grey was making every effort to find evidence to support the British Contention; F.O. 372, 601, Grey to

Procurator General, Agents of Committee on Restriction of Enemy Supplies, R.R. at the Hague, Copenhagen, Christiania and Stockholm, Oppenheimer. No corroboration was received by Grey; F.O. 372, 602, 188 Ccl., Johnstone to Grey, 23 October 1914; *ibid.*, 10Tr., 12Tr., Crofton-Lowther to Grey, 21 October, 2 November 1914. Orders were given to the navy to intercept foodstuffs for Germany but apparently remained a dead letter until March 1915; Arnold-Forster, *op. cit.*, p. 30. It may be noted that the Germans themselves had been more than slow to anticipate supply problems or to plan for anything but a short war and one in which Britain would probably implement the Declaration of London; Bell, *op. cit.*, pp. 192–7; Marder, *op. cit.*, I, 377.

27 W. N. Medlicott, *The Economic Blockade*, I, 34; Accounts and Papers, LIII (1919), *Report on Food Conditions in Germany*, by E. H. Starling (with memorandum by A. P. McDougall and statistics by C. W. Guillebaud), pp. 927–81. Cab. 37, 143, Memo., German Food Problems, 19 February 1916; R. Kuczynski, *Deutschlands Versorgung, mit Nahrungs-und Futtermitteln* (Berlin, 1927), Part IV, pp. 60–1, quoted Beveridge, *Blockade and the Civilian Population*, p. 27 and Medlicott, *loc. cit.* Starling estimated that, discounting imported fertilisers and concentrated feeding stuffs, imports represented less than 10% of total food consumed, and that, at the beginning of the war, a diminution of 15% in consumption would not have caused undernourishment. To Easter 1916, the food supply of the population as a whole was not much inferior to that of pre-war. Guichard makes an unconvincing case for Germany's retention of livestock; *op. cit.*, pp. 295–7. The perfection of a nitrogen-fixation process by Haber and Bosch enabled Germany to continue the war when Chilean nitrates were cut off and domestic production dislocated in the autumn of 1914; Medlicott, *op. cit.*, p. 30; W. Carr, *A History of Germany* (London, 1969), p. 252.

28 Arnold-Forster, *op. cit.*, pp. 37, 75; Beveridge, *op. cit.*, p. 8; K. S. Pinson, *Modern Germany* (New York, 1966), p. 223. Starch foods also had a military use.

29 Carr, *op. cit.*, pp. 250–1; Arnold-Forster, *op. cit.*, pp. 36, 90.

30 Text in A. Pulling (ed.), *Manual of Emergency Legislation* (1914), pp. 111–12; Bell, *op. cit.*, p. 723; *Foreign Relations, Suppl.*, 1914, 236. Lead and glycerine were also on the list.

31 F.O. 800, 88, Sec., Churchill to Grey, 15 August 1914, Cab. 1, 11, Notes by Hankey, January 1915; Colombos, *op. cit.*, p. 21 (6), pp. 375–6 (358–9); Bell, *op. cit.*, pp. 31–5, 43–5, 62; Davis, *op. cit.*, pp. 6–7. It may be noted that the orders to the fleet to intercept foodstuffs for Germany apparently remained a dead letter until March 1915; F.O. 372, 601, Grey circular, 29 September 1914; Cab. 1, 10, Sec., Hankey Memo., 1 September 1914; Arnold-Forster, *op. cit.*, p. 30. In November, Sir Eyre Crowe, one of the most outstanding officials, took charge of contraband negotiations generally, and the new department was supervised by Alwyn Parker. An able man, O. A. Sargent, dealt with questions touching the Scandinavian countries and Holland and R. L. Craigie with Italian and Swiss problems, while R. G. Vansittart was F.O. representative on the licencing committee, which enforced legislation on trading with the enemy. Sir Francis Oppenheimer, commercial attaché at Frankfurt, who became one of the R.E.S. committee's most outstanding agents, was sent to Holland in August. Others were appointed to Malmö, Christiansand, Esbjerg and Flushing.

32 Marder, *op. cit.*, I, 365–9.

33 F.O. 382, 12, Conf., Memo. by Grey, 22 July 1915; Grey, *Twenty-Five Years*, II, 103, 111; G. M. Trevelyan, *op. cit.*, pp. 306, 309.

34 F.O. 800, 88, Churchill to Grey, 27 October 1914; *ibid.*, 89, Pr., Runciman to Grey, 27 October 1914; See Trevelyan, *op. cit.*, p. 310. For a survey of domestic pressures on Grey see Chapter 25.

35 F.O. 800, 84, Telegrams, Spring-Rice to Grey, 28, 28, 29 September 1914; *ibid.*, Grey to Spring-Rice, 29 September 1914; F.O. 372, 601, 66Tr., Spring-Rice to Grey, 29 September 1914; *Foreign Relations, Suppl., Q14*, pp. 232–3; A. S. Link, *Wilson, the Struggle for Neutrality*, III, 112–13.

36 F.O. 372, 601, communication by Cambon, 21 September 1914; *ibid.*, Memo. by Hurst, mins., 24 September 1914; F.O. 800, 84, Memo. by Crowe, October 1914; F.O. 800, 171, Bertie to Grey, 17 October 1914; F.O. 372, 601, 21Tr., Buchanan to Grey, 5 October 1914; Lady A. Gordon Lennox (ed.), *Diary of Lord Bertie* (London, 1924), I, 52; F. Oppenheimer, *Stranger Within* (London, 1960), p. 240, nn. 1, 2. A. Pingaud, *Histoire Diplomatique de la France pendant la Grande Guerre* (Paris, 1938–40), 2, 232–7; May, *op. cit.*, p. 22; Link, *op. cit.*, p. 117. Churchill wrote, 'I agree with the French views. I consider we ought not to give in in a vital matter like this, until it is certain that persistence will actually and imminently bring the United States into the field againt us. I would not give in till the last minute'; F.O. 800, 88, to Grey, 27 October 1914; There is some evidence that the Americans did not expect Britain to make concessions so readily; F.O. 372, 602, Memo., 22 October 1914.

37 Grey reserved the right to take more effective steps against a neutral country being used as a base of supplies for an enemy army or government; F.O. 372, 601, Tel. 89, Grey to Spring-Rice, 4 October 1914. F.O. 800, 84, Grey to Spring-Rice, 29 September 1914; *ibid.*, Spring-Rice to Grey, 1, 5 October 1914; F.O. 372, 601, 117, Tel., Spring-Rice to Grey,15 October 1914; *ibid.*, Grey to Spring-Rice, 17 October 1914; F.O. 372, 602, Telegrams 129 and 131, Spring-Rice to Grey, 21, 23 October 1914; *ibid.*, Grey to Spring-Rice, 23 October 1914; F.O. 800, 55/171, Pr., Grey to Bertie, 27 October 1914; Cab. 1, 15, F.O. Memo., 28 December 1915; Davis, *op. cit.*, pp. 6, 7; Bell, *op. cit.*, 58–9; Hankey, *op. cit.*, I, 355–6. Texts of Order and Proclamation in Bell, *op. cit.*, pp. 713, 723–4; *Foreign Relations, Suppl. 1914, op. cit.*, 261–3. The Americans were also told that cotton was 'in the free list and *will remain there*'; F.O. 372, 602, 140 Telegram, Spring-Rice to Grey, 25 October 1914. Incidentally the American Ambassador (who said he would resign if told to press Britain again), told Wilson in September 1916 that ratification of the Declaration of London would have lost Britain the war; B. J. Hendrick, *The Life and Letters of Walter H. Page*, I, 373–84.

38 Arnold-Forster, *op. cit.*, p. 7. Bell does not question this, but argues that the indirect trade of Germany had hardly been checked by the previous Order in Council (of 20 August), so that the Order of 29 October involved no loss to Britain in practice; *op. cit.*, pp. 58–9.

39 Fisher, now First Sea Lord again, wrote, 'I grieve we give you trouble in closing the North Sea but the Germans were just browsing on us with mine laying trawlers and if we stopped to search them our searching vessels were bagged by the ever attendant submarine!'; F.O. 800, 88, to Grey, 7 November 1914; *Foreign Relations, Suppl.*, 1914, 466. The U.S.A. refused from the outset to concert action with other neutrals. See also Bell, *op. cit.*, pp. 128, 129, 197; Fayle, *op. cit.*, J. S. Corbett and H. Newbolt, *History of the Great War: Naval Operations*, I, 247–8. As for copper, American exports were worth nearly £30 million and it should be remembered that a depression was still possible in America, though the war had led to some improvement; May, *op. cit.*, p. 29.

40 F.O. 368, 1162, 155 Ccl. 195 Ccl., Spring-Rice to Grey, 7, 23 December 1914, min. by Crowe, 25 December; *ibid.*, 225 Conf., Spring-Rice to Grey, 24 November 1914; *ibid.*, Chandler Anderson to Crowe, 1 December 1914; *ibid.*, 122 Ccl., 123 Ccl., 143 Ccl., Grey to Spring-Rice, 6, 17 December 1914; *ibid.*, 155 Ccl., 179 Ccl., 190 Ccl., Spring-Rice to Grey, 7, 15, 21 December 1914; F.O. 800, 84, Spring-Rice to Grey, 3 December 1914; F.O. 800, 85, Pr., Spring-Rice to Grey, 15 January 1915; *ibid.*, Grey to Spring-Rice, 18 January 1915; Hendrick, *op. cit.*, I, 380–4; Bell, *op. cit.*, 129–32,

138–41. Crowe wrote, 'The State Department and, I am afraid, the President too cannot be relied upon to deal fairly with us. They believe it pays them better to obstruct this country in the legitimate exercise of its belligerent rights than to obstruct the illegitimate practices of the Germano-American contraband trades, because they find this country giving way to them whenever they parade their alleged difficulties with public opinion...

Our proper course under the circumstances is resolutely to enforce our un-doubted rights in the Prize Courts. I feel sure that, however the State Department may bluster and threaten, they will not carry with them American opinion in trying to force upon us, at the moment when we are fighting for our life, documents and theories which their own Government has always repudiated as contrary to international law. We must vindicate the rights of the Prize Courts against the endeavour of the State Department to get every case settled in their favour by diplomatic pressure outside the Prize Court.'

41 F.O. 368, 1162, 109 Ccl., Grey to Spring-Rice, 1 December 1914.

42 F.O. 372, 601, 83, Spring-Rice to Grey, 4 October 1914; *ibid.*, Matthews (B.O.T.) to Tyrell, 6 October 1914; F.O. 368, 1162, 143 Ccl., 151 Ccl., Grey to Spring-Rice, 17 November, 5 December 1914; *ibid.*, 259 Ccl., 266, Spring-Rice to Grey, 4, 10 December 1914; F.O. 800, 84, Spring-Rice to Grey, 5 October, 3 November 1914; F.O. 800, 88, Hopwood to Runciman, ? December 1914; *ibid.*, Hopwood to Grey, 30, 31 December 1914; Copper was important. Even in peace time (1912) Germany had consumed 241,000 tons, but produced herself only 35,000 tons, while 206,000 tons had been imported from the U.S.A.; Arnold-Forster, *op. cit.*, pp. 36–8. Britain actually offered to buy the whole of the American output; F.O. 800, 88, Churchill to Grey, 5 January 1915.

43 F.O. 368, 1103, 44 Ccl., Grey to Lowther, 3 November 1914, encl.; *ibid.*, 1028, 111 Ccl., Grey to Johnstone, 3 November 1914, encl.; *ibid.*, 1162, 136, Ccl., Grey to Spring-Rice, December 1914; *Foreign Relations, Suppl. 1914*, p. 466.

44 A term taken to include the Netherlands, Denmark, Sweden and Norway.

45 F.O. 800, 88, Churchill to P.M., Grey and Kitchener, 7 September 1914; *ibid.*, 84, Grey to Spring-Rice, 14 October 1914; F.O. 368, 1026, communication by Nether-lands minister, 21 August 1914; *ibid.*, Churchill to Grey, 22 August 1914; *ibid.*, 12, 46 Ccl., Grey to Johnstone, 22, 24 August 1914; F.O. 372, 86, Grey to Spring-Rice, 2 October 1914; *ibid.*, 79 Ccl., Spring-Rice to Grey, 2 October 1914; Bell, *op. cit.*, pp. 64–7; Arnold-Forster, *op. cit.*, pp. 122–3. Article 7 of the Rhine Navigation Act was normally interpreted so that goods were regarded as in transit if (A) they were sent with through bills of lading, (B) they were declared for transit immediately on arrival in a Netherlands port, or (C) if documents showed such a destination on arrival in port; F.O. 368, 1028, Tel. 14 Ccl., Johnstone to Grey, 21 August 1914. By an arrangement goods consigned to the Dutch government, which included all cargoes carried by the Holland–America line, were prevented from being re-exported; F.O. 368, 1027, note by Law, 15 October 1914; *ibid.*, 103 Ccl., Johnstone to Grey, 20 October 1914; *ibid.*, 242, Bennett (N.Y.) to Grey, 25 October 1914. The Dutch had, of course, been given an early assurance that their neutrality would be respected; Grey, *op. cit.*, II, 163.

46 F.O. 372, 601, 74 Ccl., Bertie to Grey, 29 September 1914; F.O. 368, 1028, Memo., Holland as a Base for German Army Supplies, 17 December 1914; F.O. 800, 195, Cecil to Townley, 5 March 1917; Cab. 1, 22, Memo. by Cecil, 1 January 1917, p. 4. Grey persuaded France and Russia against a protest, claiming that nothing in international law prevented the Dutch from 'exporting foodstuffs and supplies to Germany or even direct to the German army'; F.O. 372, 601, 44 and 93, to Bertie, 1, 5 October 1914; *ibid.*, from the French ambassador, 1 October 1914; *ibid.*, Bertie to Grey, 2 October 1914.

47 F.O. 368, 1026, communication by Netherlands minister, 21 August 1914; *ibid.*, 46 and 22 Ccl., Grey to Johnstone, 22, 24 August 1914; *ibid.*, 42 Ccl., Johnstone to Grey, 5 September 1914; *ibid.*, Grey to Netherlands minister, 7 September 1914; F.O. 368, 1039, Johnstone to Grey, 23 September 1914; *ibid.*, 277 Ccl., 25 November 1914; *ibid.*, F.O. memo., 17 December 1914; *ibid.*, Grey to Johnstone, 18 December 1914; Sir Francis Oppenheimer, *Stranger Within* (London, 1960), pp. 241–2, 419–20; M. Siney, *The Allied Blockade of Germany, 1914–16*, p. 40. The Dutch government opposed further guarantees, while the Foreign Office hoped to retain all guarantees possible; F.O. 368, 1027, Netherlands minister to Grey, 27 September 1914; *ibid.*, 1028, 252 Ccl., Johnstone to Grey, 14 November 1914. There were doubts whether the evidence available would justify Holland being declared a base of enemy supplies. For details of N.O.T. procedure and guarantees, see memorandum by Oppenheimer, in F.O. 551, 1, 28, 78, Grey to Howard, 23 March 1915.

48 F.O. 368, 1162, Page to Grey, 28 December 1914; *Accounts and Papers*: 1914–16, LXXVIV, 1 (Cd. 7816; Misc. no. 6, 1915, *Correspondence between His Majesty's Government and the United States Government respecting the Rights of Belligerents*). The language was less unfriendly than that frequently used in Washington in the previous months.

49 F.O. 368, 1103, 16, 44, 98, Grey to Lowther, 14 October, 3, 4, November 1914; *ibid.*, Tels. 57, 124, 129, 266, 278 Ccl., Lowther to Grey, 8, 23, 23 October, 2, 5 December 1914; *ibid.*, 124 Ccl., Grey to Spring-Rice, 8 December 1914; *ibid.*, F.O. Memo., Denmark as a Base of Supplies to the Enemy, December 1914; F.O. 800, 84, Spring-Rice to Grey, 11 December 1914; F.O. 800, 45, Andersen to Grey, 15 October, 3 December 1914; Bell, *op. cit.*, pp. 72–81, 289–90; Arnold-Forster, *op. cit.*, pp. 123, 127. Denmark was deficient in industrial raw materials, imported all fuels and earned 85% of her foreign currency through the export of agricultural produce, which in turn depended on imported nitrogenous fodder; E. F. Heckscher (*et al.*), *Sweden, Norway, Denmark and Iceland in the World War*, pp. 411–12. Lard imports in October 1914 amounted to 1,005,000 lb. as against 39,000 lb. in 1913. Large consignments of for example lard, tallow, bacon and tinned meats, vegetable oils and also hides, skins and wool were observed to proceed by rail or via Sweden to Germany, and most of them came from America. Messrs Swift and Co. of Chicago and Armour and Co. established branches to cope with enormously increased meat imports. Few established Danish firms were involved.

50 *Ibid.*, F.O. 368, 1103, 272, 275, Nil Ccl., Lowther to Grey, 3, 4, 4 December 1914; *ibid.*, 149 Ccl., Grey to Lowther, 7 December 1914; F.O. 382, 285, Conf., Memo. by Turner, 17 November 1915. There had been frequent exchanges of views between the Scandinavian governments, which led to the delivery of similar notes of protest on 13 November 1914 to Britain, France, Germany and Russia to urge the maintenance of the principle of international law (*Folkeretten*), the right to freedom on the seas and discontinuance of mine-laying. This co-operation led to the royal meeting at Malmö on 18 December 1914, when there was agreement (unknown of course to Grey) to consult on any repercussions to their notes, to consult before answering any demands from belligerents and also for Norway and Sweden to consult before granting transport facilities, particularly from one of the Allies to another; F.O. 371, 8106, 241 Sec., Findlay to Balfour, 5 July 1922 and encl., Guichard, *op. cit.*, 161–2. Details including confidential print of the negotiations leading to the agreement can be seen in F.O. 382, 282 and 284. A commentary on the agreement is in F.O. 382, 284, Memo. by Sargent, 15 September 1915. On the aims of the British government see F.O. 368, 1103, Memo. by Crowe, handed to Mr Clan, 18 December 1914. Applying article 2 was the only legal method by which Danish imports could have been stopped.

51 In August 1914, it seemed possible that Sweden, with an army of nearly half a million, might enter the war on Germany's side; F.O. 800, 78, Pr. and Sec., Howard

to Grey, 7 August 1914. Her most important exports included timber, iron and steel, machinery, livestock and meat, and in 1913 Britain and Germany were together responsible for over half her foreign trade; Bell, *op. cit.*, pp. 81–6; Guichard, *op. cit.*, pp. 139–41; Siney, *op. cit.*, pp. 49–50.

52 F.O. 382, 266, 144 Ccl., Howard to Grey, 29 March 1915. The Swedish foreign office was incensed in September and challenged British modifications of the Declaration of London, when iron ore was declared contraband, apparently not realising how little Baltic shipping the Allies could capture; but Britain then exempted Swedish magnetic iron ore from interference; F.O. 372, 601, 7, 8, 13, 9, 17, 18 Tr., Howard to Grey, 29, 29, 28 September, 5, 5, 5 October 1914; *ibid.*, 7, 9 Tr., Grey to Howard, 1, 3 October 1914; *ibid.*, Wrangel to Grey, 5 October 1914; *ibid.*, Crowe to Wrangel, 16 October 1914.

53 See n. 50; F.O. 372, 603, Hurst, Report on Visit of Admiral Slade and Mr Hurst to Paris, December 19–23, 26 December 1914.

54 The Allied governments agreed that they would not interfere with cargoes of contraband for Sweden if export was prohibited (except to verify papers), nor with the export of Swedish goods, nor with the import of allied raw materials for home consumption, nor with the export of contraband to Norway and Denmark, if export was prohibited there. Exemptions for small quantities were permitted. The policy decision was taken by Crowe. See Bell, *op. cit.*, pp. 89–92; Arnold-Forster, *op. cit.*, p. 128; Siney, *op. cit.*, p. 52. Wallenberg suggested that certain foodstuffs, important metals and raw materials should be consigned to a Swedish commission under terms even more unfavourable than the memorandum; F.O. 382, 264, 129 Ccl., Howard to Grey, 31 December 1914.

55 F.O. 382, 264, 1, 3, 10, 12, 15, 17, 19, 21, 29 Ccl., Howard to Grey, 1, 1, 9, 10, 13, 13, 13, 13, 16 January 1915; *ibid.*, Note by Crowe, 14 January 1915; *ibid.*, Pr., Howard to Crowe, 20 January 1915; *ibid.*, Grey to Swedish Minister, 20 January 1914; F.O. 382, 265, to Swedish Minister, 19 March 1915; *ibid.*, 266, 143, 144 Ccl., Howard to Grey, 27, 29 March 1915; Bell, *op. cit.*, pp. 156–9. The Russian transit trade was checked by a technicality. All Britain could do was to threaten to limit supplies to Sweden to estimated requiremens and hope that the Archangel route would soon reopen.

56 F.O. 368, 1053, 95 Conf. 71 Ccl., Findlay to Grey, 3, 20 September 1914; *ibid.*, Sec., 4th Report of R.E.S.C., 29 August 1914; *ibid.* 30 Tr., 35, 92, 139 Ccl., Findlay to Grey, 23 October, 3, 7 November, 1 December 1914; F.O. 368, 1054, 108, 150, 153, 162, 173, 190 Ccl., Findlay to Grey, 4, 6, 9, 12, 18, 24 December 1914; *ibid.*, 116, 133, 134 Ccl., Grey to Findlay, 7, 20, 21, 22 December 1914; *ibid.*, Memo. by Sargent, 22 December 1914; F.O. 371, 8115, Conf., Findlay, Report for the Years 1914 to 1920, 22 June 1922. It was impossible to prevent German companies in Norway sending Norwegian-produced copper, nickel and aluminium to Germany. Norway's most important industry was fishing, followed by timber and timber products. See also Bell, *op. cit.*, pp. 92–9, 145–7; Arnold-Forster, *op. cit.*, pp. 123, 128; Guichard, *op. cit.*, pp. 152–4; Siney, *op. cit.*, 52–6; Heckscher (*et al.*), *op. cit.*, pp. 297–302; A good account from the Norwegian viewpoint is given in O. Riste, *The Neutral Ally* (Oslo, 1965), especially Chapters 1 and 2.

57 F.O. 800, 65, Rodd to Grey, 2, 18 October, 7, 17 November, 2 December 1914; *ibid.*, Grey to Bertie, 27 October 1914; *ibid.*, to Rodd, 20, 20 November 1914; F.O. 368, 1014, Crowe to Page, 6 November 1914; *ibid.*, to Italian Ambassador, 7 November 1914; *ibid.*, 159, 171, 229, 232, 247, 261, 262 Ccl., Rodd to Grey, 14, 16 November, 1, 3, 9, 11, 8 December 1914; F.O. 368, 1011, 159 Ccl., Grey to Rodd, 29 November 1914; *ibid.*, 1018, 240 Ccl., Bertie to Grey, 13 December 1914; *ibid.*, Granville to Grey, 19 December 1914; F.O. 368, 1134, 168 Ccl., Grey to Rodd, 2 December 1914; *ibid.*, 83 Ccl., to Grant Duff, 22 December 1914; F.O. 372, 603, Memo. by Hurst, 26 December 1914, para. 29; Bell, *op. cit.*, pp. 97–105, 150. American copper exports to

Italy from the beginning of the war to the third week of December totalled 36,285,000 lbs, compared with 15,202,000 lbs for the previous year; F.O. 800, 89, Matthew to Selby, 6 January 1915; Arnold-Forster, *op. cit.*, p. 36.

58 F.O. 368, 1131, 7 Ccl., Grant Duff to Grey, 27 August 1914; *ibid.*, 33 Nil., to Grant Duff, 26, 30 August 1914; *ibid.*, 1133, 68 Ccl., Grant Duff to Grey, 7 December 1914; *ibid.*, 46, 57, 45, 82, 90 Ccl., to Grant Duff, 3, 10, 15 November, 20, 30 December 1914; *ibid.*, to Bertie, 22 December 1914; *ibid.*, 1134, 60, 67, 71, 75, 105 Ccl., Grant Duff to Grey, 27 November, 5, 10, 16, 5 December 1914; *ibid.*, 60, 83, Ccl., to Grant Duff, 2, 22 December 1914; *ibid.*, 163, 170, 191 Ccl., to Rodd, 30 November, 2, 10, December 1914; *ibid.*, 1014, 261, Rodd to Grey, 11 December 1914; F.O. 368, 1162, Memo. by Crowe, communicated to Page, 29 December 1914; F.O. 800, 65, Rodd to Grey, 18 October 1914; F.O. 372, 603, Memo. by Hurst, 26 December 1914; Oppenheimer, *op. cit.*, pp. 55, 252; Bell, *op. cit.*, p. 305; Guichard, *op. cit.*, pp. 208–11. All grain and fodder were consigned to the Swiss government from January 1915 and a little later, mineral oils. The best detailed study on Switzerland and the blockade is that by D. D. Driscoll, *Anglo-Swiss Relations, 1914–18* (unpublished Ph.D. thesis, University of London, 1968).

59 F.O. 800, 85, Persl., Grey to Spring-Rice, 18 January 1915; *ibid.*, Spring-Rice to Grey, 20, 23 January, 12 February 1915; *ibid.*, 89, Runciman to Grey, 30 January 1915; *Accounts and Papers*, 1914–16, LXXIV (Cd. 7816: Misc. no. 6, 1915), *Correspondence between H.M.G. and the United States Government Respecting the Rights of Belligerents*, 4 May, *op. cit.*, 305–6; Link, *op. cit.*, III, chapter 6, p. 183.

60 *Ibid.*; F.O. 800, 85, Spring-Rice to Grey, 26 February 1915; *Accounts and Papers, cit.*, 2, 4, 6, 7, 8; May, *op. cit.*, pp. 30, 31, 308; Arnold-Forster, *op. cit.*, pp. 7, 8, 40. 41.

61 F.O. 382, 265, Memo. communicated by Mr Chiozza Money M.P., 25 April 1915; May, *op. cit.*, pp. 305–6. At the same time British exports to the U.S.A. *fell* from 24.1 million to 14.9 million dollars. American exports to Germany and Austria fell by 30.8 million and exports to Scandinavia, Holland and Italy rose by 39.5 million, though some of the latter total may have been caused by inability to obtain all customary supplies from Germany. See also Guichard, *op. cit.*, pp. 43–4, 53; Link, *op. cit.*, III, 131; Arnold-Forster, *op. cit.*, p. 50. Allied supplies from the U.S.A., such as those under Kitchener's contract of October 1914 for the entire production of the Bethlehem Steel corporation, were a factor of increasing importance; Bell, *op. cit.*, pp. 50, 228–9; Hankey, *op. cit.*, I, 358.

62 Cab. 1, 11, Page to Grey, 22 February 1915, mins.; F.O. 800, 90 Sec., Hankey to Drummond (F.O.), 25 February 1915, encl.; C. Seymour, *The Intimate Papers of Colonel House*, I, 376, 379, 447; J. A. Spender and C. Asquith, *Lord Oxford and Asquith* (London, 1932), II, 130–1; Hankey , *op. cit.*, I, chap. 35 *passim*, 866; Riste, *op. cit.*, p. 75. Churchill wrote a strong note for the Cabinet claiming that Britain's 'blockading lines' were effective and grimly concluding that only where neutrals would not permit the stronger belligerent navy to maintain an effective blockade would they 'be driven to consider an alternative (mines) which struck blindly at commerce'; Cab. 37, 125, Conf., A Note on Blockade, 5 March 1915; Churchill, *op. cit.*, II, 284–5.

63 F.O. 382, 464, de Fleuriau to Crowe, 31 July 1915; *ibid.*, 12, Tel. 2119, Spring-Rice to Grey, 17 October 1915; A.P., 1914–16, LXXXIV, *cit.*, 12; *Foreign Relations, Supplement*, 1915, 147. The Order in Council, in making all enemy property liable to capture, was in breach of the Declaration of Paris, but the U.S.A. as a non-signatory, had no right to protest.

64 F.O. 382, 12, Page to Grey, 2 April 1915; F.O. 551, 1, 58, 75, 84; F.O. 371, 10647, Memo, on the Attitude of the United States Government towards British War Measures, 2 November 1925; Cab. 1, 15, F.O. Memo., 28 December 1915; F.O. 382, 12, 892, Grey to Spring-Rice, 21 July 1915; *ibid.*, 628 Conf., Spring-Rice to Grey,

24 October 1915; *ibid.*, Grey to Page, 22 July 1915; *ibid.*, Tel. 892, Grey to Spring-Rice, 21 July 1915; *Foreign Relations Supplement*, 1915, 152–6. 'Why', wrote Balfour to Grey, 'are the newspapers allowed to talk of "blockade"? There is no blockade and much harm is done by threats without action'; F.O. 800, 88, 22 November 1915.

65 F.O. 800, 85, Spring-Rice to Grey, 16, 29 April, 21 July 1915; *ibid.*, Persl., to Crewe, 13 June 1915; F.O. 382, 12, Memo. by Grey, 22 July 1915; *ibid.*, de Fleuriau to Crowe, 31 July 1915; Cab. 37, 130, Memo. by Crewe, 18 June 1915; House, I, 450–6; Hankey, *op. cit.*, I, 325; Link, *op. cit.*, III, chaps. 12–13 *passim*; Bell, *op. cit.*, pp. 312–14; Trevelyan, *op. cit.*, pp. 319–20, 327–8. The only ostensible chance of getting Germany to renounce the submarine campaign would have been to free raw materials as well as foodstuffs. This, of course, did much to counteract German propaganda concerning Britain's 'hunger blockade'.

66 F.O. 800, 95, Conf., Memo. by Grey, 17 July 1915; *ibid.*, Memo. by Cecil, 19 July 1915; *ibid.*, Memo. by Hurst, 28 July 1915; F.O. 382, 464, Tel. 1376, Spring-Rice to Grey, 28 July 1915; *ibid.*, de Fleuriau to Crowe, 31 July 1915 and min.; Cab. 37, 130, Sec., Notes on Lord Crewe's Memo. of 18 June, by Hankey, 23 June 1915; May, *op. cit.*, pp. 309–12; Trevelyan, *op. cit.*, p. 321. Lord Eustace Percy wrote a hard hitting minute on Britain's 'unjustified nervousness' of the United States throughout the war; F.O. 800, 95, Maurice Low to Grey, 10 July 1915. On 3 August France was told that Britain was not changing policy but justifying it to the United States; F.O. 382, 464, Tel. 1739, Grey to Bertie, 3 August 1915.

67 F.O. 800, 85, Pr., Spring-Rice to Crowe, 15 July 1915; *ibid.*, Grey to Spring-Rice, 16 July 1915; *ibid.*, 95, Pr., Spring-Rice to Grey, 15, 19 July, 3, 8, 12, 13, 19 August 1915; *ibid.*, M. Low to Grey, 10 July 1915, min.; *ibid.*, 89, Runciman to Grey, 6 August 1915; *ibid.*, 95, Memo. by Grey, 17 July 1915; *ibid.*, Clerk to Drummond, 17 July 1915; *ibid.*, Memoranda by Cecil, 19, 31 July 1915; F.O. 382, 464, Tel. 1376, Spring-Rice to Grey, 28 July 1915; *ibid.*, Tel. 1379, Grey to Bertie, 3 August 1915; *ibid.*, Memo. by Grey, 3 August 1915; *ibid.*, Tel. 1484, Spring-Rice to Grey, 8 August 1915; *ibid.*, Tels. 1062, 1079, Grey to Spring-Rice, 11, 12 August 1915; *ibid.*, Tel. Delcassé to Cambon, 4 August 1914; F.O. 382, 12, 406 Ccl., Spring-Rice to Grey, 10 August 1915; F.O. 551, 2, 75, 246; Bell, *op. cit.*, pp. 314–16; Arnold-Forster, *op. cit.*, p. 50; Hendrick, *op. cit.*, II, 63; Link, *op. cit.*, III, 605–15.

68 F.O. 800, 85, Spring-Rice to Grey, 6 September, 28 October, 21 November, 9, 12, 23 December 1915; *ibid.*, Memo. by Spring-Rice, 28 October 1915; *ibid.*, Grey to Spring-Rice, 3 November 1915; *ibid.*, 95, Grey to Drummond, 9 December 1915; F.O. 382, 12. Very Conf., and 730, Spring-Rice to Grey, 24 October, 21 November 1915, mins.; *ibid.*, Page to Grey, 5 November 1915; *ibid.*, Dixon to Cecil – November 1915, mins.; F.O. 551, 3, 84, 88, 149, 150; *Foreign Relations, Supplement*, 1916, 578–601; House, II, 78, 79, 132; Link, *op. cit.*, III, 589, 682–5; IV, 59. The American note reiterated objections to search at sea, the detention of neutral cargoes without absolute proof of enemy destination and the validity for Americans of British Prize Court decisons. When, however, Spring-Rice reported the possibility of the American Congress placing an embargo on arms to Britain, Grey minuted that the Allies could probably retaliate by cutting supplies of raw materials (F.O. 382, 12, Tel. 2989, 27 December 1915). It is significant to find someone like Spring-Rice writing by 23 December, 'The U.S. government seems now to be laying claim to the right to trade with the enemy as well as with us and neutral nations and so further to increase the immense (export) figures which are astonishing the world...But do not count on purchasing effective help by any concession. You will build on the sand' (F.O. 800, 85, to Grey). The influential Lord Eustace Percy commented on 24 January 1916, 'Americans do not love us and will not actively help us...but as a matter of fact they want us to win and expect us to "play up"' (F.O. 800, 96, Memo.).

69 The most comprehensive account of blockade organisations is still that of H. W. C. Davis, *op. cit.*, and a good survey of the system when fully developed is that of Arnold-Forster, *op. cit.*, Part II. Wartime organisations are listed under ministries in N. B. Dearle, *Dictionary of Official War-Time Organisations*. For C.I.D. influence in 1915 see Hankey, *op. cit.*, I, 353–4. Machinery created in that year includes the Enemy Exports Committee (March); the War Trade Department (February), including the Trade Clearing House (later the War Trade Intelligence Department) and, from April, a statistical section which became the War Trade Statistical Department in 1916; the Rubber and Tin Exports Committee (January); the Coal Export Committee (April); the Cotton Exports Committee (June), the Cornhill Committee (probably at the end of 1914 or soon after). Neutral shippers also facilitated identification of German exports by covering their own goods with attested 'certificates of origin'. The records of the various organisations are preserved in the Public Record Office (F.O. 902 and T.S. 14).

70 F.O. 800, 95, Memo. by Cecil, 19 July 1915; Cab. 1, 15, F.O. Memo., 28 December 1915; F.O. 551, 2, 18, F.O. to Board of Trade, 6 July 1915; *ibid.*, 322, F.O. Memo., 10 September 1915; *ibid.*, 353, F.O. to B.O.T., Admiralty, War Trade Dept., Procurator-General, 17 September 1915; *ibid.*, War Trade Dept. to F.O., 23 September 1915; Davis, *op. cit.*, pp. 13, 14; Arnold-Forster, *op. cit.*, pp. 8, 9, Chapter 10; Bell, *op. cit.*, Chapter 10; Guichard, *op. cit.*, pp. 59, 60; Medlicott, *op. cit.*, p. 21. For the legal position see F.O. 551, 3, 15, to F.O., 4 September 1915; Cab. 37, 141, Memo. by Pearce Higgins, the Policy of Rationing Neutral States adjoining Germany and its relation to International Law, 19 November 1915. The Procurator-General did not rule out the possibility of a new Order in Council authorising forcible rationing. Grey himself was absent from the F.O. with eye trouble for most of June, but Cecil, with much support, was now arguing that rationing would be necessary whichever form of economic warfare Britain chose. The *Kim* was one of four vessels which, among other items, were carrying thirteen times the normal annual import of lard to Denmark.

71 F.O. 382, 407, 697 Ccl., Bertie to Grey, 1 August 1915; *ibid.*, communication by de Fleuriau, 2 August 1915; F.O. 382, 408, Emmott to Cecil, 6 September 1915; *ibid.*, 580, 623, 625 Ccl., Grant Duff to Grey, 3 August, 28 September, 4 October 1915; *ibid.*, communication by Oppenheimer, 9 September 1915; *ibid.*, R.E.S.C. to F.O., 16 September 1915; *ibid.*, 914 Ccl., Bertie to Grey, 16 September 1915; Cab. 1, 22, Memo. by Cecil, 1 January 1917; F.O. 551, 2, 146, 163, 314, 318, 348, 360, 395; *ibid.*, 3, 21; Davis, *op. cit.*, pp. 13, 14; Arnold-Forster, *op. cit.*, pp. 8, 9, 129; Bell, *op. cit.*, Chapter 13; Oppenheimer, *op. cit.*, pp. 252–9; Guichard, *op. cit.*, pp. 211–14; Cochin, *op. cit.*, pp. vii, 12–13. For a detailed account of the negotiations see Driscoll, *op. cit.*, Chapter 3. Though the Germans used the N.O.T. they would not use the S.S.S., preferring a separate official organisation, the *Treuhandstelle*. As for the S.S.S. itself, for some time, due to antagonism and misrepresentation in Switzerland, it seemed on the verge of collapse, but vigorous British support helped to get it established.

72 F.O. 382, 206, Memo. by Sargent, 23 April 1915; *ibid.*, R.E.S.C. to F.O., 14 May 1915: *ibid.*, Pr., Johnstone to Crowe, 7 May, 24 June 1915; *ibid.*, Highmore to Crowe, 22 May 1915; *ibid.*, Grey to Bertie, 26 May 1915; *Ibid.*, Memo. of meeting at F.O., 8 July 1915; *ibid.*, 1322, 1809 Ccl., Johnstone to Grey, 20 July, 3 August 1915; F.O. 382, 207, 1856 Ccl., Grey to Johnstone, 9 November 1915; F.O. 382, 277, 346 Conf., Findlay to Grey, 14 June 1915; F.O. 382, 713, 80 Tr., Rodd to Grey, 24 December 1915; *ibid.*, Cambon to Grey, 7 February 1916; *ibid.*, Memo. from War Trade Intelligence Dept., 5 October 1916; F.O. 382, 728, 3415 Ccl., Johnstone to Grey, 28 June 1916; F.O. 551, 1, 237, 387; *ibid.*, 2, 95; *ibid.*, 3, 92, 99; *ibid.*, 6, 1; Davis, *op. cit.*, pp. 14, 15; Arnold-Forster, *op. cit.*, 60, 61, 125; Bell, *op. cit.*, 285–7, 317; Siney, *op. cit.*, pp. 83–93. Instead of detention, proscribed goods were now usually allowed

to proceed to Holland, where Britain thought they were stored by the N.O.T. for the duration of the war. In fact the trust, correctly, released them gradually for home consumption. The War Trade Advisory Committee reported directly to the cabinet.

73 F.O. 382, 282, T. 25, Grey to Lowther, 19 March 1915; *ibid.*, 283, 241 Ccl., 26 May 1915; *ibid.*, 284, Danish Minister to Crowe, 4 August 1915; *ibid.*, Sargent to Crowe, 7 August 1915; *ibid.*, T. 790, 486, T. 1100, 762,Grey to Lowther, 2, 25 August, 28 September, 23 October 1915; *ibid.*, T. 1240, T. 1363, Lowther to Grey, 20 August, 5 September 1915; *ibid.*, Pr., Lowther to Crowe, 28 September 1915; F.O. 382, 285, communicated by Foss, 15 November 1915; *ibid.*, Note by Sargent, 11 November 1915; *ibid.*, Conf., Memo. by Turner, 19 November 1915; *ibid.*, Agreement between His Britannic Majesty's Government and the Merchant's Guild of Copenhagen and the Danish Chamber of Manufacturers, 19 November 1915; F.O. 551, 2, 258, 398; *ibid.*, 3, 24, 42, 59; Bell, *op. cit.*, pp. 291–8, 318; Arnold-Forster, *op. cit.*, 127–8; Heckscher, *op. cit.*, pp. 441–2; Siney, *op. cit.*, pp. 94–104.

74 A report stated, 'It is perfectly sickening to see the piles of transit stuff on the quays here and even overflowing into the streets and public squares because there is not quay space enough. There are several public squares full of cotton bales alone, going to Germany in driblets...'; F.O. 382, 276, Gray to Consular Dept., 29 March 1915.

75 F.O. 382, 276, T. 184, Grey to Findlay, 3 May 1915; *ibid.*, Agreement between H.M.G. and Norwegian–American Line, 14 May 1915; F.O. 382, 277, 426, 346, T. 1017, Findlay to Grey, 5, 14 June, 25 August 1915; *ibid.*, Johnstone to Grey, 3 August 1915; F.O. 382, 278, T. 1121, Findlay to Grey, 17 September 1915, min.; F.O. 382, 279, 785 Sec., Findlay to Grey, 18 September 1915; *ibid.*, Draft agreement with Union of Norwegian Merchants and Manufacturers, 30 September, 1 October 1915; F.O. 382, 281, T. 2300, 2326, Findlay to Grey, 19, 27 December 1915; *ibid.*, 1853, Grey to Findlay, 22 December 1915; F.O. 382, 902, T. 282, Howard to Grey, 25 January 1916, mins.; F.O. 371, 8115, Conf., Findlay to Balfour, 22 June 1922; F.O. 551, 1, 101, 142, 167, 174, 187, 238, 387; *ibid.*, 2, 283; Bell, *op. cit.*, pp. 256–60, 318; Riste, *op. cit.*, pp. 83–94. Even by September 1915 there were agreements on cotton, whale oil, margarine and shipping. Cotton rationing agreements were made on 31 August 1915 and 29 April 1916; margarine production materials agreements on 29 April 1916 and 26 July 1916; and a more extensive list of agreements on 24 September and 5 October 1916. Until rations were fixed, there was continuing concern in London over Norway's 'excessive imports', for example over fodder, lard, margarine, meat, syrup, cotton seed oil, linseed, olive oil, corkwood and leather in February 1916 (see F.O. 382, 902, T. 391, Grey to Findlay, 2 February 1916).

76 F.O. 800, 88, Conf., Hopwood to Crewe, 15 June 1915; *ibid.*, 75, Grey to Buchanan, 29 January 1916; F.O. 382, 264, 84, Howard to Grey, 19 February 1915, *ibid.*, 265, T. 18, 16 March 1915; *ibid.*, Memo. on Sweden as a Base of Supplies to the Enemy, 25 April 1915; F.O. 382, 266, 168, 171, 209, 258, 366, Howard to Grey, 8, 8, 29 April, 12 May, 26 June 1915; *ibid.*, Memo. for Swedish Minister, 14 April 1915; F.O. 382, 267, 554, Howard to Grey, 25 June 1915; *ibid.*, to Crowe, 28 May 1915; *ibid.*, note by Crowe, 2 June 1915; *ibid.*, T. 561, Clive to Grey, 26 June 1915; *ibid.*, Findlay to Grey, 27 June 1915; F.O. 382, 268, 509, T. 835, Howard to Grey, 18 June, 3 August, 1915; F.O. 382, 270, 473, Howard to Grey, 12 August 1915; *ibid.*, 356, Spring-Rice to Grey, 22 July 1915; *ibid.*, Admiralty to F.O., 31 August 1915; *ibid.*, 1156, Buchanan to Grey, 14 August 1915; Bell, *op. cit.*, pp. 343, 350–1; F.O. 551, 1, 53, 63, 84, 90, 91, 107, 120, 127, 161, 181, 224, 384; *ibid.*, 2, 3, 223; Arnold-Forster, *op. cit.*, pp. 128–9; Trevelyan, *op. cit.*, pp. 306–7; Siney, *op. cit.*, pp. 109–20. In the summer the dominating force in the Swedish government was the prime minister, Hjalmar Hammarskjöld, a pronounced Anglophobe. Grey wrote to Lloyd George, 'It is evident that Germany is making desperate efforts to bring Sweden into the war. She may succeed in doing so' (F.O. 800, 96, 14 May 1916).

77 F.O. 382, 943, 278 Conf., Howard to Grey, 20 October 1916, min. by Sargent; Arnold-Forster, *op. cit.*, p. 11. Bell states that normal imports of food and forage were reduced in 1916 by 20%; meats and meat products by 75%; metals and ores by 85%; animal and vegetable oils by 23%, and wools and woollen manufactures by 38%; *op. cit.*, pp. 325–6. A rationing agreement for lubricating oils had been made in August 1915. Though the Swedish bargaining position was still far from negligible, Wallenberg began negotiations for a general agreement in September, even accepting the principle of rationing on a basis of pre-war imports, and discussions were still taking place when Grey left office. (See F.O. 382, 945, 227, Howard to Grey, 19 October 1916; *ibid.*, 945, Memo. by Parker, 29 December 1916.) It proved almost impossible, however, to prevent Sweden exporting her own produce to enemy countries – iron ore, wood pulp, bacon and some eggs and the withholding of British coal as a form of pressure, from mid-1915, was not very successful, as Germany made great efforts to meet the deficiency. (See Cab. 1, 22, Memo. on the Present Position of the Blockade, 1 January 1917.) There were shortages of oil and wheat in Sweden; sugar had to be rationed in the autumn, and bread and flour early in 1917; Oakley, *op. cit.*, p. 235. The index of production for the manufacturing industry and mining began to fall, being 100 in 1913, 109 in 1916, and 91 in 1917; G. A. Montgomery, *The Rise of Modern Industry in Sweden* (London, 1939), p. 229; E. F. Heckscher, *An Economic History of Sweden* (Cambridge, Mass., 1954), p. 271.

78 Cecil wrote to Asquith, 'At present several departments are concerned with the execution of the policy. There are the Contraband and Foreign Trade Departments of the Foreign Office; the Contraband Committee and the Enemy Exports Committee, which are more or less Foreign Office committees; the War Trade Department and several committees sitting under it; the Board of Trade with the Coal Committee, the Tin Committee and the Rubber Committee, and possibly others sitting under it; the Trade Department of the Admiralty; and the War Trade Advisory Committee, presided over by Lord Crewe, which is supposed to be a sort of clearing-house of the various Departments concerned, but which is too numerous and too oratorical to be of much executive value.' F.O. 800, 96, Cecil to Grey, 12 January 1916.

79 *Ibid.*; F.O. 800, 96, Grey to Lord Herschell, 18 February 1916; *ibid.*, 102, Emmott to Grey, 18 February 1916; Davis, *op. cit.*, pp. 14, 15; Bell, *op. cit.*, pp. 452–4; Trevelyan, *op. cit.*, pp. 309, 326–7. It was Crowe and Cecil who worked for unified control, with the latter first approaching the prime minister and then getting the approval of Grey, who hoped that a single minister might be able to ameliorate the controversies over American commerce. M. Denys Cochin became similarly minister of state in France in March with less power than Cecil, but voluntarily reverted to an under-secretaryship at the Quai d'Orsay in December; Guichard, *op. cit.*, pp. 68, 71.

80 F.O. 800, 89, Grey to McKenna, 25 February 1916; *ibid.*, 96, Cecil to Crewe, 29 February 1916; *ibid.*, 168, Cecil to Grey, 5 June 1916; F.O. 371, 10647, Memo. by Orchard, 2 November 1925; Cab. 1, 15, 40, Cecil, 'Two draft Orders in Council'; 20 March 1916; Bell, *op. cit.*, Chapter 21; Davis, *op. cit.*, pp. 16, 35, 175; Arnold-Forster, *op. cit.*, p. 62; Siney *op. cit.*, Chapter 8.

81 F.O. 800, 96, Memo. by Lord Eustace Percy, 24 January 1916; Bell, *op. cit.*, p. 544.

82 F.O. 800, 86, Spring-Rice to Grey, 7, 24 July, 10 August, 4, 28 September, 11, 17, 22 October 1916; *ibid.*, Spring-Rice, to Crewe, 21, 21, 25 July 1916; *ibid.*, Spring-Rice to Cecil, 11 August 1916; F.O. 371, 10647, Memo. on the Attitude of the U.S. Government towards British War Measures, 2 November 1925; F.O. 551, 5, 83, 477, Spring-Rice to Grey, 26 May 1916; *ibid.*, 6, 27, Grey to Page, 20 July 1916; *ibid.*, 6, 115, 1169 Ccl., Spring-Rice to Grey, 15 September 1916; *ibid.*, 6, 136, 1446 Ccl., Spring-Rice to Grey, 10 October 1916; *Foreign Relations, Supplement*, 1916, 362, 411–21, 447, 455–6, 462–6, 593–616; Hankey, *op. cit.*, II, 480; Seymour, *op. cit.*, II, Chapters 7 and 8; Bell,

op. cit., pp. 558–65, 609; Arnold-Forster, *op. cit.*, Chapter 25; Link, *op. cit.*, IV, Chapter 4, p. 148; May, *op. cit.*, Chapter 15; Siney, *op. cit.*, pp. 144–55. The United States protested to Britain and France on 10 January and 24 May against the right claimed to forcibly bring into port neutral vessels plying between neutral countries and to remove and censor mails. Allied rejoinders on 3 April, 20 July and 12 October pointed out that goods sent by post were not correspondence and said that the allies had never differentiated in the treatment of mails on board a neutral vessel on the high seas and those on board a neutral vessel compulsorily directed to an allied port. The allies argued that they were within their belligerent rights. (On the question of legality, see Colombos, *op. cit.*, pp. 170–5.)

83 F.O. 800, 86, Spring-Rice to Grey, 24 July 1916; F.O. 551, 4, 131, 109 Ccl., Grey to Buchanan, 8 March 1916; *ibid.*, 132, 391 Ccl., Grey to Lowther, 9 March 1916; *ibid.*, 133, 393 Ccl., 9 March 1916; F.O. 551, 5, 11, Memo. by Graham, 28 March 1916; *ibid.*, 47, 583 Ccl., Conf., Gurney to Grey, 22 April 1916; *ibid.* 69, 713 Ccl., Lowther to Grey, 13 May 1916; F.O. 551, 6, 36, F.O. Memo., 27 July 1916; Cab. 1, 22, Memo., 1 January, 1917; Davis, *op. cit.*, p. 17; Bell, *op. cit.*, Chapter 22; Trevelyan, *op. cit.*, p. 308; Guichard, *op. cit.*, pp. 164–6.

84 F.O. 800, 69, Findlay to Grey, 18 February 1916; F.O. 371, 8115, Findlay to Balfour, 22 June 1922, encl., Report on Norway for the years 1914–20; F.O. 551, 5, 50, Memo. from Norwegian minister, 3 May 1916; *ibid.*, 88, 1038 Ccl., Ovey to Grey, 2 June 1916; *ibid.*, 91, 1070, Ccl., 7 June 1916; *ibid.*, 95, 30, Wardrop to Grey, 9 June 1916; *ibid.*, 104, 1303 Ccl., Grey to Ovey, 20 June 1916; F.O. 551, 6, 2, Conf., F.O. to Treasury, 4 July 1916; *ibid.*, 109, 1807 Ccl., Findlay to Grey, 17 September 1916; Bell, *op. cit.*, pp. 481, 487–8, 496–502; Riste, *op. cit.*, pp. 101–19; Heckscher, *op. cit.*, pp. 325–41.

85 F.O. 382, 943, F.O. Memo., 25 October 1916; F.O. 800, 195, Cecil to Townley, 5 March 1917; Cab. 1, 22, Memo., 1 January 1917; F.O. 551, 4, 138, 1062 Ccl., Johnstone to Grey, 10 March 1916; F.O. 551, 5, 35, Grey to Netherlands minister, 17 April 1916; *ibid.*, 64, F.O. Memo., 15 May 1916; *ibid.*, 82, 2514 Ccl., Grey to Chilton, 3 June 1916; *ibid.*, 103, R.E.S. Dept. to F.O., 16 June 1916; F.O. 551, 6, 9, War Trade Intelligence Dept., to F.O., 10 July 1916; *ibid.*, 117, Memo., Holland as a base of enemy supplies, 28 September 1916; *ibid.*, Min. by Cecil, 4 October 1916; *ibid.*, 147, Grey to Netherlands Minister, 16 October 1916; *ibid.*, 162, F.O. Memo. 10 November 1916; *ibid.*, 172, 575 Ccl., Johnstone to Grey, 25 November 1916; Bell, *op. cit.*, pp. 473–8. After mid-1916, when the first agricultural agreement was in force, there was a considerable drop in exports to Germany. Compensation for the detention of the trawlers had to be paid by Britain after the war; Turlington, *op. cit.*, pp. 244–6. Arnold-Forster (*op. cit.*, p. 131) gives statistics which demonstrate the impact of allied policies on enemy supplies:

Exports of agricultural produce from Holland to Germany and Austria
(in thousands of tons)

	1915	1916 Jan.–June	1916 July–Dec.	1916 Total	1917
Butter	37	19	12	31	17.7
Cheese	63	46	30	76	37.4
Eggs	25	20	10	30	16.5
Meat	—	40	9	49	7.6
Cattle (head)	78	—	—	34	1.5
Potatoes	213	90	32	122	25.5
Potato-meal	71	51	6	58	9.0

The Ministry of Finance in Paris, opposed to preclusive purchase, was able to prevent French participation in the agricultural agreement with the Netherlands and seems to have only become interested in sharing available Dutch produce because of the difficulties in obtaining supplies from overseas after the German submarine campaign began in February 1917; M. M. Farrar, 'Preclusive Purchases and Economic Warfare in France during the First World War', *Economic History Review*, 2nd ser., vol. XXVI (1973), pp. 117–24.

86 F.O. 800, 66, Grey to Rodd, 17, 26 October 1916; *ibid.*, Rodd to Grey, 18, 19 October, 5 November 1916; F.O. 382, 1060, 157 Ccl., Grant Duff to Grey, 21 February 1916; *ibid.*, 1076, Memo. to French ambassador, 1 April 1916; *ibid.*, 1075, 1093, 1144 Ccl., Rumbold to Grey, 7, 17 November 1916; F.O. 551, 4, 84, Grey to Bertie, 13 January 1916; F.O. 551, 5, 20, 615 Ccl., Granville to Grey, 11 April 1916; *ibid.*, 21, 616 Ccl. Very Conf., 11 April 1916; *ibid.*, 49, French chargé d'Affaires to Grey, 2 May 1916; *ibid.*, 71, Report (Swiss Exchanges Sub-Committee), 25 May 1916; F.O. 551, 6, 65, 302, Grant Duff to Grey, 11 August 1916; *ibid.*, 126, 911 Ccl., Rumbold to Grey, 30 September 1916; *ibid.*, 169, 1123 Ccl., 9 November 1916; Cab. 1, 22, Memo., 1 January 1917; R. Pfenninger, *Die Handelsbeziehungen zwischen der Schweiz und Deutschland*, pp. 33ff, 43–55, quoted Turlington, *op. cit.*, pp. 136–7; D. Cochin, *Les Organisations de Blocus en France pendant la Guerre, 1914–1918*, pp. VII, 19–20; Guichard, *op. cit.*, pp. 214–24; Bell, *op. cit.*, Chapter 25. The Italians fell in with British plans concerning the blockade having contended vigorously until October that oranges had no food value and that the enemy was buying something useless. The French, during the winter of 1916–17, were concerned with the possible preclusive purchase of Swiss cattle, but, though recognising the advantage of purchase to the blockade, they dropped the proposal in February 1917 because of the cost involved and because of possible repercussions on French cattle-breeding; Farrar, *op. cit.*, pp. 124–9.

87 F.O. 800, 66, Grey to Rodd, 26 October 1916; Cab. 37, 143, Memo., German Food Problems, 19 February 1916; Cab. 1, 22, Memo. in regard to the Present Position of the Blockade, 1 January 1917; F.O. 551, 5, 32, 19 Conf., Gurney to Grey, 2 April 1916; *ibid.*, 33, 20 Conf., 10 April 1916; *Accounts and Papers*, LIII, pp. 927–81, Cmd. 280, 1919, comprising *Report on Food Conditions in Germany* by E. H. Starling, Memo. on *Agricultural Conditions in Germany* by A. P. McDougall, and *Agricultural Statistics* by C. W. Guillebaud; Arnold-Forster, *op. cit.*, p. 12; Guichard, *op. cit.*, pp. 83–6, 261–5, 267–99. Excellent diagrams summarising statistics showing the effect of the blockade on the trade of the Netherlands, Denmark, Norway and Sweden are to be found in Bell, *op. cit.*, Appendix IV; see also pp. 580–1, 604–6. In Germany, the guaranteed ration, equivalent to 1985 calories (or nearly 2500 per average man) could not be honoured in the autumn of 1916, when the actual ration was 1344 calories, which included only 31 grams of protein a day.

30. THE FOREIGN OFFICE AND THE WAR

1 F.O. 366/786/40089, memorandum by Crowe. The arrangement lasted until mid-September when Nicolson took the War department, Crowe the Treaty and Commercial departments handling blockade and contraband questions.

2 Nicolson MSS., F.O. 800/376, Nicolson to Hardinge, 1 December 1914.

3 M. Gilbert (ed.), *Winston S. Churchill* (London, 1972), companion volume 3, II p. 1257.

4 The evidence is found in F.O. 371/2138. Minutes by Crowe, 22 and 28 August; 371/2162, minute by Crowe, 5 August; 371/2168, minute by Crowe, 10 August. 1914.

5 F.O. 371/2168, Barclay to Grey, 8 August 1914, minute by Crowe.

6 Bertie MSS., F.O. 800/163, memorandum by Bertie, 19 December 1914.

7 Hardinge MSS., vol. 93, Graham to Hardinge, 7 January 1915; Owen O'Malley, *The Phantom Caravan* (London, 1954), p. 48.

8 F.O. 800/243, Gibson Bowles in the *Morning Post* of 2 May 1915. Mallet and Cecil came to Crowe's defence; the latter threatened to resign if Crowe was forced out of the Contraband Department. Maxse MSS., vol. 469, Mallet to Maxse, 15 October (?), 18 October (?). I am indebted to Professor Philip Quigley for this reference.

9 Hardinge, MSS., Chirol to Hardinge, vol. 97; Steiner, *op. cit.*, p. 164.

10 P. J. Cosgrave, 'Sir Edward Grey and British Foreign Policy in the Balkans, 1914–16' (unpublished Ph.D. thesis, Cambridge, 1971), pp. 52, 56, 77.

11 Nicolson MSS., F.O. 800/376, Nicolson to Hardinge, 1 and 31 December 1914.

12 *Ibid.*, Nicolson to Buchanan, 8 January 1915.

13 R. V. Rothwell, *British War Aims and Peace Diplomacy* (Oxford, 1971), pp. 29–30, 77, 124–5.

14 I am indebted to Patrick Cosgrave for information on Clerk.

15 Rothwell, *op. cit.*, pp. 45–8. Memorandum found in Cab. 16/36, 21 January 1917.

16 L. Oliphant, *An Ambassador in Bonds* (London, 1947), pp. 34–5.

17 L. Collier, 'The Old Foreign Office', *Blackwood's Magazine*, September 1972, p. 261.

18 K. Robbins, *Sir Edward Grey* (London, 1971), p. 319; see also Chapter 29, and footnote 31 below.

19 Letter from Owen O'Malley to author, 6 May 1969.

20 Lord Percy of Newcastle, *Some Memories* (London, 1950), p. 147.

21 For fuller discussion, see D. Collins, *Aspects of British Politics, 1904–1919* (Oxford, 1965), pp. 257–62.

22 See Chapter 29.

23 See Chapter 29.

24 *Ibid.*, n. 69 for a description of the blockade organisations.

25 A. Bell, *The Blockade of the Central Empires* (new edition, London, 1961), pp. 452–4.

26 The war-time Foreign Office is described in J. Tilley and S. Gaselee, *The Foreign Office* (London, 1933) and the Public Record Office Handbook, *The Records of the Foreign Office, 1782–1939* (London, 1969), pp. 22–4. It was sharply criticised in F.O. 366/787 by the Committee on Staffs which investigated the Foreign Office and Ministry of Blockade in 1918.

27 The only other department added to the Foreign Office was the Political Intelligence Department which, after a sharp dispute was transferred from the Department of Information in 1918 but was disbanded in 1920 when the News Department was also reduced in size.

28 In 1914, there were 159 males and 28 females employed in all capacities by the Foreign Office. In November 1918, there were 343 males and 361 females.

29 Hardinge MSS., vol. 22, Hardinge to Errington, 27 June 1916.

30 Collier, *op. cit.*, p. 261.

31 Hardinge MSS., vol. 22, Bertie to Hardinge, 25 June 1916.

32 *Ibid.*, vol. 23, Hardinge to Bertie, 27 June 1916.

33 *Ibid.*, vol. 24, Bertie to Hardinge, 16 October 1916.

34 *Ibid.*, vol. 22, Hardinge to Errington, 27 June 1916.

35 Warman, 'The Erosion of Foreign Office Influence,' *Historical Journal*, vol. 15, 1 March 1972, pp. 152–9.

36 This would have left Hardinge little time for Foreign Office business and the requirement was dropped. Balfour, of course, was not a member of the War Cabinet.

37 Hardinge MSS., vol. 22, Hardinge to Graham, undated; Rothwell, *op. cit.*, p. 13; Warman, *op. cit.*, p. 156.

38 Rothwell, *op. cit.*, p. 39. There had been a Committee on Asiatic Turkey headed by de Bunsen which reported in June 1915 and then the memorandum on a

'Suggested basis for a Territorial Settlement in Europe' circulated in August 1916 by Paget and Tyrrell.

39 Hardinge MSS., vol. 25, Hardinge to Bertie, 15 September 1916; Rothwell, *op. cit.*, pp. 59–60.

40 *Ibid.*, vol. 31, Hardinge to Howard, 28 April 1917.

41 *Ibid.*, vol. 24, Hardinge to Chirol, 3 August 1916; vol. 26, Hardinge to Grant, 4 October 1916.

42 Cab. 1, 22, Memorandum with regard to the present position of the blockade, 1 January 1917.

43 F.O. 800/95, Percy to Drummond, 26 October 1915.

44 E. Kedourie, 'Cairo and Khartoum on the Arab Question, 1915–1918', *Historical Journal*, VII (1964), 280–97.

45 *The History of the Times*, vol. IV, *The 150th Anniversary and Beyond* (London, 1952), p. 282.

46 Munro Ferguson to Earl Grey, 24 January 1916. This and other quotations cited in Robbins, *Sir Edward Grey*, pp. 322–3.

47 M. Swartz, *The Union of Democratic Control in British Politics During the First World War* (Oxford, 1971), pp. 70–2; *Hansard*, vol. 80., Col. 741, speech by Ponsonby.

48 These rumours, accompanied by pamphlets and speeches attacking Crowe, Oppenheimer (who was extremely sensitive on the point), Paget, Max Müller and others were not without concrete effects. Crowe's position and Müller's were both compromised; Müller could not be assigned anywhere but in the Foreign Office because of his German name and Hardinge used Crowe's German mother, wife and step-sons as yet one more reason as to why he could not possibly be permanent under-secretary.

49 For an excellent discussion of this material see, D. Collins, *Aspects of British Politics, 1904–1919* (Oxford, 1965), pp. 148–58.

50 *Ibid.*, pp. 268–95; Warman, *op. cit.*, pp. 148–9.

51 Steiner, *op. cit.*, pp. 168–70.

31. FOREIGN POLICY, GOVERNMENT STRUCTURE AND PUBLIC OPINION

1 On a number of occasions he privately expressed the view that the war was in some sense a judgment on those aspects of industrial civilization and urban life that he disliked.

2 Grey, *Twenty Five Years* (London, 1925), II, p. 70.

3 A. J. P. Taylor, *Politics in the First World War* (London, 1959), p. 70.

4 Grey, *Twenty Five Years*, II, p. 70.

5 Grey, *Twenty Five Years*, II, p. 80.

6 J. P. Mackintosh, *The British Cabinet*, University Paperback Edition, London, 1968, pp. 352–4.

7 M. Hankey, *The Supreme Command* (London, 1961), II, pp. 441–2. The Cabinet letter is cited in R. Jenkins, *Asquith* (London, 1967), p. 423. Grey to Crewe, 22 October 1915, Crewe MS.

8 Cited in J. Ehrman, *Cabinet Government and War* (Cambridge, 1958), p. 57.

9 Hankey, *Supreme Command*, II, p. 442.

10 Memorandum by Bonar Law, 4 December 1915, Asquith MS. Cited in Mackintosh, *The British Cabinet*, p. 357.

11 Lloyd George, *War Memoirs*, I, p. 584.

12 Jenkins, *Asquith*, p. 382.

13 Grey to S. Buxton, 21 March 1915, Buxton MS.

14 G. M. Trevelyan, *Grey of Fallodon* (London, 1948), pp. 276–8.

15 Cited in S. E. Koss, 'The Destruction of Britain's Last Liberal Government', *Journal of Modern History*, June 1968, p. 271. The attack by Koss on the generally accepted version of the formation of the Coalition Government is itself refuted by C. Hazlehurst, *Politicians at War*, i, London, 1971.

16 Trevelyan, *Grey*, pp. 326–7.

17 See, for example, the comments by the Editor of *The Times. History of The Times*, IV, Pt. I, London, 1952, pp. 234–5. They can be matched from a number of other sources.

18 Grey to S. Buxton, 2 February 1917, Buxton MS.

19 Grey to S. Buxton, 29 May 1917, Buxton MS.

20 Memorandum by Bertie, 19 December 1914, Bertie MS. Series A.

21 Z. S. Steiner, *The Foreign Office and Foreign Policy, 1898–1914* (Cambridge, 1969), pp. 165–6.

22 Chirol to Hardinge, 3 May 1915, Hardinge MS. 93.

23 F. Oppenheimer, *Stranger Within* (London, 1960), p. 321.

24 Comments handwritten on the introduction to the memorandum by W. S. Churchill, 6 October 1915, Asquith MS.

25 K. G. Robbins, 'British Diplomacy and Bulgaria, 1914–15', *Slavonic and East European Review*, vol. XLIX, no. 117, October 1971.

26 Trevelyan, *Grey*, p. 314.

27 E. R. May, *The World War and American Isolation, 1914–17* (Cambridge, Mass., 1959), pp. 20 ff. For a discussion of blockade policy in detail, see Chapter 24, and, for the formulation of the Declaration of London, Chapter 4, Section 9.

28 Runciman to Grey, 27 October 1914, F.O. 800/89.

29 B. J. Hendrick, *Life and Letters of W. H. Page* (London, 1924), I, p. 365. See also Chapter 24, n. 39.

30 Grey to Rosebery, 7 February 1915, Rosebery MS.

31 A. C. Bell, *A History of the Blockade of Germany* (London, 1961), p. 189.

32 J. Tilley and S. Gaselee, *The Foreign Office* (London, 1933), p. 185.

33 Bell, *Blockade*, p. 30.

34 Grey to Asquith, 15 February 1916, F.O. 800/100.

35 Grey to Runciman, 31 August 1916, Runciman, MS.

36 G. L. Dickinson to J. Bryce, 20 October 1914, Bryce MS.

37 For Bryce's attitude and the ideas of the Bryce Group, see K. G. Robbins, 'Lord Bryce and the First World War', *Historical Journal*, x, 2 (1967).

38 C. P. Scott to E. D. Morel, 24 September 1914, Morel MS.; M. Swartz, *The Union of Democratic Control in British Politics during The First World War* (Oxford, 1971).

39 C. P. Trevelyan to J. Bryce, 28 September 1914, Bryce MS.

40 D. C. Watt, *Personalities and Policies* (London, 1965), p. 42, emphasizes the appalling casualties suffered by the volunteer officers and the consequences upon middle- and upper-middle-class attitudes.

41 R. Pound and G. Harmsworth, *Northcliffe* (London, 1959), p. 475.

42 Pound and Harmsworth, *Northcliffe*, pp. 478–9. Grey made a nice point in a letter to Balfour: 'I have never seen Northcliffe and I suppose therefore it may be said that I haven't yet quarrelled with him.' Grey to Balfour, 30 July 1915, Balfour MS., 49731.

43 E. Cook, *The Press in War Time* (London, 1920), p. 31.

44 Cook, *Press*, p. 49 and p. 178.

45 P. Snowden, 'The Coalition and the Future of Politics', *War and Peace*, July 1915.

46 C. Hobhouse to W. Runciman, 28 May 1915, Runciman MS.

47 G. L. Dickinson to C. R. Ashbee, 4 May 1915, Journals of C. R. Ashbee, 18.

48 G. L. Dickinson to C. R. Ashbee, 10 November 1915, Journals of C. R. Ashbee, 18.

49 *Daily Mail*, 23 July 1915 and 21 August 1915.

50 Hendrick, *Page*, ii, p. 103.
51 House Diary, 11 February 1916, cited in May, *World War*, p. 373.
52 Grey to Sir Henry Newbolt, 31 December 1916, Newbolt MS.
53 Grey to St. Loe Strachey, 9 October 1916, Strachey MS.
54 See R. C. Lambert, *The Parliamentary History of Conscription in Great Britain* (London, 1917).
55 *The Nation*, 26 February 1916.
56 J. W. Graham, *Conscription and Conscience* (London, 1922). For a different interpretation see J. M. Rae, *Conscience and Politics* (Oxford, 1970), and K. G. Robbins, 'The Abolition of War: a study in the ideology and organisation of the Peace Movement, 1914–19', an unpublished Oxford D.Phil. thesis. The No Conscription Fellowship published a weekly journal. *The Tribunal* beginning in March 1916. The leading figures was Clifford Allen. See A. J. Marwick, *Clifford Allen, the Open Conspirator* (Edinburgh, 1964), and M. Gilbert, *Plough My Own Furrow* (London, 1965).

Bibliography

The bibliography, compiled in June 1975, is divided into:

I. Official Sources: Printed
II. Official Sources: Unpublished
III. Private Papers
IV. Autobiographies, Biographies and Secondary Sources
V. Articles

No attempt has been made to include unpublished research dissertations.

I. OFFICIAL SOURCES: PRINTED

GREAT BRITAIN

Accounts and Papers
British and Foreign State Papers.
Command Papers.
Gooch, G. P. and Temperley, H. (eds.) *British Documents on the Origins of the War, 1898–1914*, 11 vols. in 13 (London, 1926–38).
Hansard, Parliamentary Debates, 4th and 5th series.
Law Officers Opinions to the Foreign Office (Facsimile ed. by C. Parry).
McNair, Lord (ed.) *International Law Opinions*, 3 vols. (Cambridge, 1956).
Public Record Office Handbooks, Records of the Foreign Office, 1782–1939 (London, 1969).
Woodward, E. L. and Butler, R. (eds.) *Documents on British Foreign Policy, 1919–1939*, First Series, vol. iv (London, 1952).

AUSTRIA–HUNGARY

Bittner, L., Pribram, A., Srbik, H. and Uebersberger, H. (eds.) *Österreich-Ungarns Aussenpolitik von der Bosnischen Krise 1908 bis zum Kriegsausbruch 1914. Diplomatische Aktenstücke des Österreichisch-Ungarischen Ministeriums des Äussern*, 9 vols. (Vienna, 1930).

FRANCE

Documents diplomatiques français, 1871–1914, série ii and iii (Paris, 1930–1953).

GERMANY

Pius Dirr (ed.) *Bayerische Dokumente zum Kriegsausbruch und zum Versailler Schuldspruch*, 3rd ed. (Munich, 1925).

J. Lepsius, A. Mendelssohn Bartholdy, Fr. Thimme *Die Grosse Politik der europäischen Kabinette 1871–1914*, 40 vols. (Berlin, 1922–7).

Huber, E. E. (ed.) *Dokumente zur deutschen Verfassungsgeschichte*, II (Stuttgart, 1964).

Geiss, I. (ed.) *Julikrise und Kriegsausbruch 1914*, 2 vols. (Hanover, 1963–4).

Schücking, W. and Monteglas, M. (eds.), collected by K. Kautsky, *Die Deutschen Dokumente zum Kriegsausbruch* (Berlin, 1919).

Quellen zur Geschichte des Parlementarismus und der politischen Parteien, Die Reichtagsfraktion der deutschen Sozialdemokratie (Düsseldorf, 1966).

Stenographische Berichte der Verhandlungen des Deutschen Reichstags, Be. 232, XII Legislaturperiode, I Session, 9, Legislaturperiode V, Session 5.

ITALY

Documenti Diplomatici Italiani, 1870–1939 (Rome, 1952–).

RUSSIA

Adoratsky, V. V., Maksakov, V. V. and Pokrovsky, M. N. (eds.) *Krasnyi Arkhiv* (Moscow, 1922–41). See also the comprehensive index volume, *Krasnyi Arkhiv, Istoricheskii zhurnal, 1922–1941* by R. I. Zverev, ed. by V. V. Maksakov (Moscow, 1960) and the English language summary, *A Digest of the Krasnyi Arkhiv*, Part I (vols. 1–40), compiled by L. S. Rubinchek and edited by Louise E. Boutelle and Gordon W. Thayer (Cleveland, Ohio, 1942); Part II (vols. 41–106), compiled by Leona W. Eisele under the direction of A. Lobanov-Rostovsky (Ann Arbor, Mich., 1955).

Hoetzsch, O. (ed.) *Die Internationalen Beziehungen im Zeitalter des Imperialismus* (1931 et seq.).

II. OFFICIAL SOURCES: UNPUBLISHED
PUBLIC RECORD OFFICE, LONDON

Cabinet Papers
Cabinet Reports by Prime Ministers to the Crown, 1868–1916
Committee of Imperial Defence
Dardanelles Committee
Foreign Office Papers
Foreign Office Confidential Print
War Office Papers
Admiralty Papers
German Foreign Ministry Archives

DOKUMENTENZENTRALE, FREIBURG IN BREISGAU

German Naval Archives in Militärgeschichtliches Forschungsamt

HAUS-, HOF- UND STAATSARCHIV, VIENNA

Politisches Archiv

III. PRIVATE PAPERS

C. R. Ashbee Journals   King's College, Cambridge
Aehrenthal MSS.   Haus-, Hof- und Staatsarchiv, Vienna
Alston MSS.   Public Record Office
Asquith MSS.   Bodleian Library, Oxford
Balfour MSS.   British Museum
Berchtold MSS.   Haus-, Hof- und Staatsarchiv, Vienna
Bertie MSS.   Public Record Office
Bonar Law MSS.   Beaverbrook Library, London
Buxton MSS.   Newtimber Place, Hassocks, Sussex
Burns MSS.   British Museum
Bryce MSS.   Bodleian Library, Oxford: Public Record Office
Campbell-Bannerman MSS.   British Museum
Cartwright MSS.   Delapre Abbey, Northamptonshire
Chamberlain, A. MSS.   Birmingham University Library
Corbett MSS.   Bodleian Library, Oxford
Creighton MSS.   Bodleian Library, Oxford
Crewe Papers   Cambridge University Library
Cromer Papers   Public Record Office
Crowe MSS.   Public Record Office
Courtney MSS.   British Library of Political and Economic Science, London
Lowes Dickinson, G. MSS.   King's College, Cambridge
Dickinson, W. H. MSS.   Bodleian Library, Oxford
Dilke MSS.   British Museum
Grey MSS.   Public Record Office
Haldane, R. B. MSS.   National Library of Scotland
Harcourt, Lewis, MSS.   Stanton Harcourt, Oxford
Hardinge of Penhurst   Public Record Office; Cambridge University Library
Headlam Morley MSS.   New University of Ulster Library
Jordan MSS.   Public Record Office
Kitchener MSS.   Public Record Office
Lascelles MSS.   Public Record Office
Lloyd George MSS.   House of Lords Library
Lowther MSS.   Public Record Office
Manchester Guardian Archives   Manchester University Library
Maxse MSS.   West Sussex Record Office
McKenna MSS.   Churchill College, Cambridge
Mensdorff MSS.   Haus-, Hof- und Staatsarchiv, Vienna
Morel, E. D. MSS.   London School of Economics and Political Science
Murray, A.   National Library of Scotland
Murray, G.   Bodleian Library, Oxford

Newbolt MSS. (Sir Henry Newbolt)   Privately owned
Nicolson, Diplomatic Narrative   In possession of Nigel Nicolson Esq.
Nicolson MSS. (Lord Carnock)   Public Record Office
Ponsonby MSS.   Bodleian Library, Oxford
Ripon MSS.   British Museum
Rosebery MSS.   National Library of Scotland
Royal Archives   Windsor Castle
Runciman MSS.   University of Newcastle-upon-Tyne
Samuel MSS.   House of Lords Library
Satow MSS.   Public Record Office
Scott, C. P. MSS.   British Museum
Freiherr von Senden Bibran   Bundesarchiv, Koblenz
Spender MSS.   British Museum
Spring-Rice MSS. (F.O. 800/141–142)   Public Record Office
Strachey MSS.   House of Lords Library
Tirpitz MSS.   Bundesarchiv Militärarchiv, Freiburg/Breisgau, Germany
Trevelyan, C. P., Papers   University of Newcastle
Wallas MSS.   British Library of Political and Economic Science, London

IV. AUTOBIOGRAPHIES, BIOGRAPHIES, AND
SECONDARY SOURCES

Adam, C. G. F. *Life of Lord Lloyd* (London, 1948).
Ahmad, Feroz *The Young Turks: The Committee of Union and Progress in Turkish Politics, 1908–1914* (Oxford, 1969).
Albertini, Luigi *The Origins of the War of 1914*, translated and edited by I. M. Massey, 3 vols. (London, 1952–7).
Aldrovandi-Marescotti, L. *Guerra Diplomatica, 1914–1918* (Milan, 1937).
Allen, B. M. *The Rt. Hon. Sir Ernest Satow: A Memoir* (London, 1933).
Allen, H. C. *Great Britain and the United States: A History of Anglo-American Relations, 1783–1952* (London, 1954).
Amery, J. *The Life of Joseph Chamberlain*, vol. IV (London, 1951).
Anderson, E. N. *The First Moroccan Crisis, 1904–6* (Chicago, 1930).
Anderson, M. *Noel Buxton, A Life* (London, 1952).
Anderson, M. S. *The Eastern Question* (London, 1966).
Anderson, P. H. *The Background of Anti-English Feeling in Germany, 1890–1902* (Washington, D.C., 1939).
André, G. *L'Italia e il Mediterraneo* (Milan, 1967).
Andrew, C. *Théophile Delcassé and the Making of the Entente Cordiale; a Reappraisal of French Foreign Policy, 1898–1905* (London, 1968).
Angell, N. (Lane, R.) *Patriotism under Three Flags* (London, 1903).
  Europe's Optical Illusion (London, 1908).
Arnold-Forster, W. E. *The Economic Blockade, 1914–1919* (London, 1920).
  The Blockade, 1914–1918 (Oxford, 1939).
Arthur, G. *Life of Lord Kitchener*, 3 vols. (London, 1920).
Askew, W. C. *Europe and Italy's Acquisition of Libya, 1911–1912* (Durham, N.C., 1942).

Asquith, H. H. *The War, its Causes and its Message* (London, 1914).
  The Genesis of the War (London, 1923).
  Memories and Reflections, 1852–1927, 2 vols. (London, 1928).
Ayerst, D. *The Manchester Guardian, Biography of a Newspaper* (London, 1971).
Bailey, T. A. *Theodore Roosevelt and the Japanese American Crisis* (Stanford, 1934).
Baker, E. B. and P. J. Noel. See Noel-Baker.
Balfour, M. *The Kaiser and his Times* (London, 1964).
Barclay, Sir T. T. *Thirty-Years, Anglo-French Reminiscences* (London, 1914).
Barlow, I. C. *The Agadir Crisis* (Durham, N. C., 1940).
Bassett, A. Tilney *Life of John Edward Ellis* (London, 1932).
Beaverbrook, Lord *Politicians and the War, 1914–16* (London, 1928).
  Men and Power, 1917–18 (London, 1956).
  Decline and Fall of Lloyd George (London, 1963).
Bell, A. C. *A History of the Blockade of Germany and the countries associated with her in the Great War, Austria-'Iungary, Bulgaria and Turkey, 1914–1918* (London, 1937, re-issued 1961).
Beloff, Max *Lucien Wolf and the Anglo-Russian Entente 1907–14* (London, 1951).
  Imperial Sunset: vol. I. *Britain's Liberal Empire, 1897–1921* (London, 1969).
Berghahn, V. R. *Der Tirpitz-Plan* (Düsseldorf, 1971).
Bethmann Hollweg, T. von *Betrachtungen zum Weltkriege*, 2 vols. (Berlin, 1919–21).
Beveridge, W. *Blockade and the Civilian Population* (Oxford, 1939).
Birnbaum, K. E. *Peace Moves and U-boat Warfare* (Stockholm, 1958).
Bishop, Donald G. *The Administration of British Foreign Relations* (Syracuse, N.Y., 1961).
Blaisdell, D. C. *European Financial Control in the Ottoman Empire* (New York, 1929).
Blake, R. *The Unknown Prime Minister: The Life and Times of Andrew Bonar Law* (London, 1955).
Blatchford, R. *My Eighty Years* (London, 1931).
Bloch, Camille *The Causes of the World War*, translated by J. Soames (London, 1935).
Blunt, F. *My Reminiscences* (London, 1918).
Bohm, E. *Überseehandel und Flottenbau, Hanseatische Kaufmannschaft und deutsche Seerüstung, 1879–1902* (Düsseldorf, 1972).
Böhmert, V. *Die englische Hungerblockade im Weltkrieg 1914–1915* (Essen, 1943).
Bompard, L. M. *Mon Ambassade en Russie, 1903–1908* (Paris, 1937).
Bonham-Carter, V. *Soldier True: The Life and Times of Field Marshal Sir William Robertson* (London, 1963).
Bourne, K. *Britain and the Balance of Power in North America, 1815–1908* (London, 1967).
Bourne, K. and Watt, D. C. (eds.) *Studies in International History* (London, 1967).
Brailsford, H. N. *Macedonia: its Races and their Future* (London, 1906).
  The Fruits of our Russian Alliance (London, 1912).
  The War of Steel and Gold (London, 1914).
Braisted, W. R. *The United States Navy and the Pacific, 1909–22* (London, 1971).
Brett, M. R. and Oliver, Viscount Esher *Reginald Viscount Esher, Journals and Letters*, 4 vols. (London, 1934–8).

Bridge, F. R. *Great Britain and Austria Hungary 1906–14* (London, 1972). *From Sadowa to Sarajevo* (London, 1972).

Briggs, M. P. *George D. Herron and the European Settlements* (Stanford, Calif., 1932).

Browne, E. G. *The Persian Revolution of 1905–9* (Cambridge, 1910).

Bryce, J. *South America: Observations and Impressions* (New York, 1912).

Buchanan, Sir G. *My Mission to Russia and other Diplomatic Memories* (London, 1923).

Buehrig, E. H. *Woodrow Wilson and the Balance of Power* (Bloomington, Indiana, 1955).

Bueb, V. *Die 'Junge Schule' der französischen Marine, Strategie und Politik, 1875–1900.* Wehrwissenschaftliche Forschungen, no. 12 (Boppard am Rhein, 1971).

Bulow, B. von *Memoirs*, 2 vols. (London, 1931–2, English edition). *Denkwürdigkeiten*, 4 vols. (Berlin, 1930–31).

Burns, E. Bradford *The Unwritten Alliance: Rio-Blanco and Brazilian–American Relations* (New York, 1966).

Busch, B. C. *Britain and the Persian Gulf, 1894–1914* (Berkeley, Calif., 1967).

Butler, D. and Freeman, J. *British Political Facts, 1900–67* (London, 1968).

Butler, J. R. M. *Lord Lothian, Philip Kerr, 1882–1940* (London, 1960).

Buxton, C. R. *Turkey in Revolution* (London, 1909).

Buxton, N. E. *Europe and the Turks* (London, 1907).

Buxton, N. E. and C. R. *The War and the Balkans* (London, 1915).

Caillaux, J. *Mes mémoires*, 3 vols. (Paris, 1942–7).

Callwell, Sir Charles *Field Marshal Sir Henry Wilson, His Life and Diaries*, 2 vols. (London, 1927).

Calvert, P. A. R. *The Mexican Revolution 1910–1914: the Diplomacy of Anglo-American Conflict* (Cambridge, 1968).

Cambon, P. *Paul Cambon: correspondance 1870–1924* (Paris, 1940–6).

Cambridge History of the British Empire, vol. III, *The Empire–Commonwealth, 1870–1919*), ed. Sir. J. Butler and C. E. Carrington (Cambridge, 1959).

Campbell, A. E. *Great Britain and the United States, 1895–1903* (London, 1960).

Campbell, C. S. *Anglo-American Understanding, 1898–1903* (Baltimore, Md., 1957).

Camrose, Viscount *British Newspapers and their Controllers* (London, 1947).

Carlgren, W. M. *Izwolsky und Aehrenthal vor der Bosnischen Annexionskrise* (Uppsala, 1955).

Carnegie Endowment for International Peace *Official Statements of War Aims and Peace Proposals. December 1916 to November 1918*, ed. by G. Lowes Dickinson (Washington, D.C., 1921).

Carocci, G. *Giolitti e l'età giolittiana* (Milan, 1961).

Carroll, E. M. *French Public Opinion and Foreign Affairs* (New York, 1931). *Germany and the Great Powers, 1866–1914: A Study in Public Opinion and Foreign Policy* (New York, 1938).

Cecil of Chelwood, Lord *A Great Experiment* (London, 1941).

Cecil, Lady Gwendolen *Life of Robert, Marquis of Salisbury*, 4 vols. (London, 1921–32).

Cecil, L. *Albert Ballin: Business and Politics in Imperial Germany 1888–1918* (Princeton, N.J., 1967).

Chabod, F. *Storia della politica estera italiana dal 1870–1896*, vol. 1, *Le premesse* (Bari, 1951).

Chamberlain, Sir Austen *Down the Years* (London, 1935).
Politics from Inside (London, 1936).

Chapman, M. K. *Great Britain and the Bagdad Railway, 1888–1914* (Northampton, Mass., 1948).

Charles-Roux, F. *Souvenirs diplomatiques* (Paris, 1956).

Chatelle, A. *La Paix manquée?* (Paris, 1936).

Ch'en, J. *Yuan Shih-k'ai 1859–1916* (Stanford, Calif., 1972).

Chéradame, A. *L'Europe et la question de l'Autriche au seuil du XXe siècle* (Paris, 1901).

Chi, M. *China Diplomacy, 1914–1918* (Cambridge, Mass., 1970).

Churchill, R. P. *The Anglo-Russian Convention of 1907* (Cedar Rapids, Iowa, 1939).

Churchill, R. S. *Lord Derby* (London, 1959).
Winston S. Churchill, vol. 11, *Young Statesman, 1901–1914* (London, 1967).

Churchill, W. S. *The World Crisis* (London, 1923).
Great Contemporaries (London, 1937).

Clapham, J. H. *An Economic History of Modern Britain*, vol. 111. *Machines and National Rivalries, 1887–1914* (Cambridge, 1938).

Clark, I. F. *Voices Prophesying War, 1763–1914* (Oxford, 1966).

Clarke, G. S. (Lord Sydenham) *My Working Life* (London, 1927).

Clarke, P. F. *Lancashire and the New Liberalism* (Cambridge, 1971).

Collier, B. *Brasshat: A Biography of Field Marshal Sir Henry Wilson* (London, 1961).

Collins, D. *Aspects of British Politics, 1904–1919* (Oxford, 1965).

Connell-Smith, G. *The Inter-American System* (London, 1966).

Conrad von Hötzendorf, F. Graf, *Aus meiner Dienstzeit*, 5 vols. (Vienna, 1921).

Conwell-Evans, T. P. *Foreign Policy from a Back Bench 1904–1918* (London, 1932).

Cook, Sir Edward T. *The Press in War Time* (London, 1920).

Cookey, S. J. S. *Great Britain and the Congo Question, 1885–1913* (London, 1968).

Corbett, Sir Julian S. and Newbolt, Sir H. *History of the Great War: Naval Operations*, 5 vols. (London, 1920–31).

Craig, G. and Gilbert, F. *The Diplomats, 1919–1939*, 2 vols. (New York, 1965).

Crewe, the marquess of *Lord Rosebery*, 2 vols. (London, 1931).

Crosby, G. R. *Disarmament and Peace in British Politics, 1914–19* (Cambridge, Mass., 1957).

Crowthers, G. D. *The German Elections of 1907* (New York, 1941).

Cruttwell, C. R. M. F. *A History of the Great War, 1914–18* (Oxford, 1936).

Curry, R. W. *Woodrow Wilson and Far Eastern Policy* (New York, 1957).

Dakin, D. *The Greek Struggle in Macedonia, 1897–1913* (Thessalonika, 1966).

Dallin, A., (ed.) *Russian Diplomacy and Eastern Europe, 1914–1917* (New York, 1967).

Dangerfield, G. *The Strange Death of Liberal England* (London, 1935).

Davies, C. C. *The Problem of the North-West Frontier, 1870–1908* (Cambridge, 1932).

Davis, H. W. C. *History of the Blockade, Emergency Departments* (London, 1921).

Declava, E. *Da Adua a Sarajevo* (Bari, 1971).

Dedijer, V. *The Road to Sarajevo* (London, 1967).

Dehio, Ludwig *Germany and World Politics in the Twentieth Century* (London, 1959).

Dewood, D. *European Diplomacy in the Near Eastern Question 1906–1909* (Illinois, 1940).

Diamond, William *The Economic Thought of Woodrow Wilson*, John Hopkins Studies in Historical and Political Sciences (Baltimore, Md., 1943).

Dicey, A. V. *Introduction to the Study of the Law of the Constitution* (London, 1897).

Djemal Pasha *Memories of a Turkish Statesman* (London, 1922).

Dragonov, P. *Macedonia and the Reforms* (London, 1908).

Driault, É. and Lhéritier, M. *Histoire diplomatique de la Grèce*, 5 vols. (Paris, 1925–6).

Duff, A. Grant *The Life Work of Lord Avebury* (London, 1924).

Dugdale, B. E. C. *Arthur James Balfour, First Earl of Balfour*, 2 vols. (London, 1936).

Dunlop, J. K. *The Development of the British Army, 1899–1914* (London, 1938).

Durham, E. *Twenty Years of Balkan Tangle* (London, 1920).

The Struggle for Scutari (London, 1914).

Dutkowski, J. S. *Une expérience d'administration international d'un territoire L'occupation de la Crète 1897–1909* (Paris, 1952).

Earle, E. M. *Turkey, the Great Powers and the Bagdad Railway* (New York, 1923).

Earle, E. M. (ed.) *Makers of Modern Strategy* (Princeton, N.J., 1943).

Ehrman, J. *Cabinet Government and War, 1890–1940* (Cambridge, 1958).

Elliott, A. R. D. *Life of Lord Goschen, 1831–1907* (London, 1911).

Ellis, C. H. *The Transcaspian Episode* (London, 1963).

Emin, Ahmed *Turkey in the World War* (New Haven, Conn., 1930).

Ensor, R. C. K. *England 1870–1914* (Oxford, 1952).

Escott, T. H. S. *The Story of British Diplomacy: its Makers and Movements* (London, 1908).

Eubank, K. *Paul Cambon, Master Diplomatist* (Norman, Okla., 1960).

Evans, L. *United States Policy and the Partition of Turkey* (Baltimore, Md., 1965).

Eyck, E. *Das persönliche Regiment Wilhelms II* (Erlenbach-Zurich, 1948).

Fay, S. B. *The Origins of the World War*, 2 vols. (New York, 1928).

Fayle, C. E. *History of the Great War: Seaborne Trade*, 3 vols. (London, 1920–4).

Feis, H. *Europe, The World's Banker, 1870–1914* (New Haven, Conn., 1930).

Felice, R. de *Mussolini il rivoluzionario, 1883–1920* (Turin, 1965).

Fellner, F. *Der Dreibund: Europäische Diplomatie vor dem Ersten Weltkrieg* (Munich, 1966).

Fernis, H. G. *Die Flottennovellen im Reichstag 1906–1912* (Stuttgart, 1934).

Fischer, F. *Germany's Aims in the First World War* (English Translation, London, 1967).

War of Illusions (English Translation, London, 1973).

Fisher, H. A. L. *James Bryce* (London, 1927).

Fisher, Sir John (*see also* Marder) *The Papers of Admiral Sir John Fisher*, ed. P. K. Kemp, Navy Records Society, vols. CII and CVI (London, 1960, 1964).

Fitzroy, A. *Memoirs*, 2 vols. (London, 1925).

Flournoy, F. R. *Parliament and War* (London, 1927).

Forster, K. *The Failures of Peace* (Washington, D.C., 1941).

Frangulis, A. F. *La Grèce et la Crise Mondiale,* 2 vols. (Paris, 1926–7).

Frankel, J. *National Interest* (London, 1970).

Friedjung, H. *Das Zeitalter des Imperialismus,* II (Berlin, 1919).

Fry, A. *A Memoir of Sir Edward Fry, 1827–1918* (London, 1921).

Gall, W. *Sir Charles Hardinge und die englische Vorkriegspolitik, 1903–1910* (Berlin, 1939).

Gardiner, A. G. *Life of George Cadbury* (London, 1923).

Garvin, J. L. *The Life of Joseph Chamberlain,* 3 vols. (London, 1931–3).

Gaselee, S. *The Language of Diplomacy* (Cambridge, 1939).

Gatzke, H. W. *Germany's Drive to the West* (Baltimore, Md., 1950).

Geiss, I. (ed.) *July 1914* (London, 1967).

Geiss, I. and Wendt, J. *Deutschland in der Weltpolitik des 19. und 20. Jahrhunderts: Fritz Fischer zum 65. Geburtstag* (Düsseldorf, 1972).

Gelfand, L. E. *The Enquiry* (New Haven, Conn., 1963).

Gilbert, M. (ed.) *Plough My Own Furrow* (London, 1965).

(ed.) *A Century of Conflict, 1850–1950; Essays for A. J. P. Taylor* (London, 1966).

Winston S. Churchill, 1914–1916, vol. III (London, 1971).

Sir Horace Rumbold (London, 1973).

Giolitti, G. *Memoirs of my Life* (London, 1923).

Gollin, A. M. *The Observer and J. L. Garvin, 1908–1914: A Study in a Great Editorship* (London, 1960).

Proconsul in Politics: a study of Lord Milner in opposition and in power (London, 1964).

Gooch, G. P., *Life of Lord Courtney* (London, 1920).

Studies in Modern History (London, 1932).

Before the War: Studies in Diplomacy and Statecraft, 2 vols. (London, 1936–8).

Recent Revelations of European Diplomacy, 4th ed. (London, 1940).

Under Six Reigns (London, 1958).

Gooch, J. *The Plans of War: The General Staff and British Military Strategy 1900–1916* (London, 1974).

Gordon, B. K. *New Zealand Becomes a Pacific Power* (Chicago, 1960).

Gordon, D. C. *The Dominion Partnership in Imperial Defense* (Baltimore, Md., 1965).

Gordon, D. L. and Dangerfield, G. *The Hidden Weapon* (New York, 1947).

Gordon Lennox, Lady Algernon (ed.) *The Diary of Lord Bertie of Thame, 1914–1918* (London, 1924).

Görlitz, W. (ed.) *Der Kaiser: Aufzeichnungen des Chefs des Marinekabinetts Admiral Georg Alexander v. Müller über die Ära Wilhelms II* (Berlin, 1965).

Regierte der Kaiser? (Göttingen, 1959).

Gosses, F. *The Management of British Foreign Policy before the First World War, especially during the period 1880–1914,* translated by E. C. van der Gaaf (Leiden, 1948).

Gottlieb, W. W. *Studies in Secret Diplomacy* (London, 1957).

Goudswaard, J. M. *Some Aspects of the end of Britain's Splendid Isolation, 1898–1904* (Rotterdam, 1952).

Graham, G. S. *The Politics of Naval Supremacy* (Cambridge, 1965).

Graham, J. W. *Conscription and Conscience* (London, 1922).

Graves, R. W. *Storm Centres of the Near East, Personal Memories 1879–1929* (London, 1933).

Greaves, H. *Parliamentary Control of Foreign Affairs* (London, 1934).

Gregory, J. D. *On the Edge of Diplomacy: Rambles and Reflections, 1902–1928* (London, 1928).

Greib, K. *The United States and Huerta* (Lincoln, Nebraska, 1969).

Grenville, J. A. S. *Lord Salisbury and Foreign Policy: the Close of the 19th Century* (London, 1964).

Grey, Viscount *Fallodon Papers* (London, 1926).

Twenty-five Years, 1892–1916, 2 vols. (London, 1925).

Griswold, A. W. *The Far Eastern Policy of the United States* (New York, 1938).

Grogan, Lady Ellinore *Life of J. D. Bourchier* (London, n.d.).

Gueshoff, I. E. *The Balkan League* (London, 1915).

Guichard, L. *The Naval Blockade, 1914–18* (London, 1930).

Guillen, P. *L'Allemagne et le Maroc de 1870 à 1905* (Paris, 1967).

Guinn, P. *British Strategy and Politics, 1914 to 1918* (Oxford, 1965).

Gulick, S. L. *American Democracy and Asiatic Citizenship* (New York, 1918).

Gwynn, S. (ed.) *The Letters and Friendships of Sir Cecil Spring-Rice*, 2 vols. (London, 1929).

Gwynn, S. and Tuckwell, G. *The Life of the Rt. Hon. Sir Charles Dilke*, 2 vols. (London, 1917).

Habberton, W. *Anglo-Russian Relations Concerning Afghanistan 1837–1907* (Urbana, Ill., 1937).

Haberler, G. *Prosperity and Depression. A Theoretical Analysis of Cyclical Movements*, 3rd ed. (New York, 1946).

Haldane, R. B. *Before the War* (London, 1920).

An Autobiography (London, 1929).

Hale, O. J. *Germany and the Diplomatic Revolution* (Philadelphia, 1931).

Publicity and Diplomacy; with special reference to England and Germany, 1890–1914 (New York, 1940).

Halévy, É. *Imperialism and the Rise of Labour, 1895–1905*, 2nd edn. revised (London, 1934).

The Rule of Democracy, 1905–1914 (London, 1934).

The Era of Tyrannies: Essays on Socialism and War (New York, 1965).

Hallgarten, G. W. F. *Imperialismus vor 1914*, 2 vols. (Munich, 1951).

Halpern, P. *The Mediterranean Naval Situation 1908–1914* (Cambridge, Mass., 1971).

Hambloch, E. *British Consul: Memories of Thirty Years Service in Europe and Brazil* (London, 1938).

Hamer, D. A. *John Morley: Liberal Intellectual in Politics* (Oxford, 1968).

Hamer, W. S. *The British Army, Civil–Military Relations 1885–1905* (Oxford, 1970).

Hamilton, Sir I. *Compulsory Service* (London, 1910).

Hammond, J. L. *C. P. Scott of the Manchester Guardian* (London, 1934).

Hanak, H. *Great Britain and Austria–Hungary During the First World War* (London, 1962).

Hancock, Sir Keith *Smuts, The Sanguine Years* (Cambridge, 1962).

Hankey, M. P. A. *The Supreme Command 1914–1918*, 2 vols. (London, 1961).
The Supreme Control at the Paris Peace Conference 1919: A Commentary (London, 1963).
Hantsch, H. *Leopold Graf Berchtold: Grandseigneur und Staatsmann*, 2 vols. (Cologne–Graz–Vienna, 1963).
Hardinge, Lord *Old Diplomacy* (London, 1947).
Harris, W. J. A. *Spender* (London, 1946).
Harrod, R. *Life of John Maynard Keynes* (London, 1951).
Haselmayr, F. *Diplomatische Geschichte des Zweiten Reichs von 1871–1918*, Buch 5, *Die Ära des Flottenkaisers, 1890–1918*, II, *Zehn Jahre Grossflottenbau und seine Auswirkung, 1900–1909* (Munich, 1962).
Hauser, O. *Deutschland und der englisch–russische Gegensatz, 1900–1914* (Göttingen, 1958).
Hazlehurst, C. *Politicians at War, July 1914–May 1915* (London, 1971).
Headlam-Morley, J. W. *Studies in Diplomatic History* (London, 1930).
Heckscher, E. F. *An Economic History of Sweden* (Cambridge, Mass., 1954).
Heckscher, E. F. *et al.*, *Sweden, Norway, Denmark and Iceland in the World War* (London, 1930).
Helmreich, E. C. *The Diplomacy of the Balkan Wars* (Cambridge, Mass., 1938).
Hendrick, B. J. *The Life and Letters of Walter H. Page*, 3 vols. (New York, 1923–5).
Herwig, H. H. *The German Naval Officer Corps, 1890–1918* (Oxford, 1973).
Heuston, R. F. V. *Lives of the Lord Chancellors, 1885–1940* (Oxford, 1964).
Hicks Beach, Lady Victoria *Life of Sir Michael Hicks Beach*, 2 vols. (London, 1932).
Higgins, A. P. *The Hague Peace Conference* (Cambridge, 1908).
Hinsley, F. H. *Power and the Pursuit of Peace* (Cambridge, 1963).
The Causes of the First World War (Hull, 1964).
Hobson, J. A. *Imperialism* (London, 1902).
Hoffman, R. J. S. *Great Britain and the German Trade Rivalry, 1875–1914* (1933, reissued, New York, 1964).
Hoffman, W. G., Müller, J. H. *et al.*, *Das deutsche Volkseinkommen, 1851–1957* (Tübingen, 1959).
Hohenlohe-Schillingsfürst, Chlodwig, Fürst zu, *Denkwürdigkeiten der Reichskanzlerzeit*, ed. K. A. von Müller (Stuttgart–Berlin, 1964).
Hohler, Sir Thomas *Diplomatic Petrel* (London, 1942).
Hoijer, O. *Vers la grande guerre. Le Comte d'Aehrenthal et la politique de violence* (Paris, 1922).
Hollingsworth, L. W. *Zanzibar under the Foreign Office, 1890–1913* (London, 1953).
Hourani, A. H. *Great Britain and the Arab World* (London, 1945).
Howard, C. *Splendid Isolation* (London, 1967).
Britain and the Casus Belli, 1822–1902 (London, 1974).
Howard, H. N. *The Partition of Turkey: A Diplomatic History, 1913–1923* (Norman, Okla., 1931).
Howard, M. *The Theory and Practice of War; Essays presented to Captain B. H. Liddell Hart* (London, 1965).
Studies in War and Peace (London, 1971).
The Continental Commitment (London, 1972).

Hoyos, L. A. *Der deutsch-englische Gegensatz und sein Einfluss auf der Balkanpolitik Österreich-Ungarns* (Berlin, 1922).

Hubatsch, W. *Die Ära Tirpitz: Studien zur deutschen Marinepolitik 1890–1918* (Göttingen, 1955).

Der Admiralstab und die obersten Marinebehörden in Deutschland, 1848–1945 (Frankfurt am Main, 1958).

Hughes, W. M. *Policies and Potentates* (Sydney, 1950).

Huguet, C. J. *Britain and the War: a French Indictment* (London, 1928).

Hunt, M. H. *Frontier Defence and the Open Door; Manchuria in Chinese–American Relations, 1895–1911* (New Haven, Conn., 1973).

Hyam, R. *Elgin and Churchill at the Colonial Office, 1905–1908* (London, 1968).

Hyams, E. *The New Statesman 1913–63: a History of the First Fifty Years* (London, 1963).

Hyde, H. M. *Lord Reading. The Life of Rufus Isaacs, First Marquess of Reading* (London, 1967).

Hynes, S. *The Edwardian Turn of Mind* (Princeton, N.J., 1968).

Ions, E. S. *James Bryce and American Democracy, 1870–1922* (London, 1968).

Isvolsky, H. and Chklaver, G. (eds.) *Au service de la Russie: Alexandre Isvolsky; Correspondance diplomatique 1906–1911* (Paris, 1937–8).

Jagow, G. von *Ursachen und Ausbruch des Weltkrieges* (Berlin, 1919).

James, D. *Lord Roberts* (London, 1954).

James, R. R. *Rosebery, a Biography* (London, 1963).

Gallipoli (New York, 1965).

Jansen, M. B. *The Japanese and Sun Yat-sen* (Cambridge, Mass., 1954).

Jarausch, K. *The Enigmatic Chancellor. Bethmann Hollweg and the Hubris of Imperial Germany* (Princeton, N.J., 1972).

Jenkins, R. *Mr Balfour's Poodle* (London, 1954).

Asquith: Portrait of a Man and an Era (London, 1964).

Joffre, Field Marshal J. *Mémoires du Maréchal Joffre, 1910–1917*, 2 vols. (Paris, 1932).

Johnson, F. A. *Defence by Committee: The British Committee of Imperial Defence, 1885–1959* (London, 1960).

Johnson, H. *Vatican Diplomacy in the World War* (Oxford, 1933).

Joll, J. *The Unspoken Assumptions* (London, 1968).

Jones, K. *Fleet Street and Downing Street* (London, 1920).

Jones, R. *The Nineteenth Century Foreign Office: An Administrative History* (London, 1971).

Jordan, W. M. *Great Britain, France, and the German Problem, 1918–1939* (London, 1943).

Jovanović, S. *Moji Savremenitsi* (Windsor, Ontario, 1962).

Judd, D. *Balfour and the British Empire* (London, 1968).

Kann, R. A. *Die Sixtusaffäre und die geheimen Friedensverhandlungen Österreich-Ungarns im Ersten Weltkrieg* (Munich, 1966).

Kanner, H. *Kaiserliche Katastrophenpolitik* (Leipzig, 1922).

Kazemzadeh, F. *Russia and Britain in Persia, 1864–1914: A Study in Imperialism* (New Haven, Conn., 1968).

Kedourie, E. *England and the Middle East: the Destruction of the Ottoman Empire 1914–1921* (Cambridge, 1956).

Kehr, E. *Schlachtflottenbau und Parteipolitik, 1894–1901* (Berlin, 1930).

Kelly, J. B. *Britain and the Persian Gulf 1785–1880* (Oxford, 1968).

Kendall, W. *The Revolutionary Movement in Britain, 1900–21* (London, 1969).

Kennedy, A. L. *Salisbury, 1830–1903: Portrait of a Statesman* (London, 1953).

Kent, M. *Oil and Empire, British Policy and Mesopotamian Oil 1900–1920* (London, 1975).

Kim, C. I., E. and H.-K. *Korea and the Politics of Imperialism, 1876–1910* (Berkeley, Calif., 1967).

Kimche, J. *The Unromantics* (London, 1968).

King, J. C. *Generals and Politicians* (Berkeley, Calif., 1951).

Knaplund, P. (ed.) *Speeches on Foreign Affairs, 1900–14 by Sir Edward Grey* (London, 1931).

Koch, H. W. (ed.) *The Origins of the First World War: Great Power Rivalry and War Aims* (London, 1972).

Kocka, J. *Klassengesellschaft im Krieg: deutsche Sozialgeschichte, 1914–1918* (Göttingen, 1973).

Kokovtsov, V. N. *Out of My Past: The Memoirs of Count Kokovtsov* (Stanford, Calif., 1935).

Koss, S. E. *John Morley at the India Office 1905–1910* (New Haven, Conn., 1969).
Lord Haldane, Scapegoat for Liberalism (New York, 1969).
Sir John Brunner: Radical Plutocrat 1842–1919 (Cambridge, 1970).
Fleet Street Radical: A. G. Gardiner and the Daily News (London, 1973).

Kraft, B. D. E. *Lord Haldane's Tendung naar Berlin in 1912* (Utrecht, n.d.).

Krieger, L. and Stern, F. (eds.) *The Responsibility of Power, Historical Essays in Honor of Hajo Holborn* (New York, 1967).

Kuczynski, J. *Studien zur Geschichte des Kapitalismus* (Berlin-East, 1957).

Kuczynski, R. *Deutschlands Versorgung mit Nahrungs- und Futtermitteln* (Berlin, 1927).

Kurgan-Van Hentenryk, G. *Léopold II et les groupes financières belges en Chine: la politique royale et ses prolongements, 1895–1914* (Brussels, 1972).

Kuznets, S. (ed.) *Income and Wealth, Series* v (Cambridge, 1955).

Lafargue, T. E. *China and the World* (Stanford, Calif., 1937).

Lafore, L. *The Long Fuse* (London, 1966).

Lamb, A. *Britain and Chinese Central Asia: The Road to Lhasa, 1767–1905* (London, 1960).
The McMahon Line, 2 vols. (London, 1966).

Lambert, R. C. *The Parliamentary History of Conscription in Great Britain* (London, 1917).

Lamouche, L. *Quinze ans d'histoire balkanique 1904–1918* (Paris, 1928).

Lansbury, G. *Miracle of Fleet Street* (London, 1925).

Latané, J. H. *Development of the League of Nations Idea: Documents and Correspondence of Theodore Marburg* (New York, 1932).

Launay, J. de *Secrets diplomatiques, 1914–1918* (Brussels, 1963).

Lawrence, T. J. *The Principles of International Law* (London, 1895).

Lederer, I. J. (ed.) *Russian Foreign Policy* (New Haven, Conn., 1962).

Lee, Sir Sidney *King Edward VII, a Biography*, 2 vols. (London, 1925–7).

Lennox, Lady Algernon Gordon, *see* Gordon Lennox.

Leslie, S. *Mark Sykes* (London, 1923).

Lewis, B. *The Emergence of Modern Turkey* (London, 1968).

Lichnowsky, Prince *My Mission to London* (London, 1918).

Heading for the Abyss (London, 1928).

Lindberg, F. A. *Scandinavia in Great Power Politics, 1905–1908* (Stockholm, 1958).

Link, A. S. *Wilson*, 5 vols. (Princeton, N.J., 1947–65).

Lloyd George, D. *War Memoirs*, 6 vols. (London, 1933–6).

Loreburn, Lord *How the War Came* (London, 1919).

Louis, G. *Les Carnets de Georges Louis, 1908–1917*, 2 vols. (Paris, 1926).

Louis, W. R. *Great Britain and Germany's Lost Colonies, 1914–1917* (Oxford, 1967).

Louis, W. R. and Gifford, P. (eds.) *Britain and Germany in Africa: Imperial Rivalry and Colonial Rule* (New Haven, Conn., 1967).

Britain and France in Africa: Imperial Rivalry and Colonial Rule (New Haven, Conn., 1972).

Louis, W. R., and Stengers, J. (eds.) *E. D. Morel's History of the Congo Reform Movement* (Oxford, 1968).

Low, S. *The Governance of England* (London, 1914).

Lowe, C. J. *The Reluctant Imperialists*, 2 vols. (London, 1967).

Lowe, C. J. and Dockrill, M. L. (eds.) *The Mirage of Power: British Foreign Policy, 1902–1914*, 3 vols. (London, 1972).

Lowe, C. J. and Marzari, F. *Italian Foreign Policy, 1870–1940* (London, 1974).

Lowe, P. C. *Great Britain and Japan, 1911–1915* (London, 1969).

Lutz, H. *Lord Grey and the World War* (London, 1928).

Die europäische Politik in der Julikrise 1914 (Berlin, 1930).

Eyre Crowe der böse Geist des Foreign Office (Stuttgart, 1931).

Deutschfeindliche Kräfte im Foreign Office der Vorkriegszeit (Berlin, 1932).

Luvaas, J. *The Education of an Army: British Military Thought, 1815–1940* (London, 1965).

Lynch, H. F. B. *Sir Edward Grey in Persia* (London, 1912).

Europe in Macedonia (London, 1908).

Lyons, F. S. L. *John Dillon* (London, 1968).

Macartney, C. A. *The Habsburg Monarchy, 1790–1918* (London, 1968).

MacColl, R. *Roger Casement* (London, 1956).

Mach, R. von, *Aus bewegter Balkanzeit 1879–1918: Erinnrungen* (Berlin, 1928).

Mackay, R. F. *Fisher of Kilverstone* (Oxford, 1973).

Mackintosh, J. P. *The British Cabinet* (London, 1968).

MacDiarmid, D. S. *The Life of Lieut. General Sir James Moncrieff-Grierson* (London, 1923).

McKenna, S. *Reginald McKenna 1863–1943* (London, 1948).

Macmunn, Sir G. *Afghanistan from Darius to Amanullah* (London, 1929).

Macmurray, J. V. A. *Treaties and Agreements with and concerning China, 1894–1919*, 2 vols. (New York, 1921).

Magnus, P. *Kitchener: Portrait of an Imperialist* (London, Grey Arrow edition, 1961).

King Edward the Seventh (London, 1964).

Malagodi, O. *Conversazioni della guerra*, 2 vols. (Milan, 1960).

Malozemoff, A. *Russian Far Eastern Policy, 1881–1904* (Berkeley, Calif., 1958).

Mamatey, V. S. *The United States and East Central Europe 1914–1918* (Princeton, N.J., 1957).

Manchester, A. K. *British Preeminence in Brazil, its Rise and Decline* (Chapel Hill, N.C., 1933).

Mansergh, N. *The Coming of the First World War* (London, 1949).

Mantoux, E. *The Carthaginian Peace* (London, 1946).

Mantoux, P. *Paris Peace Conference, 1919* (Geneva, 1964).

Marchand, E. (ed.) *Un livre noir. Diplomatie d'avant guerre...d'après les archives Russes-Novembre 1910–Juillet 1914* (Paris, 1922–3).

Marcus, G. *Before the Lamps Went Out* (London, 1965).

Marder, A. J. *The Anatomy of British Sea Power* (London, 1940).
From the Dread Nought to Scapa Flow: The Royal Navy in the Fisher Era, 1904–19, 5 vols. (London, 1961–70).
(ed.) *Fear God and Dread Nought: The Correspondence of Lord Fisher of Kilverstone*, 3 vols. (London, 1952–9).

Martin, B. G. *German-Persian Diplomatic Relations 1873–1912* (The Hague, 1959).

Martin, L. W. *Peace Without Victory* (New Haven, Conn., 1958).

Martin, W. *The 'New Age' under Orage: Chapters in English Cultural History* (Manchester, 1967).

Martini, F. *Diario, 1914–1918* ed. G. de Rosa (Milan, 1966).

Marwick, A. J. *Clifford Allen, The Open Conspirator* (Edinburgh, 1964).

Massingham, H. J. (ed.) *H. W. M.: A Selection from the Writings of H. W Massingham* (London, 1925).

Masterman, L. *C. F. G. Masterman; a biography* (London, 1939).

Matthew, H. C. A. *The Liberal Imperialists* (Oxford, 1973).

Maurice, Sir Frederick *Haldane, 1856–1915: The Life of Viscount Haldane of Cloan, KT., O.M.*, 2 vols. (London, 1937–9).

May, A. J. *The Hapsburg Monarchy, 1867–1914* (Cambridge, Mass., 1951).
The Passing of the Hapsburg Monarchy, 2 vols. (Philadelphia, 1966).

May, E. R. *The World War and American Isolation 1914–1917* (Cambridge, Mass., 1959).

Mayer, A. J. *Dynamics of Counter-Revolution in Europe, 1870–1956. An Analytical Framework* (New York, 1971).

McCormick, D. G. *Pedlar of Death: Sir Basil Zaharoff and the Armaments Trade* (London, 1965).

Medlicott, W. N. *Contemporary England 1914–1964* (London, 1967).
The Economic Blockade, 2 vols. (London, 1952–9).

Mehra, P. *The Younghusband Mission: An Interpretation* (London, 1969).

Meyer, H. C. *Mitteleuropa in German Thought and Action, 1815–1945* (The Hague, 1955).

Michon, G. *La Préparation à la Guerre: la loi de trois ans, 1910–1914* (Paris, 1935).

Millet, A. R. *The Politics of Intervention; the Military Occupation of Cuba 1906–1909* (Columbus, Ohio, 1968).

Minto, Mary, Countess of *India, Minto and Morley 1905–10* (London, 1932).

Moberley, F. J. *The Campaign in Mesopotamia, 1914–1918*, 4 vols. (London, 1923–7).

Molden, B. *Graf Aehrenthal* (Stuttgart, 1917).

Moltke, H. von, *Erinnerungen, Briefe, Dokumente, 1877–1916* (Stuttgart, 1922).

Mommsen, W. J. *Der moderne Imperialismus* (Stuttgart, 1971).

Monger, G. W. *The End of Isolation: British Foreign Policy, 1900–1907* (London, 1963).

Monroe, E. *Britain's Moment in the Middle East, 1914–1956* (London, 1963).

Montgomery, G. A. *The Rise of Modern Industry in Sweden* (London, 1939).

Montgelas, Count Max *British Foreign Policy under Sir Edward Grey*, translated by William C. Dreher (New York, 1928).

Montmorency, J. E. C., *Francis William Fox: A Biography* (London, 1923).

Morel, E. D. *Morocco in Diplomacy* (London, 1912).

The Secret History of a Great Betrayal (London, 1923).

Morgan, E. D. *Assize of Arms* (London, 1945).

Morgan, K. O. *Wales in British Politics 1860–1922* (Cardiff, 1963).

The Age of Lloyd George (London, 1971).

Morgenthau, H. *Secrets of the Bosphorus* (London, 1918).

Morley, Viscount John *Recollections* (London, 1917).

Memorandum on Resignation, August 1914 (London, 1928).

Morris, A. J. A. *Radicalism Against War* (London, 1972).

Edwardian Radicalism (London, 1974).

Moses, J. A. *The War Aims of Imperial Germany: Professor Fritz Fischer and his Critics* (Brisbane, 1968).

Mowat, R. B. *The Life of Lord Pauncefote* (London, 1929).

Moukhtar, Pasha Mahmoud *La Turquie, l'Allemagne et l'Europe depuis le traité de Berlin jusqu' à la guerre mondiale* (Paris, 1924).

Munro, D. G. *Intervention and Dollar Diplomacy in the Carribbean 1900–21* (Princeton, N.J., 1964).

Murray, A. C. (Lord Elibank) *At Close Quarters: A Sidelight on Anglo-American Diplomatic Relations* (London, 1946).

Murray, G. *The Foreign Policy of Sir Edward Grey, 1906–1915* (Oxford, 1915).

Musulin, A. *Das Haus am Ballplatz; Errinerungen eines österreich-ungarischen Diplomaten* (Munich, 1924).

Namier, Sir Lewis *Avenues of History* (London, 1952).

Vanished Supremacies: Essays on European History, 1812–1918 (London, 1958).

Neale, R. G. *Britain and American Imperialism, 1898–1900* (Brisbane, 1965).

Nelson, H. I. *Land and Power; British and Allied Policy on Germany's Frontiers 1916–1919* (London, 1963).

Nevakivi, J. *Britain, France and the Arab Middle East 1914–1920* (London, 1969).

Newton, Lord *Lord Lansdowne: a Biography* (London, 1929).

Nicolson, Sir Harold *Sir Arthur Nicolson, Bart.: First Lord Carnock: A study in the Old Diplomacy* (London, 1930).

Diplomacy (London, 1939).

King George V (London, 1952).

Nintchitch, M. *La crise bosniaque, 1908–9, et les puissances européennes* (Paris, 1937).

Nish, I. H. *The Anglo-Japanese Alliance: The Diplomacy of Two Island Empires, 1894–1907* (London, 1966).

Alliance in Decline (London, 1972).

Noel-Baker, E. B. and P. J. *J. Allen Baker M.P. A Memoir* (London, 1927).

Noel-Smith, S. (ed.) *Edwardian England* (London, 1964).

Northedge, F. S. *The Troubled Giant* (London, 1966).

Oliphant, L. *An Ambassador in Bonds* (London, 1947).

d'Ombrain, N. *War Machinery and High Policy* (London, 1973).

Oppenheim, L. *International Law: a treatise*, ed. H. Lauterpacht, 2 vols. (London, 1961–62).

Oppenheimer, Sir Francis *Stranger Within* (London, 1960).

Orlando, V. E. *Memorie, 1915–1919* (Milan, 1960).

Owen, D. *British Opium Policy in India and China* (New Haven, Conn., 1934).

Paetow, L. (ed.) *The Crusades and other Historical Essays Presented to Dana C. Munro* (New York, 1928).

Paléologue, M. *An Ambassador's Memoirs, 1914–17*, 3 vols. (New York, 1923–5).
Un grand tournant de la politique mondiale, 1904–1906 (Paris, 1934).
Au Quai d'Orsay à la veille de la Tormente: journal, 1913–14 (Paris, 1947).

Patterson, A. Temple (ed.) *The Jellicoe Papers* (London, Navy Records Society, 1966).

Pearl, C. *Morrison of Peking* (London, 1967).

Pelcovits, N. A. *Old China Hands and the Foreign Office* (New York, 1948).

Pelling, H. M. *America and the British Left* (London, 1956).
Popular Politics and Society in Late Victorian Britain (London, 1968).

Penson, L. *Foreign Affairs under the Third Marquis of Salisbury* (London, 1962).

Percy, Lord Eustace *Some Memories* (London, 1958).

Perkins, B. *The Great Rapprochement: England and the United States, 1895–1914* (New York, 1968).

Pfenninger, R. *Die Handelsbeziehungen zwischen der Schweiz und Deutschland während des Krieges 1914–1918* (1928).

Piggott, F. S. G. *Broken Thread* (Aldershot, 1950).

Pike, F. B. *Chile and the United States, 1880–1962: The Emergence of Chile's Social Crisis and the Challenge to United States Diplomacy* (Notre Dame, Indiana, 1963).

Pingaud, A. *Histoire diplomatique de la France pendant la Grande Guerre*, 2 vols. (Paris, 1938–40).

Plass, J. B. *England zwischen Deutschland und Russland. Der persische Golf in der britischen Vorkriegspolitik, 1899–1907* (Hamburg, 1966).

Platt, D. C. M. *Finance, Trade and Politics in British Foreign Policy, 1815–1914* (Oxford, 1968).
The Cinderella Service: British Consuls since 1825 (London, 1971).

Playne, C. E. *The Pre-War Mind in Britain* (London, 1928).

Pogge von Strandmann, H. and Geiss, I. *Die Erforderlichkeit des Unmöglichen. Deutschland am Vorabend des Ersten Weltkrieges* (Frankfurt am Main, 1965).

Poidevin, R. *Les relations économiques et financières entre la France et l'Allemagne de 1898 à 1914* (Paris, 1969).

Poincaré, H. *Au service de la France*, 10 vols. (Paris, 1925–33).

Poltz, L. *Die anglo-russische Entente, 1903–1907* (Hamburg, 1932).

Ponsonby, A. *Democracy and Diplomacy – a plea for popular control of Foreign Policy* (London, 1915).

Pope Hennessy, J. *Lord Crewe, 1858–1945; the Likeness of a Liberal* (London, 1955).

Porter, B. *Critics of Empire: British Radical Attitudes to Colonialism in Africa, 1895–1914* (London, 1968).

Pound, R. and Harmsworth, G. *Northcliffe* (London, 1959).

Pribram, A. *Austrian Foreign Policy, 1908–18* (London, 1923).

England and the International Policy of the European Great Powers, 1871–1914 (Oxford, 1931).

The Secret Treaties of Austria–Hungary, 2 vols. (Cambridge, Mass., 1921).

Austria–Hungary and Great Britain, 1908–1914, translated by I. Morrow (London, 1951).

Price, R. *An Imperial War and the British Working Class* (London, 1972).

Quirk, R. E. *An Affair of Honour, Woodrow Wilson and the Occupation of Vera Cruz* (New York, 1964).

Rae, J. M. *Conscience and Politics* (Oxford, 1970).

Ramsaur, E. E. *The Young Turks, Prelude to the Revolution of 1908* (Princeton, N.J., 1957).

Rankin, Col. R. *The Inner History of the Balkan War* (New York, n.d.).

Rappaport, A. *The British Press and Wilsonian Neutrality* (London, 1951).

Rathenau, W. *Tagebuch 1907–1922*, ed. H. Pogge von Strandmann (Düsseldorf, 1967).

Redlich, J. *Schicksalsjahre Österreichs, 1908–1919. Das politische Tagebuch Josef Redlichs, 1908–1919*, ed. Fritz Fellner (Graz–Cologne, 1953).

Remak, J. *Sarajevo* (London, 1959).

The Origins of the First World War, 1871–1914 (New York, 1967).

(ed.) *The First World War; Causes, Conduct, Consequences* (New York, 1971).

Remer, C. F. *Foreign Investments in China* (New York, 1933).

Renouvin, P. *Les origines immédiates de la guerre, 28 juin–4 août 1914* (Paris, 1925).

La Question d'Extrême Orient, 1840–1940 (Paris, 1946).

La Crise européenne et la Grande Guerre, 1904–1918 (Paris, 1934).

Repington, C. *The First World War, 1914–1918* (London, 1920).

Rich, N. *Friedrich von Holstein: Politics and Diplomacy in the Era of Bismarck and Wilhelm II*, 2 vols. (Cambridge, 1965).

Rich, N. and Fisher, M. H. (eds.) *The Holstein Papers*, Vol. IV (Cambridge, 1963).

Richards, P. G. *Parliament and Foreign Affairs* (London, 1967).

Riddell, Lord *War Diary, 1914–1918* (London, 1933).

More Pages from My Diary, 1908–1914 (London, 1934).

Riezler, K. *Tagebücher, Aufsätze, Dokumente*, ed. K. D. Erdmann (Göttingen, 1972).

Riste, O. *The Neutral Ally: Norway's relations with belligerent powers in the First World War* (Oslo, 1965).

Ritter, G. *The Schlieffen Plan* (London, 1958).

The Sword and the Sceptre. 4 vols. (London, 1969–73).

Robbins, K. *Sir Edward Grey* (London, 1971).

Robertson, Sir William *Soldiers and Statesmen, 1914–1918* (London, 1926).

Robinson, R. and Gallagher, J., with Denny, A. *Africa and the Victorians: The Official Mind of Imperialism* (London, 1961).

Röhl, J. *Germany after Bismarck* (London, 1967).

Zwei deutsche Fürsten zur Kriegesschuldfrage (Düsseldorf, 1971).

Rolo, P. V. *Entente Cordiale: the Origins and Negotiations of the Anglo-French Agreements of 8 April 1904* (London, 1969).

Ronaldshay, Earl of *The Life of Lord Curzon*, 3 vols. (London, 1928).

Lord Cromer (London, 1932).

Rosen, R. R. *Forty Years of Diplomacy* (London, 1922).

Roskill, S. W. *Naval Policy Between the Wars*, I (London, 1968).

Hankey: Man of Secrets, 3 vols. (London, 1970–4).

Rothwell, W. H. *British War Aims and Peace Diplomacy* (Oxford, 1971).

Rowland, P. *The Last Liberal Governments: To the Promised Land, 1905–1910* (London, 1968).

Unfinished Business, 1911–1914 (London, 1971).

Rudin, H. R. *Armistice 1918* (New Haven, Conn., 1944).

Ryan, A. P. *Mutiny at the Curragh* (London, 1956).

Saint-René Taillandier, G. *Les origines du Maroc français; récit d'une mission* (Paris, 1930).

Salamone, A. W. *Italian diplomacy in the Making* (Philadelphia, Penn., 1945).

Salvatorelli, L. *La Triplice alleanza, storia diplomatica, 1877–1912* (Milan, 1939).

Samra, Chattar Singh *India and Anglo-Soviet Relations 1917–1947* (Bombay, 1959).

Sanders, Liman von *Five Years in Turkey* (Annapolis, Md., 1927).

Sarkissian, S. O. (ed.) *Studies in Diplomatic History and Historiography in Honour of G. P. Gooch* (London, 1961).

Satow, Sir E. *A Guide to Diplomatic Practice* (London, 1966).

Sayers, R. S. *Central Banking after Bagehot* (Oxford, 1957).

Sazonov, S. *Fateful Years, 1909–1916, Reminiscences* (New York, 1928).

Scherer, A. and Grunewald, J. *L'Allemagne et les problèmes de la paix*, 2 vols. (Paris, 1962).

Schmitt, B. E. *The Coming of the War, 1914*, 2 vols. (New York, 1930).

Triple Alliance and Triple Entente (New York, 1934).

The Annexation of Bosnia (Cambridge, 1937).

Schoen, W. von *Memoirs of an Ambassador* (London, 1922).

Scholes, W. V. and M. V. *The Foreign Policies of the Taft Administration* (Columbia, Mo., 1970).

Schottelius, H. and Deist, W. *Marine und Marinepolitik, 1871–1914* (Düsseldorf, 1972).

Schreiner, C. A. and B. de Siebert (eds.) *Entente Diplomacy and the World. Matrix of the History of Europe, 1909–1914* (London, 1921).

Schurman, D. M. *The Education of a Navy: The Development of British Naval Strategic Thought, 1867–1914* (London, 1965).

Searle, G. R. *The Quest for National Efficiency* (Oxford, 1971).

Semmel, B. *Imperialism and Social Reform: English Social-Imperial Thought 1895–1914* (Cambridge, Mass., 1960).

Serra, E. *L'intesa mediterranea del 1902* (Milan, 1957).

Seton-Watson, C. *Italy from Liberalism to Fascism* (London, 1967).

Seton-Watson, R. W. *The Southern Slav Question and the Habsburg Monarchy* (London, 1911).

Britain in Europe 1789–1914: a survey of foreign policy (Cambridge, 1937).
The Rise of Nationality in the Balkans (2nd ed., New York, 1966).

Seymour, C. *The Intimate Papers of Colonel House*, 4 vols. (London, 1926–8).

Shotwell, J. T. and Deak, F. *Turkey at the Straits* (New York, 1940).

Shuster, W. Morgan *The Strangling of Persia: a Personal Narrative* (New York, 1912).

Siebert, B. von (ed.) *Graf Benckendorffs diplomatischer Schriftwechsel*, 3 vols. (Berlin, 1928).

Siney, M. C. *The Allied Blockade of Germany 1914–16* (Ann Arbor. Mich., 1957).

Skendi, S. *The Albanian National Awakening 1878–1912* (Princeton, N.J., 1967).

Smith, C. Jay *The Russian Struggle for Power* (New York, 1956).

Smith, D. *Robert Lansing and American Neutrality 1914–1917* (Berkeley, Calif., and Los Angeles, 1958).

Sommer, D. *Haldane of Cloan: His Life and Times, 1856–1928* (London, 1960).

Sonnino, S. *Diario, 1866–1922* (Bari, 1972).

Scritti e Discorsi extraparlamentari, 1870–1920, 2 vols. (Bari, 1972).

Sontag, R. J. *Germany and England: Background of Conflict, 1848–1894* (New York, 1938).

Spender, H. *The Fire of Life* (London, 1926).

Spender, J. A. *The Life of the Right Honourable Sir Henry Campbell-Bannerman*, 2 vols. (London, 1923).

Life, Journalism and Politics, 2 vols. (London, 1927).

Spender, J. A. and Asquith, C. *Life of Herbert Henry Asquith, Lord Oxford and Asquith*, 2 vols. (London, 1932).

Springborn, A. *Englands Stellung zur deutschen Welt- und Kolonialpolitik in den Jahren 1911–1914* (Würzburg, 1939).

Steed, H. W. *The Hapsburg Monarchy* (London, 1914).

Through Thirty Years, 1892–1922: a personal narrative (London, 1924).

Stegmann, D. *Die Erben Bismarcks: Parteien und Verbände in der Spätphase des Wilhelminischen Deutschlands; Sammlungspolitik 1897–1918* (Cologne, 1970).

Stein, L. *The Balfour Declaration* (London, 1961).

Steinberg, J. *Yesterday's Deterrent: Tirpitz and the Birth of the German Battle Fleet* (London, 1965).

Steiner, Z. *The Foreign Office and Foreign Policy, 1898–1914* (Cambridge, 1969).

Stieve, F. (ed.) *Isvolski im Weltkrieg. Der diplomatische Schriftwechsel Isvolskis aus den Jahren 1914–1917*, 3 vols. (Berlin, 1925).

Storrs, R. *Orientations* (definitive ed., London, 1945).

Strang, Lord *The Foreign Office* (London, 1955).

Stürmer, M. (ed.) *Das Kaiserliche Deutschland, Politik und Gesellschaft 1870–1918* (Düsseldorf, 1970).

Sun, E-tu-zen *Chinese Railways and British Interests, 1898–1911* (New York, 1954).

Swartz, M. *The Union of Democratic Control in British Politics during the First World War* (Oxford, 1971).

Swire, J. *Albania, the Rise of a Kingdom* (London, 1947).

Sydenham of Combe. See Clarke, G S.

Sylvester, A. J. *The Real Lloyd George* (London, 1947).

Taube, M. de, *La Politique russe d'avant guerre et la fin de l'empire des tsars, 1904–1914* (Paris, 1928).

Taylor, A. J. P. *The Habsburg Monarchy* (London, 1941).
　Rumours of War (London, 1952).
　The Struggle for Mastery in Europe, 1848–1918 (Oxford, 1954).
　'The War Aims of the Allies in the First World War', in *Essays presented to Sir Lewis Namier*, eds. A. J. P. Taylor and R. Pares (London, 1956).
　The Troublemakers (London, 1957).
　Politics in Wartime and other Essays (London, 1964).
　English History 1914–1945 (Oxford, 1965).
　War by Time Table: How the First World War Began (London, 1969).
　(ed.) *Lloyd George: Twelve Essays* (London, 1971).
　Beaverbrook (London, 1972).
Tcharykov, N. V. *Glimpses of Higher Politics through War and Peace, 1855–1929* (London, 1931).
Temperley, H. and Penson, L. M. *A Century of Diplomatic Blue Books, 1814–1914* (Cambridge, 1938).
Terenzio, P. *Le Rivalité anglo-russe en Perse et an Afghanistan jusqu'aux accords de 1907* (Paris, 1947).
Terraine, J. *Douglas Haig: the Educated Soldier* (London, 1963).
Thaden, E. C. *Russia and the Balkan Alliance of 1912* (University Park, Pennsylvania, 1965).
Thayer, J. A. *Italy and the Great War, Politics and Culture, 1870–1915* (Madison, Wisconsin, 1964).
Thomas, Sir W. *Black, The Story of the Spectator* (London, 1928).
Tilley, Sir John and Gaselee, S. *The Foreign Office*, 2nd edn. (London, 1933).
The Times, History of The Times
　vol. III, *The Twentieth Century Test, 1884–1912* (London, 1947).
　vol. IV, pt. 1, *The 150th Anniversary and Beyond, 1912–1948* (London, 1952).
Tirpitz, A. von *Erinnerungen* (Leipzig, 1920).
　Politische Dokumente, 2 vols., *Der Aufbau der deutschen Weltmacht* (Stuttgart/Berlin, 1924–6).
Tirpitz, W. von *Wie hat sich der Staatsbetrieb beim Aufbau der Flotte bewahart?* (Leipzig, 1923).
Tischendorff, A. *Great Britain and Mexico in the Era of Porfirio Diaz* (Durham, N.C., 1961).
Toscano, M. *Il Patto di Londra* (Milan, 1934).
　Gli Accordi di San Giovanni di Moriana (Milan, 1936).
Toshev, A. *Balkanskite Voini*, 2 vols. (Sofia, 1929, 1931).
Trevelyan, G. M. *Grey of Fallodon; the Life of Sir Edward Grey* (London, 1937).
Trumpener, U. *Germany and the Ottoman Empire, 1914–1918* (Princeton, N.J., 1968).
Tuchman, B. *The Guns of August* (New York, 1962).
Turlington, E. W. *The World War Period*, vol. 3, in Columbia series, 'Neutrality, its History, Economics and Law' (New York, 1935–6).
Tyler, J. E. *The British Army and the Continent, 1904–1914* (London, 1938).
Übersberger, H. *Österreich zwischen Russland und Serbien* (Cologne, 1958).

Ulloa, B. *La Revolucíon Intervenida. Relaciones diplomáticas entre México y Estados Unidos* (Mexico, 1971).

Uppleger, F. *Die englische Flottenpolitik vor dem Weltkrieg* (Berlin, 1930).

Valeri, N. *Da Giolitti a Mussolini* (Florence, 1956).

Vansittart, Lord *The Mist Procession* (London, 1958).

Vigezzi, B. *I problemi della neutralità e della Guerra nel Carteggio Salandra Sonnino (1914–1917)* (Milan, 1962).

Vivier, C. *The United States and China, 1906–1913* (New Brunswick, Conn., 1957).

Vucinich, W. S. *Serbia between East and West, the events of 1903–1908* (Stanford, Calif., 1954).

Wallace, L. P. and Askew, W. C. *Power, Public Opinion and Diplomacy* (Durham, N.C., 1959).

Walton, C. C. *Kiderlen-Wächter and the Anglo-German problem 1910–1912* (Washington, D.C., 1949).

Ward, A. and Gooch, G. P. *The Cambridge History of British Foreign Policy*, vol. III (Cambridge, 1923).

Watt, D. C. *Personalities and Policies: Studies in the Formulation of British Foreign Policy in the 20th Century* (South Bend, Indiana, 1965).

Wavell, A. *Allenby* (London, 1940).

Weber, E. *The Nationalist Revival in France, 1905–1914* (Berkeley, Calif., 1959).

Webster, Sir Charles *The Art and Practice of Diplomacy* (London, 1961).

Wedel, O. H. *Austro-German Diplomatic Relations 1908–1914* (Stanford, Calif., 1932).

Wehler, H. *Das deutsche Kaiserreich 1871–1918* (Göttingen, 1973).
  Der Aufstieg des amerikanischen Imperialismus, 1865–1900 (Göttingen, 1974).

Widenmann, W. *Marine-Attaché an der kaiserlich-deutschen Botschaft in London 1907–1912* (Göttingen, 1952).

Willequet, J. *Le Congo Belge et la Weltpolitik* (Brussels, 1962).

Willert, A. *The Road to Safety: A Study in Anglo-American Relations* (London, 1952).

Williams, F. *Dangerous Estate* (London, 1957).

Williamson, S. R., Jr. *The Politics of Grand Strategy: Britain and France prepare for War, 1904–1914* (Cambridge, Mass., 1969).

Willis, E. F. *Prince Lichnowsky Ambassador of Peace: A Study of Pre-War Diplomacy, 1912–1914* (Los Angeles, 1942).

Wilson, H. *The Education of a Diplomat* (London, 1938).

Wilson, J. *A Life of Sir Henry Campbell-Bannerman* (London, 1973).

Wilson, Trevor *The Downfall of the Liberal Party* (London, 1966).
  (ed.), *The Political Diaries of C. P. Scott, 1911–1928* (London, 1970).

Wimmer, L. *Zwischen Ballhausplatz und Downing Street* (Vienna, 1958).

Winkler, H. R. *The League of Nations Movement in Great Britain 1914–1919* (New Brunswick, N.J., 1952).

Witt, P.-C. *Die Finanzpolitik des deutschen Reiches von 1903 bis 1913* (Historische Studien, Heft 415, Lübeck and Hamburg, 1970).

Wolf, Lucien *Life of the First Marquess of Ripon*, 2 vols. (London, 1921).

Wolff, T. *On the Eve of 1914* (Eng. trans., New York, 1936).

Wolpert, S. *Morley and India, 1906–1910* (Berkeley, Calif., 1967).

Woodward, E. L. *Great Britain and the German Navy* (London, 1934).
Great Britain and the War of 1914–1918 (London, 1967).
Wright, M. C. (ed.) *China in revolution, The first phase, 1900–13* (New Haven, Conn., 1968).
Wright, S. F. *Hart and the Chinese Customs* (Belfast, 1958).
Young, D. *Member for Mexico: A Biography of Weetman Pearson, First Viscount Cowdray* (London, 1966).
Young, G. *Nationalism and the War in the Near East* (Oxford, 1915).
Diplomacy Old and New (London, 1921).
Young, K. *Arthur James Balfour* (London, 1963).
Zeine Z. N. *The Struggle for Arab Independance* (Beirut, 1960).
Arab-Turkish relations and the Emergence of Arab nationalism (Beirut, 1958).
Zeman, Z. A. B. *The Break-up of the Habsburg Empire, 1914–1918* (London, 1961).
A Diplomatic History of the First World War (London, 1971).

V. ARTICLES

Ahmad, Feroz, Great Britain's Relations with the Young Turks, 1908–1914, *Middle Eastern Studies*, 4 (July 1966).
Bariety, J. L'Allemagne et les Problèmes de la Paix pendant la Première Guerre Mondiale, *Revue Historique*, 233 (1965).
Bastid, M. La Diplomatie Française et la Révolution Chinoise de 1911, *Revue d'Histoire moderne et contemporaine*, XVI (1969).
Benna, Anna A. Studien zum Kulturprotektorat Österreich-Ungarns in Albanien im Zeitalter des Imperialismus, *Mitteilungen des österreichischen Staatsarchivs*, Bd. 8.
Berghahn, V. R. Zu den Zielen des deutschen Flottenbaus unter Wilhelm II, *Historische Zeitschrift*, Heft 210–11 (February, 1970).
Bestuzhev, I. V. Russian Foreign Policy, February–June 1914, *Journal of Contemporary History*, 1 (1966).
Bosworth, R. Britain and Italy's Acquisition of the Dodecanese 1912–15, *Historical Journal*, XIII (1970).
Bougeois, A. La Mission de Lord Haldane à Berlin, Février 1912, *Revue des deux Mondes*, XXXV (October 1926).
Boyle, T. The Formation of the Campbell-Bannerman Government in December 1905, *Bulletin of the Institute of Historical Research*, LXV (November 1972).
Brand, C. F. British Labour and the International during the Great War, *Journal of Modern History*, 8 (March 1936).
Bridge, F. R. The British Declaration of War on Austria–Hungary, *Slavonic Review*, 47 (1969).
Bücher, P. Deutschlands Handelsbilanz, *Preussische Jahrbücher* Bd. 126, Heft III (December 1906).
Butterfield, H. Sir Edward Grey in July 1914, *Historical Studies*, V (1965).
Calvert, P. The Murray Contract: An Episode in International Finance and Diplomacy, *Pacific Historical Review*, XXXV (May 1966).
The Last Occasion on which Britain used Coercion to settle a dispute with

a Non-Colonial Territory in the Carribean: Guatemala and the Powers 1909–1913, *Inter-American Economic Affairs*, xxxv (Winter 1971).

Carlgren, W. M. Informationsstykken frän Abdul Hamids senare regeringar, *Historisk Tidskrift* (1952).

Chan, K. C. British Policy of Neutrality during the 1911 revolution, *Journal of Oriental Studies*, Hong Kong, 8 (1970).

British Policy in the Reorganisation loan to China, 1912–13, *Modern Asian Studies*, 4 (1971).

Cline, C. A., E. D. Morel and the Crusade Against the Foreign Office, *Journal of Modern History*, 39 (1967).

Cooper, M. B. British Policy in the Balkans 1908–9, *Historical Journal*, VII (1964–5).

Corrigan, H. S. W. German–Turkish Relations and the Outbreak of War in 1914: A Reassessment, *Past and Present*, 36 (1967).

Cosgrave, R. A. The Career of Sir Eyre Crowe: A Reassessment, *Albion*, 4 (Winter 1972).

A Note on Lloyd George's Speech at the Mansion House, 21 July 1911, *Historical Journal*, XII (1969).

Crampton, R. J. August Bebel and the British Foreign Office, *History*, 58 (June 1973).

The Decline of the Concert of Europe in the Balkans, 1913–1914, *The Slavonic and East Europen Review*, LII (June 1974).

Cunningham, A. The Wrong Horse? Anglo-Turkish Relations before the First World War, *St Antony's Papers*, 17 (1965).

Dakin, D. The Greek Proposals for the Alliance with France and Great Britain, June–July 1907, *Balkan Studies*, 3 (1962).

Delbrück, Hans, Politische Korrespondenz, *Preussische Jahrbücher*, Bd. 98, Heft, III (December 1899).

Dubois, P. Les négociations anglo-allemandes relatives aux colonies Portu- gaises 1912–1914, *Revue d'Histoire de la guerre mondiale* (1959).

Edwards, E. W. The Far Eastern Agreements of 1907, *Journal of Modern History*, xxvi (1954).

The Franco-German Agreement in Morocco, 1909, *English Historical Review*, LXXVIII (1963).

The Japanese Alliance and the Anglo-French Agreement of 1904, *History*, XLII (1957).

Great Britain and the Manchurian Railway Question, 1909–10, *English Historical Review*, LXXXI (1966).

The Origins of British Financial Cooperation with France in China, 1903–6, *English Historical Review*, LXXXVI (1971).

Ekstein, M. Sir Edward Grey and Imperial Germany in 1914, *Journal of Contemporary History*, 6 (1971).

Some Notes on Sir Edward Grey's Policy in July 1914, *Historical Journal*, XV (1972).

Eley, G. Sammlungspolitik, Social Imperialism and the Navy Law of 1898, *Militärgeschichtliche Mitteilungen*, 1 (1974).

Farrar, M. M. Preclusive Purchases and Economic Warfare in France during the First World War, *Economic History Review*, 2nd ser., xxvi (1973).

Fellner, F. Die Haltung Österreich-Ungarns während der Konferenz von Algeciras, 1906, *Mitteilungen des Instituts für österreichische Geschichtsforschung*, Bd. 71, 1963.

Fischer, F. Weltpolitik, Weltmachtstreben und deutsche Kriegsziele, *Historische Zeitschrift*, Bd. 199, 1964.

Friedman, I. The Hussein-McMahon Correspondence and the Question of Palestine, *Journal of Contemporary History*, V (1970).

Fry, M. G. The North Atlantic Triangle, *Journal of Modern History*, 39 (1967).

Gordon, M. Domestic Conflict and the Origins of the First World War, The British and German Cases, *Journal of Modern History*, 46 (1974).

Gottschalk, E. Die Diplomatische Geschichte der serbischen Note vom 31. März 1909, *Berliner Monatshefte* (1932).

Gowen, R. J. Great Britain and the Twenty-One Demands of 1915, *Journal of Modern History*, 43 (1971).

Greaves, R. British policy in Persia, 1892–1903, *Bulletin of the School of Oriental and African Studies*, XXVIII (1965).

Some Aspects of the Anglo-Russian Convention and its Working in Persia, 1907–1914, *Bulletin of the School of Oriental and African Studies*, XXXI (1968).

Grenville, J. A. S. Diplomacy and War Plans in the United States, 1890–1917, *Transactions of the Royal Historical Society*, 5th sec., II (1961).

Habberton, W. Anglo-Russian Relations concerning Afghanistan, *Illinois Studies in the Social Sciences*, XXI (1937).

Halpern, P. The Anglo-French-Italian Naval Convention of 1915, *Historical Journal*, XIII (1970).

Hanak, H. A Lost Cause: The English Radicals and the Habsburg Empire, 1914–18, *Journal of Central European Affairs* (July 1963).

The Government, the Foreign Office and Austria–Hungary, 1914–18, *Slavonic and East European Review*, XLVII (January 1969).

Hamilton, K. A. An attempt to form an 'Anglo-French Industrial Entente', *Middle Eastern Studies*, XI (January 1975).

Hargreaves, J. D. The Origin of the Anglo-French Military Conversations in 1905, *History*, 36 (October 1951).

Harris, J. and Hazlehurst, C. Campbell-Bannerman as Prime Minister, *History*, 55 (1970).

Hatton, P. H. S. The First World War: Britain and Germany in 1914: the July Crisis and War Aims, *Past and Present*, 36 (1967).

Harcourt and Solf: the Search for an Anglo-German Understanding through Africa, 1912–1914, *European Studies Review*, I (1971).

Hazlehurst, C. Asquith as Prime Minister, *English Historical Review*, LXXXV (1970).

Helmreich, E. C. Montengro and the Foundations of the Balkan League, *Slavonic and East European Review*, XV (1937).

Die Haldane Mission, *Berliner Monatshefte*, 12 (February 1934).

Helmreich, J. Belgian Concern over Neutrality and British Intentions 1906–1914, *Journal of Modern History*, 36 (December 1964).

Howard, C. The Treaty of London 1915, *History*, XXVI (March 1941).

The Policy of Isolation, *Historical Journal*, X (1967).

Splendid Isolation, *History*, XLVII, 159 (February 1962).

Hubatsch, W. Der Kulminationspunkt der deutschen Marinepolitik im Jahre 1912, *Historische Zeitschrift*, CLXXVI (October 1953).

Ikei, M. Japan's Response to the Chinese Revolution of 1911, *Journal of Asian Studies*, XXV (1966).

Iklé, F. W. Japanese–German Peace Negotiations During World War I, *American Historical Review*, LXXI (1965).

Jack, M. The Purchase of the British Government's Shares in the British Petroleum Company, *Past and Present*, 39 (1968).

Jaffe, R. Die letzen Reichstagswahlen und die Zukunft der Sozial-Demokratie, *Preussische Jahrbücher*, Bd. 128, Heft, II (May 1907).

Jarausch, K. H. World Power or Tragic Fate? The Kriegsschuldfrage as Historical Nemesis, *Central European History*, 5 (1972).

The Illusions of Limited War: Chancellor Bethmann Hollweg's Calculated Risk, July 1914, *Central European History*, 2 (1969).

Joll, J. The 1914 Debate continues: Fritz Fischer and his Critics, *Past and Present*, 34 (July 1966).

Jones, R. B. Anglo-French Negotiations, 1907: A Memorandum by Sir Arthur Milner, *Bulletin of the Institute of Historical Research*, XXXI (November 1958).

Keddie, N. R. British Policy and the Iranian Opposition, 1901–1907, *Journal of Modern History*, XXXIX (1967).

Kedourie, E. Cairo and Khartoum on the Arab Question, 1915–1918, *Historical Journal*, VII (1964).

Kelly, J. P. The Legal and Historical Base of the British Position in the Persian Gulf, *St Antony's Papers*, IV (1958).

Kennedy, P. M. Anglo-German Relations in the Pacific and the Partition of Samoa, *Australian Journal of Politics and History* (1971).

German Weltpolitik and the Alliance Negotiations with England, 1897–1900, *Journal of Modern History*, 45 (December 1973).

The Development of German Naval Operations Plans Against England 1896–1914, *English Historical Journal*, LXXXIX (1973).

Kent, M. Agent of Empire? The National Bank of Turkey and British Foreign Policy, *Historical Journal*, XVIII (1975).

Kernek, S. The British Government's reactions to President Wilson's 'Peace' Note of December 1916, *Historical Journal*, XIII (1970).

Kitch, J. M. The Promise of the New Revisionism: A Review of the Journal of Contemporary History, vol. III, July 1966, on '1914', *Past and Present*, 36 (1967).

Klein, I. The Anglo-Russian Convention and the Problem of Central Asia 1907–1914, *Journal of British Studies*, XI (1971).

The British Decline in Asia: Tibet 1914–21, *The Historian* (November 1971).

British Intervention in the Persian Revolution 1905–1909, *Historical Journal*, XV (1972).

Koch, H. W. Die Rolle des Sozialdarwinismus als Faktor im Zeitalter des Neuen Imperialismus um die Jahrhundertwende, *Zeitschrift für Politik*, XVII (1970).

The Anglo-German Alliance Negotiations: Missed Opportunity or Myth? *History*, LIV (October 1969).

Koss, S. E. The Destruction of Britain's Last Liberal Government, *Journal of Modern History*, 40 (1968).

Kumar, R. The Records of the Government of India on the Berlin–Baghdad Question, *Historical Journal*, v (1962).

Lambton, A. K. S. Secret Societies and the Persian Revolution of 1905–6, *St Antony's Papers*, IV (1958).

Persian Political Societies, 1906–1911, *St Antony's Papers*, XVI (1963).

Lammers, D. Arno Mayer and the British Decision for War 1914, *Journal of British Studies*, XII (1973).

Langer, W. Russia, the Straits Question and the European Powers 1904–1918, *English Historical Review*, XLIV (1929).

Langhorne, R. T. B. The Naval Question in Anglo-German Relations, 1912–1914, *Historical Journal*, XIII (1970).

Anglo-German Negotiations concerning the Future of the Portuguese Colonies 1911–1914, *Historical Journal*, XVI (1973).

Lehmann, H. Österreich-Ungarns Belgienpolitik im Ersten Weltkrieg, *Historische Zeitschrift*, Bd. 192 (1961).

Louis, W. R. Australia and the German Colonies in the Pacific, 1914–1919, *Journal of Modern History*, 38 (1966).

Lowe, C. J. The Failure of British Policy in the Balkans, 1914–1916, *Canadian Journal of History*, IV (1969).

Britain and the Italian Intervention, 1914-15, *Historical Journal*, XII (1969).

Lowe, P. C. The British Empire and the Anglo-Japanese Alliance 1911–1915, *History*, LIV (1969).

Mackintosh, J. P. The Role of the Committee of Imperial Defence before 1914, *English Historical Review*, LXXVII (1962).

Marchat, H. L'affaire Marocaine en 1911, *Revue d'histoire diplomatique*, 77 (1963).

Marcus, G. J. The Naval Crises of 1909 and the Croydon Bye-Election, *Journal of the Royal United Services Institute* (November 1958).

Maude, G. Finland in Anglo-Russian Diplomatic Relations, 1899–1910, *Slavonic and East European Review*, LXVIII (1970).

May, A. J. The Novibazar Railway Project, *Journal of Modern History*, x (1938).

Trans-Balkan Railway Schemes, *Journal of Modern History*, XXIV (1952).

Mommsen, W. J. Domestic Factors in German Foreign Policy before 1914, *Central European History*, VI (1973).

Die latente Krise des Wilhelminischen Reiches, Staat und Gesellschaft in Deutschland, 1890–1914, *Militärgeschichtliche Mitteilungen*, I (1974).

Monger, G. W. The End of Isolation: Britain, Germany and Japan, 1900–1902, *Transactions of the Royal Historical Society*, 5th series, XIII (1963).

Monticore, A., Salandra e Sonnino verso la decisione dell'intervento', *Revista di Studi Politici Internationali*, XXIV (1957).

Morris, A. J. The English Radicals' Campaign for Disarmament and the Hague Conference of 1907, *Journal of Modern History*, 43 (1971).

Haldane's Army Reforms 1906–1908: the Deception of the Radicals, *History*, 56 (1971).

Moses, J. A., Karl Dietrich Erdmann, the Reizler Diary and the Fischer Controversy, *Journal of European Studies*, 3 (1973).

Mortimer, J. S. Commercial Interests and German Diplomacy in the Agadir Crisis, *Historical Journal*, x (1967).

Nish, I. Australia and the Anglo-Japanese Alliance 1901–1911, *Australian Journal of Politics and History*, 9 (1963).

Remak, J. 1914 – The Third Balkan War. Origins Reconsidered, *Journal of Modern History*, 43 (1971).

Renouvin, P. The Part Played in International Relations by the Conversations between the General Staffs on the Eve of the War. *Studies in Anglo-French History*, eds. A. Coville and H. W. V. Temperley (Cambridge, 1935).

Renzi, W. A. Great Britain, Russia and the Straits, 1914–1915, *Journal of Modern History*, 42 (March 1970).

Italy's Neutrality and Entrance into the Great War, a Re-examination, *American Historical Review*, LXXIII (1968).

Robbins, K. G. Lord Bryce and the First World War, *Historical Journal*, x (1967).

Sir Edward Grey and the British Empire, *Journal of Imperial and Commonwealth History*, 1 (January 1973).

British Diplomacy and Bulgaria, 1914–1915, *Slavonic and East European Review*, XLIX (1971).

Röhl, J. Admiral von Müller and the Approach of War, 1911–1914, *Historical Journal*, XII (1969).

Rothwell, V. H. Mesopotamia in British War Aims, *Historical Journal*, XIII (1970).

The British Government and Japanese Military Assistance, *History*, 56 (1971).

Schlieffen, Alfred Count, Der Krieg in der Gegenwart, *Deutsche Revue* (Stuttgart/Leipzig, 1909).

Schmidt, G., Parlamentarisierung oder 'preventive' Konterrevolution, 1907–1914, in G. A. Ritter (ed.), Gesellschaft Parlament und Regerung (Düsseldorf, 1974).

Schroeder, P. W. World War 1 as Galloping Gertie: A Reply to Joachim Remak, *Journal of Modern History*, 44 (1972).

Selby, Sir Walford The Foreign Office, *Nineteenth Century and After*, CXXXVII (July 1945).

Seton-Watson, R. W. The Role of Bosnia in International Politics, *Proceedings of the British Academy*, XVII (1931).

Silberstein, G. A. The Serbian Campaign of 1915: Its Diplomatic Background, *American Historical Journal*, LXXIII (October 1967).

Siney, M. C. British Official Histories of the Blockade, *American Historical Review*, LXVIII (January 1963).

British Negotiations with American Meat Packers, 1915–1917: A Study of Belligerent Trade Controls, *Journal of Modern History*, 23 (December 1951).

Slade, R. English Missionaries and the Beginning of the Anti-Congolese Campaign in England, *Revue Belge de philologie et d'histoire*, XXXIII (1955).

Smith, C. J. Jr. Great Britain and the 1914–1915 Straits Agreement with Russia: the British Promise of November 1914, *American Historical Review*, LXX (July 1965).

Sontag, Raymond J. British Policy in 1913–1914, *Journal of Modern History*, 10 (December 1938).

Staley, E. Business Politics in the Persian Gulf, The Story of the Wörnckhaus Firm, *Political Science Quarterly*, XLVIII (1933).

Stavrianos, L. S. The Balkan Committee, *The Queen's Quarterly*, LXVIII (Autumn 1941).

Steinberg, J. The Copenhagen Complex, *Journal of Contemporary History*, I (July 1966).

Germany and the Russo-Japanese War, *American Historical Review*, 75 (December 1970).

The Novelle of 1908: Necessities and Choices in the Anglo-German Naval Arms Race, *Transactions of the Royal Historical Society*, Fifth series, 21 (1971).

Steiner, Z. Grey, Hardinge and the Foreign Office, 1906–1910, *Historical Journal*, X (1967).

Steiner, Z. and Dockrill, M. Foreign Office Reforms, 1919–1921, *Historical Journal*, XVII (1974).

Stomberg, R. M. Intellectuals and the Coming of War in 1914, *Journal of European Studies*, 3 (1973).

Stone, N. Moltke-Conrad: Relations between the Austro-Hungarian and German General Staffs, 1909–1914, *Historical Journal*, IX (1966).

Hungary and the Crisis of July 1914, *Journal of Contemporary History*, I (1966).

Sumner, B. H. Tsardom and Imperialism in the Far East and Middle East, 1888–1914, *Proceedings of the British Academy*, XXVII (1941).

Sweet, D. The Baltic in British Diplomacy before the First World War, *Historical Journal*, XIII (1970).

Szaz, S. The Transylvanian Question: Rumania and the Belligerents, July–October 1914, *Journal of Central European Affairs*, XIV (January 1954).

Taylor, A. J. P. British Policy in Morocco, 1886–1908, *English Historical Review*, LXVI (July 1951).

Temperley, H. M. V. British Secret Diplomacy from Canning to Grey, *Cambridge Historical Journal*, VI (1938).

British Policy towards Parliamentary Rule and Constitutionalism in Turkey, 1830–1914, *Cambridge Historical Journal*, IV (1932–4).

Thomas, M. E. Anglo-Belgian Military Relations and the Congo Question 1911–1913, *Journal of Modern History*, 25 (June 1953).

Torrey, G. E. Rumania and the Belligerents, *Journal of Contemporary History*, I (1966).

Trebilcock, C. Legends of the British Armament Industry 1896–1914: a revision, *Journal of Contemporary History*, 5 (1970).

A 'special relationship': government, rearmament and the cordite firms *Economic History Review*, 2nd sec., XIX (1966).

Trumpener, U. Turkey's Entry into World War I, *Journal of Modern History*, XXXIV (1962).

Liman von Sanders and the German–Ottoman Alliance, *Journal of Contemporary History*, I (1966).

The Escape of the Goeben and Breslau: A reassessment, *Canadian Journal of History*, VI (1971).

Turner, L. C. F. The Role of the General Staffs in July 1914, *The Australian Journal of Politics and History* (December, 1965).

The Russian Mobilization in 1914, *Journal of Contemporary History*, 3 (1968).

Tyler, J. E. Campbell-Bannerman and the Liberal Imperialists, 1906–1908, *History*, XXIII (1938).

Vincent-Smith, J. D. The Anglo-German Negotiations over the Portuguese Colonies, 1911–1914, *Historical Journal*, XVII (1974).

Viner, J. International Finance and Balance of Power Diplomacy, 1880–1914, *Southwestern Political and Social Science Quarterly*, LX (March 1929).

Walters, E. Aehrenthal's attempt in 1907 to re-group the European Powers, *Slavonic and East European Review*, 30 (1951–2).

Wank, S. Aehrenthal's programme for the reorganization of the Habsburg Monarchy, *Slavonic and East European Review*, 41 (1962–3).

Aehrenthal and the Sanjak Railway project: a re-appraisal, *Slavonic and East European Review*, 42 (1963–4).

Warman, R. The Erosion of Foreign Office Influence, 1916–1918, *Historical Journal*, XV (March 1972).

Watt, D. C. British Reactions to the Assassination at Sarajevo, *European Studies Review*, I (1971).

Wells, S. F. Jr. British Strategic Withdrawal from the Western Hemisphere 1904–1906, *Canadian Historical Review*, XLIX (1968).

Weinroth, H. The British Radicals and the Balance of Power, 1902–14, *Historical Journal*, XIII (1970).

Left-wing Opposition to Naval Armaments in Britain before 1914, *Journal of Contemporary History*, 6 (1971).

Norman Angell and The Great Illusion, *Historical Journal*, XVII (1974).

Weltman, S. Germany, Turkey and the Zionist Movement, 1914–1918, *Review of Politics* (1951).

Williams, B. J. The Strategic Background to the Anglo-Russian Entente 1907, *Historical Journal*, IX (1966).

Wilson, K. M. The Revolution of 1905 and Russian Foreign Policy, *Essays in Honour of E. H. Carr*, ed. C. Abramsky and B. Williams (London 1974).

The Agadir Crisis, The Mansion House Speech and the Double-Edgedness of Agreements, *Historical Journal*, XV (1972).

Wittich, A. von, Die Rüstungen Österreich-Ungarns von 1866 bis 1914, *Berliner Monatshefte* (1932).

Wolf, J. B. The Diplomatic History of the Baghdad Railway, *The University of Missouri Studies*, XL (April 1936).

Zechlin, E. Deutschland zwischen Kabinettskrieg und Wirtschaftskrieg, *Historische Zeitschrift*, 199 (1964).

Zotiades, G. Russia and the question of Constantinople and the Turkish Straits during the Balkan Wars, *Balkan Studies*, 11 (1970).

Index